More praise for
The Kennedy Women

"The story of the Kennedy family is a never-ending, real-life soap opera. The drama, which ranges from epic tragedy to sordid melodrama, includes dedication to worthy causes and tawdry self-destructive behavior. . . . Leamer's book offers the uncut version."
    —*The Christian Science Monitor*

"Leamer dissects the triumphs, aspirations, psychological traits, and misfortunes of Kennedy wives and daughters dating back to 1849. . . . This unauthorized chronicle, a project that required five years to finish, is imbued with the poignancy and burgeoning drama of a multi-generational novel, yet Leamer conscientiously adheres to high standards of scholarship."
    —*The Philadelphia Inquirer*

"Even those readers convinced they know all they want to know about America's first family will find themselves forced to admit that Leamer does a splendid job of weaving together the stories of six generations of women into a highly readable compelling saga."
    —*Booklist*

"A revealing, often moving epic saga of tragedy and resilience . . . Based on interviews with scores of Kennedys, archival research and hitherto untapped family papers."
    —*Publishers Weekly*

By Laurence Leamer:

THE KENNEDY WOMEN: The Saga of an American
    Family*
KING OF THE NIGHT: The Life of Johnny Carson
AS TIME GOES BY: The Life of Ingrid Bergman
MAKE BELIEVE: The Story of Nancy and Ronald Reagan
ASCENT: The Spiritual and Physical Quest of Willi
    Unsoeld
ASSIGNMENT: A Novel
PLAYING FOR KEEPS IN WASHINGTON
THE PAPER REVOLUTIONARIES: The Rise of the
    Underground Press

*Published by Ivy Books

The
Kennedy
Women

The Saga of an American Family

Laurence Leamer

IVY BOOKS • NEW YORK

Ivy Books
Published by Ballantine Books
Copyright © 1994 by Laurence Leamer
Family tree illustration © 1994 by Anita Karl and Jim Kemp

All rights reserved under International and Pan-American Copyright Conventions. Published in the United States by Ballantine Books, a division of Random House, Inc., New York, and simultaneously in Canada by Random House of Canada Limited, Toronto.

Grateful acknowledgment is made to the following for permission to reprint previously published material: DOUBLEDAY, A DIVISION OF BANTAM DOUBLEDAY DELL PUBLISHING GROUP, INC.: Excerpts from *Times to Remember* by Rose Fitzgerald Kennedy. Copyright © 1974 by The Joseph P. Kennedy Jr. Foundation. Reprinted by permission of Doubleday, a division of Bantam Doubleday Dell Publishing Group, Inc. LYNNE McTAGGERT: Excerpts from *Kathleen Kennedy: Her Life and Times* by Lynne McTaggert. Copyright © 1983 by Lynne McTaggert. Reprinted by permission of Lynne McTaggert. PRINCETON UNIVERSITY PRESS: Forty-four lines from "Ithaka" from *The Collected Poems of C. P. Cavafy*, edited by Edmund Kelley and Phillip Sherrard. Published in 1976, revised edition published in 1992. Copyright © 1976 by Princeton University Press. Preprinted by permission. SIMON & SCHUSTER, INC., AND STERLING LORD LITERISTIC, INC.: Excerpts from *The Fitzgeralds and the Kennedys* by Doris Kearns Goodwin. Copyright © 1987 by Doris Kearns Goodwin. Rights throughout the world excluding the United States and Canada are controlled by Sterling Lord Literistic, Inc. Reprinted by permission of Simon & Schuster, Inc., and Sterling Lord Literistic, Inc.

Library of Congress Catalog Card Number: 94-15361

ISBN 0-8041-1361-0

This edition published by arrangement with Villard Books, a division of Random House, Inc., New York. Villard Books is a registered trademark of Random House, Inc.

Manufactured in the United States

First Ballantine Books Edition: June 1995

10 9 8 7 6 5 4 3 2 1

To
JOY HARRIS
and
BOB TAVETIAN

Contents

The Kennedy Family Tree ....*ix*

1. "When Irish Eyes Are Smiling" *1*
2. Bridget's Journey *4*
3. The Hannons and the Fitzgeralds *24*
4. The Mayor's Daughter *60*
5. "A Marvelous Success" *96*
6. "The Prettiest Romance in a Decade" *112*
7. Rose's Blueprint *150*
8. The Salted Heart *179*
9. A Nation of Kennedys *215*
10. "London Will Be Just Grand" *252*
11. "It's the End of the World" *280*
12. "We Had Everything" *304*
13. Days of Infamy *330*
14. "The Ability to Not Be Got Down" *359*
15. Their Brother's Keeper *402*
16. Strangers in Paradise *433*
17. "When Do We Start?" *465*
18. "At Home with the Kennedys" *489*
19. "Don't Deny You Did It" *516*
20. The Women Who Had Everything *545*
21. "Say Good-bye to the President" *584*
22. "Mommy, Did They Love Daddy?" *598*
23. Kennedys Don't Cry *628*
24. "And Deliver Us from Evil" *666*
25. "Don't Tell Mother" *704*
26. The Realm of Possibility *752*
27. Family Appreciation Day *781*
28. "We Tried" *807*

Contents

Acknowledgments *837*
Notes *846*
Bibliography *939*
Index *964*

The
Kennedy
Family
Tree

Bridget Murphy M. SEPT. 26, 1849 **Patrick Kennedy**
B. 1821–D. DEC. 20, 1888   B. 1823–D. NOV. 22, 1858

Mary L. Kennedy
B. AUG. 9, 1851–D. MAR. 7, 1926

M. JAN. 1, 1883

Lawrence M. Kane
B. NOV. 29, 1858
D. JULY 19, 1905

Joanna L. Kennedy
B. NOV. 27, 1852–D. FEB. 23, 1926

M. SEPT. 22, 1872

**Humphrey Charles
Mahoney**
B. DEC. 12, 1847
D. AUG. 25, 1928

John Kennedy
B. JAN. 4, 1854
D. SEPT. 24, 1855

**Rose Elizabeth
Fitzgerald** M. OCT. 7, 1914 **Joseph Patrick Kennedy**
B. JULY 22, 1890 – D. JAN. 22, 1995   B. SEPT. 6, 1888
                                                              D. NOV. 16, 1969

**Joseph Patrick
Kennedy Jr.**
B. JULY 25, 1915
D. AUG. 12, 1944

**Rose Marie
(Rosemary)
Kennedy**
B. SEPT. 13, 1918

**Kathleen
Agnes
Kennedy**
B. FEB. 20, 1920
D. MAY 13, 1948

M. MAY 6, 1944

**William
John Robert
Cavendish**
B. DEC. 10, 1917
D. SEPT. 10, 1944

John Fitzgerald Kennedy
B. MAY 29, 1917
D. NOV. 22, 1963

M. SEPT. 12, 1953

Jacqueline Lee Bouvier
B. JULY 28, 1929
D. MAY 19, 1994

Lineage continues on following pages

The KENNEDY *Family*

Margaret M. Kennedy
B. JULY 18, 1855–D. APR. 2, 1929

M. FEB. 21, 1882

John Thomas Caulfield
B. JAN. 1861–D. JULY 12, 1937

Patrick Joseph Kennedy
B. JAN. 14, 1858
D. MAY 18, 1929

M. NOV. 23, 1887

Mary Augusta Hickey
B. DEC. 6, 1857
D. MAY 20, 1923

Francis Benedict Kennedy
B. MAR. 11, 1891–D. JUNE 14, 1892

Mary Loretta Kennedy
B. AUG. 6, 1892–D. NOV. 18, 1972

Margaret Louise Kennedy
B. OCT. 22, 1898–D. NOV. 14, 1974

Eunice Mary Kennedy
B. JULY 10, 1921

M. MAY 23, 1953

R. Sargent Shriver Jr.
B. NOV. 9, 1915

Robert Francis Kennedy
B. NOV. 20, 1925
D. JUNE 6, 1968

M. JUNE 17, 1950

Ethel Skakel
B. APR. 11, 1928

Edward Moore Kennedy
B. FEB. 22, 1932

M. NOV. 29, 1958–DIV. 1982

Virginia Joan Bennett
B. SEPT. 9, 1936

Patricia Kennedy
B. MAY 6, 1924

M. APR. 24, 1954

Peter Lawford
B. SEPT. 7, 1923
D. DEC. 24, 1984

Jean Ann Kennedy
B. FEB. 20, 1928

M. MAY 19, 1956

Stephen Edward Smith
B. SEPT. 24, 1927–D. AUG. 19, 1990

Lineages continue on following pages

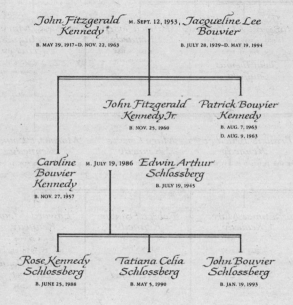

John Fitzgerald Kennedy*   M. SEPT. 12, 1953,   Jacqueline Lee Bouvier

B. MAY 29, 1917–D. NOV. 22, 1963   B. JULY 28, 1929–D. MAY 19, 1994

John Fitzgerald Kennedy Jr.

B. NOV. 25, 1960

Patrick Bouvier Kennedy

B. AUG. 7, 1963
D. AUG. 9, 1963

Caroline Bouvier Kennedy   M. JULY 19, 1986   Edwin Arthur Schlossberg

B. NOV. 27, 1957   B. JULY 19, 1945

Rose Kennedy Schlossberg

B. JUNE 25, 1988

Tatiana Celia Schlossberg

B. MAY 5, 1990

John Bouvier Schlossberg

B. JAN. 19, 1993

*Child of Joseph and Rose Kennedy

Eunice Mary Kennedy * M. MAY 23, 1953 R. Sargent Shriver Jr.
B. JULY 10, 1921   B. NOV. 9, 1915

Robert   Timothy M. MAY 31, 1986 Linda S.   Mark
Sargent   Perry   Potter   Kennedy
Shriver III   Shriver   B. JAN. 13, 1956 Shriver
B. APR. 28, 1954 B. AUG. 29, 1959   B. FEB. 17, 1964

                                                           M. JUNE 26, 1992

                                                           Jeannie
                                                           Ripps
                Sophia Rose   Samuel   B. NOV. 30, 1965
                Shriver   Kennedy
                B. JUNE 14, 1987 Potter Shriver
                                  B. JULY 13, 1992

                Timothy Potter   Kathleen
                Shriver Jr.   Potter Shriver
                B. DEC. 8, 1988   B. MAR. 9, 1994

Maria Owings M. APR. 26, 1986 Arnold Schwarzenegger
Shriver   B. JULY 30, 1947
B. NOV. 6, 1955

Katherine   Christina   Patrick
Eunice   Maria   Arnold
Schwarzenegger   Aurelia   Schwarzenegger
B. MAY 5, 1990   Schwarzenegger   B. SEPT. 18, 1993
                  B. JULY 23, 1991

                Alina Mojica M. JULY 2, 1993 Anthony Paul
                B. JAN. 5, 1965   Kennedy
(Child from Mojica's   Shriver
   previous   B. JULY 20, 1965
   marriage)
Jorge Edward Nuñez   Francesca Maria Shriver
B. SEPT. 4, 1988   B. DEC. 13, 1994

                Eunice Julia Shriver
                B. JAN. 4, 1994

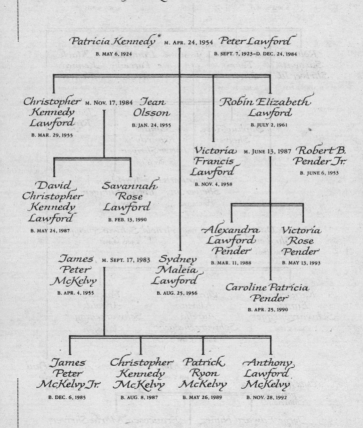

Patricia Kennedy* M. APR. 24, 1954 Peter Lawford
B. MAY 6, 1924   B. SEPT. 7, 1923–D. DEC. 24, 1984

Christopher Kennedy Lawford M. NOV. 17, 1984 Jean Olsson
B. MAR. 29, 1955   B. JAN. 24, 1955

Robin Elizabeth Lawford
B. JULY 2, 1961

Victoria Francis Lawford M. JUNE 13, 1987 Robert B. Pender Jr.
B. NOV. 4, 1958   B. JUNE 6, 1953

David Christopher Kennedy Lawford
B. MAY 24, 1987

Savannah Rose Lawford
B. FEB. 13, 1990

Alexandra Lawford Pender
B. MAR. 11, 1988

Victoria Rose Pender
B. MAY 13, 1993

James Peter McKelvy M. SEPT. 17, 1983 Sydney Maleia Lawford
B. APR. 4, 1955   B. AUG. 25, 1956

Caroline Patricia Pender
B. APR. 25, 1990

James Peter McKelvy Jr.
B. DEC. 6, 1985

Christopher Kennedy McKelvy
B. AUG. 8, 1987

Patrick Ryon McKelvy
B. MAY 26, 1989

Anthony Lawford McKelvy
B. NOV. 28, 1992

Jean Ann Kennedy *   M. MAY 19, 1956   Stephen Edward Smith

B. FEB. 20, 1928

B. SEPT. 24, 1927
D. AUG. 19, 1990

Stephen Edward Smith, Jr.

B. JUNE 28, 1957

Amanda Mary Smith

B. APR. 30, 1967

William Kennedy Smith

B. SEPT. 4, 1960

Kym Maria Smith

B. NOV. 29, 1972

*Child of Joseph and Rose Kennedy

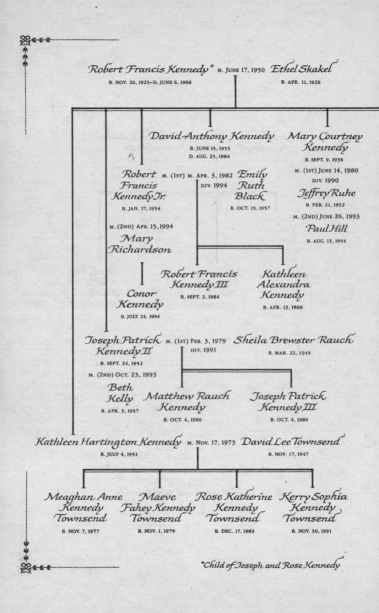

Robert Francis Kennedy* M. JUNE 17, 1950 **Ethel Skakel**
B. NOV. 20, 1925–D. JUNE 6, 1968   B. APR. 11, 1928

David Anthony Kennedy
B. JUNE 15, 1955
D. AUG. 25, 1984

Mary Courtney Kennedy
B. SEPT. 9, 1956
M. (1ST) JUNE 14, 1980
DIV. 1990
Jeffrey Ruhe
B. FEB. 21, 1952
M. (2ND) JUNE 26, 1993
Paul Hill
B. AUG. 13, 1954

Robert Francis Kennedy Jr. M. (1ST) APR. 3, 1982 / DIV. 1994 **Emily Ruth Black**
B. JAN. 17, 1954   B. OCT. 15, 1957

M. (2ND) APR. 15, 1994
Mary Richardson

Conor Kennedy
B. JULY 24, 1994

Robert Francis Kennedy III
B. SEPT. 2, 1984

Kathleen Alexandra Kennedy
B. APR. 13, 1988

Joseph Patrick Kennedy II M. (1ST) FEB. 3, 1979 / DIV. 1991 **Sheila Brewster Rauch**
B. SEPT. 24, 1952   B. MAR. 22, 1949

M. (2ND) OCT. 23, 1993
Beth Kelly
B. APR. 3, 1957

Matthew Rauch Kennedy
B. OCT. 4, 1980

Joseph Patrick Kennedy III
B. OCT. 4, 1980

Kathleen Hartington Kennedy M. NOV. 17, 1973 **David Lee Townsend**
B. JULY 4, 1951   B. NOV. 17, 1947

Meaghan Anne Kennedy Townsend
B. NOV. 7, 1977

Maeve Fahey Kennedy Townsend
B. NOV. 1, 1979

Rose Katherine Kennedy Townsend
B. DEC. 17, 1983

Kerry Sophia Kennedy Townsend
B. NOV. 30, 1991

*Child of Joseph and Rose Kennedy

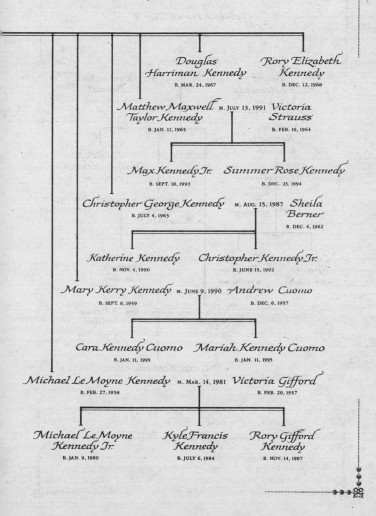

GENERATIONS IV – VI

Douglas
Harriman Kennedy
B. MAR. 24, 1967

Rory Elizabeth
Kennedy
B. DEC. 12, 1968

Matthew Maxwell
Taylor Kennedy
B. JAN. 11, 1965

M. JULY 13, 1991

Victoria
Strauss
B. FEB. 10, 1964

Max Kennedy Jr.
B. SEPT. 18, 1993

Summer Rose Kennedy
B. DEC. 23, 1994

Christopher George Kennedy
B. JULY 4, 1963

M. AUG. 15, 1987

Sheila
Berner
B. DEC. 4, 1962

Katherine Kennedy
B. NOV. 4, 1990

Christopher Kennedy Jr.
B. JUNE 15, 1992

Mary Kerry Kennedy
B. SEPT. 8, 1959

M. JUNE 9, 1990

Andrew Cuomo
B. DEC. 6, 1957

Cara Kennedy Cuomo
B. JAN. 11, 1995

Mariah Kennedy Cuomo
B. JAN. 11, 1995

Michael Le Moyne Kennedy
B. FEB. 27, 1958

M. MAR. 14, 1981

Victoria Gifford
B. FEB. 20, 1957

Michael Le Moyne
Kennedy Jr.
B. JAN. 9, 1980

Kyle Francis
Kennedy
B. JULY 6, 1984

Rory Gifford
Kennedy
B. NOV. 14, 1987

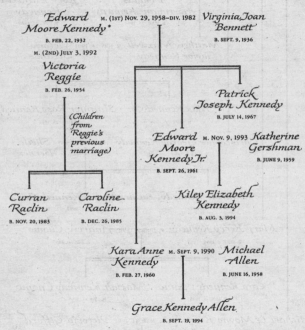

Edward Moore Kennedy* M. (1ST) NOV. 29, 1958–DIV. 1982 Virginia Joan Bennett

B. FEB. 22, 1932

B. SEPT. 9, 1936

M. (2ND) JULY 3, 1992

Victoria Reggie

B. FEB. 26, 1954

Patrick Joseph Kennedy

B. JULY 14, 1967

(Children from Reggie's previous marriage)

Edward Moore Kennedy Jr. M. NOV. 9, 1993 Katherine Gershman

B. SEPT. 26, 1961

B. JUNE 9, 1959

Curran Raclin

B. NOV. 20, 1983

Caroline Raclin

B. DEC. 26, 1985

Kiley Elizabeth Kennedy

B. AUG. 3, 1994

Kara Anne Kennedy M. SEPT. 9, 1990 Michael Allen

B. FEB. 27, 1960

B. JUNE 16, 1958

Grace Kennedy Allen

B. SEPT. 19, 1994

*Child of Joseph and Rose Kennedy

1

"When Irish Eyes Are Smiling"

*T*he tiny, gnarled figure of Rose Fitzgerald Kennedy sat in a wheelchair behind a shuttered window looking down on the 370 people gathered below to celebrate her one hundredth birthday in July of 1990. Rose had rarely spoken since her stroke in April of 1984, but on Sunday evenings when her only surviving son, Senator Edward Moore "Ted" Kennedy, and his friends sang old Irish songs in the living room, her eyes glowed with emotion, and her face lit up with recognition.

This afternoon Rose stared down on that spacious lawn behind her sprawling clapboard house in Hyannis Port on Cape Cod. Here her children had once fought fierce touch football games: Joe Jr., the eldest, running fleet-footed out for passes, scrawny John F. "Jack" tossing the ball high up into the summer sky, and Robert F. "Bobby" with his fierce intensity, blocking foes into momentary oblivion. Rose's older daughters had joined in too. Kathleen, an ebullient spirit, adored her brothers, and she asked no quarter for her sex or temperament. Eunice, lank and gawky in appearance, played a boy's game too, as tough in her competitiveness as any of them. Of the older children, only Rosemary did not take full part, pretty Rosemary who often watched her siblings in their summer games. And through it all Rose's husband, Joseph P. Kennedy Sr., sat in his bailiwick watching everything.

Rose had memories too of the years when Jack had been in the White House, and on weekends the presidential helicopter had landed on the lawn, her son striding briskly up to the house, his hair blowing in the propeller backlash, as the whole family stood there waiting for him. They had often been there then on fine summer days, Jacqueline "Jackie," the elegant first lady; Eunice and her husband R. Sargent Shriver Jr., the

1

head of the Peace Corps; Patricia "Pat" and her movie-star
husband Peter Lawford; Bobby, the attorney general, standing
beside his wife, Ethel; Jean alongside Stephen Smith, her husband; Ted, Rose's youngest, with his beautiful young wife,
Joan; and a whole brood of grandchildren.

Rose had lived her life for family and faith. She had become
one of the most revered of women, matriarch of a family
unique in American history. Her husband, the grandson of Irish
immigrants, had been ambassador to Great Britain, and one of
the wealthiest men in America. One of her sons had become
president, and three of her sons senators. Her daughters had
married the celebrated and the talented, her sons had all married women of what Rose considered worthy lineage and character, and most of the Kennedys had left bold marks on the
world.

On that grassy plain at Hyannis Port had walked other feet
though, feet ponderous with the burden of their duty: priests
with tragic messages and all the condolences of faith; a son
and daughter bearing tidings of such heaviness that they stumbled with their burdens; retainers with whispered stories so
dark and inexplicable that they challenged everything Rose believed her family stood for. Rose heard their words and took
solace in her faith but she wondered sometimes whether the
Kennedys had dared too much, dreamed dreams beyond the
pale of human ambition. "You see, we had a monopoly," Rose
reflected. "We had money, talent, relationships with one another, we boasted of good looks. We had so much that these
things just can't keep on." But that was the kind of thought
that she brushed aside, like a strand of misplaced hair, and
turned her head forward again.

In the pink-and-white-striped tent, the crowd watched a
twenty-minute film of Rose's life. Light poured in on this brilliantly sunny day, and the images on the screen appeared
washed out, like faded photographs, tintypes of a distant, half-
forgotten era. Here were photos of Boston's North End where
Rose had been born on July 22, 1890; photos of her father, the
irascible, irrepressible John "Honey Fitz" Fitzgerald; photos of
a teenaged Rose, her face in the full blush of youthful promise,
and Rose as a young mother with some of her nine children.

Rose had grown up in a culture where a woman's home was
her only habitation. Her life had encompassed the entire modern epoch in America, from an age when women had hardly

begun to agitate for the vote to an era when one of her twenty-eight surviving grandchildren, Kathleen Kennedy Townsend, had run for Congress against another woman. "Your sons have gone into politics, but you wouldn't particularly urge your daughters to go into politics?" David Frost asked, in an interview clip from the film. "Well I think their first duty is to their family," Rose said, "and I think it would be very difficult to do both."

At the end of the film an old recording of "When Irish Eyes Are Smiling" played, and a series of pictures of a perpetually smiling Rose passed across the screen. Here she was as a smiling young girl sailing to Europe. Here she was smiling with her father. Here she was smiling with Kathleen and Rosemary as they prepared to make their debuts before the King and Queen of England. Here she was a widow smiling with Ted. And always she was smiling. As the images passed quickly by, a shudder of terrible poignancy passed through the audience, and many cried or choked back emotion.

There were pictures that had never been developed, scenes that had not been shot. Rose had been raised never to look down or back, a discipline that she had imparted on her daughters and sons as well. She had called her autobiography *Times to Remember*, and that is what history was to her, a patchwork of splendid moments in brilliant color, tragedies of funereal black, and richly colored vignettes of family and home. Her history was only a cloak, beneath which lay the complex, variegated body of her life and the lives of all the Kennedy women. This was the history that Rose denied, ignored, forgot, or never knew, a history that began before her birth and would continue in the lives of her granddaughters after she died. It was women's history that had been lost not simply for her but in some measure for all women.

This history had begun in Ireland with the birth of the first Kennedy woman, Bridget Murphy. Bridget was in many respects the founder of the family, a woman forgotten by history and by the family, a woman whose life and legacy contained the fertile seeds of a dynasty. It is here that the saga of the Kennedys truly begins.

2

Bridget's Journey

Oh brave, brave Irish girls—
We well may call you brave!—
Sure the least of your perils
Is the stormy ocean wave.

The Irish Peasant Girl
by Charles Joseph Kickham

In the town of Wexford, Bridget Murphy trod cobblestone streets that had known the footfalls of half a dozen races over two thousand years. Alongside the medieval bullring, round old women in round old shawls sat selling fish out of reed baskets much as fishmongers had done for centuries. On fair days farmers rode their carts into town through what remained of the town walls, down streets so narrow that they could reach out and touch the buildings. They rarely brought their wives. The farmers stood in circles talking of politics and crops, wearing the same black wool suits they wore at work in the fields.

Bridget was born in 1821 in Wexford County on the southeast coast of Ireland. For centuries England had ruled over Ireland, a hegemony measured out in recrimination, mutual hostility, distrust, and disdain. She doubtless grew up hearing tales of the English hold over her fair and melancholy land, especially the living memories of the great revolt of 1798. In that year as many as thirty thousand men of Wexford marched in the motley rebel army, and the Orangemen were not far wrong in branding all Wexford a rebel breed. When the Loyalist troops marched into Wexford, the bridge over the Stanley River was red from the blood of Protestants butchered the day before. Here the rebel leaders were hanged, their heads severed and set upon pikes above the courthouse. Many of the captured rebels were sent to penal colonies in New South Wales, or sold

4

to the King of Prussia as slaves. Wexford was left a sullen county in a sullen land.

Wexford was a county of fertile soil and varied crops. In the summer the winds blew gently across the hills, rippling across fields of ripening wheat and barley, and pastures full of cattle. It rained half the days of the year, and the land was a palette of greens, from dark rich hues to dainty pastel shades, the landscape a verdant quilt, the green patches bordered by rows of trees or stone fences. With its varied crops, Wexford did not suffer from the great potato famine that decimated Ireland between 1845 and 1849. In all, during the famine probably about a million people died, out of a population of about eight million, and another million and a half left Ireland for good.

Disease was carried on the wings of the famine, and that blight did not pass Wexford by. Wrote one Wexford shopkeeper: "the young and old are dying as fast as they can bury them." Another plague stalked Wexford and all Ireland, a plague of evictions carried out by the British overlords and their minions. One local priest noted that "though we are . . . partially exempt from the calamitous suffering of the West of Ireland, we every day behold the cottages of the Poor levelled in the ground, & their inmates sent adrift on the World."

If the dispossessed had no money to emigrate, they frequently ended up in poorhouses, grim shelters that were often houses of death. At the beginning of 1849, there were 863 paupers in the Wexford Union Workhouse, the large majority women and children, twelve residents buried on New Year's Day alone.

In the Wexford court session that same month of January 1849, almost half the convicted felons were women. These women had committed nonviolent crimes: thefts of potatoes, sheep, meal, a bridle, a watch. One woman received three months in prison with solitary confinement one week each month for stealing potatoes. Another woman who had committed the "larceny of a goose" was sentenced to be transported to Australia for seven years.

Although Bridget Murphy's name does not appear in any of the parish and government records, in many respects the women of Ireland shared a common biography. At twenty-seven, Bridget was still single, and so were a third of the women her age in Ireland and half of the men, and they lived as apart from one another as if they were not only different sexes but different species. When they went to church, the men usually went with the men, the women with the women. On their rare journeys together to fairs, funerals, or a neighbor's house, the wife walked behind her husband. In public, married couples talked about each other in the third person, "herself" and "himself," with courtly formality and distance. The priests had come from the people, from the peasants, and they preached lessons as much from the common catechism of their lives as from the Bible. Love in the main was devilish, they said, a subtle and odious poison, designed to set young souls in the way of eternal perdition.

Few partook of that sweet poison. Young men and women had few dalliances. No matter how old they were, unmarried women were still called "girls" and unmarried men "boys." Ireland was full of "boys" in their forties and fifties. The males were the center of all things, and the boys worked the fields at their fathers' beck and call. When a father finally retired, he chose one son to inherit the lands, effectively disinheriting his other sons. And then the anointed son chose a bride with a dowry.

For the bride it was a harsh life serving her new husband and her in-laws, nurturing all the children who were sure to come, performing her daily routine. During planting season she was out in the fields with her husband. When it came time to make hay, she alone pitched and raked and built haystacks. Then she went back to the house and milked the cow, breathed life into the fire, and set potatoes cooking. No matter how tired she was, her husband wouldn't think of helping, for he was a man and that was all a woman's work. Her chores were so arduous that one observer in the early nineteenth century declared that "females in Ireland are treated more like beasts of burden than rational beings."

That burdensome life was a maiden's dream, but Bridget had no dowry, and without a dowry she would never find a husband. If she stayed in her native land, she would be a girl forever. If she had had some genteel education, she might have become a nun, or lived out her days with married brothers and their wives, an extra hand in the house. But she was only semi-literate, and her pathway led to the mills of Manchester and Lancashire, or the servant quarters of a London home. There was one other road open to Bridget, and that was to take the long, dangerous journey to America.

* * *

Bridget sailed to America on the *Washington Irving*, on March 20, 1849, from Liverpool, England. The boat was full of families, couples, single men, and forty-nine single women of Bridget's generation. Unlike the other emigrant nations of Europe where the men generally set off for America, slightly more than half the Irish emigrants were women, many of them single adults like Bridget. These women had heard that in America there was good work for them in the homes of the well-to-do. When Captain Daniel Pupton had them note their professions in the passenger registry, every woman on board, including one eleven-year-old girl, wrote the same word: "servant."

When the winds blew with untamed fury and the seas grasped the ship as if to toss it into a dark grave, the single women huddled at one end of the dark steerage of the *Washington Irving*. The women were placed there, buffered from the single men by the families and couples in the middle of the hold, each passenger with only about two square feet of space. It wasn't the Irish bachelors the women feared most, but the sailors. The *Washington Irving* was a Boston ship, but most American sailors wanted nothing of immigrant passages across the Atlantic. These ships were crewed by a motley lot, a few British tars and Swedish sailors, Kanakas from the South Seas, lascars from India, and all the scum of the ports—criminals, drunkards, and thieves. The captain and his first mate worked these packet rats at a devilish pace, but even the work, the rum, and the beatings could not always keep them from the women in steerage.

Most of the women on these ships guarded their chastity with all their strength and self-possession. A few submitted for as little as a few pieces of molasses to put on their oatmeal. Suddenly, the old values and beliefs seemed a burdensome cargo others were throwing overboard.

Bridget was on this endless ocean now, lost in this world of which she knew nothing. The Irish were an island people who loved the land, not the ocean beyond. When storms tossed the ship, by most accounts the Irish passengers quaked in terror and prayed for God's mercy. Death stalked the *Washington Irving*, as it stalked all the emigrant ships. "Ship fever" might suddenly strike, probably a form of typhus, moving through the ship like death's hand. Or smallpox. Or cholera. Or dysentery, almost endemic on the ships. About 6 percent of the passengers died at sea, their bodies dumped into the sea without benefit of priestly prayer or blessing.

One morning on deck, Bridget met a farmer from the county of Wexford. The young man said his name was Patrick Kennedy, and he came from Dunganstown, five miles from New Ross, where his family farmed eighty acres of leased land and lived in the same type of whitewashed, thatched-roof house as their neighbors. Patrick bore his father's name, but it was his older brother, John, who would inherit the farm. Twenty-six-year-old Patrick could have stayed in New Ross and leased his own land, the way his younger brother James had done. He had decided to leave, driven westward not simply by hunger and need, but by his desire for a new and better life.

In Wexford, Bridget would never have talked to a man the way she talked to Patrick Kennedy. Here on the ship there was no village priest who watched the country lanes and the bushes for couples who had gone off together. There was no mother and father to pull her away from any man who might approach her.

Irish women were not courted with sweet poems and song, and hardly knew the men they married. On the *Washington Irving*, Bridget spent more time with Patrick than she would have with her betrothed in Wexford. Patrick was as good a match as Bridget was likely to make. He was tall and handsome, with strong blue eyes and reddish-brown hair. He could read and write, whereas she could only read. If she had Patrick, she would not face the New World so alone. She was two years older and had a strength that might help them grasp hold in America.

On the fourteenth of April, as the ship neared the coast of New England, a forty-year-old passenger gave birth to a child. Three days later another forty-year-old woman died, her body cast off into the Atlantic. Then, suddenly, the coastline of New England appeared. It was green, though not as green as Ireland, and as the boat sailed along the shoreline, the woodlands seemed to go on forever.

From the deck of the *Washington Irving*, Bridget and Patrick could see the city of Boston, the yellow dome of the State House and the obelisk of the Bunker Hill Monument seeming to rise out of the very sea. Old Boston had made its fortune through the sea. This second greatest of American ports was set on a narrow peninsula that reached out to greet the Atlantic

Ocean, its harbor shielded against New England's winter winds and summer squalls. Wharfs lined the shoreline proper, buildings of Quincy granite or brick, warehouses, counting rooms, and auction halls, the rich odors of tar, hemp, and spice permeating the air.

Captain Pupton had sailed the ship across the Atlantic in good time, a month and a day. On April 21, 1849, he guided the ship past the crowded wharfs. Since Boston had no room on its docks for all the immigrant ships, the captain sailed the *Washington Irving* across the harbor. A mile from Boston proper, at the confluence of the Charles and Mystic rivers, stood Noddle Island or East Boston, the newest part of the city, its wharfs not yet bleached gray.

There to meet Bridget stood her cousin, Patrick Barron. He was earning skilled-worker's wages as a "cooper" crafting barrels from wood and staves. Patrick Barron was a success by Irish immigrant standards, but that did not mean he lived in anything but a tiny tenement apartment in East Boston. There was always room for kinfolk, though, some space on a mattress on the floor. There was room, too, almost certainly, for Bridget's new friend, Patrick Kennedy. That Irish sense of family, of kinship, had survived the travails of the journey to America. Bridget could depend on Patrick Barron, as one day others would depend on her.

As she walked up the dusty street from the wharf, Bridget was in a land where practically the only thing familiar was the language. She was from a country where history was measured in centuries, in great rare events, memorialized in song and story, a rural land of pastoral landscapes. A quarter century ago there had been nothing but pastureland on Noddle Island. Now wherever Bridget looked, she saw buildings and wharfs, and heard the sound of anvils, steam whistles, and the shouts of laborers. East Boston was becoming an industrial center, a place of cheap homes for the middle class, and quarters for the poor and the workers in the once swampy low areas, squeezed in around the wharfs, steelworks, fish warehouses, and ferry landing like caulking between bricks.

These great enterprises were built on Yankee capital, and increasingly on Irish backs, men who worked cheaper than New Hampshire farm boys and the sons of Massachusetts shopkeepers. By 1850 among the 8,552 unskilled laborers in the city, 7,007 were Irish. These Irish workers were cheap, interchangeable, and to some New England industrialists they had an added virtue: there were too many of them.

Week after week the *Boston Pilot*, the leading Irish Catholic newspaper, implored the immigrants to leave Boston. The *Pilot* had only one solution to offer, and it fairly screamed its answer: *"don't remain on the seaboard; but go at once into the interior of the country."*

There was no market for parlor maids, cooks, and seamstresses on the frontier, and for a single Irish woman, the lure of the Western land was no lure at all. Since Bridget had relatives in East Boston, Patrick had friends to help him as well. Bridget herself gave Patrick other reasons to stay in Boston, forever to link the name Kennedy with the city.

On September 26, 1849, five months after their arrival in America, Bridget and Patrick took the two-penny ferry ride to Boston. For the newly arrived immigrants a trip to Boston was always a special occasion, but today went far beyond that. Bridget and Patrick were getting married. They had no wedding party, none but Bridget's cousin, Patrick, to accompany them, along with another friend, Ann McGowan. The two couples walked from the ferry dock through the North End, the area where most Irish immigrants in Boston lived. However bleak the streets of East Boston appeared, the North End was far worse, and Bridget and Patrick could consider themselves fortunate to be living across the bay.

On Franklin Street above the squalor and the crowded streets rose the spires of the Cathedral of the Holy Cross. The priest who married them, Father John J. Williams, had been born in Boston in 1820 when there were only about 3,500 Catholics in the entire diocese. In recent years, hordes of Irish had begun to descend on the pristine city, over 15,000 in 1846; 22,250 the next year, 25,000 in 1848; and 34,000 in this year of 1849.

At twenty-eight, Bridget was old for an American-born bride, but not for Irish women, who married later than immigrants of other nationalities, and often didn't marry at all. A single woman had a chance here in America. A married woman's life was different. If she did not become a widow, she often ended up alone anyway, with a husband who deserted her. The newspapers were full of poignant advertisements from wives looking for husbands who had left them. Some of these men had died working the canals and the railroads, and some had fallen into the abyss of alcoholism, but others simply fled when they couldn't provide enough. An unskilled laborer earned between a dollar and a dollar and a quarter a day, not enough to support a family of four, even at the diminished standards of the Irish immigrants. "A married man has a bad chance here," noted one priest. "His first embarrassments with a wife and children are almost insurmountable."

Bridget was doubly blessed, for she had a new husband with a decent job. Patrick had seen his Irish brethren scuffling in the employment line, fighting to work fourteen hours a day. Thanks probably to Patrick Barron, he found steady work as a cooper.

Bridget stayed home in the tiny apartment the newlyweds rented. Irish women might emigrate by themselves and work in kitchens and parlors and factories. Yet the moment they married, the home was their one and only preserve. Nearly two years after her marriage, on August 9, 1851, Bridget gave birth to her first child. Almost a fourth of babies born to Irish immigrants died before they were a year old, and Bridget and Patrick did not want to wait to have Mary baptized in the faith, so they took the infant the day afterwards to St. Nicholas to be baptized. When Joanna, their second child, was born on November 27, 1852, they again brought the new baby to St. Nicholas for her baptism. Their son, John, was born a year and a month later, on January 4, 1854. They wrapped the infant against the winter cold and, as they had done with their daughters, carried him to the church sanctuary to be baptized.

For an Irish-American family a son was the measure of all things. John, however, lived only a year and eight months, dying on September 24, 1855, of a disease listed as cholera infantum, a scourge of the poor. By then Bridget had a new daughter, Margaret, also baptized at St. Nicholas.

In the winter months Patrick worked from dawn to dark, and if he was like many of his peers, he topped off his day with an hour or so among his friends at his favorite saloon. The burden of raising the children fell on Bridget, and a heavy burden it was.

In Ireland a woman's knowledge was passed down from generation to generation. Bridget's mother knew how best to protect herself and her children, as had her mother before. Here in East Boston Bridget faced dangers and uncertainties that were almost unthinkable in Wexford County. In Ireland, she had not had to worry about paying the weekly rent, or buying bread and meat at the local store. These were bewildering chores for some women, the weekly pay seeming to disappear in the air of East Boston. Everywhere Bridget looked, she saw dangers or worse yet the dangers found her. The wallpaper in the immigrant tenements often was "arsenical." The tiny stores where Bridget shopped had stain removers and powders for killing vermin. These were strong poisons that had to be handled with utmost care by women who often could not read the labels. The shopkeepers sold milk ladled out from open barrels, often either watered down or mixed with yesterday's leftovers. The copper pots the peddlers sold were perfect for cooking pickles or sauerkraut. However, food set too long in one of these pots picked up a poisonous compound from the metal that could kill one's family.

Groups of ruffians posed a threat to Bridget's children. Her daughters faced another unspeakable danger of urban life, from well-dressed men inviting little girls to enter carriages "to take a nice ride to Chelsea, or anywhere else they wanted to go."

These were all terrible dangers that in an instant might change her family's life, and beyond that she had the burden of her marriage. Irish-American women were taught in marital guides, religious magazines, and by their priests that the responsibility for a marriage rested primarily on the wife's shoulders. If she failed—if her husband ended up a drunk, her children wastrels—her church and her culture told her that it was her fault. The Catholic church pointed a finger of blame that would last through eternity. "Who among the children of men requires so much wisdom as the mother of a family!" asked the *Boston Pilot*. "She, *the mother*, is to be the pilot for the most important part of the voyage, and if she fails to guide it aright, dreadful will be the wreck when it dashes over the precipice of time into the abyss of eternity . . . and [through] eternity will echo and reecho the dreadful tale of a child lost through its mother's neglect!"

Bridget and Patrick and their growing family moved from house to house, apartment to apartment, all within the same few blocks, barely maintaining their modest standard of living. The Kennedy household included not only Bridget, Patrick, and their three daughters but an eighteen-year-old woman, Mary Roach, and a six-year-old boy, Michael O'Brien. Irish immigrants often shared their homes with outsiders as well as with relatives. Bridget may have simply given an orphan waif a home and taken in a boarder to help pay the rent. In any case, she was truly the matron of her home, ruling a kingdom no bigger than the walls of the apartment. In that space she had more control over her world than Patrick did in the cooper's shop.

As a Catholic, Bridget knew that if God willed it, they would have many more children, and perhaps a son to replace the child they grieved over. Bridget was supposed to have sexual intercourse with Patrick not only to have more children but to display her feelings toward him and to calm her husband's lustful "concupiscence." In their cramped tenements, sex for most immigrants was furtive coupling in the depths of night. That was just as well, for as a Catholic marital guide explained, the act should be performed quickly "to let it have its full fling" so as "to lessen its keenness, destroy its power, and to render it disgusting."

Bridget was soon pregnant again. Whatever doubts she might have had about a fifth pregnancy ended on January 14, 1858, when she gave birth to a healthy baby boy to carry on the family name. Bridget and Patrick took the newborn to be baptized not to St. Nicholas as they had their other children but to the new mother church of East Boston, the Church of the Most Holy Redeemer. The Irish might work as maids, servants, ditchdiggers, and barkeepers, but they worshipped in the grandest church on the island. The stone structure had a spire that rose two hundred feet above East Boston. It rose up higher than the mills and the factories, higher than the tenements. On Sundays the two-thousand-pound bell tolled, and eighteen hundred worshippers filled the wooden pews, looking up at the chestnut woodwork, the stained-glass windows, the high altar, the statues of St. Anne, St. Joseph, and St. Joachim, and listening to the resonant tones of the great organ.

Since their son was not worthy to enter within the portals of God's home until he was baptized, Bridget and Patrick did not walk into the Gothic-style stone building on this winter's day. Instead, they knocked and waited with their two witnesses for the priest to prepare the sacrament. Father Patrick Healy readied the balm and oil, the salt and water, and walked to the door wearing a purple embroidered stole and white surplice.

For Bridget and Patrick this was a sublime day. At the doorway Father Healy asked Bridget and Patrick what name they had chosen for their son. The Irish passed on their names from generation to generation, the most visible sign of their kinship with the past. Patrick was proud of the name that he bore and his father bore before him and they named their son Patrick Joseph Kennedy. They nicknamed him "P.J." to distinguish the boy from his father.

In the late fall, as the winter winds fell upon the city, Patrick was stricken with tuberculosis. The disease, then known as consumption, was the plague of the cities, the most common cause of death, responsible for more than 20 percent of fatalities. Consumption was a double curse for it took away not primarily the very young and very old, but men and women in the prime of life, mothers and fathers. Tuberculosis was preeminently a disease of the slums, an infection passed on in the fetid quarters, the cramped living space, the dampness, and the chill. In 1858 of the 784 people in Boston who died of the disease, 408 were Irish immigrants. Consumption was not hereditary, but susceptibility to it may have been. Patrick's illness was the first sign of a propensity for illness in a family celebrated for vigor and energy.

Patrick was thirty-five years old. He had arrived in America only nine years earlier but it was said that the average Irish immigrant lived just fourteen years in America, dying at a rate possibly even higher than that suffered by their compatriots in rural Ireland.

The disease proceeded like a dark epic poem, slowly, solemnly, inexorably, the body withering away, the spirit lightening as if casting away the ballast of worldly woes. Patrick's heart beat rapidly, and his cheeks glowed pink, a caricature of health. As he grew thinner, his eyes gleamed brilliantly, and he had moments of lucidity, then sank into dullness.

As Patrick struggled with the disease, Bridget surely realized what his death might mean. East Boston was full of widows, and though the Irish revered them in song and word, that did not feed their children. Every day there were widows at the ferry crossing and around the biggest hotel, Maverick House, huddled there begging, one hand outstretched, the other grasping a child, a pathetic and desperate sight, their widow's black proof enough of their deprivation.

For nearly a decade Patrick had sweated and struggled, but Bridget knew that her dying husband had nothing to leave her except four children, the crucifix on the wall, several sticks of furniture, pots and pans, a few dollars, and his funeral bill.

On November 22, 1858, Patrick died.

Bridget called the priest and the mourners. They carried Patrick's body across the ferry to Boston, and then across the bridge to Cambridge where they buried him in the Catholic Cemetery next to his son. Bridget was almost destitute. When a man died in East Boston without insurance, his fellow workers usually passed the hat, going door to door, collecting pennies, nickels, dimes, and dollars for the bereaved widow. Whatever help Bridget received, these wooden tenements in East Boston knew enough deaths that her moment of attention in the neighborhood was brief.

As Bridget sought desperately for a way to maintain herself, she knew what would happen if she gave up her children to a foundling home. Ten-month-old P.J. would grow up a Protestant, for priests couldn't even visit state institutions until 1879. Parish priests told stories of "orphan trains" spiriting the children into the Protestant hinterland where they would grow up without knowledge of the True Faith. The church had begun developing a series of institutions to serve their own people, but the death rate in Catholic foundling homes was extraordinary. If Bridget's son survived, at between eight and ten years of age he probably would have been shipped westward to Catholic farmers who wrote the home asking for boys who were "physically and mentally sound," boys who would be met not with open arms but with an empty milk pail or a shovel and pointed to their duties. As for her three daughters, Bridget could have sent them to the St. Vincent Asylum, run by the pious Sisters of Charity. As long as the girls were devout and attended mass, the nuns were content that almost all of them become servants or factory workers.

Bridget would not give up her son or her daughters. She would have to go to work. Everywhere Bridget looked, she saw women's bodies that bore rude testimony to the harshness of a laboring life. Seamstresses younger than Bridget walked the streets wearing blue glasses to protect what was left of their eyesight from the strain of sewing hours on end. In the factories the chosen instrument for breaking threads was not scissors but a worker's own teeth, and the city was full of middle-aged women whose mouths were a jumble of broken or missing teeth. Many of their hands bore scars too, wounds suffered on a button machine, hands impaled on a plunging needle.

Bridget had one choice that made sense. She would have to go to work in the households of the Americans. She and her four children were living in a house in East Boston with seven other families. Her neighbors would help watch over seven-year-old Mary, six-year-old Joanna, three-year-old Margaret, and her two oldest daughters in turn would have to help with their baby brother.

The vast majority of the working Irish women of East Boston worked in Yankee homes for at least part of their lives. As early as 1850, Irish immigrants made up 70 percent of Boston's servants. The Bostonians considered them practically a servant race, a fact of such sensitivity and shame that later generations of Kennedys rarely talked of this aspect of Bridget's life. These Irish women filled jobs that the native-born American women did not want. By 1870 there was one domestic employee for every three and a half families in Boston, the highest ratio in any Northern city.

Thirty-seven-year-old Bridget was old to be joining the Irish maids, cooks, nannies, and laundresses. Bridget had been named after Saint Bridget, an Irish saint, the most popular woman's name in Erin. In Boston, the name had become synonymous with maid or servant. When the Bostonians talked of *their* "Bridget," or *their* "biddy," they meant their maid. Bridget had presumably long been aware of this; none of her three daughters was named after their mother, forever branding the child with a name that to Irish ears had become as much of an epithet as an appellation. Bridget's own family name, Murphy, was also a term of derision and humor; the Bostonians had nicknamed potatoes "murphies."

Many of these women arrived with the sod of Ireland still on their shoes, ignorant of the skills of housekeeping. The Bostonians all had stories of *their* Bridget and her often feckless attempts to accommodate herself to life in America. Those women who got on often spent their entire lives in one house and were often remembered with the same fondness as a favored dog or cat. "Lizzie resembled those family slaves whom one encounters in the Greek dramatics, or in Racine," wrote the Boston-bred historian Samuel Eliot Morison, "always faithful and loyal, always jealous for the family's reputation, pregnant with sound advice and old saws."

What their masters and mistresses rarely understood was

that many of their Irish servants were full of a deep and desperate loneliness. They lay awake at night full of unspeakable melancholy. During the day they might be serving dinner to "their" family or working in the kitchen with other servants, and loneliness would be on them like a dark cloak they could not cast aside.

Sometimes what began as loneliness ended as madness. The Irish immigrant woman suffered from an extraordinarily high incidence of mental illness. As late as 1908, when the Irish tide of immigration had receded, there were more Irish than any other nationality in mental hospitals, two thirds of them women.

Working in the Yankee houses Bridget saw the Bostonians as Patrick never had. When she and the other servant women returned to East Boston they brought with them knowledge that their husbands and fathers and brothers did not possess. They achieved an American civility that set them apart not only from the boatloads of new immigrants disgorged every week on the wharfs but from the males of their family. They came back to their tenements full of stories of life among the Bostonians. As they talked they set their table as they never had before and may have cradled tin cups in their hands as if they were crystal. They were new Americans before the men, naturalized not by paper but by behavior, ready to teach their children about a world of which their husbands and fathers knew almost nothing.

Bridget eventually quit working in Boston households and took a job in a notions store at 25 Border Street in East Boston. The store was only a block from the ferry to Boston that carried thousands back and forth each day from the city. The modest establishment was a natural place for the maids, cooks, seamstresses, and shop girls to stop and buy thread, cloth, a thimble, or maybe a bit of lace.

Bridget was eventually able to buy the tiny store, an extraordinary accomplishment for a semiliterate Irish woman. Her customers were primarily women. Indeed, if one walked in the more humble streets of East Boston, it often appeared to be a city of women and children. Among these immigrants, more Irish men than women left the city in search of work. Irish women outlived Irish men in America, and here walked widows, single women old and young, deserted wives, and mothers who watched over their brood while their husbands

worked. Here too, if a representative of the church happened to
be in the neighborhood, it was likely to be a nun, not a priest.
For even the Catholic church in America was an organization
largely of women. By the end of the century there were nearly
four times as many nuns as priests. The nuns had no place in
the pulpit but they ran the schools and the charities, and they
were more a part of the everyday life of the Irish than were the
priests.

A woman did not go to the tavern, which was a man's preserve, and shops like Bridget's became women's clubs. This
was especially so in Bridget's store, since not only did a
woman own it, but her three daughters helped her, as did her
son. Bridget expanded the business into a grocery and a variety
store. Grocers frequently sold more rye whiskey than bread
and Bridget may well have sold liquor as well.

Bridget purchased the three-story duplex that was both a
store and a home. That was yet another triumph. She had become a woman of property, so rare an achievement that the
deed called her "the widow Kennedy," explaining why a
woman had her own property. Hers was a modest business,
and by the exalted standard of Brahmin Boston, she was still
a poor Irish immigrant. Nonetheless, she had become one of
the most successful immigrant women in all of East Boston.
Indeed, she may have been the most successful Irish-American
businesswoman in all of Noddle Island. The story of how she
achieved that, what other sacrifices she made, what assistance
she had in her ascent have all been lost to history, unworthy of
recollection even in the oral history of the Kennedy family.

Bridget took in a homeless youth, Nick Flynn, and he became
the brother P.J. had never known. As the first Kennedy woman
in America, Bridget had two personality traits that would become almost a family birthmark. She had what appeared to her
customers to be a generous heart. But she was also a crafty acquisitive woman who had climbed out of nearly indigent widowhood by selling thread and needles, bread and milk,
measuring out her ascent in dimes, nickels, and pennies, the
vast majority of her customers being women like herself.

Bridget kept P.J. away from bad influences by sending him
to the Sacred Heart Parochial School and keeping him near her
at the store. She had only enough money to send one of her
children to the private school, and P.J. was her unquestioned

choice. Her own life showed what a woman could accomplish, but P.J. was a boy, and all her hopes and aspirations rested on him and his future.

In immigrant homes, daughters heard the refrain "get up to let your brother sit down." For the Kennedys as for most Irish-American families of this generation, nurturing flowed primarily in one direction, from the female to the male. P.J.'s sisters acted like mothers to their little brother. His success was supposedly their success. "Look at that boy, whose sisters have made home happy," wrote the *Pilot*, "who have been his companions, his playmates and friends—and who count upon his return from school . . . and are always waiting round him with offices of love . . . Look at such a one in the progress of life, at college, in the world, and see the difference between him, and the boy who has no sister's love to cheer him . . . who has no one, if he goes wrong, who will forgive, and lead him back again."

Bridget's daughters considered it a natural part of life that their little brother should receive automatic precedence over them and their futures. These were common beliefs in the Irish-American and other families of their time. These ideas became profoundly ingrained in the Kennedy family, to be passed on to the next generation and beyond, a fundamental part of the inheritance.

When they were old enough, Bridget's two oldest daughters went to work. Mary had skills as a skirt maker, and that became her trade. Joanna ended up in a jute mill. The work was so arduous in these East Boston mills that one writer argued that "a high class locality ought to send out invitations for a plague about as quickly as a cotton mill."

This first generation of Irish-American working-class women was brought up to be servants: servants of God, servants of their brothers, servants of their husbands, servants of their employers. This upbringing was codified in the *Guide for Catholic Young Women Especially for Those Who Earn Their Own Living*, a popular handbook by Rev. George Deshon first published in 1868, reprinted thirty times in the next thirty years. For Irish maidens relegated to the scullery, to the loom, and to the shop, the priest had words of hope. "If you are under the most disagreeable and hardest foreman in the factory, or have the crossest old woman for a mistress that ever lived, or ever so hard work to do, or low wages, or poor fare, and no thanks, I don't care," the priest asserted. "I am determined to make you own up that it is all first-rate, and could not be better. . . . When the work comes hard, and you are tired out standing all day at the loom or running your sewing-machine, or scrubbing the floors, or washing the clothes or the dishes, think, 'I am doing all this for my Lord Jesus Christ.' "

Irish-American women were taught to "minister to the happiness of her husband" and succor him in "moments of professional weariness" never challenging his views. Father Deshon entitled one of his chapters "Advantages of a Life of Humiliation and Subjection," and that was his ideal of a young Christian woman's life.

That young Irish women read or heard such advice did not mean that the words were necessarily always believed, or what was believed was necessarily acted upon. However, these immigrant women were lectured to so often and in so many different places, from the pulpit to the parlor, that even if they discarded much of what they read and heard, they could not discard it all, and bits and pieces of it stuck, leaving many of them full of guilt and self-doubt, mercilessly blaming themselves for failures in life.

P.J. attended the Lyman Public School in East Boston, and then left school to go to work as a stevedore on the docks. He was "Pat's boy" to the older men, honoring his father's memory. His father had died when he was ten months old, and he was in truth not Pat's boy at all. He was Bridget's boy, his mother's boy. He was his sisters' boy. P.J. was a woman's boy, brought up by strong women who used their strength to push him ahead. If he looked to his boss like another blue-eyed, fair-skinned paddy, he was a breed apart from the men with whom he worked. He did not drink, and that alone made him a strange Irishman to the stevedores who drank away their evenings in the saloons. He had learned many things from his mother, and if temperance was one, another was not to put on airs, not to act better than his fellow man. He had learned that lesson well. Though he drank no liquor, he was not condemned as a thin-blooded, temperance-minded man. He had acquired a certain shrewdness at his mother's knee, the shrewdness that one masked, acting no better and no worse than anyone else.

For a decade or more Bridget had managed her shop and built it up. She knew about as much about her business as she could know. She wanted now to help her only son. For a man with modest capital a tavern was the most certain way to make money, as long as he didn't drink up his profits or pass them out to his friends. The tavern was an Irishman's preserve, and Bridget could hardly hope to own one herself. She had doubtless seen the wages of alcoholism in the widows and deserted wives who entered her store, and she had heard the saloon keeper condemned from the pulpit and the street. To have a son running a tavern, then, was to risk rebuke and shame from part of the Irish community. But Bridget herself may well have sold liquor at one time or another, and she was a woman with deep native shrewdness.

When one saloon was repossessed, P.J. was there to bid on it. All these years Bridget had saved. She helped finance the tavern her son opened at 2 Elbow Street in East Boston. This money, women's money since it was earned by Bridget largely from women customers, was the beginning of what one day would be called the Kennedy dynasty.

In 1882 when P.J. was twenty-four years old, the Boston City Directory listed him as a dealer in "lager beer." P.J. soon had a second tavern, down by the docks in East Boston. He bought into the Maverick House, the most famed of the island's hotels. And he started a wholesale liquor business in partnership with John J. Quigley, a water inspector.

When P.J. opened his first tavern, he read books while he poured drafts of beer, and kept running tabs. He listened, too, for now that he was successful in business he was thinking of entering politics. P.J. did not have that gift of blarney that was considered the birthright of Irishmen. He didn't like to speak in public at all. Nevertheless, he impressed the local politicians and in 1885 he won election to the state legislature from East Boston. In January 1886, at the age of twenty-eight, he took office.

Bridget was in her sixties, and she had already lived longer than most of the women in East Boston. Her son was out in the world now, one of the most successful young Irish-Americans in East Boston. All of her children were out of the house now. Of her daughters, Joanna had married first to Humphrey Mahoney, a clerk and machinist. Margaret had married best, to John Thomas Caulfield, a Boston restaurant owner. Mary had married last, to Lawrence Kane, an immigrant laborer.

Now it was P.J.'s turn. When P.J. decided to marry he did not look among the factory workers' daughters and the likes of young women who came into his mother's store. Instead, he courted Mary Augusta Hickey. A graduate of the Notre Dame Academy, Mary Augusta was deeply religious, genteel, and cultivated. To wed Mary Augusta was to gain entry into an assembly of the cultured and social elite of East Boston.

On November 23, 1887, Mary Augusta stood beside P.J. at the front of the wooden gothic Church of the Sacred Heart, its walls graced by several religious murals. Bridget watched as Mary Augusta and P.J. said their vows. Almost four decades earlier Bridget had walked with Patrick and two friends into the cathedral to be married. There had been no banks of flowers, no pews full of the notables of East Boston, no politicians paying their respects as there were this day. P.J. was marrying a woman like himself, American born, with no touch of the brogue in her voice, no hands reddened by the harsh marks of the factory or the kitchen. Mary Augusta would have her own maids and cooks and live a life that Bridget had only seen from a servant's perspective.

P.J. and Mary Augusta set up housekeeping in a frame house at 151 Meridian Street, only a few hundred yards from the apartment where Bridget and Patrick had lived soon after they arrived in Boston. Meridian Street was the proudest thoroughfare in all the town, with the best stores and shops on the island along half its distance, and substantial homes gracing the rest. Much of the street was paved and lined with sidewalks—no more plodding through mud and muck in the spring, dust in the summer heat.

Mary Augusta became pregnant almost immediately. On September 6, 1888, as she lay in her marital bed, the maids scurried back and forth from the upstairs bedroom, carrying hot water and sheets and blankets. The baby was a boy, a healthy, squalling boy.

Bridget also lay in bed now at the house on Border Street, unable to walk to her son's house to see her grandson. It had been thirty years since Bridget had taken P.J. in her arms and carried him to the cemetery in Cambridge to bury Patrick. They had been hard years, but Bridget had built a business, raised her son and daughters. She had lived to see all of them married. Her life was her son, and P.J. had gone far beyond even his mother's aspirations, carrying with him much that she had taught him. And now he had his own son, Joseph Patrick, who would one day raise his own family of Kennedys, carrying on the family name.

At the age of sixty-seven, on December 20, 1888, Bridget

Murphy Kennedy died. On the day of the funeral her body was carried from her home through streets lined with buildings and businesses that had been only empty lots when she first arrived in America. They carried her to the Church of the Holy Redeemer where her casket rested surrounded by flowers. For the first time in her life, she was the subject of an article in a newspaper. *The Argus-Advocate*'s obituary called her "a woman of many noble and charitable traits, and her loss will be deeply felt by the community."

Bridget had given up her space in the family plot in the Cambridge Cemetery so that two of her grandchildren could be buried there. Instead she was buried at Holy Cross Cemetery in Malden outside the city, far from the Patrick Kennedy she had met on a boat so many years ago.

3

The Hannons and
the Fitzgeralds

$\mathcal{F}$rom the time she was a little girl, Josephine "Josie" Hannon kept primarily to her family and to those of her own Catholic faith. That was something that Josie had learned growing up in an Irish-American family scrapping for a living on a farm in South Acton, a tiny village an hour outside of Boston. There the Hannons had been outsiders, among the poorest families in the hamlet. Not only were they one of only three or four Catholic families in South Acton but their farm lay apart from the rest of the town. The farm was reached by a footbridge over Fort Pond Brook. There in a tiny glen sat the two-story house. It had small windows and a diminutive parlor and was the kind of dwelling in which people hunkered down during the ice and snow of winter, praying for warm weather so they could spend most of their time outside.

Josie regularly made the honor roll at South Grammar and Primary Schools and despite flu epidemics and fierce storms during the winter of 1870–71 was never absent or tardy. School was not Josie's only responsibility. One day her parents told their eldest daughter to watch over her little sister, Elizabeth, and her best friend. Josie had done this countless times before. She didn't pay much attention as the two little girls wandered off down to the pond. If the day had been colder, if Josie had been older, if her father had been nearer nothing would have happened. But the day was warm, Josie was eight years old, her father was far from the pond, and the little girls drowned in the breaking ice. Her father, half mad in grief, anger, and disbelief, carried the two bodies up to the house, and the bodies of Josie's sister and her friend lay in the parlor, a cold and silent rebuke.

Two of the Hannon children had already died of illnesses,

24

and this was not the end of the Hannons' tragedies. Years later Josie's mother walked her thirteen-year-old son, John Edmond, to the train station, where he caught one of his high-laced shoes on the railroad tracks. As he tried to extricate himself the train appeared in the distance. While his distraught mother watched, the train ran over Josie's brother, severing his lower leg. Edmond went on to marry and raise a family, but his two older brothers took to the bottle more than to life and both of them died young.

The Hannons suffered not simply the common misfortunes of life. These were horrors, savage, mindless blows. Josie became steeled to human tragedy, a self-contained, self-controlled young woman who would not expose her emotions. These were lessons that she learned not only from the family tragedies but from her mother and a whole generation of Irish-American women. She must never openly display her feelings, wearing them like emblems of her own vulnerability, weakness, shame, her own supposed failures as a woman.

One Sunday in the fall of 1878, Josie was washing dishes in the kitchen when a dapper young man strutted into the room and began to talk. Josie's fifteen-year-old second cousin, John Fitzgerald, had come out to the farm to visit his country relatives, enjoy the fresh air, and pick apples. In the midst of John's soliloquy, thirteen-year-old Josie turned away and hurried upstairs. Whether Josie was merely shy, or fearful of the "condescension of the city youth toward the country girl" as Fitzgerald later thought, she did not appear anymore that day.

On the train ride back to Boston, Fitzgerald dreamed of Josie, of her satiny black hair and quizzical blue eyes that looked out on the world with an imperious stare rarely seen in a country girl. "The first time I met her, I knew," he recalled years later. "I knew this was it." He returned often during the next eleven years, arriving full of the bounty of himself. One autumn young Fitzgerald picked twelve barrels of apples, more than anyone had ever picked in one day. But much of the time, in the fields, or down by the river, he told tales of his life and ascent in Boston.

Josie listened to these tales of a world far beyond South Acton. Fitzgerald was born February 11, 1863, in the North End of Boston, the third of nine sons. Fitzgerald turned the misfortunes into part of a heroic legend that became a basis for the family history and life model. His Irish immigrant father,

Thomas Fitzgerald, had worked first as a farm laborer and then as an itinerant peddler in the streets of the North End. In November 1857, he had met and married Rosanna Cox, herself the daughter of Irish immigrants, and six years later went into business with his brother James in a small grocery store, one of the modest establishments that lined the street.

When he was five, Fitzgerald's parents sent him off to a public school. He remembered the first day "sitting in front of our house on Hanover Street and bemoaning the fact that I would have to go to school barefooted. I didn't want to go. It had rained the day before and my stockings were so wet that it was impossible to wear them. But I had to go just the same, shoes or no shoes, wet stockings or dry stockings." As the son of poor shopkeepers, Fitzgerald made the North End his fiefdom, hawking newspapers on the corner, playing baseball on Hanover Street, running races around Fort Hill Square against boys twice his size, his little feet churning across the cobblestones, winning, always winning. He attended Boston Latin School, the finest public school in America, and in 1884 was accepted at Harvard Medical School, an extraordinary achievement for a second-generation Irish-American.

Nine months later Fitzgerald's fifty-five-year-old father died of pneumonia, joining his mother who had died six years earlier, and his two infant sisters before that. In the saga of John F. Fitzgerald, the death of his father took on epic proportions. "I thought my life belonged to my brothers and that I could do better outside the medical school," he recounted. "So I gave it up and took the examination for a position in the Custom House. I took charge of the house. We had no sister and we hired a housekeeper and I kept the boys together for fifteen years."

Fitzgerald loved to muse emotionally on how he had taken care of "all six of my brothers," washing their faces, dressing them, and sending them off to school. His older brothers, James and Thomas J., were already adults, and Fitzgerald was hardly sending them off each morning with books in hand. Fitzgerald may have been privately bitter about his elder brothers' failures to do their part, but whatever arguments the Fitzgeralds might have had among themselves, in public the family stood solidly together against the world. Fitzgerald had a touch of the poet in him, and he was not about to destroy the heroic legend of his family.

* * *

For more than a decade Fitzgerald continued to take the Fitchburg Line out to the Hannon farm to see Josie. Fitzgerald's long courtship of Josie was by far the most romantic and idealistic pursuit of his entire life, an inexplicably quixotic strain in a man of impeccable realism, self-interest, and unbridled social ambition. His dogged pursuit of Josie was remarkable in several ways. Fitzgerald was a natural politician. He weighed human beings and their value to him as carefully as his parents had weighed meat in their store on Hanover Street. When he evaluated Josie, he put his thumb on the scale. She was a poor farm girl, a woman who added nothing to his social and economic weight, but she was the woman he wanted as his wife.

Josie cared deeply for her suitor, and saw in him a way out of her mundane village life, a chance to leave her star-crossed family and join a man who saw nothing in the future but promise. One serious impediment stood in the way. Josie and John F. were second cousins descended from the same great-grandfather, James Fitzgerald. For much of its history the Catholic church had prohibited a marriage of the "third degree of consanguinity" or blood-relationship extending three generations from a common ancestor. Even in the nineteenth century the church considered such a marriage incestuous unless the couple received the proper dispensation. Fortunately for the young couple, this dispensation was now considered in the "category of minor impediments," given rather routinely after "a tax for some charitable object."

First, Fitzgerald had to convince the Hannons. "Each week when John F. would visit, he would bring a letter from a different priest in his own parish suggesting that his marriage to Josie would be legitimate in the eyes of the church," said Mary Hannon Heffernan, Rose's cousin. "But still the family remained opposed. For more than canon law was at stake. Their real fear was that by marrying within the family Josie would produce retarded and weak children."

In earlier years Americans had generally viewed those with retardation as innocent victims and tried to make a place for them in society. Now they were increasingly considered a brutal and dangerous flotsam, "deficient, delinquent, defective and dependent," an underclass of beggars, feebleminded, and the institutionalized, a plague on the competitive modern world. That was the horrid, unspeakable dread that haunted the Hannons: that this union would forever taint their lineage, the bad blood bringing forth a race of the weak, the incompetent, and the doomed.

It took Fitzgerald about two years to persuade the Hannons that the marriage should go forward. Only then did he go to Archbishop Williams in Boston to make the customary one-dollar donation, and on September 7, 1889, the church granted the official dispensation. Eleven days later twenty-three-year-old Josie and twenty-six-year-old Fitzgerald stood before Father McCall and a small group of relatives and friends at St. Bernard's in the nearby town of Concord and took their marriage vows.

In a bedroom of the house at 4 Garden Court Street in Boston's North End, Josie nestled her newborn daughter in her arms. Rose Elizabeth was born on July 22, 1890, in the midst of a long torpid summer. Twenty-four-year-old Josie had arrived as a bride in Boston less than a year ago, and she knew how fragile life could be for an infant in the cramped immigrant quarters. Of the 284 Bostonians who would die in the next week, almost half were under the age of one.

Little Rosie loved her mother and knew how devoted Josie was to her, and to her sister, Agnes, born two years later. The little house on Garden Court Street was a fortress against the world and its woes. From an early age, little Rosie reacted against her mother's dour spirit, and was a bright, relentlessly positive girl. In that, Rose had the most extraordinary of models, her own father, John F. Fitzgerald.

When twenty-seven-year-old Fitzgerald came bursting through the door, sweeping little Rosie up into his arms, it was as if life and the world had entered. With her father's overwhelming love, Rose knew that she was unique and favored. She was born into an Irish-American world where fathers rarely shouted triumphantly about the birth of a daughter. Her father had grown up in a house without sisters and without a mother from his youth. By everything he did and said, Rose knew that she was special. "He seems to have regarded me as a miracle, an impression from which he never really recovered," Rose recalled.

Her father's love for Rose was like an enveloping blanket. As soon as Rose had an awareness of the world around her, Fitzgerald became to her not simply the most special person in her life but all the glories of the world. He was the drama, the color, the richness of life, the last and final authority on matters large and small. "The minute he saw me he would pick me up in his arms and twirl me around," Rose remembered. "To my mind, there was no one in the world like my father. Wherever he was, there was magic in the air."

Rose was not yet two years old when her father became a state senator and the Democratic ward boss of the North End, the beginning of Rose's education as a political woman. Fitzgerald belonged to more organizations than any other individual in the North End, and with all his political and fraternal activities her father was rarely home. Night after night he was off to the Hibernians, the Massachusetts Order of Foresters, the Knights of St. Rose, or Democratic party gatherings.

As much as Rose was drawn to the excitement of her father's life, her mother could not abide the business of politics: the vulgar camaraderie; the seemingly aimless palaver; the endless parade of supplicants, from businessmen to widows. To wall off that world, Josie made the house on Garden Court literally a woman's sphere, a sanctuary where her husband could not bring his political pals and hangers-on, job seekers, and solicitors of favors.

Little Rose saw that her mother only rarely ventured out with her father, and when she did it was usually for the great social events of Irish Boston when they dressed in their finest clothes and her mother's appearance was mandatory. They were a handsome couple, but if ever there was an example of the axiom that opposites attract, it was this marriage.

Even wearing his evening dress, Fitzgerald was a man to be glimpsed in action, his plump ruddiness and pugnacious self-confidence an advertisement for success. Practically the only time her father sat still was for official photographs, when his attempts to appear the solemn statesman often fell short, and he looked as if he wanted to burst into speech or song. He had thin, close-pressed lips; narrowly set eyes; a nose big enough to sniff any political wind; straight hair parted down the middle; and the pugnacious manner of a bantamweight fighting out of his class. Josie was a woman to be seen in repose, a woman of shy reserve. She had a dignity and carriage that suggested that she might have come from an aristocratic family, not a poor Irish-American farming family. Fitzgerald looked smaller than his height of five and a half feet. Although Josie was only five feet three, her aristocratic aura made her appear taller. Rose considered her mother "perfectly beautiful." Her skin was milky white and her hair was ebony black. She had small, delicate-appearing bones and a long, narrow nose. She weighed about 115 pounds and had a mannequin's figure that she used to full advantage in her wardrobe.

Rose's parents always attended the Young Men's Catholic Association of Boston College's annual College Ball. Fitzgerald had three times organized the ball, turning the dance into the night of nights for Boston's Catholic elite, most of whom had never graced the portals of an institution of higher learning and who spent the evening mimicking the Protestant elite of Boston and their fancy dress balls.

Josie was a stunning woman with a sense of style unusual among these ladies, with a quiet bearing that suggested she was a woman not only of shyness but of mystery. She did not have to chitchat wittily to the grocer's wife and the landlord's maiden daughter to be valuable to her husband and his ambitions. She looked as if she could be one of the upper-crust Protestant ladies of Beacon Street, and that was extraordinarily important to Fitzgerald's image. Josie's shyness might have been assuaged if Fitzgerald had spent the evening with his wife, shepherding her through the rituals of politesse, whirling her around the room to a series of waltzes. But the College Ball was *his* ball, and Fitzgerald had contacts to make, businessmen to stroke, wives to flatter.

Out on the dance floor, Fitzgerald worked the room. He had a way with the voteless women, and through them he wooed their husbands' and brothers' votes. As a bachelor he had left the pretty girls alone, not cramming his name onto their dance cards. Likewise now, he went to the line of wallflowers, and pirouetted these neglected maidens around the room on his agile, tiny feet, convincing each that she was the belle of the evening, or the belle for one song at least. And the most miraculous thing of all was that they believed him. He had discovered there was no flattery too large to be disbelieved as long as he uttered it in mellifluous phrases, pumped full of sincerity. "He got me through the women," recalled one defeated ward leader. "Every time I went into their houses, and tried to tell them the truth the women would pipe up and 'Johnny Fitz this and Johnny Fitz that' till they simply talked me down and out."

Fitzgerald had sweet words for maidens and widows, matrons and maids alike, but his pursuit of women did not end on the dance floor. Whatever Josie had expected of marriage, it

could not have been this. Over the years Josie's mouth began
to have that downward cast as if she had bitten into an apple
and found it sour. As she stood waiting for her husband at the
College Ball, she gave no sign that she was not the proud and
happy wife of the North End's most illustrious young politician.

By all accounts, Josie never talked about any problems she
had with her husband. She chose not to see what she did not
want to see, not to feel what she did not want to feel. Josie
was practicing the bittersweet craft of denial, learning to dis-
avow not only her own emotional needs, but parts of her own
history and life. She had been brought up not to expect much,
not from life, and not from a husband. In Boston she had made
a remarkable transformation, metamorphosing from a shy
country lass to a stylish matron and mother, a priceless adornment on her husband's arm, a shrewdly protective mother.

In public, Josie looked at Fitzgerald with seemingly guile-
less trust and belief, but she kept her emotional distance. In
this she was following a pattern common among Irish-
American mothers, described by Theodore Lidz as "treat[ing]
her husband like a grown-up child, pretending to believe the
fabricated tales he tells and admiring his ability to tell them;
and while she seems to defer to her husband's authority, she
holds the family reins tightly in her own hands, at the same
time ceding to the church a superordinate authority which must
not be questioned."

In 1894 thirty-one-year-old Fitzgerald won election to Congress as the "boy candidate" and was off to Washington leaving his family behind. Little Rose was already an integral
member of a political family. "My father told me as early as
five years old to stand up straight and cooperate with photographers," she said. "They have a job to do, too." Rose did not
have to be reminded. She loved standing on platforms draped
in bunting behind her father, loved the hoopla and spectacle of
politics.

As a politician, Fitzgerald endlessly repeated a series of epic
themes and heroic myths about his family, his race, and his
country that his eldest daughter believed and would one day
teach her own children. In his dramatic high-pitched voice, he
told his tales to audiences great and small, to his constituents
in their shops and homes, and to his daughter as he walked
through the familiar streets of the North End holding her hand.

Fitzgerald passionately recounted the stories of the Irish

famine years, this bedraggled, bewildered, impoverished people flooding into the historic North End. These very streets where Rose walked with her father were the crucible of American democracy. The elegant spire of Christ Church, the oldest in the city, rose from Copp's Hill. Paul Revere had lived in the North End and his house built in 1676, the oldest frame house in the city, still stood there. In the Burying-Ground lay the remains of Cotton, Increase, and Samuel Mather, Puritan leaders whose lives were the veritable history of the old city. Here too were Boston's docks and workshops, its stores and counting-houses.

As the Irish had arrived, the old Bostonians had left, turning the crowded quarter into the first modern urban slum in America. The Irish had no capital but their votes, no education but that learned in the streets of the city. This loquacious poetic people had a gift for politics, and they learned their lessons well. By 1880 the foreign born and their children made up 60 percent of Boston's population of 362,839. That meant votes and votes meant power, and in 1885, Hugh O'Brien became Boston's first Irish-American mayor.

These Irish-Americans were Fitzgerald's capital too, and he extolled the virtues of his "dear old North End" so often that its residents became known as "Dearos." Yet new waves of immigrants were moving into Boston now, and Fitzgerald's dear old North End was not even predominantly Irish any longer, but had more Italians and almost as many Jews as it did Irish residents. It was still *his* district, though, and Irish politicians controlled the ward decades after most of their compatriots had left.

The North End would always be Fitzgerald's sentimental home, but it was time for the ambitious young congressman to move to a better area, perhaps to one of the new suburbs or other parts of Boston. Josie had never felt comfortable living in the North End. She longed for her family in South Acton and the gentle country life. In the greatest assertion of her life, Josie insisted that the family move twenty miles outside Boston, to Concord Junction, near her parents' farm. "Once Mother got it in her mind to move out to Concord, nothing could stop her," Rose remembered. "It was a tough decision for Father, for he knew he'd be criticized for living away from his district and his people, but he saw how much it meant to Mother and he finally agreed."

* * *

Rose sat in the parlor of the Fitzgeralds' large, wooden-frame home listening for the faint whisper of a train whistle puncturing the still night. More than a hundred trains passed through Concord Junction each day, passenger trains full of immigrants bound for Chicago and St. Louis, freight trains loaded with wheat and corn heading to Boston and New York, local trains of farmers, mill hands, salesmen, and agents. The one train that Rose cared about was the one Friday evening that brought her father back. Her family lived in one of the finest homes in Concord Junction on a gentle rise off Main Street, a property that included a glass conservatory, a horse barn, and a henhouse and stood no more than a third of a mile from the train station.

Rose had hardly heard the train whistle when Fitzgerald burst into the house. Her father arrived in gatherings large and small with a flourish of gesture and word, as if to say nothing could occur until he was there. Fitzgerald greeted Josie and Agnes affectionately as well as the two boys, Thomas Acton and John F. Jr., and the baby Eunice. But he always had a special salutation for his first child, the daughter he called "my Rosie."

It was Friday evening and Friday evening meant lobster from Boston. At the head of the table sat Fitzgerald himself, dominating everything. As he talked, he flung his tiny fists up punctuating every point and statement, his thumbs pointing to heaven in a gesture that was his alone. At the other end of the dining room table, often in regal and enigmatic silence, sat Josie.

Rose's attention was totally on her father. In school and play her conversation was such a litany of "Father says this" and "Father says that," that her nickname became "Father says." Fitzgerald became Rose's idealized vision of the masculine function in the world. As Rose saw it, great men like her father charged out into the world seeking success, returning for precious, intense moments full of energy and emotion. Fitzgerald's frenetic coming and going were an exaggerated version of the father's role in a typical nineteenth-century family. "Young women learned, from the culture at large and from their own family situations, to expect little emotional support or understanding from men," wrote Nancy M. Theriot in her study of nineteenth-century mothers and daughters. "The role

of the male in the family involved work, or worldly orienta-
tion, and patriarchal control within the household. He was in
the family, but he was not of the family."

Whenever her father was home, Rose cherished every moment of the weekend. Sunday the family took the carriage for
the three-mile ride to Concord to attend mass. No matter how
late Fitzgerald had been up the night before, or how fierce the
weather, the family went to church.

As the horses plodded eastward, in the distance the great
golden dome of the First Unitarian Church of Concord seemed
to rise out of the ground. Soon the carriage was moving up
Main Street, a dirt road lined with great shade trees, past the
yellow Thoreau-Alcott house where Henry Thoreau died, past
Dove Cote, the clapboard house where Louisa May Alcott had
lived, past the gracious white residences along the roadway,
past the library and town hall, onto Bedford Street, stopping at
St. Bernard's Church in the center of town, the church where
Josie and Fitzgerald had married. The building had been a deserted Universalist church when the Archdiocese of Boston
purchased the broken-down structure in 1863. The Yankees
had not fancied the idea of crucifixes and saints in their cherished precincts, but since Irishmen were fighting beside their
own sons in the Civil War, the town fathers figured that they
deserved their own church.

At first farmers in town for market day had gawked unashamedly at the spectacle of a black-robed son of Rome
walking the streets. The priest was now an accepted sight on
the streets of Concord, but that did not mean that Catholics
were fully accepted. For decades no believer in the Roman
pope sat on the elected school board. Indeed, one minister advised his flock not only to register to vote to foil the papists,
but to inform their Catholic servants that if they registered,
they would lose their jobs.

Inside St. Bernard's, the Fitzgerald women entered a world
that beyond their family was the one great constant in their
life. As Father McCall intoned the Latin mass, they were hearing the same rituals that they had at St. Stephen's in the North
End, or in any church they chanced to enter. Congressman
Fitzgerald and his family were sitting among Irish maids and
Irish workers, their hands marked with toil, but inside this
sanctuary, for this moment, all were one. For the poor maid
harnessed to the yoke of service in a Protestant home as well
as for Josie and her daughters, there was not simply solace

here but romance and mystery, a faith that set them apart and above.

As Rose sat in church, she realized that here was another difference between men and women, or at least between her father and mother. As her mother sat with her head bowed deep in contemplation, her father's eyes kept darting around the sanctuary as if counting the house. "He was so deeply involved in the affairs of the world that he took religion for granted without thinking much about it," said his daughter Rose years later. "Going to mass was simply natural and normal and gave him the opportunity (I say this with love and without sacrilege) of communicating not only with God but with many of his friends and political constituents."

After church, the family rode out into the countryside in their half-open carriage behind Fitzgerald's matched pair of horses, Black Hawk and Maud. To Rose it was like a "theater box on wheels," and so it was with Fitzgerald grasping the reins, sending greetings to all within earshot.

Sunday outings were usually uneventful, even if they always ended far too soon. In the late afternoon, the horses headed back to the barn and the Fitzgerald family back to the parlor. For Rose these hours with her father were precious, and she cherished these last moments as much as she had the first. As the sun dipped on the horizon, Rose stood at the window looking for a finger of smoke in the late afternoon sky. As soon as she saw it, she called out. Like most politicians Fitzgerald wanted the world to wait for him. He tried to time it so he could step from the carriage to the train compartment without a moment's wait on the platform. At the precise moment, then, her father took his hat and bag. Rose rushed out beside her father and sat next to him on the carriage seat as they dashed down Main Street to the depot.

Fitzgerald ran for the train and he was gone as abruptly as he had arrived. Rose returned alone, guiding the horse plodding homeward. She knew almost nothing of the world that lay down those tracks where her father left in the night, out beyond that darkness somewhere. By the time Rose arrived in the house, all signs of Fitzgerald's visit were gone, and there was not even an echo of his laughter.

In physical appearance, Rose was a blend of both her parents. She was slightly over five feet tall, smaller than Josie but with her mother's delicate bone structure. Her nose was prominent

but neither as long as her mother's, nor proportionately as large
as her father's. She had large animated azure blue eyes, thick
ringlets of brown hair, and her mother's pure complexion. She
also had her mother's long chin that tilted slightly forward, a
feature that she would pass on to generations to come.

Rose appeared a pretty little girl, pretty that is until she
stood next to her sister Agnes. The two sisters had eerily similar looks, even more striking because they were often dressed
alike. In family portraits, as in person, the eye went first to
Agnes.

When Rose was seven and Agnes two years younger, Fitzgerald took his children to meet President McKinley in the
White House. As Fitzgerald presented his daughters to the
president, McKinley took out the boutonniere from his lapel
and handed it to Agnes. "I want to present this flower to the
prettiest child I have ever seen." Rose could not help that her
little sister was prettier, but she was almost lacking in sibling
rivalry. As so often in her adult life, she took a disadvantage
and turned it upside down. She realized that she would not be
able to make her way in the world with a smile and a flutter
of eyelashes. As Rose recalled years later, she "knew right
then that I would have to work to do something about myself."

Even at a young age Rose had an exquisite sensitivity to social nuances, and thus could not have been ignorant of the subtle slights of the old Yankee town. Indeed, it was a mark of
how much Rose wanted to be part of this world that she later
said she had lived these childhood years in Concord when the
family had not lived there at all but in Concord Junction. It
was not a small distinction to the residents of Concord, one of
the most historic places in America, a community "saturated
with the atmosphere of self-satisfaction." The raw, new neighboring town was not a quaint New England village, but a town
on the make with what the *Concord Enterprise* called "western
air" unlike the "air of staid old Concord." Concord Junction
was a bustling, hustling industrial and business center. The depot was a stop for three different railroad lines. To the west of
the Fitzgerald home on Main Street stood the five-story, redbrick Damondale mill.

Rose attended the West Concord Public School a few hundred yards from her house. The two-story, white frame building had been enlarged and renovated early in 1900 and
contained nine classrooms for 190 students and electric lights
over the five teachers' desks. When she left to go to school

each morning, Rose rarely had a father to whom she could say good-bye. At school she was also in a world dominated by females. Her five teachers were all single women who lost their positions if they married. They earned an average of $545 a year, less than a third of what their few male counterparts in the school system earned, and about 10 percent of Fitzgerald's five-thousand-dollar salary. Most of them made teaching their lifelong careers, and they presented models of dedication, discipline, and rectitude.

Rose was the daughter of one of Concord Junction's most illustrious citizens, but in school she was an outsider. She was a well-to-do Irish-American. The Irish in her classes, however, were poor working-class boys and girls struggling to learn enough to make their way. She was Catholic and in Concord Junction Catholicism was the religion of the poor, of maids and workers and farmhands.

The Fitzgeralds of Concord Junction kept primarily to their own family and to those of their own faith. Rose remembered her childhood here as "wonderful years, full of the traditional pleasures and satisfactions of life in a small New England town ... years of serenity, order, neighborly human relationships, family affection." She had such fond memories of her years in Concord Junction in part because her mother was probably as happy there as she would ever be. One of Rose's earliest recollections was of seeing her "mother returning from a two hour ride side saddle with her thick gorgeous long hair streaming down her back when the galloping horse had jounced her up and down to such an extent that all the hairpins had dropped to earth."

Josie's own mother lived nearby and in early 1900 moved from South Acton into a rented house on Highland Street. Her brother, John Edmond, lived with the Fitzgeralds, helping out occasionally by taking out in a carriage either John Francis Fitzgerald Jr., his father's namesake, or the newest arrival, Eunice.

Josie had much time for her children, and part of that time was spent instructing Rose and her siblings in the faith. Her children did not go to parochial school, and except for Father McCall's sermons at St. Bernard's, she was their primary religious teacher. Josie had grown up almost exclusively among Protestants in South Acton, and her faith had the strength of a belief that had to be strong to survive, buffeted by the winds of indifference and suspicion. That was the faith that she imparted to her daughters.

In the evenings during Lent, Josie led her children to a special room in the house with its little shrine to the Blessed Virgin festooned in spring flowers. Josie turned down the gaslights, and the family got down on their knees in the enveloping darkness. They held rosary beads in their hands and Josie led her children in their prayers. The rosary was a simple devotion, the repetition of a series of prayers counted out on the beads, a devotion the humblest of Catholics could perform without the benefit of priest or church.

Rose rested on her knees until they ached. "Sometimes I wondered why I should be doing all the kneeling and studying and memorizing and contemplating and praying," Rose recalled, "but I became understanding and grateful." She was drawn into the mysteries of the rosary, seeing in it, like other Catholic children, "primal images, pictures that make God, Christ, and Mary approachable." Into these prayers she could bring her joy, her sorrow, her doubts. This was the wellspring of Rose's faith, not the intellectualized religion of Augustine or Aquinas, not the theology imparted by the church fathers, but what Rose called simply "a precious gift of faith."

By the example of her own life, Josie taught her daughters other lessons of a woman's life, lessons that had been passed down like heirlooms from her own mother and family. "When she was happy everyone knew it, and there were smiles and serenity," Rose wrote in her autobiography. "But when she was unhappy (she must have been sometimes; who hasn't been) she rarely showed it." Even in the most intimate moments between a mother and daughter, Josie did not let that mask of tranquillity drop from her face. That was the lesson Josie taught her daughters.

Josie took her children on historical pilgrimages. Within a ten-mile radius of Concord stood probably more sites and shrines of American history and literature than anywhere else in the country. What Rose saw on these visits were not the events of the past as mere history but as a living force, an integral part of her life. The Revolutionary War was still recent enough that a child with a vivid imagination could almost smell the musket fire hanging in the air. The Fitzgeralds' buggy often drove past the war memorial in Concord, but the Civil War to Rose was not simply names on a monument. It was aging veterans of the Grand Army of the Republic who on

Patriots Day took out their blue uniforms and marched through the streets as a military band played "The Battle Hymn of the Republic."

Rose, then, learned her history the way she learned her Catholicism, hearing a rosary of patriotic events, where men rose to moments of heroism and self-sacrifice. This was an age of unself-conscious, unchallenged patriotism. That was how her father talked about America in his speeches, and that was the America in which she came to believe.

As Rose grew older, Fitzgerald showed in greater ways how much he adored his eldest daughter. No girl in town had the birthday parties Rose had. Her tenth birthday party merited mention in the *Concord Enterprise*. The following year the newspaper noted that "Fitzgerald gave a lawn party on Monday afternoon and evening, it being the 11th birthday of his daughter Rose," not mentioning if Josie had been there. The affair ended with a display of fireworks lighting up the nighttime sky of Concord Junction.

In the summer Rose drove her own horse and carriage to the Concord Public Library. There she picked out what she called "romantic fiction," tales that were "moral, inspirational, and sentimental." Rose's favorite novel was that most popular of young adult fiction, Louisa May Alcott's *Little Women*. The Concord author's story could have been Rose's romanticized vision of her own family. Mr. March was off doing good work, either in Washington or in his study; he made no more appearances in the book than Rose's father did in the Fitzgerald home. "To outsiders, the five energetic women seemed to rule the house," wrote Alcott, and so did Josie and her daughters. Yet Mr. March was "still the head of the family, the household conscience, anchor and comforter," and so in his own way was Rose's father.

Little Women was a universe in which self-denial always brought rewards, where sorrow turned to joy a page later, where goodness was is own reward. The March girls struggled to contain their spontaneity, energy, aggressiveness, until they became genteel little ladies. Young readers found Jo, the author's alter ego, the most appealing character, Jo who was so lively, so energetic, so full of feelings. "I am angry nearly every day of my life, Jo," her adored mother tells her. "But I have learned not to show it."

Josie reinforced the lessons of *Little Women*, and the many forms of self-discipline that stayed with Rose all her life. She had to be self-controlled. She had to be neat. She had to have her life in order. She had to be studious. She had to be devout. She had to be frugal. If she failed, her mother spanked her. That was Josie's job too, not her husband's, and yet another reason that Rose adored Fitzgerald; when she looked at her father's arms and hands, she saw only appendages that enveloped her in warmth and affection, not instruments of discipline.

Rose's father taught her another kind of discipline, and that was the public discipline of politics. One day Rose noticed her sister Agnes leaving the Fitzgerald house with some food in her hand. Agnes was a carefree little girl who wanted to eat what she wanted to eat when she wanted to eat it.

"What's a congressman's daughter doing eating bread and molasses?" Rose asked, as a classmate remembered. She was not the daughter of an Irish cook who could be sent out of the kitchen happily eating the heel of a freshly baked loaf of bread. She was a congressman's daughter and a congressman's daughter had to watch not only what she said and where she said it, but what she ate and when she ate it. She had to live her public life as if it were a biography with every moment scrutinized.

In the summer of 1900 after three terms in Congress, Fitzgerald announced his retirement. It was not for Josie to know of the internecine struggles and machinations that led to her husband's decision, not for her to know the extent of his further ambitions. Josie believed that now at last her husband would spend more time at home. Fitzgerald, though, still came booming in and out of their home, spending most of his time in Boston. He purchased a failing Catholic weekly, *The Republic*, and turned it into a lucrative business. That was not enough to satisfy him. One of the most powerful Irish political bosses and Fitzgerald's own sometime mentor, Martin Lomasney, warned him that if he wanted a political future in Boston, he would have to live there. And thus Fitzgerald decreed that the family would move back to Boston. "Father knew that Lomasney was right," Rose said. "But Mother loved Concord so much he stayed in the country as long as he could all the while keeping his voting registration in the North End."

Josie had been away from her husband's world during half a decade. Concord Junction was her home, her life. If she returned to Boston now, it would not be to the humble streets of the North End, but to a new world of prominence and a myriad of social obligations. That was not the life she wanted, but it was her husband's choice, and she could do nothing but follow knowing that her life would never be the same. As for thirteen-year-old Rose, Boston could mean only excitement, an adventurous new life in the commodious city at the end of the railroad tracks.

Fitzgerald bought a great new house in Dorchester, a prestigious suburban community that only recently had become part of Boston. The Fitzgeralds' new home at 37 Welles Avenue represented the epitome of success in a woman's sphere. The great house stood on the top of Jones Hill, above the three-story homes of the suburban community, above the soot and smoke and noises of Boston proper to the north, above the blue waters of Dorchester Bay, and the emerald islands of the harbor. The structure sat on a property of more than forty thousand square feet. The driveway curved around to the front door of the mansion, a prepossessing structure with turrets and a mansard roof. The home had high ceilings, inlaid wooden floors, a music room, a parlor, a billiard room. The rooms were richly decorated with heavy Victorian furniture and thick rugs, all emblematic of achievement in turn-of-the-century Boston.

On the stair landing of the mansion stood a stained-glass window with the Gaelic words, Shawn a Boo (John the Bold). It was indeed a bold John F. Fitzgerald who had purchased the home in February 1904. He had put the title in Josie's name, making her liable for the $10,500 mortgage on a property assessed at $16,400. Business and politics were a man's terrain. Josie probably did not think about where her husband's newfound wealth had come from, how he could afford a mansion, or why she was supposedly buying the property.

None of that was Josie's concern. She was mistress of the house, of her three daughters, of two growing sons, and of little Frederick, born in December of 1904. She was now part of Dorchester, one of the most prestigious suburbs in Boston, her neighbors the wives of merchants, bankers, and barristers. No matter what she may have expected, she spent hardly more time with her husband than she had in Concord Junction. "He was seldom, if ever, home to have dinner with us," Rose recalled.

Josie might at least have seen her husband more if she had let him bring his colleagues and cronies to the home on Welles Avenue. But this house was Josie's preserve, and the line be-

tween the Fitzgeralds' public and private life was drawn on
their front doorstep. Sometimes Fitzgerald needed his wife on
his arm, and she joined him, exquisitely gowned and coifed, a
brittle, quiet woman whose demeanor and bearing were increasingly attributed to snobbishness or unfriendliness rather
than to shyness or reserve.

Rose had not inherited her mother's taciturn quality, and she
took to this new, expanded world. Each day she walked a few
blocks down the hill to the twenty-four-room Dorchester High
School, the largest coeducational school in the city, a new yellow brick structure as utilitarian in appearance as a factory.
Upon her first day at school, Rose discovered one of the most
striking facts of coeducational high schools in Boston. So
many males had already left school to go to work that she had
twice as many girls in her classes as boys. Rose and her peers
were the first generation of women to be educated in massive
numbers. These young women studied the same books as the
young men, and they had knowledge and aspirations that went
far beyond those of their mothers' generation. When they
thought of a career, the most likely prospect stood right before
them, in their teachers, almost all of whom were women.

In her most impressionable years, Rose had two distinct female role models. At home she had her mother who watched
over her, over her brothers and sisters, over her home, a
woman who wanted nothing of the noise, the vulgarity, the
rude vitality of the political and business world beyond. Josie
kept her psychic distance from the world around her. In school
Rose had a series of women teachers who had chosen either
for a few years or for all adulthood to live in a larger world of
knowledge, learning, and authority. They were all unmarried
and many of them were second-generation Irish-Americans
who were becoming a teaching class almost the way their
mothers had been a servant class.

Rose attended school five hours a day, five days a week. In
the afternoon she carried home thick tomes on American government and civics, ancient and modern history; books on rhetoric and spelling, arithmetic, and geometry; the plays of
Shakespeare; essays by Samuel Johnson and Emerson; Dickens's *A Tale of Two Cities*; French grammar and composition.
It was a serious, uncompromising education tempered with
music and gymnastics classes.

Though Rose was a decent athlete, young women were not

allowed to participate in extracurricular school sports. For them, the main after-school activities were the dances held for an hour and a half every other Friday afternoon in the gymnasium. Teachers chaperoned these events that were as sedate and genteel as English teas, with never a vulgarity or untoward incident. Rose would have loved to attend. "I was never allowed to go," Rose recalled. "My father was a great innovator in public life, but when it came to raising his daughter no one could have been more conservative." In the Fitzgerald home her father was the final authority. It was unthinkable to challenge his commands, to argue even momentarily, or to run tearfully to her mother.

Fitzgerald's great dream was to become the mayor of Boston. In September 1905, two months before the Democratic primary, Patrick A. Collins, the popular fifty-one-year-old mayor, died of acute gastritis. Fitzgerald had been back in Boston only a year and a half, and he was far down the list of possible candidates. John the Bold announced his candidacy.

Although Rose enjoyed all the hoopla and excitement of campaigning, her father wanted her to keep her distance. Men like Fitzgerald feared that if women received the vote and entered the political arena their skirts would be dirtied and they would lose their femininity. "Do you know that my father never let me talk politics?" Rose admitted decades later. "He said that one politician in the family was enough."

Rose and her mother watched from their distant pedestals as Fitzgerald ventured out of his base in the North End, his stalwarts leading the way by foot and car, shouting his name to the heavens. The candidate roared around town in a red car, followed by two other automobiles loaded with a legion of reporters and stenographers to take down his every word. At the age of forty-two, he was indefatigable, a font of pure energy. He campaigned day and night, racing from venue to venue. He gave six speeches an evening or more, thumping, rousing, full-throated speeches. In an era before radio and television, a political campaign was a circus in the streets, the candidates filling the air with insults and verbal assaults, proud boasts and endless promises. No one campaigned with the flair of the man known as Little Napoleon, standing on a platform silhouetted against the evening sky, hurling his charges like lightning bolts, ridiculing his primary opponent as a tool of the bosses, strutting back and forth, boasting of all that he would do for the city.

The one thing missing in these *tableaux vivants* of big city politics was the candidate's wife, sitting on the platform looking reverently up at her husband. "I don't even care enough about politics to go to rallies, even when [my husband] is to speak," Josie said. "And he has always made it a point never to talk much to me about politics and to let me know the disagreeable things from time to time said about him. We try to keep politics entirely out of the home. The only public functions in which I figure are in church entertainments or something of that sort. I do not care much for society, and had rather live a quiet domestic life than any other, if it were wholly possible."

As distant as she was from the fracas, Rose could hear the charges and the taunts. Her father's opponents said that Fitzgerald had turned laborers out of their jobs because they did not support him. They said that during his six years in Congress there was "not a single line of legislation upon the statute books traceable to him." They said that his money came from "the corporations, the Boston Elevated, the gas and electric light companies." Even one of Rose's favorite periodicals, *The Sacred Heart Review*, chimed in, accusing her father of making "a business of trading on the Catholic name. He has the effrontery to appeal to the businessmen of Boston . . . as the accredited representative of the Catholic people."

Martin Lomasney, her father's mentor, had turned against Fitzgerald. During the primary Lomasney stood on campaign platforms calling him a "slippery eel," a man who "has divided families and divided friends." P. J. Kennedy, her father's old ally from the so-called Board of Strategy, the most powerful Irish bosses in Boston, had sided with her father's Democratic opponent too; as soon as the primary was over the two men embraced, and became fast friends again.

Blood was the only element that ran true. Rose's uncle Henry, her father's youngest brother, had taken over Fitzgerald's old seat in the State Senate. His older brother, James, ran the Bunker Hill Hotel and three barrooms, and contributed mightily to Fitzgerald's campaigns with advice and back-room dealings. They were all active in the campaign, a band of brothers, the loyalest of the loyal.

Fitzgerald trusted his brothers beyond anyone else, but he kept control over every aspect of the campaign. Before the primary, two of the major papers with large Democratic readership, the *Post* and the *American*, had set out to do a series of lengthy profiles on Fitzgerald and his main opponent, Edward J. Donovan. Both men came from poor, large Irish Catholic families. Both were articulate, intelligent politicians who had made their way through business and machine politics.

When the *American* reporter asked Donovan about his wife and four children, the candidate bristled. "Neither my wife nor my children are candidates for public office," he huffed. "That being the case, it can be of neither interest nor business to the public to know about them, or to look at their pictures. My campaigns are mine—not my family's." Three weeks later an *American* reporter asked Donovan if he would at least provide a picture of the family to run in the paper. "No, I can't give it to you," he said abruptly. "I don't believe in campaigning that way. I am the only one in the family running for office. I propose to guard the privacy of my home in this campaign."

Fitzgerald was opposed to giving his wife and daughters the vote and did not discuss politics with women, but he was only too willing to talk to the reporter about his beloved family and to give the *Post* a family photograph. Before the primary, the paper ran lengthy profiles of the two candidates. Over the article on Donovan was a large photograph of the candidate's house. On the other half of the page, above the article on Fitzgerald, was a large picture of his family, all of them, Josie and Fitzgerald and the six children, as heartwarming a scene as graced the papers that day.

Fitzgerald won the primary in part because he projected an image of a wonderful husband and father with a merry brood of photogenic children. Thus it was inevitable that during the general election campaign, Fitzgerald invited a friendly *Post* reporter into his parlor to talk to his family. He sat there like a lion in his lair, mournful that he ever had to step outside into the jungle of politics. Fitzgerald told the reporters that if he "thought politics interfered in any way with his career as a devoted husband and a fond father, he would drop into political oblivion." Josie listened and said little. She found such occasions excruciating, but that had become part of her woman's work, to portray herself as a devoted wife sitting with her adoring children. Rose, like her mother, was expected to sit there primly and project an image of ethereal loveliness and civility.

Rose loved the attention. To her it was marvelous fun, and she was helping her father as well in an acceptable fashion. The reporter found Rose and her younger sister "beautiful" and Josie "a handsome woman with a youthful expression." The women did not speak of politics or politicians, and only eight-year-old John Jr. had an opinion. "Papa will be Mayor of Boston," he said while his beaming, and suddenly modest, father looked on. "Then he will be Governor of Massachusetts. Then he will be President of the United States."

That article was such a great success that Fitzgerald opened his home several times for the reporters to talk to his daughters too, and the *Post* ran a story on Rose and Agnes ("FITZGERALD CHILDREN CALLED PRETTIEST BY PRES MCKINLEY"). The reporters returned again and their articles created a family image of lyrical serenity. Here, as the paper expressed it, was the "ideal American family."

Except for social obligations and photographic sessions, Fitzgerald spent little time with his "ideal American family" but it was the family duty to project that image of domestic perfection. It was the perfect form of persuasion. The press might attack his political assertions, but the newspapers let his family image sit there, without challenge.

Through all this Josie sat silently. Even the sanctity of her home was no longer inviolate, but a stage setting on which she and her children would speak the lines that were expected of them. She could not and would not express whatever resentment she may have felt.

On election afternoon, December 12, 1905, Josie went downtown for luncheon with a group of friends. There Josie heard the glorious news that her husband had won the election. She decided to celebrate over dinner with eight other women at Young's, a leading restaurant. Suddenly Fitzgerald came charging into the room, lighting up the gathering like a roman candle.

Fitzgerald had not arrived to dine with his wife but to celebrate with his associates in a private dining room. Josie prevailed on her husband to join her party. She had hardly seen her husband for weeks. Now, finally, she would have him for celebratory toasts and laughter among good friends.

As the wife of the mayor-elect, Josie and her party had been seated at a prominent table in a window looking out on Court Square. It was not long before a few curious passersby stopped and began staring at Fitzgerald. Only a few hours before he had been merely a candidate, but suddenly he had acquired a patina of celebrity and fascination. Josie had hardly tolerated the gazes of public life—the stares at mass, the photographers at rallies, the shouted questions—but this was so much more than that. More spectators joined the throng in the street—a score, two score, a hundred, two hundred, hundreds. The celebrants in the window were like birds in an atrium, and finally Josie and Fitzgerald got up and left, their departure punctuated by the cheers of the crowd.

Josie had no choice but to talk to the reporters who thronged at the doorway. "I am glad it is over," she said. "The children will now have a chance to see him and share his company. During the campaign they have seen little of him, except on Sundays, and now they have looked forward eagerly to the day when the election would be a thing of the past. We shall now have more of him."

Whatever pledge he had made to his wife, Mayor John F. Fitzgerald was a man who could not say no to an invitation. During the day he worked long hours at city hall. Then he roared through the night streets of the city, from dinner to dinner, dance to dance, affair to affair. One mathematically inclined reporter tallied up that in his first two years, Fitzgerald attended "1,500 dances, 200 picnics, and 1,000 meetings," made "3,000 speeches and gave some 5,000 girls the proud recollection of a dance apiece with Fitzy."

The mayor's grand blue touring car was seen "tearing swiftly through East Boston on a phantom trip from one precinct to another." On other evenings "startled beholders would meet it carrying a ghostly pleasure party in the parkways with the beaming apparition of Boston's Mayor sitting blithely beside the wheel."

"Me for the pretty girls, brains or no brains," he told a *Boston Post* reporter. Even during the day Fitzgerald had a penchant for attractive women. "The Mayor always had a liking for pretty girls," admitted John H. Doyle, the street commissioner, to a *Post* reporter on a slow news day when the mayor was out of town. "None of the old school dames for little Johnnie. The pretty ones get the plum every time for John F ... and he feels rather tickled to death every time a male employee in City Hall sits up and takes notice of a pretty face or a wealth of golden hair."

Josie was probably exhibiting necessary discretion in

avoiding her husband's office and evening politicking. "Fitzgerald really fell in love with Josie," said Geraldine Hannon, Rose's cousin. "He really did because they had to wait so long before they could get married. And it was funny because after that he would pick up anyone who would come along. He did it with everyone. He was a libertine."

There were some occasions that the first lady of Catholic Boston simply had to attend. The annual College Ball was such an event. When she had first married Fitzgerald, the room had been full of grocers with ill-fitting evening jackets, insurance agents on the prowl for clients, and plump homemakers sitting in the corners. Now Josie looked out on a new Catholic Boston that had achieved its own social cachet. In February 1906 about two thousand people attended the ball at Symphony Hall, the very bastion of Brahmin cultural hegemony. Fitzgerald and Josie led the grand march, and they were a distinguished couple, Josie in her exquisite gown, Fitzgerald impeccably attired in evening clothes. The Catholics were still self-consciously emulating the Brahmins, proud that their grand march was bigger than anything the proper Bostonians put together, attempting to make up in sheer ostentation what they lacked in lineage. This evening the crème de la crème were politicians and city officials who had received their higher education in the school of ward politics. Some guests were indeed college students, a better indicator yet of the advance of Irish-Americans.

The following April an event took place at Symphony Hall of transcendent importance to Boston's Catholics and to the women who were the mainstay of the church. The reception and banquet were in honor of a forty-seven-year-old priest: the Most Rev. William H. O'Connell. As the newly appointed coadjutor to the sick and dying Archbishop Williams, O'Connell would soon become the new bishop of Boston.

For half a century Archbishop Williams had been the great symbol of the church, and the lives of almost everyone in the hall had been touched by the saintly priest. He had granted Fitzgerald and Josie the dispensation that allowed them to marry. Archbishop Williams was the last living link with the era of the great famine and the Irish emigration to the city of the Brahmins. Now Boston had more Irish-Americans than Dublin had Irish men and women, and with it came a power that was as much religious as political.

O'Connell was the first high church official to whom Josie

and Rose became close, a crucial figure in the history of the family over the next four decades. The son of Irish immigrants, he had the squat build of a boilermaker, and a face that looked both pugnacious and haughty. He had a taste for fine wine, haute cuisine, and political intrigue. O'Connell represented the most conservative counsels of Catholicism, a faith that he tried vigorously to impart on all Boston Catholics, and especially on prominent families like the Fitzgeralds.

This evening, as the dinner hour approached, the immense tiered balconies on both sides of Symphony Hall filled with women, including nuns, their black habits contrasting to the rich colors of the gowns. This Boston archdiocese was largely a kingdom of women. There were three times as many nuns as priests (1,500 religious women, 560 priests). The pews were full of women. The religious sodalities and aid societies primarily involved women.

Although their names were not mentioned in the program or the extensive newspaper coverage, almost every prominent Catholic woman in Boston was present, doubtlessly including Josie, Rose, and probably Agnes. The women sat quietly looking down on the vast floor below. At precisely six o'clock the men in black evening clothes walked into the great hall and took their places at tables set for eight or nine. Then to tumultuous applause entered O'Connell and the honored guests, and speakers including the Japanese chargé d'affaires, judges, generals, former ambassadors, a United States senator, the governor, and Mayor Fitzgerald. The dignitaries sat on a raised platform, above the other men.

More than two thousand women jammed the balconies, four times as many women as the five hundred men below. The priest and the other men supped on turtle soup, fresh salmon, squab farce, and finished with frozen pudding, ices, strawberries, cakes, cheese, and coffee. Up above the women took turns going to a hall off the first balcony where a more modest buffet had been set out.

Throughout the evening the women of Boston's Catholic elite sat observing their menfolk silently from above, a position that the church told them was rightfully and eternally theirs.

Mayor Fitzgerald's rare times with his eldest daughter were often filled with public drama. For Rose's graduation from high school in June of 1906, Fitzgerald addressed the graduating students and their families. Even if fifteen-year-old Rose hadn't

been the mayor's daughter, an honor student, and the youngest
student ever to graduate from Dorchester High, the ceremony
would have been a memorable occasion in Rose's life. The
young women in the class spent weeks planning for the day. In
recent years the students had begun to compete with one another for who could have their white graduation gowns made
of the most luxurious material, and who would have the richest
ornamentation. The women graduates often carried not simply
bouquets but baskets of flowers, and presented pins or
brooches to their classmates. Some seniors had even started
giving luncheons for their classmates that cost upwards of
$250.

Rose could have worn a gown as costly as any of her
friends', and a part of her would have taken great joy in doing
so, but there was another aspect of Rose's personality that was
more serious. She realized that her public life was a political
statement. As the graduates and their parents walked into the
high school, some of the young women wore dresses of elegant refinement, richly detailed, of rare and expensive fabric.
When Rose entered the auditorium, she stood out from all the
other students in her class, the rich and the poor, the pretty and
the plain. She wore a dress like none of the others, a simple
long-sleeved muslin gown without jewel or pins or any ornamentation except a white bow that held back her brown hair.
The modest dress, the pride of bearing, the solemn demeanor,
all conveyed the image that this was not only a serious, intelligent young woman but one who had a rare sense of values.
Rose was a pretty woman but not a classic beauty, and stood
just over five feet tall. Her chin was a mite too prominent, her
nose too long, her face too round. Her complexion was pure,
though, her posture perfect, and she exuded vitality. She had a
smile of overwhelming sweetness, and self-confidence unusual
in a girl of fifteen.

The *Post* photographer took a picture of her in the dress, and
the reporter noted why she had worn the Indian muslin gown
and wrote about it the next day. With that simple gesture of
wearing a gown of muslin she had made the first political act
of her young life.

The graduates' relatives and friends jammed the thousand-
seat assembly and stood by the score in the back of the room.
The young women in Rose's class dominated the proceedings
not only by their sheer numbers but by their talents and
achievements. Although the class president and the chairman

of the class day exercises were young men, it was young women who came on stage one after another, to play the piano or the violin, to give a vocal recital, and to perform the class poem. Moreover, of the nine students on the honor roll, eight were women.

When it came time for him to present the diplomas, Fitzgerald made a short speech. "He spoke of the fact that he was to give his own daughter a diploma and that it had never happened to any other mayor," the *Dorchester Beacon* reported. "In noting the fact that his daughter was an honor pupil, being third in her class, he said that that was a great deal better than her father had ever done."

If Rose had been a son, Fitzgerald would probably publicly have been bursting with pride at his scholastic achievements, predicting a great and glorious future for the young man. Rose, however, was a daughter, and he was not satisfied simply to have a picture of Rose, his Rose, in the paper merely trumpeting her academic achievements and her unselfish act. As Rose remembered, her father persuaded one of his journalist friends to have her picture printed in another paper under the headline "MOST BEAUTIFUL GIRL GRADUATE?" and a caption stating that "her schoolmates are unanimous in their declaration that she is not only the youngest and most beautiful girl graduate . . . but that her attractiveness surpasses that of any other girl graduate of the state."

When Rose saw the picture, she was so mortified that she began to cry. She was convinced that her friends would detest her, but they were not going to let anything so silly ruin their friendship. Rose and her close friends planned to return to Dorchester High School in the fall for a fourth year to obtain a second college preparatory degree. First came the summer.

Since Rose had been a little girl, she had always looked forward to the day when the family got on the express train of the Boston and Maine railway for the journey northward to Old Orchard Beach in Maine. This summer of 1906 her father had leased a twelve-thousand-dollar oceanfront cottage known as Bleak House, considered "one of the finest summer cottages at Old Orchard." He instructed one of his underlings to drive up the mayor's big official touring car, so that the family could travel along the boardwalk in unique style.

Rose spent far more time alone with Fitzgerald at Old Orchard Beach than she did the entire rest of the year together.

It was here on these lengthy, languid days that her love for
Fitzgerald deepened and enriched, and she learned much of
what she thought not simply about one man but her ideals
about men.

Rose and her Fitzgerald took their daily plunge in the surf,
running in the water with scores of others. Rose sat royally
next to her father as the chauffeur cruised along the seashore
road. Frequently, Fitzgerald ordered the driver to pick up vacationers, giving free rides. The mayor and his wonderful car became as much an attraction as the Ferris wheel. On another
afternoon he stopped his car and took over pitching duties
from a professional player in a baseball game, and before he
left had struck out sixteen men in seven innings.

For Rose it was all one gigantic show, with her father the
principal character. Rose loved her father and saw that life
could be lived passionately and fully, and saw too that it was
men who lived life full of daring. Josie was there too at Old
Orchard Beach, and Rose's memory of her mother was of sedate passivity. "I can still picture my mother sitting in a large
porch rocker where all the mothers sat tilting their chairs so
they could see their children splashing in the water," Rose said
later.

When the Massachusetts Redberry Club came to the beach
for their annual clambake and baseball game, the mayor
pitched for the Boston side against the team from outside the
city. Playing left field for the Bostonians was P. J. Kennedy,
one of her father's sometime allies, a plump businessman with
a handlebar mustache. P.J. was one of the older players and his
athletic ability was such that the mere catching of a ball was
greeted by his teammates as a pleasant surprise. The game
ended with an eight-to-seven victory for Boston. While the
men had been playing, the women had been busy preparing a
feast, and the famished players rushed to the corn, lobster, and
clams cooking in a pit on the beach.

That summer, perhaps even that day at the baseball game,
Rose met the son of P. J. Kennedy. Rose did not remember that
she had met Joseph P. "Joe" Kennedy once before, at a family
picnic at Old Orchard Beach in 1895, when Rose was five, and
Joe a gangly seven-year-old. But this meeting sixteen-year-old
Rose did not forget.

"I shall always remember Old Orchard as a place of magic,"
Rose said decades later, "for it was the place where Joe and I
fell in love."

* * *

Tall and lanky with straight red hair, Joe was a persuasive and popular young man. As he talked to Rose about his young life, his story resonated with similarities to her own father's early years, stories she had heard endlessly repeated. Joe was a student at Boston Latin School, the same prestigious institution her father had attended. Joe was not the student Fitzgerald had been; he was having to repeat his final year, but like her father he was an outstanding leader, president of the senior class, and colonel of the cadet regiment. Joe was a formidable baseball player. Joe was a *good* Catholic, who among all his other activities served as recording secretary for the annual reunion of the Church of the Assumption in East Boston. In all of Boston, it would have been hard to find a young man who seemed better suited for Rose, a young man more like her father.

Joe was as taken with Rose as she was with him. Soon after the families returned to Boston, Joe invited Rose to the first dance of the year at Boston Latin, a teatime affair similar to those held at Dorchester High. Even though Rose was a year older now, her father would have none of it.

Fitzgerald had a fierce possessiveness about his daughter that was matched by his near disdain toward his sons' achievements, emotionally throttling them so that they would never rise up to challenge his successes. Fitzgerald was the king of the house, and he held his daughter close to him.

Although Rose adored her father, she had inherited from him a sense of daring and adventure, qualities that she had almost nowhere to employ. She was an aggressive, strong-willed young woman, a firstborn daughter with all the self-confidence that position sometimes brought. She desperately wanted to be with Joe, to talk to him. She wanted to see him, but she knew too what an extraordinary risk that would be. It was not simply her father. It was not even the fact that as the mayor's daughter, there were eyes constantly upon her. It was the fathers of the church.

To the religious guardians of her church the mere act of seeing a young man was moral Russian roulette, an act of potential spiritual suicide. From the pulpit, in religious periodicals, and in missives the priests of the church warned where such dalliance would lead. "Heed not the voice of flatterers, for you know, that the serpent which inflicts a deadly wound, likes to hide itself amid luxuriant greens and gaily colored flowers," wrote a German priest in a missive published in 1905 by members of the Young Ladies' Sodality at the Holy Trinity Church in Boston. "Don't acknowledge the company or attention of a young man without due consideration, and *never* be alone with him. In the time of temptation have recourse to prayer."

Rose had never gone against her father before. She could not confide in her mother and ask her advice, for she knew that Josie would never approve and even if she had, she would not have stood up against her father.

In her first and ultimately only successful act of defiance in her life, Rose began to see Joe surreptitiously. It was deliciously conspiratorial, and the very difficulty of their meetings made them even more exciting. When the Fitzgeralds went to Concord Junction for the weekend to visit Josie's family, Joe managed to set up a baseball game between the Boston Latin nine and Concord High School. Rose developed a sudden interest in outside lectures, and Joe developed the same interest. They met in the great halls of the Boston Public Library, for them a place of romance, not research. Their friends joined in the conspiracy, and invited them both to parties and gatherings.

As Rose and Joe talked, they discovered that they had much in common. They were both the children of politicians. They had been born into a world of security and well-being and had not a touch of the brogue in their voices, nor the sod of Ireland on their shoes. Unlike the children of many Boston Catholics, they attended public high schools. They had seen visions of life and achievement in a world beyond a solely Catholic society. And they both were full of pulsating energy.

To Rose, Joe was a young man of infinite politeness, with the sweet demeanor of a choirboy. He had grown up in a home full of female gentility and manners, and he had a well-modulated sense of the social proprieties. Rose was the mayor's daughter, as socially desirable a young Catholic woman as any in Boston. It was unthinkable that he would act improperly.

Rose was experiencing the first taste of her adulthood, and it was sweet. Even her father was not such a parental despot as to prevent her from attending her spring class prom held in the afternoon at Dorchester High School with Joe as her escort.

It was not simply her relationship with Joe that was so delicious, but that she was experiencing the world as an adult. In March she left with her father, sister Agnes, and several other members of the family on a private parlor car of the mercantile express to Philadelphia. Her mother was not present. Rose was going because her father had asked his eldest to perform a task that might normally have been Josie's assignment: to christen a ship.

Rose slipped into this new role with perfect ease. At the docks in Philadelphia, she stood poised to christen the *Bunker Hill*, watched by dignitaries from New York and Philadelphia as well as Boston. The ship began sliding into the water before the ceremony had begun. The other dignitaries jumped back, frightened. Rose quickly reached forward and broke the bottle of champagne against the bow of the ship, to the admiring applause of everyone present. Rose had succeeded better even than her proud father would have expected. "Why that wasn't anything," she said four years later. "The vessel did start sooner than we expected, but I had the bottle of champagne in my hand, I knew that it was bad luck for a boat to reach the water without a name, and—I just smashed the bottle. Anyone with common sense could have done it."

In Boston Rose could see that life for a woman of her generation would be far different than it had been for her mother. Rose took the trolley downtown by herself, an act that in the context of her mother's young life would have been not only impossible but unthinkable. These downtown streets were full of department stores like Filene's and Jordan Marsh where women shopped and had lunch together, far beyond the shadow of the home. Some of these trolleys, subway cars, and the trains of the new elevated line were full of women factory workers who made the kinds of dresses that Rose purchased at the department stores. In the depths of the night, the trolleys carried another cargo of women, almost all of them mothers— the graying, work-worn battalion of scrubwomen—who for about four hours each night, at twenty cents an hour, cleaned the great new office buildings.

When Rose thought of working women, she did not tarry on factory workers, scrub ladies, maids, seamstresses, laundresses. She read newspapers, and the new women's pages and sections, usually written by women, were full of stories of women out in the world, from picture framers to tearoom operators, builders to doctors, laundry managers to mushroom growers.

Rose believed that she wanted to embrace this modern world and all its possibilities. "I wanted to be one of the free thinkers, one of the poets, one of the testers of boundaries,"

she said. Her own idealistic vision barely nudged the parameters of this new world. The women who were, in fact, touching
the boundaries of their time were living daring lives in which
they often risked being ostracized, whether they were making
careers for themselves, advocating birth control, working in
settlement houses, expressing their own sexual freedom, parading for women's suffrage, or working for changes in the
church.

Rose knew almost nothing of those worlds, but her friends
were much the same, and she drew young women to her by the
sheer force of her personality, by her intelligence, energy, and
joie de vivre. In high school she was the leader of her set of
college-bound young women. Rose was already reaching out
into the world, and her friends were an eclectic group. Her
closest friend at school, Ruth Evans, was a Catholic who had
already studied at a convent school in France, but she had
Anglo-Irish Protestant ancestry as well. A second high school
friend, Vera Legg, was what her daughter-in-law called "a
dyed-in-the-wool Protestant." Her third close friend, Marguerite O'Callaghan, was Irish-American.

When Rose decided to apply to Wellesley College, her three
friends decided to apply as well. At Wellesley Rose would
truly begin to experience this new women's world of the twentieth century. The renowned school lay only twenty miles west
of Boston, in an idyllic setting on Lake Waban. For a Catholic
young woman, the choice was extraordinary and daring. The
church was deeply fearful of secular education.

As worried as the church leaders were about their young
men, they were more concerned about the young women. It
was not simply that many of these graduates never married,
but that in all their innocence they would be easily spiritually
contaminated.

Wellesley had been founded for "the development of Christian character, the training of the girls to become Christian
workers." The college had broader goals, but a Catholic felt
the strongly Protestant temper of the institution. There were
daily morning prayers, Sunday services in the chapel, vespers
in the evening, and a powerful Wellesley College Christian Association.

As far as Rose was concerned, Wellesley would be a grand,
glorious adventure. She would be heading off to college with
her three closest friends, and would be near enough to Boston
so that she could still see Joe and her family. Rose completed

her college preparatory year at Dorchester, filled out her acceptance papers for college, and spent the long July days preparing her wardrobe and enjoying her friends.

For Rose all that was left before heading off to Wellesley was a last idyllic summer vacation in Old Orchard Beach. In August 1907 the Fitzgerald family took up residence at Old Orchard House, the largest hotel in the Maine resort, on a plateau above most of the town. The resort was doubly magical to her because she had met Joe here. As she walked the beach with her father and swam with him in the surging surf, she was full of ideas and plans for her college life. This was Old Orchard Beach, a time for laughter and games, for the wondrous diversions of summer.

Shortly after seven o'clock on a Thursday evening, Rose and others at Old Orchard House looked down on the town where the tall ornate wooden hotels lined the streets flying American flags from their high turrets. And there they saw at the annex to the Emerson Hotel flames leaping up from a window where an absentminded chambermaid had set the draperies on fire.

The Emerson, like all the hotels in the resort, was a wooden building, dried out in the summer sun until it was like a matchstick. Within minutes the entire hotel was ablaze. From their vantage point at Old Orchard House, Rose and her family watched the fire begin to spread, leaping from building to building, hotel to hotel, the structures igniting like piles of autumn leaves. Two buildings. Five buildings. Ten buildings. Old Orchard Beach was alight in an immense conflagration. Down in the town dazed vacationers and cottage owners grabbed whatever possessions they could carry—tables, mattresses, clothes, boxes, trunks—and hauled them to the safety of the beach.

Rose's father could not stand being merely an observer to this terrible drama. As the fire spread along the restaurants and businesses on Grand Avenue, Fitzgerald hurried down into the town, the smoke hanging like a pall of fog, flames eating their way down the street. As he walked along the sidewalk on the opposite side of the street from the fire, the Horrigan and Abbott drugstore exploded. Pieces of a soda tank flew through the air. The metal missed Fitzgerald's head by a few feet, leaving his face scratched by fragments. Fitzgerald turned and saw the man next to him had been decapitated, his bloody torso ly-

ing in the street. Another man standing nearby had been fatally
injured as well.

Fitzgerald had felt death rushing past his head. Death lay at
his feet. He could have gone off with his family, as did most
others at the scene, but he was a man of physical courage, the
noblest element of his inheritance. He rushed forward barking
commands.

The flames jumped the street and spread through the business district, the finger of flame pointing up the hill toward
Old Orchard House. Many spectators pushed into the fire lines,
jostling the police. Finally, several citizens picked up clubs and
swung the wooden staves at the onlookers, driving them back.

Up on the knoll above the town, Rose and the other Fitzgeralds looked down on the fire, watching the flames through a
fog of smoke and rumor. If anyone in town was safe it was
they, and the dazed refugees from other hotels stood beside
them, staring at the onrushing inferno. The flames moved onward, fifty acres burning now. Even Old Orchard House was
no longer safe. It appeared that nothing could prevent the fire
from reaching the hotel. Rose watched The Seashore Hotel explode into flames. It was the last hotel before Old Orchard
House. Now only the Boston and Maine Railway Station stood
between the Fitzgeralds and the flames. Her father finally returned and took the time to talk on the telephone to a reporter
from the *Boston Journal*. "It is simply awful," he said. "Our
house is not at the moment in grave danger, but it is liable to
take fire at most any time and we are preparing to leave at any
moment."

Rose and the rest of the family picked up their belongings
and prepared to flee into the smoke-filled streets. As thousands
of others hurried away from the all-consuming flames, the police tried one last desperate expedient: dynamiting the railway
station. The explosion rocked the town. Then Old Orchard
Beach seemed to grow quiet. The fire began to feed off itself.
And Old Orchard House stood there, one great building above
a plain of ruins.

In the early morning hours the Fitzgeralds returned to the
hotel. All that was left of seventy-five acres of the resort were
charred, smoking remains. Of the eighteen hotels in town, only
Old Orchard House and the Boyden stood. The flames had engulfed sixty cottages and a score of stores and restaurants as
well. At least three people had died. Some of the five thousand
guests left homeless by the blaze crowded into Old Orchard

House. Most of them took whatever belongings they had managed to save and camped out on the beach, huddled together in the predawn chill. The beach was a veritable junkyard of furniture, clothes, and people. As the tide rose, it picked up the tables and trunks and mattresses and carried them out to sea.

For Rose it was not simply buildings that burned in Old Orchard Beach. The magical summers of her childhood were engulfed in the flames, and the possibility of returning, of recapturing the spirit of the place, was gone. The embers were still warm when the town fathers began boasting they would build a new Old Orchard Beach. They built the town back, but it was never the same, and the resort never regained its prominence. When the Fitzgeralds left the resort that summer, they did not return.

These events should have seared the consciousness of a person of Rose's sensitivity and youth, her first direct encounter with the tragic uncertainty of life. Rose, however, had been taught by her mother's example, by the fathers of her church, and by the lives of women around her to discard everything that was dark and negative. She sorted through her memories, tossing away experiences that were misshapen or blemished. In a pattern Rose followed throughout her years, she took this page out of the scrapbook of her life and threw it away. That terrible night was not a time to remember, and decades later she looked back on Old Orchard Beach as a "pleasant place" of "salt water and sunshine and congenial company" and did not mention the great fire that destroyed the summer resort of her youth, a place of idyllic times and joyous family life.

4

The Mayor's Daughter

O ne day in September 1907 when Rose was busy packing
for college, her father happened to meet the new Bishop
O'Connell on a street corner. They were standing, as Fitzgerald
remembered, on Union Park Street in the South End beneath
the great unfinished towers of the Cathedral of the Holy Cross.

Eighty-five-year-old Archbishop John Williams had just
died, and already O'Connell had taken firm charge of the archdiocese. The new bishop believed that Boston was at the beginning of a new era when the Catholic majority would take
over power in Boston, not simply temporal power but moral
power. As he set forth that message, the newspapers were full
of accusations against the Catholic mayor. Fitzgerald had asked
his old friend Michael Mitchell to resign from his position
overseeing the Department of Supplies, cutting him loose to
founder by himself in a sea of charges. The mayor was still
tainted by the charges, and O'Connell had let it be quietly
known that he was opposed to Fitzgerald's reelection.

Fitzgerald chatted to the bishop, mentioning in an aside that
his beloved daughter Rose was heading off to Wellesley College. He had hardly finished his sentence when the bishop
began attacking the decision. Just a few days before, on September 7, Pius X had issued a major encyclical, *Pascendi*,
condemning what the pope called "Modernists," attacking ev-
olutionism, humanism, secularism, and unfettered intellectual
inquiry. As the new bishop saw it, the church was a mighty
army, and the general to whom he swore absolute fidelity had
issued his orders. And here the mayor, without even a moment
of priestly counsel, was sending not even his son but his
daughter off to a den of modernism, a school notoriously
steeped in Protestantism, secularism, and humanism. The

bishop was setting out to create a new Catholic Boston. Catholic children would go to parochial elementary schools, from there to Catholic high schools, and then to Catholic colleges, particularly a great new Boston College.

O'Connell was as shrewd a politician as Fitzgerald. The crux of his argument was not that Rose would lose her religious faith, but that the Irish and other Catholic voters might lose political faith in Fitzgerald. The bishop reminded Fitzgerald, moreover, that Rose was not simply any young Catholic woman. She was the mayor's daughter and she set an example to other young women who might follow her, heeding the siren call of secularism.

If Fitzgerald had sensed danger to Rose's faith, her soul, or her body, he would not have allowed her to go to Wellesley. Indeed, it was the best part of the man that approved his daughter's choice. This was the Fitzgerald who had an optimistic vision of life, of social betterment, of what the individual might achieve. This was the Fitzgerald who trusted his daughter and knew that she would return to him with her honor and her religion intact. This Fitzgerald could have told O'Connell that his daughter's faith was safe and that the good bishop need not worry. He might have dissembled, shrugging his shoulders, saying what could he do about a strong-willed daughter. As O'Connell talked, Fitzgerald listened not as the father of Rose Fitzgerald, a dutiful parent primarily concerned about his eldest daughter's welfare. He was listening as the mayor of Boston in an election year. He was listening as a politician in trouble.

For Rose these were days of immense anticipation, getting her wardrobe together, secretly seeing Joe a few more times, saying good-bye to friends, preparing her trunk for transportation to Wellesley, everything in time for the beginning of her first year at Wellesley on October 1, 1907.

One Sunday evening about a week before Rose's scheduled departure, Fitzgerald gathered Rose and her mother together in the parlor. Rose noticed that her father's face was quivering. He began by talking about politics, and Rose sat back, thinking that this was once again the father she knew. Then, suddenly, Fitzgerald told her that he and Josie had decided that she was too young to go to Wellesley.

Her father was doubly dishonest. Josie had nothing to say about the important decisions outside the home. Invoking her

name was as valid as stuffing a ballot box and was a mark of
how uncomfortable he felt. He was lying too about Rose's
youth. It was a politician's gentle dissembling, slowly letting
Rose down to the fact that she would not be going to
Wellesley, not now, not ever.

The decision haunted Rose the rest of her life. In 1969 she
told a stranger at a party: "I was accepted at Wellesley, and I
wanted to go, but in those days you didn't argue with your father." Over a decade later when she was ninety years old, she
told historian Doris Kearns Goodwin: "My greatest regret is
not having gone to Wellesley College. It is something I have
felt a little sad about all my life."

Rose portrayed herself as a passive, stoic young woman who
had sat silently listening to her father, never saying a word.
This was the image that Rose wanted portrayed to the world,
a woman who from her youth had lived a life of almost saintly
rectitude and forbearance. But Rose told another story to her
great-niece, Kerry McCarthy, a family member Rose could
trust with deeper truths. This Rose Fitzgerald was not fooled
by her father's dissembling and knew immediately what was at
stake. "There was screaming and yelling, absolute madness,"
Rose remembered. "I was furious at my parents for years. I
was angry at my church. As much as I loved my father, I never
really forgave him for not letting me go."

For Bishop O'Connell and Fitzgerald there was only one religious order appropriate to educate an upper-class Catholic girl:
the nuns of the Sacred Heart. Although Fitzgerald had not
deigned to send his daughters to the convent school, he knew
that many prominent Catholics had, from Hugh O'Brien, Boston's first Irish-American mayor, to John Boyle O'Reilly, editor of the *Boston Pilot*.

The Order of the Sacred Heart, the most aristocratic order
of nuns in the church, had been born in the aftermath of the
French Revolution when priests and nuns had been exiled,
churches burned, and the clerical educational system destroyed. In the early years of the nineteenth century, Madeleine Sophie Barat, the order's founder, set out in France to
develop boarding schools to educate upper-class girls to live
in this new, uncertain, morally dangerous world. Although the
first schools were in France, the convents were now located in
several countries including Roehampton outside London, in
several cities across the United States, and in Holland.

When her friends headed off for college, Rose took the trolley downtown to 264 and 266 Commonwealth Avenue in the Back Bay, the most prestigious and largely Protestant area of the city. There Rose entered the two row houses that made up the Convent of the Sacred Heart. The convent did not look like the kind of school Rose had known before. The four-story buildings were richly furnished and had few desks and were strangely silent, the only sounds the rustling of a nun's habit as she passed in the hall, the gentle footfalls of students walking by, or the muffled noises of the world outside.

Rose's fellow students were largely the convent-educated daughters of Boston's Catholic elite, a class of women who had been neither Rose's peers nor her close friends. There were no young men to distract her, as there had been at Dorchester High, no unwieldy large classes. Instead, here the students sat in a semicircle around the teachers' desks, no more than eight or ten girls, and worked diligently under the eye of the Sacred Heart nuns they learned to call not "Sister" but "Mother."

The day began with morning prayers. There was a prayer before each class, and the day was infused with religion. The girls were not allowed to talk, except while reciting in class or recreation. The school had no playground and during the half-hour recreation period, the girls dutifully trooped out of the building and marched to the tree-lined center of Commonwealth Avenue, a mini park on the elegant thoroughfare. The *religieuses* considered the Back Bay "hostile to Catholicism" and the cloistered nuns watched from behind the convent windows as the students played beanbag, dodgeball, and other games among themselves.

The nuns provided an education that had all the rigors of a Jesuit institution. Rose was in a special senior class that was much like the first year in college. The ideal for its older students was to do "for young Catholic women much the same work that Vassar and Wellesley do for non-Catholics." Rose pursued a formidable array of subjects, some of which she had studied at Dorchester (Roman and Greek history, written French, Latin), and others that were new challenges (psychology, logic, medieval history and literature, spoken French). She knew nothing about psychology or medieval history, and spoken French was a blur of unintelligible phrases, but it was unthinkable that she would go to Fitzgerald and complain. "I never thought of remonstrating with Father," she reflected.

* * *

Rose did not devote her education simply to the Sacred Heart. She also traveled to the New England Conservatory on Huntington Avenue to study piano. The school was a serious professional institution but was also full of proper young ladies for whom music was an approved avocation. Many of them were learning to play what was known as the "thousand-dollar tune." This was a melody that a young lady could plunk out on the piano in the parlor before guests, preferably including a suitor, as well as a father reflecting on the thousand dollars in lessons that had managed this achievement. Although the term "the thousand-dollar tune" was spoken with rueful amusement, it was a symbol of social attainment.

Rose, then, was attending the New England Conservatory in part to advance her father's social position. Rose was not perfunctorily going through the expected routine. She studied hard under Alfred De Voto, a formidable musician, who was the pianist of the Longy Club of the Boston Symphony. She received A's in both sessions of the academic year.

Rose was often off in the city by herself, attending classes, a matinee at the Boston Symphony, or Burton Holmes's travel lectures. That made it easier to see Joe. He was having to repeat his senior year at Boston Latin. Until now their conversations had resonated with the commonality of their experiences. A politician's daughter, a politician's son. A Catholic girl, a Catholic boy. A public-school girl, a public-school boy. She was going off to college. He was going off to college. The vistas of their lives seemed to be opening up together.

Now Joe's life was so much larger, and almost by definition he was a greater part of her life than she was of his. In the fall he would be going to Harvard College among the best of the Brahmins, the best of the American elite, while Rose was studying with the nuns. Rose was far more scholarly than Joe. Joe was a go-getter, not a student, and if Harvard was an intellectual feast, it was a repast at which he would only nibble. Yet Joe was going out into a world where her father and her church had prohibited her from going. He would be learning things, experiencing people and ideas that she would never experience directly, but only through others.

As Rose traveled to school and back, on the street corners newsboys hawked the latest edition, yelling out the headlines of the latest Finance Commission accusation against her father's administration, or the newest issue in her father's reelec-

tion campaign. Her father's old friend, Mitchell, was featured
in many of the articles. As Rose was growing up, he had been
like a "big, comfortable teddy bear" who rumbled into their
home with his pockets full of trinkets and candies that he dispensed to the young Fitzgeralds. He had been cast out of the
precincts of the family now, eventually to be convicted of corruption and sentenced to the House of Corrections for one year
of hard labor, his lips eternally sealed. He didn't exist to Rose
any longer, part of the melancholy discipline of politics. No
matter how loud the newsboys yelled, Rose learned not to hear
them. "MAYOR TAKES CARE OF FRIENDS." The Finance Commission continued coming up with devastating accusations. "EX-
PLANATION OF THE MAYOR." No matter how black and big the
headlines, she trained herself not to see. In October after testifying before the Finance Commission, George Koch, a clerk in
the Department of Supplies, attempted to commit suicide. The
clerk admitted to accepting gifts, and overseeing a new contract for flagstone twice the price of the old, and Fitzgerald
suspended him.

For many in Boston, Fitzgerald personified the corruption
and graft that was sullying the name of democracy. On the
stormy, rain-swept night of the election Fitzgerald looked out
the window of City Hall at a crowd of five hundred shouting
his name in derision. They marched and shouted, celebrating
Fitzgerald's defeat by the Republican candidate, George Albee
Hibbard.

Even as the unruly crowd surrounded City Hall, one of the
mayor's associates asked Fitzgerald: "What of the future?"

"We held a conference a little while ago," he said, "and began our planning for the next election."

Rose had a great instructor in learning not to look at the
negative. In defeat, Fitzgerald was the same jaunty, irascible
politician he had been in victory. In the next few months the
former mayor busied himself defending his administration
against corruption charges. "Let them probe me as deeply as
they want to," he asserted, when the Finance Commission continued its investigations. "I welcome it."

In December, shortly before he left office, Fitzgerald became the first mayor of Boston to be called before a grand
jury; there he swore that his only involvement in a series of
contracts that had bilked the city was in signing documents
about which he was abysmally ignorant. In the end, despite the
massive probe, nothing was ever proven specifically against

Fitzgerald. In its final report the Finance Commission portrayed an institutional corruption where "thousands throughout the city, of all classes and conditions, rich and poor, see no harm in taking money from the city without giving in return a full equivalent."

Fitzgerald had not been indicted but there hovered over him a suspicion that never fully went away. He had entered government poor, and he was leaving office rich. He was a classic politician of his age, and in all probability his hands had left the till with coins sticking to them.

The former mayor had more time with his family now. He was not unaware that young men took a keen interest in his daughter. Fitzgerald felt that he knew the perfect young man for his Rose. His name was Hugh Nawn, the son of Harry Nawn, one of the mayor's closest friends. Nawn was a wealthy contractor and the family lived right up the street. Fitzgerald often dropped in on the Nawns' mansion late in the evenings, sitting in the kitchen with Harry, discussing politics while sharing hot cocoa and peanut butter sandwiches. It was almost like sitting in his own kitchen. Fitzgerald watched young Hugh grow up. He was a fine young man, no doubt about that, polite, deferential, intelligent, a Harvard student no less, with the prospect of one day taking over his father's business.

On the surface Joe was also a worthy suitor. P. J. Kennedy was not as wealthy as Harry Nawn, but he was a highly successful businessman and politician. Fitzgerald had had his temporary fallings out with Joe's father but that was politics, and the East Boston politician had backed Fitzgerald in his unsuccessful reelection campaign.

Young Joe had excellent prospects too, but Rose's father did not like Joe. He believed that he was not right for Rose. Fitzgerald was relentlessly determined to thwart this relationship. For a man who could make words dance and sing, the former mayor could never bring himself to talk candidly to Rose about Joe. That was the family pattern, never to deal openly with emotional matters, never to discuss candidly questions of the heart. He wanted the best for his daughter, but he would not and could not face the matter of Joe directly. Instead, he attempted to manipulate his daughter's life in a series of acts as shrewdly duplicitous as anything he did in politics. At times he attempted to keep Rose physically apart from Joe. At times he attempted to woo Rose away with other suitors. And when his efforts didn't work he banned the young man from the house on Welles Avenue.

"I was in love with Joe as he was with me," Rose recalled. "When I finally told my parents and said I was going to marry him, they sent me to Europe. It was foolish on my part to say anything. He had not asked me to marry him. He knew he was too young. But I thought it was all very romantic."

Fitzgerald announced that he and Josie would take Rose and her younger sister, Agnes, on a two-month tour of Europe and then deposit them at the Sacred Heart convent in Blumenthal, Holland, where they would study for a year. Rose was almost eighteen years old, but she had little say in all this, nor did her younger sister.

In sending his daughters away, the former mayor was giving Rose time to forget Joe and separating his daughters from continuing scandals and accusations. Equally important, sending Rose and Agnes to Europe was profoundly advantageous to the family's social position among Boston's Catholic elite. Fitzgerald's reputation was darkly sullied. Yet only the finest Catholic families sent their daughters to the Sacred Heart. To send his daughters to Europe was an even greater statement of the family's fidelity to the highest Catholic ideals, and to their social ranking. The European convent schools were so exclusive that he could not have sent Rose and Agnes to the convent of Roehampton in Great Britain where they would have had the advantage of knowing the language. There the fact that Fitzgerald was former mayor of Boston meant nothing. There a student had to be either from an old English Catholic family, or as a foreigner the daughter of a diplomat, a military officer, or of noble blood. By sending Rose and Agnes to Holland, Fitzgerald was making a significant statement about his place in this new Catholic Boston that Bishop O'Connell was building. The *Boston Post* noted that "both girls are very ambitious and musically inclined" and that the convent had educated "many of the daughters of noted families, the children being sent there from all parts of the globe."

In the education that Rose was receiving at the Sacred Heart, Europe was the center of the world, of religion, of culture. The Sacred Heart Academy at Blumenthal was not Wellesley; nor was it Harvard, and it meant being away from Joe, but it was an adventure, a journey beyond.

* * *

On July 18, 1908, Rose stood on the Boston pier with her mother and sister waiting for Fitzgerald to appear. He was at Quincy House, having lunch and a shave, conferring with his brothers and cronies. In the harbor, billows of smoke rose out of the smokestacks of the steamship *Cymric* into the darkening sky, signaling that the transatlantic ship was about to sail. On the dock stood hundreds of enthusiastic friends, supporters, several priests, and former city officials. Almost everyone who had shown up this overcast afternoon wanted it known that they had stood with Fitzgerald in his times of trouble. Joe was not among the crowd this day but his father, P.J., was there. Young Joe's sister, Loretta, was one of seventeen persons who had sent flowers to the departing family.

As the ship prepared to sail, Rose, her mother, and her sister took the launch out to the *Cymric*. They were used to waiting for Fitzgerald. Out on the *Cymric*, they stood on deck nervously watching the dock. Ten minutes. Twenty minutes. A half hour. Still Fitzgerald had not appeared, and the steamship seemed ready to leave. Suddenly the Fitzgerald women saw two tugboats moving out from the docks, one carrying Fitzgerald, and the second holding close to fifty of his friends, getting in a last good-bye, waving and shouting as he boarded the *Cymric*. As the steamship finally departed, Rose and Agnes fluttered large handkerchiefs while the ex-mayor stood nearby on deck waving an American flag to the well-wishers on shore.

For Rose's eighteenth birthday, on July 22, 1908, Fitzgerald took his daughter to visit the passengers in steerage. Here primarily were poor immigrants, many of them Irish, who had scraped together the dollars to visit their former homelands. Only two generations ago Rose's ancestors had traveled to America in conditions worse than this. For Rose, however, the distance between these dark, cramped quarters and the elegant salons of first class was so great that a visit here was like an outing into a foreign land. The day made little apparent impression on her; she made only a brief notation in her diary. Nor did she especially note the sighting of the Irish coast.

Whether it was Ireland or England, Germany or France, Fitzgerald was the tourist nonpareil, rushing from cathedral to cathedral, museum to museum, checking off each location as if he were doing an inventory. On August 22, their train stopped for a few minutes en route to Geneva. Rose had time to purchase a picture postcard of the Church of Saint-Jean and write a few words to Emily Hannon, telling her aunt she was having a "dandy time." It was one of her favorite phrases, and she used it again and again in her postcards home. Rose's postcards to her mother's family convey no longing for the streets and accents of Boston, and no apprehension at what awaited her at Blumenthal, even in her last vacation postcard to John Hannon, her uncle: "We are here at Interlaken now. It is perfectly beautiful, snow on the mountains directly in front of us. Blumenthal in less than two weeks. Oh joy!"

Rose was a diligent correspondent, and the many postcards and letters that she mailed to America were the beginning of a habit that she had all her life. There was another habit that was beginning here too, and that was never to complain. Nowhere in these cards and notes was there a hint of the anxiety and insecurity that she must have felt about to be dropped into a world in which the language and almost every aspect of life would be foreign to her American-bred ways.

The Fitzgeralds traveled to the town of Vaals, in eastern Holland near the French and German borders, an area that had passed from country to country, with the vicissitudes of war and time and power. Off the main thoroughfare the Fitzgeralds traveled up a side road that meandered through the countryside. There in the midst of a scene "suggestive of Dutch painters and Flemish mystics" sat the three-story stone building and surroundings known as Blumenthal, the valley of flowers.

Women who have attended a Sacred Heart boarding school often remember the first day as an occasion of wrenching partings and muffled tears. Rose, however, was a woman who remembered greetings, not farewells. She never spoke of what it was like that day to say good-bye to her mother and father knowing she would not see them for many months. She had learned to hold her emotions tightly clenched, and she did not let her parents or perhaps even herself know what anxiety she felt.

Rose had studied at a Sacred Heart convent for a year, but she would be a boarding student now in a European school, and it was profoundly different. "Nothing could have prepared Rose for her experience in the convent in Blumenthal," reflected Sister Gabrielle Husson, a Sacred Heart nun.

As soon as they entered the convent, Rose and Agnes were each given numbers. Among the students were members of the German nobility, *der Adel*, who bore such titles as *Frei-Fräulein* and *Durchlaucht*, girls who bore the names of the great families of Germany and France, but both the daughter of a duke and that of the former mayor of Boston were known by their numbers. Then a nun led them to the wardrobe room, where they found lockers with their numbers on them. For her high school graduation, Rose had worn a simple frock but, like her mother, she loved fashion, silks, satins, glorious dresses. All these she put away now, along with any books the nuns found inappropriate, or other personal adornments. Another girl who arrived about the same time as Rose brought with her a copy of the King James version of the Bible. "You cannot read that book without supervision," the wardrobe sister admonished. The nun took the Bible away, and gave her the *Key of Heaven*, *Introduction to a Devout Life*, and *The Imitation of Christ*.

The nuns had a subtle awareness of the foibles and idiosyncrasies of their charges. Since Rose and Agnes were so far from home, they allowed them to room together and have a rug as well as some pictures. Rose placed a photo of her father with Vice President Charles Warren Fairbanks in her austere chamber. Above the nightstand she set a photo of Joe.

They fell in line with the other students and were almost indistinguishable from the others. Most of the students were German, speaking what along with French was the language of the convent. But some girls came from France and Ireland, and four from the United States.

The students would have had much to talk about but the monastic rituals of the convent had no place for the exuberant chatter of young women. "We try to talk together at night when we are getting ready for bed," Rose wrote her mother in October. "We do not have much opportunity during meals for we have conversation only during breakfast time for a few minutes. During dinner there is German reading, and during supper, French reading, and we are silent. I am used to this regulation now, but at first it was very hard."

Before dawn the bells began to ring awakening the nuns and calling them to office. At ten minutes to six the bell sounded in the corridor of the wing of the building where Rose, Agnes, and the other senior students had their tiny rooms, apart from most of the pupils. At the first sound, they got out of their beds, dropped to their knees, and remained with their hands clasped in prayer, eyes closed. "Coeur sacré de Jésus, Coeur Immaculé de Marie," a nun intoned in the corridor. "Je vous donne mon coeur," the students replied in loud voices.

After carefully folding their nightgowns and putting any dirty linen in a sack, the girls had thirty-five minutes to perform their toilet and to dress. Even their bathing was closely regulated. For that ritual of cleanliness, the students protected their modesty by wearing special cotton bath dresses. The rules instructed: "Decency and modesty are virtues that the students must always preserve as their most beautiful possession; they must never forget that the eyes of God and those of the guardian angel are watching them all the time and everywhere. They must put on and take off their clothes behind curtains."

In silence, then, the young women dressed in long-sleeved black dresses, black shoes, and black stockings. They wore their hair in the obligatory manner, plaited down the back and tied with two black ribbons. Then they marched to the chapel in pairs for morning prayers and mass, their heads covered by veils. Still in pairs the students genuflected before the altar, and then went to the pews. The nuns, eternally observant, watched the girls in the pews, catching a student making a muffled whisper hidden behind hands clasped in prayer, another student stretching her shoulders, or nodding off half asleep, infractions that the *religieuses* duly marked down.

At breakfast the girls sat upright, and ate silently, listening to the nun's lecture. There was no time for frivolity. They were not to develop "particular friendships." They were not to touch or hug one another. The hours of the day were broken down, and broken down again, from "lever" in the morning at five-fifty to "prière et coucher" at eight-thirty at night. Study. Class. Recreation. Study. Writing lesson. Luncheon. Recreation. Recitation. Every moment of the day was regulated. Even the time of private study was broken down into periods as short as ten or fifteen minutes, so that each girl in her cubicle moved like a metronome from act to act, routine to routine.

The routine was modeled in part after St. Cyr, the school founded in 1684 by Louis XIV and Mme. de Maintenon, his devout companion, to educate poor aristocratic women to become models of virtue. Properly married, they would bring to the degenerate court of Versailles a new piety. "Learn to obey, for you will obey forever," Maintenon instructed her charges.

Mme. de Maintenon's principal advisor was Bishop Fénelon, whose methods and writings became part of the early curriculum of the Sacred Heart. Like the Humanists before him, Fénelon believed that the female sex was full of potential evil.

Even young girls would fall into vice if they were not controlled. Lust, anger, pride, idleness—there was no end to it. The Humanists believed that to control their proclivities, young girls must eat the blandest of food, wear the simplest and coarsest of clothing, and sleep in the hardest of beds. They must read only rigidly prescribed texts. They must be disciplined.

During the first weeks Rose was occupied in simply learning the routine and rituals, practicing her French, the lingua franca of the convent, trying to make sense of the German that a nun read over the noontime meal and French over dinner, watching over Agnes who was not so alertly intelligent as her older sister, and observing all the nuances of this world. Rose was faced with the melancholy prospect that this was not a short excursion, but a whole year, an eternity in the life of an eighteen-year-old. One of Rose's schoolmates, the Irish writer Mary Magiore Colum, cried herself to sleep many nights. As for Rose, as depressed as she must have been, it was unthinkable that she should protest to her parents, or ask to go home. The letters were read and censored by the nuns, and if she had dared to condemn her life at Blumenthal, her missive probably would have been returned to her.

At the end of November, she wrote a letter to her parents in which she asked special permission to mail it directly without the nuns reading it. Even in this letter, she did not rail against the unfairness of being sequestered in this remote convent, but gave full vent to her irony. One of her teachers had told her that *Les Misérables*, Victor Hugo's magnificent tale of revolutionary France, had been condemned by the church and was "a frightfully wicked book."

"I knew that we had an English translation of it at home," Rose wrote, "and so I thought perhaps you would want it destroyed. It might not look well to have it in our library. The story deals with exaggerated social conditions and that is why it is wicked. You see I am more or less acquainted with the book. Fortunately I did not inquire what grade of excommunication would come to individuals who had already read the book."

Even without the nuns censoring her letters, Rose was not the kind of young woman to complain. The most she allowed herself was to write her mother that "a year ought not to be very long in passing, and then I can go home, and never have to go away again."

Years later Rose would recall "the loneliness of waking up on those raw and chilly mornings when the only sound you heard was the rustling of garments as dozens of girls in dozens of rooms stepped behind dozens of curtains to slip off their dressing gowns." On winter mornings it was so cold that, as Rose wrote her mother, her hands turned "a purplish bluish color." In the closed world of the convent, diseases were endemic, and for several months she suffered from a sore throat. But such discomfort was only a minor cross, a lesson to be borne and learned. In the winter almost all the students sneezed and coughed with persistent colds, their hands marked with chilblains, raw itching sores. They ate food fit for penance, bread and butter and tea for breakfast, a light tea called *goûter*, supper, and a full meal at midday, the main food of the day. They were often tired when they rose at dawn to kneel on the cold hard floor of the chapel, tired as they sat in the unheated classrooms.

Rose did not question any of the myriad rules, bend them, or avoid them. She was not the kind of student who would think of smuggling in a forbidden novel. Nor was she so forgetful as to leave her walking shoes under her bed, so careless as improperly to fold her chapel veil, so brazen as to whisper in the halls, her impudence duly noted by the sound of the *surveillante's* wooden clapper.

All week long the teachers in the classes and *surveillantes* in chapel, the halls, and study hour noted conduct good and bad and indifferent. Then on Sunday the entire school marched into an assembly with the mother superior. Rose and the other girls wore special dresses and white gloves. She waited with anticipation for the mother superior to speak, and to learn if this week she had had the discipline and the focus to merit a blue *Très bien* card. Some girls never received them. A moment's laxness—that was all it took. The mother superior passed across the corridor thirty yards away, and a girl neglected to curtsy. The nuns saw everything, and that was enough, more than enough to take away a *Très bien*.

The students stood up class by class, and the mother superior called out their names while the rest of the students sat with perfect posture. Those whose conduct had been impeccable received *Très bien* cards, and those girls walked forward two by two, curtsied to the mother superior, took their blue

cards in their right hands and set them down in a box on the
table, with a careful elegant gesture. It was unthinkable to drop
the card like a milkmaid depositing an empty pail. After all,
these were the daughters of aristocratic families, and they were
learning the discipline and etiquette that would allow them to
move into the great balls and the mirrored dining halls of Europe with perfect aplomb.

Those who had stumbled the past week received brown *Bien*
cards, and they too walked forward, curtsied, and took their
cards and placed them in the box where they were gathered up
to be used the following week. The gray *Assez bien* were
marks of severe disappointment, and the girls who received
them walked forward last of all. Sometimes, though, if a girl
had spoken back to a nun or performed an act of equal infamy,
she received no card at all, and she stood alone at her chair.
She wore no further badge of humiliation, no sackcloth, for everyone knew and there was no hiding her shame.

The convent was a place of piety and penance and mortification. Mary Colum recalled how the nuns discussed how the
saints mortified themselves by "wearing hair shirts, or belts
with nails in them, sleeping little, fasting a great deal, humiliating themselves before others." The nuns had their own private world of mortification and private penance, particularly
during Lent. In *Frost in May*, Antonia White's autobiographi-
cal novel of life at a Sacred Heart convent, she wrote of "small
iron chains bound tightly around" the arms of a nun, "and
whispers of spiked belts and wire scourges." Nearly half a century later, in her nonfiction book on the order, V. V. Harrison
wrote that "nuns were still using the discipline, a whip-like device, and a small metal ring with spikes that fit over the arm
as methods of self-inflicted pain."

The system itself, in the words of Mary Colum, was a
"small, self-contained totalitarian state." The *religieuses*
watched over the girls not like jailers seeking to imprison their
charges, however, but as guides leading them ahead on their
spiritual journey and teaching them self-control. They were attempting to create a generation of young women who were
"very strong, very innocent and determined to do something
for God in their life." The austere, rigid world of the convent
was a setting of such psychological power and acumen that
most of the girls were drawn into it, a theater in which all were
players.

In this regimented convent all secular passions and emotions had been dammed up and channeled into only one outlet: the creation of heartfelt faith. Although the students received an excellent classical education, the immense, transcendent drama of Blumenthal was not primarily of the intellect but of the spirit. The more artistic, the more impressionable, the more idealistic a student was, the more likely that she would be pulled into the vortex of this drama.

In Boston, Rose had studied the lives of the martyrs, and she had heard about the oppression of the church, but it was something that had happened long ago to someone else. Here at Blumenthal she was in the midst of that history. These nuns were not mouthing abstractions about martyrdom and self-sacrifice. They had witnessed to their faith by leaving their native countries. The German government had closed the Sacred Heart convents on its soil. The anticlerical France of the Third Republic was closing the last of the French convents. These French nuns were arriving in Blumenthal too, like the German nuns, never to return to their native land, and never to leave the convent. The nuns saw themselves as living not in Catholic Christendom, but in a hostile world where their young charges would have to suffer for their faith. Here at Blumenthal each nun took her place as part of an intricate human machine devoted to the creation of faith.

"Death, and making all life a preparation for death, filled the atmosphere," wrote Colum. At the hour of Rosary, the students walked in pairs to the garden. "Hail Mary, full of grace, the Lord is with thee," a nun intoned. "Holy Mary, mother of God, pray for us sinners," the girls responded. They went into the *Friedhof*, the nun's graveyard with row upon row of graves, each marked by a small black cross. There stood an open grave, the earth freshly turned, the black cross with no name nor date, a grave ready for the next nun who would die. The nuns worked so hard, prayed so profoundly, and fasted so often that many of them died young, their bodies out here where the nuns and the children of Sacred Heart stood now and prayed for all who had gone before them.

Rose knew how she was supposed to feel and to think, but she could not help her melancholy longing for Boston and her parents. "We were terribly homesick," Rose recalled in 1911. "At Christmastime we sent cables, but there was all that water between Boston and us. If anything happened to any of the family the whole ocean had to be crossed before we could reach home—rather an appalling thought, don't you think?"

The passionate emotions of this religious drama were alien to her. To become part of the emotional tapestry of Blumenthal she would have to enter into this whole process of self-denial and lose herself within the experience. Of course, she was religious and thought herself a good Catholic.

In November Rose wrote her mother that "if I am extremely angelic, I may become an aspirant for the Children of Mary; later I may become a Child of Mary. That is the highest honor a child of the Sacred Heart can receive. So I shall have to be a model of perfection for the next few months." Becoming a Child of Mary was the most serious religious commitment a girl could make at Blumenthal, short of deciding to become a nun. The Children of Mary were supposed to take the religious life out into the world, and live lives as wives, mothers, and charitable workers that the cloistered nuns could not live. Yet Rose's letter was charged with youthful bravado, her intentions tossed off with no more concern than signing up for an advanced class in Latin.

During those difficult fall months, Rose worried primarily not about her faith but about Christmas vacation. Although Rose addressed most of her letters to her mother, this time she wrote her father to request permission to go on a chaperoned trip to Berlin and other German cities. She and Agnes "jumped and talked and laughed" when they received his positive reply.

On New Year's Eve Rose and Agnes sat in a loge at the Berlin Opera beneath the kaiserin and crown prince. The two young women took the yokes out of their girlish dresses so that they too might wear "décolleté" gowns. And they sat there in the midst of a romantic world of royalty and wealth, of grande dames and titled lords, where Rose acted as if she belonged.

When Rose and Agnes returned from their vacation early in January, one of the most important events of the year took place at Blumenthal: the annual retreat. For three days there would be absolute silence. There would be no classes. After morning holy mass, they would spend the rest of the day attending three separate sermons, reading devotional books, saying their rosary, and going to confession, all the time reflecting on the eternal mysteries of God.

For her first time at Blumenthal, Rose felt totally a part of the religious experience. As she reflected half a century later: "It was not in my nature to remain an outsider for long." She wasn't thinking about Boston or about European travel. "Deprived of everything else, I became intensely aware of all the things I had taken for granted—the beauty of the sky and the stars at night, of the birds singing and the trees in bloom," Rose said. "And with this heightened awareness of God and of His world, I emerged more at peace with myself than I had ever been before."

Rose had opened herself to the most profound experience of Blumenthal. She was deepening her faith. Beyond that, she was formulating a plan for her whole life. "I decided to forgive them all," she said years later. "All of them, my father, the bishop, the church, politics. I was not going to rebel against my faith but become its advocate, to become truly a Child of Mary. And I would marry Joe, too, no matter what anyone thought or said." In Rose's mind it all came together, her faith, her future, and her Joe. As a Child of Mary she could have them all.

To be a Child of Mary, Rose would have to live an exemplary life, beyond reproach. She was an intensely competitive person, no less so now that her aspirations had been thwarted and denied. Here was a place finally that she could compete, in the pursuit of virtue and faith. "When I got to Blumenthal and saw the severe conditions in which I lived, I could have been rebellious," Rose said. "I decided that if I could not be one of America's new thinkers, new women leaders, then I would become one of the church's deep-thinking leaders, one of the most impressive women in my faith."

The convent school did not quell Rose's exuberance, nor her abilities as a leader. When her father's birthday in February was approaching, she and Agnes decided to make fudge and mail it to their father. "The girls take cooking lessons as part of the convent course, so we got permission to use the kitchen," Rose remembered three years later. "All the girls—and the cooking mistress, too—watched us with open eyes. We packed father's in a box, and then we gave each of the girls a piece. They thought it was the best thing they'd ever tasted—why, the cooking mistress asked for the recipe herself. So I presume before long all Germany will be eating American fudge. We introduced wide hair ribbons into Germany too—and wide shoe laces."

* * *

One of Rose's American friends, Margaret Finnegan, stood behind Rose at confession when she took an hour with the priest.
Margaret could only wonder what multitude of sins Rose
might have to require so much of the priest's time. There were
sins of pride and vanity that the world outside treated at most
as blemishes, scratches on the soul that here the nuns magni-
fied into monstrous proportion. The struggle for goodness was
a struggle to deny, to contain, to repress. It was a struggle for
self-control, self-discipline, self-denial.

In May, Rose was named a Child of Mary. From now on she
would be a surrogate for these cloistered nuns, taking the Sacred Heart out into the world, into her daily life. She would be
a wife and mother, and her acts of charity would spread out
from the home, like rays of sunshine. From now on she would
attend mass every day and a special mass on the first Friday of
every month, and live with God and her faith in the forefront
of her mind.

As a Child of Mary, Rose made a series of personal promises. These were not the pledges of a young woman who anticipated that her life would go forward like a series of pictures
in the rotogravure, genteel images of upper-class wealth.
Brought up in privilege, Rose vowed that she would form her
"will to courage and patience in privations" and guard herself
"by prayer, watchfulness, a certain habit of mortification."
Rose pledged she would be "in difficult moments obtaining
from 'Our Lady of Sorrows' courage to suffer as she did,
standing at the foot of the Cross."

At Blumenthal Rose learned that self-sacrifice, self-
abnegation, and suffering were the crosses that her sex carried
through life, and she stood ready to pick up that burden. "Besides prayer and dedication to God, and frequent reception of
the Sacraments, the practical application of religion to everyday living was taught to us," Rose recalled. "Above all, a trust
and abiding confidence in the wisdom and goodness of God
were implanted in our hearts so that we might turn to Him
later when the tragedies of life threatened to overwhelm us."

For Rose it was not "if" the tragedies might occur but
"when" they would occur. These children of the Sacred Heart
were the daughters of wealth and privilege, and their education
was training for tragedy, for lives of moral and spiritual challenge. As those of a different faith stood waiting for a bounty
of goodness from their God, the children of the Sacred Heart
awaited calamity and sorrow, as if only then could they prove

their fealty to God. As Mother Stuart, the order's most articulate thinker, wrote: "The lover of the Sacred Heart knows that he has not yet believed until he has said his Credo in the midst of doubts, or hoped until he has hoped against all hope when all seemed lost, or loved until he has given all the substance of his house and counted it nothing, or served until he has served in the midst of overwhelming difficulties, or sung to God until he has sung in the night."

Rose did not want to go to Wellesley any longer; indeed, as a Child of Mary, it would have been unthinkable for her to go to a non-Catholic college. She considered herself "ignorant compared with some of the girls who have been in convents all their lives and who have been free from all the distractions of the theaters."

Nonetheless, Rose had no intention of discarding the world. In April when her father had suggested that she and Agnes should consider staying a second year at Blumenthal she had written back that "it would be too much of a sacrifice for you and for us to remain away another year or two." She was ready to leave and live her life in Boston. She was still a young woman who adored beautiful clothes, taking pleasure in the touch of a fabric or the shape of a new outfit. She felt that she had "not a thing to wear" and was inordinately pleased with the new white dress and black suede slippers that she would wear in a graduation play. She had made no vow of poverty. She still loved the things of the world—clothes and dances, laughter and fun.

Rose was still ambitious, but she had turned down the bright vision of her life to cast an intense, narrow focus. Rose's faith and her idea of womanhood had become inseparable. Her mother was unconsciously a model for Rose as well. From now on whenever Rose turned to her faith, she was turning to ideas about a woman's proper place in the world. It was in the home, ideally in a great home, a home with servants and dinner parties and formal affairs; a home with children administered to by nurses and nannies; a home in which even bishops and cardinals might come for dinner.

Rose believed that she would marry Joe one day, raise a family, and live as a Catholic wife and mother. That was what she should prepare for now. If her father ran again for mayor, Rose thought that she might help her mother at home, watch over the little ones, aid them in their studies. "There are lots of things I could learn at home," she wrote her mother. "For instance how to receive, how to write an archbishop, etc. By the way, Miriam [Finnegan] tells me you must have a special kind of paper on which to write him."

A year ago Rose would have been more interested in conveying her own ideas to a bishop. Now she was concerned with choosing the paper on which in all likelihood a man would write the words.

In the summer of 1909, Fitzgerald arrived at Blumenthal to take his daughters home with what Rose remembered as "tears and open arms." Although he was running for mayor again in the fall, Fitzgerald had taken the time to sail to Europe without Josie to escort his two daughters back to Boston. "Perhaps it is a paradox," Fitzgerald said later, "but I must have seen more of my family in my trips away from home than I have in my own house. Our trips have been picnics."

The family visited the sights of Belgium and Holland, walked the fashionable boulevards of Paris where the two young women bought velvet hats that they bedecked with ostrich feathers, and then traveled on across the English Channel to Great Britain before the voyage back across the Atlantic Ocean. "The thing I enjoyed most . . . was the day I spent aboard Sir Thomas Lipton's yacht," Rose recalled, "when the Czar and the English King reviewed the squadron at Cowes. Through our glasses we could see the jackies salute as the King and the Czar went past and at night all the vessels were blazing with electric lights and the whole harbor was illuminated, little boats were hurrying back and forth, bands playing—it was splendid."

When the White Star liner *Cymric* docked at Charlestown on August 20, Josie stood on the pier waiting to greet her daughters whom she had not seen for a year, and her husband who had been away for almost two months. "Our mother greeted us with tears in her eyes," Rose wrote in her autobiography. "She had been terribly lonely." Josie had not seen her husband for weeks, but he had no time for his wife now. He greeted her and said a few words to the waiting reporters, and then went off with his associates. That evening the *Boston Post* reported he had attended a ball in Quincy where he danced "with every pretty girl who wanted a partner."

Without Josie's two eldest daughters, the house had seemed half empty. Just as Rose and Agnes returned, her husband was running for office again, rushing in and out of the house hardly long enough to change his shirt collars, casting Josie into a public eye that she abhorred.

All her life Josie had been trained to project a smiling face to the world. She, like the other women of her generation, was admonished always to be upbeat, chipper, and happy. It did not matter what difficulties might arise during her day. She was to burden neither her children nor her husband with mundane woes and quotidian complaints. When her husband came home, he might well be "moody and selfish," and it was up to her to "study him—his needs, his moods, his weak as well as his strong points—and know how to make him forget himself."

Josie could not talk about why it was so difficult for her to project the smiling image that was her womanly duty and why she was so full of bitterness. Her inability to speak about her personal life was a pattern of behavior that her own parents had carried with them from the old country. It had become part of Rose as well and the emotional fabric of the entire family. To the world, the Fitzgeralds appeared a merry and open family, scions of that Irish race full of poets and orators and barroom bards who turned the language into a lyre on which they played melodies full of emotion. Even within the confines of the home, the Fitzgeralds were a boisterous brood, but as in many Irish-American homes that openness was an emotional façade.

Almost no one sympathized with Josie's plight, or considered it a plight at all. Her own niece, Geraldine Hannon, remembers her aunt as "a dissatisfied person. Maybe she was putting up with a lot with John F. But nothing was right with Josie. Nobody else in the family was like that on either side, and I didn't like her very well. She froze and was aloof when she met people." Others were even more harsh in their judgment of a woman who appeared to have a life of privilege and honor. To them she was "really a pill," a woman who "brought gloom into the house."

During September, Fitzgerald campaigned until after midnight many evenings. When he woke up around nine, Rose brought the morning newspapers to him. She watched as her father went through the pages looking at stories that accused him of everything from breaking up his opponent's public meetings to having "hands stuck in the treasury." These were vicious charges, and yet her father appeared totally nonplussed, sometimes nodding off for a few minutes' more sleep before rising.

It did not occur to Rose that some of the charges might even be true. "Taking my cue from his example," Rose wrote later, "I calmed down and began to accept the idea that gossip and slander and denunciation and even vilification are part of the price one pays for being in public life." In this campaign Rose had begun to train her emotions to withstand any assault, any attack, and had come to view almost any charge against her family or her kin as nothing more than lies or half truths, the petty games of politics.

During her year in Blumenthal, Rose had thought often of Joe. When she saw him in Boston, Rose believed their love had withstood their year of separation. Joe's days were full of classes. Since as a proper young woman Rose could hardly meet her beau regularly in the evenings, she saw him much less than she would have liked.

In late September, her parents sent her to the Sacred Heart boarding school on 133rd Street in New York City for a final year of finishing, similar to the first year of college. The academy had moved from lower Manhattan in 1847 to the old Lorillard estate in a village known as Manhattanville. Since then the metropolis had grown up around the school. Within the gated estate, its precincts ringed by tall trees, life was almost as minutely orchestrated as it had been in Holland. The school was as much for the daughters of the Catholic elite as Blumenthal had been.

Rose fit into this education as perfectly as into a new pair of shoes built on a last of her foot. She knew the routine, the rituals, the curriculum as well as she knew her rosary. Rose slept in the dormitory, each narrow bed shielded from the other students by white curtains the students tied up as soon as they awoke. She attended mass in the chapel each morning, walked silently down the long, narrow corridors, curtsied to the Mother Superior; sat quietly in the library among books in long rows of built-in bookcases under a portrait of the pope; and walked the grounds full of religious statues. She studied not the idioms of American English but German and Latin; not the history of this new America but of the world from 1453 to 1789; not the literature of her time but Shakespeare's *Hamlet* and *King Lear*. She took gymnastics and fencing as well.

In Boston, Bishop O'Connell had forbidden sex education as one of the "modern pagan fads," a sentiment that was almost universal among the Catholic hierarchy. At Manhattanville the only course that even touched on the human body was physical culture; students learned about good posture, a decent diet, and the deadly threats of liquor, morphine, and tobacco. If a dangerously curious girl asked why boys' voices changed, she was authoritatively informed of anything except the dark secret that it had to do with the youth's ongoing sexual development. In the end the young women learned almost nothing about sex or the human body, and they entered adulthood as woefully ignorant about this aspect of life as were their mothers and their grandmothers before them. At the age of nineteen, Rose knew nothing of men. She knew her father, that great figure strutting in and out of her life. And she knew Joe. She saw him only for intense private moments. He too strutted in and out of her life, a stalwart youth cut out of the same romantic cloth as her father.

Rose was part of the elite among the students, with a religious and social experience beyond that of most of the other young women. As a former student of Blumenthal, Rose had been close to the heart of the order. As a Child of Mary, she had been anointed a high rank in this spiritual aristocracy. As the daughter of Boston's former mayor, she was part of a political elite as well.

In January Rose returned to Boston to attend her father's final campaign rally at Faneuil Hall. As the restive audience waited for the candidate finally to appear, one of his minions soothed the crowded auditorium by singing "Sweet Adeline." Fitzgerald arrived to a burst of applause and hurried up on stage. Rose had taught her father the song, and he joined in a chorus. "Let the Mayor sing the chorus himself," shouted a supporter. Fitzgerald stood and began to sing:

> *Sweet Adeline, my Adeline*
> *At night, dear heart,*
> *For you I pine.*
> *In all my dreams,*
> *Your fair face beams*
> *You're the flower of my heart,*
> *Sweet Adeline.*

The audience cheered, and the melody became Fitzgerald's theme song. For Rose, it would always be her father's song, and playing a few chords of the melody was like calling up all the sweetest memories of her father.

In a dramatic climax to months of speeches and rallies, Fitzgerald won a second term as mayor by a margin of only 1,402 votes. It was a great and glorious victory, and Rose returned to Boston in February to sit in the balcony at Faneuil Hall and see her father sworn in a second time, this time for a four-year term. Below her sat two thousand men and women, and outside the doors five hundred others struggled to get in. The largest crowd to have seen an inauguration in Boston interrupted Fitzgerald's speech several times. As her father began his second term in office, Rose took the train back to New York City and the cloistered life of the Sacred Heart Academy.

Rose did not simply dream and pray. She studied hard those last months. Upon graduation in June of 1910 she received a prize as first in her division in German, first in Literature, and sixth in Literary Honors for the entire Academy. In the voting for the First medallion, an honor voted upon by the students signifying overall merit, she was eighteenth of the fifty-three students receiving recognition.

For two years Rose had lived this convent school life, away from Joe, away from Boston, away from the life she wanted to lead. She had obeyed and endured. When she walked through the wrought-iron gateway for the last time, she was only a month away from her twentieth birthday, a child of the Sacred Heart, and a woman ready to become, as she expressed it, "a full participant in adult life and the perils and excitements of the world."

As the mayor's eldest daughter, Rose was the undisputed leader of the young Catholic elite, but the Brahmins still ruled supreme over traditional Boston society. Rose knew about the upper-class Brahmin world primarily through reading the newspapers. Most of the Boston papers had two society pages, one for Protestants, one for Catholics.

As the Brahmins had lost political control of Boston, they had held on with great force to the reins of society and to private institutions of social and cultural betterment that traditionally were a woman's preserve. They developed a number of admirable institutions from the Museum of Fine Arts to the Massachusetts Society for the Prevention of Cruelty to Children, from Vincent Memorial Hospital to Boston Symphony. These were *their* institutions "over which they had perfect and perpetual control, which not only paralleled but in many instances overshadowed those operated by the municipality itself." Rose could never expect to be asked to join the board of the symphony or play a major role in charity work at Vincent Memorial Hospital.

To wall off the Irish tide from the civilized life of Boston, the Brahmins built their own social dikes. They joined the Somerset Club or the Union Club where they wouldn't have to sit next to an Irishman, an exclusion that rankled even the most successful Irish-Americans. "What this city needs is a lunch club where the blue bloods will eat with the rest of us," Fitzgerald said late in his life.

These social dikes walled off not only vulgarity but vitality. Without new social nutrients, the Brahmin spirit shriveled away. The race that had sired the sons of liberty now concerned itself with club elections. Descendants of that bold breed of Yankee businessman who had sailed the seas with courage now clipped coupons and worried about taxes. The intellectual class that produced historians such as Parkman and writers like Emerson now often pondered their genealogy or dreamed of ancient Greece.

In education, culture, and moral seriousness, Rose was far above the typical Boston debutante, but still the Brahmins were not about to invite her into their august precincts. Rose said that didn't matter to her. She remembered that she "had neither feelings of exclusion nor inferiority." She believed that *her* crowd was every bit as refined as *their* crowd, and to "an observer from London or Paris or Berlin or outer space there would have been no discernible differences."

Rose's social ambitions were enormous and although she was loath to admit it, the Catholics were emulating the Brahmin elite, not the other way around. Rose and her peers were full of earnest self-consciousness. These women were overcoming not simply the onus of their faith, but the stereotypes of the drunken, disorderly "Mick" hauled away in the paddy wagon. Rose did not drink, nor for that matter did Joe, and she and her contemporaries outdid the Brahmins in their sense of propriety. They were the "Proper Bostonians," even more so than the Brahmin elite.

"Some of the Irish were known as being drunkards and that generation in America decided that they wouldn't drink at all, or they wouldn't have a reputation," Rose reflected. "I remember my father saying that the typical picture of an Irish politician was a man with a glass of whiskey in his hand and a pipe in his mouth. So my father never took a drink in public, and he never smoked anyway. So I think that particular generation was an effort to counter the image of the Irish who were drunkards and boisterous."

For Rose the most important social event of her young life would be her debut on January 2, 1911. For months, she and her mother prepared for the occasion with meticulous care. These coming-out parties were increasingly extravagant affairs held outside the home. In 1907 one young woman's party at the Hotel Somerset cost more than twenty-five thousand dollars; in 1909 at another debut held at the hotel, eleven hundred guests sat down for a four-course supper during which they consumed more than two thousand dollars' worth of champagne.

Rose's father was wealthy, but he could hardly afford such expense. Even if the mayor had the money, he could not afford the cost to his political image. Thus the Fitzgeralds decided not to have a ball at the Somerset, or a sit-down dinner at another hotel, but a more modest celebration: a reception at the family home in Dorchester.

On New Year's Day in 1911, as scores of flowers were arriving at the house, a reporter waited in the reception room to talk to Rose about her debut the next day. She came running down the stairs, looking no more than sixteen years old in her severe black velvet dress with a white collar. She was a diminutive young woman, with the small, delicate bones of a bird. "Oh, I'm twenty!" she exclaimed, her pink cheeks deepening as she talked. "It's awfully old for a coming-out party, isn't it? Or rather, it seems so to me when I hear the other girls tell what good times they had since they were eighteen—two whole years! I suppose I might have come out two seasons ago, only I went to Germany to study, and—well, mother says that was more benefit than the parties would have been. Anyway, I'm coming out now—and I can't exactly describe . . ." Rose searched for the proper words, her arched eyebrows growing straight. "But everything seems—BLOSSOMING."

As Rose talked about her education and plans, she managed to exude both dignity and youthful high spirits. "Don't make me out a paragon," she cautioned. "I simply intend to have a good time for a while—and then later I expect to do some settlement work. And you know, I've recently been appointed a member of the Boston Public Library investigating committee. The work is extremely interesting, especially finding out what books the children like. I have the point of view of my small sisters and brothers for that. Then, as I say, I'm interested in settlement houses. I want to help somebody . . . for I don't think you're much good, unless you're doing good to someone."

As the journalist filled her notebook, she thought that Rose had a philosophy unlike that of the average debutante. However, when the reporter asked about Rose's dress for her party, the philosopher disappeared.

"What am I going to wear Monday evening?" Rose asked rhetorically, repeating the question. "Wait a minute." Rose bolted out of her chair, and ran upstairs, returning an instant later with a gown over her arm. "Mother says it's crepe meteor," she said, fondling the material. "There's embroidery across the bodice, you notice, I don't know its name. And— look—a touch of yellow at the neck. . . . The neck is out a little and the sleeves are short. You see, it's very simple, but, and oh, it has a demi-train. My first."

The morning of Rose's debut dawned on a springlike day of warmth and sunshine. As the four-thirty hour of the reception approached, Fitzgerald sat in his overstuffed chair, watching the activity with anxiety. Josie walked through the house with a confident manner, knowing that both she and her household were ready. She looked at Rose, her eldest daughter's countenance gleaming with excitement and anticipation, and then looked away, a shadow of sadness crossing her face.

By the appointed hour, it had begun to rain. When the first arrivals entered the house, it was as if they had entered not a home, but a greenhouse full of exquisite flowers. Mountain laurel cascaded down from the walls. Along the floor ascended a garden of flowers: roses, rare orchids, lilies of the valley, Russian violets, jonquils, sweet peas, carnations, and palms. In the midst of this garden stood Rose carrying a bouquet of flowers chosen to symbolize her life, violets for modesty and white lilies of the valley, a symbol of purity. In an age of ostentatious display, she wore no jewelry, with only a silver ribbon in her hair. Standing next to Rose and slightly back from her eldest daughter stood Josie looking so youthful that she could have passed as her daughter's older sister. Josie wore a dress of black lace and white satin, a dramatic contrast to her daughter's white gown.

Rose greeted each guest with friendly self-assurance and warmth, and a special word for each new arrival, her lilting laughter punctuating the greetings. Her manner was so impressive that *The Boston Globe* reached back to classical imagery for an analogy. "Witchery danced in eyes that matched her raven hair," the reporter wrote, "but it was not the witchery of Circe on a pedestal behind her to the right, but that of Petrarch's immortal Laura, a marble bust of whom was at the debutante's left."

In honor of Rose's debut, the city council had postponed their regular Monday afternoon meeting, and many politicians mingled with the other guests. These officials were not habitués of debutante parties, and some of them considered it the height of social grace to be able to distinguish a knife from a fork. Yet Rose greeted them with the same ease that she received her intimates. Other politicians of more distinguished cast entered the house as well, including the governor-elect, a member of Congress, several state senators, doctors, priests, and others—all of whom she received with the same self-assurance.

Rose had invited her friends as well, but this party was not simply for her. It was a social and political event in her father's career, the guest list of over five hundred names constructed with subtle calculation. It was the beginning of a pattern in her life. At almost all family events—from christenings to birthdays, weddings to funerals—the guest list would include not only friends and family, but acquaintances, retainers, politicians, the useful, the once useful, and the soon-to-be useful.

Rose had invited a group of her closest eight women friends to assist her. They presided over tiny tables in the parlor serving tea and hot chocolate from silver urns, and offering sweets and cakes. Rose's lack of a college education had not limited her in making or maintaining friendships with those who had. These friends included students at Radcliffe, Wellesley, and Trinity College, as well as a young woman who had studied with Rose at Blumenthal. Two of the women, Ruth Evans and Marguerite O'Callaghan, were the very friends with whom she had planned to go off to study at Wellesley.

Fitzgerald got up from his chair and moved around the guests serving tea and chocolate, making introductions, shaking hands. Some guests stayed only long enough to fulfill the minimal social obligation while others remained for several hours. Rose's debut was nothing if it was not eclectic, bringing together people who would never socialize together. Overall, as one observer noted, this was an "occasion when everyone seemed free of restraint" and joviality was the mood of the day. Unlike many debuts among Boston Catholics, Rose's coming-out party was not simply a self-conscious aping of highborn Yankee custom but a wedding of the Brahmin ritual and form with Irish-American congeniality and hospitality.

As the older guests began to leave, Rose and her friends gathered in the large children's room on the second floor. Christmas trees filled the room. Boughs of greenery hung from the ceiling. In the corner a gigantic mechanical Santa Claus bobbed its head in perpetual merriment. Here at dinner sat twelve couples, the educated, young elite of Catholic Boston. The eight women who had helped with the debut were joined by four others. Joe and eight other Harvard men sat next to the women along with three other males including Hugh Nawn, the young man whom her father thought was a worthy suitor for his "Rosie." Nawn had served as an usher during the reception and the Fitzgeralds treated him almost as a member of the family. After dinner the guests had their own private ball. For the first dance of the evening Rose chose neither Hugh nor Joe, but Frank Sullivan, a Harvard man, and a noted young orator, yet another potential suitor for the first young lady of Catholic Boston.

Rose's debut had been the biggest news event of the day. The next morning she awoke to find her picture on the front pages of the Boston papers. Though she was tired and the day dawned damp and unpleasant, she spent hours delivering her flowers to patients in public hospitals.

Rose's acts of charity and social concern could not compare with those of women who worked full-time in the settlement houses of Boston, the nuns who taught the children of immigrants, or activists who devoted themselves to such prominent causes as suffrage or prohibition, but she was not merely filling her days with a little charity work. As a Child of Mary and a graduate of the Sacred Heart, these were sacred obligations. She took the trolley to the North End to teach sewing to Italian children, on the very streets where her father had grown up. She did some work in the settlement houses. She taught catechism classes and Sunday school as well.

On an evening in mid-February, Rose stood at South Station waiting for her father as the *Federal Express* stood ready to depart, its engine spouting steam. She was accompanying her father to Palm Beach, an event important enough to merit her picture in this morning's *Boston Post*. As the eight o'clock departure neared, Rose was busy saying her good-byes to her mother and her sister Agnes and three young men who had come to see her off: Hugh, Joe, and Joe's roommate, Bob Fisher.

Rose should have been ecstatic to be heading twelve hundred miles south to the Florida sunshine. Instead, she was despondent. Joe's junior prom at Harvard would take place while she was in the South. She had thanked her father profusely when he invited her to Florida, but told him that she had already accepted Joe's invitation. Her father had said that didn't matter. She would be going with him. Rose was twenty years old but her father had spoken, and there was no further debate. So she stood here this evening, hoping "for a major disaster in Boston," a ferocious snowstorm, an enormous warehouse fire, something, anything that would make her father change his mind and bring them back to Boston in time for the dance.

Rose's father was always late, always rushing. For years she had seen him roaring through the streets of Boston in a touring car at breakneck speed, jumping on moving trains, or galloping a team of horses over the hills of Concord, tempting fate and then tempting it again. Just a few weeks before, a man had entered his office in Boston, insisting on seeing Fitzgerald, threatening to "clean the place out." The man was presumably insane, a possible assassin, and two police officers had to wrestle him down. It was a strange, inexplicable incident, a part of the dark underbelly of modern politics, and the mayor had shrugged it off. Rose didn't like to think about such things either.

Fitzgerald finally appeared, running up the platform. He had five minutes to go and he made his good-byes, vigorously shaking hands with a dozen or so men who had come to see him off. He made his farewells to Josie. Then he turned his attention to a group of women there to see him off. One by one he kissed them, turning aside for an instant to whisper to a reporter: "relatives." Then he turned back to the duty at hand. The train was pulling out of the station, but the mayor would not leave Boston until he had kissed the last woman good-bye, achieving what the *Boston Post* called "a new South station osculation record when it comes to bidding good-by to the ladies" before jumping on the departing Pullman car.

As much as Rose wanted to be with Joe, when she was with

her father she usually forgot everything else. A dispatch from New Haven stated that by the time the train reached the Connecticut city, the mayor had turned the sleeping-car porters into a choir whose repertoire consisted of endless choruses of "Sweet Adeline."

Fitzgerald and Rose spent the next day in Washington before continuing on to Florida. Rose was the companion her mother never could be. She was an adult now, admired by and listened to by the mayor's colleagues and peers. At lunch she sat in the Senate restaurant with her father and Senator Crane, perfectly comfortable in this assemblage of power. That afternoon she joined Fitzgerald in a visit to President William Howard Taft. Rose's father understood the value of a president's time, and after a few minutes started to leave. "It is not often I have the pleasure of receiving a pretty girl here where all the work goes on," said the amiable man who occupied the White House. "So we will keep her here awhile."

The Palm Beach that Rose arrived in for the first time that February of 1911 was the most exclusive winter resort in America. In 1894 the legendary entrepreneur, Henry Morrison Flagler, created the international resort on little more than a sandy reef, a narrow finger of an island fifteen miles long and no more than three quarters of a mile wide, connected to the east coast of Florida by several bridges. It was a sedate winter home for many of the wealthy of America and Europe, a community that regulated its poor black population by not allowing them out after dark.

For Fitzgerald and his daughter there was only one place to stay. That was the two-thousand-room Royal Poinciana, considered the largest resort hotel in the world. The seven-story-tall wooden building stretched along the beach like a gigantic white seawall and dwarfed the other hotels on the coast. The resort was full of the wealthy and the prominent, from minor royalty to major businessmen. Rose loved being around those touched with the patina of wealth, nobility, or fame. It was her father's kind of place too, where he could hobnob with the elite, making contacts and connections, spreading his name and his fame. To some he may still have been little Johnny Fitz from the North End, but these were the people with whom he sought to socialize, the world he wanted his daughter to enter.

Rose spent her days with her father much as she had at Old Orchard Beach, though here everything was on a grander scale.

Her father was a peacock of a politician, and he changed his outfits several times a day. He had come down to Florida with trunks full of new clothes, so much that one observer felt that it looked more like a trousseau than a wardrobe. His new clothes included white broadcloth suits, white flannels trimmed with lavender stripes, a rattan walking stick, a blackthorn cane, six pairs of heliotrope stockings with matching neckties, a green necktie, a red tie, pink garters, six flamboyantly colored shirts, cream gloves, and what the mayor called "a corker" of a golf outfit.

In the evening after a day of swimming and endless activity, Fitzgerald dressed in his evening clothes, and he and Rose attended the dance in the hotel ballroom. Fitzgerald's dance card was filled almost as quickly as his daughter's. "Gee, I wish I was down to the beach," Fitzgerald said after a fast dance. "Don't you, Rose?"

"A swim would be fine," Rose replied, "but I'm having the time of my life."

At precisely midnight the band struck up the "Star-Spangled Banner." Confetti fell onto the gathering. Pigeons flew up out of their cages to the heights of the ballroom. "This was the greatest ball I ever saw," Fitzgerald said at the end of the evening, referring not to elegance, beauty, or grace but to matters more tangible. "Just think of the millions and millions of dollars represented on that floor tonight, not alone in the jewels and dresses, but in the capitalists who stand for so much. All you have to do is put out your finger and you are pointing out a millionaire."

As memorable as these days were, Rose still thought of Joe and what she was missing in Boston. As close as she was to her father, this was not a matter that she could discuss with him. Her father had said what he thought of Joe. Now he was attempting to pry her away, pulling her physically and emotionally back. She could not talk about her feelings. She had to keep her dissatisfaction to herself, had to exude happiness.

When Rose returned to Boston, she started surreptitiously seeing Joe again. It was vaguely dangerous, a conspiracy of two, the clandestine nature of the romance making it even more inviting. When they went ice skating on Scarboro Pond, Rose wore a veil in a futile attempt to hide her identity. On one of their walks, they saw a man whom they were sure was a reporter. Rushing into the nearest public building, they discovered to their amusement and horror that they were sitting in a Christian Science church. At dances Joe filled Rose's dance card with such made-up names as "Sam Shaw" and danced with her all evening long. It was a joke on her mother and father, on everyone. When her mother was sitting alongside the dance floor with the other matrons, Rose made sure to dance once or twice with another partner, preferably Hugh Nawn or someone like him. She steered her unsuspecting partner toward her mother, making sure they were seen. "The others, we 'sat out,' " Rose recalled in her autobiography, "vanishing amid the potted palms or into the arcades and verandas of the hotel or country club, and in fine weather onto the terraces and paths. Some of my sweetest memories are of music floating in the night air, and the distant sounds of gaiety and laughter, while I took walks hand in hand with 'Sam Shaw.' "

It was deliciously romantic. "I had read all these books about [how] your heart should rule your head," Rose reflected. "I was very romantic and there were no two ways about it." At the same time, Rose was not acting with willful impetuousness. "I didn't stay exclusively with him. I was interested in seeing other boys too, to see someone else for comparison to see if you really love."

Rose had not grown up the daughter of John F. Fitzgerald without there being a measure of calculation even in her most romantic of temperaments. Joe appeared to be such an exemplary young man. He, like his father, considered the devotions of faith largely a woman's business, and yet he often displayed to the world a face as innocent and reverent as a choirboy. Rose was used to seeing Joe as an usher at Catholic charitable events and other occasions, the beau ideal of young Catholic manhood, relentlessly polite, deferential to the nth degree.

Joe was a baseball player and Rose loved watching him play. She treated the athletic field as a plain where young men displayed acts of comradeship, courage, and fortitude that one day they would display on a far larger field. The two baseball games between Harvard and Yale that ended the college season were among the biggest sporting events of the year, greeted with a peculiar combination of hoopla and reverence, lengthy analyses in the press, and over twelve thousand spectators for the match at Harvard's Soldier's Field.

Rose was not much of a baseball fan, but her father liked few things better than an afternoon out watching the Red Sox or the Nationals. He would have liked it even better, though, if he had a fine baseball player in the family. He had promised his own sixteen-year-old son, Tom, a gold watch if he made the Dorchester High nine. If a single event was likely to change Fitzgerald's opinion of Joe, it would be his triumph in a baseball game.

As Rose and her father entered Soldier's Field in June 1911, the stands were already filled with spectators, mainly men wearing suits and ties and straw hats, the overflow spilling onto the field and standing on the top rung of the stadium. The red, white, and blue souvenir scorecard included a team photo in which Joe sat with the other players, but he was not listed in the starting lineup. Down on the field, Harvard took an early lead on a double by Charles "Chick" McLaughlin, driving in a run. McLaughlin was not only a great hitter and the starting pitcher, but the captain of the team.

Yale scored a run in the third, but from then on McLaughlin was invincible, sending the Yalies down, often one after another. To Rose, though, that was not the drama that mattered, for Joe was sitting on the bench. Rose had an image of him as a great athlete, the youth that her father had given the award to as the best hitter in all the Boston school league. But college was a different game. He hadn't even made the varsity until this, his junior year. He rarely played, and when the coach put him in the lineup, he had played poorly. He had, indeed, played so little that the only way he would win his Harvard "H," an honor that he coveted above any academic achievement, would be to play in this final game of the season. But Joe appeared doomed to sit out the final game, humiliated before Rose and her father, his family, and friends.

Joe continued to sit on the bench. The seventh inning. The eighth inning. Yale still only had one run, and still Joe sat. The top of the ninth inning was Joe's last chance to bat. Still, the coach did not call him. Now the Harvard nine took the field for the final time, and Joe was still sitting.

For the Yalies, down four to one, this was their last chance. The first batter ground out. By now the more restless fans had begun to leave the stadium. The second batter hit a fly ball over the shortstop's head, dropping in for a single. As the Yale player stood on first base and a pinch hitter came to the plate, the remaining crowd rumbled with excitement. The batter tapped the ball to McLaughlin on the mound, who whirled and threw the man out at first. As the Harvard supporters roared in anticipation of the final out, McLaughlin called time out. With that Coach Sexton waved Joe into the game at first base, and another player into center field. The batter hit a ground ball to the shortstop, who tossed it to Joe at first base, for the final out.

The other Harvard players mobbed McLaughlin on the mound, congratulating him for the last play of his illustrious career. Only Joe was missing. He walked toward the stands clutching the game-winning ball in his hand. As those in the stands watched, McLaughlin hurried over to Joe to claim the ball that was rightfully his, but Joe shrugged his shoulders, put the ball in his back pocket, and walked off the field.

What those who watched Joe's action that June afternoon did not know was that several days before the game a group of men associated with Joe's politician father had paid a visit on "Chick" McLaughlin. The men knew that upon graduation he hoped to open a movie theater. They made it abundantly clear that if he wanted the necessary license, he had damn well better see to it that Joseph P. Kennedy won his letter. Thus McLaughlin had asked the coach to let Joe play for the final out.

Rose saw and knew nothing of that. For Rose that afternoon would always be the day that "My father and I saw him the day he won his 'H,' when he made the winning play against Yale." She shielded her eyes from Joe's world in which a man stopped at almost nothing to win the prizes he coveted. It was a life for which his mother, Mary Augusta, had prepared him.

5

"A Marvelous Success"

*J*oe was his mother's first and only son. From the day Joe
had been born in the house on Meridian Street, Mary Augusta had molded him, guided him, instructed him, pushed
him, tried to form not only Joe's destiny but part of her own.
Mary Augusta was a proud, imperious woman whose ambitions reached up to the Brahmin world of privilege and wealth.
If her husband could not achieve that world, her son would.

Mary Augusta's family, the Hickeys, were a haughty clan
who along with their cultured civility had acquired a certain
worldly cynicism. Mary Augusta herself is remembered as an
"amazingly quick-witted woman" and she had applied all that
wit and Hickey shrewdness in pursuing Joe's father, P. J. Kennedy. The first time Mary Augusta remembered seeing her
husband-to-be, she had been sitting in the parlor of her home
in East Boston. As Mary Augusta contemplated whom she
might marry, she saw a young man on the street striding ahead
purposefully. She learned that the man's name was Patrick Joseph Kennedy and that he owned several taverns and a wholesale liquor business. She heard her brothers talking about P.J.,
nodding in agreement as one of them said, "He's going to be
a marvelous success."

Mary Augusta listened and said nothing, but she remembered, and noticed P.J.'s name in the papers, and watched him
when he passed by her window. Then one day he strolled by
just after he had been elected to the Massachusetts State Legislature. He sported a new handlebar mustache and a thick
swath of beard that made him appear a decade older, a man of
substance like her father and the men of his generation. That
was the day, as Mary Augusta fondly recalled years later, that
she "set her cap" for him.

P.J.'s knowledge of women began and ended with his mother and sisters. Here in Boston Irishmen boasted of their manhood not by talking of their sexual conquests but of their lack of interest in women. When the legendary politician, James Curley, married at the age of thirty-two, he crowed that he had had "no time for girl friends," and took his bride on a honeymoon trip visiting other politicians. Martin Lomasney, another powerful politician of P.J.'s generation, bragged that he "never married, never had a romance, never attended a wedding."

P.J. had his drawbacks. He owned taverns and even within the Irish community the saloon keeper was rarely revered. When Mary Augusta was born, her Irish-born father had listed his occupation as "laborer" but he was a contractor now, and the Hickeys had forgotten their humble origins. P.J. had a roughness that Mary Augusta's brothers didn't have. His sisters were barely literate, at least by Hickey standards. She might have waited for somebody else, but as she well knew, there were few eligible young men in the parish for the likes of a Hickey woman, and born on December 6, 1857, she was fast approaching "the shady side of thirty." American women of Mary Augusta's generation married at an average age of twenty-two, five years earlier than they would have a hundred years earlier; if Mary Augusta did not marry soon, she would probably not marry at all. P.J. may not have been the ideal husband for a Hickey woman, but the first thing she had ever heard about him was that he would be a marvelous success, and that was what she wanted.

Mary Augusta was the very model of an appropriate wife for a good Catholic man. *The Sacred Heart Review*, the weekly publication read by Boston Catholics, advised that when "a young man of common sense . . . wants a wife, he wants a lady, a woman capable of elevating him by her good influence and example." That was exactly how Mary Augusta had been raised by her parents and the nuns at the Notre Dame Academy. She had never stopped on the street to talk to a man. None of the boulevardiers on Meridian Street would have dared approach her, for she had what became known in the family as "the Hickey look," a contemptuous stare that could stop a vulgarity in mid-syllable. She would never have let a man put his arm around her waist or take her for a ride. Mary Augusta was a handsome woman, with a dainty nose, fair skin, and thick brown hair. Her probing eyes were the only feature that might belie the solemn dignity of her appearance. She was

five feet seven inches tall, half a head taller than most of the
women of her time, and she walked as if her head could touch
the clouds, and sat with her back perfectly perpendicular. Mary
Augusta sang in the church choir and had a voice that was as
richly commanding in spoken word as it was in song. Mary
Augusta was a month older than P.J. She was a woman who
sought not simply fortune or prominence, but respectability
and high regard. She could sing and play the piano and was
deeply religious. As a wife and mother, she would have full
dominion over her domestic world, bringing religion to her
children and culture to her home.

In marrying Mary Augusta, P.J. was not unlike his father
marrying his mother. The older Bridget had sought Patrick out,
as Mary Augusta had set her cap for P.J. He could have found
a bride a decade younger with more time to have the large
family that was sure to come, but Mary Augusta had a strength
of character, determination, and ambition that a younger
woman might not have had.

As soon as they married, Mary Augusta and P.J. began raising
their family. For Mary Augusta, a son was the measure of all
things, and three days after the birth of their first son, on September 6, 1888, they carried him to the Church of the Most
Holy Redeemer to be baptized, the same church where P.J. had
been baptized. As the priest carried the baby into the sanctuary,
the infant wore an exquisite lace christening gown as richly ornate as the robes of the church.

Irish families generally named the firstborn male after his
father, but today P.J. told the priest that his son would be called
Joseph Patrick Kennedy. P.J. was proud of his name and his
heritage, and he likely would have wanted a son to carry his
name. But like most second-generation Irish-American women,
Mary Augusta was more Americanized than her husband, and
more self-conscious about whatever Irishness remained. She
did not want their son saddled with an Irishman's name. They
were *Americans* now.

The birth of Joe was followed on March 11, 1891, by a second
son, Francis Benedict, who died of diphtheria a year and three
months later, and was buried beside his paternal grandmother.
The mourning lifted when Mary Augusta gave birth to her first
daughter, Mary Loretta, on August 6, 1892. Not until six years
later was the final child, Margaret Louise, born.

P.J. was rarely home during the day, and at night he had meetings with business associates, friends, priests, and politicians. Sundays he was usually off with his cronies and political friends, in later years on his own yacht, the *Eleanor*, sailing to Nantasket for the day. The house was Mary Augusta's world, her preserve, walled off from the society of men and work outside. At first it was the modest home on Meridian Street but in June 1894 the Kennedys bought a new home at 165 Webster Street for $5,275 at an estate sale. The residence was one of the smallest on the street, but Webster Street was the most prestigious address in East Boston, home to the likes of a congressman, the superintendent of ferries, the alderman-at-large, and other local notables.

"Always, she [Mary Augusta] regarded herself as a preliminary antecedent to a dynasty which she co-established . . ." the *Boston Post* wrote years later. "She was the head of the household and she ruled her little domain with everlasting foresight and kindliness." She was nonetheless a stern disciplinarian who meted out the punishment in the home. P.J. was a benign and distant figure, remembered by his son as a "very quiet man who never raised his voice . . . [and] never spoke a cross word to me."

Joe's mother controlled not only the maids, the cook, the children, and the housekeeping, but the spirit of the home. It was her job, as *The Sacred Heart Review* expressed it, to "teach by example that cheerfulness is one of the first of Christian social duties!" Happiness and optimism, then, were as much disciplines as emotions, and Mary Augusta was always smiling, always chipper, always upbeat. Joe saw this sunshiny woman and considered that the proper emotional role for his mother as well as for the woman he would one day marry. Joe saw that his mother's life was directed toward making his father's career successful, thereby bringing honor on the family name.

The house had to gleam and shine, a symbol of Mary Augusta's womanhood. This was no haphazard task, for the homes of the 1890s had all kinds of dirt, dust, grime, and soot unknown to the modern home. The oil and gas lamps gave off not only fumes but residue to darken walls and rugs. The coal from heating and cooking left its own sooty remains and its own peculiar odors. The factories and mills of East Boston spewed out pollutants that fell on the homes of the island as well. Every day, then, was a battle with the broom and the brush, the carpet sweeper and the dust mop to make the Kennedy home the symbol of success that it was supposed to be.

Mary Augusta didn't cook the meals, change the sheets, or beat the rugs, but she did oversee the servants who performed these tasks. She ordained that there was always to be a fresh pot of clam chowder or another soup simmering on the cast-iron stove that she could serve to P.J. when he arrived home. A new cook soon learned that when Mary Augusta said *always* she meant *always*, and that when she said *fresh* soup she meant *fresh* soup.

The kitchen was busy from early morning until evening, activities that Mary Augusta directed. Someone had to go to the market every day. Friday meant fish, and fish meant scaling. If it was chicken that evening, the chicken probably was purchased alive, and it had to be killed and plucked. Coffee had to be ground and roasted, hams soaked, whole spices pounded or ground up, nuts shelled, oatmeal soaked, raisins seeded, herbs dried, loaf sugar pounded, and the fire stoked. Baking was something a lady did, and Mary Augusta was renowned for her pies, cakes, and cookies. The Kennedys baked their own bread, setting them apart from the working class who had no choice but to buy store-bought bread.

For Mary Augusta wash day was not the dreaded "Blue Monday" that it was for homemakers who did their own wash. In houses such as the Kennedys', the wash was generally sent out to a laundrywoman or done by a day worker. This was the kind of work that widows like Bridget Murphy performed, making sure that P.J.'s detachable collars and cuffs were so white and well starched that they were like advertisements for the quality of his home life, the tablecloths and napkins spotless and fresh, her dresses all proper and pressed.

Joe saw how much his mother was concerned with her father's well-being. When Mary Augusta realized that her husband was growing fatigued, she planned trips for him. His closest friend, Frank Lally, a bachelor, was free to travel at will. Mary Augusta called Lally's sisters, Jenny and Lottie, and developed an itinerary for the two men. "P.J. always said he never knew he was going on a trip until he would notice his steamer trunk or suitcases out for airing and his clothes all being prepared to be packed," recalled Kerry McCarthy of her great-grandfather. Off P.J. went then without his wife to Europe, across America, or to Florida.

Mary Augusta displayed no wanderlust, no desire to visit

these distant climes herself. Yet in her pursuit of culture and refinement she had reached out beyond the provincial world of East Boston, seeking the manners and mores of a larger society. P.J. was her surrogate, and she saw his successes, his journeys, his achievements as her own.

The parlor was the most important room in the Kennedy house, the symbol of Mary Augusta's stewardship of the home. Even by Victorian standards, the Kennedys' room was overcrowded with furniture and bric-a-brac. The fleur-de-lis wallpaper was hardly visible since the walls were covered with portraits of honored ancestors, landscapes, and other paintings. There were heavy chairs set against the wall as well, and lace curtains on the windows that covered up part of the wallpaper.

In the Kennedy home, the piano was a musical hearth the family stood around, singing songs old and new, the popular Hawaiian music P.J. loved to hear his wife sing as well as Irish and religious songs. Music was a great force to this generation of Kennedy women as it would be to several of their heirs, a bond that helped to hold them together. Mary Augusta's voice rose above the others, carrying the melody.

The voices of Mary Augusta's unmarried sisters, Margaret and Catherine, could be heard at the piano too. Margaret was a semi-invalid who in 1902 died of a malady listed on her death certificate as "valve disease of heart." Catherine had gone to live with her brother, Dr. John Hickey, a lifelong bachelor. Brother and sister lived together with a household staff and imperial manners in a great brick house in Winthrop overlooking the sea. When Catherine and John Hickey's chauffeur drove them to the house in East Boston and they sat in the parlor, they represented a world of civility beyond East Boston, beyond politics, beyond business.

The family and friends might all raise their voices together in song, but there were circles within the Kennedy circle, a fact that young Joe could not help realizing. Catherine did not socialize comfortably or well with the likes of Mary Augusta's brother-in-law, Humphrey Mahoney. He was a mere janitor, and the Mahoneys stood at the outer fringes of the circle. Another voice around the piano who was not accepted in the inner circle was Tom Barron, whose father had helped Bridget and Patrick Kennedy when they first arrived. Barron had failed in the liquor business. P.J. had helped his cousin out by buying his company and giving him a job as his business representa-

tive. He worked hard and long hours, ruining his health in
P.J.'s service, and he died a young man.

Mary Augusta, unlike Josie Fitzgerald, identified totally with
her husband's success, and considered it her duty to do whatever she could to further his ambitions. She, indeed, dreamed
far more grandiose dreams than P.J., and she pushed him to attain them. P.J. was so powerful in East Boston that he was besieged by favor seekers, and Mary Augusta was perfectly
comfortable having this parade of supplicants in her house.
Into the parlor, then, came the widows who turned to P.J. instead of to the streets; out-of-work fathers looking for a sinecure with the city; Irish subcontractors fighting with Brahmin
contractors; maids and cooks whose mistresses refused to pay
them; a poor young man hoping to become a schoolteacher; a
youth with a calling to the priesthood. P.J. always had time, he
usually had advice, and sometimes he had money, and here
was born the image of P.J. as an altruistic overseer of his community. When his supplicants came back to him with a job laying the streets of Back Bay, with new clients, or wearing the
collar of a priest, they would ask him, "What can I do to pay
you back?" His answer was always the same: "Say a prayer
for my mother." It was understood that he also wanted their
vote and the votes of their friends, and that was little, indeed,
for all that P. J. Kennedy had done for them.

These woes knew no time or manners, and those entreating
P.J. for help often called at dinnertime. "Tell them we're eating," Mary Augusta said.

P.J. got up and soon afterwards popped his head into the
dining room: "You'll have to go on without me." Joe remembered those evenings when his father's chair was empty, and
he knew that he wanted no life where he would be at the beck
and call of others.

P.J. was one of the shrewdest men in East Boston, quietly
amassing a fortune with hardly a public murmur against him.
He had won election to the legislature with the help of the
proliquor lobby. He was their man fighting prohibitionist legislation, and they apparently rewarded him by giving his wholesaler liquor company the accounts of major hotels in Boston.
As a state representative and state senator serving on the committee on street railways, P.J. knew where the new roads and
sewers were likely to be built, useful information for a man becoming heavily involved in East Boston real estate. After two
terms in the State Senate, P.J. retired, but that scarcely touched

his real political power. He was one of the four members of the Board of Strategy, who were the most powerful Irish bosses in Boston including John F. "Honey Fitz" Fitzgerald.

From 1889 for the next two decades, P.J. bought and sold over thirty properties. P.J. could be full of largess to a poor widow who appeared at his door, but he foreclosed on several properties, including one owned by a widow. His brother-in-law was an undertaker, and so was one of his partners, Thomas Lane. He had an uncanny ability to buy property from estates when the prices might be low, especially when sold to the town's leading politician by a lawyer serving as executor of the estate.

He was a man of the cloakroom and the corridor, not the public platform. For him politics and business were both matters that took place in the shadows, away from scrutiny. Even election day was not always what it appeared. One election Joe was walking with his father when one of P.J.'s lieutenants ran up to the political boss. "I've already voted one hundred and twenty-eight times," he said, and the day was not over. Joe always remembered that story, telling it again and again with wry amusement. Joe realized that there was a subterranean world of wheeling and dealing that took place outside the world that his mother dominated so completely.

P.J. made his way in life in part through the subtle use of contacts, using men of greater wealth and greater age to mutual advantage. He did so in becoming a banker through his relationship with one of the most powerful business leaders in East Boston, John H. Sullivan. The squat, rotund businessman was a force in Democratic politics, and P.J. probably served as his agent of influence in organizing the Columbia Trust Company.

P.J. became a board member and later the bank president. As a banker he might loan money that no one else would to an Irish widow to buy her row house, but the bank was also at the center of the commercial and residential growth of East Boston with little regard for the development of a community. Loans were made from a barroom next to the bank, where reportedly borrowers had to kick back part of their loan. The bank was at the heart of Democratic politics in East Boston. During the second Fitzgerald administration, city funds were placed in noninterest-bearing accounts in the bank that could then be loaned out at a neat profit. P.J. was perfectly conversant with the bank's activities, and through it all he rode the electric car

on Meridian Street, smiling benignly on the other passengers.
He knew this community and how to make money from it as
few did.

If her husband had to play endlessly on his Irish roots and Irish
contacts to succeed, her son would not. Mary Augusta wanted
success for Joe with a profound primordial passion that became legendary in the Kennedy family. "She guided and
stressed the success of her only living son who would be the
culmination of the wonderful things in her life if he became a
success," said Mary Lou McCarthy, remembering her grandmother. "She absolutely insisted that he become a success."
    Joe did not dare challenge the formidable matriarch who
was his mother or her demands on his life. "She left the door
open for Joe to choose from any field," said Kerry McCarthy
of her great-grandmother. "She said to him, 'You can go into
banking. You can go into politics. You can go into business.
But whatever you do, you will do it. You will do it, my dear,
you will.' "
    "She was the power behind the throne," recalled Marnie
DeVine, of her grandmother. "Joe never would have gone
where he went without his mother pushing him."
    Mary Augusta wanted Joe deeply imbued with faith, and
from an early age she instructed her son in the tenets of Catholicism. Joe could see how deep was his mother's faith.
Nuns and priests were not just distant teachers but family
friends. One nun, Sister St. Magdelen, was Mary Augusta's
closest friend, a woman she had known since childhood. The
nun often visited the Kennedy home along with other sisters
and priests who celebrated mass at the family altar.
    Mary Augusta sent her son along with his younger sisters to
the parochial school taught by the Sisters of Notre Dame de
Namur, and Joe in the upper grades to a school run by the
Xavier Brothers. The nuns taught Joe and their other charges
how to sit and how to walk, viewing slumping shoulders,
curved spines, hollow chests, and pigeon toes as the signs of
"neglect on the part of parents and teachers." They taught the
children to get up in the morning saying, "Thanks be to God!"
and before leaving their bedroom to take holy water and make
the sign of the cross. They were never to contradict their parents. When they greeted their father they were to be respectful,
always addressing him as "Father." A son was to take off his
hat in his mother's presence.

The nuns imbued every aspect of study with religion and moral training, from penmanship where children copied moral homilies ("A cheerful temper is a great blessing"), to Latin where students learned that "Mozart would have given all the Music he knew to be able to write one Preface of a High Mass."

As a Catholic mother Mary Augusta was the custodian of her children's virtue and innocence, and she taught her son to act with perfect civility inside the home. The church charged her with watching for "indecent conversation, jokes, and songs." To achieve the social success that his mother craved for him, Joe would have to learn impeccable manners. The streets were full of new immigrants—Russian Jews, Poles, Italians, Germans—carrying their bundles and their strange ways. Joe had to set himself apart from them and the immigrant world. No one must ever be able to tell by any uncouth gestures that he was the son of an Irish-American liquor dealer, a profession socially unacceptable not only to the Brahmins but to the Irish Catholic elite.

Mary Augusta did not embrace her children regularly, smothering them in affection. That was not something a mother did, especially not to a son who might be weakened by excessive affection. That was not the way a husband and wife behaved either, neither in traditional Irish-American homes, nor in an ambitious family like the Kennedys, aspiring to be accepted at the highest reaches of society. "Be, at least, as courteous toward each other as you would toward any other lady or gentleman, and do not allow familiarity to spoil good manners," advised *The Sacred Heart Review*.

As a child Joe learned ideas of womanhood that affected his relationships with other women, be they wife, lovers, sisters, or daughters. He lived in a world of women, a mother, three sisters, and female servants, a world where women served him, and in doing so, appeared to fulfill their own destinies. They served him but they expected that he would deliver the bounty of success. They did not seem to care about the niceties of how he achieved it, for that was not their world. That was what he knew about women, what he knew about his mother. And he knew that if he did not come through, he might not be loved.

When he was twelve, Mary Augusta decided that her little Joe should have a part-time job. No ordinary job was good enough for her Joe, and she arranged that he would deliver hats to highborn Brahmin ladies from their favorite millinery shop, traveling to their homes in a carriage, walking inside with the hatbox while the driver stayed with the horses. "If you are asked your name," she told her son, "answer 'Joseph.'" His nickname, Joe, was too Irish and had the rude ring of the streets to it.

Mary Augusta had never been inside those Brahmin homes. She spoke English without a brogue, but she spoke the language of culture with a strong Irish accent, caught in a world halfway between her parents who knew almost nothing of these new ways and her children who would know everything.

After his stint as a delivery boy, Joe sold newspapers in East Boston. There was a whole world of newspaper boys in Boston, pint-sized shills, toughs, bullies, orphans, and poor boys who fanned through the streets hawking their wares. They might steal a new boy's papers, kick him off a corner, or beat him up. Joe learned lessons on these rude street corners that were not taught in parochial schools, lessons that many parents of successful second-generation Irish-Americans would not have wanted their son to learn. But Mary Augusta wanted her Joe to learn them, and learn them he did.

Joe saw that in the melting pot of America, the alloys of the immigrant generation did not blend together, but rested next to one another in uneasy proximity, and a young man protected himself with whatever he had at hand: his fists, his feet, his wit, his shrewdness. "Each wave [of immigrants] disliked and distrusted the next," he said years later. "The English said the Irish 'kept the Sabbath and everything else they could lay their hands on.' The English and the Irish distrusted the Germans who 'worked too hard.' The English and the Irish and the Germans disliked the Italians; and the Italians joined their predecessors in disparaging the Slavs."

Joe and his family knew firsthand how much the militant Protestants hated the Catholics. On the Fourth of July in 1895, when Joe was six years old, thousands of members of the anti-Catholic American Protective Association marched in East Boston and a riot broke out. On the street in front of Bridget's old store, a Protestant militant fired his pistol at pursuing Catholics, killing two men. Instead of expressing sorrow, a Baptist minister in East Boston prayed that God would "hasten the day when there should not be a Catholic priest on this continent."

* * *

Joe grew up with a deep resentment against the Brahmin elite. In addition, he developed a cunning acquisitiveness that in a daughter would have been condemned as a deep moral flaw, scarring her character. One summer Joe's buddy, Ronan Grady, raised pigeons in a coop in East Boston. There was a ready market for roast squab, but by the time Grady had fattened up the birds, most of his profits had been eaten up. Joe had an idea. He told Grady to take the birds from the coop. Then, hiding the pigeons under their shirts, the two youths took the ferry to the city and walked to Boston Common. There they let the birds go. Then Joe and Grady returned to East Boston, and soon afterwards the birds returned too, usually accompanied by at least two wild pigeons that were immediately sold, the two youths splitting the profit. Joe saw that he could make as much money through a shrewd idea as his friend with his pigeons and his coop.

Joe played the same games as the other neighbor boys, but he had been brought up to think that he was a little bit better, and when he played he wanted an edge. "They used to say in East Boston that he was the only kid with bat and ball, so unless he was captain there was no game," recalled Henry J. O'Meara, Joe's college classmate. Joe organized a schoolboy baseball team called the Assumptions, and led a fund-raising drive to buy snazzy white uniforms for the team. The boys weren't bad on the field, and enough adults came to watch them play that young Joe figured they might as well pay for the privilege. He rented a baseball stadium, and sure enough the team made a profit.

The neighborhood children loved to play in the house where little Joe reigned supreme. He was the protector of his younger sisters, whom P.J. referred to as the "heiresses." He said so in a jocular fashion, but he saw his daughters as symbols of his own accomplishments; he would never have referred to Joe as his "heir," a mere inheritor, a symbol of weakness, of degeneracy.

Parochial school was good enough for her daughters, but Mary Augusta insisted that Joe take the ferry across the bay to attend Boston Latin School, then the most prestigious public school in America. "Education is no burden," she was fond of saying, an aphorism that Joe remembered years afterwards. She sent him to match brains in the classroom with the sons of privilege as he had matched wits with the sons of disadvantage on the street corners.

The elite of Boston had already begun to abandon Boston Latin for private preparatory schools such as Groton and St. Mark's rather than sit with the likes of Joe Kennedy. In their places sat row after row of earnest, intense young men studying with single-minded devotion.

Joe could not possibly best these ambitious sons and grandsons of immigrants in the classroom, but Boston Latin involved not simply academic but athletic competition. Joe's friend, Walter Elcock, was captain of the football team. When it came time to choose the captain of the baseball team, Walter was slated for that honor as well. Elcock was a poor boy, an orphan, and Joe often took him out for steak dinners. When Joe asked Elcock if he would stand aside so that Joe could be captain, the young man said yes. For two seasons Joe served as captain of the team. He was a great hitter, batting .667 his senior year, the best in the high school league, a fierce competitor remembered for "constant bickering with the umpire . . . slamming his fist in his glove."

Joe had been brought up in two separate moral universes. In the Church of the Most Holy Redeemer on Sunday, Joe was a pious young man. In the parlor on Meridian Street, he was a young man of impeccable good manners. In the secular world of the streets and the playing fields he was untamed, unfettered, concerned with little but winning. He was a young man with his eyes focused not on some vague goals, but on a life of wealth and success. He was a young man grounded in this world, not the abstractions of politics and the endless boasting of politicians, but on money, on how to get it, where to get it, and what to do with it. He was a young man who, the Boston Latin Yearbook predicted, would make his fortune "in a very roundabout way."

Joe was not a good student, but Mary Augusta would not settle for sending him to Boston College, the Catholic school developing on a new campus on the far reaches of Commonwealth Avenue. She didn't care that Boston's new bishop, William O'Connell, wanted Catholic young men to go to Catholic schools. Her son would go to Harvard University to sit and live with the social elite of Boston.

When Joe left for college, P.J. called friends in Dorchester whose sons were at Harvard and asked them to watch out for Joe. P.J. wanted to be there behind his son. Joe was a highstrung, emotional young man whose sensitivity he might mask to the world, but not to his father. P.J. questioned his son's ability to make it on his own.

That was natural enough. P.J.'s college had been the street. His toughness had been bred into him in the merciless immigrant world of East Boston. Joe had learned to be tough, taught primarily by his mother, and he did not seem as strong in the ways of the world as his father.

Whatever doubts P.J. may have had about his only son's resilience, Joe saw that the essence of Harvard, *his* Harvard, was money and power. These Brahmin sons who dominated the university could muse about poetry and literature because their grandfathers had sent clipper ships to the Orient, creating wealth now resting secure in trust funds. In college, Joe was no more preoccupied with the mundane business of studying than in high school. Although his father was well off enough to provide for a superior education, Joe was interested in making money. Joe and a friend purchased an old tour bus with the idea of giving their own Boston tours. Joe cut to the essence of things. He realized that what mattered most was the location of the bus stand, and the best place of all was outside South Station. For that he needed a license. When he went to Fitzgerald for help, despite what the mayor thought of his daughter's beau, he saw that he got his license. In two seasons Joe and his friend earned the extraordinary sum of ten thousand dollars. "He had a pal who did the work and Joe got the money," recalled Henry O'Meara, one of his closest friends.

Beyond earning money, Joe's primary concern at Harvard was making it socially. At Harvard a man was defined socially by his club, and though Joe was accepted into Hasty Pudding and D.U., it was unthinkable that a redheaded Irish-American would enter into the Brahmin preserves of Porcellian, A.D., or Fly. His roommate, Bob Fisher, an all-American football player and member of Porcellian, let Joe know that his snobbish friends were watching for Joe's inevitable display of Irish gaucherie, excess, and vulgarity. It was a reminder that Joe did not need. He was alert to every nuance. By most standards, except his own, he had been well accepted at Harvard, but he harbored within himself a deep resentment that he had not made it into the inner sanctuaries of the Protestant elite.

Joe had one special cachet, at least among Boston's Irish. That was his relationship with Rose, the mayor's daughter. It rankled him endlessly that Fitzgerald considered him, Joseph P. Kennedy, not good enough for Rosie. When the mayor pre-

vented him from seeing his Rose, he turned her picture to the
wall in his room, but he continued to see her nonetheless. She
was his Rosie too, the kind of woman whom he could marry,
a woman like his mother.

Joe had learned to divide women into two kinds, the ones
you marry and the ones for good times. He was a young man
full of sexual appetites that he fully intended to satiate. Arthur
Goldsmith, one of his Harvard classmates, remembered him as
a "fun-loving companion and ladies' man." Goldsmith was his
partner in excursions downtown to the theater district. For
some Harvard men there were few adventures to compare with
traveling from the confines of Cambridge to Boston for assignations with "actresses." In turn-of-the-century America, the
very word "actress" suggested a demimonde of lasciviousness
and bohemian adventure.

Arthur and Joe were squiring two lovelies from the chorus
line of *The Pink Lady*, a popular musical, one spring day in
1912. They were rollerskating arm in arm with them around a
popular rink when Joe spied Rose Fitzgerald skating past. "He
talked himself out of that one," Goldsmith recalled.

With Joe firmly ensconced at Harvard, Mary Augusta decided
that it was time for the Kennedys to get out of East Boston. It
did not matter to Joe's mother that P.J. was the political boss
of the island. The town was no longer a place to live. Boston
dumped onto East Boston the factories and workshops that
would have marred the landscape of old Boston.

And so the Kennedys bought a large two-story frame home
at 97 Washington Avenue in Winthrop, whose back windows
looked out on the Atlantic Ocean. The town of ten thousand
was a world from East Boston. No Irish bars stood on the
street corners; in what one historian has called "the triumph of
moral geography," Winthrop and most of these suburbs were
dry. No Jewish peddlers pushed their carts through the streets
selling vegetables, ice, and oil. No Italians stood in front of
their grocery stores, or played the accordion on the street corner.

Sunday Joe brought his Harvard friends home without anyone thinking that they were traveling into an enclave of the
Irish. In the afternoon the Harvard men, dressed in blue blazers
and blue trousers, promenaded along the Crest, the sidewalk
that ran along the beachfront. Then the college men sat down
at the round dining-room table in front of Limoges china, put

fine linen napkins in their lap, and drank water from cut-glass goblets. The food itself was good solid American fare, great platters of cold ham and sliced chicken, steaming pots of homemade baked beans, plates full of freshly baked bread. This needlepoint of family bliss was Mary Augusta's creation. Here was P.J., the amiable rotund patriarch; Mary Augusta, the matriarch, herself plump and matronly, her graying hair swept back; Mary Loretta and Margaret, both of them cultivated young women; and Joe, the Harvard man, the pride of the family, sitting properly as the nuns had taught him, his laughter cascading across the table, a youth poised for infinite success.

Joe's sister Margaret remembered these evenings as being full of "that Irish aura of saintly innocence." There were no foul jokes, no vulgarity, no drinking of wine or hard liquor. In the women's world of the home and the church, Joe and his family operated with high moral principle and Catholic puritanism. But there was another world out there, a man's world where almost everything went, where Joe would live his life, perfectly comfortable with this moral dichotomy.

After dinner, the group went into the parlor where Mary Augusta sat in her Boston rocker and P.J. in his favorite chair. Joe and his friends stood around the Steinway baby grand piano. Loretta played the piano well, and Joe led the group in singing songs old and new.

Joe could hardly carry a tune, but his voice soared out above the rest, leading the group in "Danny Boy," "Peg O'My Heart," or newer tunes from *Pink Lady*, including "My Beautiful Lady," "The Kiss Waltz," and "Donny Did, Donny Don't." Joe had told his family that he "had seen the show in New York with some classmates" and his mother never dreamed where her son had picked up these new melodies. He was her Joe. He would be a marvelous success, though she had no idea what it might take to achieve it.

6

"The Prettiest Romance in a Decade"

*A*t the end of June 1911 Rose sailed off to Europe with her father and Agnes, leaving behind a lonely and worried Joe. Fitzgerald had planned this extensive tour in part to woo her away from young Kennedy. Indeed, the group on the chamber of commerce tour included Hugh Nawn, the young man Fitzgerald hoped his daughter would marry.

One evening Rose sailed down the Danube from Vienna with Hugh. As the moonlight shimmered on the waters, they danced in each other's arms to "The Blue Danube" waltz. Everything was right—the music, the river, everything but Hugh. He was a young man of exemplary character. He would surely enter his father's business and live a predictable and decent life. On the other hand, Joe was a politician's son, a dynamic and fiercely ambitious young man, a man like her father. Married to him, Rose would surely have a more public life, employing the skills and abilities that she considered her forte.

During their weeks in Europe Rose and Agnes met several young men. The rumor that filtered back to Boston was that one of the young Fitzgeralds had attracted the serious attentions of a German baron, news that doubtlessly made Joe even more uneasy. These minor flirtations were a highlight of her younger sister's visit, but Rose was more serious. Rose saw the world as a young woman concerned with the position of her sex in society. She knew that she was a privileged young woman, and the more she saw of a woman's life in Europe, the happier she was that she was an American. "What impressed me the most was the inferior position occupied by women abroad in comparison with conditions at home," she told a *Boston Post* reporter. "Why, it is a fact that women over there work harder than men do in this country. It is a shame the way women are treated in some places in Europe." As their train moved eastward across France, Germany, and Hungary, Rose looked out on the landscape and saw that three quarters of the workers cutting hay and wheat and rye were women. In Germany and Austria, she peered out the window and watched women working on the railways, driving spikes, lifting ties, and carrying bricks. The further east they traveled the worse the conditions became. In Budapest they saw girls no more than fifteen cleaning the parks, and a poor woman and a dog harnessed to a cart loaded with milk, while her husband walked behind, smoking a pipe, and driving his team ahead.

"Why in France, marriage is a trade," Rose said, "yes, a regular trade, and the poor girls have nothing to say about it. But afterwards they practically run the family. But before marriage a girl has no freedom. She can't go out without a chaperon, and wherever she is in public she is under surveillance; that is one reason why American girls always attract attention abroad. Every American woman should be proud she is an American. There is no place in Europe where the men are so chivalrous and considerate of their women as they are here."

In England, Rose found a country in which the women's suffrage movement was a formidable force. In June forty to sixty thousand supporters had marched in London. When a reporter asked Rose what she thought of the English women, she said that she had not gotten "a very tangible impression of the suffragettes," a polite way of saying no comment.

Although Rose's intellectual sympathies were at least partially with the suffragists, she was not about to embarrass her father. Fitzgerald regularly dismissed the women activists back in the States with derision, portraying the suffragists as placard-carrying ninnies who would have been better off at home or at least not linking hands across Washington Street, holding up traffic for two hours in the mayor's beloved city. Fitzgerald loved to tell the story of the day a suffragist came to see him at city hall. "What do you suffragettes want, anyway?" asked Willie, the office boy, as he stood leaning on a broom. "Why, we want to sweep the country," the woman replied. "Do you?" Willie answered. "Well suppose you take this broom and start right here while you are waiting." And, as Fitzgerald told the story, the woman did just that.

As Rose well knew, it was not only her father who opposed women's suffrage, but the leaders of her church who feared women's suffrage as a pied piper leading women away from home and hearth. "If women stir up the volcano of man's lower nature, they must expect to suffer by the ensuing eruption," wrote *America*, the influential Catholic magazine. "It is only by being superior to man, that they can be safe from him, worshipped by him, and helpful to him; not by being equal."

Even if Rose had dared to go against her father and her church, she would not have been welcomed in the homes of some of the suffrage leaders. In Boston the movement was led primarily by well-bred Protestant women who often held ill-concealed contempt for Irish-Americans. As much as these Brahmin ladies wanted the vote for themselves, many of them could hardly abide the idea of giving it to their maids who would probably vote for the likes of John F. Fitzgerald. For that very reason Margaret Deland, a writer and prominent activist for women's rights, favored limited suffrage for men as well as women. "We have suffered many things at the hands of Patrick," Deland wrote in the *Atlantic* in March 1910. "The New Woman would add Bridget also."

Rose accepted her limited political role as her father's daughter. "Don't you wish you were a man and could enter politics with your father?" a reporter asked her.

"Well, I do at times wish that I could enter into it," she replied. "But I can go into it and I do. I follow my father a great deal. Why, when he was elected this last time I was at that last rally. So you see I enjoy it even though I am not a boy. A woman can get a lot out of life if she wants to. She can interest herself in the important things if she wishes."

As the *Franconia* finally sailed back into Boston harbor in mid-August, Rose was delighted at the prospect of seeing Joe again and assuming her role as the first young lady of Catholic Boston. Since graduating from Manhattanville, Rose had discovered that she was often the center of attention in public gatherings. The previous June the Fitzgeralds had opened up their estate for a parish party celebrating Dorchester's 281st birthday. To the young women who sold tickets for the games of fortune, cut pieces of pies, and lined up the children for the start of the potato race, Rose represented the epitome of young Catholic womanhood. They followed her directions and were only too glad to stand in a row in their crisp white summer dresses to be photographed for *The Boston Sunday Globe*. Rose sold flowers from a tray. She wore a long white dress like the other young women, but if a prize had been given for the most extravagant hat, she would have won it for her spectacular, wide frilly chapeau.

Those who had come hoping to enter the mansion itself were disappointed, for the Fitzgeralds had cordoned off their own house, a preserve for the privileged intimates. On the lawn a growing crowd milled around enjoying the various activities. While the Fitzgerald women expected that many St. Mark's parishioners would make the garden party a part of their day, they could not have anticipated three thousand people crowding onto what the *Boston American* called "the busiest two acres outside of Coney Island."

When many of these people talked of Fitzgerald and his family, it was with voices full of awe, telling and retelling the legend of the mayor rising from the cobblestone streets of the North End to this estate in Dorchester. Many of them came as they might to a palace, paying a few coins to walk through the public rooms. In his campaigns Fitzgerald had propagated the saga not only of "Honey Fitz" but of an exemplary family. And thus it was not only for the mayor himself that the multitudes had descended on Welles Avenue, but to experience what was a glamorous, celebrated, legendary family. Politically, they were an extraordinary asset to Fitzgerald. Even *Cosmopolitan*, a leading national magazine, featured the Fitzgerald women in an article that was a lyrical tribute to Josie and her daughters, calling them "the real source of his [Fitzgerald's] inspiration and perennial fitness . . . a feminine group as remarkable as any that ever blessed the life of a public man." The publication presented them as the models of womanhood, "the secret springs that feed his [Fitzgerald's] youth and optimism, the domestic 'powers behind the throne.' "

Rose, her mother, and her sisters were essentially political women who had one transcendent public function: to further Fitzgerald's career and image. Theirs was a gentle conspiracy to project an image of a civilized, cultivated family, the ideal of Catholic life. Rose knew that she must never drop the veneer, never do anything that might disgrace or blemish that image, though she knew that her father had more humble tastes than he pretended. "Corned beef and cabbage was good enough for him when he didn't have Prince So-and-So or Duke Such-and-Such to dinner," said Catherine Coffee, their cook. "For visiting royalty he had canvas duck and pâté de fois gras."

On this June day, no smell of corned beef and cabbage

wafted from the mansion. As Josie walked purposefully across the grounds, her posture erect, beautifully dressed and coiffeured, no one would have imagined how difficult she found it performing at these public functions. For Rose it was different. She had been hidden away from secular life in convents, and now she had come brilliantly alive in public life. A young woman of great social astuteness, she knew how to greet each person, a bubbly charming spirit. If she at times seemed almost too regal, patronizing in her politeness, it was a subtlety that largely went unnoticed.

The crowds continued to grow. By evening a great throng filled the property sitting under Japanese lanterns at lawn tables, properly attired in suits and ties, and long dresses, waiting for the free pop concert. Among the group of new arrivals were a hundred single schoolteachers whom Fitzgerald had admonished to be at this garden party, for "with all the fair maidens that would be present, the occasion of the first annual lawn party ought to be one of unspeakable joy for Dorchester young men, especially those who have not become a victim of Cupid. . . . The place would be an ideal spot for the darting of Cupid's arrow."

What better place for a bachelor to find a socially acceptable spouse, for a young businessman to pass out his card, or for a Catholic maiden to make new acquaintances than in the home of the most prominent Catholic family in Boston? The party was the beginning of a pattern in the lives of Rose's family. People often followed them not because they cared greatly about politics but out of sheer social ambition. The day would come when people would pay almost any price, make almost any effort to be invited into the house that Rose called home, or wait in line for an hour or more merely to shake her gloved hand.

The garden party was put on by a women's sodality at St. Mark's, only one of many organizations to which Rose belonged. These women's clubs were highly important social institutions. Young upper-class Boston women joined the Junior League, the Vincent Club, or such venerable institutions as a sewing circle, where once a week they met and sewed for the poor, maintaining membership during their entire lives. Since the turn of the century, Catholics had begun following the lead of Protestants in developing their own women's clubs as venues for self-improvement, cultural development, philanthropy, and social advancement. "They are not intended merely for a selfish benefit, or a mutual benevolence restricted to the circle of their membership," wrote *America*. "They are rather to be living centers of Catholic activity, whence shall irradiate the light of truth and the warmth of charity to the farthest limits of the world." Rose saw that her mother, despite her public reticence, took a serious and leading part in Catholic club life. She was a prominent member of the League of Catholic Women, and invited the women of the Abbotsford Club to her home to plan their winter festivities over luncheon.

Rose took club life even more seriously than her mother. Josie might be the patroness for an afternoon of whist at the Dorchester Club, but Rose declared cards were "devoid of instruction and seem to be a waste of time." She preferred to go to the German Club where she could practice her German language skills or the Alliance Française to speak French. She went to a Catholic sewing circle, where she spent her time not only talking but making clothes for the poor, and was a member of the Abbotsford Club, putting on plays for charity.

As soon as Rose returned from Europe, she formed her friends into the Ace of Clubs. The club was established to "foster an interest in the social, educational, cultural and charitable activities of its members," a series of goals that could have fit most of the prominent women's clubs. Tuesday afternoon the young women met at the Somerset Hotel to hear a lecture. Years later Rose admitted to her daughter-in-law, Joan Kennedy, that she had formed the club in part because she could not join the Junior League. The very essence of society is exclusivity, and Rose limited the membership to women who had traveled abroad, a subtle distinction that shut out many otherwise worthy potential members.

Rose saw the Ace of Clubs as a place of high-toned discussion. In the early years the speakers included Vida Scudder, a Wellesley professor, talking on St. Francis of Assisi; and Katherine Conway, a professor, author, and prominent opponent of women's suffrage, lecturing on "Italian Influence in English Literature." These were formidable subject matters that could have as easily been delivered at a university as before a group of Catholic debutantes. As she talked of the new club, Rose's voice was full of earnestness: "After we listen to a lecture we have tea and the members talk over the beauties of the places outlined by the speakers, thus enabling them to appreciate more clearly the educational importance and pleasures of travel."

Rose had something of the pedagogue in her, tempered by a self-deprecating manner. "Please don't think I am a saint," she cautioned a reporter. She was never good enough, never pure enough, almost always full of self-criticism. "I like to dance and attend shows as much as any other young girl," she said, "but a club can be made so valuable if one desires that I think it would have been a shame to have devoted this one simply to card playing."

Life, as Rose saw it, was not to be wasted in mere frivolity. "Pink teas bore me," she said. "Frivolous clubs are also uninteresting." Rose's disdain for the merely social was an implicit criticism of Brahmin society. The church had charged Catholic women to do more with their time than to amuse themselves. Rose was imbued with the ethos of self-improvement, for herself and those around her. She had not a moment for indulgence. "I get enough of the bridge and sewing clubs," she said. "They are apt to bore one, and then one doesn't get anything in return for having spent perhaps three hours of one's time."

The first time that Rose talked before the club, she arrived weighed down with pearls, as if the jewelry could give her the authority that she lacked. Her friend advised her to remove the pearls and after doing so she gave her little speech.

"Did I sound all right?" she asked afterwards. "What I said, was it the right thing to say?" She was forever asking her friends their judgments, and learning from them.

Rose's club became *the* organization for upper-crust Catholic young women. Some newer members joined because they were sincerely interested. Rose was, however, the mayor's daughter, and the same motivation that had brought thousands to the Fitzgerald home in Dorchester for the parish party brought scores of young women to the portals of the Ace of Clubs. Rose recalled: "Rather soon, inevitably, I suppose, even among serious-minded young women, the club sprouted some social activities, notably an annual charity ball, and became quite fashionable, with a long waiting list."

Rose sought to expand her life, but wherever she went and whatever she did was within a world of Catholicism. At the dances at the Somerset Hotel that she attended, she could recall meeting not even a single Protestant young man. Rose remembered, moreover, that "on one or two occasions when a

Protestant beau appeared on the threshold, my parents greeted him coldly, discouraged him, and felt that the Church would blame them if there was a mixed marriage, and they wanted no responsibility in that regard."

As Rose well knew, the true leader of the Boston Catholic society was not her father, the mayor, but Archbishop William O'Connell. In the years since his pressure on Fitzgerald had prevented Rose from attending Wellesley, O'Connell had taken firm control over Boston's Catholics. As a church leader he had a profoundly conservative view of a woman's life. He believed that it was woman's great purpose to bear and raise sons of deep faith who would go out into the world as women could not. "Those noble women have known what sacrifices loyal Catholicity requires," he said, praising Catholic mothers. "They have met the rigid demands of unswerving faith nobly, and without compromise. The flattery of public office, the miserable bartering of principles for a momentary popularity, will never take root in the hearts of those men whose mothers would rather go without bread than yield their Catholic allegiance."

In October 1911, the Fitzgerald family and almost all of Catholic Boston rejoiced when Pope Pius X named O'Connell one of three new American cardinals. These appointments, especially O'Connell, represented a watershed in American Catholicism, a victory for the conservatives that helped to define the nature of the church, its attitudes toward women, family, and social change for decades to come.

As much as Boston was a city of two peoples, the Catholics and the Protestants, living largely separate lives, so too the Catholic church was a religion of two sexes often practicing their faith apart from one another. And thus for the Boston laity the archdiocese planned two major occasions to celebrate O'Connell's return from Rome, a banquet for the laymen and a reception for the Catholic women of Boston, both to be held at the Somerset Hotel.

The seventeen hundred guests at the ladies' reception made up what was called "the largest gathering of women in a single building in the history of the city." Josie had a singular honor, chosen to stand at the head of a reception including the leaders of various charities and other organizations. Rose also had a special place, one of fifty young women to serve as ushers, all wearing white gowns and white hats emblazoned with red cardinal ribbons.

The great Louis XV ballroom at the Somerset had not merely been decorated but made over, its walls covered with white silk drapery, the room filled with yellow flowers. Except for priests the only men present were the musicians of the Boston Symphony, seated in a far corner playing sedately. At the other end of the ballroom stood a large scarlet throne in an oasis of palms. Here the cardinal stood for almost two hours as the women passed by in a continuous line, each uttering a word or two of congratulations.

When the line had finally run its course, the cardinal began his talk, looking out on the room filled with richly gowned women. Ten days before he had stood in this same room talking to the leading men of Catholic Boston, calling for a new self-confident Catholicism that would assume ascendancy over Boston. These were daring new words. The cardinal's message to these Catholic women were ones that Josie could have heard as a little girl in South Acton, or her mother before her. They were words of duty, of obligation. He spoke not of change, nor of an expanded role for women in this new Catholic society, but of what he considered the eternal verities.

"Every Christian woman ought to have two things always at heart," he said, speaking as a father to a child. "First the welfare of her husband, her children, her home, or, if unmarried, of the immediate family; their happiness must be her most sacred duty—a duty which she cannot shirk, even under the pretext of care for others, and secondly—she must every day, after the first duty is done and before she permits herself any merely selfish consideration, do something, no matter how slight, which in some even small degree will help on the happiness of someone else not of her immediate entourage."

Rose heard the cardinal's counsel. These were not simply words to her, but truths, the basis of her life. O'Connell was her cardinal, her church, her faith, and she sought to live this life of dedication and devotion. As she looked up at O'Connell, she was seeing a man whose words and judgments were setting out the limits of her life, like markers on a course.

Rose's public and private morality were the same; she had no respite from the harsh admonitions of her faith. The cardinal and her father, however, were both men who saw that what a man said and did were not always the same thing, a mark not of hypocrisy but of worldly wisdom. O'Connell admonished Catholic men to go out into the morally ambivalent world taking power and control while Catholic women stayed home, maintaining a purity both moral and physical.

Rose knew that there was a new and dangerous world out there, one that she experienced only through the newspapers, her father's cautionary words, and essays in her favorite religious publications. The daughters and sons of Irish servants, workers, police officers, and clerks as well as young people of other ethnic backgrounds went nightly to dance halls. In these smoke-filled, half-lit halls, young women were exploring attitudes toward sex, leisure, and individual gratification that would help define the modern age. As the cardinal, the mayor, and other leaders saw it, these shop girls and factory workers were using their freedom not for personal betterment, but for tawdry amusements. Women and men performed "tough dancing," steps that only a few years ago had emerged out of the whorehouses and bars of San Francisco's Barbary Coast. These weren't the sedate waltzes that Rose had learned in which the male and the female hardly touched each other. They were doing the notorious "Boston," the tango, or even the turkey-trot, intimate dances in which the partners' bodies touched each other and as one undercover investigator noted, "instantly decrease or increase the obscenity of the movement lowering the hands from shoulders to the hips."

Joe knew the banned dances, and Rose did not look too deeply into where he had picked up the steps. She found it perfectly natural that men should have far more leeway in their social lives than women. "You were never to let any boy kiss you except the one you were going to marry," Rose said. "This was my father's big advice. He said my mother never did."

Fitzgerald considered it his duty to protect his Rosie and all the women in the city from public immorality. He rigorously policed the dance halls. Fitzgerald was equally dedicated in censoring plays that he considered improper, especially those that portrayed women in what he considered an unseemly manner. During his second term Fitzgerald forbade Oscar Wilde's play, *Salomé*, from completing its scheduled performances. The mayor abhorred *Damaged Goods*, the story of a woman who unknowingly marries a man afflicted with syphilis, and did not relent even after he had thirty of the most offensive lines purged from the script.

Fitzgerald warned Rose about attending *The Playboy of the Western World* by J. M. Synge. Rose almost always obeyed her father. This time she did what she wanted to do. She knew about the play and the literary renaissance that was transforming the cultural life of Ireland, and she did not want to miss this first appearance of the famous Abbey Players of Dublin. Thus Rose was in the orchestra in November 1911 for opening night at the Plymouth theater in downtown Boston.

At the front entrance a man attempted unsuccessfully to enter carrying a golf club under his arm, asserting that he had not had time to go home after his afternoon game. Up in the balconies and galleries, the audience waited restlessly, nervously anticipating the rise of the curtain. In the back of the theater stood the leonine figure of William Butler Yeats, the poet and director. Yeats anticipated the possibility of the full-scale riot that had greeted the premiere of the work in Dublin four years before.

The curtain opened on the set of a modest cottage in western Ireland. It was as benign a scene as one could imagine, yet it set off waves of hissing pouring down from the galleries. Then from above came low-pitched, grunting noises that one theater critic realized were the first importation of a new British custom called "booing." These sounds of disapproval were met by equally vigorous rounds of applause, primarily from the ladies and gentlemen in the orchestra seats.

The theater was full of many prominent Bostonians who did not generally spend their evenings in the midst of raucous spectacle. In the second row of the orchestra sat seventy-one-year-old Isabella Stewart Gardner, the legendary patron of the arts and artists and grande dame of Boston society.

"If they start throwing things, we'll get it right on the heads," warned one of Mrs. Gardner's party. "Perhaps it would be better for us to move back." They did not change their seats, and after two men in the balcony were ejected, the play continued.

The mayor had sent his representative to decide if the play should be censored. Unlike other controversial plays in Boston, the uproar over *The Playboy of the Western World* was not primarily because of its untraditional portrayal of women. The play was the story of Christopher Mahon, a young Irishman who believes that he has killed his tyrannical father by bashing his head. When Mahon goes to another village and starts telling of the murder, the townspeople make him a hero for smiting down a villain. In the final act Mahon's father returns, his

head swathed in bandages, and the village turns on its erst-
while hero, wanting to hang him.

Synge had lived among the peasants of western Ireland, and
the play cut to the quick. He knew that the Irish gift of blarney
was at times a euphemism for endless dissembling and self-
deception. Of course the play was a satire and Synge no more
a traitor to the Irish than Mark Twain to the Americans, but
many of those in the audience with Irish blood took the play
as a savage assault. These Irish-Americans booed and sneered
and hissed. When they had their bellies full of Synge's play,
many of them got up, stomped out, and stood in a group outside the theater, railing against the "degrading spectacle" that
"outraged every idea of common morality."

In her seat in the orchestra Rose neither hissed nor applauded. She squirmed at the portrayal of vulgar Irishmen and
women, blushed at the foul language that had been banished
from her home. She was a third-generation American, and yet
the play and its portrayal of these loutish uncouth Irish peasants stung her deep and long. She knew that it was a worthy
play, a work of art, but she couldn't stop feeling grievously offended.

As she sat listening to the crude dialogue, she turned her
head away as if she had been slapped. There she saw Mrs.
Gardner and her friends. Everyone in Boston knew about
"Mrs. Jack." There was no one like her in Boston. Rose's father took the heiress to baseball games, and she sat there jaw-
ing with Fitzgerald like the regulars in the bleachers. Mrs.
Gardner was equally at home watching a Red Sox game or sitting in her box at the San Carlo Opera. She lived in a veritable
palace in the Fenway, much of which she had brought back
from Venice and filled with masterpieces, from Raphael to
Rembrandt. There she held court, as the great patroness of
Boston culture. Cardinal O'Connell was one of her regular
guests. She was a believer in a natural aristocracy of the artistic and the civilized. She appreciated merit as much in a victory by the Harvard ice hockey team, one of her passions, as
in the music of Loeffler, who arranged his work especially to
be played in her music room. When John Singer Sargent
painted her classic portrait in 1888, he showed her standing in
an austere black gown in front of a halolike damask. Around
her thin waist and voluptuous, Rubenesque hips were two
strings of pearls. Every element in the portrait was perfectly
proper, from Mrs. Gardner's visage to her hands placed de-

murely before her, from the cut of the dress to her famous pearls, but the effect was so unsettling, so darkly erotic, so beyond the circumscribed world of Boston society that the portrait was only shown in public once and now was kept in a closed gallery, viewed only by "Mrs. Jack" and her intimates. Mrs. Gardner was over two decades older now, but there was still something unsettling about her, something that created in others one desperate thought: "If only I dared."

Mrs. Gardner was not cringing at the rude language or reeling in her seat at the low humor. She was enjoying the play, at times applauding, while Rose sat looking at her hands. Rose had convinced herself that she was every bit as good as *them*, every bit as cosmopolitan and cultured and civilized. But she wasn't, not if Isabella Gardner was the measure. It was as if Rose had climbed the highest mountain she could see and reaching the top looked up and realized that the mountain had blocked her from seeing what lay beyond, an immense, distant peak that made what she had climbed nothing but a foothill.

When the play was over and the applause died down, Mrs. Gardner walked up the aisle and stood for a moment in the foyer with a great smile on her aristocratic countenance. "It was splendid," she said, as if she wanted the entire world to know. "It was a great success." She then walked over to the theater manager and told him, "I enjoyed every moment of it." Only then did she leave the theater and return to her great home.

Rose left that evening too, walking up the aisle and out into the chill autumn air. She went home to Dorchester to a house that was not as grand and a life that was not as exalted as it had been only a few hours before.

Rose was not simply the most prominent young Catholic woman in Boston, she increasingly had superseded Josie as her father's hostess and companion. Although the Fitzgerald marriage was celebrated in the press, during much of the year Fitzgerald and Josie were infrequently seen together. Josie still prided herself on her youthful appearance and mannequin's body, but she was too thin, her face hollow.

Rose was happy on her father's arm, emotionally intertwined with him, a supportive political woman acting out the public role her mother would no longer regularly play. Although Josie willingly gave up these functions to her eldest daughter, Rose's role added a new matrix to the complicated emotional and psychological life of the Fitzgerald family. For Rose these were singular and splendid times, and it was inevitable that she saw in life with her father what life with her husband might be. As for Josie, when her husband and her eldest daughter returned from these trips and speeches and gatherings, they shared a life that no longer was hers, and whatever anger or sense of betrayal she may have felt was left unspoken.

One evening Elizabeth Burt, a reporter from the *Boston Post*, arrived at the Fitzgerald home and announced to Josie that she was there to do an article on the family. Soon afterward, the mayor came bounding into the house. Josie's home was her private preserve, the one arena of her life that Fitzgerald did not dominate. She had accepted Fitzgerald's sovereignty over their public lives, and had helped to shine their family image to a high gloss. She had even accepted reporters in her parlor for interviews that she found excruciatingly painful, but not to lay out her life for display in the Sunday papers.

Josie led the reporter into the library. "I did not know you were coming, Miss Burt, or I would have been prepared," Josie told her. "Mr. Fitzgerald never told me a thing about it until the last minute. That is just like him."

Fitzgerald had begun to scent trouble in the air. He was hearing Josie's scorn and sarcasm, weapons that she kept sheathed, relegated to the boudoir, and never took out in public. The moment called for diversion. "Turn on the phonograph, Rose," Fitzgerald interjected, "and we will liven things up."

Rose cranked up the phonograph and danced an old-fashioned waltz with Fitzgerald. Rose was a willing political woman with a shrewd sense of public relations. She saw her mother's "stern face, cold eyes, and peculiar smile" and realized that her father and his image might be in for a disastrous evening. Her mother was the matron of Welles Avenue, but Rose subtly attempted to assume control over this evening. It was doubly a watershed in the history of the family. It was one thing for Fitzgerald to subject the family to controversy, sullying its name in the mud of politics. He was a man and that was his business. But here, for the first time, Josie, a woman, was risking the family image that was hers to guard and polish. Here too was the first time that Rose took a quietly confident control over that public portrait.

After the song ended, Rose led her father over to the piano to sing out of key a new ballad, "Row! Row! Row!" and then a rendering of "Sweet Adeline," the music temporarily drowning out any opportunities for her mother to elaborate on her melancholy themes.

The music could not last forever. Fitzgerald led the family in games that had the added virtue of limiting conversation with Josie. "We have quite a place here, Miss Burt," Fitzgerald declared. "It is too bad it isn't day time so you could have a better view of our garden."

Josie looked at her husband. "John, it does indeed seem refreshing to have you here," Josie began, slowly sidling into sarcasm. "I am not sorry that you are to have photographs taken to mark the evening. I am going to frame one and place a card over it on which I will write: 'Taken on his one evening at home.' "

That was a blow that hit the mayor square in the stomach. "Now you will make Miss Burt think that I neglect my family if you keep on," Fitzgerald said. He was employing one of the best defenses: restate the words of the attacker as if they weren't meant as an attack at all. "I spend every Sunday with them, Miss Burt, and I have them each in town at least once a week."

Fitzgerald was like a pitcher who has a fastball that he always throws in difficult situations. Now was a time to bear down and throw it with all his might. "I am a family man," the mayor continued, "and the reason I am such is because I was one of many children. I cared for my brothers and sisters, did all the buying for the family and was father and mother in one. . . . Why, I think nothing of buying the girls' hats and coats for them."

"They were perfect fits," Josie said. The image of Fitzgerald prowling through the women's department in search of haberdashery brought a new smile to Josie's lips. "I wouldn't be a bit surprised to see him bring me home a suit," she said. Now even she seemed to realize the danger in her words that the reporter was taking down. "I will admit that though he doesn't spend many evenings at home with us during the week, he seems to have us on his mind a great deal."

"Deal!" Fitzgerald yelled, astounded at his wife minimizing his contribution. "Why I have you all bobbing in and out of the city to see me the entire time. And you know, Miss Burt, that I never take a trip that I don't have some members of the family with me."

The reporter dutifully wrote down Fitzgerald's words and then left with plans to write a piece for the Sunday paper. That night, as Rose lay awake, she felt embarrassed for all that her mother had done and said, and nothing but warmth and empathy for her father who had to put up with it all. It did not occur to her that perhaps her mother's lot was not the blessed one it seemed, and she might have had some reason for her outbursts. The next morning at breakfast no one mentioned the disconcerting evening, and like other dramas in the family, it was treated as if nothing had ever happened.

Sunday the Fitzgerald household read the *Post* with special interest. For every one of Josie's remarks there were several of her husband's, and it was Fitzgerald's charms and ministrations that had carried the day. "There was not the smallest corner of interest that the Mayor did not show me," the reporter concluded, "and so as I left his home I had fully solved why so many seek the presence of the present Mayor of this city. He is a credit to Boston in more ways than one."

As much as Rose enjoyed serving as her father's hostess, she and Fitzgerald still were at loggerheads over Joe. Her father attempted to dissuade Rose from continuing with her Harvard beau. Fitzgerald was a man capable of extraordinary emotional deviousness, and he did not rail against young Joe in lengthy discourse. "There were no 'scenes' and no lectures," Rose recalled. "Actually, his temptation to issue Napoleonic orders gave way to sweet reason. He pointed out that I was fortunate enough to have unusual advantages and opportunities. . . . So there I was wobbly and often tearful in private, as I tried to find an equilibrium of my own."

Joe had graduated from Harvard in June 1912 and taken a position as a clerk at Columbia Trust, his father's bank. After only three months he left to become a bank examiner. These were solid positions, a worthy start for a young man, but Fitzgerald was not impressed, and continued to attempt to dissuade Rose from continuing to see Joe.

For Rose it was a terrible dilemma to be torn between the two men she loved. She was twenty-three years old now, and it was time to marry and raise the family she was brought up to raise, yet still her father attempted to bar her way. Nothing she said and nothing that Joe did seemed to matter.

In early December 1913, in the middle of her father's re-election campaign, a letter arrived at the Fitzgerald home that changed that equation forever, and gave Rose the authority to break away from her father's dictates. On that day her mother received a black-bordered letter stating that if her husband did not retire from the race, his relationship with a cigarette girl nicknamed "Toodles" would be exposed. When Fitzgerald came home that evening, Josie was waiting for him in the doorway, and Rose was standing beside her mother in strong moral support. Rose had been brought up to accept the moral dichotomy between the home and the world, and this letter challenged the moral sovereignty of the home, and everything for which Rose and her mother's lives stood.

When Fitzgerald read the letter, he claimed that he was innocent, but as a politician he knew what the words might mean. His main challenger, Congressman James Curley, was a fellow Irish-American and Democratic politician, a man eleven years his junior. Curley had risen out of the same slums as Fitzgerald, and he represented all the envy, the yearning, the anger of that world, a world that Fitzgerald had half forgotten. Curley could out-Irish him, outpromise him, even outcampaign him and outtrick him.

Fitzgerald, in fact, was innocent. In a breach-of-promise suit brought the following year, he was mentioned only as having allegedly kissed the woman on a dance floor and whispered sweet nothings in her ear, a crime that he had committed thousands of times. That was the extent of the notorious Toodles scandal, as far as it concerned John F. Fitzgerald. But this evening Josie wasn't listening. She had not wanted him to run, she had put up with his antics and absences for two decades, and now she wanted the private life that she considered only her due.

One night as Fitzgerald lay awake mulling over his alternatives, a fire swept through the Arcadia boardinghouse downtown on Washington Street killing twenty-eight men and injuring forty-four others. As the mayor spent hours walking through the charred ruins and visiting other boardinghouses, he collapsed exhausted and was carried to his home.

While Fitzgerald rested in bed under doctors' orders, Curley continued to campaign, refusing to stop even for a day, although three other lesser opponents suspended their campaigns. In his attempt to pry Fitzgerald loose from his office, Curley announced that he would be giving a series of lectures on famous men in history, contrasting them with the mayor. Fitzgerald was used to being attacked for corruption and that didn't bother him. However, Curley would soon be giving a lecture on "Great Lovers in History: From Cleopatra to Toodles" and another titled "Libertines in History: From Henry the Eighth to the Present Day." This was different. This was an attack on his home life, on the laboriously constructed image of family and home and a perfect marriage. This would bring shame to himself and to Josie and Rose, to all the Fitzgeralds. If he made a strategic retreat, he could harbor his forces for his planned campaign for the United States Senate in two years.

On December 17, Fitzgerald announced his withdrawal for reasons of health, a decision that was called "a victory for the mayor's family and friends." Although Josie was relieved, Rose saw her father's withdrawal as another name for a shameful defeat. Rose adored her father. She saw him as an epic character in a great historic drama. Now she saw that her knight errant was wearing armor of tinfoil and carrying a sword that he threw away at the first strong challenge. In later years she talked often of the time and tide in men's lives. She saw Providence, Fate, and Destiny not as abstractions, but living forces of such magnitude that she capitalized the three words in her autobiography. Her father had run from a fight, and it was now his fate or destiny that he would never recover the ground over which he had just retreated; in Rose's eyes he was never again the man he once had been.

Fitzgerald did not have the same emotional hold over Rose any longer and would not be able to prevent her from marrying the man she loved.

On one of the last glorious mornings of Indian summer, Rose stood beside Joe in Cardinal O'Connell's private chapel and took her marital vows. The tiny church was an exquisite jewel and Rose was a fitting centerpiece, dressed in a floor-length, white tulle gown, a train of white brocaded satin, a cap of princess lace, with a bouquet of lilies of the valley and orchids.

Within the precincts of this diminutive chapel stood the three men who largely defined Rose's life: Cardinal O'Connell, her father, and Joe. The cardinal led Rose and Joe in their marital vows while Fitzgerald and the other members of the two families looked on. That O'Connell was here today on October 7, 1914, to perform the marital ceremony and lead a nuptial mass demonstrated that although her father was no longer mayor, the Fitzgeralds were still Boston's first Catholic family.

For Joe this wedding was his second great triumph of the year. Earlier in 1914, at the age of twenty-five, Joe had become president of the Columbia Trust Company, proudly touted as the youngest bank president in the United States. When a rival bank had attempted to take over the Columbia Trust Company, Joe and his father had gone to his relatives to seek the money to stave off the bid. In an act of remarkable faith, his mother's three brothers, Charles, James, and John, and her sister Catherine, loaned him large amounts of their savings. This was all Hickey money. Without Mary Augusta's firm resolve, he would have come away empty. With that capital, Joe was able to coax funds out of other friends, relations, and a Brahmin banker, and to take over control of the bank. Young Joe was already an expert in the wages of human weakness. It was a time of growing strength for him, and one of decline for Fitzgerald. Joe had assumed a position of such power and honor that Fitzgerald had little choice but to accept Joe as his son-in-law.

As Joe knelt beside Rose during the nuptial mass, he was marrying not simply a woman, but a social position, hoisting himself far above most of his peers. His mother had filled him with pride in his family; Mary Augusta would have suffered half the tortures of the inquisition rather than admit that the Kennedys were not as good as the Fitzgeralds. Despite all his mother's haughtiness, this morning he, Joe Kennedy, was taking Rose's name as much as she was taking his. For Joe the prestige lay not simply in Rose's family but in the presence of a prince of the church. "I'd always wanted to be married by a Cardinal and I was," Joe reflected later.

It had been cloudy when the wedding party entered the church, but as the newlyweds left the cardinal's residence, the sun came out. Only the immediate families had been invited to the ceremony and there on the steps Rose and Joe stopped to give the newspaper photographers their moment. For the most part the journalists were interested in the Fitzgeralds, not the Kennedys. Some of them treated the bridegroom nearly as an interloper as they took the pictures that would grace the front pages of Boston's major newspapers the next morning. The *Post* photographer arranged Fitzgerald, Josie, and Rose for his shot, not even including Joe. For that picture Rose stood with a languid appearance, looking away from her parents. Then, the *Globe* photographer decided to pose the newlyweds alone.

Twenty-four-year-old Rose had been photographed hundreds of times, and in almost every photo she had a poised, professional smile, but this morning as she stood beside her new husband, she smiled with exuberant joy, her smile a dazzling flash of illumination.

Rose and Joe drove to the Welles Avenue home for a wedding breakfast and reception. Here the well-wishers were explicitly limited to "only the relatives of both families." This was a time for the two families to talk and for the celebration to begin. The press might ignore Joe, but the Kennedy women were not to be outdone by the Fitzgeralds. Joe's mother, Mary Augusta, wore a stunning outfit of taupe crêpe meteor with silver trim, and a hat set off with an ostrich plume. Her daughters, Mary Loretta and Margaret, dressed in exquisite outfits of velvet, lace, and silk.

At the reception Rose had ample time to display the diamond pendant her husband, the bank president, had given her, to admire her many other wedding gifts, and to talk to her relatives. Rose was a young woman with many friends, but almost none of them had been invited to celebrate what they told the *Boston Post* was "the prettiest romance in a decade." For a man of Fitzgerald's stature and social pretensions, his firstborn's wedding reception was shamefully modest. Rose and Joe may have wanted a small wedding, as Rose later claimed, but among the Fitzgeralds, family functions were almost always used for public purposes. The debut that he and Josie had given their daughter had been one of the largest a Catholic debutante had ever received, and the size of the debut was usually a reliable indicator of how large and impressive the wedding would be.

Fitzgerald was only grudgingly giving his daughter away to Joseph P. Kennedy, and even now at the wedding reception, a time of supposed joy and festivity, he was full of bitterness and anger. He didn't like Joe, and he liked him even less as a son-in-law. During the reception he suddenly exploded in anger, yelling at Joe. The other guests heard the loud, harsh voices of Fitzgerald and Joe, and turned to watch the two men in fierce argument. As the groom and the father-in-law continued oblivious to the scores of onlookers, Rose stood silently beside the two men. Joe was her husband and by everything she had ever learned, it was her duty now to stand with him, but Fitzgerald was her father. Suddenly, she pulled the wedding ring off her left hand, and placed it on the mantel. Rose's wedding day had been tainted by anger, a dreadful omen. In this the first crisis of their marriage, Rose had stood with her father, doubly terrible omens for "the prettiest romance in a decade."

For the guests, the Kennedys as well as the Fitzgeralds, it was a shameful moment, one never to be discussed with anyone outside the family. Rose never talked about the incident, and in her 522-page autobiography devoted only three sentences to what was supposed to have been the happiest day of her young life. By the time Rose and Joe left for their honeymoon at the Greenbriar Hotel in White Sulphur Springs, West Virginia, Rose had her wedding ring back on. As the newlyweds departed, Fitzgerald entertained the reporters waiting outside, a moment that one of them remembered as "hilarious."

When Rose returned from her honeymoon, it was to a new life as Mrs. Joseph P. Kennedy in a house in the suburbs of Brookline. For a couple with the ambitions and social aspirations of Rose and Joe Kennedy, it was inevitable that they should decide to start their married life in such a community as Brookline. Here they could live the very epitome of the suburban life-style that Joe's parents had sought in their journey from East Boston to Winthrop, and Rose's family by settling in Dorchester.

When Rose and Joe had been growing up, Brookline had a reputation as the most exclusive of the suburban communities ringing Boston. *Harper's Magazine* called the community "the wealthiest town in the U.S. Its annual income is greater than that of the whole state of New Hampshire." The Brookline residents took such pride in their affluence that the high school athletic teams were nicknamed the "Wealthtowners."

Rose and Joe were part of a great migration of middle-class Bostonians, including large numbers of Irish-Americans and Jewish-Americans in search of that rarefied life-style once limited to their economic and social betters. Back for many blocks along both sides of Beacon Street in Coolidge Corner, a commercial center, hundreds of single-family homes on small lots were going up. Here at 83 Beals Street Joe had purchased a home for sixty-five hundred dollars from Howard Kline just before their marriage. By the time Rose and Joe went on their honeymoon they had already furnished the dwelling, and with the addition of their wedding gifts the newlyweds moved into their new home. Joe left for work each morning in his new Model-T, and returned in the evening to an environment that the designer of its streets, Frederick Law Olmsted, intended to be a "delicate synthesis of town and wilderness." Great old oaks and elms lined the streets, and there were big parks and woods untouched by the developers' axes. Yet the town was at the end of the trolley line along Beacon Street from downtown Boston. Rose made it downtown in a half hour on the Commonwealth Avenue line.

The three-story frame house was on a small lot in an area where the sounds of hammers driving nails into the wooden frames of new homes were as common as the putt-putt of automobiles. Across from the Kennedys' home there stood not a single other house, and the lot next door was empty too. Entering the home, the visitor stood in a narrow hallway. There to the right was the living room with overstuffed chairs, a sofa, and an Oriental rug on the wooden floor. To the left was the dining room with its formal table and chairs, and silver flatware and the silver tea set that were wedding presents. The hallway led to the kitchen. With its black coal and gas stove, sinks, and worktable, this was a utilitarian world, the servants' domain where the mistress of the home spent little of her time. Upstairs there was a master bedroom with twin beds, a small nursery, and an even smaller room that served for guests and as Rose's study. One bathroom served Rose, her family, and the servants as well. On the third story were tiny rooms for the nursemaid and the young Irish woman who served both as general maid and cook.

On Beals Street the Kennedys were living with people of similar class. Most of their neighbors were a generation older; for them Beals Street was not a beginning but the epitome of achievement. The Kennedys had neighbors of Protestant ancestry, along with Irish-Americans, Italian-Americans, and several Jewish residents including two houses away Benjamin Stern, a furniture dealer, who kept a kosher home. These new arrivals were pursuing what Rose and Joe wanted. They sought to avoid the ethnic stereotyping of their national backgrounds and to become part of this fashionable Brookline world that by their very presence was becoming less fashionable. As the Kennedys and the others rapidly began moving in, the elite slowly began moving out, diluting and destroying the very world to which the new arrivals had aspired, the same pattern that took place eventually in Winthrop and Dorchester as well.

On this street full of salesmen, merchants, clerks, cigar makers, distillers, and other business people, Joe was the only banker, a professional status about which Rose was inordinately proud. As the Brahmins had retreated from their daring entrepreneurship to the more sedentary pursuit of contemplating and harboring their wealth, the banker stood at the center of the Brahmin world. Six-foot-tall Joe affected a banker's haberdashery, wire-rimmed glasses that perched daintily on his large nose, homburg hats, and suits cut with funereal seriousness. Beneath the calculated attire was a sinewy muscular man, with an athlete's gait, a man who outside the home could speak with the raw profanity of the street.

Rose was the banker's wife. In decorating her home Rose sent out signals to the world that hers was a home where civility was not only the norm but the imperative. In the living room she placed a piano, the very symbol of cultural attainment. She did not have much of a personal taste in art. On her trips to Europe she had seen many masterpieces of European painting, and she found prints of works by Frans Hals and Rembrandt and put them on the walls. She was the mayor's daughter. That was how she was known in Boston, and her living room contained pictures of Rose and her father and the Fitzgerald family. In her dining room she and Joe ate meals off fine china and silver prepared by an Irish maid-cook who earned seven dollars a week, a dollar more than in her previous position. She not only cooked meals and cleaned but at dinner donned a black uniform and white apron and served the Kennedys with the élan of a meal at the Somerset Hotel.

Rose's home was not full of mere products, consumer goods that she had purchased with her husband's earnings, but true belongings that tied her to her family and friends. When she took tea she lifted shamrock cups that Sir Thomas Lipton had given her; they were the same pattern he used on his famous yacht that she had visited on her trip home from Blumenthal. At dinner she and Joe often ate off Limoges china that her sister-in-law had not simply given her as a wedding gift but had laboriously decorated by hand, piece by piece. In the guest room where Joe's college friends sometimes stayed, the bedspreads were emblazoned with a harp and shamrocks, a lighthouse, and an Irish doe. Fitzgerald had purchased the bedspreads on a trip to Ireland and given them to the newlyweds, reminding them equally of him and of the sod of old Ireland.

* * *

Rose was not even settled into her new house when she became pregnant. Joe was gone early in the morning, and sometimes not back until late in the evening. Rose still had her Ace of Clubs, her friends, the frequent trips to the Fitzgerald home in Dorchester, but as Mrs. Joseph P. Kennedy her daily life had changed as dramatically as her husband's had changed insignificantly. While her husband went out into the world, Rose spent much of her day alone in the house at 83 Beals Street with the nursemaid and the maid-cook. Rose's education had been to prepare her for what she considered the sacred task of motherhood. Yet in this new age of science nothing she had learned prepared her either for pregnancy or for the day-to-day routine of life with a newborn. For Rose's ancestors an imminent birth meant a call to a midwife, the delivery exclusively the province of women. By Rose's time, childbirth was being taken over almost completely by male doctors trained in the new specialization of obstetrics, and was being moved out of the home into the hospital.

Rose and Joe spent the final weeks of her pregnancy on a summer vacation in a sprawling rented summer house on the beach at Hull. Although many modern mothers took to bed for their last month, Rose had too much energy to spend her days simply reclining. She walked on the beach, and in the evenings sat at the piano and played tunes such as "By the Light of the Silvery Moon."

On the morning of July 25, 1915, Rose told Joe that she had begun to feel the first pangs of birth. Joe called two doctors, Dr. Frederick L. Good, a leading Boston obstetrician and Harvard Medical School graduate, and his assistant, Dr. Edward J. O'Brien, whose main task was to administer the anesthetic. The special nurse was already in residence, to be assisted by the Kennedys' own maid. It was a formidable team for what if not an operation had all the clinical accoutrements of one. In the beach house the nurse laid out the supplies and medical materials.

In this scientific era of "painless childbirth," Rose's doctors gave Rose ether, sending her into a semi-sleeplike state, a procedure that sometimes caused complications and even death. For Rose, the ether meant that she had almost no memory of this birth.

As Rose lay in bed upstairs, Joe waited downstairs. Her father was on the beach in his bathing suit, playing with his son Fred and with his friends, awaiting news of his first grandchild. Shortly after ten o'clock the two doctors appeared and told Joe: "A boy, and a sound, healthy, ten-pound boy too."

"It's a boy," a messenger shouted on the beach. "A boy!" With that Fitzgerald ran to the beachfront house. Shortly afterwards, Fitzgerald opened the door to a reporter and announced: "I'm the happiest man in the world." Rose had fulfilled her immediate task, and the nurse brought the infant downstairs so that Fitzgerald could be photographed holding Joe Jr. in his arms. "Now didn't I tell you the truth?" Fitzgerald asked with rhetorical flourish, looking down at the swaddled baby. "What do you think of him? Isn't he the finest baby ever born? Doesn't he look like his grandfather?"

As the baby wailed, the nurse took Joseph P. Kennedy Jr. away. "Feeling fine and just as young as ever," the former mayor said, as if he had given birth. "Of course, he is going to be President of these United States, his mother and father have already decided that, and he is going to Harvard where he will play on the football team and baseball team, and incidentally take all the scholastic honors. Then he's going to be a captain of industry until it's time for him to be President for two or three terms. Further than that has not been definitely decided yet."

When Rose awoke more fully out of her groggy sleep, the nurse gave the infant to its mother. "When a mother holds her first baby in her arms, what awe-inspiring thoughts go fleeting through her mind and fill her heart," Rose reflected. "A child has been bestowed upon her to mold and to influence—what a challenge, what a joy. . . . On her judgment he relies, and her words will influence him, not for a day or a month or a year, but for time and for eternity and perhaps for future generations."

Rose's faith taught her that motherhood was a sacred duty, and that to fail at motherhood was to fail God. The fact that Rose felt that her every word and action could affect young Joe Jr. was not only exciting and challenging, but also daunting and intimidating.

For centuries, mothers had passed down their knowledge of raising children from generation to generation, admixtures of folk wisdom, sound advice, and superstition. In the twentieth century, that role now had been superseded by scientific experts, and they pressed upon Rose a new level of responsibility. Rose, like her husband who believed in buying the best in advice as in everything else, had inordinate faith in experts. For Rose as for other women of her generation, the great authority was Dr. L. Emmett Holt and his popular book, *The Care and Feeding of Children.* Years later Rose reflected how when she was faced with problems of child raising, she had not only called up all that she had learned from her mother but turned to books on child raising and "studied the latest advice of child psychologists." Dr. Holt's ideas and those of other proponents of modern child care were as much the common currency of the time as Dr. Benjamin Spock would be for a later generation.

The infant slept next to the nurse in a white bassinet in the small second-floor nursery. Although the nurse had hour-to-hour management over the infant, Rose was the ultimate authority, and the injunctions of these secular gods of science were as severe as the fathers of her church. The experts admonished the new mother, in the words of one popular child-care book, that "lack of precision in the mother is responsible for most of the failures we see—sad failures where the baby has suffered morally and physically. . . . She must do what has to be done for her child regularly. She must not vary so much as a minute the hours of his feeding, his bath, his nap."

Regularity. That was the key. Dr. Holt taught that the baby must be fed every two hours during the day and twice at night at precisely the same time. The infant must be put to sleep at strictly the same time each evening. Rose followed religiously the mandates of the experts, regulating every moment of her baby's life. She followed all the precepts of modern child care. Although she had a maid to help her, the days were measured out in a relentless routine.

When she had married, Rose was still full of a natural exuberance and openhearted warmth and emotion. She had maintained those qualities despite her mother's ceaseless quest for civility, the lessons taught in her favorite book *Little Women,* the training of the nuns of the Sacred Heart, and the struggles with her father over Joe. She was a mother now, and Josie and the other Irish-American women of her generation were her unconscious guides, mothers who believed that one demonstrated love not by showing it, but by holding back affection, passing it out for good behavior like an after-dinner mint. A part of Rose would have loved to have taken Joe in her arms and played with him for hours. But the experts said no. "The young mother in America is possessed of a love-madness for her tiny infant," wrote Katherine G. Busbey in *Home Life in America* in 1910, "which, while it is very poetical and picturesque, is harmful in many ways."

Dr. Holt was very specific about the damage that could be done by playing with young babies. "They are made nervous and irritable, sleep badly, and suffer in other respects," he cautioned. As a mother Rose was supposed to regulate her own emotions, or they might spill over and damage her child forever. If the infant suffered frequently from the abdominal pain of colic "the mother should take more out-of-door exercise, eat less meat and try to control her emotions; all causes of worry should be removed."

Rose's little Joe was a robust baby who thrived on life at Beals Street and seemed to validate the wisdom of Dr. Holt and his minions. A year after giving birth to Joe Jr., Rose was pregnant again. This time she decided to deliver in her own master bedroom upstairs in the house on Beals Street. Again Dr. Good made the journey to the Kennedy home and on May 29, 1917, at three in the afternoon Rose gave birth to John Fitzgerald Kennedy, named after Rose's father. Rose was so sedated with ether that she retained few memories of the birth of her second son, nicknamed "Jack." The blue-eyed baby was not only smaller, but he was a sickly child, susceptible to illnesses from whooping cough to measles.

Rose had more than an unhealthy child to worry about, for in April the United States had entered the war against Germany and the other Axis nations. Patriotism had become the national religion, and almost everyone was taking part. Fitzgerald gave a talk at Dorchester High School about the Red Cross. Rose's younger brother, Tom, joined up in the expeditionary forces to fight in France. Rose's younger sister, Eunice, was only seventeen years old. She could not go and fight like her big brother Tom, but she insisted on doing her part. She believed that if she helped out at home her big brother would return home safely to the house on Welles Avenue. She joined the Red Cross and at night went to the temporary Red Cross cottage on Boston Common to entertain the doughboys who soon would be heading to the trenches of France.

A million men were readying to go to Europe to fight with the American Expeditionary Forces in World War I. Of all Joe's Harvard friends, he was the only one not to join up in the summer of 1917 and travel to Plattsburg, New York, to take officer training. Instead, in September he took a fifteen-thousand-dollar-a-year position as assistant general manager of the Bethlehem shipyards at Fore River. A few months later, when he was about to be called into the army, he wrote a letter to his draft board asking to be allowed to keep what he considered a job important to the war effort. When the board rejected his appeal, Joe's superior used his clout in Washington to see that Joe did not have to fight.

Some Harvard men from the class of 1912 never returned from the trenches, and those who did often resented men like Joe. Rose, however, did not see that she had married a man whom some of his peers considered a coward. In her memory Joe had taken the position at Bethlehem Steel *before* America's entry into World War I, not afterwards in a blatant and calculated attempt to avoid military service. Rose's palette contained only pastels, and she painted a portrait of a courageous young man. To her Joe was heroic in the way that he pushed the shipyard to production records and in the process developed an ulcer. Joe had, in fact, hardly arrived at the shipyard when thousands of shipyard workers went on strike after not receiving promised pay increases. Joe immediately vowed that he would fire the strikers. The shipyards were crucial to America's war effort, and the young assistant secretary of the Navy, Franklin Roosevelt, personally intervened, going along with the promised pay hike. Joe's harsh precipitous action had alienated the workers and lost him the confidence of his superiors. Joe was abruptly pushed aside, into a position in which he had no authority.

Rose had grown up with a romantic ideal of a husband. Nowhere in her equation was there room for a husband who faltered miserably in the great outer world. That was the wife that Joe came home to and he was as isolated in his stereotyped husbandly role as Rose was in hers. On their wedding day, Rose had stood with her father and now in this first great failure in Joe's life, he was alone. For Joe, the shame of his debacle must have been extraordinary, but there was really nowhere he could go for comfort and reassurance. His mother had sent him out in the world to succeed. His father wanted him to be tough. And Rose was a wife.

Rose saw little of her husband during the week. By the time he arrived late in the evenings, the babies were asleep and he was ready for bed himself. In the house on Beals Street, Joe shared nearly nothing of his professional life with Rose. He didn't deign to discuss it, and to Rose it soon became nothing more than arcane minutiae.

When Rose had married Joe, she knew almost nothing about men. She had not gone to school with young men. She had danced with numerous beaux, and had her mild flirtations, but men had always been a strange and distant universe. Yet everything in her life was leading to marriage and a family. It was as if she had been trained as a chef by learning abstractions about nutrition, and then one day was led into the kitchen, set down before a strange assortment of foods and pans and recipes, and expected to prepare a fine meal.

Now Rose slept in her own bed next to her husband's, but this man, her husband, was still living in a universe beyond her reach. Rose had known nothing about the intimacies of married life, not simply the sexual aspects, but the complicated, subtle give and take of living with a man.

For Rose weekends were the best. Joe was usually home. Friday nights they often played bridge with their good friends, Marie and Vin Greene, and then ordered ice cream from Murray's on Boylston Street. Saturday dinner was baked beans, simmered in a big pot, richly flavored, and ladled out by the plateful. Joe loved music and Saturday evenings they often drove down to Boston to Symphony Hall, on Huntington Avenue near the New England Conservatory where Rose had studied piano. Sunday, of course, meant church and then perhaps a drive over to Winthrop to visit Mary Augusta and P. J. Kennedy. By now, as Rose remembered, Mary Augusta weighed between 180 and 200 pounds, so stout that "she had a little difficulty to get around."

Rose's brother came home safely from France, but the Fitzgeralds had suffered a very different kind of war casualty. Rose's sister Eunice had contracted tuberculosis on those long days in the damp Red Cross cottage on Boston Common ministering to the soldiers. Now she was fighting the malady and the life and spirit was going out of Eunice like the lights in a theater, dimming imperceptibly. Again and again she traveled to the TB sanatorium in Saranac, New York. She would come back, feverish with life, and then gradually she would fade again.

The end of the war stilled the battalions of riveters at the Bethlehem shipyards, and Joe went out seeking contracts for the building of civilian ships. In the spring of 1919 he arrived for a fifteen-minute appointment with Galen Stone, a prominent Boston broker and the chairman of a shipping line. Joe learned that the businessman had already left to take the train to New York. Joe hailed a taxicab and plunked himself down next to Stone for the four-hour trip to New York City. Joe didn't get the contract, but two weeks later he was offered a position as manager of Hayden, Stone & Co. in Boston. Joe's ten-thousand-dollar-a-year salary was soon only pocket money, as he became a member of what *Fortune* called the "intense, secretive circles of operators in the wildest stock market in history, with routine plots and pools, inside information and wild guesses. . . ."

There was a world out there, beyond Beals Street, beyond Brookline, and Rose was no longer a part of it. Women only a few years younger than Rose had begun to live lives that the nuns at Manhattanville would have considered wanton and amoral. In July 1920, *The New York Times* wrote that "the American woman . . . has lifted her skirts far beyond the modest limitation." It was not only their skirts that young women were lifting but their discretion and modesty. It was the beginning of the era of the flappers that F. Scott Fitzgerald so evocatively defined in his 1920 book, *The Other Side of Paradise*. Women were smoking cigarettes, rolling their stockings, drinking in speakeasies, and spending inordinate time in the backseats of automobiles.

For Joe the new era came as a godsend. A magazine cover announced that the clock had struck "sex o'clock in America," and when Joe heard the bell toll, he knew it was tolling for him. The man who had taken an actress ice-skating when he was a Harvard student still had an interest in the distaff side of the theater. "I hope you will have all the good looking girls in your company looking forward with anticipation to meeting the high Irish of Boston," he wrote Arthur Houghton, a theatrical manager, who became a friend, "because I have a gang around me that must be fed on wild meat."

When he told Rose of his plans, he did not speak of "wild meat." "He'd say he was going in with Arthur Houghton to watch the show for a while or something, and I'd say fine, and it was all right," Rose said. Whether or not Joe had begun his ceaseless philandering, he already had the wanderer's eye. Rose turned away from all that was black and negative, refusing to look at the shadows of life until she was confronted with their dark image. "I had heard that chorus girls were gay, but evil, and worst of all, husband snatchers," Rose said. "But nothing shocking happened. One characteristic of my life with Joe was that we trusted one another implicitly. If he had occasion to go out with theatrical people, he told me he was going and he went. There was never any deceit on his part and there was never any doubt in my mind about his motives or behavior."

What was the purpose of challenging her husband? Rose had been taught to obey her husband and her church; she was empowered only to accept or deny. Joe was a man of immense energy, full of as much lustful vitality for sex as for money and success. He had his complaints too, and he could voice them, to her or even to their friends in ways that must have been excruciatingly embarrassing to Rose. One evening when he and Rose were playing cards with the Greenes, the two couples began discussing sex. "Now, listen, Rosie, this idea of yours that there is no romance outside of procreation is simply wrong," Joe asserted. "It was not part of our contract at the altar, the priest never said that and the books don't argue that. And if you don't open your mind on this, I'm going to tell the priest on you."

Joe was not a man who easily discussed the intimate details of his married life. That he could do so, even among close friends, suggests how strong Rose's sexual reticence may have been and how deeply it hurt their marriage. It was a lament heard in many Catholic homes, where women considered the marital bed a place of procreation, not pleasure, and that sex must not take place during menstruation or pregnancy. With Rose eight times pregnant in thirteen years, Joe presumably spent almost half his early married life during times when it was unthinkable for him to have sexual relations with his wife.

Rose saw her life as a complex matrix of obligations and duties, and she would not have it said that she had failed at this wifely obligation. Decades later when Joe's adultery had become common knowledge, Rose talked to one of her young relatives about her own sexuality, suggesting that she was more understanding of her husband's desires, and perhaps even her own, than outsiders suspected. Her sexual scenario, however, had a Victorian formality. "She taught us how you're supposed to act to your husband, how you're supposed to have a chaise lounge in the bedroom," recalled Kerry McCarthy, a niece in whom Rose confided. "You put your nylons and your robe on the chaise lounge and you keep a lap robe which is folded down, and when your husband comes in, everything is perfect."

Rose had a terrible problem with her family, a problem of which she was only slowly becoming aware. When Rose's third child was due, in September 1918, the nation and Europe were in the midst of a flu epidemic called Spanish influenza after the country of its supposed origin. The disease was often deadly, eventually affecting about a fourth of the American population and killing more than half a million. It was so widespread that the Boston stock exchange closed down, and in some cities authorities required those in public to wear surgical masks. In Boston, near panic prevailed and citizens followed the advice of the health commissioner to "avoid fatigue and crowded conditions as much as possible." Doctors were inundated with the sick and the dying, and Dr. Good arrived late on September 13 to deliver the Kennedys' third child. As was the custom, the nurse had been trained to hold back the birth of the baby until the doctor arrived. Although this was supposedly done to ensure a modern delivery, the larger reason was that the doctor received his full fee only if he was present. The nurse held back the baby's head until Dr. Good finally hurried into the bedroom and Rose gave birth to her first daughter: Rose Marie Kennedy, named after her mother. Within the family, the child was called "Rose" or "Rosie," but to the outside world she became known as "Rosemary."

After several months Rose noticed that like Jack, her daughter did not seem to have the vitality and energy of Joe. Rose began to wonder if something was seriously wrong with Rosemary. Whatever activity it was—crawling, walking, talking, holding her spoon, putting on her clothes—little Rosemary was painfully slow, not like Jack, and, God knows, not like Joe Jr. She was a pretty child with green eyes that peered out on life directly, without a blink or glance. When she went out in the snowy winter streets with her big brothers, all bundled up against the cold, she couldn't steer a sled. This was her only daughter, her very namesake. The mother spent added time with her daughter, watching out for her, teaching her. "I was patient, concerned, beginning to be a little apprehensive, but not worried, partly, I suppose because of wishful thinking," Rose reflected later.

Rose tried to understand what had happened. "Nobody knows for sure," said Eunice Kennedy Shiver, Rosemary's younger sister, "but probably what happened we think is that the doctor arrived late for the delivery and the nurse did not let the baby come. He was late coming. I don't know where he was but he wasn't there. The nurse didn't know what to do so she didn't encourage the birth, and didn't let the baby arrive. Even today it happens. You don't get oxygen at the right moment."

Rosemary, then, in all probability was the victim of the worst aspect of a patriarchal modern medicine. For all of the advances of science, individual doctors at times disguised their venality under a veneer of white-coated omnipotence. In most instances, the nurses could have delivered the babies as well as the doctors, but these women learned to hold back the births, a terrible disillusionment to young nurses. Rose herself was so much under the domination of the medical profession, and so unable even to consider the idea that her own doctor may have been responsible for her daughter's plight, that she did not even think of leaving Dr. Good but retained him for the rest of her children as well.

Rose's problems did not begin and end with her eldest daughter. Increasingly Rose was full of deep discontent. At times she felt as if she had disappeared from the world. In the larger world of Catholic society and Boston politics, Rose did not exist any longer. When she had been the mayor's daughter, the newspapers had lauded her, featured her in photos and articles, and she had been invited to endless parties. Now no one cared about her opinions, not the *Post* and the *Globe*, and not her husband either. Her clubs had been serious endeavors where she and her friends tried to better themselves intellectually. Now it was her young sister Agnes, not Rose, who as the *Post* expressed it, had become "the centre around which a veritable whirl of social life has revolved." Agnes was pursued by an array of worthy suitors, but though she was at an age when most women had already married, she seemed unwilling to pull away from her single life. She had her piano playing, her singing, and the active club life that Rose had helped to establish. She appeared unwilling to venture out into the life of married women, in part perhaps because of what she had observed in her older sister's life. Agnes and the rest of the family appeared unaffected that Fitzgerald had gone through the most disgraceful debacle of his political career. In 1918 he had narrowly won election to the House of Representatives, but he and his supporters had practiced such electorial chicanery that Congress took Fitzgerald's seat away a year later. Any other politician would have spent months with his head bowed in shame, but not Rose's father. He was the same irrepressible Fitzgerald as always.

Although Rose had nothing to do with the feminist movement, the examples of what women were doing were everywhere she looked. Prohibition was beginning this month of January 1920, a triumph for America's first great women's movement. The Nineteenth Amendment giving women the vote was only a few months away from ratification. Women had advanced greatly in the workplace during the war, and everywhere Rose saw freer styles of clothes and conduct. Although she was a conservative Catholic wife and mother, Rose could not help hearing the ardent voices of her time, the women of the twenties.

Rose kept herself emotionally distant from her neighbors and their lives. If she had even walked down Beals Street and talked to the other young mothers who lived there, she would have heard tales of discontent similar to hers. At nearby Tufts College Medical School, Dr. Abraham Myerson, a professor of neurology, was seeing scores of women like Rose. In his 1920 book, *The Nervous Housewife*, Myerson wrote how he and every physician he knew were treating women going through "the commonest and saddest of transformations . . . [from] the gay laughing young girl, radiant with love and all aglow at the thought of union with her man, into the housewife of a decade—complaining, fatigued, and disillusioned."

Rose loved her father profoundly, and she had honored that love by wanting to marry a man like her father, a man who would share his life with her as Fitzgerald had shared his public life with her. Instead, she was married to Joe, who held sway over their home with patriarchal command and shared little with her except his income and his love of their children.

Rose had prepared to be mother of an exemplary family, matron in a noble house, a Catholic grande dame, her husband's helpmate and advisor. Instead, she had this life of isolation and distance, from her family in Dorchester, from her friends, and from the emotional heart of the man she had married.

Rose had three children under the age of five, and she feared that something was wrong with two of them. Little Jack was one of those children who caught every disease. In that small house on Beals Street, he sometimes woke his mother up with his cries at night, and filled many of her days with apprehension. Even more difficult than the sickly child was the "feeble-minded" child, and the idea was slowly entering Rose's mind that her daughter was not like other children. The child-raising guides told her that she was totally responsible for her children, and she was sick with worry over Jack and Rosie.

She had gone into this marriage expecting so much, with all the idealism of a child of the Sacred Heart. But she was not sharing Joe's life the way she had prepared to share it. At times her marriage appeared to be largely burdens and responsibilities, guilt and endless obligations.

One weekend early in January of 1920, Joe was away, and as usual Rose was alone with the maid and the nursemaid, and three children, two of them sick, and a fourth child due in a month. She was a woman who prided herself on her rational mind, a cautious, socially conservative political woman. Suddenly she could not tolerate her life any longer. Suddenly, she was someone else, some other Rose Fitzgerald Kennedy. She vowed that as soon as her children improved she would leave the house on Beals Street to go back to the mansion on Welles Avenue.

Rose returned to Dorchester and to the room that had been hers for most of her life.

There was one main difference in the house on Welles Avenue, and that was the condition of Rose's littlest sister, Eunice, who was slowly dying of tuberculosis. Still there was such vitality, such life in the house on Welles Avenue, especially when her father was around.

For at least two weeks no one said anything about Rose's situation. The family did not deal directly or well with such matters, and for days everyone pretended that life was as it had been before Rose's marriage. It was clear that Josie would say nothing. Nor would Rose seek out her mother's advice. All her life Rose had strived to surpass Josie and Josie's limited life. Now she seemed to be replicating that existence, with the exception of her open discontent that her mother had repressed. Josie had borne the cross of her husband's infidelities and neglect, borne them silently, borne them by never looking at them, borne them by emotionally retreating into an enclave of quietude and self-denial, borne them by repressing her anger and doubt. Josie had paid an enormous price but as she saw it everything in a woman's life, *everything*, must be directed at preserving the sanctity of the home.

Rose's act in returning to her father's home was dangerously impetuous, a mark of desperate unhappiness. After all, divorce was unthinkable. Even among Protestants a divorced woman was ostracized, but for a Catholic woman divorce was infinitely worse. It did not matter what pain she suffered, what hypocrisy she endured, her church and society told her that she must stay married.

As Rose sat in her father's house, the evening arrived for the most important social event of the year, the Ace of Clubs ball. It was not only *the* dance for young Catholics, but the first important formal dance in Catholic society since the war. Rose was not only the foundress but an organizer of the ball, and her friend from Blumenthal days, Miriam Finnigan, was the new president. Rose was eight months pregnant, and she could easily have found an excuse not to attend. It was *her* night, her dance, however, and she was not about to stay home and read about the event in the Sunday papers, not about to risk being shamed and gossiped about. Rose dressed in a gown described by the *Boston Post* as "black web net," that disguised her pregnancy. Agnes and Eunice were equally well dressed, and the three Fitzgerald sisters made a stunning entrance. Josie stood in the receiving line, along with other mothers of members. Joe was there too, dressed in evening clothes, and the room was full of young matrons and their youthful husbands as well as Catholic debutantes and their beaux from as far away as Pittsburgh, Philadelphia; Lexington, Kentucky; and Rio de Janeiro.

This annual Ace of Clubs ball was full of what the *Post* called "the buoyant spirit of optimism," and Rose was once again at the center of her world of Boston Catholic society, the esteemed foundress of the most prestigious Catholic women's social organization in the city, whose ball signaled the opening of the winter season. As she accepted accolades from new acquaintances, and renewed greetings from old friends, she was the envy of many, and a model to others, and seeing her there, so vibrant, so charming, no one imagined that when the last dance was over, she would go back home with her sisters, her husband off alone to Brookline. Whatever else Rose thought this evening, she must surely have realized that there were no divorcées laughing and drinking champagne at the ball, and that all her prestige rested on her remaining Mrs. Joseph P. Kennedy.

Rose was still her father's daughter, and finally Fitzgerald came to his daughter's room and talked with Rose. He had sensed what this marriage would be and he had tried to dissuade his Rosie from going ahead. His daughter had not listened, and she was not his Rosie anymore; she was Mrs. Joseph P. Kennedy. She had been married by a prince of the church, her marriage sanctified by God.

"You've made your commitment, Rosie," he told his eldest daughter. "And you must honor it now. What is past is past. The old days are gone. Your children need you and your husband needs you. You can make things work out. I know you can."

Fitzgerald was not about to confront Joe. Fitzgerald did not like Joe, but his daughter was married now and nothing could change that. He did not rail against Joe and vow that his son-in-law must change. It was Rose who would have to change, to accept, to acquiesce. That was the way society worked. "If you need more help in the household, then get it," he told her. "If you need a bigger house, ask for it. If you need more private time for yourself, take it. There isn't anything you can't do once you set your mind on it. So go now, Rose, go back where you belong."

During the three weeks that she was at her father's home, Rose went on a religious retreat to contemplate her faith and her future. As she prayed and reflected, the words of the nuns at Blumenthal and Manhattanville came back to her, echoes that grew louder and louder until they were like a great chorus telling her who she was. She was a Child of Mary, a Child of the Sacred Heart, and she had pledged in difficult times to obtain from Our Lady of Sorrows the strength to suffer stoically. Since she was at Blumenthal she had believed that her faith would be tested not in the crucibles of power, in the palaces of leaders, but in the womanly life of the home. Now, as Rose saw her life, this was that first time of testing, a test for her faith, her strength, her resilience.

Rose had been brought up with an astute sense of what was politically and socially acceptable, and every fiber of her being told her that her only choice was to go back to Joe. It was not simply the most spiritual aspect of Rose that was telling her to go back to her husband, to live the life of a Catholic wife and mother. Her maternal sense was pointing her homeward. Rose loved her children. They needed her, especially little Rosie and Jack. She could never abandon them, or take them off somewhere without a father to live as social outcasts. Her practical nature was telling her to return to Joe too, for what other alternatives did she have? She had a friend who had gotten divorced, and she had been so shunned, so pilloried that she had been driven out of Boston to try to make a life somewhere else. Her most cynical and calculating side chimed in as well; as Mrs. Joseph P. Kennedy she could have status and wealth to assuage her pain.

And thus, Rose returned to the house on Beals Street.

7

Rose's Blueprint

*R*ose nestled Kathleen Agnes in her arms on February 20, 1920, full of maternal pride and love for her newborn daughter. At the same time she was gripped by "frantic terror." Little Jack was sick again, this time with scarlet fever, and as so often Joe was not there. Her husband was in Palm Beach on vacation. Her second son was lying in bed at Boston City Hospital, his throat raw and red as an open wound, his fever between 100 and 103, his body covered with a terrible rash. Scarlet fever was contagious, and Rose was frightened that it might be passed on to Joe Jr. or Rosemary or even to the newborn.

The immediate worry was that Jack did not seem to be recovering. Joe returned to Boston soon after the birth, and as Rose lay in bed, Joe took control over the life and health of Jack. He was a man who knew how to take care of problems, but as he watched his tiny son lying ill in his bed, there was nothing he could do, no incantation that would lessen the pain, no way of transferring the agony to himself.

From her bed Rose observed a husband whom she had not seen before. Every day Joe left work early and came to the hospital and sat next to the bed of his two-and-a-half-year-old son, so desperately alone, away from the sheltering arms of mother and the shouts of his older brother. Joe did not have the faith of his wife, but he prayed now. "I had never experienced any very serious illness in my family previous to Jack's," Joe later wrote the doctor after Jack was out of the hospital, "and I little realized what effect such a happening could have on me."

Once Jack recovered Rose had time to think fully about her newest child. Almost from the day Kathleen was born, Rose knew that she had a blessed child, a girl who would become "really our eldest daughter." Kathleen had her grandmother Mary Augusta's ivory skin, brilliant blue eyes, and the high spirits and energy that were a match for her eldest brother, Joe Jr. Kathleen was nicknamed "Kick" because other children found her full name difficult to pronounce. It was the perfect name, for she was a kick and a half. She could ice-skate, go sleigh riding, or play tennis with her brothers, and not ask any dispensation for her sex or age. Years later, as Rose read and reread the scores of letters that Kathleen wrote to family members, her mother noted that "her early letters seemed so warm and affectionate, perhaps more so than those of the other children." She was that special blessing, a child with a perpetually bright and optimistic temperament, whose laughter and cheeriness evoked moments of happiness in almost everyone she encountered. She seemed to be naturally good, rarely requiring a mother's discipline. "Although we delighted in her," Rose recalled, "I don't think we could have spoiled her if we had tried."

There was a line of demarcation between these first four Kennedy children and their younger siblings. "My first four children were always special to me," Rose said. "I spent more time with them. I knew their every thought and each personality fascinated me." A year and a half after Kathleen's birth, on July 10, 1921, Rose gave birth to her fifth child, Eunice Mary, named after Rose's invalid sister. Eunice did not receive quite the attention of her older siblings, and was the first Kennedy baby not to be breastfed. "Years ago everyone nursed their babies, but then there was a transition period," Rose recalled. "Unfortunately, when Eunice was born she didn't get along very well because the bottle wasn't very well organized and I couldn't nurse her because I had breast abscesses."

It was a matter of wonderment to Rose that each of her children could be so different, and yet so clearly marked with the family heredity. Eunice did not have the gracious femininity of Kathleen. Indeed, she had the scrawny build of Ichabod Crane, a wiry, intense little girl with a fierce questioning intelligence. She had an extraordinary precociousness, as if she were rushing pell-mell toward adulthood full of a restless frenetic energy that she seemed hardly to be able to control. She learned to talk and to walk earlier than any of her siblings, earlier even than her bright older brother, Jack, to whom she was particularly close. At the age of one and a half she was already walk-

ing around the house, acting like a little adult, bowing and
saying, "Little Partner, dance with me." Eunice was precocious
in her humanity as well, watching out for her brothers and sisters, and especially for Rosemary, who became to her first an
older sister, then an equal, and eventually almost her child.

Eunice was born in the Kennedys' new home two blocks away
on the corner of Abbotsford and Naples Road, where the family moved in the fall of 1920. The twelve-room, Colonial
revival–style house told the world that Joe was no longer just
a young man on the make. He was a major success, building
a fortune as a customers' man at Hayden, Stone & Co., well
on his way to making his first million. He wanted this new
house to be a worthy symbol of his achievements, and he oversaw the furnishing, buying fine Oriental rugs, choosing the
proper wall coverings, picking out antique furniture.

Rose watched as the maid packed Sir Thomas Lipton's tea
set, wrapped the wedding silver, and movers hoisted out the piano and the finer pieces of furniture and transported them
down the block and around two corners to the new Kennedy
home. This was a modern house, a very model of the kind of
home to which the middle class aspired. The modern homemaker had a refrigerator, washing machine, sewing machine,
kitchen range, and vacuum cleaner.

For Rose, this new home was the beginning of a new psychological reality in which she largely carried out her father's
marital prescription. She had her bigger house, her added help
including a chauffeur, her private time, her own bedroom, and
these new "electrical servants." Here she not only had a private
nursery for the newest baby, but separate rooms for all the
children.

The Kennedys were emulating the Protestant upper class,
and Rose's own bedroom was not only a sign of privilege but
equally marked off the increasing distance between her and her
husband. This accommodation with Joe was a more complex
business than buying a bigger house or hiring a new parlor
maid or merely sleeping in a separate bedroom. It was an arrangement that developed over several years and not without
conflict. In 1921 Joe wrote a friend anticipating the arrival of
a group of actresses to Boston saying that he was having "too
many troubles around" to take part "at the present time" but he
was hoping that by the time the musical show arrived "everything may be better."

Rose and Joe began taking their vacations apart. These were not merely a few days off, a break from family life, but lengthy trips that lasted a month or longer at a time. As a wife, Rose had learned to rationalize limitlessly the realities of her marriage. In mid-January 1923, Joe headed down to Palm Beach with several friends for a long stay. Rose wrote later that she "would have been bored by going to the same place every year for a holiday." She had not been bored going with her father, and would not be bored once she and Joe purchased a winter home in the Florida resort.

In early April, after Joe had been back in Boston little more than a month, Rose and her sister Agnes set out from the house to spend six weeks in California. "Gee, *you're* a great mother to go away and leave your children all alone," Jack said, the words midway between a rebuke and a taunt. The next day the children stood on the porch telling their mother good-bye. Rose did not turn and hug her second son, assuring him of her love and of her certain return. Instead, Rose continued down the steps, never turning back. Only because she had forgotten something did she go back a few minutes later to find Jack and the other children playing with nary an apparent thought of their departed mother.

A mother who could turn away from her son might seem a thoughtless, cold, selfish woman whose children were only emotional baubles to her to be picked up and discarded at whim, but Rose had felt full of anguish. She had tears in her eyes as she walked away from Jack. As Rose saw it, she could not turn back to coddle little Jack because her son had to learn to be self-reliant and stoical, and even this moment was part of a pedagogic process and her blueprint for bringing up the young Kennedys.

Rose would literally live through her children, not through the minutiae of their lives, but by forging them into a familial battalion that would carry her name out into the world. "A mother knows that hers is the influence which can make that little precious being to be a leader of men, an inspiration, a shining light in the world," Rose said. "Women may excel in business. They may be leaders of society. They may be famous beauties. But these goals are ephemeral. You have only to compare a woman who is a great beauty, a famous writer, or a renowned scientist twenty-five-years ago, and visit her now. But a woman engrossed in her family twenty-five-years ago, now sees them grown-up, fulfilling worthwhile goals, adding lustre to her name. She feels still needed, still loved, still a vital part of life, and that is the important thing."

Rose applied all her formidable intelligence, energy, moral force, and ambition in her children's early development. The child-care authorities, housekeeping experts, and doctors told her what she was supposed to do, and she followed their advice almost to the letter, adding the moral authority of the Catholic church, and attempting to infuse her children with immense ambition and a sense of social obligation. "I looked upon child rearing as a profession and decided it was just as interesting and just as challenging as anything else and that it did not have to keep a woman tied down and make her dull or out of touch," Rose reflected. "She did not have to become an emaciated, worn out old hag, nor did she have to be a fat, shapeless, jolly happy-go-lucky individual whose only subject for conversation was as the Germans used to say, 'Kinder, kirche, kuchen,' or 'children, church and cooking.' [I saw it] not only as a work of love and duty, but as a profession that was fully as interesting and challenging as any honorable profession in the world and one that demanded the best that I could bring to it."

In the twenties that was a constant theme not only of Rose's life but of the articles and advertisements that she read in women's magazines such as *Ladies' Home Journal*, and in scores of books and pamphlets promoting the housewife as an efficient consumer and scientific mother.

Rose thought that "superior achievement or making the most of one's capabilities is to a very considerable degree a matter of habit." That was the essence of her system of child rearing: to create a series of habits so ingrained that nothing would change them; these habits would mold her children's character and much of their fate. In so doing, Rose was attempting to stamp them with her signature as Kennedys, like assay marks on bars of gold, forever branding them with their origins and value.

Rose, like the Jesuits, believed that if she integrated her children into her system at an early age, she would have them forever. Joe Jr. was five years old when the Kennedys moved into the new house, the optimal age to enter Rose's process of child development. He was not simply the first Kennedy child in age, the first to enter Rose's system, but its very model and foremost instructor. As their Irish ancestors believed that their land must go to one son impartibly, so Joe and Rose believed that the psychic inheritance, the inheritance of aspiration and faith, should go impartibly to their firstborn son. They would teach their firstborn all that they knew, and he would teach his younger siblings. If the first should falter or die, the second would pick up the legacy, and the third, and the fourth, each new bearer of the inheritance carrying a burden heavier still with all the legacy of expectation. Rose would teach Kathleen too, and she would teach her younger sister, and that daughter would teach her younger sister as well. But Joe was the central model for the girls as well as the boys. "You will find [in a large family] the older ones taking over many of the parental duties," Rose asserted. "That is if an older boy is brought up in the right way. I mean, if sufficient time and effort is paid to him inculcating ideas, first of all of high moral principles, of exemplary church habits, of care in the choosing of friends, and of responsibility towards his family and especially towards the younger members. I myself used the older children very effectively."

In Joe Jr. the Kennedys had a son who seemed a worthy vessel for all their hopes, a boy full of energy and daring and willful ambition, the standard by which they all would be judged. In the house Joe Jr. was more like a little father than a big brother, a youth who emulated Joe Sr. almost slavishly. "I think that if the Kennedy children amount to anything now or ever amount to anything, it will be due more to Joe's behavior and his constant example than to any other factor," Jack wrote in 1945. "He made the task of bringing up a large family immeasurably easier for my father and mother for what they taught him, he passed on to us, and their teachings were not diluted through him but rather strengthened."

By the time the maids had helped dress and ready the children for breakfast, Rose was downstairs to oversee the first meal of the day. She sat there and saw to it that her children ate what they were supposed to eat and in the proper quantities. If they were a mite too thin, she plied them with fats, sugars, and creams; if they looked plump, she cut down on sweets and breads. Scrawny little Jack was certain to get something extra. She watched as they marched into the bathroom to brush their teeth. She made sure they were perfectly clean. When they were old enough for school, she stood at the door inspecting their pants and their shirts and their coats. She turned the children this way and that, looking for spots, or dirt, anything that would mark them as less than perfect representatives of the Kennedy family.

If her children were to grow up properly, they had to be able to swim, play a good game of tennis, a decent round of golf. Whether they wanted it or not, she marched them off to lessons with their athletic instructors. She watched what they read too, choosing books from the P.T.A. and Boston Women's Exchange lists of proper educational and inspirational materials.

The dinner table was a lectern for Rose's courses in civilized behavior. As the family grew ever larger, Rose decided to have two separate meal sittings, one for the youngest children, the later time for the older children and adults. Rose made a point of always being present for the early meal, sitting at "the little table" directing the conversation. Here was time for Rose's subtle lessons in geography, history, patriotism, manners, and religion. At Easter she talked of Lent and the priest's special pink vestments. At Thanksgiving it was time to discuss the Pilgrims and their journey to America in search of religious freedom. As her mother had done for her in Concord Junction, Rose made her children feel a part of a gloriously sentimental view of American history.

When they were old enough, the children were expected to sit properly at the main table, intelligently answer questions posed by their father, and treat their mother with the respect and deference that was considered her due. There was no letup then, no respite from Rose's pedagogy. She sat there eternally observant of their manners and minds. Rose's concern was an exaggerated pattern of motherly conduct that was taking place in middle-class homes across America.

Rose was determinedly concerned with her children's weights. This obsession with fat came originally from Joe, whose parents in their later years had grown as portly as prosperous peasants, their Irish roots painfully evident. Joe wanted his wife and children sleek and lean, and Rose disciplined herself to lose every pound she had gained during each pregnancy. Just as Josie had kept her figure and was sometimes said to look like Rose's sister rather than her mother, so was Rose proud to be as thin as her daughters. Fat was indulgence, nature's way of displaying a lack of will and self-control, and she would have no part of it, not for herself and not for her children. She disciplined her children, shaming her daughters and sons when they put on a few pounds. In May 1927 when Kathleen was only seven years old, she wrote her mother: "I gained a pound and a half. Eunice gained some too. Rose [mary] is as fat as ever." It was an obsession with the girls from an early age.

Dinner was at a regular hour, and woe betide the young Kennedy who arrived late. One evening Kathleen and Rosemary were playing at a neighbor's house when the early evening hour was interrupted by a harsh knocking on the door. There stood a decidedly unhappy Joseph P. Kennedy. "You tell them that their father is standing on the front porch waiting to take them home for dinner and they've got to come," Joe said, skipping the expected pleasantries. With that the two girls dropped their toys and scurried out the door.

Dinner ended only when Rose had gotten up and left the room. After dinner Rose allowed the children to come into her bedroom to choose chocolate from a box next to her bed. It was a great and glorious box, full of an assortment of sweets from which any child would have gobbled up a half-dozen chocolates or more, but one chocolate was all Rose allowed them. One chocolate. They could stand and look and ponder and contemplate for minutes. It didn't matter. One chocolate.

The children would eat the right foods in the right amounts, brush their teeth twice a day, ingest only one chocolate, and go to bed at the proper time even if she were not standing over them. Rose had servants and nannies and maids and nurses for that, and in a curious way that distanced Rose from the emotional center of her children's lives.

The children's nursemaid, Katherine Conboy, or Kico as they called her, was an Irish peasant woman whose brogue was as Irish as the shamrocks on the quilt in the bedroom. She believed in a world of little people, the leprechauns and elves who made the emerald forests of Ireland their domain. The homes of Brookline and Boston were still full of women like Kico, to whom the children were drawn in search of a warmth and spontaneity that they did not find in their parents' world. Kico was an emotional surrogate mother to the young Kennedys, especially the girls. She was the woman they could rush to in tears, to be enveloped in her apron, set down in the hearthlike atmosphere of the kitchen for a glass of milk and a cookie, and allowed to talk with neither time limit nor fixed subject matter. Unlike Rose, Kico had no great vision for these children, no game plan, and they turned to her with trust and openness. She loved them unabashedly, unashamedly, in a manner that as a traditional Irish woman she probably would

not and could not have loved her own children, but love the
Kennedy children she did, and they loved her in return. As the
girls grew older they discarded Kico as they did their snow-
suits, their dolls, the other things of childhood, and followed
the road set for them by their mother.

Rose had inherited her father's pulsating energy, and she
tried to have some semblance of a life beyond the confines of
the home. For her the transcendent event of the social year remained the annual Ace of Clubs ball in January, and she continued to plan the event. It was the one evening when she was
sure to be named in the society pages of the Sunday papers,
along with a description of her gown, and she dressed with panache before Joe escorted her downtown to the Somerset. For
Rose it was a magical evening, transported out of the world of
children.

"She kept busy right up until the moment her children were
born," recalled Margaret Driscoll, a Brookline neighbor who
herself grew up in a family of nine children. "She was always
in a rush and she was always going somewhere and doing
something. And she would have her baby and she was ready
to start running again. She worked very hard, and she held up
her end. Joe and the Kennedy family would never have been
the success if Rose hadn't been able to keep up with Joe."

As her mother had been in her family, Rose was the disciplinarian, and discipline meant the ever-present prospect of a
ruler or a wooden coat hanger vigorously applied to the hand
or the bottom. In most families, the father or mother applied
corporal punishment only after a litany of warnings, then often
in a desperate moment of undisguised fury. Rose was different.
"I saw it as a duty, never to be done in anger or a fit of irritability," Rose said later. She was not one to give one warning,
two warnings, and three warnings, and then to proceed with
her spankings. "I'd just tell them not to and spank them with
the ruler if they did it," she recalled.

"It [physical punishment] is the only thing very young children understand in some cases, and it is a necessary means of
preventing accidents and bad behavior when the child is so
young that to reason with him is out of the question," Rose asserted. "If a child is walking with me on the sidewalk and runs
in front of an approaching car, I quickly paddle him then and
there, and so he is not apt to run out again. If he goes near a
stove which is hot, I hold his finger near the stove to show him
he will be burned. Or if he takes my sharp scissors, I request

that he give them back to me because the points may injure him. And in order to prove my point, I stick the point into his arm or finger in order to show the seriousness of such a point in his eye. If this reasoning does not avail, I used to have my ruler in my desk and would use it. After a few raps, the mere mention of the ruler would usually bring desired results. He was just made to understand that his father and I loved him and advised him on everything for his own good and that was it."

When her children remembered how "cruel" Rose had been when she "beat" them, she couldn't understand. She had merely spanked them, and spanked them with precision and calculation. She had come to her children, ruler or coat hanger in hand, her face emotionless, as if she were meting out abstract justice. She was doing so as part of her system of child raising, but for a child it was a process that was emotionally distancing, this mother who as she walloped them displayed so little feeling.

Rose touched her children when she spanked them. She touched them when she adjusted their collars or rubbed a spot of dirt off their cheek before they headed to school. But she did not touch them when she loved them. She did not grasp Joe or Jack, Rosemary or Kathleen or Eunice to her bosom, holding them and telling the child "I love you." Her mother had not done that to her, nor had Joe's, both of them steeped in the emotional traditions of the Irish-American woman. These children were Rose's masterwork, and to her mind it was too serious a business to indulge in the excesses of affection. That was something for the cook and the maid.

Of all her children, Jack was the most observant of the inner life of his family. "My mother was either at some Paris fashion house or else on her knees in some church," he told a friend when he was a young adult. In his early formative years, Rose had almost always been there, and on one level Jack's comment was a terrible slander against Rose. But on the level that Jack was speaking, as a young man seeking to understand the psychological realities of his family, Rose might as well have been away. "My mother never really held me and hugged me," he continued, getting at the essential truth. "Never! Never!"

Jack's lament could have been made by many young men of his class and time, in Brahmin and Irish-American homes as well. Rose did not serve up affection to her children like daily confection. She did not feel that she was depriving her children by not constantly telling them of her deep and abiding love. "We didn't talk about love and display great emotions," said Luella Hennessey Donovan, the nurse who for four decades worked for the Kennedys and was closer to them than any outsider. "Mrs. Kennedy didn't say she loved her children. It just wasn't said. It was all about respect. She respected them and they respected her. They weren't touchy people. Jack never was, not when he was a young man, not ever. Never."

Early in her marriage Rose walked into a stationery store in Coolidge Corner and purchased three-by-five file cards and index tabs. At home she sat down at her desk in her little office and noted down each child's name, birthplace, baptism. As each new baby was born, she added the infant to her list. Every Saturday night all the young Kennedys were put on the scale, their weights duly noted on their index card. If they had lost weight twice in a row, Rose added to their diet, and if she felt it necessary cut down on their exercise. She listed their illnesses, medical appointments, and eye exams. Her children had not only dentists but orthodontists. In an era when few children had braces, she had her children's teeth straightened, and the world had no idea that the famous Kennedy smile was not some hereditary blessing, but a product of dentistry.

Rose joked later that her file cards had been a matter not of "American efficiency" but of "Kennedy desperation." The cards, in fact, were a product of a movement for efficiency in the American household, and an indicator of how strongly Rose was attempting to be a modern homemaker and mother, following the precepts of her age. The very idea of the three-by-five index cards had come from Christine Frederick in articles in *Ladies' Home Journal* in 1912 and in her best-selling book, *The New Housekeeping*. "We were really organized," Eunice remembered. "It was an extraordinary thing the way she had us all . . . I guess the word is, disciplined."

In the neighborhood Rose might have found friends with whom to share a cup of tea, and talk about her life, but even early on when Rose and Joe had a small family, the Kennedys kept to themselves. From their windows the neighbors saw Rose walking the carriage, with her two boys alongside. Rose was polite enough, a smile here, a hello to someone else, a wave to a neighbor in the window, but she never said much, and when Joe was with her she often gave no sign of recognition at all.

* * *

For Rose, the church was at the center of her children's moral training. The family said grace before meals, and Rose chose a different daughter or son each time to say the prayer. Sunday mornings Rose stood at the bottom of the stairs. She checked off her children one by one, making sure they were spic and span, and attired to go to mass at St. Aidan's, clutching their prayer books and rosaries. The Kennedy children marched into church with their nursemaid in proper order. They looked, as one parishioner remembered, "like a little tribe dressed up in their velvet-collar wool Chesterfield coats." They went to the children's mass and knew that they had better listen closely and remember well. "We would talk about the sermon, what did the priest say and what was the gospel about when they got home at dinner," Rose recalled. "And if they didn't pay attention one Sunday they'd pay attention the next Sunday."

The Tudor-style church had great wooden beams and from the exterior looked like an English manor house. St. Aidan's, named after an Irish monk, was a monument to the faith and frugality largely of poor Irish-American women. It had been built primarily by the small donations of Irish servants, cooks, and maids who had lived in Brookline decades before the arrival of the likes of Rose and Joe Kennedy.

As the ground was broken in 1911, a new class of Irish-Americans and other Catholics began to move to Brookline who aspired to become part of an American gentry. They did not kneel and pray next to cooks and parlor maids. It became understood that early mass was for the working folk, and the eleven-thirty mass for the elite. For the late mass, they came then in their furs and finery. When mass was over the parishioners stood outside their church, sometimes for an hour or more, looked at each other's clothes and jewels, talked of real estate and business, clubs and children. The Kennedys, however, came out of the church, nodded to right and to left, and departed saying hardly a word. Some of the people of the parish thought that Joe and Rose had their noses in the air, and their eyes placed beyond even the highest reaches of Brookline. "I remember the beautiful squirrel coat that Rose Kennedy had," recalled May Johnson, a parishioner. "They paid no attention to anyone, just to the service."

Rose was much friendlier when she was alone, and those who knew her best realized that she was only doing what her husband wanted her to do. "They used to say that Joe was trying to get up in the world," recalled Dot Keegan, a neighbor. "He was trying to promote himself and his family."

Every morning when the children were little, Rose and the nursemaid bundled them up, and off they went for a walk, stopping along the way at St. Aidan's. On sunny days she left the baby carriage outside the church underneath a crucifix. Rose entered the main chapel, looking at the dark wood of the pews and the beams, the wood like richly worked leather, and up at the sanctuary and baptismal font where her babies had been baptized. She knelt in prayer, often alone in the warm familiarity of St. Aidan's.

Sometimes the parish priest, Father John T. Creagh, was in the church. Rose had grown up around clerics. She showed the plump, paternalistic priest much the same deference and respect that she did Cardinal O'Connell or the other princes of the church. Father Creagh was a canonist, an expert in church law, a man of formidable intellect, an austere and distant priest whose mere glance could frighten altar boys like Joe Jr. and Jack.

When Rose sat in her pew as Father Creagh said mass, she saw the glory and splendor of her church, and the purity of its vision. The priest was a perfectionist in a ritual that demanded perfection. Every moment, every gesture, every genuflection, every movement of the altar boys was performed with meticulous seriousness. That the man standing there in the resplendent robes was a petty martinet who in the words of one of his several miserable assistants "destroyed every happiness" of his priestly life, cheated workers who painted the church, and watched over the parishioners as much with the steely eyes of a warden as with the benevolent concern of a good shepherd was something that Rose did not see or feel or think. Her faith was deep and narrow, with no room for ambiguities, contradictions, or questions, no room for the morally tortured priests of a Graham Greene, or the reality of a man like Father Creagh. As for Joe, who knelt beside his wife at mass, he doubtlessly had taken the priest's full measure. He was a man who understood human weakness, and shied away from no fact of human life, be it business, politics, or religion.

When it came time for young Joe to be confirmed in the church, it would not do simply to have Father Creagh perform the rite. Rose and Joe were both out of Boston but Grandfather and Grandmother Fitzgerald were there and so was his Aunt

Agnes. Cardinal O'Connell had married Rose and Joe and now he confirmed their firstborn son. He was almost a family priest to the Kennedys. For Rose, he was a godly figure who represented her church, *the* church, at its purest and most refined. He was a formidable figure driving through Boston in his chauffeured $8,000 black Pierce Arrow upholstered in cardinal red, spending August in his $20,000 summer estate, "Villa Santa Croce" at Bay View, Gloucester, living a life-style commensurate with the $100,181.15 that he earned in one year alone.

Although Rose was blissfully unaware of it, during the early years of her marriage this church, *her* church, was tainted with moral corruption. One unhappy priest spoke of Cardinal O'Connell's "awful worldliness ... scandalous parade of wealth ... arrogant manners, his strange and unecclesiastical method of living."

Rose had probably brushed shoulders with that corruption in the person of Monsignor James O'Connell, the cardinal's nephew. The priest served as his uncle's secretary and chancellor and lived with him in the official residence, as did Father David J. Toomey, editor of the *Pilot*, a regular part of Rose's reading. Both men were secretly married to women in New York. Toomey was secretly excommunicated in 1918. The former priest claimed that the cardinal had known about the marriages for years; he had kept quiet because his nephew was blackmailing him for embezzling archdiocese funds as well as having "proofs of the Cardinal's sexual affection for *men*."

When the scandal threatened to break out into public, Cardinal O'Connell was called to Rome, where he was apparently caught lying to Pope Benedict XV claiming that the charges against his nephew were false. Monsignor O'Connell was removed, and the matter was kept quiet, from press and parishioners. Rose and hundreds of thousands of other Catholics continued to look at this prince of the church as a man of godly virtue and truth.

After mass on Sunday, the family drove either to Winthrop for dinner or out to Concord Junction to visit relatives on Rose's mother's side of the family. Rose nurtured her extended family. She considered this part of her business as a woman, remembering birthdays and anniversaries, telling her children of their grandparents' lives, seeing to it that they visited their relatives regularly.

Fitzgerald and Josie led the way out to West Concord in

their chauffeur-driven Lincoln, followed by Joe and Rose and their children in a second vehicle. At the home of their grand-mother's Hannon relatives, Kathleen, Rosemary, and Eunice stood in the backyard demure in their rose-colored coats, pushed their fingers a bit further into their fur muffs, and kept their curls properly covered in their fur caps while their brothers boxed and jumped up and down on the seesaw.

Although Fitzgerald had always favored *his* Rosie, when it came to his grandchildren he devoted most of his attention to Joe Jr. and Jack. Kathleen and Eunice sat quietly and sedately eating their meals, cutting the meat as their mother and nanny had taught them, chewing the pieces with their mouths properly closed. They were learning another childhood lesson too. Their role in life, at least around their brothers, was to stand outside the spotlight, observers to their brothers' intrepid lives.

Afterward, Fitzgerald led his grandchildren to the Lincoln for a jaunt to the countryside. The more daring of the children got to sit in the open jump seat, protected by old newspapers underneath their coats, as the former mayor ordered the driver to roar through the country roads at sixty miles an hour. This was a manly adventure too, but one in which even a girl might share.

At the dinner table, Fitzgerald talked often of politics, and to the Kennedy daughters it was the most natural topic of conversation. Their grandfather was still an active politician. In 1922, he had run for governor against the Republican incumbent, Channing H. Cox. Women could vote now, but women leaders in the Democratic Party complained that they were pushed aside, not admitted to the back rooms and the inner counsels where decisions were made. Fitzgerald was not comfortable sharing a speaker's platform with a woman, but he nonetheless needed his own wife to stand up for her husband. It was excruciatingly difficult for Josie. Her face turned red with embarrassment when she was asked to talk before a breakfast of Democratic women at the Copley-Plaza Hotel. She got up and in a "tremulous voice" asked that the five hundred women support her husband. On election day for what may have been the first time in her life, Josie went along with Fitzgerald to the Henry L. Pierce School in Dorchester to vote.

Fitzgerald had always wooed women, and through them won many of their husbands' votes. Now they had to be wooed even more, for as he saw it, women had defeated him. "Tell the people that John F. is smiling and happy," he said.

"The Republicans can thank their women's organization. . . . They were Republicans to the core and committed every minute to the Republican cause." Women had displayed an initiative and determination that Fitzgerald never imagined them to have. "The women's clubs . . . though not supposed to be political, used their organizations, not only in registering, but at the election . . . for the Republican party." In his defeat, Fitzgerald learned a lesson that he would impart to his grandsons, not that women had a rightful place in political office, but that their votes had to be courted with a determination that was as unswerving as it was subtle.

"My babies were rocked to political lullabies," Rose said. Rose and Joe were the children of politicians, natural habitués of the public arena. Even if Joe was not active himself, the Kennedys were still a political family, with both grandfathers still important public figures in Boston. The young Kennedys grew up with the idea of politics and public life as their entitlement, a natural venue. For the girls it meant lives as political women, supporting their brothers or husbands in their public pursuits.

Rose and Joe had been lucky that their older children had gotten to know all four of their grandparents. In May 1923, sixty-five-year-old Mary Augusta died in her bedroom a month after a cancer operation, leaving an estate of $13,539. For Rose and her daughters, here was a lesson about a woman's life. As soon as Joe's mother's death became known, the street for several blocks outside the Kennedy home in Winthrop filled with automobiles, as politicians, business people, old neighbors from East Boston, other members of the Ladies Sodality, the Philomatheia Club of Boston College, priests and nuns, all called at the house on Washington Avenue. Mary Augusta was no politician, no public figure, and like her own mother-in-law, Bridget Kennedy, the first and only time she was featured in a newspaper was at her death. But she had touched her community, and they came by the scores to pay their tribute.

Her funeral procession included seventy-six automobiles, and was, as the *Winthrop Sun* described it, "probably the largest funeral ever held here." This was a Kennedy family funeral, and what distinguished it was not only the immense outpouring of mourners but the presence of priests and nuns. The quartet from St. Cecilia Church in Back Bay sang the mass, the lead baritone performing one of Mary Augusta's favorite songs, "Beautiful Isle of Somewhere." At Holy Cross

Cemetery in Malden, six priests chanted a requiem. Then the mother who had so shaped the life and ambitions of her only son was buried in the family plot near Bridget Kennedy, another mother who also had lived for her only son.

That same year Rose's twenty-three-year-old sister, Eunice, returned to the house on Welles Avenue from the TB sanatorium one September day, and died the next morning. Rose mourned long and deeply for her younger sister. Indeed, almost four months later the *Boston Post* noted that at the 1924 Ace of Clubs ball "there was widespread regret that owing to a family bereavement in the death of a sister and late member, Mrs. Joseph P. Kennedy was not a participant."

Rose had complete control over the day-to-day lives of the young Kennedys. In the lives of the Kennedy children, the home, the church, and the school were the three spheres of civility, and in these worlds Rose insisted on impeccable behavior. At home the children had to eat properly, dress properly, and converse properly. In church they were to be the perfect little gentlemen and ladies, and there they rarely violated their mother's precepts. One day a neighbor girl, Helen Leahy, walked up to Jack in church where he was serving as an altar boy. "Hi, Jack," she said sweetly. "You shouldn't say anything to me in church, Helen," Jack scolded, as if she had violated a commandment. "It's wrong to speak in church and you shouldn't do it."

Rose sent her eldest children off to Edward Devotion School, an excellent public school no more than a five-minute walk from their home. Even this was a calculated gesture, part of her grand plan. Rose felt that "this rubbing of elbows with other children of lower economic levels, but higher academic accomplishments, is very important for children, especially for boys who are going to be meeting and competing with all sorts of groups in later years." Rose expected her children to behave here as well. This was an era when discipline was omnipresent and Charles Taylor, the principal, brooked no foolishness.

Beyond these three spheres—the home, the church, the school—lay the streets, and here in the playgrounds, the parks, and the alleys of Brookline was a life for her sons that had to be beyond the pale. This, too, was part of Rose's blueprint, a world where her boys could play like tough little men while her daughters stayed home and acted like angels.

When Rose's boys played, she didn't mind if they dressed "like roughnecks." They not only dressed like roughnecks, they acted like them. The nursemaid watched over the girls, but not the boys. As a father Joe wanted Joe Jr. and Jack to learn the lessons of the street, and employ them in a world of wealth and privilege. Rose wanted sons who looked like gentlemen, but who still had the brashness and bravado and daring of the Irish streets. She wanted daughters devoted to the church and faith, dedicated to their brothers and their husbands.

Rose was bringing up a race of fierce stoics who could tolerate pain without squirming, disappointment without whining, affliction without complaining. "My mother sent everybody outdoors because she wanted everybody to be healthy and robust," Eunice said. "It didn't matter if you were a little sick. The idea was that if you had a little something, you didn't go into your room and nurse it. You took care of yourself, but then you hustled right along. Except for chicken pox and maybe one or two other contagious diseases, I never stayed indoors until I was an adult. Back in those days, you weren't reared always to be saying, 'Oh, I have a stomachache,' or 'I don't feel very well today.' If you had a stomachache, you'd take your medicine, read a book, and when dinner was ready come downstairs like everybody else. You must realize my mother was never sick, and so that was her attitude. She never sat and dwelled on negative things, like being sick or having a tummy ache. If she had, she wouldn't have kept that optimism about life that she had."

In the house Rose herself was the best exemplar of that philosophy. Joe was her mentor, subtly inculcating what he considered appropriate behavior in his wife. "He didn't want to be bothered," Rose reflected. "He didn't want a cocky wife or a complaining wife." Once Rose was lying in bed after returning home from an automobile accident that left a large slash on her forehead. As she was attempting to compose herself, Joe called. Rose told him what a glorious day it was and after hanging up drove herself to the hospital for five stitches. After observing their mother's stolid demeanor, it was no wonder that her children followed suit. Rose noted in her diary on February 25, 1923, that her sons had formed a club "where they initiate new members by sticking pins in them."

In the sedate world of Brookline, Massachusetts, it didn't take much to be considered wildly rebellious. Rose's altar boy sons developed such reputations that the deliveryman considered the Kennedy boys "little devils." Joe Jr. was the leader, a bold, fearless child who led his younger brother through the alleys and over roofs. Even Eunice and Kathleen had a toughness to them, unlike most of the neighborhood girls. "My mother wouldn't let me play with the Kennedy children because they played too rough," recalled Robert Bunshaft.

Rose wasn't raising what she considered a bunch of sissies. As she watched her sons' behavior, she became increasingly concerned. She and Joe decided to take the youths out of the public school and place them in an institution where, as she wrote, "there would be afterschool supervised play" and that sphere of civility would encompass more of their hours. For Rose the obvious choice for young Catholic boys needing a diet rich in discipline was the parochial school at St. Aidan's. Father Creagh argued with Joe that his sons belonged there and nowhere else. The school was just beginning, and the priest wanted boys like the Kennedys seated at its student desks.

Rose would have delightedly sent her sons to parochial school. Joe argued that the Kennedy boys would be better off at a private school, Dexter, where they would sit next to Episcopalians, Congregationalists, and Unitarians, the sons of the Boston elite. Rose had heard such discussions before when her father had told her that she would not be going to Wellesley but to the Sacred Heart Academy. This time, however, Rose was on her father's side, arguing for a traditional Catholic education.

Up until now, Joe had left the child raising to his wife. In one of the seminal moments in the family history, Joe made it clear that he was not about to leave his sons' educations to his wife and the church. "My husband did not think it [religious training] was important, as far as the boys were concerned," Rose reflected years later. In the Kennedy home, as in the home of Joe's parents and grandparents, the children's education would be based not on their aspirations or intelligence but on gender. The Kennedy boys would be sent out to live and study and play among the American elite, to learn from them and with them. The girls would stay in the public schools, but eventually be sent to Catholic schools to be brought up in the faith.

Joe had very little to do with the day-to-day upbringing of the young Kennedys. "We were individuals with highly responsible roles in a partnership that yielded rewards which we shared," Rose wrote in her autobiography, as if she were discussing not a marriage but a business relationship. "I knew he worked hard for us, went on working hard even when he wasn't feeling well or sometimes when he was in severe pain. Yet there was nothing that he could do to help me in bearing a child, just as there was nothing I could do directly in helping him bear the burdens of business."

This was the script that they had settled upon, one in which Rose equated the "severe pain" that Joe experienced out in the business world with the pain of her own labor delivering nine children. "Child birth was something the woman had to do and the less bother she gave to anybody else including her husband the better it was, and the easier it was," Rose reflected.

Joe was not even obliged to be home when Rose delivered their babies. When Rose was ready to give birth to their sixth child on May 6, 1924, Joe was in a suite at the Waldorf Hotel in New York City involved in a battle with a group of corporate raiders attempting to take over the Yellow Cab Company. Joe hardly noticed when on the first Monday in May, Rose gave birth to Patricia. Joe finally defeated the raiders after weeks of combat. "I woke up one morning exhausted, and I realized that I hadn't been out of that hotel room in seven weeks," Joe recalled. "My baby, Pat, had been born and was almost a month old, and I hadn't even seen her."

Pat was yet another distinct variation in the spectrum of personality. As her older sister Eunice seemed to have been born with a sense of humanity, so Patricia appeared to have been blessed from birth with a natural grace and bearing. From her earliest years she was abnormally tall, not gawky like scrawny Eunice either, but a fawnlike creature that observers noted for her beauty, as the generation previous had lauded Rose's younger sister, Agnes. Patricia, like Agnes, got far enough in the world by her beauty that she didn't partake in the Kennedys' competitiveness as much as her siblings. She was a graceful creature on the tennis court, or sailing a boat with great natural ability, but she didn't care if she won or lost, not the way Eunice, Jack, and Joe Jr. cared.

Joe was away during the weekdays and often on extended trips. This was a home full of females: Rose, four daughters, a maid-cook, a nursemaid, other female servants, and only three little boys, including Robert "Bobby" Francis, born in the house on November 20, 1925, a tiny baby who as he grew up appeared the runt of the litter, trying desperately to keep up with his older brothers. Despite the home being full of women, it was steeped in masculine pursuits: boys' games, boys' sports, boys' spirit, led by Joe Jr. and Jack, and followed by their sisters.

What these girls shared was an attitude toward their older brothers that was equally an attitude about women, and about family. Their brothers were the measure of all things. "I'm sure it's normal for girls to look up to older brothers with some admiration and sense of dazzlement, but in our case it was fairly extreme," Eunice said. "To us they were marvelous creatures, practically God-like, and we yearned to please them and be acceptable. . . . They treated us in a loving but offhand way, occasionally sternly bawling us out, but most of the time considerately and humorously, and affectionately."

Rosemary was a bystander to the family drama. Rose had sent her eldest daughter off to kindergarten in the fall of 1923 to the same school she sent the rest of her children, Edward Devotion School, a few blocks from the house. Rosemary was the most beautiful of the Kennedy children, with the kind of open innocence that made adults stop and wonder. Her teacher, Margaret McQuaid, was impressed by her grace and manners. That was Rose's teaching, all those hours of chiding attention. At school politeness was not enough, and at the end of the year McQuaid could not pass her on to the first grade. So Rosemary stayed on, and in what would become a common pattern spent her days with children who were younger. She tried hard. She always tried hard. At the end of the next school year McQuaid gave her a passing C, a passing C for effort, a passing C because it did not matter, a passing C because Rosemary wouldn't be going on to first grade with the rest of the children.

This was usually the moment when a child would be labeled "feebleminded," and parents would be confronted with what they already knew. Rosemary was given the Binet intelligence test as were all children who were behind in their grade and were suspected of mental deficiency. Although the school promised that "there shall be no closing of the door of hope or opportunity" these new tests were a frightening specter that shuttled off scores of children into categories from which it was next to impossible to return. Based on the results, the school recommended children for one of the two special education classes. A low IQ was interpreted as a sign of moral deficiency, and it was not enough merely to put the "feebleminded" into their own classes. Children with low scores were given special counseling since they were considered likely to develop bad habits. Counselors went out to their homes where alcoholism and poor hygiene was suspected. After school, the students were supervised so they wouldn't get involved in smoking or in gang life.

Until recent years, Rosemary would have been considered slow or backward but not medically defined as subnormal. But Henry Herbert Goddard, the director of the research laboratory of the training school for Feeble-Minded Girls and Boys at Vineland, New Jersey, had contributed to science the concept of the "moron." These were individuals with IQs between 60 and 70, or a mental age between eight and twelve. They were less retarded than the two other standard categories: those with the mental age up to two years old, called "idiots," and the next higher category, "imbeciles," who had mental ages from three to seven. The three terms were supposedly morally neutral words of science, but they soon become epithets hurled on the playground and the street.

Rosemary was a moron then, and morons were considered a plague on American society, much more dangerous than idiots and imbeciles. Morons appeared normal but, as Goddard wrote, "they cannot be trained to function like normal people" and "they are the persons who make for us our social problems." They were supposedly the thieves and the drunkards, the prostitutes, the social parasites, the wastrels. "No one who understands feeble-mindedness, especially the moron, can expect anything else than that great numbers of these girls will fall into a life of prostitution," Goddard wrote in 1914. "They have normal or nearly normal instincts, with no power of control. . . . Some of them seek out that kind of life, others become the easy victim of the cadet, the white slaver or the madame."

In much of society there was a terrible horror of a race of feebleminded women, their ranks full of prostitutes, the wantonly promiscuous, and the amoral. They were said by science to be often "sunny in disposition and physically attractive" and they either brought forth broods of "defectives" or became "irresponsible sources of corruption and debauchery." In the name of civilization, the feebleminded would have to be either institutionalized or sterilized. The fear of such women was expressed most dramatically in the numbers of women who were forcibly sterilized under a series of new state laws. Doctors either opened up the abdominal cavity and removed a part of the fallopian tubes or they removed the ovaries. Despite the seriousness of the operation, by mid-1925 in twelve states 901 "feebleminded" women had been legally sterilized, and only 455 men.

For Rose and for any mother of a retarded child in the early 1920s, the terrible dread was that there was bad blood in her family. "Our family thought that Rosemary may have been the result of John F. and Josie's marriage," said Geraldine Hannon, Rose's cousin. The unstated, unfounded fear was that Rosemary's condition was a result of heredity, and Rose and Joe might sire other of these morons, idiots, or imbeciles.

Rose loved her daughter and wanted to shelter her. That, however, was the very attitude that the eugenics movement condemned, helping to bring about what Lothrop Stoddard called in 1922 the "dusk of mankind." Stoddard claimed that whereas in previous eras the processes of natural selection killed off individuals like Rosemary, "modern society and philanthropy have protected them and thus favored their rapid multiplication." That was the moral universe that greeted Rosemary.

Rosemary was Joe's child as much as she was Rose's but Joe was distant from his firstborn daughter. She was a girl and he did not value his daughters and their prospects as much as he valued his sons; more precisely, he saw them as future wives and mothers, a role about which Rose was perfectly adequate to instruct them. He was distant from Rosemary too because he was a man of quick intelligence and intensity, and he simply did not have the patience to deal with Rosemary. "He was much more emotional," said Eunice, "and was easily upset by Rosemary's lack of progress."

Rosemary, then, was Rose's daughter, her namesake. It was the experts who had defined Rosemary as feebleminded, and it was to the experts Rose went to seek help. Whether it was the leading psychologist at Harvard, learned medical doctors expert in the field, or a priest with expertise in the new field of intelligence testing, these men did little but throw out terms such as "genetic accident" or "birth accident." That was little solace to a mother who had a child to bring up, a child whom her school had branded as a moron. Their best advice was simply to put Rosemary in a private school where she would grow up among her own kind. As brutal a choice as that seemed, there were several excellent schools that in the words of one superintendent were for "the rich man's exceptional child" that "perhaps ... cater more to their vanity" than simply to the child.

For a family with the social ambition of the Kennedys, the idea of sending Rosemary away was logical, and Rose and Joe could have found many justifications. But Rose said no, and Joe accepted his wife's decision. It was one of the defining moments in the history of this family, and it was a moment defined by Rose. "I rejected it except as a last resort," she said later.

Rose's relationship to her eldest daughter was a complicated matrix. Though there was nobility and selflessness in her actions, there was also self-delusion and deadly pride as well. Like many parents of children with mild retardation, Rose could not fully admit that *her* Rosemary was different. As a family the Kennedys believed in blood and nurturing; if Rosemary had their blood, then through nurturing they would make her as full of the Kennedy esprit as any of the children. When Rose looked back on those years, she wondered if she had neglected the others, especially Jack, and probably she had, but it was a slight that any mother of a child with retardation would have understood.

To the world Rose pretended that her Rosie was no different from her other children. She didn't confide even in her closest friends. When Rose brought her family into the children's shop in Brookline run by Mary O'Connell Ryan, her old Dorchester friend thought that Rosemary was a little slower than the rest of Rose's nearly hyper brood, but beyond that was no different. One day Ryan told another of Rose's old friends, Miriam Finnegan: "I think there's so much made of Kathleen that Rosemary is a little conscious of that and feels a little bit in the background." Even cousins and other relatives beyond the immediate family did not know about Rosemary's condition.

Rose had an acute awareness of Rosemary. She wanted her desperately to feel like her brothers and sisters, and she did whatever she could to maintain the illusion that she was no different. She even had the maid cut her meat before setting the plate before her at dinner. Rose could have put Rosemary into a special class in the Brookline public schools, but she would not put that stigma on her daughter and on her family. Instead, the Kennedys hired a special governess or nurse, with whom Rosemary lived part of the time. Although Rose herself devoted endless hours to Rosemary, the main burden fell on an array of tutors, nurses, maids, and nuns.

As Joe prospered tremendously in business, he purchased a Rolls-Royce. The idea that a man still in his mid-thirties should have not only two cars, but a Rolls-Royce driven by a liveried driver was impressive indeed. As the great car made its stately way up Abbotsford Road, some of the neighbors were full of wonderment. One man joked over the dinner table to his family that his one claim to fame was renting his garage to Joe Kennedy's Rolls-Royce.

The neighbors began to treat the Kennedys with a mixture of awe and envy, gossiping endlessly about them. "You remembered them," said Paul Leahy. "They were very colorful people in the neighborhood, good-looking too." There were those who deeply admired the family, but there were as many who despised them. "My parents hated the Kennedys," recalled Dorothy Ogilvie, who grew up down the street. "The family had been liquor dealers. They were Irish Catholics, and they were part of the Fitzgerald family. My father thought Mayor Fitzgerald was a crook. Beyond that, my mother couldn't stand Rose. My mother thought that Rose was nothing but a social climber."

It was not only Rose and Joe but also their children who had more than the neighbors' children. "We would play with our dolls," recalled Helen Leahy Steverman, "and we would go over to their house where they had a playhouse, the only one in the neighborhood." The diminutive playhouse sat in the Kennedys' large front lawn, and was a magnet to the little girls of the neighborhood, as well as a public symbol of the family's wealth and concern for their children.

Every time Rose wheeled her baby carriage to Coolidge Corner and looked in store windows she saw new products. Every time she opened a magazine there was something else to buy. Rose was a deeply acquisitive woman, living in a developing consumer culture where advertising was turning the purchasing of goods into a sign of moral value. That Rose's daughters had a playhouse showed that she was a good mother and would spare nothing for her growing brood. The same logic followed for all her household purchases.

In the mid-twenties, shortly after the birth of Bobby, Joe took the most crucial step in the development of a family dynasty. As a banker in Boston, he had seen that what held the great Brahmin families together generation after generation was not a miraculous gene pool but trust funds, the principal protected from the will and whim of individual family members. His seven children would begin to receive income from the funds at the age of twenty-one, and one half their share of the principal at forty-five. What set Joe apart from his father's attitude toward *his* inheritance was that unlike P.J., Joe parceled the money out equally to his daughters as well as to his sons. The money grew in this and two other funds added in 1936 and 1949 so that by 1961 each Kennedy had about ten million dollars.

Kathleen and her sisters learned from their parents not simply the value of a dollar, but of a dime and a penny, and if the penny could have been broken into tenths, Rose and Joe would have wanted them to hold on to that too. "We did keep a close rein on their finances," Rose wrote. "And that, too, was part of their education." Indeed, the richer they became the more parsimonious the Kennedys appeared.

Although Kathleen and Rosemary were receiving allowances of ten cents a week, they decided that was not quite enough. "When my father came home from his work week at twelve o'clock on Saturday, all of us nine kids lined up to get our nickel allowance," recalled Helen Leahy Steverman. "Kathleen and Rosemary would also stand in line and put their little hands out and receive an allowance. My father used to get a big kick out of it. He would sit at the dinner table at night and laugh because he knew that Joe Kennedy had so much money that he could buy our entire family several times over, and yet he was the one giving the Kennedys their allowance."

By innocently standing in line with the Leahy children, the Kennedy girls were precociously displaying a family trait. The young Kennedys developed into a frugal breed when it came to *their* money, be it paying help, picking up checks, or coming up with money for taxis, and a largess and generosity when it came to spending the money of others. As the girls grew older each had her own idea of what to do with her weekly allowance. Rosemary sent hers to the Catholic missions; Kathleen bought records; while Pat quickly spent hers on sodas or ice cream. Eunice, however, saved her allowances, making a ritual of counting her savings each evening.

As much as Rose taught her children to clutch their coins with all their might, she thoroughly enjoyed spending money

on clothes. Each season she waited until the haute couture designers of Paris told her what she should wear. "Youth, slim
youth, both boyish and feminine, will be an important factor in
the inspiration of next season's dresses," wrote *Vogue* in 1925.
That was a perfect style for Rose. She took the trolley to
downtown Boston to go shopping. Even here, however, the
new millionaire's wife was a shrewd and careful shopper.
When she wanted a special gown, she would not pay the large
prices for originals from Paris. Instead, she headed to Mary
Murphy's dress shop on Boylston Street. Here eight Italian
seamstresses copied the latest Parisian fashions from fabrics
and sketches carried by ship from Le Havre to Boston and
hand delivered to the shop.

The Kennedys had to keep up appearances to match their
dramatically increasing wealth, for by the mid-1920s Joe had
become a millionaire twice over. As he grew richer and richer,
he wanted to forget from whence he had come, and those who
had helped him. In the three decades of his life, no single act
had been so generous as that of his Aunt Catherine who had
loaned him the money crucial to his obtaining control over the
Columbia Trust Company. Catherine Hickey, like the other
women in her family, was abysmally ignorant of finances and
had not even had her nephew sign a note for the loan. Several
years later Catherine Hickey went to the Columbia Trust Company to cash a check but was astounded to find that her account was empty. She never paid that much attention to her
bank account. She had assumed that by now Joe had repaid his
debt, but he had not and he never returned his aunt's money.

The more successful Joe became the more he acted as if he
had pulled himself up out of a harsh impoverished world. "It
always made my mother very annoyed when her brother Joe
acted as if he had been this boy genius, doing it all on his
own," reflected Mary Lou McCarthy. "She would say, 'He was
not Abraham Lincoln brought up in a log cabin, for the love
of God. We had servants and we had matched horses, and one
of the first automobiles. Why is he not allowing my mother
and father to be treated as successful people?'"

The more money he earned, the less Joe seemed to be at
home, and the further distance he traveled from Rose and her
world. As much as he wanted to be accepted, he was not one
to kowtow to the proper Bostonians, spending his life servicing
their money by investing for them in blue chips and gilt-edge
securities. He was not a great entrepreneur, building railroads

across the prairies or ships to cross the seas. He created no great institutions, except his wealth and his family. He was a brilliant loner, a scavenger of other people's disasters, driving stock prices down and then stepping in, making a killing, and stepping out again; buying land in Florida only after 1926 when the bubble had burst. He thrived on the economic fringes, where fortunes were won or lost in no more time than it took a rumor to travel across a telephone line. When he attended the tenth anniversary of his Harvard class at the Hotel Pilgrim in Plymouth, Massachusetts, in the midst of Prohibition, it was good old Joe who supplied the bootleg liquor, good old Joe who knew people the Brahmins didn't know, wouldn't know, and couldn't know.

Rose was as socially ambitious as her husband. When it came time for the Kennedys to take their summer vacation, they would not head up to the sunny Catholic ghettos of Nantasket where the Fitzgeralds now had a house. Instead they rented a house only a few miles away on the rocky beaches of Cohasset among the Protestant elite.

The sight of these Catholic arrivistes tooling up the coast to Cohasset in a golden Rolls-Royce was enough to set the Brahmin tongues wagging. Rose and Joe didn't seem to understand that the way you impressed the Old New Englanders was by affecting a calculated casualness, and not by ostentatiously displaying one's wealth, the printing hardly dry on one's dollar bills.

Rose and Joe were not merely content to sit on the beach in full view of the Protestants, but in the summer of 1922 applied for membership in the Cohasset Country Club. The club had a few Catholic members, including Eddie Moore, Joe's assistant who was living in a gate house attached to the Kennedys' rented home. The women of Cohasset, however, had no intention of sharing their bridge tables and tennis sets with the likes of Rose Fitzgerald, and their husbands were not about to play golf with Joe either. The men sat on the committee of the country club, and they took as much pleasure as their wives in excluding such ostentatious outsiders, their rejections couched in the euphemisms of good fellows. The summer gentry said that they had a desire "to see old faces" but Joe didn't quite get the message. June went by, and July, and now it was August, and Joe's application languished, and finally he understood.

It was a mean sport, a nasty lesson that the Brahmins taught

Joe and Rose that summer, reinforcing the family ethic that one did not get mad, one got even, though of course one got mad as well. "It was petty and cruel," recalled Ralph Lowell, one of Joe's associates. "The women of Cohasset looked down on the daughter of Honey Fitz and who was Joe Kennedy but the son of Pat, the barkeeper?"

8
The Salted Heart

The Kennedy daughters sat waiting for their father. Joe had just bought controlling interest in a Hollywood film studio, FBO, and at the age of thirty-eight was a minor movie magnate traveling back and forth from California on the *Twentieth Century Limited*. Suddenly Joe thrust open the door, his arms full of gifts, the discoverer of what to his daughters and sons was a new and wondrous world. Joe, like his father-in-law, was a father of the momentous occasion, charging his moments with his family with intensity, stamping his own mark on his children with great and persistent force.

All the young Kennedys pushed toward Joe, but none of them loved their father more than five-year-old Eunice, who talked endlessly about Joe. The other children in the neighborhood loved the movies too, but only *her* father had been there, hobnobbing with the heroes of the silver screen, only *her* father was a sojourner returning from that distant land of stars and sun and dreams and endless horizons.

As much as the children loved the glamour and romance of their Hollywood father, for thirty-six-year-old Rose it meant more months alone with her children. As Joe headed westward, Rose knew that in pulpits across America priests and pastors were portraying Hollywood as Sodom and Gomorrah on the Pacific. Cardinal O'Connell and the other leaders of the church looked down with righteous disdain on these moviemakers. This was the industry in which Joe was working, adding his energy to what the church considered a race largely of moral bootleggers, bottling wares that were lulling Americans into a spiritual stupor, filling the screens with scenes of explicit sexuality.

Rose was proud of her husband. Her Joe was not simply go-

179

ing out to Hollywood to make money but as a good Catholic family man to make films of which she and every good Catholic woman would be proud, to serve as an example of high morality and Catholic virtue. Will H. Hays, the former postmaster general, had been brought in to clean up the industry, and Hays had expressed himself delighted that a man of Joe's moral caliber was entering the industry. "Most of all," noted *Motion Picture World*, "General Hays wanted his friend to come into the motion picture business because he regarded him as . . . a man who, in his business ideals and concepts as in the fine character of his home life, would bring to the industry much that it has lacked in the past." *Photoplay*, a major fan magazine, ran a profile of Joe calling him "the screen's . . . leading family man . . ." including not only his picture but Rose's and all seven of their children. Almost every article about Joe spoke of him as a devoted husband and father and featured photos of the loving family. For Rose, this kind of adulation helped to make her life worthwhile. She was alone with the children in Brookline, but Joe was out in the world bringing wealth to the family, honor to the Kennedy name, and vicarious glory to Rose and their children.

In the summer of 1927 Joe decided that the family should move to New York. Rose was pregnant but Joe couldn't wait until after she had given birth to their eighth child. Rose had little choice but to follow. At the age of thirty-seven there was little left of that ebullient young woman who had come dancing down the steps the day of her debut, exploding in enthusiasm at a world that seemed "blossoming." Rose had become a handsome, stylish matron, an appendage to Joe's ambitions. She knew almost nothing of her husband's business dealings in Hollywood and New York, but she knew that Joe was providing for her and the children in an extraordinary fashion. When they left Boston on a day late in September, they traveled in a private railroad car. Even on this day, Rose took the time to note down the illnesses of her children. She wrote that six-year-old Eunice was suffering from a stomach illness. It may have had nothing to do with the move at all, but her third daughter was high-strung and nervous, with an almost painful sensitivity to the world around her.

Joe had rented a thirteen-room home in the exclusive suburban community of Riverdale. From their house, the Kennedys could see the vast expanse of the Hudson River flowing majestically toward the Atlantic Ocean. There were great tracts of woods, perfect for children's games of soldier, and even sheep grazing on a few of the large estates. Yet Joe could be downtown in no time on the commuter train.

For Joe the move was an unalloyed plus. He had none of what he considered his father-in-law's bathetically sentimental attachment to Boston, and he was glad to be away from the city where he was forever hearing the echoes of "Sweet Adeline" reverberating in his ears. The Kennedy children would miss their friends, but they received all the emotional sustenance they needed within the confines of the family. For Rose it was all infinitely more complicated, leaving her roots, her sense of place, leaving the city where she was still known as the mayor's daughter, home of her parents and brothers and sisters. In Brookline she had been able to tuck her newest baby into the carriage and walk to Coolidge Corner, or down the street to St. Aidan's. In Brookline she walked past many houses full of Catholic families who were members of her parish church. She knew almost no one in Riverdale, and as she grew heavy with child, she was hundreds of miles away from Dr. Good, who had delivered all seven of her children in Brookline. She was away from Joe too. Rose, like her mother moving from Concord Junction to Dorchester, had discovered that this move had not brought her physically closer to her husband. He was away as much as ever. Indeed, as the time of birth approached, Rose was alone with her children in the rented house in Riverdale, and Joe was off in Palm Beach, Florida, on vacation.

Joe stood in his tropical whites at the train station in Palm Beach waiting for the arrival of the express train. Joe had come down to the Florida resort in January of 1928 with his Irish-American aides, Eddie Moore and Ted O'Leary, men totally devoted and loyal to the man they called "the boss." The group was staying at the Royal Poinciana Hotel where a decade and a half before, Rose and her father had danced at the great balls, and Mayor Fitzgerald had regaled all within hearing with his stories and his songs.

That day Joe was waiting for the arrival of Gloria Swanson. Twenty-eight-year-old Gloria was one of the most famous movie actresses in the world, and the personification of Hollywood glamour. Joe had met Gloria a few months before in New York City where he had taken her to dinner at a roadhouse to discuss making films together. Gloria had a great sense of human character, and she caught the nuances of Joe's personality the way no woman had before. "He had the most ambitious view of pictures I had ever encountered," she recalled. "In fact, he seemed to see them precisely as a means of attaining not only wealth but also power. Like his father and his father-in-law, whom he mentioned over and over again, he was intrigued by the manipulation of people and events."

Joe was as fascinated by the diminutive actress as she was with him. She had a mysterious countenance that Edward Steichen's classic 1924 photo of her as an icon behind a veil perfectly captured. Gloria was the polar opposite of Rose. Gloria was obsessed with her own career. She had at least two abortions. She had been married three times. Her third husband, Henri de la Falaise, a French marquis, was her most recent acquisition, a weak man whose main attributes were his title and an impenetrable charm that he held up before him like a shield. Gloria had two children, one of them adopted, but unlike Rose, she did not live for them; if anything, her children lived for her, yet another part of her entourage. She was a woman who understood sex as pleasure, passion, human folly, and business tool.

As the train pulled into the Palm Beach station, Gloria's husband jumped off and introduced himself to Joe and his associates. Joe had no time for the Marquis de la Falaise de la Coudraye. After a brusque greeting, he leapt onto the train, rushed up the aisle, and kissed Gloria twice.

Joe was a man who understood perfectly well that the world is made of mixed motives. He had a lusty sexual desire for the movie star. That did not prevent him from seeing that it would be a coup to develop a business partnership with the greatest star in Hollywood. He also saw her as an invaluable social asset, one who would further him in this world of Palm Beach society. He intended to further all three of his interests.

Night after night, Joe led Gloria and Henri through a glittering array of parties. To Gloria, he seemed like "P. T. Barnum presenting Lavinia and Tom Thumb or a pair of unicorns." During the day Joe and his associates worked over Gloria's business affairs, totally reorganizing Gloria Swanson Productions, her film company. One of the pesky problems was what to do with poor Henri. Joe offered him a position as European director of Pathé studios. It was a prestigious placement for the underemployed marquis that had an added merit: The job would keep him an ocean and a continent away from his wife.

On the immediate front, however, Joe's associate, Eddie Moore, generously offered to take the marquis deep-sea fishing. Joe announced that, alas, he was too busy to join the two men, and Gloria said that she preferred to go shopping for presents for her children.

That afternoon, after her shopping excursion, Gloria returned to the hotel, put on a kimono and slippers, and relaxed on her bed. Gloria remembered years later how she had looked up and seen Joe standing in the doorway in his white flannels, sweater, and two-colored shoes. "He moved so quickly that his mouth was on mine before either of us could speak," she wrote in her autobiography. "With one hand he held the back of my head, with the other he stroked my body and pulled at my kimono. He kept insisting in a drawn-out moan, 'No longer, no longer, now.' He was like a roped horse, rough, arduous, racing to be free. After a hasty climax he lay beside me, stroking my hair. Apart from his guilty, passionate mutterings, he had still said nothing cogent."

Although Joe never recorded his own recollections of his sexual life with Gloria, her remembrances have a certain verisimilitude to them, resembling not only stories of Joe's other episodes, but an attitude to sexual matter that was typical of the men in his family. Joe approached sex like fast food, bolting it down and then getting on with the rest of the day. In Gloria's case, she was no interchangeable part of his diet, however, but a woman whose passionate demeanor, wit, and talent enormously attracted him. At times, there was a prankish joy in his relationship with Gloria that was gone from his existence with Rose.

In February Rose returned alone to Boston to have Dr. Good deliver her eighth child, Jean Ann, on February 20, 1928, at St. Margaret's Hospital. Joe arrived afterwards to her bedside. He had begun to use expensive gifts as a way to placate Rose. That day he carried three diamond bracelets he had taken on approval. Rose put all three of the bracelets on her arm, trying to decide which one to choose, as a friend stood watching. "What can you possibly think of to give her next if she has the ninth baby?" the woman blurted. "I'll give her a black eye," Joe said, frowning at his wife, and then laughing.

As she lay recuperating, Rose received scores of letters, telegrams, congratulations, and flowers including a grand bouquet from Gloria Swanson de la Falaise. Rose was living in a world where hypocrisy had been elevated to a high social form, and the congratulations from her husband's mistress were only part of it. Although Rose didn't know these people, and most of these congratulations were part of the rituals of business, these hundreds of well-wishers were paying obeisance to Rose as the matron of a celebrated family, praising her as the exemplary mother of a marvelous clan. Besides the eight children themselves, this was her greatest accomplishment, an image she carried forth in the world like a public testimony to the value of her life.

Rose saved scores of congratulatory letters, the chronicle of her life, and testimony to the rightness of the choice she had made in staying with Joe, staying with him despite everything. Rose remained in Boston for a month recuperating while Eddie and Mary Moore watched over the other children. She had trained her maids and governesses, and the seven young Kennedys did not disgrace her with misconduct.

Rose held her newest child in her arms, and thought, as she always did, of her obligations. She had been through this seven times before, and now as she told the same bedtime stories for the thousandth time, told the same historical or religious parables, she did it sometimes almost by rote. It never seemed to occur to her that if any child had a right to complain of neglect it was not Jack, but Jean.

Jean was a tender, quiet little child who would have benefitted from a mother's special care, but she sometimes appeared almost lost in the spirited games and camaraderie of her older sisters and brothers. From her earliest years, Jean was nearly forgotten in the clamorous reality of the Kennedy family, a sweetly tempered and vulnerable little girl who turned toward Kico, the Irish nursemaid, for a warmth and emotional sustenance her mother did not give her.

Jean lived distant from her parents, existing in large measure within a world of children. Joe Jr. had become a surrogate parent to his younger siblings, much as Rose had planned him to be, a hero to his younger sisters and brothers. Young Joe was not simply Jean's eldest brother, he was named her godfather. "Joe was the one who was very interested in helping us," Jean recalled in 1960. "He was so much older than we there was no irritation. He had more interest in us. Jack was more—well independent."

Kathleen was the role model for her younger sisters just as Joe Jr. was for his brothers. But she was distant from Jean too,

eight years older to the day. "Mother and Daddy always encouraged us to depend more on each other than on them," Jean
reflected. "If Dad wanted to tell me how to behave, he'd tell
Pat. He wouldn't tell me. And so there wasn't any resentment.
Pat would sort of discuss it. Like she would say it might be
good to do it this way."

The Kennedys had moved to Riverdale in part so that their
children could go to the Riverdale Country School. The school
was only a little more than twenty years old. Yet the turreted
Victorian Tower House, the white-frame master's house, the
brick dormitory, and the grassy playing fields suggested a venerable institution full of hoary traditions.

Riverdale was an excellent private school in which parents
took strong interest in their children's educations. At a building
dedication in December 1928, there were row upon row of parents. For the most part the mothers present that evening did not
work outside the home. Their husbands sitting next to them
commuted by train to New York City each morning. Lawyers,
stockbrokers, and business executives, they were busy men
who had made a point of keeping this evening free. Rose, who
had five children in the school, sat alone.

To these parents, Rose was the Kennedy family and Joe only
a rare presence. The Kennedys were considered important
enough that Rose was among those singled out as part of a
"large and distinguished audience." Another mark of that
power was the fact that Rosemary had been admitted to this
school with its proudly academic reputation. She dressed in the
same style cloth coat as her sisters Kathleen and Eunice, as if
they were family uniforms. Rosemary attended the same class
as her younger sister. "Rosemary just plugged along with the
rest of us," recalled Doris Hutchings, a classmate. "She was a
little older than we were, but it was a small school and a small
class."

Riverdale was a Protestant town with Presbyterian and Episcopalian churches nearby. Rose and her family had to make the
trek almost to Yonkers to attend mass. It was a Republican
town, and she and Joe were political outcasts, pilloried as children of corrupt Irish politicians. Riverdale was an insular community where social life revolved around private clubs and
gatherings to which the Kennedys were not welcome. "The
Kennedy family was not very happy living in the Riverdale
community," recalled Dr. Lynn L. Fulkerson, a neighbor and

classmate of Jack's at the Riverdale Country School. "They were like fish out of water because of their life-style, their close-knit family of eight children, their father's nonparticipation in neighborhood activities, and the mother's Catholic activities, which few if any of the neighborhood families shared."

Rose was isolated and alone, and she devoted herself even more narrowly to her children's development. "She was one hundred percent mother, absolutely one hundred percent," said George Duff, whose father was minister of the Presbyterian church down the street. "She had very little to do with local social activities, and all her energy was focused on her children. I was over at their house often, and I remember that quite strongly."

After school, the older Kennedy children hurried out to the field behind the Presbyterian church for games of football with their friends. These were fierce unyielding struggles. Although most little girls would not have thought of taking part in a rough football game, Kathleen played on one side, and her friend Doris Hutchings on the other. Kathleen was bonded to Jack with a profundity that mere blood seemed insufficient to describe. She would go out for passes, challenging the boys, drifting back and catching the footballs that Jack or Joe lofted to her. Kathleen may have played football but she was hardly a tomboy. Much of the time she was off with Doris and her other close friend, Margaret Duff. "We just followed around, playing little girls' games, things like that," Margaret Duff Van den Heuval recalled.

Joe was off in Hollywood producing an epic film, *Queen Kelly*, starring Gloria and directed by the legendary Eric Von Stroheim. In the luxurious bungalow on the studio lot he had constructed for Gloria, he included all the comforts that the star might possibly require. Several years later when Russell Birdwell, a leading publicist, took over Gloria's dressing room as his office, he said that he had discovered yet another creature comfort that Joe had presumably provided for his beloved: a bugging device in the ceiling.

It was not simply that Joe suspected Gloria of duplicity, but that he was a man who thought that love meant control, and control meant mastery over the substance and details of a life, be it that of a mistress, a wife, a son, or a daughter. This Hollywood world intrigued him, a fascination that never left him and that he imparted to several of his children. His mother had nurtured in him two great goals, success and power at the highest level, while maintaining an image of propriety, exhibiting exemplary character to the world. Here in Hollywood he had it all. One of the most desired women in the world was his mistress. He had the power to command the very images that millions of Americans saw on the screen. Yet he was still Joseph P. Kennedy, devoted Catholic, father of eight, beloved husband of Rose Fitzgerald Kennedy, upholder of moral standards.

On one of her trips to New York City, in October 1928, Joe invited Gloria to bring her children to the Kennedy home for a party. "When he was in control, he saw nothing as impossible or out of the question," Gloria recalled. "I couldn't even argue with him, because it would have done no good. I finally said the children could go but I would not."

Little Gloria and Joseph made the trip out to the Kennedy home. "I remember at one point when we were being taken back and forth between New York and Los Angeles that we were on their estate once," her daughter, Gloria Somborn Daly, said. "Kathleen was my age and Eunice was my brother's age. It was Halloween and I recall there were decorations around. Of course, my mother didn't talk about her relationship with Joseph Kennedy. It was hardly a subject to be talked about to an eight-year-old."

In the spring of 1929, Joe purchased a new home, a $250,000 estate known as "Crownlands" in the exclusive Westchester County community of Bronxville. The Field Real Estate Company proudly announced in *The Bronxville Review* that the purchase was "said to be the largest residential sale made in Bronxville." Rose had nothing to do with the negotiations, but the deed listed her as the purchaser of the property.

During the 1920s Bronxville had grown at what the locals considered a frenzied pace to almost sixty-five hundred inhabitants, the development fueled by the wealth and aspirations of the group the old-timers called "the stock market crowd." On weekends the Supper Club at the Gramatan Hotel was full of stylish New Yorkers dancing to Ben Cutler's band. The fast young couples might swill some illegal champagne and roar out of town in their bright red Stutz Bear Cats, but the impudent roar of a sports car was about the loudest sound in Bronxville. Sunday the movie theaters were closed down by local ordinance. The town had no room or time for the vulgar, the loud, the indiscreet, and for any who too publicly advertised that they were Catholic or Jew. Realtors assured worried clients that "the one Jew in town," a retailer, "goes home to Yonkers at night."

The Kennedys' new home was a worthy fiefdom for Rose and the family. The great redbrick Georgian house with its tall white columns was an imposing structure set on over five acres of meticulously landscaped grounds. There were twenty bedrooms, more than enough for all the children, the maids, and nurses, and any guests that Joe might invite. Joe Jr., Jack, and Kathleen had sovereignty over the third floor, which also contained an enormous playroom and the governesses' bedroom. The other children resided on the second floor. The gardener and the chauffeur had their own separate quarters as well.

Kathleen and her sisters followed the example set by Joe Jr., who from his perch on the third floor dominated the lives of his siblings. Joe Jr. was a messy youth who left behind him a trail of unmade beds, scattered socks, dirty dishes, and wrinkled pants. Kathleen was as sloppy as her big brother, dropping her clothes on the floor to be picked up by one of the maids. Eunice and Pat followed their sister's lead, though they were hardly as disorderly as Kathleen.

Rose had enough control over young Joe that she could have berated the sloppiness out of him, and his siblings would probably have grown up differently. But her children were Kennedys, and to her mind they had more important things to do than to pick up their socks. Cleaning up after themselves was not important, not to any of them. This attitude bred in them a casual carelessness, a belief that no matter what they did, there would always be someone to pick up after them.

Rose wanted her children to be unique, even in their accents. "I tried to have my children keep up their Boston accent with the broad 'A,' " Rose recalled. "However, it was quite a struggle as the children at the public school in Bronxville made fun of them and called them sissies. So they gradually applied a New York accent which they lost and now they again talk like New Englanders."

The Kennedy home was a focal point for the neighborhood children, especially on Saturday. "On the weekends we played at the Kennedys'," recalled Manuel Angullo, Jack's closest friend in Bronxville. "Everybody played. Kathleen was one hell of a football player. She was on top of everything." In the morning the children played football. As they grew older, in the afternoon they danced to music from the Victrola in the living room. "It wasn't that Mrs. Kennedy forced the boys to dance," Angullo said, "but they thought it was fun."

The Kennedys attracted a breed of friends like themselves—energetic, almost manic. The Kennedys' competitive spirit permeated everything they did. "We played the card games 'hearts' and 'go-fish' a lot," recollected Angullo. "These games were serious business. You could never cheat at anything and you had to be a good sportsman—or else you would hear from the old man. If somebody lost, everybody looked at the reasons why and it was all very carefully analyzed. But winning was what mattered."

Rosemary could not quite master the card games, and she was too slow for touch football, but her sisters and brothers made her the referee for their games, and they included her in their conversations. Eunice was always watching out for Rosemary, and Rose rarely had to admonish her other children about Rosemary. They knew. And their friends knew.

As much as Rose let her children play on their own, she was like a director standing in the darkened wings, ready to shout out a forgotten line, to encourage or deplore. "I remember going ice-skating in Bronxville," Eunice reflected. "You wouldn't go skating off into the blue yonder. She'd say use your right leg or use your left leg better. If you weren't doing well, there weren't any excuses. She'd say you just get along there, don't be stupid about it, never oh you poor thing, you may not feel very well today. Sounds like she was sort of an ogre, but you never felt that. You felt that she felt you had more in you than you thought you did. As we got older my father made it possible for us to do things, but I think that the terrific drive came more from my mother. By the time I got to know my father and he was around much more, I was eighteen or nineteen."

In Hollywood in the spring of 1929 as Joe was having a myriad of problems with *Queen Kelly*, he learned his seventy-one-year-old father lay critically ill. He took the train back to Boston. In these last years Joe had not been as close to his father as his sisters had been. Margaret had married Charles Burke, the son of their next-door neighbor, and they had come to live with the former East Boston politician in his grand house in Winthrop, along with their two children. His other daughter, Loretta, had married another young man from

Winthrop, George Connelly, a Harvard graduate who was in the marine supply business. They had one child. Both of P.J.'s daughters were devoted to him and spent endless hours with him.

Joe went immediately to the hospital to see his father and was immensely relieved to learn that P.J. was improving. Deciding that his father was strong enough, he headed back to California, at least for a short while. Almost as soon as Joe's train had departed from Boston, P.J. began to fail.

Within a few hours, on May 18, 1929, P.J. died. To his funeral three days later at the Church of St. John came the rich and poor, bankers and workmen, matrons and maids, lawyers and firemen, priests and nuns. They were all there, all the relatives and friends, everyone except for P.J.'s eldest son, Joseph P. Kennedy.

On the day after the funeral Margaret and Loretta began the sad duty of sorting through their father's belongings. Following P.J.'s last wish, they found a box full of scores of loans that he had made over the years. Some notes were for only a few dollars, but they added up to over fifty thousand dollars. Among the I.O.U.'s was a note in P.J.'s own handwriting: "Upon my death all debts are cancelled."

Margaret and Loretta took the notes, and with tears in their eyes burned them. After all P.J.'s papers were sorted, there was still the matter of the will. He divided one half to his daughters, and one half to Joe. That might have seemed a curious division, for Joe was the multimillionaire and his sisters just starting out with their families. Given the way P.J. thought, he could have easily left nothing to his daughters. Joe was the man in the family now, and he was expected to take care of his sisters, to watch out for them as long as they lived. There was nothing in the will that said that, but it was understood by everyone in the family.

Not only P.J.'s goodness but his shrewdness had survived him. His estate was publicly listed as only $55,000, though it was in fact far more than that. "I would guess that his father left an estate of between $200,000 and $300,000," said James Landis, one of Joe's closest political and personal associates. That was a fortune in the late 1920s, the most vivid evidence imaginable that Joe had hardly struggled out of poverty. It was family money, an extraordinary amount for Joe to use in his shrewd parlays in the stock market.

* * *

In the summer of 1929, Joe purchased a summer home in Hyannis Port on Cape Cod. For decades, Hyannis Port had been a favorite summer community for wealthy families from Pittsburgh, St. Louis, and several other cities. These were not the patrician families that had ensconced themselves in Newport on the coast of Rhode Island. Their hands still had the raw smell of oil, steel, and coal on them, and they prided themselves that quaint old Hyannis Port was an unassuming hamlet. People tended to put their formal manners away for the summer, to drop in on each other's homes not only without calling, but often without knocking.

The Kennedy home was a sprawling white clapboard house with green shutters, set on two and a half acres of lawn, with ample room for a tennis court, a swimming pool, and marathon football games. The Kennedys had rented the house the previous three seasons, but now that they owned it they had made a dramatic renovation. Rose furnished the summer home with a mixture of antiques and strong serviceable furniture including a long fruitwood table for the dining room and a classic old sideboard, and placed Currier & Ives and other suitable prints on the wall. For weeks before their arrival, crews had worked feverishly building an addition to the fourteen-room house that included in the basement a thirty-by-fifteen-foot private theater with its centerpiece, a fifteen-thousand-dollar RCA sound movie projector. The residential theater required two hundred ampere cable, and the residents of Hyannis Port watched as workers dug a deep, hundred-yard-long trench out from the house to the company's main power lines. The larger neighboring town of Hyannis itself had only gotten its first sound movie theater this very month of June 1929 and the local paper had proudly trumpeted that the town now had one of "2500 Western Electric Sound Systems ... installed in this country." Now as crowds stood in long lines on Main Street waiting to see this incredible phenomenon, one man, Joseph P. Kennedy, had his own sound movie system. The Boston papers called it "probably the first private installation of talking pictures apparatus in New England or in the country." It was that and more: an awesome, audacious way for the Kennedys to signal their entrance to this wealthy but determinedly unassuming community.

Soon after the Kennedys arrived, Madelaine Blackburn, their next-door neighbor, decided to go over and welcome Rose.

Blackburn went up to the front door, knocked, and was greeted by a maid.

"I live right down the street," Blackburn said brightly, "and I'm here to say hello to Mrs. Kennedy."

The servant looked up and down at the neighbor. "Do you have an appointment to see Mrs. Kennedy?" the maid asked officiously.

"Have a what?"

"An appointment."

"No, of course not," Blackburn sputtered.

"I'll get Mrs. Kennedy's secretary if you would like to make an appointment to meet with her."

Blackburn turned on her heels, muttering "The hell with that, I'm not going to bother with these people."

Within hours the story of the spurned friendship was all over Hyannis Port. Blackburn did not call at the house, and it did not take long for the people of the port to realize that the Kennedys were a people apart.

The townspeople saw the Kennedy family coming and going and wondered about events in the great white house on the sound. Other relatives arrived including Rose's cousin, Geraldine Hannon. One afternoon Geraldine returned to the house after playing a tennis match with Joe Jr. As she entered she heard Fitzgerald and Joe in the midst of a fierce argument. She cocked her head trying to hear more clearly, and realized that her Uncle Fitz was screaming at Joe about his affair with Gloria. Her uncle was threatening to tell Rose.

Fitzgerald was not about to confront his son-in-law over the kind of casual dalliance at which he was equally indulgent, but this relationship had gone far beyond that. It threatened the whole elaborately wrought family image, and might dissipate all the respect in which the family was held. Joe only laughed and said that if his father-in-law told Rose, he would simply leave his wife.

For both Joe and Fitzgerald, it was a moral convenience believing that Rose did not know about Gloria. Of course, she knew. No matter what front she might show to the world, she was no simpleminded stoic. She had her arguments with Joe. She had even been overheard by another Bronxville matron as she discussed the matter with her masseuse. Her Sacred Heart education had taught her to expect suffering, but she had not been told that it might be something as tawdry as her husband's affairs. Her anger was only partially repressed. She allowed it to come out where it could do little damage. Like many other women of her class, the hairdressers, masseuses, and maids often became confidantes that husbands and social friends could never be. But as long as nothing was said publicly then the reality did not exist and family life could go on as before. That was the unspoken family covenant that Fitzgerald vowed to break.

A few weeks later Josie purportedly confronted her eldest daughter with the reality of the torrid affair. "You see, you fool, your beloved husband is no different from your beloved father," Josie said, her words like a curse. "Now you finally know what men are really like!" In that moment, Josie had risen out of her monumental sense of rectitude, her own self-denial, to become a truthmonger shoving Rose's face into the muck of her marital life. Rose had fancied herself better than her mother, with a life better than her mother's. Josie almost seemed to have taken pleasure in her motherly "I told you so."

Rose had learned her lessons of self-denial too well, and she turned from her mother as if she had not heard her words. Later that summer on a memorable day in early August, Gloria Swanson made her first visit to Hyannis Port, descending dramatically on the tiny resort town in a Sikorsky amphibious plane, the craft landing on the water of the harbor near the white-shingled home of the Kennedys. The townspeople stood on the beach observing this unprecedented event.

Rose could have been away this weekend, but that would have only have helped to confirm the rumors. Instead, she treated her husband's mistress as if she were the most desired of guests. The star walked on the beach, though she was not about to risk her ivory complexion by swimming, and made a grand entrance into the dining room of the Craigville beach club. She also found time to visit the clubhouse that Kathleen and her friends had made for themselves over the garage. There on the wall, among movie posters, she wrote her name.

Kathleen and her younger sisters were intrigued by the glamour of Hollywood actresses. They spent hours in their clubhouse, talking about movie stars and movies. Gloria's scrawled signature gave their fantasies a substance. "We had these two fan clubs for two stars," recalled Nancy Tenney Coleman, then Kathleen's closest friend. "None of the Kennedy girls wanted to be in the Gloria Swanson Club. I was the only one. They were all in the Constance Bennett Club. Kathleen never discussed the reason she was so adamant. I didn't know what it was all about until years later." Like their mother, Kathleen, Eunice, Pat, and Jean had learned to turn their faces away from the sordid and unpleasant, to pretend to the world that their mother and father had the most blessed of marriages.

Joe had stuck the image of Gloria in Rose's face so close that she could see the pores on her skin. Rose stared at the image and said that she saw nothing. It was a performance as memorable as any of Gloria's, an exhibition before an audience that largely saw through her artful craft. For Rose, this was a new level of denial. This extraordinary willful act of negation was one that her own daughters observed, and subtly inculcated into their own belief system of how a woman should behave.

Even at the age of nine, Kathleen had known that her father had a friendship intimate enough with Gloria that he was close to her daughter as well. Kathleen loved to write letters, and she wrote to little Gloria. She also wrote her father asking how little Gloria was feeling and would her father kindly obtain an autographed photo of the actress.

A few weeks after Gloria's visit to Hyannis Port, the Kennedys spent several weeks with the actress and her husband in Europe. Rose was Joe's wife, and Gloria was his mistress, but wherever they went in public, she, Rose, was the other woman, cut out of pictures and out of attention.

In front of Rose, Gloria played the loyal wife of the marquis, treating Joe as nothing more than a business partner. Gloria's husband was a kept man, kept by his wife, and kept by Joe Kennedy, his employer, a man with a pride that men like Joe had stepped on and over, because they thought he had none. Gloria remembered Rose that summer as "sweet and motherly in every respect," a woman who "talked endlessly about her children," a woman who acted perfectly unconcerned when Joe acted "in an alarmingly possessive or oversolicitous fashion toward me." Her portrait of Joe was of a man to whom the world and the people around him were little but possessions that he owned or intended to own, including Gloria and Henri. "Joe Kennedy had compromised us both with his promises of enduring security, which Henri wanted at least as much as I did," Gloria reflected later. "But until security came, Henri was in Joe's employ and I was literally owned by him. My whole life was in his hands. . . . In addition I was genuinely fond of him. The man fascinated me. I didn't know what to do."

Rose accompanied Gloria to fittings at Lucien Lelong, the famous couturier. The actress spent a fortune on her clothes, in 1922 alone expending almost $37,000 of her $231,000 salary on apparel and appearance to maintain her image as the regal queen of cinema. In the salon of M. Lelong, Rose received neither the fawning attention given a celebrity, nor the deference merited by a regular customer. The *vendeuses* showered their concern on Gloria, ingratiating themselves with the star. Rose was only an observer. "She was the great celebrity," she recalled. "I, by comparison, was a nobody, just the wife of the producer."

Rose related later that one day on the trip Gloria mistakenly opened a letter addressed to Henri and found a letter from Constance Bennett, suggesting that they were having an affair. There is rarely such anger as that from the pickpocket who has had his pocket picked, and Gloria vowed immediately to divorce Henri. "Joe was dumbfounded and flabbergasted," Rose recalled. "We all sat around and argued the different aspects of the case. Would the picture be better box office if Gloria was in the midst of a sensational divorce, or would it do harm and detract from the picture? Finally Joe said he had put a lot of money into the picture, and he was not going to lose it all for a personal disagreement on the part of the star and her husband. Henri moved to separate quarters in the hotel, but at the opening of the picture Gloria and he were hand in hand, all smiles and to all appearances very happy."

Gloria wrote in her autobiography that several months after her return to New York City she was taken by one of Joe's associates for a meeting with Cardinal O'Connell, who attempted to convince the actress to end her affair with Joe. The cardinal supposedly told her that Joe had talked to some of the highest officials in the church, unsuccessfully seeking a dispensation so that he might leave Rose.

That meeting may have taken place only in the fervid imagination of an aging actress remembering her youth. Her own daughter, Gloria Somborn Daly, confessed that her mother's autobiography is "full of errors and wasn't primarily written by my mother." Yet the cardinal could have taken such an action. If O'Connell did, in fact, meet Gloria, it is likely that Joe's father-in-law was behind it. Fitzgerald was close to the cardinal, and to protect his Rose against her husband who dared stand against him, he would willingly have called upon the power and majesty of a prince of the church. Shortly after the supposed meeting, Hedda Hopper, the Hollywood gossip columnist, wrote an item in her column suggesting that a former mayor of Boston had taken certain measures to end his son-in-law's philandering.

Joe did not suddenly stop seeing Gloria, but he was suffering from the anxiety of the affair. His epic film *Queen Kelly* had turned into a debacle, one of the great disasters in Hollywood history, and his relationship with Gloria was heading in the same direction. Although he was a healthy man, he was losing a great deal of weight, as much as thirty pounds. He also developed an ulcer that became troublesome enough for him to have checked into Boston's Lahey clinic convinced that he had cancer.

Rose had developed her own techniques for dealing with her husband. One day she was walking along the beach in Hyannis Port with a neighbor, Alice Harrington. The woman asked Rose when a wife should act "icily" toward her husband. At first, Rose didn't quite understand. "Well, you know everybody does it in marriage," Harrington asserted. "Haven't you shown iciness toward your husband?"

Rose thought a moment. "Yes, I have," she said. "And I made him pay for that iciness. I made him give me everything I wanted. Clothes, jewels, everything. You have to know how to use that iciness."

Rose knew that in Hollywood Joe was "surrounded daily by some of the most beautiful women in the world, dressed in beautiful clothes." She would be forty years old on her next birthday, and she could hardly compete with such women. She vowed to maintain her petite figure, to watch over her complexion, and to wear stylish clothes. In the next seven years, Rose returned to Paris seventeen times almost always by herself making the rounds of the great salons.

Joe had had enough of Hollywood. He sold his film interest to R.K.O., for an estimated five-million-dollar profit. Rose believed that Joe took something from Hollywood more important than mere money. "My husband said, 'I don't care what they [my sons] think about me. I will get along all right, if they stick together,' " Rose reflected. "He sort of planted that idea and when they went into politics they thought they should stick together. I always thought that he got the idea from the Jews in Hollywood because at the time he was the only Christian in the motion picture business. And I believe in the Jews there is a close family relationship."

Gloria discovered that she had ended up with little but debts from her time with Joe. In her contract with Joe for *Queen Kelly*, he shared in any profits with her fifty-fifty, but she had the honor of paying any debts all by herself. Even a fur coat he had given her had been charged to her account now that their affair was over.

This was Gloria's bittersweet tale. It would not do to admit that her affair with this man who had so mauled her financially would continue for at least half a dozen more years. As Rose herself later admitted, Gloria and her daughter came to visit them in the mid-1930s, half a decade after Gloria said their relationship ended. Then Pat took Gloria's namesake with her to school and introduced the movie star's daughter. "Nobody believed her," Rose recalled. "They all just grinned, thinking it was a joke."

Over the next five years, Gloria made periodic visits to Joe's homes. During the summer those in the quiet, watchful community of Hyannis Port several times observed Gloria arriving in Joe's Rolls-Royce shortly after Rose left town, the two women's passages so closely timed that they might even have passed on the road. "Soon after Mrs. Kennedy left for Europe, always so beautifully dressed, then sooner or later Gloria Swanson would swing by," recalled Nancy Tenney Coleman. "We didn't think of it as anything other than exciting, the big red Rolls and two dogs and the chauffeur jumping out."

In Bronxville the twenties had been, in the words of a local historian, "a gay and wicked period in which husbands and wives lightly exchanged partners, 'companionate' marriage was fiercely advocated by young people and embraced by a few." Discretion, however, was the eleventh commandment, the one commandment that was never broken. Joe was different. Another man would have kept his mistresses in New York, but not Joe. He flaunted himself and his women in front of the townspeople, and many residents developed a contempt for Joe and his life.

The parents' views of Joseph P. Kennedy filtered down to their children. "The story around school was that the old man would go away on a trip with another gal once he had gotten his wife pregnant," recalled Alan Gage, who was in Jack's class. "Whether that was truth or fiction I don't know, but that was the word around the school."

"When Joe Kennedy used to have his women come into town, he would keep them at the Gramatan Hotel," said Paul Morgan, whose family lived next door to the Kennedys. "Gloria Swanson was there, of course, but there were other women as well. In fact, I recall Greta Garbo being there. In any case, Mrs. Kennedy knew what was going on. There was no doubt of that. My friend Jack Slattery had a car, and when the old man went to drive down to the Gramatan Hotel to see his women, we used to hop in the car and go chasing after him."

Kathleen's and Eunice's friends knew about Joe and his women too. They, however, would never have thought of piling into a car and following him down Pondfield Road to his latest assignation. "Of course, all of us kids growing up were very well aware of the father and all of his activities with women, with Gloria Swanson and all the others," said Jane Cash, Kathleen's friend in Bronxville.

"Gloria Swanson was over at the Kennedys' house quite often," recalled Angullo. "He blatantly and publicly welcomed his mistress into his home. I remember that she was there because we used to take dancing lessons and frequently I was the dance partner of his daughter. But Gloria was very much around the Bronxville house."

Rose became the preferred subject of gossip, tittering asides about poor Rose and her randy unreliable husband. Mr. Ryan, a local plumber, told a story that was soon passed from ear to ear until all Bronxville buzzed with the delicious tale. The plumber had supposedly been called to the Kennedy home by Rose, who made the most unusual request: to place a screen far down in the toilet bowl where it could not be seen. The next day Rose called the plumber back to the estate. When he arrived, she asked the man to retrieve a diamond ring from deep within the innards of the toilet and to remove the screen. Joe had been off on one of his romantic sojourns with Gloria, and when he returned home he had performed his act of penance by presenting Rose with a diamond ring. When Joe handed Rose the gift, she threw the present into the toilet, and then flushed it away, to all appearances bidding the ring an eternal farewell. The story may have been apocryphal, but it was told and retold behind Rose's back.

The women of Bronxville had no use for Joseph P. Kennedy, and Rose was the victim, not her husband. Their favorite venue for rumor mongering, as well as more elevated cultural pursuits, was the Bronxville Women's Club. Almost every woman of good station belonged. The Bronxville Women's Club could have provided an interlude of cultural and civic activities that would have immeasurably enriched Rose's daily life. Rose, however, was not invited to join. "I remember my mother telling me how awful she thought it was that these women wouldn't invite Mrs. Kennedy to join in their activities," said Angullo. "But they wanted nothing to do with her. The Kennedys were treated just awfully by the town's socially prominent people. It was her husband. He was just so blatant about his affairs. Rose Kennedy was judged and condemned by the people in town because of her husband."

Joe knew that he had paid a high price for the involvement with Gloria. In July 1939, after the relationship had ended, Joe attended the fortieth birthday of one of his closest aides, Harvey Klemmer. Joe took the younger man aside and gave him a serious warning.

"Forty is a dangerous age," Joe declared, looking intently at Klemmer. "Look out boy. Don't get in trouble. When I was forty I went overboard for a certain lady in Hollywood of which you may have heard."

Joe stopped, smiled a moment, and turned back to Klemmer. "It ruined my business. It ruined my health, and it damn near ruined my marriage."

In the early months that the Kennedys lived in Bronxville, the great bull market of the twenties slowly began to expire. The stockbrokers, advertising men, and executives of Bronxville paid their chauffeurs and their nannies and their butlers on the profits of the market, and they were sure that the market would right itself and go roaring off into the thirties. Joe was one of the few to smell death in the air, and he had gotten out in time. In the weeks that followed Black Tuesday, he sat at a desk at Halle & Steiglitz and calmly figured out which stocks to sell, which stocks to short, which stocks to buy.

As the Depression descended upon America it reached even into Bronxville. At the railroad station every week there were fewer and fewer chauffeurs, and in the village FOR RENT signs started popping up where once there had been expensive dress stores and tailors. Many houses were empty, and others were dark because their inhabitants couldn't pay the electric bills. People who had once had it all, or seemed to, simply disap-

peared, off to eke out their days in summer cottages, off somewhere where no one would see or know.

For Joe Kennedy, though, these were banquet years. In 1933
he purchased a second vacation home in Palm Beach—a classic South Florida Mizner house, a sparkling white, walled
Spanish-like villa, with a red tile roof, tennis courts, a large
pool, and a stretch of private beach. With both a summer home
and a winter vacation home, the Kennedys didn't need to be
entertained by the people of Bronxville.

To several of the neighborhood children, Rose was not just
another mother, one of those wealthy matrons who performed
the rituals of motherhood as if by rote. "She was just terrific,"
recalled Angullo, "very likeable, very feminine, very pretty,
and that was what I thought at the time."

Paul Morgan echoed the same view. "She was quite a
woman," he said. "She really was the one who held the family
together."

On February 22, 1932, the year after Joe ended his business in
Hollywood, Rose gave birth to their ninth child. Rose knew
that Edward "Ted" Moore Kennedy would be her last baby,
and he was very special to his parents, a plump adorable tyke
spoiled by his sisters, especially by four-year-old Jean.

"My earliest memories of my mother are in Bronxville,"
Ted said. "I can remember one day walking home from school.
I think it was prekindergarten. And everybody was looking for
me because it was just after the Lindbergh kidnapping. But the
point that I remember most is that every single night just before going to sleep, I'd go up to her room and she would read
the syndicated Peter Rabbit story of the day and sort of act out
the little characters and the voice. And then we'd say prayers,
and I'd go back to bed."

Rose cared profoundly for her children, but the neighborhood children sensed that Rose kept a psychic and emotional
distance from them. Only Rosemary did she embrace, only
Rosemary did she reach out and hold and try to shelter from
the fierce winds of life. "She wasn't a bring-them-to-the-
bosom kind of mother," said Morgan. "There was a reserve between Mrs. Kennedy and her children, except for the case of
Rosemary, who received most of her affection."

Every day Rose took Rosemary for a long walk down tree-
lined Pondfield Road. The Morgans had two enormous great
danes that bounded out at the first glimpse of Rosemary. Rose

stood there and waited while her eldest daughter played with the dogs, talking to them and petting them.

The neighborhood children who roamed the estate with the young Kennedys admired Rose, but as much as they esteemed her they felt sorry for her. They were a bright, precocious lot and they knew about Joe and his other lives. "When it came to her husband," reflected Angullo, "I think she must have had a salted heart."

For their twentieth wedding anniversary, Joe gave Rose a gift of a European vacation. It was a thoughtful tribute to his wife of two decades, though it was missing one item usually considered indispensable at a wedding anniversary: the husband. Rose had a public face that she wore even to greet her husband, and she allowed herself no bitterness that again she was alone. Joe had his excuses. On that special day Rose cabled her husband in Bronxville from her room by herself at the Ritz Hotel in Paris: "THANK YOU. TWENTY YEARS. RARE HAPPINESS. ALL MY LOVE ALWAYS. ROSA."

When Joe was home, Rose usually made sure that her father wasn't around. Joe couldn't stand Fitzgerald's endless tales, the thickly sliced blarney, the Irish hokum. When Joe showed up, the old man sidled away, taking his tales with him. Kathleen and her sisters enjoyed Honey Fitz but it was Joe Jr. and Jack on whom the old man lavished his stories and attention. To the youths the anecdotes were a song of life, sentimental and funny, full of wonderful characters and all the pratfalls of politics, attracting the youths to politics as an arena of human personality. Their grandfather *was* politics, this glorious circus of life, all these outsized personalities, tales of betrayal, corruption, and shenanigans that in the masterful hands of Fitzgerald were nothing but wondrous private anecdotes.

Fitzgerald had another sort of lesson to teach his grandchildren, and that was about women. Age had not dimmed his propensity to admire the female sex. In the early 1930s, when he was in his late sixties, he invited a sixteen-year-old niece for an afternoon at the theater. The convent-educated girl was delighted that her renowned uncle cared so much for her that he would even send a chauffeur-driven Cadillac to pick her up at her home and take her to the Copley Plaza Hotel where he was waiting. At the hotel, Fitzgerald introduced the young woman to his friends and cronies as his niece. "When he did that everybody laughed, and I couldn't understand why," the woman remembered.

The young woman had rarely been to the theater, and she was excited to be sitting there. "Study the plot," Fitzgerald said, as the curtain opened. She attempted to follow her uncle's advice, but it was difficult to concentrate, for he kept putting his hand on her thigh. Afterwards, in the Cadillac, Fitzgerald continued his explorations. "I kicked him in the shins," the woman said, who half a century later remembered the incident with pain and humiliation. "That was the end of it. I learned later that he did it with everyone."

This was precisely the kind of incident that in the hands of the Kennedy males became a picaresque tale of manly roguish adventure. Decades afterwards, when Joe Sr. was in *his* sixties, he chased a young woman in a shed at the Hialeah Race Track in Miami. When Jack heard the story, he roared with laughter and said: "When I'm sixty I hope I'm just like my father."

"The father and grandfather were heroes to young Joe and Jack," said one Kennedy relative. "They bought them beautiful clothes and took them to ball games. They did everything. And they were adored. They were their idols. And it was terrible because they were anything but idols. Think of the wives and everything, how they felt."

Kathleen and her sisters loved their father as profoundly as their brothers did. That they saw him so infrequently only deepened the intensity of their feeling. In talking about their father, the Kennedy girls sounded very much like Rose at the same age, constantly quoting her father. "Pat and Eunice were always saying, 'Dad says this' and 'Dad says that,' " recalled Ann Kelley, a Bronxville neighbor. "But if I hadn't finally met him, I never would have known he existed."

To love their father as unabashedly as they did, they had to deny so much of what he was and did and to ignore the manner in which he treated their mother. Ignore it they did. Deny it they did, though no more than Rose did herself. In Bronxville, they had stood face-to-face with the reality of Joe's affairs, but they did not see it or feel it or smell it. Her daughters learned from their mother's example that a woman did not have to forgive what she did not see.

"If Daddy was running after all these women all the time and doing this and that, we weren't aware of it," Eunice said.

"And we weren't buzzing in the back room saying, 'My God, Daddy is doing this and that.' "

Kathleen was by far the most emotive of the Kennedy girls, a deeply and openly affectionate daughter. As she grew older, it was not simply her father but her mother who was often gone, off to Europe or down in Palm Beach, anywhere but Bronxville. In February 1932, as Kathleen looked forward to her twelfth birthday party, Rose was in Boston giving birth to her youngest brother, Ted, and her father was probably in Palm Beach. "Daddy did not come home last night," she wrote Rose. "We do not know when he is coming." She asked her mother to tell their nanny if Rosemary was coming to her birthday party, and reminded Rose to send games to be played at the party. Kathleen trusted her mother enough to tell Rose of her growing interest in boys. She had her hair waved and attended a party where she had danced with a boy.

"You were in charge of us and raised and trained us while we were children," Eunice told her mother years later. "And, then, when we began turning into young people, Dad took charge the rest of the way." Rose was in charge of manners, character, discipline, and religious values and now Joe took over the intellectual, political, and secular moral development of their children. This division was doubly damaging, for Joe shunted his daughters aside into a narrower world. An acquaintance saw it accurately: "What Joe said, in effect, was: 'I'll send my girls to the Church to believe, my sons to the marketplace to know better.' "

Joe Jr. had left Riverdale Country School to attend The Choate School, where he developed into an outstanding scholar-athlete. Jack attended Catholic Canterbury for a year before, in the fall of 1931, joining his brother at the exclusive prep school in Wallingford, Connecticut.

Joe and Rose both rained down upon the headmaster at Choate a constant barrage of letters, telegrams, and notes, a correspondence unprecedented in the history of the school. At Choate, Joe was concerned primarily with the academic success of his sons, and the further development of their character. Rose's preoccupations were more maternal and modest, primarily their health. Joe Jr. was strong and outgoing and he required little direction to lead him down the road his parents wanted him to go: to Harvard, and to a life of leadership. Since he was a baby, Jack had been sickly, and Rose watched over him with obsessive concern, as if she could will her son to full health. When he was sent to the infirmary early in 1932, as soon as Rose learned about his mysterious lingering cold, she wrote the school that three years previously Jack had had "a condition similar to the one you now describe." A few days later Rose suggested that "you procure from the local druggist a bottle of Kepler's Malt and Cod Liver Oil and give him a teaspoonful after each meal." Time and again Rose wrote. Jack was too thin. He wasn't eating his green vegetables and lettuce. He had a knee problem. In the summer of 1934 Jack was sent to the famous Mayo Clinic in Rochester, Minnesota, for some inconclusive tests, and she had more letters to write.

In all her letters, only one note dealt with the learning that her sons were receiving. Even that was a concern over the teaching of social niceties. "The fact has come to my attention," she wrote Mr. George St. John, the headmaster, "that some of the boys at Choate do not seem to know how to write a letter correctly or how to address it. It seems to me it would be a very practical idea and a very useful one if a short period could be given demonstrating the different forms etc."

Rose rarely, if ever, visited her sons, and not because they cringed at the idea of shepherding their mother around the campus. Indeed, Joe Jr. wrote asking Rose to visit, gently chiding his mother: "I can easily understand how busy you must be buying antiques and clothes." Rose wrote their headmaster regularly; her unwillingness to visit Choate was not in her mind the mark of a negligent mother. She had given the education of her adolescent sons over to Joe. Beyond that, this was the mother who had not turned back to hug her sensitive five-year-old son when he called out to her as she left on a trip. Jack continued to cry out psychologically for a mother's succoring, and Rose was perhaps still concerned that her visit might emotionally weaken her sickly son and make him more vulnerable to what she considered the inevitable assault of a manly life.

Rose had brought up her son and her other children to ignore all but the most serious health conditions. When they were sick they gritted their teeth stoically. "I never even heard that Jack was sick at Choate," Eunice said. "Did he have an ulcer or something? In our family sickness was not a big deal. You just didn't pay attention to it. We have a long tradition of nobody really complaining very much about illness. Usually we passed the information back and forth, somebody's sick, and you'd send them a card, make a phone call or something. Jack had stomachaches a lot. And he'd often get flu. And then he'd come back, so everybody was kind of used to that."

When her daughter graduated from the Riverdale Country School, Rose sent Kathleen to the public schools in Bronxville. Rose herself had had a public school education, but this was no longer the sedate, chaperoned era of her Dorchester childhood. At thirteen years old, Kathleen was sitting in classrooms with boys Rose did not know, boys who were primarily not Catholic, boys who were calling the house. As her eldest sons became teenagers, Rose was perfectly content to have Joe Jr. and Jack off dating girls. It was expected, even desirable, but she had different expectations for her daughters. Rose began to worry and to plan. "Joe and I had agreed that the responsibility for education of the boys was primarily his, and that of the girls, primarily mine," she said. "My conclusions were easier to reach. She was quite pretty and was getting altogether too popular with boys, which she enjoyed. She was on the telephone with them for hours at a time. They distracted Kathleen from her school-work and other duties by boys inviting her to the Saturday-afternoon movies and so forth. My answer to the situation was to send her away to school."

Rose refused to deal with the morally complex world in which Kathleen was growing up, and she forbade her daughter from dealing with it either. Instead, she decided to send Kathleen to the Noroton convent of the Sacred Heart, the most exclusive and most rigid of all the order's American schools. Rose had been educated by the sisters of the Sacred Heart, and as deep and rich as that education had been, it had left her as impaired as the elite women of China walking on bound feet. Rather than her feet, her mind had been bound up to appeal to her husband. And now she attempted to shape her daughter's mind to be a replica of her own.

The first time Kathleen made the journey from Bronxville to the convent in Greenwich, Connecticut, in the fall of 1933, she was traveling not simply through space but through time, back to the era of her mother's youth at Blumenthal. Noroton, like the Dutch convent school, was set off behind walls but was even more isolated, sitting on a tiny peninsula, surrounded on three sides by the waters of Long Island Sound. The imposing ivy-covered sixty-six-thousand-square-foot main house, the ten acres of grounds rich with vibrant foliage, and the massive log

guest house built over the water had once been part of an estate called "Journey's End." The nuns had turned the ballroom
into a chapel, the large high-ceilinged bedrooms into classrooms, sold off the secular paintings and the more ornate furnishings, filled the walls with religious art, each alcove and
niche with statues of Christ and saints. Yet something of that
aura of unbounded wealth hung in the air like a lingering perfume.

Kathleen soon discovered that the sixty girls in the four
classes at the boarding school included the daughters of the
wealthiest and the most publicly devout Irish-American families in America, notably the McDonnells and the Cuddihys
from New York, and the Coakleys from Cleveland. Even the
scholarship students were hardly the worthy poor, but largely
upper-class girls whose families had fallen on hard times during the Depression.

Kathleen adored pretty clothes, and most of the costumes at
Noroton were as appealing as a hair shirt. In the morning she
put on the student uniform, a nondescript brown wool jumper.
For swimming Kathleen donned a heavy woolen bathing suit
that covered her down to her knees, and over that a short skirt.
In the winter when she went tobogganing with her schoolmates, she was forced to wear her gym tunic over her ski
pants. Kathleen thought it absurd that in the name of decency
she was weighted down with layers of clothes. "I had ski pants
on and Mother Fitzgerald wouldn't let me appear without a
coat over the pants," Kathleen wrote her mother, telling of her
role in a school play. "She thinks pants are immodest. Ski
pants, mind you. If she only knew."

Thursday afternoons and Sundays Kathleen and the other
girls dressed in their more appealing wine-red jumpers. Thursday was considered "free" day, but even those hours were full
of a ceaseless stream of activity, in part to forestall the girls
from weaving melancholy daydreams. The students had classes
until ten o'clock in the morning. Then a parade of outsiders descended on the school: the hairdresser, the art teacher, the dic-
tion coach, and the dancing teacher. In the afternoon between
two and five, the students wore their more formal dresses and
high heels, and were served tea, *goûter*, in the cavernous cabin
by the sea. This was the hour when visitors were allowed, and
the Kennedys made frequent appearances. "The whole family
would come, and sometimes they would just send Rosemary,"
remembered Mary Lyon Chatfield-Taylor. "And Kathleen

would ask, 'What is the message you were supposed to bring?' And Rosemary would have a hard time remembering."

Sometimes Kathleen had other guests, including Jack and his closest friend, Kirk LeMoyne "Lem" Billings, a youth of perpetual good humor and playfulness. Lem descended on the sedate precincts of Noroton like a whirlwind, his visits previewed by his weekly letters to Kathleen. "I hope Mother Superior enjoys my letters," he wrote in a typical note, knowing that the all-seeing eyes of the nuns were reading his words before Kathleen saw them. Both Kathleen and Jack had a raucously frivolous side to their personalities. Lem played the court jester always ready to puncture a scene of seriousness with his ready wit. Lem adored Kathleen, and Kathleen adored him in turn, not as a beau, but as a confidant and coconspirator in boisterous good times. Kathleen joshed and kidded with Lem and her other friends, listened to their tales of football games at Harvard, parties, and dances, for a moment sharing vicariously in their times, wishing that she could go and be with them and their world. And then suddenly the visiting hours were over, and Lem and the others trooped dutifully out of the cabin by the sea, and Kathleen remained.

After the guests left it was time for sewing lessons. While the students stitched away, Mother Tack read aloud from *The Scarlet Pimpernel*, her eyes managing the formidable feat of jumping down the page, previewing the words. "Oh, oh, girls you wouldn't believe," Mother Tack said confidentially, her voice dropping to a whisper. She turned the pages until she found a passage that she could safely read and then began reading again. After sewing the girls gathered for the weekly politeness class, sitting at their desks wearing white gloves. On special occasions the students saw Hollywood films that Joe had graciously provided. He was careful in his selections but nonetheless a nun sat next to the film projector, ready at the mere hint of an unseemly scene to put her hand in front of the lens.

"I miss you all like anything in fact worse than I ever have. . . ." Kathleen wrote after returning from her Christmas vacation in Palm Beach. "A week ago today I was basking in the sun and now I am in a fire trap trying to study. It's a great life if you don't weaken."

In her mother's house Kathleen had learned how to obey, and in this intense decorous regimented world, she attempted to fall into step with the other girls. She did her best but Kathleen hated the endless, windswept winters in what she called "the dear old fire-trap." She lived for the vacations. She wasn't feeling that well, either, and when the other students went for a mile-and-a-half walking race, she did not take part for she knew that she "would get out of breath." She was sent into New York City to see a doctor who prescribed a series of injections for her asthma, an ailment that in a milder form plagued her the rest of her life.

Despite their veneer of ruddy good health, the young Kennedys suffered from a myriad of mysterious illnesses and health problems. Of the eldest children, Joe Jr. was the only truly healthy Kennedy. As she grew older, Rosemary's condition was not only more apparent, but she was more easily rendered emotionally distraught. Jack had been patched and poked at by doctors so many times since his birth that it was a wonder he even attempted athletic play. Like Kathleen, Pat had a series of allergies to ragweed, horses, and dust that required her to take injections. Eunice was the most high-strung of them all, nervous and ill-at-ease, plagued by sleeplessness. Her stomach condition was so severe that at the age of twelve she spent a week in a New York hospital. Joe Jr. had visited her there "about four days out of seven," winning a ten-dollar bet when he wagered Eunice that even now in this hospital bed she could not lie quiet for ten minutes.

Kathleen's illness was serious enough that her doctors recommended in the fall of 1934 that she take the winter semester off, spending months in the healing sun of Palm Beach rather than the damp clime of Noroton. Kathleen contemplated leaving the convent. She was having a hard time even sleeping at night. But her father's favorite daughter did what Joe would have expected her to do, to tough it out and not leave Noroton, to exhibit to him and the world what he called "a very fine spirit."

Most of the other students had no idea of Kathleen's condition. "Wherever Kathleen went, sunshine followed," recalled one of her schoolmates, now a nun. She was full of infectious joy. The other girls vied to be her friend, though the order had the same rigid proscription against "particular friendship" as when Rose had gone to school.

Kathleen was a decent athlete, but she was too full of fun, too apt to laugh and joke, too likely to go tearing off and begin "doing something crazy" to be the captain of the Noroton field hockey team. Out on the point where the sound of the crashing surf was a perpetual melody, four big trees stood in the midst of the playing field. When Noroton took on other convent schools, the trees were like four extra Noroton players, and Kathleen ducked adeptly behind the massive trunks, losing her opponent.

"Our wickedness was so innocent," recalled Elizabeth Rivinus Augenblick of events over half a century ago. "We'd walk down the big beautiful staircase with vigil lamps on the side, and we would take the warm wax and have a chew."

The nuns censored the girls' letters, excising candid perceptions of themselves and the convent as well as comments about other students. The nuns purged the improper and the vulgar from any correspondence, returning one letter because the writer had been so unladylike as to use the word "swell." It was all done in the name of high morals and ladylike good taste, but Kathleen and the other students learned a subtle self-censorship, sometimes developing into women of such discretion that they could not tell the difference between reticence and deception. Kathleen was already covering up for her father and his philandering, pretending to the world that her parents had the ideal Catholic marriage, and Noroton was merely further training in lessons that had begun at home.

Kathleen learned to practice the same moral duality as her mother, always keeping appearances proper. She wrote her parents regularly, occasionally bypassing the nuns' censorship by mailing a letter directly. She was full of love for her family, but her love for her mother was like Rose's love for her, proper and civil. Her love for Joe was more intimate, openly and deeply felt. From her earliest letters to her parents when she was no more than seven years old, she had addressed Rose as "Mother" but Joe with the more familiar "Dad." It would always be "Mother" or "Dearest Mother," but Joe was soon "Daddy" and at Noroton he was "Dearest, Darlingest Daddy" and "Daddy dearest."

Beyond the salutation, Kathleen rarely could tell Joe how she *felt*. Kathleen, like her father, was full of deep emotions that in the psychological matrix of the family found no outlet. She adored Jack, loved him beyond love, but it was something that she could only tell him by humorously deriding him, by jokes and endless tomfoolery. Only to her father could she admit how much she admired Jack. "She really thinks you are a great fellow," Joe wrote Jack at Choate in February 1935. "She has a love and devotion to you that you should be very proud to have deserved. It probably does not become apparent to you, but it does to both Mother and me. She thinks you are quite the grandest fellow that ever lived and your letters furnish her most of her laughs in the Convent."

After Christmas vacation, Kathleen spent a few hours with Jack and Lem. They had lunch together and then went up to Farmington, the exclusive girls' school, for a visit. The girls could have "callers" on Saturday, proper young men from Harvard, Princeton, or Yale like Jack and Lem. That was the kind of school that Kathleen might have attended if her mother had not insisted on a religious education. Then in the evening, she had to return to her place behind the high walls of Noroton.

"Here I am back in this_____I had better not say," she wrote Rose. "Its [sic] lovely here now but its [sic] awful to be back."

In their way, the Sacred Heart nuns had a deep understanding of their charges. The nuns did not traffic in the new interest in Freudianism with its emphasis on the sexual being. Janet Erskine Stuart, the sixth Mother General of the Society, and one of the order's deepest thinkers, went unapologetically back to the Middle Ages and the long-discarded concept of body humors (phlegmatic, sanguine, choleric, melancholic). In a subtle, sophisticated, and deeply perceptive analysis, Mother Stuart divided girls into four types of personalities, the clay with which the Sacred Heart had to work.

Kathleen's large, ebullient personality fit Mother Stuart's model of the softly sanguine personality, "the richest group in attractive power . . . there is a fund of energy which, allied with the power of charm and persuasion, with trustfulness in good, and optimistic outlook on the world, wins its way and succeeds in its undertakings, making its appeal to the will rather than to the mind."

Eunice arrived at Noroton in Kathleen's footsteps, a perfect example of another of Stuart's types: "There is the unquiet group of nervous or melancholic temperaments, their melancholy not weighed down by listless sadness . . . but more actively dissatisfied with things as they are—untiringly but unhopefully at work—hard on themselves, anxious-minded, assured that in spite of their efforts all will turn out for the worst, often scrupulous, capable of long-sustained efforts, often of heroic devotedness and superhuman endurance, for which their reward is not in this world, as the art of pleasing is singularly deficient in them. Here are found the people who are 'so good, but so trying,' ever in a fume and fuss, who, for sheer goodness, rouse in others the spirit of contradiction."

Eunice was a much better candidate for life at Noroton than Kathleen. Although Kathleen was an excellent student, Eunice was the most intelligent of the Kennedy daughters, a deeply religious adolescent who easily identified with the nuns of the Sacred Heart and had the spirit and the faith that could have made her a Sacred Heart nun.

There was an aura of romantic self-sacrifice about the women the students called "Mother." The nuns were well educated and carefully selected, including daughters of some of the most privileged Catholic families in America. Before they had entered the order many of them had had legions of beaux, and large trust funds, and had left distraught suitors behind, or so the students whispered. They had given it up to live a cloistered life, their hair shorn, wearing one of two black handmade habits, fluted white bonnets, a gold double wedding band on their right hands, ornate silver crosses around their necks.

Within many of these women faith burned brilliantly, and in the intense, rarefied atmosphere of Noroton, many students vowed that they too would become nuns of the Sacred Heart. That rarely happened, and if it had in large numbers the upper-class Catholic families would have stopped sending their daughters to the school.

Eunice learned many lessons from the nuns of the Sacred Heart, some of which were not part of the stated doctrine. The nuns were charged to create a woman whose "special influence depends upon her distinctively feminine qualities: tact, quiet courage, and the willingness to subordinate her will to another's gracefully and even gaily." The nuns were projecting a different lesson as well. They were powerful women running a formidable institution. "As I knew it, the Sacred Heart was really a feminist institution as well as one of the most conservative institutions in the United States," stated Suzannah Lessard, a Noroton graduate and writer. "Except for the gardener, you were in a female world, and the priest who came in to say daily mass was more or less like the gardener. You weren't that conscious of the Catholic male hierarchy of Rome and the pope. And you did not feel like a second-class citizen because you were a woman. It's hard to see through the curtsying and all, but these nuns are incredibly arrogant women, and in their femaleness they really felt very well of themselves. The Sacred Heart taught me that I was going to be very powerful, that I was a soldier. Noroton's motto was noblesse oblige. It was on our rings, a part of our school song, on our martyr's picture. They were very serious about it."

Eunice studied much the same curriculum that Rose had studied, and spoke French during meals as well. Within this narrow curriculum, the students learned to write clearly and to think abstractly. Eunice developed a fearless intellect. Except for questions of faith, there were few questions she would not ask, few places she would not go in search of answers.

At Noroton as at the other convent schools of the Sacred Heart, the order still had two classes of nuns, the "mothers" who did the teaching, and the uneducated "sisters" who performed manual work, cooking and cleaning. Eunice was used to servants picking up after her, and it was only natural that the nuns of the Sacred Heart had their servants too. Eunice learned that the business of goodness was a rarefied one in which the mundane chores of living were relegated to a silent legion of drones.

Eunice and her sisters did not consider Joe Jr. and Jack simply older brothers, distant siblings who descended on their lives, disrupting their routine. For the girls, they were archeypes of what men should be, and how life should be lived. "To us they were heroes, young gods," said Pat.

Jack and Joe Jr. were even more godlike to Rosemary, who caught only glimpses of them far beyond her world. As she grew into a teenager, her distance from her brothers and sisters was greater still, but she tried to be one with them. She had a fresh, freckled face, and a seemingly uncomplicated openness.

Rose's other children were all good athletes, and she left them to their coaches, their friends, and their family competitions. Only with Rosemary did she play, spending hours on the court, methodically hitting the ball back and forth to her. She helped Rosemary to write better, to spell, and to count. This was her Rosemary, her daughter, and she never seemed to grow short of temper with her. She hired a procession of teachers and special counselors.

Rose sent Rosemary off to Elmhurst, the Sacred Heart Convent at Providence, Rhode Island. The convent had no program for the retarded, but the Kennedys were generous to the church, and fifteen-year-old Rosemary was taken apart from the others, and set down before two nuns and another special teacher, Miss Newton, who worked with her all day long. Rosemary wore the same uniform as the other girls, but she studied in a separate classroom, a solitary student. By any definition, it was an extraordinary effort, and the Kennedys gave the school a new tennis court.

In her studies Rosemary had reached an impregnable barrier. She read, wrote, spelled, and counted like a fourth-grade student. At times, Joe sounded almost as frustrated with his eldest daughter as she was with herself. "I had a firm talk with Rosemary," he wrote Miss Newton, her special teacher, "and told her that something must be done and I am sure she really wants to do it. It is something else besides herself that must be blamed for her attitude. By that I mean, it is her inherent backwardness, rather than a bad disposition."

Joe knew Rosemary's condition. Yet he had admonished his daughter to be and do something that he knew she could not be and do. He had taken the daughter to whom he was the sun and the moon and the light, and used that love like a bludgeon. Rosemary wanted so to please her mother, and her father even more. Joe was the world to her, the world to which she aspired, the world she so much wanted to please. "I would do anything to make you happy," she wrote her father after he visited her at the convent. "I hate to disapoint [sic] you in anyway. Come to see me very soon. I get lonesome everyday." She studied and studied, but the mathematical tables, the vocabulary words, the historical dates rolled off her mind like raindrops on a windowpane. As her Latin exam approached, she wrote her parents: "Pray very hard that I will get someplace, I tried as hard as I could."

During that year Rosemary looked forward anxiously to the tea-dance to be held on a Friday afternoon in January. She was fifteen years old, and she knew nothing about young men, nothing about the life that her popular sister Kathleen was leading.

Rose wanted her daughter to be like all the other girls at the convent. She wanted to protect her. The older Rosemary grew, the more difficult and challenging that task became. Rose took what for her was an extraordinary step. She wrote a letter to George St. John, the headmaster at Choate, to ask that Jack be given permission to leave school to travel to Rhode Island to attend the dance with his sister. Rose would not reveal Rosemary's condition to the headmaster nor to anyone else outside the family. "The reason I am making this seemingly absurd request is because the young lady who is inviting him is his sister, and she has an inferiority complex," she wrote. "I know it would help her if he went with her." By now the headmaster was used to receiving frequent missives from Rose and Joe. He could always tell Rose's letters in that she printed out the words, letter by letter. Most upper-class women sent handwritten notes. What the headmaster did not know was that as a young woman Rose had beautiful handwriting, her letters and words elegantly sculptured. Since Rosemary could not make out her mother's handwriting, printing was the only way Rose could communicate with her eldest daughter in a letter, and what had begun only for Rosemary had become a general habit.

Jack was at the age of self-consciousness when most adolescents would have cringed at the idea of escorting their sister to a dance, especially a sister whom the world labeled as "different." Jack went to the dance that day with Rosemary, as he and his brother went with her to other dances on Cape Cod and elsewhere. She was *their* sister, a member of *their* family, and they danced with her, waltzed her around the ballrooms, brought her punch, stood with her and shared a quiet laugh, stayed with her so that she appeared not different at all.

9

A Nation of Kennedys

"Years ago, we decided that our kids were going to be our best friends and that we never could see too much of them," Rose said in 1939. "Since we couldn't do both, it was better to bring up our family than to go out to dinners. My husband's business often took him away from home and when all of us had time to be together we didn't want to share it with outsiders. As a result the Kennedy children became natives of the Kennedy family, first and foremost, before any city or any country."

This nation of Kennedys to which the children owed allegiance beyond city or state was largely formed in Hyannis Port. Here, as at no other time during the year, the family was one. Jack called his mother "the glue that held the family together." She fused together the foundation stones of her children's lives. She cemented together the bonds of family and belief. Now that the two oldest boys, Joe Jr. and Jack, were teenagers, Joe took over his children's lives with a deep sense of concern. Rose considered her husband "the architect of our lives" and it was here on this sandy soil, in this air pungent with the scent of seaweed, that most of the building of the young Kennedy lives took place.

The Kennedy daughters peered up at their father, who sat on a deck outside his second-story bedroom, an area known as the "bullpen." He had one of the largest long-distance telephone bills in America, and all day long he talked to brokers, politicians, business people, cronies, and others. As he sat, the phone receiver propped on his neck, he watched his children on the beach, out in their sailboats, or on the tennis courts, and even what he could not see he somehow sensed. "He ruled the roost," said Mary Francis "Sancy" Falvey Newman, whose family was one of only two other Catholic families in the village. "And, oh God, did they love him. But they were scared to death of him too. The girls would say, 'Have you called Daddy today?' 'Did you talk to Daddy?' 'Did you do what he told you to do or not?' It was unbelievable. You just don't hear of people like that anymore—or even then."

"Joe knew what he wanted," said the late Thomas "Tommy the Cork" Corcoran, the New Dealer and lobbyist. "He wanted status and money for his children. To Joe his children were an extension of himself, and if you have this progenitor's sense, you play the game differently than if you want only for yourself. You have to look at the sheer animal vitality of the man, this piece of energy adapting itself to its time. He was a man not afraid to think in a daring way. He had imperial instincts. Mrs. Kennedy had them too. She had to have them to put up with what she put up with."

Joe was not a shouter, and almost never did a curse or profanity cross his lips when he was at home. In the evenings when he had gone to bed, if the children's noises were drifting up to his bedroom, he pounded his shoe once on the floor. One single thud. That was enough to quiet the children, the older ones hushing the others into frightened silence. During the day sitting high on his vantage point, he exuded authority over the world below. "We don't want any losers around here," he told his children. "In this family we want winners."

"He always trusted experience as the greatest creator of character," Eunice reflected, as contrasted with her mother who "believed religion was." Hyannis Port was a school for experience that was like endless Outward Bound training. Joe saw these games and sports of summer as metaphors for the life his children would lead. He urged them on with a psychic lash that propelled them forward as no sting of hand or word could have ever exhorted them. "Don't come in second or third," he admonished his children. "That doesn't count—but win."

Joe hired "skippers" to oversee his boats and provide sailing lessons, athletes to teach tennis and swimming. Every summer the children took two swimming classes a week, serious training for swim meets. "I remember racing fourteen times a week when I was twelve-years-old!" Eunice recalled. "We did well—but I hesitate to think about the consequences if we had lost them all!"

The young Kennedys hit tennis balls for hours, swam lap after lap, sailed in weather fair or foul. Then they ventured out to test their mettle in swim meets and sailing competitions, sweeping away medals and trophies. The rest of Hyannis Port was merely an audience for the Kennedys, a foil, fodder for them, provider of applause, trophies, and ribbons. These were, indeed, not games at all, for Joe had as clear an idea about the development of his teenaged sons as Rose had had for their earlier years. As he looked out on the sun-dappled grounds of his summer estate, Joe had a dream for one of his sons of such grandeur that it was only to be whispered. His assistant, Eddie Moore, a man of such loyalty that Joe named his last son after Moore, was one of the few who had heard these dreams. That year of 1932 Moore was on a boat with several men whom he trusted. "If we live long enough and he is spared, the first Irish Catholic in the White House will be one of this man's sons," Moore told the others. The men laughed and forgave the Irishman his reveries.

Hyannis Port was a boy's world where the Kennedy sons were always the quarterbacks, always first on the tennis court, and Kathleen and her younger sisters watched and waited their turns. "The older boys would always play with us," Pat recalled. "The boys were terrific. They taught us sailing and tennis and nurtured a terrific interest in sports."

Joe Jr. was a fearless youth, almost six feet tall, weighing 175 pounds, with the best features of both his parents. He was his father's son, a virtual Platonic ideal of what Joe thought a young man should be. He wasn't cracking books at Harvard any more than his father had. He was a football player too, and when he didn't win his letter, his father blamed the coach. If he was quick in temper and took pleasure in pummeling his young brother Jack into the ground, he was quick to defend his family and his friends, a young man to whom the world beckoned with infinite promise.

Jean was too young to take part in the sailing and swimming races, but she identified completely with her older brothers, especially Joe Jr. He was her godfather, an unusual role for an elder sibling, one that created a special bond between the little girl and her big brother. He was forever teasing her especially about getting fat, but then he would call her "Jeanah Darlin' " and all would be right.

At the dinner table that same relentless preparation for life continued as on the athletic fields. Rose set up a bulletin board to which she tacked clippings from newspapers and magazines

that her daughters and sons were supposed to read, in readiness
for mealtime discussions. "Rose was like a Hollywood mother,
terribly pushy, always pushing her children to succeed," said
Harry Fowler, who as a youngster spent many days at the
Hyannis Port home. "Rose didn't have the normal emotions
that most people have. I never saw her exhibit any emotion, including anger. I never saw her once pat a child's head or put
her arm around a daughter. She was concentrating on the children. She was pressing them to make good. Even at the meal
Rose was sitting there trying to give history lessons. She had
questions written out. I mean she wasn't going to let you sit
there and talk about what you were doing or talk about racing.
It was all my mother could do to get me to finish half of my
required reading for the summer, and here Rose was giving us
instruction in history. I thought to myself, 'My lord, this is a
nice summer afternoon, what in the hell is she doing anyway?' "

Rose prodded her children but she did not provide a secular
moral framework for their lives large enough and strong
enough to take out into the world. That was left for Joe. Their
father was the world. Their father smelled of the world, of its
accomplishments and fascinations, and about the world he was
his children's teacher. When Joe was at the head of the table,
he totally dominated the conversation. He asked more intellectual questions than Rose, penetrating queries that depended not
on a yes or no answer. He had taught his children not to be
afraid to pronounce their own judgments, as long as they could
defend themselves.

Joe's greatest gift to his children, beyond even his immense
wealth, was the sense of empowerment that he gave primarily
to his sons. They were not simply passive observers of the
world around them, but participants knowing that one day they
would stamp their own mark on the events of the day. Joe Jr.
and Jack read newspapers not only as public documents but as
a series of problems and situations over which they might one
day have an impact. Of the Kennedy daughters, only Eunice
shared this sense of herself as an active player in the world beyond her family.

With her fierce questioning intelligence, Eunice was precociously adept at her father's dinnertime queries. "Father wasn't
awfully interested if you didn't know what you were talking
about or if you said something kind of stupid," Eunice said. "It

was up to you to find out before you went in and started talking."

During the summers in Hyannis Port, the Kennedy daughters had playmates who enjoyed talking about movie stars or boys, and in the evening perhaps watching a romantic Hollywood movie, all worlds where females acted with gentility and grace, and never with that unseemly cutthroat competitiveness of a man's world. The Kennedy daughters were different, but it was only on the field of athletics where they could allow their own ambitions full play. In the sailing races on the Cape, the Kennedy girls gave their challengers no more quarter than their brothers did, and took away award after award, trophy after trophy, even more than their brothers. Out on these waters, beyond sight of society and its restraints, they were as fiercely driven to win as their male siblings. Of all the daughters, none of them sailed with the fierce intensity of Eunice, with wild daring recklessness, shooting ahead at the starting flag, rashly turning at the windward buoy, carrying full sails when the less daring reefed, and with her brother Joe Jr. the last to seek the shelter of the harbor in a summer's squall.

At the end of the 1934 season at the Hyannis Port Yacht Club, three Kennedys won trophies, two of them girls, fourteen-year-old Kathleen and thirteen-year-old Eunice, and Joe Jr. as well. The next year the young Kennedys led by Eunice, Kathleen, and Pat, who was sailing in races for the first time, plus Rosemary, Jack, and Joe Jr. came away with fourteen first prizes, thirteen seconds, and thirteen thirds in seventy-six starts.

When they descended on the yacht club, the Kennedys seemed a race apart. They traveled in a pack, enough of them to need no others. When Jimmie MacClean, their summer skipper, drove the youngsters down to Hyannis, they were often barefoot wearing threadbare shorts, looking like a race of beggars. They usually carried no money and they trooped into Megathlin's Drug Store en masse, putting ice cream cones on the family expense account. On these sojourns to Hyannis, the townspeople noticed that the young Kennedys had a peculiar, almost belligerent attitude toward the rest of the world. One summer day a Kennedy girl had a family dog, a fox terrier, in her arms as they all marched into Megathlin's. The drugstore had a long soda fountain replete with wire chairs, shelves carrying such essentials as Bude's Pepto Magnan and Wyeth's

Sulphur, and a cat that had the run of the store. As soon as the
Kennedy dog spied the cat, the terrier leapt out of the girl's
arms and charged after his victim. "There wasn't any real damage
done, but the whole window display was wrecked,"
Megathlin recalled. "The Kennedy kids—being kids—got a
big laugh out of it." In most families the children would have
been filled with unholy dread as to what their parents might
think, but the young Kennedys knew everything would be
taken care of, and the incident would give their father a good
laugh.

One afternoon as Eunice set out on the *Tenovus* in stormy
waters, she decided she had better leave her wristwatch ashore,
handing it to Jimmie, who put it on his wrist for safekeeping.
Almost immediately, the Kennedys' terrier and another dog
started a fierce brawl on the pier. The skipper grabbed up both
dogs with the idea of throwing them into the water. As he
started to give them the heave-ho, Jack gave Jimmie a shove,
sending the skipper, the two dogs, and Eunice's precious wristwatch
into the drink. Standing above the bedraggled skipper,
Jack said he was only "trying to help." And everyone laughed,
for it had only been the skipper, only a watch, and was yet another
summer anecdote.

July and August in Hyannis Port were days of comradeship
and good times. For the final race of the summer the entire
family trooped over to the Wianno Yacht Club, and each of the
children, except for Rosemary, sailed in a race for his or her
age and class. Eunice was the best sailor among the girls, but
they all were good, every one of them. They raced as if their
lives depended on it, and for seven years in a row the Kennedys
took away more prizes than anyone else, carrying away a
bounty of loving cups, silver trays, bound books, clocks, and
desk sets as they left the port at the end of the summer.

Over the dinner table at Hyannis Port, the family frequently
discussed President Franklin D. Roosevelt and the New Deal.
Joe was one of a relatively few wealthy men in America who
actively supported FDR. In his own way, Joe was as deeply
conservative as the portly gentlemen in *The New Yorker* cartoons
sitting in their club libraries, smoking cigars, berating
Roosevelt as a traitor to his class. Joe had seen the ravages of
the Depression, and, unlike the burghers of Bronxville and
Palm Beach, realized that the very future of the society that
had so richly benefited him was at stake. In these desperate

times Joe was willing to give up half his wealth if he could save the other half, save it not only for himself but for his children. "I'm as much concerned to hold on to what I've got and to protect my nine children as anyone could be," Joe said. "I'm interested in establishing a system that will make my family secure." He understood that Roosevelt was a reformer not a revolutionary, not the scourge of his class, but perhaps its savior. Joe had worked for FDR in the election, made major financial contributions and employed skillful flattery, all with the idea of obtaining a major position in the administration, to be a player himself in the great drama that was Roosevelt's Washington.

Although Joe was disappointed at not being initially named to a position, in July of 1934 he was a candidate to be named chairman of the new Securities and Exchange Commission, pledging to rid Wall Street of the very excesses that his whole life and fortune exemplified. "I can well remember Joe saying goodbye in the morning on his way to Washington," Rose recalled. "His last words were, 'I shall probably be back tonight, for I shall not stay unless I get the chairmanship.'" Joe received the appointment, headed down to Washington, and leased a twenty-five-room estate outside the city in Potomac, Maryland, for himself and his cronies. During the day he worked diligently at his new task. In the evenings there on the Potomac River west of Washington, Joe gave some of the most memorable parties of the New Deal years. One of his guests, Senator Harry Truman of Missouri, was in positive awe. "It is the finest home I've ever seen," Truman wrote his wife, Bess, "a grand big house a half mile from the road in virgin forest with a Brussels carpet lawn of five acres all around it, a swimming pool in the yard, and . . . a motion picture theater in the sub-basement."

Rose was left behind in a conservative Republican Bronxville and a conservative Republican Hyannis Port that had found yet another reason to dislike Joe. Rose not only accepted her husband's absence, she lauded his attainments and basked in the glow of his celebrity. He continued to dominate her life as he dominated the lives of his daughters and sons, by the sheer titanic force of his personality.

Despite all her husband's affairs, Rose maintained a bedrock of concern for her husband. "I think of you often—my darling—and I love you more every minute," she wrote Joe from the *Bremen* on one of her innumerable trips to Europe.

"Be sure to take good care of yourself. I only wish you could get away soon too."

In September of 1935 Rose and Joe sailed to Europe on the *Ile de France* with eighteen-year-old Jack and fifteen-year-old Kathleen. Jack was to follow the lead of his older brother who in 1933–34 had spent the academic year studying at the London School of Economics under the tutelage of the renowned Professor Harold Laski before he entered Harvard. Now it was Jack's turn. As for Kathleen, she was to emulate her mother's education even further, spending her year at a Sacred Heart convent school in northeastern France.

As soon as she arrived at the remote, austere convent of St. Maux, Kathleen realized that she could not tolerate a year there. She had complained to Rose about Noroton, but those grievances were aimed at letting her mother know what she was going through with little hope of changing schools. This time Kathleen stood up against her mother and pleaded that she be sent instead to the convent at Neuilly, in the suburbs of Paris, where she might experience something beyond the routine and rituals of the nuns. As Rose saw it, St. Maux was no more remote, no more disciplined, no more rigid than the Blumenthal convent where she had spent a year. Rose wanted Kathleen to follow her pathway, to learn the stoic discipline that she felt had served her so well as a woman. Her daughter was a different young woman, unwilling to tolerate what Rose had quietly accepted. Thus Rose agreed to allow Kathleen to study in Paris.

Kathleen departed for Neuilly, leaving her American friend alone at the convent with one other student from Noroton. "Mother, Hope looks simply ghastly," Kathleen wrote Rose in November 1935 after her friend's visit to Paris, her comments a vindication of her obstinacy. "She hates the convent like anything and when she had to go back last nite [sic] she was crying terrifically. It is a crime to leave her there. . . . If she stays there much longer she will honestly kill herself. Every night I thank God I am not there. The head nun is also always trying to turn Hope against me because I left and didn't have the spirit to stay."

Kathleen had so much looked forward to spending time in Europe with Jack. He was her kindred spirit and had that same quick wit that she dared unsheathe fully only with him and a few others. Now he would be only a channel crossing away, and she began contemplating the times they would have together. She had hardly unpacked at Neuilly when she learned that Jack had fallen ill and was returning to the United States, where he entered Princeton University as a freshman. Kathleen was not that well either, taking injections for her asthma, and it did not help matters to have Jack sailing back home.

The nuns noticed that Kathleen was homesick. It was difficult for her to speak always in French, her limited vocabulary without words for all she saw, felt, and wanted desperately to say. She tried to will herself to speak fluently, but still she spoke in the simplistic sentences of a child.

Kathleen was upbeat and chipper in her letters but her world was full of maddening uncertainty. At home her emaciated-appearing brother was in the hospital suffering from hepatitis, the latest of Jack's constant round of maladies, the specifics of which her parents were vague about in their letters. Her one close friend, Hope, was miles away. And now Kathleen learned that Hope was sick too, returning to the United States. "I do not know all the details," she wrote Rose in December, "but she will rest for awhile and may have to wear a belt on her stomach for two years. All I can say is a fine lot I came over with. First Jack, then Hope. I shall probably contract something sooner or later." As she sat in her tiny room, she wrote that "every time I think of that darn brother of mine I burn."

Neuilly was in some ways more like a conservative finishing school than a rigid convent. "It was a very liberal school," remembered one American woman there that year. "We weren't so restricted, but when we went out we were admonished not to act like Americans. I think that meant not to be loud. Kathleen had a great sense of humor. The nuns called her 'Mademoiselle Pourquoi' because she was always questioning the rules."

Rose and the nuns had taught Kathleen to make almost every moment of her day a time of self-improvement. One afternoon a nun asked Kathleen to accompany her as she distributed notices about Sunday school to some of the less savory addresses in Paris. For most of the students, the mere idea of getting out of the convent for a few hours would have made the excursion worthwhile. Kathleen, however, wanted her parents to know that she and the nun had "talked French all the time so it was not a waste of time." Beyond that, it had hardly been an idyllic afternoon. "I have never been in such

little, smelly places before," she wrote. "I honestly don't see
how the French survive."

In her hours alone in her room, Kathleen dutifully worked
her way through a French edition of *A Tale of Two Cities* and
spent most of her free time writing letters. She wrote all her
brothers and sisters. In her letters, irony was the highest feeling
she allowed herself. In the emotional language of her family,
she could never say directly what she felt about Jack, how she
had worried, how relieved she was that he was finally out of
the Boston hospital, or how deeply she appreciated his rare letters. "Thanks awfully for your letter which I was glad to receive," she said. "Thought you might have died off."

Among her sisters, Kathleen was closest to Eunice, who was
back at the "old fire-trap" at Noroton. Kathleen wrote her in
that same style laced with sarcasm, an emotional shorthand,
disguising how deeply she missed the sister whose nickname
was "Puny Eunie." "You should write your lonely little sister
at least once a week," Kathleen wrote, though the real loneliness that she was experiencing was something she would never
write about. "Boy, I could just see you over here. Lots of times
I wished you here. Now isn't that sweet of me."

Kathleen was obsessed with the idea that she was gaining
weight. There was so much food at Neuilly, soup, potatoes,
tea, cakes. She wrote her parents that she planned to try on her
evening gowns, fearing that she hardly fit into them any
longer. Kathleen was petite, far smaller and slimmer than most
of the French girls, and she felt that Reverend Mother was trying to fatten her up. No matter what the nun said, Kathleen
vowed that she would not return to the States so fat that she
would immediately have to go on a diet.

Two years before, Rose had sent Kathleen to Noroton to get
her away from the baneful influence of young men. If anything, she was even more interested in young men now, and
they in her. With her two American friends at Neuilly, she discussed the merits of a number of well-born Catholic young
men with a sophistication beyond her fifteen years. Both
Kathleen's friends were struck by how aware their younger
friend was of the social backgrounds of the men and how important that was to her. One name that Kathleen kept mentioning was Robert Sargent Shriver. He was from an old Maryland
Catholic family. Kathleen had a fried from Noroton, whom she
visited in Baltimore, and she knew all about young Sarge. His

family had fallen on lean times, but he was a student at Yale University, an admirable suitor for a child of the Sacred Heart.

In a letter home Kathleen had declared herself "rather sad at the prospect of Xmas in Switzerland without any of the family" but in Paris she seemed delighted at the trip. Her father was one of the wealthiest men in America, but Rose had trained her daughter to think of frugality as a regular form of penance. Kathleen dutifully wrote Rose and Joe that the trip would cost two hundred dollars plus eight hundred francs or so for ski clothes, and she sold her parents on the vacation by telling them the excursion was to *French* Switzerland where she would be able to practice her language skills.

The little group with their chaperon traveled to the Winter Palace Hotel in Gstaad. After midnight mass on Christmas Eve, Kathleen called down to the desk and in her best French ordered five egg sandwiches. The German-speaking clerk took the order, and twenty minutes later a waiter knocked at the door carrying a tray laden with sixteen ham sandwiches. Kathleen and her companions proceeded to eat the sandwiches, and woke up the next morning sick to their stomachs.

One day at the resort she chanced upon a young American, Derek Richardson, a student at Cambridge University in England, whom she had first met at her friend Charlotte McDonnell's house in Southampton. Fifteen-year-old Kathleen considered Richardson a sophisticated and charming young man. He immediately invited her to come to England for the Cambridge-Oxford hockey game on January 22. If Kathleen had had more time, she doubtless would have properly garnished her request with a whole series of edifying reasons to go to London, perhaps visiting monasteries or the London museums. But time was short and Kathleen wrote a gushing impulsive letter to her parents. "I suppose this sounds fantastic," she admitted, which of course it did, "but it would be so much fun and I wouldn't miss anything." Her father wired back immediately vetoing the trip, followed by a more formal letter telling her bluntly: "Mother and I have no objection to your seeing as many things as you can over there . . . but the idea of merely going over for a game was not quite the thing to do."

Richardson was impressed enough with Kathleen to invite her as his date for May Week, the legendary end-of-the-year celebration at Cambridge that despite its name took place early in June. It was an event that almost any young American woman would have been delighted to attend, a wonderful ending to Kathleen's year in Europe.

Unfortunately, Rose was planning to visit Kathleen during precisely the dates that Kathleen hoped to be in Cambridge. Kathleen could not afford the luxury of candor, asking her mother to come to Paris, but please not in early June when she hoped to go to Cambridge. Thus Kathleen created other reasons why Rose should come earlier in the spring. "School lets out the tenth of July and by that time think I shall be quite ready to get home," she wrote. "So it would be rather silly just to come over and go right home, for you."

Kathleen casually mentioned in a letter to Rose that Richardson was writing her. Even an ocean away Rose could smell the scent of a man near her daughter. Kathleen had been warned about the nefarious conduct of French boys, but after one brief conversation with a young French man she had decided they "really are not as bad as they are made out to be." Her daughter stayed away from French men, but Rose had hardly imagined that Kathleen would meet an American in Switzerland.

A few days later, in anticipation of her birthday on February 20, Kathleen cabled her parents telling them the time they could telephone her. Cables were expensive, and Kathleen left off the word "birthday," thinking that her parents would know why she wanted them to call her. Rose did not even wait until Kathleen's birthday, but telephoned immediately, her voice charged with anxiety. "When you said you thought I had eloped I didn't know what to think," Kathleen wrote her mother after hanging up. "Hope you don't think I am gallivanting like a chicken over here. Thought something dreadful had happened when I heard you were calling."

Rose agreed to visit in April, as Kathleen had proposed, perhaps because she felt it imperative to learn about her daughter's life at Neuilly. After all, Kathleen had written her again mentioning Derek Richardson, this time saying that the young man and his mother would be visiting Paris and that Kathleen was *sure* it was all right for her to go out with them. With Derek and his mother, Kathleen climbed to the top of the Eiffel Tower, had lunch at a marvelous little bistro, went to the races at Saint Cloud, all in all as memorable a day as she had experienced in Paris.

As soon as Derek departed, Kathleen left Paris with a student group led by a chaperoning nun for a four-week trip to

Italy. In the canals of Venice a gondolier sang Venetian melodies, his voice wafting out across the water. The nun sang along with the Italian, when she wasn't terrified that the boat was going to turn over. "Never have I seen such a night," Kathleen wrote home. "We have all decided to come back here on our honeymoon." What she couldn't abide were the Italian men. She was properly dressed and chaperoned but the boulevardiers of Venice didn't let the mere presence of a nun dissuade them from their manly games. "It is not very funny here as all the men talk to the girls on the street," she wrote her parents. "We had about 6 in a cavalcade following us all over Venice today."

In the streets strutted the black-shirted minions of Fascism, but to Kathleen it was all part of the pageant of Italy. Returning veterans of Ethiopia walked proudly by, the names of the towns they had attacked stitched on their military caps. "Just saw a parade celebrating victory of 'Gondar' which was taken tonight," she wrote from Florence. "Shall be very Fascist by the time I get home." In the Bay of Naples she saw a troop ship bound for Ethiopia. She was shown around Rome by a friend of her father's, Enrico Galeazzi, the Vatican's financial advisor, who gave Kathleen his Fascist pin as a going-away present. "The girls are very jealous," she wrote her father.

As soon as Kathleen returned to Paris, a cable arrived for her: "SAILING TODAY ILE DE FRANCE SEE YOU RITZ TWENTYNINTH. MOTHER."

Kathleen was extraordinarily excited. "Mother shall be here in three days and just can't wait to see her," she wrote Bobby. "I haven't seen any beautiful Kennedy faces for seven months—long, long time that."

It had, indeed, been seven months since Kathleen had seen her mother. In preparation she went out and bought a stylish new suit and hat. "She looked so pretty and sophisticated," Rose recalled, of the moment she first saw Kathleen at the Ritz, "but the moment she saw me she dissolved in tears of happiness as if she were still a little girl. I will never forget what I felt when I saw her. I realized so clearly how lucky I was to have this wonderfully effervescent, adorably loving and extremely pretty child as my daughter and friend."

Rose had been a dutiful, diligent mother. Now her relationship with her daughter was like Joe's had always been to his children, with these intense special moments, all the more pregnant with meaning because of their rarity. Paris was a city that Rose knew and loved. She usually traveled alone on her annual trips to the haute couturiers of the Right Bank. This time was different, as if she were finally receiving a glorious reward for her years of child rearing. "Traveling with Kathleen was such a joy," Rose remembered. "It reminded me of all the wonderful trips I had taken with my sister Agnes."

After a week in the City of Light, Rose took Kathleen on an epic journey to Russia. Joe Jr. had made the trip the year before. For the first time in their lives, Rose and Kathleen were taking what in the lexicon of the Kennedy family was a man's adventure. Rose cabled Joe a nonchalant message as if she were setting out for no more than a jaunt around the neighborhood: "EXPECT LEAVE FOR MOSCOW WEDNESDAY NIGHT TRAIN BERLIN. PLANS UNCERTAIN. SEND BROWN WHITE DRESSY SHOES PUMPS LONDON OR PARIS. LOVE YOU ALL LOTS. ROSE AND KICKS."

Rose and Kathleen flew by commercial plane as far east as Latvia, where they boarded a four-seat craft with a fuselage and wings apparently held partially in place by two ropes. The pilot flew only a few hundred feet above the thick, seemingly endless forests, broken only by occasional fog and clouds.

In Moscow, the American ambassador, William Bullitt, was a "perfect host." They saw the Bolshoi Ballet, visited the Hermitage in Leningrad. Every time they left the embassy, they were followed by a car. Despite the surveillance, Rose was positive about aspects of the Soviet system, as Joe Jr. had been the year before. "The masses really were better off in a good many ways than they had been under the czarist system," she wrote in her autobiography. "Many of its aims, if not many of the methods, were worthy of respect and discussion and study in some of our Western societies."

As much as Kathleen moaned to her mother about rigid old Neuilly, she had little more than a month left at the convent school. More than a week of that time would be spent traveling to England to attend May Week, an excursion that she had been anticipating for months.

"Well, darling, I miss you and wish you were along," Rose wrote Kathleen from the *Queen Mary* on May 27, "but I am so glad you decided to stay." As Rose sat penning her note to Kathleen, her daughter was off to England with her friend, Eleanor "Ellie" Hoguet, a Noroton student who was spending a year at the Parisian convent school.

Kathleen and Ellie stayed at a vicarage in Cambridge, the two young women sleeping on the floor, Kathleen on an air mattress on which she felt she "was rolling all night." Kathleen watched Derek rowing in a race on the Cam, and during their four evenings together attended two different balls. At the Trinity Ball held overlooking the Cam in a great tent lit by a multitude of lanterns, Kathleen wore a glorious chiffon evening dress. Derek waltzed her around the dance floor, but young man after young man asked her to dance, spinning her around the floor. She was an American Cinderella, so long hidden away in the convent. Fresh from her adventures in Moscow, at ease with young men, her conversation punctuated by laughter and wit, she was pursued by a brigade of Cambridge students. She seemed so open, so gay, approachable yet distant, whirling from one partner to another. "There is something wrong with the English girls," she wrote her mother afterwards. "Hardly any pretty evening dresses or girls." Kathleen's only regret was that suddenly it was dawn and it "seemed rather funny to be walking around in evening clothes in broad daylight." It had been a splendid four days. Before she left, she was invited back for another weekend. Her primary regret was that she was missing her mother and younger sisters in Paris, but she wrote them telling them what to expect. "Don't eye the Frenchmen or they will be hot on your trail," she warned. "Another thing Frenchmen are never satisfied no matter how much you tip them and that goes for everything."

As soon as Kathleen returned to the United States to enter Noroton for a final year, her string of male conquests continued. Lem Billings's admiration had turned into love, and another of Jack's close friends, Torbert Macdonald, fell in love with her as well. For these young men, Kathleen was tantalizingly alluring. They could only catch glimpses of her, standing in her red jumper at the *goûter* among a room full of similarly garbed young women; at chaperoned balls or other affairs, a dance or two on her card, a few laughs, a story or two; or in witty, warm letters in which laughter seemed somehow to pour out of the envelope, all innocence and joy.

These young men pursuing Kathleen divided females into either women of virtue and godliness, or dames of momentary pleasure. That was how society presented women to them, and as long as they did not mix the two categories up, all was right with society. They knew better than to attempt to have sex with the likes of Kathleen or to make lustful boasts about her. They knew not even to think of bringing home to their family a woman who lived outside this sacred circle of virtue and innocence.

Kathleen had grown up close enough to Joe Jr. and especially Jack to see how their sexual lives had developed, so dramatically different from hers. Kathleen had become interested in boys when she was no more than twelve years old, and she had known how to deal with them, to flirt genteelly but always to keep her emotional distance. She had watched Joe Jr. and Jack begin their dating with shy ineptness. Then they approached girls not with lust, primed for a momentary pleasure, but with tender sensitivity. Kathleen had been there in Hyannis Port in 1929, the summer of Joe Jr.'s fourteenth year, when he had fallen in love with a girl from California. He took her sailing four times and never did he even give her a kiss good-bye. As for Jack, he had been so shy that he could have been the definition of the word. Kathleen enjoyed her dancing class but Jack had had to be dragged down to Miss Cuvington's Dance School at the Gramatan Hotel Ballroom in Bronxville, all gussied up in Buster Brown collars and shiny brown shoes. Jack darted back to the men's room where he hid until the teacher dragged him out to face the music. The girls chose the boys they would dance with, and handsome Jack was a popular partner. He was chosen inevitably by a girl at least a head taller, whom he waltzed around the room, holding her with the same stiff caress as if dancing with a broom handle.

As a young teenager Jack developed more interest in the opposite sex, especially in one pretty girl, Betty Young. He was terrified at the prospect of asking her out. So he finagled his friend, Manuel, to call and arrange a double date but Jack could not even bring himself to talk to her on the telephone.

As Kathleen and her younger sisters watched, Jack eventually overcame his shyness. "Jack was a very naughty boy," little Jean wrote her mother, betraying her older brother. "He kissed Betty Young under the mistletoe down in the front hall."

Jack was, indeed, a naughty boy, and Kathleen knew just how naughty. One evening Lem, Jack, and Kathleen headed up to the legendary Cotton Club in Harlem. Jack was not unfamiliar with the streets of the black ghetto. It was here at the age of seventeen, as his friend Ralph Horton Jr. recalled, that Jack had lost his virginity to a white prostitute for the magnificent sum of three dollars after several of the women had put on what passed as a show. Since then he had gone to The Gypsy Tea Room, a brothel in West Palm Beach, several times, and had developed much the same taste for show girls, actresses, and "easy" women as his father. Kathleen knew all about Jack's taste in women, but he was her brother and a man and her deep admiration for him was not affected. She knew all about men and their ways. In the abstract she was as remarkably sophisticated and knowing about men and their habits as she was personally innocent and inexperienced.

When Joe learned that Lem and Jack had taken Kathleen to Harlem, he was white with rage. His sons were one thing, and his daughters quite another. He would not have Kathleen taken on what he considered manly adventures.

That fall Lem wanted to take Kathleen to a Harvard football game. Kathleen was eager to go because the Crimson eleven was captained by none other than Torbert Macdonald, who kept her picture atop his bureau. As Kathleen well knew, the students could not leave on weekends at Noroton and Harvard football games would have to wait.

Kathleen was at an age when it was natural for her to spend most of her time with friends. Yet she felt morally obligated to miss her family. She could not admit to Rose and Joe that she wanted to be around her friends. Even when she went to Palm Beach, she felt guilty when she didn't spend sufficient time with her parents. After a visit over Christmas in 1936, she wrote her father, signing the letter with her nickname:

> *Dearest Daddy—*
> *I didn't have any time to see you before I left but after thinking about Sat. night I realize what a low trick it was; after you and mother had done so much for me already—I'm sorry it had to happen and like it did, as it rather left a very unpleasant blot on the holidays ...*
>
> > *Love from a daughter*
> > *who needs more*
> > *sense*
> > *Kick*

Kathleen had been taught to be respectful of her mother, so much so that she and her siblings stood up when Rose entered and left the dining room. As she grew to adulthood, Kathleen respected Rose twofold, as mother, the institution epitomized in the saintly life of Blessed Virgin Mary, and as *her* mother.

For Mother's Day in 1937, Kathleen wrote a letter to Rose in her careful script:

> *Dearest Mother—*
>
> *Hope this reaches you before Mothers Day which is now and always will be a special day for all the little Kennedys.*
>
> *Wish I could be with you today but mothers are happier when their obedient children are where they should be (so I hear).*
>
> *You have all my prayers whether it be mass or just an ejaculation. And now your darling daughter should study. My love to all and especially to the most wonderful mother in the world.*
>
> *Kick*

When Kathleen graduated from Noroton in the spring of 1937, she was ready to accept those invitations to which she had for so long had to say no. Her closest friend was still Charlotte McDonnell, who introduced Kathleen to the upper-crust New York Catholic society that had not invited Rose through its portals. In person, the prominent Catholic families treated Rose and her offspring with perfect grace, while behind their backs they condemned the family. The McDonnells and the other families of New York's Catholic elite might have admired the Kennedys and their intrepid life-styles if not for Joe. In New York these elite Catholic families were more socially accepted than their Boston counterparts. They saw themselves as both a moral and social elite, and they had little use for Joseph P. Kennedy, so prominently identified as one of the two leading Catholics in the Roosevelt administration. He and his family were the very thing they abhorred, pushy upstarts trying to buy their way in, led by what they considered an abominable father.

Once Charlotte went to meet Kathleen at the apartment her father kept at the Waldorf Hotel. Charlotte knew all about Joe's reputation. Still, she found it strange that when the Kennedys were in New York, Joe stayed there while Rose had a room at the Plaza. It was not a matter that a sixteen-year-old child of the Sacred Heart was supposed to notice. In the suite, Joe called out from the shower that Charlotte should leave her coat on the chair and go across the hall where Kathleen and Jack were waiting.

While Charlotte chatted across the hall, Will Hays, the Hollywood "Czar" and censor, walked into Joe's room through the open door. It hadn't bothered Hays that the man he had touted as the very exemplar of moral family life was living apart from his wife in New York City. As he spied a woman's coat, he assumed that Joe was carnally occupied, a matter about which the only emotion this preacher of celluloid morality could evoke was embarrassment. As quickly as he entered, he hurried back out of the room.

After a few minutes, Kathleen, Jack, and Charlotte returned to Joe's suite. "You'll never guess what happened," Joe said, standing with a towel around his waist, laughing and looking at Charlotte. "Will Hays came in and saw your coat and turned around and walked away, thinking I had a girl in the bedroom."

Jack and Kathleen laughed as loudly as their father, but Charlotte cringed with shame. If her father had said something like that to *her* friend, she "thought she would have left home." But it was unthinkable that James McDonnell would ever speak like that in front of his daughter. Joe had not only done so, but Kick had laughed right along with her father and brother.

Charlotte was a frequent guest at all the great houses of Catholic New York. One evening she took her closest friend to a dinner at the home of Michael Grace, one of the heirs to the W. R. Grace and Company and the Grace Lines shipping fortune. Charlotte's sister, Anne, was there as well. Anne was dating Henry Ford II, a Protestant, and heir to one of the greatest fortunes in America, who had visited her at Noroton.

Michael was a Notre Dame man, and he had invited many of his college friends. During the evening his twenty-three-year-old big brother, Peter, arrived at the house. Peter was already working in the family business, and he had little time for frivolous evenings like this one.

"You don't dare to tackle this guy, do you, Peter!" Michael asserted, pointing to his hefty friend, a 240-pound tackle on the Notre Dame football team.

The Kennedys were not the only family in America in which the two eldest sons had a fierce rivalry. Peter was a hockey star, not a football player, and this lengthy hall seemed hardly the place to begin to learn the sport. Peter, however, was captivated by Kathleen. He guessed correctly that Kathleen was impressed by tough men. Her brothers were football players, and stayed away from what she considered a sissified sport like soccer. Peter knew that if he wanted to have a chance with Kathleen he would have to go through with it.

"Give him the ball," Peter said.

The tackle walked back up the hall, grasped the football in his ham hands, and charged down the corridor. Peter stood waiting in his business suit, his briefcase to the side. As the football player reached him, he suddenly faked left. The man lunged by, and Peter blocked his knees, sending his gargantuan opponent to the ground with a broken leg. As the group stood speechless, Peter picked up his briefcase. "If you don't want your friend hurt, don't bring him around here," he said, turned, and walked upstairs.

"That was a nice little victory," Peter recalled. "And I think the girls were impressed."

Peter could have recited love sonnets under Kathleen's window until doomsday without half the impact of smashing up a Notre Dame football player in the living room. Kathleen esteemed men like her brothers, gentlemen from good families who were as tough as street urchins.

Kathleen was definitely impressed, and she and Peter began what was her first serious relationship. He could have been one of her brothers. His grandfather had started out as a singing waiter and dockworker, and not only had ended up immensely wealthy but had been the first Irish-born mayor of New York. A Yale graduate, Peter was full of energy and enthusiasm, and traveled far beyond the parochial world of Catholic society. "The Catholic girls in those days were considered second rate," Grace reflected. "I thought they were all very attractive and had a much better religious background, much better." Grace may have admired Catholic womanhood, but it was an altar that he worshipped at only from a distance. Kathleen was the first Catholic he had ever dated.

Grace was serious about Kathleen, and serious meant marriage, and marriage meant a Catholic woman, and a Catholic woman meant a big family. He was six years older than Kathleen, but he had never had to stay more alert to keep up with a date. The couple simply didn't go to parties and dinners. Often they attended sermons by Father James Keller, who spoke passionately about the duty that wealthy Catholics had to society, ideas that resonated positively within both of them.

Peter drove out to Bronxville, arriving on time for his frequent dates, and always Kathleen was late, after a half hour or more bounding down the stairs. Joe was almost never at home, and the young man sat in the living room talking to Rose. "Mrs. Kennedy was very interested in who the boyfriends were," he recalled. "Whenever I went to pick Kathleen up, her mother was there."

Peter never talked to Kathleen about getting married. He didn't think he had to talk to her. He was a man with an orderly sense of things, and he figured that the following year, when Kathleen was eighteen, would be the appropriate time to ask for her hand. He didn't seem to notice that Kathleen was flitting emotionally out of reach and did not seem ready for family life.

After serving as chairman of the SEC for a year, Joe had resigned with almost universal praise for his efforts. In the spring of 1937, Roosevelt named him chairman of the Maritime Commission, asking him to mediate between militant unions and intransigent ship owners. He arrived back in Washington, in the words of *Fortune*, "surrounded by critics, moving in a great cloud of legend, speculation, mystery, and gossip that forms as naturally around him as fog forms when a warm current of air passes over a cold surface." It was a thankless task and after several months he resigned, with his reputation fully intact.

During the summer Joe joined the rest of the family in Hyannis Port. The days on Cape Cod were as full of activity as in past years. Joe had taught his children that it was not money or gold but time that was the most precious quantity in their lives. Joe wasted as little of it as he could, flying back to Washington on the Fourth of July weekend on a chartered plane.

Joe stood on the veranda of the house one afternoon watching as Kathleen sped past the shoreline on a board pulled on the back of a motorboat, gliding over the smooth blue-green sea. As she passed the house, the boat began a series of inexplicable moves, first right, then left, then right again, twisting back and forth. Joe thought that Kathleen would be crushed against the back of the boat, cut to pieces by the motor. Suddenly, though, Joe realized what Kathleen was doing. There in the trailing surf, she was spelling out her nickname. K I C K. She was showing off for her father. K I C K. It only lasted an instant and then she disappeared almost as quickly as her name in the surf.

Among his daughters, Kathleen was Joe's favorite, carrying into the world a message of what women in the family were to be. "All my ducks are swans," he would say, but Kathleen was "especially special." Her younger sisters grew to be tall angular women who were often called handsome not beautiful, with abrupt features that defined them as Kennedys. Kathleen was, as one friend called her, a "soft Kennedy." Unlike her younger sisters she was petite. She had tiny feet, long auburn hair, and skin of creamy perfection. Her nose was a little large, her eyes expressive but too deep set, her body tending to squatness. She was not especially photogenic. Her grace and appeal was something that a camera could not capture. She had a personality of such vivaciousness that she was like quicksilver, skewing her older brothers with her wit, filling a languid afternoon with laughter and humor so that the hours overflowed with life. She was a girl, and then a woman, whom no one ever forgot. Now that she had graduated from Noroton, she wanted to embrace what she saw as a woman's life, to enjoy all the possibilities that her family position allowed her. After those years in the convent life to her meant not politics and books, but matching skirts and sweaters from Saks Fifth Avenue in New York City, the latest swing records, and on the weekends dances at the Wianno Yacht Club.

Almost every friend Jack brought home from Harvard became infatuated with her, even more captivated by the way she danced away, always out of reach of their emotions. She exuded an extraordinary sensuousness of which most of the Kennedys' young male friends, knowing her innocence, hardly dared speak. "I think she probably had more sex appeal than any girl I've ever met in my life," recalled Tom Egerton. "She wasn't especially pretty, but she just had this appeal."

Eunice was only a year younger than Kathleen, but in the family she was of a different generation. Eunice was an often sickly girl. When her daughter was younger, Rose recalled that "Eunice [who] was not very strong went to a day school in Bronxville and came home for her meals, a necessity in her case on account of her low weight." Now Eunice often stayed home while Jack and Kathleen went to the dance at the yacht club. Unlike her older sister, she was not a teenager whom young men swooned over as if she were the very model of womanhood. Eunice's words spurted out of her in a nervous staccato, the sentences crunched together, the ideas compressed, as if she could never say all that she would like to say.

"Puny Eunie," they called her, and puny she was—gawky, rail thin, a scarecrow of a girl, thin nearly to the point of emaciation. She was so intense that she could rarely sit still. She was sickly, like Jack, suffering innumerable mysterious ailments. She slept with eye pads and earplugs, and guests were warned not to flush the toilet or the sound would wake Eunice up.

Of all the nine Kennedy children, she and Bobby were the most deeply religious, and many thought that Eunice would one day become a nun. She asked her friend, Nancy Tenney, after they had gone to church together, "Listen, Ten, don't you think you ought to become a Catholic?" She took her faith with her into peculiar corners. Once before a sailing race, she told her boat mates: "All right, now: everyone say a Hail Mary."

Pat did not have that competitive fire that burned so fiercely in her siblings. Although she had formidable skills at tennis, she didn't seem to understand that for a Kennedy what mattered was winning not playing, results not style. She was more of a daydreamer, a romantic.

As for Jean, the youngest daughter was often forgotten in the rough and tumble life of Hyannis Port, and not praised and petted like Teddy, his big brothers' mascot, pampered by his older sisters, adored by his mother, spoiled by his father. Even at the age of nine or ten, she was precociously aware that she was special as a Kennedy, a realization that made her both inordinately proud and suspicious. She was fond of measuring her ankles and wrists, noting their diminutive size. "Your ankles aren't slim enough to be really aristocratic," she told a younger cousin. She was constantly telling her less blessed relatives how rich she was and how she would have to choose her friends and her husband with extreme care to avoid those interested primarily in her money and her name. "Because I'm so wealthy, people will want to be close to me," she told a cousin one summer day.

Jean was always watching out for her little brother but she seemed almost to get lost, yet she also understood there was only one way to make her presence felt within the family. Thus, in 1937, nine-year-old Jean made her dramatic and extraordinary entrance into the racing scene, winning five races, coming in second ten times, and finishing third in nine other contests. Jean, too, was a Kennedy.

Jean always had another little girl to play with because Rose saw to it that through the summer each young Kennedy had a

relative as a special friend. Rose was the impresario of the
family, not only inviting them to Hyannis Port but paying for
the educations of her forty-five nieces and nephews. "Each of
us was given between two weeks and a month at Hyannis Port,
whether we wanted it or not," recalled Mary Lou Connelly
McCarthy. "Some of us were quite happy at home. But my
mother was told, 'Have Mary Lou ready on the fifteenth
because she's coming down.' It was like a command performance."

At the age of seven, Mary Lou was sent off into the competitive regime of Hyannis Port, expected to be the companion of
her eight-month-older cousin, Jean. "I didn't like Jean at all,"
McCarthy said. "There was no congeniality there. Somebody
decided that Jean and I would play one another in tennis. And
of course she beat me terribly. I took a lot of razzing. It was
my first summer there. I was homesick. I just hated the whole
darn thing. I was on the servants' back stairs sleeping, holding
my teddy bear, and Bobby came thumping along and asked,
'What's the matter with you?' He said, 'Well, Jean's a pest. I'll
teach you. We'll show her.' And so for the next week he gave
me lessons and then he told his sister that he had missed seeing the first marvelous match and he would like to see us play
again. Of course, she thought that was a wonderful idea. And,
of course, I licked her and it was marvelous. Bobby came over
and gave me a very darling boyish kind of halfway bear hug
and said, 'We did it. We did it. That's good. Give it to her.
That's fine.' And he had my total admiration forever."

Eunice made a special point of spending time with Rosemary,
her older sister, integrating her into their lives. She was there
behind Rosemary, whether it was a game of dodgeball or duck
duck goose, making sure, as her brother Ted remembered, that
"Rosemary would have her fair share of successes."

"I would take her as crew in our boat races, and I remember
that she usually could do what she was told," Eunice said.
"She was especially helpful with the jib, and she loved to be
in the winning boat. Winning at anything always brought a
marvelous smile to her face."

On occasion specialists arrived at the house to treat Rosemary. "I think she was partly epileptic as well as retarded,"
Eunice said. "I can remember at the Cape the doctors coming
in and giving her shots and then disappearing, not often but
enough to know what was happening."

Rose did not have to chide Jack and Joe about taking Rosemary with them to the dances at the Yacht Club. When the evening began, Jack put his name at the top of his sister's dance card and then went around the room, getting his friends to help fill out the rest of the card. Jack was a young man of too many easy gifts—charming and handsome and bold. His own sister's life was his own touchstone with the unfair wages of human existence. His mother didn't have to upbraid him about the sister that he called "Rose" or "Rosie." "Rose seemed to enjoy the Stork Club and acted *very* well," he wrote his mother on Harvard stationary. "She seems to be much better when alone and when the attention is chiefly on her. Her dancing was *much* better."

Jack and Joe Jr. put off their adventures with the women of the port until they had seen Rosemary home. "Why don't other boys ask me to dance?" she asked her mother. Rosemary was, in fact, an immensely pretty woman, and Joe Jr. and Jack presumably warned unwary men to stay away from their sister. When Rosemary saw her little sisters Pat and Jean off in a sailboat by themselves, it didn't make sense why her mother would not allow her to set off by herself alone in a boat too. For Rose it was terribly painful, seeing Rosemary, so stolid and slow, trying to keep up with her sisters who were like gazelles, running through long summer days, their feet hardly touching the ground. As much as Rosemary felt the pain, Rose believed that "a mother suffers more for a child who's affected than the child itself sometimes."

For the most part Rosemary did not have her own friends. She would have felt comfortable playing with younger children but that would not have looked right. So Rosemary was usually sent off with her sisters to play. As Rosemary grew into a teenager she desperately wanted praise. She was happy for hours with a mere scrap of approval, and forlorn and discouraged at the hint of criticism.

"Rosemary, you have the best teeth and smile in the family," Rose told her daughter, motivating her with an endless stream of compliments. "Rosemary, that's the most beautiful hair ribbon."

Rosemary was slow and plodding, living among the swift and nimble. Wherever Rosemary looked, whatever she did, there were people prodding her to keep up, or by deed or word reminding her that she was so far behind that she could hardly see those ahead of her: the nuns at Elmhurst standing behind

her back, overseeing her painfully printing out letters in a notebook, off by herself away from the other girls; her father at the
dinner table asking Jack and Joe and Kathleen a question that
she could not quite understand, and when she finally grasped
it, or part of it, they were on to something else; her mother hitting yet another tennis ball at her until she returned it; her sisters waving at her to catch up, way up ahead on their bicycles;
her brothers shouting at her from the shore, out on the sound
of Hyannis Port in their sailboat. Rosemary was slow, but she
was not stupid and sometimes she would erupt in an inexplicable fury, the rage pouring out of her like a tempest from a
cloudless sky. It was an anger that among the Kennedy daughters and their girlfriends seemed masculine in its uncontrolled
force. Then just as suddenly, Rosemary would grow quiet, and
life would go on, with Rosemary watching and trying to take
part.

At Hyannis Port the cook served up enormous helpings of
plain, healthy food, washed down with pitchers of milk, twenty
quarts a day or more. On cold, windswept days the children
stayed inside, nestling in the warmth of the veranda, playing
Monopoly, twenty questions, or charades. Sometimes Eunice
and her friends put on plays in the theater, charging admission.
In the evenings Rose at times sat at the piano and played old
songs, and the family gathered around and sang in voices that
were almost universally off-key.

For the Kennedy daughters, as for their brothers, family was
not the quotidian routine of most upbringing but these moments of supercharged intensity, when everyone and everything
came together. "There was so much to be thankful for," Eunice
reflected passionately. "Everything was so wonderful most of
the time. Most of our relationships were so wonderful within
the family and with our parents. If you had a little problem, so
what? That's what comes with a large family. It's a great advantage. You can see other people's problems and they don't
complain. You don't see your mother complaining. My brother
Jack was the same. He didn't complain, so what's to complain?"

Joe Jr. and Jack brought friends to Hyannis Port. They were
often better athletes than the Kennedy youths or finer scholars,
but they had an ardent, sometimes subservient loyalty to the
young Kennedys. They were drawn to the Kennedys, as if
among them life was lived with an intensity beyond anything

they had experienced, every moment cherished and charged with passion.

"They were golden years, probably too golden," reflected Nancy Tenney Coleman. "Probably nobody had anything on their minds but Mr. Kennedy, who was setting their course—and he did. He wanted to see his sons succeed."

And always there was the sight, sound, and smell of the ocean. Rose did not like to sail, but she loved the sea, and there was not a day that she did not walk the shore. The house looked out upon the sound, out upon the wild dune grass and a private beach. She was most at peace in her moments of aloneness, deep within her own thoughts, walking by herself along the rock-strewn beach.

The evenings often meant a first-run Hollywood film, shown even before it had opened in the theaters. "Joe was the high honcho who would tell the projectionist what film was going to be shown and when," recalled Bill Mulcahy, who worked for one of Joe's companies in Boston and selected the films. "Sometimes the projectionist would sit there waiting for hours and nobody would ever show up."

Joe wanted to make sure that the film was appropriate for the children. "I would have been fired if I had brought down something that was really bad," said Mulcahy. On the rare occasion when the film had its risqué moments, Joe ordered the projectionist to stop the screening and waited while the young Kennedys duly trooped out.

Rose was not always present for the screenings. "I can remember Joe would walk in wearing a terry-cloth bathrobe and slippers with a statuesque female on his arm," recalled Harry Fowler. "They would always claim to us children when we would ask about these beautiful women, 'Oh, they are Daddy's secretary and they are here because he is working at home and he needs their help.' It was pathetic as I look back at it because I was even aware at this time, and this was 1936 and 1937 when I was twelve or thirteen years old. Joe and his 'secretary' had two seats in the front of the screen, and the two seats in front of them would be turned around so that they could rest their feet up on these chairs. Rose would come in and stand in the doorway and look around at all the kids and then she would look over at her husband and some woman and just turn around and walk out. I remember thinking to myself, 'Wow, that's too bad. Mrs. Kennedy can't go over and sit down with her husband and watch the movie with the rest of us.' "

When their mother wasn't there in Hyannis Port, Joe blatantly brought in his show girls and "secretaries." When he was alone in the darkened theater, Joe took pleasure in pinching Kathleen's friends. Afterwards, he acted as if nothing untoward had happened. Young women who stayed overnight learned that they had best lock their bedroom doors at night and not go wandering in the halls. And when he bid his daughters' overnight guests good-bye, he kissed them on the mouths.

Those who observed Joe watched in bewilderment. "I think only a Roman Catholic could possibly describe how you could be amoral and still religious," reflected Joe's close friend, Arthur Krock, the *New York Times* columnist. "That is, how you can carry an insurance policy with the deity and at the same time do all those other things. . . . It was a way of the world as far as I knew it and the way of *his* world. . . . It never bothered me at all because Rose acted as if they [the other women] didn't exist."

Joe Jr. and Jack had no problem with their father's blatant infidelities. To them that was simply the way a man acted. For Kathleen, Eunice, and their younger sisters, however, their mother's and by fiat their own lives were in question. They became agents of their father's duplicity. The Kennedy girls treated these secrets like a thread on a suit that if pulled at would unravel their entire outfit, leaving them and their whole family standing naked before the world. They learned not to see. They focused instead on what they saw as the fabric of their lives, a rich mosaic of cloth on which family and faith were emblazoned.

Rose's children were respectful to their mother, deferential even. In the afternoon when she took her nap, they tiptoed through the house and kept their conversations to a whisper. In the evenings when one of the Kennedy daughters was late from a date, a party, or a dance, Rose headed out looking for her in her small blue car. She knew the haunts as well as anyone. When the headlights approached, the girl knew that it was Mother and when Rose said, "Dear, it's time to come home," there was nothing to be done but say good-bye and hop into the little auto. The daughter might find a little note on her pillow: "The next time be sure to be in on time."

Kathleen did not challenge her mother's edicts, nor did her

sisters; for they knew if they did, it would bring the wrath of their father down on them. Instead, they learned to go along with Rose, to humor her, to put in their time. Rose insisted that her daughters develop the distaff side of themselves with the same rigor and discipline that they approached everything else.

"Now, Kathleen, I want you to learn how to arrange flowers," Rose said one sun-filled afternoon when the beach beckoned.

"Arrange flowers?" Kathleen asked, as if this were an arcane business in which she could have no possible interest.

"Yes," Rose replied, "I want you to take these scissors and the basket and I want you to go out and pick flowers and arrange them." Kathleen did as her mother told her. She cut the flowers the wrong length, left them sitting outside until they dried out, and it was all a disaster, though not to Kathleen.

"Mother thought it was a wonderful idea to teach the girls how to arrange flowers," Pat recalled. "So one week one of us would have to arrange flowers, and the next week another child. We all hated the whole idea. I was very fortunate because I tried it once—and I get terrible hay fever—so I never had to arrange the flowers, much to the consternation of Kick and Eunice."

Late that summer of 1936, Rose's forty-four-year-old sister Agnes died in her sleep from an embolism, the obstruction of a blood vessel. She left a husband, Joseph F. Gargan, a son, Joseph "Joey" Jr., and two daughters, Mary Jo and Ann. Rose was shrouded in grief. Her other sister, Eunice, had died at the age of twenty-three. Her brother, Fred, had died too, drinking himself into the grave at the age of thirty-one. And now Agnes. Rose's sister had a wealth of women friends, but at her funeral the *Boston Post* did not list a single woman present. A long list of male notables appeared—priests, politicians, and others including Joe who "had been travelling in Europe, returned on the Queen Mary and flew to Boston to attend the funeral."

In Hyannis Port, Rose took the three young Gargans in during the summers and made them a part of the Kennedys' extended family. "Aunt Rose was marvelous," Joe Gargan reflected. "She had nine children of her own, and she could have sent us to a camp for the summer. It was a very nice thing to do." The Gargans were family but they were not *the* family, and Joey became a playmate for Teddy, a little older, a little more mature, expected to watch out for his cousin.

When Rose was at Blumenthal, she had worried about what kind of letter paper was proper on which to write to a bishop. She wrote not only to bishops now but to cardinals. Indeed, in November of 1936 when Cardinal Eugenio Pacelli made his visit to the United States from Rome, the Kennedys were invited to travel with the cardinal as he rode from New York City to the Hyde Park home of President Roosevelt.

As the Vatican's Secretary of State, Cardinal Pacelli was the second most powerful priest in the world. The American government did not recognize the Vatican. The cardinal's visit was viewed with trepidation by many Americans who considered the Vatican a shadowy sovereignty that controlled the lives and loyalty of American Catholics. Thus Roosevelt could not formally welcome Pacelli to the White House; instead this visit to Hyde Part was arranged.

Rose was the bearer of the faith in the Kennedy family, but it was Joe who, as she wrote, was considered "one of the nation's leading Catholic laymen." It did not matter that he was known as a notorious philanderer and a ruthlessly predatory businessman. Joe, the leading Catholic layman, was the reason that they had received this invitation.

The Kennedys were becoming the very model of an American Catholic family, lauded for their fecundity, praised for their faith, honored for their generosity to the church. Rose had long since learned not to look down where her feet stood in the muck of an adulterous marriage, but up at the ideals of faith and family. This was her life, then, these glorious moments. Decades later she could remember every detail of this visit the way she would recollect few other events during those years in Bronxville. She recalled the color of the clear November sky, the hue of the autumn foliage, the bright smiles of the Catholic schoolchildren who stood along the road, waving their American and papal flags. She remembered the look on the cardinal's face as he stopped to greet the children, intense, compassionate eyes that stared out from behind wire-rimmed glasses. "Who would ever think to see a Roman Cardinal in his red robes walking in the middle of the road of a country town of the State of New York?" she reflected. "Truly a never to be forgotten experience."

Most of all, however, Rose remembered how on the way

back from Hyde Park, the cardinal had gotten off his private rail car in Bronxville and come to the Kennedy home for tea. It was an honor for Joe in his world of power and ambition, but it was tenfold, a hundredfold, greater an honor for Rose in her universe of faith and family.

The cardinal sat in the living room on an overstuffed chair. After a while four-year-old Teddy ran up to him, hopped on his knee, and played with his pectoral cross. The priest was the greatest of the princes of the church and from then on whenever Rose looked at the chair, she thought of the visit. Wherever her family moved, the chair moved with them until it came to reside in a large front room of their home in Hyannis Port. It was the one seat on which no one was allowed to sit.

At the end of July 1937 Rose left on the United States liner *Washington* with Kathleen and Joe Jr. for a European tour. Rose had chosen to travel to Europe when her six younger children were together, and Joe was only in Hyannis Port for weekends. Most mothers would have relished days with their family and put off their European vacation until their children were in school. "Mother always took trips, with Daddy, with her friends, and with us," Eunice said. "I remember going down to the *Normandie* seeing my parents off one time, and having a ball and at the same time being sad like all children when they're ten or eleven and their mother is going away for three weeks with their father. And then as they got older my father didn't like to travel, but my mother was enormously curious and liked to go places. She wasn't running away from my father, running away from all of us. She'd come back and say, 'Now, you children have to go too.' She was the one who pushed all of us, and we were delighted."

Rose, however, often seemed to be somewhere else, even when she was at Hyannis Port. One of Jack's friends remembered how each time he arrived at the home, as a joke he was introduced to Mrs. Kennedy by a different name, and each time she thrust out her hand and greeted him as if it were for the first time. Years later when Bobby rushed into the house after a trip to Europe expecting a warm greeting from Rose, his mother nonchalantly walked past him asking, "Bobby, have you seen Jack?"

Rose was in Paris when thirteen-year-old Pat was rushed to St. Elizabeth's Hospital for an emergency appendectomy. For Pat it was a time of fear and loneliness, her father in Washington, her mother an ocean away. If ever there was a moment in her life when she needed her mother, needed her standing beside her as the nurses wheeled her into the operating room, needed her as she woke up in a strange white room, it was then. As an ambulance carried Pat to Boston, the hospital telephoned Luella Hennessey, a young nurse, and asked her to come to the hospital. Luella had been working nights for a month and she was worn out. When she heard that not only was it an emergency operation but that it was a little girl and she was all alone with her parents off somewhere, she said that she would come.

Pat's operation was hardly finished when eleven-year-old Bobby was carried into the same Boston hospital stricken with pneumonia. Although Rose was returning to Boston, she was still days away from her children. In the hospital the two Kennedys took a special liking to Luella. Although always firmly professional, Luella had a gentle warmth and humor that their own mother infrequently conveyed. She had a bouncy, optimistic personality, a wonderful bedside manner. Luella found the two Kennedys special as well. "Patricia was such a loveable, beautiful child, and so grateful for the smallest thing I did for her," Luella recalled. "Clouds of chestnut hair emphasized the blue of her wide, trusting eyes, and sick as she was, she seemed like one of the happiest little girls I had ever known. Her smile was almost perpetual."

Rose arrived from France when Pat and Bobby were still in the hospital. She let her two children choose the nurse who would accompany them back to Hyannis Port during their recuperation. They agreed upon Luella, to whom Rose had only one question: "Do you smoke?" Already determined and left unsaid was the more crucial matter of Luella's religion and family background. The dark-haired young woman was Catholic and from a good family, one sister a nun, another married to a doctor, and her brother a Harvard graduate. She didn't smoke and Joe asked her not to wear makeup. She was exactly the kind of young woman Rose desired to have around her children.

In Washington Joe was busy angling for an even more important position in the Roosevelt administration: secretary of the treasury. That job was in the capable, politically astute hands of Henry Morgenthau Jr. and Rose knew that the position was out of the question for her husband. As a political woman,

Rose understood instinctively that politics was a complex matrix of relationships and interests. Morgenthau was friendly with Eleanor Roosevelt, and Rose sensed that "dispensing with Henry could have resulted in friction . . . in the Roosevelt home."

Rose felt that the chairmanships of the SEC and the Maritime Commission had not been prestigious enough for her Joe. The position that appealed to Rose as well as to Joe was that of ambassador to Great Britain. The current ambassador, Robert Worth Bingham, was seriously ill. Over the years some of the most distinguished names in American public life, including two presidents, John Quincy Adams and James Monroe, had served in London. For the United States it was the most important diplomatic post in the world. That was even more true now, as the shadow of Hitler rose out of a renewed Germany, Mussolini's armies marched through Ethiopia, and civil war raged in Spain. Joe, unlike his wife, knew no foreign languages and had shown little interest in Europe except as a market, but Rose saw London as a spectacular opportunity for her family and herself.

"What has the President said?" Rose quizzed her husband when he returned to Bronxville. "Couldn't you tell him what you want?"

"Well, I can't just walk into the office of the President of the United States and say 'I want to be ambassador to England.' "

When Joe was officially named ambassador to the Court of St. James's, both Rose and Joe took pleasure in the positive reception his appointment received. The papers treated the appointment as if the president had named not simply a man but a glorious American family. The Boston press treated the Kennedys as if they had never left the city. *Life*, the popular new picture magazine, ran a full-page photo of the photogenic group ("THE KENNEDY FAMILY: NINE CHILDREN AND NINE MILLION DOLLARS"). This time the entire family would be going with him, unlike Joe's two other Washington appointments.

Rose was preeminently a political woman. In London she would finally be in a position that would allow her to play a speaking part in the family drama. As Joe's wife she had a rich sense of public manners, in fostering the intricate and subtle network of relationships that were the essence of the political life. One of the first things she did after learning of the appointment was to send a handwritten note to Roosevelt. With his insight into human motivation, the president had sensed that Joe would be a worthy public servant because it would bring honor to his family. Rose further confirmed Roosevelt's judgment by thanking him not only for Joe, but for her, and for the family:

> *My dear Mr. President:*
> *I do want to thank you for the wonderful appointment you have given to Joe. The children and I feel deeply honored, delighted and thrilled, and we want you to know that we do appreciate the fact that you have made possible this great rejoicing. All we can do is to pray for you, and as the little children in the Convent seem especially near to God, I am sure their prayers will bring you continued blessings.*
> *Love from us all to Mrs. Roosevelt and love to you, too (in spite of Emily Post.)*
> *I am, dear Mr. President,*
>
> > *Yours*
> > *faithfully,*
> > *Rose Kennedy*

As the ambassador's wife, Rose would be in a position of the highest social visibility. Her duties included choosing the American debutantes to be presented to Queen Elizabeth and King George. That power made her the most important woman in America to a number of women who only a few weeks ago would have snubbed her. "Boston blue bloods, social registerites from New York, Philadelphia and Washington will be presented next June to Queen Elizabeth in Buckingham Palace by a Boston woman who was never invited to join the exclusive Junior League or Vincent Club," wrote *The Boston Globe* in December. "American debutantes of 1938 cannot stick three white feathers in their hair and drop three curtsies before the Queen of England without the sanction of Rose Fitzgerald Kennedy."

Her Sacred Heart education and her youth as the mayor's daughter had prepared her for just such a role. She was proud and honored that her family would be going to London, but she was deeply insecure. At the age of forty-seven, she looked amazingly youthful, dieting constantly to maintain her 115-pound figure. She purchased clothes with meticulous concern. "I have to buy 200 dresses and suits a year," she angrily told a clerk in a Boston store, who had given her the wrong dress and had no idea of the work involved in maintaining her daughters' wardrobes. Rosemary, Kathleen, and Eunice were reaching the ages when she wanted them to be as well dressed and turned out as their mother. "I think you owe your store better attention to the details of such trade."

Rose didn't trust herself any longer. She blamed it all on her life as mother. She had been beaten down not by years of preoccupation with children's games and tales, but by years of Joe's treating her as a mother not a wife, cordial to her yet largely dismissive of her mind and sensibilities. She was well and deeply educated. She was a woman of high refinement, conversant in three languages. She looked youthful and stylish and had a beautiful wardrobe. Yet she didn't feel comfortable out in the world.

Rose's closest friends were primarily nuns, and as she always did in moments of crisis, she turned to the church, in this instance to Mother Patterson, a Sacred Heart nun whom Rose had known when they were students at Manhattanville. At Noroton, Mother Patterson had been a legendary teacher, a woman of brilliance and originality, with a quick wit and rapid-fire speech. She had suffered a stroke that left her right side paralyzed and she was able to speak only with painful slowness. "Mrs. Kennedy asked Mother Patterson to give her practice in conversation," recalled Sister Mary Quinlan. "She said that she had spent so many years looking out for her children and led such a retiring life that she didn't feel that she was up to socializing with adults. Mother Patterson said that she and Mrs. Kennedy did canned conversations, and sat around and discussed cultural things, current events, and things like that."

Those who saw Rose out in the world could not imagine that this was a woman full of insecurities about her public role. Shortly before the Kennedys were scheduled to leave for London, Rose returned to Boston in late January 1938 to attend a special afternoon meeting of the Ace of Clubs, the organization that she had founded a quarter century before. This was *her* day, and Rose's parents accompanied her.

Rose lived for moments like this, moments that sanctified all her sacrifices, occasions that celebrated her and her family as the perfect exemplars of Catholic values. To the two hundred Catholic women at the Somerset Hotel, Rose was a great symbol of all that was possible to a Catholic mother and matron, and all the distance their forbears had traveled from their Irish roots.

Rose had an image of her family as exalted and superior, one that she would not besmirch with the melancholy truths of her daily life. As she spoke to these women, Joe was not the notorious womanizer who was whispered about; he was the noble head of a great Catholic family. And Rosemary was not slow. There were those in the audience who knew the truth about Rosemary, but Rose told the group that her daughter Rosemary was off in New York City studying music. It was all so perfect: Rose, Rosemary, Joe, the family, the future, everything.

"Of course we are excited and honored and thrilled to be going to London," she said. "At first it seemed as if we'd have to leave the children on account of their schooling; so when my husband told me that it could be worked out to take them, I was so happy I decided to make the flying trip to Boston to celebrate." Then Rose stepped off the podium, sat down at the piano, and began playing "Sweet Adeline." Her father needed no introduction to stand up and sing the song he had sung a thousand, ten thousand times before, and sing it he did as the guests hummed along.

After this memorable afternoon, Rose was stricken with appendicitis. At St. Elizabeth's Hospital, Luella Hennessey took care of Rose as she had watched over Pat and Bobby. At the end of the two-week stay Luella agreed to go with the Kennedys to England "to keep the children healthy and happy." For Luella it was the opening of a universe of new experiences, but for Kico, the Kennedys' faithful retainer, it was the end of her two decades of service. "I had had an old family nursemaid who conscientiously and successfully took care of the babies after they were four weeks old," Rose reflected. "But this faithful Irish soul could not take a temperature, nor talk intelligently to a doctor, and I decided that I should have a trained nurse with me instead of her."

The illness meant that Rose and the children would leave for England a few weeks after Joe, but Rose was a woman of such stoic discipline that she did not even tell her children about the operation. At Noroton Eunice had to learn about her mother's illness by reading a newspaper account while Rose was recuperating. "Of all the surprising things that occurred in the Kennedy family within the past few months the greatest shock came when I heard that you had your appendix out," Eunice wrote Rose.

If you were a Kennedy woman, you did not cry out with pain or complain. That was Rose's lesson to all her daughters, a lesson they carried within them as they prepared to leave for their great and glorious adventure in England.

10

"London Will Be Just Grand"

When the *Washington* stopped in an Irish port on its journey to England in March 1938, Rose remembered that she had been here once before in 1908 with her father. Then the quays of Queenstown had been full of young Irish women and Irish men saying good-bye to family, friends, and the Irish sod before sailing off to a new uncertain life in a new uncertain world. That day her father had sung his Irish songs, spouted his Irish poems, and waxed sentimental over the land that their own family had left in steerage not so long ago carrying with them little more than their hands, their minds, and their faith.

This day, Rose's sentiments were more complicated. Rose thought how incredibly far her family had come from its roots in Ireland. The day they left on the twenty-four-thousand-ton liner, they had faced a legion of photographers, newsreel cameramen, and journalists on the dock, treating not only Rose, but the five children traveling with her—Kathleen, Pat, Bobby, Jean, and Teddy—like movie stars, taking down their every word, capturing them at their most photogenic. Standing there the Kennedys exemplified all the possibilities of this nation of immigrants. "We're just going to act natural when we get there," Rose said. It was as if the entire family had been named ambassador to the Court of St. James's: youthful, optimistic emissaries of America to an old and tired world. Rose didn't know what to expect, and felt relieved to have the nurse Luella traveling with her and Elizabeth Dunn, the governess.

It was a stormy crossing and a deeply troubled Europe to which Rose and her family were sailing. Even as they sailed across the Atlantic, Hitler's armies were marching into the streets of Vienna, raising the swastika over Austria. "As I approached London, the embassy, and the Court of St. James's as the wife of the American ambassador, I freely admit to feeling a bit nervous," Rose recalled.

Kathleen shared none of her mother's anxieties. She had simply adored England when she had been there for May Week at Cambridge. She was through with drab schoolgirl uniforms, and as the ambassador's daughter she would be invited *everywhere*. In the weeks before they had left New York, Peter Grace had done everything possible to impress her. He had even scored three goals in a Yale hockey match, when he was usually a goalie and had never scored before. Peter's name had gotten into the headlines, but no matter how many goals her beau scored, she wasn't ready to marry and give up her time in London.

When the *Washington* arrived in Plymouth, Joe was waiting for his family, as were a number of reporters. Rose could have anticipated a vague question or two about her first impressions of England, but not about Peter's love for Kathleen, a story that had just been published in the *New York World-Telegram*. For the first time in Rose's life, she found the intimate details of her family life being scrutinized by the press. "Peter is a nice boy," Rose said. "Really, I don't know very much about it." Kathleen blushed when the reporter asked her about Peter: "I can't think how that started. It's so silly, but he's awful nice. I like him a lot, but I do not know anything about him at all."

Joe slammed the whole matter shut. "It's rubbish!" he exclaimed. "Why she's only eighteen." Joe put his hand on Rose's shoulder, and looked at his five children as if they were the universe. "Now I've got everything," he said, "London will be just grand."

England took to the Kennedys with rare delight, savoring the saga of this unpretentious forty-nine-year-old ambassador, his even more youthful forty-seven-year-old wife, and their nine exuberant children. Joe was the most undiplomatic of diplomats, and the British press celebrated his brusqueness. He sat with his feet on his desk at the embassy on Grosvenor Square, pontificating off the record on the world and its ways, in words shucked of their protective diplomatic gloss, passionately proclaiming his intention to help keep America out of any European conflict.

Everyone in England wanted to meet the Kennedys, especially Rose, the mother of the nine Kennedy children. One publication described Rose "as vivacious as a screen-star, as wise as a dowager." Another called her a "remarkable woman responsible for much of that rare harmony and unity which is both the central theme and leitmotif of the Kennedys."

The British genuinely liked the Kennedys, but there was an element of calculation as well. Joe was from an Irish-American family, and the British upper class generally disliked the Irish almost as much as the Irish disliked the British. Joe was a man of crucial importance, and the word went out among the British establishment that Joe and Rose Kennedy were to be hosted and toasted, wooed and lauded. "The men usually know it's because they represent a most powerful nation," reflected one diplomat, "but sometimes it goes to the women's heads. Mrs. Kennedy arrived a thoroughly down-to-earth type, but after a few months, she thought she was rather grand."

Upon arriving at the six-story embassy residence at No. 14 Prince's Gate, Rose first helped to organize the household. She had lived in mansions in America, but this was a great European home of the sort that the nuns had talked about at Blumenthal. The great ballroom was laid with Aubusson carpets, its walls lined with French panel paintings. On the first floor there were also two reception rooms, one a copy of a chamber in Versailles, the other, the Pine Room, an elegant apartment that Rose chose as her own office.

The house contained twenty-seven bedrooms in all, for family, visitors, and servants, and an elevator that Bobby and Teddy at first treated like their own private toy. Rose soon had that stopped, and with the help of Luella and Elizabeth Dunn, she soon had life organized.

Eunice and Rosemary arrived in England in April, and with Joe Jr. and Jack scheduled to arrive in the summer from Harvard, the family was complete. Rose sent Eunice, Pat, and Jean off to the Sacred Heart convent at Roehampton on the outskirts of London, a school of such exclusivity that in her youth she would not have been accepted.

Behind the formidable gothic walls sat a sprawling country home that had once been the home of the lord chief justice. The nuns had left many of the original decorations including paintings by European masters and the finely wrought furniture in the drawing rooms. The students included the daughters of the royal families of Europe from Luxembourg, Bavaria, and France, to whom the three Kennedy girls were a rare and different breed. To one of their schoolmates, "they were like birds of paradise, bringing a glamour and worldliness that contrasted with the attitude of the dour daughters and displaced European aristocrats and English girls in tweeds." It was much the same impression that many of the European girls had once had of Rose and her American compatriots at Blumenthal.

Seventeen-year-old Eunice was one of the older students. She had an alert, angular face that looked out on the world with a rare intensity. In her first field hockey meet, she dashed up and down the field shouting "hey, hey" with an enthusiasm and passion rarely seen on the playing fields of Roehampton. She was acting no differently than when she played football with Joe Jr. and Jack. Afterwards, her teammates took her aside and told her that nice girls didn't act that way. Eunice didn't leave her intensity on the playing field. She plunged into the life of Roehampton. In dressmaking, she proved a remarkable seamstress, making a coat and skirt that she could have worn anywhere. Even in this convent, Eunice's religious fervor appeared extraordinary, even excessive. In the chapel she prayed with her arms out in front, her head bowed to the floor, as if she were imitating one of the paintings of a saint. She was so perfectly a child of the Sacred Heart that the following year she was named not only the most popular girl at Roehampton but the student who had done the most for the school.

Eunice insisted on cabling Jack to remind her less-than-devout brother that he had best not forget to attend mass for his first Friday obligation. Jack was the world to Eunice, a gay, witty presence whom she admired beyond admiration. "She was a clever girl, devoted to her brother," recalled one of Eunice's teachers, Mother Binney, half a century later. "They were totally united as a family."

Fourteen-year-old Pat was neither as pious as her older sister, nor as intense, but she had a beauty that reminded her admirers not of her mother and father, but of a legendary Irish lass, her hair dark, her eyes violet, her smile a flash of illumination. Although she was ahead of her class in some of her work, her American education had left her woefully behind in algebra and geometry.

Pudgy little Jean was having her trouble with mathematics as well. On the first day of class, when her teacher pointed out an error, ten-year-old Jean said boldly: "Well, five goes into nine in America; I don't see why it doesn't in England." In the play period, Jean donned blue overalls over the blue serge uniform and romped about with the eight royal princesses who were her schoolmates. Jean might smile in school, but she was going through a period of intense private anguish. The Kennedys' nursemaid in America had been like a second mother to her, a warm, emotionally generous woman enveloping Jean in her affection. After Rose had discharged Kico, Jean suffered and felt so terribly alone. She sat by herself in the great house, tears filling her eyes, crying to Luella, "I miss Kico."

The three Kennedy girls came home on weekends as did Rosemary, who had been sent off to a Montessori school in Hertfordshire. Bobby and Teddy stayed at home, attending the Gibbs Preparatory Boys' Schools on Sloane Street about a mile from their home.

In March Rose sat with Joe in the queen's sitting room wearing a stylish two-piece blue suit, talking to the British monarch. Rose had been terribly nervous about what she might say to Queen Elizabeth, but decades before she had perfected an inoffensive social patter not unlike that practiced by the royal family. Princess Elizabeth and Princess Margaret were roughly the same ages as Bobby and Jean, and for thirty-five minutes the two mothers talked about children, schools, and family.

Soon afterwards, the British monarchs invited Rose and Joe to spend a weekend at Windsor Castle with them. Nearly half a century later, Rose still remembered the details of what to her was "one of the most fabulous, fascinating experiences of my life." The master of the household showed Rose and Joe to their rooms. They were flawless chambers in a tower of the castle, looking out on the park below. They had hardly settled into their rooms when a servant arrived with sherry. "Rose," Joe said, looking at the resplendent furnishings, "this is a helluva long way from East Boston."

Rose wanted to memorialize this historic weekend not only in her diary but in letters to her children. There in the drawer of the desk was a neat stack of stationery. "Look, Joe!" she said pointing to the paper embossed with the royal coat of arms. "Let's write to each of the children on it tonight. They will be surprised and pleased."

At dinner in the Garter Throne Room, the other weekend guests included Prime Minister and Mrs. Chamberlain, and the foreign secretary, Lord Halifax and Lady Halifax. The king sat in the middle of the lengthy table, with Rose seated on his

right and Mrs. Chamberlain on the left. Across the table sat the
queen, with Joe to her right and the prime minister to her left.

In London as in Washington, social and political life blended
imperceptibly into one another. This weekend was not merely
an exquisite introduction to royal hospitality, but a subtle probing of American policy. During dinner, the queen gently
nudged the conversation into a discussion of international politics. Although Joe dressed like the other men in a black suit,
the new ambassador was not about to cloak his words in
formal garb. "What the American people fear more than anything else is being involved in a war," he said bluntly. "They
say to themselves 'Never again'! And I can't say I blame
them. I feel the same way."

"I feel that way too, Mr. Kennedy," the queen responded.
"But if we had the United States actively on our side, working
with us, think how that would strengthen our position with the
dictators."

As Joe and the queen conversed, Rose talked at some length
to the king about the children. Her husband was the ambassador, and she had nothing to say about political matters. She listened as Joe suggested that the king and queen visit the United
States. Then Lady Halifax asked Joe to describe Roosevelt, the
kind of question that in such a gathering Rose would never
have dared ask. Joe characterized the president as a gallant, indomitable figure struggling heroically against the bondage of
his crippled body.

After dinner the queen led the party into a drawing room.
The men bowed to her and then went to another room for cigars, brandy, and gentlemanly discussion. Rose talked alone to
the queen for about fifteen minutes as she stood in front of the
fireplace. A Scottish bagpiper roamed through the castle playing the haunting, lilting music of the pipes. Rose was supposed
to call the queen "Ma'am" but she kept stumbling over the
phrase, and the queen told her to stop worrying about addressing her that way. Then Lady Halifax came forward to talk
alone to the monarch, followed by the other women.

Rose drank in the elegant scene, the queen in her regal
gown, the other ladies so beautifully garbed, the attendants, the
bagpiper. On the wall she looked up at Van Dyck's portrait of
the eldest five children of Charles I. Although the painting
could have hung in a place of honor in any museum in the
world, this evening Rose looked at the portrait as a mother.
These were cherubic faces looking out on the world with inno-

cent eyes. Rose remembered that the king was beheaded, and two of these children were murdered, and the other three were plunged into all the bloody horrors of the English Civil War. And yet here these children sat so serene, so unaware of the tide of blood and death that roared toward them.

Beneath the portrait Queen Elizabeth chatted amiably with one of her guests, all charming pleasantries. Rose kept thinking of the painting. She recalled years later: "There was something about seeing those children frozen for that moment in time, blissfully ignorant of all the pain of the years ahead, that made me shudder inside and suddenly feel afraid."

The next morning was Palm Sunday. The king and queen and all of their guests, except Joe and Rose, attended services at St. George's, whose spires reached high above Windsor. It was almost unthinkable that the guests would have stayed in their rooms this morning, or passed the time by taking a constitutional on the manicured grounds. The Church of England and its rituals were a central part of this aristocratic society, and the castles and great estates often had an Anglican chapel on their very grounds. As for Rose and Joe, they were driven to mass in a small Catholic church in Windsor, in the shadow of the castle.

Over luncheon, Rose sat next to Prime Minister Chamberlain. Since her husband's most crucial relationship would be with Chamberlain, she subtly attempted to ingratiate herself with the prime minister. Sixty-nine-year-old Chamberlain was a stern ascetic, a man without small talk, hardly the most congenial luncheon partner. Rose, ever the dutiful wife, suggested to Chamberlain that he and Joe were very much alike. They were both former businessmen, both enjoyed music and walking, leaving unsaid their greatest similarity, that they shared the same darkly pessimistic vision of the Western world.

Monday morning when the Kennedys motored back to London, they could view the weekend as a triumphant success, the beginning of what boded to be an extraordinary tenure in London. Joe might have congratulated his wife particularly for her astute efforts with the prime minister. After all, Joe was proud that he could "talk Chamberlain's language." In telling the prime minister about the similarities between the two men, she was making a point that Joe made repeatedly. Instead of appreciating what a socially and politically astute woman he had married, Joe berated his wife. As Rose wrote, "Joe later told me I could compare him with anyone I wanted to, but to keep such opinions private." It didn't matter to Joe that the queen had led the political discussions over dinner and another woman, Lady Halifax, had asked Joe pointedly serious questions. Joe wanted his wife to stay out of the manly business of diplomacy and to retreat into that gilded enclave of ritual, ceremony, manners, and dress where he believed women belonged.

Joe expected Rose to be a cordial and efficient hostess. At one party Rose didn't recognize Harvey Klemmer, Joe's speech writer and longtime associate, when he came through the reception line. The ambassador became so upset that he yelled at Rose in front of Klemmer and several others. Rose did not make that mistake again. "She was absolutely remarkable on the surface," said Page Huidekoper Wilson, then a young, socially prominent Baltimore woman working as a secretary in the embassy. "She had great aplomb, great poise, if only she hadn't had that unfortunate voice, so tiny, tinny, no one could help her with that."

When Rose and Joe were together in public as a couple, Rose was sometimes cast in a shadow so dark and deep that she could hardly be seen. "She was a rather shadowy figure in London," said Jane Compton, then Jane Kenyon-Slaney, one of Kathleen's closest friends. "I think she must have had a pretty wretched life with Joe. I'm sure she knew what was going on. Of course she knew. She was very shrewd." Another debutante remembered her as "a dreadful simpering idiot." Sarah Norton Baring, one of the most intelligent and beautiful debutantes in 1938, had her own occasions to observe the Kennedys. "I found him extremely aggressive, very rough mannered, not at all the type to be an ambassador," Baring recalled. "And Rose? She always seemed to me like a fluttering little sparrow, a little nervous and probably overpowered by him."

When Joe was not around, Rose was especially gracious to Kathleen's and Eunice's friends. From her own insecurities, she could empathize with how difficult it was for some of these young women to enter this public world. One evening Ursula Wyndham-Quin arrived at Prince's Gate to see her friend Eunice. She entered the front door and found herself in the midst of a large party. "Oh, Eunice, I'm going to be terrified out of my wits," she said. "Oh you must come and meet my mother," Eunice replied, taking her friend by the hand, and passing her on to Rose. Rose spoke to her like a mother to a daughter, made her feel at ease, and helped her to enjoy what she thought would be only an ordeal.

"Mr. Kennedy was the center of the family, not Mrs. Kennedy," recalled Luella Hennessey. "She was so busy socially, and she'd probably have a little shopping to do in the morning, then a luncheon and a tea, she was so busy. He'd go out to dinner if it was really important, but he didn't care for all of that. Definitely, Mr. Kennedy was the top man and quite a disciplinarian. Mr. Kennedy told me never bring any complaints about the children to Mrs. Kennedy. He would handle them. He didn't want her to worry. Of course, she worried plenty over his shenanigans. But he was so polite to her when we were sitting at the table. Then he showed her the greatest respect."

When Joe looked down that dining-room table, he insisted that his children treat their mother with deference, but he shuttled Rose and her opinions aside, as he did his daughters. "He paid more attention to boys," Luella said. "With the boys it was talking about world events, politics, long conversations. With the girls it was 'What are you doing tonight?' 'How was the party?' kind of fluffy talk. But he was very strict on the girls' image outside, that they act properly."

Rose accepted her diminished role in the family. When Charles Lindbergh came for dinner Rose did not ask him about his leadership of the America First isolationist movement in America and his views of the Nazi Luftwaffe or at least she did not note such a discussion in her diary. Instead, she talked about the authenticity of flight scenes in the motion picture, *Test Pilot*, that they saw after dinner. The Luces came to dinner as well. Henry Luce's publications, *Time*, *Fortune*, and *Life*, were sympathetically chronicling the rise of the Kennedys. His wife, Clare Boothe Luce, was an acerbic, elegant writer whose celebrated play, *The Women*, portrayed a group of bitchy, self-involved New York sophisticates, a world away from Rose and her life. Clare could have been a character in her own play, a gutsy woman who barged into a man's world with style and impunity and made it her own. When Rose talked to Clare Luce, the American journalist employed her lady talk, inoffensive traditional patter for wives. But with Joe and other men she was at least their equal, expressing her fiercely held opinions on the major questions of the day. Joe enjoyed Clare's company, as would his son Jack, but her behavior wasn't something the ambassador would have tolerated in Rose. Wit, banter, and subtle irony were tolerable in mistresses and occasional women, amusing in small doses, but hardly behavior Joe wanted in a wife.

Joe and Rose were invited to all the great events of the Season, the series of events that included a week at Ascot, Private View day at the Royal Academy, Founder's Day at Eton, and innumerable balls, parties that defined Britain's aristocratic society. To Rose it was a wonderland of cordial dukes, lovely ladies, exotic maharajahs, liveried butlers, and fawning footmen in which she paraded forth in one new Paris creation after another. She had a splendid sense of occasion. For Gold Cup Day at Ascot most of the other women dressed in lavender, pink, and other springlike pastels, but they merely provided a background for Rose, stunning in a black organdy dress from Patou and a matching black hat.

Joe viewed the king and the queen as regal impresarios and when he saw the royal procession at Ascot, he exclaimed: "Well, if that's not just like Hollywood!" Although Rose thrilled at the sheer spectacle of the monarchy, she did not simply romanticize the king and queen but saw the extraordinary effort that went into their public performances. She considered the royal family the very model of public life. Disciplined, stoical, eternally gracious, they went through life wearing impenetrable masks of civility, masks that they never dropped. Public life meant remembering: birthdays and anniversaries, names and dates, handwritten notes and small kindnesses. This routine was a matter not of sentiment, deeply felt emotion, but of training, deeply ingrained habits. Rose made a point of telling her sons about "such things which are so important in public life." These months in England, and the example of the British monarchs, reinforced Rose's own ideal of public life and how she and her family should carry themselves.

Rose's primary obligation as the ambassador's wife was to be a cordial hostess and to maintain the image of a partner in a deeply devoted marriage. "The whole thing was a façade," said Klemmer. "He was in truth a great family man, he loved his family, he boasted about them all the time. When we wrote speeches, we always had to work the family into his speeches. But Rose and Joe didn't live together, not in any real sense, not for twenty-five years."

In London, Joe was no longer humiliating Rose by bringing

his women home, as he had at Hyannis Port, Bronxville, and Palm Beach. Joe had not suddenly become aware of Rose's sensibilities; he simply did not want to be caught in an assignation. As the ambassador to the Court of St. James's, he could hardly bring show girls and actresses to 14 Prince's Gate. Instead, he occasionally used his staff to set up clandestine rendezvous. He had developed a belated taste for wealthy women, even bragging about a supposed affair with the king's sister-in-law, the Duchess of Kent. "I could feel a surge when Joe discussed women," recalled Klemmer. "He was always talking about women, saying who was the best lay in the United States, who was second best. He would lay anything in sight. I think he was pleased when his name was connected with a lot of famous people. Once he even said that the queen was the greatest woman in the world, even leaving open speculation about her, though it was absurd."

That was fine for Joe and his sons, but woe betide any young man who had the same idea about his daughters. Joe became obsessed with any young man who became close to *his* daughters, and he learned everything he could about them. "He even watched over *my* boyfriends," Luella said.

Joe insisted that Kathleen be properly chaperoned at the Wimbledon tennis matches, but he arrived that spring afternoon with a young blonde woman on his arm. "I remember it very well," said Jane Compton. "We were plunked here and he was around the corner with his girlfriend." Joe's conduct was a topic of frequent gossip. "He was a filthy old man," said Lady Maureen Fellowes, who also knew Kathleen in London.

Kathleen had scarcely arrived in London when she received her first important invitation. Lady Astor asked her to spend a weekend at Cliveden, her country home. That was a notable honor, for the American-born Lady Astor was not only the first woman member of Parliament, but hostess to the most famous house parties in England. The British upper class considered leisure one of the great prerogatives of wealth, from the week at Ascot and the tennis matches at Wimbledon to shooting in Scotland in the fall, and weekend house parties. Nancy Astor had given the legendary parties of the age. Over the decades she had mixed an impeccably eclectic group of guests, from Edward VII to Charlie Chaplin to Rudyard Kipling. After a weekend at Cliveden, George Bernard Shaw described his visit with Lady Astor like "spend[ing] Sunday with a volcano." It was a setting where the socially inept had full opportunity to embarrass themselves, and poseurs words enough to stumble over their syntax or to expose their ignorance.

Kathleen was brought up to believe that she could go anywhere and be with anyone, intimidated by neither wealth nor lineage nor achievement. Thus as she was driven up to the immense house sitting on four hundred acres on the Thames, she was hardly numb with awe. Cliveden, like the other great houses of England, was in essence a small community with coachmen and carpenters, dairymen and electricians, butlers and maids. In the main house itself there were thirty servants to take care of the seven family members and their guests.

Lady Astor, whose social acumen was a matter of details small and large, delegated a British debutante to watch over Kathleen. It was hardly necessary. Kathleen had grown up in a family that to outsiders often seemed like a perpetual house party—spirited conversation over dinner and hours of games and merriment—and she was a natural at the social minuet of the British aristocracy. The liberal press had dubbed Lady Astor and her political friends as "the Cliveden set," envisioning the estate as the center of the pro-Nazi, defeatist movement in England. Like her mother, Kathleen saw none of that. She was here in England to enjoy her life, and political intrigue and formalities and protocol be damned. She didn't even care that Lady Astor was notoriously anti-Catholic, muttering to Kathleen's coreligionists as they left for mass on Sunday: "How can you stand all that mumbo-jumbo!"

In the evening the group played charades and musical chairs. Lady Astor was a celebrated mimic, and in charades she threw herself into her characterizations. Kathleen shouted out her questions, and played with the same boundless enthusiasm that she did in the living room at Hyannis Port. "Very chummy and much gaiety," Kathleen wrote Billings. "Dukes running around like mad freshmen."

Astor soon realized that the new ambassador's daughter was far from a typical debutante, relegated to silence by the fear that she had nothing to say. Kathleen was brash, irreverent, fresh. Only "Kick" would dare call the formidable Duke of Marlborough "Dukie Wookie." Only she would come bouncing up to some young earl or lady and say, "Oh, kid, what's the sto-o-ory?" The young men loved it. They were used to shepherding debutantes around the dance floor whose conversations ran the gamut from azaleas to begonias, ancestors to descendants.

Kathleen was devoid of the vapid self-consciousness of so many seventeen- or eighteen-year-olds watching their own image in the world. She exuded life, knocking the stuffiness out of aristocrats with a flick of her wit. She was irreverent, yes, but she had a scrupulous sense of the appropriate, knowing not only that she could say things that a British woman could not say, but knowing also the precise point when the naughty became vulgar, the irreverent insolent. She seemed to live in the eternal present, focusing all her attention on the person with whom she was speaking. On this stage, she played a role in which she was wonderfully confident, never speaking lines of great emotion, never having her feelings plumbed and questioned. Like her brother Jack, she was uncomfortable with personal emotions, and pushed back those who got too close. In this upper-class British world, that was not only tolerated, it was the norm, and Kathleen made this society her own. It seemed to almost everyone who met her that she belonged here at the center of this world. In this upper-class English society, she had found a stage where her every line was applauded and her grace, wit, subtlety, and calculation had full play.

Kathleen had just arrived but it was the twilight of an age and a manner. In the darkening shadows faces looked fresh and innocent, laughter carried out into the void, and no features were so etched in memory, no gay laughter carried further than did Kathleen's. Indeed, half a century later, the mere mention of Kathleen's name brought tears to the eyes of elderly men who once danced her across gleaming ballrooms, and wistful melancholic silences to women who so long ago shared evenings of laughter.

The Kennedy women had arrived in London just in time for the Season. At the center of the Season was the annual parade of seventeen- and eighteen-year-old debutantes that signaled their arrival into adult society by their presentation to the monarch.

Each year the American ambassador named about thirty upper-class American girls living in the United States to come to London and be presented to the king and queen. The selection was generally made by the ambassadress and would have been Rose's first important duty in London. Joe, however, called the practice "undemocratic" and ended the spectacle of scores of American mothers and fathers lobbying senators and members of Congress over the transcendent matter of having their daughter on the list. Rose would have had the privilege of choosing the American debutantes, and by doing away with the custom, the new ambassador was doing away with part of his wife's social power.

The American press lauded Joe for ending this supposedly unseemly obeisance to British royalty; the Associated Press said that for this one act he would "go down in history as one of the heroes of United States diplomacy." This champion of egalitarian democracy decided that despite his edict, American women living in England could be presented at court, which meant that his own daughters could go ahead and make their debuts. In his first public act as ambassador, then, Joe had dramatically enhanced his own image as a plainspoken, no-nonsense democrat, while maintaining those privileges for his family, privileges that by his act were now even more exclusive.

Kathleen was a natural for the social scene of aristocratic London, but it was a daring decision for the new ambassador and ambassadress to present Rosemary to British society. Part of that ritual of the Season was a week at Ascot, where the British aristocrats celebrated the sport of kings, a triumph of good breeding. The debutantes who watched the races were themselves thoroughbreds with lines registered and documented, and the Season resembled a mare's auction, the horses paraded through the ring, to be appraised, evaluated, bid over, and mated. Virginity was not only a matter of contemporary mores and religious training, but of social morality. There could be no clandestine seductions, no questionable paternity, no twisted bloodlines. All of their upbringing—the governesses, the finishing schools, the elaborate coiffures—furthered their one high purpose in life: to marry properly and to provide a male heir. For generations this system had maintained one of the longest surviving elites in the modern world, casting aside those who would challenge its prerogatives and rituals. "We were expected to keep totally chaste and virginal, and with one or two notable exceptions did," recalled Juliet "Mollie" Acland Tabor, a 1939 debutante. "We were meant to get married and were told quite bluntly and rightly that decent men didn't marry second hand goods!"

These were blue bloods who prided themselves on the purity

of their lineage. And it was obvious to anyone who spent much time with her that Rosemary was "slow," the contemporary euphemism. That such a young woman made her debut was simply not done. The British upper class had a deep and largely hidden horror of what might be considered hereditary defects. There were whispered stories of "slowness" in other families, daughters who did not make debuts but disappeared forever into distant country homes, and sons never seen. Queen Elizabeth's grandfather, Lord Strathmore, had an older brother who had been born with a strange egglike shape, tiny, brittle legs, and a body that as he grew older became covered with hair. For decades he was hidden away in a small room, his existence known only to his brother, his brother's eldest son, and two hirelings. There were whispers about two of the queen's nieces, Katherine and Nerissa Bowes-Lyon. The two girls were retarded, an embarrassing predicament for the royal family. In 1941 their deaths were duly recorded in *Burke's Peerage*, the authoritative reference of British nobility. In fact, they had been secretly locked away in a mental hospital, where they lived for decades. In this world, Rosemary's debut was a daring and courageous step.

For Rose, as for her daughters, the preparation for their debut was a time of ceaseless activity. Every debutante gave a ball or a party, and the Season consisted of three months of constant socializing. It was unthinkable that a mother would send her seventeen- or eighteen-year-old daughter off to a private ball if she had not met the girl's mother. Thus there were meetings called "Mums' lunches" or "Mums' teas" when Rose and the other mothers got together, arranging for their daughters' coming-out dances, and exchanging names of "debs delights," socially acceptable young men to be added to their invitation list. For Rose this was an opportunity to meet some of the most prominent women of the realm, and to meet them on terms in which she felt comfortable, discussing matters of mutual and deep interest. It was her "coming out" too, in a way that would have been impossible without her daughters' debuts.

Rose and her daughters needed a wardrobe full of fine gowns and dresses, enough for three months of events. Rose was a worthy guide to the haute couture houses of Paris. On several weekend trips, they brought home trunks full of glorious outfits, including for the court presentation white gowns from Molyneux for Rose and Rosemary, and a white Lelong dress for Kathleen.

The presentation at Buckingham Palace was a ritual that had changed little in a hundred years. Rosemary and Kathleen had learned to curtsy at the Sacred Heart convents, but this curtsy was different. Many debutantes traveled to the Vacani School of Dancing near Harrods to learn to perform the deep court curtsy taught by the Vacani sisters or the equally formidable Miss Betty. The debutantes first stood holding the barre, as if they were in ballet class, practicing bending deeply almost to the floor, their left knee crooked, foot behind, and back perfectly straight. Then they practiced with a curtain affixed to the shoulder to approximate a train, a few bedraggled feathers and a bit of net approximating the ostrich feathers and veil they would be wearing, and some fake flowers as their bouquet. Then with Miss Betty playing the queen, they walked forward. Giving a quick kick so that their foot would not get caught in their gowns, they curtsied, a smile pasted on their mouths to match the one that they were assured the queen would give them.

As much as they practiced, most debutantes felt anxious even thinking of curtsying before the king and the queen in a room full of princesses and nobles, diplomats and others. Kathleen, however, had nicknamed the king and queen "George and Lizzie" and she took it all in stride. "Have to practice up on the curtsy left over from convent days," Kathleen wrote Lem Billings.

For Rosemary it was a different matter. She had never been exposed in public before, out there by herself. Whenever she had gone to dances, Joe Jr. or Jack had been there to shelter and guide her. As her mother watched her, Rosemary practiced hour after hour. No matter how often her daughter tried to do it right, Rose feared that she might not be able to curtsy properly. Rosemary was forced to spend days practicing for this evening, the family bit so tightly in her mouth that she felt pain if she even glanced to right or left.

The American ambassador and ambassadress would have attended this royal court even if their daughters had not been making their debuts. This was their first court too, and for Rose this evening was a fairy tale. After her maids carefully inserted her in a regal white lace gown, all embroidered with silver and gold, the representative from Molyneux pinned on the Prince of Wales plumes, her hairdresser affixed the diamond tiara borrowed from Lady Bessborough on her coiffure, and the maids helped her into her shoulder-length, skintight kid gloves and attached her jewels, she looked into the full-length mirror and "felt a little like Cinderella."

In another bedroom Luella and Miss Dunn helped Rosemary put on her gown and makeup. They were not simply dressing Rosemary, but preparing her mentally for this public ordeal. Luella feared that at Buckingham Palace Rosemary might suddenly turn around and walk out of the ballroom. "Oh, Rosemary, you're going to be the best-looking one," Luella told her, as she applied her makeup. "Even more than your mother." As Rosemary looked in the mirror, Luella realized that it was true: Rosemary was absolutely beautiful. Rosemary stared at her image and smiled. "Oh, you're so beautiful," Luella half whispered in her soothing voice. "So beautiful." Rosemary seemed at peace with herself. As Hennessey escorted her downstairs, the nurse felt that everything would be all right.

Rosemary and Kathleen both wore gowns of ethereal white tulle and trains of gossamer-thin net. Kathleen was stunning, but she was only a shadow of Rosemary's beauty. This should have been their night, the night of the three Kennedy women, but it was not their night alone. For generations American ambassadors had appeared at court functions wearing the customary costume of knee breeches, silk stockings, and formal black coats. When reporters asked Joe if he would continue the custom, he replied, "Not Mrs. Kennedy's little boy." Thus this evening he wore a black tailcoat, white tie, and long trousers, while the other diplomats, including the other Americans, dressed in breeches.

After the photographers and newsreel cameramen finished taking pictures, the Kennedys entered two large embassy automobiles to be driven to Buckingham Palace. As they traveled through the evening streets of London, sitting back in the plush seats, they made a resplendent appearance. The fleeting image that they created was a picture of splendor, beauty, and a peculiarly American virtue and courage. Here was Rosemary, not simply pretty, but beautiful, with this sweet blossoming youthful femininity, Rosemary who appeared the very perfection of civility and class and breeding, Rosemary who was being brought up to be a Kennedy like all of them. Here in the other automobile was Joe sitting upright in his formal clothes, daring to confront the social customs of the British aristocracy, daring to be his straightforward Irish-American self, casting off the wigs and frocks of diplomatic livery.

The cars neared the palace at nine o'clock where crowds lined the streets, waiting to catch even a glimpse of the elegantly attired participants in their Roll-Royces, Bentleys, and Daimlers. As the two cars carrying the Kennedys rolled slowly through the great gates, the spectators waved and Rose waved back. As the Kennedys' autos made their stately passage into the immense court in front of the palace, other vehicles were entering, including one driven by a debutante, her three ostrich feathers nudging the roof of the car, while her chauffeur and footman sat in cushioned comfort in the backseat.

Rose and Joe descended from their automobile and walked slowly into the palace, up the red-carpeted Grand stairway lined by resplendently costumed retainers and guards, the gentlemen-at-arms wearing scarlet coatees and plumed helmets, the yeomen of the guard in Tudor uniforms. Passing through a series of anterooms, their way heralded by powdered footmen, they finally reached the great Throne Room and took their place among the diplomatic corps.

This immense gold, red, and white ballroom was a jewel in whose regal surroundings protocol and court ritual took on aspects of absolute law. In this setting Joe's tails and white tie appeared as out of place as if he had come in shirtsleeves. No one sneered, however, or looked disdainfully at Joe. He was the American ambassador, and in this Nazi-threatened world, Joe and his country might hold the future of the empire hostage. When Queen Mother Mary looked at Joe, there were those who saw a momentary frown cross her studiously expressionless visage. A writer for the *Evening Standard* noticed one irony: "Mr. Kennedy's desire to shield himself from the charge of 'flunkeyism' achieved the somewhat paradoxical result that the only trousers at last night's Court were those worn by himself and some of the less important waiters."

At precisely nine-thirty the king and the queen entered the ballroom, signaling the beginning of the two-hour ceremony, the debutantes two by two walking gracefully forward to bow before the monarchs. When it finally came time for Rosemary and Kathleen to be presented, they stood with the other debutantes in an antechamber while the court usher rigorously scrutinized them, finally taking the trains that they held over their left arm, and placing the lengths of white tulle on the floor where they trailed along the floor a precise eighteen inches.

Then as the Lord Chamberlain announced their names from
their pink Cards of Command, they entered the Throne Room.
The debutantes were so well trained that this parade of curtsying had all the precision of a military ritual.

"Miss Rosemary Kennedy," the Lord Chamberlain called
out. "Miss Kathleen Kennedy." About twenty debutantes had
gone ahead of them, and except for their sponsor or mother,
the rest of the assembly watched the proceedings with the desultory interest of observers at any lengthy awards ceremony.
Kathleen and Rosemary walked side by side up the red carpet
to the royal couple sitting on their raised golden chairs. They
looked for the little gold crown on the carpet, a few feet in
front of the king in his field marshal's uniform. The mark told
them where to stop and curtsy. Then with smiles on their lips
and after quick kicks to make sure their skirts were free, they
curtsied deeply, holding their bouquets of lilies of the valley in
front of them. Continuing to smile they took three gliding steps
sideways to the right, and curtsied again to the ever-smiling
queen. At that point they were to glide off to the right, never
turning their back on the monarchs, and slide discreetly out a
side door.

It had all proceeded perfectly, and Rose could finally breathe
a sigh of relief. Suddenly, just as Rosemary was attempting to
glide off, she tripped, nearly falling. It was a debutante's worst
horror, at the most important social moment in her life, in front
of the king and queen, to make a public spectacle of her awk-
wardness, her ineptness. The king and the queen smiled as if
nothing had happened, and there was not even a murmur from
the assembly, and indeed, it was all over in a few seconds.
Rosemary recovered and followed Kathleen out the door.

Rose never talked about the incident, and treated the court
ceremony as an unalloyed triumph in which nothing out of the
ordinary had happened. Rosemary did not have the awareness
of social nuances that her mother and sisters had, and she may
not have realized how badly she had stumbled.

For Kathleen the most important evening of the Season,
other than her presentation at court, was her own coming-out
party at Prince's Gate. The engraved invitations listed Rosemary's name alongside her younger sister's, but the letters
were addressed to debutantes and others who were Kathleen's
friends and acquaintances. Kathleen had only been in London
a little over two months, but she had the unerring instinct to
become friendly with the most socially prominent of the Brit-

ish debutantes. For dinner that evening she invited eighty
young people, the so-called "maximum people," the crème de
la crème, to be joined by three hundred more guests later in
the evening.

For three months the debutantes feasted evening after evening on a regimen of balls and dances, a repast of social life
so rich and overladen that except for their own party they
could hardly remember one night from the next evening. Only
a few evenings did they savor in their memories, and the Kennedy ball was one of those occasions. The mother of Lady
Maureen Fellowes sensed that it would be a notable evening,
and onto her daughter's delicate lace gown she sewed a splendid brooch, a family heirloom designed by Prince Albert.

After the dinner party at the embassy, the guests entered a
ballroom decorated with pink and delicate purple flowers. The
Kennedys had hired the popular Ambrose band, which most
evenings played their signature song "When Day Is Done" at
the Mayfair Hotel. Harry Richman, a well-known vocalist,
sang "Thanks for the Memories" as scores of couples danced,
and others watched.

Rose had arranged that an embassy official would spend the
evening as Rosemary's escort. His name was Jack Kennedy,
and he was known as "London Jack" so as not to be mistaken
for the ambassador's son. Rosemary was a marvelous dancer,
as if she and the music were one, and London Jack spent the
evening whirling her around the ballroom. She never seemed
to tire, and dance after dance, Rosemary stayed out on the ballroom floor.

In most homes the nurse and the governess might have been
allowed to peek into the ballroom, or stand in the background
among the former nannies and other chaperons. Rose, however,
insisted not only that Luella and Dunn attend but that they enter the ballroom as if they were arriving with the other guests.

This was Kathleen's evening, though, and the young men
took turns dancing with her—Viscount Newport, Prince Frederick of Prussia, the Duke of Kent, one after another. Among
the young men present were a few impecunious souls who had
little but good breeding and decent evening clothes as their inheritances, but their names rarely graced Kathleen's dance
card. Each dance lasted about twenty minutes, and she tried to
get the men to cut in, picking up the pace of the evening, but
they would have nothing of that act of supposed American

gall. Except for that, as she wrote Lem, "everything was wonderbar."

For Kathleen the evening after her coming-out party meant another dinner party, another ball, another evening of witty repartee with supremely eligible young men. Unlike many of the debutantes' mothers, Rose rarely chaperoned Kathleen herself but had another woman friend or embassy associate attend the evening ritual.

Sometimes Kathleen stayed at the dance for a while, and then she would be gone, only to return before the playing of "God Save the King" in the early-morning hours. She and her friends headed off to the Four Hundred Club or Café de Paris. Though these clubs were considered dangerous environments for an eighteen-year-old, they were hardly dark places of assignation. They were the most reputable of London night spots. The maître d' guarded the tables against an onslaught of vulgar riffraff. For a debutante the most unseemly act was likely a stolen kiss on the way back to the ball. It was, nonetheless, an adult world, and that was daring enough for most of the debutantes.

Kathleen's own vision of the male sex, based on her father and her brothers, doubtlessly reinforced by the dark muttering of the nuns, was of a species incapable of fidelity. One evening at a dinner party, a guest commented disdainfully about a married acquaintance who was in the midst of an affair. "That's what all men do," Kathleen said, as if she were discussing not a weakness but a fact of nature. "You know that women can never trust them." Kathleen and her debutante friends were for the most part abysmally ignorant about sexual matters. Of course, there were a few debutantes who were "getting up to mischief," debutantes who were "naughty," debutantes who were "wicked." Everyone knew who they were and what they did, though not exactly. "I knew what happened to animals, I just didn't associate it with human beings," said Sarah Norton Baring, one of Kathleen's acquaintances. "We thought you could get pregnant with a kiss. We discovered the truth eventually through conversations with people who had crossed the Rubicon. When we heard we thought it was disgusting."

The young men the debutantes danced with had gone to all-male schools and they were often as innocent as the young women. Sometimes the debutantes heard whispered conversations that after the dances some of their gentlemen friends headed off to the Net, a fancy brothel, but those were only rumors. A few of these young men pressed them too closely on the dance floor, or tried to embrace them; these were the dreaded "taxi tigers" or "NSIT's." (Not Safe in Taxis). To protect one's reputation, they were studiously avoided. For Kathleen and the other debutantes, however, almost all of their escorts were clean, scented young men who ideally wore white gloves so their sweaty hands wouldn't touch a bare back or a fragile gown. That was just as well, for Kathleen had an absolute abhorrence of a man touching her in an untoward manner.

During the Season Kathleen and her friends often drove through the London night to parties at private homes. They walked up to the house along a strip of red carpeting placed from the front door to the road so that their feet would not even touch the common pavement. As Kathleen and her friends hurried into the brightly lit home, they sometimes moved past a gauntlet of shabby bystanders, looking for the most part not with the fiery eyes of envy or radical distaste, but as if observing a strange and wondrous species living lives eternally beyond them and their kin.

Many debutante balls were held at 6 Stanhope Gate, a large fashionable house owned by a catering firm. There was no curtain in the large window where the elaborate buffet was laid out. It was always a feast of succulent dishes: sides of roast beef and legs of lamb, whole fish, cauldrons of soups, platters of vegetables, pyramids of cakes, silver platters laden with pies. As the guests filled their plates, they were watched by a silent army of onlookers, their faces pressed against the windowpane. "One could see pathetic faces looking in," recalled Lady Chichester, one of the few debutantes even to notice. "I remember trying to sit far away so that I couldn't see or be seen—it quite put me off my supper!"

Kathleen was high-spirited, full of that Kennedy ethos that every moment was to be squeezed of its life. When she met Jean Oglivy, now Lady Lloyd, she wasn't about to go through the tedious expected formality of sending an embossed invitation inviting her to lunch. The next day she simply called her new friend and invited her to the embassy that very afternoon where they spent hours listening to American jazz on the Victrola. It was something no upper-class British lady would have thought of doing, but with Kathleen, it seemed so very right.

Another evening at a dinner party, Kathleen threw a dinner roll down the table at one of the other guests. It was a provocation that was met by another roll winging its way back up the table, and soon the party was one gigantic artillery battle, the bread whizzing through the air. "If someone else had done that, it might have been rude or shocking," Lady Lloyd reflected. "But she had this way about her that made it seem an absolute liberation."

One of the many men who pursued her was William Douglas-Home. He was waiting for Kathleen one evening at 14 Prince's Gate when a man in white tie and tails carrying a tray of whiskey entered the room.

"Could I have a small one?" Douglas-Home asked, motioning the butler over.

"You could if you poured it," said the man, introducing himself as Joseph P. Kennedy.

Douglas-Home had the artistic sensibilities of a man who a decade later would become a prominent playwright, and he saw in Kathleen a woman unlike any of the British debutantes. "Kick was the merriest girl you ever met," he remembered. "She had the same witty conversation that Jack had."

Early one morning next to a fountain at Hever, Kathleen supposedly promised Douglas-Home that she would marry him. By next morning she had forgotten it all, and asked him to drive her to meet another beau. Kathleen was like a firefly, illuminating a scene, and then suddenly disappearing, to shine for a brilliant moment somewhere else.

Even before the Kennedys had arrived in England, *Queen*, a magazine that covered royal and upper-class social life with fawning reverence, named Kathleen as a prominent debutante in the upcoming 1938 season. In May the magazine featured Kathleen in a separate article, calling her in its headline "AMERICA'S MOST IMPORTANT DEBUTANTE." Kathleen seemed so born to this life that inevitably she aroused jealousies. "How could I have so envied her, her glamour and her beauty?" recalled Helen Long decades later.

Kathleen filled her scrapbook with mementos of her conquests, intense missives from a score of young men, clippings from newspapers celebrating her social emergence, ticket stubs and calling cards. The young men wooed her in words that were more fervid than their actions ("Your devoted lover, Prince Ahmed Husain, Oxford"), in fervent pleas for attention

("Darling Kick. When—oh when"), pledges of eternal devotion ("You'll always mean everything to me, Peter").

Even as Kathleen appeared totally attentive to each beau, she was standing back evaluating them not with acidity but with social acumen. These were judgments that she kept largely to herself, candidly noting them primarily in letters to Lem. He was a gossip, and he relished their correspondence. Billings adored Kathleen. He was an ocean away and to Lem she could afford to be candid. "I so often think of you when I meet a guy who thinks he is absolutely the tops and is just a big man," she wrote, her American penchant for knocking the pretentious in full play. "What laughs you and Jack would get. Very few of them can take any kidding at all." The Americans were hardly better. She wrote Billings that one Princeton man was "rather too polite and too sweet." She found Byron "Whizzer" White, who one day would sit on the Supreme Court, at a disadvantage because he had not "gone to an eastern college." Billings seemed to think it his mission to keep Kathleen's suitors at bay, warning her that Peter "Grace is wildly in love with you and is heading for England this summer in order to clinch the romance—so watch it, Kick."

Peter had not forgotten his moments with Kathleen, and he kept up a regular correspondence with her. Her warm, witty replies gave him the impression that he still had a chance with Kathleen. He wrote her that in July 1938 he would be sailing to England on the *Queen Mary* to visit her. Kathleen gave Peter every reason to believe that he would be welcomed in London. Upon arrival in Southampton, Peter took the boat train to London and arrived at Prince's Gate full of anticipation at seeing Kathleen "always bubbling over and that wonderful smile."

When the butler opened the door, Peter wasted not a moment getting to the matter at hand. "I'm Peter Grace," he said as if that should be introduction enough. "And I'm here to see Miss Kathleen Kennedy."

"I'm afraid that's quite impossible, sir," the butler said, looking down at Peter with polite disdain and incredulity. "Miss Kennedy is in Sussex at the races."

Peter turned on his heels, took the boat train back to Southampton, and sailed back to New York City on the *Queen Mary*.

"We were close," Grace recalled. "I had taken her out every night in New York, but I don't blame her. She was a young girl, extremely attractive around all these dukes and princes. She was getting around in the highest circles in England. To some people if you get in with all the highfalutin people in London, that sweeps you away. I sort of figured she was caught up on that glamour, and you can't fight that."

Kathleen would have been at Prince's Gate to meet Peter if she had not attended the king and queen's annual garden party at Buckingham Palace a few days before. She was there that sunny day along with thousands of other guests wandering around the little lake, taking tea in the gaily colored tent. As Kathleen was walking with two of her London friends, she was introduced to William "Billy" Cavendish, the Marquess of Hartington, perhaps the most eligible young bachelor in England. He was of such impeccable lineage that he had even been mentioned as a potential husband for twelve-year-old Princess Elizabeth, the future Queen of England.

Even if Billy had been a shameless lout, many debutantes would have relished his attentions, for upon his father's death he would become the Duke of Devonshire, one of the wealthiest and most prominent men in the kingdom. Far from being a boor, Billy was the very model of a young British gentleman. A product of Eton and Trinity, Cambridge, where he was completing his bachelor's degree in history, Billy had a manner that was unassuming and self-deprecating. At six feet two and a half inches tall with a lean sinewy frame, he towered over the diminutive Kathleen. He stood with a stooping stance, as if he were afraid he was taking up too much space. Standing next to Jack or Joe Jr. he might seem almost fey in his gracious manners and demeanor, but the debutantes appreciated his gentleness. He was not one of those young men like Joe Jr., who was stigmatized as NSIT.

As Kathleen stood talking to Billy for close to an hour, the future Duke of Devonshire was as intrigued by the ambassador's daughter as she was by him. Even as he walked through the great halls of the ancestral house at Chatsworth, he saw his forebears' portraits on the walls, and knew the heritage of which he was a part. The Cavendish family had become one of the great political families of England in large measure through its opposition to Roman Catholicism. The painting of the First Duke, William, displays the long Cavendish nose and imperious demeanor of a leader who in the seventeenth century opposed the ascension of the Catholic king, James II, and fought him in bloody rebellion. The Third Duke, William, was "plain in the manners, negligent in his dress," and his portrait hardly suggests an aristocratic manner; in the eighteenth century he served as Lord Lieutenant of Ireland, sovereign over a Catholic people, his name long remembered in the huts and hovels of the Emerald Isle. The family tradition continued in the nineteenth century, when the Eighth Duke, Spencer Compton, a sinewy figure with a long thin gray beard, stood in the House of Lords vehemently opposing Home Rule for Ireland.

Over the centuries the men of the family had increased their wealth primarily by the largely painless expedient of marrying rich women. With each marriage came new lands and new homes, and over the year the family migrated from estate to estate. Billy was born and brought up in Churchdale Hall, a gloomy country estate in Derbyshire. The family properties he would inherit included Chatsworth, a magnificent palace in Derbyshire where much of the winter season was spent; Lismore Castle in Ireland, which was visited in February, March, and April; a great house in London for the Season— May, June, and most of July; then on to Bolton Abbey for grouse shooting during August and part of September; and finally Hardwick Hall for the partridge season in October.

Billy's grandfather had just died, elevating his own father to the dukedom. For a duke Billy's father was a frightfully poor show. Although the official portrait of the tenth Duke of Devonshire shows a figure of austere, regal bearing, Billy's father was, as Andrew, the eleventh and current duke, phrased it, "the worst dressed, the most unostentatious, and least ducal figure."

"He was a frustrated man, hated being a Duke and was really a bit bored by all his possessions and palaces," wrote Sir Henry Channon in his celebrated diary. As the head of perhaps the greatest English family after the royal family, the duke was expected to perform his ordained role in what was a public theater, but he mumbled his lines and shuffled to the back of the stage. He was a rotund, rumpled man, who when he roamed the verdant fields of Chatsworth could easily have been mistaken for a gamekeeper. He enjoyed sitting with a grocer's apron over a suit that hardly needed protection, creating salmon lures from feathers collected from the hats worn by some of the finest ladies of the land. If he had a passion, it was for port, and at Chatsworth he managed to play the good host while getting three glasses to every one glass for his guests. If he had a hatred to match, it was for Catholicism, proud that the Cavendishes were the most famously anticlerical families in all of Great Britain. "I think it's fair to say that my father was a bigoted Protestant," said Andrew, Duke of Devonshire. "My father and mother both felt very strongly that Catholics prose-lytized and that our family had a long tradition opposed to Catholicism."

One day the mantle of the dukedom would fall on Billy's lean shoulders. As he contemplated his future, there was a curiously disengaged quality to Billy, as if life itself had been nearly refined out of him, a man passionate only in his lack of passion. As he got to know Kathleen, he saw something untamed and daring that he lacked. Life seemed to course through her, vitality and energy to bubble out of her. For Kathleen's part, she saw in Billy the epitome of the aristocratic man of noble values whom her whole life and education had prepared her to marry.

Though even casting a yearning eye toward Kathleen bordered on betrayal of the Cavendish heritage, Billy talked to her for nearly an hour. A few days later he invited Kathleen to visit the family house in Eastbourne, Compton Place, to attend the Goodwood races. Kathleen knew that accepting Billy's invitation meant that she would miss Peter. Yet she accepted and did not even leave a note for Peter. She was no good at good-byes. Her life was where she was, not where she had been. Her absence was good-bye enough.

At the races, Billy and Kathleen joined his younger brother, Andrew, and his date, Deborah "Debo" Mitford. Andrew was more mercurial than Billy, but the two men shared the Devonshire taste. Taste is acquired as much by osmosis as by instruction, and spending time in great homes like Chatsworth, its walls lined with paintings by artists such as Rembrandt, Holbein, Van Dyck, Sargent, and Reynolds, and exquisite decoration, one learned to recognize what is best and displayed it in the women they courted as much as in the art they collected.

As the two couples sat for an elegant picnic lunch, it was clear that the two brothers had a more daring, eclectic taste in women than in art. Debo's five sisters were among the most controversial women in Great Britain, including Diana, married to the British Fascist leader Oswald Mosley, and Unity, a Hitler sympathizer, as well as Jessica, a Communist. Debo had avoided the family passion for politics and to all appearances had enjoyed making her debut in the 1938 Season alongside Kathleen.

Billy had an even more controversial date, for Debo at least was not a Catholic. Both young men had grown up hearing their father's deeply felt fear of Catholics, viewing the religion not simply as a faith but a conspiracy. To the tenth Duke of Devonshire, the Church of England was, indeed, *the* Church of England, as much a part of a loyal subject's life as fidelity to the crown and belief in the empire. The duke did not have to lecture his sons on marrying within their faith. To marry a Catholic was not only unspeakable, it was unthinkable. The Catholic church insisted that the children of such a marriage be brought up in the popish faith. It would have been outrageous if Andrew married a Catholic, but for the firstborn Billy, the next Duke of Devonshire, to do so would be a betrayal of three centuries of family history.

Kathleen was so intrigued by Billy that she began putting every newspaper clipping of Billy that she came across into her scrapbook, even those that showed him with other young women including Lady Irene Haig and Lady Mary Fitzroy. If Billy had known about the scrapbook, he doubtless would have been as startled as flattered, but he did not know that Kathleen had become a chronicler of his youth. She gave him no hint of her feelings, and she was going out with other young men, her popularity only making her more desirable.

11

"It's the End of the World"

$\mathcal{I}$n early September 1938 Rose was taking a vacation on the French Riviera in a villa above Cannes. The rest of the family had already left, but she wanted a few more days strolling along the seaside boulevards, shopping in the boutiques, looking down on the city as the sun set over the blue waters of the Mediterranean. As she relaxed at the villa, Joe phoned, his voice nervous and intense, telling Rose that she should return to London the next day. He said that Hitler was about to carry out his threat to send his armies into Czechoslovakia to take over the Sudetenland.

In those ominous days of September, Joe was standing close enough to the bonfires of Nazi Germany to see the flames cast gaudy shadows across the faces of his sons, and to fear that the flames would sweep westward, devouring everything in their path. Joe watched as Chamberlain flew twice to Germany attempting to negotiate a settlement with Hitler, but his concessions were merely scraps of paper to be fed to the flames.

Rose might have provided good counsel to her husband. From her year at Blumenthal, she could remember the bitter pride of the French girls whose nation had lost to the Germans in the Franco-Prussian War. She had watched the French students refuse to stand up for the singing of the German national anthem. In Europe politics often seemed to be blood and memory, and she had a sense of the perils of this European world. She wanted to keep her sons out of war as much as Joe did, but on the rare occasions when she talked of politics, she tempered her feelings with a greater awareness of the world in which they lived.

As for Joe, his isolationism was visceral, a deeply felt sense of foreboding, an intense, intimate fear for the future of his family and his nation. It was just the sort of emotionalism of which men often accused women, deriding them and their involvement in politics. Joe, in fact, saw politics as many women did, not as distant abstractions but as a force that could affect the most intimate part of one's life. Joe's problem, however, was that for him the world began and ended with his family. He could see Joe Jr. and Jack, so bright and youthful, see them dead, soldiers in a needless war. He could envision Prince's Gate a bombed smoking ruin, Rose, Kathleen, Rosemary, all of them gone. But he could not see, not truly see, the frightened faces of Europe, the 400,000 German Social Democrats in the Sudetenland who faced extermination or imprisonment in a Nazi regime, the haunted faces of the Jews of Germany, or if he did see them, he did not consider them his business.

Rose was not with her husband in London, but like almost everyone in Europe, she too watched the flames rising above Germany. There had been no seats on the plane to London, and she had been forced to take the night train to Paris. There the papers and the talk was of Chamberlain's flight to Berchtesgaden to meet with Hitler. As Hitler's October 1 deadline neared, war appeared inevitable if Hitler carried through on his threat to march into Czechoslovakia.

Nonetheless, Rose stayed at 14 Prince's Gate only long enough to refurbish her wardrobe. Then she was off to Scotland where many aristocrats enjoyed the fall season of grouse shooting. In the bracing climate of the Scottish autumn, Rose attempted to find pleasant walks through the wooded highlands. She listened to Chamberlain on the radio telling the British people to remain calm and to hope. She had sat next to him over lunch half a year ago, and now his voice sounded "filled with sadness, with loathing of war." The next day she journeyed to the Scottish shipyards to watch Queen Elizabeth christen the great 1,031-feet-long liner that was named in her honor.

On the morning of September 28, Joe called and said that Rose should return to London; war was only a few days away. In Scotland it was the day of the annual Perth races. Most years this picturesque city was full of tourists, and clansmen in their colorful kilts. Rose's hotel was nearly empty, however, and as she drove into town to visit a well-known tweed shop, the mood on the streets was somber and subdued. The shopkeeper told her that Chamberlain had decided to make a dramatic flight to Munich in search of peace. There was no reason

to believe that the prime minister would be any more successful this time, but everywhere there was an inexplicable rush of
emotion, and unbridled hope that this time Chamberlain would
accomplish a peaceful settlement.

Rose decided that she would stay in Scotland at least for a
few more days. Kathleen was in Scotland as well, but she was
off with some of her new British friends. That afternoon
Kathleen attended the races wearing a tweed outfit without the
obligatory hat. She was photographed and the papers credited
her as being part of the new "hatless fashion." Rose's other
younger children were in London, and Rose had heard the rumor that workers were digging trenches in Hyde Park. Yet she
stayed in Scotland, as if questions of war and peace were not
her business, leaving it to Joe, Luella, and Dunn to prepare the
children for immediate evacuation. In the evening she chanced
upon Kathleen at a cocktail party at the castle of Lord Forte-
viot. Kathleen was so involved with her friends that she didn't
even know about Chamberlain's flight.

In Munich, while Kathleen and her mother were at their
cocktail party, Chamberlain and French Prime Minister Edouard Daladier signed an agreement with Hitler giving over the
Sudetenland to Germany. William Shirer, a young American
correspondent, wrote in his diary that the prime minister
looked less like a diplomat than "like some bird—like some
black vultures I've seen over the Parsi dead in Bombay," but
in London the church bells rang out, and the crowds cheered
Chamberlain for bringing what he believed would be "peace
for our time."

"Everyone feels relieved and happy," Rose wrote in her diary. "Chamberlain's words, from Shakespeare's _Henry IV_: 'Out
of this nettle, danger, we pluck this flower, safety,' "

When Rose arrived back in London Joe took her in his
arms. As she recalled, he repeated over and over again like a
mantra "what a great day this was and what a great man
Chamberlain was." Joe viewed Munich as his triumph too, and
at the first chance he sought to drive home the message. He
had an immediate opportunity in a speech to be given in October before the Navy League on Trafalgar Day, memorializing
Lord Nelson's great victory. It was a day for patriotic paeans,
for toasting the supposedly indomitable British spirit. Joe had
a very different sort of message that he intended to give: De-
mocracies and dictatorships will "have to live together in the
same world, whether we like it or not."

When Rose read Joe's speech, she saw that her husband was about to create a totally unnecessary controversy. She had a sense of the rightness of things, and she knew that the message would bring down a wrath of abuse upon him. "Have you thought how this would sound back home?" Joe quoted her as counseling him. He did not listen to his wife, but went ahead and gave his speech. And Rose was right. He found himself at the center of a firestorm of controversy that scarred him and his reputation.

Rose's advice had been shrewd and wise, and the Trafalgar Speech should have taught him to crook his ear toward his wife and listen to her good counsel. But he did not do so. "That was the beginning and the end of my entire career in international politics," Rose wrote later. And it was the beginning of Joe's time of trouble.

At the end of 1938, Rose and the children traveled to St. Moritz for a holiday in the Swiss Alps while Joe flew back to Washington for consultations and a vacation at Palm Beach with his cronies. The Kennedys had scarcely arrived at the resort when Bobby sprained his ankle on the nursery slope. Joe Jr., who was spending the year observing the workings of diplomacy and traveling through Europe, went careening down the biggest slopes, heedless of life and limb, making spectacular runs until he made an equally spectacular spill, breaking his arm. Joe Jr., like his brothers and sisters, viewed physical pain as a test, and he laughed off his distress. "It sure looks awful, doesn't it?" he asked with perverse pride. And he was soon off again skating with his arm in a sling. Little Teddy did his best to follow his brothers' lead, managing to collect a wrenched knee for his endeavors, making it a perfect three for three in injuries for the boys. While he was convalescing Ted amused himself in part by playing with matches, setting a wastebasket on fire at the Palace Hotel.

Eunice and Pat skied as well, taking the lift to the top of the mountain, while Jean stayed below and went skating on the lake with her mother. Rose was used to Joe being far away, emotionally if not always physically, and she was not full of self-pity or anger as she rang in the new year without her spouse as all around her couples toasted each other and filled the night with merriment. Even now Rose was forever thinking of Joe and the family and their social and political advance. She sat down in her room at the ski resort, and on the station-

ery of the Suvretta House wrote a note to Roosevelt, thanking
the president for all that he had done for the family.

> *My dear Mr. President:*
> *The children and I saw the old year out here at St.*
> *Moritz, and we thought of all the interesting and stimulating*
> *experiences which we had enjoyed during 1938. We appre-*
> *ciate the fact that it had all been made possible through the*
> *honor which you had conferred upon Joe. And so we want*
> *to thank you again for 1938 and we want you to know that*
> *we are hoping and praying that you may enjoy every happi-*
> *ness of 1939.*
> *I have the honor to remain, dear Mr. President,*
>
> *Yours sincerely,*
> *Rose Kennedy*

As a political woman, Rose had learned to be eternally alert
to a misspoken word, a public stumble that might bring them
all down. She had a subtle wariness toward journalists and
journalism, and unlike her husband she almost never popped
off to them in words that would later haunt her. Her family
was famous and even here in St. Moritz photographers were
taking pictures of Rose and her illustrious brood. While in the
Swiss resort, Rose received a telephone call from a London
Daily Express reporter. The journalist asked about rumors that
Joe was resigning and that Rose and family would soon be returning to the United States. Joe had, in fact, talked about quitting, but Rose was not about to give credence to a rumor that
had most likely been fanned by her husband's enemies in
Washington, especially when she was so happy with the prestige as the ambassadress in London. "We hope to stay in London for a long time, perhaps years," Rose said, squelching the
story. "We like England and we just love the English. I've had
some of the happiest times of my life in England. All the children like it too."

Beyond the series of injuries, Rose's main concern at St.
Moritz was her eldest daughter. At twenty, Rosemary was a
picturesque young woman, a snow princess with flushed
cheeks, gleaming smile, plump figure, and a sweetly ingratiating manner to almost everyone she met. Rose knew that she
could depend on Eunice to spend much time shepherding her
older sister around the Swiss resort. Rosemary, however, was

attracting the attention of young men who took her cryptic silences and deliberate speech as feminine demureness. Rose
wanted Rosemary to enjoy at least something of the social life
that filled her sisters' days, and she agreed to let Rosemary go
out as long as she had Joe Jr. to chaperon.

"Well, why does Joe have to come?" Rosemary asked.

"Oh, they're just foreigners, dear," Rose replied, brushing
the matter off, "and Joe is not going to bother you. He'll just
be in the room."

Rose and the rest of the family formed a closed circle
around Rosemary, not simply to protect her from the world,
but to protect the family image from the reality of Rosemary.
The Kennedys had become one of the most celebrated families
in America and England too, lauded in lengthy magazine articles, applauded as flawless exemplars of American life, called
by *Reader's Digest* "one of the most interesting family groups
in the world," described by *Parents Magazine*, the bible of
family values, as "the natural expressions of a fundamentally
happy family, each youngster a personality at peace with himself."

Rose and Joe felt that they had to lie about Rosemary, and
lie they did, constantly changing their story, as if trying to find
some tale that would work. They told *Woman's Day* that Rosemary was "studying to be a kindergarten instructor." *Parents
Magazine* learned that although Rosemary had "an interest in
social welfare work, she is said to harbor a secret longing to go
on the stage." When two *Boston Globe* reporters wrote requesting an interview, Eddie Moore prepared a response that Rosemary then copied. "I have always had serious tastes and
understand that life is not given us just for enjoyment," she laboriously printed out, letter by letter. "For some time past, I
have been studying the well known psychological method of
Dr. Maria Montessori and I got my degree in teaching last
year."

Almost as soon as Rose returned to London, she prepared to
set off again on another lengthy trip, this time by herself. Rose
was the ambassadress to the Court of St. James's at one of the
most crucial periods in American history. Her role was so minimal in her husband's life that she could leave on a lengthy trip
to the French Riviera, southern Italy, Athens, the Greek islands, Turkey, Palestine, and Egypt. There was a poignant
quality to this tiny, brittle forty-eight-year-old woman, so proud
of her station as the ambassadress, so insistent on the prerog-

atives of that position, and yet so alone, traveling from first-class hotel room to first-class hotel room, city to city.

Years ago she had made her truce with Joe and marked off the territory on which she would build her life with her husband. It was only a spit of land, family, and social ambition, but build it she did and she was proud of her husband, and their creations, the nine Kennedy sons and daughters. The letters that she wrote Joe whenever she was away were affectionate missives to a man who was her partner in the making of an extraordinary family. "I am going to Egypt," she wrote Joe shortly before she left. "It is going to be wonderful, and if it is half as good as I think, I shall try to send the youngsters next summer. You know we get twenty-five per cent discount!"

Rose was in Egypt when she heard the news that Pope Pius XI had died and that Cardinal Eugenio Pacelli would become the new pope. Pacelli was a family friend and had taken tea with the Kennedys at Bronxville. Now the president had chosen Joe to represent the United States, the first time an American diplomat had ever officially attended a pope's inauguration. All she had as writing paper was a piece of brown wrapping paper, but that would have to do to write her old Brookline friend, Marie Greene, and tell her the news: "Have just had a cable from Joe that we are to represent the United States at Pope Pius XII coronation."

Rose considered the appointment an honor to her and the children as well. She headed immediately to Italy from the Middle East. She made it in time to be at the train station in Rome as the train carrying her family from Paris arrived. Joe had engaged a special private railroad car, and as the children disgorged from the wagon-lit, Rose was first elated and then suddenly alarmed. Joe Jr. was nowhere to be seen. When Rose asked her husband what had happened to their eldest son, Joe told her that he had sent a cable to Joe Jr. in Spain where he was traveling, but in the bloody turmoil of the civil war the message had not reached him. The truth was that Joe had been exchanging cables with his eldest son, and apparently had agreed that Joe Jr. could stay in Madrid. As Joe saw it, religion was a woman's preserve, and politics a man's. He could not think of ordering his son out of Madrid, even for the coronation of a pope, no more than he could think of telling his wife the truth. It was perhaps a gentle, harmless dissembling, but Joe was teaching his children that they could tiptoe around their mother's values as long as they did not wake her up.

In Rome, Rose found a "special joy" that the aged Cardinal O'Connell had journeyed to Rome for the ceremonies. Rose had not an iota of anger or doubt about the role that O'Connell had played in her life, indeed just the opposite. She thought about how he had married her and Joe, and that although he was growing feeble, Rose felt that he "retained his kindness and wisdom."

Joe had taught his children to shove themselves forward, to stand in the forefront of any gathering, and to walk at the front of any parade. In Rome Joe set a splendid example. There were only a limited number of seats at the papal ceremony in the Vatican, and he, the ambassador to the Court of St. James's, not his entire family, had been invited. But he wanted his family to be there, and that was that. Cardinal O'Connell was intimately familiar with the ways of Joseph P. Kennedy, and when he learned of the size of the Kennedy contingent, he exclaimed: "Oh, will Joe never learn!" Count Ciano, Italy's foreign minister and Mussolini's son-in-law, arrived at his seat for the coronation in St. Peter's to discover it occupied by a young Kennedy. The diplomat was about to stomp out of the cathedral when another seat was found for Ciano.

Rose would remember these days as one of the greatest moments of her life. For her the most extraordinary experience of all was their private audience with the pope. The pontiff generally remained seated for his audiences, but as Joe entered, Pius XII stood up and greeted the American ambassador. After Joe and the pope spoke privately for a few minutes, the rest of the Kennedys and associates left the antechamber and entered a private room. The pope walked over to a table with a silver tray of rosaries and medallions, gifts to the Kennedys. The pope chatted amiably with Rose, remembering the day he had taken little Teddy on his lap in Bronxville, and the boy had asked about the cross he wore around his neck. "I told my sister Patricia, I wasn't frightened at all," seven-year-old Teddy said afterwards. "He [the pope] patted my hand and told me I was a smart little fellow. He gave me the first rosary beads from the table before he gave my sister any."

Two days later the Kennedys returned to the Vatican, where Pius XII gave Teddy his First Communion, the first American to receive such an honor. For Rose family and faith were always together, like two hands in prayer, and it was an honor beyond honor, a gift to her, to her family, to her faith.

* * *

On the ides of March, while the Kennedys were still in Rome, Nazi troops entered Bohemia and Moravia. As the flames of war grew closer to London, Joe had one transcendent task: to determine the will of the British people and report accurately to Washington.

Joe used Kathleen's and Eunice's young friends as a gauge of the moral strength of the young generation. One evening at an embassy party Kathleen sat next to Billy Hartington. Joe showed the assembly a film that dealt with the trench warfare of World War I. "See that?" Joe yelled over the sound track, as if he would stick their youthful heads into the bloody wounds. "That's what you'll look like if you go to war with Germany!"

"Will you fight the Germans?" Joe asked the young men. The British are not much given to abstract declarations of courage, and it was unlikely that the young men would unfurl their banners of patriotism, particularly not in the living room of the isolationist American ambassador. Moreover, there was something about the boldness of his questions, the veiled challenge that lay behind the words, that rankled.

"Oh, I know when it comes to it you won't fight," Joe said furiously, as Kathleen Ormsby-Gore and others watched.

"Of course, we won't," one of the young men answered. "Why should we?"

The other young men embroidered on the answer, portraying themselves as a race of knaves, laggards, and social parasites. It was great putting old Joe on, and they outdid one another in professing their cowardice. That many of them were already in the reserves, and even full-fledged officers, including Billy in the Coldstream Guards, didn't matter, and Joe never seemed to catch on.

"You mustn't pay any attention to him," an embarrassed Kathleen told Billy after her father's diatribe during the film screening. "He just doesn't understand the English as I do." Kathleen had a gift not simply for talking but for listening, and she knew that Billy and her friends were full of anxieties and fears, retreating into black humor, joking that they would get America on their side in the coming war by shooting one of the Kennedys and pretending that the Germans had done it.

In the drawing room at Prince's Gate no one was more angry at Joe's disregard for the evil of Nazism, no one more outraged at his arrogant dismissal of the British will, than

Kathleen's and Eunice's debutante friends. As part of their "finishing" many of them had spent several months in Germany, and knew more about Nazism than did the young men. Kathleen Ormsby-Gore quietly fumed, hardly able to contain herself, listening to Joe railing against her worthless effete generation. His cynical disregard endlessly rankled her. She had spent time in Vienna after the Nazi takeover that Joe said didn't matter. There she had broken her foot and had it set by a Dr. Rosenblatt, a Jewish physician in the apartment across from hers. Then one night he and his family were gone, and the door was left blowing in the wind. "It was so frightening and those of us who had been there talked to our contemporaries and anyone who would listen," she recalled. "I was a terrible bore on the subject."

While other women debated the prospects of war, Rose had retreated into a world of ritual and appearance, and was consumed with the idea of doing everything in the proper fashion. The great social occasions dominated Rose's imagination. During the Kennedy's second year in London no event so concerned Rose as the dinner party for the king and queen in the first week of May 1939. She ordered Baltimore shad roe, Virginia ham, and Georgia pickled peaches flown in from the United States. Orchids were imported from Paris, but she thought that orchids might sound a bit extreme, so she told the press that they were "phalaenopsis," the scientific name for moth orchids. When the flowers arrived the afternoon of the dinner, she supervised as they were arranged in the appropriate colors in all the main rooms at Prince's Gate. She decided that strawberry shortcake would be a homey touch, a patriotic finale to the dinner, but she felt that British strawberries weren't quite good enough, and she had the fruit flown in from Paris as well. The dessert proved to be an enormous success with Their Majesties, the exotic confection making its way onto the menus of some of the city's finest restaurants.

Dinner menus were always printed in French, the language of civilized discourse. But Joe had said "not in my house" and had the menu printed in English. It was a gesture that the American reporters celebrated, applauding him for following "his own bent rather than custom." The Kennedys again managed to appear populists while approaching the monarch as if they were their subjects. There was yet another unusual touch. Almost any other diplomatic family would have had their children make an appearance for a quick curtsy and greeting; Rose and Joe set out a small table in the dining room so that the six young Kennedys could be a full part of this evening along with their older siblings.

Rose believed that punctuality was a sign of moral character, and she took it as proof positive that the king and queen were as timely as Big Ben. She and Joe stood waiting at the foot of the steps when, as Rose remembered, "about twenty-seven minutes of nine, they told us the automobile was approaching." Rose considered Queen Elizabeth the very model of regal behavior, a personage to whom life had become a never-ending parade of decorum and ritual. The queen was a miracle of manners, emotionally impregnable. Tears did not dim her eyes. Vulgarities did not touch her lips. Distasteful emotions never clouded her countenance. "I think the queen was quite remarkable and this queen too," she said decades later, "because they have so many responsibilities. They always have to be on time. They always have to be beautifully dressed and meticulous. They have to meet people of different countries with a smile and say something gracious, remember whom they're meeting and what the interests of the other party are, and they do that day after day and month after month. In politics, we . . . know that there will be an end and that we can relax. But they have it from birth, so I admire them very much. I admire the queen."

In the spring of 1939 Rose traveled to the United States in part to help prepare for the historic visit of the king and queen to the United States. Millions of Americans looked at Britain as a land of empire and privilege whose quarrels with Nazi Germany were the intramural spats among residents of a tired and decidedly old world. Roosevelt was attempting to mold the inchoate, volatile mind of America to a different understanding, an endeavor greeted frequently by deep and indeed justified suspicion that he was preparing America for the possibility of entering a great and distant war.

A king was a king and a queen a queen, especially in the egalitarian world of the United States, and there was a deep fascination with the appealing royal couple. This pointedly nonpolitical visit had a major political impact. "THE BRITISH RE-TAKE WASHINGTON," said one headline the day after the royal couple left the nation's capital.

Rose adored the glamour and ritual of monarchy, but she understood instinctively that Americans liked even their royalty to have a humble democratic side. After all, she had served American strawberry shortcake to the royal couple at Prince's Gate, and that had been a great success. And now after a "great argument" hot dogs were served to Their Majesties at a picnic at Roosevelt's home in Hyde Park, New York, and as Rose noted, "Their Majesties were delighted and it all caused a great sensation in the press."

The visit was a triumphant success, Rose in her quiet way helping to undermine Joe's politics of isolation. "To Mrs. Kennedy, of whom we did not hear enough during the Royal tour, must go much of the credit for the overwhelming success of the American visit," the London *Daily Express* wrote.

By the time the king and queen arrived in Hyde Park, Rose was gone, traveling back to Hyannis Port for a few days. Rose had stood apart from the endless social life of a resort community. Now her visit was, as the *New Bedford Standard Times* triumphantly expressed, "spelled out in capital letters . . . NEWS, not alone for Cape Cod, but for the country at large." Rose couldn't find the energy to talk to the local reporters. It was an exhausting endless ritual always playing the dutiful wife and hostess, never having anyone in whom to confide, always looking so chic and young and thin, and sometimes she felt worn out. Her father knew his daughter, and when she arrived at the Cape, Fitzgerald could see that she was not quite his beloved Rosie. "She isn't seeing anyone," Fitzgerald told a reporter. "She came here from England for a complete rest. She is tired and wants to get back into condition before she returns to England."

Rose had been there in London during the three months of Kathleen's Season, but just as Eunice began attending the ritual of events her mother was in the United States. As the world lumbered and lurched toward conflagration, in the great houses of London the lights often burned late for the dinners, dances, and parties of the 1939 Season. Those who were connoisseurs of British social life felt there had rarely been a Season as brilliant as this Season of Eunice's debut. "Despite the none too good news from Europe, the social racket still goes gaily on," the *Tatler* reported, "and quite right, too, for what is the use of squealing before you are hurt!"

Kathleen had been one of the most lauded debutantes of the previous Season, and Eunice was entering a society on which her older sister had engraved her signature. Seventeen-year-old

Eunice was not the gawky, awkward adolescent of a few years ago. She had a high-strung intensity, and a smile that suddenly would flash, a triumph over her shyness. "Eunice would never take anything for granted," Luella recalled. "She thought like a man. She had her mind set whether it was going to a dance or a party, what she was going to wear, and who was going to be there, and what was the purpose. She was so organized in her mind."

Eunice spoke in a nervous staccato, the words jumping out of her. She was quick to challenge others, ready to dismiss stupidity and intellectual sloth. She was an interesting young woman but next to her vivacious sister, the very model of charm, Eunice could seem almost forlorn. "Kathleen and I got along well," Eunice said. "There wasn't any jealousy because in a big family everybody has a different kind of talent and if somebody is good at one thing then somebody else is better at another."

All her life Eunice had lived within the security of her family, and of her older brothers whom she adored, and of a father whom she idolized. And now she was going out by herself to dances and balls, lunches with other debutantes, Wimbledon, and Ascot—all the events on which Kathleen had left her mark.

Eunice was far more popular among women than men. Often her dance card was not filled, and she spent much time in the cloakroom or the powder room, talking anxiously with other debutantes. The debutantes off in these rooms, the muffled sounds of music and laughter wafting into their retreats, shared a gentle illusion that they were here to powder their noses and apply fresh lipstick, and were not hiding away from a world that seemed beyond them. "I'm not sure I'm looking forward to tomorrow night's party," Eunice told Ursula Wyndham-Quin, as if she were having a marvelous time at this evening's dance.

"I hated those parties," Eunice recalled. "They were terrible. I'd go into the ladies' room and wait for the dance to get over and talk to somebody. You'd go hide in there, anything to fill in the twenty minutes of the dance. Then you'd go back and maybe your card was filled for the next dance. Then you're all right for a while, and then bam you'd go back into the ladies' room."

While their mother was away, Eunice and Kathleen assumed Rose's role as hostess with great élan. At an embassy tea party they had the tea and cakes set out at a number of small tables instead of the customary large buffet. It was only a minor innovation, but it was different enough to be commented upon.

Eunice could not hope to match her sister's memorable coming-out party. The other debutantes knew one or another, at least they seemed to, but Eunice had been away at Roehampton with the nuns. The *Times* listed the party on June 22, 1939, as a "small dance," a definition that meant primarily that the king and queen would not be attending. Though it was hardly the grand occasion of Kathleen's event, the affair was small only by the exalted standards of the Season. As was the custom Eunice gave her own intimate dinner party, while half a dozen other women gave dinners as well for guests who would later come to Prince's Gate for the dance.

Eunice dressed in a glorious peach-colored dress from a French designer, Paquin, and greeted guests that included Viscountess Astor and Baroness Ravensdale, an impressive gathering of the British nobility and elite. Three other debutantes had their dances this evening as well, but Eunice's was the place to be. Elizabeth Leveson-Gower, a debutante and the future Countess of Sutherland, attended the dinner party. "They [the Kennedys] all had this quality of liveliness—Eunice too," the Countess of Sutherland reflected. "She wasn't classically good-looking, and certainly not as attractive as Kick, but she was so lovely and energetic, and *that* was attractive. She had a rather wide face, but her figure was good and she was tremendously good company."

Like many debutantes, Leveson-Gower did not feel comfortable carrying on a serious political conversation. She found it unsettling talking to Eunice's older brother, Jack. He was too intense, too consumed with politics. She was happy to be sitting next to Joe and although she knew his reputation as anti-British found the ambassador "easy to talk to and a good host." Billy Hartington was among the guests, obviously smitten with Kathleen. "I remember going to a dance and sitting next to Billy," recalled the Countess of Sutherland, "and he spent the whole dinner telling me how wonderful Kathleen was."

Even the Duke of Marlborough had asked if he might attend, though the fathers of the debutantes rarely accompanied their daughters. "Dukie Wookie" not only showed up but in the early-morning hours led the guests in doing the Big Apple, the line dance that was all the rage.

"It was a wonderful ball," the Duchess of Northumberland recalled. "I remember having a dance with Jack. It was a lovely ball."

In mid-July the last two court presentations took place. On July 12, two days after Eunice's eighteenth birthday, she drove with her mother and father to Buckingham Palace. It was an evening that would not happen again, an evening of splendor and magnificence including many of the most prominent of the debutantes. Even in that company, Eunice and Rose stood out as stunningly well dressed. Eunice wore a splendid Paquin creation of ivory tulle crinoline with an ivory satin train while Rose stood out even more in a dramatic ice-blue satin gown, diamond tiara, ostrich-feather fan, and long blue gloves. There were jewels almost beyond comprehension. The Bolivian ambassadress wore a tiara studded with emeralds that Mrs. Alan Kirk, the wife of the American naval attaché, thought looked "each one as big as a hen's egg."

As this great gathering of princes, princesses, diplomats, and debutantes took their places, an usher sidled up to Rose. "I'm very sorry, Madame," he said, "but you must have a pair of white gloves."

Her daughter Kathleen would have brushed the whole business off with cavalier detachment, another tale about the Brits and their peculiar ways. But Rose lived for moments like this. She prided herself on having a superb sense of protocol and manners, and now to be singled out in Buckingham Palace for her gaucherie. "Oh, there was great distress about that!" Mrs. Kirk recalled. The ushers were always ready with sundry items—extra bouquets, buttons, long white gloves—and Rose put on the poorly fitting gloves and went ahead wearing an outfit that was proper but not right.

Eunice didn't approach the occasion with the offhand unconcern of Kathleen, or the determination of Rosemary, but with breathless fervor. Afterwards, as she wrote down her reflections on the evening, there was a childlike innocence to her recollections of a girl of ten or twelve, not a fiercely bright young woman whom her father called the most intelligent of his daughters:

> The day I had planned and hoped for had come at last, but I was unable to realize that I was about to make my appearance before Their Majesties and the titled families of En-

gland. I, who had lived for eighteen years like any ordinary American girl was to be presented tonight to King George VI and Queen Elizabeth at Buckingham Palace!

As I entered the Palace more excitement and joy seized me than ever before in my life. . . . I had the honor of being the first debutante presented after the most honorable matrons. . . . During the first moments of waiting, I was breathlessly excited; then a strong rich voice called MISS KENNEDY and I started to walk alone toward their Majesties, I glanced upward and wondered if ever I would reach the throne thirty feet away; but somehow, I did. As I made my curtsy . . . I realized that at this moment I was the center of interest of this King and Queen and all the pompous ceremony that England holds so sacred.

Shortly after midnight, I left the Palace for home, happy in the realization that I had achieved the aim of every young girl—that of being presented at the Court of St James's—the world's greatest empire—"The Empire upon which the sun never sets."

Those languid days of June and July were filled with parties, balls, luncheons, tennis matches, and maddening inconsistencies and contradictions. Lady Astor, who had cried shame when Churchill had condemned the Munich agreement, was now preparing Cliveden as a hospital in the event of war. On the Fourth of July, Rose gave an Independence Day garden party. That evening at an Independence Day banquet and ball, the four young Kennedys sat together at one table. The Duke of Kent told Rose that "he had seen Kennedys at every table at the 400 Club." Joe Jr. and Jack were squiring around several of the most beautiful women in the capital, and their father had no objection to their spending evenings at the exclusive nightclub. Joe, however, couldn't abide Kathleen going there. He took his daughter aside, and as Rose wrote in her diary, he "reprimanded Kick for being there."

A few days later Eunice drove to the Eton and Harrow cricket match, with her friend Elizabeth Leveson-Gower. Eunice knew nothing about cricket, and little enough about this annual match that Eton had won thirty years in a row. At Lords, Eunice and Leveson-Gower found a place in Billy Hartington's box and looked out on one of the most picturesque scenes of upper-class English life. The Eton boys wore double-breasted gray waistcoats, carried black canes, and sported blue carnations. The Harrow lads sported top hats, cut-away coats, coffee waistcoats, and silver-topped canes.

Billy had been an Eton boy, and dressed in his proper topper and coat he cheered on his alma mater. It was not to be Eton's day, and after three decades of humiliation, Harrow defeated their perennial tormenters by eight wickets. While Eunice watched from Billy's box, the triumphant Harrovians ran onto the field, and within minutes a melee was taking place, insti-gated by the old graduates.

Eunice attended the last great dance of the Season held on July 7 in honor of Lady Sarah Spencer-Churchill, eldest daugh-ter of the Duke and Duchess of Marlborough. A thousand guests attended the largest party that the Duchess had ever given at Blenheim Palace. Jack, who was in England working on his Harvard senior thesis, had been invited as well. He pro-nounced Blenheim "nearly as big as Versailles" and wrote Lem Billings that he had "never had a better time." Even the sar-donic diarist Chips Channon found himself stunned. "I have seen much, travelled far and am accustomed to splendor, but there has never been anything like tonight," he wrote in his di-ary. Lady Sarah's grandmother had seen much too, and she too was awestruck, sensing something not only magnificent but ominous. "I suffered the same unease that had afflicted me once in Russia when, surrounded by the glittering splendor of the Czar's Court, I sensed impending disaster," she recalled. "For again, in this brilliant scene at Blenheim, I sensed the end of an era."

Even before the guests arrived at the golden palace in the Oxfordshire countryside and drove through the bronze gates, they could see illumination ahead of them, shining above the dark and cloud-strewn night. As they were chauffeured up to Blenheim, the palace appeared in luminous relief, searchlights highlighting its surfaces, the light playing off a lake that seemed to move and shimmer. As they walked up the great stairways, the guests moved through a gauntlet of powdered footmen and into the regal rooms of the main house. Every-where there were flowers, not diminutive roses and posies but rare pink malmaisons and huge pink carnations, a cascade of flowers, as if every plant had been grown to flower on this very evening.

The older dinner guests dined in the Saloon, but Sarah, Eu-nice, and the young set sat on the terrace in front of the arti-ficial serpentine lake. Behind their table stood a series of six-foot-tall trees, and before them searchlights played against the trees and the building, a kaleidoscope of colors. From the Long Library in the Palace, the sound of Viennese waltzes carried out across the terrace, the lilting melodies punctuated by the sounds of laughter and the clinking of champagne glasses.

After dinner, hundreds of other guests arrived, and the ball took place in the great rooms of the palace, the dancing centered in the Long Library, a 180-foot-long room with exquisite stucco decorations. It was an evening for waltzes, and magnificently gowned and jeweled ladies whirled around the room in the arms of their partners. Some ladies did not even bother leaving their minks and fox stoles and capes in the cloakroom but draped them on the marble statues.

Through the night Eunice danced as if in the midst of a fairy tale. At one point she and her escort walked toward Sarah's father. There was a breathless intensity to Eunice. "Let's ask this man the time!" Eunice exclaimed, as if asking a stranger on a train platform, not the Duke of Marlborough in Blenheim Palace.

Out on the terrace liveried waiters served supper to the ball guests, and strolling Tyrolean musicians wandered across the lawn. There too sat Winston Churchill in intense conversation with Anthony Eden. One of the debutantes, Mollie Acland, was sitting a dance out with a young man who had visions of becoming a politician. "Oh look at that poor old has-been," the man said, throwing a dismissive glance toward Churchill. "My father says he's still a potential trouble-maker, but he won't get any more public life now!"

There was dancing on the terrace as well, on a floodlit floor that had been laboriously put down. Nearby sat scores of wraps ready for the ladies in case they became chilled. The guests looked up and saw the sky darkening, and it began to rain, the drops refracted through the brilliant light of the searchlights looking like snowflakes. The wind picked up, and the footmen, valets, musicians, and chefs scrambled to cover the food and the instruments and to bring whatever they could inside.

The dancers poured into the rooms, but the palace did not seem overcrowded, and the guests waltzed on. In the predawn hours one of the ladies went to fetch her fur coat, but it was gone, and it seemed someone had taken her stole by mistake. Then a second and a third garment was missing, seventeen coats in all, and the women knew that while they had danced and drunk and eaten, thieves had been busy in the night.

Eunice and the other debutantes slept in the palace, and while they were still asleep the footmen took off their livery and started tediously removing the gritty mass of caked flour from their hair, collars, and necks, a task that took several hours. And out on the darkened grounds electricians began taking down the wiring for searchlights that soon would be scanning something other than trees and palaces.

In late July Kathleen left London with Joe Jr. and Hugh Fraser for a trip to Spain. Kathleen had always idolized her older brother, even more so now that he had so daringly served as an eyewitness to the siege of Madrid. She was proud that Joe Jr. was willing to travel with her, to show her *his* world where he believed courage was the common currency. "What fun we had!" she recalled. "I remember thinking then of how brave Joe was when different Spaniards told me of how he, the only American there, used to walk about the streets during the horrible, bloody days of the siege of Madrid." This was the first time that Kathleen had seen the ravages of war, buildings toppled to the ground, the line of the trenches still visible around the outskirts of Madrid. She wrote her family how she had met General Mossarch, the Nationalist officer who had held the fort of Alcázar for three months, and who, when his son was captured and threatened with death unless Mossarch gave up the fort, "told his son to die like a Spaniard."

Kathleen, like her older brother and her church, viewed Franco as a largely heroic figure, and the war not a complex harbinger of World War II but a struggle between the "Reds" and the forces of Christian civilization. Franco's Fascist government had quickly begun policing the morals and customs of the Spanish people. At the beach of San Sebastian, Kathleen had worn the required long bathing suit, but Joe Jr. had gotten in trouble with the police when he had neglected to put on the top of his swimming suit.

From Spain Kathleen and Joe traveled to the villa of Domain de Ranguin outside Cannes, where Rose and the rest of the family were spending a month. It was a grand home including one of the most splendid rose gardens on the entire Riviera. Kathleen enjoyed the French Riviera, but soon after she arrived she wanted to return to England to attend twenty-one-year-old Billy Hartington's coming-of-age party at Chats-

worth, the great house that one day would be his home. It
would be a two-day-long celebration, with a traveling circus of
trained dogs and ponies, music played by the band of Billy's
regiment, the Coldstream Guards, and gifts for the three thousand employees and tenants. Kathleen knew that the event
would be as memorable as the Blenheim Ball.

Rose would have none of it. It didn't matter that once long
ago Rose's father had acted in a similar fashion, preventing her
from attending the Harvard prom with Joe, but forcing her to
go with him to Palm Beach. Rose forbade Kathleen from returning to England to attend. Kathleen was nineteen years old,
but she would not disobey her mother, and she stayed with the
family on the Mediterranean.

On the very day of Billy's party, a story appeared in *The
Boston Globe* titled "KENNEDY GIRL MAY WED PEER." Both families immediately denied the story. "Kathleen and Billy were,
in fact, discussing marriage," recalled Jane Compton. "But it
wasn't that serious. We were all sort of young and gidderish
and involved with having a good time." As much as Kathleen
enjoyed Billy's company, she was still Catholic and he a member of the Church of England, and to their parents the differences appeared insurmountable.

Kathleen was not one to moan, to mope endlessly in the
summer sun, especially when almost everyone around her was
having such a marvelous time, and Jack had arrived with his
friend "Torby" Macdonald, one of Kathleen's innumerable
flames. The two friends had had a dramatic journey from Paris
in which Jack had wrecked their dilapidated rented car, ending
up upside down on the side of the road. Although Jack dismissed his mishap with humorous bravado, his mother took it
far more seriously. Rose ruled that her twenty-two-year-old son
as well as his twenty-four-year-old older brother would only be
allowed to drive the tortuously curving road from their villa
down to Cannes when Luella was in the backseat. Luella was
amenable, as long as Joe Jr. and Jack gave her some francs for
gambling, and picked her up at the casino after their dates.

At Eden Roc, Rose watched the Kennedy sons dive off the
high rock into the water far below. As a girl, eleven-year-old
Jean was not expected to make the spectacular dive, but her
brothers chided pudgy little Ted until he made the jump. Another mother would have called a halt at the mere idea of making a seven-year-old attempt such a dive, but to Rose these
were the rites of passage to manhood. "I could barely swim at

that point," Ted recalled. "I think I was pretty scared but they all seemed to be doing it."

Rose enjoyed taking lunch where the diminutive bathing area was so crowded that there was hardly room for another sun mat. Marlene Dietrich descended to the beach from Hotel Du Cap wearing a stunning white-skirted bathing outfit, covered by a knee-length coat. Norma Shearer, another Hollywood star, was expected at any moment. Over in Monte Carlo the Duke and Duchess of Windsor had arrived in a black Buick for the National Sporting Club boxing tournament. In Cannes, the American hostess extraordinaire, Elsa Maxwell, was planning another season of parties. Many of the young Kennedys' friends had come down to Cannes too, and there was hardly an evening without a party. In mid-August Jack and Torby set off to visit Germany, yet another adventure.

In this glamorous, exclusive Riviera society, the Kennedys were a much-desired addition, deluged with invitations. Despite the anger that some Britons felt toward Joe, for the most part he was still being lauded as an attractive representative of his country, praised regularly and extravagantly in the popular press. "He is the most popular Ambassador that America has sent us for many years," wrote the *Star* in June. "He is popular because he seems to the London crowd to embody the sparkling vitality of a continent." The *Tatler* also often wrote about the Kennedys. The magazine was largely full of short gossipy items, small pictures, and rarely ran even a half-page photograph. In August for the first time, the *Tatler* ran a full two-page photograph. There across two pages of the magazine were the eleven Kennedys with a caption stating that Joe "is stupendously popular, and so is his very charming wife, and his not inconsiderable family, numerous enough for two polo teams and a 'spare.'" The Kennedys stood in a line arms linked, with smiles that appeared not grins staged for a photographer, but manifestations of sheer ebullient optimism. They looked like an impregnable force marching into a future that they knew was theirs.

On August 21 the Nazis and Soviets announced that they had signed a nonagression pact, an agreement that left Poland locked within the arms of a vise. Joe immediately returned to England to meet with a disconsolate Chamberlain who told him of "the futility of it all" and that "all that the English can do is to wage a war of revenge that will mean the entire destruction of Europe."

Joe called Cannes to tell Rose that the family must leave immediately. The children heard the news on the beach, and the Kennedys did not so much leave Cannes as flee, with Kathleen and her friend and guest, Janie Kenyon-Slaney, still in beach clothes, their baggage to follow later.

At dawn on September 1, 1939, the first of a million German troops began their march into Poland, and the German bombers droned eastward to bomb Warsaw.

Two days later Chamberlain called Joe to Ten Downing Street. The prime minister showed Joe the speech that later in the day he would give declaring war before Parliament. The two men had stood together holding up the tattered banner of appeasement. With tears in his eyes, Joe read the tragic words that would prove his political epitaph as well as Chamberlain's: "Everything that I have worked for, everything that I have hoped for, everything that I have believed in during my public life has crashed in ruins." Joe returned to the embassy and called Roosevelt, and in a voice choking with emotion, repeated again and again, "It's the end of the world . . . the end of everything."

Rose, Kathleen, Joe Jr., and Jack ventured forth into the gloomy streets to hear Chamberlain's speech to Parliament. Everywhere they looked passersby were carrying gas masks, slung over their shoulders as nonchalantly as if they were the latest fashion accessory. As they walked toward the Palace of Westminster, a photographer snapped a photograph of the three young Kennedys, Kathleen in her white gloves, pearls, and big hat, and the two men in impeccably tailored double-breasted suits, the threesome marching forward with a jaunty air as if they had good seats at the Royal Opera, rather than being observers at the beginning of World War II.

As they hurried home after the speech, the air-raid sirens sounded and the four ran into the nearest shelter. Rose recalled: "When the sirens sounded my first thought was: 'That's Hitler's efficiency—having a raid as soon as war is declared.'" As they huddled in the darkness, Rose realized that they were hiding not in a cavernous bomb shelter but in the basement of Molyneux, the French couturier whose dress Rose had worn the year before at Kathleen's court presentation. "I thought later, what an ironic way for a woman to begin her war experiences," Rose recalled.

Kathleen wanted to stay in England. Billy was being called up, and all the antique furniture, artifacts, and paintings of Chatsworth were crated away, the great house turned into a girls' school for three hundred students and teachers. Her friends were no longer carefree, careless debutantes but were joining up too, planning to work in factories, as nurses, whatever was needed. Until now in her political thinking, Kathleen had largely followed her father's and Joe Jr.'s views. The mouth that a few months ago had spouted the slogans of Franco's Spain now pledged her support to a Britain her father said was doomed. But her father would hear nothing of it, and ruled that Kathleen would be traveling back to America with the rest of her family, leaving only Rosemary alone with him in London. Luella wanted to stay as well, to be with her beau, a British banker, and Rosemary. Joe would hear nothing of that either and said that he had brought Luella to England, and he would be damned if he did not return her to America from whence he had brought her.

The Kennedys had been loaned an estate in the country away from the expected bombing of London. On the final weekend before they left for the United States, Joe and Rose brought their children together. Sunday dinner the young Kennedys were all there: Joe Jr., Jack, Rosemary, Kathleen, Eunice, Pat, Bobby, Jean, and Teddy, and one outsider, Tom Egerton. "They were all so gay and they never stopped talking, chatting away sometimes even over the top of each other," remembered Egerton. "Kathleen was so unhappy to be going back, but what I recall most of that afternoon was the sheer exuberance, the happiness, the enjoyment in each other and the moment."

And then they were gone. They left not as they had arrived with fanfare and welcoming committee and photographers, but on vessels crowded with refugees and others desperate to reach the sanctuary of America. The Atlantic was full of Nazi submarines. The Kennedys traveled on several different ships. Rose, Eunice, Bobby, and Kathleen sailed on the *Washington*, while Luella traveled with the three youngest children on the *United States*, and Joe Jr. took passage on the *Mauritania*. Jack flew home on a Pan Am Clipper.

The Kennedys were sailing away from war, but the war was with them. The *Washington* carried 1,746 passengers, sleeping on cots in the swimming pool, cots pushed one next to another in the post office, cots set up even in what had been public rest rooms.

Eunice had an eleven-inch-long bandage on her left arm, the result of nothing as dramatic as a bombing raid, but a mere bicycle accident. Her mother was going through life fluffing up reality like a pillow on a sofa, and Eunice had a double measure of her mother's esprit. Eunice was relentlessly optimistic about life, her attitude a matter of denying the unpleasantness of much that was around her, as well as a natural optimism. She found the trip home "all great fun." She wrote her father: "Everyone we have met on the boat, even the young people, think you have done and are doing a marvelous job."

Eunice was partially correct. One of the passengers, Sol Hurok, the Russian Jewish impresario, had been astounded to hear on board passengers supporting Hitler and Mussolini. They at least would have approved Joe's policy of appeasement. The ship was full of women and men who were witnesses to Nazism, and the more they had seen the more resolute they were in their opposition to Hitler. Thomas Mann, the great German writer sailing into exile, said to any who would listen that "the aim of the war must be the destruction of the present German regime." Mann and Hurok and the hundreds of refugees on the ship were unlikely to have praised Eunice's father for his "marvelous job."

In 1938 when Rose had departed the first time, she had talked to the reporters at length. Now when the ship docked in New York harbor, Rose hurried off the boat without making any comments to the press. She and her children could not avoid one of the photographers. The picture that ran the next day in *The New York Times* showed a sophisticated family wearing the latest hats and fashion. Gone were the smiles that had almost always graced their photographs.

12
"We Had Everything"

𝓘n the house in Bronxville, the sounds of their London life echoed through empty rooms. Kathleen wrote a friend that it was like "returning to a house you lived in as a child and being surprised at how shabby everything suddenly seems."

Rose had supped with kings and queens, and here in this land without royalty, life seemed strangely provincial. As Rose settled back into the mansion in Bronxville in the fall of 1939, she realized how precious that year and a half in England had been, and all that the experience had done for her family. All those months the newspapers and magazines in America had been full of stories about the glorious Kennedy family, stories that acclaimed Rose and the children as much as they did Joe. The Kennedys had been anointed with the patina of celebrity, and those who once had disdained her now walked across crowded rooms to shake the hand of the ambassadress. The McDonnells might still call Jack a "moral roustabout" and his father a "crook and a bounder," but it was Rose who in October on her twenty-fifth wedding anniversary received congratulations from King George and Queen Elizabeth, greetings that were duly noted in *The New York Times*.

To Rose, the church hierarchy was a religious nobility, and it was only natural that she would become a confidante of the most powerful Catholic leader in the city, The Most Rev. Francis J. Spellman, the archbishop of New York. The archbishop became not simply the family priest, though he was that, but her priest, her confessor, her advisor and friend. The fifty-year-old Massachusetts-born priest was on his way to becoming a cardinal and one of the most powerful figures in the history of American Catholicism, a political priest wielding the

304

kind of influence to which the aging Cardinal O'Connell had once aspired.

Rose was one of the most admired Catholic women in America. She was in demand as a speaker at women's clubs from Boston to Richmond. To the ladies who sat reverently listening to Rose's recollection of life in London, Rose seemed almost royal herself. She had taken on certain upper-class London mannerisms, a slight British flavor to her accent, an imperious attitude toward her maids. Rose referred to Joe as "the ambassador," a title by which he would be known the rest of his life.

At the end of September, while Rose lectured about teas, court presentations, and wondrous balls in Richmond, Virginia, the Germans were subjecting Warsaw to a merciless bombardment. As she recalled her weekend at Windsor Castle, the Nazis and Soviets were completing the destruction of Poland. Rose was lecturing about a world that did not exist any longer, not for her, not for anyone. Even if she had wanted to speak of the terrible events in Europe, Joe would never have permitted it, and Rose was eternally relegated to this world of ritual and form, and expurgated times to remember.

Kathleen had hardly gotten off the ship in Manhattan before she was in the midst of the New York social whirl. In her first week back in the United States, she went to the World's Fair at Flushing Meadows twice, and took up with Peter Grace all over again. Peter had gotten over being so dramatically stood up in London, and took her to a polo match where she watched him play. He took her to the theater as well. Kathleen found him "just the same."

Nineteen-year-old Kathleen had a will and independence all her own, and she was not about to be shuttled off to Manhattanville where her mother had gone. Kathleen was not exactly scholarly. When she was turned down by Sarah Lawrence, a fine women's college, she decided to attend Finch, a junior college that was a glorified finishing school. That gave her plenty of time for her social life. Even Kathleen was socially accepted at a level that would have been unthinkable before her years in London. This November of 1939 she was a sponsor of "a series of Gotham subscription dances," which the top layer of young Catholic society attended.

Kathleen and her sisters had a newfound celebrity. "One evening in Cambridge, we went out on the town, Lem Billings,

Kathleen, and Eunice," recalled Richard Edwards, a friend. "What I do remember vividly is that wherever we went the Kennedy girls were recognized by almost everyone."

Fifteen-year-old Pat was too young to share in her older sisters' adventures. Pat was a tall, lanky, sweetly tempered young woman of striking good looks bound to have her full share of male admirers. Rose had long ago decided that Noroton was the proper venue for her teenaged daughters, away from teenaged males and the assorted dangers of secular society. Pat had heard quite enough about Noroton from Kathleen and Eunice to know that she must do *anything* to avoid being sent there. Pat knew that her mother was so narrowly focused on her moral maxims, repeating them like catechism, that as long as she pretended to obey, she could do as she pleased. When Pat learned that she had to take an entrance exam for Noroton, she knew that she had come upon her way out. All she had to do was to fail the exam.

Instead of being sent off to Noroton, Pat stayed home and along with Jean studied at Maplehurst, a Sacred Heart school on a magnificent former estate in the fringes of the Bronx only a quarter-hour ride from home. Pat began the school year repeating the work of the sophomore year of which she had seemed so abysmally lacking. She made a miraculous intellectual recovery, and within two weeks was pushed ahead into the junior class. "By then Mother decided it was too late to send me off to Sacred Heart at Noroton," Pat recalled. "In fact, I never went to boarding school until college. I never told her what I had done."

Although Pat felt relieved not to be subjected to the rigors of life at Noroton, at Maplehurst she was exposed to the same discipline as at any Sacred Heart school, the silences in the classrooms and the hall, the drab uniforms, the prayers and vigils. The main difference was that the regimen had a beginning and an end each day, and on weekends Pat could forget the nuns and their rules. The other difference was that she and her younger sister, Jean, were chauffeured to the school by a liveried driver, sometimes with seven-year-old Teddy accompanying the driver. Although the students dressed alike and were treated alike, everyone knew that the Kennedys were different, their legend reaching down even to the elementary grade that eleven-year-old Jean attended. In a family of such public and private distinction, Jean knew that she too must be different and special, though the one certain distinction was her name and her family, and she developed a precocious, protective snobbishness.

Of the nine Kennedy children, Jean had been the youngest in London to be sent off to school, living in Roehampton in an intimidating world primarily of much older children. And now again she was the only Kennedy child to spend no significant time in a public elementary school, but to be sent off immediately to the nuns.

Eunice could have gotten into a top secular college, but Rose sent her off to the nuns of the Sacred Heart at Manhattanville. It was so much *the* school for graduates of Noroton and other Sacred Heart academies that sometimes the nuns would not even forward a student's grade to a secular school. Since Rose's time, Manhattanville had become a full-fledged college. The high walls shut out the world of black Harlem that had grown up around the school. Inside the grounds nuns still walked silently, wearing the same crenellated veils and long dresses of a hundred years ago, and the students still studied a curriculum half of which consisted of Bible, religion, ethics, philosophy, psychology, Greek or Latin, and a modern language. All that was the same, but thanks in good measure to one person, Grace Cowardin Dammann, the president of the college, Manhattanville was a very different place now from the school Rose had attended. Mother Dammann was a formidable woman of great intellect, social consciousness, political awareness, and deep Catholicism.

Mother Dammann had admitted Manhattanville's first black student in the fall of 1938, a daring step for a conservative Catholic institution. She not only invited the world into Manhattanville but she sent the students out to work as part of their educations. They took the subway down to the Bowery and walked among alcoholics and bums to the Barat Settlement House. They volunteered at Casita Maria in East Harlem. They traveled down to Dorothy Day's Catholic Worker to experience the leftist Catholic movement.

Most of these young women were the progeny of the wealthiest, the most socially prominent Catholic families in America. Like the Kennedys, their ancestors had fought their way out of the slums of cities from Boston to San Francisco, or broken the sod of the prairies, struggling to provide the affluence that allowed their heirs to have the leisure, the culture, and the refinement that they did not have. Mother Dammann believed the modern task of the Sacred Heart education was to see to it that the children and grandchildren of these pioneers "must never be separated from the roots from which they spring. When this separation is made we have a false and parasitical aristocracy—'upper classes' whose logical downfall we have seen in history too often not to recognize signs of it in our own times." That was the drama of Manhattanville as it was of the Kennedy family. Would the great wealth that Joe had obtained be passed on to an energetic, disciplined generation full of purpose? Or would it end up a gigantic albatross, dissipated among a brood of the self-indulgent and self-involved?

The eighteen-year-old Eunice who arrived at Manhattanville in September 1939 seemed dispirited, distanced from the educational drama unfolding at the school. She roomed by herself in a tiny room near the chapel where the lay sisters chanted mass. Eunice had no intimate friends and it seemed by choice. Almost everyone at the school knew that she was one of the celebrated Kennedys, her father one of the most prominent, most admired Catholics in America. Eunice was polite and made the best of her long legs and stamina on the field hockey team, but she was not an integral part of the school. Occasionally, she would flash alive, astounding the other students with her mind. "I remember her brilliance," said Margery Mullen Tracy, two years ahead of Eunice. "In economics she always had a concept that was way beyond the rest of us."

On the weekends when Rose picked her daughter up in a chauffeured automobile, Eunice always sat in the front seat with the driver, not completely comfortable with her life of privilege. She dressed poorly, her hair a thicket of knots, as if she could hardly bother to brush or comb.

At the Christmas dance Eunice brought her sister, Pat. Paul Leahy attended the ball as well, escorting another Manhattanville student. "Now point out to me which ones are the Kennedy girls because we used to live right next to them in Brookline," Leahy said. Leahy walked over to the two young Kennedy women and introduced himself. "How did you like it in London?" he asked.

"Well, it was terribly fun over there and we just had a marvelous time," Eunice said, in what Leahy took to be something of a British accent.

So much of Eunice's life was to please her father, and she

wrote him letters full of pride in Joe, in her family, and her own accomplishments, which were achievements for the family as well. When she played in several tennis tournaments, she wanted her father to know that she had gotten her name and picture in the paper. On a tennis trip to New York, Pennsylvania, and Cleveland, Ohio, she could talk to the other players the way she could not back at Manhattanville. "The chief topic of conversation during the trip was your brains and what a wonderful job you were doing," she wrote her father. "Also how young looking Mother was. You can imagine how upset Mother was when I told her this. She almost jumped over the table in her excitement."

Joe was a world away in England, but even from that distance he dominated the lives and thoughts of his wife and daughters. Rose knew how desperately Joe wanted to return to the United States to see his family, so much so that "he couldn't stand it anymore." She knew how depressed and distraught he had become. As always, in the family, it was his psyche as a man, his emotions that were considered paramount.

Rose had an exquisite sensitivity to her husband's mood, and she wrote Joe a letter that was a rarity for her, a passionately felt missive, a letter to a man whom she sensed was suffering in his aloneness. "My darling," she began, an appellation that she hardly ever used:

> I am wondering when I shall see you and what is happening! It is all so heartbreaking. . . . Of course I am not complaining. I just hope and pray daily that you are taking care of yourself and are not too terribly lonely. When the children and I start to think and talk about our experiences there [England], we realize what a superlatively inspiring position it was. I just wish I might be along with you. As I say—all I can do is pray very hard that I shall see you soon. All my love always.

Rose understood her husband's mood better than he understood it himself. In mid-September he wrote his friend Arthur Krock asking him to call Rose for "after a while she is bound to get a bit depressed." It was Joe, however, who was dispirited and six weeks later he wrote the journalist admitting his feelings: "The job is now terribly boring and with all the family back in America, I am depressed beyond words." He wrote his daughter Pat of his feelings as well: "Between you and me it is pretty lonesome."

All the young Kennedys corresponded regularly with Joe, and between his sons and daughters there was an extraordinary intellectual and emotional dichotomy. The father and his sons wrote of politics and world events, in words no more emotional than those in a newspaper story. The father and his daughters discussed feelings and personal family events.

Kathleen wrote her father a letter those first weeks as well. She had her own precise awareness of her father's mood, and her letter was full of melancholy for a time and a place and a life that were gone. "It all seems like a beautiful dream," she wrote. "Thanks a lot Daddy for giving me one of the greatest experiences anyone could have had. I know it will have great effect on everything I do from here on in."

Joe sat in the movie room in the residence at Prince's Gate viewing the latest newsreel with its pictures of Rose and the children leaving on the *Washington* for America. As he watched the flickering images on the screen, his eyes filled with tears.

Only a few weeks ago the house had been alive with the laughter, conversations, and gentle quarrels of Joe Jr., Jack, Kathleen, and the others, and now the house was shrouded, the windows cloaked in black-out curtains, the great rooms and hallways enveloped in silence. Outside the skies were still silent and in the blacked-out streets the cabs and cars nudged ahead, shadows in the night.

Joe lost fifteen pounds in three months, and his hair had begun to turn gray. His digestion was so troubled that in the fine restaurants of Mayfair he occasionally frequented the waiters knew that the ambassador would ask for special dishes. Joe frequently dined alone. Until the end of August, the ambassador had been invited into the great salons of power, his judgment sought, his words weighed. The invitations grew fewer and fewer, and some who had once listened to every nuance of his words now turned their backs on him.

Joe's mood swept from the bleakest despair to a manic hope that was another form of desperation. There was a near hysteria in Joe's voice, full of a dark apocalyptic vision that the Western world stood on the brink of extinction. One perceptive British diplomat wrote that the ambassador's views were "based on some fundamental and emotional attitude of mind [rather] than on reason." Joe believed in a visceral way that when Britain lost, and he was sure she would lose, that the British empire would be lost, the world economic system would be lost, and the world plunged into a morass to which the Depression was only a tiny overture. He believed that he and his family would lose in some terrible way.

Joe spent much time at St. Leonard's, the large estate near Windsor Park that had been taken in case the expected German bombing forced the closing of the London embassy. He was largely alone except for Eddie Moore and his wife, Mary. But on this occasion, Klemmer's assistant and the youngest member of the embassy staff, Page Huidekoper, stayed at the estate. She was a good friend of Kathleen's, a well-bred, well-spoken young woman who had made her debut in Baltimore before coming to London. Joe knew that the young woman's father had died recently.

"Wouldn't you like to call your mother?" Joe asked.

"I don't think I can," Page said, shrugging her shoulders. Calling the States was not only outrageously expensive, but in wartime it was next to impossible.

"Just pick up the phone and call her and talk as long as you want," Joe said.

That was invitation enough. Page dialed her Baltimore home and talked extensively to her mother, who could hardly believe the voice on the phone.

When she finished, Page returned to the living room where Joe sat slumped in a chair.

"God, I'd give anything to talk to my mother," Joe said. Mary Augusta was dead, long gone, but it was her vision, her ambition, her unswerving drive that had pushed him and pushed and pushed him again, helping to bring him here to London. Page was in her early twenties, and she was startled that the ambassador would talk so intimately.

"I've had a wonderful life," Joe said, as if he were talking in the past tense. "If I died tomorrow, I could leave each one of my children a million dollars."

Joe paused and looked out into the British countryside. "And you know they'd never never have as exciting a time as I've had."

Although Joe had written Krock that "all the family [was] back in America," Rosemary was still in Great Britain. To her father

Rosemary had always been an afterthought, even now when she was the only young Kennedy in England. Joe and Rose had sent twenty-one-year-old Rosemary to a convent school that served as a training center for Montessori teachers. For Rosemary, life had always been something that was done to her; she was the receiver of endless rounds of advice, instructions, admonitions, praise, and warnings. Here in this idyllic countryside of Hertfordshire, Rosemary was doing something for someone, and in doing something for others, she was finally a person in her own right. It was not a great thing, perhaps, not compared to what her brothers and sisters were doing, but it was something. Every afternoon she read stories to the children. Always before, she had become irritated at the idea that she had to take a nap in the afternoon, but she didn't complain any longer. "It will be good, won't it," she told Dorothy Gibbs, who served as her companion, "as I shall be refreshed to read to the children afterwards." Sometimes she became upset with the children, but she and Miss Gibbs had a little talk and Rosemary vowed not to be "fierce" with the children whatever happened, because it is "not 'Montessori.'"

Like many of those with retardation, Rosemary exuded an innocent goodness that could make an observer wonder if evil were carried on the wings of intelligence. She was happy with so little, her day made by a word of praise, or a group of little children listening attentively as she read them a fairy tale. With her mother gone, Joe was at the center of Rosemary's world, and she cherished his occasional visits and her trips to the home in the Windsor countryside, while the rest of the time she followed her father's life in the newspapers and radio.

Rosemary had neither the energy nor the self-consciousness of her sisters, and she was forever putting on weight. She had the plump, pink-cheeked looks of a milkmaid. Her father was appalled. As he wrote to her tutor, he had told her "in no uncertain words" that she was "getting altogether too fat." Her mother would be disappointed, and he would not "have her picture taken for America if she remains as stout as she is."

Her father was Rosemary's one hold on her family and her home. Yet when Joe decided to go to America for three months at the end of 1939, he did not take his eldest daughter with him to share Christmas with the family. Years later Rose attempted to rationalize this, asserting that "it seemed wise" for "it would have been an unpleasant trip for her, possibly a complicated one for Joe."

Rosemary learned about her father's return from reading a newspaper. "I see in the papper [sic] where Daddy ... attends [sic] to leave for London," she wrote Eddie Moore on February 13, 1940. "There was a pice [sic] about him in the sketch. I have ordered it for myself. I have heard Daddy [sic] name on the radio. About world affairs."

Rose stood in a long mink coat and hat behind a chain fence as the Pan Am Clipper landed in the bay at Manhassett on Long Island on December 6, 1939. She ducked under the chain, ran to Joe, and embraced the husband she had not seen for three months. The two Kennedys walked arm in arm toward the port building, their way lit by illumination bursting from flashbulbs. Inside the building, Rose stepped back out of the glare of lights and the verbal thrusts of over a hundred reporters, and let Joe take stage center alone.

Three decades before, Rose had watched as her mother had stood on the Boston docks to greet her father in warm and public embrace, and then watched as the former mayor had left with his cronies for a night on the town. Joe saw the lights of Times Square that evening with Rose and a group of family friends, and, then, the next day he was off by himself to Washington for meetings with President Roosevelt, leaving Rose alone.

Rose did not see her husband again until three days later when she and Joe flew into the airport at East Boston on separate planes. Rose's father was there to greet the couple, as were Joe Jr., a Harvard Law School student, and Jack, completing his senior year at Harvard. Rose was a deeply honored and admired woman in Boston, more now because of Joe than her father, and she was ever more the prisoner of her husband's image and reputation. Rose knew how distraught and deeply fatigued Joe was, how indiscreet and impetuous.

In Boston Joe went for his annual physical at the Lahey Clinic. For a decade he had had an ulcer and chronic stomach problems. Dr. Sara M. Jordan, the clinic's leading specialist in gastroenterology, diagnosed Joe as having acute gastritis and more seriously acute colitis.

In Washington the president had told Joe that he wanted him back to his post soon after the Christmas holidays. With Joe's prompting, Dr. Jordan wrote Roosevelt that the condition was serious enough to warrant hospitalization but that she recommended instead that Joe go to his Florida home for a rest

"which to be effective should be of at least two months' duration." Roosevelt granted Joe his stay, and not until early March
did Joe sail back to an England that he had not seen for a crucial three months.

As soon as Joe arrived in London, he could feel the bitter rancor of a public opinion that had turned against him. "You
would be surprised how much anti-American [the English]
have become," he wrote Rose in March. The British still had
a great, almost obligatory hope in Roosevelt, and they were not
so much anti-American as anti–Joseph P. Kennedy, anti–
Charles Lindbergh, anti the fervent legion of American
isolationists. "I feel it strongly against me," he confessed to his
wife. "If the war gets worse which I am still convinced it
will . . . I am sure they will all hate us more."

Again in a crucial moment in her subtly ingratiating way,
Rose attempted to calm her husband down, to purge him of his
public excesses. "Joe dear," she wrote in her wifely way, "I
have a definite idea that it would be a wonderful feat if you
could put over the idea that altho you are against America's
entering the war—still you are encouraging help to England in
some way. [Most Americans would be sympathetic,] and it
would endear you to the hearts of the British."

In a few sentences Rose had laid out an appropriate policy
for the ambassador. Most Americans didn't want their country
to enter the war either, but they were sympathetic toward the
British and their desperate plight. "It is easy enough to say we
should do something," Joe wrote back, "but the real difficulty
is—what?" At the bottom of the letter, he scrawled a personal
message: "Its [sic] Hell to be here without all of you. . . . I get
news that you are more beautiful than ever. Maybe you do better away from me. All my love."

As much as Joe was tired of life in London, his second eldest
daughter wanted desperately to return. Kathleen wrote passionately felt letters to her many friends in England, and they responded in kind, but it was as if they had moved beyond her
life of frivolity and fashion and endless good times. If not for
this great and terrible war, many of them would have soon cal-
cified into rigidly snobbish matrons measuring out their lives
by the Season. They knew now that they had lived and danced
through the last Season, and the world would no longer be the
same, and neither would they. Whether they built jeeps on an

assembly line, worked breaking German codes, nursed soldiers
back to health, or nursed their own babies while their husbands
served in uniform, they became women of a different sort.

Kathleen read their letters and knew that she wanted to be
there. As her father's isolationism was a visceral thing, so too
was Kathleen's support for the British. It was love not thought,
impulse not calculation, the British not Britain. When a vote
was taken at Finch College as to whether America should get
into the fight against the Nazis, only two students voted yes,
and one of them was the daughter of the isolationist ambassador to the Court of St. James's. Not only did Kathleen vote in
favor of the war, but she wrote and told her father what she
had done.

In her first public stance, Kathleen had done just the opposite of her two older brothers. Joe Jr. was a fervent isolationist,
parroting his father's view all over Cambridge. Jack was not so
fervent, but in his first public statement on the transcendent issue of his time, he wrote a pro-isolationist editorial for the
Harvard *Crimson*.

Kathleen wrote no editorials, gave no speeches. She simply
wanted to be there with the British in what she sensed would
soon be an American war as well. Kathleen wanted desperately
to return to England and play her own part, do something. Jack
thought of his sister as a kindred spirit. He wrote his father:
"Kick is very keen to go over—and I wouldn't think the anti-
American feeling would hurt her like it might us—due to her
being a girl—especially as it would show that we hadn't
merely left England when it got unpleasant." Jack's letter was
perceptive. Though Jack would have liked to have spent the
summer in England himself, he understood that if he or his
brother had gone over, they might have looked like shirkers or
voyeurs, picking up a few more scraps of experience. Since
Kathleen was a woman, the British would not judge her the
same way. Many of the British considered Joe no better than
a coward, chauffeured out of the city to his country house, his
wife and children all safely sent away. As Jack perceptively realized, Kathleen's presence would help on that score as well.

Joe would not change his mind. At the very time that Jack's
letter was arriving, he decided that while he stayed alone in
England, the Moores would escort Rosemary back to America.
In late May of 1940 they flew back on a Pan Am Clipper from
Lisbon. The reporters were told that Rosemary had stayed in
England "to continue her art studies." Soon after she arrived in

Bronxville, Fitzgerald talked to his granddaughter over the phone. "She mentioned the terrible things that are going on abroad," the former mayor said, contributing to the duplicity surrounding Rosemary, "but she seemed sorry that she could not have stayed over in London with her father."

Those eerily quiet days of the phony war were over, and the Battle of Britain was about to begin. France had fallen, Chamberlain was gone, Churchill was prime minister, and all that stood between England and the Nazis was the English Channel and several thousand young, inexperienced pilots. "It would be difficult for an impartial observer to decide today whether the British are the bravest or merely the most stupid people in the world," wrote Mollie Panter-Downes in *The New Yorker*. "The way they are acting in the present situation could be used to support either claim."

In May 1940 Kathleen joined her friend Charlotte McDonnell, Jack, and a group from Harvard for the Maryland Hunt Cup. The steeplechase race attracted the horsey set from New York to the Carolinas and was as close to an event in the British Season as anything in America. Kathleen adored her brother, who shielded her from one side of his attitude toward women. In the fall when he had been interested to "get something that likes lovin' " at Hyannis Port, he had written his friend Lem "preferably therefore not Kick this weekend." Charlotte was Jack's date this weekend, and she saw only Jack, the choirboy. Years afterwards she remembered how it was not unusual for him to postpone a dinner and theater date by having Lem call giggling over the phone: "Well Jack's tied up. He's having a massage." Charlotte waited for Jack's late arrival, accepting as Kathleen did that men needed their "massages," and when he arrived he wouldn't even think of pawing her.

This was Kathleen's weekend. One of the young men, Zeke Coleman, was infatuated with Kathleen; he was, as Eunice wrote her father, the "first boy completely approved of by all the Kennedys," approved that is by everyone but Kathleen.

That evening Kathleen dressed in a gorgeous gown and Jack in white tie and tails, and the party headed out to the ball. The dance went on until dawn, and while most of the guests went to bed, Kathleen, Charlotte, and Jack drove to a nearby Catholic Church to attend seven o'clock mass. For the other guests, this had been a weekend of pure gaiety and endless high jinks. But Kathleen knew that for her, as well as for Jack, the world had darker hues. Her brother had a deeply serious side that he rarely exposed to socialites like those this weekend. He had just completed his first important intellectual work, a 147-page senior thesis titled "Appeasement at Munich," a manuscript that by inference criticized his father's position on the war in Europe.

When the Kennedys arrived in Hyannis Port in June 1940 for the summer, their coming was an event of such importance that it merited a front-page headline in the *Barnstable Patriot*: "J. P. KENNEDYS ARE EXPECTED ON CAPE." The family had hardly settled into their airy home by the sea when they were off again to attend the wedding of Anne McDonnell to Henry Ford II.

Just as Joe's appointment as ambassador to the Court of St. James's signaled the emergence of Irish Catholics into the American political establishment, this marriage symbolized their social ascendancy. Kathleen was a maid of honor at what the newspapers called "the wedding of the century," this marriage between a Catholic heiress and the grandson of Henry Ford. Kathleen had gone to school with Anne at Noroton, and her sister, Charlotte, was her closest friend. Henry, so debonair, so charming, had come out to Noroton on Thursday afternoons, so desirous of Anne's hand that he was willing to convert to Catholicism, turning his back on his grandfather's fierce anticlericalism.

There were few wealthier, more renowned families than the Fords, and the wedding was a magnificent affair in which sixteen guards had been hired to protect the wedding gifts alone. There were scores of photographers and reporters sending the story not only all across America but all over the world. For Kathleen, Eunice, and Pat, the marriage suggested that there were few limits any longer on whom they might marry, and to how high they might aspire socially.

The Kennedys traveled back together from Long Island to Hyannis Port. For Jack it was a wondrous summer, for with the help of his father's friend, Arthur Krock, his senior thesis had been prepared for possible publication, and not only was it accepted, but had been rushed to print and was climbing the best-seller lists. One of Jack's close friends, Charles Spalding, recalled the scene in Hyannis Port that summer: "Jack was autographing copies of *Why England Slept* while grandfather Fitzgerald was reading to him a political story from a newspaper. Young Joe was telling them something that had happened to him in Russia. Mrs. Kennedy was talking on the phone with Cardinal [sic] Spellman. A tall and very attractive girl in a sweatshirt and dungarees turned out to be Pat who was describing how a German Messerschmitt plane had crashed near her father's home outside Windsor. Bobby was trying to get everybody to play charades. The next thing I knew all of us were choosing up sides for touch football and Kathleen was calling the huddle for the team I was on.

"These were still days not too far away from the depression, you know, when most everybody was more or less pretty well depressed about what they were going to do. And so here you see people who weren't worried at all. But then I thought to myself, 'Well, this is really the best possible way to approach life.' "

To impressionable visitors like young Spalding, the Kennedys appeared to be free spirits. They never let on to outsiders the inner dramas playing out that summer of 1940. Joe was still an ocean away in the midst of danger, never far from thoughts of his wife and daughters. Eunice worried frequently about her father, and the high point of her small nineteenth-birthday celebration was the cable that arrived from Joe.

Kathleen's thoughts were in England, with her father, Billy, and all her friends. All the news she had been receiving was dreary and pessimistic, and for months she had been pumping up herself and her friends by "telling everyone 'the British lose the battles but they win the wars.' " Now on August 13, 1940, the "Day of the Eagle" had arrived, the Nazi code name for the Luftwaffe bombing of British bases, airfields, aircraft factories, and the London docks. Day after day waves of German bombers pounded Britain as Hitler attempted to bomb the British into submission. In Hyannis Port, Rose could do little but read the papers and worry, passing part of her time pouring tea and sewing for war relief.

For Kathleen it was all terribly frustrating. She could do little except knit a scarf for Billy, aid the Red Cross, and put together a fashion show and luncheon to help disabled British sailors. Twelve-year-old Jean copied her elder sister by vowing to knit a scarf for a soldier, and considered it "really awfully nice" making bandages at the Red Cross two days a week. As for sixteen-year-old Pat, she was at that self-conscious age when she was more concerned with her diet than volunteering down at the Red Cross.

* * *

Rosemary barely understood what was going on in England. She had only just returned, and she hadn't been with her brothers and sisters and mother for close to a year. Rosemary remembered the years before the war at Hyannis Port when Joe Jr. and Jack had always taken her to the dances. But they seemed to have no time for her any longer, and of all her siblings only Eunice was always watching out for Rosemary. "It was embarrassing to be around Rosemary sometimes," recalled one guest of that summer. "She would behave in strange ways at the table, and I think they all were at pains not to seem embarrassed. She was an awkward member of the cast. She would appear there standing in her nightgown when everyone else was moving ahead so rapidly. I don't think she really existed in the lives of Jack and Joe Jr., not any longer."

If Rosemary still imagined that she could be one with her brothers and sisters, she learned otherwise. For part of the summer, Rose sent her twenty-one-year-old eldest daughter to a special camp in New Hampshire. Rosemary tried so hard, and at camp she reportedly did not complain about the tightness of her shoes until a counselor noticed that her feet were bloody.

During the summer Rose planned a big party with guests from out of town. Rose didn't feel comfortable having Rosemary around. So she asked Luella if she could possibly take Rosemary to her sister's house in North Falmouth. As she drove in the chauffeured automobile along Cape Cod, Rosemary seemed so much different than at Hyannis Port. She acted as if she belonged here, an elegant young lady with her driver on a summer day.

When the car arrived at Falmouth, Rosemary greeted Luella's sister, brother-in-law, and four children with impeccable manners. "Please, I don't want to sleep in the room with Laura," Rosemary said. Rosemary found it easier to pronounce Luella's name "Laura." "She bosses me so."

Luella's sister could hardly believe that Rosemary was "slow." At tea she was the perfect lady, holding her little pinky finger out as she daintily sipped from her cup. When the family went down to the beach, Rosemary took charge of the four children. She craved the idea of being a useful person, whether it was at the Montessori School in England or here on the beach at Cape Cod. She lined the children up on the beach, and one by one took them out into the surf, returning them to sit next to their siblings. Then after all the children had had their swim she told them: "Now it's reading time." Then she laboriously and devotedly read from *Winnie-the-Pooh*, one of the few books that she could read.

When it was time to leave, Rosemary bid the family good-bye with the same grace that she had greeted them. "Dave, the chauffeur, came back to get us," Luella recalled. "And you'd think she was Mrs. Astor, the chauffeur opening the door for her, waving at everyone." As soon as she got back to Hyannis Port, she went to her room and in pencil laboriously wrote out a thank-you note and took it down to the post office. And then when she got back to the house she exploded, all the anger and pent-up emotion surging out of her in uncontrolled fury. "Whenever that happened I always called Eunice," recalled Luella. "She was the one who knew how to calm her, no matter what."

At the beginning of the summer Eunice had written her father that there were so few people at the Cape that it looked as if the Kennedys might end up having to race themselves. As the days wore on, more summer residents arrived and at the end of the summer the seven young Kennedys, everyone but Joe Jr. and Rosemary, won most of the annual sailing awards, an achievement noted on the sports pages of *The New York Times*.

Joe sat in his office in London feeling "plenty homesick" as he looked at a *Life* magazine picture of his children sailing on Cape Cod. Although Joe had been living most of the time in his country house, in August he decided to start spending the work week at Prince's Gate. The house had been closed up, the furniture covered, the windows shuttered, and it was an eerie feeling staying in this cavernous house. He was so consumed with the enveloping war that he noticed one evening that he had "forgotten to shave for a couple of days."

On the seventh of September a great wave of German bombers flew over London, dropping their deadly cargo, leveling street after street of East End slums, immolating the docks and the warehouses, filling the late-afternoon sky with smoke so intense that it blotted out the sun. It was the first day of Hitler's strategy of Total War against London, waging war against the mother in her home as much as the pilot in the sky, against the conductor in his bus as much as the Tommy in his foxhole. Four days later the attacks shifted toward the West End where Joe resided, reaching a terrible crescendo on the eleventh of

September. In Buckingham Palace King George watched as six bombs fell on the palace, one landing "about 30 yds. away."

As the bombing of London intensified, Joe began working and sleeping at his seventy-room country estate, communicating with his office by telephone. As he sat in the countryside, he wrote a series of letters to Rose and the children. His message to his wife was a perfunctory, businesslike affair telling her that he was hoping to buy the china and chintzes that she had requested. To Jack he played the fearless man of the world ("Haven't the slightest touch of nervousness. But I can see evidences of some people beginning to break down."). To Eunice, he wrote a deeply felt, emotional message. "There has been plenty of bombing going on," he wrote. "I can't tell you what my state of mind would have been if any of you had been over here. . . . I think I should have gone mad." It was a peculiar man who could tell his daughter not his wife of his dark fears and call Eunice, not Rose, "old darling." Eunice adored her father, and if she had slept fitfully before this letter, startled awake by the slightest rustle, the letter surely filled her sleep with new nightmares, new worries.

During the worst of the blitz, Joe sent a notice to the embassy staff that "the Chancellery would operate on a reduced staff tomorrow to give all hands a chance to sleep." Joe had begun to panic, calling the embassy on September 22 from his estate announcing that the invasion of Britain would begin that afternoon at three P.M. Even some members of his staff believed that the ambassador "had lost his nerve." A more charitable estimate was that Joe was showing the courage of his lack of convictions. "Kennedy has the speculator's smartness but also his *sharpshooting* and *facile* insensitivity to the great forces which are now playing like heat lightning over the map of the world," wrote the estimable General Raymond Lee, the United States military attaché in the embassy, in his diary on September 17 after a night of deadly bombing.

Joe didn't think this was his fight, and he wasn't about to die in another man's battle. But behind his back the American correspondents who daily braved the Nazi bombs to report home, and the British officials who tallied up the deaths and destruction, considered Joe a coward. More than ever, however, Joe believed that if this war continued not only these streets but all Britain would be little but rubble above which would fly the swastika.

* * *

In September Kathleen went off for a month with three close friends, Nancy Tenney and newlyweds Francis and Cynthia McAdoo, to the Flying Cloud Ranch at Wise River outside Butte, Montana. Cynthia was a talented artist, and she painted a series of vivid watercolors chronicling their trip. The Old West was alive in Montana, with stagecoaches rotting in the side streets, false fronts on the buildings, and in the bars tall, lean, handsome cowboys who mumbled unintelligibly when presented to the two pretty Eastern women.

Like other members of her family, Kick had an extraordinary ability to compartmentalize her life. When her worries became too intense, too real, her sense of foreboding a dark curtain over her life, she drove it all away, and played and laughed and seemingly thought of nothing but good times. On the ranch Kathleen was unpretentious to a fault, walking around in curlers. "Kick and Jack both had this enormous vitality, this will to live and enjoy," recalled Francis McAdoo.

Cynthia McAdoo noted one peculiar aspect of her friend. "Kick talked about her father all the time that month, but never mentioned her mother."

At three o'clock in the afternoon on October 27, 1940, Rose, Kathleen, Eunice, Pat, Jean, and Teddy stood outside the customs office at La Guardia Airport looking into the sky where the silver figure of a Pan American Clipper soared westward above the Atlantic Ocean. More than two thousand spectators craned their necks as well, gathered in the airport gallery to watch the arrival of the ambassador to the Court of St. James's. The seaplane droned on, passing near two giant dirigibles, guardians of the World's Fair, and then landed in the tranquil waters of the bay.

Rose waited for her husband with a certain trepidation. She knew how tired, anguished, and irritable he had become. "Joe felt that at home people around Roosevelt were sniping at him personally, that the President was against him to a certain extent, because the Jewish influence in the press was strong and against anything called appeasement," Rose recalled. Roosevelt had lost all confidence in his ambassador to the Court of St. James's. The president considered Joe an obstacle that he had subtly to detour around, sending his own emissaries to London, serving as his own ambassador to London by corresponding directly with Churchill, no longer even deeming to send the letters through Joe.

Earlier in the month Alsop and Kintner, in their widely syndicated column, had predicted that Joe would betray Roosevelt by giving his unvarnished "opinions to every available American listener the instant he got through customs." The scores of journalists who waited for Joseph P. Kennedy to walk down the ramp knew that it was evident, as *The Boston Globe* correspondent expressed it, that Joe "will not be returning to England as Ambassador." And they waited impatiently, expecting one of the greatest political stories of the election year.

Joe walked briskly down the ramp and into a room full of reporters. "I am going right on to Washington now, and I won't make any statements," Joe said. "After I have seen the President, I will make a statement."

As Joe continued sparring with the disappointed journalists, Rose and the children entered the room and rushed up to the ambassador, five women swathed in exquisite fur coats, and little Teddy trailing behind. Even to the professionally jaded sensibilities of the journalists, there was such extraordinary passion in this greeting that they stopped shouting out their questions. "In a moment the ambassador was smothered with kisses," the *Boston Post* reported. "Tears of joy flowed freely, and the ambassador wiped his own eyes. . . . Mrs. Kennedy's youthful face was buried in her husband's shoulder and her tall daughters alternatively wept and thumped their dad on the back. It was one of those spontaneous displays of emotion which touched all present."

Rose could not help but be aware of the headlines ("KENNEDY ANGRY AT PRESIDENT") and the swirling controversy engulfing her husband and ultimately her family and the Kennedy reputation. In London she had seen her husband's willful disregard for the proprieties of his position, indeed, for a diplomat's diplomacy, and where her husband's reckless candor had led him and his reputation. Now she saw herself as a bulwark of sanity and dispassion that might hold Joe back from the worst of his excesses. She was not the only one to understand that was the role that she must play now. Roosevelt saw Rose the same way, and the president asked that Joe bring Rose with him, an extraordinary request that Joe believed was "because of her great influence on me." For half a decade Rose had written a series of warm ingratiating letters to FDR, and the president appreciated Rose as an astute political woman. The president had felt that Joe would do a good job in government because he cared about his family's prestige, and the president knew that Rose held sacred that reputation.

The plane left almost immediately for Washington. On the flight to the capital, Rose listened as her husband poured out his story of Roosevelt's supposed perfidy and how he was about to have his exquisite revenge. In London Joe had mulled over Roosevelt's apparent betrayal and duplicity, his deep fears that the president was "going to push us into the war." He had written an article that he called "an indictment of President Roosevelt's administration for having talked a lot and done very little." Joe wasn't about to resign and be made to look a coward, but he wasn't about to sit in London either. If Roosevelt wouldn't recall him, and let him return to the States with his honor intact, then he would have the article published on November 1, a week before the election. It would be Joe Kennedy's November surprise, an article of such revelation and intensity that it could throw the election to the Republican candidate, Wendell Willkie, denying Roosevelt a third term.

Rose could understand Joe's anger, but what her husband proposed to do was sheer folly, anathema to everything in which she believed. She was the daughter of a Democratic politician, and the party was her secular church, the political institution to which she gave her complete loyalty. Moreover, after all these years she had achieved immense social status as the wife of the ambassador, recipient of anniversary messages from the king and queen. In one great dramatic gesture, Joe was going to throw that away, possibly even becoming responsible for electing a Republican president. He was going to take the Kennedy name and perhaps turn it into a curse word to every Democrat from the North End of Boston to the docks of San Francisco.

Rose listened intently to her husband venting months of spleen as the government transport plane flew southward. "The President sent you, a Roman Catholic as Ambassador to London, which probably no other President would have done," she told her angry husband. "He sent you as his representative to the Pope's coronation. You would write yourself down as an ingrate in the view of many people if you resign now."

Rose put Joe's ambassadorship in deep perspective, relating it to Catholic and American history, and her own family's social emergence. Although Joe did not dramatically change his mind, Rose's cautious words sobered him up and gave him pause.

The plane landed in Washington on a black and cloudy evening. A White House chauffeur stood waiting, carrying a heavy gray overcoat in case the chill evening air bothered Joe. Rose followed along behind her husband, and ducked into the limousine that took them immediately to 1600 Pennsylvania Avenue.

While Joe and Rose sat waiting for the president in the family rooms at the White House, they were met by Senator and Mrs. James F. Byrnes. The senator, who had been brought up as a Catholic, was a leading Southern liberal and Roosevelt loyalist. Joe reflected later "that Roosevelt didn't want to have it out with me alone." FDR had a brilliant sense of mise-en-scène, and he had orchestrated this meeting to perfection. Joe had blistered Roosevelt's ear over the transatlantic phone, and with others present, particularly women, the president's angry ambassador was likely to be more subdued.

The president sat at his desk "shaking a cocktail shaker," Rose recalled, "and reaching over for a few lumps of ice with his powerful hands." Roosevelt presided over this modest familial Sunday dinner, serving eggs, sausage, and toast to the two couples and Missy LeHand, his secretary.

Just before leaving London, Joe had visited Chamberlain on his deathbed, and Joe told about the visit. Joe had been deeply moved by the sight and words of the ashen-faced former prime minister. Chamberlain had clasped Joe's hand and said: "This is goodbye. I remember you always said you would stay after me. But we will never see each other again."

Joe talked about the blitz and life in London. Then Byrnes brought up a new subject. "I've got a great idea, Joe," the senator said, as if listening to Joe's morose reminiscences had triggered a brainstorm. "Why don't you make a radio speech on the lines of what you have said here tonight and urge the President's re-election?"

This was exactly what Roosevelt and his advisors had been discussing for several weeks, but the president wanted Byrnes to be the one to float the idea. If Rose had had her way, Joe doubtlessly would have immediately agreed to the request. It was an honor to give a nationwide radio address for the president on the eve of the election, an honor for her and the family as well as Joe. But several years of anger and frustration had built up in Joe, and he sat there sullenly saying nothing. Roosevelt agreed that Joe's speech could indeed be crucial in his reelection campaign. Still, Joe said nothing.

The president sensed the danger in pressing the subject. Turning to Rose, he began telling her a series of colorful anecdotes about her father. He told Rose that on his last trip to South America, scores of Latins still remembered her father and his rendering of "Sweet Adeline," an event that had taken place over thirty years ago. Rose had a father who could charm the clouds from the sky, and she saw that the president also had a charm so infectious that as Rose admitted later, "even while I knew I was being charmed, the charm was difficult to resist." As for Joe, he had been trying for a quarter of a century to distance himself from his father-in-law's emerald-green blarney, and there were few things he detested as much as having to listen to the twice-told tales about Honey Fitz.

Joe assumed that once the president had his fill of this small talk that he and Roosevelt would go off to another room for their private discussion, but the president was playing a different game, and went on and on with his anecdotes.

"Since it doesn't seem possible for me to see the President alone, I guess I'll just have to say [it] in front of everybody," Joe exclaimed, setting off a torrent of anger and self-justification, "I am damn sore at the way I have been treated." For months he had been collecting his slights real and imagined, and he paraded them before the president, punctuating his words with profanity. He was not a man who swore in front of women, but this evening he didn't care what Mrs. Byrnes, Missy LeHand, or Rose heard or how brutally he burned their ears.

"Joe did most of the talking," Rose recalled, as if anyone else had a choice. "The President looked rather pale, rather ashen, and I always noticed the nervous habit he had of nervously snapping his eyes."

The president sat white-faced, listening to the tirade. For Rose it was almost incomprehensible what her husband was doing, to himself, to her, to the family image. For the first time in her life, she was sitting eating a casual dinner with the president of the United States, and Joe was talking to Roosevelt as if he were an incompetent underling.

Rose could hardly burst into the midst of this tirade, silencing her husband with some benign remark about Windsor Castle or the queen. Instead, in the midst of Joe's monologue, Rose attempted to mediate the matter, making the reasonable suggestion that it was difficult evaluating a situation from three thousand miles away. Joe only glared at his wife, and charged onward with his attack. As Byrnes listened to this singular diatribe, the senator wondered "what the President could possibly say in his defense."

Roosevelt was not engaged in a schoolboy debate this evening. He was in the most difficult political race of his life, and he needed Joe. He needed that speech. And so Roosevelt did what he often did in private with his critics. He agreed with Joe, blaming the faceless, nameless bureaucrats for all these affronts to the ambassador's power and prestige. After the election there would be a clean broom sweeping out the stuffed-shirt bureaucrats who had stymied such an esteemed public servant as Joseph P. Kennedy.

The president now turned to a more pleasant subject, the Kennedys' two eldest sons, praising them to the skies and beyond. "I stand in awe of your relationship with your children," Roosevelt said. "For a man as busy as you are it is a rare achievement. And I for one will do all I can to help you if your boys should ever run for political office."

This was Roosevelt's final masterful touch. Nothing meant more to Joe, nothing, than his sons' lives and futures. It was unthinkable that he would risk holding their careers hostage. And thus when Roosevelt asked Joe directly if he would give a speech endorsing him, Joe said: "All right, I will. But I will pay for it myself, show it to nobody in advance and say what I wish."

Rose left the White House with her husband that evening knowing that she had perhaps helped save the family from calamity, a public spectacle that probably would have destroyed the Kennedy family fortunes within the Democratic party, and left Joe in public league with the America Firsters and other isolationists.

Two days later Joe gave his speech to a national radio audience. Other than Roosevelt's own addresses, it may have been the best, the most important speech of the whole campaign. "During this political campaign, there has arisen the charge that the President . . . is trying to involve this country in the world war," Joe said. "Such a charge is false. . . . I have a great stake in this country. My wife and I have given nine hostages to fortune. Our children and your children are more important than anything else in the world. The kind of America that they and their children will inherit is of grave concern to us all."

Rose went on the radio as well and said that she too was

voting for Roosevelt, and she was sure he "would not lead my sons and their sons into war." A week later Roosevelt won the election and Joe could legitimately claim to have been a crucial factor in the victory.

Joe might have savored that victory, and reaped his reward, but he was too bitter for that, and too unwise. After the election Joe met Louis Lyons of *The Boston Globe* and two *St. Louis Post-Dispatch* reporters in his suite at Boston's Ritz-Carlton Hotel. In London Joe was used to putting his feet up on his desk at the embassy and talking candidly with reporters. The journalists always protected him. And thus today in Boston he sat in his suite in shirtsleeves, his suspenders dropping around his waist, eating apple pie and a wedge of cheese, talking in what Lyons said sounded "like a campaign speech but not for Roosevelt."

"I'm willing to spend all I've got left to keep us out of the war. . . ." Joe told the furiously scribbling reporters. "Democracy is finished in England. It may be here." Eleanor Roosevelt was a fine woman but "she bothered us more on our jobs in Washington to take care of the poor little nobodies who hadn't any influence than all the rest of the people down there altogether. She was always sending me a note to have some little Susie Glotz to tea at the Embassy." "Glotz" was Joe's code word for "Jew," and the reporters took down his every word.

Lyons published Joe's remarks in the *Globe*. Though Joe tried to deny them, his critics hung them on him like a badge of shame. Rose knew her husband could not be quiet. The month of November wasn't even over before Drew Pearson and Robert S. Allen reported in their syndicated column that Joe had told a group of Hollywood moguls that "England was virtually defeated" and that "Hollywood producers should stop making films offensive to the dictators."

Shortly before Thanksgiving Roosevelt invited Joe to Hyde Park. Joe followed the president in his wheelchair into his study, and Joe had the private discussion with Roosevelt that he had sought for so long. After only ten minutes, Roosevelt asked Joe to leave the room, and called Eleanor into his presence. She had seen Roosevelt on good days and bad, full of great joy and equal anger, but she had hardly ever seen him so enraged, his face a white sheet, his voice a tremulous whisper.

"I never want to see that son of a bitch again as long as I live," the president said. "Take his resignation and get him out of here!"

* * *

Among the millions of Americans who supported Roosevelt, Joe was an outcast now, in league with the most vociferous, most intemperate of the isolationists. In the White House, Roosevelt received scores of letters vilifying Joe. As long as FDR sat in Washington, Joe's political career was over. Joe always spent January in Palm Beach, but since his resignation, he could spend all season in Florida. Rose was in the resort as well. Eunice was also in Florida, having dropped out of Manhattanville because of what she called "stomach problems similar to Jack." And Jack was there after having completed a semester of lackluster study at Stanford University in California. Later in the spring, they joined their mother on another one of her trips, this time a month-long journey through South America.

Jack's friend, Chuck Spalding, visited the Kennedys as well. Spalding could tell as soon as he entered the Kennedy home that the veneer of civility between Rose and Joe had stretched thin. As he watched the couple walking on the beach, he didn't have to hear their conversation to tell that something was wrong. Their body language spoke volumes, so rigid, awkward, distant.

Many years later on a summer afternoon, Rose sat in the living room of the house in Hyannis Port, the brilliant sun shining into a room filled with pictures of her sons and daughters, each photo illuminating one memory or another. It was the past that was left now, and as she did so often she talked of days long ago. "We had everything," the old woman said. "Everything. But Joe didn't have an ounce of humility, and in London he refused to learn anything. After a while I tried to tell him what I felt. He didn't listen, though—Joe never listened—but maybe I should have said even more.

"Afterwards I was very angry at him. I felt that he had not accomplished what we could have accomplished as a couple. He had not accomplished what he should have as a world leader, and I was made to suffer for it. I lost my friendships. We lost our prestige, and within a few years we began to lose our children. And I wonder if he ever knew how much I lost because of him."

13
Days of Infamy

"For God's sake can that thing!" Page Huidekoper whispered. "It just doesn't look right for a nice tough newspaper person." Kathleen was wearing an enormous straw hat. It might have been quite the thing in Palm Beach or Newport. But it was decidedly out of place in the grubby confines of the newsroom of the *Washington Times-Herald*, especially for a young woman applying for her first job in journalism.

Kathleen took off her hat and the two women continued through the hectic newsroom, reporters pounding away at typewriters or yelling for copyboys, while photographers rushed out to cover the latest story for the capital's only all-day newspaper. Since Page had left London, she had been working for the *Times-Herald*. When Kathleen had called during the summer of 1941 saying that her father wanted her to have a paying job, Page had told her to come right down.

"You couldn't have come at a better time, Kick," Page said, as the two women stopped in front of the office of Frank Waldrop, the executive editor. Waldrop, a Southerner of studied cantankerousness, shouted out orders from his open office door. He considered it a prerogative of office life to have a pretty young thing as his research assistant, a position that since her arrival from London had been filled by Huidekoper. Waldrop had just named her a reporter, joining the other women on the paper covering society and social life.

Waldrop was expecting Kathleen. Her father was not going to have his cherished daughter working for just anybody. He had asked Krock to call Waldrop, a fellow isolationist who had no more use for Roosevelt than Joe did. The editor decided that Kathleen seemed attractive enough for placement outside his door. He didn't care that she could hardly type and was to-

tally ignorant about reporting. Waldrop made Kathleen his secretarial assistant, offering her a salary of twenty dollars a week
for what the former editor later described as "a hey-you kind
of job."

Kathleen took a small one-bedroom apartment in northwest
Washington. For the first time in her life, she was on her own,
in a city in which questions of war and peace and politics were
the common parlance. Kathleen knew that as the prospect of
America's entry into war increased, Joe Jr. and Jack would
never simply sit on the sidelines, watching others play the dangerous games of war, heralded as heroes and patriots, winning
essential credentials for any man thinking of entering public
life after a war. Despite his isolationist views, Joe Jr. dropped
out of Harvard Law School in the spring of 1941 to begin
training as a Navy pilot in Florida. As for Jack, he would probably never have passed a regular military physical, and despite
the veneer of health, aided by regular sessions underneath a
sunlamp, he was a sickly young man. With persistent, stabbing
back pains, he was a candidate for disability, not for combat.
Joe used his contacts to get his son a commission in naval intelligence and Jack donned a uniform as an ensign in the U.S.
Naval Reserves.

Jack was assigned to the Office of Naval Intelligence in Washington, taking up residence in Dorchester House on Sixteenth
Street, not far from his sister's apartment. Kathleen saw her
brother all the time. There was yet another Kennedy resident in
Washington; unknown to almost anyone outside the family,
Rosemary had been placed in a convent school in the nation's
capital.

One evening Kathleen invited her new boss, Waldrop, to
spend an evening with her visiting father and Jack. The two
young Kennedys sprinkled the adjective "terrific" through their
conversations: a terrific day, a terrific movie, terrific this, terrific that, everything was terrific. The editor was a fiercely energetic man himself, but even he was worn down by the
ceaseless banter and the determinedly upbeat tempo of the conversation. Kathleen and Jack felt comfortable teasing their father about his isolationist views. "Oh, Mr. Ambassador, tell us
again your argument," Jack said with exaggerated deference.
And when he finished Kathleen took over. "Now that the ambassador has stated his position we can go on," she said mock-
ingly. As Waldrop listened, he sensed that beneath the joshing

lay a deep affection. "When they joked with him it didn't make him mad, it tickled him," Waldrop reflected. "I mean they loved the old son of a bitch for what he was because they knew he loved them. They liked putting up their dukes with the old man. They were very much at ease with him although they were careful to keep it all within safe bounds. They knew how to get along with him."

Kathleen traveled in a social world far above most of her colleagues on the newspaper, and when she had an invitation to an embassy party or dinner at the home of one of Washington's old families, she carried her mink into the office stashed away in a shopping bag. She didn't want to set herself apart and was fascinated by the universe of human personalities spread out across the newsroom at the *Times-Herald*. They were an idiosyncratic, individualistic, hard-talking, hardworking, often hard-drinking breed.

Almost as soon as she arrived at the paper, Kathleen became friendly with twenty-eight-year-old Inga Arvad, who wrote a daily column profiling government officials. Inga was blonde with sensuous good looks. Seven years older than Kathleen, Inga was an intense, intelligent woman who had lived the kind of life that Kathleen had only read about, a passionately adventurous life, led through men, with men, by men. The nuns had taught Kathleen that divorce was unthinkable and unspeakable. Yet Inga was already on her second marriage, and was acting in Washington as if she were not married at all. Her forty-six-year-old husband, Paul Fejos, rarely visited Washington. The nuns had taught Kathleen that a decent woman dressed with modesty, and treated men with wariness and distance. And yet Inga had been a beauty queen in Denmark, starred in her film director–husband's film, and, while working as a newspaper correspondent in Berlin, used her feminine charms to obtain interviews with Himmler, Goering, Goebbels, even Hitler himself. Now in Washington Inga had a seemingly endless array of admirers, men of power and position.

Kathleen decided to introduce Inga to Jack. Inga met this "boy who was supposedly brilliant, who laughed the whole time" and was immediately attracted to him. For his part, Jack was mesmerized by Inga's rich bounty of beauty, charm, wit, sensuality, and insight. He did not care that this woman four years his senior was still married any more than Inga did, and they began a passionate affair.

* * *

At the *Times-Herald* Kathleen met John White, the paper's star reporter. He was as different from most men she knew as Inga was from the women. Despite his hopelessly rumpled appearance, and the tattooed serpent on his right arm, White was a Harvard graduate and the son of an Episcopalian minister. He was tall and wiry with a prominent nose and large expressive lips. His features were just short of handsome, with the intense look that women deemed interesting, a judgment that his personality more than justified. A sardonic, witty, cynical observer of life's foibles, the thirty-year-old reporter had one great ambition: to go through life without ambition. John's cynicism was the protective veneer of a tender, sentimental, self-obsessed man who found it impossible to commit to anything, from a woman to an idea to a faith.

Kathleen had gone her entire Catholic education without having to defend her beliefs, or to have them directly confronted or challenged. And here, almost as soon as she met him, this strange irascible man was mocking what she held most sacred, teasing her, attempting to dislodge the foundation stones of her beliefs. She called him a "big bag of wind." She could not let his arguments just stand there unchallenged, resting in her brain. Late at night after one of their first dates, Kathleen telephoned him. "Birth control is murder," she yelled into the phone.

"It's the Catholic church's way of keeping membership," White yelled back.

One evening in mid-October on their second or third date, Kathleen accepted John's invitation to come to his apartment. John lived in the basement of his sister and brother-in-law's home in Georgetown, in quarters he had aptly dubbed "the cave." As they sat on a sofa talking, Kathleen enjoyed the banter. Later in the evening John reached over and tried to kiss her. Kathleen recoiled from his embrace. She did not like men to touch her. "I don't want any of this, John," she told him. "You must understand. Please don't try. I don't want the thing the priest says not to do."

John thought anything and everything was worthy of discussion, and he debated with Kathleen. He found it hard to believe that this vivacious young woman could be not only puritanical, sexually reticent, but seemingly totally uninterested. He talked to her frankly about the possibility of at least some kind of physical relationship, just hugs, and occasional kisses, some sign of physical warmth and affection. But Kathleen said no and could never say the word "sex," as if verbalizing it would somehow soil her.

John did not give up. He realized he loved her too much for that. He continued to confront Kathleen about everything in which she was supposed to believe, from her father's isolationist politics and her conservative social beliefs, to her Catholic faith. "It delighted her to see people somewhat careless of appearances who were still not bad people," White recalled. "It was as though we were breaking the rules and not being thrown out." John was a Jesuit of disbelief, casting forth his doubts, little seeds that he hoped would one day sprout. His ideas had a deep impact on Kathleen's faith. Several years later, White said that Eunice accused him of "talking my sister out of her religion." That he did not do, but he talked her out of her easy certainties, her slavish acceptance of the church's authorities, her belief in every nuance of doctrine.

In Washington, Kathleen and the rest of her family were confronted with a far different kind of dilemma. For years Rose and Joe had been putting Rosemary in schools and situations where she did not quite belong. She had just had her twenty-third birthday in September, and here in this new school she was so much older, so different from the other students. Always before her father or mother had come to visit, always before she had been part of her brothers' and sisters' world. Kathleen was only a few minutes away, but Rosemary was not much of a part of her life. Jack was nearby too, but he was no longer taking her to dances the way he always had in Hyannis Port. She had no invitations to Georgetown parties, no adventures on Capitol Hill, no walks with a young man in Rock Creek amid the brilliant autumn foliage, no polite teas with her sister and her friends.

Sometimes all the emotions burst out of Rosemary, a great rage of inchoate feeling. In the convent the nuns had been charged to control and contain Rosemary's life, and control and contain it they did, with days of endless routine that stretched on and on. Joe had sometimes raged against Rosemary for failing at her studies, but Rosemary was not stupid, not stupid in the way some demeaned her, not stupid at all. She knew that life was not here within these walls, but outside, out where Kathleen and Jack lived.

Rosemary figured out how to escape from the convent, and

at night she walked out into the dark streets looking for the light and life of the city. Although her father had often berated her for being fat, her body had ripened to sweet voluptuousness, and she was a beautiful young woman, looking no more than seventeen or eighteen. She had been warned about men and what they wanted. She was a healthy woman whose sexual appetites had been denied her, pushed back into her, unmentioned and unmentionable. The nuns would find her wandering in the streets, her story disconnected and vague, and they would bring her back to the convent, ask her to bathe, and warn her never again to walk into those nighttime streets. Soon she would be off again, another evening, another adventure, out there in the streets where the family worried there were men who wanted her and men she may have wanted.

When Rose and Joe talked about Rosemary's situation, he told his wife about the possibility of curing their daughter with a new surgical technique. Rose had never heard about the surgery, and she asked Kathleen to learn what she could about this new procedure. John White happened to be writing a six-part series on St. Elizabeth's Hospital, Washington's federal mental hospital, and Kathleen quizzed him about new approaches without ever telling him why she was so interested. White was a fine reporter, intensely involved with his work, and he detailed for Kathleen an experimental surgery on severely mentally disturbed patients in which the surgeon cut the fibers at the front of the brain. White told Kathleen that the results were "just not good" and that afterwards the patients "don't worry so much, but they're gone as a person, just gone."

Kathleen discussed the surgery with Rose. "Oh, Mother, no, it's nothing we want done for Rosie," Kathleen said.

"Well, I'm glad to hear that," Rose replied. Rose had always said no to the doctors who had wanted to institutionalize Rosemary, specialists who had nothing to offer but resignation.

For years, Joe had left Rosemary's problems largely to Rose, but this was a matter too important to leave to his wife. This was Joe's problem, affecting the family reputation. Joe had consulted Luella on all other family health issues, but this time he did not ask the nurse her opinion. "I think he knew what I would have said," Luella said.

The family feared that Rosemary had lost all control, and she and her sisters had been brought up to live lives of transcendent self-control. They feared that she was going out into the streets to do what Kathleen called "the thing the priest says not to do," the thing Kathleen could not even talk about. For Kathleen, her mother, her sisters, and the nuns of the Sacred Heart, it was a shameful, unspeakable thing for a Catholic maiden to do. If Rosemary had been a man, Joe likely would have felt proud that his child was at least not backward in that department. But Rosemary was a woman, and there was a dread fear of pregnancy, disease, and disgrace.

For a father thinking about the most serious and radical sort of treatment for his daughter, and a man who always sought the finest experts, in Washington it was almost inevitable that Joe would go to Dr. Walter Freeman, one of the best known doctors in the country. Besides his appointment at St. Elizabeth's where John White had learned of his work, Freeman was a professor of neurology at George Washington University and had his own extensive private practice as well. Freeman was a flamboyant man, just the kind of no-nonsense, hyperactive, wildly ambitious, self-confident professional whom Joe considered a kindred spirit.

Five years before in the spring of 1936 Freeman had sent for an article in a French medical journal by a Portuguese neurologist, Dr. Egas Moniz, on a new surgical procedure called prefrontal leucotomy. Moniz had first employed it in November of the previous year. Since then Freeman and his surgeon associate, Dr. James Watts, had become America's greatest proponents and largest practitioners of an operation that Freeman dubbed a "lobotomy."

In the fall of 1941, when Joe was contemplating what to do with Rosemary, the era of psychosurgery was in its infancy. In the entire world only 350 to 500 lobotomies had taken place, about eighty of them performed by Freeman and Watts. Their surgical techniques were primitive. It would not be until half a dozen years later that Freeman would develop the well-known "ice pick operation" usually associated with lobotomies. "The doctors told my father it was a good idea," Eunice reflected. "I have reviewed it since that time with a number of doctors, and they said it wasn't successful in any case."

Despite the extremely experimental nature of lobotomies in 1941, articles lauding the operation were appearing in the popular press, from *The New York Times* to *The Saturday Evening Post*. Most of the attention was due to Freeman's extraordinary skills at self-promotion. Freeman had a "psychosurgery exhibit" at the AMA's annual meeting. There he buttonholed reporters, and according to his partner Watts, "often behaved like a barker at a circus, using a 'cricket' noisemaker to attract people to his booth." Despite Freeman's articulate and persuasive defense of lobotomies, the medical profession was of two opinions. Joe would not have had to look very far to find passionate opponents of Freeman and his magical operation.

Rose had given Joe no encouragement to take such a drastic step, and it was incumbent upon him to learn everything he could about such psychosurgery. Freeman kept meticulous records of the eighty patients upon whom he and Watts had operated. These were all seriously disturbed human beings, chronically depressed, schizophrenics, or chronic alcoholics, suffering from the most acute mental problems facing medical science at that time. Almost all of these patients were far older than Rosemary, and only one was younger. They had often been brought to Freeman after years of treatment, distress, and disappointment, seeing the neurologist's technique as a last desperate hope. None of these patients was retarded. Freeman had his own caveats about lobotomies and knew that the patients had to be chosen with great care.

Having such an operation performed on Rosemary, a mildly retarded young woman with ill-defined emotional problems, was by any definition an extreme measure, but Joe was a pragmatic man who saw life as a series of problems waiting to be solved. He decided to go ahead, convincing the doctors that his daughter was a perfect candidate. Thus Rosemary became probably the first person with mental retardation in America to receive a prefrontal lobotomy.

"Mr. Kennedy was a powerful man who could talk anyone into anything," Luella said. "The operation erases any active thinking, and I think Mr. Kennedy decided it would be better for Rosemary not to be exposed any longer to the general public in case she ran away. It would be better to almost 'close the case.' Then there wouldn't be any more trouble and it would be easier to have her in a home somewhere."

Freeman and Watts performed their lobotomies at George Washington University Hospital, only a few blocks from Jack's and Kathleen's apartments. In Freeman's experience "some patients have been much more concerned about the loss of hair and whether the scar would show than they have been about their prefrontal lobe." Thus the doctor directed the nurses to shave the hair on only the front of the skull "so that women can arrange it without too much apprehension."

Freeman and Watts performed their operation at eight o'clock in the morning, and at the appointed hour the patient was wheeled into the operating room. Although mildly sedated, she was very much aware of her surroundings. She was given local anesthetic, Novocain, and was awake lying on the operating table, her head placed on a sandbag.

Watts drilled two burr holes in each side of the cranium and inserted the tubing from a large hypodermic needle about two and a half inches into the brain. Then the doctor took a spatula that looked like "a blunt butter knife," pushed it into the cavity left by the tubing, and twisted upward destroying the white matter of the frontal lobe. The surgeon made three other cuts, reinserting the spatula each time. Although the doctors called this Freeman-Watts standard lobotomy a "precision operation," it was a matter of art as well as science. Each operation was different. The more serious the condition, the more likely the doctors would cut into the posterior regions of the brain, and the more likely the patient would end up tragically changed. The doctors kept talking to Rosemary, getting her to sing or count. When the patient became sleepy and disoriented, the two doctors could tell that the operation was working. As long as she continued to sing out and to add and subtract, the doctors kept cutting away, destroying a larger and larger area of the brain. When the doctors were finished, they closed the incision with black silk sutures, and she was wheeled out of the operating room.

Rosemary had been Rose's child, Rose's burden, and her daughter was now like a painting that had been brutally slashed so it was scarcely recognizable. She had regressed into an infantlike state, mumbling a few words, sitting for hours staring at the walls, only traces left of the young woman she had been, still with those flashes of rage. This was a horror beyond horror, an unthinkable, unspeakable disaster. Rose and her children had repressed so much, and now they repressed what Joe had done to his daughter, repressed it all and pretended that it had never happened and that Rosemary no longer existed.

Rosemary was shipped off to several private institutions. She lived a number of years in Craig House, a private psychiatric hospital an hour north of New York City. The institution sat on a hill outside Beacon, New York, and housed no more than twenty or so patients at a time. Craig House was famous for its discretion in handling the wealthy and the prominent, and the townspeople whispered among themselves about the movie stars, and the scions of famous names who were said to have spent time there. There were several houses and cottages and a mansion with barred windows for patients who might try to escape. Craig House was by no means a residence for a young woman with retardation, but it was here that Rosemary lived, among alcoholics, potential suicides, schizophrenics, and manic depressives. In the forties it was often considered poor therapy for psychiatric patients to have their treatment interrupted by visits from family, and Rosemary spent years largely by herself, without a glimmer of awareness of what had happened to her and her life as a Kennedy woman.

Almost no one outside the family knew Rosemary's whereabouts. Eunice said that she did not even know where her sister was during that decade. From that day on, in all the letters that Rose wrote the family in the next few years, she began "My darlings" or "Dear Children." Then she mentioned Joe and each of her children in turn, Joe Jr., Jack, Kathleen, Eunice, Pat, Jean, Bobby, and Ted, everyone but Rosie, her namesake. Rosemary was gone, gone from the family letters, gone from discussions, gone.

In late November of 1941 as autumn winds stripped the last of the leaves from the trees around the great house, Rose directed the help in closing down the mansion in Bronxville for good. Joe had sold the house that was the one place that most of the Kennedy children thought of as home. Rose knew that it didn't make any sense to keep the house any longer. Everyone was gone. Joe Jr. and Jack were in the service. Kathleen was working in Washington, and the others had all been sent off to school. Eunice was at Manhattanville, while Pat had begun her first year at Rosemont College. Bobby was at Portsmouth Priory in Rhode Island. Jean and Teddy were off at boarding school too.

When the last photograph was packed, the last piece of furniture shipped off, it was all over and she turned away from the house for a last time and traveled into New York City. On the first weekend in December she sat down in the hotel and wrote a letter to her children to be mimeographed and mailed out. With the family all gone and spread out, her regular letters chronicling their whereabouts would have to suffice to hold the family together, except for the holidays and special occasions when they would all be together. "The house was no longer a necessity," she wrote. "So today I feel quite relieved and very free with nothing on my mind except the shades of blue for my Palm Beach trousseau."

In Washington that Sunday Kathleen was sitting in a Hot Shoppes Restaurant having lunch with John White and his sister Patsy White Field. In the midst of their spirited repartee, a special announcement came over the radio. Japan had attacked Pearl Harbor. As they left the restaurant, smoke was rising up from the garden behind the Japanese embassy as the diplomatic staff burned box after box of papers and documents. Outside on Massachusetts Avenue a menacing and growing crowd formed, its mood tempered only when Washington police and FBI agents arrived.

Everywhere people were full of a sense of betrayal. In this mood of paranoia and suspicion, those who had yesterday parroted the slogans of isolationism sought immediately to reaffirm their patriotism. Joe sent a wire to the president: "In this great crisis all Americans are with you. Name the battle post. I'm yours to command."

Joe was an outcast. As he waited for a reply that never arrived, the family gathered for Christmas and New Year's in Palm Beach. When the children were younger, Rose had dominated their movements, but they had moved beyond her control. They dashed from party to party, event to event, not only beyond her supervision but oftentimes beyond her knowledge. "When you all were little and I could regiment you and have you all come and leave at a certain time and at the same time," she wrote her children, "and when I was sure of what clothes you were going to wear and how you were going to have your hair cut and what hat you were going to wear ... it seemed to me much more simple. However, time marches on and I suppose I must get used to the new uncertainties and excitement."

Then they were gone, all except Jean and Teddy. Her youngest son traveled down to Palm Beach with Rose on the train. "We got sidetracked and went through West Virginia," Ted recalled. "It was terribly, terribly cold and there weren't enough blankets and we slept together. The train was running low on food, and Mother got off at a sort of trestle and walked into this little town and got some oatmeal and some milk. And then—I have this clear recollection, it's burned in my mind—the train started to move. And Mother running up with the milk and the oatmeal and I remember not being able to stop the train, and trying to get my mother. She just came right up to the moving train and said 'Hold onto these, Teddy' and pulled herself right up and [it] never sort of even fazed her."

Rose wanted twelve-year-old Jean down for the winter season as well, and thus she was taken out of school in the North and along with Ted sent to the Graham School in Palm Beach. Rose accompanied her daughter to dancing school and declared that Jean "will go along and get quite a lot out of the season here." Even nine-year-old Teddy was not immune from his mother's eternal quest for civility. Rose sent him off to dancing school as well, the youngest boy in the class. "He dances very well, has remarkable rhythm, and shakes his head like a veteran when he does the conga," Rose wrote. "He only fell down once last week, so he is improving."

Jean was four years older than Teddy, but they were kindred souls, shuttled from one boarding school to the next, both teased and pampered by their older siblings, and disciplined by their mother. Ted admired his older sister so much that when his teacher asked for nominations for class treasurer, the newest student raised his hand: "I nominate Jean Kennedy." Jean and her younger brother were like seedlings that had been uprooted so many times that they learned never to set their roots too deeply into the soil. Jean and Teddy had hardly made new friends when Rose sent them back up North, Jean to the Sacred Heart nuns at Eden Hall and Teddy to the Riverdale Country School.

Ted was moved between boarding schools, often not even staying the whole year. Years afterwards Rose reflected that her youngest son had "changed too often," an opinion with which her youngest son concurs. "That was hard to take," Ted reflected. "I mean at that age you just go with the punches. I finally got through school where I spent some time trying to find out where the dormitory and the gym were located."

When the rest of the family was celebrating New Year's 1942, twenty-year-old Eunice was traveling westward to San Francisco. For her the last months had been fraught with pain and difficulty. Eunice had loved and cared for Rosemary more deeply than any of her brothers and sisters. For the deeply religious young woman, the operation betrayed everything in which she believed, the sacredness of human life, the sanctity of family, the deep worth of every human being. Her fellow students at Manhattanville knew nothing about the lobotomy, but they thought that in the last months of 1941 Eunice had begun to act strangely. She was often sick and distanced herself even more from life and study at the college. She missed so many classes that one of her schoolmates, Barbara Dunn, tutored her in chemistry. After the Christmas recess, the students returned and saw that Eunice's room was empty. Some students whispered that Eunice had contracted tuberculosis and had gone off to a sanitorium. Others gossiped that her father was worried that if she stayed at Manhattanville she would become a nun and had ordered her to leave. Still others knew that for inexplicable reasons in the middle of the year Eunice was transferring to Stanford University in Palo Alto, California, three thousand miles away. None of them knew about Rosemary's operation and how much Eunice loved her eldest sister. "My mother wanted me to go out there," Eunice recalled.

"We sent her out there because we thought that the mild climate would be better for her during the winter, as she was not very strong during those college years," Rose said later.

The Stanford campus with its graceful, Spanish-style tiled buildings, its tennis courts, playing fields, and immense grassy venues was a world away from the walled confines of Manhattanville. Jack had spent a desultory semester there and Eunice had first learned about the campus from her older brother. Her father and Jack had not given Eunice a terribly high estimate of the California university, but initially she was impressed. "When I think of Manhattanville's five acres!" she wrote her parents. There was not a nun to be seen at this private university, the coeds dressed not in uniforms but in skirts and sweaters, clutching their books as they strolled between classes. Eunice knew that she still had serious health problems. Even before she registered for classes, she arranged to see two different doctors and assured her parents that "everything is well under control."

As idyllic as the campus appeared, Stanford was far closer to the war than Manhattanville. Some of the male students were dropping their studies to enlist, and already men in uniform were walking across the quad. In February, *The Stanford Daily* reported that an enemy submarine had shelled a refinery in Santa Barbara on the coast of California, and the more alarmist girded themselves for a Japanese invasion.

Eunice roomed by herself in Lagunita Court, a dormitory that consisted of a series of two-story, interconnected houses at

the center of campus. She had hardly arrived before she was
writing Rose asking for more blankets against the rain and the
cold, though it was a temperate clime, far different from winter
in Manhattanville. Eunice's housemates at Lagunita were a resolutely friendly lot, but they soon sensed that Eunice didn't
want to get close to them. "Hi, girl," she would call out as
they passed her in the hall, "Hi, girl." Although Eunice thought
she had fooled her dorm mates into thinking that her habit of
shouting out this generic greeting was "an Eastern custom,"
the students understood perfectly well that their newest dorm
mate didn't know their names.

The other students learned not to knock on Eunice's closed
door. They gossiped about how she supposedly kept her nail
and hair clippings in a box in her room. Eunice studied with
great intensity. If she did not write Rose regularly, her mother
noted that fact in her frequent mimeographed letters to her remote children. Late in the evenings when the young women sat
around talking behind blacked-out air-raid curtains, Eunice occasionally rushed in to ask in her tense, hyper way if anyone
had anything to eat. The students could hardly believe it. Eunice looked absolutely emaciated, yet she had such an incredible appetite that she could have sat at the training table for the
football team. They learned to avoid sitting with her in the dining hall. Stanford prided itself as a civilized place, and in the
dining room the rule was that no one could leave a table until
everyone had finished eating. Eunice went back for seconds
and thirds, and picked leftover food off the other students'
plates.

When she went off on a ski trip to Sun Valley, Idaho, with
a group of students, she was inexhaustible, running from skiing
to skating to swimming to sleigh riding, hardly stopping the
entire time. "I didn't really have a very good time at Stanford,"
Eunice reflected. "I wasn't mad about the school and, I don't
know, I just didn't click."

The students laughed about Eunice's peculiar ways, but as
time went by it became a tender laugh since they realized that
she was sick. "All I heard at the time was that she had some
kind of glandular disorder," recalled Mrs. Charlotte Cecil Walter. "She was like a starving person, so skinny. She was in real
trouble. I think she wasn't well enough to be friendly."

One of the few friends Eunice made at Stanford was Virginia Carpenter, a student from San Francisco with whom she
spent several weekends and vacations. "Eunice was hell-bent

to learn, and that was very commendable," Carpenter recalled. "She was quite loyal and very serious minded and deeply religious. But she was careless about her person, extraordinarily so, and generally careless about lots of things. And she had serious health problems. She made very frequent trips to the Stanford Hospital in San Francisco for gynecological problems. I was surprised that she had children from what I knew of her problems."

Eunice had never been so far away from home for so long. She had no intimate friends outside the family, especially not here in this school where she was such an outsider. Yet she would not think of writing whining letters of complaint to her mother, letters asking to return to the East Coast. Instead, she wrote Rose making Stanford out to be "an interesting and varied experience."

Across America the air was alive with rumors and suspicions that infiltrators, fifth columnists, and spies might have burrowed themselves in almost everywhere. On the West Coast the great fear was the Japanese-Americans. When Eunice arrived at Stanford the Japanese-American students were locked into their rooms at eight o'clock each evening, but they were soon sent away to be kept in camps for the duration of the war.

In Washington, anyone with past dealings with Nazi Germany was immediately suspect. Page came up to Kathleen and told her that Inga might be a spy. A man in the purchasing department at the paper had shown the young reporter a picture purportedly of Inga with Hitler in the dictator's box at the 1936 Olympic games. (After the war Waldrop said that he learned that the purchasing department employee was an undercover FBI agent being used to discredit the isolationist newspaper.)

When Kathleen told Inga the accusation, she was outraged. She went to see Cissy Patterson, the *Times-Herald* owner. That was a daring gesture. The isolationist publisher, pilloried in the liberal press, could scarce afford to be rumored harboring a suspected Nazi spy. Patterson sent Inga, Page, and Waldrop off to the FBI, where Inga indignantly demanded "a letter from the Federal Bureau of Investigation, stating that she was not a spy." Not only did the FBI refuse to give her the requested statement, but agents burglarized her apartment and began an extensive secret surveillance.

Suddenly, not only Inga but Jack and Kathleen had been

sucked into a dark world of suspicions and shadows. Kathleen would do almost anything that Jack asked her to do, no matter how dangerous to her own reputation or status. Jack was passionately in love with Inga, and he asked Kathleen to help him maintain his romance. Kathleen commandeered John White to double-date with Inga and Jack to give the impression that her brother was not so intimately involved with the Danish beauty.

As Inga and Jack coupled nightly in her apartment in a love affair as passionate as it was deluded, the shadows of the world were already passing across their romance. On January 12, 1942, Walter Winchell's syndicated column contained a short item phrased in the gossip writer's telegramlike style: "One of Ex-Ambassador Kennedy's eligible sons is the target of a Washington gal columnist's affections. So much so she has consulted her barrister about divorcing her exploring groom. Pa Kennedy no like."

Later in the day, Joe arrived at the newspaper and closeted himself with Waldrop. Joe was a man who believed in taking care of problems, and he saw a major problem here. Joe felt that he had made a fool of himself over Gloria Swanson. Now his precocious, precious son was following even further down that pathway than Joe had ever ventured. Inga was no match for Jack, an older, soon-to-be-twice-divorced woman, in a society where even one divorce was enough to drop one from the social register. She was an adulterer. Beyond that, Inga had happily cavorted with America's enemies in Germany, supposedly saluting Hitler and dancing at Goering's wedding. It was hardly a résumé likely to end in marriage to a son of Joseph P. Kennedy.

The next day Jack received orders transferring him to the Navy base in Charleston, South Carolina.

On a cold, rainy evening after Jack left to spend a few days in Palm Beach before taking on his new assignment, Inga sat writing a letter to her lover. She thought of him in the warmth of Florida, "one of the very rare people born to sunshine and happiness." She *knew* him, and through him she knew his family, and she realized that behind Joe, whom she considered "a typical slick politician, a good handshaker with a flashy smile but cold eyes, sly, intelligent and too sure of himself," stood the impenetrable, formidable presence of Rose Fitzgerald Kennedy. To friends like Chuck and Lem, Jack sometimes made fun of his mother, putting her down. But Inga, who knew Jack more intimately than his adolescent male friends, realized how deeply he cared for his mother, and what a crucial role she played in his life and the life of the whole Kennedy family. And in this letter it was of Rose she spoke:

> But of course we have to live our own lives, and even then a mother will always be a mother. (I am happy you love yours so much, and I understand why she is so fond of you. In the telegram I sent her, I said you were looking forward to seeing her. Hope you dont[sic] mind.) ... I admire the way "big Joe" brought you all up. How nice to be able to be proud of your children. I do know though, that your mother is the quiet power behind the thrown [sic].

When Jack left, Kathleen took over his apartment, sharing it with Betty Coxe, Chuck Spalding's girlfriend. Inga noticed immediately that "Betty is more or less the boss, and Kik [sic] is already a little sad about the whole arrangement" but it was not in Kathleen's nature to confront anyone. However, when Betty bought a bottle of rye for the apartment, Kathleen told her pointedly that "Daddy wouldn't approve." Her main decorating touch was to display pictures of her British friends, a presentation that Torb Macdonald described as "a living room full of lords and ladies."

One of Kathleen's first overnight guests was her sister Pat, who had come down from Philadelphia where she was in her first year of college. Again Pat had outsmarted her mother. Just as she had avoided being sent to the austere regimented precincts of Noroton, she managed to replace the conventlike atmosphere of Manhattanville with Rosemont College. This small Catholic women's school of four hundred students was literally on Philadelphia's Main Line, the Pennsylvania railroad line stopping directly in front of the school with its collegiate gothic buildings.

Pat had made a grand entrance at college, arriving late for her first year, bringing with her not only trunks of clothes but her own bed. Students had to wear stockings as well as hats when they went off campus, and Pat wore stylish sweaters and skirts, but her dormitory room looked as if it had been looted. "When the dorms were being shown to visitors," recalled Mrs. Thomas Joyce, "her room was always 'off limits' because of the mess."

As Pat had settled into her dormitory in the months just before Pearl Harbor, there had been no great debate about war and peace, isolationism, or intervention, as was taking place at many schools. The most important outside speaker, Father James Keller of the Maryknoll fathers, talked not about Nazism but "the Communistic program of bitterness and hate."

Pat soon discovered just how much more sedate and circumscribed her existence was than her brothers had experienced at Harvard. One of the first big social events had taken place in October, when the entire first-year class from St. Joseph's, a nearby Jesuit school, descended on campus for a two-hour afternoon tea-dance in which Pat and her classmates served punch to their guests.

By the time of this first dance, Pat was one of the best known first-year students, with her picture in *The Rambler*, the student newspaper, as the Rosemont tennis champion, beating out all the senior women. Pat was nearly a head taller than most of the students, with a lithe, athletic body, square shoulders, and thick brown hair. She had what her classmates took to be a soupçon of a British accent. She had inherited the pure complexion and beauty of an Irish colleen. She was a lovely young woman, yet she saw herself as gawky, plump, and unappealing, and her brothers, especially Jack, as splendid, gorgeous manly creatures. "Write me sometime when you can move that beavtiful [sic] body of yours to a pen and ink," she wrote Jack from Kathleen's apartment, picking out the words on her sister's typewriter. "Loads of love," she ended her letter, signing herself "Fatty Patty."

In Washington, Kathleen was still seeing John White. They would often go over to his sister's house, where people that her parents knew, such as Jimmy Roosevelt and Lord Halifax, the new British ambassador, were often present, sitting on the floor, eating plates of spaghetti, ardently discussing the war. Her father came occasionally too, once bringing one of his women friends with him, her presence more offensive to Patsy White Field than to Kathleen, who hardly seemed to notice.

Since he had returned from London, Joe had become ever more flagrant in his philandering, a fifty-two-year-old rake. One evening when she and John were at a party at the Mayflower Hotel, Kathleen overheard another guest joking about her father's sexual prowess, and she had become terribly upset. Her father could do whatever he wanted with his women, but she couldn't stand anyone criticizing him.

Before she had met John, Kathleen wrote her friend Janie Lindsay in London that she felt she might never marry: "Sometimes I feel that I am never going to take that on. No one I have ever met ever made me completely forget myself and one cannot get married with that attitude." Kathleen cared for John but she did not care for him that way either. "Tonight for the first time, I held her hand," White had written in his diary November 30. "I held the hand of Kathleen Kennedy . . . feel very friendly towards her and do now wonder what will become of us."

Kathleen let John come back to her new apartment, where he sat in her bedroom while she got undressed in the bathroom and put on her nightgown. She didn't care if he saw her putting night cream on her face and putting up her hair in pin curls. That only emphasized the asexuality of their relationship. Then she got in bed and John rubbed her back, or read a few pages of a novel to her, leaving as soon as she was asleep.

Kathleen had decided she liked to be hugged, as long as it remained a warm affectionate gesture and had nothing to do with the thing the nuns said not to do. It had taken her weeks of subtle manipulation so that John would hug and caress her in a sweet brotherly way, never touching what he wasn't supposed to touch, never pressing his body against her, never attempting to seduce her or lull her with some subtle sexual lullabies until she was doing what she shouldn't do and wouldn't do and couldn't do.

For Kathleen, sex was not simply this rude coupling that she disdained as a Catholic lady of good upbringing. It was an emotional commitment, it was giving of herself in some deeply dangerous way. It was an abyss. One night John sat on the edge of Kathleen's bed rubbing her back. Seeing Kathleen there in her long flannel nightgown, John thought of her as Claudette Colbert in *It Happened One Night*, and himself as Clark Gable, sharing a room with her while protecting her honor. Usually, Kathleen lay there like a contented kitten, gently falling to sleep. This night, however, Kathleen suddenly roused herself out of her half slumber and turned toward John on the verge of tears. "Listen, the thing about me you ought to know is that I'm like Jack—incapable of deep affection."

On the afternoon of the first Friday in February, Jack drove in his Buick convertible to the Fort Sumter Hotel, where Inga was waiting for him in room 132 registered under the name

"Barbara White." He went up to Inga's room, where the couple spent almost the entire weekend.

FBI and Navy intelligence monitored Inga's and Jack's movements, including a listening device in their hotel room. As a chronicle of Jack's sex life, this weekend was memorable. He was a man whose passion was generally spent quickly, disposed of like an itch, but this weekend he was almost insatiable, endless in his passion, consumed with emotion. Inga realized how differently Jack was acting. "Inga was much wiser, and a little bit older, with a European sophistication, and she had him sized up very well," John White recalled. "With Jack if the girl wouldn't go to bed with him, that was okay. But if she did it was under the terms that afterwards she gets out and goes. That's it. No in between. No affection. No lasting relation. But Inga said that with her things didn't go exactly to plan, and as they became more and more involved he began to fall apart, and it was a little embarrassing to have this powerful personality suddenly become groping and unsure of himself. This intimacy with Inga was awkward for him, and she wasn't sure if she wanted to have him that way. She was honest. She liked him immensely but she didn't necessarily want him on these new terms of him being human, so to speak."

"To you I need not pretend," Jack had told her in an intimate moment. "You know me too well." But in all those hours together, all those intense conversations, never once did he mention Rosemary and her tragic operation. Whatever pain he felt and whatever guilt he might have suffered over his own failure to stop his father were matters not to be discussed, not with a lover, not with anyone outside his family, and probably not with his own kin either. He was a young man facing war. Yet never in all that night and day wrapped in Inga's arms did he talk about his own fears and doubts. That was nothing to talk to a woman about, even a woman he loved. He was a young man with health problems of such seriousness that he should not have been wearing a uniform, much less contemplating going into combat. But Jack wanted to be treated like everyone else, not like some semi-invalid, to be pitied, set off on life's sidelines, and he mentioned not one word about his back problems and his agony.

Jack was a Kennedy and Kennedys did not complain or whimper or expose themselves. Yet as Inga wrote Jack, "a man or woman who thinks and makes others believe that he has no weakness in him or her, well they are like diamonds cut by the unskilled hand," and her Jack was a diamond that shone brilliantly. She saw, however, how profoundly he feared the wages of the human heart. "Maybe your gravest mistake handsome . . . is that you admire brains more than heart," she told him, "but then that is necessary to arrive. Heart never brought fame—except to Saints—nor money—except to the women of the oldest profession in the world, and that must be hard earned."

Inga was a connoisseur of powerful men, almost all of them far older than Jack. She saw all Jack's ambition and cunning and shrewdness, qualities that he camouflaged with his wit and his nonchalance. "You have just sufficient meanness in you to get along and enough brains and goodness to give to the world and not only take," she told her lover.

Inga was wise about the wages of power. "Anyone as brainy and Irish-shrewd as you cant [sic] be quite like a white dove. . . ." she wrote him. "You have more than even your ancestors and yet you haven't lost the tough hide of the Irish potatoes."

She saw what he might do and be with all his gifts, and if he did not use those gifts, well, she feared what he might become. "If you feel anything beautiful in your life—I am not talking about me—" she wrote him in a letter that was almost a plea, "then dont [sic] hesitate to say so, dont [sic] hesitate to make the little bird sing. It costs so little; a word, a smile, a slight touch of a hand . . . in the near future . . . life is going to be tough, and doubble [sic] hard for the people who have ideals, who have hopes, who have someone they really love, who understand humanity."

Inga was a peculiar mentor for the convent-educated Kathleen. As Kathleen and Inga strode rapidly down the sidewalk on their daily walk to work, the two women talked often about Kathleen's brother. Inga wrote Jack that she loved Kathleen "for admitting that what gets her goat is that she is jealous of me." Inga wanted her lover to know that Kathleen could never be to Jack what she was. "What I give you—if I give you anything—and what I take—which is plenty—that is something she couldn't do for you anyway," Inga said. "But she is young and as yet intollerant [sic]."

Kathleen loved Jack, and if she was jealous, admitting it was the beginning of healing. She cared for Inga and saw her as a guide to a sophisticated secular world. Kathleen and Inga had become close friends and they had what to all appearances were frank and honest talks. But they had lost what, as Lyn Mikel Brown and Carol Gilligan write, so many young women lose: "their ability to distinguish what is true from what is said to be true, what feels loving from what is said to be love, what feels real from what is said to be reality." Inga did not tell her friend that she had at least one other lover and feared that Jack would leave her. Kathleen said nothing of how much she doubted that Inga was good for Jack, and how much of those doubts she had told her father.

Kathleen flew down to Palm Beach to spend a few days with Joe and Rose. Two days later Jack called Inga and told her that his father had just called and convinced him what he must do about their relationship. Jack obtained special permission to fly to Washington for one night, and when he flew back to Charleston he did not return to Inga again.

"Inga seemed very sad yesterday," Kathleen wrote her brother. "She says she isn't going to see you anymore. I haven't inquired into the story but I certainly would like to. If there is anything you think I should know don't be afraid to tell me."

Then Kathleen turned to the great lesson of the affair, for Jack and for herself as well. "As for your words of advice Brother I'll take 'em," she wrote. "Boy the only persons you can be sure of are your own flesh and blood and then we are not always sure of them."

At the *Times-Herald*, Kathleen had been promoted to reviewing plays and movies in her own bylined column. Rose was proud of her daughter, but this was something she wanted too, though nobody knew it. The year before when she had traveled to South America along with Eunice and Jack, she had kept a diary and secretly harbored the idea of writing an article, perhaps for *Ladies' Home Journal*, but she hadn't dared to say anything. "Please do not mention this to anybody," she cautioned Mother Patterson, to whom she confessed her aspiration, "as my sons and my husband scoff at the idea, in fact, you are the only one who has ever given me any encouragement." Her sons had learned the same intellectual disdain for their mother that their father harbored, and Rose didn't dare talk of her own private dreams, especially not to her author son.

Rose decided that she could at least further her daughter's journalistic career. She told Kathleen that she should use a nom de plume and have a new picture taken to run beside her stories, but Joe and Kathleen had decided that wasn't necessary. Kathleen was a part of her father's world now, and Rose sometimes seemed to be shunted aside. "I am quite crushed to think that my three or four children got into print with works of their brains and I was never allowed to edit one word," she wrote the family. She tried to have an impact on the lives of her adult children. Joe Jr.'s sloppiness had not been regimented out of him in the Navy, and when on several occasions he received demerits for having a dirty wastebasket, Rose vowed to write the Navy Department, the War Board, perhaps even the president himself, but Joe quickly squelched that. "Your father again has restricted my activities," Rose wrote, "and thinks the little woman should confine herself to the home. Personally, I think it shows [an] antiquated system with emphasis made on the unessentials, and after all, there are times when a woman should show initiative . . . (This, of course, is all in fun, and don't discuss it outside of the family circle.)"

In the middle of April Rose flew out to California to visit Stanford. Other mothers visited their daughters. Few of them, however, stayed for several weeks in the dormitory as Rose did, sitting in the reception area typing letters, going off to class with Eunice. The two women kept to themselves, Rose, a gracious, impeccably groomed matron, and beside her Eunice, unkempt, scrawny, and sickly. At meals they sat uneasily with the other students, Rose making the benign small talk of which she was a master. "Oh, we just love the Bard," Rose said when one of the students mentioned her class in Shakespeare, and proceeded to monitor the class that afternoon. Another day Rose arrived late for a class in art appreciation watching a series of slides in the darkened room. As she attempted to slip into the room, she managed to switch on the light. "Oh that's Eunice's mother," someone yelled, as Rose quickly doused the light and sat down.

Rose was a professional optimist, and in her letters to her children she never let on that Eunice was not healthy, nor that beyond her studies she was making no mark on Stanford. When Joe Jr. and Jack had gone off to Harvard, they had made themselves presences on campus, joining the best clubs, playing athletics, dating young women who made them the envy of their peers. With so many young men leaving campus, there were more opportunities for women, but Eunice was not active on the War Board, the Women's Conference, Cap & Gown, or any of the organizations she might have joined. She played tennis and skied, but the overwhelming impression she left on her classmates was that of a sick and troubled young woman who belonged somewhere other than Stanford.

Now that the Bronxville home was gone, Rose moved between two resort homes and hotel rooms, often alone, with Joe off somewhere else. She could do little to cure his moroseness, her husband so vital, so energetic, relegated to the sidelines in this the epic struggle of their time. He wanted desperately to be part of the war effort. Deluded about his reputation, he wrote Lord Beaverbrook, the British press magnate, volunteering his services to England.

That spring of 1942 Waldrop came down to Palm Beach. The editor and his wife drove out to the mansion for a luncheon with the Kennedys and Cissy Patterson, the *Times-Herald* owner. Rose greeted her daughter's employers with cordiality and graciousness. "It was all very gay and informal," Rose wrote her children afterwards, with the publisher and editor praising Kathleen, and Rose and Joe in turn praising Patterson and Waldrop for being so helpful to their daughter. Behind his gruff persona, Waldrop was a man of great insight and awareness. Though the luncheon seemed pleasant enough, when Waldrop spoke a few sentences to Joe, he could tell that the former ambassador "was in despair emotionally."

In the psychological matrix of the Kennedys' marriage, Joe was allowed to express passionate and deep emotions, where it was his wife's role always to hold herself together, emotionally aloof and contained. As her husband became more distressed, Rose increasingly appeared almost bloodless in her feelings. In fact, she worried now not only for her family's honor but for the lives of her two sons who she knew would soon see combat. "I was caught in events and forces and circumstances utterly beyond my control," Rose recalled. "There was nothing I could do but put on a cheerful face, to hope, and to pray."

Since Kathleen was a little girl, Jack and Joe Jr. had been her heroes, Jack even more than his older brother. She wrote him almost every week, calling him by innumerable different salutations. Brother. John F. Brother. Jack. Twinkle-toes. Jackie. Johnnie. All the nicknames of affection.

Kathleen was as intense and high-strung as her brothers, but she knew that they faced something that she presumably did not: the possibility of wartime death. Joe Jr. got a few days off from his training and came to visit. Kathleen wrote Jack that she had had "dinner with future Pres. of the United States . . . at the Metropolitan Club."

"I don't know which one of you is the worst," Kathleen wrote. "You might have chewed gum but he chewed his nails and it wasn't from excitement."

Kathleen wanted to be part of the war, to go to London with a correspondent's credentials. She talked to officials at the State Department, but it was clear that she wasn't going to get official approval. The fact was, as her roommate Betty Coxe realized, Kathleen "hadn't any ambitions to work, but she wanted to marry well—socially well. She was not a serious journalist. It was a way to get jollies, a great way to get around and meet people in Washington."

Kathleen showed Betty letters from her British admirers, not only Billy but Tony Rosslyn, William Douglas-Home, and Hugh Fraser, asking her which of the men seemed the most attractive. John White thought that *he* was the one unwilling to commit, but Kathleen's women friends knew that John wasn't even a consideration. Socially, he was nobody. Kathleen enjoyed repeating her father's axiom that "one shouldn't marry a girl for money but there's no sense in knowing any poor girls," a rule she considered as appropriate for women as for men. Indeed, when Page told Kathleen that she was marrying a man of no great background, she appeared stunned. "But I thought you were ambitious," Kathleen said.

In March 1942, Kick received a letter from one of her debutante friends saying that she had received a letter from Lady Astor imploring Kathleen "to stop all this foolishness and come right over and marry Billy." Kathleen talked to Jack about the possibility. After ending his affair with Inga, Jack viewed romance and marriage with detachment. Love had nothing to do with it. "I would advise strongly against any voyages to England to marry any Englishman," he wrote his sister. "For I have come to the reluctant conclusion that it has come time to write the obituary of the British Empire."

The First World War had been a man's war in the trenches, but the Battle of Britain was a war waged as much on women as on men. Kathleen had always expected one day to visit the Café de Paris again, that favorite haunt, to sit in that dark basement room listening to the music of Snakehips Johnson and his band. On the night of March 8, 1941, at about ten-thirty two of Kathleen's fellow debutantes, Sarah Norton and Virginia Brand Polk, had arrived separately at the popular club. Norton spent most of the war hidden away in MI-6 in Bletchely working at breaking German codes, while Polk worked as a jeep mechanic, but tonight they wore evening clothes, stunning young women out for an evening of frolic.

On her arm Sarah had Billy Hartington, to whom she was for a short time engaged. Whenever Billy got a pass, the couple braved the bombs and fires of the night. The Café de Paris was so far underground that it was considered as safe as a bomb shelter. As they turned into the block before the famous club, they saw that the building that housed the café lay in smoldering ruins. Less than a half hour before, a fifty-pound bomb had penetrated eighty feet underground and exploded before the bandstand in the crowded nightclub, killing Johnson and thirty-three others as the musicians played "Oh, Johnny." As the two former debutantes stood there, scavengers picked through the smoking ruins by candlelight, carrying off sequined evening bags and diamond necklaces. Billy and another man hurried into the building as bodies were being carried out, the wounded bandaged with cloth ripped from ball gowns. After a while Billy returned through the grim ruins. "Well, then, let's go to the Four Hundred," Sarah said, as if they had merely been turned away by the doorman.

"You had to go out," said Lady Ford, the former Virginia Brand, remembering that night. "Life had to go on. You had to behave in what to a later generation would have seemed an uncaring manner. But dear heavens if you didn't do that you would have gone mad."

In America there were no bombs in the night and always there were the parties, parties touched not only by laughter but now by the melancholy moments of good-byes. In March Kathleen went to New York for Lem's farewell party, off to Africa as an ambulance driver for the American Field Service. Then in April, Kathleen and Betty traveled to Aiken, South Carolina, where all the old friends converged for a glorious going-away party for George Mead. George had often come to Washington to visit Kathleen when he was in Marine officer training nearby at Quantico, Virginia. He had joined the Marines even before Pearl Harbor, and of all Kathleen's friends he would be the first one going into combat. George's father was the founder of the Mead Paper Company, and the Meads' winter home was a plantation with all the antebellum charm of Tara in *Gone With the Wind*. Jack was up for the weekend from Charleston. Chuck Spalding made it, and so did another of Kathleen's former beaux, Zeke Coleman.

Kathleen loved being with Jack. She cared for him as a vital, witty, sardonic young man charged with life, and that was the role Jack played this weekend for Kathleen and for everyone else. No one would have guessed that in Charleston he was having to spend days in bed because of his bad back, lying there in excruciating pain. It had gotten so bad that in March he had taken ten days' leave to seek treatment at the Mayo Clinic in Rochester, Minnesota, and the Lahey Clinic in Boston as well, where it was recommended that he have surgery: "fusion of the right sacro-iliac joint." He was now in the midst of more tests that in May would lead to authorization to travel to Boston for further examinations at the U.S. Naval Hospital in Chelsea. But in Aiken, joking with Kick and the others, Jack appeared the very definition of good health.

During the weekend the young men endlessly kidded each other, joked about the Navy and the Marines. Although George put on his own display of good humor, Kathleen thought that he was acting rather strange. She and her friends had gone to such an effort to come to Aiken for the weekend, and she couldn't understand why George "wouldn't show he was pleased." He seemed so distant, so reserved.

Neither George nor Jack could talk to women about their fears and doubts. During the weekend George took Chuck aside and said that he was afraid. The American soldiers were still holding onto Corregidor, but that was all that was left of the Philippines, a beleaguered fortress, all the rest gone, overrun by the Japanese. All over Asia the Japanese were on the move, and George knew that the politicians boasting of quick victory did not know what these Japanese soldiers were like. He had heard the tales. He was an officer. And he was afraid, afraid he wasn't ready, afraid he couldn't lead, afraid he was a coward. Chuck said that Jack had figured it all out; if you didn't think you were going to be killed, you'd survive. You just couldn't let it get to you. And then Chuck did what they all did when things got too heavy, too emotional, too deep, too personal. He turned to laughter, saying how they were all so glad that good old George was the one going out there winning the war for them. Then George and Chuck went back with the others. They joined in the joking and the playing of games, and Kathleen and the other young women never knew what George and Chuck and Jack and the other young men were thinking and feeling and fearing. The guests said good-bye to George, and in May he was gone with the Fifth Marines on a troop ship sailing to the Pacific.

Always before, summer had meant weeks at Hyannis Port, but this year was different. Joe was finishing his flight training. Jack had been accepted for Naval Reserve Midshipmen School at Northwestern University in Chicago, and he headed west to train to become a torpedo (PT) boat captain. Kathleen spent part of the summer on the Cape. Pat was now the oldest member of the family still at home. For her it was a strange, dispirited summer. The young men had gone off to war, not only Jack and Joe Jr., but most of the young men of the port. Pat was so used to being around her brothers, and adored them so intensely, that by her estimate other young men always came up short. Her brothers were smarter, more handsome, more athletic, and potential beaux soon left, weary of Pat's constant references to Joe Jr. and especially to Jack. "Well how's every little thing with you good looking? . . ." she wrote Jack in July. "The Cape is smaller than ever and your sister more unpopular (if that's possible)." That was far from true, but it was part of the self-deprecating humor of the family.

That summer too the war had begun to strike home. On August 7, 1942, George Mead was one of nineteen thousand Marines who landed on the tiny island in the Solomons called Guadalcanal. On August 18 the Marines began their first thrust against the entrenched Japanese. The next morning Mead was killed, a bullet striking him in the face.

The Meads, like the Kennedys, were a family that had what was said to be everything. In her time of mourning, George's mother wrote a letter to Kathleen and Jack and all the friends. "The love in our hearts for George certainly is there stronger, if possible, than ever before and always will be," she wrote. "What is death, then, but a physical change which does not interfere in any way with our power to love? With that power and love and George in our hearts, how can we be unhappy! We can't."

Kathleen was profoundly affected by the letter, as she was by George's death. She wrote Mrs. Mead a letter memorializing a young man who lived up to his family name, as she knew that she and her brothers had been taught to live up to theirs. "Your words to us meant more than all the things I have ever read, learned or been taught about death, war, courage, strength . . . ," she wrote George's mother. "I know that everyone who talked to you cannot help but know that what George did was just an act of obedience to you and Mr. Mead. You had already taught him love of duty and obedience to it. He was killed living up to that heritage. Future days may bring bad news to all of us, but remembering your words, and the way you have acted, one cannot but feel—Please God, let me act in a similar fashion."

────── 14 ──────

"The Ability to Not Be Got Down"

*A*t seven in the evening on a sweltering summer day in late June of 1943, Kathleen walked up the gangplank of the *Queen Mary*. She was wearing her heavy winter Red Cross uniform and a raincoat, and had a tin helmet on her head. She carried a canteen, gas mask, and a first aid kit strapped to her waist and was hefting thirty-five-pound musette bags full of her belongings.

As Kathleen pushed her way through thousands of milling G.I.'s, she hardly recognized this as the graceful vessel that her parents and Jack had sailed on in the thirties. Then, movie stars and politicians and gangsters and millionaires and journalists and ambassadors and the sons and daughters of ambassadors had all traveled on the splendid ship. For dinner the ladies in their gowns and jewels and gentlemen in evening dress entered the massive first-class dining salon, then danced the evening away on the polished wood floors.

No one was dancing on this ship. Everywhere Kathleen looked, she saw soldiers sitting or standing. The *Queen Mary* appeared not a great vessel about to sail the Atlantic, but a gigantic rescue ship that had just picked up all the flotsam of the seas. To Kathleen the overburdened ship was "the most pathetic sight in the world." The ship had been camouflaged a ghastly gray. It had just been totally refitted to house not the two thousand passengers of its halcyon civilian days, or even the five thousand she had carried as a troop ship to Australia, but fifteen thousand American soldiers. Workers had affixed standee bunks, often six berths high, not only in the cabins but in the cocktail bar and the swimming pool. The soldiers slept in shifts, two or three to a bunk each twenty-four hours, and a third of the men slept on the decks each night.

Kathleen picked her way along corridors packed with G.I.'s, every crevice full of soldiers. She finally found her own cabin, which she shared with seven other women in standee bunks. Kathleen fancied herself a woman of the world, but not *this* world. There were 160 Army nurses on board, and Kathleen pronounced them "a lot of tough babies." Her friend and fellow Red Cross volunteer, Katherine "Tatty" Spaatz, was rooming with several young women from the USO. During the voyage these entertainers performed for troops on a one-to-one basis, carrying what Tatty considered the ideal of "personal service" to an extreme. These were the "bad girls" that Kathleen and Tatty knew existed in the lives of their brothers and other men. They did not, however, socialize with such women, much less sleep in the same room with them.

Kathleen quickly learned that there were three hundred officers on board. They were the only men with whom she would even consider socializing. She wrote the family that "most of the Red Cross girls don't pay attention to them as it isn't any compliment to be sought after when the ratio is so uneven. . . . The girls are quite nice but you certainly get sick of a lot of giggling females and they still like to sit up until about 1:30 A.M. every night."

Although it was a wet, windy crossing Kathleen tried to get in a walk every day. She paced back and forth on the tiny, forty-foot-long stretch of free deck space. Once, as she walked back and forth, the ship swerved sharply as the *Queen Mary* avoided a submarine somewhere off the starboard.

During the five-day crossing, Kathleen had many hours to think. Kathleen knew that she could have stayed in Washington and made a career of journalism. She was no Clare Boothe Luce, but her work was going well enough. When Inga left for New York City in July, Kathleen had taken over her column and was making a success of it. Yet as the months went by, Washington had become the capital only of Kathleen's malaise.

Everyone was leaving. Despite all his cynical boasting, John White had entered the Marine Corps. In August she had gone up to New York to see him. John had taken her out to Jones Beach, the great new state park where over a million New Yorkers congregated on torrid summer weekends. She had never been anywhere like that before, lying half naked cheek by jowl with thousands of others, John's brown Marine Corps blanket almost touching the blankets and towels of other groups of summer sojourners.

The air was full of the scent of hot dogs, suntan oil, and playful sensuality, and there before all these strangers John had reached over and kissed her passionately. She could hardly believe it was happening, hardly believe that John would try something like that, hardly believe that she would allow something like that to occur. She worried that she was losing control. That evening she and John had gone to visit Inga, who had just been divorced and was living with another man. It was as strange and disturbing an encounter as John's lusty embrace. Inga took Kathleen aside and confided that she still loved Jack. That dangerously illicit romance was still alive, and Kathleen had another forewarning about where uncontrolled passion might lead: directly into a doomed marriage.

A month later John had telephoned her that he was shipping out for Northern Ireland. Kathleen had hardly said good-bye before he was back in Washington, incarcerated in the Navy brig. In Londonderry John had blithely gone out photographing British destroyers and he had been arrested as a possible spy. After Inga's experiences, John might have been more cautious, but that was not John White. Kathleen visited him in prison before he was released and transferred to the West Coast. Nonetheless, this episode ended Kathleen's last residues of romantic sentiment for John White. This was not a time for puckish insouciance, at least not in the men Kathleen admired. She wanted a man like her brothers, a man who played a hero's game.

Despite his health problems, Jack had gone through training to captain a PT boat. As Kathleen sailed to England, her beloved brother was already in the South Pacific taking PT-109 out on night patrols. "As a matter of fact this job is somewhat like sailing," he wrote Kathleen, "in that we spend most of our time trying to get the boat running faster—although it isn't just to beat Daly for the Kennedy cup—it's the Kennedy tail this time." Joe Jr. had completed his flight training and was piloting a flying boat first out of Puerto Rico and now from Norfolk, searching the waters of the Atlantic for elusive German submarines. And now Kathleen in her way would be joining her brothers, playing her own part in the war.

As a Red Cross volunteer, Kathleen would be following in a family tradition set by her late Aunt Eunice in World War I. All over England and the allied territories, wherever American G.I.'s went for a few days of rest and recreation, Red Cross clubs were being set up. Her father had made sure that

Kathleen would not be treated like most of the twenty-seven hundred professional staff members from the United States sent off first for six months to Northern Ireland, some dreary provincial town in Wales, or the more obscure reaches of the Mediterranean. His friend at U.S. Army Headquarters in London, Tim McInerny, reported to Joe that "by putting the squeeze on a few people" he saw to it that Kathleen was posted in London. Another young woman was summarily transferred to Londonderry, Northern Ireland.

When Kathleen arrived in London, she spent several days at the home of an old friend, Sylvia "Sissy" Ormsby-Gore, and her husband, David. Kathleen sat in their garden sunning herself and writing letters. "Everyone is very surprised and I do mean surprised to see me," she wrote Jack. "There's much more anti-Kennedy feeling than I imagined and I am determined to get my stories straight as I think I'll get it on all sides."

The Red Cross assigned Kathleen as the program assistant at Hans Crescent, an exclusive officers-only club situated in an exquisite Victorian hotel in the center of London, Knightsbridge, only a block from Harrods. Kathleen settled into her work, providing a momentary illusion of intimacy to an endless series of young men. The long days started at ten in the morning and often did not end until after the evening dance, when Kathleen checked in the women guests before dancing with the soldiers. "The job is a little more than I bargained for but life is full of surprises [sic] so I guess one more won't hurt me," she wrote Waldrop, her former boss. "As we get a day and a half off a week I am here recuperating from five and a half days of jitter-bugging, gin rummy, ping-pong, bridge and just being an American girl among 1500 doughboys a long way from home. (I'm not sure yet but I don't think this is what I was born for.)"

Before the war, Kathleen would scarcely have talked to most of the G.I.'s who frequented the club. The war had tempered Kathleen's snobbishness, as it had most of her fellow debutantes. "You wouldn't recognize old Kick," she wrote Lem, in a letter filled with humor, "who used to walk around with her nose quite far in the air if she had to go in the subway to get to the Automat with you. I'd give my two tiny hands, covered as they are with warts for a meal in the Automat and I wouldn't care if I had to sit with two dirty truck drivers. As a matter of fact they are probably the only people I know how to charm now."

The young officers usually had eight-day passes every five or six months and they strutted into the Hans Crescent ready for a good time. They spent their free time eating ersatz American home cooking for twenty cents, bathing, having their shoes shined and khakis pressed, dancing to the jukebox, sleeping on one of the fifteen hundred cots, taking in West End theaters, getting loaded on scotch or beer, or experiencing their first rich taste of English women. Kathleen didn't go out with the soldiers, but she spent much time talking to them. "The boys around the club are very nice," she wrote the family, "but most of them are so homesick and heartily dislike the British and everything about them." As American soldiers poured into London, Kathleen could hardly walk on the street without being stopped by G.I.'s making small talk. "We are very nice but I hop on my bike and away I go," she wrote home.

On her second Saturday night in London, Kathleen saw Billy for the first time in almost four years, several lifetimes in the life span of most youthful romances. When Kathleen saw him, so austerely handsome in his uniform, she could tell that Billy still cared. They were a splendidly matched couple, with that aura of rightness about them that few missed. "It really is funny to see people put their heads together the minute we arrive any place," she wrote the family after that first evening. "There's heavy betting on when we are going to announce it. Some people have gotten the idea that I'm going to give in. Little do they know. Some of those old Devonshire and Cecil ancestors would certainly jump out of their graves if anything happened to some of their ancient traditions. It just amused me to see how worried they all are."

Two weeks later Billy invited Kathleen to spend a weekend at the Cavendishes' seaside home in Eastbourne. Before the war Kathleen had loved the weekend house parties, these exquisite moments of pleasure and palaver, good talk, good food, games and camaraderie, and brilliantly honed repartee. It was not quite the same now, but for a few hours Kathleen forgot the war, forgot the yearning faces of American G.I.'s, forgot the routine of Hans Crescent. As for Billy, Kathleen saw that he had become "a bit more ducal" but he was the same old Billy, and they hit it off as if she had never left.

Billy's whole life had been set out for him as his batman laid out his clothes. Everything lay before him perfectly fitted and ready—military service, perhaps a bit of politics, and then the dukedom on his father's death with all its obligations and rituals. He was full of a young man's insecurities, though, uncomfortable in the uniform of wealth and power that would be his to wear. He was a young man who had never wanted for anything, but he loved Kathleen. In loving her, he was experiencing emotions he had not known before, feeling joy with her and within that joy all the possibilities of sadness.

As Kathleen saw Billy this weekend, she understood what he felt, and what she felt, or what she did not feel. She did not love him, at least not in the way Billy loved her. She doubted if she would love anyone, not that way. There was only one person in the world who could understand what she was feeling, not her mother, not even loyal Lem, but Jack, that kindred soul. "I can't understand why I like Englishmen so much," she confessed to Jack, "as they treat one in quite an off-hand manner and aren't really as nice to their women as Americans, but I suppose it's just that sort of treatment that women really like. That's your technique isn't it." That wasn't Billy's technique, however. She wrote that Billy would never give up his religion and, of course, neither would Kathleen. "It's all rather difficult as he is very, very fond of me and as long as I am about he'll never marry," she wrote Jack after the weekend. She was not bragging to her brother of another romantic trophy to add to her endless list. She understood Billy.

In her long, intense, intimate letter Kathleen wrote not one word about her feelings toward Billy, as if that had nothing to do with it. "However much he loved me I can easily understand his position," she went on. "It's really too bad because I'm sure I would be a most efficient Duchess of Devonshire in the postwar world, and as I'd have a castle in Ireland, one in Scotland, one in Yorkshire, and one in Sussex, I could keep my old nautical brothers in their old age."

When Kathleen had arrived in England in the spring of 1938, she had descended on London with a fresh breathless intensity that charmed almost everyone she encountered. There was still an untested youthful optimism to her, the pages of her life as unlined as her countenance. To the other former debutantes, it appeared that Kathleen lived a blessed life that they had long since given up.

These women had to make do. They created mascara out of shoe polish. They melted down old lipsticks and mixed them together like medieval alchemists. They donned wool stockings on legs that had once known silk. They put up their hair in utilitarian Victory rolls so they could get by without permanents. As they pulled on their overalls for another shift in the tank factory, or nursed a dying Tommy, some of them envied Kathleen and thought it wasn't quite fair. "There was such resentment about her and some of the other American girls," one former debutante recalled. "We resented awfully that they didn't have to do anything except for the odd stint at a canteen, and they had access to clothes and makeup that we didn't have. Sitting in our factories in our uniforms, we used to say good heavens, it wasn't fair."

It wasn't just Kathleen's clothes and her nonchalance and her gaiety that upset the British women. Her greatest sin was that she was dating Billy, the most eligible bachelor of their generation, and had half a dozen other young men pursuing her including Richard Wood, who had lost his legs in the war; Tony Rosslyn, who considered her his ideal of a wife; and William Douglas-Home, still carrying a torch. But it was Billy who was by far the most upsetting. "She was after Billy," said Rhona Wood Peyton-Jones. "He had a nice big fat title and estate coming and all that. That was not a nice thing to say, but it was well known and so terribly obvious."

Kathleen's coworkers had their own reasons to be less than delighted with her newest colleague. She received so many personal phone calls that she had to be admonished to cut them down. Kathleen took more time off as well, a day and a half off every week, while they had days off only every two weeks. That would have been rankling enough. Then the *Daily Mail* took a picture of her in a uniform pedaling a bicycle. The picture was published not only in Britain but all across America, as if Kathleen were the epitome of a Red Cross worker. In America, Joe worked at promoting his daughter as the very model of a Red Cross worker. "As you said you would like to do an article on her sometime," Joe wrote Waldrop at the *Times-Herald*, "I thought I'd send along a copy of the last picture that we had taken of her."

Kathleen wrote her father about the hostility she had engendered. Joe replied: "You must remember that those pictures of you in the paper and in fact that everybody in England who is worthwhile is on your team is bound to affect a lot of those pompous bosses of yours as well as doing something to your associations."

Kathleen wasn't about to give up her social life, even if she was working five and a half days a week. Life at Hans Crescent was not all routine, not for the officers who wanted to live every moment of their short-lived passes. One evening during a carnival party at the club, Lord and Lady Astor made their own appearances. They walked into a scene of revelry, drunkenness, and buffoonery the likes of which they had not seen in the rarefied precincts of Cliveden. Lady Astor had taken a special liking to the newly arrived American. Kathleen believed that she reminded Lady Astor "of herself when she first came to England."

Kathleen cherished letters from her family that kept her up on the whereabouts of her far-flung sisters and brothers. Rose filled her pages with gentle gossip about her children and friends, leavening the mix with occasional humor and rare displays of emotion. Rose had been deeply moved when Jack remembered her for Mother's Day 1943 even though he was already thousands of miles away in the South Pacific. "I was amazed and very much delighted yesterday on receiving a lovely basket full of the sweetest spring flower," she wrote her children from the Plaza Hotel. "It seems Jack had written to Paul Murphy [at the Kennedy office in New York] and asked him to send it to me for Mother's Day. He also enclosed a card, 'To Mother with Love. Sorry I am not there to give them personally.' It was in his own handwriting so imagine how thrilled I was. He certainly is having a great experience. I suppose you all read the article on the P.T. Skippers which was in LIFE on May 10."

Kathleen knew that Jack was already in the South Pacific, and she had her own vision of her brother out there captaining his stalwart sailors on PT-109. "Well, take care, Johnny," she wrote him. "By the time you get this so much will have happened. The end looks nearer now than ever."

While Kathleen's letter was in the mail, Jack's boat was sliced in two by a Japanese destroyer in the dark straits and was reported lost. In Hyannis Port when Joe received the message that his son was missing in action, he did not show it to Rose. Such notices were usually the precursors to an even darker message, or to months or even years of uncertainty. Joe considered it his burden to keep his terrible worries to himself, saving Rose from the news until he knew something for sure. A few mornings later Rose happened to turn on the radio and heard that the previously reported missing Lieutenant Kennedy had been discovered alive. As happy as Rose was to hear the news, it was like so much of her life—overheard conversations, cryptic phone calls, half-understood business letters. She was like an inquisitive child listening into adult conversations from another room, even when it was her own son's life or death that was at stake.

As for Kathleen, she was ecstatic when she learned of her brother's heroism. After losing two of his men, he swam with a third to a tiny island, probably saving the sailor from drowning. Then he swam out along the reefs in search of rescuers. She did not think of the danger, of the possibility of death, or that Jack's own nonchalance might have been one reason why his was the only ship in the entire war to be rammed by an enemy vessel. He was her brother, her Jack. Only then when it was all over, the dangers gone, did Kathleen become, as she wrote Jack, "worried to death about you."

The Kennedys were enthralled by the idea that Jack was a hero. In October, seventeen-year-old Bobby emulated his older brothers by signing up for the Naval Reserve, entering the V-12 training program at Harvard the following March. Across America not only men but women were serving in the war effort. Already by the end of 1942, an estimated four million women were working in war plants. Millions of others were working in nonwar factories and offices, on farms, volunteering for the Red Cross and other service organizations. Roosevelt had signed a bill creating a Women's Army Auxiliary Corps (WAAC) of up to 150,000 volunteers between twenty-one and forty-five to serve in noncombatant positions all over the world.

For Rose and Joe it would have been unthinkable to have Eunice, Pat, or Jean wearing the khaki of a WAAC. The following March Joe visited Pat at Rosemont, where he gave an informal lecture saying that both houses of Congress were opposed to the drafting of women.

At Rosemont, Pat learned that a woman's role in the war was to stand and to wait. The conservative church leaders feared that with women in the military and others joining the lunch-box brigades to factory and office, a "New Woman" would be spawned out of the exigencies of war.

Pat was urged to contribute blood to the Red Cross, money to War Bonds, her time to the First Aid or Home Nursing courses. At morning mass on Friday the women knelt wearing their long white chapel veils and prayed especially for the "soldiers, sailors and flyers"; Pat prayed for Joe Jr. and Jack at the far ends of the world. Her brothers and her nation were involved in a war against fascism and Russia was a crucial ally. Pat, however, learned from visiting lecturers that the great struggle in the world was between Christianity and Soviet communism. Every year Msgr. Bishop Sheen, the passionately theatrical radio priest, lectured and led a retreat. He filled the minds of impressionable students full of a dread fear of Godless communism, a red-tinged plague on the world, a vision that was as compelling to Pat as it was to her sisters.

Pat had inherited her father's interest in dramatics, and she directed and acted in various plays and theatrical spectacles. There was a paucity of young men at nearby Villanova College, not only to date but to take the male parts in plays; in 1944 tall and leggy Pat played Hortense in *Taming of the Shrew*, dropping her voice to do a memorable job wooing Bianca.

Pat was captain of the tennis team too, important enough a figure on campus to be profiled in the pages of *The Rambler*:

> Pat is a study in contrasts—a spontaneous jokester to those who know her and rather reserved to those who don't. Her diets are famous and her nightly exercises well done and unending. . . . Her abbreviated language with matching gestures has swept the campus. . . . Listening to Pat you'd think her life was one constant problem, but we know better for there's no one with more method in her madness. She can concentrate amid hilarity and sleep through any bell. . . . She is our tall sophisticate—the girl who knows her mind and can use it. For the most dual of all dual personalities, Pat takes the prize with her unbelievable combination of poise, joie de vivre, and, at odd moments, her complete urge for the nonsensical.

By all external measures, Pat was a success at Rosemont. She arrived at her final class one Friday afternoon ready to rush off for the weekend in an elegant black sheath dress, a magnificent three-quarter-length leopard coat draped over her arm. She appeared a creature of some great sophisticated world beyond that of her fellow students. Yet there was a quality that seemed missing, a connection with her fellow students she appeared unable to make. "She seemed very mature and very sophisticated," recalled Sister Caritas McCarthy, a classmate. "But Pat always struck me as not simply reserved but lonely."

Jean was studying at the Sacred Heart Convent at Eden Hall. She sat one day hidden behind a curtain on a window seat reading a book, *The Education of a Princess*, the memoirs of Marie, Grand Duchess of Russia. Another student, Joan Mulgrew, discovered Jean sitting there hidden away, and the two of them began a conversation. The two girls became close friends, and Jean invited Joan to Hyannis Port in the summer. "Mrs. Kennedy ran the most orderly house I have ever seen," Mulgrew recalled. "So pleasant. Not only did she have all her own children, they had all their friends there. No roughhousing, no yelling, no fighting—zilch. When the butler rang the little triangle for dinner, you were there or you didn't eat. Punctual, orderly, and very well run. Mrs. Kennedy was a frugal woman and knew how to run things. A wonderful atmosphere. And I'm not overbaking this."

Mulgrew felt herself picked up and brought into this vital, energetic family, friends with all the Kennedys. "I think because of her place in the family, Jean might have seemed shy," Mulgrew reflected. "Because when they were all blossoming, you know, she was like eleven or twelve, but she is the wittiest of the Kennedys. I mean she just makes you fall down laughing. And she always has."

Jean had been sent off to school at an early age, and much of her sense of family came from legendary stories of her elder siblings. "He [Ted] and I were the babies, kind of the last gasp, so we don't remember the close family life the other children had," Jean said. Jean had finally found a close friend in Mulgrew, but Rose, nonetheless, transferred her youngest daughter to Noroton. There several of her schoolmates thought that she was full of a deep and overwhelming loneliness. When Kathleen and Eunice had studied at the convent, Noroton had been isolated from the outside world, but that was even more true now during the war. There had been rumors of German submarines in Long Island Sound, and the nuns rigorously followed the blackout rules, covering the windows with dark shades. "There was no gas and we couldn't go anywhere," recalled Ann Fitzgerald Farrell, one of Jean's fourteen classmates in the class of 1945. "Every time we went home we had to struggle with the ration coupons to take back. There weren't many vacations with the trains cut off."

Jean did not have beaux motoring down from Yale or Harvard to visit her for congé Thursday afternoons. Father James Keller came to lecture occasionally, talking about the obligations of Catholic women in society. Joe came to lecture one afternoon as well. "His speech was on what you should do in life, how because you were privileged you should do good in life," said Renee de la Chapelle Perna, a classmate. "Nobody liked him at all."

Other than Joe's one visit, Jean's family rarely came to Noroton. "Jean always received these carbon copy letters from her parents," a classmate said. "And she would eat the letters up. I mean she would relish them incredibly. She was a nice, agreeable person, low-key, really kind of a loner. Looking back on it, she must have been frightened about what might happen to her family."

When the class picture was taken, Jean stood in the middle of the back row, as little visible as possible. "Jean just wanted to be left alone," another former student reflected. "She was a nice person, but she just wanted to be left alone."

At Noroton, Jean made another close friend in Mary "Dickie" Mann, her roommate. "I think what I got mostly from my religious education were very strong friendships with girls that I see today who are still my best friends," said Jean. "You connect and your value system connects for the rest of your life, and that is invaluable." Mann saw a private Jean far different from the quiet, diffident girl that she appeared to most of her peers. "She was a lot of fun," Mary Mann Cummins remembered. "She might have been shy with adults, but she was more on the mischievous side than the serious."

There was a lonely quality to Rose and her life as well. Her children were either grown up or in boarding schools and colleges. She shuttled between New York and Palm Beach and Hyannis Port, living primarily in the two largely seasonal, transient resort communities. She could not give her benign reminiscences about London to women's clubs when there was a war on, and she had no place for all her energy and ambition. She was a deeply thoughtful woman about her family, sending money to cousins and nephews, overseeing an extended clan that existed almost solely because of her interest and Joe's money.

Rose was by herself much of the time. One day in New York City when she was staying at the Waldorf-Astoria, she noticed a young woman standing on Fifth Avenue crying, tears running down her cheeks. For three days the woman had been waiting for her soldier husband to arrive on leave. Rose bid the crying woman to enter her chauffeured automobile and took her to the Waldorf-Astoria for tea, where she offered her a room. "You took my hand and squeezed it, with a sign of love, and said leave everything to God," the woman wrote Rose a quarter century later.

For Kathleen the best news of all late that summer of 1943 was that Joe Jr. had been assigned to London. She really didn't know her eldest brother that well. She did not know the extent to which the news of his younger brother's heroics had only stiffened Joe Jr.'s resolve to wear a hero's laurels as well. Before he left for England, he had driven to Hyannis Port to celebrate his father's birthday with his parents and several guests. During dinner one guest, a Massachusetts judge, had proposed a toast: "To Ambassador Joe Kennedy, father of our hero, our *own* hero, Lieutenant John F. Kennedy of the United States Navy." Joe Jr. raised his glass and smiled as if he had no role in life but to cheer his younger brother on. That night he shared a bedroom with his father's old friend, former Boston Police Commissioner Timilty. And as Timilty lay in the bed next to the Navy pilot, he heard Joe's muffled tears.

Kathleen did not know this Joe Kennedy Jr. Kathleen saw Joe Jr. as another intrepid hero, swooping down on England to rescue her from the banal and ordinary. He piloted his VB-110 across the Atlantic carrying not only his full crew and gear, but a crate of fresh Virginia eggs for his kid sister. Stationed in Cornwall on the coast of southern England, Joe was still 250 miles from London and his sister. In late October Joe Jr. wrangled an assignment to fly some matériel to northern England, taking a neat detour that landed him at an airfield outside London.

Joe Jr. bounded into the Hans Crescent town house carrying a crate of not-so-fresh eggs, an enormous smile, and exuberant greetings. He settled down for a few hands of gin rummy and bridge with Kathleen and some other officers, shouting out his bets over the sound of the jukebox. "Everybody makes mistakes, Kick, but you make too darn many," he admonished his sister. "I don't want to be her partner and I feel sorry for any sucker that has her." He couldn't tolerate Kathleen as a bridge partner. "Gee, Kick, aren't you ever going to learn?" He soon

was up three pounds and decided that was enough of cards and
that nothing would do now but the Four Hundred Club.

The two of them headed off to the hallowed club off Leices-
ter Square. The Four Hundred Club was as dark as it had been
before the war, but every evening it burned with the bright intensity of American and British pilots on leave, socialites ready
for an evening's entertainment, even Kathleen's old favorite,
"Dukie Wookie," the Duke of Marlborough. Kathleen would
have stayed all night, but she had already used up her free
weekend and had to be to work the next morning. In the shadowy deserted streets, she simply flagged down an American
MP in his jeep and talked him into chauffeuring her back to
Hans Crescent. The young American may have had ideas of a
detour of his own, but when Joe Jr. appeared out of the blackness and jumped into the vehicle, the soldier started mumbling
about the court-martial he was likely to receive for serving as
a jitney taxi and headed off toward Hans Crescent.

The next evening William Randolph Hearst Jr., a war correspondent, invited Joe Jr. and Kick to join him for dinner at the
Savoy, the legendary hotel that despite all the restrictions remained an elegant respite from wartime England. Hearst had
further brightened their table with two British women. One
was Lady Sykes, the former Virginia Gilliat, whom as a debutante Joe Jr. had the misfortune to be kissing when her father
walked into their living room. Sykes was not only very married but very pregnant, and Joe Jr. turned his attentions to the
other woman at the table, Patricia Wilson. Wilson's hair was
dark black, her eyes were blue, and her personality scintillat-
ing. Joe Jr. and Kathleen learned that Wilson was the daughter
of an Australian sheep rancher. In 1931 at seventeen she had
come to London to be with her mother to make her debut and
shortly before her eighteenth birthday had married the twenty-
one-year-old Earl of Jersey, in what was considered the marriage of the year. They had one child and in 1937 the marriage
was formally dissolved, London society abuzz with rumors of
the Earl's relationship with a movie actress. That same year
Patricia married Robin Filmer Wilson, with whom she had two
more children. Wilson was a major in the British army stationed in Libya. Like hundreds of thousands of other wives,
she hadn't seen her husband for two years, and couldn't expect
to see him until the war was over.

Theirs was a gay, youthful table at the Savoy. Patricia's
laughter cascaded like a shower of sentiment and amusement.

Kathleen was full of wry commentary. Joe Jr. joked to his sister while learning everything he could about this new acquaintance. They were joined by General Robert Laycock, the head of the British commandos, and his wife, Angie. As they talked, American and British troops were fighting their way up the boot of Italy. While soldiers lived and died, some of their wives were drinking champagne with American officers. As much as the British appreciated the American G.I.'s, the common saying was that they were "overpaid, over-sexed, and over here." The general liked none of it. To him it was a double betrayal, Americans like Joe Jr. far from the trenches, and women like Patricia Wilson flirting outrageously while her husband was perhaps in mortal peril.

Joe Jr. cared nothing about the British general's disdainful glances. The man was nothing to him, and he went right on talking to Wilson, giving an enthusiastic yes when she invited him and some of his friends to spend a weekend at her country home. They soon began a fervent affair.

Kathleen had already lived through Jack's affair with a married woman. She had little of her mother's moralizing, and living here in Britain she had even less. Soon after Kathleen arrived, she had penned a letter to Waldrop. "Dear Ex-Boss," she began, "I am stationed very near where I once lived and need I add that this life is very different from those good old days." Her friends still had gay times and moment of frivolity, but there was a manic intensity to it all.

For British women the war not only meant new jobs and new responsibilities, but new freedoms too, and many women lived for the moment. It was no different for an upper-class woman like Pat Wilson than for a cockney barmaid off with a G.I. on his two-day pass with nothing to show for it but a pair of silk stockings and half-drunken sentiment. They might as well, for in the broken streets of London there was nothing chivalrous about the German bombs that killed women as easily as they killed men.

While Kathleen lived in a world of pristine cleanliness, Joe Jr. was stationed at Dunkeswell in conditions he dubbed "Mudville Height," camped out in crude Nissen huts, two officers to a room, in the midst of an ocean of mud. As far as Joe Jr. was concerned, it was hardly heroic stuff, long cold flights scanning the seas for submarines that never surfaced, then sitting in the dank coldness worrying about how to keep his feet dry.

After a few weeks of that uninspiring duty, Joe Jr. wangled a week's pass, and Kathleen arranged to give a big party for her big brother and his crew. In his frequent telephone calls to London, Joe Jr. treated his sister with a brotherly bossiness that sometimes rankled Kick. "You talk to me like I was a member of the crew!" she accused him, though his crew members wouldn't have put up for long with these nagging admonitions. Kathleen didn't need Joe Jr. to tell her how to give a party. She wasn't about to have the festivities at the Hans Crescent in the midst of all the flotsam but asked her mother's old London friend, Marie Bruce, if she might use her home. "People swarmed in," Kathleen wrote her parents. "It was the first party London had had for the young for two years." It was perhaps the first party for *her* kind of people, and a memorable evening it was. As she was dressing, Bruce received a phone call from Irving Berlin. Kathleen knew serendipity when she saw it, and she invited the famous songwriter to the party. Berlin had composed some of the most famous songs of the twentieth century, songs like "God Bless America" and "I'm Dreaming of a White Christmas," songs that crystallized the sentimental yearnings of a people.

Kathleen asked Berlin to sing a few of his compositions. He sat at the piano and in his high-pitched voice belted out song after song with the guests joining in. Kathleen and her brother could scarcely carry a tune, but they joined in too, making up in enthusiasm what they lacked in talent. "Kick handled herself to perfection as usual and made a terrific hit all around," he wrote their parents. "The girls looked very pretty and made quite an impression on the love-wan sailors whom I brought."

Early in 1944 Kathleen spent a weekend at the country home of Lady Milbanks. The house was crowded. Kathleen shared a room with Ursula Wyndham-Quin, who had made her debut with Eunice and was now serving as a nurse. Saturday evening after the two young women prepared for bed and chatted a bit, Kathleen got down on her knees and prayed. What struck Wyndham-Quin as so extraordinary was not simply that this American woman was praying, but that she stayed on her knees for fifteen minutes, lost in prayers. The next morning she prayed again, and then headed off to a Catholic church for mass, while the other guests either went to services at the nearby Church of England or merely stayed in the house.

Kathleen was praying a great deal these days, spending hours in deep thought. When she had flown home over the Christmas holidays, a privilege almost unheard of among Red Cross workers, she had not even mentioned to her parents that she was pondering the idea of marrying Billy. She could scarcely envision herself measuring out the rest of the war ministering to an endless series of lovelorn, homesick, boisterous American soldiers. At Noroton she had been trained to function as a hostess, wife, and mother in a great and noble family, and there was no greater, no more noble family in Britain than Billy's. Kathleen could have found that life in America too, among her myriad pursuers, but among the British upper class she had found a perfect fit for her life. She had the soul of an expatriate, finding in England richness, vitality, and stimulation as well as a freedom that those born into its rituals and rules and responsibilities could never know.

Kathleen wanted to be here, to make her life here as the Duchess of Devonshire, one of the great ladies of the land. She faced the same serious religious questions that had haunted the relationship before the war. The Cavendishes could not abide the idea of their son, the future Duke, marrying a woman who would insist that their children be brought up as Catholics, ending the centuries-long reign of one of the great Protestant families of England. The Kennedys were one of the great Catholic families of America. They could not abide their daughter marrying into such a notoriously anti-Catholic family, breaking the laws of Rome by allowing her children to be raised in the Church of England. So there it stood. During the early months of 1944 intense religious and diplomatic negotiations took place. These involved not only both sets of parents, but Archbishop Spellman and Pope Pius XII seeking some way to let the marriage proceed within the strictures of both faiths.

"I want to do the right thing so badly and yet I hope I'm not giving up the most important thing in my life," Kathleen wrote her parents. "Poor Billy is very, very sad but he sees his duty must come first." In late January she went to see Bishop Mathew seeking a dispensation, but even before she went to see the Catholic leader she knew that it would be "practically impossible."

Her father was a man who believed he could solve any problem by applying the appropriate amounts of power, money, persuasion, or threat. He adored his daughter. To Joe,

Kathleen's own happiness meant more than the mere edicts of the Church. "You're tops with me," he wrote her. "I'll bet on your judgment anytime for any amounts." Joe went to Archbishop Spellman and Spellman went to the pope but they could get no further than had Kathleen imploring Bishop Mathew in London. For Joe, finally, it was a matter between Billy and the daughter whom he loved so much; as for everyone else "let all the rest of us go jump in the lake."

As the dialogue continued, Kathleen realized that it was not "Archie Spell" who was her most formidable foe but her own mother. Rose had sacrificed so much not simply for her faith, but for the strictures of her faith, the appearances of her faith as dictated by a patriarchal hierarchy. Kathleen wanted to marry into one of the greatest families of all England, and that flattered Rose's overweening social ambition, but to Rose the image of faith transcended everything. It was unthinkable that Kathleen should marry Billy. "When both people have been handed something all their lives, how ironic it is that they cannot have what they want most," Rose wrote her daughter on February 24, 1944. "I wonder if the next generation will feel that it is worth sacrificing a life's happiness for all the old family tradition."

Rose approached Kathleen with gentle deviousness, subtly manipulating her away from marriage with Billy. In her own mind, Rose had already lost one daughter whose fate she could hardly bear to think about. If Kathleen should marry Billy and bring up their children in the Protestant faith, she would be an empty shell, spiritually devoid, as lost to Rose as Rosemary.

Kathleen understood her mother well enough to know that it would do no good to harangue her with maudlin appeals about human happiness. She might, however, listen to an upper-class British lady whose respect she desired. Thus in January 1944, Kathleen had Marie Bruce write Rose: "She thinks you would not approve. I think if you saw the pair of them together you certainly would."

Rose was a woman who followed every nuance of good manners, and the fact that she did not answer Bruce's letter was a response of the strongest kind. Bruce had innocently walked into the midst of a fearsome family battle, and she feared rightfully that she had angered Kathleen's mother. Rose was waging her own form of psychological warfare on Kathleen, withholding not simply affection but dialogue. Kathleen was living in a wartime world where women and men went off together to spend the night as casually as her beaux had signed her dance cards. This was a world where her own brother was having an affair with a married woman while her husband fought in the Mediterranean, a world where Billy's regiment would soon be a part of the invasion of Europe, and God alone knew how long he might live. All her life Kathleen had done almost everything her mother, her church, the Sacred Heart nuns, and her father wanted her to do. Now she sought only this: to marry one of the wealthiest and most prominent young men in England, a man who needed no title to be called noble, a man who loved her as had no one else. The waiting, the negotiation, the duke's disdain for anything Catholic, and most of all her mother's psychological games were becoming too much. "I think something will have to be decided one way or another before we both go nuts," she wrote her parents on March 4. "Somehow I can't make myself see that the Lord in Heaven (not the one in question) would make things so difficult."

Kathleen's and Billy's parents dominated their lives, by their examples, their overwhelming presences, and the multitude of obligations that came with their family names. "Billy wanted to marry her badly and absolutely didn't want to think about the implications," said Lady Lloyd, a British friend. "It was the most definite thing in his life." What Billy truly wanted was outside the endless stream of obligations.

In the army Billy had found something that he cared about as well. As an officer in the Coldstream Guards, Billy was not simply the future Duke of Devonshire, scion to one of the most famous families in England. He was a man among men. His loyalty was to his troops that he knew would see combat in the impending invasion. His father, however, wanted Billy to leave his command to run for the House of Commons in the by-elections of 1944. Billy's father considered the seat almost as much family property as his twenty thousand acres at Chatsworth. He felt it perfectly appropriate for his twenty-six-year-old son to come home to West Devonshire to claim the seat. It was much the kind of thing that Joe might have done to Joe Jr., if he had been a duke, but Joe Jr. envisioned a political career for himself and Billy did not. "He never should have come back," Lady Maureen Fellowes reflected passionately. "He should have stayed with his regiment. He was just too nice. He would never have said, 'Go to hell, Dad.' He didn't want to hurt anyone."

And so Billy came home in January and ran for the House of Commons. "The by-election was a grave error of judgment on my father's part," said Billy's younger brother, Andrew, Duke of Devonshire. "My family treated it like a rotten borough. I suspect my brother was pushed into it, but it wasn't something we talked about when I got home."

Kathleen spent the last days of the campaign with Billy, traveling with him from one picturesque village to the next. Kathleen knew it would not do to be seen campaigning openly with Billy. "I was known as Rosemary Tong, the village girl," she wrote her parents. She traveled from village to village, town to town, sitting in the back of the audiences, attempting to gauge the reaction to the young aristocrat.

For Kathleen politics was a matter of heroes and scoundrels. Billy's opponent, Charlie White, was the kind of scrappy, socialist politician that she considered anathema. "He hates the Cavendishes like poison . . ." Kick continued. "He looks absolutely repulsive." Kathleen had picked up her political catechism from the nuns and her father. To her these Labourite politicians were a dreadful crew "preaching socialism . . . they know just what the working people want to hear and they give it to them."

Her Billy stood in the town squares amid the ancient motorcars, the farm carts, hay wagons, and high gigs with their yellow wheels, and tried to make himself heard. "Young man, you ought to be in the front line, not standing there talking politics," an engine driver's daughter yelled at him.

"I've been in the army five years and have seen action overseas," Billy said, smiling as he spoke. "I hope to take my place in the front line shortly."

"But what can *you*, the son of a Duke, do for the working man?"

Billy's opponent couched the election as a contest between the spoiled ducal heir and a common peddler's son. Charlie White drew Billy down into the vicious assaults of class politics. "Can you milk a cow?" Billy was asked. "Yes," he replied. "I can milk a cow, and I can also spread muck. Some of my opponents seem rather good at that too."

White and his workers portrayed Billy as a coward whose father had wangled his eldest son's resignation from the Coldstream Guards so he could gallivant around the countryside while British soldiers died in combat. White told an audience, "Lord Hartington will have to explain to the parents and relatives of serving men and women in West Derbyshire how he can more or less please himself so far as military service is concerned while men and women in the ranks must comply with the rigid military requirements and discipline."

Billy had only agreed to run to please his father. Now day after day, speech after speech, he had to stand before his countrymen and countrywomen defending his honor, his courage, and his name. Billy was Kathleen's hero, and she marveled at how well he answered the questions when for four years he had been serving in his regiment, hardly ever thinking about these issues. "Why isn't the park at Chatsworth plowed up?" they asked. "Why didn't your father pay more death duties?" Kathleen could envision herself as Billy's political wife, astutely standing behind her husband, gauging public sentiment, praising him, pushing him onward. "I must say I haven't ever spent such an interesting week," she wrote her parents. "That's really the way I like to spend my time."

For all that Kathleen admired Billy, she could not see that her blind admiration was itself another burden to him. He was loaded down with expectations, his father bulling his way into the campaign, his mother out giving speeches too, the whole weight of the family heritage resting on Billy's youthful shoulders. He could perhaps shrug off the assaults against his family name, but the questioning of his courage was a wound that festered, poisoning his whole system. For all that Kathleen cared for Billy, and sat looking pridefully up at him as he talked, she simply could not see how these attacks against his honor as a soldier so brutally wounded him. He was a man, however, like Jack or George Mead, who did not admit his doubts and fears, not to a woman, especially not to Kathleen, who saw him as a man largely without flaws.

On election day, Kathleen went with Billy and the rest of the family to the Matlock Town Hall for the counting of the ballots. Although both sides thought the election would be close, White won in a landslide, sixteen thousand votes to Billy's eleven thousand. Afterwards, the candidates walked out onto the balcony to address the multitude spread out in the town square. Kathleen stood there as White harangued the crowd, condemning Billy. "This is West Derbyshire's answer to political dictators," he said, and his supporters cheered.

When White finished, Billy said a few words. He did not

care about the loss as much as he cared about the way he had lost, and the charges that hung on him like badges of shame. He spoke about returning to his regiment with passion and intensity as if he were making a fearsome pledge. "It has been a fierce fight," he began. "Now I am going out to fight for you at the front, to fight, perhaps die, for my country."

On weekends in the spring of 1944, Kathleen and her friends all converged on a quaint cottage on Crastock Farm outside Woking in southern England. It was here that Pat Wilson was living with her three children, not far from Billy's new quarters at Alton and Joe Jr.'s Naval air base, and less than an hour's train ride from London.

They all brought something, a few nuggets of chocolate, fresh eggs, a half kilo of beef, the latest war gossip, usually descending on the diminutive cottage late Friday. Kathleen hurried into the tile-roofed house with hardly a greeting before rushing upstairs. "Don't bother," she admonished Wilson. "I'll go upstairs and wash my hair!"

Kathleen was a world and a war away from the exquisite and elegant weekends at Cliveden and other country estates of her debutante days. Now she was spending her weekends in what was the gardener's cottage, but these were precious times, full of the games and spirited foolishness that Kathleen adored. It was a peculiar menage: proud Joe Jr., first heir to the Kennedys' next generation, now living in his younger brother's half shadow, and in love with a married mother of three children; Billy, as adamant as ever about the Church of England, and yet so much in love with Kathleen, and so sexually reticent; and Kathleen, trying to desperately to decide what to do, knowing, as they all knew, that summer would bring that great and awesome and inevitable event, the invasion of Nazi Europe, and the end to all this.

On these weekends, Kathleen got to know her eldest brother as she had not known him before. He was a man of deep faith himself, not ashamed to get down on his knees to pray among the hard-bitten Navy pilots. That he had learned from his mother, but his was a practical Catholicism that allowed him to enter into adulterous relationships and to live in a morally imperfect world. He wasn't about to support his mother in her campaign. Instead, he lent his strong steadying arm to Kathleen. "Never did anyone have such a pillar of strength," she wrote later.

In the Kennedy family, the women were supposed to carry out their duties with stoic disregard for their own happiness. Thus if Kathleen went against the dictates of her parents, Rose could only conclude that a man must be providing the backbone behind her daughter's decision. "Moral courage he [Joe Jr.] had in abundance," Kathleen said, "and once he felt that a step was right for me, he never faltered, although he might be held largely responsible for my decision."

With desperate urgency, Kathleen sought out guidance. In London she went to her Mayfair parish church on Farm Street to see Father Martin D'Arcy. The Jesuit was a priest of such subtle persuasion that he had converted many British intellectuals including the darkly sardonic novelist, Evelyn Waugh. If Kathleen expected this worldly priest to show her singular understanding, she was mistaken. The priest attempted not persuasion but moral intimidation, painting for her an appalling portrait of the empty life and godless eternity that lay before her if she married Billy. He took her back to her childhood and those catechism classes at Brookline, and reminded her of the ideas that had been etched into her young mind.

For Kathleen God was real, present in her daily life, and it was a terrible vision the priest set out before her. If she married Billy, she would be living in sin, unable to make an act of confession, unable to receive Holy Communion, ostracized from the one true faith. When she died, she would die eternally damned. Her only chance was if Billy died before her. Only then might she be absolved. It was a fearsome vision that her mother held as well, a vision of a doomed life.

For Kathleen the idea of living her life outside God's house was a terrible thought. Fifteen years before, the Catholic church in England had allowed a compromise: to bring up the daughters as Catholics and the sons as Protestants. But now the Catholic hierarchy would hear nothing of that solution. She thought that perhaps it might be best to convert to the Church of England and live her life resting secure under the shelter of Christian faith. That at least would allow her to have a church wedding, something that mattered deeply to her, and not be sent off into some dismal register office, shuttled in and out for a quick ten minutes between divorced people, atheists, agnostics, and sundry others. When she went to see Father Torbert, an Anglican monk, she saw that was no answer either. If she converted to Anglicanism, her mother would die a thousand deaths.

* * *

Billy would not yield and neither would Rose. Kathleen had to choose between them, between everything she had learned and believed as a girl in America, and everything she felt and cared about as a woman in England. Finally, on the fourth of May, Kathleen made her choice, and Billy and Kathleen announced their engagement.

Even before the announcement, Rose had entered New England Baptist Hospital in Boston for what the press was told was "a routine physical checkup." In reality the hospital was a place where the deeply distraught Rose could hide not simply from the press but from what she considered the terrible prospect that loomed ahead. On the day before the wedding, *The Boston Traveler* noted that the marriage "will bring her [Kathleen] into a family prominent in the defense and spread of Protestantism throughout the British realm." This was the kind of commentary that was a stake through Rose's heart, a public airing of her shame. She was on the border of a nervous breakdown.

When Rose heard the news of the engagement in the hospital, she cabled her daughter: "HEARTBROKEN. FEEL YOU HAVE BEEN WRONGLY INFLUENCED—SENDING ARCH SPELLMAN'S FRIEND TO TALK TO YOU. ANYTHING DONE FOR OUR LORD WILL BE REWARDED HUNDRED FOLD." Rose was convinced that Kathleen could not possibly have decided this on her own. Only the nefarious influences of others could have seduced her daughter away from her duty.

Rose's rejection of the idea of her daughter marrying outside the faith was the received doctrine of the church. She was merely repeating what she knew to be the truth. Her husband and her eldest son saw that such rigidity risked creating a kind of prayer-wheel Christianity in which the mechanics of religion were more important than the essence of faith. They knew Kathleen's deep faith and goodness, and they could not believe that a just and forgiving god would bar the gates of heaven to such as Kathleen.

Rose was not worried simply about faith, but about the appearance of faith. In her life of social ambition, she had been driven in part by a terrible fear of shame, the dread that one day her family might be exposed and the elaborately wrought structure brought down. "I thought it would have such mighty repercussions in that every little young girl would say if

Kathleen Kennedy can, why can't I . . ." she said. "Everyone pointed to our family with pride as well-behaved, level-headed and deeply religious. What a blow to family prestige."

This was the same argument that Bishop O'Connell had made to Rose's father that September afternoon in 1907 maintaining that Rose could not go to Wellesley because it would look bad and other young women might follow her lead. Appearances were everything, everything because appearances were so great a part of the life that Rose had left. It did not matter that Joe was living an adulterous life, flagrantly and willfully violating God's commandment. It did not matter that Rosemary's lobotomy had violated the church's belief in the sacredness of each human life. It did not matter that having returned to the United States, Jack had briefly resumed his affair with the now twice-married Inga or that in England Joe Jr. was involved with a married woman. These were the wages of men, and Kathleen was her daughter and her conduct was held to a different standard.

Kathleen indeed had a pillar of strength in Joe Jr. He took the train up to London to meet with the Cavendishes' solicitor. Her brother convinced the attorney that it was unnecessary for Kathleen to sign a paper agreeing to bring up their children as Anglicans as she had given her verbal promise. More important, as much as Joe Jr. loved his mother, he was not afraid to confront Rose with his own hard truths, understanding that with his mother it was a question equally of religion and social status. "As far as Kick's soul is concerned, I wish I had half her chance of seeing the pearly gates," he wrote. "As far as what people will say, the hell with them. I think we can all take it. It will be hardest on Mother and I do know how you feel Mother, but I do think it will be alright."

On the morning of May 6, 1944, only two days after she and Billy announced their engagement, Kathleen rushed breathlessly up the stairs into the redbrick building that housed the Chelsea Register Office, accompanied only by her brother. Kathleen had wanted her wedding to have some semblance of style and signal significance, even if it had to take place in a tawdry government office. She wore a new pink matte crêpe dress, an outfit that had taken the combined efforts of three people, two of whom Kathleen did not even know. Only the day before Marie Bruce had set out to have the new dress made for the twenty-four-year-old bride. Bruce purchased material in part with ration coupons contributed by her milkman, then took the cloth to her dressmaker, who stayed up all night completing the dress in time for the ten o'clock Saturday morning ceremony. Kathleen had come up with a half hat of blue and pink ostrich feathers and a pink veil. Thus she had something new and something blue, but to be a proper bride she needed something old and something borrowed too; Marie Bruce's gold mesh bag and diamond brooch were exquisite choices for those bridal necessities. In her hand Kathleen carried a bouquet of pink camellias fresh from the gardens of Chatsworth. Even her underwear was borrowed, dainty feminine Portault underclothes given her by Bruce.

As Kathleen entered the drab office, she saw Billy wearing the khaki uniform of an officer of the Coldstream Guards. The creases of his wool pants were sharply pressed, and the coat fit perfectly on his lean frame. Since the war began twenty-six-year-old Billy had aged tremendously. He no longer looked the sweetly androgynous boy-man so attractive to debutantes. His hairline had slightly receded, giving his face a definition and maturity, and he appeared like a man who might be a leader of men. This morning, though, he was the delighted young groom, seeing the fulfillment of a great and glorious romantic dream that had begun six years ago at a garden party at Buckingham Palace.

Billy's parents had come up from Chatsworth for the ceremony. His aunt, Lady Salisbury, and younger sisters Anne and Elizabeth were present as well. Billy's friend, Charles Granby, the son of the Duke of Rutland, was there too, serving as best man. Kathleen could have invited any number of her London friends, but she chose only two guests, Marie Bruce and Lady Astor, both older prominent women whom she greatly admired.

The ceremony was hardly more than a civic formality, involving no exchange of vows and promises of fidelity. Joe Jr. gave his sister away. Billy slipped an old family ring on his bride's finger, and Joe Jr. and the duke signed as witnesses. It was all over in ten minutes.

In wartime England, all the events of life—births and deaths, marriages and mourning—were truncated, cut down to their essences. Kathleen could have been married before a thousand guests at Chatsworth and worn a white gown embedded with half the jewels of the kingdom, and there would have been no greater feeling than on this day marrying in this modest room. "You would rejoice in their young happiness," Mrs. Bruce wrote Rose. This wedding had not been merely another day on her social calendar, as it would have been in peacetime, but a commitment of time and emotion. She had dared to write Rose her own feelings about the prospective marriage, had spent Friday seeing that Kathleen had a new dress, gave them a gift of an Augustus John drawing that she said was from Rose and Joe, and stood there now witness to this love.

In all the British Empire there was no more vociferous a hater of the Church of Rome than Lady Astor, but she loved Kathleen even more than she hated her church, and she too had arrived to witness their love. As for Joe Jr., he was not merely giving away his sister in some mundane ceremony, but risking displeasing not only his mother but Boston's Irish-Americans. He fully anticipated returning to Massachusetts to run for office, and he was only half joking when he told his sister that after the Irish Catholics saw his picture in the paper at the wedding he was "finished in Boston." Billy's sisters too saw something in this ceremony that they would never forget. "I was only fourteen," Lady Anne Tree recalled. "But Kick was a shining light of gaiety and pleasure and enthusiasm. She was absolutely nonpareil."

Rice was nothing to be thrown away, so the guests showered the newlyweds with rose petals. The bride and groom stood on the steps outside the register office posing momentarily for photographers. During his campaign for Parliament, Billy had been sickened by the onslaught of journalists and photographers. All he wanted now was his privacy and his bride, and as the photographers snapped away, he managed a smile that was half a grimace. Kathleen grasped Billy's arm, standing close to him. From the register office, the newlyweds drove to a reception with two hundred of their friends. "Listen, you God damn limey," an American sergeant swore, accosting Billy at the wedding reception, "you've got the best damn girl that America could produce." Bruce had pulled another minor miracle, bribing the readily bribable headwaiter at Claridge's with a five-pound note to produce an icingless chocolate cake.

After champagne toasts, Kathleen and Billy boarded the train for Eastbourne, where they walked the half mile from the station to the family estate at Compton Place. An Anglican priest blessed the couple and their marriage, and they began a short-lived honeymoon.

Kathleen had not married Billy in some half-crazed romantic

frenzy. She had married not simply a man but a life, and she was prepared for it all: Kathleen, Marchioness of Hartington; gracious wife; compassionate mother; matron; noblewoman. But first there was the war, and for Kathleen these were moments of preciousness beyond value and name. Everyone knew that in a few weeks the British and the Americans would begin assaulting the German army in France with the greatest amphibious invasion in history. Billy's regiment would be part of that invasion force, perhaps not the first day, or the first week, but they would be part of it. Kathleen knew that once Billy was gone, she might not see him again until the war was over and the Allies marched into the rubble of Berlin.

Even in these priceless moments, Kathleen had other thoughts than her new husband and their new life together. She had scarcely spent her first night with Billy when the letters began arriving, not notes of congratulations and blessing, but ugly messages condemning her. Evelyn Waugh took his own full swipe at Kathleen—there was nothing more Catholic than a convert. "Her heathen friends have persuaded her that it is a purely English law that her children must be brought up Catholic, and that she can get married in U.S.A. after the war," he sneered condescendingly. "It is second front nerves that has driven her to this grave sin and I am sorry for the girl."

In the newspapers Kathleen read not joyous accounts of her wedding, but speculative articles saying that Rose was in the hospital because of her daughter's marriage. It was a terrible thought to her. On her daughter's wedding day, Rose had left the hospital to fly to New York City and from there to travel to Hot Springs, where her father said she would go for a "much-needed rest."

Rose was accompanied to the airport by Joseph F. Timilty, the former police commissioner, an elderly friend who aroused no gossip when he often accompanied Rose. As she stood fending off reporters, she looked terribly wan, dressed in what could have been mourning clothes: black suit, black beret with black veil, black pumps, black gloves, and a silver fox draped over her arm. The reporters wanted only a word or two of congratulations, a sweet anecdote or two about the daughter who would one day be the Duchess of Devonshire. "I'm sorry, but I don't feel physically well enough to grant an interview now," Rose said, as she turned to go into the plane. "I'm sorry it has to be this way."

The Boston Globe ran two full stories on Kathleen saying

that as the next "Duchess of Devonshire, [she] will take rank, next to the Queen, as the most powerful woman in England." To the reporters at La Guardia Airport, Rose might have given Kathleen her blessing. Instead she said ominously: "I am not making any statements."

Joe Jr. knew what his sister was suffering and the day after the ceremony he cabled his father: "The power of silence is great." It was indeed great, and it was haunting Kathleen's honeymoon. Her father immediately sent his reply to his daughter: "WITH YOUR FAITH IN GOD, YOU CAN'T MAKE A MISTAKE. REMEMBER YOU ARE STILL AND ALWAYS WILL BE TOPS WITH ME."

For Kathleen, the cable was the blessing she so desperately wanted. She hurried down to the telegraph office to answer her father: "YOUR CABLE MADE MY HAPPIEST DAY. MOST DISTRESSED ABOUT MOTHER. PLEASE TELL HER NOT TO WORRY."

On the third day of her marriage, Kathleen sat down in the library at the estate to write her mother. Kathleen, like Rose, was a political woman, with immense social ambition, astute judgments of human personality, and deeply felt religious beliefs. She understood her mother as Rose did not understand Kathleen. "[Now] every morning letters arrive condemning my action," she wrote. "They don't bother me at all and I only hope and pray that things will not be too difficult for you and the rest of the family with the McDonnells etc." Kathleen was devoid of that rancorous self-pity that might have linked her mother to those who so viciously condemned her. She was acutely aware that her marriage might affect the family's relationships with other leading Catholic families, and she was sorry if that were so. She did not want her mother to feel any blame, any sense of failure as a mother, any sense of shame or embarrassment. "Please don't take any responsibility for any action which you think bad (and I don't.)" she wrote. "You did everything in your power to stop it. You did your duty as a Roman Catholic mother. You have not failed, there was nothing lacking in my religious education."

If Rose had been able to distance herself from her shame, she might have seen that Kathleen was not in the grips of a Protestant Svengali, but had matured into a deeply thoughtful young woman who was honoring her mother's values, not debasing them. Rose continued to blame herself. On the surface she seemed to acquiesce. She went shopping for clothes for Kathleen. She had Joe send Bruce a cable, but she was unwilling to send one herself. She hoped that Kathleen would realize her terrible error. It was still not too late. In private, she discussed with Archbishop Spellman how Kathleen might go about getting an annulment.

Kathleen and Billy's honeymoon lasted hardly more than a long weekend, when they were off to the Swan Inn, a tiny country hotel in Alton, only a motorbike ride from Billy's regiment. The Marquess of Devonshire and his bride were given the prized suite, a room that at Claridge's would have been used for brooms.

Kathleen had the frenetic energy of all the Kennedys. She had scarcely spent a day in her life simply sitting around. Here in this country town she had little to do once Billy set off on his little motorbike but sit around and gossip with other war wives. "At the moment I am a camp follower . . ." she wrote Mark Soden, one of Joe Jr's. fellow Naval aviators. "I spend my days listening to all the old ladies talking about what a hard war that they are having. It's rather a change from G.I. conversations to say the least."

Kathleen roamed the countryside on her bicycle and wrote to friends in America, who had sent letters of congratulations. She had always been a woman who made friends, and in this moment they were there for her, in letters full of sweet memories and endless joshing. Her old boss, Frank Waldrop, wrote and so did the entire staff at the *Times-Herald*, and, of course, John White sent a message. "At the moment I am living in a pub," she replied, "but don't worry, things will get better and I've been in worse places (mainly with you!)."

And so the days passed, as each evening Kathleen waited for the putt-putt of Billy's motorbike returning up the country lane. They talked of many things, of going to America after the war and how all the Kennedys would greet the Marquess of Hartington. The top secret documents concerning Operation Overlord had reached even Billy's battalion by now, and there was hardly a soldier in all England who did not realize that the invasion was imminent. At 9:34 A.M. on June 6 the radio broadcast a message from Supreme Headquarters Allied Expeditionary Force that "Allied naval forces, supported by strong air forces, began landing Allied armies this morning on the northern coast of France." The invasion of Europe had begun.

A week later in the early morning hours of June 13, a great and terrible new weapon appeared over the coast of England, twenty-six-foot-long V-1 rockets. Only one rocket reached London, plunging earthward and creating havoc, killing six people. It was the first of many rockets and many nights and thousands of deaths, a weapon that left people, as Kathleen wrote in her diary, "absolutely terrified."

Later that day Billy told Kathleen that the time had come and that his regiment was leaving. They had shared much those five weeks, and now they shared even Kathleen's diary. It had been "the most perfect month" of his life. He knew that it would end, but that made his leaving no less difficult. "How beastly it is to be ending things," he wrote in his meticulous hand. "This love seems to cause nothing but goodbye. I think that that is the worst part of it, worse even than fighting."

For Joe Jr. the fighting was ending. His first thirty-five missions were over, and all he had to show for it were endless dark and empty seas. He had volunteered for another tour, hoping this time to get his submarine, but since the Allies had driven most of the U-boats out of the English Channel in part because of flights like Joe Jr.'s, he was having no more luck than before. As he counted out his last missions, he flew with reckless daring, swooping down on a grounded Nazi E-boat on the Brest Peninsula until driven away by the rat-tat-tat of anti-aircraft batteries; on his final mission he flew against orders so near the German-controlled island of Guernsey that he returned to base with bullet holes in the fuselage from Nazi fire.

Jack was the hero, but he had never courted heroism the way his older brother did now, wooing danger like a lover. As the day for his return to the United States loomed, a new secret weapon was being prepared at the air base at Dunkeswell to combat the dreadful onslaught of V-1 rockets on London. Navy workers had stripped a PB4Y plane of everything from the guns to the copilot's seat, added new electronic gear, and filled the plane with explosives, turning the PB4Y into the largest single bomb ever created. The pilot and the standing copilot would fly the plane over England, then parachute out, leaving the mother plane to guide it across the channel, exploding into the concrete bunkers in France above Calais that were said to be the launching sites for the V-1 rockets. The Army had tried the scheme and they had one dead pilot and another wounded airman to show for it, but that did not dissuade the Navy from the attempt, nor Joe Jr. from volunteering to pilot the plane. "I am going to do something different for the next three weeks,"

Joe Jr. wrote home on July 26, 1944. "It is secret and I am not allowed to say what it is, but it isn't dangerous so don't worry."

Rose had reasons to give prayers of thanks. Jack was back home now, sallow, emaciated, his ribs sticking out of him, but he was alive. Joe Jr. would be home soon too. As for Kathleen, that moral debacle was an ocean away, and Rose still had hopes that the marriage might be annulled and that she would have her Kathleen back within the sacred precincts of the church.

Her other daughters were back with her too, all except for Rosemary who was not talked about. Eunice had just graduated from Stanford. She had seemed almost to disappear off campus one day, a silent, sullen presence leaving almost no deep mark on the lives of women with whom she had lived for three years. That last semester she had suffered from the tragic loss of a friend, a death that shattered forever any youthful assumptions of invulnerability. One of Eunice's only real friends at Stanford was nineteen-year-old Ann Clare Brokaw, only daughter of Clare Boothe Luce. Ann was herself at times a forlorn young woman, living in the deep shadow of her extraordinary mother. She and Eunice had much in common. In January Ann had been riding back to school in an open convertible driven by one of Eunice's other friends when the vehicle was struck by a car, throwing Ann out of the automobile, killing her instantly. Pat had known Ann as well, and her classmates at Rosemont could tell how stunned she was by the accident.

Even on Cape Cod, a day did not go by that Rose did not see or feel or hear something of the war. Joe continued to give occasional speeches, but he did not hold quite the same sway over the daily life of Hyannis Port. Luella, who spent much time there, found Hyannis Port had "become a different place, quiet, lonely and, in time, a very sad one."

There were blackout curtains on the windows. In the windows of stores in Hyannis, Rose looked up and saw the names of young men who had died in places far away. Soldiers were stationed throughout the Cape. The Hyannis airport had been used first to train Naval Air Corps cadets, and then turned into an Army Air Corps antisubmarine base.

Pat often served as a hostess at affairs for the soldiers, be it a clambake at the West Beach Club, or a dinner dance at the

Hyannis Port Club. She was witty and vivacious and few who met her realized that she was deeply insecure about everything from her weight to her appeal. Pat, like her sister Kathleen, would have considered it unthinkable to socialize with anyone but officers. Eunice was a year older and might have been expected to take part as well, but she appeared to need these long summers as respites, to recuperate for another year in what to her had become a difficult and distant world.

The days were as long as ever, and there was time for sailing and swimming and marathon games of tennis. And always was the hope that soon the young men would all be back, and life would be as it had been before.

On the second Sunday in August, Rose went to mass as she always did, and afterwards the family sat on the porch for a lunch. The family was largely grown up now. Jack, Eunice, and Pat were all in their twenties. Eighteen-year-old Bobby was old enough to fight, sixteen-year-old Jean old enough to leave school, and only twelve-year-old Teddy was still a child.

In the early afternoon, Joe went upstairs for his nap, Rose read the Sunday papers, and the other members of the family played quietly in the living room or talked out on the porch. Rose heard a knock on the door and when she opened it saw two priests standing there. During the war years most mothers or wives seeing two unknown clergymen standing in their doorway would have shuddered, fearing that they were the dark angels of death. Rose, however, was used to priests soliciting her family. She showed them into the living room, expecting that she would be asked to help build a new sanctuary somewhere, or add to the coffers of one charity or another. The priests asked to see Joe. That was usual too, for he controlled the finances on any but modest matters. "This cannot wait," said Father O'Leary, a Naval chaplain. "It concerns your son Joe Jr., who is missing in action."

Rose fled up the stairs, as if she could outrun the news, and stood over the sleeping form of her husband. She woke him and told him what the priest had said. Joe hurried downstairs and led the two priests to an anteroom off the living room and asked them enough questions to know that Joe Jr. was gone forever.

Joe and Rose went out on the porch. Standing there holding Rose, he told his children who were not children anymore that their brother had died. Although Joe did not know the details

of Joe Jr.'s top secret mission, he knew that his son had died
a hero's death, died tempting the gods of fate and chance and
the terrible laws of probability, died living out all the family
laws of courage. As Rose retreated into the truths of her faith,
so Joe fell back on these certitudes with which he had inspired
his children to live, and which his son's death either justified
or proved its utter paucity. "We've got to carry on," he said.
"We must take care of the living. There is a lot of work to be
done."

Joe and Rose had taught their daughters and sons to live
lives of ceaseless stoicism, never showing their pain, never
stopping out of weakness, never giving in. He told them to go
out and sail in the Sunday race as they had planned to sail.
They followed their father's direction, except Jack, who
walked by himself on the beach.

While his sons and daughters sailed on the placid waters of
the sound and Rose stayed huddled with her prayers, Joe telephoned his sister, Mary Loretta. For an hour and a half he
cried, terrible terrifying sounds welling up out of some dark
place of eternal sadness, cried as he would never cry in front
of his own wife.

And by herself Rose cried too, and at night she lay awake
thinking of her firstborn son, haunted by his loss. She had been
told that her son's plane had blown up, and in one instant he
was no more, this firstborn son in whom she had vested all her
knowledge and wisdom and faith, all her ideas and aspirations
and mortal dreams, her firstborn son "splintering into a thousand pieces," filling the sky with an instant illumination.

On the day that Kathleen learned Joe Jr. had died, Mark Soden
telephoned saying that before her brother flew on his last mission, he had apportioned out his mortal goods to family and
friends. Kathleen and Joe Jr. had squabbled over the ownership
of an Underwood typewriter, and he willed that to her along
with a Victrola, a Zenith radio, and a Zeiss camera. As Soden
ran down the list, she began to cry, sobbing into the phone. Almost immediately, she wrote Soden, apologizing for her tears.
"I'm so sorry I broke down tonight," she wrote, as if she had
violated some fundamental matter of protocol. "It never makes
things easier."

As a Kennedy, Kathleen wasn't supposed to cry openly or
shroud herself in mourning black, but she knew that in this
moment she wanted to be only one place, and that was with

her family in Hyannis Port. Her father arranged for her to take an army transport plane back to the United States, and Kathleen left almost immediately. Kathleen was the wife of Billy Hartington now. There were those in Britain who considered it an unseemly business that she should leave now while her husband fought in the great battle in France.

The army transport plane carrying Kathleen flew from London on August 16, 1944. A wan, emaciated Jack was there on the tarmac at Boston's Logan Airport. Kathleen stood there a moment in her neatly tailored blue American Red Cross outfit, and then ran into Jack's arms weeping. They held on to each other, and Kathleen dried her tears and walked forward arm in arm with Jack. Kathleen learned that Jack had managed to get out of Chelsea Naval Hospital for a few hours; the very next morning he had rectal surgery that lessened his back and leg discomfort but did nothing to alleviate his "abdominal symptoms."

In Hyannis Port, Kathleen found herself in a house where the deepest words were left unspoken, the most passionate emotions held back. She could not talk about her brother as he was any longer—the raw vitality, the anger, the quixotic generosity, the endless teasing—but had to view him as a heroic icon, a flawless exemplar. She could not mourn her brother, but was supposed to honor his memory by pretending that life was somehow the same. She showed to the world that same chipper, upbeat personality. "It's a great treat to be back in the land of 'the free!!! & the brave'—No place like it," she wrote Waldrop at the *Times-Herald*.

Rose shuffled off to St. Xavier to mass each morning, lost in her own solitude. The woman whom Kathleen had called "the dearest mother in the world" could not forgive Kathleen, and, in her silence, condemned her daughter. It was her father, though, who dominated the house, not an exuberant inspiring presence out on the second-floor deck any longer, but a dark shadow hovering over the long summer days.

To Kathleen, Jack appeared a sadly diminished young man, thin beyond thinness, his back an open wound after a failed operation, his skin touched with the yellow pallor of malaria. His condition should have filled a father with worry, but Joe thought almost exclusively of his martyred son, and paid little attention to Jack or his visiting friends. Hours on end he sat by himself in his room, hardly venturing out even when Jack brought his old PT-109 colleague, George "Barney" Ross, another PT-boat veteran, Paul "Red" Fay, two other Naval officers, James Reed and Leonard Thom, as well as the two married officers' wives, Jewel Reed and Kate Thom, back to the house for Labor Day weekend.

After Joe Jr.'s death, Joe had admonished his sons and daughters to live these summer days as they had always lived. Twenty-four-year-old Eunice set out with a vengeance to follow her father's mandate, as if by sheer will and frenetic activity she could remake the family lives. Tennis. Golf. Touch football. Charades. Game after game. Challenge after challenge. Competition after competition.

Eunice needed a crew for her boat in the Labor Day race, and she commandeered poor pregnant Kate who had never even been on a boat. Eunice shouted unintelligible orders to the flustered landlubber. "I remember how cruel I thought she was because she kept barking orders at me and if I did something wrong, she'd scream," recalled Kate Thom.

Sixteen-year-old Jean tried to keep up with her older siblings, but she appeared lost. Joe Jr. had been her godfather, and she adored him the way a kid sister could adore an older brother. She was at an age when most young women did not confront death, and in a sense her youth ended this summer.

Kathleen was usually the exuberant extrovert, but she had grown silent and thoughtful. Kathleen joined Jack's buddies out on the golf links of the Hyannis Port Country Club. Humor was the great leaven among these veterans of the Pacific, and they laughed from hole to hole, telling jokes, recounting tales. The young Kennedys always had at least one court jester among their friends, and today the irascible Red Fay had taken that role. A perpetual cutup, he wasn't about to merely stand there waiting when two local women played a painfully sedate game in front of these impassioned combat veterans. "Excuse, the Marchioness of Hartington is trying to get through," the red-haired, freckle-faced Fay yelled, as the woman turned to look at an embarrassed Kathleen.

In England Kathleen knew many young men like Jack's friends. They were a different breed once they had seen combat, once they had seen wounded and dead friends and colleagues. They didn't put up easily or well with the trivia of civilian life. Neither did Kathleen.

After their round of golf, Jack's friends wanted a few stiff drinks. Rose and Joe allowed only one cocktail before dinner.

Kathleen and Jack snuck into the kitchen looking for the hidden bottle of scotch. As they stood pouring stiff drinks for the Navy men, Bobby entered the room wearing his white Navy uniform. He was old enough to know that if a man wanted two drinks before dinner that was his own business. But he was full of the same awe and trepidation as his siblings were toward his father, and he vowed that he would tell their father. Kathleen had no use for such a snitch, and she abruptly told him to leave the kitchen and mind his own business.

Over the dinner table, Jack and his friends continued telling their own tales of the Pacific, punctuating the meal with laughter. Joe went from Red to Jim to Barney to Leonard asking each of them how he had fared at the day's sports, chiding anyone who had disgraced the family by finishing worse than second. Kate took high honors, for Eunice's boat had won the sailing race. Through it all Rose sat silently. "The humor bypassed Rose," Fay recalled. "She was simply out of the loop. I don't think that she really could stay abreast of what was going on. And I thought she was a very lonely person, and kind of sad."

After dinner, the group headed outside the house to sit there and reminisce, telling more twice-told tales. It had been a sentimental reunion, and as the sun was setting, they laughed and laughed some more, each story climaxed with guffaws and belly laughs. As the merriment pealed forth, the upstairs window burst open. "Jack, don't you and your friends have any respect for your dead brother?" Joe shouted. "You get in here! You're making a nuisance of yourselves with the neighbors."

Jack was a twenty-seven-year-old veteran of the Pacific, and his father shouted at him as if he were a naughty ten-year-old. He meant no disrespect to his brother, unless life and laughter itself would forever be a mark of disrespect. He knew he wasn't supposed to cry, and he wasn't supposed to laugh either. His friends sat there in stunned silence. Suddenly, Bobby rushed out of the door and said in a stage whisper, "Dad's awfully mad."

Kathleen had had quite enough of her father's incivility and craziness. She did not need to have her kid brother reiterating the obvious, and she turned on Bobby. "You're frightening our house guests out of their wits!"

Thus ended Labor Day weekend.

* * *

Kathleen had been so proud of Jack when she learned of his exploits in the Solomon Islands. Now while she and Jack rested at Hyannis Port, millions of people were reading about her brother and PT-109 in the pages of *Reader's Digest*. The article by John Hersey had originally run in *The New Yorker*. Jack was proud and also mildly embarrassed by all the attention. His sentiments weren't far different from his PT-boat comrade, Barney Ross, who said that the article had made him and the other crew members "sound like some kind of hero because you saved your own life. . . . I had always thought it was a disaster, but he made it sound pretty heroic, like Dunkirk."

To Kathleen, Jack and Joe Jr. were both heroes, and she didn't make any distinction between them. Jack, however, had not willfully risked his life. Jack understood that distinction perfectly well. He had thought about it a great deal and why the Japanese were better jungle fighters than the G.I.'s. "An American's energies are divided," he had written Inga from the Pacific. "He wants to kill but he also is trying desperately to prevent himself from being killed." Joe Jr. had not been that kind of a soldier. Neither was Billy.

In the fierce fighting in Normandy in August, Billy had led his troops with heedless courage, as if there were no danger he would not court, no challenge he would not attempt. "I can still see his dismay when told that his company had done enough and must hand over the lead to another," a fellow officer recalled.

Half a year earlier in the town square of West Derbyshire, a portly Labour politician had as much as called Billy a coward for leaving his regiment, and now it was as if he had to prove his courage again and again. Early in September, his battalion crossed the Somme River in northwestern France, scene of two of the bloodiest battles of World War I. Billy could have been an officer in the Great War, an upper-class Englishman with a quaint sense of chivalrous courage that had been largely killed in the trenches of the Somme and the Marne. When he wrote Kathleen, he even called the Germans by the World War I term "Hun." As an officer, he was allowed to wear a different uniform than his men, and he donned a white mackintosh and bright pants, as if he dared the German snipers to shoot at him. When a fellow officer visited his company, Billy had his batman, Ingles, bring out the rum, not rude swigs from a bottle either, but proper glasses and toasts. Despite sleeping in trenches and bombed-out villages, he managed to look almost spiffy, each morning pulling out his steel mirror from his left breast pocket and giving himself a proper shave.

As the Germans retreated pell-mell, victory seemed in the air. Whatever town or village the British tanks and soldiers passed through, they were met by cheering multitudes, heralding them as saviors, singing songs of celebration, garlanding the Tommies with flowers. Billy's armored company was one of the first units to liberate Brussels, and he rode into the Belgium capital on top of a tank. As the army moved eastward from the elated capital of Brussels, Billy felt, as he wrote Kathleen, "so unworthy of it all, living as I have in reasonable safety and comfort during these years. . . . I have a permanent lump in my throat and I long for you to be here as it is an experience which few can have and which I would love to share with you."

On September 8, the rain began and the air was touched with autumn chill, and suddenly the Germans were not retreating any longer. On that day in attempting to capture the village of Beverlo, Billy lost a quarter of his men. The next morning the rain was gone, the sky was clear, and Billy's Number Three Company set out to capture the town of Heppen. Along with his batman, Billy walked out ahead of the tanks, carrying a pair of wire cutters, wearing his white mackintosh and bright pants, with no helmet. "Come on, you fellows, buck up," Billy said as he led his company forward.

In the afternoon when the fighting was over and the town was taken, a farmer and his son returned to their farm in what had been the middle of the battlefield. They saw six smoldering British tanks. They came upon their farmhouse where the Germans had holed up and there they found more than a score of bodies. They saw soldiers who had been killed with bayonets and spades. They saw a German and a British soldier lying next to each other where they had strangled each other to death. In front of the house they saw five dead soldiers, two Germans and three British. And by the back door they found two more bodies, including one lying on its back, with feet propped against the kitchen door. It was a body unlike any of the others, for it was wearing a white mackintosh and bright trousers, and was unblemished except for one small bullet hole through the heart.

On September 16, Kathleen was on a shopping spree at Bonwit Teller's on New York's Fifth Avenue. The shelves of the stores in London had long since been stripped of any but bare necessities, but in America there appeared to Kathleen to be an overwhelming cornucopia of goods. Washington had banned full skirts and knife pleats, but there were plenty of ballerina-length gowns, small hats, turbans, and leather shoes in the six approved colors: black, white, navy, and three gradations of brown.

Kathleen was working her way through the second floor of the department store, clutching her purchases, when Eunice appeared for their luncheon engagement. "Before we go, I think we ought to go back and talk to Daddy," Eunice said.

"Something's happened," Kathleen said, her voice halfway between a question and a statement.

"Why don't you go talk to Daddy?" Eunice said.

Eunice's voice was thin, her words halfhearted. As the two sisters hurried back to the family suite at the Waldorf, Eunice kept to herself the news her father had just told her. At the Waldorf, Joe led Kathleen into his suite, shut the door, and told her that Billy was dead. Kathleen stayed by herself in her room, and at dinner the family talked of everything but Billy. Around her family Eunice usually could hardly stop talking, but this evening she spoke barely a word to her grieving sister.

As the evening progressed, Joe asked Kathleen if there was any friend she would like to have with her. Unhesitatingly, she said the name of John White's sister, Patsy Field. Kathleen had many more intimate friends than this older woman, but Patsy had a quality of strength and understanding that Kathleen needed. Joe knew Patsy. He had attended the quasi-salon in the living room of the Fields' Georgetown house. He hadn't liked Patsy or her anthropologist husband and any of what he considered their half-baked progressive ideas. But that didn't matter now. At midnight, he placed a call to the Field residence. "I hate your guts, as you well know," he told Patsy. "But I have to ask a favor of you. Will you come and stay with Kathleen?"

Patsy came up to New York the next day, where she was met by one of Joe's associates. Her brother had told her all about the strange domestic customs of the Kennedys. Thus she did not find it amiss that she was driven first to see Joe in his suite at the Waldorf before being take to see Kathleen, who along with her mother and the rest of the family was at the Plaza.

Joe was uncomfortable dealing with Patsy. After he thanked her, he gave her a pair of nylons, as if this was nothing more than a transaction, and then he had one of his retainers drive her over to the Plaza.

As Patsy met Kathleen, her mother, and the rest of the family, she had a feeling that "a great cloud of misery was hanging over everything." The women in the family had strewn their clothes over the suite, and in the middle of the room sat Kathleen, her face ghastly pale, her eyes darkly ringed.

"What have you been doing since you received the news?" Patsy asked, when she was finally alone with her friend.

"Mostly going to mass." Kathleen shrugged, barely looking up. "Mother keeps saying, 'God doesn't send us a cross heavier than we can bear.' Again and again she keeps saying it."

The two women spent hours together talking. They talked about girdles. They talked about Jack and life in Washington. They talked about Billy too, and what he had been, and Kathleen said that her only regret was that she was not pregnant with their child. "The amazing thing was that Billy loved me so much, Patsy," Kathleen said. "I felt needed. I felt I could make him happy." That was exactly what she had written Jack a little over two years before. She, Kathleen, future Duchess of Devonshire, would have been everything for Billy—loyal wife, gracious hostess, noble matron, loving mother. Everything. And yet she had had only five weeks as Billy's wife. Five weeks. Billy had been nothing but a brilliant moment flashing across her life.

"Have they given you anything to sleep?" Patsy asked, looking at those haunted eyes.

Kathleen shrugged, and Patsy took a vial of sleeping pills out of her purse and gave them to her friend. Not only would she be able to sleep now, but Patsy felt that Kathleen was trying to numb herself, preparing for the ordeal of the memorial service in England.

Joe believed that Kathleen had better start getting over Billy, shaking off her grief like a football player gritting out an injury. That evening he insisted that Kathleen and Patsy join him and the family for dinner at a French restaurant. Joe was the impresario of the evening, offering tickets to Broadway shows to everyone in the family, leading the conversation. Kathleen sat buried within her mournfulness, occasionally offering a word or two.

"So ends the story of Billy and Kick," Kathleen wrote in her diary on September 20. "I can't believe that the one thing I feared most should have happened. . . . Life is so cruel."

Kathleen flew back to Britain and on the last day of September sat with Billy's family and a few friends in the Anglican church at Edensor, down the road from Chatsworth, for a memorial service. Although the Cavendishes had for centuries been buried here behind the church in a dank, mossy cemetery, shrouded under thick shade trees, Billy would rest forever in a foreign field among his fallen comrades.

When Kathleen walked away from the church at Edensor that autumn day, she was taking almost nothing away from her short-lived marriage but memories and a small five-thousand-pound inheritance. Since she had borne Billy no male heir she had lost all claim to Chatsworth and the Cavendish fortune. She had no reason to stay in England any longer, no reason except that she felt she belonged here.

Here in England away from Rose and Joe and the stern mandates of the family, she gave her grief full sway, not feeling her tears were a betrayal of her family. For weeks she stayed with Billy's parents and his sisters. She was haunted by her memories. She could not sleep in a room by herself. Kathleen would be fine for a while, and then suddenly, day or night, alone or with friends, tears would come flowing out of her eyes, as if she had tapped a deep spring of sadness. The nights that Billy's sister, Elizabeth, slept with Kathleen, she felt that she had "never met anyone so desperately unhappy. Her mother had tried to convince her that she had committed a sin in this marriage, so in addition to losing her husband, she worried about having lost her soul."

Kathleen returned to the Catholic church, but even as she knelt before God, there was irony in her act of contrition. Her mother could see God's plan in the fiery explosion in the sky that took her eldest son, and surely Rose saw that same master plan in the death of her Protestant son-in-law. Kathleen wondered what kind of moral accounting could only absolve her sins once her brave and blameless husband was dead. "I guess God has taken care of the matter in His own way, hasn't He," she wrote a friend.

From London, Kathleen helped Jack to prepare a privately printed book of reminiscences about Joe Jr. She penned her own recollection of her brother, but what she remembered most deeply about Joe Jr. was his support regarding her marriage to Billy, and she was not sure that belonged in the memorial book. "Do what you think," she told Jack, and he let the sentences stay.

Kathleen didn't like to go out in public often for she felt that people were "looking to see how I'm taking it." When she decided that she was going to make her life in England, she went to Caxton Hall to sign on for rationing. The line looked endless, and Kathleen plopped herself down in a chair at the end, next to a poor woman who stared at her. "You look like Mr. Kennedy's daughter," the woman said, continuing to stare unashamedly.

"I am," Kathleen replied.

"Of course, the likes of you would never speak to the likes of me," the woman said.

"We are all the same in the sight of God," Kathleen said, and the woman sat stony faced as if to say she doubted it.

Kathleen had been brought up to believe that her family had a special blessed destiny. She knew now that God had prepared no charmed fate, not a God who could take her brother and Billy from her. What she knew she had as a Kennedy, as she wrote Lem, was "the ability to not be got down." That gift sustained her now, that gift slowly gave her strength.

The next summer when the war in Europe was over and the sun was shining over London, Kathleen looked out on the city and felt life return to her. "It's such a wonderful day," she said to her friend Jane Compton. "You don't think Billy would mind if I wore a really flowery dress, do you?"

15

Their Brother's Keeper

When Jack announced his candidacy for Congress in Massachusetts's Eleventh district in the spring of 1946, the Kennedy women returned to Boston to work in the campaign. Eunice gave up her position at the State Department in Washington, where she had been dealing with problems involving POWs returning from Germany. Having graduated from Rosemont the previous spring, Pat arrived to help Jack win the seat their grandfather Fitzgerald had held four decades before. Jean came from Manhattanville, where she had just completed her first year. Only Kathleen was missing, and that was by calculation; her presence would have conjured up untenable images of wealth and infidelity to Catholicism.

Rose was startled at the sheer audaciousness of twenty-nine-year-old Jack attempting to start his political career with a run for Congress. "I was surprised at the leap to go over to Congress first thing because my father had gone up through the legislature and had been into other things first," Rose said. "But his father was always for getting the top place, if you could." Joe was a shadowy presence unseen by most of the press, a formidable figure managing the strategy and writing the checks, but Rose was also crucial to her son's campaign. "Rose was so important to Jack in 1946 because she was better known than anyone else in that district," recalled Dave Powers, who began working for Jack that year.

Rose's father had never allowed her to speak at rallies, but she was a natural campaigner. At the VFW hall in Brighton, she talked not about issues or her would-be congressman son, but about life at the Court of St. James's and bringing up a big family. The audience was mesmerized listening to this fifty-five-year-old Gold Star Mother, who looked as if she had just bathed in the fountain of youth. When she sat down to a thunderous burst of applause, Jack stood up. He was a sallow-faced, reed-thin young man with a self-deprecating manner, and he gave a speech that was a pallid contrast to his mother's spirited remarks.

Jack had been ambivalent about running. "I can feel Pappy's eyes on the back of my neck," he had told Red Fay. He knew that he was supposed to pick up the fallen banner and carry it forth. "Red, when the war is over I'll be back here with Dad trying to parlay a lost PT-boat and a bad back into a political advantage. I tell you, Dad is ready right now and can't understand why Johnnyboy isn't all 'engines ahead full.' "

The three sisters were as much strangers to Boston as Jack was. The candidate had taken up residence in a dank little suite at the Bellevue Hotel on Beacon Street. His sisters were not running for office. They stayed a few blocks away in the Ritz-Carlton, Boston's premier hotel.

During the day the three Kennedy women worked in the campaign office answering phones, writing letters, sending out campaign material. In the evenings the two older sisters often headed out to a series of house parties in which Kennedy supporters gathered groups of friends to meet the candidate. In the first house party in Charlestown, twenty-four-year-old Eunice stood behind her older brother. Eunice identified with Jack so completely that she even took on his mannerisms, the quick slash of her hands in exclamation, the staccato rhythms of her voice, the frenetic pace of her activities. Eunice repeated every word of his speech along with him. Afterwards, Jack turned on his sister. "Eunice," he said, "you made me very, very nervous. Don't ever do that to me again."

"Jack, I thought you were going to forget your speech."

Despite her own sometimes excruciating shyness, Eunice was better than Jack at the casual glad-handing of politics, so adept that she was sent to houses in Cambridge, the territory of Jack's strongest opponent. She was more the natural politician and far more intrigued by the process of politics than Jack, who still sometimes daydreamed of making his career as a journalist. "Eunice would have loved to be the one that father picked to run," said former Senator George Smathers, one of her brother's closest friends. "If she'd been a little older, and if it had been like today, when a lot of women are running for office, I suspect the history of the Kennedy clan would have been quite different. You might have seen Eunice as the first woman Congressman from that district."

At each house campaign workers set up a movie screening or entertainment. Then Eunice or Pat kept the groups sufficiently diverted that they hardly realized that Jack, as always, was late, finally arriving to sit in the living room to be ogled by the young women, and mothered by the old.

Jack knew how to count well enough to realize that women were the key to the primary that in heavily Democratic Boston was tantamount to election to Congress. "Women compose the majority of voters now," he had told the League of Catholic Women the previous November. "Women not only have political power, but they have financial power." He made an important campaign speech at the Brighton Women's Club, a largely Catholic organization considered by his aides perhaps the most important political institution in that entire community.

Jack and his advisors feared that the women of the district might utilize their power by sending Catherine Falvey to Washington. Far from being a token female candidate, she was arguably the best qualified of all the ten candidates to deal with the complicated realities of the postwar world. Falvey was the first woman veteran of the war to run for Congress. The thirty-five-year-old lawyer had twice been elected to the Massachusetts legislature from her native Somerville. A stylish brunette, she was as attractive a woman as Jack was a man. A major in the Women's Army Corps, Falvey had recently served at the Nuremberg war trials as chief of the interrogation analysis division. "We thought there was a little danger . . . because she was a woman," recalled John Droney, a campaign aide. "We didn't know how the women would react. They may go for her."

As the primary approached, Falvey's candidacy had not taken off. The sophisticated, witty major apparently appeared a threat to many women voters, to whom careers were anathema, an abrogation of their responsibilities as women, wives, and mothers. To numbers of the men she seemed equally out of place, an uppity female who had no place in the manly business of politics. "Falvey was a fresh face, but at that time I don't think the people were ready yet for a woman in Congress," said Samuel Bornstein, then a reporter on the *Boston American*. "Sort of something insincere about a woman running for national office at that time."

"We were overwhelmed by the Kennedy ladies who vigorously campaigned," recalled Eddie Jaffe, who handled public relations for Falvey. It was not simply the Kennedy women who overwhelmed Falvey, but a whole network of women who were the silent understructure of the entire Kennedy campaign. They were traditional political women, the consumers of politics, the archetypal little woman behind the man. "Perhaps the best ticket for the campaign was Rose Kennedy," said Billy Sutton, the first person hired to work on Jack's campaign. "Everybody wanted to see her as much as they wanted to see Jack. Jack wasn't from Boston and they knew him largely because of Rose and the Fitzgeralds. She didn't give very many speeches but she was around here with the Ace of Clubs and was highly connected with the church and Archbishop Cushing. She knew what to do with these people. She was always a part of it, a big seller."

In every community women worked for Jack, telephoning their friends, talking him up after mass, lobbying their husbands, boyfriends, and brothers. Their names were not in the paper, and they sought no bounty except Jack's election, a quiet army slowly building support for the young veteran.

Jack's appeal had little to do with traditional politics. His modest, predictable, indifferently delivered remarks were not creating this excitement among women from Brookline to East Boston. Jack was not only a veteran but a hero, and his brother a martyred hero. He had a boyishly adorable quality that made the Catholic maidens of Boston dream of wedded bliss with young Kennedy, and their mothers want to fatten the poor lad with soup and encouragement. Part was an inexplicable excitement that Jack and his family created. These women identified with Jack, Eunice, Pat, Jean, Bobby, and little Teddy. Although Joe's reputation had diminished elsewhere, in Boston the Kennedys were that most legendary of families. Their achievements, triumphs, and sorrows were tales told and retold in thousands of Boston homes. The Kennedys had become Catholic Brahmins, seemingly as sophisticated and worldly as any of the old families. They were people with whom the socially aspiring identified, hoping to rub shoulders with members of this exalted family, if only in a political house party or at a campaign rally.

As primary day neared, Jack was apparently leading, but he needed a special boost, an adrenaline shot of publicity. One of those trying to come up with an idea was Lawrence "DeGug" DeGuglielmo, a young Italian politician working for Jack in

Cambridge. DeGuglielmo observed the Boston Irish with the clinical detachment of an anthropologist. He noted that these daughters and sons of Erin had one overwhelming hidden characteristic: They were a race of "social climbers." And thus he suggested to Eunice that the campaign have a fancy reception for the women of Cambridge. "We'll do it," Eunice said, not listening to the old pols who thought the idea silly, effete, and worthless.

"Any guy who would suggest such a thing would have been looked at rather strangely, a beer party yes, but not a tea," Sutton reflected. "Up to then there had been only one tea party in Boston that mattered politically. But it was a pretty good gimmick because you got all these people who wanted to be important to go there."

Eunice set out to make the reception three days before the June primary a main event. She took twenty volunteers and set them down to address engraved invitations to thousands of women in Cambridge, Somerville, and other parts of Boston. Most of the recipients had never received an engraved invitation in their lives. It was not dinner in the White House, not a presentation before the queen, not a ball in Palm Beach, but for all the excitement and anticipation it might have been. As the day approached the beauty parlors of Cambridge were busy from morning till night, and the dress shops had rarely done such business in party dresses in the middle of June.

On the evening of the reception, the Kennedys arrived early at the ballroom of the Commander Hotel in Cambridge. There were arrays of flowers; pyramids of dainty, crustless sandwiches; silver urns of tea—all the food and amenities for a wedding reception or a fiftieth-wedding-anniversary party. As Jack looked out on the vast and empty ballroom, he expressed himself dubious of the whole gigantic venture. Rose was cautiously optimistic, envisioning an event like the Fourth of July garden party at the embassy in London.

Well before the scheduled hour, the women of Boston began walking into the lobby of the Commander. They took their places in the reception line, shaking first Rose's hand, then Jack's and finally Eunice's, who quickly moved the women on into the ballroom. On and on they came, five hundred, a thousand, fifteen hundred women before the room could hold no more: garrulous, stout old ladies in bifocals and flowered hats; stunning Irish-American women, wearing up-to-the-minute dresses with padded shoulders; matrons in stylish suits; a full cross section of Boston's womanhood. On and on they came jamming the hotel lobby, flowing out into the sidewalk, their cars creating a traffic jam in Harvard Square, the drivers and bystanders waiting for even a glimpse of Jack. Those who made it inside the ballroom reception were pushed together like sheep in a holding pen, a profusion of colorful hats bobbing up and down over the permed heads, many of the women hoping to have their picture taken with Jack or to get his autograph.

Jack's opponents might rail against him and his millionaire father. They might ridicule Jack and his "negro valet and chauffeur." But he and his mother and sisters had won the hearts of thousands of Boston women and many of the men as well.

Three days later on election evening, Eunice and Jean joined their father and Bobby at election headquarters listening to radio station WBZ reporting the returns. Thanks to the new voting machines, returns were coming in far earlier than in previous elections, and already at nine-thirty two of Jack's wards had reported. "It looks like Jack's winning it easily," Joe said.

"Eunice, you look like Jack," John Droney, the campaign aide, said as the celebration began, a remark that she took as the highest of compliments.

"Who do I look like?" Jean asked.

"Bobby," Droney replied.

As the results kept coming in foretelling a landslide victory, Jean argued bitterly. She, too, wanted to look like Jack.

During the summer the Kennedys gathered at Hyannis Port, a family with grandiose dreams for the future, yet haunted by the past. With all that Joe was doing to memorialize his eldest son, the world at times appeared like a gigantic mausoleum, the daughters as much as the sons commissioned to memorialize their brother. Jean had christened a destroyer in her brother's honor, the *Joseph P. Kennedy Jr.*, which sailed the seas now. Years later Rose looked back and realized how much her youngest daughter's life had been changed by family tragedy. "Jean was about sixteen when we lost our son and all these tragedies started," Rose reflected. "And so Jean probably didn't have as much joy in her life at sixteen as perhaps some of the others had."

During the summer Jean and Eunice joined their parents and

grandfather Fitzgerald at a solemn high mass dedicating a new main altar at St. Francis Xavier Church. There carved into the dark wood in bas-relief were Joe Jr.'s plane; George, patron saint of England; and Joan of Arc, a trilogy of saints. This was the church the family attended when they were in Hyannis Port, and from now on whenever they looked up at the altar, they would likely think not only of God but of Joe Jr. and of the family legacy.

Joe Jr. had ascended into perfection, and there was the nagging thought in all the young Kennedys that whatever they did it would not quite measure up. "I'm just filling Joe's shoes," Jack said during the primary campaign. "If he were alive, I'd never be there." As for Eunice, Pat, and Jean, their role in life as women was not to attempt to fill Joe Jr.'s shoes, but to polish and prepare them so that Jack could step into them.

Eunice, Jean, and Pat sailed on Nantucket Sound while Jack spent much of the time reading books on the veranda, wearing an unwieldy brace to protect his back. Although he was away much of the time, Joe was the architect of the great public family that the Kennedys were now becoming, and that affected the daughters as much as the sons. That summer of 1946, as Jack made his political debut, Joe started the Joseph P. Kennedy Jr. Foundation, the major Kennedy philanthropy, a further attempt to honor his son's name. As its first contribution, the foundation gave $600,000 to the archdiocese of Boston for a convalescent home in Joe Jr.'s name; Joe made sure that his son, the candidate, gave the check to Archbishop Cushing.

That year Joe sold his interest in his father's bank, Columbia Trust, for a half million dollars. He took that money and pledged it to development in Massachusetts, an act for which he was portrayed as a noble son of the Commonwealth. Joe's sisters, however, considered that money to be as much theirs as Joe's, and they felt robbed of their inheritance. Their father had trusted his only son with legal control over most of his estate, and doubtless if Mary Loretta and Margaret had fallen on hard times, he would have helped them out. He saw himself as the unchallenged patriarch of the family, who had control over the family money as over everything else. "When we were growing up there were three gods," said Mary Loretta's daughter, Mary Lou McCarthy. "There was God in Heaven. There was FDR in Washington. And there was Joe. And they controlled our lives."

* * *

In the fall Jean returned to Manhattanville. Her first year in college seventeen-year-old Jean had developed what became one of the closest friendships of her life. Jean and her roommate, Ethel Skakel, had that rare bonding that sometimes happens between two young women. They were as inseparable as the rigorous rules of the college permitted, finishing each other's sentences, laughing at the mere suggestion of their friend's joke, attesting to the virtue of the other to all who would listen.

When the two women talked of their families, their anecdotes often sounded interchangeable. Ethel came from a big family too. She was the next to the youngest of the seven Skakel children. The Skakels, like the Kennedys, were a family of great wealth who in their Greenwich, Connecticut, estate had created their own familiar universe. Ethel's mother was an Irish Catholic of Falstaffian proportions, her father a taciturn Dutch Protestant, who had made his fortune with the Great Lakes Carbon Corporation. They had raised an exuberant, flamboyant brood, with neither the restraint nor the discipline of the Kennedys. Ann and George Skakel were not about to spend their lives painfully and quietly obtaining what the haughty Protestants considered good taste and civility. What was wealth for if it was not only to be spent but to be flaunted?

Although at first hearing Jean's and Ethel's childhood recollections sounded similar, the Skakels appeared like the Kennedys blown up to cartoonlike size. Where the young Kennedys' friends found something inspiring and enviable in the intrepid, adventurous young scions, the Skakels' friends often found the Skakel family "scary." Jean and her brothers and sisters had sailed daringly in the Hyannis sound, but they knew to come into port in the most foul and dangerous weather. The young Skakels knew no such limits. Ethel's brothers swung from the trees on the estate like a race of Tarzans, tied Ethel on a rope and swung her from the second-story window, greeted her beau with a withering and alas accurate barrage of pellets from air rifles; played "King of the Castle" in which one of the Skakel boys stood on the roof of the car while another drove through the wooded byways of Greenwich, trying to find a branch low enough to knock the king off the castle; took guests on a tour of the estate in an old station wagon that ended with a roller-coaster–like ride down a hill and into the middle of a pond.

Ethel's personality was itself a roller-coaster ride, carrying

Jean along with her. At Manhattanville, there were always
women who enlivened the monastic routine with practical
jokes, but there had rarely been such puckish pranksters as
Jean and Ethel. They were fearless in their frontal assaults on
decorum and cant. One evening when the students were discussing what the nuns wore to bed, Ethel said that there was
one way to find out; she rang the fire alarm, sending the Sacred Heart mothers scurrying out into the halls in their night-
wear. Another evening she was bemoaning the fact that
because of all her marks in the demerit book she would not be
allowed to leave campus for her big date. "This is ridiculous
to ground us at this age," Jean said. "We're too old to be
grounded." Jean concluded that the only thing to do was to
swipe the book from the office and toss it down the incinerator
chute, freeing Ethel and several others from the walled campus.

When Monsignor Hartigan arrived for a visit in his fancy
new Cadillac, Ethel thought that was the height of hypocrisy.
She neatly affixed to his windshield a hand-printed message:
"Are the collections good, Father?" The priest was so irate at
that audacious guerilla attack on his integrity that no one could
leave campus until a few days later Ethel came forward to admit her crime. Ethel was fanatically attached to horses, and at
the International Horse Show in New York she became infatuated with a member of the Irish team. Ethel and her friend,
Mary "Dickie" Mann, invited the young Irishman out for a
soda. The next day he ignored the two Manhattanville students,
a snub that Ethel found intolerable. As revenge, she and Mann
snuck into the stables and painted the Irish rider's horse green.

In most secular colleges, Ethel's high jinks would have led
to expulsion, but the mothers of the Sacred Heart had a different sort of measurement to apply. The deeply religious Ethel
was full of not only mischief but religious joy. Ethel became
a Child of Mary at Manhattanville, and was serious enough
about her faith to consider becoming a nun. Beyond that, the
more outrageous Ethel's conduct became, the wider her father
opened his purse to the nuns of Manhattanville.

Rose, however, was distressed that her youngest daughter
would become friendly with a young woman of such unruli-
ness. "Mother didn't think we were studying," Jean recalled,
"and Mother thought that Ethel was a bad influence. I had had
honors when I graduated from Noroton, and my marks went
steadily down. So she put a wall between us."

In these years that Jean and Ethel attended Manhattanville, the college was an almost schizophrenic amalgam of the most progressive and most conservative aspects of American society. At Harvard, where Bobby was now a student, his professors lectured about social problems. At Manhattanville, the students not only heard academic discussions, but they worked a few hours each week in settlement houses, hospitals, and other institutions. The college's Interracial Forum introduced the students to questions of racial justice in America. Some students went even further than simply listening to lectures or volunteering in their social activism. Ethel's older sister, Pat, who was a senior during Ethel and Jean's first year, was a highly serious woman, the president of the student government. At a time when blacks rarely ventured below Harlem for social activities, Pat and a black student went to lunch together at Schrafft's in midtown Manhattan, effectively desegregating the popular restaurant.

Ethel was as much in the shadow of her older sister as Jean, forever being compared to her exemplary sibling. When Ethel and Jean were seniors, Pat Skakel returned to lecture to the student body about her work for the Christophers, the Catholic activist organization founded by Father Keller. As Ethel and Jean looked up at Pat from the audience, she told the student body: "You may feel that you don't know enough to teach Christian ideas," she lectured. "Don't let that bother you. If the Communists had the truth we have, the world would be converted in ten years."

At Manhattanville there were many teachers who had suffered the ravages of Nazism personally, and students who were themselves refugees. When Joe Kennedy came to the school to speak criticizing the Marshall Plan for aid to devastated Europe, he was applauded politely, but privately there was much condemnation of his isolationist view.

As much as the students learned about the world beyond their walls, their great goal and obligation in life were to marry and raise good Catholic families. This was the other inner drama of Manhattanville: how to find a husband. "We had a Happy Husband Hunting Club, where we learned such things as how to take care of trees and flowers so if we had an estate we would know how to manage it," recalled Charlotte Murdoch Hogan.

In the postwar era, the age of marriage was dramatically dropping, and even at the age of seventeen or eighteen, the students worried about their marriage prospects and what would happen if they didn't find anyone. "I can remember Jean announcing at one point that if she didn't have an engagement ring by the time she was twenty-five that she was going to buy a gold ring and go all over Europe as a merry widow," said Betty Street Vanderbilt, a classmate.

Beneath the banter and the bravado, Jean was playing a deadly serious game in which *any* husband, as long as he was a practicing Catholic from a good family, seemed preferable to a life of spinsterhood. As she set off on one of her dates, Ethel yelled at her friend as she headed down the dormitory corridor: "Get him to put a ring on your finger."

Her older sisters had made their debuts before the king and queen in London. If Jean could not do that, she could at least be presented before Catholic society in New York. But eighteen-year-old Jean could hardly abide the idea of marching into a ballroom on the arm of a young man she didn't know, to be scrutinized by a society about which she cared not at all. "Mother said I could come out in New York at Christmas," Jean recalled, "or I could go skiing. I went skiing."

For years Jean had watched as her older brothers' friends had become infatuated with Kathleen, romances that were at least partially love affairs for the family as well. Now Jean found that one of Jack's closest friends, Red Fay, the proverbial older man, was taken with her. "Jack wanted me to fall in love with one of his sisters," Fay said. "He was kind of lining me up with Eunice. There was no one else around for her, and I was the logical one, close to her age. And I kept saying, 'God, Jack, if you want me to pair up, why don't you let me pair up with Jean?' And that caused a little embarrassment. Jack said to his father, 'Well, I think maybe Red and Jean would be a better go.' And the old man said no way."

When Red stopped seeing her, Jean presumably had no idea that Joe had vetoed the fledgling romance. Even if she were having no luck with romance, Jean could at least find a husband for her closest friend. Jean set out to play the matchmaker. During the Christmas holidays in 1945–1946, Jean just happened to bring Ethel on a skiing trip to Canada. And Ethel just happened to spend hours skiing with the uncommunicative and terminally awkward twenty-year-old Bobby. Ethel and Bobby looked as if they could have been brother and sister. With his scrawny build, antennalike ears, great unruly mop of brown hair, and high-pitched voice, Bobby was hardly the beau of which the students at Manhattanville dreamed. Seventeen-year-old Ethel had a long, triangular face, widely set eyebrows, high forehead, large teeth, and a maladroit tomboyish quality. Bobby invited Ethel for a Harvard weekend, but when he met Ethel's older sister, Pat, he decided that the Skakel he was interested in was not named Ethel. Pat was not an adolescent prankster.

Ethel was totally taken with Bobby. It was endlessly humiliating to her that of all the women in the world, Bobby should be dating Pat. Ethel did not give up, and neither did her friend. Jean invited Ethel to come to Boston in the spring of 1946 to work on Jack's campaign. Ethel rang doorbells and passed out literature as fervently as anyone, spending as much time with Bobby as she could manage. Still, Bobby did not seem to think of Ethel as more than an amusing, sometimes annoying girl.

During Christmas Bobby invited Pat to spend the holidays at the Kennedys' home in Palm Beach. That was almost a declaration of intent, but Jean and Ethel plotted their own strategy. Jean invited Ethel to come as well, in yet another attempt to pry the romance apart. In the end, Bobby and Pat parted, not because of Ethel's overwhelming allure, but because Pat considered Bobby immature and too young. As Bobby rebounded, Ethel was there to catch him. By Ethel's junior year the two were said to be "serious." Jean, though, still had no one.

In January 1947, Eunice traveled to Washington with Jack and moved with her older brother into a three-story town house on 31st Street in Georgetown. This was the same quaint district of narrow streets and historic buildings where Kathleen had spent so many evenings with John White. The Kennedys brought with them their longtime housekeeper, Margaret Ambrose. Bill Sutton, one of Jack's campaign aides from Boston, lived in the house as well, working on Capitol Hill as Jack's assistant.

Eunice was not arriving in Washington to fill a mundane, interchangeable secretarial job or to write up social notes at the *Times-Herald* as Kathleen had done. Joe wanted more than that for *his* daughter, whose intelligence and ambition he often praised. "If that girl had been born with balls she would have been a hell of a politician," he said.

Joe had seen to it that Eunice would be one of the most prominent twenty-five-year-old women in the capital. A few months before, representatives of Attorney General Tom C. Clark had come to Joe to seek help in funding a government bureau to implement a series of programs recommended by a national conference on juvenile delinquency. Joe said that he would pay for the bureau with one condition: his daughter, Eunice, must be given a staff position. Thus, the first executive secretary in juvenile delinquency arrived at the Justice Department in a burst of publicity surpassing even the attention received by her older brother, who, after all, was merely another new member of the House. A picture of Eunice greeting the attorney general was in *Newsweek*. She appeared the very model of a socially committed woman of her times. At the *Times-Herald*, John White was back at his desk, among other duties writing the "Did You Happen to See—" column that Inga and Kathleen had once written. Early in 1947, he wrote an article about Eunice:

> She is a pretty girl with big blue eyes which sparkle as big blue eyes should. She also has mahogany-brown hair, a merry smile and quick, engaging ways. Very attractive . . . Eunice Mary Kennedy . . . is energetic and ambitious with a lot of her old man's ability. And she has that Irish enthusiasm and enjoyment of life. . . . She is serious about her work and conscious of its importance, but doesn't let it get her down. In fact, "it is fascinating," she says. Right now she finds there is hardly time enough to get through it all, but keeping busy-as-a-bee comes fairly naturally to a Kennedy.

Neither Eunice nor Jack seemed to have time or concern for keeping the house on 31st Street in order. The rooms sometimes looked like a fraternity house after a particularly riotous weekend. There were rugs heaped up in the corners, clothes strewn heedlessly on floors and chairs, women's underwear forgotten under the sofa pillows.

Washington is the most punctual of cities. Arriving for a dinner party, Joseph Alsop, the columnist, was startled to discover no Kennedy yet at home. That gave him ample time to survey the "complete disorder" of the living room, discovering the ancient leavings of a hamburger behind some books on the mantelpiece.

Jack didn't care about such matters, and neither did Eunice. He wore mismatched socks, rumpled pants, and ties spotted with food. She wore stockings with runs in them, unironed skirts, blouses with buttons undone, and disheveled hair. He had a weak stomach and subsisted on cream of tomato soup,

creamed chicken, and other bland food. She had a stomach that
was no better. He carried no money with him, sent all bills up
to the Kennedy office in New York, and was constantly hitting
his friends up for minor loans that he never repaid. Eunice was
in a perpetual state of emotional disarray, running late for
meetings, dictating letters and memos to her frenzied assistant,
full of such frantic urgency as if all life were on deadline.

Eunice was not one of those who believed that the profession of virtue is the same thing as its enactment. She brought
home troubled girls for dinner, not sociological case studies,
but adolescents she was trying to help. Sunday evenings Eunice often sat down with as many as fifteen or twenty delinquents from a girls' home. "We want you to be happy
children," she told them as they ate fine meals prepared by
their housekeeper. "Happy children become happy men and
women."

Jack was the member of Congress, but as their friend
Charles Bartlett observed, "Eunice was really more interested
in what she was doing than Jack was interested in what he was
doing. He was never fascinated by the House of Representatives. And she was working very hard." Jack tolerated Eunice
and her brigades of troubled girls, but he did not have his sister's visceral concern for the poor and underprivileged. When
he could manage it, he was elsewhere when Eunice filled their
house with delinquents. "It's fair to say that then I was more
concerned with social problems than Jack," Eunice admitted.
"He was challenged mentally and emotionally by it, but he
wasn't running around concerned with things such as housing
for the poor. His early years he was more of a searcher. He
wasn't totally engrossed in what he was doing."

Although most of Eunice's friends and classmates were already
married, she was in no rush to join them. Indeed, Kathleen was
more concerned about her sister's marital prospects than Eunice. The year before on a visit to New York, Kathleen had
told her about one wonderful possibility, Sargent "Sarge"
Shriver. Kathleen had discussed him at great length as early as
1935 when she was at the convent in Neuilly. He sounded almost too perfect, as if he had been groomed from birth to
marry a Kennedy woman. Sarge came from an old Maryland
Catholic family that had lost its money during the Depression.
He had spent the war years as a combat officer in the Navy,
not on PT boats as Jack had been but on destroyers and sub-

marines. At Yale he had played second base well enough to think about a professional career. As editor of the Yale *Daily News*, he had proudly presented his intellectual résumé, describing himself as "Christian, Aristotelian, Optimistic, and American." The postwar world was full of possibilities for a Christian Aristotelian Optimistic American, especially one who with his upper-class accent could sell himself or his ideas with all the unabashed fervor of a carnival huckster.

Sarge was unhappy with his current position as assistant to the editor of *Newsweek* and was looking to become the "right-hand man" to a prominent businessman. He told his friend Peter Hoguet of his aspirations. Hoguet, whose sister had gone to Noroton with Kathleen, thought immediately of Joe Kennedy. He was having dinner with Eunice and Kathleen in a few days at the St. Regis when their father would be in the hotel as well.

That evening Sarge just happened to drop into the St. Regis, his date on his arm. "My goodness, there he is, the most divine man over there," Kathleen whispered to Eunice. She had no idea that Sarge was here on a mission that had nothing to do with romance. "He's just right for you," she whispered into Eunice's ear as Sarge approached their table. Hoguet introduced Sarge to Eunice as "a fellow who would like to work for your father." She led him over to Joe, who looked him over and set up a breakfast appointment a few days later.

Eunice simply worshipped her father, and any man who could appreciate the values of her estimable father was a worthy man indeed. Sarge was six feet tall, handsome, with wry good humor and an intense, passionate interest in the world around him. "He was bubbling, bursting with energy, and very attractive," Eunice recalled.

A few days later over breakfast in his suite at the Waldorf-Astoria, Joe asked Sarge to evaluate Joe Jr.'s letters for possible publication. Sarge told him honestly that they were not worthy of publication. Instead of being upset, Joe immediately offered him a position as his representative at the Chicago Merchandise Mart, the enormous building complex he had recently purchased.

Sarge dated Eunice a few times before he headed out to the Midwest to begin working for her father. He had hardly settled into his new position when Joe asked him to go to Washington to help Eunice in organizing her office. Eunice was overwhelmed by the magnitude of her responsibility and the paucity of resources she had been given to do it. The soothing, enthusiastic hand of Sarge was the apparent answer.

Sarge's housemate in Washington, Walter Ridder, could tell that he was "smitten." Sarge was in a curious position, part employee, part friend, and part suitor. At the advanced age of thirty-one, Sarge knew that he had little to offer Eunice financially except for a rich old name. Eunice was an heiress and Sarge sensed that Eunice "wanted some assurance that whoever she married loved her for herself." Eunice was not so sure that she was romantically interested in Sarge, but she was not fickle in her demands. She worked with him all day calling out his name again and again—"Sarge . . . Sarge . . . Sarge . . ."—in a voice that was less a request than a command. She was so emotionally overwrought and had such a weak stomach that at meals she could hardly eat. She thought nothing of calling his apartment in the middle of the night, considering Sarge the best available cure for her insomnia.

"In those days it was almost pathetic the way Sarge hung around," recalled John White. "She would ignore him or kick him or whatever. He was patient and I suppose loving, but it was all a little embarrassing, the cruelly whimsical way she would treat him, like a little animal you know is going to come back no matter what you do."

Eunice was in no rush to marry. Her family life was all-encompassing, and she and her siblings seemed neither to need nor to want anyone else. Often when she and Jack were alone, they talked about "being so old and not married and how to change that, with Jack arguing more vigorously than I." Jack was not very impressed by Eunice's new suitor. Sarge was full of exhausting enthusiasms, and had a boyish earnestness that was anathema to Jack's intellectual and emotional detachment. Sarge's courtly respect for Eunice was proper for Jack's own sister, but he treated all women that way, hardly an attitude likely to make him a close friend of Jack Kennedy.

Eunice had learned to compartmentalize her life, to enclose her love for her father and brothers in the impregnable recesses of her soul, letting nothing they did affect her feelings. The same appeal that had brought Jack the women's vote was equally evident on a personal level. Jack was constantly bringing women back to the house. Some of them were pretty stenographers and secretaries, women with whom Eunice would not think to socialize. Others were postdebutantes and other socially prominent young women. Rich or poor, married or single, for Jack their primary virtue was their sexual availability, coupled with the willingness to be gone, with no attempts to ensnare him emotionally. One evening Jack went to the movies with his old friend, Rip Horton, and a gorgeous blonde from West Palm Beach. "Well, I want to shake this one," he told Horton back at the house. "She has ideas." The fair-haired woman was hardly out the door when another woman arrived. Horton went to bed assuming that this was Jack's woman for the night, but the next morning when he came down for breakfast, he discovered still another woman sitting at the table. "They were a dime a dozen," Horton recalled.

Eunice's father visited the house often. At fifty-eight, Joe was still his randy self, but he had become a largely intellectual voyeur, preoccupied with his sons' and daughters' dates and friends. Mary Pitcairn, one of Eunice's close friends in Washington, occasionally dated Jack. On one of his trips to Washington, Joe took Pitcairn out for dinner at the Carlton Hotel, where he asked her "a lot of personal questions— *extraordinarily* personal questions" and then confided in her about his relationship with Gloria Swanson. "He did something that I heard he did to everyone," she recalled. "After dinner he would take you home and kiss you goodnight as though he were a young so-and-so. One night I was visiting Eunice at the Cape and he came into my bedroom to kiss me goodnight! I was in my nightgown, ready for bed. Eunice was in her bedroom. We had an adjoining bath. The doors were open. He said, 'I've come to say goodnight,' and kissed me. It was so silly. I remember thinking, 'How embarrassing for Eunice!' But beyond that, nothing. Absolutely nothing."

Eunice was the host for many parties in the house on 31st Street. She and Jack liked to be around the youthfully energetic and those with the sheer glint of ambition in their eyes. They had an array of friends including two other freshman legislators, both of them conservative Republicans, Representative Richard Nixon and Senator Joseph McCarthy. The Wisconsin senator was a great favorite, whom Eunice was dating. McCarthy was a Catholic and a conservative. His fiercely anticommunist views were compatible with what the Sacred Heart nuns had taught the Kennedy sisters. They were seemingly compatible too with the positions Jack was taking in Congress.

The parties that Eunice and Jack gave were more fun than the stuffy affairs that filled most Washington evenings. Eunice was a unique hostess, at one gathering pouring a quart of milk into a goldfish bowl. "One night they had us doing charades," Waldrop recalled. "Eunice is quite funny and she was acting something out, patting her ass, and you were supposed to link that up with whatever word was involved. But I had to laugh at this prudish little Catholic girl putting on this raunchy performance. I wondered to myself if she had any idea what she was inviting people to think about. I don't think she did. I don't think she had a prayer of an idea." Eunice took impish delight in creating socially untenable situations to enliven Washington's painfully predictable dinners and cocktail parties. One evening during these Washington years, Jack arranged for Eunice to go out with Peter Lawford, a rising young Hollywood star. Jack had met the British-born actor in Hollywood at the end of the war. Lawford was an exquisite escort: famous, charming, with an appealing British accent. Peter was going around the country promoting his latest film, *The Red Danube*, which was about a Russian ballerina so terrified of being repatriated to her Communist native land that she commits suicide. Despite the fact that the film was not likely to be a hit in the USSR, Eunice marched her date to the Soviet Embassy for a cocktail party. "I never thought I'd get out of there alive," Peter recalled. "A couple of Russians came over to us with their remarks on the picture [and] I told Eunice that we'd better get out of there."

In late August 1947, Jack traveled to Ireland to be with Kathleen before setting out on a congressional junket to Europe. Kathleen was staying at Billy's family's castle in Lismore, a great walled structure that looked as if it still could harbor knights and ladies, not just Kathleen's sophisticated London friends. For Kathleen it was, as she wrote Lem, "the most perfect place" in the world, even more so now that Jack was here for a few days. As house guests, Kathleen had an eclectic collection of the socially and politically prominent, including Anthony Eden, Churchill's foreign minister; a former beau, Tony Rosslyn, now a member of Parliament; Hugh Fraser, another politician in the making; and Pamela Churchill, a beautiful divorcée who thought Jack looked "skinny, scrawny, actually Kathleen's kid brother. Not eligible, so to speak."

Jack's back was bothering him so much that he could not join the others playing golf. "I researched before I came over where the original Kennedys come from," he told the group.

"And it's not so far away, only about one hundred miles or so. And I'd like to go there."

These were Kathleen's ancestors too, but she was at heart an Anglophile and had no interest in celebrating her Irish roots. Pamela Churchill agreed to join Jack, and the two arrived back late in the evening. Jack was full of excitement. "We found the original Kennedys," he said enthusiastically. He had touched his humble Irish past with his own hands, and his family achievements suddenly seemed even more miraculous. Kathleen listened to her brother's tale with only mild interest. "Well, do they have a bathroom?" she asked, picturing her ancestors wallowing in deprivation.

"No, they did not have a bathroom," Jack said, though that was hardly the point. As they walked through the verdant Irish countryside, ambling along the Blackwater River, she talked about her life in England. Kathleen had taken a long-term lease on a three-story Georgian town house at 4 Smith Square. She had a cook and a housekeeper and had filled the house with antiques. On a prominent table sat a framed eight-by-ten picture of the eleven Kennedys marching happily forward, a picture taken just before the start of World War II.

Kathleen was tired of a society in which life itself seemed rationed. She burst forth onto gray old postwar London, the gay young widow, banishing the wartime gloom from her thoughts and her presence. She drew people to her, making the colors of life more vivid, more intense. She had an inexplicable, almost magical way about her that enchanted men, not simply youthful pursuers but prominent married men who adored simply being around her. Fifty-year-old Anthony Eden was positively smitten by Kathleen. He loved receiving letters written in her intimate, vivacious style that were almost like talking to her. "For then I can imagine that you are here," Eden wrote. "How I wish that you were, and I do believe that you would enjoy it too."

These upper-class English men and women did not endlessly analyze Kathleen's esprit, authoritatively attributing her joviality to a grief syndrome, or an attempt to get away from what they considered her dreadful father. They simply appreciated it and her, and realized how unique Kathleen was. "Gaiety, like honesty is a kind of social courage," wrote Angela Lambert. "It is not easy to be unfailingly charming, lively and original.

It requires energy and generosity always to make the effort to be on one's best form."

Kathleen soon grew tired of her set. She turned to a slightly older group to whom pleasure was an avocation and frivolous good times the one thing worth seriously pursuing. They were primarily married couples in their thirties. They had set out to recreate the pleasure-filled world that Kathleen had known as a debutante, traveling from house party to house party, fox hunting to horse racing, the Riviera to Scotland. They had a genius for diversion. The women were pretty and the men were debonair, and there were games to be played between men and women that were never out of season. It was a seductive world, and Kathleen was drawn into its sway, savoring its transient delights.

No one so epitomized this sophisticated hedonism as did thirty-seven-year-old Earl Peter Fitzwilliam. Evelyn Waugh called him "king dandy and scum." He was the reincarnation of an Edwardian rake, totally given up to personal pleasure. As Kathleen and Jack sat beside the Blackwater River, she told her older brother about the man with whom she had fallen in love and planned to marry. She had met Peter at the Commandos' Benevolent Fund Ball at the Dorchester Hotel the previous June. Kathleen had been the chairwoman of the ball, greeting guests including Princess Elizabeth and such honorees as Peter. During the war Captain Fitzwilliam had won a Distinguished Service Order. He had captained a torpedo boat mission that had burst through the German blockade to obtain desperately needed special ball bearings from Sweden.

Peter was a dashing figure, impossibly tall. He was still in his thirties. When he was tired, his handsome, refined features could suddenly look terribly old and jaded, the despairing looks of one who had danced every dance, played every game, wagered every bet, drunk every drink. Fitzwilliam appeared to Kathleen as the most debonair and dashing figure at the ball. Kathleen had lost weight since Billy's death. At twenty-seven she was at her most enchanting, at a moment appearing a girlish debutante, the next moment a sophisticated, stunning matron. She wore a pink gown set off with diamond clips, and all evening long Peter whirled Kathleen around the dance floor.

Peter's wife, Olive, was the president of the ball committee. Peter might have been expected to dance with her, but almost everyone at the ball knew the story of their lives together. Peter came from a family that before the war had been consid-

ered wealthier than the Cavendishes. They had estates in
England and Ireland, and at Wentworth a house that dwarfed
even Chatsworth. The 606-foot-long structure was said to be
the largest home in all Europe, an edifice so enormous that
guests were given wafers to crumble along the pathway leading to their bedrooms so they might find their way back for
dinner. Whereas Billy's home had an intimate quality stamped
with generations of individual taste, Wentworth Woodhouse
was not only grand but grandiose, an amalgam of styles, from
Baroque to Palladian, which loomed over the South Yorkshire
countryside like a monolith.

Other than his only son, Peter's father had cared primarily
for sport, from big-game safaris to polo to treasure hunting in
his four-thousand-ton liner. Peter had proven his father's son,
racing cars and horses and chasing women. During the early
1930s, Peter had dated eighteen-year-old Olive "Obby"
Plunkett, a blonde heiress. They seemed suited to each other,
not simply burning the candle at both ends, but running their
hands so close to the flames that they risked singeing themselves. There was no car too fast, no dare too extreme, no
challenge too mad. At a house party shortly before their wedding date in 1933, Obby rushed toward the dining room and
ran into a plate-glass door. She had sought the best plastic surgery available, but even with makeup the scars still ran across
her youthful countenance.

Peter married Obby, but he turned to other women and she
turned to drink. During the war Obby nursed her loneliness
with liquor. When Peter finally returned, she was wedded more
to a bottle than to him. Peter had excellent business instincts
and he developed a premier thoroughbred racing stable, turning
an avocation into an immensely profitable business. He won
the lucrative Coca-Cola concession for northern England, and
set out to live the same life of privilege as he had before the
war.

Peter was a dangerous man who often left unhappiness in
his wake. Almost from that first dance at the Commandos'
Ball, Kathleen was maddeningly in love with him, lost in her
emotion as she never imagined she could be. Surely, she had
loved Billy but it had been a sedate genteel love, not this erotic
passion that led her to visit Peter's house in London. Peter was
a man of willful indiscretion. Even he knew that this affair between a married British lord and the titled Catholic widow of
a war hero had to be discreet. They kept their public appear-

ances to proper lunches at the Ritz, dinners at Kathleen's new home, and parties where they both just happened to be.

Upper-class England is like a small town in which the idiosyncrasies of all its residents are known and richly commented upon behind their backs. There was not a person among Kathleen's acquaintances who did not know Peter's sorry reputation, not a friend who did not fear for her name and her happiness. "I liked Peter very much, he was so charming," said Andrew, Duke of Devonshire. "But if they had married there would have been a reaction." Her close friend, Jane Kenyon-Slaney Compton, was concerned not with what others might think but what Kathleen might feel. "You don't know him," Kathleen repeated again and again. "You don't know him."

Compton thought that she knew Peter only too well: "I think there would have been problems and I don't think she would have been happy with him." But Kathleen's friend could do nothing to stop her sexual and romantic obsession of this first affair of her life. Compton believed that Kathleen found Peter "like Joseph Kennedy himself—older, sophisticated, quite the rogue male. Perhaps in the last analysis those were the qualities required to make her fall deeply in love."

As Jack listened to Kathleen's story, he knew nothing about Peter's reputation. He heard only about this war hero, this charming, stellar gentleman who had completely mesmerized his sister. Jack told Lem Billings later that he was somewhat envious. Except possibly with Inga, he had never been passionately in love, and Kathleen made it sound like a wondrous spice without which life had little taste. He promised Kathleen he would keep the whole matter secret.

The Kennedys were a family with secrets within secrets. When Rose and Pat unexpectedly arrived at Lismore later in the month, Kathleen acted as if she had nary a thought of love and marriage on her mind. Rose spent time in Kathleen's new house in London, on several occasions visiting with Kathleen's former in-laws. No one who saw them together would have imagined that only three years before Rose had seen the Duke and Duchess of Devonshire as the enemy, bearers of an alien faith, a threat to the Kennedys' religion.

Jack collapsed in London. That had happened before, but on this occasion the physician, Dr. Daniel Davis, discovered a new and potentially fatal illness. Jack was suffering from Addison's disease, an incurable malady that involved a deficiency of the adrenal glands. The symptoms of the disease involved some of the problems he had been having for years with other illnesses. The disease made the skin look tan. That was the strange pigmentation blamed on wartime malaria that Jack had tried to cover up by frequent use of the sunlamp. The disease caused weight loss, and often a nervous condition, queasy stomach, and a disregard for food and eating. The patient was usually given hormone treatment, though a new, highly expensive synthetic compound, cortisone, had recently been developed that showed great promise in treating the debilitating disease.

It was a grim joke on the thirty-year-old member of Congress who had promised to bring a new youthful vigor to Washington. "That young American friend of yours, the brother of Lady Hartington, he hasn't got a year to live," the examining physician told Pamela Churchill bluntly.

Jack's medical record was already long enough for a whole ward of maladies. "He used to turn green at intervals, and I mean really pea soup green," recalled Alsop. "And I asked him why, and he told me that he was taking injections for something that he'd gotten in the war . . . and unless I'm very mistaken, he said that as a matter of fact, he had a kind of slow acting leukemia and that he did not expect to live more than ten years or so, but there was no use thinking about it and he was going to do the best he could and enjoy himself as much as he could in the time that was given him."

Jack was extremely ill. "He had leukemia at one point," Rose admitted in 1972, confirming a rumor that has been suggested for years. "I remember because there was one doctor that could cure or, or who had specialized in it, and we searched for him. They don't get over that [leukemia] very often."

Jack's diseases were yet another family secret that might destroy his image. No one held that secret closer or saw more clearly her brother's anguish than Eunice. She saw in his daily life a quiet heroism that the world did not see. She knew why his attendance record in the House was so abysmal. She saw his pain and understood why he pushed the dinner plates back half eaten. She saw the women who came at night who thought that his dark skin and lean body were signs of health, not its opposite. She saw that to her brother sex was both a diversion, his chosen opiate, and an assertion of life.

In the late winter of 1948, Kathleen lounged by the pool at the house in Palm Beach harboring her momentous secret. She had decided to marry Peter and nothing anyone was going to say would stop her, not the church, not her parents, not her friends, no one. Kathleen realized that Peter's divorce would be a nasty bit of business. In England, as in much of the United States, adultery was the one generally acceptable grounds for divorce, a category in which Peter and probably Obby both eminently belonged.

Kathleen knew that Peter wasn't about to trumpet his wife's infidelity to a world waiting for the latest scandal. Instead, he would be named as the guilty party, with some woman other than Kathleen listed as his partner in adultery. That would keep Kathleen's name out of the court papers. Peter's threat to disclose his wife's own conduct might keep her quiet, but inevitably Kathleen's name would be drawn into the whole sordid business. In a diminished Britain where the foibles of the upper class were becoming a staple of the daily press, Kathleen's love affair with Peter was bound to become public entertainment, the Kennedy family's first great public scandal.

Before she had flown to the United States, Kathleen had gone to talk to the Jesuit priest who had counseled her against marrying Billy. Then the man she was marrying was a bachelor, probably virginal, a man of the highest moral principles, sympathetic to Kathleen's dilemma as a Catholic. The man she was contemplating marrying now was a notorious roué, still married, father of a twelve-year-old daughter, adamantly opposed to bringing up his daughter or further children in the Catholic church. The Jesuit told Kathleen that she would again be cast out of the sacraments of the church, to live her life unsheltered by the faith. In its moral absolutism, the church had been unable to make a distinction between the two men, and Kathleen could not make that distinction either. As she saw it, the church had been wrong before. It was now twice wrong.

Kathleen had vowed that nothing would stop her from marrying Peter. Those weeks at Palm Beach she could not bring herself to talk to Rose and Joe about her plans. Week after week she amused herself in Florida, attending dinner parties, playing golf, and talking of everything but Peter.

As spring approached, Kathleen headed north to visit friends in Washington and New York, still clutching tightly onto her secret. There only to Jack could she talk of her intentions, not to Eunice, so much a child of the church and its mandates. Jack listened attentively to her plans, giving her what she so desperately sought, a sympathetic nonjudgmental hearing.

In New York City, Kathleen confided in her old friend, Charlotte McDonnell Harris. Charlotte had sensed some wild quality in her friend, untamed by all the ministrations of the nuns of the Sacred Heart. She was not surprised that Kathleen should fall in love with a man like Peter. But Charlotte realized that there had always been a self-protective shrewdness in Kathleen's choice of beaux. She was startled at the mindless, reckless way in which she was proceeding, as if the sheer illicitness of the affair gave her love a special flavor. "It was passion. It was hysterical. It was all 'I gotta do, I gotta go.' If she couldn't marry him, she was ready to run off with him. She just wasn't concerned about consequences."

Before returning to face her future in England, Kathleen had one last weekend with her parents at the grand reopening of the Greenbriar Hotel in White Sulphur Springs, West Virginia. The hotel was full of celebrities, prominent businesspeople, social reporters. All weekend long Kathleen anticipated the moment when she would tell her parents, when she was sure her father would explode in indignation.

On their last night at the Greenbriar, Kathleen told her parents of her marital plans. She had expected her father's opposition, but not Rose's merciless and terrifying judgment. Rose said that she would disown her daughter, never seeing her again. She would disinherit her as well, leaving her financially stripped. Beyond that, Rose was willing to pull the whole temple of the family down around her daughter. If it came to that, Rose would leave Joe or embarrass him publicly, bringing a terrible shame down on all the Kennedys, and a guilt on Kathleen that would taint the rest of her life.

Kathleen had thought that she was prepared for almost anything. As she rode northward to Washington the next day, she was shaken, reflecting on this mother she had not known before. In Washington she turned to John White's sister, Patsy, who had been so understanding when Billy had died. As Patsy listened to Kathleen's tale, she thought of her conversations with her after Billy's death. She realized that for the first time Kathleen was truly in love, "more fulfilled with Peter than in her short marriage to Billy."

Patsy understood what it meant to Kathleen to be cast out of the family, sent off into perpetual exile. "She never wanted to be separated from her family, even if she were living in England," Patsy Field recalled. "I never heard Kathleen criticize her father or mother or brothers or sisters. She was completely happy with them, happy being a Kennedy, happy with all of them."

For the first time there was a break in the family's solid front, not yet to the world but among themselves. Eunice could not abide the thought of her sister's marrying a divorced man outside the faith, while Jack sided with Kathleen. It was a volatile situation potentially creating what Alsop called "a perfectly hair-raising family row."

Eunice was equally passionate in her feelings, and desperately seeking someone else to blame for leading her sister off God's chosen path. "*You* made Kathleen leave the Catholic church!" she accused John White one evening at a party, her voice charged with unrelieved fury. "It's all your fault."

Kathleen turned to Patsy and John White for solace and support. John's feelings for Kathleen had mellowed into gentle platonic affection, but he was startled by the intensity of her passion, emotions of which he never dreamed she was capable. "As she talked of Fitzwilliam, the man sounded like the hero of *Out of Africa*, a professional Englishman, a devastatingly charming rogue," White said. "But I was overjoyed to see that she had finally been awakened. Rarely in life do you see someone so bubbling over with love, everything that love should be, every bit of it. Poor old Billy Hartington. But again he probably would have been blown away if she had felt that way about him. Very few people could stand that much love, the sheer blast of emotion."

Kathleen spent her last night in Washington at Patsy's house. The two women shared Patsy's king-size bed and talked most of the night away. Joe had come upon a legalistic solution: he would convince the Catholic church in England that Peter had not been baptized, and voila, in the eyes of the church he had never been married. It was silly and impossible, and showed, if nothing else, how much Joe loved Kathleen and how desperately he was searching for a solution that would satisfy his wife and daughter.

Eunice had her hand in a different solution, setting up a meeting the next day in New York City for Kathleen with Bishop Fulton Sheen. The bishop was one of the most charismatic, persuasive figures in the whole church. He would work Kathleen over emotionally and intellectually, confronting Kathleen with her Catholic upbringing, and a future without God or church.

"I just don't want to do it," Kathleen kept repeating. "I just don't want to do it."

"Then don't, honey," Patsy said. At two in the morning Kathleen called the Manhattan rectory and canceled her appointment.

As they talked on into the morning hours, Kathleen expressed how much she was looking forward to the weekend she and Peter would be spending on the French Riviera in May. There they would have peace and privacy, and she could share a few quiet days with the man she loved so passionately.

Rose was not about simply to allow her daughter to sail off into the dark night of life with Fitzwilliam, leaving both her church and her reputation behind her. All those years she and Joe had worked to create a family of shared values and common aspirations. She would not have her daughter deserting her family and her faith. Rose had made her own sacrifices that her willful daughter could barely understand, and without which Kathleen would have nothing of the life she had. Happiness? Rose sniffed her nose at the idea of human happiness when it conflicted with the dictates of the church and the strictures of society. Then happiness was nothing more than a euphemism for self-indulgence. Only four years ago Rose had been driven into the hospital by the sheer shame and embarrassment of Kathleen's marrying Billy, but this would be tenfold worse. The Kennedys were so esteemed, the scandal so juicy, that rumors of the affair had already even entered the walled confines of Manhattanville. "We all knew that Jean's sister was carrying on with someone," recalled Margaret Hutchinson, "and that gave us a lot of scandal to talk about. We all felt that what we called a holy runaround was going on."

Soon after Kathleen left on the *Queen Elizabeth* for England, Rose booked her own passage to England and arrived at the house on Smith Square to confront her daughter. As the housekeeper, Ilona Solymossy, overheard the conversation, Rose threatened Kathleen again with ostracism from the family, and disinheritance. Kathleen was not a child, but a twenty-eight-year-old widow. Yet she cowered at her mother's words like a naughty little girl. Hour after hour Rose raged at her daughter, her tongue lashing out at her, scarring Kathleen with her fury.

Kathleen cried and cried but she did not yield. She did not

yield in part because in opposing good and gentle Billy so adamantly, Rose had squandered much of her moral capital with Kathleen. Moreover, Rose could not talk to her daughter any longer. She could only lecture. She was a woman of such moral rigidity that she could not possibly suggest a sophisticated compromise, such as Kathleen's continuing her affair with Peter while pushing off the idea of marriage well into the future. After four days of a merciless, unyielding assault Rose left the house and Kathleen was as determined as ever to marry Fitzwilliam.

To Kathleen, her father was still a wondrously protective figure who had always been there for her emotionally, always ready to solve her problems. It so happened that Joe was to be in Paris the very weekend she and Peter planned to be at a villa in Cannes. Kathleen called her father, arranging for a luncheon in Paris on May 15, 1948. When she hung up the phone, Ilona noticed a sudden radiance about her, as if now everything would be fine.

Peter had swept Kathleen up into a life in which one approached pleasure with the same intensity that others pursued politics or business. He chartered a DeHavilland Dove to fly to southern France on Thursday. The couple would spend Friday on the Riviera, and then fly back the next morning for luncheon at the Ritz with Joe.

For Peter the unexpected was the expected. Kathleen loved the pace of life with her fiancé. On the morning of May 13 she was waiting for him, looking smashing in a navy-blue suit and string of pearls, with two big suitcases containing clothes for any occasion. She had jettisoned the formally cut suits and grandmotherly nightgowns of yesteryear for a wardrobe of tightly fitting gowns, a filmy negligee, a lacy garter belt, and a pink peignoir.

At Croydon Airport outside London, the pilot, Peter Townshend, told his two passengers that there was a squall over the Rhône Valley along their route. He said that he thought that they would be able to avoid the worst of the weather and make the trip without problem. In Paris Townshend landed the plane at Le Bourget, where he planned to stay for a half hour before continuing directly to Cannes. Peter called some of his friends from the French racing set, and he and Kathleen set off in a taxi for a leisurely, pleasurable lunch at Café de Paris.

At the airport, Townshend read the latest weather report, predicting a great thunderstorm over the Rhône at around five P.M. It was two o'clock, two-thirty, three o'clock and still his two passengers were not back. Townshend had flown for the RAF during the war. Then flying was a matter of life and death, not the indulgences of wealthy, irresponsible patrons. As each minute went by, he became more infuriated at the predicament he and his copilot were unnecessarily facing.

Suddenly, Kathleen and Peter showed up along with their luncheon guests, a gay crowd, full of the flush of a fine meal and jolly conversation. All commercial flights had been canceled. Townshend told Peter that he was not about to fly up into that menacing sky. Peter was a man who was used to getting his way, and he was not about to be grounded by a timid pilot. He was as charming as he was self-indulgent, and he finally talked Townshend into going ahead.

At Kathleen entered the plane, she doubtless would have liked to have sat next to Peter. To balance the weight, he sat in the front left seat of the ten-seat plane, and she in the back left-hand seat. For the first minutes, the plane flew through a calm sky. Then as they passed above Valence, the dark clouds of the thunderstorm rose before them like a black curtain. As they entered the storm, the currents of air tossed the plane up and down thousands of feet at a time. Kathleen sat alone, enveloped in the storm, held tightly by her seat belt. She had entered this plane trusting in Peter and their future together. Now she sat here yanked through the dark heavens. She had no sense of whether they were flying south or north, up or down. She was sitting a few feet and an eternity away from the man she loved. For endless minutes, the plane was yanked through this black abyss. Suddenly, the cloud bottomed out and they were no more than a thousand feet above a mountain ridge. Townshend tried desperately to pull out, but the starboard wing ripped off, sending the fuselage earthward.

Joe heard the news of the crash from a *Boston Globe* reporter early the next morning at the George V Hotel. He said that they must hope that there had been some mistake and it was not Kathleen at all. He traveled from Paris to Lyons, and from there along the Rhône River to the village of Privas, at the foot of the mountainside, and he went to the *mairie* where the four disfigured bodies lay in makeshift coffins. He asked them to open the coffin of the one they said was Kathleen, and when they opened it he asked them to close it again. That night he called Hyannis Port and he said how "beautiful" Kathleen looked, and how she lay there as if asleep in her stocking feet.

When Eunice first heard the news on the phone from one of Jack's assistants, she wished for a moment that the Lady Hartington who had died was not Kathleen at all, but Andrew Hartington's wife, Debo. Eunice looked at Jack, who lay on the sofa listening to a record of *Finian's Rainbow*, a popular musical that took place in a magical hidden land in Ireland. Jack cried when he heard the news, then after calling Rose who was in Hot Springs, Arkansas, secreted himself in his bedroom. That evening as Eunice and Jack prepared to join the rest of the family in Hyannis Port, they were full of frenetic, manic energy as if by the sheer rush of activity they could outrun the shadows of memory that haunted them.

Kathleen had been plucked out of the sky and cast against the earth. Billings said that Rose regarded the death "as a matter of God pointing his finger at Kathleen and saying *no!*" For the family's reputation, the story had to be cleaned up for public viewing. As far as the Kennedys were concerned, Peter was twice dead, his life severed forever from Kathleen. The *Boston Post* reported that Kathleen had stayed in England only to be near her dead husband, a noble widow shrouded eternally in black. Under the headline "CHANCE INVITE SENDS KENNEDY GIRL TO DEATH," the New York *Daily News* story ended embarrassing speculation over Peter by saying that Kathleen had chanced on Lord Fitzwilliam in Paris and had merely hitched a ride on his plane.

Rose stayed in Hyannis Port with the rest of the family and let Joe handle the delicate matter of the burial. Joe agreed that Kathleen would be buried in the land she loved in the mossy, shaded Cavendish family burial grounds of the small picturesque church at Edensor, down the road from Chatsworth.

On May 20, about two hundred of Kathleen's close friends traveled with the casket from London. They had loved her in life, but understanding their loss, they loved her more in death. "No American, man or woman, who has ever settled in England was so much loved as she, and no American ever loved England more," an anonymous friend wrote to the *Times* of London. "Strangely enough it was those in London who are most disenchanted with this day and age who perhaps derived the greatest comfort and light from her enchanting personality."

Kathleen's casket was covered with flowers including a

wreath and a note from Winston Churchill. Around the grave stood men and women who as youths had frequented the house at Prince's Gate that Kathleen had often filled with gaiety.

Joe was the only Kennedy there that day at the funeral. As they lowered his daughter's body into the ground, he stood a man apart. He turned and walked away, not even acknowledging the duke and duchess or the other mourners, not even paying the priest for his services.

It was left to the duchess to decide what words to place on the gravestone. Kathleen had left no descendants. She had held no political office. Her name had not been stamped on business or the arts. She had founded no noble institutions. Her family had endowed no foundation to carry on her name. She had died in a plane crash, flying off for an adulterous weekend.

The duchess's chosen words were chiseled into a gravestone and placed in the cemetery. Decades later the Anglican priest at Edensor often looked out his window at the cemetery. And sometimes, especially in the summer, he saw people walking through the graveyard searching for Kathleen's grave, then standing there reading the words on the stone:

JOY SHE GAVE JOY SHE HAS FOUND

16

Strangers in Paradise

*I*n the spring of 1949, Joe traveled to the St. Coletta School for Exceptional Children in Jefferson, Wisconsin. Joe had learned about St. Coletta's through his friend, Archbishop Richard Cushing. The Catholic institution run by the Sisters of St. Francis of Assisi had opened in 1904 as "St. Coletta Institute for Backward Youth." Over the years St. Coletta's had developed into a boarding school and residence for over three hundred of those with mental retardation. Those only mildly affected left after finishing their schooling, but others stayed on, working on the large farm, or if more severely disadvantaged, simply institutionalized.

Jefferson had no decent hotels, and visitors usually stayed in Serra Home, a guest house overseen by the nuns. Joe could rest assured that out here in this town an hour west of Milwaukee, almost no one had ever heard of the Kennedys. He was taken to Alverno House, a building set off in a grove of trees about a mile from the main campus. Alverno House was an institution for adults who required lifelong care. It was here on these grounds that Joe oversaw construction of a private house.

One day in the early summer of 1949 two nuns arrived at Craig House and took Rosemary away on the train, arriving at her new home on the first of July. "They say Rosemary was very uncontrollable when she first got here," said Sister Margaret Ann, the nun who is primarily responsible for Rosemary's care. "She had been sent out here alone from an institution."

In her first years at St. Coletta's Rosemary was generally kept apart in her little house, watched over by several nuns. For Joe it was the end of his problem. As much as Joe and Rose had attempted to exorcise Rosemary from the family history in letters and conversation, her uncertain plight was a pall

433

that hung over all the Kennedys' endeavors. The secret of Rosemary had been a major impediment in the rise of his sons to positions of power and prestige. The story of the botched lobotomy could have had a chilling effect on the Kennedys' public image. His sons and daughters would soon be marrying into prestigious families, where the onus of Rosemary's condition could prove an embarrassment. "I am still very grateful for your help," Joe wrote Sister Anastasia Mueller, the superintendent at St. Coletta's in 1958. "After all, the solution of Rosemary's problem has been a major factor in the ability of all the Kennedys to go about their life's work and to try to·do it as well as they can."

Soon after Rosemary was sent to St. Coletta's, Rose visited Rosemary. She recoiled at what she saw and what her daughter had become and hardly ever traveled to Wisconsin again for two decades. Rose saw that the past was alive in Rosemary, bursts of memory, suddenly appearing and disappearing, like lightning flashing across a troubled sky. Joe had hoped to quell her violent rage, but that the surgeon's knives had not totally excised, and she still could suddenly erupt in inchoate rage. When Rose arrived, her daughter turned away from her mother, wanting nothing to do with this woman who stood before her so beseechingly. Rosemary seemed to know that this was her mother, and the nuns believed that Rosemary blamed Rose for abandoning her. "In the back of my mind is the idea that Rosemary had had this surgery and her mother didn't show up," said Sister Margaret Ann. "And that she was taking it out on her mother. The way I understand it is that Mrs. Kennedy would come out and would go back very upset. I wasn't here when Mrs. Kennedy was here, but they said that Rosemary never accepted her."

In June of 1950, twenty-four-year-old Bobby married twenty-two-year-old Ethel in a spectacular and opulent wedding given by the Skakels in Greenwich, Connecticut. Bobby had a small man's need to prove himself a match for his brawnier brothers and friends, even on an occasion such as this. The evening before at the bachelor dinner, the Kennedy and Skakel men wreaked such damage on the august precincts of the Harvard Club that Joe was presented with a special bill. But on the appointed morning all was sedate, and Ethel looked the spectacular bride in her fitted gown with Pointe Venise lace and pearls, and her full-length veil. A crowd formed outside St.

Mary's Roman Catholic Church on Greenwich Avenue, watching guests enter a church filled with peonies, lilies, and dogwoods. The reception was a lavish one, even by the exalted standards of the wealthy Greenwich community.

Joe danced with his new daughter-in-law, welcoming her into the Kennedy clan, spinning her around the dance floor. Ethel could have been his own daughter: deeply religious; blissfully ignorant of such traditional wifely skills as cooking, sewing, and housekeeping; treating money like water from a spigot that never ran dry; and totally devoted to her Bobby. After their Hawaii honeymoon, the newlyweds settled into Charlottesville, Virginia, where Bobby was attending law school.

The family got together again in October of 1950 for another rite of passage, the funeral of Rose's father. Eunice, Jean, and Pat sat dressed in black from their shoes to their veils in the Cathedral of the Holy Cross. At their Grandfather Fitzgerald's funeral, the mourners came by the thousands to mark the old man's passing. The governor of Massachusetts was there, the mayor of Boston, the secretary of labor, a United States senator, and former Mayor James Curley, who so long ago had snatched the laurels of power from Fitzgerald's head.

Jack and Bobby sat next to their three sisters, along with a multitude of other Fitzgeralds and Kennedys. From this vast assemblage there were only two notable absences, Josie, who had not felt physically up to attending her husband's funeral, and Rose, who was on a trip to Paris. In the past weeks Rose had known that her eighty-seven-year-old father was weakening, but she let little stand in the way of her constant sojourns. The *Boston Post* reported that a grief-stricken Rose had tearfully told her family over the phone that "she probably wouldn't arrive in Boston in time for the funeral." And thus as Joe had missed P.J.'s death and funeral, so Rose missed Fitzgerald's, his death haunting her. "In spite of his age," she said years later, "it was impossible to conceive of life without him."

With daily doses of the new drug cortisone, Jack's health had stabilized and he was already contemplating running for a higher office. Bobby was headed up the same path as his brother once he completed his law degree. As for Teddy, he was a first-year student at Harvard, a gregarious football player, the inheritor of his grandfather's gift of political blarney and backslapping camaraderie.

Life was moving on, but the three Kennedy sisters appeared

reluctant to march down the one road clearly open to them toward an altar visible in the distance. Both twenty-nine-year-old
Eunice and twenty-six-year-old Pat were older than their new
sister-in-law, and twenty-two-year-old Jean was the same age.
Not only was Ethel married but soon afterwards she was pregnant. Most of their contemporaries were either married or contemplating wedlock, but the transcendent power of the family
pulled them inward and made the idea of marriage seem not a
joining of families but a separation. There was a seven-year
difference between Eunice and Jean, and growing up they had
been sent to different schools. Only now as adults were they
discovering each other and realizing the commonality of their
experiences. "We had such a very good time with each other,"
Jean reflected. "My family were my best friends, and I was
very close to Bobby and Teddy. I mean, we all had such a
good time that we didn't really want to marry."

Upon graduation from Manhattanville in 1949, Jean wanted
to travel in Europe with a woman friend. "My father was very
wary of that," Jean recalled. "But my mother pushed very hard
for it. She always said that when you're young, you should do
everything before you're saddled with a lot of responsibility.
She encouraged us to stay, to see museums and such. That was
her great strength for me, her belief in her children that we
should answer life's challenges, that we should always be
ready to go out and do it, to have an adventure."

Eunice was the most daring of the three women and seemingly the least likely to marry. In her position in Washington,
she had become deeply intrigued not simply by juvenile delinquents, but by women criminals. Early in 1950 Eunice headed
down to the Federal Penitentiary for Women in Alderson, West
Virginia, to observe the institution for two months, living on
the prison grounds. She had initially hoped to arrive at the
prison pretending to be an inmate, but the authorities were
afraid that she would be considered a stool pigeon.

These robbers, counterfeiters, drug addicts, jewel thieves,
traitors, murderers, and spies treated Eunice not as a slumming
heiress, but as a straightforward, straight-talking woman who
wished them well. She didn't flinch at their language, and
matched them vulgarity for vulgarity. "Miss Kennedy, you talk
tougher than me," one inmate told her. The nuns had warned
against "particular friendships" with other women, but it didn't
bother her in the least that lesbianism was rampant. "Lots of
sex among the girls," she wrote in her notebook. "Girls give

each other bracelets or put their initials on arms or leg with a razor." She was not easily conned by the women either. She knew that when the women asked to paint their rooms, they were probably more interested in obtaining paint remover that they drank as alcohol, along with volatile mixtures of fermented garbage and orange peels.

Eunice took her hastily scribbled notes and mailed them to New York to James Landis, her father's associate, where a secretary typed them out as best she could. Jean was living in New York and Eunice told Landis that if anything was illegible, Jean would be able to puzzle it out. Eunice's secret agenda was, as she wrote Landis, to write "a good article for the *Reader's Digest.*"

Eunice spent her days and evenings with the women prisoners in the cottages where they lived, each with her own room. The tougher, the more incorrigible, the more infamous the prisoner, the more fascinating she was to Eunice. She was as comfortable talking to Alderson's most famous prisoner, Tokyo Rose, the collaborator to whom no job was now too menial, as she was to the queen of the Washington numbers racket. She wasn't even frightened by the violent woman who three times had escaped from the federal penitentiary. To Eunice the woman was just a "fantastic case."

It was a strange, inexplicable world where there was as much misfortune as evil, as much resignation as tragedy. Beauty sometimes occurred in the most unexpected places. One morning Eunice heard a prisoner playing a Mozart sonata on the piano. When the woman wouldn't even tell her what her crime had been, Eunice scribbled in her notebook: "See her more and help her get job."

"I didn't know quite what I was doing at the beginning," Eunice said. "But the prisoners were wonderful. It's the same old story you get always in life. I see that people are so much smarter than people think they are."

Sarge drove down to West Virginia to visit Eunice. "I used to say that I'm the only guy I know who went and courted a woman at a federal penitentiary," said Sarge. One day on the softball field, Eunice talked to one young attractive redheaded player who was totally involved with the intramural game, laughing and cheering as if this were the World Series. The young woman was not a prisoner at all but a member of the United World Brethren, a Protestant sect in which many young members volunteered a period of service. The nuns of the Sacred Heart had taught Eunice that she should make some kind of contribution to society. This idea of tithing one's life, giving up a year or two, was new and exciting to her. "Never in my life have I seen a more inspiring example of Christian service," Eunice told the Congress of Catholic Women in Boston a few months later, reflecting back on the three Brethren volunteers at the prison. "They were superb examples of what can be done by the average citizen to help those whose distorted and shattered lives have brought them within the confines of a reformatory."

Eunice was a woman of spectacularly good intentions. In May 1950 at the Conference for Youth of the League of Catholic Women in New York City, she attempted to start an organization in which young Catholic women would work with juvenile delinquents. Eunice never settled down long enough to begin to accomplish her noble purposes, like the never-written *Reader's Digest* article and so many of her other glorious ideas and intentions. She had the metabolism of a hummingbird. She dropped her idea on the Catholic women, had an organizational meeting, and then soon was off again. She lived with Bobby and Ethel in Charlottesville for a while. Then she was off to Chicago where Jean was working for a short time in public relations at the Merchandise Mart. Pat was spending a good deal of time as well in the midwestern city. Eunice decided that she would work as a social worker at the House of the Good Shepherd and do graduate study in social work at the University of Chicago.

Eunice knew only a few people in Chicago including Sarge, who was back helping to manage the Merchandise Mart, and her cousin, Mary Lou Connelly. Soon after she arrived, Eunice descended like a whirlwind on her more sedate cousin. Mary Lou had recently married Matt McCarthy, and Eunice wanted to know all about married life. Mary Lou was not completely happy with her celebrated relatives; Joe had her betrothed investigated by private detectives, bestowing on her intended the same honor as his own daughters' possible husbands.

"Do you like *him*?" Eunice asked.

"Are you out of your mind?" Mary Lou exclaimed.

"I mean are you in love?" Eunice asked.

"I more than like him or I wouldn't have married him," Mary Lou said forcefully.

"I do *like* marriage," Eunice said, as if she were talking about an exotic dish. "It's very different."

"There's someone on the horizon," Mary Lou asserted.

"Oh, well, maybe," Eunice said.

Eunice had work to do in Chicago. She was a cheerleader of altruism. She convinced her pregnant cousin to volunteer with her at the House of the Good Shepherd working with so-called "wayward women" and teenagers by teaching an art course. Occasionally Eunice would come swooping in from the Ambassador East Hotel where she was staying, back from New York or Washington, full of praise for her cousin. "Everybody is just raving about it, Mary Lou," Eunice said. "And I'm so excited, I've told Daddy."

"Well, I'm thrilled Uncle Joe is thrilled," said Mary Lou, now obviously pregnant. "But until I see a Kennedy beside me in this building, I don't want you guys getting all the credit. Now, by gosh, you get in here and help me."

And with that Eunice swooped off again. "Jack needs me," she responded. "I've got to go."

On her next visit to Chicago, Eunice discovered that Mary Lou was no longer at the House of the Good Shepherd. "Mary Lou, why aren't you there?" Eunice asked accusingly over the phone.

"Didn't they tell you?" Mary Lou replied incredulously. "The nuns told me I was in danger. I'm seven months pregnant, Eunice. Some of those girls are criminally insane and there were some razor blades missing."

"What?" Eunice said in disbelief, then suddenly changed the subject. "Well don't worry, Mary Lou, *we'll* find something else."

Although Eunice was too much of a gadfly for Mary Lou's taste, Eunice did spend months as a social worker at the House of the Good Shepherd. "I learned a lot," Eunice recalled. "They were all sexually abused. The ones that I got along with very well were pregnant from their own fathers. I had a feeling for them, and I helped them."

While Eunice was setting her frantic pace in Chicago, Jean and Pat were both traveling from place to place, excitement to excitement, trying to find a role that suited them. In their franticness, the three Kennedy women developed an extraordinary casualness toward belongings and to those outside the sacred confines of the family. One evening in 1950, Eunice had left an eighteen-thousand-dollar necklace with 240 diamonds and twenty-four sapphires in her hotel suite at the Ambassador East in Chicago, where it was stolen. That was so typical that it was hardly commented upon. Two years later in January 1952, Jean parked her Cadillac in front of Jack's house in Georgetown and walked in to visit her older brother. A group of teenagers passed by and noticed some jewels sitting in the car. The youths took what they thought to be costume jewelry, not even imagining that they were running off with thirty-three thousand dollars' worth of exquisite gems.

Mary Jo Gargan considered her older niece, Pat, the model of what she wanted to be. "I just started going to college," Gargan recalled. "Pat said you'll have a much better time if you don't drink. Pat was my idol. She was a beautiful girl and just had everything as far as I was concerned."

Pat moved to southern California to work as a production assistant in television. Of the three Kennedy sisters, Pat was the most likely to win acceptance in Hollywood. She did not have the beauty to compare to the never-ending parade of stars and starlets, but she had undeniable glamour as she swept into a room, as tall as most of the men, greeting others with the quick wit and short attention span that were family trademarks. Pat, like her father and older brother, was fascinated by Hollywood. She was a Kennedy woman, and it would not do for her to work in the morally dubious enterprises of the film industry. Instead, she went to work as a production assistant on Kate Smith's radio program; the rotund singer was the epitome of patriotism and good old homespun American values. Pat later took up a similar position on Father Peyton's *Family Rosary Crusade*, the program that made "the family that prays together stays together" a household phrase.

Pat didn't spend all her time promoting patriotic and religious programming. The young Kennedy women had Rolodexes in their heads of all the possible eligible men. There was hardly a more celebrated bachelor on both sides of the Atlantic than Peter Lawford. Eunice had been the first Kennedy sister to meet Peter, and she had introduced him to Pat. Nothing came of that meeting, nor again in London at a party in 1949. Peter's image of suave congeniality made him the heartthrob of thousands of women. Peter was dating another socially prominent American woman, Sharman Douglas, the wealthy daughter of the American ambassador to the Court of

St. James's. Peter paid no more than nodding attention to Pat. Months later Pat chanced upon Peter one day in Los Angeles at the NBC Studios. He invited her to go to a party with him. They discovered that there were not even a few watts of electricity between them, and they separated even before the evening was out.

Eunice had yet another potential suitor to pass on to her younger sister, and that was Senator Joseph P. McCarthy in Washington. The Wisconsin senator had been a regular guest in Eunice and Jack's house in Georgetown. McCarthy was forever trying out his ideas on friends and casual acquaintances, the wary and the unwary, tinkering with his rhetoric until he was ready to roll it out into public view, speaking passionately about the cancer of communism eating away at America. Joe and much of the church leadership supported McCarthy, while Jack affected a studied neutrality, and a few politicians had begun to speak out opposing the Wisconsin senator as a vicious demagogue who was destroying not communism but liberty.

Pat and her sisters had all largely accepted the political catechism of the Catholic hierarchy and were sympathetic to McCarthy. In 1950 the forty-one-year-old junior senator from Wisconsin was dating Pat. McCarthy was hardly as handsome as Jack, or Peter, but he was full of a certain raw wit and charm when he had not had too much to drink. Moreover, he was admired by Pat's father. Joe invited McCarthy to the Cape and to Palm Beach, and appeared to be delighted that his daughter was attracted to a man with such a brilliant future.

In the fall of 1951, Eunice and Jean took a lengthy trip to the Middle East and Europe. Unlike their brothers' worldly sojourns, they did not travel with assignments from an American newspaper, or spend their days familiarizing themselves with a new generation of leaders in anticipation of their own political careers. Like their mother, Eunice and Jean were fascinated with royalty, with noble families and ancient bloodlines, a heritage passed on generation after generation, the great families intermarrying. In Athens, they were delighted beyond measure to be invited to meet Queen Alexandria, in whose veins flowed the German blood of her grandfather, Kaiser Wilhelm, and whose husband, King Paul, had Danish blood.

Jean and Eunice wore hats and black gloves, and chatted amiably with the lady-in-waiting before being shown into the queen's sitting room. Rose had taught her daughters well, and they were almost as adept as their mother in the social patter of a royal audience. "We came away convinced that we had met one of the greatest women in today's world," Eunice wrote in the *Boston Post*.

After their European trip, Jean decided to join Eunice in her social work at the House of the Good Shepherd. Her elder sister had become a liaison officer with the juvenile court, working with the same kind of troubled adolescent girls as she had in Washington. Jean had been with Eunice only a couple of weeks when one of their charges attempted to escape, bolting from an automobile. For Eunice it was all in a day's work and she held the young woman down. This was not Jean's idea of social work, and she decided that if she wanted to do good work in the world, it would not involve wrestling with female criminals.

Jean finally found something that mattered to her, and it was her brother's career. When Jack decided he was going to run for the Senate against Henry Cabot Lodge in 1952, the sisters dropped everything. Jack knew how crucial his mother and sisters might be in his underdog campaign. At the beginning of the campaign he asked Eunice for "photographs of yourself with children, possibly in connection with your work with the House of the Good Shepherd in Chicago." In May he wrote his mother at the Greenbriar in West Virginia reminding her to be there later in the month for teas in Worcester and Springfield. "I've written to Pat and Eunice about them, and am counting on three of you being there," he admonished.

Jean was the quietest and the least adept of the sisters at the life of a political woman, but she was the first to journey to Massachusetts to begin working for Jack. Jack, like all the Kennedys, had a Manichaean view of the world, of who could be trusted and who could not. He told his youngest sister to get a list of everyone who volunteered. "I don't want anyone saying, at a later date, that they worked in the campaign, when possibly, they did not," he alerted Jean.

"At first, I went up and stayed in the office—index cards, things like that," recalled Jean, who worked on the campaign for nine months. "We sort of got involved gradually."

For Jean it was endlessly difficult, being polite to people she didn't know, always having to be wary, alert, running, always running. "You never meet anyone you can really talk to—you meet people very superficially and constantly. After four or five months you get into the routine, but it is never easy."

Jack set his own sisters on pedestals placed to the side of the main stage of life. As his campaign manager, he did not even consider choosing the most obvious candidate: the articulate, energetic, politically astute Eunice. Instead, he named twenty-six-year-old Bobby, an inarticulate neophyte whose most obvious virtue was his gender.

Bobby proved to be a determined champion of his brother's political career, fixated completely on Jack's election. He sent the three Kennedy women and their mother out on the campaign trail. Even Ethel campaigned on occasion ("I'm crazy about Jack, and I'm only an in-law"). She had already given birth on July 4, 1951, to the first Kennedy woman of the next generation, Kathleen Hartington, named after Kick. During the campaign Ethel gave birth to the first Kennedy man of the new generation, Joseph Patrick, who became known as Joe II, though he was the third Joseph in the family line. The only Kennedy missing was Ted, who was serving in Europe in the Army. The previous spring he had been thrown out of Harvard when he had a friend take his Spanish exam for him. He considered one of the rare benefits of life in the military the fact that he had lost fifteen pounds, but other than that he had found the voyage on the troop ship *Langfitt* to Europe less than edifying. His sense of humor remained intact, and he wrote his parents that when he had the misfortune of being one of the relatively few soldiers chosen for KP duty, he had contemplated jumping ship in Norfolk. "However, upon considering my welcome back in New York by my family . . . I concluded that to make the crossing now was the only thing left to do."

Senator Henry Cabot Lodge Jr., the patrician Republican candidate, found himself outspent, outnumbered, and outgunned, campaigning against a veritable onslaught of Kennedys. Jack was the Kennedy who was running for office, but it was the whole family, especially the women, who provided a dramatic new element in the campaign. Rose was the genteel matriarch whom the pope had recently named a papal countess, a legendary and distant figure who descended on the campaign like a royal visitor. For one of Jack's early campaign appearances in Quincy the campaign ran an ad in the *Patriot-Ledger* in which Rose took precedence over her candidate son.

Reception To—
Mrs. Joseph P. Kennedy
and
Congressman John F. Kennedy
SUNDAY, JUNE 1ST, 1952
MASONIC TEMPLE
QUINCY
3 to 5 P.M.
All South Shore Ladies Invited

With Rose attending there was no need to indulge in the sordid minutiae of politics, charges and countercharges, rhetoric and promises. She went from rally to rally, tea to tea, an exemplary presence. Only once in the campaign did that perfect veneer of civility and distance ever drop from her face. She was speaking to a rally in Worcester at Pemberton Square. She had a natural politician's gift for extemporaneous speech, but she did not trust herself to speak off the cuff, and she read from a prepared speech. "Certainly I can appreciate what is happening to the mothers of the boys in Korea—I who lost one son. . . ." She stumbled on for a few more words before breaking down into tears and walking off the platform.

When Jack appeared one day in the North End he had been swooned over by young women the way the bobby-soxers attacked Frank Sinatra. Jack had an almost incandescent sexual appeal that could be translated into the hard currency of votes. *Cosmopolitan* noted that few politicians "have been kissed, hugged and generally mauled by their female constituents to the extent sustained by John F. Kennedy." His back was acting up and he was on crutches during much of the campaign, but he still projected this irresistibly virile image.

Rose went around the state lecturing on such matters as "her visit to Paris," hardly a subject intended to educate the voters. The women of New Bedford and other towns didn't care. They sat quietly listening to Rose discuss marvelous places where they would probably never go. As for Jean, she did not like to speak publicly as a surrogate for Jack, but Eunice and Pat were both formidable campaigners. Pat was content merely to relate the epic story of her illustrious big brother, but Eunice gave a political stump speech dealing with issues in as rigorous a manner as Jack ever did.

One evening the three Kennedy women hurried along

School Street, past city hall, dressed in neat shirtwaists and skirts, looking like three secretaries heading home after a day in front of the typewriter. On a stoop sat a group of young men, the sort who might whistle at an attractive woman or call out a compliment. "There go the Kennedy sisters," one young man said reverentially. Then they stood up, took off their hats, and bowed toward Jean, Pat, and Eunice. "We are all one hundred per cent with your brother for the Senate," one of them yelled.

Eunice adored public life. Pat's striking good looks and patina of glamour were enough to get her by on the political circuit. When they were not working in the campaign office, Pat and Eunice talked to groups large and small, both alone and together. They were so young and personable that it seemed almost unthinkable not to vote for Jack. They didn't simply lecture these groups of women, but presented them with "work kits" of campaign material. As the weeks went by, they helped develop an extraordinary network of women working for their brother's election.

Either Rose or one of her daughters was present at the thirty-three teas held for women voters throughout the state. These were not rude rallies but elegantly appointed receptions with lace tablecloths and candelabra, creating an image that Polly Fitzgerald, the organizer, said was "as if it were an exclusive party in someone's estate." The turnouts were unprecedented, a thousand women in Brockton standing in the sweltering July heat to greet Rose, Eunice, Jean, and Bobby; two thousand greeting Rose, Pat, and Jack at the Hotel Kimball in Springfield; a thousand women to meet Jack, Eunice, and Pat in Salem; seventeen hundred women in Fitchburg where Rose, Eunice, and Pat heard Jack call upon women to be the "watchdogs of government."

Jack and his advisors were not about to listen to the columnist who wrote that Jack "better let go of his 'tea' parties and get on with the 'rough and sassy' politics more adept to men." Kennedy's campaign was based more on the women's vote than any other element, a realistic appraisal of politics in the Bay State. In postwar America women had become the largest of all voting blocs; Massachusetts had the highest percentage of voting-age women in the nation, 52.6 percent. Win the women and you win the race. Jack understood, but when Lodge turned his Brahmin gaze on Massachusetts voters he saw everything but women; in September as the race tightened, he polled Boston voters, Irish voters, French voters, Italian voters, and Jewish voters, but he did not poll women.

The Kennedys worked fervently for the women's vote. On October 4, more than two hundred volunteers gathered at the Parker House in Boston. This was a crucial organizational meeting, and as such, the campaign workers, many of them women, were addressed not by Rose or her daughters or by any other woman, but solely by men: Jack, Bobby, and two other top campaign officials. One of the volunteers at the meeting was Edward C. Berube, a Falls River bus driver. "He gave the pitch on what he was running for and how he wanted his campaign run," Berube recalled. "Of course, his theme was to hit the woman vote. Of course, he indicated this to me when I met him . . . that he was going to come out for the women, that he figured the woman was the one that was going to put him in. And he wanted coffee hours and tea hours and arranging coffee hours in homes."

The women left that evening to go back to their cities and towns and organize forty-five thousand other women to open up their homes on the morning of October 15 for "Coffee with the Kennedys." At eleven that morning women across the state watched Jack, Rose, Pat, and Eunice on WNAC-TV. Jack was as telegenic as any politician in America. Rose, Pat, and Eunice were all spectacularly adept at presenting an irresistible compelling image of family and faith to tens of thousands of women voters. The women called in questions about socialized medicine, federal scholarships, the whole gamut of issues, and Jack answered with detail and often with wit. But those answers were not what made Jack's dramatic rise in the polls. "Maybe you don't know it, but politics in Massachusetts have gone social—*we mean high society!*" reported one Massachusetts newspaper. "The Kennedy family is principally responsible for this politico-social revolution—*teas, we mean.* . . . Mrs. Kennedy and her equally charming daughters appear to be well on their way toward electing John F. Kennedy to the United States Senate."

Although General Dwight Eisenhower decisively defeated the Democrat Adlai Stevenson for the presidency, in Massachusetts Jack won by 68,753 votes.

As Rose had said so many years ago, the Kennedys were like a nation unto themselves, with their own private language and customs. They invited friends into their lives, but there was always a distance between them and others, even if their friends did not realize it. Except for Bobby, the young Kennedys found it difficult to marry. For Eunice and Jack, the two eldest, the time had come when it would be almost embarrassing to remain single much longer.

Sarge had chased after Eunice for more than a decade. Finally, early in 1953, she relented and agreed to marry him. She was thirty-one years old. If she were ever to marry and raise a family, the time was now. As it was, Sarge's attentions had become something of a joke among the Kennedy entourage. It was a minor party game guessing what hoop Eunice would have poor Sarge jumping through next. Sarge had a courtier's solicitousness, toward both Eunice and her father, and he jumped and jumped some more. Joe not only approved of thirty-seven-year-old Sarge, but he actively promoted Eunice's marriage to his business lieutenant.

For Rose and Joe their daughter's marriage was to be a great public event, celebrating not simply a wedding, but the family celebrity and power. Ethel's family had set a high standard, but that was virtually an elopement in comparison with Eunice's affair. Jack gave a reception for his favorite sister in Washington inviting the crème de la crème of political power, including the new vice president, Richard Nixon, and Senator Joe McCarthy.

The Kennedys' official press release for the May wedding at St. Patrick's Cathedral called it "one of the most important and colorful weddings ever held in America." Cardinal Spellman officiated assisted by three bishops, four monsignors, nine priests, and an apostolic blessing in absentia from the pope. Rose helped to direct the decorating of St. Patrick's Cathedral, placing a multitude of tall white candles and great sprays of white flowers throughout the immense church. Everything was white, an advertisement of purity: Eunice's Dior gown of white mousselline de soir, her bouquet of orchids and lilies of the valley, the bridesmaids in gowns of white satin. The seventeen hundred guests included senators, mayors, Supreme Court justices, industrialists, socialites, a list that *The Boston Globe* called "a directory of Who's Who in the nation."

At the reception held in the starlight roof room, the guests sat down to dinner and later danced. The wedding cake was so tall that Eunice had to stand on a chair to cut the first piece. Eunice told the guests, "I found a man who is as much like my father as possible." Although the Shrivers were a distinguished old family, there was no question this evening but that Sarge was marrying into the Kennedy family. As the newlyweds waltzed on the shiny dance floor, the early edition of *The Boston Globe* featured on the front page a wedding photo of Eunice and her father, a photo with eerie similarities to the photograph of Rose and her father that had appeared on the front page on her wedding day.

It was an exquisite, resolutely decorous evening, almost until the very end. "Somebody decided that in honor of the Shrivers, everyone should sing 'Maryland, My Maryland,' " recalled Red Fay. "That was fine until the Kennedys started singing 'Marilyn, My Marilyn,' in honor of Marilyn Monroe, and the Shrivers were appalled."

After their month-long honeymoon, the Shrivers settled into a splendid duplex apartment overlooking Lake Michigan and began their married life in Chicago. They were a stunning couple. Sarge was a man of wide intellectual and aesthetic interest, with a taste for abstract art; he was a collector of beautiful things, from paintings to pottery to ideas. Eunice shared her family's indifference to art but the two were both deeply religious Catholics who believed that to do well in life, one must also do good. They were both collectors of people, and their friends were as eclectic and interesting a group as was to be found in Chicago.

The Shrivers' new friends learned that Eunice had her idiosyncrasies. Eunice and Sarge gave wonderful parties, full of repartee and gaiety, though she did like to go to bed early. One mirthful soiree, the guests still had not left at midnight. "A new game!" Eunice shouted, directing everyone to form a conga line. "Close your eyes and follow the leader!" Eunice led the dancers through the dining room, past the great windows with their panoramic views of Lake Michigan, then through the living room and out into the hall, an enormous serpentine. Eunice led the party onto the elevator, murmuring a quick "thank-you" and retreating before the door slammed shut.

Eunice's marriage was not the only Kennedy wedding in 1953 billed as "one of the most important and colorful weddings ever held in America." Jack had decided to marry too. At the age of thirty-five, Jack had all the attributes essential for political success in America in the 1950s except one item: a wife.

In Eisenhower's America an unmarried woman in her thirties was considered a spurned spinster, a bachelor not quite right, or at least lacking a sense of responsibility. And thus the junior senator for Massachusetts decided it was time to get married.

Jack's friends were forever seeking to match him up with one woman or another. One evening in May of 1951, Charles Bartlett, the Washington correspondent for the Chattanooga *Times* and a Yale man, arranged a dinner party for Jack to meet Jacqueline "Jackie" Bouvier at the Bartletts' Georgetown home. Jack abhorred the stilted dinners of official Washington, but an evening at Bartlett's house was different: intriguing conversation, party games, and a stunning young woman as his companion. Even at the age of twenty-one, there was a strange dichotomy to Jackie that was as inviting as it was occasionally unsettling. She had a gaminelike demeanor, at times almost childlike in her queries, and then suddenly out of this wispy voice would come a literary or cultural allusion of the utmost sophistication, and an almost dangerous wit. She was not sexy like Inga or Gene Tierney, the actress who was another of Jack's conquests, but she had a sweet sensuality of her own. She was tall and lithe like Pat, with wide-set dark eyes that set off her exquisite ivory skin. Jack was attracted enough to walk out with her into the Washington night, only to find one of her other admirers camped out in the backseat of her car.

The Bouviers, unlike the Kennedys, had felt no stigma from their Catholicism; Jackie had grown up on estates in Newport and Southampton perfectly comfortable with her social position. Her father, John "Black Jack" Bouvier III, was a member of the New York Stock Exchange. He was a man of inordinate charm, a legendary womanizer who made more conquests in the bedroom than on Wall Street, a classic bon vivant of the roaring twenties, brought down by the great Depression. Jackie adored her father and his seemingly chivalrous, dangerous charm. Her mother, Janet, was a woman with twenty-twenty eyesight for trust funds, inheritances, and property. She gave her daughter an advanced degree in social calculation. She had divorced Bouvier when Jackie was only a little girl, and had married Hugh Auchincloss, a tweedy retiring gentleman with a good name and a fortune.

In the 1930s and 1940s when Jackie was growing up, divorce was uncommon, especially in a Catholic family, and that fact alone set her apart. Jackie had the psychological distancing that was common among divorced children, always shielding her emotions. "We were a gang of girls at Farmington," remembered Sally Roche Higgins, who went to school with Jackie. "The powerful and the simpering, and then there were the outsiders like Jackie. She was so shy, so insecure, removed from everyone and everything, interested primarily in her horse."

Jack didn't begin dating Jackie at all seriously until the following January when the senator-elect took her to Eisenhower's inaugural ball. As their relationship grew more serious, Jackie was supposed to fly with Jack to New York. That afternoon she was in Middleburg, Virginia, riding horses, while Jack fumed at National Airport. In his senate office, Evelyn Lincoln knew that the cardinal rule in dealing with Jack was not to keep him waiting. She found it extraordinary that this woman should dare to be so late.

Jackie finally sauntered into the office, looking fresh and relaxed. "Where's Jack?" she asked, as if she expected him to come popping out of his inner office.

"He's at the airport waiting for *you*," Lincoln said, her loyalties perfectly apparent.

"Oh," Jackie said, in a voice that was a perfect wedding of innocence and steel.

Jackie had a position as the inquiring photographer at the *Times-Herald*. Waldrop was still the same curmudgeonly self as he had been when Kathleen and Inga had worked for him, with his eye as much for a well-turned ankle as for a finely honed phrase. "Now listen to me," he remembered telling her. "I hear you're running around with Kennedy."

"I'm seeing Jack," Jackie replied, in that enigmatic whisper of a voice that was her signature.

"I want to tell you something. He's older than you and he's smarter than you and he's been around and half a dozen women have had their shot at him, so you watch yourself."

"Yes sir." Jackie then turned and left the office.

"The next thing I knew I got an invitation to the wedding," Waldrop recalled. "She was a clever little girl. She didn't want to spend the rest of her life being humble because Black Jack had blown it. And who can blame her?"

Evelyn Lincoln, Jack's executive secretary, spent time every day answering phone calls from women seeking to get through to the senator. From actresses to secretaries to socialites, Lin-

coln found many of these women almost shameless in their aggressiveness. She had learned how to shield Jack from an un-
wanted or no-longer-wanted admirer. "The women chased
him," Lincoln recalled. "I had seen nothing like it in my whole
life. Half my telephone calls were women." Since the engagement announcement Lincoln had noticed no diminution in the
number of female phone calls.

Lincoln's sense of it was that on their wedding day, Jack and
Jackie were not in love. "I think old Joe had a lot to do with
their marriage," Lincoln said. "I think he persuaded her. He
thought that a candidate for President had to have a wife.
There was no love there. That I'm sure."

Jack was rather cynical about the prospects of married life.
He told Fay that he was "both too young and too old for all
this." He wrote Fay that "after the breakup with the bad and
the beautiful," mentioning one of his other women, he was
"getting married this fall. This means the end of a promising
political career as it has been based up to now almost completely on the old sex appeal."

Jackie could hardly afford to be as jaded as her betrothed.
Marriage would almost inevitably be more a source of fulfillment to her than it would be to her husband-to-be. As she contemplated the man she was about to marry, the duality of her
personality was perfectly evident. In her feelings toward Jack,
she seemed to be giving both her emotions and her calculations
full play. She was not a woman of overt passion, but she could
talk about Jack with girlish enthusiasm, in a voice alive with
affection. She also could stand back from him and the other
Kennedys and consider the merits of marrying the most eligible bachelor in Washington as if she were thinking of purchasing an expensive painting of uncertain value.

When Jackie met Joe during a weekend at Palm Beach, she
was immediately taken by Jack's father. She appreciated him
and savored his personality. "You're all black and white, Mr.
Grandpa," she told him later. "You have no nuances." Rose
wasn't there that weekend, and Rose's relationship with her future daughter-in-law began inauspiciously even before they
met. Rose thought that the charming thank-you note signed
"Jackie" was from one of Jack's male friends; after all, Jackie
was one of her son's nicknames. The more she heard about
Jackie, however, the more she thought that she might be right
for her eldest son. She was Catholic, and given the kinds of

women Jack had been dating that was a relief and an enormous plus. She was young, a proper age to raise a big family. She was from a socially prominent family. Another plus. And she was not only well educated but properly so. She had gone to Miss Porter's School in Farmington, Connecticut, an exclusive private secular academy. She had attended fashionable Vassar College for two years, then had studied at the Sorbonne in Paris for a year, and later at George Washington University in Washington, D.C.

Jackie had a sense of feminine style far different from the three sporty Kennedy sisters. On her first visit to Hyannis Port she *dressed* for dinner, entering the room in a sophisticated outfit that would have been appropriate at a New York supper club, not the Kennedys' home-style dinner table. "I remember she was so sweet to me," Jackie recalled. "It was my first weekend in the Cape. I had sort of a dress to wear to dinner—I was more dressed up than his sisters, and Jack teased me about it, in an affectionate way, but said something like, 'Where do you think you're going?' She said, 'Oh don't be mean, dear, she looks lovely,' or something like that. Anyway, I liked her enormously. I saw that this woman did everything to put one at one's ease."

Rose treated Jackie with cloying affection, but the two women had little in common except their devotion to Jack. Both women fancied themselves interested in the arts, but the moment they began talking it was obvious they had totally different viewpoints. In 1951 Jackie had won *Vogue*'s Prix de Paris contest in part by writing an essay naming Sergei Diaghilev, Charles Baudelaire, and Oscar Wilde as the artistic figures she wished she could have known. Rose's father had banned Wilde's *Salomé* in Boston, and to devout Catholics Wilde and Baudelaire were pied pipers of sin, neither to be read nor discussed. Rose wanted to appreciate an uplifting piece of theater or a poem, she didn't want to hear or see her most cherished ideas challenged or attacked.

Jackie arrived in Hyannis Port to go through an almost merciless hazing, the Kennedys' rites of passage. "They were like carbonated water and other families might be flat," Jackie reflected. "They were talking about so many things with so much enthusiasm or they'd play games—they had so much interest in life. At dinner or around the table on a weekend with everybody telling something from someplace else, it was so stimulating." The three Kennedy women would have found it difficult accepting anyone as their beloved brother's bride but at least someone like Ethel, a tomboyish, perennially pregnant earth mother, who gave no quarter on the tennis court or in the dinner-table conversation, and was already pregnant with the third Kennedy of the next generation. That was the model for a sister-in-law, not this Jackie Bouvier whom they dubbed "the Deb," mimicked her childlike voice, which they thought more appropriate for a geisha than their brother's wife, and led her on to the turf for a football game where she could be blocked into oblivion. Jackie eventually broke her ankle. The game stopped long enough to cart Jackie off the field, and that was the end of her short-lived football career. "She wasn't as fast afterwards," recalled Richard Clasby, who was there that day.

Jackie didn't seem to appreciate the fraternity-house atmosphere at Hyannis Port where the Kennedy women matched their brothers in put-downs, athletic competitions, party games. "My sisters are direct, energetic types and she [Jackie] is more sensitive," Jack said later. "You might even call her fey. She's a more indirect sort."

Jackie's mother had dealt with her father's monumental indiscretions by obtaining a divorce. In the Kennedys, Jackie was observing a family that lived on an emotional scale far beyond that of her stepfather's family, or anything else she had seen in life. These Kennedys were the most generous and philanthropic of people and the most niggardly and selfish. They were the most outgoing and gregarious and the most withdrawn and insular. They were the most spiritual and yet full of the most worldly cynicism. In the Kennedys these did not seem like contradictions, but integrated on some high plane that only they could understand.

In the high Catholic circles in which the Kennedys traveled, Joe was neither ostracized nor barely tolerated but embraced. He sat on the board of Notre Dame, the premier Catholic university in America, and frequently invited its president, Rev. John J. Cavanaugh, to his homes. Father Cavanaugh was a sophisticated churchman of the modern age. He didn't consider it amiss to have on his board not simply a celebrated adulterer but a man who in the priest's opinion was "not in the usual sense 'religious.' " That made Joe's behavior understandable, since the priest thought that "if you don't believe that there's something sacred about your fellow man, about adultery, let's say, if there is no sanctity to marriage, what is adultery?"

* * *

For their engagement party, Jack decided that a scavenger hunt was in order, hardly Jackie's idea of a good time. It was not just an ordinary scavenger hunt but one in which the various Kennedys outdid one another in their ingenuity. Pat was supposed to bring back "something big." So she rushed over to Hyannis and drove off with a bus while the driver was in the station. Bobby and Joe Gargan had to display "a show of courage." So Joe ran up to a policeman patrolling downtown Hyannis, whisked his hat off his head, jumped into Bobby's car, and the two of them zoomed away. By the time Pat, Bobby, and the other participants returned to the Kennedy house, there was an irate welcoming crowd including a busless bus driver, a hatless cop, and several other fuming police.

Those weeks before the wedding, Jack's sisters tried to outdo each other in Kennedyesque antics, as if to set themselves even more apart from their future sister-in-law. Jackie's style would have been to skew her enemies with a word or two, remarks of such coy calculation that it would be impossible to tell whether she was naïve or deeply nasty. That summer of 1953, however, Jackie was only a fiancée, and with her future mother-in-law she carefully set out the parameters of her own turf. At sixty-three, Rose was a woman of compulsively regular habits, the most important being the sacrosanct hour of meals. Jackie liked to sleep late, and she particularly seemed to like to sleep late when she was at Hyannis Port, arriving downstairs sweetly demure and innocent well after mealtime.

Rose and her daughters and sons were not psychologically insightful. They did not look into themselves, and they were openly disdainful of lives of deep introspection. Jackie was different. She was a young woman who at times fell into brooding self-analysis, and was capable of subtle analysis and insight. She had deep perceptions about Rose and her life as a woman. "I always thought if she'd let herself go when Mr. Kennedy was there—and Jack and all the brothers," said Jackie. "I think she was trying too much to keep up with everything. Whenever she was relaxed and not trying to keep up with everything, she has this wit and this mischief, she's like a little girl and she says some quite irreverent things. It's so disarming and beguiling. It's the upbringing. I mean you can see those pictures of her mother with the whale bone and the high collar—you're brought up like that and you don't reveal yourself. I mean to reveal yourself is difficult and almost dangerous for people like that. I'd say that Jack didn't want to reveal himself at all. Rose would be terrified to do it. Occasionally they do manage to get in an unprepared question and she can answer anything—very deeply. I think it must have been difficult for her to be married to such an extremely strong man . . . whose life was like a roller coaster zooming, accelerating, going up and down. To be doing this, having nine children and having them all grow up and doing all these things, it almost took her breath away."

Jackie was not entering her marriage as some mousy naif, a Catholic convent maiden who had lived her twenty-four years with her head bowed. She had heard all about Jack's sexual exploits. She had seen in the diminished figure of Rose Kennedy where such a life might lead. A few weeks before her marriage she talked to a friend and asked her: "How can you live with a husband who is bound to be unfaithful but whom one loves?" Four decades later the friend recalled the intimate conversation. "Jackie was a very vulnerable young girl," the woman reflected.

Jackie could see that Rose had sacrificed so much for the idea of family that she had mortgaged the value of her life on the lives of her children. Rose had sent her daughters off to obtain the Sacred Heart education that she had considered a destroyer of her own broader aspirations. Now Rose went to Jackie and sought to prepare her to live the same kind of married life that she had lived for almost four decades with Joe, to accept the onslaught of rumors and gossip as the price of public life married to a Kennedy.

"I warned them [Jackie and Ethel] in the beginning," Rose said. "There would be rumors. There would be letters, anonymous letters. There'd be all sorts of stories. That was part of the political spectrum. I tried to explain to them as soon as they were thinking of getting married. I told them both. I didn't tell my daughters. They grew up with it. It was my daughters-in-law I warned. They were in a complete new atmosphere. They had never been touched by politics.

"Jackie didn't want to have reporters at the wedding. Her mother was so sensitive to having publicity of any kind. She thought it was demeaning and vulgar. Mr. Kennedy said in our case there'll have to be reporters at the wedding because he was a public figure."

By their actions Rose and her daughters were making it clear to Jackie and her mother that to their minds Jack was not marrying into the social elite of Newport and Southampton;

Jackie was marrying into the Kennedys. When Rose went to meet Mrs. Auchincloss, she dressed for social combat in an exquisite blue silk dress and hat. Jack felt that Mrs. Auchincloss had "a tendency . . . to think I am not good enough for her daughter," and he had his own statement to make. "My mother asked Mrs. Kennedy to come over to Newport," Jackie recalled. "Jack was thirty-six at the time and he was grown up and he was a Senator. And his mother was coming over to have lunch with my mother, and we were going to the beach. We were sort of sitting in the backseat like two bad children. Mrs. Kennedy was all dressed up. She had on a beautiful, light blue silk dress and a big hat, and Bailey's Beach was terribly dressy then anyway. Jack had on some undershirt and a pair of bedroom slippers, so she was rather mortified, anyway it was, I'm sure, one of his least favorite days, the two mothers sitting there talking about the wedding. So we went swimming. I came out of the water early. It was time to go up for lunch and Mrs. Kennedy stood on the path, calling to her son in the water. It was just like the little ones when they know their mothers are calling. Then she or I started down to get him and he started coming up saying, 'Yes, Mother.'"

There was an irresistible quality to the romance chronicled from its beginnings in the pages of *Life*, the immensely popular picture magazine. Jack and Jackie seemed as wedded to the camera as to each other. The cover photo that July showed the two of them sailing in the waters of Hyannis Port, breathlessly attractive and casual, with toothy smiles and windblown hair, adventurous and gay. Inside the magazine one photo showed Jackie gazing at "photographs of Kennedys and of royalty," the two categories hardly distinguishable from each other.

For the September wedding the Kennedys traveled to Newport like a great feudal family, with retainers, servants, and jesters. It was nothing as piddling as a romance that was being solemnized here but a dynastic marriage. Just before the wedding dinner Joe took Jack's old friend, Senator George Smathers, aside and asked him to be sure to show up the Bouvier clan: "Now you're going to have to speak for the groom. I want you to be funny, to make Jack look good. I don't want the Bouviers to be outshining us."

The wedding guests at St. Mary's Church were equally prestigious as those who had attended Eunice's wedding. As Jackie walked down the aisle, her face seemed to glow with happiness and expectation, showing not a sign of her dismay that her beloved father was not there to give her away. Black Jack had girded himself with so much liquor that he was still back at the Viking Hotel, with a bottle of whiskey as his primary companion. Outside the church Jackie threw her bouquet into a crowd of single young women. Pat was taller and more agile than most of the others, and she reached out and grabbed the flowers, signaling to the world that her marriage would be next.

Jackie and Jack had Archbishop Cushing of Boston officiating, assisted by several other ranking priests, and an apostolic blessing from Pope Pius XII. Nonetheless, their wedding was hardly imbued with that nearly medieval sense of religiosity that had marked the Shrivers' nuptials with its cardinal and multitude of priests. After the ceremony Jack whispered to Fay: "I couldn't help feeling that Archbishop Cushing considered himself the key figure in this ceremony. There is a man I'd hate to follow on the podium."

The newlyweds had hardly arrived in Acapulco when Jack wrote a lengthy letter to Evelyn Lincoln instructing her on myriad political and personal matters. After a few days alone on their Mexican honeymoon, the newlyweds flew to Los Angeles, where for a week they secreted themselves in the Beverly Hills mansion of Marion Davies. There they were watched over by the former film star's employee, Ingo Dauth. The newlyweds insisted that Dauth call them by their first names, and Jack spent hours reading books from Davies's library. Afterwards, both Jack and Jackie penned personal notes to Dauth. For Jack the time was so precious that he said that he would "never forget our week together" and implored Dauth: "Let's keep it our secret!" Jackie sent her own note thanking her "for being so wonderful to us."

These had been idyllic romantic days alone together, but by the time the couple drove up to San Francisco to spend a few days with Red Fay and his bride, Anita, there was another Jack Kennedy on view. In Jack's emotionally compartmentalized life, Red was his prankster court jester, to whom Jack played the sardonic, fun-loving man-about-town. On this stage there was no room for Jackie, and it was here that the young bride received her first major marital lesson. "The pressures of public life . . . too often intruded on the kind of honeymoon any young bride anticipates," Red reflected. It was not public life that was intruding but Jack's private preoccupations. He had

had quite enough of honeymoon bliss, even supposedly suggesting to Jackie that she return to the East Coast by herself. Jackie was not Rose Kennedy, and she stayed in California, visiting Marin County with Anita while Jack and Red went to a 49ers football game and visited Stanford and sundry other places before the newlyweds flew back home together.

The newlyweds did not have a home yet. During the first weeks of their marriage Jackie spent her weekdays alone in the house in Hyannis Port while Jack remained in Washington. Jackie eventually moved down to the capital, living for a short time at Merrywood, her family estate, and then in a rented home at 3321 Dent Place in Georgetown.

When Eunice had shared a house with Jack, they had lived like two bachelors, tossing their clothes in the corners, nursing their weak stomachs over hurried dinners, running from engagement to engagement. The new Mrs. Kennedy set out to impart to Jack a sense of style and manners, and an appreciation for what she considered a more civilized life.

For her first dinner party, Jackie invited ten or twelve guests including Senator and Mrs. John Sherman Cooper, Bobby and Ethel, but most important and most critical, her own mother. Jackie, by her own admission, "was not sure I had it all together" and if she did not, Mrs. Auchincloss was only too delighted to point it out. Jackie was a natural hostess, with a flair and conviviality among people she knew, and the evening proceeded with ease and grace. The dinner was perfect. The service was perfect. Even the background music was perfect. Finally, however, Jackie's mother noticed a gaucherie of the first order, a faux pas so grievous that she interrupted the dinner to tell her daughter.

"Jackie, isn't the record player broken?" she said, an accusation more than a question.

"Oh, no, Mommy," Jackie replied sweetly. "It's just Fred Astaire tap dancing."

Jackie had home-cooked meals delivered to Jack in his Senate office for lunch, and she set out to transform his haphazard postpreppie clothing into an elegant wardrobe appropriate for a United States Senator. Even Rose was impressed, though she attributed it as much to Jackie's sister as to her own daughter-in-law. "Jackie contributed a lot which is natural because I think Lee's first husband was rather well groomed all the time. I think that had an influence too."

Jackie's sisters-in-law were initially less than enchanted with this elegant exotic who had entered the sacred precincts of the family. "She would switch to French in their presence and converse solely to one or two intimates," recalled Kerry McCarthy, Rose's niece. "Her selling and trading in of carefully chosen wedding gifts irked many who heard about it. 'Why didn't she just have "please send cash" engraved on the invitations to the wedding,' some would say."

In this first year of marriage, among all the Senate wives, it would have been hard to find another woman more adoring, more single-mindedly devoted to her husband's well-being than twenty-four-year-old Jackie. When she sat in the gallery listening to Jack speak on the Senate floor, she called it one of the most exciting moments in her life. "The more I hear Jack talk about such complex problems the more I feel like a complete moron," she told one reporter. She realized that she knew little about politics, and she set out to rectify that by enrolling at the Georgetown University Foreign Service School, only a few blocks from her home.

Neither Jackie nor Jack had much liking for the tedious rituals of Washington social life, the mammoth cocktail parties and the dinners where political posturing took precedence over conversation, and the scent of deal-making was the richest aroma. "Jack would be traveling a lot so we just liked to stay home, and there were a couple of houses that you'd go to for dinner or else you'd have . . . close friends over rather informally," she recalled. "You know, you work hard all day, and then you like to be with a few [friends]. . . . At least that was the way Jack operated and it's the way I liked to live too."

Jackie's notable lack of athleticism was duly noted and commented upon by her sisters-in-law and other family members. "She didn't play tennis, football or golf and of course the rest of us did those things," Rose recalled. "Then suddenly one day she brought this poem she had written about Jack, and of course nobody in the family had ever written a poem. So we all began to sit up. Lem Billings said, 'Gosh, this gal has something that nobody else has.' "

Jackie often played the fluttering gamine incapable of hardly anything more than signing her name to occasional checks, but occasionally she dropped that feminine façade. The Kennedys loved to play party games, especially "Categories," a game of intellectual trivia. If the "category" was literature, a player would name a subgroup, modern Italian literature, say, or medieval literature, and then each contestant would have to name an author starting first with the letter A, and working their way through the alphabet. "Jackie was phenomenal at this," recalled Father Cavanaugh. "I would play to beat her and I'd put down theologians and every kind of thing I could think of, and she would roll me out of there like nobody's business!"

On one occasion, Jack invited a group of diplomats from the Spanish embassy over to his Georgetown house. Jackie had very undiplomatically beaten at Categories everyone else in the living room four or five straight times. Between games Jack managed to take his wife aside in the kitchen. "Gosh, Jackie, you can't afford to do this to your husband when he is in public like this. It is not good to do that sort of thing."

Jackie turned and looked at her husband with those enormous innocent eyes. "Why, Jack!" she said, "I thought all of the Kennedys liked competition."

Jackie had hardly settled into married life when Jack's back began acting up, and he was in constant, debilitating pain. Jackie had married what she thought was a vibrantly youthful man, and she found herself with an invalid on crutches. By the summer of 1954, even Jack's will was no longer enough, and he met with specialists from Lahey Clinic. The only hope to restore his back was a complex operation on his spinal discs. For a man in stellar condition, the operation would have been dangerous enough, but for a patient with Addison's disease, there was no better than a fifty-fifty chance of survival. Jack had weathered worse odds, and after consultations with his father told the doctors to go ahead.

Jackie's sense of life had not been tempered by a series of tragedies and misfortunes. It was as if she had been handed the life of a woman a generation her senior. In this time of crisis, however, she saw her father-in-law's strength and grew closer to Joe. No matter how deep his despair, Joe was always there for Jack. "It was very difficult for all of us, especially for Jackie who was a new bride," recalled Rose. "His father kept encouraging Jack though Joe was heartbroken at different times. There again he was with him. He went to the doctors. He made the decisions or gave him the advice or he decided what to do or whether he would go. I was not consulted because I didn't know enough of all the circumstances."

Jack was operated upon at the New York Hospital for Special Surgery on October 21, 1954. He developed a urinary tract infection and was put on the hospital's critical list. Joe called his son's Boston secretary, Grace Burke, and told her: "The only thing that will save him now is prayer."

Jack lay there barely alive. Lem Billings could decipher his friend's hidden emotional language the way no one else could, and he sensed that Jack was almost gone, not his life, but his spirit. Jackie was there, however, fanning whatever coals of vitality remained, feeding him, playing with him, reading poems, bringing him silly toys and silly talk and silly friends.

In Washington the rumor was that he was dying, and Jackie and Joe joined in a gentle conspiracy to hide from the world how terribly sick he was. Jackie had a superb sense of public manners, and she wrote a handwritten letter to Senator Lyndon Johnson, the new majority leader. In three graceful pages, she managed to flatter Johnson, subtly ingratiate herself with the Texas politician, and suggest to him that Jack was "feeling better now."

Jackie was quickly learning about a perverse political world, where one man's tragedy is another man's opportunity. Johnson could smell death in the air, and the day after Jackie's letter arrived, Johnson called Joe. "How is Jack?" Johnson asked.

"Getting along very well now," Joe said, though death's door was still ajar. "In spite of all the rumors around there."

"I got a sweet letter from Jackie," Johnson said. "I thought that in the interest of putting a stop to these things maybe wisdom would indicate that somebody say something."

"He has neither of the things he is supposed to have," Joe replied, attuned to Johnson's careful probing. "He hasn't cancer; he hasn't Parkinson's disease. I think a lot of these things started with the wish fathering the thought. They are already talking about his successor in Massachusetts. There is nothing to that. He is better—much better—now. I think if *you* wanted to, you could talk with him on the telephone."

"I would be the last one that would want to take away an ounce of his strength," Johnson said, his words pumped with sincerity. "Tell him for me how much we all love him."

"You have got a tough job on your hands," Joe said, flattering the most powerful politician in the Senate. "But I can tell you this—at least you have got one boy that not only has a brain but has got real affection for you."

Jackie was with her husband in the hospital room early in December as the historic censure motion against Joe McCarthy came to a vote on the Senate floor. In Massachusetts, Jack was feeling pressure both from the heavily Catholic pro-McCarthy groups, and from liberal organizations and individuals fervently opposed to the Wisconsin senator. It was a politician's worst nightmare: a vote that might signal an end to a political career. It was also a vote that separated the principled from the expedient, the courageous from the merely shrewd. Jack was the shrewdest of them all, for he managed not to vote at all, pleading illness. Jack was sick but he could have paired his vote with another absentee senator who was voting the other way. He did not do so. For several years the rank odor of expediency hung over him, which liberal Democrats could sniff the moment he appeared over the horizon.

Jackie knew little of the Kennedys' long-term relationship with McCarthy, the money that Joe had given him, the times that Eunice and Pat had dated him. She knew nothing of political reality in Massachusetts. Jackie went with her husband when he was flown down by private plane to Palm Beach to recuperate. She was with him too when he was flown back to New York in February 1955 for a second operation, and returned with him again to Florida.

Jack was an emaciated stick figure, lying on his stomach, his back swathed in bandages. "It's nothing serious," Eunice said when she saw him. "It's nothing serious, just Jackie's cooking." That was Eunice's humor, the way she handled her own illnesses, a part of the Kennedys' private language. Jackie was the one who often changed the dressing, exposing an ugly, oozing, open wound in his back. And she was the one there day after day, week after week.

One of the visitors was Oleg Cassini, the European-born dress designer, who was as well known as a Don Juan as he was a couturier. He flattered a woman with his interest in her, and he devoted endless hours talking with Jackie. If Cassini had been a vindictive man, he surely would have fancied the seduction of Jackie under the eyes of her invalid husband and her father-in-law as sweet revenge. When Cassini had returned after World War II, he had found his wife, the actress Gene Tierney, having an affair with Jack. And several years later when he introduced his new fiancée, Grace Kelly, to Joe, the Kennedy patriarch had looked on the blonde movie star with lustful eyes, and had helped to talk her out of marrying Cassini.

Cassini thought that everything was fair in love and lust, and he bore no grudges. Joe, however, had the common weakness to think that men he admired thought the way he did. He was convinced that Cassini was either having an affair or about to have an affair with his daughter-in-law. One evening Joe sat next to Cassini on the porch. "Look, Oleg," Joe said, as Cassini recalled, suddenly changing the conversation as the two men looked out on the sunset. "I wouldn't be surprised if you have some ideas about Jackie. If the situation were different, I might have some ideas about her myself. But the question is: essence versus perception. I don't care what you do, but it must not be perceived. The worst thing, to my mind, would be to have the perception but not the reality—that would be silly, a real donkey's game. You understand."

"When the moment came to reciprocate, it could have happened," Cassini said, "but I had no interest because I liked Jackie and the past was the past and I'm sure that Jackie had no interest in me and we were friends."

Slowly Jack began to recover. He took some of Rose's favorite paintings out on the lawn, and sat there with palette and oils, making copies. "It was disastrous," Rose recalled, not at all appreciative of *her* paintings becoming part of Jack's recuperation. "It might have been disastrous for the paintings, but that didn't worry him. So it was lucky I didn't have old masterpieces."

As Jack improved, old friends such as Red Fay flew down to Palm Beach to spend a few days with their friend. Red was still the same clowning, mocking cutup he had been a decade before, and had the same enthusiasm for almost everything Kennedy. Even he, however, was taken aback by a voluptuous and mysterious house guest, who wandered through the estate saying almost nothing. "Where does she fit in?" Fay asked. "Well, she's a friend of Dad's," Jack said, as if it were the most natural thing in the world for his father to have his mistress and his wife living under the same roof.

At Palm Beach, Fay watched one day as Jack injected himself with cortisone, a procedure that he performed twice a day. "Jack, the way you jab that in looks like it doesn't even hurt," Fay said as Jack pushed the needle into his body.

Jack looked up and quickly jabbed the needle into Fay's leg, the former Navy man screaming in pain.

"It feels the same way to me," Jack said, his voice devoid of emotion.

When Jack wasn't painting or reading, he set to work on a book, a series of profiles of courageous politicians on which his assistant, Theodore Sorensen, did much of the work. When he was moved up North to Merrywood to continue his recovery, Jackie helped in his research, diligently going through books at the Library of Congress and staying with him until he was finally able to be on his own.

In any marriage, these many months of illness would have been a time of testing. That was infinitely more true in this marriage, where Jackie seemed so different from the Kennedys. Whatever complex matrix of reasons had drawn Jack and Jackie together, she had come through, and by the way the family defined itself she was now truly a Kennedy woman.

In the summer of 1955, as Jack was finally feeling himself again, he happened into the Wianno Beach Club. He wasn't a member but that had never stopped him or his family from using the facilities. There sat Harry Fowler along with a woman whom Jack had dated during his bachelor days in Hyannis Port. The woman prided herself on the fact that she had never slept with Jack. She was married now and it had been years since she had given him any thought. Everyone in the Port knew about Jack's illness, and she was delighted to see that Jack was healthy again.

"Why don't we go to a motel, huh?" Jack importuned her, as Fowler listened incredulously. "It's practically next door."

The woman sat speechless.

"Come on, let's go," Jack continued, not even minding that Fowler was listening. "It'll be fun. What does it matter anyway?"

"I'm *married*," the woman said finally.

"What does it matter? Come on, you know there's that cheap motel right up the street."

"No, Jack, absolutely not."

With that the senator from Massachusetts shrugged his shoulders and walked away.

——— 17 ———
"When Do We Start?"

*A*t Jack's wedding Jean talked to Father James Keller, the founder of the Christophers and one of the most prominent priests in America. The Maryknoll priest had taken the Chinese proverb, "Better to light one candle than to curse the darkness," and turned it into a motto and ideal, and an organization. To an impressionable young woman like Jean, educated by the nuns of the Sacred Heart, there was an irresistible quality to the charismatic father and his message. Her parents had impressed on her that as a child of privilege she was obligated to do good in the world. "The idea of doing something for other people came from my parents," Jean said. "They both believed very strongly that those to whom much is given have responsibility. They both felt that we had a real responsibility for some kind of public service."

At the wedding when Jean said good-bye to the priest, she asked if she might come to see him. "Certainly," Keller said, though Jean thought he "looked a little puzzled." The following week Jean walked into the Christophers' offices at 18 East 48th Street in New York City and told the priest of her desire to work for him without pay at whatever task he chose to give her. "I knew Father Keller's work," Jean recalled, "and when I met with him, he was just beginning his television show and I thought that I was fairly interested to get into television." Keller questioned Jean about her motives. As noble as Jean presumably appeared, the priest was also not unaware what a strong bond to the Kennedys might mean to his organization. There was Jack in the Senate, Bobby who had been fighting Communists with Joe McCarthy in Washington, Rose one of the great Catholic laywomen, and Joe with the family foundation dispensing hundreds of thousands of dollars.

Jean quickly moved into a position of considerable influence as Keller's "girl Friday." "She has the maturity of a person of forty," Keller told a reporter from the *Boston Post*. "Her judgment is very good—and I rely upon it, to a considerable extent, probably more than she realizes."

Father Keller had a six-day-a-week newspaper column, a monthly newsletter sent out to over a million people, a radio program on 585 stations, and a TV show on 202 stations. For Jean the most exciting aspect of the work was Father Keller's connection with Hollywood and the new universe of television. "She's getting stuff together for our Hollywood trip," the priest said. "It's all in order, so that for the first time we will be able to face the cameras with material with which to work."

For Jean, this world around Father Keller was a comfortable and familiar one, largely priests and devout upper-class young women who thought of the work as a worthy prelude to marriage and family life. Jean's first trip to Hollywood with Keller led to her assignment to Los Angeles and work as a production assistant on *The Christopher Hour*, a weekly television program. This was *her* life now, and in Hollywood she made new friends and for the first time in her life was known not simply as a Kennedy. Yet it was not simply her abilities but the financial resources that stood behind her that gave Jean her considerable clout. The Joseph P. Kennedy Jr. Foundation was essentially a *Catholic* foundation giving out its money almost solely to Catholic groups. In 1954, for instance, the foundation donated $620,000 exclusively to Catholic organizations, including ten thousand dollars to the Christophers.

Jean and her sisters saw the world as divided into those who were loyal to her brothers and family and those who were not. The women dressed up their emotions in the abstract language of politics, but it came down to a simple logic: You were either with the Kennedys or you were against them. That was the Christopher view of the world as well, and Jean and her colleagues not only helped to choose who would go on *The Christopher Hour* but who would not. "We lined up people and shot these Christopher people for a couple of months straight in California," Jean said. Lucille Ball and Desi Arnaz were two of the most famous performers in television, but they were notoriously liberal, and though they wanted to appear, they were turned down.

"Jean worked behind the scene," said Ann Denove, whose husband produced the program. "The Kennedys were great backers of the program. Jean at her own expense paid for half the cost of the films. She would come out here and work and work until eleven o'clock at night. Her clothes were beautiful and she always carried this same exquisite alligator purse."

There was yet another Kennedy with a great interest in Hollywood, and that was Pat. At the age of twenty-nine, she was a woman with as much flair as energy. She had her father's business acumen. "The one with the best business head is Pat," her father said. "If she put her mind to it, she could easily take over this business."

More than any of her sisters, Pat had inherited from her mother a certain graciousness that she drew upon like a line of credit. She had been at the Hotel Edelweiss in Switzerland on a skiing trip in February of 1953 when she had read about the death of Peter Lawford's father, Sir Sydney Lawford. She wrote a note to the star that managed to be comforting while also suggesting to Peter that she hoped that their relationship might develop further. "Do let me know if you come to New York," she wrote in her schoolgirl script, "so we can do a better job of meeting than our last crossing!"

In November Pat was hurrying along Madison Avenue when she ran into Peter. She was wearing a long mink coat and might have been off to a smashing party somewhere, but was on a more banal mission: grocery shopping. Peter was a man of immense personal charm who could cover over forgetfulness or impoliteness with a few gentle words and a smile. He immediately invited Pat out for a date.

Pat and Peter soon began seeing each other regularly. Wherever they went heads turned, maître d's fawned, and there was always someone there to deal with such banal chores as getting to the airport, finding a ticket to a sold-out show, or being seated in the best banquette at 21. There was not much difference between the way Peter was greeted in New York and what she experienced traveling in Massachusetts with Jack. To Pat this was simply life, and she was as attracted to Peter's sophistication and fame as he was to her mixture of innocence and worldliness. "She was one of the *purest* people I'd ever met," Peter recalled. On first meeting they both seemed so strong, full of a joyous appreciation of life that overflowed, bubbling over all those around them.

Peter happened to be spending the Christmas holidays in Palm Beach, a place that for him resonated with memories more melancholy than happy. It was here that the Lawfords had arrived after Peter had made his Hollywood film debut in a minor part in the 1938 film *Lord Jeff.* The resort community was full of not simply the wealthy but the artfully impecunious trading on titles, looks, names, or accomplishments, and the social leaders of the resort community had taken immediately to Sir Sydney and Lady Lawford. When war was declared in 1939, the Lawfords lost whatever source of money they had in England, and no longer had even enough resources to put up a decent appearance. Lady May still dreamed that her handsome son would one day be a great Hollywood star. Peter parked cars on Worth Avenue, accepting tips from notables including a generous Ambassador Joseph P. Kennedy, dropping quarters on the youth.

The young man who strode into the Kennedys' Palm Beach villa to meet Joe that Christmas of 1953 had fulfilled his mother's wish and had just costarred alongside Judy Holliday and Jack Lemmon in the MGM film *It Should Happen to You.* Joe looked the six-foot-tall actor up and down, from his blue blazer and his white pants, to his luminous red socks. For the most part Joe considered actors a narcissistic, fraudulent breed. After Peter left, Joe's only comment was that "He seems like a nice man."

Peter was a successful actor and had managed to save a hundred thousand dollars, but he did not have anything like the wealth of the Kennedy heirs. That didn't bother Pat. She did not have the common obsession of heirs, believing the only way to be sure a suitor was not pursuing her money was to marry someone equally wealthy. The other man whom she was dating seriously was Frank Conniff, a foreign correspondent with INS stationed in Tokyo, with whom she shared travel and adventures, not wealth.

In May, Pat would have her thirtieth birthday, an ominous occasion for a still-single woman in the fifties, marking her with the sign of spinsterhood. Pat wanted desperately to marry. She told one friend that she was planning to fly to Japan to convince Conniff that *he* should do the honors. As she prepared to set off for Tokyo on her worldwide trip, she had an opportunity to spend a few more nights with Peter in his Hollywood haunts.

On their last night together, Peter leaned across the candlelit table at Frascati's and said: "I'm crazy about you. I'd like to marry you eventually."

The operative word was *eventually* but Pat heard only the violins and the sweet amour. "How about April?" she replied.

"You're pulling my leg," Peter exclaimed incredulously. "April what?"

"Next April."

Peter said nothing. He could perhaps hear the clanking of a cell door in the background. When he finally spoke, it was to sputter out a few apologetic words, attempting to push any marriage into a vague and hazy future. Pat was amused at her supposed suitor's discomfort. She let Peter know that Frank was still available, and if he couldn't be more specific she might ride off into the sunset with the foreign correspondent.

Peter said good-bye to Pat, but the more he thought about her, the more he felt that perhaps he had made a dreadful mistake, and he called Pat when she arrived at her hotel in Tokyo. "Okay, Pat," Peter began, signaling both victory and defeat. "Please come home. April it will be."

"I accept your eloquent proposal of marriage," Pat said, and returned to Los Angeles on the next flight.

A few days before the Kennedys announced the engagement, Peter had proclaimed he "had no intention of marrying anybody." Peter was taken in hand by the Kennedys and their public relations firm. As a youth he had been under contract for MGM, and the Kennedys were as controlling of their image as the studio had been of its stars. "I had promised the Kennedys not to say anything to anybody," he told a reporter, apologizing for his remarks lauding bachelorhood. "I guess I was just nervous, and I had said all those things so many times about preferring freedom to marriage that it was easy to repeat them."

Pat and Peter did not know each other's foibles. They had only been dating for two months when they became engaged, and they were marrying these immensely appealing images of each other. "Peter was being courted by everyone, society and Hollywood types," recalled Joe Naar, then one of his closest friends. "Pat was only one of many, and Peter was terribly impressed by who she was. This doesn't presume to say that he wasn't taken with her as a human being, but the fact that she was who she was didn't hurt. He didn't want to marry Lana Turner or Ava Gardner, but somebody outside of the business who meant something socially. I hate saying that out loud but it's true."

Peter's longtime manager and most intimate friend, Milton

Ebbins, talked almost daily to Peter. "The spark was never there, on her side yes, not on his," he reflected. "He thought it was time for him to get married and she was appropriate. He liked her, but I never thought he loved her."

Two decades later when Peter reflected back on his life to Patricia Seaton, the woman who would become his fourth and final wife, he expressed a far different opinion. "I think he loved her a great deal," said Patricia Seaton Stewart. "It was their first marriage and there was a strong friendship. But he was incapable of loyalty and she was innocent."

As a young girl Pat had devoured the issues of *Variety* that her father brought home. She adored movie magazines and dreamed of Hollywood. Her short courtship with Peter was like a movie, full of witty dialogue, enough romantic suspense to keep things interesting, and fade to a happy ending. The fact was, however, that Pat knew hardly more about Peter than some star-struck fan in Omaha. She was far more sophisticated and more widely traveled and better educated than most of the stars and starlets of Peter's professional life, whose world was confined to the parameters of the studio lot and who were rarely as interesting as the roles they portrayed. About the world of sex and male-female relationships, she was not only innocent but dangerously uninformed. She had met some of her father's other women, but she, like her mother and sisters, simply denied their existence. She was a virgin and had a convent-girl's reticence on matters sexual. Peter, on the other hand, was a sexual epicurean. To him sexual preference as to gender, number, or technique was no more a matter of morality than choosing between fish and meat for dinner. His mother had dressed him in girl's finery in private until he was almost ready to enter puberty. He was about ten years old when his nanny began fondling him, performing fellatio on the pretty little boy, an experience he considered not molestation but a pleasant initiation. "Then my nanny I loved her skirt," he wrote in a poem years later. "An early start for such a squirt." He wrote no poem to the uncle who may have fondled him.

In Hollywood, Peter was in a society where love affairs often lasted no longer than the shooting of a film, or the staging of a publicity shot or two. Peter cut an erotic swath among the stars and starlets, having affairs with Lana Turner, Ava Gardner, Judy Garland, and Judy Holliday among others, but always returning to his beach buddies and to a life without constraints and commitments.

Peter and Pat flew to New York to meet Rose and Joe. Joe had made his opinion of Peter well known. "If there's anybody I'd hate worse than an actor as a son-in-law, it's a *British* actor." Joe had a special affinity for Pat, the most lighthearted and vibrant of his surviving daughters. As he had with all his daughters' suitors, he had Peter's background investigated. Joe talked both to sources at MGM, and to his friend, J. Edgar Hoover, the director of the FBI. The resulting dossier was full of the most sordid speculation. The unsubstantiated rumors of Peter's bisexuality were the least of it. The FBI report dated January 29, 1954, stated that Peter had been investigated in 1946 involving "White Slave activities in Los Angeles." He had contact with a Hollywood madame that year, and four years later the report noted a call girl was "reportedly a frequent trick for movie actor Peter Lawford."

Peter was a man of professional charm. As he walked into Joe's suite he was determined to impress the Kennedy patriarch. In their initial meeting, Peter took a strong liking to his future father-in-law, appreciating Joe's sense of humor. Joe decided that the report was nothing serious enough to prevent the marriage. Joe was no innocent when it came to the sexual practices of Hollywood. He may well have figured that Peter's dossier was no longer than Jack's or his own. The fact was that Peter's friends were not movie people, but *sportifs* who lived an outdoor Los Angeles life of surfing, swimming, and endless good times. They were heavy social drinkers, the clink of glasses was background music for good times, but there was hardly an undercurrent of decadence to their daily lives.

Joe knew how much his willful, high-strung daughter wanted to marry Peter, and he probably did not want to risk losing a second daughter, the way he had lost Kathleen. "Pat's father couldn't control her," said Peter's manager, Ebbins. "If she wanted to do something, she did it. He couldn't stop her from marrying Peter. He tried to but he couldn't."

Not surprisingly, Rose was concerned with Peter's future religious practices. The nominally Episcopalian Peter agreed to have any children brought up Catholic, and that was sufficient to assuage her doubts about the match.

Peter may have passed muster with Joe and Rose, but Pat discovered that she had larger problems with her future mother-in-law, Lady May Lawford. Peter's mother was a tart-tongued, narrowly snobbish woman who lived through her son's accomplishments. She had groomed him for stardom and marriage to European royalty, not the ersatz American variety. Lady May played the game of publicity with verve, and her statements to reporters were full of praise for Pat. In private, Lady May unsheathed her vicious tongue, lashing out at the Kennedys in invective that struck at the Kennedys' sensitivities. To her the family were "barefoot Irish peasants," and Pat was "a bitch" who had "trapped" her beloved son into marriage.

Pat attempted to pay proper obeisance to Lady May, arriving at the Lawford house in Los Angeles accompanied by Cardinal Francis McIntyre. Lady May considered Catholicism the peasant church of a peasant people, and she was hardly impressed with Pat's chaperon. "Do you think Peter will rape you?" she asked.

Pat was full of a Kennedyesque pride in her family. She had stood as close to Lady May's foul mouth as she intended to stand. Pat, like Jackie in her initiation at Hyannis Port, knew that it was not her womanly role to openly confront Peter's mother. She must employ more subtle, less direct means. Pat politely accepted Lady May's invitation to give an engagement party to introduce Pat to her future mother-in-law's friends in Los Angeles. On the appointed day, Lady May recalled that Pat not only arrived two hours late, but she wore sports clothes, and, feigning illness, left with Peter almost immediately.

Lady May was taken aback that Pat was drinking every bit as much as her son and his friends. "Lady May never shut up about Pat's drinking," said Buddy Galon, who wrote her delicately titled autobiography, *Bitch*. "Lady Lawford was not used to a young girl drinking. I think that Pat took an immediate dislike to her. Lady Lawford was pointing out all these things that were wrong, from the drinking to the wedding plans, but the Kennedys had no use for these leftover Victorian ideas on how to behave."

Whatever the private dramas, to the public this marriage between the suave British star and the lovely heiress was the stuff of movie magazines. Everywhere the couple went they were pursued by photographers and reporters, whether it was wandering through Central Park or walking hand in hand at the Palm Beach Country Club.

Pat had wanted an April wedding, and an April wedding she had, though nothing as grandiose as Jack's or Eunice's. Since

Peter was not Catholic, the marriage took place in New York not at St. Patrick's Cathedral but at the Church of St. Thomas More. There were only three hundred relatives and friends invited, and no coteries of priests and no chorus as had blessed Eunice's nuptials.

Outside the Upper East Side church stood a largely female crowd of three thousand. For the most part they had come straining to see even a glimpse of Peter, but this was a Kennedy wedding in which Pat's family dominated almost every moment. Peter invited only a half dozen of his old beach buddies, and they were lost among the Kennedys and Fitzgeralds and their family friends.

Pat made a splendid, beauteous bride in a stunning gown of pearl-white satin that set off her thin, athletic frame. The portrait neckline could have been approved by the nuns at Rosemont, set off by the single strand of pearls high around her neck. As for the bridegroom, unlike many former child actors, he did not look like an aging boy-man. His thirty-year-old countenance was now gently touched by lines of maturity that only strengthened his debonair good looks. He was the very dream of a leading man, and as Pat and Peter walked back up the aisle and out into the April sunshine, cheered by the adoring multitudes, they were the picture of newlywedded bliss.

For the reception at the Plaza Hotel, the grand ballroom was made over into a veritable spring garden, a provision of pink snapdragons, delphiniums, and tulips gracing the room, with the bridal table fronted by a hedge of white hydrangea. Peter danced with his bride to the song "Strangers in Paradise," and then Joe danced with Pat, and Peter with Rose, and soon the floor was full of dancers.

The only untoward note was the decidedly sour presence of Peter's mother. Lady May was busy counting up the Kennedys' supposed assaults on good taste, which included inviting her to a dinner alone with Joe and later alone with Rose, being seated at the prewedding dinner in a corner chaperoned by a priest, and having a strange man as her escort at the wedding.

For their honeymoon the newlyweds flew to Hawaii, a favorite haunt of Peter in his bachelor days. Peter still had good friends in Honolulu, and they were there to greet him at the airport. Jackie had discovered on *her* Kennedy honeymoon that being married to a Kennedy man seemed to mean that you were married to him, but he was not so married to you. In Hawaii, Pat had *her* itinerary including a visit to the state legislature and rounds of golf, while Peter was more interested in surfing. It was a curious honeymoon. They could both be gracious and thoughtful, and yet they each had their own willful self-centeredness, a part of their personalities that sooner or later their acquaintances discovered.

One day Peter borrowed his friend Rab Guild's red convertible and managed to wreck the vehicle, driving it into a ditch. "You're lucky I didn't get killed," Peter told his friend, totally unconcerned that he had destroyed his friend's cherished auto.

On one of their last evenings in Hawaii, the gay boisterous group went to the movies, arriving after the newsreel had already been shown. After the main feature, the manager showed the newsreel again to the little group, and Peter watched as the words "Pat Kennedy Marries Actor" filled the screen. "Peter was crushed," Rab Guild said. "He was just *crushed*. They hadn't even used his *name*."

It was a most peculiar marriage, an amalgam of Peter's British upper-class customs learned at his mother's knee, Pat's Catholic schoolgirl reticence and her Kennedyesque ideals of family, the laid-back beach culture of southern California, and the social mannerisms of Hollywood. In their first months in Los Angeles, they each sought to establish their own marital turf. Peter made it clear that he was not going to be stamped with the Kennedy imprimatur. He refused his father-in-law's offer to buy the newlyweds a house, and instead rented a beach house in Malibu, just north of Los Angeles. The two-bedroom home with its twenty-four-foot glass window had the homey, casual feel of the Kennedy house in Hyannis Port, opening out onto the beach where Peter loved to surf and play volleyball, seeking to replicate the best parts of his life before his marriage.

Peter and Pat had good friends, but they had the manner common to politicians and actors alike, of appearing to be gregarious comrades and then suddenly dropping the person seemingly with nary a thought or regret. As Pat set out to establish her own sovereignty over their rented house, the less educated and the more rowdy of Peter's gang of beach friends felt that they were no longer welcome. If they took umbrage it was in part because Peter did not set boundaries for them or provide some other role in his new life. It was Pat, however, who took the blame. "She cut most of the guys off," recalled Royal Marcher Jr., one of Peter's friends. "Wives do that. They fear the guys are going to take the husband out and get him laid. But you couldn't take Peter out and do anything that he didn't want to do. If he was madly in love with Pat, he wouldn't do it."

Most of Peter's old friends viewed Pat as an unwelcome intruder who had broken up a marvelous scene. "I'm one of the few people who really have nothing bad to say about Pat," said Dick Livingston, another of Peter's close friends. "Once in a while she was moody, but if you moved someplace and then all of a sudden all your husband's old beach buddies are coming through the house, you'd go 'wait a minute.' In fact, she put up with a lot more than probably a lot of women would have."

Pat was used to social life that was either serious discussion or madcap revelry. She added her own touches to Peter's social life—party games and witty repartee during high-stakes poker games. When there was a small dinner party at Livingston's tiny house on Beverly Glen, she sat on the floor cross-legged, laughing and eating spaghetti as happily as if she and Peter were in the favorite banquette at Frascati's.

Pat and Peter were both charged with energy, and they burst into parties and dinners full of vitality and laughter. They were enamored enough of each other that their foibles were subjects of gentle ribbing, not endless argument. Pat could be terribly cheap, while Peter had a movie star's largess, tipping lavishly, considering price tags a vulgarity not to be thought of when he bought a suit or a sweater. Pat was well organized, her days planned, but for Peter life was nothing if it was not full of uncertainty and a flurry of last-minute decisions. Both needed plenty of space, and they didn't consider that an embarrassing necessity, but good fortune that they had found one another. "Pat's the only girl I've ever met that I could be married to," Peter proudly admitted. "Actually, I never could stand domesticity. And neither could she, as a matter of fact. Pat hadn't wanted to get married either."

It pleased Peter to believe that Pat would have remained unmarried forever, her single status continuing through her life. It pleased Peter to believe many things about his wife that were not always true. "Pat's the most understanding girl in the world," he continued. "I trust her completely and she trusts me. There's no possessiveness or jealousy. That's for the immature, anyway. . . . If I should call now and say, 'I'm not coming home for dinner,' she wouldn't say a word. I wouldn't have to say why—or where I was going. You call that 'understanding,' I suppose."

Pat had a mother who was nothing but "understanding" to her husband. Pat sought to make her way with Peter and his life, three thousand miles away from her sisters and family. Eunice had given birth to her first baby, Robert Sargent III, in April, and Pat knew that the goal of her whole upbringing was to have her own family. From what she knew of her new husband, she might have considered waiting until he got used to the idea of marriage before they started a family. The church told her that was unthinkable, and she and Peter had scarcely been married four months before she was pregnant.

Peter viewed the prospect of a baby as an unblessed event, harbinger of his decline as a romantic lead, a deadly drag on his good and free life. As Pat's stomach began to swell, he seemed almost to be blocking off the idea that he was married.

On the morning of their six-month anniversary, Pat told her husband: "Let's have a few people over this evening."

"Fine," Peter said.

By the time he returned from the studio, Peter had totally forgotten that the party was in their honor. When Pat brought out a cake, and the group started singing "Happy Anniversary to You," Peter looked totally nonplussed. "It seems like thirty years," Peter said finally, intending the remark as a compliment.

As Pat grew even more obviously pregnant, Peter spent less time at home, during the week staying with the Ebbinses in their Los Angeles home. Peter's manager did not want to be part of breaking up his client's marriage. He pleaded with Peter to return to his home in Malibu, but Peter would hear nothing of it. Finally, Pat showed up at the Ebbins home and told Peter: "I'm going to move in here." She stayed until the middle of her seventh month of pregnancy, when she flew to Canada for a ski trip.

In the mid-1950s, pregnant women did not roar down the Canadian Rockies, but Pat was not going to allow her pregnancy to interfere with her sporting life. On March 29, 1955, soon after she returned from skiing, her premature six-pound thirteen-ounce baby boy was born. They named him Christopher Kennedy Lawford so that he might carry both family names. Rose happened to be in Los Angeles on a visit, and for the first and last time Rose served as a nurse and helpmate at the birth of one of her grandchildren, a role that Luella

Hennessey performed for the other grandchildren. Her servitude did not last more than a few days. Early in April she was gone, continuing a round-the-world tour with her niece, Mary Jo Gargan. They traveled to Japan where she was entertained at the embassy; Hong Kong; Thailand; India where she briefly met Prime Minister Jawaharlal Nehru. Rose was an inveterate traveler, taking immense pleasure in her long voyages. Finally, two and a half months later, she arrived in Paris, where she spent a few days with Joe. She was there when she learned that in Washington on June 15, 1955, Ethel had given birth to her sixth grandchild, David Anthony.

Pat had a hard enough time suddenly having this new mother's role thrust on her without having a husband who could not stand the wailing of an infant, the changing of diapers, or the disruption of his sacred beach routine. Peter rectified matters by renting an apartment two doors away where his little son and his nanny could spend their days. Pat not only put up with the banishment, but she too enjoyed handing Chris off to the nanny for hours.

The birth of a Kennedy grandson was a great occasion in the family. Joe flew out for the christening at the Church of the Good Shepherd in Beverly Hills. Peter Sabiston was the godfather, and he stood proudly next to Peter and Pat, with his gorgeous actress friend properly in the background. Peter's other close friend, Dick Livingston, was there, with his attractive young wife. As Grandfather Kennedy surveyed the scene, his interests were not solely on Christopher Kennedy Lawford, his new grandson. In the space of a few minutes, he managed to invite both Peter's friend and the new Mrs. Livingston to visit him in his villa in southern France. At the party afterwards at the beach, Joe was even more persistent in his invitation. "How should I handle this?" asked Peter Sabiston's date.

Sabiston sidled across the room toward Joe. "What a wonderful invitation you've extended," Sabiston said, fairly gushing. "But I'm sorry I can't make it."

Joe was a connoisseur of pulchritude. When he watched the well-endowed dancers on *The Jackie Gleason Show* on television, he knew not only their names but their phone numbers. When he came to Los Angeles, he expected to see not only his daughter and his grandson, but a starlet or two. That was considered Pat's daughterly role as well. "Pat tried on a couple of occasions to fix Joe up with various ladies I know," said Sabiston.

Pat had a far better sense of financial matters than Peter, and she sat next to her husband at meetings discussing his future roles. When Peter was approached to star in the TV series *Dear Phoebe*, about a male lovelorn columnist, he first rejected the idea. Television was still the enemy in Hollywood, and no ranking star would consider appearing weekly on the tiny screen. Pat saw matters differently. "This sounds good, Peter, why don't you do it?" Pat told Peter at their meeting with his manager Ebbins. "You're gonna get paid, aren't you?"

"Sure he is," Ebbins said, "five thousand dollars a week."

"What!" Pat said. She hadn't been brought up a Kennedy without knowing the value of a dollar, no less five thousand of them. "Peter, you *have* to do this!"

If Peter produced the program in association with a partner, he stood to earn even more. He and Pat had achieved equality when it came to money matters, and they each put up $12,500 to become coproducers and share in the profits. Pat told Peter almost nothing about her own wealth. Each year accountants shoved blank tax forms in front of the actor, which he signed without comment or complaint. One year, however, the accountants returned the joint returns addressed to Mr. and Mrs. Lawford, and Peter was startled to read that his wife had earned $265,000 simply in interest income.

During the shooting of *Dear Phoebe*, Pat was often on the set, even taking a walk-on role in one episode. Pat tried to make herself part of Peter's life and career, but she was at her happiest whenever her family was around. Once during her first year of marriage, not only was Jean in town working on *The Christopher Hour* but Eunice had flown in for a few days, and Ted was there too along with his college roommate, Claude E. Hooton Jr., who had a crush on Jean.

"The three sisters hadn't seen each other in a long time, and they were absolutely darling," Hooton recalled. "No one got a word in edgewise. They didn't care who else was around. Peter would come up and try and interrupt the conversation, but they were like sorority sisters off among themselves. It was just incredible. They had all been around the world, done all kinds of things, but they just came together like three kids."

For Claude it appeared to be a wonderfully loving family, but others observed the same scene and felt only sorrow for

Peter, living in the eternal shadow of the Kennedys. "I think that Peter just felt inadequate," said a woman who was one of Pat's closest friends. "When the sisters would come out here there was a bond the likes of which I've never seen before, and then there was Peter. The family was in one place emotionally, and Peter was somewhere else. The sisters had their own dialogue, their own language. They laughed together and had their own little secrets. And anyone who wasn't the most secure had to feel very intimated and to feel less than great."

Christopher was not even six months old when Pat flew off with Jean to Moscow. Pat and Jean approached Russia with far greater intellectual curiosity and openness than had Rose, Kathleen, and Joe Jr., who had all been there before World War II. They attended a fashion show at the Dom Modeli, where hefty models in squeaky patent-leather shoes walked back and forth on the platform wearing clothes that they felt "would be compared more to a Sears Roebuck catalogue than any of ours shown in fashion houses." They went into a cosmetic store and sampled perfumes named Red Poppy and Jubilee of the Soviet Army. They went to a state farm and a school, and the Bolshoi where instead of an elegant theater crowd, there were "men in open shirts and women in flat shoes."

"We left Russia with a vast admiration for the women," Jean and Pat wrote in an article for United Press. "They will pave the streets, work in the factories and labor on the farms. But it seems regrettable that they have so little time for any home life or for any real enjoyment of life which, here in America, comes natural to us."

Twenty-seven-year-old Jean was still unmarried, and she was suddenly feeling rather aged and alone. She cabled Pat in May of 1955 from Paris for her birthday, asking her older sister if she felt as aged as Jean looked. She, however, had found an appropriate beau as well, a twenty-seven-year-old New York businessman with a résumé perfectly suitable for elevation into the Kennedy family. Stephen Edward Smith was a graduate of Georgetown University, and was an executive at the family transportation firm, Cleary Brothers. Smith could sing the old Irish songs with heart and soul and listen attentively to the twice-told tales of immigrant life; his grandfather William Cleary had worked on the Erie Canal and had scrimped and struggled to buy a tugboat that became the fleet managed by the family company. His grandfather had been a three-term congressman, and in Smith's veins flowed the blood of business and politics. Smith had a full measure of charm, an Irish-American ebullience often fueled on liquor, and a raw toughness that he rarely displayed among women. In sum, Smith was a man whom his father-in-law sensed immediately was an appropriate husband for his youngest daughter.

"Daddy gave me the choice of a big wedding and a small present or a small wedding and a big present," Jean recalled. She had been given much the same alternatives when it had been time for her debut, and she made the same decision. She had little use for public spectacles in which she was the center and she chose the gift, an enormous diamond pin.

Jean's wedding on May 19, 1956, did not have the grandeur of Eunice's spectacular nuptials, but by most any standards except the Kennedys' it was a grand occasion. The ceremony took place in St. Patrick's Cathedral, presided over by Cardinal Francis Spellman. Jean wore a long gown of champagne satin and a tulle veil held by a coronet of orange blossoms, as she stood in the immense cathedral, with Eunice as her matron of honor. Jean flashed an ebullient bridal smile as she walked out of the cathedral on Steve's arm, and was radiant when she danced with him at the Plaza Hotel.

There were about a hundred and fifty people at the reception, and it was a time for toasts and speeches and remembrances. When she was growing up Jean's closest friends in the family were not her older sisters but the two family members closest to her age, Bobby and Ted. Her youngest brother had a special affinity with Jean. Ted was the most sentimental and emotional of the siblings, a spirit that he often masked in humor. He was at his funniest recalling the sometimes dubious distinction that he shared with Jean of being the two youngest in the family.

Ted began by telling what it was like always being the one to be shuttled out of *his* room to make room for one guest or another. Once he had passed a memorable night sleeping on the rubbing table in Palm Beach. "I was up at Hyannis Port and the same thing happened," Ted continued. "Jean said to me once: 'Listen, Teddy, I know that you've been going through all this and we're going to sail up to Maine. I want you to have a room by yourself and come along.'

"I got into the boat and I had my room decorated and I thought: 'That was awful nice of old Jeannie to do a thing like that for me.' We were just about to cut away, we were actually in motion already, and a couple came down to the dock waving: 'Hey, Jeannie. Hey, Jeannie! We finally made it.'

"'My gosh!' Jeannie said. 'We're going to have to change. You'll have to sleep with me.'

"That was the first time in my life I slept with my sister, or with any woman! That's good old Jeannie."

As the audience rolled in laughter, Jean held her head in her hands, laughing through her embarrassment.

Jean had hardly settled into married life when she and her sisters were abuzz with extraordinary news. Jack's name was being bandied about as a possible vice-presidential candidate to be named at the 1956 Democratic convention in Chicago. This was an occasion not simply for Jack but for the entire family, and the women arrived in the midwestern city in the humid heat of August. The only Kennedy woman missing was Pat, who was eight months pregnant. By that rule, Jackie should have stayed home as well. She had a miscarriage during her first year of marriage. She needed to spend these months in tranquillity, but it was politically important for her to be seen at her husband's side. The Kennedy people had prepared a dispassionate analysis of possible vice-presidential candidates and their prospects. After eliminating potential candidates who didn't want the nomination, and those who opposed the putative presidential candidate, Adlai Stevenson, the third criterion was that the nominee "should be married, and with no previous divorce—five candidates out." Stevenson himself was divorced, and the former Illinois governor needed to be mated with a vice-presidential candidate who had an exemplary family life. An obviously pregnant Jackie was a walking advertisement of Jack's marital status, his marriage a necessity if he were to achieve national political office.

Jackie arrived in Chicago, not staying with her husband, but off with Jean and Ethel in Eunice's apartment overlooking Lake Michigan. To make room for them, Eunice sent two-year-old Bobby and her new baby, nine-month-old Maria Owings, to Hyannis Port.

Eunice was one of the two heads of the Entertainment Committee. Although this was considered an important post for a woman, it was nothing of great consequence to the largely male politicians preoccupied with choosing a slate to run against President Dwight D. Eisenhower. In less than half a decade, Eunice had become so much a part of Chicago life that she could be chosen for such a highly visible task, seeming like a real Chicagoan and not an interloper from the East. "This brings a lot of money to Chicago," she said. Even if her accent marked her as an outsider, she was an enthusiastic booster of *her* city. "We'd like to get both conventions again in 1960. We certainly want people to enjoy coming here."

Eunice was a Kennedy woman and she saw her role in politics as boosting Jack as far as time, money, ability, and good fortune would boost him. Her own husband, Sarge, was a man of exemplary moral values with a prescient awareness of the problems that would immolate American society in the sixties. Through his work on the board of education and on Chicago's Interracial Council, he was concerned with questions of race and poverty a whole political generation before any of the Kennedy men. That week the national spotlight shone on Chicago. Sarge could have stepped forward, taken a prominent public role the way Eunice had, and made his own national political debut. But Eunice was devoid of political ambitions for her husband. "I'm perfectly satisfied leaving him remain president of Chicago's Board of Education," she told a reporter as the convention began, as if she controlled Sarge's future. Jack was different. "We think that public office is a natural field for him and that he'd be terrific as vice-president. But he says, 'Nobody has asked me.' "

Eunice and her two sisters watched on the first evening of the convention as Jack narrated an emotionally powerful film about the Democratic party. Afterwards, the Massachusetts delegation staged a rousing, placard-raising demonstration, attempting to ignite a firestorm of support for their favorite son. On the third night of the convention, the Kennedy women had yet another opportunity to see their older brother in the limelight, giving a nominating speech for Stevenson.

Instead of choosing his own vice-presidential candidate, as was the tradition, Stevenson threw the nomination open, and for a day Jack, his brothers, and brothers-in-law worked fervently to win delegates. Reporters saw Jackie, Ethel, Eunice, and Jean all "bustling around the corridors." For the Kennedy women it was a moment of great emotional intensity—the nominating speeches, the hectic politicking, the thunderous floor demonstrations, the voting, the first ballot with Jack behind Senator Estes Kefauver, the second ballot where Jack surged into the lead, only sixty-eight votes short of the nomination, and then Jack falling back with the Tennessee senator triumphing. Afterwards, the disconsolate group went to a steak house near the convention center where Eunice and Jackie did not conceal their tears.

"Don't feel sorry for young Jack Kennedy," wrote the *Boston Herald*. "Despite his defeat after a magnificent race here this mid-afternoon, he probably rates as the one real victor of the entire convention. His was the one new face that actually shone."

After an exhilarating, exhausting week, Jack and Jackie flew back together to New York. They had not had any privacy for at least a week, and Jack had hardly slept for three days. Jackie was tired too, tired from her pregnancy, tired from all her efforts in Chicago. For her, spending a week at the convention had been like venturing down into a mine where in the sweat and darkness, men struggled to haul out nuggets of gold. She had attended breakfast with the Massachusetts delegation, held up a Stevenson banner standing with Jean in their convention box while the photographers clicked away, said all the sweetly appropriate things, applauded for Jack with refined moderation, and cried when Jack lost. As much as she wanted her husband to succeed, it was to her still a world of almost unspeakable vulgarity, commerce, and incivility, a world from which she sometimes wanted to flee. When one particularly persistent journalist, Maxine Cheshire, pursued her relentlessly at the convention, the seven-months-pregnant Jackie bolted from her box, scurried down the stairs and into the parking garage, sprinting away from the reporter.

The John F. Kennedy who was so proudly touted at the convention as a family man would surely have flown back to Newport to spend the last months of her pregnancy with his twenty-seven-year-old wife. But Jack Kennedy bid his wife of three years good-bye at the New York airport and two hours later got on a plane for Paris, en route to a vacation in southern France. Jackie took an air-taxi to Newport to stay with her mother at Hammersmith Farm, where news reports said she would be "expecting a child soon."

In Chicago, Jackie had discussed the idea of Jack's going off with George Smathers and Ted, now a student at the University of Virginia Law School. "Why don't you and Jack take a trip to the Mediterranean?" Smathers remembered her saying. "He wants to go." In the Senate, Smathers had almost as great a reputation as Jack for being a ladies' man. Jackie presumably knew that she was not sending her husband off to explore the riches of the Louvre, or an archeological study of the Roman ruins of the Midi. She had a sense of manners that she carried with her into the intimacies of marriage. Her offer was a magnanimous gesture that Jack did not have to accept. In private, she asked her husband to stay with her, but Jack was not about to give up his good time.

Jack was often intellectually and emotionally dismissive, not only of Jackie but of most women. A few months before while rereading one of his favorite books, *The Young Melbourne*, he had jotted down some notes explicating his attitude about women. He found European women such as Lady Melbourne and Mary Queen of Scots interesting because they were "women of leisure" but in America "women [were] either prostitutes or house wives [and] do not play much of a role in [the] cultural or intellectual life of [the] country." That was the same attitude he had had since adolescence, dividing women into two categories, the good and the bad.

Jack's and Jackie's fathers thought much the same. Indeed, Black Jack Bouvier had given tacit approval to Jack's trip, and dreamed wistfully of making his own flight to European shores. "I would like to see that English nurse of yester-year," he wrote Jack as if he were not his son-in-law but a worthy competitor in the eternal quest for women, "she of my twenty minute romance, which you and your gang so rudely but effectively interrupted."

In southern France, Jack and his comrades visited Joe and Rose, who had rented a villa on the Mediterranean. Rose thought her son looked "bronzed and smiling." They talked about the convention and how "people upon whom he depended failed him." That was one of the great themes of the family, and Rose listened empathetically to her son. Out there were duplicitous sycophants and fair-weather allies who insinuated themselves into the counsels of the family only to betray them.

Jack didn't come to the Côte d'Azur simply to talk politics with his parents. If Jack needed any further reinforcement that the way he was treating Jackie was appropriate, he had only to look at his parents' lives. Though his father was spending a few weeks with his mother, Joe continued to live a totally free sexual life. When his parents left for Paris, they planned to stay at different hotels, Joe at the Raphael Hotel and Rose at the Ritz.

At Cannes Jack and his friends chartered a forty-foot boat, and sailed off into the Mediterranean with a contingent that reportedly included a French starlet and other young women. Smathers said that he did not go along but sent a friend instead. While Jack was relaxing on the sea, Jackie began hemorrhaging. On August 23, 1956, at Newport Hospital doctors performed a cesarian, but the baby was born dead, the mortality attributed by the hospital to "exhaustion and nervous tensions following the Democratic National Convention."

When she awoke after the operation, Jackie saw Bobby sitting there. He had quietly arranged for the burial of the baby, and he was there to do whatever he could do for his sister-in-law. "You knew that, if you were in trouble, he'd always be there," Jackie said.

Rose was sitting at the Villa Les Fal Eze writing a letter to Clare Boothe Luce when Bobby called from America, saying that the baby had died. "Jackie lost her baby!" Rose added in a hastily written postscript. "Heart broken. I am sure Jack is on a boat and we expect to contact him soon—Pray—please—dear Clare."

Not until several days later did Smathers finally reach Jack at sea. "She [Jackie] was very emotional, you know, and you couldn't tell just why," Smathers recalled, though the loss of a second baby was presumably ample cause for emotion. "But anyway, I got him to come back. I told him 'you ought to come back,' which he did. But nobody had actually told the guy a lot about it. So he came back. . . . They had really a great time."

In his book *Profiles in Courage* Jack had described those rare transcendent moments where one vote, one speech, one action defined a politician's entire career. There are such moments in a marriage too. Jack in his terrible obtuseness, his awesome, willful insensitivity had defined the emotional parameters of his marriage. He had shown what he truly felt, more accurately what he did not feel. Even after he heard about the miscarriage, he had initially wanted to stay on the boat, to enjoy himself, to relax. He had little apparent regard for Jackie and her anguish.

Despite his great intelligence, his fascination with human personality, his overwhelming charm and wit, Jack simply didn't understand that while Jackie might ignore the betrayals of the flesh, she would not accept a betrayal of the spirit. Jackie's arsenal against Jack and his emotional disdain was limited largely to the weapons of passivity and withdrawal, weapons that not only hurt Jack but produced their own self-inflicted wounds. She displayed her unhappiness to such an extent that Drew Pearson, the gossip columnist, reported rumors of a divorce. "I know it must have been difficult for her," Rose reflected. "But I never knew that they had a serious break or that they were contemplating divorce."

Divorce was unthinkable. Joe had a talk with his favorite daughter-in-law. He would not allow Jack's prospects for the White House to be smashed apart on the shoals of a broken marriage. Jackie agreed to continue living with Jack, but on her own terms. She had put up with the fraternity-house communality of the Kennedys, but she would attempt now to step back from them as best she could. She had decorated a house in McLean, Virginia, where she had wanted to live with her baby, but she had no desire to remain there any longer. Jackie and Jack moved into a house in Georgetown and sold Hickory Hill to Bobby and Ethel.

Jack saw nothing wrong in his behavior and neither did his father. When Joe was in New York City, he had a Tuesday-evening dinner with Oleg Cassini at La Caravelle where he discussed the Kennedys with considerable candor. Cassini considered the pursuit of women the ultimate game, an avocation that had brought him in close contact with several Kennedys. "The old man had an eye out for every woman that walked," Cassini said. "In the Kennedys' sense of morality that was all right. I don't think that Joe loved anybody. He was a predator who wanted a symbolic success in life and thought that women were one of the ways of showing power. In his way Jack loved women. He interrogated women. He had tremendous charm and his aim was to disarm women with this interest, whether real or not. But he was incapable of a lengthy relationship with a woman. Joe told me that Jack was not a good lover. But he certainly was a conquering man."

That fall of 1956 several Kennedys were out on the campaign trail. Bobby traveled with the Stevenson campaign, a wily mole learning everything he could about running a presidential campaign. He grew so disdainful of Stevenson's lassitude that he voted for Eisenhower. Jack stumped for Stevenson in twenty-six states, arguably working harder for the ticket than anyone other than the two candidates themselves. As he did so he ingratiated himself with local leaders and spread his name to the farthest reaches of the nation. He left Jackie behind as he traveled from speech to speech, on occasion creating the kind of pandemonium associated in the fifties primarily with Elvis Presley. At Ursuline College in Louisville, the Catholic young women screamed, "You're better than Elvis Presley," and practically threw themselves in front of his car. Three weeks later at the "Ladies Day" Rally in Queens Village, mothers, grandmothers, and matrons mobbed Jack, swooned over him, yelled for his autograph, reached out to stroke his hair, screamed out his name. "Just as their teen daughters mob Presley, the women swarmed around the young man with the unruly hair," a New York paper noted. "No matinee idol ever had a greater reception on Long Island than did Kennedy yesterday."

The same week that Jack was being mobbed in Queens, Eunice received a more subdued reception in South Bend, Indiana, to a deeply thoughtful speech. In part her address was a devastating criticism of the emerging politics of personality that was sweeping her brother into the national consciousness. "Even his friends admit . . . that Stevenson rarely creates much bobby-sox appeal," she said. "His opponent for the most powerful office in the world is different. He has the greatest smile since Maurice Chevalier; but his friends admit he is no student or philosopher."

The candidate with "the greatest smile since Maurice Chevalier" won in a landslide in November. As the Kennedys gathered at Hyannis Port for Thanksgiving, they spent hours discussing the political future. All were there, Rose and Joe, the children, the nine grandchildren, including the two newest additions, Sydney Maleia Lawford, and Ethel's fifth, Mary Courtney.

Eunice had as deep a sense of politics as anyone in the family. "Eunice is the one most nearly like Joe," said Smathers. "And Eunice was ambitious as hell, and bright, and persuasive and dogged. She encouraged Jack, in my judgment, more than Rose did, I think as much as Joe."

When it came time for Jack to discuss his political future, it was a matter simply between Jack and his father. After dinner one evening the two men went into the study. Joe had opposed Jack's run for the vice-presidential nomination, but he felt differently about the 1960 presidential nomination. "Just remember, this country is not a private preserve for Protestants," he told his thirty-nine-year-old son, who bore the family legacy on his lean shoulders. "There's a whole new generation out there and it's filled with the sons and daughters of immigrants from all over the world and those people are going to be mighty proud that one of their own is running for President. And that pride will be your spur, it will give your campaign an intensity we've never seen in public life. Mark my word, I know it's true."

"Well, Dad," Jack said, his whole countenance igniting in a smile. "When do we start?"

18

"At Home with the Kennedys"

*I*n the spring of 1957 Ethel and Jackie often sat in the front row of the Senate Select committee hearings investigating the Labor movement in America. Jack had reluctantly agreed to be on the eight-person committee, hearing testimony damning elements of one of the most important Democratic constituencies, but it was Bobby's show. The thirty-one-year-old chief counsel was a badgering inquisitor, tearing through the self-justifications and homilies of corrupt officials such as David Beck, president of the Teamsters. Sometimes Ted drove up from Charlottesville, where he was attending law school at the University of Virginia, sitting next to his two sisters-in-law watching what was an extraordinary spectacle. Rose did not sit there along with the rest of the family, but she was acutely aware of the proceedings, and especially of Bobby's critics. She sent down a newspaper quotation ("Honest and fair criticism hurts nobody") and wanted to be sure that Bobby saw it. She was fluent in the family's emotional language of humor, sending her third son a short note when Mother's Day arrived:

Dear Bobby:
   If you can find me, send large expensive present. No flowers.

                                                          Love,
                                                          Mother

Above all else, the Kennedys were a family, and the men advanced together almost in lockstep, their paths opened often by the nearly invisible hand of their father. "One of his slogans which Joe often quoted was 'Things don't happen, they are made to happen,' " Rose recalled. "As for instance when Jack got the Pulitzer Prize for his book [*Profiles in Courage*], or when he or Bob were chosen as outstanding young man of the year. All of this was a result of their own ability plus careful spadework on their father's part as to who was on the committee and how to reach such and such a person through such and such a friend. However, Joe was lucky because his sons were good material to work with. They behaved well, they were intelligent, and best of all they always had confidence in their father's judgment, because it had been vindicated so many times."

The Kennedy wives often sat and watched their menfolk in their public roles, and helped them in countless ways. For the Kennedy women, even birth had become a political act, signaling the family's commitment to the traditional values of home and hearth. In February 1958 when Ethel gave birth to Michael LeMoyne, her sixth child, a Kennedy operative made sure that a portrait of the happy parents and their tiny son appeared in the *Boston Traveler*. Once a Kennedy child could talk, he could learn lines to advance the family. Joe wrote Bobby that he should have a reporter ask three-year-old Bobby Jr. "where his Daddy is and what he is doing" and Bobby's answer should be " 'he's chasing bad men like a cowboy.' "

The Kennedy women were largely the creators of the home life, and images of that home life were packaged up and peddled to a ready public. Journalists by the score were attracted to these handsome, energetic Kennedys; they needed little prodding to shine their spotlight on the family; they were rewarded by access and invitations and ersatz intimacy. Ethel and Bobby's Christmas list in 1957 alone included thirty-seven reporters, ten photographers, and sixteen radio and television technicians. Ethel and Bobby were careful in what they gave these journalists, noting on the top of the list: "Did not send liquor."

Bobby and Ethel followed the Kennedy pattern, sending their eldest daughter Kathleen to the nuns of the Sacred Heart day school outside Washington. On a September morning Ethel took six-year-old Kathleen's hand and led her into the classroom. "Kathleen arrived kicking and screaming, throwing the worst temper tantrum I've ever seen," remembered Anne Coffey, who would become Kathleen's closest friend. "I sort of decided to strike up a friendship with this little gem who had arrived to make my life better in the first grade." Ethel gave

Kathleen's hand to the nun and hurried out of the room leaving a little girl who was not going to submit easily to the disciplines of the good sisters of the Sacred Heart.

Except for Rosemary, twenty-five-year-old Ted was the only young Kennedy left to be married. Now he felt pressure to take a bride and to begin to raise a family. At Harvard, where he had returned after his stint in the Army, he had proven himself a better athlete than a scholar, catching a winning touchdown against Yale. He had lived with a group of jocks at Winthrop House. He was a good and generous friend who did not act as if his last name won him special merit.

Ted was not nearly as obviously intelligent as Jack, nor a quick intellectual study like Bobby. At law school he had to pore over the law books hour after hour, day after day, trying to retain enough to get by. "I've got to go at a thing four times as hard and four times as long as some other fellow," he told his biographer. He would work and work and work, and then suddenly he would become the locally celebrated "Cadillac Eddie," the big-drinking, big-talking, big-spending party animal. It was Cadillac Eddie who outraced a Virginia police officer at ninety miles an hour. And it was Cadillac Eddie who when he was finally run down a week later, sat doubled up behind the wheel, looking to the officer "weak as a cat."

Ted had a gift for people. He was at his best not at some deep intellectual endeavor, but in oral arguments; politicking for his brother and shaking hands; or out with his friends, lifting a few drinks and telling a few tales. As the youngest male in the family, he too was being groomed for a public life. In October 1957, Rose asked her youngest son to speak at the dedication of a new physical education building in Kathleen's honor at Manhattanville College on its new campus in Purchase, New York.

The Sacred Heart was as important to the Kennedy women's education as Harvard was to the men. If ever there was an occasion for Rose or one of her daughters to speak, this was the one, but a great public occasion when the Kennedy name would be honored in newspapers was not an occasion to waste on a woman. On a Sunday afternoon in October, twenty-five-year-old Ted arrived at the campus from law school to give his first important public address. It was truly a family occasion, and not only Rose and Joe were there, but Jean and Steve; and

Ethel, with Kathleen's six-year-old namesake and five-year-old Joe II.

Ted was a good speaker, and it did no harm that the auditorium was full of single young women. One of the few Manhattanville students who was not present was Joan Bennett. She had just arrived back at college from a weekend at Yale and was more interested in typing up her term paper than attending a dedication ceremony. Five-foot-seven-inch-tall Joan was a woman of stunning beauty, a blonde of breathtaking voluptuousness, wooed by any number of young men. During her summer trip to Europe with eight other Manhattanville students, she had been pursued down the streets. A smile, a word or two, and the European boulevardiers appeared instantly infatuated with her.

Joan was so stunningly attractive that during other summers she worked as an actress-model on live national television. "It was so exciting," Joan recalled. "There was like a little countdown from ten to one. I had to be ready to do my little spiel when Perry Como finished his song. I was on Eddie Fisher's *Coke Time* and I drank Coke. I was on *The Sixty Thousand Dollar Question.*"

Despite her allure, twenty-one-year-old Joan was one of the most popular young women at the school. In a school full of privileged young women, Joan was the woman who seemed to have everything: looks, intelligence, an appreciation of music and the arts, and an inner goodness. Joan was sitting in her dorm room laboriously finishing her paper, when a friend, Margot Murray, came bursting into the room. "Teddy's here," she said urgently, "and you've got to meet him."

Life at Manhattanville was full of tender collusions like this one, women arranging just accidentally to meet a desirable young man. That was the great game for Joan and her friends, the winning prize matrimony in some vague and distant future. Joan had grown up in Bronxville only three blocks away from the Kennedy mansion. This world of prominent Catholic families was a small one and Joan seemed to know almost everyone by reputation if not by name.

Joan had another reason to turn away from her term paper. Manhattanville was still rife with so many rules that a senior like Joan who wanted to have at least some fun and freedom learned to evade the most onerous edicts. If Joan went to the reception, the nun taking names would figure that she had been there all along, and she wouldn't go down in the demerit book.

At the reception Joan looked out on the gathering and recognized Jean, whom she had met the previous summer at a party at the Skakels' house in Greenwich. Jean not only greeted Joan with great friendliness, but took her by the hand and walked her over to meet her little brother. Jean had already been responsible for introducing Ethel into the family, and she thought that Joan was proper dating material. "I want you to meet my little brother," Jean said. Joan looked up at a six-foot-two-inch-tall, two-hundred-pound baby brother whom she found a "darn good-looking fellow."

Ted suggested that he might need a ride to the airport, and Joan said that she and her friend Margot might be available. It didn't matter that she and her friend Margot could be expelled for leaving without permission.

"May I call you?" Ted asked as he squeezed out of the little car. "Yes," Joan said. With that Ted rushed into the airport, totally unaware that this was all part of a romantic intrigue in which he was the only innocent.

Ted telephoned the very next evening, and several calls later invited Joan out Saturday evening during the Thanksgiving holidays. She already had a date that evening, and Teddy settled for Sunday brunch. As Ted knew by intimate experience, when some of these convent-educated maidens left the convent, they left all the rules behind. Joan was different. Her mother insisted that she couldn't even take the train into New York by herself, and Ted had to drive out to Bronxville Sunday morning.

Ted drove Joan to the Sherry Netherland for brunch with Pat and Peter. Joan was roundly impressed by Ted's movie-star brother-in-law, and she fit in well with the convivial group. Later, when they got back to the Bennett home in Bronxville, Joan's date for the evening had just arrived. "I couldn't have planned it better," Joan reflected later.

Joan was living hundreds of miles from Ted. The rest of the academic year she saw him only twice, on a ski trip to Stowe in the winter, and for a weekend trip to Charlottesville in the spring. Although Joan was continuing to date other young men, she had been touched by the hand of the Kennedys, and other young men were wary. "A friend of mine was dating Joan," said Dan Burns, whose father was once one of Joe's closest associates. "Someone told him that she was dating Ted Kennedy, and he said, 'I'm just taking the painting out and I'm leaving it intact at the Kennedy gallery.' "

After her June graduation, Ted invited Joan to spend another weekend with him, this time at Hyannis Port. Rose was the only other Kennedy in residence. Joan had brought a splendid wardrobe with her. She, unlike Jackie, sensed immediately that she should dress as casually as possible and kept her stylish sporty outfits in the suitcase.

Rose considered the proper marriage of her youngest son a matter of the highest urgency. Ted was dating a sundry group of young women that included a French ballerina, a series of sensuous young women, one of whom Rose feared Ted might actually marry. The longer he remained single, the more likely he would troll in dangerous waters. Rose wanted her Teddy wedded, married not simply to a proper woman but to a proper life of faith and family.

On her first meeting with the Kennedy matriarch, Joan recalled that she "wasn't at all put off by her asking me questions, but she seemed very interested in what I thought." Joan was a child of the Sacred Heart. That was immensely important to Rose, and the two women talked at length about Manhattanville and the nuns. Rose gently probed Joan, learning about her background, her faith, her values, her attitudes toward family, never letting her guess that she was in the midst of an oral examination, results of which might determine her entry into the family. "She asked me about Bronxville, about Manhattanville, about the nuns, but mostly we talked about music," Joan recalled. "My mother-in-law played the piano very well, and she asked me to play. I had to give a big recital in order to graduate, and I played some of that music, some Brahms, and she played a Chopin étude for me. There was something that first week I met her that really connected. There was so much in common and the nuns and mostly our piano.

"She told me later that she had been saying her rosary all the time that Teddy would meet a nice Catholic girl and settle down and have children. Apparently, he had brought other girls home, but she hadn't approved. I guess she said something to Eunice, 'I can't believe *our* luck.' I was a nice Catholic girl with a nice upbringing, upper middle class or upper class, and the fact that I was gorgeous. It was too good to be true, that I was somebody that Teddy could be attracted to, a beautiful young woman, with the other qualifications."

As impressed as Rose was by Joan, she didn't let her investigation stop with Joan's words alone. She called Manhattanville

The Kennedy Women
The Saga of an American Family

$\mathcal{M}$ary Augusta Hickey Kennedy, whose stern admonitions to her only son, Joseph P. Kennedy, were the steel of his ambition.

(John F. Kennedy Library)

$\mathcal{A}$ youthful Patrick Joseph "P. J." Kennedy, Boston political leader and shrewd business-man.

(John F. Kennedy Library)

$\mathcal{M}$ary Augusta and P. J. Kennedy with their two daughters, Margaret (*left*) and Loretta. In her later years, Mary Augusta became very heavy.

(John F. Kennedy Library)

$\mathcal{P}. \mathcal{J}.$ Kennedy (*second from left*) playing cards with a group of his friends in 1899. Even by Victorian standards, the Kennedy parlor was heavily decorated.

(John F. Kennedy Library)

*A*gnes and Rose Fitzgerald, the two sisters, in 1894.
(John F. Kennedy Library)

*M*ayor Fitzgerald presents Rose her high school diploma in 1906.
(Boston Post)

*J*osie Hannon Fitzgerald, the austere first lady of Boston.
(Boston Post)

Sixteen-year-old Rose (*third from left*) and seventeen-year-old Joe Kennedy (*second from right*) meet again at Old Orchard Beach during August of 1906.

(*John F. Kennedy Library*)

The Fitzgerald family in 1910: Rose (*left*), Eunice, John F., John F. Jr., Thomas, Frederick (*seated*), Josie, and Agnes.

(Boston Globe)

*R*ose Fitzgerald in Boston, 1911.
•◆•
(*John F. Kennedy Library*)

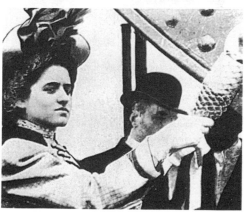

*T*he mayor's daughter, Rose Fitzgerald, christening a ship, about 1913.
•◆•
(*AP / Wide World Photos*)

$\mathcal{R}$ose Fitzgerald playing the piano in 1913 while her father sings and mother and sisters listen.

(Boston Post)

$\mathcal{R}$ose Fitzgerald and her mother Josie at Rose's debut in 1911.

(Boston Globe)

$\mathcal{A}$ smiling Rose Kennedy with Joe on their wedding day.

(Boston Globe)

$\mathcal{I}$n 1920, the Kennedys moved into their large house on the corner of Naples and Abbottsford roads in Brookline, Massachusetts, c. 1925.

•◆•
(John F. Kennedy Library)

$\mathcal{R}$ose Kennedy with her first child, Joseph P. Kennedy Jr., 1916.

•◆•
(John F. Kennedy Library)

*R*osemary and John F. Kennedy in Cohasset, 1924.

*T*he three eldest Kennedy sisters, Eunice, Kathleen, and Rosemary, in Brookline, c. 1925.

*K*athleen with her beloved brother Jack at Palm Beach.

(John F. Kennedy Library)

*T*he Kennedy family in 1936 at home in Bronxville. Left to right, seated: Eunice, Jean, Edward, Joseph P., Patricia, and Kathleen. Standing: Rosemary, Robert, John F., Rose, and Joseph Jr.

(AP / Wide World Photos)

*T*he Kennedys off to England, 1938. Left to right: Kathleen, Robert, Rose, Patricia, and Jean, with Edward M. in front of his mother.

•—◆—•

(AP / Wide World Photos)

*K*athleen, Rose, and Rosemary Kennedy are presented at Buckingham Palace, 1938.

•—◆—•

(Keystone)

*K*athleen with Billy Hartington (*center*) at the races in Great Britain in 1939.
•◆•
(*British Library*)

*I*n March of 1939, all the Kennedys except for Joe Jr. attended the coronation of Pope Pius XII. Left to right: Kathleen, Pat, Bobby, Jack, Rose, Joe, Ted, Eunice, Jean, and Rosemary.
•◆•
(*John F. Kennedy Library*)

𝒯he Kennedys on the eve of World War II, marching into an optimistic future. Eunice (*left*), Jack, Rosemary, Jean, Joe, Ted, Rose, Joe Jr., Pat, Bobby, and Kathleen.
—•—
(*Dorothy Wilding / John F. Kennedy Library*)

𝒥oe Jr., Kathleen, and Jack en route to hear Great Britain declare war on Germany in 1939.
—•—
(*John F. Kennedy Library*)

*E*unice Kennedy dancing distantly from her partner in Palm Beach, 1942.

(Bert and Richard Morgan)

*R*ose and Eunice Kennedy in Palm Beach, 1941.

(Bert and Richard Morgan)

*E*unice (*left*), Bobby, Ted, and Jean Kennedy on the tennis court in Palm Beach, 1941.

(Bert and Richard Morgan)

A smiling Rosemary Kennedy.
•◆•
(*JPK Enterprises*)

*E*unice Kennedy and the
father she adored, at
Hyannis Port, 1940.
•◆•
(*John F. Kennedy Library*)

*J*acqueline Bouvier with her
pony, 1939.
•◆•
(*Bert and Richard Morgan*)

*I*nga Arvad, the great
love of Jack Kennedy's
early life.
•◆•
(*John White*)

*T*he Kennedy sisters, Pat, Kathleen, Eunice, and Jean, at Hyannis Port.

•—•—•
(John F. Kennedy Library)

*J*ackie with her father, John "Black Jack" Bouvier, in 1947 (*left*) and 1949 (*right*).

•—•—•
(Bert and Richard Morgan)

*Th*e Kennedys at Hyannis Port. From left: Jack, Pat, Rose, Joe, Jean, Bobby, and Eunice, with Ted kneeling.

(*John F. Kennedy Library*)

*P*at Kennedy and Peter Lawford on their wedding day, 1954.

(*Peter Lawford Collection*)

*B*illy Hartington and Kathleen Kennedy on their wedding day, 1944.

(*Associated News*)

*J*ack Kennedy and Jacqueline Bouvier on their wedding day, 1953.

—•—

(John F. Kennedy Library)

*E*unice Kennedy cuts the wedding cake with her new husband, Sargent Shriver, while Jean and Bobby Kennedy look on, 1953.

—•—

(AP / Wide World Photos)

*J*ean Kennedy and Stephen Smith on their wedding day, 1956.

(UPI / Bettmann)

*J*oan Bennett and Edward Kennedy on their wedding day, with Jack Kennedy standing behind, 1958.

(AP / Wide World Photos)

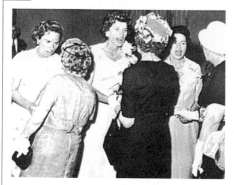

$\mathcal{E}$thel Kennedy and Eunice Shriver campaigning with Lady Bird Johnson in 1960.

•—•—•
(*John F. Kennedy Library*)

$\mathcal{T}$ed, Eunice, Pat, and Ethel watching the presidential election returns in Hyannis Port, November 1960.

•—•—•
(*Photograph © 1994 Jacques Lowe*)

$\mathcal{E}$unice, Jean, and Pat with Jack on Boston television the night before election day, November 1960.

•—•—•
(*Photograph © 1994 Jacques Lowe*)

$\mathcal{T}$he Kennedys pose for a family portrait the day after Jack's election as president. From left, seated: Eunice, Rose, Joe, Jackie, and Ted. Standing: Ethel, Steve Smith, Jean, Jack, Bobby, Pat, Sarge Shriver, Joan, and Peter Lawford.

(Photograph © 1994 Jacques Lowe)

$\mathcal{J}$oan Kennedy and Jean Smith with assorted children at Hyannis Port, 1961.

(Photograph © 1994 Jacques Lowe)

$\mathcal{E}$thel with seven of her children at Hickory Hill, 1961. Left to right, seated: Bobby, Joe Jr., Kerry Kathleen, Michael. Standing: David and Courtney.

(Photograph © 1994 Jacques Lowe)

A pensive Eunice with her two eldest children, Bobby and Maria.

(Photograph © 1994 Jacques Lowe)

*E*unice working with her brother Jack, the president, at Hyannis Port.

(Photograph © 1994 Jacques Lowe)

*T*he Kennedy women. From left: Joan, Jean, Eunice, Jackie, and Ethel.

(Photograph © 1994 Jacques Lowe)

*E*thel Kennedy, Jean Smith, and Eunice Shriver at a press conference given by Sargent Shriver, 1961.

(UPI / Bettmann)

*P*at and Peter Lawford with their dear friend, Frank Sinatra, and Nat King Cole. Man in center is unidentified.

(Peter Lawford Collection)

*R*ose and her son, the president, at a 1962 dinner of the Kennedy Foundation honoring research in the field of mental retardation.

(AP / Wide World Photos)

*J*ackie and Caroline
in the White House.
•-•-•
(AP / Wide World Photos)

*J*ack and Jackie
Kennedy arriving at
the Palm Beach estate
after mass, 1963.
•-•-•
(Bob Davidoff)

A pensive Pat Lawford.
•-•-•
(Peter Lawford Collection)

*P*at Lawford and Jackie Kennedy taking their daughters, Victoria (*left*), Sydney, and Caroline to school at the Convent of the Sacred Heart, 1964.

•◆•

(AP / Wide World Photos)

*J*ackie at Arlington National Cemetery for the burial of her husband, November 25, 1963. With her are Bobby, Rose, and Eunice.

•◆•

(UPI / Bettmann)

*J*ackie Kennedy aboard the yacht *Christina* with Aristotle Onassis and Franklin Roosevelt Jr., 1963.

•◆•

(AP / Wide World Photos)

*J*ackie Kennedy and Peter Lawford in Hawaii.
(Peter Lawford Collection)

*M*ass at St. Edward's Church in Palm Beach, 1972. From left: Timothy and Maria Shriver, Sydney Lawford, Bobby, Rose, Sargent, Mark, and Anthony Shriver.
(Bob Davidoff)

*R*osemary Kennedy swimming with Caroline Kennedy and Maria Shriver, 1975.

•◆•

(*Bob Davidoff*)

*R*osemary Kennedy and her helper, a nun, in Palm Beach, 1975.

•◆•

(*Bob Davidoff*)

*R*osemary Kennedy's home at St. Coletta's, where she has lived since 1949.

•◆•

(*Laurence Leamer*)

$\mathcal{R}$ose Kennedy nestles her first great-grandchild, Meaghan Townsend, while David Townsend and Kathleen Kennedy Townsend look on, 1978.

(Bob Davidoff)

$\mathcal{M}$aurice Tempelsman and Jackie Onassis hailing a cab in Manhattan.

(Brian Quigley)

$\mathcal{S}$ydney Lawford and her father, Peter, on her wedding day, 1983.

•–•–•

(*Peter Lawford Collection*)

$\mathcal{T}$he Smiths at home. From left: Steve Jr., Amanda, Steve, Jean, Kym, and Willie.

•–•–•

(*Frank Teti*)

$\mathcal{J}$oan Kennedy returned to her alma mater, Manhattanville College, in 1984, to give the commencement address. From left: Ted Jr., Joan, Patrick, and Kara.

•–•–•

(*Brian Quigley*)

$\mathcal{E}$unice Shriver.
•◆•
(*Special Olympics*)

$\mathcal{P}$at Lawford and her four children at Christopher's 1983 graduation from Boston College Law School. From left: Sydney, Pat, Christopher, Victoria, and Robin.
•◆•
(*Brian Quigley*)

*J*oan Kennedy, May 1991.
•◆•
(*Brian Quigley*)

*E*unice and Sarge Shriver at the European Special Olympics games in Scotland, 1990.
•◆•
(*Special Olympics*)

*M*embers of the young generation at play. From left: Kerry, Courtney, Max, and Ted Kennedy Jr.; Victoria and Robin Lawford; Kara and Christopher Kennedy; and Anthony Shriver.
•◆•
(*Frank Teti*)

Three generations of Kennedys at Rose's 100th birthday celebration, July 1990.

(AP / Wide World Photos)

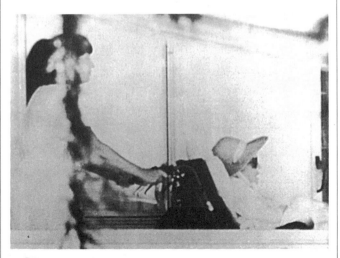

Rose Kennedy on the afternoon of her 100th birthday.

(AP / Wide World Photos)

C a r o l i n e
K e n n e d y
Schlossberg
kneels at her
mother's coffin,
May 1994.
••••
*(AP / Wide World
Photos)*

R ose Ken-
nedy prays at
St. Edward's
Church in Palm
Beach, 1979.
••••
(Bob Davidoff)

and talked to Mother Elizabeth O'Bryne, the president of the college, with whom Rose had a close relationship. The Kennedys were the greatest benefactors of the school, and it would be the worthiest of recompenses to provide a second daughter-in-law to the Kennedys. Moreover, it would tie the family even closer to the school. Although Joan was a mediocre scholar finishing sixty-seventh in her class of 108, Mother O'Bryne praised her as a good student, a commendable young woman, eminently worthy of marriage to young Ted.

Joan's emotional life resonated with many of the same themes as the women in the Kennedy family. Her mother, Virginia "Ginny" Bennett, was a woman of great social ambition who considered her daughters her capital. A stark disciplinarian, she had applied the hairbrush to Joan and her younger sister, Candy, for the most minor of offenses. When Ginny brought Joan back to Manhattanville one September, one student, Delayne Dedrick Gold, recalled her as a classic stage mother, an upper-class Catholic version of Rose in the musical *Gypsy*. To Joan, however, as to the young Kennedy women, her father was the measure of all things. Harry Bennett, a charming and debonair advertising man, doted on his two beautiful daughters.

Joan was a woman who carried the Kennedy pattern of self-denial and relentless positiveness to a plane beyond even that of Rose. Her mother had a serious drinking problem, and her father was a heavy drinker as well. But the family maintained a veneer of perfect civility. To Joan, everything in life was perfect. She recoiled from anything negative or nasty, as if its mere touch would taint her. One night she had gone down to Greenwich Village to see Eugene O'Neill's *Long Day's Journey Into Night*. Joan had found the play so dark, so unnecessary, nothing one wanted to sit through. She wasn't one to talk about anything negative, and Ted wasn't the sort of man who sat around discussing emotions. He was always on the move, charging ahead.

Joan spent two more active, communal weekends with Ted that summer, ending the season with a final weekend in Hyannis Port. Joan was still a virgin. No matter how much she might have been sexually attracted to Ted, she was not about to give up her virginity before her wedding day. That only made Joan more desirable. "All our dates were well chaperoned," Joan recalled. "It was sort of romantic. You got to know each other with other people around."

One day the couple walked alone along the seaweed-strewn beach. Whenever Ted got nervous or unsure of what to say or respond, he fell into mindless mumbling. "What do you think about our getting married," he asked, as if he were discussing nothing more romantic than establishing some kind of business partnership.

"Well, I guess it's not such a bad idea!" Joan replied. With that Ted plopped down on the sand.

"What do we do next?" he asked. He told her that he wanted to marry right away.

Joan met Joe that evening and then headed back to Bronxville. "I was young and naïve then," Joan recalled, "but looking back, there were warning signals. We didn't see each other from the time of his proposal until the engagement party." Ted was busy as the nominal head of Jack's reelection campaign to the Senate. During the week he studied law in Virginia. On weekends he traveled from one end of Massachusetts to the other. Ted, like the rest of the Kennedys, was not deeply introspective. He had learned that the best way to deal with intractable emotional problems or uncertainties was to run from them. The closer they came, the harder he ran.

Joan was engaged to the celebrated youngest Kennedy, yet Ted had not even given her a ring. He did not even arrive in Bronxville on time for *their* engagement party. The celebration was half over before Ted finally roared in, sneaking into the house through the maid's quarters and up the back stairs to avoid embarrassing Joan's mother. Upstairs Ted handed Joan a package containing the engagement ring that Joe had purchased and that his son had not even bothered to open.

Then the couple descended the spiral staircase to greet adoring family and friends, and suddenly everything was okay. Ted had inherited his grandfather's Irish charm by the bucket load, and there was hardly a woman or man in the Bennett house to whom Teddy didn't have a few affectionate words that seemed uniquely crafted for her or him. Joan was on his arm, looking stunningly beautiful, and they were a tableau of young love. In public moments like this, everything was fine, and the marriage seemed as splendid an idea as it was inevitable.

Joan and Ted were both the children of privilege, sheltered from the world of work and difficulty that was life to so many others. For Joan it was unthinkable that she should marry anyone but a socially prominent, well-to-do young Catholic who would provide for her as well as had her adoring father. For all she knew of marital life, it would be like playing doll's house. In a wife, Ted needed a woman of formidable strength, a woman who would stand up to him and to his indulgences, stand up to his family as well, and be both his partner and his goad, not someone with a psychological neediness greater even than his own. Beneath their handsome exteriors, Joan and Ted were both people of terrible vulnerability who were living the scripts of life others had prepared for them, reading lines that they pretended were their own. In the weeks before their marriage, Ted had no time to spend with his finacée and learn about Joan. As the November wedding approached, the couple hardly ever saw one another.

Joan was increasingly despondent at the prospect of marrying a man she scarcely knew. "Joan's father, Mr. Bennett, arranged a meeting between himself and Ted and Joe," recalled Mary Lou McCarthy. "And Mr. Bennett said that his daughter had second thoughts and that they should either cancel the engagement and the wedding plans or perhaps put things back a year. Joe became furious and said they're not going to put in the papers that my son is being tossed over. He forced this issue. He was God."

What had begun as a college romance had become in part an arranged marriage. "But the funny thing is that everyone thinks this is a marriage made in heaven," Joan reflected. "Both my mother- and father-in-law, and my parents and me, and all my girlfriends and Ted's friends. Everyone thinks this is a marriage that will just be perfect."

Jack knew that he would handily win reelection. He wanted to show that he was the Bay State's favorite son sent off into the presidential sweepstakes with an overwhelming vote. It was a time of testing too, a trial run, not only for Jack but for the family.

Joe and Jack and Bobby, the triumvirate of power, were discovering that Jean's husband Steve had the visceral instincts of an oldtime Irish pol. He liked to stand just out of the spotlight, deftly manipulating whatever happened in the glare of publicity. Jean and her sisters were not invited in the back rooms where men talked the unvarnished argot of politics, a rude and often vulgar shorthand, the language of deal making, but the Kennedy women were sent out on the campaign hustings. Now that they were wives and mothers, they could not travel to the extent they had in Jack's previous campaign.

Jackie felt especially limited since on November 27, 1957, she had given birth to a healthy baby girl, Caroline Bouvier Kennedy. Her enlarged family moved into a new home in Georgetown. Jackie took immense pleasure in her baby and hired a gray-haired British nanny, Maude Shaw, to watch over Caroline.

Jackie accompanied her husband, and when she was not with him spent much time at the couple's house in Hyannis Port, across from Rose and Joe's. That was a double burden to her. "It was always Mr. Kennedy who wanted to keep everyone here [at Hyannis Port]," she recalled. "I really fought against it. I wanted to get away from the compound. He had this house for us for two years before we lived in it." Jackie was there the week before the election for the most unusual event of the campaign. Massachusetts television viewers that morning turned on their sets to see the title "At Home with the Kennedys" on their screens. The camera scanned across the faces of Rose, Jackie, Eunice, and Jean, sitting with one-year-old Steve Jr. on her lap. The four women sat there in a living room set with their backs arched, hands folded in their laps, legs crossed at the ankles, dressed in conservative dark dresses, wearing pearl necklaces, the very uniform of matronly civility. "Good morning friends," Rose began, reminding viewers that six years ago there had been a similar program. "We have a charming addition in the person of Jacqueline, Jack's wife, who has been campaigning with him during the last few months and whom many of you have met," Rose said, enunciating each syllable. "Won't you tell us, Jacqueline, a little about your experiences?"

"I've enjoyed campaigning so much, Mrs. Kennedy," Jackie said, addressing her mother-in-law as if her appellation were a royal title. Jackie's voice was as peculiar as Rose's, an accent full of the upper-class resonances of Newport and Southampton, along with a breathy, almost lisping manner that together made her sound both childlike and sophisticated. It was a voice not calculated to win many votes in the Irish bars of the South End, but this was a weekday morning, and many women viewers at home considered Jackie a veritable princess. "Since September fifteenth Jack and I have been traveling through the state trying to meet as many people as we can. Your son, Teddy, who as you know is campaign manager, set up the schedule for us last summer. We visited 184 communities. . . ." Jackie's mini speech suggested that among her many attributes was a good memory, and an ability to read the words that were written for her.

"Well, congratulations, Jackie," Rose said, as if bestowing a high honor, "and congratulations to Jack for having found a wife who is so enjoying the campaign."

"Jack has been so ungallant as to suggest that you have been campaigning for sixty-five years," Jackie said, smiling slightly as she looked at a Rose who appeared no more than a youthful and stylish forty-five. "You were a tiny baby."

"That is not quite true because in those days women didn't have the vote, and so we did not go to rallies."

"I'm surprised that Jack hasn't insisted on taking Caroline on this trip," Jackie said. "She's back in Boston now but she was very lucky to be with you at the Cape."

"Speaking about the Cape, Jean, how did it go?" Rose asked, taking a sedate sip of water, and neatly segueing to her daughters.

Jean had a wicked sense of humor and could have told her mother a thing or two about life at the Cape, but this was not the occasion. "Mother, Bobby was there with his six children, and Eunice with her two, and Jackie at times," Jean said. "And of course I was there with Steve Jr. It was great fun, all next door to one another."

Eunice and Jean and Jackie all had their own homes in Hyannis Port now.

"Well, what did you do, Eunice?" Rose asked, as Eunice sat dutifully there, her hands still clasped.

"Well, we learned to ride and swim," Eunice said. "And Bobby took them out to sail."

"Tell me, did you have a chance to take them up to Plymouth?" Rose asked, though she surely knew the answer.

"They're a little young," Eunice said.

That gave Rose the entree to lecture her daughters, daughter-in-law, and the women of Massachusetts on developing a sense of history in their children. Then she introduced a series of home movies, all with generic background music and narration by Eunice and Jackie. Here were Eunice and Sarge taking their children to the zoo in Chicago, and teaching little Bobby Shriver and Maria geography. And here was Ethel's and Bobby's brood in Hickory Hill. Then came footage of Pat and Peter at their beachfront home in Santa Monica. At the end of the film, the scene returned to the Kennedy women in the living room. Only now Jack stood behind them. He reminded the audience to vote on November 4, and then took questions from viewers calling in to phones answered by the Kennedy women.

In this last week of the campaign, this television program was the great final salvo, an appeal directed at Jack's largest constituency. Although most of the program had nothing to do with matters crucial to Massachusetts or the nation, Jack had an astute understanding of his appeal to women. This morning he had given the women voters several reasons to vote for him: as a champion of family values, as the scion of Massachusetts's royal political family, as an articulate spokesman for the state and the nation, or as a politician of pure sexual charisma. On election day, the voters turned out in the record numbers that Jack hoped they would. The electorate gave him 73.6 percent of the vote, the greatest victory any senatorial candidate had ever received in Massachusetts.

The family had one other important event in November 1958, and that was Teddy's wedding. As the date approached, both twenty-two-year-old Joan and twenty-six-year-old Ted had their moments of doubt. Sometimes it was as if they had stumbled onto the wrong train together, and as it picked up speed they wondered if they dared to jump off. For Joan it was not one thing, but a series of events. She was a woman used to being courted, but Teddy couldn't be bothered any longer.

Ted could not possibly tell Joan what was troubling him. A few days before the wedding Ted and Joan were out with a group that included one of his best college friends. As the evening progressed, Ted sent Joan home in a limousine and continued out for a long night of carousing with his drinking buddy. At a nightclub the two men spotted the Aly Khan at a nearby table. If ever there was an expert on the perils of matrimony, it was this legendary playboy. Ted didn't know the man, but he walked over and told Aly Khan of his doubts. Aly Khan looked at the flush-faced young man and shook his head: "It's too late now for advice." On the evening before the ceremony, Ted confided to his friend that he was worried that he was making a terrible mistake.

Joan might have broken off the engagement herself, but after the meeting with her future father-in-law, she had steeled herself to go ahead and to put aside her doubts. Joan had wanted an intimate wedding for family and friends. She soon realized that Joe "wanted to invite every political crony he'd ever met, and others he wanted to impress." She slowly comprehended that even the most intimate family occasions might be witnessed by important supporters, worthy retainers, amenable journalists, and others, and that the glare of publicity would reach into all but the most intimate recesses of her life. Joan's mother had invited Ethel and Bobby, but not their children; nonetheless, Kathleen, Joe Jr., Bobby Jr., and even two-year-old Courtney showed up at Bronxville for the ceremony.

One of Joan's father's friends gave the bridal couple a gift of a film of the entire wedding. The film crew had placed tiny microphones in the pockets of several members of the bridal party. After the honeymoon Joan watched the film of her wedding. It was wonderfully candid. There were the bridesmaids putting on their gowns. Here she saw herself getting ready. And there was Cardinal Spellman, who officiated. And there behind the altar waiting for the ceremony to begin stood Ted and Jack, his best man. Jack didn't realize that he was being recorded. As Ted waited to take his vows promising fidelity to Joan, Jack was giving his baby brother a lecture on married life. It was hardly the kind of marital sermon heard in church, and when Jack found out about it Joan recalled that he "blushed scarlet." Ted adored his older brother, and was prepared to do and be whatever was necessary to merit Jack's praise and honor, even if it meant intending to betray his own marital vows before he had taken them.

Joan managed to laugh, but it was an ominously haunting moment. Here was Cardinal Spellman talking about the sacredness of the marital vows, and behind the altar Jack giving a different sort of sermon on what marriage meant to a Kennedy man. And then the whole offensive business had been cut away, as if life itself were nothing more than raw footage to be edited for public consumption.

All her life Joan had been a pampered daughter of privilege, but in Charlottesville she found herself spending hours alone in their modest quarters. "I had to clean house, cook, do the laundry, and I really learned a lot," Joan reflected. "It was fun—for a while!!" When Ted graduated the following spring, he sent Joan up to Boston to find an apartment while he flew off to Africa with a group of senators. Joan found an apartment with bad plumbing at Lewisburg Square, a gamy neighborhood for a debutante from Bronxville. Rose took one look at the apartment and the neighborhood and pronounced it improper and unsafe. "I admire your wanting to save the Kennedys' money," she told her newest daughter-in-law, "but my dear you have to be careful."

Soon afterwards Joan and Ted moved to a better apartment in a better neighborhood.

While Jack crisscrossed the country giving speeches, energetically promoting himself, Eunice and Sarge were making their own journey across America. As her father and brothers grew preoccupied with Jack's political future, Eunice realized that no one was watching over the future of the Joseph P. Kennedy Jr. Foundation. She went to her father and said: "Daddy, I'd like to do something for the foundation. I'd like to see if I could help it get a kind of focus."

"Fine," Joe said. He had unlimited faith in the abilities of his children, and he wanted Eunice to have this opportunity.

"Well, you know I'd like to go out and really find out what the big need is," she continued, enthused with the prospect.

Joe left it to Eunice to decide where she would go and what she would see. Eunice and Sarge were a political team. When Eunice got through talking to her father, she called her husband and asked him to join her on their quest.

As she and Sarge quizzed the leaders of the philanthropic world, medical researchers, academicians, and researchers, Eunice became convinced that mental retardation was the one compelling issue for the foundation. Eunice had a special empathy for those with retardation because of her own sister. It was not as much what the experts said as what they did not say. The great foundations of America were concerned with social problems and cultural patronage, not the thankless task of helping to pay for the warehousing of a hidden, forgotten population. Medical researchers were trying to cure cancer, heart disease, and other maladies, not attempting to alleviate what was considered a largely hopeless condition. Social workers were faced with the ravages of poverty and neglect, and in a moral triage, they turned away from this needy sector of society. Educators in the public schools felt they had enough to do with the challenge of Sputnik, and they had no time or place for those with retardation. Government officials on the national, state, or local level had almost no interest in funding programs for these Americans who did not vote and did not clamor for attention. All across America there was not one university prior to 1956 with a major research program dealing with mental retardation. For many Americans, mental retardation was not simply a condition but an embarrassment, and those who worked with the developmentally disabled were as much pushed off to the side as their clients.

Eunice was serving on the board of the Menninger Foundation in Topeka, Kansas, where she sat in splendid surroundings discussing the development of medical science. America was full of boards where social ambition was as much a motive as philanthropy, and self-congratulation more common than self-examination. Eunice had a desperate urgency to do something, to perform great and lasting good. She could hardly sit still listening to the social chitchat and the tales of triumphant medical research.

Eunice resigned from the board and returned to her father and outlined for him a new direction for the Joseph P. Kennedy Jr. Foundation, focusing almost exclusively on mental retardation. Joe listened intently. Until now the family foundation had been largely a Catholic charity, donating money to groups and organizations approved by the newly named Cardinal Cushing. Among its other gifts the foundation had given money to institutions that housed those with retardation, including the St. Coletta School in Wisconsin where Rosemary lived. Eunice was suggesting something dramatically different: to hone in solely on this one problem and to finance research and diagnostic care.

Joe and his sons were brilliantly exploiting the family name to promote Jack's political career. Her father could easily have used the foundation to fund a series of highly visible projects that would bring immediate glory to the Kennedys. But Joe actively supported his daughter and her husband. "If we had wanted to promote my brother, mental retardation is not the issue we would have chosen," Eunice said passionately. "You go where the bigwigs are where there's a social thing. You give it to Massachusetts General in hopes of having your name on the hospital or the New York Public Library. And then you get on the board, this whole route until you end up a bigwig."

Eunice was a doer, a goad, and she set out to make things happen. Eunice sought to have the foundation fund multidisciplinary research centers at leading universities to develop programs to prevent or ameliorate mental retardation. Since the federal government had not yet begun to pour hundreds of millions of dollars into research, the university presidents and deans listened to her carefully. The foundation was giving away only one or two million dollars a year, a minuscule amount by later standards. Research was still relatively cheap, and it was enough money, if properly and carefully parceled out, to have a seminal impact on a problem that affected more than five million Americans.

Although Eunice's commitment exceeded that of everyone else in the family, Sarge was named executive director of the foundation and Eunice was put in charge of midwestern operations. But it was as a team that they traveled the country, with an entourage of academic consultants. Eunice had inherited the family faith in experts. They advised setting up programs at the University of Wisconsin, at Johns Hopkins University, and at Santa Monica Hospital in association with UCLA.

As enthusiastic as Eunice was about the proposals, she went back to her father for approval. She needed continually to prove herself worthy to him. She was consumed with doing right and doing well and doing good. During these months Dr. Robert Cooke, then of the Department of Pediatrics at Johns Hopkins, and a lifelong consultant to the foundation, first met Eunice. As he watched her constantly returning to her father for advice and assurance, he felt that this relationship, more than anything else, was the key to Eunice's life. "I don't think it's her Catholicism or anything that she learned that motivates her," said Cooke. "Take all that away, and you have a woman who all her life has sought to be the daughter her father wanted her to be."

Mary Ann Orlando, who was Sarge's secretary, had much the same sense about Eunice. "I think that Eunice was at one point in time terrified of her father," Orlando reflected. "I shouldn't use the word 'terrified,' but she was so anxious to please. Let's put it that way. She would go through hoops trying to be what he expected of her."

Eunice and her sisters and brothers loved their mother, but they knew that their father provided the ample funds that removed them from the mundane concerns of most Americans. Joe and Rose had seen the dissipation of many wealthy families. He was appalled that his children had so dismally failed that lesson, that they spent money as if his coffers were limitless and not replenished from his shrewd business dealings.

"I don't know what is going to happen to this family when I die," he said one evening at Hyannis Port as Jack, Bobby, Ethel, and the Fays listened. "There is no one in the entire family, except Joan and Teddy, who is living within his means.

No one appears to have the slightest concern for how much they spend."

All their lives money had been the one taboo subject at the dinner table, and the family members sat in stunned silence listening to Joe's outraged monologue. "I don't know how long it will take all of you to exhaust the principal after I'm gone."

Joe stopped a moment and looked at his daughter-in-law. "Ethel, you are the worst," he said. "There isn't the slightest indication that you have any idea what you spend all your money on." Ethel sat there crunched up like an old paper bag as Joe continued his sermon. "Bills come in from all over the country for every conceivable item. It is utterly ridiculous to display such disregard for money."

Bobby could not sit there any longer. "Dad," he interjected, "I think you have made your point." With that a chastened, tearful Ethel ran out of the dining room, with Bobby close at her heels, and the others sat there as if they had weathered a great storm.

Ethel and Bobby finally reappeared. "Ethel, don't worry," Jack said. "We've come to the conclusion that the only solution is to have Dad work harder."

In Los Angeles, Pat served as the western head of the foundation; although she made some efforts with the Santa Monica Hospital, she was hardly as committed as Eunice. Pat was the only Kennedy sister to wed not only a nominal Republican, but a man who lived outside the pale of politics.

In the fall of 1956 Peter purchased a sprawling mansion along the Pacific Coast Highway in Santa Monica owned by Louis B. Mayer, the legendary producer. The ten-thousand-square-foot home included an elevator and a projection screen in the living room. With its spacious living and dining rooms and four bedroom suites set apart from the body of the house, as well as a guest house, it was an environment ideally suited for the kinds of casual entertaining that dominated Pat's and Peter's social lives. The Lawford home became a recreation center for the other members of the family. For Jack especially it was a hideaway from the electorate and the press, a place where he could relax with the sun and the surf and nubile young things. "I was around when he was dating a number of women," recalled Peter Sabiston, Peter's close friend. "I used to pick these girls up. For a while Jackie never came out here, and I thought maybe she was forbidden to come out."

Peter did not need his brother-in-law's example to guide him in his own casual dalliances. Pat had the sexual reticence that was a mark of her upbringing, and that may have set her husband's eyes wandering. "Peter was a little kinky in his sex, and I'm sure Pat wouldn't do what he wanted her to do," said Ebbins. "He talked about sex with Pat, or rather the lack of it. He was with some pretty good women, some proficient women, but you're married, she's the mother of your children, and you live the life."

Peter could sit there and watch his father-in-law setting up his assignations in front of his daughter, but he was far more circumspect with his own wife. He was too much the gentleman to parade another woman in front of Pat, who was no Rose, ready to shield her eyes with the veil of faith. "When Peter married Pat, he did not screw around," said Ebbins, who had his own Hollywood definition of infidelity. "He'd go out of town and there would be a masseuse, or something like that with whom he had his way, but what's wrong with that? That's not screwing around. When Pat was pregnant, he had a few alliances. Just stop and think about it. You don't become celibate because your wife is pregnant."

Fred Otash, a former Los Angeles police officer, was a private investigator for *Confidential*, a notorious magazine specializing in writing about celebrity scandals. Otash and his employers practiced a technique that some might consider closer to blackmail than to journalism. They held back many scandalous stories in hopes of getting other stories, or at least dissuading the studios from filing too many lawsuits. "These stories kept coming in from pimps and madames about Peter, whores, and hash," Otash recalled. "One of Peter's friends came to me screaming. It was a story about a couple of black broads and Peter, and they had sold the story to *Confidential* for thirty-six hundred dollars. I had to fight to kill the story. That kind of thing happened two or three different times. He was fucking around on the Kennedy girl from day one."

For Pat, proximity to Hollywood had not brought immediate disillusionment, the portraits of celebrities looking blemished and wrinkled at close view. For her the glamour and magic of the film world was still there, personified in Frank Sinatra. The scrawny singer had the same impact on women as Jack did. Pat was obsessed with meeting him. Since costarring in *From Here to Eternity*, Sinatra's career was again on the ascendancy. Wherever he went, he traveled with a protective entourage.

Pat kept insisting that Peter introduce her. "Boy, did you come to the wrong window," he told her. He then recounted the story of how in his bachelor days at MGM, he had been friendly with the volatile entertainer. When Sinatra mistakenly believed that Peter was dating his estranged wife, Ava Gardner, he had phoned detailing the ways in which he was going to have Peter's legs broken. As much as Peter had enjoyed Sinatra's considerable charm and camaraderie, he knew enough to stay away from the awesomely temperamental crooner.

Pat had her opportunity to meet Sinatra at a dinner party given at the home of Gary and Rocky Cooper in August 1958. Peter had a minor accident on the set of a television show in which he was guest starring. That delay allowed Pat to spend the entire dinner talking animatedly with Sinatra. Pat was six months pregnant, but she hid her pregnancy, still looking impossibly lean. Pat was knowledgeable about the world of politics, and she was a decided change from Sinatra's typical dinner partner.

Peter came rushing into the drawing room after dinner holding his bandaged hand up. "Guess what?" Pat said, uninterested in Peter's tale of a burnt hand. "I just had dinner with Frank Sinatra. He's charming."

Frank accepted an invitation to the Lawfords', and the quarrel was forgotten. Pat was taken with Sinatra, not in some hopeless romantic crush, but in unabashed admiration. Frank had a charm of such incandescence that when he shined it at Pat it blinded her from seeing anything else about the man.

Sinatra was a man of courtly thoughtfulness to the wives of his friends, and he was wonderfully gracious to the now obviously pregnant Pat. When a friend and a member of the group became pregnant, Sinatra flew the woman and her husband to Las Vegas, gambled with her saying that she brought him luck, and later sent the new mother an extravagant arrangement of flowers. Sinatra was such an outsized personality that he swept people into his life, transforming them. Sinatra suddenly stood at the center of Pat's and Peter's lives. They saw him usually twice during the week, at his home for a screening and then at the Lawfords'. Weekends they often drove to the singer's home in Palm Springs. The Lawfords always had the same bedroom, and felt so at ease with this new life that they left their casual sportswear in the closet.

Pat had known Sinatra only three months when she gave birth to her second daughter on November 4, 1958. She decided to name the child in part in honor of her newest and dearest friend. The girl's first name would be Victoria, memorializing Jack's electoral triumph on this very day. But the girl's middle name would be Francis, forever linking the Kennedys and Sinatra.

Pat had little interest in the chores of motherhood, and as soon as Victoria Francis was back home, she was handed over to a nursemaid. Pat was more interested in involving herself in the world of filmmaking. Only eleven days after giving birth she and Peter purchased the rights to a screenplay titled *Ocean's Eleven* for ten thousand dollars.

Sinatra was interested in producing the script, another link that tied the threesome even closer together. Pat was enamored with the idea of Sinatra, this man so Kennedy-like in his intensity and energy. Wherever Pat and Peter went with Sinatra, there was an underlying tension. The singer could change in a matter of minutes from a sweet boyish comrade to a spoiled, petulant prima donna, or to a violent street tough. Pat undoubtedly had heard the stories of him slapping women around and roughing up photographers, but there was a layer of danger here far beyond that. Pat had almost never entered the back rooms of either politics or entertainment. She had no idea that Sinatra had grown up near some of the most notorious mobsters in America. He not only knew these men, he prided himself on these associations.

On New Year's Eve, Pat and Peter drove to Mike Romanoff's celebrated restaurant for the owner's private party. She sat at the most desired table in the room, with Sinatra, Natalie Wood, and Robert Wagner. Pat had given birth only two months before, but boring holidays at home were not for her. She and Peter planned to spend the day with Frank in Palm Springs.

Pat wore a low-cut gown that on most occasions would have been perfectly comfortable, but the new year was blowing in with a cold vengeance. The group was supposed to drive down to Palm Springs in the middle of the night. The two women made the reasonable suggestion of waiting until the morning sun to head south.

Sinatra treated his sojourns with his friends like military expeditions in which he was the general whose orders were to be smartly obeyed. "Happy New Year's, my ass," Sinatra said before stomping out of Romanoff's and heading out into the night by himself.

Late in the morning Pat and Peter were at their house after a restful and warm sleep, wondering whether they should drive down to Palm Springs. Peter decided to call first. "Well, I guess Mr. Sinatra . . ." said George Jacobs, the butler, finding it difficult to find the right word, "I guess he's really pissed off about something."

"How so, George?" Peter asked.

"He came in and had a couple of drinks. Then he went into the room where you and Mrs. Lawford stay and took all of your clothes out of the closet."

"What'd he do with them, George?"

"Tried to make a bonfire out of them by the pool. When the fire wouldn't get going, he threw everything into the pool."

As he hung up Peter laughed out loud and then thought about the loss of his favorite aged jeans. "What will that sweet man do next?" Pat asked rhetorically, her words dripping with irony. Her husband looked as if he had lost an irreplaceable heirloom. "We'll age another pair. Just make sure you don't take them down to Frank's."

When Sinatra exploded his friends scurried off in all directions, returning once the volcanic entertainer had simmered down. He called three weeks later, and Pat and Peter were back with him again. Peter and Sinatra had a psychological quirk common among entertainers: the inability to be alone.

As her friends and acquaintances, Pat had known only proper young Catholic women, but around Sinatra and his entourage she was introduced to another kind of woman. Wherever they went there were sexy young "actresses" or "models" whose most obvious means of support were the men they serviced with obvious dispatch. Pat was perfectly comfortable with these women; she had been brought up to believe that there were two kinds of women, and these were the other kind.

When Pat and Peter traveled with Sinatra to Hawaii in November 1959, they stayed in adjoining penthouse suites. They were soon joined by Judith Campbell, a young woman who looked like an erotic, voluptuous version of Jackie. Campbell fancied herself a cut above the ersatz "actresses" of Hollywood. She had never dated Sinatra before accepting his ticket to Hawaii. Before her first day in Hawaii was over, she admitted that she was in bed with the entertainer.

Campbell's recollection of Pat that week is of a strong-willed, mildly disheveled woman, relegated to playing a walk-on role in this drama dominated by men. One evening the two couples went out to a Japanese restaurant, where two Japanese women prepared the dinner at their table. The women flirted with Peter and Sinatra, totally ignoring their two companions. While the food cooked, Pat simmered. She grabbed a cocktail napkin, and as Campbell remembers, boldly wrote a note and shoved it over to Campbell: "I still think they're full of shit!"

For many bachelors, one of Hawaii's great appeals was the Oriental masseuse, to whom a massage was often only foreplay. When two pretty Japanese women walked into Frank's suite, prepared to give the two men a "massage," Pat was outraged. This was behavior that her own mother had tolerated. Pat was of a different generation, and Campbell recalled that Pat could not hide her fury. As angry as she was, Pat was making her own moral compromises as well. Another woman would have broken off the friendship with Sinatra, blaming him as the instigator, but Pat wanted to be around Sinatra, and Peter was hardly an innocent. Campbell said that later in the week Peter made a pass at her saying, "But darling, don't worry, Frank will never know." He did not mention whether Pat would ever know.

When Pat and Peter were out with Sinatra or other friends, they appeared an exemplary couple. Peter and Pat were both performers, Peter an actor, Pat skilled in the public role of a political woman. Increasingly, they performed as much for each other as for the world. In private, their relationship had begun to turn sour, the bitterness seeping out in asides and barrages of irony that their friends duly noted. Pat had a wicked tongue, and she seared Peter's ego with her words.

Pat had been unable to satisfy her husband sexually, though even if she had had all the skills of a courtesan, Peter probably would have sought out other women. As it was, Peter's dalliances had destroyed the sense of intimacy and trust that had been at the center of their marriage.

Pat had grown up in a world where sex was the great unmentionable. She found herself in a marriage to a man who wanted his lovers to perform what to women of her background was the unthinkable and the unspeakable. "Her Catholic upbringing, her nightly prayers, and her other acts of devotion were unnerving for him," said Patricia Seaton Stewart, Peter's last wife. "They had not had sex before their marriage, Pat probably being a virgin. He could not reveal to her that he liked to be restrained and abused. He could not show her that intercourse gave him less pleasure than sensual experiences involving less physical and emotional commitment. He could not tell her that he wanted to see two women fondling each other, then having oral sex with him. Those were both the high points of his sexual pleasure and the dirty little secrets about which he felt uncomfortable."

Peter told one intimate that Pat attempted to please him in some of his favorite sexual pursuits, but she had been repulsed, and panicked. Nothing Pat had ever seen or felt or learned or knew or believed prepared her for this new world in which Peter lived. She had been taught to live for and with a man, a husband, as a wife and mother, but not as part of a sexual menagerie in which nothing was too bizarre, too outré if her husband sought such pleasure.

Pat had never been much of a drinker, but she began matching Peter, using liquor not as a social stimulant but as an anesthetic. Her father worried enough about Pat that on June 26, 1956, he wrote admonishing his daughter to "take very good care of yourself, don't drink too much Scotch, nor smoke too many cigarettes and stay up so late at night. How . . . you stay so beautiful doing all these things is the eight [sic] wonders [sic] of the world."

Unlike Jackie, Pat was not financially dependent on her spouse, and she was simply not about to hunker down emotionally within her marriage, providing a shield for Peter's affairs. Instead, she did something that was unthinkable for a Kennedy woman. She began to have her own relationships with other men.

When Peter began to sense that Pat was having affairs, he did not shrug his shoulders figuring fair's fair, but became deeply possessive. Peter was consumed with suspicion, and Otash said that the actor called him seeking to wiretap his wife. "He was so cheap he didn't want to pay for a guy to go do it for him," Otash recalled. "I gave him the equipment and showed him how to install it and hide it."

Peter never told Ebbins of his alleged wiretap, and his former manager did not believe that Peter would be quite so duplicitous. "Peter was my closest friend, and there wasn't anything in his life that he didn't tell me about," Ebbins insisted. "What happened is that Peter heard Pat talking to her lover on the phone. He didn't pick it up accidentally. He heard her talking on the phone at different times when he was in the room—guarded, cryptic conversations. And so he simply listened in. They were arranging a rendezvous in Texas. It was the usual, 'Oh when I see you, this is what I'm going to do. . . .' And Peter said, 'I'm sorry that I picked it up.' He was destroyed, not destroyed maybe, but disappointed. But he knew. A man knows."

Pat spent much time with Peter in Las Vegas where he was costarring in *Ocean's Eleven*. It was now Sinatra's film. He had bought the script from Pat and Peter, and he had turned the movie into an employment bureau for his friends. Peter, Dean Martin, and Sammy Davis Jr. were all costars, and their buffoonery didn't end when the cameras went off. In the evening the five performers headlined in the Copa Room at the Sands Hotel. There was a boisterous boys-night-out ambience, with each performer playing his public persona to the nth degree, from a self-deprecating Joey Bishop to a boozy Dean Martin. The audience loved the idea that they were being let in on the private argot of Hollywood's celebrated clan, and laughed knowingly as Bishop lampooned Peter's famous brother-in-law. They put one another down with the same wit and bravado while taking their sauna in the morning as they did on stage, sitting there wrapped in towels nursing hangovers with gin fizzes before heading over to the set.

This was a man's world, and Pat stood just outside the charmed circle. She had one thing, though, that none of them had, not even Sinatra, and that was Jack, who in January 1960 had announced his presidential candidacy. In the equation of power within their own marriage, the balance had tilted.

Pat knew her brother and how Jack lived with laser-focused intensity, compartmentalizing his friends and colleagues, taking from each person whatever he considered his or her best. Pat was Jack's Hollywood sister, whose primary function was to provide diversions from the rigors of the campaign. She and Peter had done that for Jack in Los Angeles before. Now early in 1960, as Jack crisscrossed America, they had an opportunity to do that in an even more fitting environment.

When Jack descended with Ted in his private plane into the gambling capital of Las Vegas, Pat was already there waiting for him. It was Pat, then, who was responsible for introducing Jack to this world. In the entourage around Sinatra that weekend, there were several women, including Judith Campbell. Pat considered Judith just another pretty face to be quickly superseded by other equally available young women. As she sat at a table with Campbell that weekend, she had no idea that there were dangers to her brother's ambitions and reputation far exceeding anything he encountered in Washington or on the campaign trail.

In her recollections of her initial meeting with Jack in her book *My Story*, Campbell assumed the persona of her Catholic schoolgirl past, reticent and proper. She said that she first met Jack and Ted, his brother's western campaign manager, at Sinatra's table in the lounge of the Sands Hotel. Later that evening she recalled that Ted made a pass at her that she rejected. The next day Jack supposedly had an almost three-hour lunch with Campbell, largely devoted to seeking her views on Catholicism and politics. That evening Campbell attended the show at the Copa Room with Jack, Pat, and another woman. Then she said good-bye to the departing candidate. Although they had not even kissed, Campbell woke up the next morning "feeling like Scarlett O'Hara the morning after Rhett Butler carried her up the stairs."

Campbell said that Jack sent her an airline ticket to visit him a month later at the Plaza Hotel in New York. There in Jack's suite she initially resisted his advances before finally succumbing to his persevering passion.

Ebbins had a shorter remembrance of the initial meeting between Jack and Campbell that evening in Las Vegas. "I was there the night she met him," Ebbins recalled. "Pat and I were there at the Copa listening to Sinatra performing. And all of a sudden she showed up. I didn't know who she was. She sat there. And I subsequently found out that she was a hooker and she went upstairs with Jack for two hundred bucks. That's why Frank Sinatra said, 'Hell hath no fury like a hooker who becomes an author.' "

To Ebbins the word "hooker" was a generic term for women who sleep with men in return for a variety of favors. Campbell was what in the fifties would have been called a "party girl." Blair Clark, then a radio journalist, was there that evening in Las Vegas as well, and his recollection paralleled Ebbins's account. "There were all these bimbos and showgirls standing around," he recalled. "And then there was one woman, quite attractive, with blue eyes and raven hair, whose name was Judith Campbell."

Shortly after her assignation with Jack at the Plaza, Judith was in Miami at another meeting of Sinatra's "clan" for the singer's show at the Fontainebleau. At this gathering, Campbell met a nondescript, rumpled fifty-two-year-old Chicago businessman who gave his name as Sam Flood. The businessman was Sam Giancana, the boss of the Chicago syndicate, a man whose character was such that he was rejected for the draft in World War II as "a constitutional psychopath." To Campbell he was a gentleman, and in her recollections of life with the mafia chieftain, she reverted again to her schoolgirl reticence, claiming "it was almost a year and a half before we became intimate."

Jackie knew about her husband's compulsive womanizing, endangering not simply the threadbare fabric of their marriage, but his whole political future. She had grown so disgusted with Jack's behavior that she had begun to talk about it to her intimates. One Sunday in Washington she was at a luncheon given by Walter and Marie Ridder. As usual, Jackie was by herself.

"He's gone." Jackie shrugged, as she sat alone with Walter Ridder. "He's somewhere and I haven't heard from him. He's campaigning, but I bet he's off with some dame. I've got to divorce him."

"Well, Jackie," Ridder replied, as he told his wife, "I can understand this, but do you want to really ruin his chance of being president?"

"No," Jackie replied, making the choice that any of the other Kennedy women would have made.

Pat may have been present not only when Campbell met Jack, but in Miami at the party where she met Giancana. "If Pat Lawford was there, I just don't remember," Campbell wrote later. "She became the kind of person that I didn't see even when she was sitting at the same table."

Pat would do almost anything to help her brother reach the White House. If that included providing Jack R and R by helping to set him up with women, that was fine. She had no idea that partially through her good services, her brother was sharing the affections of Campbell with one of the most powerful criminals in America. Jack was an imprudent man. For him it was merely another dalliance, but his relationship with Campbell was indirectly connecting him with a dark criminal world.

Pat's concern for Jack intruded into the most intimate recesses of her marriage. She and Peter were both seeing other people, and a separation may have been in the offing. Catholicism aside, a separation was unthinkable politically, since it would be sordid fodder for Jack's opponents and the dregs of journalism.

Pat and Peter not only decided to stay together, but their friends noted a change in their marriage. "Somebody said you can't make waves now, you're going to make this work until he's president," said one of their close friends. "We would play poker every weekend with the Lawfords, and all of a sudden the two were calling each other 'bunny,' and 'baby,' all kinds of sweet names. Our group was their closest friends, and yet they were doing this. I remember it so vividly. I had a feeling it was just for our benefit so that no one would pick up on the fact that they weren't living as husband and wife."

19

"Don't Deny You Did It"

*A*lthough Jack was the Kennedy on the campaign trail, all the Kennedy women were under scrutiny. The television cameras and the reporters pressed close. Friends and acquaintances pushed closer too, seeking to join the inner circle, treating the women with deference and sometimes with jealousy. The world outside the family was increasingly a public theater, where the women played the roles that were expected of them and mouthed predictable lines.

Jack was unapologetic in his insistence that Jackie's transcendent task in life was to promote his career. "Since I'm completely committed, and since she is committed to me, that commits her," Jack said, his masculine logic irresistible. In public, Jackie meekly concurred, presenting herself as an abjectly obedient young wife. "The most important thing for a successful marriage is for a husband to do what he likes best and does well," Jackie said. "The wife's satisfactions will follow."

Jackie was expected to stand on the podiums across America sweetly promoting her husband. She proceeded doggedly, usually spending no more than three days at a time campaigning, putting in twelve- to fifteen-hour days. In this era before women's liberation, a candidate's wife could be just that, a wife, a helpmate, and Jackie expressed few opinions except avowals of devotion to her husband. Jackie's friends in the social elite of New York knew all about Jack's marital habits. The whispered story was that Jackie's expression of eternal love was a performance that would soon draw to an end. On one of the few off days during the campaign, Red Fay told Jack about the rumors. That evening, Jack told Jackie what was being whispered in New York. "Jackie," he said, "out on the golf course today Red asked me if there was any truth to the rumor that you were going to divorce me after the campaign. Your good friend who married the fellow with the Russian name in New York is spreading the story."

"That little bitch!" Jackie exclaimed, bristling like a cat. "And she always acts like such a dear friend."

Wary about so-called friends, Jackie sought to isolate herself and her family. In Hyannis Port, she ordered a fence built around the compound of Kennedy homes. If Jack won the nomination it was a necessary security. The residents, who had always respected one another's privacy, were offended, feeling that the Kennedys, and especially Jackie, wanted to turn their backs on them and their lives.

Jackie was equally wary about the reporters who pursued her, and she rarely dropped a candid word. During the campaign it was her sister-in-law, Jean, who was the most straightforward about Jackie, telling a writer: "I don't think she's mad about politics. She's been brought up in a different kind of world. She's terribly bright, very cultured and not particularly gregarious. It takes a real effort for her to mix with people she doesn't know."

Jackie attempted to create a semblance of a normal home life for Jack and her baby, Caroline, a charming, precocious little girl who needed her mother's attention, but Jack and his advisors saw his wife and daughter as formidable parts of the campaign, an appealing image that had to be exploited. Jack was nearly as consumed with politics when he was home for a few hours or days as when he was out on the hustings. Rose was fond of saying that her sons had been rocked to political lullabies, and so was little Caroline. Her first spoken words were "plane," "good-bye," "New Hampshire," "Wisconsin," and "West Virginia."

"I am sorry so few states have primaries," Jackie said, her irony so faintly spoken that it could hardly be heard, "or we would have a daughter with the greatest vocabulary of any two-year-old in the country."

Jackie had made her decision to stay with her philandering husband. If there was an element of cynicism in her conclusion, she was more than an elegant American courtesan, making her way in the world on her beauty and style. She spent his money with abandon, but much of it went, as she saw it, to make their home "the greatest haven for him."

Jackie felt that she and Jack were both like icebergs—"the

public life above the water—the private life is submerged."
She was not about to open herself to anyone, not expose her
anger, her wit, her exquisite sense of irony. Her brother-in-law
Steve saw that mask of tranquillity and knew that other emotions lurked underneath. "I'm sure there must be some turmoil
that we never see," he said. "But if she is depressed, she just
goes off by herself."

Jackie was not going to expose herself, not to her sisters-in-
law, and especially not to journalists ready to feed her most intimate emotional secrets to the public. She agreed to answer a
series of questions about Jack from Fletcher Knebel, a writer
friendly with the Kennedys, as long as he did not quote her
directly. As she portrayed herself, she was the one always
waiting for Jack, always trying to make his time with her
memorable. She found some of the questions "too corny" even
to merit a reply and others of his queries almost too "dreary"
for words. She could hardly tolerate what she considered his
silly inquiry about whether Jack worked around the house.
"Really Fletcher!" she replied. "Do you think I welcome my
husband home after ten days in West Virginia or wherever—by
telling him he has to mow the lawn?" In her own way she was
trying to make a home for her husband apart from his "crazy
campaigning life for the past fourteen years." She knew how
much Caroline missed her father, how much she adored jumping up on his lap. "She is at the age now where she misses
him," she wrote. "I think he probably suffers as much as she
does (though neither of them are probably as aware of it as I
am) from his absence."

None of Jack's opponents could create anything of the excitement among women audiences that Jack effortlessly inspired.
To win he needed women's votes, but he had almost none of
them at his side in key positions. Although women were the
majority of the population and of the voters, they were treated
primarily like a minority group to be wooed and placated. In
Chicago, Sarge, not Eunice, wrote a letter to Edith S. Sampson, a black lawyer and a leading Democrat, asking her to
serve on a committee for his brother-in-law. He told her that
the hour had arrived "for the ladies to become active," writing
in the kind of language that one day would be considered
wildly patronizing. Jackie was the only Kennedy woman to sit
on the campaign's Women's Committee. "He [Jack] thought it
was great," Jackie said when the group of twenty-five distin-

guished American women met at her Georgetown home. "He said to me a long time ago that one woman is worth ten men," Jackie said. "They have the idealism, they have the time to give, and they work without making demands."

Rose and her daughters headed out into the chill winter of New Hampshire, the isolated towns of Wisconsin, and the mountainous roads of West Virginia seeking votes for Jack. Rose began the campaign in New Hampshire, maintaining a schedule that would have tested the stamina of a person half her age. Rose knew all her efforts were minuscule compared to what Joe was accomplishing. She could see, as she wrote in her diary, that Jack became annoyed at mentions of his father's wealth and influence, "as remarks of Grandpa Fitzgerald used to annoy Joe in the old days." She knew, though, that without Joe, her eldest surviving son would not be on the verge of the presidency. "The efficiency with which it [the campaign] is run—the amazing results it achieves—all this because it is first a purely family team at the center," she wrote in her diary. "Jack, his brothers, his brothers-in-law, and the overall strategy of their father, who I doubt will ever get credit for the constant, unremitting labor day and night which he had devoted to making his son President."

Jack won decisively in New Hampshire, but Wisconsin was a more difficult testing ground. As formidable a campaigner as sixty-nine-year-old Rose had proven in New England, the campaign initially made no effort to bring her and the other Kennedy women into the state. "Everyone assured me she looked like a woman of fifty," recalled Patrick J. Lucey, the state campaign director. "And how could you possibly convince people that a man is old enough to be president when he has such a young looking mother?"

Rose did come into the state to do her part for Jack. Rose descended on the little towns like an exquisite little piece of history, endlessly repeating her stories of Jack's youth and the years in London. She talked of everything except the one fact that linked the Kennedys to Wisconsin, the fact that Rosemary was a resident of the state. Jack made a campaign stop in a heavily Republican town a few miles from Jefferson as part of a plan surreptitiously to visit his sister. At the last moment the plans changed and Jack never saw Rosemary.

* * *

Rose's daughters and daughters-in-law had a more difficult time deciding what to say and how to campaign than their mother. Jackie hardly had the soul of a campaigner. Her days started late and ended early. The three Kennedy sisters worked far more energetically for Jack. Each of them attended eight or nine teas or coffees each day, talking almost exclusively to other women. Eunice gave rousing stump speeches, explicating Jack's platform with passion and intelligence while Pat and Jean settled for merely asking the farm people and town folk to vote for their brother.

Pat and Jean wanted to help but they didn't know quite what to do or say. They were not great legendary personages like their mother, and they didn't feel comfortable talking about issues the way Eunice, Ted, and Bobby did. "I could get in trouble doing that," Jean admitted shortly before she left for Wisconsin. "I don't know enough about the issues. I think I'll just answer questions on the family." Even though the two women shied away from saying anything political, their mere presences made a statement signaling the nascence of an era when women would not be relegated to the sidelines. "All this massing of the family clans in Wisconsin raises interesting questions," wrote William S. White, the columnist, who sensed that something dramatic was happening. "It used to be that in politics the kinfolk, and especially the women folk, were those whose duty was only to stand and wait."

In the tiny towns and villages of rural Wisconsin, the Kennedy sisters expressed their own commonality with the women who were their main audience. "You wouldn't think that they came from Massachusetts," a farm woman said after the Kennedy women had left, echoing a frequent comment. "You'd think that they came from Wisconsin." That was the highest of compliments, signaling the down-to-earth, unaffected qualities that Jean and Pat projected. What was most striking to the campaign workers was the unalloyed devotion the women had for their brother. "It just seemed that they were one person, and the one person was Senator Kennedy," reflected Marguerite Benson.

For Jack and the Kennedy men the presidential campaign was a mixture of repetition, tedium, and never-ending work occasionally interrupted by exhilaration, drama, controversy, and ample doses of sex. For the Kennedy women, there was exhilaration at times, but there were also embarrassment and humiliation. They traveled not with Jack in the *Caroline*, the families' private plane, but more often with strangers in cars, driving across the frozen American landscape. Jean was pregnant and she might have been better off in Georgetown than traveling these endless country roads. In Prairie Stacks, Wisconsin, Jean arrived to give her talk and discovered only four people in the audience. She wanted so desperately to help Jack, and she considered the pathetic audience her failure. Driving out of the town, she saw a crowd of people at a livestock auction. She ordered the driver to pull over, and she walked into the crowded arena full of farmers in overalls, their wives bundled up against the cold.

If you were a Kennedy, everyone assumed that you were a public person, adept at speaking. Jean was a woman of the deepest reticence, a private person whose wit and charm were gifts she bestowed only on her intimates. And yet she was a Kennedy. She marched over to the auctioneer and asked permission to talk to the farm audience. The auctioneer motioned for a cow to be prodded out of the ring to make room for Jean's appeal. These farmers looked at her with no more sympathy than at the cattle they were buying and selling, and waited to see what she would say. She stood there, for a minute, two minutes, and still she could find no words. Finally, she spoke: "My brother is running for the presidency. I hope you will vote for him." That was all she said, all she could say, and she hurriedly exited the arena and headed toward her car. "Well, get a load of her," one woman said loud enough for Jean to overhear. "She's as common as dirt."

Pat returned to Los Angeles in time to give a party on the evening of the Wisconsin primary. Judy Garland, Sid Luft, and Mrs. Milton Berle were among the guests that evening. When it came to her brother, Pat didn't care about expenses and she had a direct phone line to Wisconsin. She talked first with Jack and then Bobby, and to her father back in Massachusetts as well. Pat set up a large map of the state, and assembled the election returns as the districts came in. "We've lost that one," she shouted out at one point, though the guests did not know one district from the next. "We took that district," she said excitedly. As the results kept coming in, Pat understood the one salient fact: Jack had won but he had not won in the massive numbers that would have buried the religious issue. The battle would go on, for Jack and for the Kennedy women as well.

From Wisconsin, the campaign moved on to West Virginia, a state presumably not much more friendly to a Massachusetts

Catholic than the rural Midwest. The Kennedy forces arrived with thousands of dollars to dispense to the amenable county bosses; Franklin D. Roosevelt Jr., to recall the days of the New Deal; and the Kennedy women as well. Dorothy Tubridy, an Irish friend, drove with the women along the winding, treacherous roads, and up the hollows where the cabins perched on tiny plots of cleared land. There they knocked on doors and talked to women who greeted them with a natural reserve and impassivity that outsiders often labeled suspicion, and that to Tubridy reminded her of the Irish poor. "Oh, he's the Catholic, I don't want to hear anything about that," they said sometimes, half hidden behind the front door. Usually, however, they took the campaign literature, and gave no sign whether they intended to vote for Jack or for Senator Hubert Humphrey, or even vote at all.

For the first time, Joan took part in the campaign, traveling into the Appalachian towns and villages with the presidential party. "Jack liked to have a female member of the family with him," Joan remembered. "I think it was probably pretty smart politics to have a female member of the family standing close right next to him because there were a lot of other women that wanted to stand right next to him and this looked better." Joan was a woman of such stunning attractiveness that when she had gone down into a West Virginia coal mine, she had set off a near riot of shouts, whistles, and merriment. That was the last time she traveled with Jack, drawing attention away from his utterances. After the election, Jack gave his youngest sister-in-law a silver box engraved: TOO BEAUTIFUL TO USE.

On primary day in West Virginia, Jean flew back to Washington with Jack. When Jack won so massively that he forced Humphrey out of the race, Jack and his sisters began to celebrate. Humphrey had been worn down by a constant assault of energy, money, and family. "I don't have to fight one," he complained. "I have to fight a family of them."

Jack could reach out and almost touch the golden prize, and as he stood so close, the glaring lights of attention fell on him as never before. The aura of success, celebrity, and power embraced the Kennedy women, and they too were under the kind of scrutiny they had never experienced before.

In the spring of 1960, *Time* decided to do a cover story on the Kennedy family. The cover of *Time* was one of the great icons of success in America, and everyone in the family had to take part. In June probably for the first time and certainly for the last, Jack candidly discussed with a journalist on the record the intimate life of his family. Hugh Sidey, the *Time* reporter, asked Jack to discuss certain legends that had grown up about his family. These "myths" included such accusations as Rose having had almost no impact on the family, that "the family was run like a Ford assembly line with the life tour of every member plotted and planned," and Joe being a bloodless martinet who ruled "by cold threats and brutal scorn of failure."

"It makes you wonder about history," Jack mused, as he listened to the litany. "About Lincoln and men like that—just how much can you believe?" As Jack listened to Sidey's recitation, he had no idea that these themes would resurface later as the basis for revisionist history defining the Kennedys as a dysfunctional family. He was terribly uncomfortable talking about his family. The Kennedys were a conundrum within a conundrum, and if these accusations were a myth, so too was the family myth of this happy band of brothers and sisters marching together into the future. Jack was a man of fierce intellectual honesty—that was one of his father's gifts to his son—and he did not deny that there was some truth to these ideas. As he saw it, these themes had been exaggerated into such caricature that he could hardly recognize his family. What the outsiders never seemed to understand was that, despite the often merciless put-downs of one another and the awesome pressures Joe and Rose applied to their children, the Kennedys deeply loved one another and were fully cognizant of the uniqueness of their family. Jack recalled how his mother had spent hours with him as a boy. "She was great on self improvement," he said. "She always saw to it that we read good books, had good conversation." He portrayed a family dominated by Joe and his sons. "It was just a matter of fact that only the boys talked at the dinner table," he reflected. "But that has ceased. The girls talk now."

The most damaging myth of all was Jack's relationship with other women, and that was no myth at all. Infidelity was the vice of choice among politicians, and Jack's problem was not his affairs but the daring indiscretion of it all, as if he were taunting fate. In politics, information is capital, and all across America there were those gathering whatever information they could about the possible next president, from J. Edgar Hoover at the F.B.I. to the Republicans, from gossip columnists to mobsters.

Judith Campbell was not Jack's only dangerous liaison. The month before at a rally at the University of Maryland, an irate middle-aged woman had burst out of the crowd. She had confronted the senator with a large photo she had supposedly taken of him leaving the Georgetown home of Pamela Turnure, one of his secretaries who bore a startling resemblance to Jackie. Florence Mary Kater was obsessed with Jack. During the campaign she claimed to have picketed the Eisenhower White House, marched in front of Harry Truman's residence in Independence, Missouri, and written letters to fifty prominent Americans claiming that the Kennedys had tried to stop her by threatening to have her husband fired, all without receiving one iota of publicity.

The press was a model of discretion, believing that it was not their duty to enter the candidate's bedroom, and Sidey wasn't about to confront Jack with the accusations. The journalist spent a few hours with Jack and Jackie and on that basis decided there was no truth to the stories about theirs being "a marriage of convenience."

Jean talked to a *Time* reporter as well. She was a startling combination of spontaneity and caution, a woman who would instinctively speak with full candor and then would often seem to regret her words even as they came out of her mouth. Like Jack she had an exquisite sense of irony, but one that she rarely dared unsheathe. "In the last year I got to know a lot of famous people—senators and so on—very well, and I found that they are not always what they should be," Jean candidly admitted. Jean had taken the measure of Washington's frauds and fakirs, but it was the kind of remark that could be used as a bludgeon against Jack and the family, and that she would rarely make again.

Jack was a decade older than thirty-two-year-old Jean, and she had hardly known him when they were growing up, but she was immensely proud of her big brother. "I feel Jack is terribly bright, terribly well balanced," she said. "I think he is terrific. He is well qualified—though I suppose that sounds sisterly."

As Sidey and the other *Time* reporters interviewed the Kennedy women, there was a kind of casual innocence to the game, each woman asking what her sisters said, musing openly about family matters, knowing that nothing terribly offensive was likely to get into the story. When Sidey interviewed Joe, however, the Kennedy patriarch had a matter of utmost seriousness to divulge. Until now the family had persistently lied about Rosemary. Most recently, in Jack's 1960 semiauthorized campaign biography by James MacGregor Burns, the Kennedys had led the author to believe that Rosemary "helped care for mentally retarded children," a subtle bit of duplicity.

Although Joe was relatively candid, *Time* wrote merely that Rosemary "was a childhood victim of spinal meningitis," its own euphemism for mental retardation.

Los Angeles was Pat's city. Pat personified the casually energetic life-style of southern California. In the summer of 1960, her tan and tall lithe body appeared an advertisement of good health. At the Democratic National Convention she zoomed from one venue to another, the one delegate to the convention with dual celebrity, the wife of a movie star and the sister of the likely presidential nominee.

Pat and Peter were about the most celebrated couple in Hollywood. In the excitement, Pat hardly had time to contemplate her problems with her husband. On the Saturday evening before the convention opened, Pat and Peter gave a party ostensibly for Eunice's thirty-ninth birthday at their Santa Monica home. "We said it was for Eunice," Pat recalled, "but it was really just an excuse to give a gigantic party for Jack and everyone in Hollywood we wanted to invite. We even had a real live donkey."

The gathering was by far the most desired social invitation of the evening. The party was a synergistic mesh of politics and entertainment, the stars of politics and the stars of entertainment, from Sinatra to Judy Garland, Nat King Cole to Henry Fonda. The Kennedys were all there, except the pregnant Jackie, who had stayed on the East Coast.

The Kennedy women made their public debut at a reception for delegates at the ballroom of the Biltmore Hotel, an eleven-story hostelry in Pershing Square, the closest thing Los Angeles had to a city center, a home to transvestites, junkies, and two-bit hustlers. On her way into the hotel Rose badly twisted her ankle. Her escort, former Massachusetts Police Commissioner Timilty, tried to talk Rose into leaving, but she would hear nothing of it, and she stood for two hours shaking hands with delegates. She was a head shorter than her daughters, but she stood tall in her example of how a Kennedy woman must behave. She approached the public like her model, the Queen of England, never complaining, never uncivil, with neither a hair, a seam, nor her demeanor out of place. Pat had her marital troubles, and Jean's husband had begun to emulate his father-in-law and brother-in-law in more than politics, but the women had a public role to perform and they did it well. Pat and Jean were there that afternoon along with their sister-in-law Joan, shaking hands, signing autographs, holding the delegates captivated until Jack descended on the gatherings. As always, Jack arrived late, with Eunice, who was serving as a stand-in for the absent Jackie.

The dichotomy between the Kennedy women and men was vividly apparent during the week-long convention. The women played public ceremonial parts in the drama whereas the men had roles as much private as public. Bobby, Sarge, Steve, and Ted worked gathering delegates for Jack. Joe kept away from the convention, knowing that he was a controversial presence who would only hurt his son. He stayed in Marion Davies's mansion in Beverly Hills, which had been loaned to the Kennedys, remaining a disembodied voice on the telephone. Jack had a wily disregard for the supposed limitations of public life. He escaped from his police escort as if they were not his protectors but his warders and went his own way. His campaign headquarters were at the Biltmore, but he kept a decidedly private hideaway on North Rossmore Boulevard. For most of the week the press did not discover the apartment. Daniel Stewart, a young Los Angeles police officer helping to guard him, was startled at the parade of young women moving in and out of the apartment on the back stairway.

The press finally discovered the apartment and staked out the street, the CBS and NBC cameras focusing on the third- and fourth-floor windows like artillery. Jack escaped out the back way, down a fire escape, over a five-and-a-half-foot wall, and set out in a chauffeur-driven car to his parents' temporary home in Beverly Hills.

The evening that Jack was nominated, he waited in a large upstairs room in the Sports Arena. "The girls are in there, and Bob kept going in and out, and Mrs. [Joseph P.] Kennedy was there," recalled James J. P. McShane, a former New York detective who was guarding Jack. "I never saw her look lovelier—that is the mother—or absolutely more composed. This is another thing that, for the first time, impressed me with the Kennedys: that this was to happen, and why get so excited about it? It's inevitable, and there's no use throwing yourself into each other's arms and kissing and crying with joy and cheer. Subsequently, Frank Sinatra came in the room. He was the only one outside the family that I saw in the room."

The evening after Jack was chosen as the Democratic standard bearer, the family gathered at the Davies mansion waiting for the nominee to make his appearance. Although this was something they had all worked for, Jack's nomination had already begun to change them. As the butler announced that Jack was arriving, the Kennedy women and men unthinkingly formed a semicircle facing the front hallway, waiting for the man they were sure now would be the next president of the United States. Jack hurried through the door in that almost self-deprecating manner of his. The other Kennedys clapped and cheered, and Red Fay, one of the few outsiders, let out a piercing whistle. Jack greeted his family and his closest friends with affection and a word or two, but everything was different.

Rose and her daughters and daughters-in-law spent much of the summer in Hyannis Port, and after the convention most of the family returned to their residences. The village was a Republican bastion, and many residents were bothered by Jack's nomination, and by the hordes of tourists who descended on the peaceful community.

Jackie kept herself at a psychic distance from all the sweaty maneuvering and planning, and observed the machinations of politics as if she had dropped into a foreign land. On those long New England summer days, Jackie read Henry Adams's novel of nineteenth-century Washington, *Democracy*. It was a book of such cynicism that Rose would surely have slapped the book shut after a chapter or two. Jackie read on, appreciating Henry Adams's dark wit, expressing herself "enthralled by it." She was so interested in the literature of politics that she asked Arthur Schlesinger Jr. to bring Edwin O'Connor over to Hyannis Port for a visit. O'Connor had written *The Last Hurrah*, a classic political novel of a corrupt Boston politician patterned after Jack's grandfather's nemesis, James Curley. O'Connor was a worthy teacher of American politics, but he was hardly the guide that most potential first ladies would have found edifying.

During those precious summer weeks, Jack and his advisors planned the campaign. For Eunice her brother came before everything else, including her own husband's political future. Sarge had been widely talked about as the Democratic candidate for governor, but there could not be two family members

running for office in the pivotal state of Illinois, and Sarge had
stepped aside. Sarge was barely tolerated in the inner circles of
the campaign. Jack treated his brother-in-law with a modicum
of civility, but Bobby could hardly contain his disdain. "Bobby
always spat on Sarge," said Charles Peters, who worked with
Bobby during the 1960 campaign. "His people considered
Sarge weak, a nonplayer. Before I got to know him, I thought
he was a jerk, and I wasn't alone. That was what he had
bought into by marrying Eunice."

There were over three million more voting-age women than
men, and Jack's success or failure would inevitably rest in part
on how well he did with women voters. They swooned over
him, the young and the old, jumping up and down, running after his car. On the press bus the reporters tallied up the score
after each speech, from the jumpers and the bouncers to the
leapers and the lopers.

Jack appointed Margaret Price vice chairman of the Democratic National Committee and director of Women's Activities,
but she was merely a token. "There was really no room for
women in the hierarchy," said Barbara Coleman, who worked
as a press aide. "We were all sort of a class of secretaries. You
didn't necessarily do secretarial work but, so what, you're still
in that role."

There was no more room for the Kennedy women in the inner
councils of the campaign than for other members of their sex,
and they each performed modest roles. Jackie was a subject of
endless public fascination that was potentially as much a det-
riment to the campaign as an attribute. A presidential candidate
had to convince the voters that he was one of them, and yet the
moment the elegant, cultured Jackie opened her mouth it was
clear that the Democratic nominee had chosen a wife as foreign to most Americans as a finger bowl. That was doubly apparent when contrasting Jackie with Pat Nixon, the wife of
Jack's Republican opponent, Vice President Richard Nixon.
From the soles of her sensible shoes to the collar of her cloth
coat, Mrs. Nixon appeared the kind of middle-class matron one
might meet at the PTA meeting, or in the next pew in church
holding one half of a hymnal while her husband held the other
half. Pat Nixon not only had more in common with most voters than Jackie, but she was a woman of more appealing hu-

man dimensions than her husband, and the Republicans set out to promote her in their "Pat for First Lady" campaign.

The Democrats had no such campaign for Jackie. Jack had not even mentioned Jackie in his acceptance speech in Los Angeles, a slight that had not gone unnoticed. The campaign leaders believed that not only did Jackie have to be brought into the campaign but that her image had to be democratized. Jackie's penance included donning the sackcloth of frugality, a $29.95 maternity dress worn for an interview with the Associated Press. "I'm sure I spend less than Mrs. Nixon on clothes," said Jackie, who when she heard the word "sale" usually thought of a boat. "She gets hers at Elizabeth Arden, and nothing there costs less than $200 or $300." Jackie had to be humanized as well, and that meant allowing reporters to come trooping into her life, catching a few moments of supposed intimacy. For Jack's historic first television debate with Nixon, Jackie sat sedately in her living room in Hyannis Port, watching her husband on television. Twenty-five reporters, cameramen, and photographers sat in a semicircle watching Jackie, reading her facial expressions as if they were tea leaves. "Except for the celebrities present, the pleasant, homey living room of the Kennedy home looked much like millions of others last night," reported *The Christian Science Monitor*, the very idea that Jackie was trying to project.

For Jackie the most threatening moment of the whole campaign was her first meeting with the women of the Washington press corps at her Georgetown home. The women reporters worked in a tiny ghetto of journalism, for the most part relegated to covering women's issues and society. They could not even join the National Press Club, though they were allowed to watch important proceedings from a balcony if they made a polite written request. The women had taken on many characteristics of any ghetto population. Some of them exhibited a fawning acquiescence while others displayed a surly resentment at their plight. They were often jealous and petty toward one another while clenching on to whatever prerogatives they had achieved.

The women reporters had threatened and complained until Jackie was made available to them. They trooped into the house at 3307 N Street for their tea. Jackie had good reason to be fearful. As the journalists sat down, however, a remarkable and totally unexpected transformation took place. "They were all just as gentle as lambs with her," recalled Barbara Coleman, who helped to organize the tea. "They fell all over themselves. It's almost as if—this is perhaps being unfair to the women reporters—she was so much of a lady, you know, that that's what put them in kind of a deferential position."

The women reporters were exhibiting a trait that Charles Peters, a campaign leader in West Virginia, had noticed when he had twice compaigned with Jackie in his impoverished state during the primary. "There was no question that instead of identifying with the woman who was like them—Murial Humphrey—they identified with the Princess," Peters reflected. "You could just tell they wanted Jackie. They had a wondrous look in their eyes when they saw her."

Americans fancied that they lived in an egalitarian society in which the great goal was to be rich and unequal. Voters wanted their leaders to be like them, yet infinitely better. Like any great politician, Jack had a cunning awareness of the emotions of his constituents. His campaign did not so much create the idea of Jackie as the Kennedy princess in America's royal political family, but provided the spectacle that millions of Americans seemed to want. Pat Nixon could walk down every political runway in America wearing her modest cloth coat, but she could not compete with the glamour and excitement of Jackie.

Even some of the more jaded journalists treated Jackie with awestruck reverence, creating for her the same glass prison in which more traditional royalty lived, a public arena where she felt she could never be herself. "She had a kind of image of herself or what she thought a politican's wife ought to be," said Barbara Coleman. "But she'd want to impress the women reporters with her interest in her husband's campaign. She'd come across sometimes with this sort of breathless air about her that made her seem insincere sometimes, I thought. But I've seen her, you know, in talking casually with her friends or acquaintances—she was a different person from when she sort of came on for a reporter."

There was an inevitable tension between Jackie and her sisters-in-law. "They adore Jack and would do anything to get their names in print," Jackie confided to Joseph Alsop. They had no use for Jackie's fey reticence to jump into the political fray with both feet. Jackie was at least partially right as well about publicity. Peter Dugal, who shepherded Pat Lawford through northern Wisconsin, thought that "as hard as the girls worked it might not have really been politically a gain proposition. But it was giving them exposure; that's something that they needed." Publicity was the best measure of their impact on the campaign, and they saw the articles as promoting Jack, the most tangible evidence of the help they were giving their brother.

Even among the Kennedy women there was not a single pattern, and not all of them counted up their press clippings. Joan was the most reluctant, frightened by the glare of the media, sad in her vulnerability. Joan had a six-month-old baby at home, Kara Anne, but she was expected to join her sisters-in-law on the campaign hustings. In September, she joined Ethel on a campaign trip to Chicago where in three days the two Kennedy sisters-in-law attended a dozen teas in private homes, and rallies and meetings with primarily female voters. Joan was asked to appear as the representative Kennedy woman on a television program that would include prominent political women such as Lady Bird Johnson, the wife of the Democrats' vice-presidential nominee, and Murial Humphrey. "I don't know if I'll know what to say," she fluttered, looking positively terrified, as she turned down the request. Ted was running the campaign in California, and she did what her husband wanted her to do. "My husband says I am to go with him today," she told a San Francisco reporter, not sensing that she sounded like Ted's chattel. Other days she joined Pat attending teas and coffees through California, shaking hands and making small talk, retreating into the background when the women asked questions, always letting Pat or one of the other Kennedy women respond. "All she has to do is look pretty," one observer noted. That was all she had to do for much of her life, and now the act of looking stunning, photographing like a blonde siren, had become a political act, her own contribution to Jack's campaign. She was also busy learning not to see what she wasn't supposed to see, and not to feel what might bring her pain.

So far, Joan's life with Ted had largely been one nearly endless political campaign, with Ted treating his home as little more than a pit stop where he slept, changed clothes, and momentarily relaxed before he headed out. He had his own reckless disregard for proprieties. During the campaign he flew out to Hawaii alone to meet Peter and Sinatra for a fund-raiser. During the flight Ted walked back from his first-class seat to talk to a European beauty queen sitting in tourist class. Peter had already heard about Ted's little secret, and while the plane was still in flight, Peter called Dick Livingston, who was in Honolulu helping on the campaign. Peter, hardly a loyal husband, believed that he owed Pat and his brother-in-law's campaign at least a modicum of discretion, and he was appalled by Ted's antics. "Could you go to the airport?" Livingston recalled him saying. "That goddamn Ted is flying over here with this beauty queen and he thinks he's fooling somebody."

Livingston hurried to the airport, met the young woman, and registered her at a hotel away from Ted. "That night Frank is having a dinner party at Don the Beachcomber," Livingston remembered. "We have a long table and Teddy hasn't shown up, and Frank is getting pissed. And finally Teddy arrives with this beauty queen on his arm. I thought Frank was going to get up and whack him, he was so pissed off."

Jackie perceived Peter and his friends—Sinatra, Dean Martin, and their celebrated Rat Pack—as being dangerous. That set her against Pat, her sister-in-law. Jackie complained that the Hollywood group was in bad taste. She did not want to share the same campaign stage with Peter's friends, and thought that neither should her husband. Jackie's apparent snobbishness was an astute political judgment of the damage that Sinatra's reputation might inflict on her husband's administration. Although the Rat Pack kept their distance from Jackie and Jack, Sinatra campaigned actively for Jack at fund-raisers in Hawaii and New Jersey.

While the pregnant Jackie remained at home, the other Kennedy women journeyed across America in pursuit of votes. They still attended "teas" or "coffees," but these were now often sessions to instruct other women how to hold their own events. "You may think it just a small thing," Eunice warned, "but it may mean a difference of twenty or thirty votes."

Eunice would have been far happier venturing down into the coal mines of West Virginia soliciting votes, as Ted and Bobby had done, than balancing a tea saucer while talking inanities with socialites. The woman's world was left to her, and she put on her pearls and her tweed suit from Bonwit Teller's, and headed out into such politically uncontaminated surroundings as the Englehard estate in Far Hills, New Jersey, and the Elks Club in New Philadelphia, Ohio. Eunice had to deal with queries that reporters would not have asked Bobby or Teddy. They were dying to know about Jackie's new hairstyle. "She changes her hair," Eunice replied as seriously as if she had been asked about the future of communism, "but I don't think she does it to appeal to voters. She does it just because she likes to."

Jean gave birth to her second son, William Kennedy, on September 4, and could have easily excused herself from further campaigning. By mid-October, she was out with Ethel on a hectic tour of Florida. Ethel had seven children, compared to Jean's modest accumulation of two sons, but together the two women made such a svelte appearance it was as if they had turned childbirth into a form of exercise and weight control. They were a formidable team, Ethel warming the almost exclusively female audiences up with humorous anecdotes and then Jean speaking with deeply felt sincerity about her big brother. "I'm not here because Bobby or Jack asked me to be," Ethel said in Tampa. "I believe in Jack's courage and integrity and I feel I'm a better person for having known him."

As the campaign drew to an end, Jack was exhausted, pushing ahead on a burst of adrenaline, half mumbling some of his speeches. Rose, however, looked as fit and fashionable as the day she had set out in New Hampshire ten months before. In her suite at the Statler-Hilton, she met reporters, impeccably dressed in a stylish black dress, white kid gloves, and a white mink hat, a double strand of pearls around her neck, her only other jewelry a small gold model of Jack's PT boat. She had traveled over thirty-five thousand miles, and what she had seen primarily was the women's unheralded campaign, a campaign by women and to women. "It is true that the women seem to feel an affection for him," Rose said. "The women tell me: 'I just love your son.'" She thought of the campaign headquarters she had seen all over America, with volunteers, so many of them women, working far into the night. She talked about her own family, especially her daughters and daughters-in-law and all the places they had gone, all the teas they had attended, all the talks they had made, all the hands they had shaken. She said that Jackie was sorry she had not been able to join them. "But the girls have gone out and tried to take up the slack," Rose said, as she sat with perfect posture in a straight-back chair. "Of course, I don't know yet the country's reaction to them."

Rose stopped for a moment and looked out at the reporters and photographers. "But it won't be long."

On election evening the Kennedy family sat around a small portable television watching the first of the returns. Eunice,

Pat, and Jean were almost giddy as the first positive returns came in, rushing manically around the house. As Jack sat impassively watching the flickering images on the screen, he heard a correspondent in Hyannis Port report that his sisters said he was "jumping up and down for joy," a statement so ill-timed and so unfounded that he scolded them. The results in the East got better and better, and at ten-thirty, even Jackie could not contain herself, turning to her husband and saying, "Oh, Bunny, you're President now!" Jack turned away from the screen for a moment: "No ... no ... it's too early."

Jack's dismissal of his sisters and his wife was like a father shushing a child speaking out of turn. Except for Eunice, they knew almost nothing about the arcane minutiae of politics, and had no understanding of the ominous pattern of votes the men in the family had detected. At three in the morning as Jack left the command post set up in Bobby's house, Pat said to her brother: "Good night, Mr. President."

As the hours went by, the voting grew closer and closer. It became for the family, as Jackie said later, "the longest night in history." Not until nine-thirty the next morning was it clear that Jack had won in the closest presidential election in American history. It was in essence a dead heat; Jack had received only 112,881 votes more than Nixon.

After the election, Jack signed a photograph to his youngest sister: "To Jean—don't deny you did it. John Kennedy." "It was a joke," Jean said. Since the first tea in 1946, Jack had known that he had an extraordinary appeal to women; in this election he had at times generated the electrical intensity of a rock star. His mother, sisters, and sisters-in-law had diligently campaigned almost exclusively to the women voters. There had been a kind of schizophrenic quality to Jack's appeal to women, and for every woman who voted for the dynamic, youthful Kennedy, there was another who preferred the more comfortable, comforting image of Nixon. In the end, in the great irony of the campaign, women had voted in larger numbers for Nixon than for Jack, by a margin of 51 to 49 percent.

Not until noon did the president-elect and his family journey in four automobiles to the Hyannis Armory. There Jack told the reporters and the nation that he and his wife were preparing "for a new administration and a new baby." From the bunting-draped stage, Jackie looked at her husband with apparent serenity, and relief that the campaign was finally over.

Rose knew that in politics the campaign was never over, and

that a political woman could never relax. When Jackie walked over to stand next to her mother-in-law for the family photograph, Rose looked at her with quiet dismay. Jackie was wearing a scarlet dress, and Rose's dress was cerise. "Our dresses clash horribly for color photography," she told the new first lady, and Jackie moved away.

When the election was over, Eunice collapsed and was in Boston Hospital for a week. She was like a mechanical toy wound up so tightly that it almost exploded with tension, and then played down in frenetic movement until there was only a quiver of action, only to be wound up again. It was in this period, the early 1960s, when it was discovered that Eunice, like Jack, had Addison's disease, and she too began cortisone treatment. She was not only psychologically like her big brother then but, as Sarge said later, "physiologically alike." They were as similar as twins, but one brought up as a Kennedy man, one as a Kennedy woman.

Eunice could not possibly relax, and as she lay in bed she read *The New York Times*, seeing each article as a problem that would soon be her brother's. As she read an article about a congressional report on mental health, she was appalled that the lengthy article did not mention mental retardation even once. "There was nothing," Eunice recalled. "It just made me mad to think about it."

All her life Eunice had been struggling to find one issue, one cause in which she could focus her immense inchoate energy and intelligence, one cause great enough for all her passion and faith and intensity. Her work with the Joseph P. Kennedy Jr. Foundation was a start, but Eunice felt that mental retardation merited the most serious attention. In Palm Beach, Eunice discussed the subject with her father and Jack. The president-elect was a man of profound emotional disengagement, and if Eunice's intensity sometimes amused him, he appreciated her concerns. In this instance, Eunice's father was her best advocate. "Yes, we really ought to do something," he said. "This has been a terrible situation in the country. The Foundation can't go on trying to lick this problem alone. It affects too many families in this country."

Eunice suggested that Jack form a national committee to study the problem. Such committees were often political ploys, a way of saying no while saying yes, pushing away controversial and intractable problems into unread reports. That was not the kind of committee Eunice was suggesting, nor that Jack had approved. "That's a good idea," he told his sister. "Get hold of Mike Feldman [an aide] and see if you can get something going on it."

Pat and Peter had flown back to California right after the election in time to attend the wedding of Sammy Davis Jr. to May Britt, a Swedish actress. Until the election, none of the reporters would have taken any note of Pat, especially not with Sinatra, Janet Leigh, and Milton Berle among the famous guests. Since Jack was now president-elect, everything Pat did had potential political impact. The most reactionary politicians of the South had fought civil rights laws in part by playing on the fears of miscegenation. Some of them saw Pat's presence at the wedding as a way to paint the Kennedy administration as the amoral proponents of race mixing. Thus copies of the story with Pat's remarks underlined were placed on the desks of all the members of the Louisiana legislature.

Pat had gone to the wedding because Sammy was her friend, and she had kissed him as the happy groom. Sammy was an integral part of Sinatra's clan, and of course the diminutive performer expected to perform in front of Jack at the inaugural gala. Sammy decided that he should not appear. "Sammy called Sinatra in Hawaii and said he's not going, and that the press was mad because he and Pat had this picture where they had kissed," Dick Livingston recalled. "Frank got so mad. He was furious."

In Los Angeles, Pat helped Peter, Sinatra, and others in putting together a gigantic fund-raising gala to be held the evening before the inauguration at the Washington Armory. Hollywood knew a star when it saw one, and a glorious lineup of talent agreed to perform, from Leonard Bernstein to Sidney Poitier, Laurence Olivier to Ella Fitzgerald.

In her house in Georgetown, Jackie attempted to plan for her life as first lady.

Jackie occasionally sat in on Jack's political meetings and at times had astute comments to make. "I remember a meeting right after the nomination between the President and Jackie and Lyndon Johnson and Lady Bird Johnson," recalled Meyer "Mike" Feldman, a Kennedy aide. "Some of her contributions were very perspicacious. She could see what was needed. She wasn't a political animal. Her husband, the president-elect, was the best politician I've ever seen, but even he didn't like politics the way most highly successful politicians do."

As the pressures and obligations grew ever larger, that peculiar duality of Jackie's personality became even more evident. There was part of her that wanted no exalted life as the first lady. "What I wanted to do more than anything [was to] keep my family together in the White House," Jackie said. "I didn't want to go down into coal mines or be a symbol of elegance. I just wanted to save some normal life for Jack and the children and me. My first fight was to fight for a sane and normal life for my babies and their father." She had already lost a baby and she knew that all the excitement and turmoil of the campaign was a threat to the life of her still unborn child. Her doctors had warned her explicitly: If she did not want to lose another child, she was not to move.

Jack had been away when Jackie had lost their firstborn child. Now for all that she had sacrificed during the campaign and how rarely he had seen his wife, he might have chosen to remain near her. As president-elect, he had the excuse of excuses for his frequent absences, and his nighttime jaunts. After Thanksgiving dinner in Georgetown, he left Jackie and Caroline to fly to Palm Beach with his aides. Jackie was not due for almost a month, but Jack had hardly left when Jackie began to hemorrhage and was rushed to Georgetown University Hospital, where on November 25 she gave birth to a six-pound, three-ounce son, John Fitzgerald Jr.

Even in the sanctuary of the maternity ward, Jackie had no respite from the bombardment of publicity. Just as Jack created excitement wherever he went, drawing spectators and cameras to him, so now the public had an insatiable desire to learn about Jackie, to feel her, to see her. As she was wheeled into the nursery to see her son for the first time, a photographer bounded out of a storage closet and attempted to photograph her.

Jackie was exhausted physically and emotionally. As she lay in her hospital bed, she read a letter from Eleanor Roosevelt. There was no one in America who had a better understanding of what she would be going through than the former first lady. Mrs. Roosevelt advised Jackie that "most things are made easier, though I think on the whole life is rather difficult for both the children and their parents in the 'fishbowl' that lies before you." Despite her illness, Jackie immediately replied to Mrs. Roosevelt's note. To Jackie letter writing was not simply

a mindless social obligation, but often an occasion to craft
handwritten, exquisitely felt missives. She was knowledgeable
enough of political history to know that the Roosevelts had
hardly had an exemplary marriage, and she wrote Mrs. Roosevelt that her remarks were "a great comfort." She had already
felt the solicitousness of others, and it gave her solace to think
that such kindness would make it easier to be in public view.
But, as she admitted to Mrs. Roosevelt, all those long months
of the campaign she had been terribly frightened that she
would "panic" as first lady.

Luella, who had come down from Massachusetts to nurse
her, knew how emotionally and physically vulnerable Jackie
had become. She warned Jackie that if she got up on her feet
she might die. Even as she heard the nurse's admonitions, and
part of her sought to have the most private of public lives,
there was another part of Jackie that was brilliantly creating
her own public persona. Before she had entered the hospital,
she had started writing the story of her life for *Ladies' Home
Journal.* The pages did not have her name on them, but that of
her friend, Mary Van Rensselaer Thayer, and they allowed her
to wax romantically and lyrically about her early years and
background, pretending to a noble French background.

That was the past, however, and the future lay ahead at 1600
Pennsylvania Avenue. While she was still in the hospital, Jack
called Oleg Cassini and asked him to fly immediately to meet
with Jackie to discuss her wardrobe as first lady. As Cassini
entered Jackie's hospital room, he saw spread around several
sketches by the best known American designers. Cassini saw
life as a matter of creating glorious illusions, swathing reality
in a fabric of cloth or words, and then moving on to the next
illusion, the next design, the next lover, the next idea. He knew
Jackie, and to him she was still a girl. As he showed her his
sketches, he was displaying for her his greatest illusion, this
new woman, this resplendent glorious Jackie, a woman of regal, youthful, simple elegance, the emblem of the new age.

"You have an opportunity for an American Versailles," the
couturier said, and told her that he wanted to design not one
dress, or ten, but all her clothes. She would live within his illusion, wearing nothing but his dresses, gowns, furs, shoes, and
handbags. He would become Jackie's own self-styled
"designer-courtier." As Jackie agreed to Cassini's ambitious
plans, she spoke not of haute couture. To her, clothes were
merely symbols of the style and excellence that she intended to

bring into her White House. As she saw it, the fifties had been a dowdy decade personified in the grandfatherly image of President Dwight David Eisenhower and the rotund, grandmotherly figure of Mamie Eisenhower. All that would be swept away, and as first lady Jackie would create these glorious tableaux, immortalizing herself as an empress of style and manners. There would be great artists and fine wine. She would redecorate a house that she thought looked "like a Statler hotel" and invite intellectuals and authors into a White House where they had not been welcome nor perhaps even known.

"I think she was under great pressure," Cassini recalled. "Jack was selecting people for the government and she had a lot of imagination and she was already thinking of her own responsibility, and she could not wait. She knew that no matter what the pressure of the moment, she had to think of tomorrow and of next week. She only had a few dresses. She knew that to have a decent wardrobe when she entered the White House, she had to think of it. And thus the new Jackie was an image in a way created by her and me."

Joe was the third partner in this creation. Jack had little awareness of the potent political magic that Jackie represented, and had an exceedingly bourgeois attitude toward his wife's clothing bills, viewing them as thoughtless extravagance. Joe appreciated Jackie's persona in a way that her husband did not, and he authorized Cassini to spend whatever had to be spent to create an incomparable image. "Just send me an accounting at the end of the year," he told Cassini. "I'll take care of it."

With Joe's money, Jackie and Cassini would create their own illusions, but dreary reality kept intruding, all the mundane obligations of her life. As the new first lady, she was supposed to submit to a tour of the White House conducted by Mamie Eisenhower. Jackie did not care about the visit. "I really just wanted to see which rooms would be ours and the children's rooms when we moved in," she recalled. The visit, however, was one of the endless series of new responsibilities. Jackie knew that it was sheer folly for her to go ahead with the White House tour on the very day she left the hospital. But Jack insisted. "I knew I wasn't up to it," Jackie recalled. "But Jack said I should go." He would not have his wife violate protocol; she must live the stoical life of his mother and sisters. Jackie could not walk more than a few feet without feeling faint. She agreed to the tour as long as she could sit in a wheelchair and be wheeled through the multitude of rooms.

Jackie's first visit to the White House was her coming-out party as the next first lady. Photographers, reporters, and staffers waited to meet her along with Mamie Eisenhower. Luella had warned Jackie that if she walked up and down the stairs at the White House she might well die, and as she greeted Mrs. Eisenhower she looked desperately for a wheelchair that was not there. She asked for no wheelchair, made no excuses, walked the long corridors and up and down the stairs, posed for photographers, and finally stepped back into the car.

If she were not ill before, she was ill now, and she took John John and the nurse and flew down to Palm Beach, where she thought she would find a time and a place of serenity. For all the fabled allure of the Kennedy house in Florida, the structure had not been upgraded since the 1920s. The Kennedy home was not only without air conditioning, but without heating.

For Jackie these were excruciatingly difficult times. "John's health wasn't doing so well," she recalled. "There was, thank God, this brilliant pediatrician in Palm Beach who really saved his life, as he was going downhill, then, premature. I was ill and recuperating in the room I shared with dear Jack. The house was so crowded. He was writing his inaugural speech in the room. I remember the yellow pages being strewn all around the room. And when he left I would get up and try to keep them all together under some weight on the desk. Someone would come in the room and have conferences with Jack. So I would go sit in the bathroom till it was over. I didn't come to meals. I couldn't hold any food down."

As ill as Jackie felt, she had all the burdens of the future bearing down on her, in a world where illusions were sometimes deadly fictions. In her public persona, she sought to become a great democratic queen, elevating America with her style and grace. As she left with Jack for church the second Sunday in December, it was no claque of admirers waiting at the gate on North Ocean Boulevard, but a single man, Richard Pavlick, carrying not roses but seven sticks of dynamite. Pavlick believed that Jack had bought the election and he planned to drive his car into the president-elect's limousine, detonating the dynamite simultaneously, but when he saw Jackie he had second thoughts. "I did not wish to harm her or the children," he told the Secret Service later. "I decided to get him at the church or some place later."

Jackie had probably saved her husband's life as well as her own. As she and Jack were driven to St. Edward's, secure in this cocoon of secret vehicles, she had no idea that her husband was being stalked and that security itself was sometimes as much an illusion as the ball gowns and dresses that Cassini and his minions were so frantically creating.

This was Rose's house, not Jackie's, and for the seventy-year-old matriarch these were days of almost overwhelming complexity. Rose had lived a life of compulsive regularity, but suddenly nothing seemed the same and her most private sanctuaries were no longer hers. "If I go into the study, Jack probably is in there in conference," she wrote in her diary. "If I want to go out the front door to the street, the door is locked behind me almost before I get out. The back door is also always locked now. None of this makes too much difference to me except I am a bit confused as to where I should come and go."

Both Rose and Jackie were going through weeks of terrible uncertainty and inner chaos, which they could not openly admit, not to each other, not to their husbands, not to anyone. They forged onward pretending that everything was the same. "Your house was in turmoil," Jackie finally admitted a decade later. "And I never let you know what was happening to me. . . . Heaven knows you must have been under so much more strain."

Rose needed no personal designer to create a new image for the president's mother. Rose was proud that her clothes were timeless, timeless in part because she had always considered it unseemly to stand at the forefront of style. She decided that for the inaugural balls she would wear the same Molyneux gown that she had worn for her presentation at court in 1938, a tribute to her style and discipline.

For Rose there was only one model for how a Kennedy woman should behave, and at times she could hardly contain herself from commenting to Jackie when she fell short. When she saw an improper neckline on one of Cassini's half-finished dresses, she simply had to say a word or two. And when she looked out the window and saw someone swinging Caroline through the air like a top, she was upset. Her granddaughter was scheduled to be photographed. Caroline had to be fresh and alert for the camera.

One evening when Rose and Joe were dining with Jackie

and Jack, the subject of Caroline came up. To Rose, there was only one way to educate a girl and that was by the nuns of the Sacred Heart. Jackie wanted a different sort of education for her daughter, but Rose hardly listened, outlining Caroline's future. "Well, the trouble is you want Caroline to be like you," Jackie said finally. "And I want her to be like me."

Jack had few evenings sitting peaceably over dinner. Palm Beach had always been one of his playpens, and he saw no reason that should not continue. His best-known dalliance was with Florence Smith, the wife of Earl Smith, the American ambassador to Cuba. The Smiths lived in a house just down the beach from the Kennedy estate, and Jack was seen hurrying up the back stairway.

Jackie had no time or place to worry openly about Jack's casual romances. She was still sick, close to a breakdown. She spent most of her time in bed, occasionally calling or writing Cassini. As she lay there, she prodded Cassini onward in a masterful piece of psychological manipulation. She knew that Cassini thought of himself as an aristocratic couturier, not some meek tailor with pins in his mouth, and she referred to him as a "gentleman," who must come and "amuse the poor President & his wife in that dreary Maison Blanche," flattering his conceit that he was "an intellectual—and social—equal." She understood his massive male ego, and she challenged him as if his very manhood were at stake ("Are you sure you are up to it, Oleg?"). Jackie and Cassini were both snobs of the first order, an occupational necessity in a couturier, and an intolerable vice in a first lady, and only privately to Cassini could Jackie vent her spleen against the vulgar masses: "I want all mine to be original & no fat little women hopping around in the same dress." She played Scarlett O'Hara as well, poor helpless little thing if Cassini did not take care of the details. She would "be a wreck & not strong enough to do everything I have to do."

As the January inauguration approached, the gowns, dresses, furs, and shoes arrived, all exquisitely finished and detailed. They were beautiful outfits, but to Jackie and Cassini they were not simply clothes but costumes to be worn in the greatest drama of Jackie's life.

In those last weeks in Palm Beach, Jack was choosing his cabinet and other appointed officials. In these discussions Jack and the other Kennedy men employed a private political language, a brutal and vulgar barracks-room jargon. The men would not have spoken such language in front of their wives or other women. For them these inner sanctums of power were places women did not belong. Indeed, they just barely included Sarge, to whom profanity did not come trippingly off his tongue.

Jack named Sarge head of the Peace Corps, a do-good organization, but Bobby was a problem. "What am I going to do about Bobby?" Jack asked George Smathers one day. "He worked his ass off, but he hasn't really made a record. What the hell can I do?"

"Make him assistant secretary of defense," said Smathers, who disliked Bobby. "In a couple of years you can move him up to secretary of defense. He's kind of military minded and belligerent anyway."

"Well, now do me a favor," Jack said. "Dad is not for that. He wants him to be attorney general. Just go over and suggest it to Dad at the pool."

Smathers screwed up enough courage to walk over to Joe, who was reading the newspaper and sunbathing at the east end of the pool. "Mr. Ambassador," Smathers began, and went ahead with his suggestion.

"Did Jack tell you to come over and tell me this?" Joe said, suddenly alert.

"Well, Mr. Ambassador, this is my own idea."

"I don't believe that," Joe said, looking past the Florida senator to his son, the president-elect, sitting at the other end of the pool. Joe rose and strode over to Jack: "Goddamn it, Jack, I want to tell you once and for all. Don't be sending these emissaries to me. Bobby spilt his blood for you. He's worked for you. And goddamn it, he wants to be attorney general, and I want him to be attorney general, and that's it."

"Yes sir," Jack said.

When Jack discussed the appointment with his younger brother, Bobby said, "If you announce me as attorney general they'll kick our balls off." Two days later Jack announced the controversial appointment to his aides. "So that's it gentlemen," he told them. "Let's grab our balls and go."

At the Palm Beach airport, Jackie stood waving good-bye to Jack as he flew to Washington in January. The photographers took her picture, and no one had any idea that Jackie had not been out of her bed for days, lying alone in the bedroom. "I guess I was just in physical and nervous exhaustion," Jackie recalled, "because the month after the baby's birth had been the opposite of recuperation."

Jack's physician, Dr. Janet Travell, told Jack of the seriousness of his wife's condition and he ordered the *Caroline* flown back to Florida to bring Jackie back to the capital. She flew back alone and while Jack, Eunice, Jean, Pat, and the other Kennedys attended the first of the inaugural events, Jackie lay alone in her bed in the dark, disordered house in Georgetown.

20
The Women Who Had Everything

The Washington Monument seemed to rise out of verdant spring, but the dormant grass had only been painted green, and the earth was still frozen. On the afternoon before the inauguration, snow began to fall in Washington, burying the painted lawn, covering the streets, seven inches in all, great swirling windstorms of snow, the Washington Monument an ivory spire rising like a marker above the thick covering of snow.

Rose was a woman with the natural conservatism of age, and she would normally never have thought to go out into this frigid, storm-swept city, but this was the morning of her son's inauguration as the thirty-fifth president of the United States. To her it was as much a spiritual as a political event, the highest possible testimony that she had been right in everything she had lived for and believed as a mother and wife. She knew that she must attend mass. She headed out of the Kennedys' rented Georgetown house, a tiny sparrowlike woman in her winter coat, scarf, and galoshes, picking her way through the snow, crossing the empty streets in the half light.

When Rose arrived finally at Holy Trinity Church, she saw many police cars and security officers. She knew that Jack had come to mass this morning too, and felt blessed. She was still all bundled up against the winter, in her mind not properly dressed to approach her son, and she sat alone in the back of the church. After Jack left surrounded by a phalanx of Secret Service, she walked up to one of the remaining security men. "I am Mrs. Kennedy, the president's mother," she said in her tiny voice, "and would you ask one of them to send a car back and pick me up?"

The man nodded politely, but presidents' mothers did not

walk to church, especially not on a day like this one, and the automobile never arrived. Rose turned and left the empty church and walked alone back to her house through the deserted streets.

At noontime, Rose was there along with Joe, her daughters, and her daughters-in-law on the Capitol Plaza as Jack was sworn in as president. Rose wore a fur coat and cap, and sat under a thick gray wool blanket on the far end of the front row. "That day I was going to suggest that they put the father and mother nearer to their son," Rose recalled. "We were way at the end of the row and in a lot of pictures you couldn't see us at all."

After taking the oath administered on the Fitzgerald family bible, Jack gave one of the most memorable of all inaugural addresses. To Rose, Jack's words resonated with the ideas that she and Joe had instilled in their son. As she sat listening to his clear, energetic voice, she thought of the words of St. Luke that she had so often spoken to her young son: "Of those to whom much has been given, much will be required." That was what she had taught Jack, and now he instructed the citizens of this rich and powerful nation: "Ask not what your country can do for you—ask what you can do for your country."

As Rose watched her son, an overwhelming series of emotions coursed through her. "Thanksgiving to almighty God that I, out of all the millions of mothers in the world, on this day I was the mother of the president-elect. The wonder. The thrill. The price, . . . the humble gratitude of a mother to her God for endowing her son with the courage, determination, dedication which made it possible for him to be elected to that great office."

Later in the afternoon Rose sat in the reviewing stand in front of the White House along with the other notables. The stand was closed on three sides, but the fierce winter cold poured into the enclosure. When Jack arrived to review the parade, Joe rose to greet him, and the two Kennedys, father and son, stood there together. To Rose and her children this was as great and memorable a moment as any on this extraordinary day.

There was no greater symbol of the new Kennedy era than the resplendent, elegant Jackie dressed in one glorious outfit after another, her head often cocked toward Jack in public adoration, her photo gracing almost every newspaper and magazine in America. The photos, however, were essays in deception. "The period . . . was not a happy time in my life that it looks like in all the pictures," Jackie reflected a decade later. Jackie was physically and mentally exhausted, facing a life of merciless, unrelieved attention stretching before her for at least the next four years. Her life had become largely a series of photo opportunities, and she girded herself for the requisite public appearances before collapsing again in her upstairs bedroom in the cluttered Georgetown house.

Jackie was on Jack's arm when they walked into the preinaugural gala, but she left after the first intermission when the evening had hardly begun. She had not gone to mass on inaugural morning with her husband either, though she had wanted so much to be there. She had ridden with Mamie Eisenhower up Pennsylvania Avenue to the swearing-in ceremony. "Mrs. Eisenhower said to me in the car on the way to the inauguration that President Eisenhower looked like 'Paddy the Irishman in his Top Hat,' " Jackie recalled. "Then she realized she had made a slight gaffe."

Jackie stood next to Jack at the swearing-in ceremony looking at her husband with eyes as much dazed as devoted, and rode with him back down Pennsylvania Avenue to the White House. Jackie left the frigid parade reviewing stand after scarcely an hour. She was without the fierce constitutions of her husband's family, who sat watching the bands, floats, and soldiers as if they were basking in the summer sun. As distraught as she felt, Jackie had put on her own performance, *The New York Times* reporting authoritatively that she "seemed genuinely to enjoy the ceremonies" and "appeared in glowing health."

Later that afternoon at the family reception in the White House, the Kennedys, Fitzgeralds, and Bouviers eyed each other like hostile clans until the liquor and the forced proximity drew them together. The most notable emotion that the three groups had in common, other than pride in Jack's success, was their disappointment that the new mistress of the house did not even deign to make an appearance. Jackie stayed upstairs in the Queen's Room on the second floor, lying in bed, a heating pad warming her lower back.

Jack was in the most exuberant of moods, but Jackie didn't even join her husband for the receptions and parties early in the evening; she remained in the White House until Jack picked her up at ten-thirty. "I had been in my room for days, not getting out of bed," Jackie recalled. "All the details were getting too much. . . . I guess I was just in physical and nervous exhaustion because the month after the baby's birth was just the opposite of recuperation. . . . I missed all the gala things. . . . I always wished I could have participated more in those first shining hours with him [Jack], but at least I thought I had given him our John, the son he longed for so much."

Jackie attended the first few inaugural balls with Jack, but as much as she wanted to continue and share the rest of this glorious evening with her husband, she was so exhausted, so emotionally drained, so overwhelmed by the burdens she faced that she insisted she be taken back to the White House while the new president went off alone. "Then I had to stay in bed for a week," she remembered.

For Jack's sisters and sisters-in-law the idea of resting during the week of inaugural events was unthinkable. Eunice could well have gone to bed. As she had rushed to catch a plane to Washington, she had so badly sprained her ankle that she had sought first aid at the Chicago airport. She limped her way through the inaugural events, beginning her week carrying a cane at the reception for distinguished ladies.

Jackie was supposed to have been there at the National Gallery of Art as well. The other Kennedy women made up for her absence, a formidable group greeting six thousand Democratic women from across America who moved down four receiving lines before sipping their drinks beneath Tintorettos and El Grecos. Rose, Eunice, Pat, Jean, and Joan all wore black dresses, the uniform of courtly civility. Ethel, the exuberant mother of seven, greeted the women wearing a sleeveless pink dress that stood out against the somber hues as much as did her shrieks of laughter.

The Kennedy women had a more intimate coming-out party at Jean's preinaugural party for her big brother on the evening before the gala. Jean had constructed a two-hundred-person guest list that was a mesh of the new elites of Washington and Hollywood. Sinatra was there and Nat King Cole and Gene Kelly along with other Kennedys and Vice President–elect and Mrs. Johnson. It was a celebrated event, for that evening the party of parties.

The Lawfords were responsible for the Hollywood contingent, and for Pat this should have been a triumphant time. The

preinaugural gala had been her glory almost as much as it was
Peter's and Sinatra's for bringing together this glittery retinue of
the stars of culture and entertainment. She had stood next to
Jack during part of the evening. She wore an alluring, low-cut
gown, but her body appeared too thin, like a tiny object
wrapped in far too large a package. She sat there during the
long evening as a parade of performers paid their tribute to the
president-elect in song, melody, verse, and finely wrought word.
At the end of the long evening, Pat listened as Jack said a few
concluding words. "The happy relationship between the arts and
politics which has characterized our long history I think reached
culmination tonight," he said, standing in his black tie, a spotlight illuminating his handsome features. "I know we're all indebted to a great friend—Frank Sinatra. . . . And I want him
and my sister Pat's husband, Peter Lawford, to know that we're
all indebted to them, and we're proud to have them with us."

As Pat and Peter listened proudly to Jack's accolades,
Bobby, the attorney general in waiting, turned toward Red Fay
and other companions. "I hope Sinatra will live up to the public position the President has given him by such recognition,"
he said in a voice scarcely above a whisper. Bobby had little
use or time for Pat's Hollywood friends and what he considered their self-indulgent high jinks that might end up harming
the president-elect. In preparing for the gala, Peter, Sinatra, and
other Hollywood entertainers had flown to New York for a
meeting to coordinate the gala. A prostitute had supposedly
ended up dead, her body dumped far from the hotel, the matter
hidden away. It was only one story among many stories, but
Bobby hoped that would be the end of the stories, the end of
the rumors, and that Pat's friend would not prove a deadly albatross to Jack and the New Frontier.

As much as Pat reveled in her brother's triumph and basked
in the reflected glory, she was still alone with her husband in
a shell of a marriage. In recent months Peter's philandering, indeed, his separate life, had become notorious, even in a Hollywood community blasé about such matters. His father-in-law
believed that in marriages it was appearances that mattered, but
Peter didn't care enough to put up a decent façade. "Hey, come
on, you should be with her," Ebbins admonished Peter when
he told his manager that he was going to stay at the Statler-
Hilton Hotel during the inauguration, and not out at Hickory
Hill with Pat. "You're married, Peter."

"Oh, *she* doesn't care," Peter replied. "Don't worry."

* * *

When Peter and Pat spent a few days in New York in their apartment in the Savoy Hilton, thieves stole her thirty-thousand-dollar brooch. The Lawfords did not report the loss to the police and one officer charged that the crime was being "covered up." A few days after the inauguration, police arrested four international thieves, three men in their thirties and a twenty-three-year-old woman, for shoplifting. When officers searched their apartment, they discovered a brooch matching the description of the gem stolen from Pat and Peter's apartment. The police were delighted that they had apparently recovered the property of the new president's sister, and had broken a notorious gang of international hotel thieves.

The police held the suspects on a lesser charge of shoplifting and immediately sought Pat out. "She certainly knows we are looking for her," Detective Chief James Walsh told reporters. "But she doesn't want to see us." Her cooperation was "vital" if they were going to be able to prosecute the group, but for several days Pat avoided the police. Peter stayed in New York but pregnant Pat flew off with Jean for a skiing holiday in Switzerland while the three Lawford children remained in Palm Beach.

In Klosters, Switzerland, Pat told a reporter that her gem would be returned. "The police told me I'll get it back," Pat said. Two days later while Pat was skiing down the slopes of Klosters, Frank S. Hogan, the New York district attorney, issued a strange and confusing statement, contradicting both Pat and his own detectives. Hogan announced that only about a thousand dollars in cash, a few credit cards, a charm bracelet, and a watch had been stolen from the Lawfords' apartment.

On February 15, Jack Anderson wrote a memo to his boss, Drew Pearson, the syndicated columnist. A reliable source had told Anderson that a drunken Peter had picked up an attractive woman after the inauguration and taken her back to his hotel room. The woman was a member of a ring of jewelry thieves, and she let in her accomplices who had walked out with Pat's highly expensive diamond brooch. That explained why Pat was not interested in pursuing the matter, and that she was apparently royally miffed at her husband. "I am told that District Attorney Hogan knows the whole story, but is holding it as political blackmail," Anderson wrote. "I understand that Hogan is supporting Carmine de Sapio (a Democratic political boss) in New York's factional fight and expects to use the brooch incident as a bargaining point."

The formal investigation had ended, and with it the stories in the newspapers. This secret had been wrested away potentially to be used by others as political capital, not by enemies but by those who were supposedly friends.

Washington was their city now. Jackie lived in the White House, Jean in Georgetown, Ethel at Hickory Hill, and Eunice in a rented estate in Maryland. Jack considered his male relatives a natural pool of talent for his New Frontier. Both Sarge and Bobby had high-ranking positions, and Steve was working as a consultant to the Development Loan Fund. Jack did not even consider naming any of his sisters to office. His administration considered power and politics almost completely a masculine pursuit. Jack and his aides were for the most part not comfortable having women other than secretaries around them in cabinet meetings and important discussions in the Oval Office. He did not send out a secret directive excluding women; it was simply that, as he and his minions saw it, the female candidates didn't seem quite up to snuff.

Margaret Price, the new vice chairman and director of Women's Activities of the Democratic National Committee, sent the president-elect a list of several potential women qualified for high office, none of whom Jack chose. Eleanor Roosevelt called on the new president and gave him a three-page letter of women qualified to hold ranking government jobs. As she left, she commented that some "men sometimes needed to be reminded that such women exist." India Edwards, the most prominent political woman in the Truman administration, believed that members of her sex had been shut out by Kennedy's close aides, and that Jack himself considered women "nothing but sex objects." Other prominent Democratic women came knocking at the barred gates of the White House and wrote letters of protest, but none of the Kennedy women lobbied their brother or brother-in-law in the name of their sex. None of the Kennedy women identified with their own sex as a political entity. None of them pushed for the advancement of women within the administration.

Even by the modest standards of the Eisenhower administration, Jack's New Frontier fell short in this regard. In March, Doris Fleeson, a political columnist, added up the number of women in the top two hundred political jobs. "Mr. Eisenhower named eight women to bonafide, top-level jobs," she wrote, "while [in the Kennedy administration] half or more of the population must be content with six not really powerful jobs."

Women made up only 2.4 percent of all appointed officials. The one member of the new administration specifically involved with women's issues was Esther Peterson, head of the Women's Bureau in the Labor Department. "I talked President Kennedy into doing this commission on the status of women," Peterson recalled. "I had no support from any of the Kennedy women. When we worked on this women's committee on civil rights, we didn't even think about bringing in the Kennedy women. President Kennedy didn't care deeply about women's issues. To him it was a political matter. It was, 'We've taken care of women.'"

Jack took further care of women by establishing the President's Commission on the Status of Women chaired by Eleanor Roosevelt. The commission would have been a natural venue for Jackie or one of his sisters or sisters-in-law to take part, but the Kennedy women were conspicuous only in their absence. In October 1963, Myer "Mike" Feldman, a special assistant, wrote the president, detailing the administration's accomplishments for women. He listed the commission, the equal pay law, the extension of the Fair Labor Standards Act, but significantly he did not list the appointment of women to office.

For Jack, on a deep emotional level women simply did not belong in his White House. It was a man's world, an atmosphere that Walter Rostow, deputy special assistant for national security, described as one of "tremendously suppressed affection on both sides." These men loved Jack as their commander in a setting that Rostow described as "like the atmosphere of a unit at war." Feldman believed that at least a half dozen of the cabinet members would instinctively have taken an assassin's bullet in the president's place, throwing themselves across his body.

Women did not belong in the front lines of this war. Barbara Ward, the British author and political figure, was one of the few women with whom Jack felt comfortable carrying on an intellectual discussion. Even she was struck by his inability to look beyond a woman's sex. "My impression of President Kennedy is that on the whole, he had little empathy for the trained, intelligent woman," Ward reflected. "I think the coolness was mutual. . . . I don't think he would have been happy in a team that had included women at an operating level."

Jack's sisters cheered on the endeavors of men, eternally vigilant to those who might dare to stand against their brothers' efforts. At a White House dinner, Pat was seated next to John Hersey, the author who had given Jack his early fame by writing about PT boat 109 in *The New Yorker*. He would not have been invited if he were considered an enemy of the family, but Pat was on edge.

"John Hersey, John Hersey," she said, searching her memory. "There's something bad about you. You were for Nixon?"

"Oh, no, Mrs. Lawford. Never! I was for Stevenson right through the convention."

"Oh yes," Pat said, knowing that she was right. "I knew there was something bad about you."

Jack had hardly taken office when he suffered arguably the greatest single defeat of his administration: the thwarted invasion of Cuba backed by the United States government. The plan had been put in place by the Eisenhower administration, but Jack had gone ahead in part to prove his political manhood. "Phoned Joe who said Jack had been on the phone with him most of the day . . . as well as Bobby," Rose wrote in her diary. "At the end I asked him how he was feeling and he said 'dying'—the result of trying to bring up Jack's morale after the Cuban dibacle [sic]."

That evening Rose accompanied Jack and Jackie to a dinner at the Greek embassy. Afterwards, she returned to the White House with her son and daughter-in-law. "Jackie walked upstairs with me and said he [Jack] was upset all day," she noted in her diary. "Had practically been in tears, felt he had been misinformed by the C.A.A. [sic] which Alan [sic] Dulles was the head of. Felt so sorry for him. Jackie seemed so sympathetic and said she had stayed with him until he had lain down as she had never seen him so depressed except once at time of his operation."

Jack had been in office for less than two months when thirty-nine-year-old Eunice became ill and was flown from her Chicago home to Boston for an hour-long gynecological operation. With all her illnesses and operations, Eunice might have justifiably become a hypochondriac, endlessly poking herself for suspected ailments, running from specialist to specialist. Instead, she treated her body the way she treated her automobiles, driving them at reckless speed, with total disregard for law or logic, mindless of such tedious necessities as oil changes and tire pressure, driving them until they sputtered to a halt.

In the fall of 1961 the Shrivers moved to a rented estate, Timberlawn, in suburban Maryland just outside Washington. Sarge was occupied with the development of the Peace Corps, the idealistic centerpiece of the New Frontier. It was an idea that resonated with Eunice's intense concerns, and she was ready with advice and scolding. She became a frequent visitor to the Peace Corps headquarters in downtown Washington, bounding into the offices shouting out Sarge's name. The overburdened staffers learned to steer a course far away from their director's wife. "They would say, 'Lay low, hunker down, Eunice is in the building,' " recalled Coates Redmon, an early staff member and author of a book about the Peace Corps. "She terrified everyone. I, stupid fool that I am, wanted to see it. The legend had grown so strong. She just came in and created havoc. This day she charged into Sarge's office. She says, 'Sarge, I don't understand why you said what you said in your last speech. My brothers never would have set themselves up to look like such a fool.' "

Eunice may have been married to Sarge, but her highest political loyalties were to Jack. Her brother's enemies were her enemies. Her favorite instrument of attack was the bludgeon. As president, Jack could hardly speak candidly about what he thought of Prime Minister Jawaharlal Nehru of India. During Nehru's state visit of November 1961 Eunice marched right up to the leader of the world's largest democracy, eyed him like a piece of overpriced sculpture, and said: "So that's what you look like, you old rascal, you."

Of all the Kennedy women, Eunice was the most qualified for a position in the new administration. Her brother undoubtedly would have named her the chair of the President's Panel on Mental Retardation, a committee making recommendations to the president. Instead, by her own choice and calculation, she was listed merely as a consultant. Eunice knew that she stood at the right hand of her brother, and that was title enough. She believed, moreover, that she could get things as a woman that she perhaps could not achieve as a man. "I think I had my maximum impact the way I had it," she reflected three decades later, rejecting the idea that to a woman like herself, her gender had been a prison. "I couldn't have done more as a man, or in some position. You know I don't know what else I could have done. I was perfectly happy where I was.

And I think I just had a very wonderful relationship with my brother, and he was wonderful to this cause. I don't say that blindly."

As Eunice looked out on the world of medicine, medical research, and social services she saw great fiefdoms devoted to mental health, the aged, or childhood illnesses. Each institute or discipline had its own good reasons why mental retardation was a matter to be dealt with somewhere else. Within the federal government, there was one bureau within the Office of Education—the Department of Special Education—specifically dealing with mental retardation. "It took me three days to find out where the department was," Eunice recalled. "I couldn't find what floor it was on, or the office it was in, or where it was, or anything about it. It was just a laughing, roaring joke."

As Eunice began her work, she knew that Washington was full of commissions and committees whose primary accomplishments were a few press releases, largely unread reports, and effusive self-congratulation. Eunice wanted her commission to be the beginning of a revolution in the understanding and treatment of those with mental retardation. She set out to people the presidential panel with some of the most outstanding doctors, scientists, and other experts in America.

Eunice knew that ideas meant nothing unless they were linked to power. Thus she arranged for the first meeting to take place in the White House where Jack greeted the group in the Rose Garden. Jack did not spend his days greeting commissions and panels, but he could hardly deny Eunice. Jack's presence signaled to Washington that this commission was something other than volunteer work for his sister. It signaled equally to the panel members that the presidential eyes would be on their efforts.

As chairman, Eunice chose Dr. Leonard Mayo, director of the Association for the Aid of Crippled Children. At the White House Mayo went up to Sarge to tell him how delighted he was to be heading the panel. "Mr. Shriver, your wife is listed as a consultant," he told Sarge earnestly, "but as far as I'm concerned she's chairman."

Sarge looked down paternally on the diminutive doctor. "Dr. Mayo, I see I don't have to draw any pictures for you," he said. "You're very smart. She's the closest member of the family to her brother. They're like peas in a pod. This panel was really her idea."

Eunice was so single-minded, so determined, so convinced

of the value of what she was doing that she used that as her droit du seigneur to be merciless in the demands she made on her subordinates. In the White House office, Edwin R. Bayley had the unenviable assignment of publicizing the presidential commission. Bayley found Eunice "insistent" and "unreasonable." He used every chit he had, begged every reporter within calling distance to write something, anything about the panel's first Saturday White House meeting.

At nine Sunday morning, Bayley was awakened by a "livid, screaming" Eunice. "There isn't anything in the paper," she yelled, berating the press aide because there was no story in *The New York Times*. Eunice listened to Bayley's explanation and excuses and hung up. When Bayley read his copy of the *Times*, he discovered a six-inch-long story on the panel and felt vindicated enough to dare to call Eunice back. "The story is in the *Times*," he told Eunice. "It's on page fourteen."

"Well," Eunice sniffed, "I know that little story, but I meant the big story. Why wasn't it on page one?"

Jack's staff could be mildly patronizing to Eunice and her associates. "The big problem was that mental retardation with the people right around Kennedy had a low priority," said Dr. Patrick J. Doyle, then of the Public Health Service. "Sometimes you had the feeling that they were very condescending because Eunice was involved, and that they were going along with you because of this, not because they had any real substantive interest in what you were doing."

As much as Jack cared for his sister, even he was sometimes worn down by her constant assaults on his time and political capital. She pressed him relentlessly. "Jack, this group interested in mental retardation is coming to Washington," she told him one day on the phone. "Could I have them at the White House for a reception?"

"Well, Jackie isn't here," Jack said, though that was hardly sufficient deterrent to his sister.

"Well, could I *still* have them at the White House?"

"Fine," Jack said, signaling defeat. "Have them at the White House. But don't run up a big liquor bill on me. Serve some kind of punch."

"Fine," Eunice said, though by then her brother had already hung up.

Eunice felt such a kinship with Jack that she thought nothing of calling him up on the slightest whim or impulse. One evening she called the president when he and Jackie were having a gay private dinner with their friends Tom and Joan Braden, and Leonard and Felicia Bernstein. Jack listened as Eunice prattled on. "You talk to her," Jack said finally, turning the phone over to the astounded Bernstein, who had never even met Eunice. "I can't talk to her anymore."

"Oh, come on, what are you all doing?" Eunice said, talking on for another twenty minutes. "You have all the fun, and I'm never asked when it's fun. What did you have for dinner?"

Jack tolerated his sister's eccentricities and her devotion to those with mental retardation. But he was a politician, not a social activist, and to him it was simply another issue competing for his attention and for federal funding. He attempted to push her off on his assistant Feldman and Wilbur Cohen, the assistant secretary for legislation at the Department of Health, Education and Welfare.

Eunice argued frequently with Cohen, even in the corridors of the White House. "Hello, Wilbur," Jack said, as the assistant secretary walked into the oval office. "Has my sister been giving you trouble again?"

"How do you know?" Cohen asked, amazed at the president's seeming knowledge of a disagreement that had just taken place.

"Why, I know my sister," Jack said.

"If she [Eunice] hadn't nagged the hell out of Sarge Shriver and her brother, there wouldn't be a mental retardation program. . . ." reflected Cohen, two decades after his battles with Eunice had ended. "The drive came from Eunice, not from Jack. I think quite frankly if I had to put it, he wanted to get Eunice quiet—and he was working on other things, and if Eunice wanted it, for God's sake, Wilbur and everybody else, do it! So get her off my back!"

A columnist suggested that a television newscaster should sign off his program with the words: "Good night, Mrs. Kennedy, wherever you are." Jackie was wherever she wanted to be, and it was not next to her husband in the traditional role of a first lady. It was off with the horsey set in Virginia, off in Palm Beach during the Season, off seeing plays and ballet in New York, off on a private trip to Europe.

Even when she was on Jack's arm at various functions, Jackie didn't quite grasp the subtle social pas de deux of politics, creating the illusion of politeness while moving constantly through groups of well-wishers. She stood and talked to people. Jack grew so irritated waiting on Jackie that he complained to his mother. "The girl can't just rush away from people," Rose replied. "You ought to have a Secret Service man there or someone like that who would say, 'your husband is waiting or you have this other engagement, Mrs. Kennedy.' Otherwise she can make a bad impression."

In the White House, Jackie was not ready to spend her days observing the abominable rituals delegated to the first lady: attending luncheons with the wives of senators and representatives, meeting ambassadors' wives from obscure nations, promoting one charity or cause after another, mouthing banal comments. She had almost as many excuses as she had invitations, and she avoided all but the most public and important functions. She did not want to live her life as if it were an autobiography, her every gesture and step to be memorialized. "So many people, you know, hit the White House with their dictaphone running," Jackie asserted. "I never even kept a journal. I thought, 'I want to live my life, not record it.' "

While Jack was in Washington, Jackie did not simply spend her days in languid retreat. The White House was divided into the West Wing and the East Wing, and it was a division as much sexual as physical. Jack ruled over the West Wing, a manly preserve of power and politics. Jackie worked out of the East Wing, an almost exclusively feminine bastion, from Jackie's staff to the reporters who covered the first lady's activities.

Years later, in reflecting back on the White House years, Jackie told the journalist Laura Bergquist: "You know, you were always part of *his* wing." To the Washington world of 1961, it seemed like a natural division of humanity and human endeavor, the women of the East Wing concerned with culture, charity, and social life, while the men in the West Wing wrestled with matters of war and peace, economics and commerce. Even within her own wing, Jackie had no use for the more déclassé of the female scribes, ruthlessly snubbing those women whose only stylebook came from the UPI or the AP.

Jackie set out to create a White House that was a court of such splendor that its rays would radiate through the great cities of America, to the furthest hinterland. Jackie had Arthur Schlesinger Jr. as her great ally in the West Wing. She treated the historian like her minister of culture, inundating him with messages about her various projects. Schlesinger was the esteemed presidential biographer of Roosevelt and Jackson. Jackie had the professor working on a guide to the White

House that she insisted be suitable for children. She understood that Schlesinger craved intimacy with power more than he desired its essence, and her sweet insistence was a melody he longed to hear. She wrote him handwritten missives, complete with pen sketches, goading him on.

The men of the West Wing considered Schlesinger not quite one of them. After the botched invasion of Cuba, Jack read an interview that Schlesinger had given purporting to have gotten the president to change his mind on Cuba. "Look at that damn interview," Jack said, swearing half to himself. "I'll tell you what Artie can advise on. He can devote all his mental capacity to advising Jackie on the historical significance of the furniture she puts in the White House."

In 1961 many Americans looked upon the arts as a dead European language, relic of a continent that had little to teach except bad examples. Jackie thought differently. She had lived and studied in Paris, and she considered Europe the fountainhead of culture and style. She looked naturally toward Europe for culture and couture, a direction in which her head could no longer even be caught glancing. From now on she would have to focus on America. As this most Europeanized of first ladies sought what was best in her native land, she discovered and heralded much that was good and fine and worthy. In doing so she helped to change the way Americans thought about their own culture and in a sense about themselves.

Jackie's first impact was on the most accessible aspect of culture and style: dress. She had hardly entered the White House when millions of women began to emulate her, from the pillbox hat and the classic lines of her dresses, to her hairstyle. This was American style, and if Cassini's competitors bitterly backstabbed him, this was their victory too. All her adult life, Rose had made twice-yearly journeys to Paris in search of the finest styles; Jackie was doing the same but she had stayed at home.

Jackie set out to redecorate the White House, filling the house with American antiques, creating a living museum of the evolution of American style. She was unswerving in her pursuit of bequests and gifts. She was concerned with the smallest detail, creating what to the more proudly philistine aides in the West Wing was a revolutionary idea: that a chair was not only something to sit on, and a painting not simply something to fill a blank space on the wall.

Jackie wanted to look out on a world of beauty. That imbued all her political and cultural activities, from redecorating the White House with the artifacts of the nation's past and developing a pamphlet for tourists to the White House so that Americans could have a richer esthetic and historical awareness, to affecting the clothing styles of millions of women. She wanted to look out on a world of beauty when she looked out of the White House across Pennsylvania Avenue to Lafayette Square, an exquisite rendering of nineteenth-century residences, many of which were about to be demolished to make room for executive branch office buildings that were themselves exquisite renderings of Washington's bureaucratic soul.

There were other preservationalists in Washington who, day after day, memo after memo, meeting after meeting, were fighting the good fight to attempt to save such jewels as Decatur House, Dolley Madison's House, Blair-Lee Houses, and the Renwick Gallery. Jackie, however, was the first lady, and it was her subtle, spirited efforts that became the very soul of the movement. "Unfortunately, last summer the president okayed some plans for the building," she wrote Bernard L. Boutin, the General Services administrator, in March 1962. Jack understood that once he signed his name to a document, the force of bureaucracy was often as irreversible as the incoming tide. "You can't stop until the bulldozers roll," she admonished Jack, as their friend, the artist William Walton, listened. In the end the new buildings were set back a block, the square was saved, and the modern preservation movement had one of its first important victories, and its first great symbolic champion.

Jackie was instrumental, too, in inviting great artists to the White House. On one memorable evening eighty-five-year-old Pablo Casals played in the White House for the first time since 1904 when he had performed for President Theodore Roosevelt.

"I couldn't help comparing it with the last time I had been at the White House, which had been during the reign of Eisenhower when I had played with about thirty members of my orchestra," recalled Leonard Bernstein. "To compare that dinner with the Casals dinner, is to compare night and day. In the case of the Eisenhower dinner, it was very stiff and not even very pleasant, and the food was ordinary, and the wines were inferior, and you couldn't smoke. Compare that to the Casals dinner. It's all like having dinner with friends. The food is marvelous, the wines are delicious, there are cigarettes on the table, people are laughing, laughing out loud, telling stories, jokes, enjoying themselves, glad to be there. It was like a different world, utterly like a different planet."

Jackie's solicitousness that evening included her own mother-in-law. Rose had stayed up late with Casals, and afterwards Jackie wrote her a note on White House stationery addressing her "Dearest Belle Mere," and thanking her for adding "immeasurable lustre" to the event.

Early in the administration, Jack was more worried about his wife's health than any contribution she might make to his New Frontier. He had an idea of how to perk Jackie up and stop her endless moping. During the campaign he had noticed that one of his closest friends had a new lilt to his walk, a heightened spin to his wit, and an enviable energy. The friend attributed it all to a marvelous East Side physician, Dr. Max Jacobson. The physician usually limited his treatments largely to one mysterious injection that Dr. Jacobson said included a variety of elements including the blood of a young lamb. Whatever it contained, to most of his patients it seemed the pure elixir of youth. The first time the friend had taken the injection, he had stayed up for three days. Jacobson's fame was such that his tawdry waiting room was a Who's Who of culture and entertainment, including Alan Jay Lerner, Truman Capote, Tennessee Williams, and Marlene Dietrich.

For Jack's visit the Secret Service had cleared the office, and he stayed long enough to get his first treatment. Jack had had enough experience with doctors to know that miracles rarely come out of a hypodermic needle, but the doctor seemed so convincing, so conservative in his emphatic disapproval of any alcohol that it was easy enough to believe that he had found one of the secrets of the age. He *had* found one of the secrets of the age; the age was the late sixties and early seventies, and the secret was amphetamines and steroids, a short-lived miracle in a syringe for which people lived and sometimes died.

At Jack's request Jacobson flew down to Palm Beach in May to meet with Jackie. He wanted the doctor to decide whether Jackie could go on a stressful visit to Canada and then to Europe for an extensive state visit. "He was very much concerned about Jackie's condition following her last delivery," Jacobson wrote in his unpublished autobiography. "She suffered periodic depression and headaches." The doctor was led to his new patient, who appeared unhappy, suffering from a severe headache. "After a brief conversation I said, 'The least I can do for you is to stop your migraine,' which I did," Jacobson recalled. "That broke the ice. Her mood changed completely."

Jacobson had performed another little miracle, and Jackie flew with her husband to Ottawa for a state visit. There as Jackie sat in the visitor's gallery, she heard Senate Speaker Mark Drouin tell the House of Commons that "her charm, her beauty and her vivacity of spirit have captured our hearts." The tribute was unprecedented and for the first time signaled the extraordinary impact Jackie had, not simply on America but on the world, and made Jack aware of the overwhelming political benefits of his marriage.

On the Canadian trip, Jack joined Jackie in a symbolic planting of trees at Government House. Jackie lifted dainty little mounds of dirt, but Jack, the manly young American president, had to do more, and he hefted ten hefty shovel loads. In the process, he reinjured his back. The pain was excruciating, and the timing was impeccably bad, for he was about to embark on what might be the defining moment of his presidency: a state visit to France where the imperial President Charles de Gaulle was seeking to reassert an independent and often defiantly nationalistic voice; and then a summit meeting with President Nikita Khrushchev in Vienna. Jack had to impress the Russian dictator with his vigor, strength, and determination, or as he saw it, the results might be a devastating escalation of the Cold War.

Jack invited Dr. Jacobson to the White House, where he met first with Jackie. "She was apprehensive about the pending European trip and its strenuous schedule," Jacobson recalled, a matter that the good doctor dispatched with another of his "treatments." As the doctor went on his appointed rounds, he usually left his patients with a secret smile on their lips, and he proceeded to the president's bedroom, where he gave another "treatment." "I feel very much better," Jack said afterwards.

Before leaving Washington, Jacobson said that he had several more meetings at the White House. Jackie showed the doctor Demerol tablets that she had discovered in Jack's bedroom. She sensed that something of great and compelling danger was going on, and Jacobson confirmed her apprehension. The pills had been given to him by a Secret Service agent, presumably at Jack's request. In his determination to mask his pain, Jack was mixing the opiate-based Demerol with Jacobson's mysterious injections, risking a secret addiction. Jacobson said that he warned the president saying that "Demerol was not only highly addictive, but it would interfere with his function." It was that latter warning that perhaps was the most telling, and Jack asked the doctor and his little black bag to join him on the European trip.

The Parisians have always had a bare tolerance for visitors from the provinces, be they from Avignon or Washington. In Paris the new president and his wife could anticipate a glacial civility that masked a certain disdain. As Jackie and Jack stepped off Air Force One onto the tarmac outside Paris to meet President and Mme. Charles de Gaulle, the crowds pressed behind fences began a hypnotic chant: *"Vive Jacqui! Vive Jacqui,"* a phrase that echoed along the avenues of the city as the motorcade passed by in stately procession. It was Jackie's city, and to the Parisians it was as if she were coming home.

At lunch Jackie sat next to de Gaulle, discussing in impeccable French the reign of Louis XVI and the later Bourbons. De Gaulle had a facile contempt for what he thought passed as culture in America. He was, nonetheless, impressed with a woman who, as he admitted, knew more French history than most French women. For his part, Jack had always been proud of his wife's interest in culture as long as he did not have to indulge her by sitting through appallingly long concerts. Jack was elated that Jackie was such a hit; it was subtle one-upmanship, a mark of his own manhood, power, and achievement.

That evening after the state dinner at the Elysée, Dr. Jacobson said that he was called to the Palais d'Orsay where the presidential party was staying. The doctor met first with Jackie, who "was so loquacious in contrast to her usual reserved attitude toward me." In the morning Jacobson returned and "ministered to the President" to prepare him for the rigors of another day.

At the final state dinner given by President de Gaulle at the Palace of Versailles, Jackie wore a Givenchy gown, a tribute to the haute couture of Paris. If there was one symbol of the role she envisioned for her White House it was this opulent, grandiose palace under the reign of Louis XIV. The Sun King had fostered the arts, crafts, and taste, and the rays of his vision had spread to the furthest reaches of the kingdom.

This evening, Jackie sat between Jack and de Gaulle, interpreting for the two men. The French president continued to talk about French history. Whatever subject he broached, whatever epoch he traveled, Jackie went with him, and talked with insight and detail and depth. "I now have more confidence in your country," he told the American president, a result doubtless due as much to Jackie as to her husband.

Jackie was almost as much a triumph in Vienna and London as she had been in France. She had done her duty as she saw it, and from England she flew to Greece for a private vacation. For Jacobson the trip had been a triumph as well, though he had come close to an unseemly altercation with Dr. Janet Travell, the president's personal physician. Travell's concern was more than professional jealousy. She may have guessed what Jacobson's ministrations involved. On the return flight Jacobson returned to his seat to find his wife, Nina, talking to Eunice. There was no one in the world more honestly and deeply concerned for Jack's well-being than his sister. She had been subtly attempting to worm out of the doctor's wife what he was doing on the trip. Nina said nothing, and Eunice had finally gone on her way.

Shortly before he took office, Jack was talking to his old friend, Charles Bartlett. "I'll tell you something," Jack said. "I'm going to keep the White House white." In one sense at least, he had not done so. Jack had continued to have his desultory affairs, continued to insist that married or not, president or not, he could live the life he wanted to live.

Jackie sought to get away from the White House as often as she could. Her attitude toward her husband was one of almost infinite complexity. There was hardly an emotion that she had not expressed, from love to hate, passion to indifference, joy to dejection.

"I think Jack was a hard kind of guy to be married to," reflected Bartlett. "He really wasn't a good choice for Jackie. She is an extraordinary person, a romantic who came from a cold family life. I think that Jack in his way was enormously proud of Jackie. I think he really adored her in his way. But it was in his way. It wasn't exactly what Jackie needed. I think she needed a warmer, cozier husband, more constant. Jack was difficult, easily bored, and he liked to be amused—not what she needed."

Bartlett was a man with the kind of pristine moral sensibilities that some of the Kennedy men considered vaguely unmanly. He thought that he knew Jack well, but he knew nothing of Jack's philandering, nor the more sordid machinations of White House politics. Bartlett fit in one neat little compartment of Jack's life, as did everyone else from his wife to his sisters to his political associates. And in that compartment, Bartlett had seen and felt Jack's magical sway. "I never expect to know anybody who had this sort of light and this marvelous wit and a great generosity of spirit," Bartlett reflected. "Jack was selfish too, and he was spoiled and he had a lot wrong with him. But there was something that was very luminous about Jack. You just think about him and you have a lightbulb go off in your head—Jack this unique, strong being who was sort of dropped on earth."

In the White House, Jackie experienced her own ineffable magical moments. Her husband had no interest in classical music. When Jackie arranged for some of the greatest classical musicians in the world to play at the White House, Jack's performance in pretending to enjoy the music was almost as great as those of the artists. Jack preferred show tunes. His favorite music at the time was the score of *Camelot*, the Lerner and Loewe musical playing on Broadway, the Arthurian legend of lords and ladies, princes and knights, bowdlerized, Americanized, and fitted with memorable if sentimental melodies. Jack loved to play the music when he was shaving in the morning and just before he went to bed at night, and Jackie thought it would be a treat for her husband to meet Frederick Loewe, the composer.

Loewe came to the White House for a small dinner party with a few of the president's friends. Afterwards, he agreed to sit at the piano and play some of his music. The guests asked him to play selections from *My Fair Lady*, the classic Lerner and Loewe musical based on George Bernard Shaw's *Pygmalion*. Jack requested that Loewe play the music from *Camelot*. Jack knew all the music almost by heart, from "I Wonder What the King Is Doing Tonight" to the haunting lyrics of the final song: "Don't let it be forgot, that once there was a spot, for one brief shining moment that was known as Camelot."

Jackie had understood how much the Lerner and Loewe music meant to her husband, and it had been a memorable evening, the echoes of the music lingering long after the guests had left.

* * *

Summer still meant Hyannis Port, and for the long Fourth of July weekend, the Kennedys converged on the village for several days of activity.

Joan often spent time with Jackie, the two youngest Kennedy women of their generation finding they had much in common. "Jackie would say, 'They have no idea what we do when we're alone. I know you go over to Squaw Island by yourself and play the piano and I go off alone and paint and they think we're weird because we're alone. They can't stand to be alone.' "

Jackie and Joan at times went off together by themselves. "We would get a Secret Service man to drive her speedboat and go water skiing," Joan remembered. "Jackie would go first and then she would rest and I would go, and that was enough for me, but she was very very good, and she would go again. Then the two of us were dropped off a mile away from the harbor and we swam in together. We did this the whole time she was first lady, and almost nobody knew about it."

The photographers and reporters were herded away, kept far back from the compound of three Kennedy homes. Jackie was the most insistent on protecting the privacy of her children, in part because Caroline and little John had so little of it. In May *Newsweek* had even put Caroline on its cover in an article that paradoxically portrayed the extent to which Jackie was attempting to shield her daughter from just such publicity.

Eunice was not nearly so reticent about publicizing her children, and she had agreed to allow Stanley Tretick, a photographer for *Look*, to take pictures. The tiny photographer knew how to ingratiate himself with his subjects. He sat on the Kennedys' porch talking with Bobby Shriver and his sister, Maria, until Caroline suddenly appeared.

Tretick took the obligatory pictures of the Shrivers, but he had no doubt that his pictures of Caroline would be the master coup of this assignment. At lunchtime Jack, Joe, and Jackie arrived in a golf cart. Jack detested anyone who associated him in word or picture with a golf game, or even a golf cart. Golf had an image of a rich man's leisurely avocation, and the Democrats had often made fun of President Eisenhower's love of the sport. Tretick, a photographic politician, knew that he should not even try to shoot the president. Caroline was different. Tretick owed his access primarily to the president, and Jack considered it useful to have Caroline's and John's photographs appear regularly in newspapers and magazines.

Jackie stood there on the back of the cart, looking like an avenging Valkyrie. "You are not going to photograph us, Stan, are you?" Jackie had little use for Tretick. He was one of Jack's people, a creature of the West Wing. As her photographer, the first lady preferred more cultivated artists such as Richard Avedon or Mark Shaw, not an ungrammatical, dogged little man like Tretick.

"It's up to you," Tretick replied.

"I'd rather not. Caroline either."

"Okay," Tretick said, not bothering to tell her that his camera was already full of candid shots of her daughter at play. That afternoon the photographer tagged along as the Shrivers, Ethel, Bobby, and a horde of children including Caroline sailed across the sound for a picnic. "Caroline, will you stop spitting in the boat?" Bobby admonished his niece. Through much of the picnic, Tretick kept shooting away.

In a few hours Tretick had amassed a collection of wonderfully vivid photographs of Caroline. *Look* put the photos together in an album, and Laura Bergquist, their premier reporter on the Kennedys, went to see Jack seeking his approval to publish the photographs. As a journalist Bergquist was unique in successfully straddling the world of both the East and the West wings, one day reporting on Caroline and John, the next day flying to Cuba to interview Che Guevara, the Argentinean revolutionary.

Jack was on his way up to Hyannis Port for the weekend, and he sat in shorts, his shirttail out, leafing through the album, occasionally making a comment. If there had been a photograph of him playing golf, or grimacing with back pain, he might well have slammed the book shut. He had no problem, however, with millions of people looking at pictures of his adorable three-year-old daughter. The problem was Jackie. Jackie believed that "some people are made for public life and some are not," and her children were not.

Jack discussed the photos with Jackie that weekend, but she was not ready to change her mind. She did not have to do so, but she wrote a letter to Bergquist. "You are right—they are such good pictures . . ." she said in her handwritten note. "It is partly because they are so good I must sadly tell you I just can't give you permission to publish them. Caroline was being recognized wherever she went. That is a strange enough thing to get used to at any age—but pretty sad when one is only three. Every article just increases interest in her—her little friends and cousins see it and mention it to her and it is all bad for her."

Unlike a political pattern that had begun in the family with Jack's grandfather Fitzgerald, Jackie did not believe that children belonged in the public arena of politics. She believed in families, however, and she was proud when administration members brought their children to the White House, or placed them in Caroline's little school on the White House grounds. "We had a reception for all the Cabinet members and there were children there," Jackie recalled. "Every time we could ... I always tried to have their children there. Like we had the Johnson girls to a steak dinner when Vice President and Mrs. Johnson were there. Any time you knew of someone who had someone young, you'd try to have them."

Pat was the one Kennedy woman who was not spending time in Hyannis Port that summer. She was far from her sisters and brothers, in the isolation of a marriage that was going terribly wrong. To the world Pat was a woman who had everything. She was a sister of the president, the wife of a matinee idol, the mother of three healthy children and pregnant with a fourth.

To the Kennedys Peter was the extra guest at the dinner table, amiable host, source of gossip, but the eternal outsider. He appeared unable to handle his isolation and distance from the Kennedys and even his wife. He sought solace equally in liquor and women, masking his own vulnerabilities.

Pat seemed no longer willing to tolerate his indulgences or to pretend that they did not exist. In this she was not her mother's daughter. She would rage at Peter, great tidal waves of emotion. "You know when a dog knows you're afraid of him, he'll bite you," said Ebbins. "When Pat found out Peter was weak, that finished them. Because Kennedys can't stand weakness. Boy, forget it. She'd rear up and instead of commiserating, she'd attack."

Ebbins was Peter's manager, and he was paid to be quiet, but the couple had begun fighting even in front of their friends. "Pat would get mad and throw some expletives at Peter and then go to bed," Dick Livingston said. "She went to bed a lot."

"Kid, this is the pits," Pat laughed to a woman friend one day, before retreating into silence.

Pat could not afford to trust anyone outside the family with her intimate emotional secrets when there was no telling what use might be made of them. Unlike anyone else in the family, she had a sorrowful sensitivity to life that became a wound that never closed. She was private in a painful way, eternally suspicious of outsiders and what use they might make of her and her family. She had what one friend, Leonard Gershe, called "a psychotic need for privacy."

Although Pat had begun to drink heavily, her drug of choice was not alcohol but constant, ceaseless activity. She was the least maternal of women, and she handed off her babies to the nurse and went on her way. During the White House years she took innumerable trips. Off on these hectic jaunts she had little time to think or reflect on what her life had been, what it had become, or what it might be.

Pat was pregnant with her fourth child, keeping pace with everyone but Ethel. No one could complain that in this aspect she was anything less than an exemplary Kennedy woman. Pat, unlike Ethel, took no delight in parading around in maternity clothes, being treated with deference by friend and stranger alike.

On July 2, 1961, Pat gave birth to a five-and-a-half-pound baby daughter, Robin Elizabeth. Pat, Peter, and Bobby, the infant's godfather, arrived twenty minutes late to the Santa Monica Catholic Church for the christening. Pat stayed seated during most of the ceremony, but she was soon up again, handing her latest child off to a nurse.

Summers had always been special times for Pat. She was not going to allow the mere birth of her daughter to upset her plans. Robin was not even a month old when Pat flew to the capital to serve as a surrogate hostess for Jackie, who was staying in Hyannis Port. From Washington, Pat traveled to the Cape for a week, and then on to southern France where her parents had rented a home in Antibes.

After visiting with her parents, Pat joined Peter and a group of his friends on a chartered yacht sailing from Nice. The ancient, steam-driven *Hiniesta* was beautifully appointed inside, but it looked like a freight ship among the sleek and elegant crafts of the port. Stavros Niarchos, the Greek tycoon, and his wife Tina were possibly going to join the group, but Pat was so embarrassed being on the homely ship that she didn't want them anywhere near the *Hiniesta*. "You can't park this goddamn scow where they can see it," she told Peter's friend, Bob Neal, when the group went to the Niarchos villa for luncheon.

The ship had the styling of a tugboat, but the larder was full of champagne, liquor, liqueurs, caviar, steaks, and seafood. The group made their necessarily slow and stately way from port to port eating and drinking. In the midst of their cruise, Pat and Peter received a cable that five-week-old Robin had been taken to the hospital after a choking episode. Pat was told that the infant was doing well. Pat's most traumatic childhood moment had been that summer day when she was rushed to the hospital for an appendectomy while her mother was in Europe. Yet Pat and Peter decided to continue the cruise.

Three days later a second cable arrived saying that Robin had been taken back to Children's Hospital and required abdominal surgery. Pat and Peter gave permission for the surgery over the phone, and flew back to Los Angeles. By the time they arrived on August 16 the surgery was over, and tiny Robin was recovering.

There was such a willful desire in Pat to live her own life unhindered by obligations of home and hearth that even the sight of Robin in the hospital bed did not keep her in Los Angeles for long. She decided against joining Eunice and Jean on a trip to Poland and Yugoslavia, as she had originally planned. Instead, she flew back to France with Peter on August 26, where he was scheduled to play Lord Lovat, a war hero, in Darryl F. Zanuck's epic film of the Normandy invasion, *The Longest Day*.

Pat knew from her own bitter experience that the long days on location were natural spawning grounds for short-lived affairs. This time there was a sweetly ironic twist to the pattern. The "real" Lord Lovat was on hand, an idiosyncratic Scot, addicted to turtlenecks, berets, and bagpipes. Lovat watched as Peter sought to inhabit his life; after a while Lovat decided that he should inhabit Peter's life as well.

"Say, Pat, let's go off somewhere," the lord said, with the same boldness he had exhibited leading troops across Pegasus Bridge during the D-day invasion.

"You're joking," Pat replied, as Ebbins recalled. "I am *married*. Remember who he is."

"I'm married too," Lovat replied, as if mutual adulteries canceled each other out. Pat only laughed.

If Pat had wanted an assignation with the Scottish lord, it would indeed have been short-lived, for she was soon gone from the coast of Normandy. On September 26 while Jack and Jackie were vacationing at Newport, Pat stood on the south lawn of the White House with the six-year-old Poster Girl of the Leukemia Society. This was one of the chores that Jackie abhorred, the sort of thing that Pat and her sisters had been taught to perform with dignity and aplomb. Pat smiled and held the child, and the photographers snapped their pictures. Back home in Santa Monica, Pat's four children had not seen their mother for many days.

Ethel was often gone too, but when she left Hickory Hill it was usually with Bobby. When she was in Washington, life progressed at a manic pace. Hickory Hill was a lab school for the sixties in all its glories and excesses. The stern admonitions that Rose had learned from Dr. L. Emmett Holt in the 1910s had been thrown out, replaced by the permissiveness of Dr. Benjamin Spock with its emphasis on the character of the individual child. For Ethel's children all life was to be experienced. If that meant dumping a live fish into the swimming pool in Palm Beach, or turning the basement at Hickory Hill into a menagerie, well that was just fine. Whatever messes resulted, the latest maid, nanny, lackey, or Kennedy hanger-on would clean it up. Her children were Kennedys too, and the grounds were a boot camp where the children competed in everything from football to tree-climbing to running with all the competitive fervor of their father.

Ethel had a schedule that would have driven most cabinet members to distraction. On one October day in 1961, she appeared at the Junior League Christmas Shop before hurrying over to the Washington International Horse Show to take part in the competition. Ethel had not ridden in a show for fourteen years, and the day before had practiced on Sky's Pride for only five minutes. Nevertheless, her children sitting in the Kennedy box predicted that their mother would win, so compelling was Jack's and Bobby's preaching that Americans could do more than anyone ever thought they could do. They watched intently as Ethel put the chestnut horse through its paces. She wore a borrowed riding coat and borrowed pants and a borrowed hat on her borrowed horse. She not only did not win, she did not even place, but she finished and that was victory enough, at least for this day. Ethel, Bobby, and their five oldest children were off immediately in a chauffeured car, and less than an hour later she was back in a velvet gown to watch the international jumping competition and to present the Joseph P. Kennedy Jr. Memorial trophy to the winning Argentinean rider.

Jean brought up her two sons in a more sedate manner. Only

occasionally did she take the boys out to Hickory Hill to spend afternoons with their more raucous cousins. She was more comfortable shepherding four-year-old Stephen and one-year-old Willie to the White House to play with Caroline and John. "I had a baby boy then," recalled Jean. "And with a new baby, that was my life. Jackie's children were the same age, and so I went to the White House a lot and we played together and I did a lot of things. We went up to Camp David. My husband and the president got along very well. They were good friends, and so we did much stuff together. It was that kind of life."

Jean enjoyed the prerogatives of being the president's sister, traveling with Vice President Johnson on a tour of Southeast Asia. Like her sisters, Jean had learned the craft of letter writing, and wrote an effusive, handwritten thank-you note to Johnson signing it, "Love and bunny hugs from 'Baby Sister.'"

It was her Jack who was president now, but in public Rose insisted on treating her son with courtly formality, calling him "Mr. President" to his face and to others. When she visited the White House, she was like the queen mother, keeping her emotional distance from Jack. She was deeply aware of the nuances of protocol, be they that of a mother-in-law or the mother of the president. Sometimes she walked out on the White House lawn and peeked at her son at work in the Oval Office. She didn't want to get in the way. She didn't spend lengthy periods in the White House. She even made a point of not passing the entire summer in Hyannis Port where she could have spent days with her grandchildren; instead she and Joe went to southern France.

There had always been an emotional formality to Rose's life with her husband and children, and her behavior toward Jack only codified the way she had behaved for years. "It's sort of a leitmotif that has run through my life in my relations with my son, [and] my husband," Rose reflected later. There was no room for dark thoughts and ponderous discussions, no room for the petty unpleasantness of life. Even when she was staying in the White House, she saw her two grandchildren only infrequently and on a rigid schedule. "My room was on the second floor, and they [Caroline and John] were on the top floor," Rose recalled. "They had their hours. Then I had a great deal to do. I was there for a short visit and during that visit I had specific occasion to be with the president and Mrs. Kennedy.

None of that informal storytelling or hearing prayers [of my grandchildren] like there would be at the Cape."

Rose treated her own son with extraordinary deference, as if there were some terrible fragility in their relationship that might break by a mother's emotion. "I never wanted to intrude on his time or the time of my husband," she said. "I always thought they had a lot of responsibilities, a lot of things on their minds and I would keep out of the way and leave them uninterrupted. I wouldn't think of going to talk to Jack. I think if he had something particular to say he'd come to me or ask them to tell me if he was coming. . . . But to expect to see him at lunch or dinner, no I never expected that. I knew if it were possible he would send for me, but otherwise he would be engaged and he had a good deal on his mind. That was my attitude in my whole life, whether it was my father, my husband, or my son."

Rose was seventy-one years old, and Joe a vigorous seventy-three. Joe made a point of staying away from the White House. That might prevent a spate of stories about the *éminence grise* of the Kennedy administration, and although Jack called his father regularly, Joe did not have the influence that some had expected.

Joe was a man of monumental force and authority, and it was not easy for him. Cassini, one of the few men with whom the Kennedy patriarch talked at all candidly, watched his old friend with a certain dismay. "He was a man of great talent who made a president out of his son," said Cassini. "The liberals didn't want the old man at the White House. He had thought he was going to get even with his enemies but wisely Jack and Bobby dispensed with him totally. He was a nonperson at the White House. That really hurt him."

In Palm Beach late in the fall of 1961, Joe was talking to Frank Waldrop, the newspaper editor he had known since the isolationist years of the late thirties. Joe was not a man to confide the emotional truths of his life to others, certainly not to Rose. He wasn't a man to let others get anything on him that might be used against him, but there were a few men to whom he sometimes exposed glimpses of his inner self. As the two men walked on the beach, Waldrop turned to Joe and said admiringly: "It's so incredible about Jack as president. You must just feel so great."

Joe turned and looked at his old friend. "I get awfully blue sometimes," he said, and continued down the beach.

Joe was reaching an age where his favorite indulgences were no longer so pleasurable or so possible, and he was spending more time with Rose. Even when they were together, Rose went her own way, and Joe his own. "I don't think they ever communicated with each other about running the house," recalled Frank Saunders, the chauffeur. "Mrs. Kennedy would tell me to do something, and then Mr. Kennedy would repeat the exact same instructions."

Joe had never had time for the endless social niceties of life in a resort community: the kibitzing on the golf course, the lassitude of lying on the beach without a phone, the interminable parties with the same faces. He headed off first thing each morning at eight o'clock to meet his friends for a game of golf, the competition spiced with a few bets and the latest gossip. He had no time for Rose with her game of short drives. Rose understood, as she had understood so many things, and headed out later. She could have gotten someone to accompany her but she was usually by herself, her face protected against the tropical sun, a tiny dot of a woman scurrying along the fairway. She wasn't out for the sport but for the exercise. Rose started play in the middle of the course somewhere, inserting herself between groups, placing three balls on the ground, and hitting them one after another. Three balls; that was her regimen. She would hurry out onto the fairway, hit away, play three holes, then tuck her club under her arm and head back to the house in north Palm Beach.

The best times were still when the family was together. In mid-December Joe drove to the airport to meet Caroline and John accompanied by their nurse, who had flown down on the *Caroline* from Washington. Jackie and Jack were on a trip to South America, and on their return Jack's plane touched down in the Florida resort. Jack could spend only one day relaxing, a decent respite in the life of a president, and Joe saw his son off the next morning, December 19, 1961, while Rose went Christmas shopping on Worth Avenue. It was always something of a letdown when Air Force One lifted off from the tarmac taking Jack away.

As his companion, Joe turned to his niece Ann Gargan. Ann was one of the lesser Kennedys. She and her brother Joe had been looked after by Rose and Joe after the death of their parents. Ann had wanted to become a nursing nun. After three years in the convent she developed multiple sclerosis and had left the order. Joe had always had a special liking for Ann. He sent her to the Lahey Clinic to see the finest specialists. At the dinner table he cut her meat to spare her embarrassment, and encouraged her in other ways. Ann recuperated and became a useful person to have around, nunlike in her solicitousness and life-style, a woman who performed sundry duties for Rose and Joe and exhibited a constant congeniality. She had a giddy sense of humor that her Uncle Joe especially appreciated.

While playing golf with Ann after Jack's departure, Joe felt a little weak on the sixth hole, but thought nothing of it. Though he felt queasy, he was sure his problem would soon go away. Then he began to wander drunkenly around the golf course. Ann shepherded him into a golf cart, and then a car, and brought him back to the house.

"Was he able to walk into the house?" Rose asked as she returned from her shopping trip and learned that Joe was in bed. That was always the way she asked questions, seeking the positive.

"Yes, but I had to help him," Ann said.

Rose went into her husband's room and had a little chat with Joe. Rose asked Joe how he felt. She knew what he would answer, what she would answer in the same situation, and she left saying that he would be fine after a little nap.

Rose returned to Joe's room after lunch. He was deteriorating now and a physician was called. The doctor arrived immediately and requested an ambulance from the Ambulance Service of Palm Beach. The attendants wheeled Joe into the ambulance and Ann jumped in beside him.

Rose stood there as the ambulance pulled out of the driveway, its siren blaring. Always before in these great and terrible moments of death and disease, Joe had been there, shielding her from the unpalatable truths. Rose was alone now, and she had no intention of going to the hospital, not now, not yet. What she did not see did not exist. What she did not feel did not touch her.

"There's nothing I can do except pray," she told Frank Saunders. The chauffeur saw that her face was a deadly pale, denying her words, advertising her unspoken fear. "He'll be all right. Ann's with him. He'll be fine, you'll see. I just cannot let this get me down. I must keep up my schedule. I have my routine. I'm going to play golf now, Frank, yes, I will play."

Rose went to the Palm Beach Golf Club course and drove her three balls up the fairway as she always did. And in the perpetual sun of the impeccable greens, life went on as it al-

ways did. Denial and routine: They had always been her
friends, and they were her companions this day. Joe made fun
of her little drives, but she hit the ball repeatedly, and always
she got to the green. Again and again she hit the three balls
until she looked up, startled, as a golf cart headed right at her.

"Mrs. Kennedy, the hospital called and they want you to
come," Saunders said, his voice charged with emotion.

"Oh, what is it?" Rose said irritably. She could not understand why they didn't leave her alone.

"It's the hospital."

"What can I do?"

"They need you to sign some papers."

"Oh, very well."

The chauffeur insisted that Rose go immediately to St.
Mary's Hospital, but she would have nothing of it. She ordered
Saunders to take her back to the house. "He'll be all right,"
she said, half a supplication. "I am going to take a swim first,
Frank."

Rose changed into her swimsuit and slowly let herself down
into the pool and began doing her laps across the shallow end.
She swam the same way she played golf, without any exhilaration or intensity, but with methodical strokes. She had kept
herself so fit and trim, not indulging like so many Palm Beach
matrons, never eating too much, never getting tipsy on liquor,
never any excesses. Back and forth she swam. As Saunders
watched her, he thought that Rose was trying to wear herself
out.

Rose lifted herself out of the pool finally, her face as emotionless as when she had entered. "Now I must have my
shower," she said, and off she went to bathe and dress as she
always did.

It was nearly dusk now, hours since Joe had been taken
away, and as the car made its stately way along North Ocean
Boulevard, police appeared at the intersections to stop traffic;
other police vehicles led the way, their rotating blue lights illuminating the dusk. Her two friends, denial and routine, were
gone now. Rose sat alone encased in the backseat of the Chrys-
ler heading inexorably toward Joe.

Joe had suffered a massive stroke. His right arm and leg were
paralyzed, and when he tried to talk, words came out that had
no meaning. The right side of his face was paralyzed too, and
he could not control his mouth, saliva dripping down his chin.

Rose went into Joe's room, but he did not recognize his wife, and she went to the chapel to pray. Soon afterwards Jack arrived from Washington, and the president, Jackie, and Bobby walked into the chapel. The Kennedy women were all there now, or on their way, descending on the resort, full of desperate urgency.

For all their lives, the Kennedy women had depended on Joe. He had given Rose, his daughters, and his daughters-in-law wealth to live as few lived, but that was only the beginning of their inheritance. They depended on him in ways that outsiders could hardly fathom, ways that in this great and terrible sickness they themselves were only realizing. His daughters loved their father with a deep and fearful love, and they loved him now in this moment of terrible need as they had in his years of incomparable strength.

They brought Joe home and laid him in his bed. The nurses dressed him and fed him, and wheeled him outside. He could not walk and he could not talk, but his intellect remained alive. His wife and daughters could see in his eyes, and hear in his fitful shrieks, and feel in the flailing of his arms that Joseph P. Kennedy was all there, imprisoned in this condition, struggling to wrest his way out, and then collapsing back into seeming despair.

The Kennedys faced a predicament unlike any in their lives. "They want to concentrate only on good things," said Dr. Henry Betts, one of the specialists involved with Joe. "If anything bad happens, forget it and move on to something good. . . . And they've done that all their lives. . . . And here was something bad that they couldn't get rid of. . . . For a group of people who don't want to face bad things, it was hard, harder than death because with death they always went on. They'd go in the morning and then they'd go home, find God, find diversions and then they'd find fun and work and things like that. They go on because they repress it in a way. But how could you [repress] this, because he was around all the time, horror and death."

Joe had lived his life in a world where women were largely objects and possessions. Now he found himself imprisoned in a world of women. In the early months of 1962, four powerful women waged a subtle, emotionally complicated struggle over the control of Joe's rehabilitation. "Anyone who could interpret what Mr. Kennedy was saying could control that family," reflected Dr. Betts. Rose was Joe's wife and her authority was obvious. Ann Gargan considered her Uncle Joe's illness an opportunity not simply to repay the Kennedys for their generosity, but to assert herself, never again to be the poor relative. She was, in Dr. Betts's phrase, "totally fixated." Ann had some nursing training. She did not so much nurse as baby her Uncle Joe, endlessly solicitous to his every need. Rita Dallas, the primary nurse, was the strong-willed voice of medical wisdom. She was ministering to the president's father, a fact of which she was deeply aware. She sought her own control over what she called "the Kennedy case." Luella had flown down to Palm Beach as well, as she did in any Kennedy birth or medical emergency. Luella was much beloved by the family, and her presence was an optimistic sign; she too thought it was her natural right to be the authority.

Rose walked briskly into Joe's bedroom to see her husband. "No! No! No!" Joe screamed, his voice like a terrible curse, the sound echoing through the room. "No! No! No!" he yelled, beating the side of the bed with his left arm. "I'm going dear, I'm going," Rose said, hurrying out of the room as if it were perfectly natural to have your invalid husband curse the sight of you.

Rose blamed Joe's attitude on his condition, but he did not scream when anyone else entered his room. "His children told me that he did not like having her around before his stroke," said Dr. Betts. "She made him nervous. That's what I've been told, because she always had something else—she was always upset about something else and she wanted to change something." Her frequent presence now, in the early weeks of his illness, may have symbolized the narrowing of his own world, and Rose's final dominance over him.

As the weeks went by, Joe stopped shouting at his wife and seemed to enjoy her visits. "She was awfully good to him when he had his stroke," Luella recalled. "It wasn't what one would call a normal relationship between husband and wife. . . . Rose took care of him but there was very little feeling left. It had gone so many years ago."

Rose wanted Joe's life to go on as it always had. Early in his illness she had Dallas wheel her husband down for breakfast, where he sat between his wife and niece. The maid served while Rose read the day's paper out loud to Joe. Rose droned on, her face hidden behind a newspaper. In the midst of this, Ann slid out of her chair, got down on her hands and knees in front of Joe, and began mimicking Rose reading the paper.

Rose read on, oblivious to the scene, until Joe let out a shriek, a sound that began as a hardy guffaw, but became a constant mindless screech. Rose pulled the paper aside, overturning a water glass, and looked at her screaming husband. Their whole life together had been a symphony of discipline and self-control. That life was no more. She had no idea what the next moment with Joe might bring, no idea what she should do or be. "What have I done?" Rose asked, though she had done nothing. She tried desperately to control her own emotion. "Oh, Joe, please God, tell me what I've done."

Joe gave out more incomprehensible shouts, pounding his good arm on the table with such force that the dishes fell to the ground. He yelled in seeming hysteria. Rose bolted from her chair and ran from the room as Joe sat there sobbing uncontrollably, his head wobbling on his chest. "Oh, Uncle Joe," Ann cried, holding her arms around his neck. "You'll never have to go through anything like this again. I promise you. You're a Kennedy and you don't have to do anything you don't want to do."

The old man was wheeled back to his bedroom. He watched television and lived for the visits from his family and especially for the calls to Jack. "I called the White House every morning and said that Mr. Kennedy wanted to talk to the president," Luella recalled. "When Jack came on the phone, he would say what was going on, and Mr. Kennedy would say 'ahh,' or 'ohhh,' a kind of grunt, acting either pleased or not pleased. And then the next day Jack would tell him how it came out."

By April Joe had improved enough to begin serious rehabilitation. Rose, Ann, Luella, and Rita flew with him on the *Caroline* to New York City, where he entered the Institute of Rehabilitation Medicine. Joe and Rose had brought up their children to come together not simply on great public occasions and sundry holidays, but to encourage one another in public and private endeavors. This was a family moment, then, and they all came to New York City this day. It was a time to do something positive. They grasped at it as if it were not simply Joe's rehabilitation at stake, but the family's optimistic sense of itself.

The Kennedy women arrived at Joe's private bungalow at the new residential rehabilitation center, Horizon House, bursting with enthusiasm as if they could will Joe back to good health. Pat had her own private way of communicating with her father, and she was, as Dr. Betts recalled, "absolutely fantastic with him." Jean cooed sweetly into her father's ear, telling him that now he would get better and be his old domineering self. As for Eunice, she too attempted to bolster her father, but her concerns went beyond that. She had already visited the center, marching through the facility with a cascade of questions pouring down on the doctors. Today she strutted back and forth, issuing orders, demanding a consultation with the doctors.

They all had to do something, and Bobby and Ethel paraded through the tiny bungalow, flushing the toilet, turning the shower on, making minute inspections. "Everything works, Dad," Bobby said. Rose was not convinced. She insisted that the *Caroline* be flown immediately to bring back the cook and serving maid. The Kennedys ran back and forth, a great blunderbuss of emotion and activity, until suddenly Joe erupted in a shriek, banging his feet on the ground, and the women scattered, running from the bungalow in a burst.

Quiet had descended on the little house, and Joe was sitting alone in his wheelchair in the living room when Jackie arrived, sliding silently into the room. At times the first lady was a woman of the most willful manipulativeness, selfish and self-absorbed. There was also a Jackie who was a woman of exquisite sensitivity and concern. It was this woman who knelt on a footstool in front of Joe and whispered, "I'm praying for you every day, Grandpa, so you work hard while you're here." She knew how Joe had dominated the world around him, and she placed her head in his lap, as if she needed his solace. Then she kissed his crippled hand and his crippled face. As she whispered to Joe, he grew peaceful and relaxed, until his face did not look contorted at all.

Joe wanted to get better, and the Kennedys applied all the resources and energy imaginable to that task. In Dr. Betts, Joe had his own full-time physician devoted to his rehabilitation. Rose was there along with Ann, Luella, and Rita Dallas. Eunice put her other interests to the side, and she too visited frequently along with her sisters. Eunice came bursting into the room, throwing her arms around Joe, her laughter filling the room. "Oh, Daddy, Daddy, you're a real Whooper!" she shouted, fluffing her father's mood up like a pillow, never letting him know all the time she was spending learning about his condition. "You can do anything you want to do," she insisted. "Anything at all."

Joe had been a man of such dominance that the mere inflection of his voice was usually enough for him to get his way. Now he could scarcely do more than grunt, and these hours of rehabilitation were endless lessons in frustration. He tried and tried again, sometimes flailing out with his arm, sometimes screaming incomprehensibly, but slowly he improved. Jackie brought him an exquisite walking stick, and for the first time he walked, moving down the hall and back. He sat down exhausted and Jackie kissed his hands. "Grandpa, remember when you told us that you didn't believe in coming out in second place? . . . You came out first today, Grandpa. You had yourself a victory."

Rose agreed with the doctors to establish rules that during the hours of rehabilitation no outsiders, not even family, could visit. This was in part to keep Ann away from her uncle. She meant well, but she was constantly hampering the rehabilitation by telling Joe that he did not have to do anything he did not want to do. "Ann did not make him happy," Dr. Betts recalled. "She was devoted to him but she was much more manipulative. He loved and hated her. She was not relaxing to him and she stirred him." Ann was bonded to Joe's neediness, to the invalid within him, and she was obsessed with staying at Horizon House. Rose not only told Ann that she could not be around during the day, but pushed her to leave and to visit her sister in Detroit.

Now Rose had her days to herself and her evenings largely alone with Joe. His favorite New York restaurant was La Caravelle, and Rose arranged for catered dinners served by *his* waiter on a candlelit table, with fine china and silver. Rose again had routine and discipline in her life, and she no longer sat nervously ready to flinch at Joe's next outburst. After dinner, she took off her shoes and they watched television. "They'd sit there just like any elderly couple you might see, as nearly as I could see very content," said Dr. Betts.

Rose did not spend all of her days ministering to her husband. She started again giving her lectures on her years as the ambassadress in London, a subject blissfully free of even a hint of tragedy or unhappiness. In late April she traveled to Paris for clothes shopping, returning afterwards to Joe's room at Horizon House.

On Father's Day, Ann called Joe from Detroit, and when he

got off the phone he exploded in rage. Rose shuddered at the outburst and hurried from the cottage. "I don't understand, Mrs. Dallas," she cried to the nurse. "I simply don't understand. I thought he was getting along so well, but now this. It's like it used to be."

During the next few days, Ann called repeatedly, beseeching Joe that she be allowed back into the sacred fold of the family, back ministering to Joe. The old man could not talk but he could understand, grunting out his responses into the telephone.

Rose didn't know what to do. Dr. Betts had gone off to Long Island but Rose knew where to find him. "Now I can stay here now with Mr. Kennedy or I can go to the Cape," Rose said over the phone. "I could tell Ann to stay in Detroit and I could stay here or I could go to the Cape and let Ann come back. Now what should I do?"

The young doctor found himself caught up in this psychodrama. Rose's daughters had told him that their father became nervous around Rose. Yet everything he had seen suggested that Joe enjoyed his wife's company. This was a pattern that he had often seen among elderly and paralyzed patients. They were frightened of dependency, yet they were ready to settle into reliance on others. That was even more true in a man of such power and independence as Joe Kennedy. Over the weeks this awesome struggle had been waged within his psyche, its ending signaled by his acceptance of Rose. "I don't know," Betts said, though he thought he knew the answer, at least from Joe's perspective. The doctor, however, was astute enough not to want to be drawn into making the decision. "I don't think it's for me to tell you what to do, but I can tell you that your husband is most happy when you're there."

Rose hung up. She was in the midst of her own terrible dilemma. For most of the over four and a half decades of their marriage, Rose had lived her life and Joe had lived his life. She had laboriously constructed an existence for herself. That was the way Joe had wanted it, but now it was *his* life they were both living. She was there with this shadow of a man, there for his rages, there to witness this mumbling, stumbling shadow of a self, there for the regimen of pain and memory. All her life she had pushed away all the pain, be it Joe Jr's. death, Kathleen's marriage and death, Rosemary's condition, or the realities of her marriage, but coming here each day—this she could not push away.

Rose's life was as regulated as the seasons. It was time for her to go back to Hyannis Port for the summer, back to her own routine of daily mass, swims, walks on the beach. Rose called Betts back. Rose was asking Betts not for advice as much as to confirm what she wanted to do. She called him three times, but each time he only reported his observations, and there was no point talking to him any longer. She knew what she wanted to do. She only had to do it now, to put it behind her.

Rose returned to Horizon House. She stood there in front of Joe and told her husband that she would be going back to Hyannis Port and Ann would be returning to take care of him. "No! No! No!" the old man shouted, his arm flailing out as Rose stepped back to avoid his attack. "You can come home for a couple of weeks during the Fourth of July," she went on, trying to placate him. "Oh Joe! Oh Joe! We're trying to do what's best; and you know we have to take care of Ann."

Joe continued screaming, like some primordial curse, the sound rising out of a deep reservoir of pain and anger and disbelief. As she turned to leave the house, he picked up objects and threw them at her.

By the time Dr. Betts returned from his weekend, Rose was gone for good, and Ann was back ensconced in the cottage. From then on Ann was her uncle's constant companion, with him night and day. There were other nurses, but Ann had sovereignty over Joe's life, and he collapsed into her care, as if he were exhausted by the struggle to regain his independence.

Soon afterwards Joe left the rehabilitation center for some weeks on Cape Cod. He was supposed to return, but he never did. "Mrs. Kennedy changed a great deal after her husband left Horizon House—perhaps because a decision had been reached that not only relieved her, but also left her conscience intact," recalled Dallas. "She was nervous and uncomfortable around illness of any kind, and she had gone through severe shock in trying to cope with her husband's condition. I believe she was sincere in feeling that she had made the right choice by putting Ann in a position of authority. She knew she was neither physically nor emotionally able to take care of her husband."

Joe began a life of being shuttled between Hyannis Port and Palm Beach under the observant, all-seeing eyes of his favorite niece. There were nurses around the clock too, but Rose could not stand them flitting through the house in their starched white uniforms, angels of disease and death, and she insisted that they wear casual clothes, though not her favorite shade of rose.

21

"Say Good-bye to the President"

*E*verywhere the Kennedy women looked, they saw that if you were a Kennedy man, anything was possible. No prize was too grand, no challenge too immense, no goal too lofty. Jack was the most popular president in modern times. Bobby, his brother's closest confidant, was the second most powerful man in Washington. Thirty-year-old Teddy was positioning himself for a triumvirate of power by running for the Senate from Massachusetts. No three brothers had held major political offices in America simultaneously in modern times. The Kennedys had the makings of a great political dynasty.

The Kennedy women were as much a subject of awestruck fascination in the media as the men. Jackie was the Democratic queen, as regal as any monarch, her every gesture chronicled by the popular press. In March 1962 she traveled with her sister, Lee Radziwill, to India and Pakistan for a "private" visit. *The New York Times* reported that the "tour has turned into an Asian caravan of such proportions as to make even a latter-day Marco Polo bugeyed."

Ethel left with Bobby on a world tour as well. Ethel was the prankster of the family, living at a fever pitch of exuberance. Life to Ethel was a series of dares. To the jet-lagged news reporters, Ethel was not simply good copy but an endless source of entertainment. At a luncheon in Rome commemorating the end of the trip, the journalists presented her with a shiny green Vespa. Ethel had never driven a scooter before. Nonetheless, she jumped on as if it were one of her children's ponies, and set out circling the block at a wobbly uncertain pace. The next time around she stepped up her speed, roaring around faster and faster until she careened into a small car, denting the scooter, the car, everything but herself.

In Washington, where most social life is formalized and studiously uninventive, Ethel considered protocol something to be stomped on. In June Ethel gave a party for Pat and Peter in which the dance floor pushed dangerously close to the swimming pool. Ethel toppled into the water, evening gown, high heels, and all. Later in the evening, Arthur Schlesinger Jr. fell into the pool with his evening clothes on, joined by Mrs. Spencer Davis, another Kennedy friend.

Joe could hardly speak, but when he heard about the celebrated party, he yelled and ranted and stomped. "The swimming pool thing was poor publicity and their father bawled them out about it, but as I said the president did not go," remarked Rose. "Bobby and Ethel were uninhibited and gay and happy and there wasn't any harm if they threw two people in the swimming pool. Nobody objected very strenuously."

In Boston, Joan gave no swimming parties at her home at Charles River Square. She had enough to do keeping up with Ted, the newest Suffolk County assistant district attorney, and their two children, Kara, born in February 1960, and Edward Moore Jr., born in September 1961. Joan and Ted were a couple of such attractiveness that they seemed to belie all the laws of time and nature. Jack liked to make fun of his kid brother but even the president looked enviously at Ted's sheer joy of life and his perpetual good health. "Teddy was less inhibited than Jack," Rose recalled. "Teddy had the strength and the vitality and Jack rather envied him his health and capacity to take part in all these sports."

Ted and Joan had contemplated moving to the West and starting a life for themselves in the distant reaches of the family shadow. But Ted was a Kennedy man, and his obligations lay elsewhere. When he announced his candidacy for the Senate, the train of life on which Joan had embarked with her husband picked up even more speed. Since she had married Ted, her life had been one campaign after another. Just as Jack entered the White House, the campaigning began again with an intensity and immediacy greater than anything she had known. He had to win the tough primary even before going up against the Republican candidate. "We started campaigning in January or February of 1960, two years before Ted announced," Joan recalled. "We went to every little town in Massachusetts. We would go together or we would go separately. Ted would go to the big cities and I would go to the small towns. That's where I learned the ropes, in the small towns."

Joan was only twenty-three years old when she and Ted set out to give speeches across the state. She had to act with all the social decorum of a matron of an older generation. When she was with her husband she sat there at gathering after gathering looking up at Ted with adoring eyes, hearing him repeat the same phrases a thousand times. She did not have the deep fascination with politics that Eunice had. Rather than say a few predictable words, she preferred playing a short selection of classical music, a language in which she was far more fluent and comfortable.

This time there were no tea parties and no multitude of Kennedy women crisscrossing the state. "Ted explicitly asked us not to engage in campaign activity in Massachusetts," Jean said in mock horror. "We feel like being expelled from the state where we spent the greater part of our lives but Ted is determined to fight the campaign alone."

Ted was already under merciless assault for having no credentials other than his name. He did not want to appear to be gaining office not simply by hanging onto his brother's shirttails but also by grasping onto his sisters' skirts. Jean made one magnificent contribution: the services of her husband. Steve came up to Massachusetts to manage the campaign, spending much time away from his wife and two children. Jean didn't mind. This was all for Teddy, Jean's favorite and closest brother. She was as proud as she was protective of him. She could not stand to hear his opponents criticize Teddy unfairly. The Republican candidate, George Lodge, was the son of the man Jack had defeated for the Senate. Jean considered Lodge "an old friend," and she bristled when he had the bad taste to employ "unpolished language" against her brother.

Ted's sisters may have been personae non gratae in the campaign, but the candidate could scarcely exile his own mother. Rose did not so much campaign as present a historical tapestry of her life. The audience was impressed not simply by the tales of lords and ladies, princes and kings, but by the youthful mother of the president, whose age, listed as seventy-two in the programs, seemed clearly a misprint. Since the election she had added slides of the Kennedy presidency. It was a seamless transition from Windsor Castle to the White House.

At Cardinal Cushing Central High School in South Boston, Rose told evocative stories of visiting the district with her father, the mayor. As Rose stood there pointing out popes and princes on her illuminated slides with a flashlight, Joan sat in the darkened auditorium. As often as she had heard these stories, Joan still found it awesome, particularly hearing that the Holy Father had given Ted his first communion.

"I hoped that Ted would grow up and become a priest or even a bishop," Rose told the Catholic audience, "but he met a beautiful blonde one night." Then in one deft movement, Rose turned her flashlight down into the audience where it illuminated a blushing Joan. "And that was the end of my hopes for Ted for clerical life."

The women in the audience chuckled approvingly. Even the nuns nodded understandingly at the church's losing a priest to such a beautiful and exemplary Catholic woman. Joan knew the story was not true, but like so much of politics it was amiable fiction, far less complicated and far more morally edifying than the truth.

"My mother-in-law campaigned with me often and she loved it and I learned a lot from her," Joan recalled. "She showed me how to sit on stage poised. You have the Sacred Heart way of sitting. You don't have your legs crossed. She always sat that same way. She got after me about my poor posture. I was five feet eight when I was twelve, one of those tall girls who are always scrunched over. And she would say, 'Stand up straight, you have a beautiful figure. Stand up and show it.'"

Joan had married the best instinctive politician in the Kennedy family. Ted had inherited his maternal grandfather's gift, and he took delight in the sheer game of politics. He was so much like Fitzgerald that at an Irish dance, he belted out a chorus of Honey Fitz's theme song "Sweet Adeline." Joan sat and watched as her husband answered charges and accusations that would have rendered her speechless. Ted turned them away with neat flicks of rhetoric, and went on to say why he could do more for Massachusetts. It was an opinion with which the voters massively concurred, sending him to Washington as their new senator.

Jackie told her youngest sister-in-law, "Live in town if you want to see very much of your husband." Joan and Ted moved immediately into a rented home in Georgetown. Joan had what by most criteria would be considered a life of enviable ease and circumstance. She had a French-speaking cook, a nurse for the children, and enough other help so that the mundane chores of housework were banished from her life.

In Washington, Joan discovered that the life of a senator's

wife was full of endless waiting, half-eaten meals, half-spoken conversations, and excuses within excuses. She had hardly arrived when Ted pushed her forward to attend the thousand-dollars-a-ticket dinner commemorating the second anniversary of the inauguration. Ted was at another fund-raiser, and she sat by herself at a table near the presidential party. Jack and Jackie were supposedly the main draws of the evening, but the largest crowd of well-wishers swarmed around her table. She rose and for forty-five minutes worked the room as deftly as Ted ever did. Ted called it "Meet and Greet." He turned on automatic pilot and worked his way through a room, hardly ever stopping, hardly ever remembering, one of the mindless spectacles of politics. Joan talked to everyone with natural sincerity, carrying on lengthy conversations. She was a generation younger than almost everyone else in the room, but she gamely pushed on doing her best to talk Washington talk. "I can't get over it," one guest said, startled after his encounter, "a beautiful child like that talking so soulfully about some bill in Congress. It just doesn't seem right."

Wherever she went in public, Joan led with her beauty. She rarely had to say anything witty, wise, or provocative to be a focal point of interest. In private, Joan had on occasion begun to drink. Although she insisted that she did not have a drinking problem until the early 1970s, several of those who knew her then have different recollections. One former staff member remembered a party at the Kennedys' home in early November of 1963 celebrating the first anniversary of Ted's election, in which Ted alerted this staff member to lock the liquor cabinet. Another staff member recalled Joan asking her to pour her straight vodka and pretend that it was merely water. If Joan had on occasion already learned to anesthetize herself against the pressures of it all with a drink or two or three or sometimes more, her problem was largely hidden, from herself and from the rest of the Washington world. Almost everyone in the political community thought that Ted had the perfect political wife, the envy of the capital.

Ted had married a beautifully wrapped package. When he opened the package up the person inside was not quite what he had expected. Joan was an immensely vulnerable woman to whom the stress of Washington and the ambiguities of this Kennedy marriage were sometimes too much. It was nonetheless true, as in later years Ted told his children, that they had been "conceived in love," both his and Joan's. On a campaign platform Joan often looked up at her husband with swooning eyes of adoration, and she loved and admired what was best in her husband. Ted, for his part, was immensely proud of his beautiful cultured wife, a hostess of impeccable taste.

If the Kennedys had known how soon and how easily Joan would become a problem drinker, Ted may well not have married her; and if Joan had realized with how many other women she would share her husband, she too might have called off the wedding. Ted tried to understand his wife. He was a drinker too, but no matter how much he drank, how late he stayed up, he was up the next morning. Though he followed the womanizing habits of his older brother, in his own way he felt that he was deeply concerned about Joan. He gave her cleaners, cooks, nannies, governesses, chauffeurs. He came home in the evenings, even if a few hours later he was off to a meeting or a party somewhere.

Ted made his way to Washington largely because of his name. Now by the sheer force of diligence, he would have to perform well enough to merit both his name and his office. Joan increasingly became a problem to be locked away, hidden behind the benign dissembling of politics, to be brought forth on public occasions, duly photographed and admired, a smiling beautiful icon of family bliss.

In Los Angeles, Peter was slowly sliding down into an alcoholic haze. Pat tried to live as she had before Jack became president, but her life was slipping away too. She was drinking too much and she was drawn into a shadowy nexus of politics. Pat had an almost pathological need for privacy. When she picked up the phone and talked intimately to Jean or Eunice or Jack, or argued with Peter in her powder room, she assumed that no one else was listening. Yet her words were probably being captured by surveillance experts. Fred Otash and two of his former associates said that he was hired by Jimmy Hoffa, the corrupt Teamster president, to gather information on the Kennedys and had bugged the Lawfords' home.

Pat adored the genial camaraderie of the Hollywood celebrities, but one by one they were leaving. Sinatra was the first to go, taken away by the exigencies of politics. Peter asked Sinatra to be the president's Palm Springs host on Jack's trip to southern California in March 1962. Sinatra put in a helicopter pad, cottages for the Secret Service, even a flagpole on which the presidential flag would be unfurled.

As attorney general, Bobby was making the most single-mindedly attack on organized crime in American history. He warned Jack time and again about Sinatra's unsavory connections. "Everybody complains about my relationship with Sinatra," Jack confided to Charles Bartlett. "Sinatra is the only guy who gives Peter Lawford jobs. And the only way I can keep this marriage going is to see that Peter gets jobs. So I'm nice to Frank Sinatra."

Jack, then, may have compromised himself in large part to help his sister. When Bobby heard about the proposed stay, he became incensed. He was his brother's keeper. He could not abide Jack's associating with a man with such connections. Peter had the unenviable task of telling the singer that Jack would not be staying with him.

Lawford recalled that Sinatra vented his spleen by destroying the concrete landing pad with a sledgehammer. He applied a different kind of sledgehammer to his friendship with Peter and Pat, banning them from his company. Pat had wanted nothing more from Sinatra than the pleasure of his presence in her life, but nothing was simple anymore, not even friendship.

On his trip to Palm Springs, Jack ended up staying at the home of Bing Crosby. Marilyn Monroe flew down to be with the president, spending the night in his bedroom. She was Hollywood's reigning sex goddess, and there was almost an inevitability that Jack would have an affair with the actress.

On another of Jack's West Coast trips, Otash said that with their electronic surveillance of the Lawford house, they had heard the sounds of Jack making love to Marilyn. Joe Naar, Peter's closest friend in Hollywood, had his recollections as well of that house on the beach. "I recall a party there and I'm dancing with Marilyn," he said. "And Bobby wants to dance with her, and makes some lewd remark, and she turns to me and makes a sign as if she's throwing up. He kept hitting on her all the time."

Peter's life was reduced to being a Kennedy in-law, relegated to walk-on parts in the family drama. He had never been a strong man, and as his career faltered, he became beset with self-doubt, his weakness glaringly exposed to his wife and the other Kennedys.

Even Jack felt sorry for poor Peter. He became infuriated reading a column by Drew Pearson suggesting that he had become bored having the actor around. "That god damn Pearson," Jack said. "The whole article is a filthy lie. It's so unfair. Now that Peter is having a rough time, this is plain cruel. Here I am, President of the United States, and I can't do anything to stop a bum like Pearson."

Pat might have been more supportive of Peter, but any reservoir of goodwill she maintained for her husband had been drained. When Peter costarred in a television play with twenty-seven-year-old Lee Remick, he began a passionate affair with the talented actress. Peter had had his flings before, but he was deeply serious about Remick. She was married to the director Bill Colleran, with whom she had two little children, but that didn't matter. Peter was so taken with Remick that he did not practice the necessary public duplicities, and the relationship became common knowledge in Hollywood. In her column, Hedda Hopper wrote: "The big news in Hollywood is a romance that can't be put into print. I don't like blind items, but I guarantee if this one hits the papers it will curl hair from Washington to Santa Monica." Even such a public notice as that did not serve as warning to Peter, and four days later the columnist ran a second item: "Regarding my blind item of the other day about Hollywood's most hush-hush romance, the two parties evidently don't seem to care who knows. They dined in a popular restaurant, and if he's not careful he may lose his million-dollar baby."

Soon afterwards when Pat and Peter planned an elaborate party, Lee Remick and her husband were invited. As the guests began arriving at the beach house, Pat stood near the front door. "Hello, Pat, I'm Lee Remick," the actress said, as if Pat did not know her identity. Pat took Lee's proffered hand and replied: "And I'm the million-dollar baby."

For the most part, Pat's triumphs were at best petty one-upmanship. As anyone around them knew, the marriage was becoming an elaborate charade. Pat still had her family, and as her marriage deteriorated, her brothers and sisters became more than ever the center of her life. In April of 1962, she flew to France with Jean. For fifteen days they stayed in the Alps in the village of Courcheval. There the two sisters could talk about their lives the way they could to no outsiders, as Jean's marriage was hardly idyllic either; and she was herself at times full of the most inexplicable sadness. "Jean would suddenly start crying," Ebbins recalled. "You'd say, 'Oh, gee, come on not now,' and she'd just cry. And I'd say, 'Something I said?' And they'd say, 'Oh, no, she just bursts out.' No reason."

The two women talked together for hours. They spoke an

emotional shorthand. From Courcheval Pat wrote Peter a long handwritten letter in her neat Sacred Heart script. She wrote of the kinds of intimate concerns that a husband and a wife usually discussed between themselves in person.

Pat told her husband that she strongly suspected that he was on the verge of alcoholism. She reminded Peter that she had tried to talk to him for a year and a half about his problem but he had curtly dismissed her. When she had first married him, she told him, he would have a few drinks and then he was fun to be with, full of laughs. Now it was different. She was relieved that at least she didn't have to see him during the day when he slowly sank into a silent, dark mood, but in the evenings she was with him and that was almost as bad.

Pat told her husband that she understood the frustrations that he was going through with his marriage and career. She felt, however, that he should deal with these problems differently, perhaps give up his daytime drinking. Pat had been brought up to acquiesce to the demands of men, and that seemed a worthy compromise to her. She had no complaints to make about his other women and his life apart from her. That she could accept, but not this deadly, self-destructive drinking.

Pat's letter had the formal appearance of a document that she had written and rewritten, almost certainly with the advice of her sister. It was not until the last sentence that Pat displayed her own pain. "I am sorry to have to write this letter (and probably very badly)," she concluded, "but I loved you once very much and I feel strongly that this is the main problem breaking up our marriage."

Jack was everything to the Kennedy sisters, and they would go to any length to defend and shelter him from damage. In her early years in Hollywood, Pat had known Marilyn Monroe with the ersatz intimacy common to celebrities, a gushing friendliness behind which lay almost nothing. Marilyn was Jack's plaything, and that was about it, but now Pat developed an intense intimacy with the actress.

Pat's burgeoning friendship with Marilyn Monroe was at least partially in service of her brother, yet there was something deeper that drew the two women together. On the surface they had little in common except their gender. Pat came from the most celebrated family in America, Marilyn from a broken home and a childhood rich only in deprivation. Pat was considered "handsome" in Hollywood, a mildly dismissive description, while Marilyn was a woman of eye-stopping, heart-throbbing beauty. Pat was a child of the Sacred Heart; Marilyn practiced the contemporary religion of therapy and liberal humanism. Pat was married to her first husband, while Marilyn had had a series of husbands, and innumerable lovers. Yet they were both women whose public lives were veneers behind which they struggled for stability and meaning.

On May 19, 1962, Pat was sitting in the presidential box at Madison Square Garden for a Democratic fund-raiser celebrating Jack's forty-fifth birthday. Rose, Ethel, and Eunice were there, a goodly contingent of Kennedy women, but not Jackie. On this day, instead of flying to New York to be with Jack, she had participated in the Loudoun Hunt horse show, taking a third-place ribbon. This evening she was staying in the Virginia hunt country at Glen Ora where Jack and Jackie had rented an estate.

Pat looked out on the massive arena. She watched as one star after another paid tribute to Jack, from Jack Benny to Maria Callas to Ella Fitzgerald. In the midst of the evening Peter came forward, looking flushed and overweight. "Mr. President," he began, as he stood hunched over the podium, "on this occasion of your birthday, this lovely lady is not only pulchritudinous but punctual. Mr. President—Marilyn Monroe!" To the fifteen thousand Democrats, Marilyn was the ultimate American sex symbol, and they roundly applauded her. Marilyn, however, made no appearance, and Peter walked off stage in seeming bewilderment.

In Hollywood, Marilyn had been working on a troubled picture, *Something's Got to Give.* She had developed a reputation as a difficult and irresponsible performer. It was crucial to her career that this new picture go forward without major problems. Nonetheless, the Kennedys had insisted that the actress leave the set to come to New York for the birthday celebration. When the studio said no, Bobby had called one executive, Milton Gould, and acted "both disturbed and abusive" when Gould refused to excuse Marilyn.

Jackie had acquiesced in her husband's little conspiracy, but that did not mean that she would sit here as Jack was serenaded by one of his occasional mistresses. That seemed hardly to matter to Jack. He had his sisters and his mother around him, and they buttressed him against any suggestion that his birthday celebration was a bachelor's affair. Pat was used to providing such a service, and so was Eunice, and after another of Peter's false introductions Marilyn made her spectacular entrance. She minced forward wearing a shimmery silver gown so tight that the thousands of sequins appeared riveted to her skin. This was how Hollywood had outfitted her. She had taken on the role of Hollywood sex goddess for so long and so singularly that she had begun to mock it. "Happy birthday to you," she began singing breathlessly, an erotic put-down, the audience laughing and roaring. "Happy birthday to you . . ."

Marilyn returned to Los Angeles. On the first weekend in June, depressed and hysterical, she took an apparent overdose of sedatives. The following week the studio fired the actress from *Something's Got to Give*, and the studio filed a $500,000 lawsuit against her. Everywhere the actress turned, there were those ready to use her body, her talent, or her name. She saw her psychiatrist almost daily and her doctor several times a week.

In the next few weeks, Marilyn called Bobby in Washington at least eight times, and she spent a number of nights at the Lawfords' palatial beach house. Don Pack, a photographer friend of Peter's, remembered one evening observing Marilyn passed out on a sofa at the Lawfords' house.

"Pat became very close to Marilyn those weeks," said Peter's widow, Patricia Stewart. "Peter told me that Pat was wonderfully understanding, good listening to Marilyn's endless monologues." Peter told Stewart years later that Marilyn had become distressed because she was being pushed out of Jack's life. Pat was in a situation of immense emotional complexity. Her own marriage was a sham. She had her own problems with liquor and pills. She could have used her own counselor. Yet here she was listening to a deeply disturbed and lonely woman who represented danger not simply to her and Peter, but to Jack and the whole elaborately orchestrated family image.

Sometimes during the night Peter and Pat heard Marilyn's footfalls in the dark corridors. "Are you okay?" Peter recalled asking her once as he saw her there, her face streaked with tears. And then Pat and Peter spent hours talking with the actress.

Another day Marilyn stood talking to Peter and Pat as they lay in bed. "How come I can't be as happy as you two?" she asked. It was an irony beyond irony that Marilyn would find in their empty marriage a model of bliss.

In June Pat and Peter flew up with Marilyn for a weekend at the Cal-Neva Lodge at Lake Tahoe. Sinatra was the half owner of the casino resort in the High Sierras, but Sam Giancana and the mob had a purported interest as well. For Pat and Marilyn, these were the games of men, and to them the resort was a respite in the mountains. The threesome stayed in Chalet 52, a rustic cabin, and spent most of the weekend by themselves. Marilyn may have become dangerously ill on liquor and barbiturates. At the end of the weekend, Pat flew off to Hyannis Port while Peter and Marilyn boarded a private jet for Los Angeles.

Pat always spent part of the summer on the Cape. Now that Jack was president and her life in Los Angeles such a mockery, these days had even more meaning to her, resonating with memories of summers past. Her father was no longer the indomitable figure who could brush her problems away like a crumb on the tablecloth. Her mother was the same mother she had always been, off to mass in the morning, off on her long walks. Rose was not a mother who could possibly understand the world of which Pat had become a part. Pat could truly confide only to her sisters, but she could have good times with Jack and Bobby and Teddy too, and be ensconced in this enclave, away from Peter, away from Los Angeles, away from everything.

Pat had been in Hyannis Port for only a week when the news came that Marilyn had died of an apparent overdose in her house in Brentwood. On the Saturday afternoon of her death, Marilyn had called Peter and asked how she could locate Pat. "Pat's in Hyannis golfing or water-skiing," Peter replied, as he told Earl Wilson, the columnist.

"Then could you give me a number for her?" Marilyn asked.

"Sure," Peter replied, thinking that nothing was untoward.

On August 4, 1962, the last afternoon of her life, Marilyn wanted to talk to Pat, but she never made the call to Hyannis Port. Early in the evening, Peter telephoned Marilyn and heard a woman who seemed lost in some dark cavernous place, slurring her words. "Say good-bye to Pat, say good-bye to the president, and say good-bye to yourself, because you're a nice guy," she said. Peter was no stranger to drugs and liquor in deadly combination. He had seen Marilyn passed out in his house. He sensed that Marilyn was in mortal danger. He might have simply jumped into his convertible and driven over to

Marilyn's house, but he was a star, and a star was a person who did nothing on his own. Thus he called Milt Ebbins. "Let's go over there," he said. "I want to go over there right away—I think something terrible is happening to Marilyn."

Ebbins was his manager and as he saw it a manager's job was to protect his client, not to run around trying to play God. "Peter, don't do it!" Ebbins said emphatically. "If there's anything wrong there at all, you're the last guy that should be there. You're the president's brother-in-law!"

Ebbins called Marilyn's lawyer and Marilyn's lawyer called Marilyn's housekeeper and Marilyn's housekeeper said that Marilyn was fine, and that was that. Peter was worried enough that later in the evening he made several other phone calls including one to Joe Naar, asking him to go over and check on Marilyn. Even before Naar was dressed, Peter called back and told him to forget it. By then Marilyn was probably already dead.

Pat flew back to Los Angeles to pay her final respects. Joe DiMaggio, Marilyn's former husband, claimed sovereignty over her remains. He decided to invite only thirty relatives and friends to the services at the Westwood Village Mortuary, not including the Lawfords. Peter and Pat were among Marilyn's closest friends, and it was a chilling rebuke. "I am shocked," Peter said. "Pat flew in Monday night from Hyannis Port where she had been vacationing with the kids, just to attend Marilyn's funeral."

Marilyn was dead, but her memory haunted Pat and Peter. "I blame the changes in Peter and his final decline into the bottle on Marilyn's death," Naar said. "Peter kept saying, 'I should have let you go. I killed her.' "

For Pat, Marilyn's death was only a way station on a downward path. She had spent endless hours with Marilyn in part probably to make sure that the actress's affair with Jack did not become known, but she had no one to watch over her. In September, Pat had a minor traffic accident in which police charged her for driving with an expired license. Although the offense usually merited nothing more than a fine, Judge W. Blair Gibbens sentenced Pat to visit children in hospitals injured in traffic accidents. It appeared an inexplicably harsh judgment, but in reality the judge had treated Pat leniently. "At the accident the cop had smelled liquor on her breath," Ebbins said, "and she got in front of the judge and of course the big Kennedy machine did its thing."

Pat's and Peter's lives were drenched in liquor. At Matteo's on Westwood Boulevard, the couple downed drink after drink, their arguments overheard by Matty Jordan, the owner. Pat was at least as good an actor as her husband, but it had reached the point where neither one of them could tolerate staying together any longer. It was not Rose who had to be told, but Jack. Peter flew to Washington to tell his side of the story. Peter could not even do this by himself; he had brought Ebbins along to help manage this occasion as he managed everything else.

As Ebbins remembered the meeting in the Cabinet Room with Jack, Peter sat holding his head in despair, weeping openly. "Sorry, Jack, so sorry," he cried.

"Peter, listen," Jack said, sympathizing with his brother-in-law, "don't worry about it. If it's going to happen it's going to happen. Let me tell you something—it's not all your fault. I know Pat better than you do."

Jack did perhaps know his sister better than Peter. Jack knew that she had been brought up to accept Peter's behavior. Her husband's womanizing was no worse than Jack's or Steve's or Ted's, and they were all still married. Perhaps Peter drank too much, but so did many men. He had caused no public embarrassment to Jack and the presidency. Jack liked Peter better than did anyone else in the family, and he deeply sympathized with him. "You and I will always be friends, Peter," Jack said. No mere divorce from his sister would undo their relationship. "You're not going to lose me."

Ebbins mentioned the adverse publicity that the divorce would cause. He warned that it would inevitably spill over onto the president. As Jack heard that, he reflected a moment: "Maybe we'd better wait."

And thus Peter and Pat agreed to remain married until after the 1964 election. That they would do for Jack, for the family. In public they would mouth words to each other that they did not believe, playing roles that no longer had any meaning.

said, and she got in front of the judge and of course the big Kennedy machine did its thing.

Pat's and Peter's lives were drenched in liquor. At Frances's on Wilshire would Booze and the people downed drink after drink, their arguments overheard on at Jordan, the owner Pet was at Chasen's good a people could could could it had wasted the point where where could could could it had wasted the any longer. He gave it a go at could plant was wasting up, they flew to Washington to tell his story. the story Peter could not even get him could his his his his is there was along to help manage this occasion....

A his books remembered the meaning in the Cabinet Room while Bob Peter all looking boy he'd in despair. Where's did anyone else in the family and he deeply sympathized....

_____ 22 _____

"Mommy, Did They Love Daddy?"

As much as Eunice cared about events in the political world, her children and her family were at the center of her life emotionally, philosophically, and religiously. "I don't think of my parents as having spent 'quality time' with us," her daughter Maria reflected. "I mean I don't buy into that whole quality-time nonsense. I mean maybe when Bobby and I were very little, my parents traveled and worked an obsessive amount, but they were home a lot more when my younger brothers were older. And so I don't have memories of like being left home alone without my parents. I have, in fact, an image of my parents having practically no social life at all other than us."

To Eunice it would have been unthinkable to have a favorite among her children, but their only daughter Maria held a unique place in both her parents' lives. She was a darling, dark-haired child, the kind that adults pampered and praised in a way that would make any little girl believe that she could spend her life trading in the currency of her beauty and femininity. But Maria was raised differently. "I remember growing up when people would come up and say, 'Oh, your daughter is so pretty.' I can see my mother going, 'Stop it, Stop it,' to them, and then turning to me to say: 'Don't pay attention to that. It's your mind.' And I always said to myself, 'She's so weird.'

"Now I think for her to have done that when I was little was really pioneering. She was always pushing me to do boys' activities, you know, to speak up when boys were there. My father would say, 'I'm going to the baseball game,' and she'd go, 'Maria is going along.' And I came to believe I was a boy or one of the boys."

* * *

In the summer of 1961, Eunice began a camp for those with mental retardation on the Shrivers' rented estate in Maryland. Here for a month each summer was Eunice Kennedy Shriver in the one role that fit her to exquisite perfection. She had once thought of becoming a gym instructor, though that was hardly possible for a Kennedy woman. And here she was with her own camp, a rumpled woman running back and forth, working with children, giving instructions.

Eunice's children grew up knowing that this was part of their summer. "Nobody else's mother was doing anything like that," Maria recalled. "It was always my mother following her own gut. It was always going against the grain. People saying to her, 'You can't do this.' It was like, 'I'll show you.' It was all that incredible energy. People think, 'God, it would be such a horror if your mother had really great health. What would she have been like?' I can't even imagine."

The camp was only for four weeks, and it would have been understandable if Eunice had largely chosen children like the youthful Rosemary, with only mild disabilities, brought up in private schools or by their parents. A few of the children did come from such backgrounds, but for the most part the campers were institutionalized children brought by bus from Washington. Some of them could hardly walk or speak even a few words, and they required an enormous amount of individual attention. For her counselors, Eunice went to the elite private schools of the Washington area and involved privileged youths who mostly had never known anyone with mental retardation.

These youthful volunteers represented one extreme of human possibility and circumstance, and the campers represented the other, and yet for the most part the two groups worked well together. Eunice did not simply parade around like a matron of virtue, but got down with the children, joining in the tugs-of-war, helping the campers ride on a pony, passing out sandwiches. Eunice did not expect miracles, but the miraculous did happen, measured in inches not miles. "One Down's syndrome boy was at the age of puberty when the institution decides the level that you'll be the rest of your life," recalled Chris McNickle, a volunteer. "He could only crawl. He couldn't feed himself. He couldn't do anything. He was a candidate for the back wards, thrown in there where they were hosed off. After four weeks at the camp he was talking and dressing himself. He wasn't speaking in complete sentences, but he was making an effort to talk. And thus at the end of the camp he wasn't put in the back ward, but one of the cottages. It was pretty neat."

Many of those in the mental retardation community knew about Rosemary and privately criticized the Kennedys for being unwilling to talk about her condition. It was only a matter of time before the whole matter surfaced. Indeed, already in December of 1960 a one-sentence caption in *Children Limited*, the publication of the National Association for Retarded Children, had acknowledged Rosemary's condition ("The President-elect has a mentally retarded sister who is in an institution in Wisconsin"). In August of the following year, Luella alluded to Rosemary's condition in an article in *Good Housekeeping*. ("Rosemary is happiest in the nursing home in Wisconsin, where she has been a patient for many years.")

Eunice decided that it was time to talk about Rosemary, in effect rebutting three decades of lies. She would do so in the largest public forum available to her, an article for *The Saturday Evening Post*. She could not think of taking such a major decision without the counsel of both her father and her brother, the president. "I spoke to my father and Jack and I had no opposition," she recalled. "I told my mother as well, who said, 'It's all right.' They couldn't have been better about it."

In September 1961 millions of Americans read Eunice's startling revelations in her article titled "Hope for Retarded Children." "Early in life Rosemary was different," Eunice wrote. "She was slower to crawl, slower to walk and speak than her two bright brothers. My mother was told she would catch up later, but she never did. Rosemary was mentally retarded." It was a historic moment in the history of mental retardation in America. It was not simply the coming out of the Kennedys, but an attempt to use Rosemary's condition to further the evolution of concern about the developmentally disabled and their treatment. By any measure, the article represented the Kennedys at their most exemplary, taking this deep family tragedy and turning it into activities of the highest social usefulness. "Because of Rosemary, our family has been deeply involved," Eunice wrote. Eunice avoided any suggestion of Rosemary's lobotomy by saying simply that the doctors had said "that she would be far happier in an institution."

When Luella showed the article to Joe, he looked at the page with its caption—"How the Kennedy family's own misfortune spurred the fight against a widely misunderstood affliction." He looked at the picture of a young beautiful blossoming Rosemary standing with Jack and Eunice. And then the old man flew into a terrible rage, grunting and moaning, seeming to curse the very pages on which the words were written. Joe had known about the article beforehand. As Eunice rightfully suggested, he probably was reacting not to the article itself but to being confronted with this family tragedy in which he had played such an unfortunate role.

For Eunice the article was just one weapon in her single-minded attack on mental retardation. She knew that the great battles in Washington were often fought far from public awareness—in the bureaucratic trenches, where words mean power. She got down into those trenches with administrators and waged internecine warfare over a sentence or a phrase. Many health professionals, especially psychiatrists, linked mental health and mental retardation together, considering retardation a disease, not a condition. It was an immense struggle to break the two apart, first in Washington, and then later in the minds of Americans. There were struggles over the funding with the Bureau of the Budget, and squabbles with those interested in money for other important health issues.

These issues coalesced in the first presidential message to Congress on mental illness and mental retardation, delivered on February 5, 1963. On the Saturday beforehand, Mike Feldman drove out to the Shrivers' home to go over the draft of the speech with the Shrivers and Dr. Leonard Mayo, chairman of the President's Commission on Mental Retardation. For Eunice, this was no perfunctory chore, no delicate rubber stamping of a speech already approved by her brother. Instead, for six hours straight she went over every word, every nuance, struggling to advance her cause.

Feldman was a brilliant negotiator. He was not here merely to please Eunice but, by protecting the speech, to protect the president's other commitments as well. On and on they went, until finally Feldman and Eunice came to loggerheads over one phrase. Eunice insisting on a change, Feldman just as adamantly refusing.

Mayo had seen Eunice in dozens of meetings, and as he sat there he watched her perform each of her techniques. She made rational arguments and when that didn't work she invoked her brother's sacred name. She beseeched and she threatened. None of it changed Feldman's adamancy, and Mayo thought to himself, "Eunice, the only way you're going to carry your point is to cry." And as he sat there, Eunice burst into tears. Feldman looked at her, sitting there crying, and with that all his argument collapsed, and Eunice got her way.

Eunice had scarcely wiped her tears away when she became her old resolutely dissatisfied self. For her any achievement was only a beginning, any mountain she climbed only a way of providing vistas of a distant higher peak. In May of 1963, she gave a speech to the Women's Committee of the President's Committee on Employment of the Handicapped, pillorying the federal government for not hiring any individuals with cognitive disability. "Of the two hundred thousand handicapped hired by the Federal Government since World War II, there is no record of the employment of a single mentally retarded man or woman," she said firmly, her voice duly amplified by its proximity to the president.

Eunice was the conscience of the Kennedy family, calling upon the finest qualities of her brother. "You should put more fire into your speeches," she admonished him.

"And, you," Jack replied, "should put more of your speeches into the fire."

Eunice's political concerns were not limited to mental retardation. She felt free to go to almost anyone in the administration with her requests. She became passionately concerned with the idea of a domestic Peace Corps, having young men and women volunteers working with the developmentally disadvantaged, with the economically disadvantaged in the ghettos of American cities, and among the rural poor in Appalachia. Eunice kept pestering her brother about it, boring him with her impassioned monologue. "That's a good idea, Eun," he said the fourth time she had beaten away on him. With what he doubtless took as brotherly concern he came up with his presumably chivalrous response. "Why don't you go to Sargent about it?"

Jack considered Eunice's husband a prissy man who would have made a better priest than a politician. He was, nonetheless, developing a grudging admiration for the superb job his brother-in-law was doing over at the Peace Corps. Sarge was sending volunteers to Asia, Africa, and Latin America. He was not ready to take on America as well, and Eunice headed back to talk to her brother again. "Well are you ever going to do this?" Eunice said one evening. "It would be wonderful for the young people. It would be wonderful for you. It would be a great boon to all these underprivileged kids."

"Are you ever going to get off my back on it?" Jack said, flaring with irritation.

"Well, Jack, I think you're just missing a great bet."

"Well, why don't you call Bobby? It's not a bad idea."

Bobby was a man who listened. He heard his sister out and passed the idea onto David Hackett, a close aide and a boyhood friend. Hackett proposed a cabinet-level committee that in three weekend meetings developed plans for a national service corps. It had been Eunice's idea, and now it was Bobby's. He traveled up to the Hill to give testimony in support of his brother's bill for the establishment of a domestic Peace Corps. Not once did he mention Eunice's name or contribution. As attorney general, Bobby cared not simply about law but social justice. He traveled out of the sanctuaries of government and privilege, into the other America of poverty and social deprivation. This was a world that Eunice had discovered and had cared about years before anyone else in her family.

Bobby made dramatic, passionately felt visits to the ghettos of Washington and New York, the sharecropper cottages of Mississippi, the Indian reservations of the West, places where cabinet members had rarely ventured. In his testimony in support of a domestic Peace Corps, he talked about a state hospital for the mentally retarded in which "patients were left naked in cubicles, which suggested kennels"; migrant workers "living in their car for three months"; the deprivation of Indians, Alaskans, and illiterates. Many of these outrages he had witnessed with his own eyes on his lightning visits, and they were all areas in which young American volunteers would find ready service.

As impassioned as Bobby spoke, and as deeply as he cared, his words contained the seeds of a deadly romanticization of the poor and the underprivileged, deadly because it turned circumstance into nobility, and deadly too because like most romances it could grow cold and disillusioned. Eunice was now no more than a cheerleader for her brother, and it was a pity, for she had seen the underclass, the disadvantaged, the disabled as Bobby had not. At Alderson Prison, she had caught on to the inmates and their cons, and knew that to help them was not to excuse them. She had worked with Rosemary the way none of her brothers and sisters had bothered, and she knew that it took patience beyond patience to work with the mentally re-

tarded. In Chicago, she had wrestled down a juvenile delinquent, and her concern was tough and if need be almost merciless. "There is no lady bountiful in Eunice," reflected Sarge.
"No Christmas baskets. Not even slightly in her character. No
guilt complex. Zilch."

The bill for the domestic Peace Corps passed the Senate in
1963, but it lost in the House of Representatives.

Behind all Eunice's efforts stood Sarge, an omnipresent advisor,
sitting in on meetings, making phone calls on his wife's behalf,
providing an emotional ballast to his often overwrought wife. As
a political couple, the Shrivers were sometimes compared with
Eleanor and Franklin Roosevelt. Unlike the Roosevelts with
their separate agendas and constituencies, the Shrivers were
ideologically and politically bonded, and had an emotional
closeness that the Roosevelts had lost early in their marriage.

"My mother wanted to have a man who would allow her to
do all that she wanted to do and be supportive of it," said Maria. "She's capable of doing all of the things she does because
of my father. A lot of other men would have said, 'Sit down,
I'm not going to have a hundred retarded children running
around on my lawn. I don't want you traveling from here to
there. I don't want you talking to professionals about mental
retardation and testifying, doing all that.' To my father's credit,
he saw my mother's potential and instead of suffocating it or
putting it down like I think the majority of men would have
done then and still do today, he allowed her to flourish and he
actually helped her blossom. She never would have been able
to do what she does if my father were possessive or insecure
or a high-maintenance guy."

Eunice and Sarge had something else in common. They
were both users of people, not in some mundane, grasping exploitation, but in service of their ideals and ambitions. At the
Peace Corps, Sarge took seriously the sign on his desk: GOOD
GUYS DON'T WIN BALL GAMES. Like Eunice, he was a person
who was better at demanding than praising, concerned with accomplishment, not who accomplished it. "Shriver doesn't give
a damn about people," one of his loyal aides said, half face-
tiously. "He uses them. He uses me. When I can't produce out
I go. You don't get two chances here."

In June of 1963 Jack flew to Europe on a state visit. The Eu-
ropeans expected that he would have Jackie at his side, repli-

cating her triumphs of two years before. Since she was six months pregnant, with a history of miscarriage, Jack invited Eunice and Jean to go along for part of the journey as his hostesses.

In Bonn while Jack met with the German leaders, Eunice visited a home for those with mental retardation. This was not merely a desultory stop, a photo-op with a few inspirational words, and then a quick exit. Eunice took the time to visit with the children, hugging several of them. She tried to learn from the administrators and then pushed her concerns forward to the reporters.

This trip was not simply a state visit but a private journey into the emotional center of the Kennedys. That later journey took place primarily during the presidential visit to Ireland. The Kennedys had always had an ambivalent attitude toward their Irish roots. They had managed to forget that their ancestor, Bridget Murphy, had worked as a servant in Boston. They all remembered Fitzgerald, however, and loved to tell stories about the irascible Honey Fitz. They did not reflect that as soon as he could manage it, he had moved out of his old Irish neighborhood. Jack, with his ironic detachment and fascination with English political history, was something of an Anglophile. In 1947 when he had returned to the old family homestead in Dunganstown he was more intrigued by the family past than any of his sisters and brothers. Jack knew that there were those so prejudiced against anyone of Irish background that even now he would be socially ostracized. "Do you know it is impossible for an Irish Catholic to get into the Somerset Club in Boston?" he told Red Fay one day. "If I moved back to Boston even after being President it would make no difference."

Jack was far enough from his peasant ancestors to look at such attitudes with more wry amusement than anger. As he returned to Ireland, he was unabashedly proud that he was returning to his roots. Jack's visit was a gigantic homecoming, a family reunion. He was the surrogate for the millions who had immigrated to America, and were still immigrating, and in cheering him they were cheering themselves, their own victory and courage. "The outpouring of love was really overwhelming," Jean recalled. "I mean, it's very exciting to have somebody leave Ireland and have their descendant, the president of the United States, one hundred years later come back to visit. It's really tear time. And he was so great, you know, responding to everybody. And he was so thrilled himself. He was just thrilled how they responded. I never saw him so excited. Oh, yeah. It was so touching, such a poetic experience."

For the three Kennedys, the most emotional part of the journey was not the tumultuous greeting in Dublin, but the trip by helicopter to Wexford County and the old Kennedy homestead at Dunganstown. In New Ross a children's chorus sang the stirring patriotic ballad "The Men of Wexford." Jack was so moved that he asked the children to sing it again, and joined in with them. When the presidential party arrived at the homestead, Mrs. Mary Ryan, a cousin, stood waiting to greet her relatives. For days she had suffered at the hands of the Secret Service and Irish security people. Workers put a parking lot in her fields and since the nearest telephone was several miles away had added a new temporary line. The thatched-roof cottage from which Patrick Kennedy had departed a hundred and fourteen years ago stood empty, and next to it a modest farmhouse. Mrs. Ryan was a plump, plain, outspoken woman who could have been one of those legions of Irish women who cleaned the Brahmin homes and kept the immigrant families together. She greeted Jack with a hug and a buss on the cheek and introduced him to her two grown daughters, Mary and Josephine. Jack invited the three women to the White House and Eunice and Jean joined their brother in greeting their numerous cousins.

For the three Kennedys, these moments with their relatives were the most vivid testimony of what their family had become, the saga of which they were all a part. Rose had taken them to Plymouth Rock and Bunker Hill, but she had never brought them here, and here was the living monument to their family history.

The group moved out into the barnyard where the Ryans had set up some tables with sandwiches and tea. As Jack raised his teacup, he looked out on his relatives and proposed a toast to "all the Kennedys who went and all the Kennedys who stayed." And then he and his sisters were off, flying above the green pastures in a helicopter. The Kennedys guarded themselves against sentimentality with a shield of wit and irony, but Jack had been not only deeply moved, but deeply happy with the sojourn into the Kennedy past.

As he left Jack vowed that he would return in the spring. On the flight from Ireland to England, the presidential plane stopped at Waddington Royal Air Force base. From there Jack and Jean took a helicopter, soared over the patchwork fields, and landed in a small field in the hamlet of Edensor. For several days the residents had known that Jack would be visiting, but they had said nothing, and there were no crowds, no cheers as Jack and Jean walked along a country lane and into the tree-shaded cemetery. There they stood and looked at a headstone bearing the words "JOY SHE GAVE JOY SHE HAS FOUND." Jean took the three bouquets of roses and placed them on Kathleen's grave while Jack stood there in silence.

Eunice scheduled her camp to end just in time for her to fly up to the Cape for the Fourth of July to be with the whole family. Jack and Jackie were there too in their rented house on Squaw Island only a short ride or walk from the Kennedy compound. Ethel had already arrived with her seven children, pregnant with an eighth, and the other Kennedys were there as well.

The film of Jack's visit to Ireland had just arrived, and the president sat mesmerized watching the footage. "It was magic to him," Frank Saunders, the chauffeur, recalled. "John Kennedy was happier than I'd ever seen him. He was just like a kid." He was so taken with the film that he insisted on watching it again and again, until his brothers and sisters dreaded the thought of yet another rerun.

There were now twenty Kennedy grandchildren in all, a camp unto themselves each summer, with their own tennis and swimming instructors. Occasionally they would shyly look into their grandfather's bedroom, the old man immobile in bed, and then rush down the stairs. As much as anything those summers, they loved the excursions on the *Marlin*, their grandfather's boat. Their mothers each had lunches prepared, fancy sandwiches and rare delicacies from Ethel's cook, exquisitely prepared picnic fare from Jean and Pat, and dainty tea sandwiches and French desserts from Jackie. "Aunt Eunice" was the last to arrive, her shirt hanging out, sneakers untied, hair uncombed, rushing up the dock holding a paper bag full of Wonder bread and big jars of peanut butter and jelly. As the boat headed out, the staff laid out the buffet on a tablecloth while Eunice sat on the deck spreading thick coatings of peanut butter and jelly onto slices of bread and slapping second slices on top. The children looked at the sandwiches with the same wide-eyed, envious stares of Tom Sawyer's friends the day he whitewashed his aunt's fence. Eunice passed her sandwiches to Robert, Maria, and Timothy Shriver, and they grudgingly exchanged their plebeian fare for a share of their cousins' elegant repast.

It was a summer of women and children, but on the weekend the Kennedy men were there, and often they would go out on the *Marlin*, the boat weighted down with Kennedys. One day the boat ended up so overloaded with family that Jack decided to take out the presidential yacht, the *Honey Fitz*, as well. As the two boats raced side by side, Jack shouted at his dog riding on the *Marlin*: "How's it going with you, Charlie?" With that the dog leaped into the ocean and was swept toward the propellers. Bobby jumped in and swam toward the dog, reaching him only a few feet from the propellers. Bobby and the dog disappeared under the enveloping sea. The others watched in tense silence. Suddenly, Bobby and the dog surfaced, their emergence heralded by cheers, shouts, whistles, and tears of relief.

The two ships continued their race, but a lesson had again been taught, to the women as well as the men, the children and the adults. Some might have considered Bobby's action a fool's bravado, the attorney general of the United States, the president's brother, the father of seven children risking his life to save a dog. But that was not how the Kennedys saw life. Bobby's physical courage was not an intellectual process, an act taken after weighing risks and alternatives; it was instinct, and in Bobby that instinct was at times pure and primitive. Ethel adored her husband in part because he was a man who would risk his life over a dog. Ethel and the other Kennedy women were not expected to have the same instincts, but rather to succor their husbands, to applaud their endeavors, and to teach their children, especially their sons, to behave as their fathers behaved.

During these long summer days, Rose flitted through the events with an agenda that she kept to with the regularity of a metronome. She pinned to her dress a series of notes to remind her of all her obligations. She had an excellent memory, and she took obvious pleasure in pulling off the note of an assignment she had completed and tossing it away. Her life was a matter largely of preservation and preparation. She was consumed with the idea of remaining youthful. That was her one great vanity. Her secret fear was that she would one day end up like her senile mother, who spent her summers in a tiny house in Hyannis Port sitting in a chair. Rose could hardly stand to visit Josie. She pushed the whole matter aside, letting her brother Thomas take care of their mother, doubtless paying for her nurses but not even attending Josie's ninety-eighth birthday celebration.

Rose could tolerate only so many moments with Joe. In Hyannis Port she had come waltzing into Joe's bedroom one day proud to show off a gown that she would be wearing to a ball. She stood there in her finery and the old man lashed out at her, spewing venom and disdain. As she fled from the sunny bedroom he had suffered a minor seizure. She knew that Joe might not last much longer and hanging in her clothes closet she had a black mourning dress to wear when her husband died.

For the most part her grandchildren observed and respected and obeyed Rose and tiptoed around her life as if she were an exquisite piece of porcelain. She had led such a decorous life, blocking out the untoward, the ugly, and the unacceptable, that her eyes no longer saw the darker colors of the spectrum. "Pat drank a bottle of wine in the morning," Rose was told.

"That's impossible," Rose replied. "Pat doesn't drink."

It was a summer of pregnancies. On the Fourth of July, the Kennedys celebrated not only Kathleen's twelfth birthday, but the birth of Ethel and Bobby's eighth child, Christopher George. For Joan the occasion was streaked with melancholy. She couldn't seem to keep up with her sisters-in-law, not with births nor with anything else. In May she had been five months pregnant with her third child when she had miscarried. Eunice's three children were hardly matches for Ethel's brood either but she had just learned that she was pregnant again. Thirty-three-year-old Jackie had kept her pregnancy secret for five months, but the news was out that she was due in August.

They were a fertile clan, then, and those who visited that summer had a sense that they were in the midst of an explosion of life. The children ran across the lawn, led usually by members of Ethel's unruly brood, heading for the tennis courts, the pool, or the beach. The adults congregated in one house or another, their number supplemented by friends, celebrities, and administration officials. The high point of any weekend was Jack's arrival, the presidential helicopter setting down on the lawn, and Jack emerging, rushing toward the house.

Jackie was still not completely comfortable as a member of this raucous tribe. She didn't want to explore too deeply into the psychological matrix of the Kennedys. "Everybody asks me about Jack's complexes," she commented privately.

"Doesn't Jack have a complex about his father? And doesn't Bobby have a complex about Jack? That's all anybody ever asks." She had decided that this was to be her last summer at Hyannis Port. Next year she and Jack had made plans to rent a house in the more sedately civilized Newport. Off in their rented house on Squaw Island, she and Jack were distant from the rest of the family. In many respects it was a congenial surrounding in which to wait for the birth of their child.

Jackie planned to give birth to her third child at Walter Reed Army Hospital in Washington. While she rested on the Cape, she directed that a baby's room be prepared in the White House, the white crib, curtains, and rug set off against the blue walls. On the morning of August 7, she felt birth pangs. Extraordinary measures had been taken for just such an emergency. Eight minutes after her physician, Dr. John Walsh, made his request a helicopter landed on Squaw Island to fly her to a special ten-room suite at Otis Air Force Base hospital. There by cesarian section Jackie gave birth to a premature four-pound, one-ounce boy. The infant was so sickly that Patrick Bouvier Kennedy was immediately baptized. His condition worsened and he was flown to Children's Hospital in Boston and placed in a unique high-pressure chamber. Jackie remained in her suite at Otis, far from her child. At 6:25 A.M. on the third day following the birth, Dr. Walsh entered Jackie's room and told her that Patrick had died. He placed her under sedation and she remained in bed, unable to attend the funeral in Cardinal Cushing's private chapel, or to witness the burial at the Kennedy family plot at Holyrood Cemetery in Brookline.

Summer was over for Jackie, and in early September she and Jack celebrated their tenth wedding anniversary in Newport. Summer was over for the rest of the Kennedy women too, and in the second week of September Eunice left Hyannis Port with a suntanned contingent of children. They were a remarkable sight at the Hyannis Airport, at least fifteen cousins with their dogs and a turtle or two, pouring out of three cars, and rushing across the tarmac to board the *Caroline*.

Jack was the center of the family, adored by his sisters, unabashedly admired by his brothers, their model of humankind. It would have been totally incomprehensible to them that he would one day become the first president whose sexual life was as much a matter of public scrutiny as his foreign policy. His defenders would argue that the tales were blown up into grotesque caricatures. "Did John Kennedy have any affairs when he was in the White House?" asked Mike Feldman rhetorically. "I'm sure he did. Did he have anything like the number of affairs attributed to him? I'm certain that's not true. One of the stories is that John Kennedy had to have sex every day. I've been with him almost continuously sometimes for three or four days at a time. And he was all business. And there just wasn't any opportunity. I knew pretty much what his schedule was. I think it would be pretty difficult, given his schedule, to do the things that are attributed to him."

As his personal secretary, Evelyn Lincoln knew more about Jack's daily schedule than anyone. She too asserted that the stories are exaggerated. It was not the number of Jack's affairs but their nature that made his indiscretions so dangerous. Whether it was one of Jackie's assistants, a socially prominent Washingtonian, a starlet introduced to the president by Peter, or the consort of a Mafia chieftain, Jack didn't care. They were all momentary pleasures to him, diversions walled off from the world of politics and complex decisions. The most dangerous of these liaisons was with Judith Campbell, whose relationship with Sam Giancana provided a potential conduit for the Mafia directly into the Oval Office.

"They were trying to blackmail Kennedy," Lincoln said. "Hoover came to the White House and he said to the president, 'I just wanted to tell you that your girlfriend is connected with Giancana and has called your secretary eighty times. Did you talk to her?' And the president said, 'No, I didn't. I put her off.'

"I kept the log of the telephone calls and the fact is she did call eighty times and I didn't put her through. I have the logs showing where he didn't talk to her. But J. Edgar Hoover had come over with the purpose of blackmailing Kennedy. He'd use it against him if he wanted something. I tell you Hoover was no good."

By his willful indiscretions, Jack had put his own presidency in deep and secret jeopardy. "Hoover hated Kennedy," said Edwin O. Guthman, Bobby's press secretary at the Justice Department. "Hoover was not bashful about using the raw files on people and leaking stuff out on people. There's no question in my mind absolutely that if Jack Kennedy had lived and run for a second term, the Judith [Campbell] Exner thing would have been a factor. And even if his opponent, Senator Barry Goldwater, had said, 'I'm not going to use that crap,' it

would have been leaked out by the FBI or by others and it
would have been an issue in the campaign. I have no question
in my mind."

Jack was just a year away from his reelection campaign, and
it was not just the president but all the Kennedys who were positioning themselves for the election. Jean had moved with her
family to a duplex apartment on Fifth Avenue in New York.
Steve had given up his employment as a special assistant in the
State Department to work full-time as Jack's political agent.
For now he was overseeing efforts in New York, Pennsylvania,
Ohio, and Michigan, crucial industrial states. Soon Steve
would be running the whole campaign, running it with the energy and savvy and devotion that he had shown managing Teddy's victory. On the weekends when Steve was in town, his
family often traveled outside the city to Westbury where they
had a second house. Jean was proud that Steve was so helpful
to Jack, but she had no deep interest in politics herself. She
filled her days managing her nurse, cook, and maid, trying almost every day to take Steve Jr. and Willie for a romp in Central Park. She sought no publicity and relished the relative
anonymity of life in Manhattan. "I've no idea if I'll help in
1964," she told a reporter, "although I doubt it."

Eunice's seven-year-old daughter, Maria, saw her mother
running from one activity to the other, serving as executive
vice president of the Joseph P. Kennedy Foundation, teaching
a class in calisthenics at a school for those with retardation, attending a meeting at the White House, and wondered why Eunice wasn't the president instead of her uncle. But Eunice had
no political ambitions for herself, content to be known always
as the "sister of . . ."

Everything was Jack, and as far as Sarge's political future
went, he would simply have to wait. "He'd make a wonderful
governor of Illinois, but I wouldn't want to see him run in
1964," she said. As for now, Sarge would have to use every
ounce of his political astuteness and energy to further Jack's
triumphant reelection.

In that sprawling beach house in Los Angeles, Pat's whole
life was on hold, willfully held hostage to Jack's political future. She wanted no more of Peter's life. He began his days
with a medicinal bottle of beer, then vodka throughout the
morning, gin in the afternoon, and whiskey at night. She threw
him out of the house several times, but he always returned,

smelling of booze and women. She could bear the shame of being part of the first Kennedy divorce, but not the onus of embarrassing Jack. She worshipped her brother, and almost no sacrifice was too great to make, even this, a drunken husband, a façade for a life. It was all worth it to protect Jack, to honor the family, to hold on until after the election.

Joan was holding on as well. Ted had won the election in 1962 but only to fill the last two years of the six-year Senate term. Thus he was running again from the day he entered office, meaning that she was running again. She could see the extent that her husband was bonded to Jack, and how he adored him with a purity and devotion that he showed to no one else. Even to her and his sisters, he referred to his brother not as Jack but "President Kennedy," loving the way the very sound rolled off his tongue. Just as the great wealth of the family flowed from Joe, so the political capital flowed from the vital, youthful man in the White House. If Jack was reelected, then surely Ted would win again as well. Then Joan would have some peace, a recess from this constant campaigning, a chance to get control of her life.

Of all the women in the family, Jackie was the least concerned with Jack's reelection. The death of Patrick had left a shadow over her life. She had never even seen the baby in its three days of life, nor been there beside Jack for the funeral. Though the nursery was gone from the White House, the pain of loss was not.

Jackie's attitude toward her husband was full of the most intricate paradoxes and contradictions. She had more in common now with Rose than perhaps she would ever admit, accepting her husband's sexual betrayals as much as her mother-in-law had Joe's. Yet on another level, she did not give in totally to this life.

Evelyn Lincoln observed Jackie's disdain for all the obligations of a political wife, her extravagance, the parade of sophisticated, jet-set friends alien to the world of the White House, her emotional disengagement from Jack. Lincoln had become convinced that the Kennedys' marriage had reached such a nadir that after the election there might be the first divorce in the White House.

Jack's secretary may have misread Jackie's demeanor or underestimated what Jack and Jackie would accept of each other's behavior. What was clear was that Jackie felt immensely fatigued by her life as a first lady, and she used first her pregnancy and then her mourning over Patrick as an excuse to avoid much of her life in Washington. When she arrived back in Washington the fourth week in September, she had already been away from the White House for almost three months, and had been recuperating on Squaw Island and Newport for well over a month. Even that she did not consider respite enough. On her return to Washington, she announced that she would have no official engagements until the end of the year.

Her sister Lee arranged to have Aristotle Onassis, the Greek shipping tycoon, invite Jackie to come to Greece to use his splendid 325-foot-long yacht *Christina* for a lengthy cruise. Jack and Jackie had met Onassis on his yacht in the 1950s, when former Prime Minister Churchill was a guest. Onassis had risen from a penniless boyhood to become immensely wealthy and famous by applying ruthless business techniques while ingratiating himself with men and women of substance and celebrity. Onassis gave his guests gracious hospitality, endless gifts, and never-ending charm, and his guests gave him credibility and status.

Jack had no use for Onassis. Several times he had been under investigation from the Justice Department and had once been indicted for fraud. When Jack was on his recent European trip, Onassis had sent a ship model to the American embassy in Rome. Jack knew nothing about the gift until he had come into his office in the White House to discover the model sitting on his secretary's desk. "Where did you get that?" an aide asked.

"Aristotle O—"

"Take that out of here," Jack said even before Evelyn Lincoln could say Onassis's full name.

Jackie could have chosen other vacations, but she insisted on accepting Onassis's invitation. "Kennedy said to me, 'Onassis is a pirate. He's a crook,'" Lincoln recalled. "He didn't want any part of him. And he didn't like Jackie going off with Onassis on his yacht. He didn't like it at all, and he sent along Franklin Roosevelt Jr. so it looked reputable."

Roosevelt, the under secretary of commerce, did not consider chaperoning among his official duties, but the president commanded him along with his wife, Suzanne, to join the cruise. It was hardly front-line duty, sailing forth on the most luxurious ship in the world, ministered to by a crew of sixty, two coiffeurs, and a dance band.

On the *Christina*, the favorite games were those of sexual flirtation and assignation. Onassis had the ship's barstools made of the scrotums of whales, but he played his sexual games with far more sublety and nuance. Jackie's sister was present with her husband Prince Radziwill, but she was carrying on her own liaison with Onassis, whose longtime lover, Maria Callas, had stayed in Paris. Jackie and Lee had always competed with one another. As Onassis saw and talked with Jackie, his ardor for Lee fell away. Onassis may have looked more like a toad than a prince, but it was not simply his money that drew women to him. He was fascinated by women in a way that Jack was not, and he lavished on Jackie his attention, flattery, and charm.

Jackie strolled happily through the ancient streets of Smyrna, guided by Onassis. On the last evening he presented her with an exquisite diamond-and-ruby necklace. For the first time since Jack entered the White House, she was a target for the Republicans, who asked if it was "improper for the wife of the President . . . to accept [Onassis's] lavish hospitality." Her activities had even irritated the White House journalists who for over two and a half years had put up with her constraints and demands. "Touring with her sister, Lee Radziwill, Mrs. Kennedy allows herself to be photographed in positions and poses which she would never permit in the United States," wrote Merriman Smith of the UPI, one of the most influential White House reporters. "The results at times are quite charming, but they serve to point up the fact that she's almost a different person when traveling, as it were, on her own. . . . If Onassis is in this country for any length of time it would seem almost required that the Kennedys entertain for him at the White House. That would be only simple courtesy."

Soon after Jackie returned to Washington she and Jack invited Ben Bradlee, the *Newsweek* correspondent, and his wife, Tony, to the White House for dinner. Jackie had seen the avalanche of publicity her cruise had created, but remained a proud defender of her host, calling him "an alive and vital person" who had made his way up from poverty. Jack had seen how the Republicans were already using his wife's European jaunt to portray the Kennedys as a frivolous clan of pleasure seekers. He was not about to have anything to do with the Greek businessman. He made it clear that Onassis would not be welcome to enter the United States until after the election.

"Maybe now you'll come with us to Texas next month," he said, as if that were only a fair exchange.

"Sure I will, Jack," Jackie agreed, as Bradlee listened.

Jack knew how important Jackie was in the equation of his reelection campaign. When Jackie was in Washington, she was concerned more with the upbringing of her two children than with politics. She had her nanny, Maude Shaw, handling the minutiae of child rearing. That was the way Jackie had been brought up and, as she saw it, her attitude was hardly an abrogation of her motherly duty.

Jackie had started a private little school in the White House for Caroline and a few others. Now she felt it was time for her five-year-old daughter to begin religious instruction. She sent out the headmistress of the school to choose an appropriate catechism class for her daughter and the five other Catholic children in the school.

For the first class Jackie went with her daughter to the Georgetown Visitation Convent. Jackie sat in the back of the class while Sister Joanne Frey of the Mission Helpers of the Sacred Heart began her instructions by talking about God's creation of the world. The nun asked the children to put their heads down on the desk, to think about the story of creation, and then to draw a picture of what they had thought.

Caroline took a thick black crayon, drew a large square on the white paper, and filled the square with blackness. Although Sister Frey tried to treat the children the same, she could hardly forget that Caroline was the president's daughter. Sister Frey was appalled. "Oh what a terrible image of religion I have given to these children," she thought. "What have I done?"

She turned from Caroline to her other charges. "Now does anybody want to tell us about the story of what they drew?" the nun asked.

Caroline raised her hand. "In the beginning there was nothing but darkness," the little girl said, looking at her drawing. "And God put a light up in the sky and he put a big moon." The nun looked down at the picture and saw there were holes in the blackness that were the stars and a moon.

After class, Jackie came forward to talk to Sister Frey. "Sister, this was just adorable," she said. "If I had been taught my religion this way, I am sure that it would have made a great difference to me. I know that Caroline's dad would like to see her drawing. May I take it home to him?"

"Well, of course you may," the nun said.

Caroline came to class every week, sometimes with her mother, sometimes alone. Her brother often came rushing into the room with the Secret Service agents to bring Caroline home. He marched in one day carrying a stick. "Do you know what he is doing, Sister?" Caroline asked Sister Frey. "He is acting like he is a soldier. That's what he is doing. He is marching and he is pretending to be a soldier and he doesn't even know how to salute."

Jackie kept her promise to go off with Jack to Texas, though on the morning of their departure, November 21, 1963, she was late. As Jack nervously drummed his fingers on his leg, aides were dispatched to find the first lady and bring her to the waiting helicopter. For Jack the trip to Dallas was an unpleasant necessity. The liberal and conservative wings of the Texas Democratic Party fought each other with more vigor than they attacked the Republicans. Jack felt that he had to bring them together in time for his reelection campaign.

Jackie knew little of the complex matters consuming her husband. The next morning in Dallas she was twenty minutes late again for Jack's breakfast with the Dallas Chamber of Commerce. She had been puzzling over the transcendent matter of choosing between short or long white gloves. Twenty minutes was an eternity in the life of a president, but when Jackie finally walked into the ballroom with Jack in a stunning pink suit and pillbox hat, that wait seemed justified, at least to the Texans spread throughout the room. "Two years ago I introduced myself in Paris by saying that I was the man who had accompanied Mrs. Kennedy to Paris," Jack told the business audience. "I am getting somewhat the same sensation as I travel around Texas."

As much as she smiled and graciously accepted the accolades, this trip to Texas was for Jackie a descent into a netherworld. Between Jack and his aides, she heard snatches of conversation about the Democrats' vicious internecine warfare that Jack was trying to mediate, but there was a mindless vulgarity about the whole business. When she left the ballroom, Jack showed her a full-page, black-bordered advertisement in that morning's *Dallas News*. The right-wing organization accused Jack of being responsible for imprisoning and starving thousands of Cubans, and perhaps reaching a secret agreement with American Communists. It made her sick. "You know, last night would have been a hell of a night to assassinate a President," he said, as he stood before Jackie.

Jack had scarcely ended his dark ruminations when they were out together in the presidential limousine riding through the streets of Dallas, along with Governor and Mrs. John Connally. Whatever that ugly advertisement had said, these Texans were cheering with endless enthusiasm and goodwill. To Jackie the motorcade reminded her of the presidential trip to Mexico City, where the affection was as warm as the tropical sun. She had been in this limousine with Jack so often before, and it was always blurred images, half-read signs, snippets of conversation, faces full of exhilaration and excitement. On and on they went, through the well-wishers, the hot sun beaming on the great black open car. There ahead lay an underpass behind which lay a building called the Texas Book Depository. As the auto approached the shadow, Jackie thought: "How pleasant the cool tunnel will be."

In her house at St. Coletta's, Rosemary sat in front of the television set. She loved television and could sit for hours staring at the screen, watching the images. She had been here in the home for nearly a decade and a half now, and though she had not seen Jack for so many years, she saw his image on the screen or in magazines, and the nuns talked endlessly about him. As she sat there, the program was interrupted and an announcer said that Jack had been shot.

As Rosemary watched the television screen, Eunice sat in the dining room of the Lafayette Hotel with Sarge and four-year-old Timmy, the youngest of their three children. She had driven downtown for an appointment with her obstetrician, Dr. John Walsh, and on a whim had called her husband for lunch. Eunice had heard the scientific naysayers warning a woman not to have children after the age of forty, but she hadn't listened. At the age of forty-two, she was pregnant for the fourth time and looked the perfect image of motherly vitality. She had discovered that black appeared slimming and she had a whole wardrobe of black outfits to wear, including the suit she was wearing that day.

The Shrivers hardly had time to look at a menu when Sarge was called to the telephone. Eunice sat with Timmy waiting for Sarge to return before they ordered. Sarge was gone only a few minutes before he hurried back into the dining room.

"Something's happened to Jack," Sarge said, looking at his wife.

"What?" Eunice asked, suddenly alert.

"He's been shot."

"Is he going to be all right?"

"We don't know."

"There have been so many crises in his life," Eunice said after only a moment's reflection. "He'll pull through."

Eunice felt so bonded to Jack that it was almost as if she could feel her brother's pain. Sitting there looking at Sarge, Eunice was like the victim in a serious accident who shouts out "I'm not hurt," and stumbles to her feet. Eunice ordered her lunch from the menu. Everything would be all right. Everything. She and Sarge would eat their meal and life would be the same. Eunice usually picked away at her food, but today she ate a thick slice of bread and took spoonful after spoonful of soup.

While Eunice sat at the Lafayette, Jean was Christmas shopping in New York, walking along streets that had not yet been festooned for the holidays. "Haven't you heard the news?" a woman shrieked. Jean learned on a car radio that Jack had been critically injured by a would-be assassin's bullet in Dallas. She could have hailed a taxi to drive her home to the ringing phones and the unthinkable realities, but instead she walked twenty blocks to her duplex on Park Avenue. As she walked the news passed from person to person, from ear to ear, and the shrill sounds of commerce grew quieter, and the whole great city seemed to shudder in disbelief.

"Please turn the TV down, Ann," Rose said, her voice rising in irritation. "I'm taking a rest."

"Aunt Rose," Ann Gargan cried. "Jack's been shot."

Rose thought to herself, "These things happen. It's not going to be anything serious." Then she raised a trembling hand to her forehead and looked at her disconsolate niece. "Don't worry," she said. "We'll be all right. You'll see."

Rose returned to her bedroom in Hyannis Port and began to pace. As she walked back and forth, she thought, "Jack is having some more hard luck, another problem about his health but he'll surmount." That was the same thought Eunice had, that all the Kennedy women had, not a thought really but a protective instinct. Everything would be all right. Everything.

Then Rose was called to the phone. "It looks bad," Bobby

said from his home in Virginia. "As far as I know Jack can't pull through."

When Rose learned that Jack was dead, she donned her old black coat and went for a long walk alone along the cold, windswept beach. Hunched against the wind, she moved in and out of the fog and the mist, a tiny figure lost in the immensity of the landscape. After a while her nephew, Joe Gargan, joined her and the two of them walked along paths they had trod for decades. "Joey, we must go on living," the old lady said. "We can't look back. There are a lot of people who need us. Joey, you have to think about your future, your family, your education more. We must go on, Joey. We must."

The Kennedy women had at first clapped their hands to their ears, but they had all heard the news now. Eunice and Sarge fell to their knees in prayer in the Peace Corps offices. "Hail Mary, full of grace . . ." they intoned, words that Eunice had learned in catechism class so long ago. "Holy Mary, Mother of God . . ." At Maria's third-grade class in her Sacred Heart academy, a nun came into the room to tell the eight-year-old that her uncle was dead.

The Shrivers ran out of the building and drove to the White House, entering the West Executive Avenue by the wrong one-way entrance, and parked by the Diplomatic Reception Room. Ted had arrived as well. He understood his wife's emotional vulnerability, and his first instincts were to find Joan, who was having her hair done at Elizabeth Arden's on Connecticut Avenue; an aide had found her and she had gone to bed, stricken by the force of the tragic news. After Eunice talked to her younger brother, her one thought was Pat, poor distant vulnerable Pat. She tried to call her sister, but the maid said that she was not talking to anyone.

Pat had been with her maid changing her outfit when Bobby had reached her to tell her that Jack was dead. Eunice had been right to worry. Pat was so alone. Peter was up at Lake Tahoe performing at Harrah's with Jimmy Durante, spending his nights with a variety of chorus girls. He was returning now to Los Angeles. People wanted to be with others now. This was as true of the Kennedys and their acquaintances as it was of everyone else. A multitude of people descended on the Santa Monica beach house: the next-door neighbor, a priest, two nuns, a psychiatrist who sedated Pat, and other friends and celebrities including Judy Garland.

The others cried and told their twice-told tales of Jack, and hung onto one another. In the midst of the gathering sat Pat as silent and emotionless as if her personality had been consumed in the initial flame of agony. Peter arrived along with Ebbins, landing on the beach in a helicopter, and Pat went off to her bedroom.

Ebbins walked into Pat's bedroom and saw her lying there looking like a "zombie." He knew that Pat and Peter's marriage was over, and with Jack's death there was no need to pretend anymore. "Pat," the manager said gently, "Lem Billings is on the phone and he was told to fly out here and get you and bring you back to Washington."

"I'm going back to Washington with my husband," she said definitively, and turned her face away.

In the White House Eunice thought not of her own grief but the grief of others, commiserating with stricken aides, asking about the condition of Governor John Connally, who had been wounded riding next to Jack. She thought about her parents too, especially her father, who lay in bed shielded from the news. The strength of the family had passed to Eunice's generation now. It was not Rose to whom would fall the terrible duty of telling Joe that his son was dead, but to Jack's brothers and sisters. And thus Eunice and Ted took a helicopter to Andrews Air Force Base and flew up by Jetstar transport to Hyannis.

"Oh, Jesus. Oh, Jesus help me," Eunice whispered as the chauffeured car pulled into the driveway as nighttime descended on Hyannis Port. To Eunice had fallen a triple burden, not simply her brother's death and this duty of telling her father, but that of supporting Teddy. He was the man and by all the rules of the family he should have been the strength and the fortitude, but he was full of such an excess of pain and sentiment that he was mute. His virtues and faults were so allied that one could not touch one without grasping the other. As he sat slumped in the backseat of the car both images of her brother were there, the sentimental, emotional Irishman struck dumb in the face of tragedy.

Eunice threw her fur coat over a bannister and spoke to the nurses outside her father's door. She knew far more about the medical aspects of Joe's case than anyone else in the family. As she talked Ted seemed to shrink back into the stairs behind her, his face wet with tears, emitting a half-audible sigh. Eu-

nice gave her brother the stern look of an older sister. He
pulled himself together and followed her into Joe's bedroom.
Joe had no idea that his son and daughter were in the house.
He looked at them with bewildered eyes. Eunice took her fa-
ther's gnarled hand in hers, kissed him, and whispered:
"Daddy, Daddy, there's been an accident. But Jack's okay,
Daddy. Jack was in an accident, Daddy. Oh, Daddy. Jack's
dead. He's dead. But he's in heaven. He's in heaven. Oh, God,
Daddy. Jack's okay, isn't he, Daddy?"

Eunice's faith and her belief in eternal life were a solace beyond solace. Her father, however, was not what his friend Father Cavanaugh considered "in the usual sense of 'religious,' "
and he found no such deep consolation in his faith. The old
man looked at Eunice and then at Ted.

"Dad, Jack was shot," Ted blurted out.

Eunice buried her head in her father's hands. Ted kissed his
forehead, put his hand on Joe's shoulders, and then fell to his
knees, covering his face with his hands, blotting out the world.
"He's dead, Daddy," Eunice said. "He's dead."

Jean had spent less time in the White House than her sisters.
She stood uneasily looking into the Oval Room, holding her
overnight bag that contained her black dress. She had flown
down from New York on the four P.M. shuttle. None of her sisters or brothers were there, and Mr. West, the chief usher at the
White House, gently told her that the first lady would not be
coming directly to the White House, but would be traveling
with the president's body to Bethesda Naval Hospital. Jean decided to go out to the Maryland facility along with Jackie's
parents.

Jean had never been comfortable with all the panoply of
power and the attention it brought. Normally she would have
been appalled to find herself stepping into the waiting limousine, sitting there behind a phalanx of motorcycle police. Like
almost everyone else, the police wanted to retreat into what
they knew, into the comfortable and the familiar. The motorcycle officers sounded their sirens, breaking their way through
the traffic, and the great black car roared up the suburban
streets at ninety miles an hour. Jean was tossed back and forth
in the backseat. The landscape passed by, the streets lined with
grim spectators, a blur of color. Jean hardly noticed when one
motorcycle overturned, throwing an officer into the hushed

masses standing along the route. It was a tiny madness within the great madness of the day.

At the hospital Jean waited, anxiously applying lipstick, standing by herself, withdrawn and isolated. Jackie had arrived, her pink suit caked with blood, her stockings streaked with red. No one could talk her into changing her clothes, and no one tried any longer, as she spoke endlessly about the events in Dallas. The room was full, almost too full, and it was as if Jean existed somewhere else in a room by herself. Bobby was on the phone making arrangements, but Jean had little to do with this terrible business of death except to ask that Jack's favorite suits and ties be brought from the White House.

A few hours ago Dr. Walsh had been examining pregnant Eunice, and now the Kennedys' obstetrician was administering another kind of medicine. He gave Jean a sleeping pill and she staggered off to a bedroom to lie down. Then he prepared a shot for Jackie, a hundred milligrams of Visatril. It was enough to put anyone out, but for all its impact on her he could have been injecting her with saline water.

"I think Miss Shaw should do exactly what she feels she should do," Jackie told her mother, Janet Auchincloss. Mrs. Auchincloss called the White House from Bethesda and told Miss Shaw that she would have the task of telling Caroline that her father was dead. The nurse believed that it was better for children to be told bad news before they went to sleep so they wouldn't be shocked in the morning. And thus the nurse, who had been with Caroline since she was only eleven days old, went to her bedroom and told the little girl that her father was dead. Caroline put her head in the pillow and cried herself to sleep.

Early in the morning at around seven o'clock Caroline and John Jr. came into their father's bedroom, where Janet and Hugh Auchincloss were resting. Caroline walked over to the bed, pushed her stuffed giraffe in front of her, and noticed the front page of the morning papers.

"Who is that?" Caroline asked, pointing at her father.

"Oh, Caroline," Mrs. Auchincloss said, "you know that's your daddy."

"He's dead, isn't he?" she said thoughtfully. "A man shot him, didn't he?"

"Well, Father," Jackie said to Father Cavanaugh when he entered her bedroom in the White House. She was still wearing

the outfit she had worn in Dallas, lying in her bed in her stocking feet. She sat up on the side of the bed, looked at the old
priest, and shook her head back and forth, tousling her hair.

Cavanaugh knew that it was not the time to seek to comfort
Jackie by saying "Wasn't this horrible?" or some other banal
bromide. He had known her since Jack's first years in the Senate, and he reached out to her and took her hands. "Jackie,
what can I do for you?" he asked.

"Father, where do you think our Mass should be?" In the
early morning hours Jackie had accompanied her husband's
body back to the White House, where it rested in state.

"I think it should be at the East end where the body is resting," the priest said.

"I told them that," Jackie said. "I wish you would make the
Mass as fast as you can."

Saturday evening the family and friends gathered in the family
dining room for dinner and told tales both bawdy and irreverent. Someone plucked Ethel's wig off her head, and the false
hair was passed from guest to guest, ending on the pate of the
secretary of defense, Robert McNamara, a man of impenetrable dignity. The Kennedy women shared as much as the Kennedy men in this raucous evening, determined that no tidal
wave of despair would come crashing in, overwhelming them.
Milt Ebbins sat uncharacteristically quiet. Earlier in the evening Peter's manager had stood in the East Room and seen
Bobby enter by himself, throw his arms around the coffin, and
talk quietly to his brother. The image of that moment haunted
Ebbins. He turned to Pat and started to tell her about Bobby
and Jack, but Pat cut into his conversation. "We don't want to
hear about that," she said and turned back to the laughter.

In all this interminable weekend there was but one abuse to
Jack's memory, and that was not this determinedly raucous
evening, but the presence of Aristotle Onassis. He was no
friend of Jack's, and he had been invited by Angier Biddle
Duke, the chief of protocol, doubtless at Jackie's request. The
following evening Bobby harangued the magnate mercilessly
about his wealth, and drew up a supposed document for him to
sign giving away half his fortune to the poor of Latin America.

Jackie rose out of her grief and disbelief to give part of the
direction to the funeral preparations. It was her last gift to her
husband, to memorialize him not in all his flawed humanity,
the Jack Kennedy of the family wakes, but as the saintly young

president, husband, and father, stricken down in the midst of great heroic endeavors. It was a gift not only to her dead husband's memory, but to her children, to Caroline and little John, creating their images of Jack as well. Jackie was an artist of grief, adding exquisitely poignant touches to the mosaic of mourning: an escort of seamen for the horse-drawn carriage bearing the coffin of the Navy man who had been her husband; the bagpipers of the Scottish Black Watch Regiment, whose music Jack had so recently appreciated; the funeral services at the more intimate St. Matthew's, not the gigantic Shrine of the Immaculate Conception; walking by herself behind Jack's body to the church; a mantilla for her head; choosing Jack's words to be read at the funeral.

Rose had flown in with Eunice and Ted on Sunday, and all the Kennedy women were there in the White House now. The public ceremonies were beginning that would test their composure nearly to a breaking point. The women stood in the rotunda of the Capitol when Jack's coffin was carried there to stay while tens of thousands of Americans passed by paying their final respects. The Navy band played "Hail to Chief" as a slow stately dirge, each note lasting a long poignant moment. Jean and Eunice worried that Pat might collapse and instinctively they moved close to her. Pat stood erect, girding herself by thinking, "If Jackie can do it, I can."

It was their brother's funeral, and they were to be spectators at his death as they were spectators to his life. That evening passages were chosen for Bobby and Ted to read at Arlington National Cemetery where Jack would be buried, but no words were selected for his sisters to speak over their brother's grave. In the morning the two brothers walked on either side of Jackie to St. Matthew's Cathedral, and behind them came two other Kennedy men, Sarge and Steve. Then came the leaders of the world twelve abreast, and lost among the foreign delegates were the three Kennedy sisters while Rose followed in a limousine. Rose was on the verge of a physical breakdown and had not walked to the cathedral. But in the dim and crowded cathedral, she stood and waited until the last moment before taking her place in the front pew wearing the dress she had intended for her husband's funeral.

Cardinal Cushing cried out, "May the angels, dear Jack, lead you into Paradise." Eunice thought to herself that "the service was sad instead of hopeful, and Jack was never sad in his life." That was not how others experienced this day. Jack was a man who loved language. Jackie had chosen the Scriptural passages and the words from Jack's inaugural address, and they were words of hope, strength, and majesty. And then it was over and they bore the casket out into the gray day.

"John, you can salute Daddy now and say good-bye to him," Jackie said to her son, as the band played "Hail to the Chief" for the final time. And the little boy raised his hand, and held it to his forehead, looking like a little toy soldier.

At Arlington National Cemetery, Eunice looked at the blanket of flowers that graced the embankment below which Jack's body would lie, and thought that if he were here he would look beyond the people and see the floral beauty. Ted was supposed to give the first reading, but he was as mute this day as he had been in his father's bedroom, and there were no family words said over the grave. Jackie took the taper that was given her, walked forward, and lit the eternal flame. Bobby moved forward too, and touched the taper to the flame. It was Rose's turn now, but she was lost in silent prayer, and Bobby passed the taper to Ted instead.

After the burial the leaders of the world, the American dignitaries, and the family and friends returned to the White House. Jackie could not possibly meet everyone, but she talked to de Gaulle, Haile Selassie, and to Mary Ryan, a distant cousin whom Jack had met on his visit to the old Kennedy homestead in Ireland. "It was Jacqueline who requested that I go," Ryan recalled. Jackie had never met the woman, but she knew how Jack felt, and an aide had called Ryan to invite her. The woman had borrowed a black dress and hurried to Shannon Airport, where a plane stopped, carrying among others the prime minister of Romania. The Irish woman had arrived so late in Washington that she and Martin Luther King Jr. were the last two mourners to be seated.

Jackie took Mary Ryan aside and talked of her husband's visit to Ireland five months before. "It was the one thing in his life that he enjoyed," she said. Jackie wanted to give the woman a gift. The White House was full of possibilities, from picture books to signed photographs, memorabilia and antiques and exquisite artifacts. Jackie wanted none of that. Instead, she gave her Jack's rosary beads and a set of his Navy dog tags and wished her a safe journey back to Ireland.

When they had all left, the great and the powerful, the friends and the distant relatives, the intimate family gathered in the Oval Room for the last time. Jackie was standing talking to Rose when Caroline came rushing into the room.

"Mommy, did they love Daddy?" she asked, looking up at her mother.

"Oh, yes, they loved Daddy."

"No, Mommy," Caroline insisted. "They didn't love Daddy. If they loved Daddy, they'd never done what they did to him."

Jackie said nothing. "Mommy, do they love you?" Caroline asked insistently. "Do they love you?"

"Caroline, I didn't quite give you the right answer to your first question," Jackie replied. "They did love Daddy. Far more of them loved Daddy than love me, although many people love me too. But I know what you are thinking and I don't think we should be so surprised that some people did not love Daddy. After all, not everybody loved Jesus, did they?"

Caroline stood looking up at her mother. Then she smiled suddenly and ran out of the room.

——— 23 ———
Kennedys Don't Cry

*T*wo days after the funeral Sister Joanne Frey arrived early for her weekly religion class and was astounded to find Caroline there waiting for her. "Sister, we were just riding around and we didn't have any place to go," Caroline said, as a Secret Service agent stood nearby. "So we came here."

Sister Joanne tried to contain her surprise. The White House had telephoned and told her that Caroline would not be coming; even without that call Sister Joanne had considered it unthinkable that Caroline would be here. "I have something to show you," Caroline said as she took off her diminutive trench coat, exposing a large medal around her neck.

"Caroline, what is this?"

"Haile Selassie gave it to me," Caroline replied. The nun thought that Caroline mentioned the Emperor of Ethiopia's name as if she were talking about Mickey Mouse or Bugs Bunny.

"Sister, I have to tell you that I did something that you asked me not to do, something I wasn't supposed to do," Caroline continued, suddenly apprehensive. "During the last few days I just needed something to do, and my mother told me that I could open my religion book. So I went ahead and I did several pages."

"That's fine, Caroline," the nun said tenderly. "That's fine."

Soon after the class, Jackie and her diminished family flew up to Hyannis Port for Thanksgiving. Friday morning Jackie contacted Theodore White and told the journalist that she had a message she wanted to convey in the pages of *Life* magazine. That evening White arrived in the rain-swept village. The former first lady took White off into a room alone for a long impassioned talk, the words sputtering out of her in an intense, repetitious monologue.

White's instincts were to write about the late president empathetically yet realistically. Jackie, however, had a different vision of her martyred husband that she wanted to convey. "History!" she exclaimed contemptuously, as if the very word were an epithet. "History . . . it's what those bitter old men write." Her Jack must not be memorialized with such melancholy exposition. She would create the world's memories of Jack, and she would walk with him in memory as she had not always walked with him in life. She would likewise create her children's own images of their father, her gift to them and their lives. She knew Jack's flaws and weaknesses. She knew his other women and his other lives. That was not her Jack anymore. Her Jack was a youthful man who had sailed through life unsullied by the tawdry compromises and truths of adulthood. Her Jack Kennedy had become the great and noble king in a place like the Camelot of the musical Jack had loved so deeply. "I want to say this one thing," she half whispered in her wispy voice. "It's been almost an obsession with me, all I keep thinking of is this line from a musical comedy, it's been an obsession with me." As she talked to White, Jackie was a more persuasive figure than any of the presidents and potentates he had interviewed. He had allowed none of them to dictate his words, but when he called in his story late that dreary Friday night, Jackie entered the room with her penciled edits covering his typewritten words. Millions of readers the next week learned that "once there was a spot, for one brief shining moment that was known as Camelot," and that spot was the White House when Jack and Jackie had lived there.

In late March Rose flew to Paris to attend a ceremony renaming the Quai de Palsy "Avenue du President Kennedy." From morning until night she heard the well-intended condolences. Each heartfelt message was another tiny knife in her heart, and she left the City of Light to go to Normandy to visit Loel and Gloria Guinness, Palm Beach social acquaintances. "Strange for someone to want to be with a stranger right after her son had died," Gloria Guinness reflected. The Guinnesses had turned the pursuit of pleasure into a modest craft, and they were what she needed now, a couple full of wit and graciousness and the rare good sense to know enough not even to mention Jack's name.

The Guinnesses offered to send a car for seventy-three-year-old Rose, but she insisted on making her way to the train station by herself, baggage and all. "How can I find out what time is mass and where?" Rose asked immediately after her arrival. She attended mass every morning, but she did not wear her religion in public view, never alluding to her faith in casual conversation. She was amiable company, and when she learned that Loel Guinness had a serious back problem, she had advice to offer. "Loel, what you should do is get one of those heating pads that sticks to the back," she said enthusiastically. "You know Jack had the same problem, and I sent him a heating pad . . ." Rose's voice trailed off into tears. "I'm terribly sorry," she said, and changed the subject.

The Kennedys were all trying to move on. Just after the assassination, Jackie had vowed to Charles Bartlett: "I will tell you one thing. They will never drag me out like a little old widow like they did Mrs. Wilson when President Wilson died. I will never be used that way."

Jackie attempted to distract herself. In the summer at Hyannis Port, she took sailing lessons from John Linehan, who had taught many of the young Kennedys. "Noon was the only time I could sneak away to give Mrs. Kennedy her private lessons," Linehan recalled. "I used to go with her and Caroline and John. They were just buttons at the time. They would bring their little lunches along with them. I would just sit and look at Mrs. Kennedy and listen to her. The tears would just start trickling down her face. Out there alone away from everyone where no one could see, she would talk a lot and cry a lot. She reminisced about her husband and the boats they had gone on. I felt sorry for her."

Jean was closer to Jackie than any of the other Kennedy sisters. She spent much time with her sister-in-law going over plans for the John F. Kennedy Library in Boston, talking to architects, criticizing scale models. Her husband, Steve, was the central figure in the development of the library, and the Smiths' conversations were often dominated by talk of Jack and the library.

As for Joan, her life too was full of memories of Jack. She saw now that she would have no recess from the exigencies of politics. Ted began his own reelection campaign, and the weight of his brother's legacy rested on the two of them.

For Pat it was simply too much. Her nerves were raw and

open, her resiliency gone, and a darkness descended on her that never fully lifted. Her friends walked gingerly around her life, trying to stay out of her shadow.

There was one other Kennedy who had fallen down this black shaft of despair out of which he could not extract himself, and that was Bobby. He sat for hours lost within his memories. He was a man who needed help, but his family had been trained to look onward and not within. Rose never talked to her son about his despair.

Ethel still loved her husband with girlish adoration, but she did not have the deep philosophical and emotional reservoirs on which Bobby could now draw. One evening at a dinner party at Hickory Hill, Bobby talked to his dinner partner incessantly about his fallen brother while Ethel prattled away at the other end of the table. Bobby raised his head and said mournfully, "There was never anyone quite like Jack. Nobody."

"We don't have to worry," Ethel said breathlessly, inserting her voice into the deep and pensive silence. "We know that Jack is up there in heaven, Bobby, and he's looking down on us and taking care of everything."

Bobby looked at Ethel with disbelieving eyes. "Those words were spoken by the wife of the attorney general of the United States," he said, spitting out the words disdainfully.

To help her through her endless grieving, Jackie invited Dr. Jacobson to Washington. He found her sitting in an upstairs bedroom in her Georgetown house, her countenance as dimly lit as the room, slouched in an upholstered chair "with eyes wide open gazing at the wall." She told the doctor that "life had become empty and meaningless." The doctor tried to minister to her with words of encouragement and solace, a technique he used far less than the chemical philosophy he carried in his black bag. He talked to her for three quarters of an hour, when suddenly Jackie stood up. "I hear Bobby coming up the stairs," she said. "Please leave through this door."

Often in those mournful days, Bobby went over to Jackie's house in Georgetown. He sat before the fire in her drawing room reading the Greek tragedians or Albert Camus, seeking shards of understanding. At Easter Jackie and Bobby flew to Antigua with a few friends. Jackie could give him an intellectual and spiritual solace that Ethel could not, and he developed an intimate emotional relationship with Jackie. Their friendship had begun as that of a loving brother-in-law for his brother's widow, but had developed into something far more intense. "He was terribly devoted to Jacqueline and he took a lot of responsibility of helping her adjusting in her new life, and she was very grateful," Rose recalled. "He was with her a great deal because she was adjusting to her new home and circumstances. But that was public knowledge."

Jackie's relationship with Bobby was a matter of intense speculation among the family intimates. "After Jack's death, Jackie kind of went into hibernation and Bobby was practically over there every day with her," said Red Fay. "I don't know if he became infatuated or not. She's a fascinating woman. If she'd throw her charm at you, why you'd be emotionally swayed. Bobby was a controlling individual, and I think that probably if Bobby felt something, why she was going to go along."

It was indeed public knowledge and had reached the ears of even those journalists who turned their ears away from the more squalid gossip. "I was talking to Bobby one day about Jackie," recalled Murray Kempton, the columnist who wrote about the Kennedys with the same grace that he wrote about everything else. "I was saying something—it wasn't a probing question—and Bobby said in that sad voice of his, 'Oh, she'll never be happy.' You can say that about someone with whom you've slept. But that's one thing I could not imagine Bobby doing—knowing what he felt about his brother—that he would sleep with his widow. To the extent that he was a very Catholic person, I think he would regard it as a cardinal sin. This was like the fire department in New York that for years had a rule that no woman could come inside the firehouse and go beyond the public part except the widows of firemen. They came and cleaned. That was a way to take care of them. They would come in twice a week and clean up, and they were like nuns. They were widows of our great dead. It was a very Irish department and I think that's the way it was with Bobby."

Bobby considered President Johnson a vulgar usurper who had taken his brother's mantle and wore it with gaudy excess. Johnson was a man of the highest deviousness. As much as he sought to place his own indelible mark on this new American age, he knew that he could not risk alienating the Kennedys. Thus he wooed the Kennedy women as much as the Kennedy men. With Jackie he exchanged personal notes of the deepest sentiment, while his aides collected every scrap of negative information about the former first lady. Eunice had a relationship with the new president as well. Eunice had not let even a week pass after her brother's death before she announced her plans to see President Johnson and push him to have the new administration play a major role with mental retardation. She saw in Johnson's Great Society the opportunity to build on the foundation stones set in place during her brother's administration. She was especially well situated, for Johnson had appointed Sarge head of the War on Poverty, the massive series of programs including VISTA, the domestic volunteer program that Eunice had earlier promoted. The other Kennedy loyalists were all leaving the administration, and Sarge's prominent presence was a demarcation point, setting off Eunice and her family from her brother.

Johnson was forever invoking Jack's holy name, but each of his legislative initiatives, each of his successes only deepened Bobby's despair. As for Jackie, the streets of Washington resounded with memories of Jack and her years there, and finally in the middle of 1964 she moved to New York City. That September she walked hand-in-hand with six-year-old Caroline, taking her to her first day at the Convent of the Sacred Heart school on Manhattan's East Side. Pat accompanied her, along with eight-year-old Sydney and five-year-old Victoria, who also were students at the Catholic school. The three little girls were dressed in the regulation gray flannel jackets and pleated skirts, and white blouses, setting out to receive the same education that two generations of Kennedy women had already received.

Caroline's way to school that first day was chronicled by photographers and reporters, but the moment she and her two cousins stepped inside the door of the school at Fifth Avenue and 91st Street, they were treated as much as possible like the other children. For Caroline especially, these elementary school years at the convent were a determined attempt to blend in anonymously with the other girls. Her peers were the daughters of stockbrokers, diplomats, prominent journalists, and others, and they were hardly likely to treat Caroline with deference and awe. On occasion, a reporter stood outside the school, attempting to wrest an intimate anecdote or two from her schoolmates, but they did not have to be instructed to move silently on.

"I don't ever remember Caroline getting special treatment from the nuns," recalled Patti Blair Brown, a classmate. "And why should she? There were so many people from special families who were there. I completely forgot about Caroline's background. I remember once bringing in a film that my brother had done on the assassination of President Lincoln. It wasn't until after I showed the film that I remembered that Caroline was there. I thought, 'God, she sat there and watched the whole thing along with the rest of us and didn't have anything to say about it. If she was going through some kind of anxiety, she had a poker face about it. Imagine, to have to deal with your life and your family and your father being such an incredible part of history."

For the Kennedys there was no greater affirmation than the birth of a new child. In February 1964, forty-two-year-old Eunice gave birth to her fourth child, Mark Kennedy Shriver. Joan, also pregnant, was doubly happy since she had miscarried within the last year. The period of official mourning was over, and Joan and Ted had begun to accept social invitations again, and pregnant or not she resumed her obligations as Ted's wife. In April she flew up to Boston with Jackie and Ted for meetings dealing with the John F. Kennedy Library. On the last day of May, when Joan began to feel not quite right, her husband was off in New England. Ted flew home immediately by private plane, and was in Washington the next day when Joan lost their child.

A miscarriage merited no period of bereavement, and Ted was immediately off again. Joan was expected to be at his side, especially at such events as the Massachusetts Democratic convention in Springfield, even if it had only been two weeks since she left the hospital. She was there in a private house in West Springfield waiting for Ted to arrive from Washington, where he was casting his vote for the historic Civil Rights Bill. Waiting. That was the life of a political woman. Waiting in dreary holding rooms. Waiting at cocktail parties while Ted conversed. Waiting for dinner. Waiting on this damp, dreary, foggy evening. Waiting.

Joan sat watching the eleven o'clock news on the local television station when she heard that the private plane carrying Ted and three others had crashed while landing at the fog-shrouded airport. She was driven to the hospital, lost in her own silent reflections, the only sound the news reports on the radio. As the car drove through the blackness, Joan attempted to steel herself to the fact that Ted might well be dead. At the hospital, Joan ran up the corridor in her suit of shocking pink and found her own way to her husband's bedside. He lay under an oxygen tent, receiving a blood transfusion. "Hi, Joansie," Ted said, calling Joan by her nickname. "Don't worry."

The pilot and one of Ted's aides were dead. He had suffered two cracked ribs, a punctured and partially collapsed lung, and three injured vertebrae. Pat arrived at the hospital, an angel of concern, sitting outside her brother's door. Joan returned to Washington. For Ted months of tortuously difficult rehabilitation lay ahead. For Joan there also lay ahead a difficult regimen, going out on the hustings in her husband's place, campaigning in scores of venues. Whatever apprehensions Ted's aides had about his wife, there was a very different Joan out on the campaign trial.

For Joan there was renewed meaning. "She's the first candidate's wife to take over her husband's campaign from start to finish, substituting for him not only at gatherings of women voters, but everywhere," a reporter noted. She worked with diligence and endless goodwill. Ted's landslide reelection was a tribute to his own hard work in the Senate, his brother's name, and Joan's efforts.

Eunice was running her own campaign, not for political office, but to minimize the number of babies born with mental retardation and to improve the lives of those with the condition. In July after her summer camp at Timberlawn, Eunice flew to Sweden and England to learn about European methods of treating those with mental retardation. In August Eunice traveled to Philadelphia to visit the Kenniston Day Camp for those with retardation. She donned a bathing suit, jumped into the pool, and taught swimming strokes. Eunice believed that the mentally retarded needed the same physical training and exercise as everyone else. It was a lesson she had learned from Rosemary.

Eunice treated herself like a mechanical toy, wound up until the spring nearly exploded, and then played until not a tick of motion remained. At the Philadelphia airport, she collapsed and was flown to Boston to be treated for a kidney condition. She was up within a few days, telling reporters she was "feeling fine."

Bobby had resigned as attorney general and was himself running for the Senate in his newly adopted New York State. His campaign against Republican Senator Kenneth Keating in 1964 was a far more difficult business than Ted's race. Steve Smith headed the campaign, and his tough professionalism was a necessary tonic. In his quest for anonymity, Steve was a perfect match for his wife, called by the press "the member of the Kennedy clan whom nobody knows." By now Steve had taken on all the attributes of a Kennedy man except the name and the certain prospects of elected office. He made little attempt to hide his affairs from the staff. "He was having an affair with this fashionable brunette in her early twenties," recalled one campaign staffer. "Everyone knew. It was that open. It was unbelievable. I can't believe that Jean didn't know. The woman would come around, right into our office. Bobby must have known Steve was playing around."

Bobby's relationship with Jackie had become a matter of intense speculation as well. Staff members saw the candidate and Jackie walking hand-in-hand and whispered about the twosome, hoping that no photographer managed to take their picture. "Jackie would call all the time and ask, 'Is Bobby there?' " recalled one of his secretaries. "The word we got was that she was shell shocked. She would ask if something bothered Bobby. I think they needed each other, both trying to recuperate. Bobby never smiled, and in private he would cry."

Only once did even a hint of their closeness reach the papers. "The former First Lady and the former Attorney General have been seen all over New York, and elsewhere together," the *New York Express* commented, explaining why Jackie had not been active in the campaign. "It was felt the genuine family relationship, cemented by the mutual suffering over the loss of the man they both admired and loved, should not be publicly displayed in the fever of a political campaign. Gossips would be only too eager to distort the relationship and injure the unblemished reputation of Mrs. Kennedy."

At the beginning of the campaign, Bobby had reportedly vetoed not only Jackie's appearance but Pat's and Eunice's as well. Bobby was having enough troubles defending himself against charges of carpetbagging, and it would hardly help to have his sisters jetting in from California and Washington. Even after his two sisters arrived in the midst of the heated campaign, an aide reported in a private memo that "RFK does not want much coverage on Kennedy sisters."

In the end, Bobby decided that he needed the Kennedy women, and once again they joined the campaign. At moments it seemed like the good old times. The *New York World-*

Telegram reported that "Robert F. Kennedy's secret weapon, may turn out to be his three sisters, wife and mother. . . . They have poured tea for, drunk coffee with, made speeches to, shook hands with, signed autographs and been 'at home' to an estimated 50,000 New York women." Pat had purchased a co-op on the East Side in July, and she could easily refute any charges of being solely an outsider. That was not the kind of question she was likely to be asked as she attended elegant teas and receptions. Jean hated campaigning, but she was a good sport, visiting shirt factories, homes for the aged, alumni meetings, as well as the more familiar turf of a party at El Morocco. She was endlessly self-deprecating, publicly acknowledging that she was the least celebrated of the Kennedy women. "I know you were expecting Ethel," she told a group of Bronx Democrats in late September. "But that's the story of my life. They always want Jackie first, then Ethel, then Pat Lawford—but they usually get me."

The aura of royalty spilled over on all the Kennedys and the women did not have to campaign as much as hold court. Ethel invited groups of women to her new home in Glen Cove where the guests cast admiring gazes at the furnishings before watching a campaign film and hearing Ethel's few enthusiastic remarks. The Kennedy women appeared in supporters' homes. It was much the same approach that Jack's sisters had used in his first congressional race, only these were hardly the modest homes of Charlestown, but often estates on Long Island or upstate New York.

Rose was treated as a precious heirloom. On the day that she filmed an interview with CBS, the seventy-four-year-old matriarch spent the morning at Kenneth's having a shampoo, set, and manicure, and then an hour with a makeup artist before the two o'clock filming. The next day she attended two exclusive campaign gatherings, a tea at the residence of Countess Ilinska on East 57th Street, and a second reception at the Dakota, the fashionable apartment building on Central Park West.

Bobby's campaign was an impassioned cry to the downtrodden and the despondent, but that was not how his wife, mother, and sisters campaigned. Only Eunice headed out into the electorate without the protective foliage of teas, films, and canned remarks. She stood alone before some of the most critical audiences making an impassioned plea for Bobby's election in a voice eerily reminiscent of Jack's. She spoke as easily before

college women as part of a series on "Women in Politics" at
Barnard College as she did before an audience of Puerto Ri-
cans at the Fez Ballroom, or a luncheon in the strongly Republican communities of upstate New York. No one who saw her
or heard her would have realized that her life was almost as
shrouded in illness as Jack's had been.

Eunice and her mother, sisters, and sister-in-law may not
have been crucial factors in Bobby's November victory. Nonetheless, as the race tightened the women played a significant,
and by now traditional, role in Kennedy politics. They took
justifiable pride when Bobby was sworn in as the junior senator from New York State. For Eunice there was yet other
good news. She was pregnant again, at an age when most
mothers were contemplating an empty nest. In July of 1965,
forty-four-year-old Eunice gave birth to her fifth baby, Anthony Paul Kennedy Shriver.

Pat had been staying married to Peter to maintain the family
image, but now that Bobby was elected she decided she didn't
have to pretend any longer. To turn her back on everything the
nuns had taught her about married life was unthinkable, but for
Pat the marriage was ten times over. For Peter the news was
devastating. The presidential helicopters were no longer landing on the beach at Santa Monica. Nothing was left any longer,
not his glorious association with Jack, nor the celebrities who
had crowded around the president's brother-in-law, not the
good times with Sinatra, not the young man's roles, nothing
but booze and memories, and Pat and the children. And now
not even Pat.

Peter had a weak man's gift for persuasion and was willing
to use pity or shame to beg Pat for another chance. He called
Hyannis Port to talk to Pat, believing that he could convince
her to continue the marriage, but Bobby came to the phone instead. Pat's younger brother despised the actor. Peter personified everything Bobby hated about the Hollywood world that
he wanted to be rid of forever. Bobby had his father's pitiless
anger, and it was that voice of cold fury that Peter heard now.
Bobby may not have lived the life of moral purity that his fol-
lowers assumed he did, but he was a religious man, and if his
love came out of the New Testament, his anger came out of
the Old; it was harsh judgment he meted out to his brother-in-
law.

"You mean I'm never to see her again?" Peter asked, not
even daring to attempt to refute Bobby's litany of charges.

"I'm never to call or come there? And she's never coming back?"

Peter set down the phone and turned to his two friends with tears in his eyes. "When that family tells you you're not going to do something, you're not going to do it."

"Why?"

"Because you'll suffer sooner or later. You learn that very quickly. If they say don't do it you don't do it."

In December, Pat and Peter met in New York City to sign a separation agreement that was the legal manifestation of Bobby's voice on the phone. Pat was an heiress, her wealth protected by a retinue of lawyers and advisors. The idea that Peter would pay her alimony was not only laughable but unthinkable. Pat had no intention of ever living in Los Angeles again, and she was divorcing not only Peter but her California life. She received custody of the children, with visitation rights for Peter that he was unlikely to employ except during summer vacations or during Christmas. The only property they held together was the great beach house with all its ghosts and memories. That was to be sold now in part to pay the fifty-two thousand dollars that Peter owned his wife.

Pat signed the ten-page document in her neat Sacred Heart script, and Peter wrote his name in a flourish, underlining his signature. Steve Smith served as a witness for Pat, and Royal Marcher for Peter, and then it was over.

Soon after Peter returned to Los Angeles, he called his old friend, Dick Livingston. "I think I did the best joke I've ever done in my life," Peter laughed.

"What?" Livingston asked.

"Well, you know how frugal Pat is. I had fifty bottles of water delivered to her apartment in New York, and I wrote a note: 'Dear Pat, you forgot to drain the pool.' "

Peter still had residues of his sense of humor left, but his jokes frequently turned mean. "He would come over to my house a lot," Livingston recalled. "But it wasn't the same Peter because he would get drunk and nasty. One day he said to me, 'Dick, I've got to stop drinking.' He'd have a Bloody Mary to wake up, before lunch a Dubonnet and gin, and then wine with lunch, and then cocktail hour, drinks before dinner, wine with dinner, and then cordials after dinner. Peter said, 'I'm drinking a quart a day.'

"So he knew he had a problem, and he started smoking a little pot, and only wine. And it was just so difficult seeing Peter who was so terribly dignified sitting there smoking pot and using the jargon that I hated. His whole attitude seemed changed, and his sense of values changed, and I don't know about his ambitions but he wasn't working very much. Milt Ebbins told me, 'Dick, if Peter hadn't gone like he did, he'd be making more money and having more work now than he ever had in his life.' But Peter just sat there drinking and smoking pot."

That evening after Peter signed his separation papers, Marcher happened to be in P. J. Clarke's, the famous New York saloon, when he spied one of its habitués, Steve Smith, across the room. He had met Pat's brother-in-law for the first time that afternoon in the lawyer's office. Marcher called over a waiter and asked him to send a drink over, but Steve refused the offer and turned his back.

Steve was hardly such an exemplary husband that he could rightfully shun Peter's friend. "I can't believe that Jean didn't know what was going on," recalled a woman who was then working for the Kennedys. "Bobby must have known too that Steve was playing around. Steve was dating this very pretty woman with short blonde hair and a great figure. I used to go out with them in a group sometimes on a double date to clubs or restaurants. Steve would order champagne and always pick up the tab. He was boisterous. He didn't try to hide his affairs. It was incredible. One night Steve rented a yacht on the East River. We sailed up the river to Westchester, and the next morning we went down the river. I remember my date had these Gucci loafers. He and Steve were joking around. Steve picked them up and threw them into the river. That was Steve."

Jean had put up with her husband's sexual antics for many years as if they were part of the obligatory penance of a Kennedy woman. She was portrayed in the press less than her sisters and sisters-in-law; in the few articles about her, Jean was inevitably depicted as the loyal loving wife and commendable mother of two sons, the very model of wifedom.

Jean was imprisoned in this image, unable to move out into a different world. She was not deeply interested in politics or business. She did not have the social concerns of Eunice. She was not willing to subjugate her life totally to her husband's career the way Ethel had, especially not to a husband who had his own separate life. She was a woman with an exquisite sense of irony and wit, qualities of limited value in a political woman. She had always been considered the cute, pert Kennedy, but now at the age of thirty-seven, the five-foot-seven-and-a-half-inch-tall Jean was a handsome, stylish woman, with a quick repartee that was as threatening to men as it was to women.

Jean was a woman of immense pride, quick to anger, and only she knew the psychological costs of maintaining an image of marital perfection. Whatever Steve gave her it was not enough, and she began a dangerously close relationship with Alan Jay Lerner, the famous lyricist.

Friends, Lerner's assistant, and others believed that Jean was having an affair, but Jean insists adamantly and passionately that it was nothing more than a friendship. In any event, it was a dangerous friendship for a married woman. As a man, Steve could stride into Bobby's headquarters with his mistress on his arm, but Jean had to be far more furtive in her involvement. That was difficult with Lerner. He was not simply the most celebrated musical lyricist of his times, but he was a dashing public figure, an extravagant man to whom a Rolls-Royce was the vehicle of choice, a man whose charm and wit were not simply something to be lavished in his lyrics. More than any other subject, his lyrics were about the romance between men and women, songs with gentle irony, whimsical sentiments, deep emotion. Lerner was as adept at creating romance off the stage as on. A man of refined good looks, Lerner's ever-present cigarette seemed less a habit than a prop. He was also one of Dr. Jacobson's most devoted patients, a man who thought it was his natural condition to live at a fever pitch of intensity.

When Jean met him, Lerner was going through his fourth divorce, and Jean was totally taken with him. "It seems Frances [Jean] has never been in love until now," he told Doris Shapiro, his assistant, who called Jean "Frances Douglas" in her memoir. "Even during the divorce proceedings the intimate bond that had developed from his Kennedy connection turned into a romance," Shapiro wrote.

"In public you would never think she could be so simple about love," Lerner told his assistant. "So open." It was an extraordinary statement to make about Jean. She was the most deeply suspicious of all the Kennedys, eternally vigilant about those who would misuse her or her family. If she trusted Lerner, it was a small miracle. "Everything she does conveys a meaning," Lerner said. "No empty gestures. Even her funny Freudian slips. We were walking down Madison Avenue one day, and we passed the American Primitive Museum, she said to me, 'I just read that as the American Punitive Museum.' "

Jean had not left her skepticism at the door to this romance. Doris Shapiro remembered the time that Lerner took Jean to Dr. Jacobson's famous emporium of chemical dreams. She sat "regally" on a stool as Jacobson spun his fantasy of the entire United States Army hopped up on his magical shots. As Jacobson talked on, Shapiro "could see her smile turn to a slight, mocking sneer." That was Jean's most notable look, a stare of such disdain and dismissal and coldness that it could stop a conversation in mid-sentence.

Unlike the Kennedys, Lerner believed that money was to be spent when you had it, and even when you did not have it. He loved beautiful things—cars, houses, boats, women—and he introduced Jean to a whole new level of luxury. He was not a man who worried about the costs of things, be they romances or houses. He had a barber to shave him, a tailor to design his clothes, a clerk to hold his paper, a clerk at Battaglia to watch fawningly as he picked up sweaters eight or ten at a time, a boy to deliver his toiletries from the drugstore.

Jean and Lerner flew off for two days in Venice. It rained on them in that grand romantic city, and they walked through St. Mark's under an umbrella. When they returned, the lyricist brought with him a secret as extravagant as the man himself. In August of 1965, his new show, *On a Clear Day You Can See Forever*, would have its tryout in Boston. Lerner whispered to Jean that he would charter a yacht to sit out on the Charles River as a secret rendezvous for his meetings with her.

There were few scenes in Lerner's musicals as romantic as that image of Lerner ferried out into the great white yacht where Jean would sit waiting for him, the skyline of Boston rising up behind them. It was irresistible in its attractions and its dangers. Lerner was contemplating his summer of work and romance when he received a call frightening in its implications.

"Who was it?" Shapiro recalled asking.

"I think it was Robert Kennedy. He said he was calling to warn me. He said, 'Listen, buster, we've got a file on you. You're to stop seeing Mrs. Douglas [Jean]. Or we'll fix your gondola.' "

"What are you going to do?"

"Marry her," Lerner said anxiously. "After all, this isn't *Anna Karenina*."

Lerner might momentarily pretend that he would marry Jean, but that was hardly his style. The lyricist lived in a world of make-believe where the blood was never real, and he could not envision the idea of sacrificing himself for her. Jean was used to being endlessly solicitous to men. That summer of 1965 she sat in a darkened theater in New York as Lerner went through a run-through of his play. In Boston she was beside him too, as he worked on every moment of the show, attempting to create a compelling musical narrative that would pull the audiences and the critics into reverie. The yacht lay at rest in the Charles River, but Lerner was spending most of his time at the Ritz-Carlton working on the musical. It was there that Dr. Jacobson arrived with his magical satchel to keep Lerner and his chosen friends vitally awake and stimulated.

A pre-Broadway tryout is not unlike a political campaign in its self-absorption, merciless schedule, and recriminations when it does not seem to be going right. Jean was used to winning campaigns, and Lerner did not want her around to see what he considered a deeply flawed play. She was there, however, at the Mark Hellinger Theater on West 51st Street for the opening, along with Pat. Later that evening at the opening-night party at Luchow's, Jean sat next to the lyricist at the head table.

One of the less prominently displayed guests at the party was Karen Gundersen, a statuesque, dark-haired journalist who during the tryouts had come to interview him. Lerner had a penchant for younger women. He began an affair with the vivacious reporter who found him "a very romantic figure" and was taken aback by his habit of midnight phone calls. By the following summer this newest affair had reached a point at which Gundersen was living with the lyricist in his home on Center Island outside New York City on weekends, while Jean continued to see him during the week.

Jean had been brought up to believe that the highest of goals was not to bring shame or embarrassment on her family. She had seen how her mother had lived, putting up with her father's affairs, sacrificing everything for the family. She loved her children, and wanted them to bear the family name with righteous pride. She wanted her own life too, and during the summer of 1966, she got a plane to Paris, leaving Steve, and expecting Lerner to meet her. It was a gesture of such daring, sacrificing reputation and position in the name of love, flying off into the unknown. It was unlike anything her mother, her grandmother, or her sisters would have even considered.

The lyricist was a man of grand romantic gestures, never one for the mundane nitty-gritty of life, commitments, obligations. He had enjoyed his sentimental interlude with Jean, but he was not ready to become the corespondent in a divorce, or assume the burdens of a Kennedy in-law.

When Lerner failed to arrive in Paris, Jean flew back to New York City. Lerner was adept at avoiding creditors, be they of money or romance, and he was not ready to rush to the airport to be confronted by an irate Jean. Instead, he sent his chauffeur. "What Jean got was a note from him, and that was an ending," recalled an intimate observer of the event.

Jean returned to her husband and a married life that would never be the same. Despite those difficulties, in the next years Jean and Steve adopted two daughters, Amanda Mary, born in April of 1967, and Kym Maria, born in November of 1972. It was a matter of great sensitivity to Jean that her two youngest daughters were constantly referred to as "adopted." Kym's Vietnamese parentage was obvious, but Jean integrated the two girls into her family with love and devotion, attempting to make them a seamless part of the Kennedy family.

Steve continued to have his outside relationships, including one fifteen-year friendship with Jan Cushing Amory, a stunning New York socialite. "I think Steve loved the kids and he loved Jean and he was seeing other people and so was she," said Amory. "I think he felt a sense of responsibility to the family and to the Kennedys. What was on the side was on the side. When I saw him from time to time, he made it very clear that he would never leave Jean. Jean even had me for dinner. I was the devil you knew. I think Jean knew I would never break up the family and he saw several other women as well. I think he wanted true companionship, someone he could truly talk to, and I always wondered how much either one talked to the other. What they had in common was the love for their children."

At the age of seventy-four, the Kennedy matriarch was still looking out for the family image in myriad ways. In May of 1965, Rose wrote her children reminding them that she had taught them "the importance of who and whom" and giving them an example from the Queen of England's recent address.

In September she wrote Bobby about a more serious matter. "I thought you should see this," she wrote her oldest surviving son, "but I did not want to upset Jackie too much and did not send it to her." She enclosed an interview with Oleg Cassini about Jackie from a French newspaper. The headline exclaimed: "LE CRI D'ALARM DE SON MEILLEUR AMI" ("Her Best Friend Cries an Alarm"). "Jackie is imprisoned by the Kennedy clan," Cassini was quoted as saying. "She knows that for now she is the only celebrity in the family, and everything the Kennedys are doing with her is to further the political designs of her brother-in-law, Bobby."

Jackie knew that Bobby was using her, but that was the nature of politics. Bobby asked her to petition the president to have the Space Center at Cape Canaveral renamed Cape Kennedy. Jackie only reluctantly agreed. "I'm so embarrassed," she told Bartlett. "Bobby keeps making me put on my widow weeds, and I go down and ask Lyndon for something else." She had begun to take off her suits of mourning, making social appearances at society balls and exclusive dinner parties. Wherever Jackie went with the other Kennedys, the attention of journalists and the public was simply overwhelming. Even such a matter as arriving at the Hyannis Port airport for the summer brought a crowd of three hundred to stand gawking on the edge of the tarmac. When she and her two children went to Aspen for the Christmas holidays in 1964 along with Steve and Jean, Bobby and four of his children, and Pat and Peter, it was not simply the tabloids but respectable publications such as *Time* that reported on every aspect of the trip, including that Jackie had a "Bloody Mary and a cheeseburger" for lunch at the Aspen Alps Club.

Jackie, Jean, and the other Kennedy women learned to tolerate the perpetual onslaught of the journalists and the merely curious. Thirteen-year-old Kathleen was the oldest of the young Kennedys. She and her siblings and cousins, used to a world where there were spectators to their most innocent games and play, let only a few special friends into a sanctuary of trust.

On April 1, 1966, one of Johnson's top political aides, Liz Carpenter, wrote a confidential memo to the president about Bobby Kennedy. The new senator from New York had left his barb in Johnson, pushing it deeper and deeper by musing mysteriously how he could achieve peace in Vietnam. In so doing, he had won many in the youthful armies of protest to his side. Carpenter's suggestions included having the administration "start working to soften up the Kennedy columnist set . . . subvert them from 'buying' everything Bobby does" and that "we can include some of the jet set, even though they are personally obnoxious, at the next glamorous White House evening." When Johnson saw the memo at nine-thirty that evening, he wrote: "Tear this up and flush it down the toilet."

Johnson and the Kennedys were involved in a game of subtle deviousness in which words such as Carpenter's were to be whispered and never committed to print. The women in the family were primary players in this game. If in part they matched Johnson disingenuous gesture for disingenuous gesture, there were elements of honest sentiment in their exchanges. It was as if women among themselves might sometimes transcend the manly games of politics. Sarge was a crucial member of President Johnson's cabinet, and Eunice's message of concern for those with mental retardation found a listener in the Oval Office; the president named Eunice to the President's Commission on Mental Retardation that she had instigated during Jack's presidency. Jackie knew very well Bobby's feelings about the president, but she maintained her own relationship with the Johnsons. Only a week after Carpenter's memo, Jackie wrote a four-page handwritten letter to Mrs. Johnson about the upcoming Fine Arts Committee meeting concerning the restoration for the White House. Jackie had an almost painful aesthetic sensitivity, and it rankled when even one detail was misplaced or misguided. "I was just wondering if Mrs. Roosevelt's portrait outside the East Room didn't bring the 20th Century in so much that it really jars the unity of that whole floor," she wrote, in one of many suggestions.

The president sent letters to Caroline and John Jr. on their birthdays. "How incredibly thoughtful of you," Jackie replied in another handwritten letter. The Johnsons sent flowers to Joe when he was hospitalized in November, and Rose replied to Mrs. Johnson in her own apparently genuinely felt letter: "I am sure he was deeply moved as was I by your thought of him." President Johnson grew livid at the mention of Bobby's name, but Johnson sent flowers to Bobby's children when they were sick, and Ethel had her children write ingratiating replies, worthy social training. Fourteen-year-old Kathleen penned her own cloying note to Mr. and Mrs. Johnson thanking them for writing her a letter.

* * *

Within the Kennedy family, the women had become the great protectors of the eternal flame of emotion and sentiment that kept Jack's memory vividly alive. They watched carefully over the books being written about Jack.

Schlesinger began work almost immediately after the president's death, preparing what the Pulitzer prize–winning historian intended as one of the seminal histories of the Kennedy White House. Schlesinger had been Jackie's closest ally among her husband's aides. In what was an unusual gesture for a work of objective history, Schlesinger sent the manuscript of *A Thousand Days* to Jackie for her comments, criticisms, and corrections. Schlesinger feared that Jackie might find it too painful to read the pages, but she considered that part of her obligation to Jack's memory.

Jackie edited the manuscript not for herself but for Jack. She let stand statements about her own life that almost anyone else would have neatly expunged ("Jacqueline often feared that she was a political liability and that everyone considered her a snob from Newport who had bouffant hair and French clothes and hated politics.") For the most part, Jackie edited out the intimate, personal details of her married life. "But the world has no right to his private life with me," she wrote the historian, in an impassioned plea. "I shared all these rooms with him—not with the Book of the Month Club readers—and I don't want them snooping through those rooms now—even the bath tub—with the children—Please take all these parts out."

She didn't want emotional intimacies displayed in Schlesinger's pages even if the author's words honestly reflected what they had been. In his manuscript Schlesinger wrote that when Jackie had told her husband, "Oh, Jack, I'm so sorry for you that I'm such a dud," he had replied "that he loved her as she was." Jackie crossed out the latter passage, writing "too corny" in the margin.

Schlesinger was hardly the only author writing a book. Like his two younger brothers, Jack had that rarest of attributes in a politician: a gift for friendship. Inevitably, these friends began writing books about the deceased president. Red Fay was the first, turning out a modest, engaging, and deeply human memoir of his long friendship with Jack. Bobby and Jackie had both known that Red was writing the book. Bobby had sent Red to Evan Thomas, an editor at Harper & Row, with the stipulation that the Kennedys be allowed to read the manuscript before publication. When Bobby and Jackie read the pages in the spring of 1966, they were appalled by the casual anecdotal nature of the book, considering it a betrayal. Bobby went through the typewritten pages, purging the text of anything that might prove politically damaging, Jackie was more concerned with what she considered vulgarities. In one anecdote, Red had Jack bemoaning a pulled muscle. "I don't want to read anything in the papers about my groin," the president was quoted as saying. "We can attribute it all to the back." Jackie found the word "groin" offensive, and agreed to allow the anecdote to remain if Fay changed the word "groin" to "leg."

The widow who had continued to wear her blood-splotched dress so the world could see what had been done to her husband was still full of unrelieved fury at those who would denigrate her husband. "Leave it," she wrote of one passage. "Don't you see it makes Red look awful. . . . Let these pathetic men criticize him. I think it makes them look like the awful people they are."

Jackie's anger at Red was only a tiny overture to her wrath a few months later over the publication of William Manchester's account of the assassination, *The Death of a President*. By hiring the young author, the Kennedys had hoped to prevent other books from mercilessly exploiting the subject. Manchester had received the kind of cooperation with family and friends that no outside author had ever obtained. Eunice was instrumental in helping the author gain access to President Johnson; the matter was of such sensitivity to the new president that not only were Manchester's questions written out in advance, but his aides prepared the suggested responses.

In the end, Manchester's sin was to have listened too long and too well and to have written a compelling novelesque account of those November days. Bobby and his aides were concerned about Manchester's truthful account of Bobby's tortured relationship with Lyndon Johnson immediately after the assassination. Jackie, for her part, was distraught over matters of emotional intimacy. She had trusted Manchester and had told him the most painful details of the assassination when, in her words, "the floodgates were open," and he had dutifully portrayed all that in the most private detail.

The floodgates were shut down now, and Jackie could not tolerate the idea of this gush of emotionality hawked in magazines and books across the world. Jackie and her minions insisted Manchester excise such matters as the details of her placing her wedding band on Jack's body in the casket, Caroline's letter to her dead father, and Jackie's tearful outbursts.

Jackie sued Manchester. Suddenly, she found herself portrayed in the press not as the noble widow of the martyred president, but as a willful and arrogant woman attempting to control her dead husband in death as she could not control him in life. In the end, Manchester and the Kennedys compromised, and the book was published, but the bitter taste remained. "It is not difficult to understand Jacqueline Kennedy's desires," wrote James Reston of *The New York Times*. "No President's family has ever approved its biographers. She can do nothing now about the death of the President. What she is faced with is the death of Camelot, the killing of the myth. It is intolerable but also inevitable. . . ."

That was all true, but what Jackie had attempted to do was not ignoble. In this instance, she had sought to control not history, but only the intimate details of her family's life. Her chosen memories were the jewels of her life with Jack, and she felt that they were being taken from her one by one. To Jackie, as to the other Kennedy women, their lives had become a part of other people's commerce, peddled on the newsstands, the magazine racks, and in the bookstores, lives that they sometimes could hardly recognize.

Rose's life had changed less than the other women's in the family, though she too had a new celebrity. "Do you know what has happened to me?" she asked Gloria Guinness. "I've been elected as one of the ten best-dressed women in the world." To Gloria her friend sounded "like the child that had gotten the biggest doll."

As the mother of the martyred president, Rose was called upon time and again to lend her presence to various events in Jack's honor. Rose traveled to several European cities to open the Kennedy Library's traveling exhibit of Jack's life. She spoke French in Paris, where in three days fifty thousand Parisians viewed Jack's desk and doodles and other memorabilia. In Bonn she amazed the audience by speaking in an apparently fluent German. Jean and Joan made their own separate appearances in others of the fifteen countries where the exhibit was shown to large, awestruck crowds, from Dublin to Warsaw, Rome to Belgrade.

Rose's public life was not simply a matter of memorializing

Jack. Eunice had involved her mother in her latest "Flame of Hope" project: the selling of candles and later also perfume to aid those with retardation. Rose was in her mid-seventies. She stood there before crowds of spectators in department stores across America. She often appeared on television or granted interviews to local papers. The journalists all wanted the intimate details of life among the Kennedys, and she was brilliantly adept at throwing out an innocuous anecdote and then turning the conversation back to the Flame of Hope. When she had given what she intended to give, she left and flew back to Hyannis Port or Palm Beach.

When Rose returned to the house, she always went to Joe's room to see her husband. Joe's mind was still lucid, and each member of the family attempted to find ways to connect emotionally to the Kennedy patriarch. Rose was full of upbeat tales of her latest travels, the words cascading out. Ted sometimes got down on his hands and knees, mugging for his father, playing the buffoon to bring a smile to Joe's lips. For Christmas in 1967, ten-year-old Caroline wrote a poem for her grandfather about a tiny blue mouse and sparrow who had everything in life except "someone as nice as Grandpa who they missed more every day." For his birthday the grandchildren sang songs they had written especially for the occasion, often with darkly satirical lyrics.

> Oh you'd better watch out
> You'd better take care
> We're just like honey to a certain old bear
> Gram papa is coming to town.
>
> He sees you when you're sleeping
> He knows if you're awake
> He knows if Ted's campaigning
> For his own, or, for Jack's sake.
>
> He knows if Sarge is the Cape
> Or with Wally at the Mart
> Or if Pat's in Vegas gambling
> Or finding Frankie's heart.

Visitors came to see the old man as well. Wyatt Dickerson, a family friend, was asked to bring Jean, Pat, and Odile Rodin Rubirosa, the beautiful widow of the late diplomat and playboy, to Hyannis Port from Boston. Dickerson had been warned not to stop for a meal at the Locke-Ober Café, the celebrated Boston restaurant, for Steve was there with his mistress. Instead, he drove directly to the Cape. Joe had known Mrs. Rubirosa before she married her husband. She wore a widow's black, the dress exquisitely sculptured on her voluptuous figure, her legs in black silk. As Mrs. Rubirosa entered Joe's room, he rose up in a great paroxysm of emotion, reached out toward the widow, his voice a deep groan of yearning and agony, and fell back into the wheelchair.

For the family it was painful beyond pain to watch this man of such strength struggling with his condition. Several times he had been given the last rites, but he always recovered. Rose would take him to one of the balls in Palm Beach, his wheelchair resting on the edge of the waltzing couples, or out to dinner, or would simply watch television with him in the evening.

"You were always tense in those years because you never knew when he was going to have a stroke," said John Ryan, who watched over Joe every day. "He was always known as Grandpa. The kids always came up and kissed him on the forehead. He would make his feelings known by a yes or no movement of the left hand or a smile or frown. When you were talking, you had to look him in the eye. He had the strongest eyes. A lot of those times she would just go for walks. I think Mr. Kennedy's condition was probably one of the biggest trials of her life. And you can't just sit back and die. I think that is something that has inspired Mrs. Kennedy all of her life. You have to keep going forward."

By the end of 1967 over half a million American soldiers had been sent to Vietnam, hundreds of them dying each week in the steamy jungles of Southeast Asia. The ghettos of the great American cities were festering with unrest, and on many university campuses the American flag had become a symbol of derision and shame. Johnson had become largely incarcerated in the White House, his sojourns outside the gates met by the unruly brigades of protest. Senator Eugene McCarthy of Minnesota had entered the presidential primaries to take on the seated president.

For months Bobby sat on the sidelines, his attacks on Lyndon Johnson limited to the fire of his rhetoric. The cold-eyed professionals around Bobby—Ted Sorensen, Pierre Salinger, Fred Dutton—argued against Bobby's entering the race. Ted, the best politician in the family, argued against it as well.

Ethel listened to Sorensen tick off reasons against Bobby's entering the race. "Why, Ted!" she exclaimed. "And after all those high-flown phrases you wrote for President Kennedy!" Ethel wanted her Bobby to run. Her Bobby was a savior to the disenfranchised and the impoverished. Her Bobby could quell the fire in the ghettos and the firefights in Vietnam. Ethel was not invited into the councils of war, but she stood at the edge of the room shouting her message. Jean was not invited either but this most nonpolitical and wary of the Kennedy women repeated Ethel's refrain, calling for her brother to challenge Lyndon Johnson.

Ethel and Jean were nagging goads, calling up everything noble and idealistic in the Kennedy heritage. Pat was not so vocal, but she too passionately prodded her brother to enter the race. "This is going to cost you a lot of money," Bobby told Pat and Jean over dinner, and they were as ready to open their pocketbooks as their mouths. Jackie was not quiet either, sending her former brother-in-law a searing essay by William Graham Sumner attacking the pretensions of nations that worked their will on others in the name of civilization. Only Eunice said nothing. Her husband was a crucial part of the administration, and the voice that would have been the most persuasive and persistent of all was stilled.

Never before had the Kennedy women so single-mindedly pursued a political issue. They spoke as mothers opposing a war fought largely by the sons of the poor. When Bobby stood up in the Senate caucus room in March of 1968 and announced his candidacy, he did not mention his wife, his sisters, and sister-in-law, though he might profitably have recalled their anguished, heartfelt entreaties. Instead, he ordered reams of Kennedyesque prose laced with portentous, overweening, apocalyptic phrases ("At stake is not simply the leadership of our party or even our country—it is our right to moral leadership on this planet").

Rose heard her son's impassioned address and she watched with dismay and foreboding. She called Gloria Guinness and told her friend, "If Joe were himself today, he wouldn't have allowed it. It is too soon and it is the wrong moment." Guinness recalled that Rose "was very unhappy about it. She was terrified. And everybody was terribly sentimental about it and everybody wanted Camelot to go on."

As much as she had wanted Bobby to run, Jackie had that same terrible presentiment of disaster as Rose.

"Do you know what I think will happen to Bobby?" she asked Schlesinger a few days after the announcement in the Senate caucus room. "The same thing that happened to Jack. . . . There is so much hatred in this country, and more people hate Bobby than hated Jack. . . . I've told Bobby this, but he isn't fatalistic, like me."

Bobby Kennedy headed out on the campaign trail, stopping only for a respite at Hickory Hill or Hyannis Port. On his first trip to the Cape, much of the family was there. In the evening, Jackie walked over from her house to toast her brother-in-law. As the world saw it, and as she had lived these last four and a half years, she was as much a Kennedy as any of them, the enthusiastic booster of Bobby's campaign, a guiding force behind the new library in Jack's honor. Bobby was bubbling over with positive reports, from the newest polls to the enthusiastic crowds in city after city.

"Looks like we're going to make it," Bobby said.

No matter what Bobby said on the speaker's platform, Jackie knew how rare it was for him to speak in private with such unalloyed optimism. And she matched him, enthusiasm for enthusiasm. "Won't it be wonderful when we get back in the White House?" she fairly gushed.

"What do you mean 'we'?" Ethel replied, her words like a pinprick to a balloon.

Ethel often spoke with a raw bluntness that her admirers called a sense of humor, but was full of curt meanness. Jackie was used to being treated with courtly civility, and she flinched at this rude stab. But Ethel was right. Jackie might revel in the collegial atmosphere of the Kennedys, the air rich with memories of Jack. Nonetheless, Ethel would be the first lady, and that would only underscore Jackie's distance from the days of Camelot.

Jackie got up to leave. On another occasion Bobby might have walked her back to her house, but he stood there and watched her go. He had been entranced by her, but that was over now, and the world beckoned him. The next day Jackie spent many hours walking the familiar haunts of Hyannis Port, from the horse barns where Jack had stood with Caroline, to the beach on Squaw Island where they had their home one summer. She appeared to be retracing her life with Jack, imbedding those times and scenes so deeply in her memory that even if she never saw them again they would be there. Not until the evening did she return to go to Joe's room. "I've had a lot of thinking to do today," she told the old man. "You'll always know I love you, won't you, Grandpa?"

As enthusiastic as Ethel had been about Bobby's announcement, she dreaded the prospect of constant campaigning. For all her extroverted exuberance, Ethel was painfully insecure about talking in public or granting interviews. She never seemed to say just what she meant to say, or what she was supposed to say, and she sometimes made statements embarrassing to Bobby. As much as possible, she limited her speeches to a few words praising her husband, before sitting down as quickly as she had stood up. She was pregnant with her eleventh child, and nobody seemed to mind that she said so little.

Ethel's family, the Skakels, lived with wealth, health, vitality, and fertility almost without measure, and then many of them died in inexplicable tragic accidents. Ethel's parents had died in a plane crash in October of 1955, and her brother, George Jr., in another plane crash in 1966. In February of 1967 George Jr's. eldest daughter, seventeen-year-old Kathleen, drove over a bump, sending a child in the backseat hurling out the window to his death. A few months later George Jr's. widow, Patricia, was having dinner with her family when she choked to death on a piece of meat.

Ethel pushed the dark tragedies to the inner recesses of her mind. After nearly eighteen years of marriage, Ethel still loved Bobby with the unabashed adoration of a newlywed. All she wanted was to be with Bobby every day on the campaign trail, but often that wasn't possible and sometimes she was led onto the tarmac to board small planes whose short hops were an eternity to her.

The mere sight of a plane terrified Ethel. Richard "Dick" Tuck, an aide and celebrated wit and prankster, realized that something had to be done to divert her. On the main campaign plane, he got the stewardess to agree not to make an announcement heralding the plane's taking off and landing. Instead, they simply passed drinks around, and at a signal the passengers sat on the floor or quickly took a seat. The family dog, Freckles, went along as well, primarily to make Ethel feel more relaxed.

The press celebrated forty-year-old Ethel as a chic, youthful "super woman," adeptly juggling the tasks of a mother, wife, hostess, and friend with aplomb and grace. "I believe in discipline and when I say 'don't do something,' the kids know I mean it," she told *The New York Times*. There was at least one man who had a different view of life at Hickory Hill. He was Jack Kopson, a seventy-one-year-old maintenance man who had the misfortune of living in a small house across from the back of the estate. Kopson claimed that thirteen-year-old David Kennedy and several of his brothers had destroyed his tranquillity by late at night attacking his house with firecrackers. Kopson had retaliated by firing a shotgun blast at the retreating youths. "I think Mrs. Kennedy ought to come on home and watch her children instead of traipsing all over Indiana," Kopson said. "She ought to be here looking after her children instead of wearing those hippie clothes. There is only a colored maid over there to watch these children and apparently she does not know what is going on. No one is controlling those kids."

A few weeks after Kopson's complaint, David and a friend went to a nearby highway and began pelting automobiles with rocks, eventually smashing the windshield of one vehicle. The police apprehended the youths. Their parents came to take charge of the other youths, but only a governess arrived to retrieve David.

Ethel campaigned almost exclusively alongside Bobby or among members of her own sex. She returned from campaigning in Indiana in time for a massive reception at Hickory Hill for the wives of men attending the convention of the American Society of Newspaper Editors. The journalists covering the campaign were almost all men, but several of their wives were Kennedy hostesses, including Mrs. Roger Mudd and Mrs. Sander Vanocur, whose husbands were network political correspondents, and Mrs. Ann Buchwald, whose husband was a humor columnist. There was, indeed, an enormous social cachet associated with being around Ethel, ideally as one of her ladies-in-waiting or at least visiting Hickory Hill even for an afternoon. "Most of the wives didn't really want to go," wrote the columnist James J. Kilpatrick, "which is why a thousand of them lined up 35 minutes early, dressed to the teeth and fighting to get on the first bus."

Eunice and Joan were among the hostesses as well. Eunice had just flown back from campaigning in Indiana. That was an extraordinary act of devotion to her brother. Sarge had just been named the ambassador to France by President Johnson.

Earlier in the day he had appeared before the Senate Foreign Relations Committee, and had been asked pointed questions about his loyalty to the administration. Johnson had dramatically withdrawn from the presidential race, but he still occupied the White House, and the war raged on in Vietnam. Sarge had vowed his fealty to Johnson, pledging to defend policies that his brother-in-law considered abominable.

For Eunice, when it came to her brother what was political was personal. She believed she was campaigning not against anyone but for her brother. Eunice's campaigning was a daring affront to the unity of the administration, but that did not come close to what Bobby's aides considered the action of choice: for Sarge to resign and lend his support to Bobby. "I felt a little torn about going to Europe versus staying with my brother running for president," Eunice said, "but the idea of representing the United States was so exciting, and I thought there was so much Sarge could do as ambassador."

For all Rose's doubts, her loyalties were to her son and her family. As she headed out on the campaign trail, no one who heard her imagined the dark doubts that filled her mind. The other Kennedy women headed out too, but the traditional women's politics of tea parties and endless politesse no longer seemed to work as well. In his speeches Bobby was confronting questions of race, class, and inequality with a rhetoric that had not been widely heard in America since the Great Depression. Ethel had been in Indiana the day Martin Luther King Jr. was assassinated in Memphis, where Bobby had spoken so passionately, so deeply of violence and its consequences, to him, to his family, and to them, to this crowd of grieving blacks in Indianapolis. These were not days to serve tea and little sandwiches. Bobby used his sisters as best he could, introducing them at every campaign stop, joking about who received the most applause. ("Jean did better in Salt Lake, but Pat seems to be getting over better here.")

Of all the Kennedy women, Rose was by far the most effective campaigner. Her sweet anecdotes of Bobby's childhood were antidotes to charges that he was a ruthless politician. At the age of seventy-seven, Rose could still run sprightly through the mine fields of politics, rarely making a mistake. Her only error of the campaign came when she told *Women's Wear Daily*: "It's our own money, and we're free to spend it any way we please. It's part of this campaign business. If you have money—you spend it to win." That was one of those impalpable unspeakable truths. If Bobby had spoken so candidly, the words would have been hung round his neck by McCarthy like a badge of shame. Not even the proudly sardonic Minnesota senator was about to criticize the sainted mother of the martyred president, and Rose continued her campaign journey talking about her son and family.

The campaign in the crucial Oregon primary was run by Rep. Edith Green, one of the few women in positions of power in the Kennedy campaign. "Oregonians couldn't care less about sisters and in-laws," Green recalled. "I think Rose Kennedy was probably a plus, but the others were not. There were lots of adverse comments about the teas that the sisters had. . . . There was an awful lot of feeling among the people that . . . that was taking time and money, and effort away from what really ought to be done. . . . I do not know of any other campaign that's ever been held by anybody where the family, you know, moved in by the dozens and had teas, and you know, receptions, etc., etc., etc. . . . Oregonians wanted to talk to the candidate—not his sisters and cousins."

Oregonians were serious about politics and the Kennedy women had become unwieldy appendages to the campaign. Rose could get away with her sentimental recollections of Bobby and life in the London embassy. Her daughters and daughters-in-law were expected to talk about issues, and they were terrified to talk about substantive, controversial matters. No one had pushed more eloquently, more passionately for Bobby to enter the race than Jean and Pat, but they considered themselves little more than members of a family claque, trained to root for their brothers. They found it humiliating sometimes to go door to door talking to people who didn't know or didn't care or were voting for McCarthy. Joan attempted to do her part, trying with unswerving devotion to follow the intricate pattern of Kennedy life. She not only visited lumberyards and canneries but took down hundreds of names and addresses and composed handwritten thank-you notes.

Bobby lost to McCarthy in Oregon, the first Kennedy defeat of his generation, and he headed south to California for what had become the most crucial primary of all. The alarm had gone out, not to Rose and the other Kennedy women, but to the men around Kennedy. Steve Smith and John Seigenthaler reorganized the campaign for the final days while such intellectuals and writers as Adam Yarmolinksy, Daniel Moynihan,

George Plimpton, Arthur Schlesinger, and Roger Hilsman campaigned on the campuses, the great bastion of McCarthy support. Bobby campaigned to frenzied crowds, the white, brown, and yellow faces a polyglot vision of Bobby's America. He yelled his message until he could hardly shout out his perorations any longer.

Diane Broughton had volunteered to work in the campaign, but on the final day she found herself at the Beverly Hills Hotel watching over six of Ethel's children. That wasn't quite what the recent college graduate thought she would be doing when she first offered her services. But she was delighted at the prospect of meeting some famous Kennedy women.

"Aunt Jean is in a bungalow," four-year-old Christopher said. "You want to meet her?"

Diane had clippings of all the Kennedys, and she wasn't about to miss an opportunity to see an adult Kennedy woman in the flesh. Jean greeted her with a dismissive stare that could have frozen the Queen of England in her tracks, and marched the group over to the children's bungalow. "Why are these clothes here in a pile?" Jean asked, looking at a mound of soiled laundry.

"That's all for the washing machine," Diane replied brightly.

"And what about *those*?" Jean said. "Why aren't they in the pile?"

"I was going to wash them by hand."

"Well, then do it," Jean said, throwing the dirty pantyhose in her face and stomping out of the bungalow.

That morning eleven-year-old Courtney returned from swimming in the hotel's famous pool shrieking in pain, crying for her mother. Ethel and Bobby were staying at the Malibu beach house of director John Frankenheimer and the children had seen their pictures on television. Diane put through a call to the Malibu house, and Ethel called back agreeing to allow her children to spend the day with their parents. Soon after Courtney put down the phone, Jean came rushing into the room. It was her job to oversee Ethel's and Bobby's children, and she was infuriated at this attempt to run around her authority. "Jean literally pushed me against the wall as she passed," Broughton recalled. "Perhaps I've led a sheltered life, but never before or since has anyone else ever deliberately pushed me against a wall. I felt like a character in an overacted B movie."

* * *

It was a gray forlorn day. The fabled coast of Malibu looked washed out and dismal, but the Kennedy children intended to enjoy the beach. Bobby was still bone tired, but he romped on the foggy beach with his offspring, and pulled David out of an undertow before catching a nap by the pool.

In the evening John Frankenheimer drove Bobby and Ethel to campaign headquarters at the Ambassador Hotel in downtown Los Angeles in his Rolls-Royce Silver Cloud. The other two Kennedy sisters-in-law, Joan and Jackie, abhorred these campaign scenes of groups milling around hotel suites, but Ethel plunged into the room, throwing her greetings and cheery asides right and left. The candidate suite was full of an eclectic group of supporters and journalist friends, people who not only fed off the energy around Bobby but added to it. Kennedys were always together for the important moments in each other's lives, and Jean and Pat were here this evening, as well as Steve, who was downstairs warming up the audience for Bobby. The three older Kennedy children were still in school on the East Coast, but David, Michael, Courtney, and Kerry all were at the hotel for the early part of the evening, before joining their younger siblings, Chris and Max, back at the bungalow at the Beverly Hills Hotel.

Ethel did not like to be alone, and she felt safe in the gathering. These were their friends. Just days before in San Francisco's Chinatown, she had been standing with Bobby in an open convertible when she had heard a loud report; she had instinctively crunched down in the car, pulling her body around her in the fetal position. Bang. Bang. Bang. Bang. The sounds rang out, and still Bobby stood looking down at his wife curled up. It was only a string of firecrackers. Everyone laughed and the motorcade moved on.

Ethel dreaded that she would make another mistake. When she had arrived in Los Angeles, she had bubbled enthusiastically to the reporters that she was delighted to be in "Anaheim." "For Christ's sake, Ethel," Bobby had admonished her, "if you're going to get the name of the town wrong, at least say it in a whisper."

The early returns strongly suggested that Bobby was going to win. Ethel decided to rest for a few minutes in a bedroom that had been set aside for her. As she opened the door, she saw Bobby and Budd Schulberg, the novelist, sitting on the bed in discussion. That was typical of Bobby, sitting hunched

over, his ear bent listening intently to someone's earnest entreaties. "Can't even get in my own bedroom," Ethel said in
mock horror, delighted that the returns were growing stronger
and stronger by the minute.

Ethel lay down finally and tried to collect her energy for the
pandemonium that was bound to await them in the Embassy
Ballroom downstairs. "Ready?" asked Bobby.

"Ready!" Ethel replied.

Bobby entered the ballroom surrounded by advisors, union
officials, politicians, all vying for honored places behind the
successful candidate on the podium. Ethel had the most honored place just behind her husband, and she stood there as she
had in so many rooms, listening to Bobby. She listened
proudly to Bobby as if she were hearing him for the first time.
He began, as always, with a joke or two, a few words of passionate encouragement, and finished with a challenge to move
on to the next contest. "And now on to Chicago, and let's win
there."

Before Bobby plunged back into the crowd he turned to Bill
Barry, his one security person, and told him, "Take care of
Ethel." Normally Barry would have been in front of Bobby,
like the bow of a ship, breaking his way through the massed
humanity, his eyes scanning the faces, but Ethel was pregnant
and Bobby wanted nobody jostling her or knocking her down.
He knew what the crowds could be like. Since his brother's
death, his presence had stirred an almost uncontrolled frenzy.
He had played to the sheer emotionalism, standing on the hood
of a convertible as it pushed through crowds from Indianapolis
to Los Angeles, reaching down and touching. He had turned
down all suggestions for increased security that would wall
him away from the crowds. When that emotionalism was not
there, his aides tried to create its illusion by such measures as
building breakaway fences that would collapse at the touch,
sending hundreds of supporters spilling around him. There was
no need for exhortation or calculation this evening. These were
Kennedy people, exulting over the triumph, believing that the
road to Chicago was an open one and that in August Bobby
would be nominated to be the next president.

Ethel was safe within this cocoon of Kennedy men. As long
as she kept pace, she would not be jostled or pushed, and
Bobby would be just ahead. She knew nothing of the logistics
of this evening. She followed along as she was led out of the
gesticulating crowds chanting, "We want Bobby," into a corri-

dor, her sight of the dirty walls blocked by her dark-suited protectors. Pop. Pop. Pop. Up ahead. A firecracker. A car backfir-
ing. Anything but the sound of death. Pop. Pop. Pop.
Seventeen-year-old Irwin Neal Stroll fell on Ethel trying to
protect her when he was struck by a bullet in his left leg. "Oh,
my God, no!" Ethel screamed. "Get his gun!" It was all chaos
and screaming and bodies. "Get his gun." Whatever fear Ethel
felt was nothing compared to her maternal instinct to succor
Bobby, to shield him from any harm. Then she saw Bobby. His
injured head lay in a pool of blood. He had bullet holes in his
head, neck, and below his right armpit. His hand held a rosary
placed there by a busboy. "Oh, my God," she murmured almost soundlessly as she knelt beside him, touching his face,
pressing ice cubes on his cheek.

Back at the bungalow at the Beverly Hills Hotel, all the children had gone to sleep except David, who sat up with
Broughton watching television. He was the fourth eldest child,
and he had not yet been sent off to school like his three older
siblings. He was privileged to stay up, and sat there staring at
the screen as the journalists spoke of the shooting of his father.
Broughton put a blanket around his shoulders and tried to comfort him.

Ethel would let nothing, no one hurt Bobby anymore. When
the ambulance attendant and driver pushed their wheeled
stretcher up to her husband's stricken form, Ethel said, "Keep
your hands off him. I'm Mrs. Kennedy," and tried to push the
attendant away. The two men lifted Bobby onto the stretcher.
In the elevator carrying Bobby down to the waiting ambulance,
Ethel told the man: "Please lower your voice." Jean forced her
way onto the cramped elevator, but as the attendants pushed
the stretcher rapidly forward toward the ambulance, Jean was
left behind.

"Just for the record, please, what happened?" the ambulance
attendant asked, making his obligatory inquiry. Ethel would
have no more of this intrusive man. To her this ambulance
driver had become the surrogate for all Bobby's assailants and
foes. As the driver lifted Bobby's stretcher into the back of the
ambulance, she yelled at him: "I don't give a damn what you
say," and then, according to his recollection, threw the ambulance record book out of the back of the vehicle. Then during
the two-minute ride to Central Receiving Hospital, she struck
the man on the face. At the entrance to the emergency room
stood a lone photographer. To Ethel he appeared a merciless

predator, and she cried out, pushed her shoulder down, and blocked the man, sending him skittering backwards.

"Please help him! Please help him!" Ethel implored Dr. Victor F. Bazilauskas, the emergency-room doctor. "Please don't hurt him, please don't hurt him," she said, repeating the words over and over, like her rosary. The doctor knew that the kind of crisis medicine that he performed sometimes appeared like brutal indifference to the patient's pain. He explained to Ethel that he would have to massage Bobby's heart. Finally, after an injection of Adrenalin, the heart began beating again. "His heart is going now and now we do have some hope," the doctor said.

"I don't believe you," Ethel said softly. "He's not moving. He's dead. I know he's dead."

Ethel went with Bobby in the ambulance when they took him to Good Samaritan Hospital for brain surgery. She was with him as they prepared him for the operation, first performing a tracheotomy. She was with him as they wheeled him into the operating room. Then she waited, pacing the corridor. Pat and Jean were there now too, and they succored their sister-in-law as best they could and got her to lie down. After three hours and forty minutes, the operation was over, but the brain was a shattered remnant. There was, however, a life force within Bobby of terrifying resilience, and the heart beat on.

The family worried about Rose. Rose awakened a little after dawn and turned on the television set. When she heard the news she knew that she must go to morning mass, as she always did. She dressed in a black shawl and coat, and was driven to mass. She hurried into church, past the flash of cameras, past the brutal intrusions of the shouting journalists ("Do you feel as badly as when the president was assassinated?"). She sat in the front of the church, a look of deep serenity on her face. Then she returned to the house and went into Joe's room and told her husband, and they cried and cried, tears from a boundless ocean of pain.

And still the heart beat on. At Putney, when Kathleen learned of the shooting, she packed up her books and left to join her eldest brothers, Joe II and Bobby Jr., to fly to Los Angeles. In Paris, Eunice kept her scheduled appointment with Madame de Gaulle and then went to the airport to fly with Sarge and their house guest, Joan, to the United States. The Shrivers and Joan did not cry, their emotions encased during the interminable plane flight. Joan sat there thinking about

"Ted more than anyone else, and his family burdens." In her New York apartment, Jackie was awakened by a phone call from her sister, Princess Lee Radziwill. "No, it can't have happened. No! It can't have happened." As soon as it could be arranged, she boarded a private plane at Kennedy International Airport and flew to Los Angeles.

And still the heart beat on. In the hospital they had all gathered. Ethel, Jean, Pat, Jackie, and Ted, in the board of directors room. Ted stood in the bathroom, the door half open, doubled up in agony, his pain as palpable as if he had been brutally punched in the stomach. A medicine cart filled with liquor was wheeled in, and they drank and drank and drank some more, never managing to get drunk. Only Jackie did not imbibe. "The Church is . . . at its best only at the time of death," Jackie told Frank Mankiewicz, the press spokesman. "The rest of the time it's often rather silly little men running around in their little suits. . . . We know death. . . . As a matter of fact, if it weren't for the children, we'd welcome it."

By six-thirty P.M. the machine that monitored Bobby's brain waves no longer showed any activity, and still the heart beat on. The Kennedys had achieved a terrible adroitness at the business of mourning. As they ate and drank they planned the funeral, from services at St. Patrick's Cathedral, then a train from New York City to Washington, and burial in Arlington National Cemetery, near Jack. At one-thirty A.M., the heartbeats began to slow. Ethel was in the room now, and she held onto Bobby's hand, the other members of the family standing back, giving her this last moment of intimacy. The only sound in the intensive-care room was the beeps on the cardioscope. And then the beeping stopped.

Ethel walked up and down the aisle of the government plane that carried Bobby's body back to New York, talking and occasionally joking to family members and friends. That was the stalwart image of a Kennedy woman that sixteen-year-old Kathleen saw on the long flight: her mother, Jackie, Jean, and Pat, all of them acting with resolute strength. Her mother sat there next to the mahogany coffin, finally falling asleep.

The Kennedy women mourned, but it was the men who assumed the public duties, the men who grabbed the torch. As the plane landed at La Guardia Airport, Ted appeared at the front door along with Joe II and Robert Jr. The fourteen- and fifteen-year-old youths were young for the duty of helping to lift the coffin, and one of them almost fell off the platform. Even here there was bitter anger among Bobby's aides. When the casket was lifted out of the plane, they pushed Sarge away, Sarge who had gone to Paris as ambassador, Sarge who had not been there.

At St. Patrick's Cathedral, the men stood over the casket in shifts, including two of Bobby's sons. The Kennedy women sat in the pews in mourning. At the funeral services, Ted stood before the vast assemblage and spoke in words of matchless eloquence of his dead brother. "My brother need not be idealized, or enlarged in death beyond what he was in life [but] remembered simply as a good and decent man who saw wrong and tried to right it, saw suffering and tried to heal it, saw war and tried to stop it. . . . As he said many times in many parts of this nation, to those he touched and who sought to touch him: 'Some men see things as they are and say, why. I dream of things that never were and say, why not.' "

Even here this contagion of violence and death, a plague on the Kennedys, did not fully leave them. One guest arrived with an unloaded pistol in his briefcase, while at the side door to the cathedral another man was stopped trying to carry several bullets into the Gothic structure. As hundreds of thousands stood along the tracks between New York City and Washington to pay their final respects as the train carrying Bobby's body passed by, two of the mourners were killed, hit by a passing train.

Ethel walked through the twenty-one cars greeting the thousand mourners. So did Joe II, assuming the mantle of authority that would have been Kathleen's if she had been a boy. Rose sat in her suit of black with a look of almost eerie serenity on her countenance. Among the mourners was Andrew, Duke of Devonshire. After her son's death left Kathleen a widow, the duke's mother had become friendly with Rose. Now almost a quarter of a century later, she had said to her son that he must go to the funeral and that he must stand in the background. And so he had. On that train ride south, he decided he should pay his respects personally to Rose. "I came away from this with the sense that her religious faith was so profound that even the death of her third son did not touch it, that the things of this world didn't matter in comparison to the next world," Andrew recalled. "If ever I saw an example of faith, that was it. We didn't dwell on the death, on the immediate. We talked more about my family than hers."

At Arlington National Cemetery on a dark spring night, they buried Bobby, buried him without the salute of cannons, without a phalanx of soldiers. John Glenn, a former astronaut, handed the folded flag to Ted, and Ted handed it to Joe II, and Joe II handed it to Ethel. Then the pallbearers, led by Bobby Jr., carried the casket to the place where Bobby would lie, sixty feet southeast of his brother's grave. And then the other Kennedys came forward, first Ethel, and behind her Kathleen, Rose, Pat, Jean, and Eunice; each knelt and kissed the mahogany casket.

As the family left Arlington that moonlit night, Bobby entered the sacred pantheon, alongside Joe Jr. and Jack. Ethel carried from the grave memories of laughter and dreams and of promises beyond promises and hope beyond hope. Like Jack, her Bobby would be eternally young, unsullied by compromise and the blemishes of experience, her Bobby, against whom no mortal man would ever measure up. Bobby's sisters all mourned him deeply, but for Eunice no one would ever replace Jack, no pain as great, no memory as deep. Pat and Jean were younger, and they knew Bobby as a good brother and good friend whom no one could ever supplant, and they mourned him deeply, rarely able even to speak of his death.

Of the young generation of Kennedys, no one knew her father better, loved him more, admired him so boundlessly as did sixteen-year-old Kathleen. She had gone to the casket with the other women of the family, not with the children. She kept her love and memories of her father in a secret region of her heart, to draw on not in pain and despair, but in hope and aspiration.

24

"And Deliver Us from Evil"

*E*thel's mood swept from deep private despair to manic ir-ritability to frenetic highs of ceaseless activity. Joe II was Bobby's eldest son, and as Ethel saw it, he and his younger brothers were Bobby's true heirs. Joe II was a mediocre student at Milton Academy. He had neither his father's quick intelligence, wit, nor seeming compassion, but he was the eldest male. Ethel told him that he was to occupy his father's seat at the head of the table. He did so with the willful authority of a sixteen-year-old deemed an adult well before his time. When he slapped Kerry for making too much noise, Ethel ordered her eldest son to walk up and down the stairs a hundred times.

The three eldest sons—Joe II, Bobby, and David—bore the brunt of their mother's capricious temperament, the daughters largely spectators to the drama. During that summer of 1968, the girls were sent off to mass, offering prayers for their father's soul. It was understood by almost everyone that the boys needed father figures, while the girls would take care of themselves. Ted was now the head of the family, and he assumed that role with Joe II, spending time with the young man. Lem Billings became a surrogate father for fourteen-year-old Bobby Jr. He took the youth to Africa that summer on a photographic expedition, a great adventure memorialized in the boy's journal. Joe II traveled on his own Hemingway-like quest in Spain. He was slightly gored fighting a small bull. He and his friend roared around the Andalusian countryside on motorcycles. Thirteen-year-old David and his thirteen-year-old cousin Chris Lawford flew to Austria to a tennis and ski camp, where David had his first sexual experience with a girl who sought the honor of sleeping with a Kennedy.

Before her father died, Kathleen had promised to work in

the summer on an Indian reservation in Arizona. She and a close friend from Putney flew to the Southwest. The volunteers were for the most part the privileged sons and daughters of the American elite, students at Princeton University, and members of the radical Students for a Democratic Society.

Kathleen taught English to Indian children in the mornings, and in the afternoon worked planting pistachio trees and building a science center out of adobe bricks. In the evenings the students sat around planning how *they* would foster a "Red Power" movement. Soon the summer was over and the students returned to their dormitories, and there was no one left to water the trees and teach English, no one left to plan the Indians' revolution.

If there was something silly and dangerous about privileged youths planning a revolution for someone else, Kathleen had a heartfelt need to find for herself a socially useful life of intellectual and physical adventure. That summer of 1968, she honored her father's memory in a far deeper way than did her brothers.

At the end of the summer the family gathered back in Hyannis Port. They were joined by an endless parade of friends, almost all of them men, including famous athletes Roosevelt Grier, Rafer Johnson, and John Glenn, worthy role models for Ethel's sons. When the boys were not around their celebrated guests, they were trying to top each other with stories of their adventures in Europe and Africa. The boys went out on the grass where their father and uncles had waged their legendary football games. They played too, blocking each other with brutal abandon, seeking to drive their opponents into the earth. When Joe II's knee went out and he lay thrashing in agony, his younger brother Bobby stood over him. "Oh, has our sister hurt his knee?" he said, spitting out the word as if it were a foul epithet. These were masculine games of passage to the manly Kennedy world that was their endowment.

The family had expected to go to Chicago in the summer of 1968 to watch Bobby nominated as Democratic candidate for the president of the United States. Instead, only Eunice flew into the torpid midwestern city seven weeks after Bobby's death, not to attend the convention, but to oversee the first "Special Olympics" games for over a thousand participants with mental retardation from twenty-six states and Canada on July 20, 1968.

Earlier in the year, Anne Burke, a physical education teacher in the Chicago park system, had come to the Kennedy Foundation with the idea for summer games for those with retardation. At the foundation Eunice had been listening to the ideas of Dr. Frank Hayden, a Canadian expert who envisioned an expanded athletic role and competitions for the developmentally disabled. With her typical large vision, Eunice had suggested making the games national, and had the foundation put up the funding to do just that. For several months, a small, dedicated staff had worked putting the Special Olympics together to take place at Soldier Field, the great Chicago stadium on the edge of Lake Michigan. There workers constructed a swimming pool in the end zone of the football field. Since these Special Olympians were not generally allowed in public pools and other athletic facilities and often did not know how to swim, the ninety-foot-long pool was less than four feet deep.

For the opening ceremonies, Eunice stood in a nearly empty stadium, wearing a green short-sleeved dress on her bony frame. No more than a thousand spectators dotted the massive brown stands, a seeming rebuke to the grand scale of her vision. She didn't look up at the empty stands, but out on a field filled with boys and girls from all over America, and coaches that included Olympic-medal-winning athletes Rafer Johnson, Jesse Owens, and Bob Mathias, football legends Paul Hornung and Howard Cassidy, members of the Notre Dame football team, and the Chicago Bulls basketball team. "In Ancient Rome the gladiators went into the arena, with these words on their lips," Eunice began, her voice nervous and intense, her left hand jabbing the air like a conductor, so reminiscent of Jack. " 'Let me win but if I cannot win let me be brave in the attempt.' Today all of you athletes are in the arena. Many of you will win but even more important I know you will be brave and bring credit to your parents and your country. Let us begin the Olympics."

Most of these boys and girls had never competed in anything before. None of them had ever participated in an event of such magnitude, with gold, silver, and bronze medals for the winners, and ribbons for all the participants. The three-hundred-yard run was the longest event, and some contestants could not run that far without stopping, but they were cheered onward to the finish, and the last was applauded as much as the first. Eunice didn't sit up with the V.I.P.'s but walked down on the field. At her own home at Timberlawn, she had seen what these young people could do, how they could swim and jump and run, so much more than almost anyone realized, and she cheered the athletes on, lost in the excitement of the moment. At the end of the day she stood saluting the Special Olympians as they marched around the field a final time.

The event didn't get the attention Eunice had hoped it might receive. *Life* magazine had semiofficial status as chronicler of the lives of the photogenic Kennedys, but the editors were not ready to run pictures that they thought might upset their audience. On the day itself there had been all kinds of glitches. It could be better. With the establishment of Special Olympics Inc. as part of the Kennedy Foundation there would be a next time, and Eunice was convinced that it would most assuredly be better and bigger.

Ethel carried Bobby's eleventh child in her womb, a gift of preciousness beyond measure. Although almost six months pregnant, she was tearing around the tennis court in Hyannis Port playing doubles with Jim Whittaker, the Everest climber, against Art Buchwald and singer Andy Williams. For Ethel there was no such thing as a social game, and losing a crucial point, she fell to her knees and hammered the court with her head.

In October, Ethel almost lost the baby. From then on, she spent her days in a great bed in her upstairs bedroom at Hickory Hill. "The baby means so much to her," Ted said to Luella when he asked her to come down. The nurse flew down on the next plane from Massachusetts to spend the remaining days of Ethel's pregnancy in the house. The seven youngest children still at home ran into Ethel's bedroom bringing buttercups or daisies, a story or two from school, a gentle hug or a kiss. Ethel did not even leave bed when Ted came out to the house to give a press conference announcing the formation of the Robert F. Kennedy Memorial Foundation. She didn't leave until December 11, when she arrived at Georgetown University to deliver the next morning by cesarian section an eight-pound four-ounce girl named Rory Elizabeth Katherine Kennedy.

In the eyes of the American people, Ethel was a tragic widow, supplanting even Jackie in the public mind. A Gallup poll named her the most admired woman in America, and Rose the second most admired. Ethel approached her widowhood far differently from Jackie. The former first lady had understood that the public sought to turn her into a national symbol of mourning, held aloft the way Mexican peasants carried their plaster saints through the streets on feast days. She had moved to New York with her two children, taken up with old social friends, and not allowed herself to be eternally garbed in widow's black.

Ethel intended to spend the rest of her life honoring her husband's memory. "Why can't we stay right here at Hickory Hill?" Kathleen had asked, and Ethel had agreed, though the estate was a mausoleum of memory, every inch full of her life with Bobby. Ethel had the wealth, the energy, the strength of ego to create her own universe around her. Her martyred husband had been a man of relentless optimism. She and her family would mourn him by banishing mourning. It would be their laughter, not their tears, that would reach to heaven to remind Bobby of how much they cared. When friends came out to the Virginia house for dinner, they no longer sat around the dinner table for intense, eclectic conversations as they had when Bobby was alive. That might lead to morbid speculations, and Ethel had never been comfortable with mere talk. Instead, Ethel led the group in games, if not charades then a quiz based on news events, or some other contest. "OK, everybody, let's have a race," she said after one dinner, and led the guests outside for a sprint on the lawn.

Ethel had no life other than Bobby, few friends who had not been both their friends. They came out to Hickory Hill, as they had before, and they learned not to cry but to laugh, and laugh loudly. "If she's downbeat, she never lets on," said Buchwald, the resident clown. Wherever she went, there was not hushed silence but often forced laughter. She was imprisoned in a cell of solicitousness. She had always been demanding of the women who traveled with her and ran her errands, swept up into the energy and excitement of Hickory Hill. Ethel continued to call but the road from Hickory Hill no longer led to the White House, and the shrewder, more socially ambitious of the women became busy elsewhere. Even many of the women who cared deeply for Ethel learned that you were Ethel's friend, but she was not always yours, and slowly one by one they too began to leave her. She was notorious for her treatment of maids and cooks and gardeners and such, and they rarely stayed, but they were replaceable, and these women and men became interchangeable parts of life at Hickory Hill. The main exception to this was the Costa Rican–born Ena Bernard, who watched over the children like a second mother and was there for the children when Ethel was not.

When Ethel was planning a memorial mass for Bobby, a group of women went out to Hickory Hill to help. Ethel scrutinized every detail of the coming event, objecting to the colors on the program, criticizing almost every detail. The women had been there for almost six hours. All Ethel had offered was a soft drink, and none of the women had dared to ask for anything to eat. "That's fine to sing 'The Battle Hymn of the Republic,' " Ethel said, "but in the program we will call it 'Glory Glory Hallelujah.' I simply won't have a battle hymn for Bobby."

With that Ethel jumped up and ran upstairs. "Isn't she coming back or at least saying thank you or good-bye?" one woman asked. "No, I think that's it," another woman said.

There was at times a graceless quality to Ethel that she imparted to her children as Kennedy inheritance. She hired a young tennis pro to teach her children. He not only taught her children but Ted's youngest son, Patrick, and Jean's youngest, Willie. One day he had the group out on the court, hitting scores of balls to the boys. "Now what we're going to do now is to pick up the balls, boys," the tennis pro said, "and whoever picks up the most gets to hit with me for an extra half hour. How about that?"

"We Kennedys pay people like you to pick up balls for us," Patrick said sullenly.

Once, the pro was working alone with David, playing a game with the youth. The coach had the obligatory deviousness of a good tennis pro, letting his client appear a worthy competitor, keeping the score close. There are few venues better for the quick judgment of human character than a tennis court, and the pro realized that David was cheating on the line calls. A ball might be in the court a good six inches, but David called it out.

The pro motioned Ethel over and asked her to watch. Ethel was a good player and she could scarcely miss what her son was doing. "Did you notice anything special, Mrs. Kennedy?" he asked.

"No," Ethel said.

"Well, David is taking all these calls when they go the other way."

"I pay you to teach them strokes, not morals," Ethel said, and turned on her heels.

* * *

One afternoon in October of 1968, Rose received a phone call from Jean. Her youngest daughter was still very close to Jackie, and she had some extraordinary news to tell her mother: Jackie would be calling to tell Rose that she was marrying Aristotle Onassis. As Rose put the phone down, she was totally nonplussed. "I was really rather stunned," she wrote in her diary. "I knew he had been here but she has had different guests since Jack passed away and so I didn't take him too seriously." It seemed impossible. She had known that Jackie was dating again, including Lord Harlech, one of Jack's old friends. The Greek magnate had visited the Cape once or twice, and she remembered this short stocky man sitting in a flaking, faded wicker chair on the porch. He seemed a totally inexplicable choice for the widow of her martyred son.

Jean told her that the marriage would take place in two days. Rose had been pushed aside from any of the family's crucial decisions. Although she had no idea, her whole family had known about the impending marriage for months. In August Ted had traveled to Onassis's home on the Greek island of Skorpios to negotiate the prenuptial agreement. The other members of the family had spent hours discussing the marriage, all away from Rose's hearing. Rose's dear friend and confessor, Cardinal Cushing, had known. Even some of the neighbors had known. "She romanced him right on the street in front of my house," recalled Larry Newman, whose Hyannis Port house gave him a front-row seat to activities at the Kennedys'. "They used to have a champagne lunch here and then they would go dancing up the hill in front of my house and then would go whistling down the street to their house. And I just kept asking myself, 'How in God's name could she love that guy?' "

Rose had no time to face that enigma. "Later Jackie called," Rose noted in her diary. "By that time I was quite composed." There are few cruelties like those that come coated with a balm of kindness. By trying to shield their mother from unpleasantness, her children had jolted her with this inexplicable, startling news. Jackie was not expected to immolate herself on her husband's funeral pyre, but she was still Jack's widow. Rose might have given Jackie some cautionary counseling, or in the end might have congratulated her for marrying one of the world's wealthiest men. There was no time for anything but to accept, and to pretend that everything was being done as it should have been done.

When her chauffeur asked her about the wedding, Rose told him: "I've known about it for some time. Ari asked my permission."

"Of all the people, she was the one who encouraged me, who said 'He's a good man' and 'Don't worry, dear,' " Jackie recalled. "She's been so extraordinarily generous. . . . Here I was married to her son and I have these children and she was the one who was saying, 'marry Ari.' "

Rose might support her daughter-in-law, but millions of Americans considered that Jackie had befouled the image of Camelot. She was not marrying a man of noble bearing and stature, after all, but a rudely spoken Greek billionaire, who was carrying her off to his island like a spoil of war. "THE RE-ACTION HERE IS ANGER, SHOCK AND DISMAY," headlined *The New York Times*.

For Jackie, though, the violence of America had become a plague that stalked those who bore the Kennedy name. Onassis offered her untold wealth, and a security beyond anything her Secret Service detail could possibly give her. As a wedding bauble he gave her a $1.25 million set of heart-shaped rubies framed by diamonds, and on his island of Skorpios brought in trained attack dogs to tear apart anyone who attempted to violate Jackie's privacy.

Sixty-two-year-old Onassis was a man who collected people, and thirty-nine-year-old Jackie was a trophy of incomparable value. She was as beautiful as a star, as regal as a queen. Though she joked that she brought no dowry, she did, in fact, bring a dowry of priceless value. One man who knew that aspect of the marriage was John W. Meyer, who described himself as Onassis's "aide de camp." Meyer was a talker, and when he stayed in his apartment in Palm Beach, Florida, he often talked to Rita Whitely, a socialite who had the virtues of being beautiful and circumspect, never passing on the telephone conversations she overheard, or his whispered confidences. "Johnny loved to talk and I loved to listen," recalled Whitely. "Johnny told me, 'You know, Rita, Onassis knows that Jackie is an icon and he feels that if he marries her, the U.S. government will get off his back.' The government was after Onassis, and he felt that not only would he be left alone, but he wanted to build this super port in New Hampshire, and he figured he could get that, too."

When Onassis had begun seriously wooing Jackie, Bobby had still been alive. Bobby had no use for Onassis. Indeed, in the spring Jackie had called Bobby to tell him of her intentions, and he had at first been full of rage. Onassis knew that as president, Bobby might well have had Onassis's dealings pursued to the point of indictments, but not if it would destroy his former sister-in-law's new marriage. Bobby was gone now, and with this marriage Onassis was at least partially immunized against the worst legal attacks on his business life. In comparison to the money Onassis thought this marriage might bring him, his gifts of diamonds and rubies were no more than paste jewelry, Jackie's extravagances like a few copper coins that Onassis might leave for a waitress in a bar.

Keeping her house in Hyannis Port, Jackie maintained her relationship with the Kennedy family. Beyond anything else, Jackie was a devoted mother and she was not about to yank Caroline and John from the context of their lives. She had married a Greek billionaire, but she wanted Caroline and John never to forget their father and their Kennedy heritage, and to think of their cousins as among their closest friends. 'Now each house [at Hyannis Port] has parents with children in it," she said. "The children will go away and get married but they'll always come back. You always have to have a place that you think of as home, even if it's gone."

Rose visited Jackie in Greece. Onassis took her up to visit the Acropolis in the evening, and as they walked down the hill, their way was illuminated by the light of flashbulbs from photographers hidden in the bushes. Whatever Rose might initially have thought about the marriage, she was deeply understanding about Jackie's decision to marry Onassis. The Greek ship owner was not unlike her own husband. Both men were business buccaneers who delighted in beating those who fancied themselves their betters. Both men doted on their families, and yet were notorious for their various affairs; indeed, both men had known Gloria Swanson's favors. Both men had rude exteriors yet were capable of the most subtle charm and graciousness.

Both men had married their social betters. Rose had been the mayor's daughter, but she was hardly the prize that Jackie had become. To Onassis, Jackie was an exquisite gem that had to be placed in the proper setting for all of its glitter to be fully appreciated. As the marriage began Onassis treated his wife like a queen, and at times Jackie began to act like one. When the couple visited Palm Beach, a group of models was ferried out to the *Christina* to provide a fashion show for Jackie alone on the yacht; the young women were warned that as they paraded in front of Mrs. Onassis they were to look only at her feet, never daring to glance at her countenance. Once, Jackie told James Connor, a Palm Beach police officer who moonlighted for the senior Kennedys, that she wanted to return to the yacht. "Just a minute, I have to wait for Mrs. Kennedy," Connor said, referring to Rose.

"I want to go right this minute."

"No, ma'am, I have to wait for Mrs. Kennedy."

"You are fired!" Jackie said. Rose arrived in time to hear her employee dismissed. "You can't fire him, Jackie," Rose said, speaking no less than the truth. "He works for me."

Rose continued to worry about her children's lives. She had been delighted that Sarge was named ambassador, but she had been worried about her bedraggled daughter flying into the capital of style looking like a charwoman with runs in her stockings, hair uncombed. When she learned that Gloria Guinness was helping with the redecoration of the ambassador's residence, Rose wrote her friend requesting that she please forget buying sofas and focus on choosing dresses for Eunice. Eunice was an astute enough politician to realize that in Paris she should pay attention to her appearance. Few who saw her elegant style realized what a metamorphosis that represented.

Eunice called her mother regularly from Paris full of exuberant tales of life as ambassadress. Pat telephoned often as well, presenting to her mother a solid front of upbeat conversation and good cheer. Pat finally had a project that had meaning to her, putting together a privately printed book of reminiscences about Bobby. To her Bobby was not an epic figure striding boldly across the stage of history, but a brother and friend, a person of infinite concern, "a warm and loving man," and that was the sort of recollections that filled *That Shining Hour*. Pat's recent years had been filled with unhappiness, her emotions only partially deadened by liquor. She wanted this book filled not with sadness but joy, the way she wanted to remember everything—her childhood, her father, Joe, Jack, everything. Her memories were vague, a half-recalled anecdote here, a snapshot in time there, memories disappearing and reappearing in the miasma of sentiment and time.

Jean did not have the time for her mother that the others had. There was an irritability in Rose's youngest daughter, an implicit criticism of Rose and her family.

As for Ted, he was his mother's favorite, both as her youngest child and as her only son. He was a good son who spent much time at Hyannis Port, not in his own house on Squaw Island but with his parents. Rose doted on her Teddy. To her he was fulfilling with consummate concern all the mandates of life as the last Kennedy son. This spring alone he had attended five or six fund-raisers paying off Bobby's campaign expenses, from one end of the country to another. He still wore a back brace from the airplane crash, but he didn't complain. He had been there for Ethel and her children, and he was there for his other sisters and Jackie as well. To his mother's eyes, her youngest son was the noble scion of a noble brood.

Ted was his father's favorite too. Since the stroke, his eyes had always lit up when Ted came striding into the room full of life. During the early summer of 1969, the old man had begun to decline. Rose noticed that even when Ted came bounding into his father's upstairs bedroom, Joe was, as she put it, "bereft of even that minimal spark." Joe hardly ever came downstairs any longer. He lay in his room unable to eat anything but ice cream or baby food. She sat next to him sometimes.

Rose and Joe knew almost nothing of the Ted Kennedy who in April, flying back from a trip to Alaska as chairman of the Special Subcommittee on Education, had gotten drunk. Reporters heard him muttering: "They're going to shoot my ass off the way they shot Bobby." They knew almost nothing of the tattered marriage between Ted and Joan, and how the previous Christmas one of Ted's closest friends had confronted the couple with their destructive behavior, Joan and her drinking, and Ted and his other women. Rose didn't see that much of her youngest daughter-in-law any longer. Joan knew that she had to look right and act right when she talked to her mother-in-law. She rarely visited the house, and when she did she sat there fidgeting, full of nervous insecurity.

Rose went to mass every morning, played her three holes of golf, walked on the beach. She rarely went out to social affairs. On the afternoon of July 19, 1969, she accepted an invitation to attend a church garden party at St. Francis Xavier. She was getting ready when Ann Gargan told her that there had been an accident on Chappaquiddick involving Ted in which a secretary had drowned. Shortly after Rose heard the news, Ted arrived in the compound, having been flown by private plane and chauffeured to the house.

Ted rushed upstairs to his mute father, and with his hand on Joe's shoulder told the old man the news. "I'm telling you the truth, Dad," he said with terrible solemnity. "It was an accident." Joe took his son's hand and pressed it tightly against his chest. This was a moment that called for all Joe's power, cunning, strategy, and strength, but all that was gone. He could offer his son nothing. Joe closed his eyes, and Ted left the room.

Ted did not rush to his mother to tell her the tragic news. "I never discussed it with him," Rose said two and a half years later. "No, I've never discussed it." A woman was dead, and Ted had been driving the car, and from the television and newspaper accounts and talks with other family members, she learned the bare outline of what had happened. Ted had flown up from Washington to sail in the Edgartown Regatta on Martha's Vineyard and then to attend a weekend party across the inlet on the tiny island of Chappaquiddick for six of Bobby's "boiler-room girls," the dedicated young women who had worked impossible hours for his brother. Friday afternoon Ted had begun drinking, downing some beers on the *Victura* during its ninth-place finish in the regatta, rum and Coke on the victorious boat afterwards, more beer at the Shiretown Inn in Edgartown where he was planning to spend the night.

Ted's chauffeur, John "Jack" Crimmins, then drove him to the ferry and across to Chappaquiddick for the party. Although the guests included six married men and six single women, the party was not one of the senator's extramarital romps but an occasion to honor those who had served his brother. Ted had more to drink at the party. At approximately eleven-fifteen P.M., Ted asked Crimmins for the car keys. Then he left with one of the young women, Mary Jo Kopechne, whose last name he did not even know. He said later that he was merely offering Mary Jo a ride back to Edgartown. He roared back up the road. The paved road curved sharply left toward the ferry. Ted, however, turned right onto a washboard-like gravel road that led to a tiny bridge across Poucha Pond, and from there to a private beach. As he drove along the tiny road and up onto the narrow bridge, the car plunged into the water. Ted said that he dove repeatedly to attempt to save Mary Jo, but she died entombed in the car in the black water. Although she was considered a drowning victim, the diver who discovered her body believed that she had died with her head pressed against the roof of the Oldsmobile sedan, gasping for oxygen after she had used up the pocket of air.

A woman had died, but there was a reputation, an honor, a future to be saved, and the old Kennedy aides arrived at the compound. Sorensen, Jack's alter ego; Robert McNamara, the former secretary of defense; Richard Goodwin, a speech writer; and others. One of Ted's closest friends, Claude E. Hooton Jr., flew from Paris where he was working. Sunday Pat phoned her mother to say that she was flying in from California. "I always try to be optimistic and view news in a quiet, composed, calm way," Rose wrote in her personal notes of the accident. "So when she first said she was coming I tried to persuade her that all was well and it was not necessary to take the long trip. . . . But when she arrived, I was so glad to see her and I know Ted was, as she went up there at once, ate there, and spent nearly all the time with him. Ethel and LeMoyne Billings later phoned Jean and Eunice and told them they had better come. Jean was at Majorca in a house for a month . . . but she came along a few days earlier."

The family always gathered in times of crisis and tragedy, and the Kennedy sisters and their mother were all in Hyannis Port. Jean and Steve arrived together, but Steve took command. Pat had already arrived, her sleepless eyes deep hollows. Eunice rushed into the house, and shouted irritably, "Where's Teddy? Where's my brother?" She hurried out of the house looking for her brother, not even stopping to greet her mother and father. Jackie considered herself still part of the family, and she returned as well.

The Kennedy women were all there but in the ethos of the family, it was not time for womanly counsel, but for the words of men. Except for Hooton, these advisors were ambitious political men who saw the Kennedy name, their own futures, and the dream of a Kennedy restoration drowning in those murky waters on Chappaquiddick. Here then was the small horror within the larger horror. Not only Kopechne's death but Ted's life was lost in the frenetic search for a way out. His advisors argued over him as if he were a product that had been recalled, trying to devise a campaign to regain market shares.

Rose wanted to speak with her son, but even here among the family's most trusted counselors and servants, she dared not speak where her words might be overheard. She led the dazed, bewildered Ted over to the flagpole in the middle of the lawn for talks the content of which she apparently never discussed with anyone.

As Ted walked the beach, he mused about leaving the Senate and going off with Helga Wagner, a voluptuous blonde model with whom he was passionately involved. She had been the first person he had called, not Joan, not one of his sisters, but Helga, who was planning to travel to Europe to join Steve and Jean on a vacation. To Jean traveling with your brother's lover while you treated your alcoholic sister-in-law with distant disdain was perfectly permissible behavior.

Joan was an indispensable part of this scenario of grief. She traveled with Ted to the coal-mining town of Plymouth, Pennsylvania, to attend Mary Jo's funeral. Ethel was there in the little church as well. Ted was a man not simply of deep sentiment but of deep sentimentality. When emotion overwhelmed him, words sputtered out of him incoherently. After the funeral he talked privately to Mary Jo's parents. "I couldn't understand a word he said, he was so emotional," Joseph Kopechne recalled. Joan was here then through all of this: the sound of Mrs. Kopechne's quiet weeping in a full church, a gauntlet of photographers and reporters, the discussions in the car and the private plane, through it all, a necessary political appendage, the loyal wife. She wanted to be more than a symbol, but back in Hyannis Port Ted closeted himself not with his wife, but with his sisters.

Friday morning, Joan was with her husband again at the courthouse in Edgartown. There the court clerk read the charges against her husband that he "did operate a certain motor vehicle upon a public way in said Edgartown and did go away after knowingly causing injury to Mary Jo Kopechne without stopping and making known his name, residence and the number of his motor vehicle."

The clerk then turned to Ted. "How do you plead? Guilty or not guilty." "Guilty" was a word that did not exist in the lexicon of the Kennedys, not in Rose's and Joe's upbringing of their nine children, not in their public life. In his moments of deep public doubt, Ted always turned to his advisors; though everything had been decided beforehand, he looked at his lawyers as if they might yet devise a magical solution. Their faces told him nothing, and he turned back. "Guilty," he said, the word forced out of him in a half whisper. "Guilty," he said again, the word audible.

Judge Boyle sentenced Ted to two months at the House of

Corrections at Barnstable, but suspended the sentence. That evening Ted requested time on television. The American people were the real judge and jury of his future. Ted appeared tense as he sat in the living room in the family home to broadcast a speech on all three networks. He had asked his mother and sisters and wife to be with him watching from an adjoining room, a part of the now-familiar family pattern. Eunice entered the living room before anyone else. She was the most morally concerned of the sisters. Even when this tale was stripped of all the suggestions of sexual misconduct and drunkenness, it was still unthinkable conduct for a Kennedy, an unspeakable shame on the family name. Yet Ted was her brother and blood was everything. Eunice did not reject Teddy but embraced him and sought to lighten his burden. She looked at all the retainers and advisors standing around, and ordered them out, out. It would only be the family here. When Joan arrived, she walked into the room where Ted waited to offer her own encouragement; he quickly directed her to leave and join the other women.

"My fellow citizens, I have requested this opportunity to talk to you . . ." he began in a speech crafted primarily by Sorensen. "Only reasons of health prevented my wife from accompanying me," he said. Joan was newly pregnant, but she was healthy enough that on the day of the accident her neighbor, Harry Fowler, saw Joan and her daughter, Kara, going off to play tennis. Pregnant or not, she would have abhorred being dragged to a nostalgic evening of drinking and oft-told anecdotes in a remote cabin.

Ted asserted that he had not been drunk that evening, and had made a wrong turn returning to Edgartown with Mary Jo and had driven off the bridge. "I remember thinking as the cold water rushed in around my head that I was for certain drowning; then water entered my lungs and I actually felt a sensation of drowning." He told how he had made "immediate and repeated efforts to save Mary Jo by diving into the strong and murky current." He admitted that his actions afterwards "to the extent that I can remember them, made no sense to me at all." After his own futile attempts, Ted said that he returned to the cottage to ask Joe Gargan and Paul Markham to attempt to rescue Mary Jo. They failed also and the three men then had gone to the shut-down ferry.

"I suddenly jumped into the water and impulsively swam across, nearly drowning once again in the effort," he said. In the end, Ted asked the people of the Commonwealth of Massachusetts to decide whether he should continue in the Senate. Ted concluded: "Whatever is decided, whatever the future holds for me, I hope I shall be able to put this most recent tragedy behind me and make some future contribution to our state and mankind, whether it be in public or private life. Thank you and good night."

Ted had read the words that others had written for him, and when he was finished he walked up the stairs to his father's bedroom. "Dad, I've done the best I can," he told the father who had wanted so much from him and his brothers. "I'm sorry." He had been such a bonny boy, whose pure unmitigated joy had lit up his father's heart. He had run for the Senate as much to please his father as himself. He had taken on the burdens of politics and family one after another, but he was not Jack and he was not Bobby, and sometimes he was afraid and sometimes he strayed. He had done the best he could.

Among the millions of viewers, there were those who heard the heartfelt words of a tortured, honorable man whose service to his state and his nation should continue. Others listened to what they perceived as more of Ted's endless dissembling. His sisters were eternally loyal to their brother, and so was Joan. Less than three weeks after the accident, Joan narrated "Peter and the Wolf" with the Boston Pops Orchestra at the Berkshire Music Festival in Tanglewood, Massachusetts, and afterwards vowed to be in the family gallery in the Senate to watch Ted oppose the antiballistic missile bill.

In those terrible weeks, Joan played the noble spouse, always on Ted's arm, always the supportive wife, and almost no one knew that her worries now reached even further than Ted. Shortly before the accident at Chappaquiddick, Joan's mother, Ginny, had gone off on a European tour with a friend. Ginny, like her daughter, was a perfectionist to whom life was a vision of expectations unmet, and goals fallen short. Ginny had a drinking problem, and just before she left on the trip, her husband, Harry, told her that he wanted a divorce. "She'd been a beautiful woman, but her appearance shocked me," recalled the woman who accompanied her on the trip.

Her impending divorce was curse enough. Then in the middle of the trip she learned about Chappaquiddick. "In England the hotel maître d' passed the word that one of the party was ill," her companion recalled. "Ginny was out cold on the floor as if she'd had an epileptic seizure. When we finally got word to Joan and Ted around 2:00 A.M., they said to send her back with a doctor and to be sure she was taken care of." She was sent off to a sanitorium in White Plains, New York, where the Kennedys paid the two-thousand-a-month bill.

At the end of August Joan suffered her third miscarriage while Ted was off on a camping trip. "It was after Chappaquiddick that it became worse," Joan reflected. "For a few months everyone had to put on this show and then I just didn't care anymore. I just saw no future. That's when I truly became an alcoholic."

Rose viewed her son's speech and everything about the tragedy at Chappaquiddick as a loyal mother and the matriarch of a great political family. She acted as if her family had acquired vast amounts of moral capital that they should be able to expend on this accident, and then get on with life. In her public utterances, she seemed unable to realize that what set this death off from all the earlier family tragedies was that this time it was not a Kennedy who had died. "It was a very sad experience," Rose said in September. "But I've always brought my children up with the idea that you have the great moments, the ordeals and the triumphs. Some people call them the agonies and the ecstasies, the ups and downs. I call them the ordeals and the triumphs."

One of Rose's persistent themes, and that of several of Ted's associates, was that the blame lay largely in a failure of staffing. "Of course, I was surprised that none of the men went with him that night," Rose admitted later. "Mr. Kennedy told me years ago he always had this man, Eddie Moore, with him so that no matter what happened Eddie Moore would be there. And that night it would have been so easy for one of the men to step in the front of the car with Teddy, and I didn't understand why one of them didn't have the gumption enough—or why he didn't have gumption enough—to think of that. Teddy had had that experience before. Somebody wants their picture taken with the candidate. Someone will grab him around the neck and embrace him and then have a friend take a picture. And they have all had those experiences. They all were standing around there. I thought that was quite stupid, the way that Teddy had been brought up, and all of them knew enough about politics—or anybody else—if you go out with a woman, you or the chauffeur at night and there is an accident, you are sure to be blamed. It's very sad and dreadful for the family. I felt very badly to think he was responsible. The girl was a wonderful girl. It was so stupid, so stupid for the people who were with him to allow it to happen. Really!"

Rose saw the accident as a double failure of staffing, before the death and afterwards. "I did not understand why Joe Gargan or Markham did not report the matter to the police even if Ted did not have sense enough or control enough to do so—especially when the body of the girl was in the car," Rose wrote in her personal memoir of the accident. "That is what seems so unforgivable and brutal to me, and I suppose it is one of the questions which the press says is unanswerable."

There was no point, as Rose saw it, to muse endlessly about what might have been. "This is what I say is life," she reflected. "Teddy has everything for him. He goes out one night in an accident and everything is smashed. It just seems—as I was reading last night from Shakespeare—just how much destiny decides."

In one sense, no punishment could be more merciless than that made upon Ted: to have shamed the legacy of his family and his brothers with a mark of such blackness that nothing could ever cover it over. Yet there remained the bewildering paradoxes of the man who after Chappaquiddick, continued his open involvements with other women, his wildness untamed and unfettered.

Soon afterwards, Ted made a trip to Paris to visit Eunice and Sarge. "You'd think that there would be some remorse," recalled Dr. Herbert Kramer, who also was staying at the ambassadorial residence working on a project with Sarge. "But no. He walked around the living room naked, drunk most of the time. There was a brilliant guy there, an economist, and we took a walk near Notre Dame and I said, 'What Teddy ought to do is to resign from the Senate and take a year, two years to do some good work to redeem himself, to suggest that night at Chappaquiddick had been an aberration.' And this man said, 'You got to be kidding. This isn't a moral animal. It's a political animal. He's not going to leave the Senate.' "

Remorse, however, takes many shapes and can be buried in flesh as much as in prayer, drowned in whiskey as well as in tears. Ultimately no one knew—not his defenders and not his critics—what Ted truly felt and how the burden of Chappaquiddick rested on his shoulders.

* * *

For years his daughters and son had called him every night, and for years he had lived for their voices on the phone. Eunice. Pat. Jean. Ted. Voices full of life. They called wherever they were, whatever they were doing, but Joe fell in and out of sleep now, and when he was dozing the calls were not put through. Since Chappaquiddick, he hardly ate anymore. He was almost blind but his reddened eyes were full of tears, and it was as if he were perpetually crying.

Rose was with him now as she had rarely been with him during his halcyon days. In the evenings she sat next to his bed as his beloved classical music played, the sounds wafting down the stairs filling the old house. The end was near, and on November 15 Jackie arrived at the compound. In her marriage to Onassis, Jackie had become a woman of unseemly extravagance, measuring out her life in shoes purchased by the hundred, dresses by the score; when Onassis looked at her bills, he thought he was reading the litmus test of her character. Yet this woman of such apparent capriciousness and frivolity was here kneeling at the bedside of her former father-in-law. She no longer carried the Kennedy name, but she had always loved Joe, and she loved him still. "It's Jackie, Grandpa," she said, kissing that gnarled old face, ignoring the oxygen tube.

Pat and Jean flew into Hyannis and then Eunice and Sarge arrived from Paris. Eunice not only adored her father, but so much of what she had done in her life was to honor the best part of Joe: his admonition that his children go out and do good in the world. She loved him beyond love. It was unthinkable that he could not hear what she was saying and see what she was doing, and how she was bringing honor to the family name. She was a woman of resolute strength but when she saw him lying there so helpless, it was all too much. She stooped to kiss him and rushed out to cry in another room.

Rose spent all of November 16 sitting with Joe. There was nothing she could say or do now, but she sat there, a silent vigil, honoring the nearly five and a half decades of the marriage. He was comatose, but he had an incredible life force. The next night Jackie stayed in the room with him along with Ted, and in the early morning hours they left, leaving Joe with the nurse, Rita Dallas.

At ten-thirty, the nurse rang the alarm bell, the sound carrying out of the great house and across the grounds, disappearing into the gray endless ocean. The family knew that the bell was tolling for Joe, and one by one they arrived. Pat was first.

There was no longer any reason not to cry in front of her father. She reached down and kissed him, her tears falling on his dormant figure, his pulse hardly beating. Jackie had not even stopped to put on shoes or a jacket before running out of her house. She rushed into the room in bare feet and a short-sleeved shirt.

They were all here now, all except Rose. Ted left and brought his mother into the room, his arm wrapped around her. She sat next to the bed and placed her head there next to Joe's hand, and cried with unspeakable anguish. Her daughters and son had rarely seen their mother cry, and never like this, an outpouring that seemed it would never stop.

Ethel, Joan, Jackie, Steve, and Sarge stepped back and now only Rose, Eunice, Pat, Jean, and Ted stood around the bed. Rose looked up a moment and took Joe's rosary from the nurse's hand, and her tears grew quiet. She touched the cross to Joe's lips, put the rosary in his still hand, and suddenly the room was silent.

For Eunice religion had been a solace beyond solace, and as she stood there, she began almost soundlessly to speak the infinitely comforting words of the Lord's Prayer.

"Our Father, Who art in Heaven, Hallowed be Thy name."

Ted did not practice his Catholicism the way his sister did, but he too found comfort in the words of faith. "Thy kingdom come, Thy will be done," he said softly.

Jean did not have to think to speak the next words of the familiar prayer. "On earth as it is in heaven."

Pat picked up the natural cadences of the prayer. "Give us this day our daily bread."

"Forgive us our trespasses," Ethel said, the words softly passing her lips.

"As we forgive those who trespass against us," Jackie said.

The room was silent. Rose sat with the others, her head bowed in prayer. Finally she spoke: "And deliver us from evil. Amen."

The family looked up from the prayer. Joe had died.

Rose was alone now. She had had her difficulties with Jackie when she had been first lady, but since then the two women had grown closer, full of mutual respect and the kind of intimacy that expressed itself often in unspoken gestures. After Joe's death Rose had gone to visit Jackie, and one day something triggered all her grief, a word, a memory, and she began to cry. She grabbed Jackie's hand as if she were trying to hold on to a support, and quieted her tears. "Nobody's ever going to feel sorry for me," she said, and then they continued with the conversation.

Jackie marveled at Rose's strength. "She taught me so much . . ." she said. "I think I have a tendency to go into a downward spiral of depression or isolation when I'm sad. To go out, to take a walk, to take a swim, that's very much what the Kennedys do. It's a salvation really."

Jackie continued to serve as an elegant surrogate for the other Kennedys. *Newsweek* had been particularly harsh on Ted's role over Chappaquiddick. When the editors decided they should mend fences with the family, they arranged a luncheon with Jackie. Katharine Graham, the magazine's publisher, came up from Washington, where she was publisher of *The Washington Post*. When Jackie had known her, Graham had been simply a Washington wife. Not until her manic-depressive husband committed suicide did she become a formidable public figure in her own right. The two women could have found much to talk about. Jackie retreated into that fey, wispy voice of hers and during the meal managed to say everything about nothing.

At *Newsweek* the writers were almost all male, and the researchers who served them female, and there was a rising tide of discontent among the women. One editor began talking about the burgeoning of feminism in the workplace. "I don't go for all that," Jackie said, her voice barely audible. "I had no trouble finding a position in journalism as a photographer."

Graham turned her head toward her old friend. "Oh, Jackie, don't you remember," she said half in amazement, "when we would be in the White House sitting at the feet of Jack and Phil, saying nothing, just looking up to them?"

Jackie didn't come back to Hyannis Port every summer any longer. She had a different life, and her house was almost too full of memories. Time was a blessed balm. She couldn't even remember the precise cadences of Jack's voice any longer. After all these years, she still couldn't bear to look at his picture. This house in Hyannis Port was a trove of memories. It was the one house that had truly been theirs, and everything had the smell of Jack on it. Even the pickle jar reminded her of the day she had purchased it in a tiny store on the Cape, purchased it when Jack was alive.

One evening she walked across to the sprawling house and

sat and talked to Rose awhile. "It really hits you, doesn't it?" Jackie said. That was all she had to say. Rose knew. Later that evening Rose called Jackie and asked her if she would like to go for a walk on the beach. As Jackie listened to Rose, she thought "that woman who has so many reasons to be sad—for her to be thinking about calling me up—it shows you what else she's like."

Jackie was awed by the concern that Rose showed. She noticed something else about her former mother-in-law. All those years the colors of Rose's personality had been muted, lost in Joe's shadow. "Now that she's all alone, you have so much more chance to see what she was," Jackie said. "I thought in the years before Mr. Kennedy's stroke—I mean he was always the dominant one—she was nervous, I think."

Jackie was not the only person who observed the changes in Rose. "[Before] she behaved like an older woman," recalled Gloria Guinness. "She wasn't this gay, divine person she became. She was surrounded by tremendous publicity for others. Everybody around you has always been in the papers. They all achieved something. Now it's too late for her to achieve a career, so she has to achieve something. And pain and prayer are not enough. So what does she do? She becomes one of the best-dressed women in the world and she takes great care to see that she remains one of the best-dressed. From this moment she has gained all this publicity: Rose Kennedy, the wonderful mother, the courageous personality. She gives it all tremendous thought. Rose isn't going to be caught like Jackie many times when she looked like hell. Rose is always going to look trim and tidy. A beautiful woman for her age."

For Rose the world outside was a stage in which she performed with subtle grace and nuance. She had never been considered a beautiful woman, but the beautiful women of her generation were almost all gone now or had sunk into old age. She had the beauty of her own age now, a beauty appreciated primarily by other women. Those years of self-discipline and restraint and exercise were apparent in her posture and her figure, and the youthful illusion that she could still engender in the forgiving, half-lit rooms where she spent her social evenings.

Few outsiders saw the backstage Rose, without her makeup and regal presence. Guinness was one of the few friends who knew both the public and the private Rose. Once the two women went off on a cruise on a private yacht in the Greek is-

lands. "We went ashore one day and we walked up to this castle on the beach," Guinness recalled. "Rose sat on the beach
and pulled her pants off. And I said, 'Rose!' And she said,
'They can beat me up. I am so hot.' And so we found the
church and we went in and sat on the end of a bench. She took
off her makeup and started making up her face all over because she had been sweating so. I mean this is what I think
helps her a lot, not only prayer, though she feels at home with
God and the Virgin, but there was the mirror and the powder
box and the lipstick too. It was the best thing I have ever seen
in my entire life."

Rose found it no sacrilege to use the quiet church as her
powder room, for these were her two consolations: her faith
and her vanity. During the summer of 1969 she was in Paris
when Kathleen arrived at the Ritz looking for her grandmother.
Rose's eldest granddaughter and her friend, Anne Coffey, had
been spending the summer backpacking around Europe. They
marched into the hotel in blue jeans, backpacks, and rain gear,
and the concierge looked at them with a withering gaze. Rose
asked the concierge if he had heard of Kathleen's hotel, and
the man acted as if the very name of such an obscure domicile
were enough to soil him. With that Rose ordered a cab to investigate Kathleen's disreputable lodgings.

When Rose had been Kathleen's age, she had been at
Blumenthal, her every action monitored by the nuns of the Sacred Heart, her uniforms extreme only in their demureness.
Kathleen was dressed like a homeless waif. She had eschewed
a religious education for Putney. Now she was heading off to
college in the fall not to Manhattanville, where Rose thought
Kennedy women belonged, but to Radcliffe, to sit cheek by
jowl with Harvard men. Rose could hardly believe the way
these two young women were dressed, though their scruffy
clothes perfectly matched the shabby hotel where they had
taken a room.

Rose patrolled the dark corridors of the hotel, as if she had
stumbled onto a den of vice. "Maybe boys can sleep here," she
said as she paraded back and forth in her elegant Dior dress.
"But can girls?" The hotel was reputable, the kind of place frequented by tourists on a tight budget and students. "Is there a
shower?" she demanded, speaking in French. "Will these girls
be safe?"

Kathleen and Anne were perfectly safe, but Rose insisted
that they pack up their motley belongings, and she moved

them to a far better hotel. Kathleen enjoyed talking to Rose, but when Kathleen was growing up Rose was not the kind of grandmother who believed it her right and pleasure to spoil her grandchildren. Kathleen found that Rose was "always very nervous." During her childhood Rose had not enveloped her granddaughter in love, but admonished her to act well and proper, and cast critical glances her way. How many times she had told her, "You stand up straight and keep your right hand away from your body because it makes you look thinner, and always stand at an angle with your feet close together, it's like the Greek statues." Often, by word or gesture, she had let Kathleen know what it meant to be a Kennedy woman.

Rose and Kathleen both visited Eunice at the American embassy. One day, Rose came walking in from the garden in a cool silk dress and white hat that shielded her from the sun's rays. Kathleen entered the room asking, "Where's Eunice?" That was often not an easy question. Eunice could be practically anywhere in the enormous embassy residence, off on the tennis court, or out somewhere on one of her innumerable campaigns.

Eunice and Sarge worked in tandem in Paris. Eunice knew little about France, but unlike many Americans, she was hardly intimidated by the rarefied world of French culture and high society. Sarge was frequently confronted by demonstrators vehemently opposed to America's role in the Vietnam War, but he argued with them as he would detractors in America. Many French intellectuals took facile pleasure in condemning materialistic American culture, their venom sometimes only exceeded by their ignorance. Instead of hunkering down in their elegant home, the Shrivers turned the official residence into an island of American values and culture. Sarge was a devotee of modern American art, and the walls of the embassy residence were graced with abstract art, except one salon that they filled with American antiques. Rock and roll blasted at receptions. Guests ranged from Nobel prize winners to obscure Parisian intellectuals; middle-class French families to Vanessa Redgrave, notorious for her nude scenes in the film *Blow-Up*; those with mental retardation and experts in the field.

"A French secretary at the embassy was overheard saying, 'Well, if you're not mentally retarded, you can't even get invited to this embassy. You have got to be mentally retarded to get any real attention from this ambassadress,' " recalled Sarge. "Eunice worked classes and got people from the U.S. to teach them and got French people interested. By the time we left, there was a cadre. French don't pay attention to teenagers. And the idea that French teenagers would be in the U.S. ambassador's home, it was a real shocker too. The French are highly intellectual and they thought, 'What are they fussing around about the mentally retarded, a little odd, quirky interest of the ambassador's wife?' "

The Shrivers went everywhere, from Lille to Marseille. They filled each day with so many activities that almost everywhere they went they were late. That was as serious a failing in French society as it would have been in Washington. That was the primary criticism against them, except from such as Betty Beale, the society columnist for the *Washington Star*. "One gathers that when he [Sarge] finally leaves France, there will be disappointment only among the young," Beale wrote, her criticism ample evidence of how dramatically the Shrivers affected the staid diplomatic rituals. "The old guard will probably celebrate."

Before anything else, the Shrivers were a family, and the embassy resonated with the sounds of the five Shriver children. "We lived in the vast marble embassy, where my bedroom looked out to the Eiffel Tower, which I thought was pretty neat," Maria recalled. "My father threw me into a school where nobody spoke English, and I had to learn how to adapt myself pretty fast." Eunice was not a mother simply to parade her brood before guests and then send them upstairs. She wanted her daughter and sons to experience their parents' world. Guests were astounded to find as their dinner partner not the ambassador or at least an embassy official, but Timmy or Mark or Maria or Bobby.

Eunice had brought her campaign for the retarded to Paris with her, and she was as determined as ever, discussing the matter even with President de Gaulle, who had a retarded child. The concept of volunteering was almost as alien to the French as rock and roll, and Eunice attempted to show them through the example of her own life. Every Monday morning she taught 140 mentally disabled children. For the most part the children had no idea who Eunice was but they followed her lead as she directed them in her fractured French. "All right," she yelled, as she took one child by the hand. "Un jeu maintenant."

* * *

At Radcliffe Kathleen was presented with new gods, from Erikson to Freud. Kathleen had decided that conventional religion was a crutch that solved too many moral dilemmas for people that they should work out for themselves. Kathleen felt uncomfortable with Rose's somewhat self-satisifed sense of altruism, the way she quietly boasted: "My husband can make it through business—we helped these poor people." That was not the way the world was any longer, not Kathleen's world.

Whenever Kathleen was around, Rose was forever questioning her. "What are you doing? What are you studying in school? What book are you reading?" Kathleen gave her answers and then Rose related it to something in her own life, and Kathleen saw that her grandmother was "always pulling things together—into a sort of wholeness." Kathleen confessed to her grandmother the difficulties of being a Kennedy woman. Anybody else could go madly running down the beach and nobody would say anything, but if she did it they would say, "Isn't that obnoxious?" and blame it on her being a Kennedy. Sometimes at Radcliffe she didn't know if she were being accepted for herself or simply because of her name. That set her grandmother off reminiscing. "Well, you know my father was the mayor of Boston and I had the same thing, maybe not on the same scale. . . ." Kathleen had heard it all and she found it "a little maddening at times—you want your own experience." Then she reflected on how unusual it was to have an octogenarian grandmother who was not only healthy and alert, but a woman with whom you could argue and discuss almost anything, and decided that she was fortunate to have her.

At times Rose journeyed by herself to places that a woman a quarter century younger might not have ventured even with companions. In the summer of 1970, she visited a health spa in Switzerland, then Jackie and Onassis in Greece, before flying on to Ethiopia to celebrate her eightieth birthday on July 22 with Emperor Haile Selassie, whose seventy-eighth birthday was a day later. "Mother was a great traveler," Jean recalled. "And I went to Ethiopia with her, along with my two sons. She just called me up and said that Haile Selassie had told her that they should celebrate their birthdays. She said she was going to Africa, would I meet her in Addis Ababa, which I thought was pretty daring at eighty years old. And so she went and that's when I went to Kenya and I met her there. We had a great time."

* * *

Rose spent most of the summer in Hyannis Port, but she almost never went to Ethel's house. Rock music blared out from speakers, the sounds wafting across the expanse of lawn, and that was the least of the affronts to the decorum of Rose's world. Joe II and Bobby Jr. were the presumed heirs to their father's legacy, the leaders of the pack. It was a boy's world at Ethel's, the girls mere observers. It was a world that had begun like *Tom Sawyer* but was ending, as Chris Lawford recalled, more like *Lord of the Flies*. The two oldest Kennedys, several neighborhood youths, sometimes their little brother David, and often Chris Lawford and Bobby Shriver became a plague on Hyannis Port. They untied boats from the docks and took perverse pleasure in seeing them lying beached in the high tide. They sent water balloons soaring high into the sky, landing on the top of moving automobiles, preferably police cruisers. On the Fourth of July the youths were accused of knocking on the door of an eighty-two-year-old neighbor, and when the old woman opened the door they threw lit firecrackers into the house.

Harry Fowler recalled the time that Ethel's "children tied up the family cook and hung her up in a tree and threatened to set her on fire." Sancy and Larry Newman discovered that food was missing from their kitchen; they learned that Ethel had locked her sons out of the house and for several days the youths had holed up in their basement, fed by the Newman children. By the time the Newmans discovered their guests, the boys had left and were living in the woods in a hole they had dug and covered over.

At a birthday party, the boys pulled out a knife and stole a birthday present from a little girl. "Those kids didn't see that there was anything wrong with what they had done," Larry Newman recalled. "It was just a big joke to them."

One summer evening the boys ran through the dark streets of the village shooting off BB guns, leaving holes in the plateglass windows of a church. Fowler was deputized to go over to Ethel's house along with members of the civic association to have a talk with her. Ethel listened politely to the list of outrages real and suspected that her sons had perpetuated on the quiet village, the litany sounding more like a police blotter than the résumé of a young Kennedy.

"I am a widow here alone," Ethel said finally, choking with tears. "It is just so hard for a mother in this day and age to bring up children. I'll do the best I can. That's all I can say."

Ethel and her sons were becoming notorious, and not only in Hyannis Port. When the family went skiing in Vail or Aspen, they left rented homes so trashed that it was as if some barbarian horde had rampaged through the rooms. In their wildness, the Kennedy youths were attempting to outrun the family legacy, willfully reckless, heedless of counsel. Rose had endlessly preached that as Kennedys her progeny must exhibit caution in public for there were people out there who would want to exploit them. But the boys were not listening.

Eunice tried to be some support to Ethel, but she saw her own eldest son drawn into this ominously threatening world. With President Nixon in the White House, Sarge had been recalled from Paris, and the family was spending much of the summer in Hyannis Port. One summer evening in 1970, Eunice had Ethel and her children over for dinner when the doorbell rang. Several police officers stood there, informing the Shrivers that sixteen-year-old Bobby Shriver and sixteen-year-old Bobby Kennedy Jr. were accused of possession of marijuana. Millions of young Americans had taken a puff or two of marijuana, and the two youths had been set up by an undercover cop, but that did not diminish the onus of the charge. Ethel raged at her son, chasing him into the backyard, pushing him into the bushes screaming: "You've dragged your family's name through the mud."

Eunice and Sarge were strangers to the psychedelic world of the sixties, and they might have pointed the finger of shame at their eldest son. They were parents with the deepest sense of compassion and empathy for their children, and after their own anger subsided, they took Bobby aside. Sarge cautioned his eldest son that the way he was headed he was going to end up with a prison record and a ruined life. Bobby listened to his father and realized that he had better avoid his dangerous cousins.

With her manic mood swings and hidden anger, Ethel was hardly able to give her sons the good guidance they so desperately needed. They continued down the road they were headed on, traveling into a wilderness where young Kennedys had never ventured before. Joe II wandered desultorily from place to place, misadventure to misadventure, from MIT to Berkeley, from encounters with purported drug dealers to sessions with psychiatrists. He was not smart and he was not wise, and wherever he went he seemed to leave wreckage in his wake. One Sunday in Nantucket he borrowed a friend's Jeep and went for a crazed joy ride with his young brother David and David's girlfriend, Pam Kelley. It was like a drug high, turning the vehicle around and around again in circles, spinning it like a top, laughing and screaming, a mindless exhilaration, and then suddenly there was a station wagon coming toward them. Joe II swerved and ended up in a ditch, and they were tossed out. They were okay, all except Pam, who was paralyzed from her neck down, all except Pam who would be taken care of by the family while Joe's life moved on.

Bobby and David Kennedy and Chris Lawford continued their journey. Bobby and David's father was one of the few white politicians who in the sixties had felt welcomed in the black ghettos of America, and the brothers traveled up to Harlem to score heroin. That was the new frontier, sticking a needle into your arm, taking them to places no Kennedy had ever ventured before.

Ethel practically disowned her prodigal sons, banishing them from the sight and sound of her fury. Bobby Jr. had the strength of ego to attend Harvard, even as his drug use continued, but David sank into a netherworld of drugs, lost from his mother and his family. Pat was little better with her Chris. She was an alcoholic herself, and she sought to distance herself from the omnipresent family legacy by moving to Paris, far from Chris, far from all of them. In 1972 Chris wrote his father seeking to move out to California with Peter, promising not to tell his mother about his request. The teenager did not move permanently to Los Angeles, but he often visited his home, sharing such father-son activities as smoking pipes of hashish together and discussing drugs.

Four years later Peter flew in to New York to attend Christopher's twenty-first birthday in Pat's apartment in New York. Pat was in an apparently jovial mood, and she asked to try on his slacks, leaving her ex-husband pantless in her bedroom, forced to return to the party with a towel around his waist. Everyone had a gift for the young man's coming of age, but Peter had the gift of choice: a vial of cocaine. Chris wrote his father thanking him for the gift but saying that alas "it was not one I could hold on to for very long!"

Rose continued to spend the winter months in Palm Beach. The home had not been redecorated in decades. The windows still had the blackout curtains from World War II, and the whole house looked as if time had ended in the forties. Rose went to dinner at the Guinnesses' every other Saturday night, but she kept away from the nightly social life of the resort community. Jim Connor worked part-time as a bodyguard, driver, and security man. The Palm Beach police officer was a massive, blunt-spoken man who often escorted Rose on her daily three-mile walks, occasionally pleading for a momentary halt as his octogenarian companion strode briskly along. Of all her family Rose was the most personally generous. She loaned Connor five hundred dollars to pay off some debts, and arranged for his daughter to attend an expensive Catholic academy. When he was five minutes late to drive her to mass one morning, she marched out on North Ocean Boulevard, put her thumb out, flagged down the next car, announcing: "I'm the president's mother. Take me to St. Edward's Church."

Connor overheard her talking frequently to Jackie, joking with her with an openness she rarely had even with her daughters. "Rose didn't talk too much about personal events except like the time Jackie got caught nude sunbathing," Connor recalled. "She laughed and said, 'I told Jackie she was going to get caught and they caught her good.'"

"Do you love your mother?" Rose asked the police officer one day.

"Yes, ma'am, I do," Connor replied.

"What could I do to make her happy?" Rose asked.

"Probably, Mrs. Kennedy, if she could meet you."

That was a price Rose considered reasonable. "I'll tell you what. We'll set up a tea at noon on Sunday."

"Okay," Connor said, growing thoughtful. "Would you mind if my mother-in-law came too?"

"Are you friends with your mother-in-law?"

"Yes, ma'am."

"Well you know a lot of people don't like mothers-in-law," Rose continued. "Yes, you have both the ladies come and you treat them with respect, just like any other guest that comes here."

When the two women arrived at the appointed hour, Connor held their car doors for them with the same panache as if they were some of Rose's famous guests. Rose's maid, "Mademoiselle," served the women tea and cookies, and Rose chatted amiably, acceding with queenly forbearance to their request to be photographed with her.

The two women were in their best Sunday finery, wearing their best manners as well, nibbling genteelly on the cookies, sipping sedately at their tea. Rose kept the conversation moving along, but something was bothering her. Connor's mother and his mother-in-law were sitting in *her* house with their legs crossed at the knee. To Rose that was nearly an invitation, an advertisement of indiscretion. "You cross the legs at the ankles," she said suddenly. "You don't cross them at the knee. You cross them at the ankle."

The two women immediately unlocked their knees, and moved their legs into positions that the nuns of the Sacred Heart would have found acceptable. And when they left that afternoon they talked and laughed for days about how the great lady had given them an etiquette lesson.

Kathleen did not see her grandmother very often any longer, but she still received Rose's round-robin letters to the grandchildren, counseling them to act in the approved Kennedy fashion. "Drugs are terrible and you children are forerunners and you have national status and you should maybe start an anti-drug routine," Rose wrote early in 1970.

Kathleen expected to hear her octogenarian grandmother raging against her drug fiend grandsons, but she was amazed at Rose's attitude. Rose had an irresistible gift for the positive. "Well maybe there's something there," she mused to her eldest granddaughter.

"Grandma, do you want to try some grass?" Kathleen asked wryly. The idea of eighty-one-year-old Rose toking on marijuana was tempting.

"Yes, sure, do you have some right with you?" Rose replied, calling Kathleen's bluff.

"Well, I don't have any on me," Kathleen said, not about to become her grandmother's dealer.

"Well, I have to watch my diet," Rose mused, apparently having heard that the weed sometimes increases one's appetite. "I don't know if it's very good for my diet."

Rose was intrigued enough about the drug to discuss it with her friend Mary Sanford, the doyenne of Palm Beach social life. "Have you ever smoked marijuana?" she asked her worldly friend.

"No," Sanford replied, taking it all as a joke.

"I haven't either," Rose admitted. "What do you think it's like? Do you think we ought to try one?"

* * *

At Harvard, Kathleen was living among a race of intellectual nomads, setting down in one place, and then pulling up their tent and moving on to the next oasis of belief. Two years before when she had come down to Harvard from Putney to visit a boyfriend at Harvard, she had to leave his dormitory at seven o'clock. To her mother's generation that would have been scandalous enough. Now, she was in Harvard-Radcliffe's first coed dormitory, Eliot House, living in the same corridor with Harvard men, sharing the same bathroom.

Since Putney, Kathleen had started going to mass again, at least occasionally, but it maddened her to hear the priest tell the congregation that they should obey the police on God's authority. If she obeyed the officer, it was going to be because she had figured out for herself that she should. That was the existential quality that her father had imparted to her: You had to go out and do it and figure it out for yourself. Her home in Hickory Hill had been full of controlled and uncontrolled chaos. "Nobody ever sits down and has a heart-to-heart conversation about your future life," she said. "That's just not the way the family works."

For a young intellectual Catholic woman in the early seventies, no issue was of such overwhelming moral and psychological complexity as that of the abortion question. Harvard-Radcliffe was not the WASP enclave it had been when Joe, Kathleen's grandfather, had attended in the 1910s, and Catholicism had been considered little more than a euphemism for superstition. But the dominant secular liberalism of Cambridge still looked askance at those Catholics who fancied themselves educated and yet accepted the church's militant stance against abortion.

Kathleen knew where the other Kennedy women stood on the issue, notably Eunice. Kathleen had spent one summer working at Eunice's summer camp, and she had boundless admiration for her aunt. Eunice had spoken frequently on the issue. Eunice was a woman of determined optimism. She believed in the potential of human life, and she was not simply opposed to abortions, but in favor of structuring society so that women could more easily keep their babies, or at least have them easily adopted. Eunice was a social liberal and a moral conservative, and most of those who applauded half her equation condemned the other half. She feared the devolution of America into what she called the "Hard Society." "I would define the Hard Society as one without love—where everyone takes care of himself, where people use one another to satisfy their desires, but do not get involved with one another, because they do not want the responsibilities that go with permanent or deep relationships . . ." she wrote in *Vogue*. "It is a society characterized by separateness between rich and poor, between whites and blacks, between an intellectual elite and the unlearned masses, where both individuals and blocs are concerned solely with maximizing their own comforts and enforcing their own prejudices."

Kathleen was herself in a quandary. Along with Eunice her own mother had proudly declared herself "the friend of the fetus," a stance that brought the women public castigation for being "stupid" and "inane." Kathleen had read some of Eunice's articles and interviews, but she was not ready to pick up the banner opposing abortions.

Kathleen didn't know what to believe. She wanted to experience life and come to her own decisions. She saw how privilege, be it of intellect or of wealth, could become a velvet prison, incarcerating ignorance and calling it knowledge. She loved the woman she called "Old Moms" but she saw how hopelessly remote Ethel had become from many realities of society. One day she sat talking to her mother about the importance of day-care centers for working mothers. "Okay, Kid," Ethel replied, "but if women with children have to go out to work, then let them hire a maid!" "Oh Mummy!" Kathleen groaned. Even Eunice was distant from the day-to-day life of most Americans. She trumpeted the cause of the family, yet she didn't know how to cook and had always had maids and nannies. She spoke authoritatively about birth control and abstinence. But until a Kennedy Foundation official informed her, she believed that men strapped on condoms each morning. That was her vision: millions of men heading off to the office or the plant each morning, as ready for play as for work.

Kathleen couldn't look simply at her mother and aunt for her own way. Kathleen's own brothers were searching for meaning too, but the road in the family had divided long ago. For her brothers drugs had begun as a great, unfettered adventure, their initiation into a land beyond that traveled by the men of their father's generation. Kathleen had no mentor like Lem Billings, who devoted himself to Bobby, doing drugs with him and traveling with him, including a wildly dangerous journey down the Apurimac River in Peru along with David, Chris Lawford, and a journalist chronicler.

Kathleen had her own adventures too, but they were of a different sort. She couldn't stand the abstract intellectualism of Cambridge. One summer she went on an archaeological dig in Greece. Another summer she traveled to Alaska to work teaching in a Head Start program. She was a natural outsider who felt uncomfortable with some of the dominant themes of her generation. She was painfully aware that at Radcliffe she was part of an American elite, segregated from the needs and aspirations of most Americans.

The women's movement was becoming the kind of energetic political and cultural force it had not been since the suffrage days when Rose had been young. Kathleen's life in the Kennedy family might have turned her into an avid feminist, but there was part of her that didn't go fully along. Her mother had brought her up to be a socially conservative Catholic woman. "It was never expected that I would go into politics or be a lawyer, or have a job, or do any of those things," Kathleen reflected. "It was not even dreamed about, talked about, thought of. It wasn't in the realm of possibility."

Years later Kathleen could look back and see that she "was lucky to be in a situation after women's liberation that allowed people to dream differently than they would have otherwise been able to." As a college student she was deeply torn between her belief that she could be and do anything her brothers could do, and her realization that she wanted to have a family. It was difficult for her to reconcile these two ideas. "I guess I'm a big advocate of the family," she said at the time. She had read an article by Joan Didion criticizing the "women chauvinists" who thought it more creative to be a potter than a wife and mother, and she agreed completely. "I'm glad women are working hard in politics," she said, "not just giving coffees like Mummy used to do. None of the girls at school want just to get married. They have a good feeling they can be anything today, not just a teacher or a secretary. What a pain that is, though, wondering who am I going to marry."

Kathleen had a very good idea of whom she might want to marry. His name was David Townsend, and he happened to be her tutor and mentor at Harvard. David was four years older than Kathleen. He was a sincere, quietly brilliant young man with a shyly ingratiating smile, full of an intellectual introspection that to those outside the academic world looked like a daze of befuddlement. To David, though, ideas were not pallid substitutes for life, but life itself. David, like Kathleen, was a deeply questioning Catholic, with the kind of moral concerns that made it unthinkable to date a student over whom he had academic authority.

For all David's brilliance, he was a hopeless naïf when it came to women and the complex games of romance and mating. Kathleen had an idea of stunning audaciousness. She had been reading Mark Twain's *Life on the Mississippi* as part of her course work. She thought about retracing the journey, only it would not be Huck and Tom on the raft, but David and Kathleen. David agreed to the summer journey, unaware that he would be embarking on two great uncharted adventures, only one of which was taking place on the Mississippi. "I didn't say so but the reason I did the trip was because I had a crush on David," Kathleen admitted. "He was very straight and to my great dismay didn't think you should go out with your student. And so I tried to think of a way to get to him. And he had a girlfriend. So I thought, 'What can I do? Well why not suggest that we float down the Mississippi?' And so we built a raft."

And so in the summer of 1972, Kathleen, David, and three other friends set off on a five-hundred-mile journey down the Mississippi. "I wanted to get away from all that talk, talk, talk," Kathleen recalled. "I loved sawing that raft. I even liked the river mud." It was indeed a great adventure. In the languid July days the twelve-by-twenty-foot-long raft floated south, but when storms came up the tiny craft tossed and turned, heaving their belongings overboard. Captains of the great river barges seemed to take pleasure in running the raft down, considering it great sport nearly to cut it in two. The other great adventure of the summer was equally a success, for by the time the raft reached its journey's end in Louisiana, David and Kathleen were a twosome.

Kathleen arrived at the 1972 Democratic National Convention in Miami in blue jeans, her luggage a cardboard box held together by a rope. If not for Chappaquiddick, this would have been Ted's year for the nomination. Even with that onus hanging over him, he probably would have been the Democratic candidate, a prospect that Rose had found frightening. When she had read in Gail Cameron's 1971 biography of Rose that she had a "burning desire" for her youngest son to become president, she had written in the margin "NEVER." She was so glad that he had said no, so glad that Ted did not have the monumental ambition for the White House that had motivated his older brothers. "I don't want him to be president," Rose said. "I couldn't stand another one. There is always a chance. You have kooks around right at this house in Palm Beach. They come up to stare and they come up to look for him. I mean you can't tell what it is in these people's minds. People have said to me 'Don't let him run.' I mean it is not a question of courage. It is just a question of losing another son as far as I am concerned. Then having all of these children left without any father. You have eleven of Bobby's children left without any father. A man who is president of the United States can't give very much time to his nephews and nieces."

It was McGovern's turn then, but when his vice-presidential choice, Senator Thomas Eagleton, resigned after admitting to shock treatments for manic depression, Sarge was chosen to take his place. Suddenly the Kennedys were again in the midst of a presidential campaign.

Eunice had always put her brothers before her husband in politics, but this was Sarge's race this time, even if he was McGovern's seventh choice. Eunice made a few campaign junkets on her own, but for the most part she traveled with her husband crisscrossing America in a marathon of fifteen-hour days. Eunice sat behind Sarge when he spoke, and walked beside him on the streets of American cities. Sarge was an indefatigable spokesman for a renewed liberalism. If his patrician manner and tailored suits seemed off-putting to many Americans, he won voters with his sincerity and enthusiasm. For the most part, however, it was a dispirited, dispiriting race, McGovern at times turning the clarion call of liberalism into a whine, and Nixon brilliantly manipulating the fears and doubts of millions of Americans who once had been Democrats.

As the polls predicted the worst Democratic loss in modern history, Sarge prophesied that the McGovern-Shriver ticket would win on a massive upswing in support that only he had detected. "He is tearing through the countryside telling Democrats that it's not all over," wrote newspaper columnist Mary McGrory. "To rouse his audiences he does everything but administer open-heart massage."

Through all this, Eunice sat observing the Democratic debacle. At the age of fifty-one, Eunice had the leathery face of a sailor, her face full of lines and wrinkles that she was not ready to camouflage with elaborate makeup or the black magic of cosmetic surgery. Although on the campaign trail she sometimes wore her Parisian designer clothes, albeit with a button missing or her slip showing, for the most part she had relapsed into such unconcern about dress that her more fashion-conscious friends considered it an achievement when her shoes matched. She always ran until she could run no more, but as the days of the campaign wore on, even she exhibited strain and fatigue, her eyes bloodshot, her shoulders slumped.

In mid-October, in Baltimore, Eunice attended a beer party for state Senator Joseph Staszak. Eunice was a Democrat the way she was a Catholic, eternally wedded to its verities. To her a man like Staszak, who had just announced that he was supporting Nixon, was a political traitor. She could hardly abide the sight of this room festooned with banners and posters emblazoned DEMOCRATS FOR NIXON. She boldly marched up to the stage, took a microphone, and started to speak to the nine hundred guests. "Good afternoon," she began. Eunice had not even gotten into her pitch for Sarge and McGovern when John Jakubik, a Democratic committeeman, tried to yank the microphone out of her hand. "I haven't finished yet," she said, and wrested the microphone back.

"I'm from a proud Irish family and I know you're proud of your heritage," she said, her voice barely carrying to the back of the hall.

"I came here to dance not to listen to this garbage," a man shouted.

Eunice finished her little speech and left. Eunice couldn't help but be discouraged at the failure of Americans to understand her husband's message. "It's just the mood of the country right now," she rationalized in mid-October. "They're not listening to anyone."

On election day Eunice played a marathon game of touch football on the great lawn of Timberlawn, the teams including her children and friends, campaign staffers, and journalists who had covered the long campaign. That evening she sat on the sofa, her face emotionless. "This will be quite a night," she said. "The night the Kennedys lost."

That was the only murmur of discouragement she allowed herself, and she was soon up bounding around. She had a cocktail party and dinner to host. After that she sat next to Sarge listening to some skits making fun of the campaign.

Eunice was not immune from the gentle ribbing. She was presented with the "Staszak Award," a microphone symbolizing her tug of war in Baltimore. During McGovern's concession speech, the gathering turned somber. A campaign was a life compressed into a few weeks—friendships, love affairs, jealousies, passions, heroes and goats, careers made and lost—and then suddenly everyone packed up and it was gone. The guests left, and journalists went to new assignments, the politicos on to new candidates and new campaigns, and Eunice turned her attentions where they always were: on tomorrow and not yesterday.

25
"Don't Tell Mother"

*T*he Kennedy women did not spend the long summers together at Hyannis Port any longer. Jean and Steve had sold their place and Pat was often in Europe or off somewhere else, and it was a memorable event when the three sisters got together. One evening Rose and her daughters were sitting over dinner in the old family house. The long dining room table was large for the room, and with the Atlantic Ocean outside, there was a feeling of being on a ship crossing, lost somewhere in the midst of time.

There had been so many memorable moments over the years at this table, and the conversation turned, as it often did, to sweetly tempered recollections. Each sister had her stories to tell, and they laughed until they thought they could laugh no more, remembering one wondrous moment after another. "What more could you have, Mother?" Jean exclaimed, over the laughter. "Your daughters all around you like this and all of us laughing and having such a good time."

"My sons," Rose said softly. "My sons."

Rose knew that most of her life was in the past, and now in her eighty-first year she decided to write her autobiography. She was proud that she had received more than a million-dollar advance from Doubleday, the money to be given to the Joseph P. Kennedy Jr. Foundation. The family took the project very seriously, hiring Robert Coughlan, a talented, stylish writer, to work with her. Coughlan rented a home near the estate in Palm Beach. Every morning during the winter of 1972, he arrived at the house at precisely ten o'clock to work with Rose in an office that had been set up in Joe's old bedroom. Then for two hours she spoke about her life into Coughlan's tape recorder, as the author occasionally prodded her with questions. Rose had never talked so much about her life before to anyone, and it came pouring out of her in great waves of memory. Rose had endured in part by never thinking much about the past. To relive her life for this book, she had to journey back through regions in which she risked running emotionally aground. For Rose it was an act of disciplined will to sail back through her life, skirting the shallows, warning Coughlan away from the dangerous shoals of memory.

"Mr. Coughlan, I think it's time for a swim," Rose said every day exactly at noon. "Would you like to go?"

"Mrs. Kennedy, that would be delightful," Coughlan inevitably replied.

Coughlan took Rose's arm as they walked down the stairs to the beach. "Watch your step, Mr. Coughlan," Rose said.

"Mrs. Kennedy, may I help you in the water?" Coughlan asked.

"Oh thank you, Mr. Coughlan," Rose answered, taking the writer's elbow. She swam for fifteen minutes. Coughlan helped her out of the water, and then she went upstairs for her lunch.

"I think Rose realized that she had had an extraordinary life," Coughlan said. "She felt image conscious and wanted to get things right. That plus a very severe case of vanity made her decide to do the book. I think that part of it was mythmaking. She wanted to keep the myth going. Part of her life she had blocked out, a kind of mental and emotional amnesia, a kind of self-hypnosis.

"It's a tangled thing, her life. Nothing was cut and dried and easy. The circumstances. The psychological convulsions. All of that. I think she handled the thing pretty well with a certain degree of hypocrisy or what you might call understanding. She didn't want to bust up the family. She liked Joe. She admired Joe. She had brains enough to know he wasn't the perfect husband but he was a pretty damn good father, and she respected him, I think. She was a very competitive person."

Rose presented to Coughlan the image of a self-contained, self-controlled matriarch, a woman of persistent, impenetrable civility and emotional control. He did not see what she was like after he left, clutching her loose-leaf notebook, remembering details of half a century and quickly jotting them down, or noting some change or other. "She relived every damn page of it," Connor said. "And it hurt a lot to remember each individual detail. I mean that book was written from the heart."

Rose called the book *Times to Remember*, and that was what

she wanted it to be, a selective recollection. Since Joe's death she had developed a wickedly subtle sense of humor that on occasion she allowed Coughlan to see. One day in January of 1972 the author showed Rose a passage in which he described her as always calm and composed and never complaining.

"That was a great mistake," Rose exclaimed. "There were a lot of things I'd like to complain about and now I don't. I'll ruin my reputation if I start to complain, so I rather resent that. I suppose I can start. They'll say 'She didn't complain when her husband was alive, but afterwards she made up for it.' "

Almost none of Rose's humor made its way into the massive manuscript that a year and a half later was read by the entire family. The Kennedys got together one summer day in Hyannis Port to go over the text, each with marked-up pages. They criticized the pages not as if it were their mother's life there, but as if they had the right to burnish the family images until they gleamed. Eunice didn't like the fact that there was a lot in the book about maids and governesses. That was not the image she wanted of her family. She didn't like her mother quoting Rosemary's letters so much; she was sure that the nuns had helped her write them, and they made Rosemary seem too normal. She thought there was too much about Rose's father and not enough about her parents' marriage. Eunice showed the manuscript to her friend Barbara Walters, the television journalist, who had her own comments and criticisms. Pat felt there was too much on Gloria Swanson and her mother often sounded too negative and apologetic. "Don't put yourself down," she wrote in the margin of several pages. Jean didn't want her mother to talk about her father being absent at their children's births; she felt that would give Steve the idea that such behavior was appropriate. Ted was most worried about political matters. He wanted it made clear that his "Dad cannot be blamed for misreading Hitler's intentions." Moreover, he wanted his mother to say that "perhaps one of the granddaughters might one day be in the Senate."

Coughlan listened to Ted and Eunice picking away at his work, and then at Rose sitting there silently looking so tiny and fragile in her chair. "Mrs. Kennedy, this is *your* story," Coughlan remembered saying. Rose said nothing and Coughlan had the feeling that Rose "was the captive of her family."

These were not Rose's words on the paper either, and in the weeks that followed she had her own extensive list of changes.

She wasn't about to talk about "Ted's emotional turmoil" after Chappaquiddick, problems with her eyes, her "chronic digestive activity," or paragraphs where she went on too effusively about Ted. All that had to be excised.

Coughlan finally finished the book, and just as it was going into galleys, he had appendicitis and was hospitalized. Although he had been working with Rose for two years, he received not one phone call, neither from Rose nor from anyone in the family. Weeks afterwards when he received a finished copy of the book, he discovered that even more material had been cut out. He noticed too that someone had added a few pages of religious devotions to the ending.

Times to Remember was a best-seller in several countries, and it brought Rose fame she had not known before. For Rose, the book had been an immense emotional strain. Afterwards, when she returned to Palm Beach, Connor thought that she had dramatically aged and was never quite the same again.

In November of 1973 Kathleen stood beside David Townsend wearing a long white dress in Holy Trinity Church in Georgetown. For all her sixties bohemianism, Kathleen had accepted the idea of a traditional wedding. She had bridesmaids, wedding bouquets, four-year-old Rory and six-year-old Douglas as ring bearers, and her Uncle Ted to give her away. Her mother's friend Andy Williams sang "Ave Maria," as five years before he had sung at her father's funeral. The wedding had its own untraditional touch as well; everyone sang "When Irish Eyes Are Smiling," everyone from her aunts, her cousins, to Grandmother Rose. Afterwards twenty-two-year-old Kathleen and twenty-six-year-old David departed for the reception at Hickory Hill in the rumble seat of a borrowed 1932 Packard.

Of all the friends and relatives, only Ted did not go to Hickory Hill, but drove back to Georgetown University Hospital where he and Joan had spent the night. Earlier that morning surgeons had removed the cancerous leg of twelve-year-old Ted Jr. just above the knee. At the hospital, Joan sat waiting, suddenly a woman of somber sobriety.

"I would get there at nine in the morning," Joan recalled. "Ted would come later. Little Teddy had to prepare for big Ted, to be on stage. He had to be strong for his father. He had to be a man for his father. He had to be a Kennedy. The whole Kennedy philosophy is not to dwell on your pain, and for god's sake don't be introspective, don't feel sorry for yourself. Ted would bring in the whole front line of the Washington Redskins and they would slap little Teddy on the shoulders and say 'tough guy, you're going to be fine.' And in the afternoon big Ted would parade all these dignitaries and nurses and this stream of people through the room to meet little Teddy. Ted really believed that we can't let the kid have one moment to himself to rest. He should be kept entertained. And this went on until finally about five or six days later little Ted said, 'I'm so tired but I can't tell Dad.' And so I had to do it.

"My whole marriage I was put in the position of being the spoilsport, but I did it for my children. I promised I wouldn't tell Ted that his son was tired, that he just wanted to watch TV. Ted got mad at me and said I was no fun, that I didn't want my son to have a good time. I had to take it. I guarded the door and I was the traffic cop. When little Teddy was going through the chemotherapy, I would stay with him and he would barf all over me. But I wasn't a very popular lady. Even Ted's sisters didn't understand. I've never told anyone how hard it was. It was awful. Ted was doing what he knew how. He thought he was doing a good job. My son was intimidated by his father. With me Teddy Jr. could feel sick, he could cry and fall apart and be a baby and I would hold him in my arms. But he wouldn't let anyone else know that. He was a Kennedy."

For Joan and Ted that anguish continued not simply during the operation, but for Ted Jr.'s eighteen months of chemotherapy. Whatever weaknesses Ted had as a husband, he was a profoundly caring father. Ted flew with his eldest son to Boston on weekends once a month and sat with him at Boston Children's Hospital. Often he slept in the chair next to his son's bed, waking up to give Ted Jr. his medication. He learned how to use a hypodermic. That way he could give Ted Jr. his injections and get him out of the hospital earlier. "There are times of real despair," Ted Jr. recalled, "where you think it would be better to live with the disease than to go through one more session. In the midst of them you think to yourself, 'I'd rather die.' But that's when my father and my friends were so important to me. They were always there, and that presence was enough to get me through."

Ted Jr. was a Kennedy male, and he had this image of his time of illness as one of masculine bravado that could have been scripted for a Hollywood war film, brave comrades facing dangers. He forgot that someone else had been there for much of the time, and that someone else was his mother.

"It's strange, but for some reason in times of crisis and expectation I could rise to the occasion and not take a drink," Joan said. "But then the show is over, and you are left with no goal to go back to and you feel desperately let down and un-needed. . . . I was in okay shape while he [Ted Jr.] was in the hospital. I was the mother by the bedside. But as soon as he was well and back in school, I just collapsed. I needed some relief from being so damn brave all the time."

Joan's alcoholism had become serious enough to warrant intense discussion within the family. "When I started having a drinking problem in the early seventies, Eunice would come out to the house and talk to me," Joan remembered. "It was a time when nobody in the family would talk about it, and only the people in the family were aware of it. Eunice was sympathetic to me. She knew how her little brother Teddy was probably being unfaithful to me, and she knew how much that hurt me and that probably contributed to my wanting to anesthetize myself. And she was very supportive. But Jackie was very good too. I could talk to Jackie. She was a real confidante, very sympathetic. When you think about it we had a lot in common. We were both married to attractive Kennedy men who were in politics and who were womanizers."

Joan had been taught all her life to live by her beauty, through her beauty, and with her beauty. That was what she brought to the Kennedys, to Ted and the others, what they paraded before the public. And now with Ted's endless involvements, she had begun to doubt even that which she had never doubted before. She thought that maybe she wasn't sexy, not sexy the way Ted's women were sexy. She began to dress more flamboyantly, calling attention to her splendid figure, advertising her beauty. She wanted to make Ted want her and need her. She went on trips to New York where she flirted with other men, hoping that once he saw what other men saw he would not wander so far from the home. She hoped that her scheme might work, but when she returned home from one of her trips she could smell the scent of a woman in her marital bed.

The Kennedys were desperately worried that Joan's condition would become public knowledge; the alcoholism that they could no longer deny to themselves they at least would deny to the world. Ted's associates treated Joan like a recalcitrant child who had to be perpetually watched over. They found a psychiatrist priest who flew down each week to Washington to meet with Joan. "As both a priest and a psychiatrist, they were doubly sure he wouldn't say anything," Joan reflected.

Joan had several friends who were recovering from their addiction to liquor thanks to Alcoholics Anonymous. The program was anathema to the Kennedys, for Joan would be expected to stand up and talk about her problem in front of other members. Joan was so desperate that she didn't care what Ted and the others thought. She arranged for a meeting with Del Sharbutt, a Washington broadcaster and prominent member of the organization.

"They have council meetings of all the Kennedy folks, and they talk about what are they going to do about me as if I'm a nonentity," Joan confided. "They don't want any part of AA. That means public to them. And of course all I want to do is go to AA. They say no, you'll do it with this priest psychiatrist. I talk to him and all I do is wait until he leaves to go into my closet and get a bottle of vodka."

Christmas was the longest holiday of the year. The memories of Christmases past resonated through the great empty house in Palm Beach, memories of days when there was not an empty room, the days filled with laughter, discussions, and endless good times. This year Ethel had agreed to come down with her children. Rose knew that she would not be alone and the home would echo with laughter and good times. She directed her secretary to buy gifts for her grandchildren and she helped to wrap the presents. She told Connor to go out and buy a big Christmas tree, and he returned with a ten-foot-tall tree that was set up in the living room.

Three days before Christmas Rose called Connor. "Are you working tomorrow, Jim?" she asked.

"No, Mrs. Kennedy, you know I'm taking a few days off to be with my family."

"Well, I'd like to ask you a favor, Jim. I want you to take my Christmas tree and find some needy place that needs it. And I want you to find someone who would like those presents."

"What's wrong, Mrs. Kennedy?"

"Ethel's not coming. They decided to go skiing in Colorado."

For all the much-heralded closeness of the Kennedy family,

Rose was often alone. Relatives and family friends who visited the Kennedy homes in Hyannis Port and Palm Beach were startled by what an isolated life Rose was living. Her nephew Charles Burke spent more time with his aunt than he ever had. "I think she welcomed us because her children were all involved in other things and were too busy," Burke said.

In his last years Joe had been treated as well as any ailing king or Arab prince; in comparison outsiders thought that the aging Rose was living shamefully. "They weren't going to spend the money to give her the kind of care she deserved," reflected Herbert Kramer, who was involved with both the foundation and the Special Olympics. "When I went down there to Palm Beach, I was just appalled. First of all the house was coming apart, and second of all she had nobody taking care of her except for a secretary and a bunch of old ladies."

It was Rose herself, however, who was niggardly when it came to maintaining her homes. Like many aging people, she saw her surroundings as they once had been, not noticing that the decor had become threadbare, the fixtures decrepit, and there was still no air conditioning. The historic family photos were set among cheap plastic flowers. Yet any dramatic renovation would have hauled away what she considered part of her own self. She wanted no nurses or enlarged staff, symbols of increasing dependency.

Rose continued writing checks to relatives who beseeched her for funds. She still took her twice-annual trips to the fashion houses of Paris. If money wasn't spent on something that was going to show, she considered it a waste. When she returned from Paris, Barbara Gibson, her secretary, wanted to have a limousine waiting, but Rose insisted on taking a cab. "Mother's saving all her money for her relatives so they can ride around in limousines after she's gone," Eunice remarked.

Rose's daughters had their lives filled with obligations, and at Palm Beach it was Ted who made the most extraordinary efforts to visit his mother. He spent one New Year's Eve not with Joan and his children, or one of his mistresses, but waltzing his octogenarian mother around the dance floor at the Poinciana Club in Palm Beach. Connor recalled, "Whenever he could, he got down here to see his mother. I mean he would go out and party, don't get me wrong. But I mean this was usually after his mother had gone to bed. And he would bring girls to the damn house and Rose wouldn't even know the damn girls were in the damn house. But the Senator came down mainly to see his mother. I mean, he really loves his mother. He cherishes her. I mean, he's the baby."

Since Joe's death Rose had begun flying out to Wisconsin to visit Rosemary. Her eldest daughter was the great unrelieved tragedy of Rose's life. In Rose's mind, her departed sons never grew old. Joe Jr. would always be a brave young lad; Jack his witty, vital self; and Bobby, impassioned, brimful of life. Rose had youthful images of Rosemary too, teaching her tennis on the courts at Hyannis Port, standing with her as she and Kick prepared to be presented to the King and Queen, watching as Jack and Joe Jr. took their pretty sister with them off to a dance at the Wianno Yacht Club.

As Rose entered the little house at St. Coletta's, she was confronted with a Rosemary who was not anything like these memories. Although the operation had severely limited Rosemary's intelligence, she was not a simple, gentle child eternally destined to be five or six years old. She was not a child at all but a tall, hulking woman of emotional complexity far beyond whatever formal intelligence was left with her. For those who had known her before the operation, her face could be a haunting vision, her eyes deep set, her once glorious smile looking more like a grimace, her hair thick and black, with the unlined skin of a woman half her fifty-some years. She still had remnants of the Kennedy physiognomy, a prominent chin and sharply etched features, but at first glance no one would have recognized her as a Kennedy. Rose had always harped on Rosemary to lose weight, but she had grown into a muscular, hefty woman, who at five feet eight inches tall physically dominated the diminutive Rose.

In the quarter century since Rosemary had arrived, her little house on the grounds at St. Coletta's had become her only home. She had been brought up in a family where achievement was the only norm. She had become, in the words of Sister Sheila Haskett, the chief administrator, no longer "goal oriented." Instead, "her whole life is wrapped up in doing things she liked, like taking trips into town."

At St. Coletta's in what the nuns called "the Kennedy cottage," Rosemary lived far better than the other residents. Rosemary, like her brothers and sisters, had her own trust fund that provided for her generously. Two nuns lived with her, constantly overseeing her activities. She had a dog and a car that the nuns used to take her for rides in the countryside.

Often Rosemary and a sister walked a hundred yards up the gravel road to Alverno House. Here lived the residents who were unable to move out in the community and for the most part would spend their entire lives at St. Coletta's. The residents went to mass every morning and had various kinds of play activity and physical therapy, but they spent much of their day merely sitting around, watching television or staring at the walls.

Rosemary enjoyed visiting Alverno House. One of her friends, a woman named Gloria four years her junior, was in some respects similar to Rosemary. Gloria had been a precociously talented musician with hopes of becoming a concert pianist. Then on the night of her senior high school prom, she had been in an automobile accident, leaving her severely brain damaged. Gloria had been at St. Coletta's since then. Rosemary loved to listen to Gloria play. She played only music she had learned before her accident. At mass Gloria recited by heart a passage from the Scriptures, and then could not find her way to her pew.

In the mid-1970s, Rose invited Rosemary to Palm Beach for the first time and to Hyannis Port as well. For Rose it was an extraordinary decision. "Her mind is completely gone," Rose had told Coughlan in 1972. "And we sent her to Wisconsin because if she were here there would be a lot of discussion and a lot of comparisons. I have thought of bringing her back sometimes but I don't think I will because she is used to it out there."

When the nuns told Rosemary that she was going home for a visit, she said the word "Bronxville." That was home to her, the home she remembered before the operation. "European" was another word she kept saying, the word some strange talisman of memory.

Connor waited at West Palm Beach Airport to greet Rosemary and the two nuns who accompanied her. "When we returned they opened the gate and let us back into the estate," Connor recalled. "Rosemary came bouncing up the steps there and she said, 'Mommy. You momma, me baby.'" Bob Davidoff, a Palm Beach photographer trusted by the family, was in the home that holiday. "I saw them in the living room doing the Christmas picture," he recalled, "and they were trying to decide whether to put Rosemary in it because she was so fidgety."

Rosemary did not take easily or well to the new or unfamiliar, and she could not stand when someone crept up behind her. She could tell who felt comfortable with her, and those were the people with whom she developed rapport. Caroline had a special way with her aunt, and in the winter of 1975, she and Maria Shriver went for ocean swims with Rosemary.

As Rose grew older it was easier by far to have Rosemary make annual trips to Palm Beach and Hyannis Port than for Rose to travel to Wisconsin. For Rose these visits were the most emotionally harrowing of times. Days before, she became nervous, unable to relax or settle into her routine. During her oldest daughter's stay, Rose appeared perpetually on edge.

One evening at Hyannis Port Rose went up to her bedroom, leaving Rosemary sitting in a replica of Jack's White House rocking chair. She turned back a last time to look at her daughter sitting in the darkness, the room lit only by the light of the television screen. Near Rosemary sat a nun from St. Coletta's and Kerry McCarthy, Rose's great-niece.

A while later Rose came down the stairs. "I couldn't sleep without giving Rosie an extra hug," Rose said. Rosemary did not even look up. Rose walked behind the rocking chair, ran her fingers through Rosemary's black hair, and kissed her on the back of the neck. Rose slowly walked up the stairs and a few minutes later returned to stand behind Rosemary, who was rocking and shuffling cards. Rose was in her mid-eighties, a tiny wisp of a woman, looking in the half light a child behind the massive figure of Rosemary.

"Kerry, look at Rosie's hair," Rose said, as she ran her fingers through the hair of her eldest daughter. "She doesn't have any gray in it. Rosie? . . . Rosie? . . . Rosie, do you remember Aunt Loretta, Kerry's grandmother?" Rosemary stirred with some vague sense of recognition. "Rosie . . . Rosie . . . Rosie . . . Remember when you learned to write and you wrote Aunt Loretta from England? Remember that, Rosie? Remember?"

Rose began to sob uncontrollably. Kerry led her back upstairs and Rosemary sat there in the shadows shuffling and rocking, shuffling and rocking.

These visits were no tribulation at all to Eunice. She had watched over Rosemary since they were little girls, and she watched over her still. She visited St. Coletta's far more frequently than anyone else in the family, at one point almost every six weeks. She took Rosemary with her to places she

had not gone before. In October of 1975 while Eunice was in
Chicago for a dinner, she invited her elder sister down to the
Illinois metropolis along with two nuns. She planned to spend
a long Sunday holiday with Rosemary, walking along Lake
Michigan, and having lunch together. Eunice took Rosemary
to eleven o'clock mass at St. Peter's. Afterwards, Eunice
was standing in the vestibule perusing some religious books
when she realized that fifty-seven-year-old Rosemary was
gone. Rosemary had blended into the crowd of shoppers and
tourists, disappearing into the crowd with her slow, determined
walk. Not only was Rosemary unable to say her full name and
address, but she had no identification. Eunice flagged down a
patrol car, and for the next several hours frantically scanned
the streets, her search aided by foot-patrol officers. Not until
almost five hours later did Peter Nolan, a television reporter,
see Rosemary looking into store windows five blocks from the
church.

"Are you looking for Eunice?" Nolan asked.

"Yes," Rosemary replied, though she appeared perfectly
content to go on looking in the store window.

On Rosemary's visits to Hyannis Port, Palm Beach, or the
Shrivers' home in Maryland, Eunice integrated her into the life
of the family, taking great joy in the smallest sign of recognition. She was Rosemary's true guardian, keeping a vigilant eye
on her treatment at St. Coletta's, overseeing her medical care.
She believed that everyone could do more with their lives than
they did, everyone, and she pushed Rosemary to swim and to
walk and live a more active life. She spent an hour or more
with Rosemary in the swimming pool, her sister giving no
more recognition to Eunice than a smile or a nod.

Eunice took her older sister everywhere with her, from daily
mass to family dinners, from treks on the beach to weekend
sails with the family. Once she headed out with her teenaged
son Anthony and his friend, Brad Blank, on the Shrivers' motorboat, *Lucky 7*, for a jaunt over to Baxter's, a fish restaurant.
As a little boy Anthony had been a pest at the summer camps
at Timberlawn, but he had long grown out of that, and no one
in the family had a better rapport with Rosemary than Anthony. "I just find Rosemary to be a very moving and inspirational figure," Anthony said. "It's hard to describe. But I think
her smile and her efforts just from point A to point B, as little
as that may be, it's very motivational and energizing and it re-

orients you back to sort of the presence of your heart in a lot of ways."

The group was having lunch when it began to rain. The judicious plan would have been to wait the storm out, but that was not Eunice. It was no easy task getting Rosemary into the boat and settled down. "Damn, Anthony, get away from me," Rosemary said, one of her few sentences. By the time they headed out in the twenty-five-foot boat a great driving storm had fallen on the ocean. Anthony steered the boat, pressing onward. Brad tried to shield Rosemary's face from the fierce onslaught. But it was hopeless, and they seemed lost in the trackless storm. Anthony was an able sailor, and suddenly the dock appeared out of the gray.

"You're just like Jack and PT-109," Eunice told her youngest son.

Blank cringed for a moment, finding the comparison corny to the extreme. But the more he thought about it, the more he sensed how Eunice was trying to motivate her son, and make him feel part of an epic and ongoing history.

In these years of slow decline, Rose suffered from the fear not of death but of lingering, debilitating disease. She did not sleep well, her rest consisting primarily of fitful naps and a few hours of sleep at night. On a few occasions she panicked, thinking that she had suffered a stroke, but she was soon her same resolute self. Rose slept fitfully, and she grew dangerously dependent on sleeping pills, using them to regulate the rhythms of her life.

Rose's life was not consumed with constant intimations of infirmity. Even as she approached her ninetieth year, she still had a youthful vanity, priding herself equally on her looks and her fame. "Sometimes when I get all dressed up and think I look rather young and glamorous, then Sarge Shriver, my fifty-seven-year-old son-in-law, shouts across the room 'Grandma' to me and I am rather discouraged, rather dispirited about it," she had told Coughlan when she was already eighty-one years old. She continued worrying about her hair, her cosmetics, and her figure, eating tiny portions of chicken and rice, often only a baked potato.

In Hyannis Port Rose grew close to her great-niece, twenty-five-year-old Kerry McCarthy, whose family had moved to Hyannis Port. In the summers during the mid-seventies, Kerry gradually began spending more time with Rose, walking with her in the afternoon, talking with her often in the house. Rose's own daughters had no interest in, and practically no knowledge of, their family history. Kerry and her mother were the family historians, and Kerry loved to talk to her great-aunt about her past.

One afternoon Kerry chanced into Rose's bedroom, where the Kennedy matriarch stood in front of a full-length mirror admiring herself in tailored blue slacks and a matching turtleneck. "I want to maintain my posture, otherwise my bust will droop," Rose said matter-of-factly before taking a disapproving look at her plump young relative. "Oh, dear child," she admonished her great-niece. "Stand up straight. Your posture's fine but I'll show you some exercises, and we'll discuss brassieres."

"Heavens, that does wonders for my ego," Kerry said.

"Don't be silly, we've all got them. We just have to help them stay where they should be."

Rose was equally aware of the power of her fame. The tour boats sailed so close to the breakwater that she could hear the guides' commentary, a sound that sometimes woke her up during her afternoon naps. Strangers, some of them obviously psychotic, showed up at the house, drawn there by some mystic need to touch Rose, to commune with the spirit of the Kennedys.

When Rose went on her daily walks, she took pleasure in seeing the frisson of excitement her presence created in tourists and passersby. She invited a family from Colorado to drive their large recreational vehicle into the compound for a personally guided tour of the house, and to camp overnight. Usually, she preferred that her well-wishers keep their distance and not pepper her with impertinent questions. She created a little speech that she would happily recite if outsiders pressed too near to her.

One evening Rose and Eunice were going for their brisk evening walk when a vehicle slowed to a near stop and trailed along with the two walking women. "I appreciate your interest," Rose said firmly, "but I have to have some quiet time and privacy and I am sure you will understand because I am getting older."

"I appreciate your interest . . ." a voice in the car began, repeating back her words to her. It was Kerry's parents, the McCarthys, and her great-nephew, Kevin, not another group of tourists. "This is not good if the only ones that are going to stop and see me are my own family," Rose insisted, her words drowned out by Eunice's laughter.

Rose considered her family a broad all-encompassing clan including the Fitzgerald and Kennedy cousins. For decades she had held them together with letters, cards, scholarships to colleges and private schools, and invitations to Hyannis Port and Palm Beach. Her own children had a far more narrow view of family, and they could be disdainful toward what they presumably considered a poor and distant relative. Jean treated relatives such as Kerry as interlopers, expected to pay for their proximity to the "real" family by acting as virtual servants.

Shortly after Kerry's family arrived in Hyannis Port, she and her brother Kevin were invited to a "Young People's Party" at the Shrivers'. Eunice was Rose's only child to be deeply concerned with holding the family together. Eunice greeted all her young relatives, and led them into the dining room. The Shriver five were here, most of Ethel's brood, Chris Lawford, and Lem Billings. The family had their own hierarchy, and Kerry had already heard some of Ethel's children taunting their cousins: "We're Kennedys, you're only Shrivers or Lawfords." As Kerry looked around the room, she observed that the teenaged Maria stood out from all the other blonde and sandy-brown-haired cousins.

"What are you all doing?" Eunice asked, as the cousins attacked their lamb chops. "Now who likes the New England Patriots? Who's in college?" Eunice was attempting to pass on her parents' tradition of quizzes over the dinner table, but she spoke so fast, and rarely gave anyone a chance to finish. The boys ran off on the nightly adventures in the streets of the village, and the girls sat there with Eunice, Ethel, and Lem.

Kerry observed that many of the young Kennedy males were deeply troubled. Ethel's three oldest sons, Joe II, Bobby, and David, along with Chris Lawford, had created the most embarrassing and public of problems. Others of the young men were obviously struggling, having lost much of the connection to everyday life.

One morning Kerry came running into the kitchen when she heard a loud argument. "Stop it!" she exclaimed to Jean's youngest son, Willie, and the cook. "You're going to upset Aunt Rose. Now what's the problem?"

"This lazy bum comes in here, it's ten o'clock, and he wants me to cook him breakfast."

"Okay," Kerry said, turning to nineteen-year-old Willie, a student at Duke University.

"Well, I'm hungry." Willie shrugged.

"For God's sake, can't you have cereal and toast?"

"Well, yeah, I guess, but I don't know how to fix it."

Kerry explained how toast was made, and pointed to the boxes of cereal in the cupboard. Willie looked at the big box of cereal with amazement. "I always thought cereal only came in those little boxes like you know in the restaurants," Willie said.

As Kerry observed the young Kennedys, especially the males, she decided to talk to Rose. "Your grandchildren are destructive," Kerry remembered saying. "They're unhappy children. They're without focus. They think their folks died, so they'll die and there really is great sadness. It comes out in a way that's so unappealing and so hard to reach."

"Why doesn't anyone tell me?" Rose asked.

"Because they always hide everything from you, Aunt Rose," Kerry replied. "You can have a fight with one of your children. And they'll say, 'I disagree vehemently with my mother, but whatever we do don't tell mother.' Aunt Rose, you're bright enough that you could have handled these things over the years, but that's always been their attitude."

Rose was shielded from much that was unpleasant, including the fact that Jackie's marriage to Onassis was ending. In its first months, the marriage had brought out much of the best in both partners—Onassis's generosity, warmth, and hospitality and Jackie's gracious style and taste and courtesan-like ability to please. Now it was bringing out the worst. Onassis, the acquisitive businessman, became bitter that he was not receiving full value. Jackie was retreating into a sanctuary of selfishness, self-regard, and emotional distance.

These were tragic times for Onassis. His son, Alexander, died in a mysterious air crash. His former wife, Athina Livanos Onassis Blandford, died of acute edema of the lung, in what was a suspected suicide. His great business enterprises stood threatened. He did not have the strength any longer to fight to maintain his empire, and he did not have the consoling wife he needed.

Onassis was a vindictive man. In New York City he had lunch at La Caravelle with Jack Anderson, the syndicated columnist. Over the meal he was circumspect, but afterwards

Onassis introduced the columnist to several of his aides who railed against his wife's extravagances, giving information that Onassis surely knew would appear in Anderson's column. He also set out to have his wife wiretapped, through his associate Johnny Meyer. "I met with Onassis and Meyer at P. J. Clarke's in New York," recalled Fred Otash, the surveillance expert who years before had allegedly wiretapped the Lawford home in Santa Monica. "Onassis sits down and orders a hamburger. He says, 'Johnny told me that you're a guy that can do this and this and this. I got a problem. I'm married to Jackie Onassis.' Of course I knew that. He says, 'I have reason to think she's fucking around and I have to find out. And keep in mind that there are Secret Service and other people around but I have access to the building.' So I said, 'Let me think about that.' I didn't want to get involved because I wasn't going to be in that area that much. But I told him I'll set it up so I put him in contact with Bernard Spindel, who was one of the best. We had a meeting. He gave Onassis the stuff and the next time that Onassis was going there, he told Onassis where to put it."

Onassis wrote a will, providing an income of not more than two hundred thousand dollars a year for his wife, a pittance when weighed against his fortune of close to a billion dollars. The dramatic divorce would take place as well, smearing Jackie's image with indelible stains. Revenge takes far more time than forgiveness, and Ari had little time left. As he sank into deeper illness, he flew to Paris to have his gallbladder removed. After the operation, he lay in intensive care at the American Hospital connected to a respirator and kidney machine. Three days later, on March 15, 1975, Onassis died.

Jackie had not been there for much of the marriage, and she had not been there at his death, arriving only in time for the funeral. Jackie kept the name Onassis, and after a lengthy legal struggle she ended with a settlement of twenty-six million dollars, leaving her a woman of independent wealth, financially free of any ties to the Kennedys.

Although the Kennedy women deferred to Ted, the family had largely become a matriarchy with Rose as the titular head and Eunice dominating her generation. Eunice, Pat, and Jean were well into middle age but they were still known as "the Girls," and so they would be considered as long as their mother lived.

Rose admired Eunice for all the good she was doing. Yet she could laugh in bewilderment at Eunice's idiosyncrasies.

Rose had been brought up in an era when a lady didn't smoke; Eunice puffed on long narrow black cigars. Rose had lived a sedately disciplined life; Eunice ran from activity to activity with all the grace of Chicken Little.

Rose and Kerry were taking their daily walk at dusk one summer day when they saw a strange apparition in front of them, a scarecrow in pants and a thick cloth coat falling below the knees. "For heaven's sakes who is that?" Rose asked.

"Mother," the scarecrow said, sounding amazingly like Eunice.

"It's Eunice," Kerry said.

"Oh, no, it couldn't be," Rose exclaimed, half laughing. "Oh, Eunice dear, who chooses your clothes?"

"What's wrong with them?" Eunice asked. "I'm cold."

"You're dressed for the North Pole," Rose said. "It's embarrassing. Oh, well, walk behind us dear. Maybe people won't recognize you."

"No, I won't," Eunice said, hurrying down the street. "You two aren't nice tonight."

Rose might laugh about Eunice's strange ways, but she knew that Eunice was a self-confident woman making a strong mark on her family and on the world. Unfortunately, Pat seemed beaten down by life. Pat did not get along with one of Rose's cooks, and she allowed that fact to keep her away from Hyannis Port, visiting usually only when the woman was on vacation. "Sometimes I just want to shake Pat," Rose confided to Kerry, "and tell her *try*, just *try*." She continued to correspond occasionally with Peter, but she said that she would never forgive him for the way he had treated Pat, blaming Peter for Pat's condition. As isolated as Pat's life appeared, Rose wrote in her diary that she hoped her own daughter would not marry again. "She's divorced," Rose said, as if that were reason enough. "And plus the fact that she is older now and a man would be fifty odd years old, and I think a man fifty odd is much more difficult than a man twenty odd."

Jean was troubled in a very different way, and she was as vocal in her distress as Pat was quiet. Rose worried about her youngest daughter's drinking and her seeming unhappiness. One day as she was swimming in the pool in Palm Beach with her mother, Jean said suddenly: "I was shuffled off to boarding school at the age of eight."

"Well, what was I to do?" Rose replied, her remarks overheard by her secretary, Barbara Gibson. "Your father was always gone, or we were having dinners at the embassy or attending formal affairs. I had no time to spend with you children."

"That's why I'm still trying to get my head on straight."

This was not some random outburst, but a persistent theme of Jean's life. It did not matter how old her mother became or how much disappointment Jean suffered, her mother was still the font of all her unhappiness. "I don't see why you continue to blame me for your problems!" she told Jean in Hyannis Port the summer of 1978, when Rose was eighty-eight years old and Jean fifty.

Jean simply could not let up. The two women were swimming in the pool in Hyannis Port when something Rose said set off her youngest daughter. "Listen, Mother," Jean said in exasperation as she got out of the pool. "It's just this type of thing that makes me so screwed up."

Afterwards, Rose talked to Kerry about the altercation. "Imagine!" Rose exclaimed, shaking her head in disbelief. "Speaking to me that way. 'Screwed up' is such a coarse expression. I told her I didn't know why after years of analysis and thousands of dollars, she was still blaming me. . . . I'm too old to have a daughter who continuously harps on old hurts."

Although Jean did not deny that she had such conversations with her mother, she had an interpretation of her comments different from both her mother's and those who overheard. "That's supposed to be funny," Jean said. "If I were really wacko, I wouldn't say that."

Rose explained to Kerry how she thought she was helping her own daughters and her nieces by sending them off to various Sacred Heart academies, giving them the same education she had received. Rose had sent Kerry's own mother off to a Sacred Heart boarding school when Mary Lou was eleven years old, and Kerry had heard the tales of lonely nights, but her mother could laugh about it with her cousins, trading stories like war veterans. Jean had been a difficult person even before the nuns got hold of her.

Rose never tolerated disruptions to her own life of persevering discipline. She went to mass each morning and sat in her favorite pew, with a clear view of the priest. No matter what the weather, she walked her three miles. She practiced her German and French. She wrote down new words that she wanted to learn. She kept a little book in which to write important thoughts or quotes. Rose had her own standards of how the family should live and behave, and neither time nor age had changed them. When she read a book in which Ted was quoted as using the word "ass," she was upset enough to write him. ("I am sure you realize it really does not look very well in print.") When he said "if I was President" in a speech, she wrote him correcting his grammar, lecturing him that he should have said "if I were President." ("The reason is the old, what used to be known in Latin as 'condition contrary to the fact.' ")

As she reached her eighties, Rose was fighting the same fight for independence that Joe had fought in more dramatic circumstances. Gibson noticed that "by 1974 the house had changed, in reflection of the personality of the octogenarian Rose Kennedy. It was dominated by routine, orderly and organized, and was somewhat closed to social activity. . . . Mrs. Kennedy . . . erected more and more barriers between herself and the frenetic flow of family life around her."

In the summer at Hyannis Port, Jean invited her mother to a party in New York City. It was hardly the most onerous of requests, but Rose turned her youngest daughter down. In 1974, Jean had started an organization called Very Special Arts to involve those with retardation and other disabilities in painting and crafts, and she wanted her mother to be there at an important social occasion. Again and again she called, and again and again Rose said no. "I've gone to so many parties in my life, I wish Jean would understand," Rose confided to Kerry. "I don't need that anymore."

Pat and Jean both called inviting Rose to come to Long Island to see the new weekend and summer home the Smiths had purchased to replace their house at Hyannis Port. Rose could hardly abide the idea of leaving the Cape. After several persistent requests, she finally agreed to spend three days with her daughters in New York.

The next day she returned to Hyannis Port.

"Aunt Rose, you were gone less than twenty-four hours," Kerry said.

"I don't care. The girls can come and see me if they miss me."

Jean and Pat seemed not to understand how much they drained their mother. "My daughters are nice women," she told Kerry. "However, I tire of them."

In many respects, Rose's daughters were privileged women

who could not perform part of what their mother considered the basic functions of running a home and a family. "During one period in Hyannis Port, we used to let all the maids off in one night," Rose recalled. "We'd all go into the kitchen and cook a little bit of something and sit around the kitchen table and gossip and try out something. It was a very good experience because some of them didn't even know how to cook even eggs. They'd take them out of the ice box and think they should be cooked in three minutes, which of course they weren't. Eunice was apt to be involved in telephoning or something and she wasn't there very often when the dishes were to be washed. But everyone just laughed and tasted a little bit of everything. It was just a general happy time."

In May 1973, Eunice gave a commencement address at Newton College, a Catholic school outside Boston. At this date the subterfuges of Watergate were still only partially unraveled. The most judicious voices of Washington had not yet begun to cry out for the impeachment of President Nixon, and almost no one in power spoke with the moral passion and Cassandra-like musing of Eunice in her address:

> These are most bitter days, and yet, as our leaders stand revealed, we see not evil men but shallow and pathetic men. The final charge against these men, I think, will not be their shabby deals, their frantic cover-ups. No, it will be simply that having been given the extraordinary power and opportunity to make life better in this nation and the world they scarcely tried. And to justify their selfishness, their paltry goals, they told us there was no dream, no moral cause, forget about generosity and love. Their message was grab what you can and run. Let them run now, and let us see if we can make something grow in the desert they have left behind.

For Eunice family came first, and when it came to politics that meant her brother before her husband. "Family friends insist that Eunice has always put the political careers of her three brothers ahead of that of her husband," wrote columnist Marianne Means. "In 1970, Shriver campaigned across the country for congressional candidates in hopes of sparking a presidential campaign for himself. But when he returned home, friends say, his wife was more interested in hearing about grassroots comments about Teddy than about him."

In 1975 Sarge decided that he wanted to seek the Democratic nomination for president, but first he had to go to Ted and seek his approval. Everyone deferred to Ted in the family. Not until Ted definitely told his brother-in-law that he was not running could Sarge consider entering the race. "If you're not going to run, how about me?" Sarge asked Ted in Hyannis Port in June of 1975. "I wish you well," Ted told Sarge, though his well-wishing was studiedly neutral.

Sarge had never run for public office on his own before in part because he had stepped back to make room for other Kennedys. Although Jean, Pat, Jackie, Ethel, and Rose all signed on as members of the Shriver for President Committee, they did not head out en masse onto the campaign trail. Moreover, Steve did not help run the campaign as he undoubtedly would have for Ted, to whom he had become like another brother.

Ted watched the campaign from a calculated distance. "Poor Sarge, I hope he doesn't stay in it too long because it's going to be hard on Eunice's health," he remarked within hearing of Massachusetts Congressman Paul Tsongas, a former Peace Corps volunteer who was considering supporting Sarge. Ted might display heartfelt solicitousness for his beloved sister, but he was full of the professional jealousies of most politicians, and appeared hardly able to abide the idea that Sarge might actually win.

Although Sarge campaigned vigorously, often with Eunice at his side, he was the wrong man at the wrong time. In the aftermath of Watergate, obscurity was a high virtue, and the nomination went to a man largely unknown in Washington: Governor Jimmy Carter of Georgia. Even with the family's total support, Sarge probably would not have won, but a foul taste remained in the mouths of the Shriver supporters. "Teddy didn't do shit for my father in 1976," Bobby Shriver said later with unrelieved bitterness.

Nothing in Eunice's public life meant as much to her as Special Olympics. Eunice and Sarge had a brilliant understanding of the uses of celebrity, their own and increasingly that of Special Olympics itself. They could pick up the phone and reach almost anyone in America. They talked the three television networks into giving them millions of dollars' worth of free time to make people aware of Special Olympics. They knew how to inveigle corporate sponsors to sign on, giving them an opportunity to advertise their noblesse. They invited famous athletes and Hollywood stars too, and the cameras that panned across the faces of the famous included the countenances of Special Olympians as well.

Those who attempted to work with Eunice on this noble quest sometimes found that humans were trampled in the name of humanity. She could reach down to a child at Special Olympics and play a game with her as if that moment were the beginning and end of her life. Then she could return to her office and be brutally curt with her secretary or assistant, unforgiving for the most minor lapse, unwilling or unable to praise. "I think my mother does put the fear of God in most people," reflected Maria. "She's a perfectionist. She's very demanding of herself and therefore, I think, demanding of people around her. My father has had two executive secretaries, and each one stays with him for like twenty-five years. My mother is lucky if she can keep one for two weeks."

Eunice acted at times as if being part of this noble movement were reward enough, and if people could not give full measure of themselves, they should move on. The foundation consultants and advisors learned to keep a subtle distance from Eunice, or they risked being drawn totally into her sphere, their ideas and energy dissipated, recipients of demands and requests at any hour of the day or night.

No one received more of those demands and no one was more devoted to furthering Special Olympics than Herb Kramer, the director of communications and assistant to the chairman both of the foundation and of Special Olympics International. In his previous position at the Travelers Insurance Company in Hartford, Kramer had invented the company's famous red umbrella, and he was even more full of ideas for an organization that he considered partially his own creation. He wrote most of Eunice's speeches and articles, and he was brilliantly effective in creating an exemplary image for the Shrivers and Special Olympics.

As a youth, Kramer had seen the J. M. Barrie play *The Admirable Crichton*. He had identified with the story of the noble servant, a man of enviable taste and total devotion. Eunice was as ready to play the master as Herb to play the slave, and he slipped naturally into this role with the Shrivers, wearing everything but liveried finery. Kramer had a Ph.D. from Harvard, a prima donna's ego, and he had learned to stand up to Eunice, to argue with her as did no other employee, but after his moment of temper he was again back in his little office as "The Admirable Kramer."

"The old man told them they could hire good people cheap on the strength of their name and use them and that's what they did," Kramer asserted. "I remember at the International Special Olympics Games in 1979 at Brockport, New York, I had done everything—publicity, television, everything. And during the third day I got sick. I thought I was going to die. I crawled out of there and an ambulance took me to Rochester Memorial Hospital. I had a kidney stone. And nobody came to see me. Nobody. I had to make my own travel arrangements. I landed at New York in a wheelchair. My son met me. Even then I didn't hear from Eunice or Sarge. I wrote a letter to Eunice. I said at least the aristocracy had some sense of noblesse oblige. When their servants were sick, they took care of them. I said, 'you don't even have that grace.' "

Eunice had an unflappable ability to ignore what she chose to ignore, and she treated the letter as if she had never seen it. Soon after Kramer's letter, he was back at work.

Eunice believed in the family as the moral and spiritual center of life, and she was as much a goad to her own five children as she was to the world beyond. Maria was her only daughter, and she attempted to impart to her everything she knew and believed about a woman's role in life. Eunice's older sister, Kathleen, and her youngest sister, Pat, had been the Kennedy sisters praised for their feminine beauty. And thus like her own mother, Eunice had known from an early age that she could not make her way on her looks. Her vivacious brunette daughter, however, had been the kind of baby and child whom friends and strangers constantly praised for her beauty.

Maria considered it strange sometimes the way Eunice pushed her to play boys' games, talk and argue as much as her four brothers, and drive over to Baltimore with her dad to watch the Orioles play. No one had a mother anything like Eunice, and at times Maria cringed, wishing her mother could be like all the others. When she stood outside the door at the Sacred Heart Academy waiting to be picked up after school, she watched the other mothers, impeccably garbed, dowagers of style. Eunice came roaring up the driveway in her Lincoln convertible, two of Maria's brothers and a couple of dogs by her side, her hair an unbelievable tangle, combs sticking into the back of her hair, a disheveled gypsy of a mom, and Maria thought to herself, "I hope nobody sees her."

Eunice was strict with Maria, but not, she often pointed out, half as strict as Rose had been. "I'm letting you off easy," she said, "because you know what my mother used to do. Take a clothes hanger and hit us." For four generations, Kennedy women had been obsessed with food and diet, and as Maria entered adolescence, she put on a great deal of weight. "She was about as wide as she was tall," recalled Connor. "She used to love to eat chocolate mousse cake and Coca-Cola. She'd take it in her hands and just throw it in her mouth."

Eunice saw fat as the physical manifestation of moral sloth. She could not tolerate having an overweight daughter. One day at the swimming pool at Timberlawn, Eunice and Maria were sitting with General Robert M. Montague Jr., the president of the Kennedy Foundation, and his wife, Chris, a svelte athletic woman. Eunice could hardly abide the comparison with her overweight daughter. "Why can't you be thin like that!" Eunice berated her. Even a few years later when Maria had lost a good part of her fat, Eunice still felt her daughter was overweight. For Maria's twentieth birthday, Eunice walked into a Georgetown shop and told the saleswoman: "My daughter wants a skirt that makes her look thin."

Eunice would have no moping, no excuses, no rationales, not for herself and not for her children either. "I think Mother has struggled through many, many things in her life but no one knows about it," reflected Anthony, her youngest son. "She's very, very good at covering up her problems, covering up any physical or mental anguishes she may be experiencing. People in my family, none of us really knew what her health situation was because it had never come up. And I think that has carried over to us to some extent.

"I remember when I was growing up we were never really allowed to stay home from school even if we were sick, unless we were practically dying. It used to drive me crazy because I would have friends that would get a little cold and they'd be home. I'd say, 'God, Mother, you know, even my cousins, they'd stay home from school.' And we never would stay home from school. Just never. I mean, we'd be dead. Because it was just a mentality that, 'My God, it could be worse' and because she was always over here fighting and struggling, it was never something, you know, 'if you have a little cold or a sniffle, I mean, you've got to be kidding me if you think you can stay home from school for that.' Her attitude was you need to just stick tough and move through it and everything will be fine."

In September of 1972, Caroline arrived as a sophomore at Concord Academy accompanied by Jackie driving a large yellow station wagon. Station wagons were the vehicles of choice among parents bringing their children back to the exclusive Massachusetts school, but Caroline was the only student with her own retinue of five Secret Service agents. Rose was in Paris but she wrote her granddaughter asking her to think of her as she passed the Concord Library. It was there almost seven decades before that the teenaged Rose had searched for the novels of Louisa May Alcott and had driven past in a horse and carriage.

Before Caroline's arrival an editorial appeared in the weekly newspaper calling her "probably the most adored, criticized, maligned, harried kid of this century" and implored the citizenry to "give the kid a chance to live and grow up as you would wish your daughter or niece or granddaughter to grow up." It was a message that most of the townspeople took to heart, but it was almost impossible not to take special note of the most famous fifteen-year-old student in America. "I remember this one mean-spirited person talking about how she had seen Caroline Kennedy grabbing a bunch of grapes at Anderson's Market and eating them without paying and saying, 'Who does she think she is anyway?' " said John Sheehan, a lifelong resident. "Well, I don't know of anybody who grew up in Concord who *didn't* steal a handful of grapes without getting caught." Caroline often walked across the street from the school to the Concord Library. Caroline was known by the librarians for being at times loud, whispering with her friends, treating the book-lined precincts as her social club. On at least one occasion, she had some overdue books, a crime of such felonious import that it reached the pages of the *Chicago Tribune*.

Caroline, like her cousins Maria and Kara, had a teenaged weight problem, and the same ravenous, almost uncontrollable appetite. Jackie came to visit her daughter at Concord. She took her daughter to the dining room of the Ritz-Carlton in Boston for dinner. After a hefty meal, Caroline happily contemplated the idea of dessert. "You're not going to have dessert," Jackie told her firmly. "You'll be so fat nobody will marry you." As Caroline sat there sullenly looking down at the table, she was hearing an admonition that was a familiar theme of Kennedy women. It was a warning that could as easily have been made by her own great-grandmother Josie Fitzgerald to her grandmother Rose, by her Aunt Eunice to Maria, by her Aunt Joan to Kara, as by Jackie to Caroline.

Caroline had been in the audience the day that Rose had gone on *The David Frost Show*. "The people behind me thought she was terrible," Caroline recalled. "They said she was 'dead to the world' because she was saying everybody should get out and work and help everybody else and stuff like that. They were just a little bit older than me, and they didn't like being told they should go out and work."

Rose feared that wealth and celebrity might dissipate the strength and purpose of her family. Joe II was the oldest grandson, and since the tragic accident that had left a young woman an invalid, he had seemed to straighten out. In 1976, he had run his uncle Ted's reelection campaign, a position that in the family was considered the preferred political training ground. Joe II was in his mid-twenties, an absolute neophyte in life as in politics, but he was already being approached by Massachusetts politicians to run for statewide office, perhaps lieutenant governor or treasurer.

Joe came to his grandmother's house to seek her approval. "Joe exited her home in an angry and teary state," said Kerry McCarthy. "On our walk that day Aunt Rose told me she had point-blank 'forbidden Joe' from running for office. She told him he was 'too young and inexperienced' and that he owed the voters and citizens of Massachusetts 'more maturity and training.' She continued stating that she didn't want anyone in the next generations to 'demand' support of those who had trusted in other Kennedys for generations. She also acknowledged that Joe would have his chance if he proved himself worthy. She firmly held to this dictate."

Rose rarely walked across the grounds to Ethel's house full of her noisy, unruly brood, and she rarely went to Joan's house either. On one occasion she accepted an invitation for dinner at Joan's and Ted's on Squaw Island. Joan's house was very different from Rose's. The living room, decorated in blue, white, and green, seemed to blend into the colors of the ocean out the great window. Every aspect of the evening, from the linen napkins to the dinner courses prepared by her cook, met the highest standard of entertaining.

Ted was delayed in Washington and, although there were

only family members here this evening, Joan was noticeably nervous. Just before the group moved over to the dinner table, the new German governess marched Patrick into the living room to say a proper goodnight. Patrick was a sickly looking boy, an asthmatic who at times required oxygen. Patrick broke the governess's tight grip, and ran crying toward Rose. "Grandma, Grandma," he cried uncontrollably, as the governess tried to pull the boy back.

Rose brushed the governess aside and held Patrick in her arms. "This child is burning up," Rose said, looking accusingly at Joan.

Joan, in turn, looked toward the governess. "Well, Mrs. Kennedy," the German woman said authoritatively, "the boy has just had a normal day." Rose asked enough questions to learn that Patrick's "normal day" consisted of over six hours of exercise, exertion, obligations, and demands.

"That's ridiculous!" Rose exclaimed. "This is a little child, not an Olympic trainee. He is hysterical and physically exhausted from what has been demanded of his body."

Rose insisted that little Patrick be put immediately to bed. Over dinner she turned her accusatory gaze back to her daughter-in-law. Joan was always trying to please someone, Ted, her mother-in-law, her sisters-in-law, somebody, and the German governess had been her husband's idea. Ted didn't want Patrick growing up a wimp. He thought a regimen of Teutonic discipline was just what his frail, often sickly son needed.

Rose listened to Joan and then called the governess back into the dining room. "Tomorrow, I want Patrick to rest, eat lightly, and spend a good part of the day in bed," Rose told the woman. "I'm going to tell the Senator about this, and I'm going to call tomorrow and check on Patrick's condition."

Although Ted had hired the woman, Joan was the one who always seemed to come up short, no matter how hard she tried. "Patrick was a severe asthmatic, and Ted would say, 'Joan, you're making a baby out of him,'" Joan recalled. "Patrick would go out to these exciting functions with his father and he would come back breathing so hard, and I would run for the medication and bring him into a corner and hook him up to the asthma machine and Ted would say, 'You're giving in to him.' He made it seem that the asthma was a weakness, not a disease."

When Joan was around her mother-in-law, she appeared not

simply awestruck, but frightened. Rose had a curiously ambivalent attitude toward her youngest daughter-in-law. She criticized Joan the way she did not her own daughters or Ethel. At times, she seemed jealous of Joan's still-youthful beauty.

By the standards by which Rose had lived, Joan had everything a woman needed. It was beyond her why Joan was so lacking in the stoic strength of the other Kennedy women, so unable to stand beside Ted and support him in all her son's obligations and duties. In McLean, Virginia, she had a house with a staff that included a French chef who once had cooked for the Duke of Windsor, a maid, a nurse for the children, and a social secretary. She had a marvelous home on Squaw Island, and the money and the freedom to go off traveling in Europe and elsewhere, to study piano, to go and do whatever she wanted to do.

Yet Joan drank. For years it had been the great unmentionable. "I tried to talk about it, but I was embarrassed about it," Joan said. "Everybody was embarrassed, but nobody would really talk about it." For years they had tried to pretend, though when she went off on her binges, there was no telling what might happen or where she might end up. After visiting her father she arrived drunk in Palm Beach on a bus, and was immediately flown to Washington. Another time in Palm Beach, Connor recalled finding Joan and a prominent Palm Beach man lying together in a car in the parking lot at the Kennedy estate.

Joan took great pleasure in wearing the newest and most daring fashion. In 1969 at an evening reception at the Nixon White House when floor-length gowns were de rigueur, Joan wore a silvery mini-dress. The outfit brought forth a chorus of anonymous catty comments from Republican matrons. For the Democrats, Joan had committed the unforgivable sin: She had upstaged her husband. A year later at a luncheon reception at the White House, she appeared in a silvery leather midi-skirt, black boots, and a lacy see-through blouse. The following year she created another sensation in the society pages by wearing hot pants under a short, slashed skirt for a party at the Kennedys' home.

Clothes gave Joan pleasure. If she had been living in New York or Paris, she would have been considered a style setter, not an unhappy woman on a sad quest for attention. Washington was a resolutely conservative town, where the little black dress was almost as ubiquitous as the Mao coat in Peking. Joan was a senator's wife in her mid-thirties, and as much as her friends defended her, the matrons of the capital tittered mercilessly about her costumes.

Joan was not the dumb blonde her critics thought her to be. Her outfits may have been, as Laura Bergquist observed, "small signs of rebellion" in a marriage in which she had few weapons. "That business of wearing outrageous clothes was perhaps her way of getting back at Ted and asserting her own individuality," suggested one intimate. "She had a good sense of the jugular and what mortified him."

"I would go on these trips to New York and spend time with Lenny Bernstein, people like that," Joan recalled. "I would flirt with men, trying to make Ted see that other men found me attractive, making him want me. That was as far as it went." Other friends and associates have other memories of Joan's short involvements with men, relationships fueled on liquor that she may not even remember. She told her secretary, Marcia Chellis, how she had set up a meeting in Europe with an old lover, but when she met the man in her hotel room, she was so drunk that she could hardly walk, and he greeted her with pity rather than romance.

In 1972 Joan gave an interview to *Good Housekeeping*, admitting to feeling insecure in such a powerful family and saying she was seeing a psychiatrist. She described how she was overcoming her problems and was on her way to leading a happy, fulfilling life. Later that year she told Boston's *Herald-American* that she was "bored to tears with gossip about Ted and his so-called illicit romances." She was specifically refuting stories alleging that Ted was having an affair with Mrs. Amanda Burden, a New York socialite. "Amanda was supposed to be aboard a yacht with Ted and Senator Tunney in Maine," she said. "Gossip columnists said another woman was along too. But the two women turned out to be my sisters-in-law, Pat and Jean." The presence of her sisters-in-law was hardly indisputable proof of Ted's innocence, and by now she presumably knew it. Pat and Jean were loyal to Ted, not to any ideal marriage.

As much as she publicly defended her husband, Joan was bothered by Ted's affairs. "When one grows up feeling that maybe one is sort of special and hoping that one's husband thinks so, and then suddenly thinking maybe he doesn't," Joan told one interviewer, "well, I didn't lose my self-esteem altogether, but it was difficult to hear all the rumors. And I began thinking, well, maybe I'm just not attractive enough or attractive any more, or whatever, and it was awfully easy to then say, well, after all, you know, if that's the way it is, I might as well have a drink.

"It wasn't my personality to make a lot of noise. Or to yell or scream or do anything. My personality was more shy and retiring. And so rather than get mad, or ask questions concerning the rumors about Ted and his girl friends, or really stand up for myself at all, it was easier for me to just go and have a few drinks and calm myself down as if I weren't hurt or angry. I didn't know how to deal with it. And, unfortunately, I found out that alcohol could sedate me. So I didn't care as much. And things didn't hurt so much."

Early one afternoon in October of 1974, thirty-eight-year-old Joan was driving her 1971 Pontiac GTO convertible near her home in McLean when she rammed into the rear of a vehicle waiting at a traffic light. She hit the automobile hard enough to send it into the back of another car. When she got out of the car, she kept saying how sorry she was. She pled guilty to a charge of drunk driving, and had her license suspended for six months.

Repeatedly during the next years Joan gave interviews to sympathetic writers who described her alcoholic despair in detail, and then ended by writing that Joan was on her way to recovery and a happy life. When she talked to the reporters, her hair gleamed and her makeup was impeccable. Then she would begin drinking again, and end up looking haggard and bedraggled, a shattering apparition. She would go off to a clinic somewhere, and eventually return to her home life in McLean and another reporter for another magazine would write an article about the rebirth of Joan. In one sense, Joan was acting courageously, confronting the truths of her existence in the approved psychological fashion, doing so with the approval if not instigation of Ted's advisors. Yet there still remained an unsettling aspect of self-promotion in it all, as if Joan had decided that if she could not have her husband's love she would have the world's.

In America, self-revelation was becoming a common currency, exchangable for attention and celebrity, but it was almost unthinkable for a Kennedy woman to expose herself. Rose was appalled. When she saw the latest reincarnation of Joan on the cover of a women's magazine that her cook was reading, she exclaimed: "Oh really, don't they have anyone else they can interview?" She leafed through the pages as Kerry looked on. "They always rave about how beautiful she is. Do you think she is?"

"Yes I do, Aunt Rose. She has a natural beauty. Most girls want to grow up and look like that."

"Perhaps, but I'll tell you now what I've thought about all this. I see no need for such public confessions."

In her interviews, Joan never criticized Ted. Yet to his detractors, Ted was the villain of the piece, driving an innocent young woman to drunken despair. "It may be self-evident, but the fact is that Ted Kennedy has held the reins of information," Joan argued. "I'm married to a powerful man who has control of the knowledge of the family. He's had all the power. When he was in trouble with his womanizing, he fed certain trusted journalist confidantes. He would feed them through his press secretary Richard Drayne, and the whole idea was that people would say poor Ted because she drinks. The irony is that maybe I drank because there was another mistress."

Drayne had a drinking problem himself, and may have mused melancholically to certain journalists, but it is unlikely that he did so under Ted's firm direction. Joan was the loving mother of his children, and in exposing her he would only degrade his own family. It would not do to point out that Joan's mother was an alcoholic, and thus his wife may have had a genetic predisposition to alcoholism. It would be equally unseemly to suggest that Ted was not the only one having a series of affairs.

Ted was emotionally dead to his wife, and even in public he could hardly steel himself to display the appropriate husbandly affection. He had tried everything to help her, from priests to psychiatrists, even for a time involving Luella Hennessy and her husband, George Donovan. "We helped Ted out an awful lot," Luella said. "Joan would do anything my husband would ask her to do. We played a big role in her rehabilitation. But when old Johnny Barleycorn gets a hold of you, it's tough. She has to have somebody close to her that watched, an older person who will keep her in line. She's such a sweet innocent lovely person, so bubbly and open. And people try to take advantage of that."

Within the tight confines of the family, Joan was shuttled aside, largely ignored by the other women in the family. Only Eunice reached out to Joan. "Eunice has always been so supportive of me," Joan said. "I talked to her on the phone. We've stayed in touch and I really feel close to her. She's a wonderful lady. Whenever I had problems and went and talked to her about her brother, she would listen and give me advice. She sticks up for me. That's her way. I always felt real cozy with her."

Eunice felt fiercely protective toward Joan, treating her like a wounded fawn. In February of 1976, Joan committed herself to the Smithers Rehabilitation Center in New York City. The center followed the approach of Alcoholics Anonymous; at meetings and meditations individuals stood before their peers and talked with terrible frankness about their problems, knowing that their remarks would never go beyond the group. Thus Joan hardly imagined that two other patients would sell her story to the *National Enquirer*. One of them, who called himself a free-lance writer and public relations consultant, made a point of sitting with Joan after meals, sidling up to her emotionally, getting her to confide in him. For Joan this was a nightmare within the nightmare, discovering that she was living in a house without walls.

Eunice considered the tabloids the gutter press, but she was appalled that the *Washington Evening-Star* ran a story based on the tabloid's reporting. Long ago the Kennedys had learned not to give negative stories a second life by condemning them. Eunice was so outraged, however, that she wrote an article for the *Star* railing against the paper for having "violated every canon of honorable journalism" by printing "unadulterated gossip."

Joan's alcoholism was hardly gossip. One day at their house on Squaw Island, Ted walked a journalist around the side of the house to meet his wife. Joan lay there passed out in the backseat of a car. "She was a rag mop," the reporter recalled. "I've seen drunks often enough, but what I was looking at there was the result of a two- or three-day bender. I think Kennedy just wanted me to see what he was up against. If something got printed, he was prepared for that."

The fact that Ted would show an outsider the pathetic scene was a symbol of his own emotional disengagement from his wife. He had stumbled into this marriage, and he had never given his wife the loyal romantic love that she so deeply desired. Each time Joan returned from her stays in hospitals and rehabilitation centers, she tried to make Ted the loving center of her life, but he was not there for her. He could give her everything but what she wanted, and no amount of family counseling, therapy, or psychiatric intervention could change that.

In the fall of 1977, Joan moved up to an apartment in Boston's Back Bay. It was not simply Ted and politics and Washington that were too much for her, but the demands of her children. She became a mother of the special occasion, taking little Patrick off to Disney World for a few days, spending a weekend with Ted Jr. and Kara at Squaw Island. She made it clear to her family that none of them, not Ted, not the children, were to "barge in" without calling and setting up an appointment. She signed up to work for a master's degree in education, and made room in her schedule for thrice-weekly visits to her psychiatrist.

Joan may have been "searching for herself," having "a growth experience" in the approved seventies fashion, but she was a woman of the fifties with her sense that life was anchored in husband and family. In Boston, she was a mother without her children, and a wife without her husband, and it was as if in these months she could will her life back to the innocent days when she had first met Ted. Her husband visited, but he did not stay over. "Ted comes up often, and he'll say, 'How about dinner?'" Joan said. "In Washington, when we were out for dinner, it was always with our children or my inlaws or his friends, or invariably in a large group. Now we go out alone together. It's almost like having a date."

Joan agreed to talk to Joan Braden for an article in *McCall's*. Braden praised Joan's "courage, her understanding and her self-reliance," and concluded that Joan's stay would end with her living "happily ever after." When the article appeared in August of 1978 with Joan's radiant face on the cover of the magazine, she was at home drunk. Soon afterwards she was back in McLean Hospital in Belmont, Massachusetts.

To the women's magazines, Joan's tortured pursuit of sobriety didn't seem to matter. She was being held up to the world as an icon, her face gracing the cover of one magazine after another, that heroic mask a new level of burden pushing in on Joan. In the April 1979 issue of *Good Housekeeping* Dr. Joyce Brothers, a pop psychologist, weighed in with her pithy optimism ("Admitting her addiction was only the beginning of Mrs. Edward Kennedy's courageous story"). A month later *Ladies' Home Journal* had its article by Lester David on "Joan Kennedy: Her Search for Herself." David asked Joan whether Ted still loved her. It was a question that no reporter would ever have asked Rose Kennedy, but Joan's whole life had taken on such a soap-operatic quality that she was expected to sing these arias of self-revelation. "I don't know," Joan admitted. "I really don't know." The journalist asked her if the marriage would continue. "I don't know," she said. "I know that sounds like a cop-out, but I just don't know. . . . I don't think it will end. There is no reason for it to end right now. But we don't talk about it."

Joan's marriage with Ted had reached such an emotional impasse that she communicated with him in part on the pages of magazines read by millions. Ted and his staff read these utterances and revelations like tea leaves, trying to divine Joan's emotional state, which had become crucial since, for the first time since Chappaquiddick, Ted was contemplating running for president, taking on the roundly unpopular President Jimmy Carter in the Democratic primaries. Ted had become the most powerful voice of liberalism in the Senate, a passionate spokesperson on such issues as health care and refugees, admired by his colleagues for his legislative finesse. The personal issues, Chappaquiddick and Joan, dogged him, making his potential campaign vulnerable.

In the spring of 1979, Joan flew down to a meeting with Ted and the family to discuss the possible presidential run. Ted had assembled four psychiatrists including Joan's Boston therapist, and leading experts in substance abuse from Yale, the Mayo Clinic, and California. These psychiatrists were not soothsayers, predicting Joan's future, and the best therapeutic help in America had not pulled Joan away from the bottle. "There is nothing we can prescribe that will cure her," one doctor said, as recalled by Richard Burke, then Ted's administrative assistant. "If she wants to get better, she'll get better, but she's got to do it herself. She's got to have the support of the people who love her."

If Joan could not tolerate the stress of a political campaign, her very life might hang in the balance this morning. There was another life that would stand at risk during a presidential campaign, and that was Ted's. That too was part of the equation they were all working with this morning, Ted, Joan, the entire family. He had been implored by several of his closest advisors not to run, that the risks were far too great, but he had decided he was ready to go ahead if his family agreed. He had already gone to his three children, and he had decided that they were old enough and strong enough to manage. That still left Joan.

Jean, Ethel, and Eunice sat listening to the doctors. They all knew the wages of politics, but Ted was the head of the family, and both Ethel and Jean suggested that if he ran, they would support him. Only Eunice stood back from it all. "Eunice was outspoken and clearly rallying to Joan's side," Burke recalled. "She wondered openly whether a presidential campaign was in Joan's best interest."

"I want to be president," Ted said, a statement that he never before had made with such firmness and certainty.

"I want Ted to be president," Joan said. Joan was Mrs. Edward M. Kennedy, an identity that she clung to like a life raft in a turbulent sea. If she denied him, she would be denying all the Kennedys, denying everything in her past, and Mrs. Edward M. Kennedy wanted her husband to be president. In September she would be forty-three years old. As much as she spoke bravely about her life in Boston, it was at times lonely being cut off. In Boston she had her own affairs, some of them with younger men, but nothing deep enough or romantic enough to anasthetize her pain. She had always dressed for men, and now she often dressed in extravagantly bright plumage as if that could restore her youthful bloom. Jackie often wilted under the merciless glare of publicity, but the thwarted performer in Joan thrived under the ceaseless attention, as long as the camera remained tightly focused on her visage. In her apartment on Beacon Hill, she had pretended that she and Ted were off on dates together. Now fantasy and reality were mixed together in a heady brew. She and Ted would be together again on the podium, and perhaps in the White House as president and first lady. It was hardly all fairy tale, for she still loved her husband and there was a terrible unspoken dread that Ted could be killed out there, and all the merciless burdens of the family would fall on her. Beyond that, Joan considered the campaign an opportunity to show that she was truly a Kennedy woman, a strong political partner who could carry her full share of the burdens of the campaign. "The 1980 campaign was my high water mark," Joan recalled. "I was sober. I was intent on proving to Ted and my family and to everybody that I was okay, that I was as good a campaigner as ever and that I was an asset to the campaign. I had been doing it before, but not out there by myself."

Joan was there beside Ted on October 20, 1979, for the dedication of the John F. Kennedy Library in Dorchester. The building with its whalebone white exterior and high glass walls looked like I. M. Pei's postmodern rendering of some ancient tribal lodge, a structure that would have fit almost as well at Stonehenge as it did here, standing on a lonely pinnacle of land, looking out on Boston Bay.

Although Rose had had a serious operation for a strangulated hernia a month previously, Jean had pushed her to be here today. When Eunice arrived at the house in Hyannis Port, she listened to the nurses who said that her mother might die if she attended. Eunice told her mother that she would have to hear about the dedication upon the family's return.

The three Kennedy sisters sat in the brilliant autumn sunshine along with Jackie, Ethel, and Ted. Of the twenty-nine grandchildren, only Kathleen was missing, about to deliver her second child in New Mexico. Although it was a day to honor Jack's memory, the dedication was equally a family memorial, an opportunity for Ted to display himself as the legitimate heir to his brother's legacy, and a political coming-out party for the young generation of Kennedys.

As her father's oldest child, it would have been appropriate for twenty-two-year-old Caroline to have given the major address for her generation. She was a woman of surpassing shyness, with long brunette tresses, the Kennedy visage softened into a sweet and gracious femininity. She fled publicity. It was difficult enough for her to stand up and introduce her brother, John. He had inherited both of his parents' good looks and even without the Kennedy name might have had a career in Hollywood or as a male model. Young John didn't even remember his father. For the dedication, he read a poem by Stephen Spender titled "I Think Continually of Those Who Were Truly Great."

Bobby's life was also memorialized in the library and Kathleen was the logical choice to speak. Kathleen, however, was a woman. Among Ethel's children, another son would stand up today to speak of greatness gone and greatness yet to come. Young Joe had pushed his way forward in the family and was chosen as the family representative this day. He was an intemperate young man who acted at times as if rudeness were the same thing as truth. He was upset that his father was not being treated equally with his Uncle Jack at the ceremony, and gave a wildly unrestrained speech, attacking special interests from banking to coal to oil. "One day it may be different here, but only if we acquire what my father called 'moral courage,'" he shouted, as President Carter sat there like a sinner in a lowly pew. The older generation of Kennedys looked on with acute embarrassment, while Joe II's cousins shrieked and stomped their approval.

The Jackie who attended the opening of the new Kennedy Library was a far different woman from the widow who had envisioned a glorious temple of learning and knowledge to memorialize her husband. She had gone to work as a book editor, first at Viking Press in 1975 and then two years later at Doubleday. There were those who imagined that it was nothing more than a hapless publicity stunt, the dilettantish Mrs. Onassis descending on the precincts of publishing for a few hours of excitement, Mrs. Bountiful of Culture. She worked in her modest office only three days a week, and was far removed from the endless cabals, game playing, and relentless pressures of modern publishing. But she cared deeply about her books, and had a shrewd awareness that she was the sweet bait that attracted many authors and celebrities to her publishing house.

Jackie did not give interviews, and she attempted to distance herself from the onslaught of publicity that continued to surround her. "The sensational pieces will continue to appear as long as there is a market for them," she wrote Laura Bergquist in 1978. "One's real life is lived on another private level."

There was an important event in her personal life: her growing relationship with Maurice Tempelsman. Tempelsman had endeared himself to Jackie by managing her $26 million inheritance from Onassis, reportedly managing to quadruple the sum. Maurice was the same age as Jackie. On the surface, that was all they had in common. Although he dressed in impeccably tailored suits, he looked like yet another portly New York businessman, perhaps in the garment business or municipal bonds, but he had eyes of sharp intensity, and a warmth that ingratiated him to secretaries as well as to secretaries of state, and deep interest in the world in which he lived.

Tempelsman had been born in Belgium into a Yiddish-speaking family of Orthodox Jews and had escaped the holocaust by fleeing to the United States in 1940. The millionaire businessman traveled in high circles of politics and business, and had known the Kennedys since the 1950s. He was a man who believed that discretion was among the highest of virtues. He had managed the not inconsiderable feat of maintaining a major business relationship with the DeBeers diamond cartel in South Africa, importing jewels into the United States, while developing contacts with the African National Congress led by the imprisoned Nelson Mandela.

Tempelsman, unlike Jackie's two husbands, was a man with a deep interest in culture and the arts. He spoke fluent French, and Jackie could speak that language with him. A collector of African art, he had three grown children and a wife, Lily Tempelsman. Mrs. Tempelsman maintained her Orthodox faith. It was unthinkable that he would divorce his wife of more than three decades. Instead, he became in the nomenclature of the eighties Jackie's "significant other."

"What is the present state of your marriage, Senator?" asked Roger Mudd as part of the *CBS Reports* documentary on Ted. Mudd was an old friend of the family. This was hardly the kind of question Ted had expected a few weeks before he announced his presidential candidacy. The fact was that he and Joan had separated when she moved to Boston, doing everything but sign a formal legal document.

"Well, I think it's a—we've had some difficult times," Ted began uncertainly. Since his youth his stratagem had been: When in doubt mumble. "But I think we'll have—we've—I think been able to make some very good progress and it's—I would say it's—it's—it's—I'm delighted that we're able to share the time and relationship that we—that we do share."

Mudd bored in again. "Are you separated or are you just . . . what?"

"Well, I don't know whether there's a single word that should . . . have a description for it. Joan's involved in a continuing program to deal with the problems of . . . of alcoholism, and . . . and she's going magnificently well, and I'm immensely proud of the fact that she's faced up to it and made the progress that she's made. And I'm—but that progress continues, and that . . . it's the type of disease that one has to . . . to work."

Ted was equally inarticulate in discussing Chappaquiddick, and his reasons for taking on the seated president of his own party. In the end, the program left many viewers disquieted. That was only the first of many debacles in a doomed campaign. Soon after Ted announced his formal candidacy with Joan at his side in Boston, an article appeared in *The Washington Monthly* by Suzannah Lessard titled "Kennedy's Woman Problem: Women's Kennedy Problem." The magazine was a serious policy-oriented periodical read by an elite audience.

The provocative essay was the talk of the capital, legitimizing questions about Ted's sex life and marriage that only the tabloids and gossip columnists would previously have written about.

Ted and his staff decided that Joan was too vulnerable to head out with him on the campaign trail. Instead, she stayed in Boston, where early in December she held a press conference in her apartment for a carefully selected group of reporters. In the past, Joan had frequently committed the political sin of candor. Since the campaign could not afford another debacle of the magnitude of Ted's interview with Roger Mudd, she was prepped for every aspect of her appearance. Her psychiatrist prepared a tape of what she should say about her drinking. A team of advisors peppered her with the queries she was likely to receive. Joan assimilated all of this the best she could. Her advisors were satisfied when her responses had become largely rationales she had picked up from various therapists, pat phrases suggested by aides and honed to innocuous perfection, the mix unleavened by spontaneous moments of reckless candor.

"That was ages ago," Joan told the little group of reporters when they asked her about her feelings of inadequacies as a Kennedy. "All that was out of the dark ages."

"The senator's number one love is politics," a reporter declared. "How does it feel to be second?"

"I am not," Joan replied, blushing, her hands trembling slightly. "Ask Ted Kennedy."

"What about your relationship with the senator?"

"It's better than ever," Joan declared firmly. "I have been through such an ordeal. I'm glad it's over."

The Boston Globe headlined its front-page story "JOAN STRIDES OUT OF HER DARK AGE." That was exactly the image Joan was supposed to project. A few days later she headed off with Ted on the campaign trail. She had never thought that she would now play Rosalynn to Ted's Jimmy Carter, advising her husband on policy matters, sitting in on strategy sessions. Nor did she imagine that she would be the new Nancy Reagan, who looked up gooey-eyed at the Republican front runner, and walked hand in hand with the husband she called "Daddy." Ted, however, could not even muster up the minimal public signs of affection toward his wife required in a political marriage. "The senator looked embarrassed by the whole procedure," wrote Myra MacPherson in *The Washington Post*. "He did not talk to his wife, did not touch her arm or laugh with her. . . . Even some staff members worried at how distant they seemed as a couple."

Ted's behavior proved that he was less the consummate artiste of hypocrisy than his opponents imagined him to be. He had other matters on his mind, and like his brothers he was embarrassed by such public affirmations of his husbandly concern. Beyond that, sex was his momentary amnesia, his great release, not with his wife but, as Burke recalled, with numbers of women along the campaign trail.

In February 1980 in Concord, New Hampshire, Joan gave a speech applauding the women's movement, a speech unprecedented in the history of the Kennedy women. Joan's mother-in-law, Rose, had stood on the sidelines when the suffragists had marched in the streets of Boston, and none of her sisters-in-law had ever publicly supported the reborn feminism of modern America. "My own life experiences in the last few years brought me to an increased awareness of the central importance of the women's movement," Joan told the audience. Her speech was no more the pure product of her own mind than her Boston press conference had been. It was intended by her speech writers not to have Joan lock arms with Betty Friedan and Gloria Steinem, but to attempt to authenticate Ted as "the man for the women of 'America.' " Her feminism, then, was at least partially a dress she wore for her husband.

Joan was not the only Kennedy woman out on the campaign trail. Eighty-nine-year-old Rose was frail and brittle, but she made campaign appearances for Ted in Florida and Iowa, an inestimable testament to her love for her youngest son, and to her family ambitions. "I know you helped my sons when they aspired to the great position of president of the United States," she told an audience in Iowa. "So I am delighted you are going to help my younger son—my last child."

Eunice was a forceful, occasionally controversial figure in the contest. She was a goad and a nag, pushing her ideas on Ted as she pushed them on everyone else. A few years back when Ted had been holding hearings on teenage pregnancy, Eunice had called him at five-fifteen in the morning. "Do you know what time it is?" Ted had asked, half asleep. "Oh, I thought it was eight-fifteen," Eunice replied.

Even before the campaign began, Eunice came up to Boston to advise her troubled sister-in-law on how she should handle the media. "And that night, for Ted's benefit and for the family, she seemed to be encouraging Joan to shade or evade some unpleasant truths," recalled Marcia Chellis, then Joan's assistant. Eunice was fifteen years older than Joan. She could not abide the spectacle of Joan regurgitating her life with Teddy. She considered it time for Joan to play the supportive wife, praising her husband.

Over the years, Eunice had inundated her kid brother with requests, position papers, and advice. She was at her most persistent over the abortion issue. As Ted's aides viewed it, Eunice didn't appear to care a whit about the realities of politics in liberal Massachusetts, or whatever Ted's personal beliefs may have been. She lobbied him so mercilessly that his staff came to dread her phone calls. And yet now that the campaign had begun, Ted saw a certain usefulness in Eunice's position.

"I want Eunice with me in Iowa as much as possible," he told Burke, his administrative assistant.

"Why?" the administrative assistant asked.

"She'll help me with the anti-abortionists."

Pat served largely as a surrogate for Joan when she couldn't stand next to her husband, a human placard advertising that Ted was a family man. Jean headed out with a small entourage. She was not a natural campaigner, but she was closer to Ted than anyone in the family, and she would do what she could do. Jean was sent not to the auditoriums where thousands chanted the Kennedy name, but to the political backwaters, where she scoured for votes by the tens, not the thousands. Jean had the unenviable task of campaigning in Carter's home state of Georgia, where press coverage proved as rare as Kennedy voters, and she took little away but a sense of humiliation. In New York City, Jackie appeared before an ecstatic gathering of Greek-Americans in Queens, preparing them for Ted's speech.

Pat was the least comfortable of the three sisters on the political platform, but even she was available. One day an agitated campaign worker called her in her New York home. "Mrs. Lawford, we promised a family member at this meeting and we have nobody," the woman said.

"Well, how soon is it?"

"In an hour," the aide said urgently.

"In an hour!" Pat exclaimed. "Why my hair is a fright. I don't have any makeup on. I've got this old dress. I look like a total wreck. Why it's impossible."

"But, Mrs. Lawford, what are we going to do?" the woman implored.

"All right, then," Pat said finally. "I'll just come as Eunice."

The young generation of Kennedys headed out on the campaign trail as well. Caroline made herself available on occasion, as did her brother. Kathleen left her newborn at home in the care of her husband. Maria took a leave from her position at *PM Magazine* to help her uncle. The young Kennedy men took part as well, but what was the most striking was that the young women were as articulate and well versed in the issues as any of the males. Indeed, John H. Davis, working then on a family biography, noted that it was not even a blood Kennedy at all but Joe II's wife, "Sheila Rauch Kennedy, [who] was considered the best of all."

When the young Kennedy men made headlines, it was not for their glorious political triumphs or victories on the football field. In September of 1979, twenty-four-year-old David had driven up in his brown BMW to Harlem to score some heroin when he was beaten up and robbed of thirty dollars in the Shelton Plaza Hotel, an establishment known primarily as a place for buying or shooting up drugs. A narcotics detective said that David was known in the hotel as "White James." And "White James" was hustled to Boston, where he was committed to a drug rehabilitation program at Massachusetts General Hospital. From there he was sent West, away from the family, where by April of the next year, in the midst of Ted's campaign, David was sitting in a dreary room by himself in Sacramento hallucinating. Chris Lawford started out the campaign in exemplary fashion, his handsome magnetic looks as much an asset as his name. He had graduated from cocaine to heroin, and was trying to kick the habit. In a break from the campaign over the Christmas holidays he had been arrested in Aspen trying to pawn off a fake prescription for Darvon to a suspicious druggist.

Joan was not the only Kennedy to begin the campaign with dreams of a new life. The young generation had their own visions too, full of the romantic idea of Jack's presidential race, memorialized in Theodore White's classic book, in films, and in the display cases at the Kennedy Library, this merry band of brothers and sisters fighting their way to the White House. It was not 1960 anymore, and as the primary losses mounted, Steve Smith stepped aside from the day-to-day running of the

campaign, his place supplanted by a new generation of professionals. The young Kennedys had been brought up to believe
in their family destiny, but out on the hustings they heard their
uncle pilloried and ridiculed. For Kara this was not a politician
but her father, and in Philadelphia when a priest introduced her
by railing against a man "who does not deserve to be president," she ran from the building in tears.

Neither Kara nor any of the young Kennedys perhaps knew
how heavily the burden of his brothers' legacy rested on Ted's
stout shoulders. Ted was a Kennedy man, and he could hardly
let it be known that his deepest fear was not that he would lose
but that he would die. He had received numerous death threats,
most of which had been kept quiet, but during the interminable
primary campaign, he was an open target. A hand that reached
out to him might carry a gun. A slap on the back might be a
knife's steely thrust.

Whatever failure of nerve he had shown at Chappaquiddick,
he did not show on the campaign trail. "One of the things I admire about him is his extraordinary personal courage," said
Melody Miller, a senatorial staffer who has worked longer for
the Kennedys than anyone else in Washington. "I was one of
several people who implored him not to run. We were afraid
for his life. We knew about the death threats. But he has told
me he doesn't intend to live his life looking over his shoulder.
He pushes it back in his consciousness, but there is no way hu-
manly to forget it. He was the one candidate in 1980 for whom
the Secret Service had an armored car shipped ahead at every
stop. At times the Secret Service asked him to wear a bullet-
proof vest. That brings it all back to the forefront of consciousness."

In Chicago, on the day before the Illinois primary, Ted
insisted on marching in the St. Patrick's Day parade. Ted, unlike any other candidate or even the president himself, drew
the kooks and the crazies. The Secret Service dreaded the idea
of his walking in that raucous brawl of a parade, the sidewalks
jammed with gesticulating, celebrating Irish-Americans and
Irish-for-a-day. A helicopter flew overhead and the crowd was
laced with Secret Service and Chicago police. Joan was with
him on the snowy day, and so were their three children, and
Eunice and Maria, all of them proudly carrying Irish walking
sticks. Only Ted wore a bullet-proof vest.

There were no more fervent Kennedy supporters than the
Irish-Americans, and Ted and the family were greeted with

whooping shouts and applause, the kind of sound he had not heard often enough these past weeks. He and Joan were marching on when suddenly a series of cracks rang out. Bang! Bang! Bang! Bang! Ted fell to the ground as Secret Service agents formed a ring around him. It proved to have been nothing more than firecrackers, and Ted and Joan and the rest of the family moved on. He rushed into the crowds, shaking hands, ignoring the occasional taunts, then moving on again. In the evenings, when Patrick wasn't with him, he called his young son to tell him that his father was fine; if he forgot to call or was late, Patrick filled with dread, fearing that Ted had died.

In Illinois, Ted won fourteen delegates; Carter won 165. The Kennedys had no experience losing, and not simply losing but going down often to humiliating defeat. In Iowa where Ted had employed everyone from Eunice to his mother in his behalf, he won approximately half the votes of Carter, 31 percent to 59 percent. Eunice and Jean soldiered on, continuing with their brother to the end as they had been there at the beginning. At the time of the New York primary on March 25, Eunice and Jean had become among their brother's closest advisors. They told Ted their assessment of his prospects, as Joe II and young Bobby looked on. "So, what's the good news?" Ted said, his irony bringing much needed laughter to the dour family gathering.

Ted won the New York primary decisively. There were other victories, but not enough, and the Kennedy women and men arrived in New York City for the convention in August knowing that Ted was far short of the votes needed for nomination. For all the Kennedy women, but especially for Joan, it was a time of immense uncertainty. She had entered this campaign with vague yearnings to be reunited with her husband in this mutual quest, and then go on living with him in the White House. During the months of the primaries, they had shared little except podiums. Ted could return to his seat in the Senate, a man of power and prestige and honor. For Joan, the future opened up to her like a chasm. She started eating, gulping the food down. And then it was time to fly to New York.

Joan was in a room near the podium when Ted addressed the delegates Tuesday evening. This was still her husband out there, in this his final moment as a presidential candidate. In the final weeks, Ted had campaigned as an unreconstructed, unabashed liberal, and that was the way he talked this evening, calling for national health insurance, passage of the Equal Rights Amendment, and economic justice. "And someday, long after this convention, long after the signs come down, the crowds stop cheering, and the bands stop playing, may it be said of our campaign that we kept the faith." His eloquence and passion and idealism took flight on the wings of rhetoric, and for thirty-two minutes both the future and the past stood still. Among the delegates there were tears and cheers and sighs of what might have been and what yet might be. "For me, a few hours ago, this campaign came to an end. For all those whose cares have been our concern, the work goes on, the cause endures, the hope still lives and the dream shall never die."

The convention erupted in cathartic applause, the waves of emotion rolling over Ted as he stood there in the lone spotlight. This was the Ted whom Joan loved, and she came forward and hugged and kissed him on the podium, and he embraced her. And then it was over, and Joan went to her own bedroom in the Kennedy suite at the Waldorf-Astoria, and Ted went his own way.

Ted asked Joan to have lunch with him the next day, and she prepared like a high school girl on her first date, dressing in a sweetly innocent dress with ruffles and puffed sleeves. Ted came to pick her up. At the age of forty-eight, he was still a handsome man and he led her out into the New York summer. She could still be shyly demure with Ted, and she saved her serious conversation for their table at The Box Tree on the East Side. When they entered the restaurant, it filled with reporters.

Joan felt betrayed, set up, relegated to yet another photo opportunity and a few adoring quotes from the loving wife. That she would imagine Ted would do such a thing to her suggested how little was left of their mutual sense of intimacy and trust. He wanted to be alone with Joan as much as she did. He wanted to discuss their marriage and children, but the reporters had dogged their steps.

As upset as she was, Joan flew down to the McLean home, where she and Ted gave a party thanking the campaign staff and Secret Service. In the midst of the festivities, Ted came up to Joan and told her that they would be leaving immediately for the Cape. As the private jet soared northward, they were finally alone, but Ted opened his bulging briefcase and went to work. Joan was half asleep when the plane descended, landing in a strange airport. Ted told her that they were on Montauk Point on the end of Long Island, and though he was leaving her here, the pilot would fly her on to Hyannis. And so she flew on alone through the dark sky, back to a world where she no longer belonged.

Two years later when the family gathered at Hyannis Port for Thanksgiving, Joan was not there. Ted's divorce, like Rosemary's lobotomy, was a subject not to be discussed, and as the family sat down for the holiday dinner, her absence was not commented upon. The family had gathered this holiday in part to discuss whether Ted should run again for the presidency in 1984. The clear sentiment was that he should not, and it was a time when the past had become a series of gigantic markers that might not ever be reached again.

Rose was ninety-two years old. She had days when she appeared lost in a mindless daze, and others when she was like an ancient seer, full of the most exquisitely detailed memories of events of over a half century ago. Rose was still a woman with a sense of the great occasion, and as she looked down the long table at Pat, Jean, Ted, and their children, it was as if suddenly she was the young mistress of this home. "Have you all had enough for dinner?" she asked, though that was never a problem at the Kennedy home.

"Thank you, Mother," Pat said, with that curious formality that marked Kennedy family affairs. "We're all stuffed."

Ted stood and made a toast to his mother and all that she had done and meant. Then he asked her: "Mother, would you care to make a toast?"

Rose stood up from the table, bolstered by her youngest son's hands, and began to speak. "I want you to remember that you are not just Kennedys," she said, enunciating each word. "You are Fitzgeralds too." She cared for *her* history, for *their* history the way none of her children or grandchildren did, and she wanted them to know from whence they had come.

"And who was the greatest mayor of Boston!" Rose exclaimed, her voice carried on some hidden font of energy and strength. "Honey Fitz," they yelled back.

Rose stood there, and all the barnacles of age seemed to drop away. She told the stories they had all heard so many times before, of her father's life and ambitions, of the day she met Joe, of her debut, and of the glorious days of youth.

"And who was the prettiest girl in Boston?" she asked.

"You were!" they shouted.

"At first I liked Mr. Kennedy, but I didn't love him," she said. "In time, I came to love him very much. Very much!"

The darker memories of Joe had been interred long ago. Instead, Rose brought forth the family history like a series of exquisite gems carried out of a vault of memory, the family's most valued inheritance. On and on she went this day, and then she faltered, words and sentences strangers to her. She looked toward Ted, seeking in him strength and comprehension. "I'm so happy when you're here, dear," she said finally.

Later in the evening the family went into the living room. Everyone had a glass of champagne and Rose sat down at the piano. She played "Sweet Adeline," singing the song as she had seventy-two years ago when she had taught her father the tune.

> Sweet Adeline, my Adeline
> At night, dear heart
> For you I pine

Rose had a tiny, distant voice that sounded like an old recording, a voice rich in pathos, carrying all the shards of memory. In the stillness of a November day, the sound carried through the house, and out onto the beach, lost in the eternal sounds of the surf and the sea.

> In all my dreams,
> Your fair face beams
> You're the flower of my heart,
> Sweet Adeline.

26
The Realm of Possibility

Sydney Lawford had seen how her parents had lived their lives, and she wanted nothing of celebrity or celebrities. If she had her way, she might simply have eloped with James Peter McKelvy, but she was a Kennedy woman and inevitably her wedding would be a great public event, her walk into Our Lady of Victory Church in Centerville on Cape Cod observed by reporters, photographers, and hundreds of Kennedy watchers.

Sydney faced one other difficulty as she approached her September 17, 1983, marriage to McKelvy, a Boston television producer. She wanted her father to be there, but Peter was in terrible shape. Wherever she had been, from the Foxcroft School in Virginia and the University of Miami, to Franklin College in Lugano, Switzerland, she had kept in touch with her father by letter, telephone, and occasional visits. Another daughter might have been appalled by all the pratfalls of her father's life. For her twentieth birthday, Peter had taken Sydney and Christopher to Trader Vic's in New York for dinner, but even on that occasion he had brought a young model as his date, and gave both women jewelry from Van Cleef & Arpels.

In the two decades since Peter and Pat's divorce, sixty-year-old Peter had been married to two much younger women and was living now with Patricia Seaton, a woman two years younger than twenty-seven-year-old Sydney. Her father had become notorious for his drunkenness and drug problems. None of that diminished Sydney's love for Peter, and her mother made a point of reminding her children to remember their father on his birthday and holidays. Over the years Sydney deluged him with telegrams, postcards, and letters, beseeching him to write or to visit. In March of 1980, for instance, when she was twenty-three years old, she wrote Peter: "When I'm introduced it's not 'Senator Kennedy's niece' it's 'Peter Lawford's daughter' and people almost pass out!! You're really loved and admired by so many people Daddy. It makes me feel so proud."

Peter knew how deeply his eldest daughter loved him, and he knew that he should be there for her wedding day, but he felt that the Kennedys considered him a pathetic failure. After Pat Seaton's earnest entreaties, he decided to attend. He was an actor, after all, and he prepared himself to cut the *bella figura* among the Kennedys. He kept off drugs and liquor for a few days, and planned to carry himself not simply as the father of the bride, but as Peter Lawford, star of film and television, the father that Sydney liked to remember.

Sydney saw her father at the rehearsal dinner. Despite all the weight he had put on, and years of abuse to body and mind, Peter still had a shadow of that handsome face of years ago. It was one of those faces that created a shiver of recognition when he walked through a hotel lobby. People recognized that he had been *somebody* but were not quite sure who or when or why. Peter was so apprehensive among the Kennedys, so embarrassed at his decades-long decline, that he began to drink. The next morning as he put on his gray morning suit, he continued downing straight vodka.

Peter walked downstairs to the limousine pursued by a clerk from the local tuxedo rental establishment insisting that the father of the bride pay in advance. Peter forgot that minor embarrassment when he saw his daughter. Sydney was one of the least known of the Kennedy women of her generation. She had her mother's tall, spindly frame, a faintly androgynous handsomeness, deep-set eyes, and a shy, endearing smile that she flashed only occasionally. Sydney was wearing a stunning gown of appliquéd lace by Jean-Louis Scherrer, a Frenchman who was one of her mother's favorite designers. The gown fit beautifully on Sydney's thin body, and she could as easily have been a runway model as a bride. For Sydney the rehearsal dinner the night before had gone wondrously well, a fact that she kept repeating as if she could hardly believe what a good time she was having.

When Sydney got out of the long gray limousine, the crowd gasped and applauded. Most times Sydney treated even the most innocent of journalistic inquiries like a flashbulb going off in her face. This time she was nothing if not a good sport, hefting up her own train, and mugging happily for the photographers. Then Peter led his eldest daughter down the aisle of the diminutive white church.

The church was already full with about three hundred family members and friends. It had been several years since the Kennedy family had gotten together for such a festive occasion, and almost everyone was here this afternoon. Joan had been one of the first to arrive, on the arm of her son, Ted Jr. Now she looked back up the aisle to catch the first glimpse of the bride. Jackie had seemed almost to float into the church, oblivious to the throng of bystanders, wearing a businesslike two-piece suit, with a white jacket bordered in black, and a white skirt. It was a professional woman's outfit, appropriately so since Jackie had become a successful book editor, using her own literary judgments and celebrity to acquire books. She sat in an honored place in the third pew. Pat sat on the aisle just in front of Jackie. Pat looked almost ethereal in a royal blue silk dress, her hair dyed red. Pat's face had a strange sweet look on it that masked any emotion. Jean and Eunice were in the church too, sitting with their husbands. Ethel had shown up as well, but she had other matters on her mind than her niece's wedding; just a week ago Bobby Jr. had been arrested on a heroin drug charge in South Dakota, after the stewardess on a Republic Airlines flight had found him in the toilet "white as a sheet, cold as an ice cube, large beads of sweat pouring off him . . . eyes wide open and fully dilated."

At the age of ninety-three, Rose was shrunken, and was helped up the church steps by Ted and Pat as if she were climbing over a series of barricades. The young generation of Kennedys was here as well, the young women serving as bridesmaids, including Caroline, Maria, and Sydney's two sisters, Robin and Victoria. They were women well into their twenties now, and the light blue gowns and nosegays that they wore seemed throwbacks to another more innocent era, relics of high school proms from the fifties.

When Pat and her sisters and brothers had married, the ceremonies had been grand political-social-religious events, with princes of the church presiding, the pews full of political notables. Although there were a number of famous guests here today, from Oleg Cassini to Norman Mailer, this was a wedding for two members of a new generation.

The young priest was not here as part of a clan's ambitions, but to speak to the young woman and young man standing and kneeling before him. As part of the wedding service, Sydney's brother Chris came forward to read a scriptural passage chosen by the bride and groom. Chris had a stooped posture that made him appear older than his twenty-eight years, but he had a firm youthful voice, and his resonant phrases sounded throughout the church.

"If I have the faith to move mountains but without love, then I have nothing at all."

Sydney and McKelvy both came from broken homes, and they had been dating for seven years. They knew the wages of divorce and marital unhappiness, and their friends believed that they had waited until this day so that they could be as sure as they could possibly be that their marriage would not end like their parents'.

"Love is always patient and kind. It is never jealous."

Out in this church among their relatives, there was little to inspire the couple that love was likely to last until death do they part, nor perhaps even into middle age. Rose sat motionless. She had given Sydney lectures on morals and manners, but all the young Kennedys knew about their grandfather's life and loves. Pat listened to her son reading these passages about love. Her life was a cautionary tale. She had hardly known *her* Peter when she had married him. Her life suggested that if a woman sought everything in a marriage, she might end with less than nothing. Joan listened to these words too. Her life with Ted was over. Since the convention in 1980, they had gone ahead with a formal divorce. Though she was invited to family gatherings, she was no longer legally a Kennedy. Despite everything, she had loved Ted deeply. She still loved him. Ted had wanted to continue the façade of their marriage, with each of them living their own life, but as she saw it, for her "own state of mind," she had had to end it.

Jean was still married, sitting beside her husband, but Steve's lovers were rebukes to the idealistic words that Chris was speaking. Indeed, most of the Kennedy women there this day had husbands who considered that as Kennedy men they had open mandates to roam sexually free, while their wives presumably stayed home, keeping warm the hearth of family virtue.

"It does not take offense when it is not successful. Love takes no pleasure in other people's sins."

Jackie sat there listening too, her lips slightly pursed in a

smile. She would have been as comfortable in the cathedrals of
the Medicis as in this country church. She knew as much about
love as any of them here, love with Jack, love with Onassis,
and now love with Maurice Tempelsman. The wealthy New
York businessman was a married man; if this was love, it was
not the kind of love of which the priest spoke here today.

"To hope and to endure whatever comes."

When it was time for Sydney and Peter McKelvey to take
their marital vows, Peter did not give his daughter away, and
Sydney did not promise to love, cherish and obey her husband.
That was something her mother and her aunts had all done, but
the world and women were different now, and so were many
men. Sydney and Peter McKelvey took a different kind of
vow. They stood alone before the priest, holding hands, and together spoke the same vows.

"I, Peter, take you Sydney to be my wife," he began. "I
promise to be true to you in good times and in bad, in sickness
and in health. I will love you and honor you all the days of my
life."

Then it was Sydney's turn to repeat the vows. The audience
applauded, and as the ceremony ended Sydney walked back up
the aisle beside her new husband, stopping for a moment to
kiss her father but ignoring her mother, a pattern so familiar in
the family.

It was one of those brilliant days of New England Indian
summer, and the guests gathered on the lawn at the compound
for a reception that included a dinner in the two blue-and-
white-striped tents. Jackie wanted to be next to Peter. She
switched the place cards, a gesture that infuriated Pat. As
the mother of the bride, she wanted to sit next to Peter, and
she could hardly believe that Jackie could so cavalierly
change the wedding dinner.

Sydney and McKelvy had some friends videotaping the
wedding, and they went around an increasingly inebriated
group asking questions. For their generation the wedding night
had become as archaic a custom as bundling boards, and provided an occasion for some raunchy sexual humor, led by the
women more than the men.

Pat had not spent the time with Peter she had wanted to
spend. Not until late in the day did they stand alone on the immense lawn, looking out on the gathering.

"Do you have any advice for the newlyweds?" Peter was
asked.

"Be as happy as you can and free and compatible and loving and that's about it," he said as Pat looked on, her face a mask of inexpressiveness. "I wish them love and happiness. Joy. What else is there?"

The band played on but the guests began departing, drifting away. There was almost no one left by the time the bandleader announced that the group would play a song in Rose's honor. The Kennedy matriarch had been too weak to attend much of the reception. And as the music of "When Irish Eyes are Smiling" wafted into the old house, outside the first chill of autumn was in the air.

Three months after Sydney's wedding, Peter entered the Betty Ford Center in Rancho Mirage, California, supposedly to deal with his addictions. The one aspect of Peter's life that was still working well was his addict's duplicity, honed to such a fine point that he managed to fool even the center. Peter took lonely long walks in the desert, out to a spot where a rented helicopter landed to deliver his latest hits of cocaine. As part of his therapy, Peter was supposed to write honest letters to those he had hurt in his life, whether they were alive or dead. He might have written Sydney and his other children but there was no one to whom he needed more to write that letter to than Pat. Two decades before she had warned him so lovingly about his alcoholism and how it had destroyed their marriage, and now Pat herself was an alcoholic. He was not ready to write a letter to Pat, for he would have had to write on the parchment of truth. Instead, he penned a chatty note to Jack that he wouldn't like the center because there was "not a pretty girl within miles," and asking how Marilyn and Bobby were doing.

Peter left the Betty Ford Center after five weeks looking remarkably fit. Three days later he was so drunk that he could not even leave a bar by himself, and had to be helped home.

In April 1984 Sydney flew down to Palm Beach to see her aged grandmother. Rose had not appeared in public since Sydney's wedding. She had grown so feeble that she could not even attend the memorial services on the twentieth anniversary of Jack's death in November.

The nurses who took care of Rose observed the three Kennedy sisters arguing over who would have sovereignty over their mother's care. When it came to the care of Rose, they were all strong, willful women each with her own ideas over what should be done. None of them seemingly understood how seriously ill their mother had become. The nurses and doctors knew that Rose would never again be that great and formidable matriarch that she once had been, but her daughters and son could not let go of that image of their mother.

Eunice believed in the salutary benefit of exercise. She insisted that her mother be put in her bathing suit, wheeled down to the pool, and walked back and forth through the water. "Look, you're all trying to kill your mother," the nurse said. "She needs bed rest. Leave her alone."

The nurse called Ted in Washington. "Senator, if they don't stop they're going to kill her."

"Okay," Ted said. As the last surviving son, he was the final arbiter. "You've got control."

Rose collapsed during dinner on Good Friday. Her nurse immediately gave her oxygen and took her to her bedroom. The Palm Beach Mobile Intensive Care Unit sat outside the mansion most of the evening, but Rose seemed to revive, spending time talking to Eunice and Sydney.

Rose had helped to instill in her children optimism that had become an impenetrable shield, and they needed to believe that Rose would be herself again. On Easter Sunday, Rose had a stroke of such seriousness that it appeared certain that she would die. The priest read the last rites over her motionless form as the family members stood saying the rosary. It was then that her heart stopped, and the nurse, trained in emergency-room procedures, gave her an injection, and her heart began beating again.

Two of Rose's other grandchildren, David and Douglas, were in Palm Beach that same Easter weekend. Although Douglas would have been welcomed at the Kennedy estate, David was no longer trusted. He had not been watched over when he had stayed in Rose's apartment in New York in recent years, and he had cut the lamp cords to use as tourniquets for shooting up drugs.

That was one reason David was staying not at the estate but at the Brazilian Court, a deluxe hotel in the center of town. David and his younger brother looked out of place at the old hotel, which featured a sedate, genteel international clientele. The rooms were set around an open court. As Ethel's two sons traipsed back and forth from their suite they were observed by guests and staff members.

Monday afternoon David and Douglas went out to the house on North Ocean Boulevard to see Rose. They were far less able to confront disease and death than were their sisters or female cousins. They were startled by the sight of Rose lying there helpless, so tiny that it was as if she had reverted not simply metaphorically but physically into a helpless child, and they stayed no more than two minutes.

David fled, tears streaming down his face. He was a twenty-eight-year-old Harvard dropout with a big drug problem, a small trust fund, and a famous name. He had just gotten out of a treatment program at St. Mary's Rehabilitation Center in St. Paul, Minnesota. He had attempted everything to straighten out, from psychiatrists to group therapy, methadone to "neuro-electric therapy." He had tried even the least likely antidote of all, talking to a journalist, David Horowitz, coauthoring a book on the family. David had hoped that it might help free him of the burden he felt as a Kennedy. He had just read the first results of that exercise in the April issue of *Playboy* and was appalled. To him the graphic presentation of his drug problems was not an exorcism but a betrayal, only increasing his mother lode of guilt and his sense of failure.

These few days in Palm Beach had hardly given credence to the family hopes that David had at least found his way. He cut an aimless swath through the clubs and restaurants of Palm Beach, drinking vodka and snorting cocaine. He had long since concluded that his famous name was an albatross, but he could still wave the name Kennedy like a magical talisman, getting a free suite at the Brazilian Court, amenable bellhops to score some cocaine, and women to listen to his tales.

Douglas left Monday to return North to school. That evening, David reportedly had dinner with Marion Niemann, a forty-one-year-old German woman, at the Rain Dancer Restaurant in West Palm Beach. He hardly touched his dinner, and Niemann counted him drinking as many as seven vodkas. Later in the evening they returned to David's room in the Brazilian Court, where he began talking about the night his father had died.

"David, this is very sad," the woman remembered saying. "You are so nice and you are such a nice person. You make the people around you unhappy."

"I cannot forget when I see my father on this, in this television and this time I can, I never find peace inside. I've been full of pain. . . ."

The following afternoon David went up to the clerk at the Brazilian Court to cash a hundred-dollar check. The employee looked at him standing there, his hair dirty and uncombed, his head hanging down, wearing a pair of wrinkled shorts, slurring his words, and she thought at first that he was a derelict who had wandered in off the street. But when she learned that he was a Kennedy, she cashed his check and David took a cab out to the Kennedy estate. He had come out to see his relatives but was so inebriated that the security guard turned him away.

Shortly after David left the Kennedy home, a Palm Beach attorney, Howell VanGerbig Jr., received the first of several phone calls from Ethel. The attorney had never met Ethel before, but she began pouring out her emotions to VanGerbig. She told him that her son "really was in bad shape and she didn't know what to do, that he had been very abusive to members of the family and was upsetting them. . . ."

That evening Sydney drove out to the West Palm Beach Airport to meet her cousin Caroline, who was flying in to see their grandmother before she died. Back at the estate the talk over the dinner table among the Kennedy women concerned not simply Rose's illness, but David and his desperate condition. This pattern in the family of the women protecting the men was at least three generations old. Rose had devoted her adult life to maintaining the family honor and reputation. Now she lay semicomatose upstairs, but that mandate lived on in her daughters and granddaughters.

Caroline and Sydney had been brought up to believe in family honor. They were close to their cousin David, and they knew that it was their duty to protect not only him, but the family name. The next morning at about ten-thirty Caroline arrived at the Brazilian Court looking for David. She called his room, but nobody answered. An hour later a woman called the hotel saying she was "Mrs. Kennedy from Boston" and asked that someone go up to Room 107 and check on her son's condition.

The staff did not know that there was no "Mrs. Kennedy from Boston" and Douglas Moschiano, the bell captain, and Betty Barnett, a secretary, walked up to the room. They paused when they saw the DO NOT DISTURB sign hanging from the doorknob. They entered the room, and saw that the shades were still drawn and that the message light on the phone blinked insistently. The twin beds had not been slept in, and there were dollar bills scattered on top of the bedspread and on the floor. Then they saw David facedown between the beds. He was wearing a long-sleeved shirt, shorts, shoes and socks, and he was dead.

A little later Caroline and Sydney arrived back at the hotel in Rose's blue-and-white Cadillac. They looked as if they had just come from a swim. Their hair was wet, and they were in beach outfits and bare feet. A police officer told the two women that their cousin was dead. Caroline remembers that they said, " 'Oh, my God,' or hugged or something." An observer watched as Sydney began to cry and Caroline displayed no obvious emotion. In the hotel the two cousins then began the arduous task of calling relatives and friends. Almost immediately, the Kennedys attempted to close out the tragedy from public view. Ted talked on the phone to Bill Miller, the medical examiner, and requested that David's body be moved to a hospital "as quickly as possible . . . so that the investigation could be conducted in a less public setting." When Miller tried to talk to Caroline and Sydney, he found the two young women "reluctant to answer questions." Soon afterwards the two cousins left the hotel; they were still in their bare feet when they joined their Aunt Jean at the Palm Beach County medical examiner's office to identify David's body.

The next day Caroline and Sydney joined Joe II on the flight carrying David's body back to Hickory Hill for funeral services before burial in the family plot in Brookline. As the plane flew northward, Ethel and a group of family and friends drove in two limousines to Arlington National Cemetery. There before Bobby's and Jack's graves, Ethel spent a half hour seeking solace, and perhaps some link between these deaths and that of their third son.

Sydney returned to Palm Beach two weeks later to take yet another difficult flight. She was there when Rose was carried out of the Palm Beach house on a stretcher and taken in an ambulance to Palm Beach International Airport where a special ambulance plane stood on the tarmac. It was a journey hauntingly reminiscent of the flights Rose had taken with Joe after his stroke. Joe had still been mentally alert, while Rose was capable only of fleeting moments of lucidity and comprehension. Ted and Jean had also flown down to Florida to make the flight north with Rose, and they and Sydney sat in the plane, along with two nurses and a doctor.

The plane lifted off and flew to Barnstable Municipal Airport on Cape Cod, where another ambulance carried Rose to her house at Hyannis Port. Her room had been prepared for her, a team of nurses hired, and she was carried into the house and put to bed, never to return to Palm Beach.

David's death was a jarring, dark image that did not fit into the heroic mold of the family saga. It did not fit the courtly image of Palm Beach either, and two bellhops at the Brazilian Court, David Lindwood Dorr and Peter Marchant, were arrested and indicted for selling David cocaine, charges for which they faced up to twenty years in prison. They were not notorious drug dealers, and they had gotten involved primarily to be associated with a Kennedy. Previously, Dorr had performed manual labor for the Kennedys in Hyannis Port and Ethel in McLean. Although David had not remembered the thirty-year-old bellhop, Dorr had eagerly volunteered to find cocaine for his acquaintance with the famous name.

The charges were draconian, especially so since the medical autopsy revealed that David had died not simply from ingesting cocaine but of a "combined drug intoxication" of cocaine, the painkiller Demerol, and the tranquilizer Mellaril, the drugs or some of them injected into his groin. The tranquilizer had been prescribed for David, but the powerful painkiller had not been. The trail of the Demerol led directly back to the Kennedy mansion, and was probably more a factor in his death than the other drugs. Doctors had prescribed Demerol for Rose's heart condition. In recent days a large vial of the powerful and dangerous medication had disappeared from the nurse's table.

All the force of law fell on the two bellhops. A year and a half later, when the publicity had died away, and the journalists had pulled up the stakes of the media circus and moved on, both men pleaded nolo contendere, were fined two hundred dollars each, and sentenced to eighteen months probation.

When the police first examined the bedroom at Brazilian Court, they found the prescription medicine Mellaril, but no illegal drugs except a small packet of cocaine secreted in David's wallet in a drawer in a night table. The analysis of the water in the toilet bowl, however, revealed significant traces of cocaine and Demerol. The authorities also found that David's sock on his right foot was inside out. These several facts led the investigators for the Palm Beach County state's attorney's office to conclude that someone may have attempted to "clean up" the death scene. It was a chilling image, then, someone finding the nude or half-nude body of David lying there, perhaps with the syringe sticking from his groin, clothing the corpse, frantically flushing the evidence away, cleaning up any other traces of drugs, and quickly exiting the room.

"Do you know if anybody got into that room before you and Betty [Barnett]?" Moschiano was asked during his deposition.

"Could have been Caroline Kennedy," the bellhop replied. "She called the room; there was no answer. She walked back toward the room, knocked on the door; this is what I heard. This is when I saw her coming out from the south wing area, this was the only time I saw her."

In her deposition, Caroline stated that she did not go anywhere near the room. Caroline and Sydney were never seriously interviewed by Palm Beach authorities, and with the plea of the two hapless bellhops, the case ended. The matter had besmirched the reputation not simply of the Kennedys but of David Bludworth, the Palm Beach County state's attorney, who had been so reluctant to release the depositions and other court documents. "It sounds like [by the way] you're running the office, you're governed by what the Kennedys want you to do," he was told by Circuit Judge John Born.

Jackie had kept Caroline and John away from the dangerous antics of the young Kennedy men, and Caroline's days with David were the only time that she brushed closely against the dark side of the family. As she had grown up, Caroline had come to see herself as a bearer of her father's legacy. In her mind that had nothing to do with a lost character like her deceased cousin. David was the first Kennedy of her generation to die, to die not to enemy fire, nor to an assassin's bullet, but to a self-inflicted overdose of drugs. His life was not memorialized in a private book, nor in a foundation that bore his name. His life was an episode that she and the whole family tried to forget.

Caroline had only the sweetest memories of her father. She could recall how she had ducked under Jack's desk in the Oval Office, hiding there with her little brother, and how she had stood watching her father taking off in the presidential helicopter. Over the years she had seen photos and films of herself with her father, and some of her memories were probably only her recollections of these images. She remembered the stories that her father had made up and told her at bedtime. These memories nobody would take from her, not parceled out in an-

ecdotes to journalists, not melded into some speech. Her father's friends and associates had told her all sorts of stories
about her father too, tales of heroism and nobility and political
courage and wit and grace, and that was the John F. Kennedy
she remembered.

In the years since his death the great tapestry of her father's
life had been pulled down, trampled upon, befouled with revelations, ripped apart with revisionist interpretations, but Caroline's head still looked up, seeing a profile in courage and
grace and wit, and nothing anyone could say or do would turn
her head downward. Jackie had taught Caroline to revere that
vision of her father, and it dominated her young life. Caroline
had been slower than most of her classmates in developing an
interest in boys, slow in part perhaps because there were intimacies she did not want to exchange, slow in part too perhaps
because no youth could measure up to the yardstick of her father. At Concord she infrequently saw her mother, and she was
consumed with her father's epic life.

Although Caroline was near Hyannis Port, she rarely saw
Rose, and when she did, her grandmother was full of instruction and advice. "Every time I see her she tells me about the
last picture she saw of me," Caroline said. "And things like I
shouldn't put my teeth over my lip because it might give me
buck teeth, and you should stand with your hands away from
your side because it makes you look thin. Every time I send
her a poem I've written, she says, 'We know you're not only
an artist, but also a poet.' "

Caroline had grown up knowing that wherever she went she
received the deference of name not of achievement. Even the
most fledgling steps into the world beyond her cloistered life
were greeted with such outrageous applause that she quickly
drew back into her sanctuary. When she was still at Concord
Academy, she spent her summers not in holiday amusements,
but attempting to experience life beyond the pale of wealth. At
fifteen she spent six weeks among the coal miners of East Tennessee, working on an oral-history documentary film, accompanied by three Secret Service agents. As she recalled she had
"interviewed miners, miners' wives and widows, many with
black lung disease, children, mine operators and officials."
During the summer Caroline took still photos of her own. The
following February *The Washington Post* reported that the Associated Press was buying some of the photos for a reported

ten thousand dollars and that Caroline would be having her own show at the Lexington Art Gallery in Manhattan.

Jackie had been a photographer herself in Washington, and Caroline's talents may well have exceeded her mother's; however, it was not her daughter's photos that were being purchased but her Kennedy name. The switchboard at Concord was inundated with agents and editors wishing further to exploit the modest collections of photos. It was a heady business for a sixteen-year-old, but Jackie knew that as painful as it was to call a halt to the sale and the gallery opening, it would have been more painful to proceed, and to be a partner in helping to create a daughter who was a creature of celebrity, a young monster of ego.

The following summer Caroline traveled to Hong Kong, where she had visited drug rehabilitation centers and the courts. The same vacation she worked as an intern in Ted's Washington office. Her senior year she worked part of the summer for NBC doing documentaries on the Middle East and Sweden. She had these opportunities in large measure because her name was Caroline Kennedy, but once she was there she sought nothing but to be treated like her peers.

What was most striking about Caroline was not that she had a sense of entitlement, but that this sense was not even larger. She suffered from social schizophrenia that was the disease of all the Kennedys of her generation, but in her it was the deepest. She wanted to be the princess and the pauper, to live a life both of privilege and of experience. She worried that people liked her because she was a Kennedy, and she worried that people *didn't* like her because she thought of herself as a Kennedy. "Everyone hates me! They all think I'm a snob," she exclaimed to one friend. She was no beauty like her mother, and she worried about her looks, shaving off an eyebrow in one desperate moment of self-criticism.

After graduating from Concord, Caroline spent a year in London studying art appreciation at Sotheby's. She stayed at the home of Hugh Fraser, a member of Parliament and an old friend of her father. Fraser had attracted a measure of controversy because of his calls for the death penalty for terrorists. In October 1975 Caroline came within minutes of being killed when a bomb placed in Fraser's parked car went off prematurely, killing a passerby. That brush with death would have

been enough to have sent many young persons home, even if
her last name had not been Kennedy, but Caroline stayed on.

There is no better place in the world to be rich and young
than London, a world in which wealth brings no pestering guilt
nor any sense of obligation. For a while Caroline enjoyed going to balls and parties, whirled through the night by a succes-
sion of titled young men. This was the life in which her Aunt
Kathleen had so brilliantly sparkled, but Caroline was of a different generation, and it was unthinkable that she would make
her life as an expatriate in Britain.

Caroline followed in her father's path by attending Radcliffe
Harvard College. There she had the same feelings that her
cousin Kathleen had experienced, wondering whether friends
liked her merely because her name was Kennedy. Caroline,
like her mother, was drawn to a career in journalism, and the
summer after her first year she worked as an intern for the
New York Daily News.

Caroline made several attempts at journalism, but the light
shone on her more than on her subjects, and it was clear she
would have to make a career elsewhere. After graduation, she
took a position working on television and media projects at
the Metropolitan Museum of Art. There she met Edwin
Schlossberg, a cultural historian thirteen years her senior. At
Columbia Schlossberg had written his Ph.D. dissertation by
imagining a conversation between Albert Einstein and Samuel
Beckett. It was the kind of project that some viewed as
daringly brilliant, and others considered an academic con.
Schlossberg had his own company that designed multimedia
video projects for museums and industry. He was a man of notable erudition opening up a new intellectual world to Caroline.
He was Jewish. In her mother's generation, it would have been
highly unlikely for a well-brought-up Catholic woman to have
dated a Jewish man, and unthinkable that she should marry
him, even if he agreed to bring their children up Catholic.
Jackie was deeply involved with Maurice Tempelsman, who
was not only Jewish but still technically married, and Jackie
not only accepted Schlossberg but wholeheartedly approved.

In July of 1986 twenty-eight-year-old Caroline married
Schlossberg in a great family wedding on Cape Cod. Her marriage to forty-one-year-old Schlossberg was an exquisite rendering of her and Jackie's sensibilities, and the onlookers took
on the mood of the moment, watching with almost reverential
concern. Many of Jack's stalwart old New Frontiersmen were

present but they no longer walked with the quick pace of the White House years.

Jackie had planned the ceremony, and everything from her daughter's breathtaking Carolina Herrera gown to the groom's blue-gray linen suit was in subdued taste. As the ceremony ended, the newlyweds emerged from the church and waved to the cheering spectators. Behind them stood Jackie, perfectly elegant in a lime-green dress. Jackie smiled too, but as the sun glistened it was obvious that she had tears in her eyes.

Ever since they had been children, the lives of Caroline and her cousin Maria Shriver had been linked. As they were growing up, Caroline was the most celebrated Kennedy woman of her generation, and Maria had been jealous of her younger cousin. It was not that Caroline sought publicity or gave interviews, but her life was constantly chronicled in magazine and newspaper articles. When Caroline was seventeen, she was on the cover of *McCall's* in an article that quoted not Caroline but Maria talking authoritatively about her cousin. ("Although Maria doesn't think Caroline will ever run for office herself, she believes her cousin will definitely work for others who do.")

Caroline had only memories of her father, but Maria had two parents who absolutely doted on her. She was full of a pride beyond pride in her parents. She wanted to achieve her own successes, without being lifted above the crowd by her parents. She had begun her college education at Manhattanville, and like her mother had lasted only a year before transferring to the American Studies program at Georgetown University. Although Maria had a Catholic education and attended Sunday mass, she was not nearly as devout as her brothers. Among this young generation of Kennedys, then, religion was no longer the business of women, but of personal faith.

Maria was losing weight, and was on her way to becoming a sleek, stunning young woman. She enjoyed a much more eclectic dating life than did her cousin Caroline, and was not beyond having her boyfriends stay overnight at her grandmother's house in Palm Beach.

Upon graduation from Georgetown, Maria decided that she wanted to work in television journalism. "I saw the impact television was having in politics," Maria recalled. "In our family everyone assumes, 'Well, I'm going to go out and be involved in politics or some kind of social justice or something.' And I always had the desire to go against the crowd. I wanted to pick something different, yet I wanted to see what I had been brought up to believe in but in a different field."

Maria began her career as a production assistant at a small station in Philadelphia and moved from there to WJZ-TV in Baltimore. One of her new colleagues at the station was a young black woman, Oprah Winfrey, and they became friends. A new generation of women was moving into television now, who belied any idea that they were weaker in ambition, initiative, stamina, or drive than their male counterparts. They worked as long hours and they made sacrifices in their personal lives that few men would make. Maria put in her fifteen-hour days, but on weekends she managed to get away, attending family affairs and seeing friends.

In the fall of 1977 shortly after she began work in television, Maria met Arnold Schwarzenegger at the Robert F. Kennedy Tennis Tournament in New York. The celebrated bodybuilder had been a hit at the celebrity tournament, burlesquing his embryonic tennis skills on center court, losing along with his partner Rosie Grier to two ten-year-olds. Maria was taken enough with Schwarzenegger that he was invited to fly back with the family to Hyannis Port. Arnold was not only a Republican and a foreigner, but was champion of a sport that was as alien to the tennis-playing, sailing clan as stock-car racing and bowling. The former Mr. Universe was the most celebrated bodybuilder in the world. He was the star of a documentary, *Pumping Iron*, and was even more adept at pumping his own career. The Austrian-born Schwarzenegger had dreams of becoming a movie star, considering his thick accent, his four-syllable name, and his supposedly rudimentary acting skills hardly detriments.

At first, Eunice was dismayed at this hulking presence escorting her only daughter. Eunice was nothing if she was not realistic. She wanted to be what she considered "with it," and the more she saw of Arnold the more she realized that in early 1980s America, Arnold might be the very definition of "with it." He was not only ambitious, but he was smart, and he was not only smart but he was thoughtful, and he fit comfortably into the Shriver home and life-style. He was a man of such monumental ambition that among the Kennedys, he was most like Eunice's father, Joe. In 1977, for instance, when he was known only as a bodybuilder, Arnold told *Stern*, the German newsmagazine: "When one has money, one day it becomes less interesting. And when one is also the best in film, what can be more interesting? Perhaps power. Then one moves into politics and becomes governor or president or something."

Eunice signed Arnold up as the weight-lifting coach for Special Olympics. He took to it not simply to stamp his growing celebrity onto another letterhead, but in a serious and dedicated way, working with individual athletes and developing the general program. Maria did not fly off to California, joining her would-be movie-star lover in Hollywood. She was as ambitious as Arnold, and her career kept almost apace with his. With his leading role in *Conan the Barbarian*, Arnold had the stardom that he had told Maria would be his. Maria moved to Los Angeles not simply because of Arnold but to become an on-air personality and interviewer on the celebrity-oriented *PM Magazine*, and from there to do celebrity interviews on the *CBS Morning News*.

Eunice worried about her only daughter and how she could possibly combine her career with a family, making decisions about her life that would have been unthinkable for a woman of Eunice's generation. Maria and Arnold had scarcely announced their engagement, when in August of 1985, twenty-nine-year-old Maria flew off to New York to take what was by far her most important assignment, to become the coanchor on the *CBS Morning News*. Practically her whole family had gotten involved with the negotiations, including her brother Bobby, Eunice, and Sarge, who thought that his daughter merited not simply a half-million-dollar salary but an apartment in New York, purchased for her by the network.

The *CBS Morning News* was last in ratings, last in prestige. The show was such a failure that CBS had attempted some of the more bizarre experiments in anchoring. They had gone from Sally Quinn, the acerbic and witty *Washington Post* writer who had given new meaning to the term "amateur," to the recently deposed Phyllis George, a former Miss America, and now to Maria. It all suggested that when the network signed women as on-air talent they thought more of casting than hiring. Maria was almost as hopelessly inexperienced as her predecessors, but she worked with diligence and good cheer, up to eighteen hours a day. "Maria was first-rate with celebrities, but sometimes she didn't grasp an issue or would see it only from the peculiar perspective of a privileged Catholic woman," recalled Peter McCabe, the producer. "Every morning after the show, she and her mother Eunice would talk on the phone, and at times it seemed to me we were getting an input we didn't need."

At the troubled program, rumors were the weapons of choice, Maria had always made it abundantly clear that one day she wanted to have children, an admission that in the career-oriented world of television made her vulnerable. As Maria's April 1986 wedding approached, the whispered story was that Maria was pregnant, or would soon be pregnant, and would give up her position to be a wife and mother. Maria could easily have parlayed her impending marriage to Arnold into a bonanza of publicity, joking about him on the show, granting interviews to magazines and other television programs. Just as she did not traffic in her Kennedy background, merchandising it to advance herself, neither did she exploit Arnold. "I think I was obsessive about not exploiting the Kennedy connection," Maria said. "It was almost to a ridiculous extent. But it was very important to me because people would have doubts that I had gotten the job because of my name or because of my looks or because of my parents. So it was really important to me that I worked twice as hard, that I did jobs that did not reflect my family connection."

Maria's nuptial was a Kennedy wedding, with the whole family arriving for the ceremonies at St. Francis Xavier in Hyannis. Thousands of onlookers stood behind barricades attempting to glimpse Maria in her stunning gown by Christian Dior's Marc Bohan and Arnold, her thirty-eight-year-old movie-star husband. Maria was thirty years old, and had dated Arnold for nine years, a pattern reminiscent of her mother's long relationship with her father. She was of a different generation, and this was a different time, and the guest list was as brilliant a mélange of the media and Hollywood and the political elite as her parents' wedding had been of a political and business world. Maria had kept her old friends, and they were here too, names unknown to the media. From Tom Brokaw to Quincy Jones, Diane Sawyer to Professor Laurence Tribe, Oprah Winfrey to Edward Bennett Williams, Barbara Walters to Andy Warhol, the guest list was in part a cross section of a new American media elite, celebrating the nuptials of what was potentially one of the most powerful couples in America.

Of the young generation of twenty-eight surviving Kennedys, Kathleen was the least willing simply to accept the given truths of her family or her generation. She sought to live what was truly *her* life, an authentic existence in which she confronted the moral and spiritual challenges of her age, her sex, and her class. In that she was the spiritual descendent of her Aunt Eunice. Her life was an adventure that did not depend on a needle in her arm or a journalistic chronicler to celebrate her daring.

After graduation from Radcliffe, Kathleen traveled with David out to Sante Fe, New Mexico, where her young husband taught classics at St. John's College, and Kathleen commuted to the University of New Mexico Law School in Alburquerque. David was the least Kennedyesque of men. His father was an elementary school principal, and he had spent his childhood not in football games and ersatz Olympic competitions but "following the stream or railroad tracks to the source, catching turtles and snakes, trying to educate myself and to learn how to love the things I liked." To David life was an open adventure, and ideas about sexual roles and masculinity and feminity were just that: ideas. They could be thought about and experienced, and experimented with, as could everything else in life.

David was the rarest of beings in modern academia: a true intellectual. He sought neither his name on the spines of books, nor the accolades of distant colleagues, but knowledge. That was a legitimate quest at St. John's, an unusual college whose curriculum was based on reading the Great Books in a largely chronological fashion.

David's quest did not end when he left campus. When Kathleen became pregnant, she and David decided that she would give birth to the first Kennedy child of the young generation at home using natural childbirth assisted by a doctor and two midwives. Kathleen was no mock hippie believing in the stars or fate. She and David seriously investigated the subject and decided that it was safe. "I didn't want to be knocked out during one of the most profound experiences there is," Kathleen explained. "Also, I don't like to be told what to do. Hospitals tell you how to act." For two generations, the Kennedys had given up sovereignty over many decisions to experts. This decision was an attempt to return birth to the intimate confines of the home, to be controlled not by doctors but by a wife and husband.

Kathleen didn't even tell Ethel about her plans until she gave birth to her healthy daughter, Meaghan Anne. The new grandmother arrived soon afterwards, making the trek to the austere primitive house in the mountains overlooking Santa Fe. Ethel opened the refrigerator. "What is this?" she asked.

"A placenta," Kathleen replied matter-of-factly.

"What's it doing there behind the milk?"

Kathleen explained that there was a tradition in New Mexico to bury the placenta and plant a tree above it. Ethel immediately purchased a piñon tree and buried the placenta.

After four years in New Mexico, Kathleen and David moved to New Haven, where Kathleen finished her law degree and David began his studies at the Yale Law School. Kathleen became pregnant again, but in all of New Haven they could not find one doctor willing to countenance a home birth. They did eventually locate a midwife, but she had not yet arrived in the early morning hours when Kathleen was ready to give birth. David had read a police manual on giving birth, and he proceeded to deliver their second daughter, Maeve Fahey, by himself. The infant arrived in an amniotic sac that David bit through with his teeth. The baby was not breathing. "David massaged her the way they said to and everything was fine," Kathleen recalled. "The pediatrician came to help afterwards. We were slightly hysterical."

After David finished his law degree in 1981, the Townsends moved to Boston, where Kathleen sought an active role in politics. The family had a tradition of introducing its young men into the higher reaches of politics by having them run the campaign of an older member. The practice had begun with Kathleen's own father running Jack's campaigns. Kathleen wanted her own chance, but in 1976 her younger brother Joe II was named to run her Uncle Ted's campaign. Six years later Kathleen believed that it was not only her turn, it was more than her turn. Ted was an impassioned supporter of women's issues in the Senate, but that did not mean that he wanted a woman to run his campaign, least of all his niece. He could hardly turn down her appeal. "It takes a while to change attitudes," reflected Kathleen. "And this family is like many Irish Catholic families. It's very male dominated. But, nonetheless, they have to change. The men in the family who have gotten involved in politics, Teddy and Joe [II] might be better than those who haven't gotten involved because they have to become more aware."

Kathleen was a hands-on operative, fully meriting Ted's congratulatory statement after his victory that she had "made all the difference." After her uncle's victory she went to work for Governor Mike Dukakis as a policy analyst in his Office of Human Resources while David stayed home watching

Meaghan and Maeve and writing a novel. Kathleen was trying her hand as a writer too, not fiction, but several serious, prophetic articles published in *The Washington Monthly*, the publication that had so savaged her Uncle Ted and his attitudes toward women.

These were not the articles usually written by fledgling politicians, flashy diatribes shouting "hey me," but provocative, controversial, deeply thoughtful essays. In 1982, she was one of the first persons to see that the Far Right in America had usurped issues of moral value and patriotism and religion and made them their own. She called for "A Rebirth of Virtue," a plea that would have made many members of her generation cringe in embarrassment. At the beginning of the Reagan age of supposedly enlightened selfishness, she saw that her generation was joining the parade and realized where the drumbeat was leading America. "A professor with a Harvard Ph.D. teaches at a small college for $11,000," she wrote of David without mentioning his name. "He is considered an outcast, an oddity. When he decides to attend Yale Law School, suddenly his opinion is sought, and his advice valued. Now he can earn big money, therefore he must be smart." Kathleen wrote that among her generation "the idea of a wife and husband who commit themselves as selflessly to each other and to their children is almost an anachronism."

In an essay titled "The Forgotten Virtue of Voluntarism," Kathleen preached to a readership full of Democrats who saw volunteering as a Republican attempt to abrogate governmental responsibility, and career-oriented women who considered volunteering largely make-work for society ladies. Here again she sought to rescue one of the more noble aspects of American society, and place it as a centerpiece of contemporary values.

Charles Peters, the editor of *The Washington Monthly*, was so impressed by Kathleen that he was fond of saying that "she could be the first female president of the United States." Of all the young Kennedys, she had the best credentials to run for Congress. Her younger brother, Joe II, was the other obvious candidate in the family to run for the vacated seat in the Massachusetts Eighth Congressional District that Jack had once held. Since the accident that had left a young woman physically crippled, Joe II had founded a nonprofit organization to buy oil for the disadvantaged, and around him there was a coterie of ambitious advisors and Democratic state politicians who considered him a shoo-in.

Hardly anyone thought about Kathleen's candidacy, either in the family or out of it. "When we were young, my mother used to say women shouldn't run for office," Kathleen reflected. "That's why the women's movement has been so helpful." That Kathleen was not considered was partly her own reticence, for she still had something in her of that traditional political woman of her mother's and aunts' generation. "It took me a longer time to figure out that's what I would be good at and that's what I should do. My father was attorney general and a politician but it had never occurred to me until after I had graduated from college," Kathleen reflected. "It never occurred to me that that was what I should do."

Kathleen and David had a marriage in which they shared their obligations to their children and made room for each other's ambitions. They did not do this as in some modern marriages in which the two partners monitored each other's behavior like gender police, rigorously dividing duties, but with tender regard for each other's lives. David was neither a novelist nor destined for a stellar career in a law firm, but was a natural teacher. When he received an offer to teach at St. John's College in Annapolis, he and Kathleen decided he should accept. In the summer of 1984, the family moved to a seventy-year-old Victorian house just north of Baltimore. They filled their home with books, Kennedy family pictures, toys, and a nursery for their third daughter, Rose Katherine.

Kathleen had been old enough to know her father the way none of her younger siblings could, and she saw herself endowed to carry on his legacy. Just as her Aunt Eunice was intellectually open to discuss anything but her Catholic faith, so was Kathleen's mind unfettered except when it came to discussions of her father's life and legacy. Bobby was sacred to her. To further his memory, she was instrumental in creating the Robert F. Kennedy Human Rights Award. There were many awards given out in America whose primary purpose was the self-aggrandizement of the giver. This award was not one of them, although the Kennedys squeezed on the stage for their moment of applause. In November of 1984 the first annual award was given to the Co-Madres (The Committee of Mothers and Relatives of Political Prisoners, Disappeared and Murdered of El Salvador), a largely illiterate group of women fighting the violence in their native land. In Reagan's America, the Co-Madres were considered a dangerous, subversive group. Four leather chairs sat empty on the podium at Georgetown

University, symbolizing the fact that the women had been denied visas by the State Department for having "personally advocated acts of violence and have actively participated in terrorist activities" in El Salvador. In later years, as the violence of the military government in El Salvador became widely known, the Co-Madres women were no longer objects of such controversy, and their bravery was justly celebrated. The award often went to such individuals whose activities challenged the comfortable American assumption that their government always put human rights at the forefront of foreign policy.

Kathleen didn't want simply to celebrate the activism of others. On February 1, 1986, she declared her own candidacy for the House of Representatives in Maryland's Second Congressional District, the first Kennedy woman ever to run for public office. Joe II had already announced his candidacy for the House of Representatives in Boston. As Kathleen looked northward, she knew that her brother had by far the easier task. He had announced earlier, seeking to overwhelm his opponents in the Democratic primary that was tantamount to election. The other Democratic candidates had neither his name nor his money, and the Boston papers at times treated him as if he were being anointed rather than elected. Kathleen had to face charges that she was a Marylander-come-lately who had hardly registered to vote in the state before she had decided to run for Congress. The fact that she had little opposition in the Democratic primary had little to do with her perceived clout and a great deal to do with the strength of the Republican incumbent, Rep. Helen Bentley, a tough-talking, sixty-two-year-old former journalist.

Kathleen spoke from platforms in union halls, country clubs, fraternal lodges, and campaign forums. She tried to lower her voice. She even practiced speaking with a cork in her mouth. But she still sometimes emitted a squeaky sound and tended to rush her sentences, as if by sheer intensity she could convince her audiences. Those who came seeking resonances of her father and uncle usually came away disappointed. As a woman her appearance was scrutinized the way a male candidate's attire would not have been. She wore enormous glasses and with her short-cropped hair and utilitarian suits appeared more the academician than did her husband.

Kathleen simply didn't care about her looks. She was perfectly happy to accessorize her new Lord and Taylor suit with a pair of running shoes. That bothered Ethel, whose main contribution to her daughter's campaign was to arrive at important speeches with ropes of pearls to throw around Kathleen's neck, thereby hoping to soften her image.

Kathleen's concern for ideas often conflicted with the realities of a political campaign. At Radcliffe, she had been comfortable neither standing with the pro-life activists, nor with the militant pro-choice forces. As a candidate she was expected to pick up one slogan or the other, and carry it as if it were the truth. In the end, she stood against the beliefs of her mother and the other Kennedy women of the older generation by taking a pro-choice position. She did not shout her stance from a bullhorn and make it a major issue, but it was there. "I'm obviously pro-choice, but the issue is not one of my great loves," Kathleen reflected recently. "I'm clearly Catholic and the church is not in favor of abortion. But it's not something that I want to speak about loudly. But when it comes down to it, I don't think the government should tell women what to do."

People remembered the noble passion of her father's speeches, but Bobby for most of his public life had been a poor speaker, his high-pitched voice an unworthy vehicle for his sentiments, his nervous intensity catapulting his words ahead. As a Kennedy man, he could get away with speeches and manners that a woman could not. Kathleen simply didn't have the charisma of the male Kennedys.

Her opponent condemned Kathleen as a carpetbagger, although she pointed out rightly that she had followed her husband's career to Maryland, a sacrifice that the conservative Republicans should have applauded. Others considered it unseemly that a thirty-five-year-old mother of three would run for office, particularly since she talked so often about the noble value of the family, a criticism that a male candidate would not have received.

Kathleen's daughters rarely saw their mother during the long months of the campaign, and they had a role model for a mother unlike any in the Kennedy family. Kathleen seemed devoid of the endemic guilt of mothers with careers. "The other day someone said to my oldest daughter, 'Meaghan, you're really tough,'" Kathleen said. "And she said, 'Yup, just like my Mom.' Isn't that great? I'm just in seventh heaven. I couldn't be happier."

Kathleen's campaign was caught up in all the contradictions of her family and her gender and her own life. Sometimes in her speeches she attempted to cover over these contradictions with a veneer of rhetoric, but at her deepest, most intellectually honest she did not. She knew that she had privileges that most women did not have. She was uncomfortable with the way many feminists looked disdainfully at women who stayed home to bring up their children, and believed that at the center of the women's movement stood not simply women but families. "What we need and want are an ethics and an environment that supports a parent's choice to both work and care for her children," she told one group. "Only if women directly confront the question of who shall raise America's children will we take power as women."

Kathleen knew that she had won this nomination because her name was Kennedy, and yet she had to fight the charges that it was her name alone that mattered. As much as she tried to deny it, she was on the surface the quintessential yuppie candidate, with a family income in 1985 of $174,434, mainly from trust funds and partnerships. *Vogue* wrote that "the challenge for Kathleen Kennedy Townsend is to get elected, so that bright young mothers like her and her supporters will finally have a strong and understanding voice in Congress." That was partially true, but Kathleen was painfully aware of the privileges of class and circumstance, and all her life had been attempting to fly out of the gilded cage of her birth.

In the suburbs of Baltimore, Kathleen ran from house to house, street to street, jogging down the macadam, followed by panting staff and reporters, a hyperkinetic caricature of an energetic politician. By her estimate she knocked on more than ten thousand doors. On the way to a fund-raiser for the Women's Campaign Fund in Washington, D.C., she had no time to change into a suit. "Forget it. I'll change in the car," she said as she took off her blouse. "Any niece of Eunice Shriver's ought to be able to change in the front seat. It never bothers Eunice—she shows her bare bottom to the world."

By mid-September Kathleen and her staff had the feeling that they were closing the gap, that she might just pull off this extraordinary upset. It was then that Joe won his primary, and members of his ragtag army of supporters drove down to Maryland to help Kathleen. Most of them knew little about the state except its name, and they managed to alienate a good number of voters. Kathleen could read the ending of her dream in the declining polls. Two weeks before election day she knew that Bentley would defeat her, and Kathleen would have the distinction of not simply being the first Kennedy woman to run for office, but the first Kennedy to lose a general election.

Kathleen had entered the race idealistically emulating the most noble aspects of her father, but those beliefs had been tempered in the fierce fires of politics. She had had her moments of exhilaration and euphoria but those times had been matched by embarrassment, rejection, and indifference. She had entered the race enjoying the rhetoric of politics, the public profession of virtue. That was what politics was to her mother, and most of the other Kennedy women of her generation. But there was another side to politics, as there was another side to her father, the merciless fighter in the dark alleys of public life. In her race, Kathleen felt betrayed by the Democratic candidate for governor, William Donald Schaefer, the popular mayor of Baltimore, who supported the Republican Bentley, even attending Kathleen's opponent's fund-raiser. That was something she did not forget. Kathleen would never be as adept as her father at that brutal part of politics, but there was a toughness to her now, and a hunger to return and run again. She admired Eunice beyond any of the other aunts, and Eunice alone of the women of her generation had that political toughness that was thought to be the endowment of the Kennedy males. Eunice understood that the world was made of mixed motives, and that one had to exploit them. Eunice used people. She used their desires to get near the Kennedys. She used their desires to be praised for their goodness. She used her celebrity, and the celebrity of others. These were all things that Kathleen was learning as well.

In the wake of her defeat, Kathleen became the president of the Maryland Student Service Alliance. This was an obscure program within the state's Department of Education that monitored community-service programs for high school students across the state. It was Kathleen's vision to make Maryland the first state in which these programs became a mandatory part of high school education. As she walked into the tiny warren of offices at the Department of Education in downtown Baltimore where she worked initially with a part-time secretary, she was in an unlikely venue for such radical reform. This was government, not the stirring rhetoric of a campaign speech, but monotonous endless offices, tiny fiefdoms of power, all the crushing weight of entrenched bureaucracy. Even within these walls Kathleen had as many enemies as friends, her ideas op-

posed by the educational establishment of school superinten-
dents and teachers' unions.

As Kathleen went out and visited scores of schools, she saw
that so often words had been separated from deeds and a terrible timidity had come over public education. School after
school she found hallways littered with refuse, and rarely a
teacher who dared to tell a student to clean up his or her
school, or not to litter in the first place. Kathleen had gone to
a parochial school where the nuns had taught a long specific
list of moral strictures. These she had rebelled against, but she
saw that the modern public school had gone to the opposite extreme. In the name of moral neutrality, she found the schools
had retreated from teaching any values at all.

To Kathleen these service programs were a way to teach
what she called a "crucial ethic." This was not mindless incul-
cation of moral slogans, not some innocuous values clarifica-
tion, but a hands-on experiencing, a concern for others that
connected one to the larger world. This was what her father
had taught her, what it meant to her to be a Kennedy woman.
She sought to make service not the dilettantish avocation of a
few, but an integral part of the life of every young woman and
man in Maryland. When she went out across the state, she saw
how dramatically such service could change young people.

Kathleen had been roundly defeated in her first race, but this
attempt to make a mandatory requirement for high school
graduation to give at least seventy-five hours of service was a
campaign too. She, like her sisters and brothers, lacked a certain public grace, and she sometimes appeared impolite when
she was simply uncomfortable and nervous. She was a dogged
proponent of her cause, however, crisscrossing the state, traveling with her one associate, Maggie O'Neill, often writing and
working in the car. She wooed editorial writers and journalists
from the *Baltimore Sun* and *The Washington Post*, achieving a
bounty of positive editorials and clippings. She garnered the
support of corporate and civic leaders and attempted to neutral-
ize the opposition of much of the educational establishment.

Kathleen talked in schools from the suburbs of Washington
to the southern reaches of the Eastern Shore, but not in the parochial schools of the Baltimore diocese. She had attempted to
announce her pro-choice position as softly as she could, but
her voice was heard loud and strong in the counsels of the
church. Kathleen was one of the outstanding Catholic laywomen in Baltimore, but the archdiocese had unofficially

banned her from talking in any of their schools. It was a chilling rebuke to a woman whose early years had been spent under the stewardship of the sisters of the Sacred Heart, and whose mother was a daily communicant. It forced Kathleen to look squarely at what she believed the church had become, and her deeply felt belief that she had not left the church, the church had left her. "The church is very chauvinistic," Kathleen said. "And I think the priests are getting worse because so many have left the church. And the people going in are much more misogynistic than they were thirty years ago. I've talked to a number of priests who are in their fifties, and they agree. A lot of these new priests are gay and just don't like women. The hypocrisy! But I guess the church has always been filled with, you know, all these popes who weren't paragons of virtue either, having children and starting wars. But the nuns are terrific. They can't believe in this church either. But they understand there's something deeper than the church itself."

Kathleen worked with fierce diligence, and in 1992 the state board of education voted to make Maryland the first state in which these programs were mandatory. It was not the kind of vote that garnered massive publicity, but it was a great achievement for Kathleen and for the family legacy she was attempting to keep alive.

— 27 —

Family Appreciation Day

For Rose's hundredth birthday in July of 1990, the Kennedys planned a great celebration, commemorating not simply a century of life but a family. Congress passed a resolution making July 22 "Rose Fitzgerald Kennedy Family Appreciation Day." As the day approached, Rose's youthful picture graced the covers of several major magazines including *Life, Parade*, and *McCall's*. That was the Rose everyone wanted to remember, especially the family. Rose's daughters and son were so used to their mother as this overseeing matriarch that they could hardly deal with her diminished condition.

Soon after Rose had been flown back to Hyannis Port from Palm Beach, the nurse had brought Rose down to dinner. "Go ahead and eat, Mother, go ahead and eat," Pat said as she pushed spoonful after spoonful of food up to Rose's mouth, pretending that Rose was ingesting the food. Afterwards the nurse wheeled Rose back to her room and gave her nourishment through feeding tubes.

Rose knew nothing of David's death, and it was unclear what other events in recent years she comprehended. "We didn't tell Rose about the divorce," Joan said, her words carried on a laughter both impish and embarrassed. "She loved me always, and we didn't tell her. I don't think she ever knew and then she had the strokes. And you see even after the divorce and the stroke, I spent a lot of time there. I'd have dinner with Ted and the kids and my mother-in-law. We'd have Thanksgiving every year with Ted and the kids. We had Christmas every year. I don't think she ever knew."

Ted and Eunice often took their mother for walks, wheeling her down the old familiar lanes and byways. They continued to celebrate her birthdays as great family events, an occasion for

Ted to tell the press some pithy remark that Rose had supposedly made. Shortly before her hundredth birthday, Ted told a reporter that when his mother saw him taking out his tennis racket, she had said: "Are you sure this is yours, Teddy? I've been looking all around the house for mine."

Ted was the great sentimentalist of the family, and he was inventing these sentences. "Ted made these quotes up," Eunice said. "I had nothing to do with it." Ted was not engaged in a grand duplicity to hide some evil secrets from the media. This was his vision of his mother, and he willed his mother into coherence.

"There's a presence about her," Ted reflected. "A radiance that has an extraordinary impact on others, particularly on children, and so her presence is still an extraordinary force." Ted could turn a murmur into a phrase, a flash of her eye into recognition, a nod of her head into approval. His sisters and his nieces and nephews joined him in his deception, pretending to the world as in a way they pretended to each other. Ted continued to make up these remarks. "I'm like old wine—they don't bring me out very often, but I'm well preserved" he had her saying just before the birthday.

On the evening before the public celebration, the family and intimate friends got together for a private dinner. There were five surviving children, twenty-eight grandchildren, and twenty-two great-grandchildren, and most of the adult Kennedys were here this evening, the largest family gathering since Bobby's death. Spread out in the living room, the Kennedys seemed not simply a family, but a great clan of remarkable fecundity and variety. Twelve of the grandchildren were females. They were growing up believing in family and home as their grandmother did, but knowing that they could have a life outside as well. Among her granddaughters Kathleen, Maria, and Caroline juggled careers and families, and Sydney exercised her freedom by staying home with her three children.

Kathleen had set the standard, and she was bringing up her three daughters to believe that they could do anything a man could do. Caroline was the second Kennedy woman of her generation to have children. She had two daughters, two-year-old Rose named after her great-grandmother, and the infant Tatiana. Caroline was not only a mother but was active on the board of the Kennedy Library, completing a book with a coauthor on the Bill of Rights, and helping to oversee a new Profile in Courage Award, given each year to an American who best represented the political courage her father had written about in his book. Kathleen's younger sister, Kerry, had taken over as the head of the Robert F. Kennedy Memorial Center for Human Rights. She was not content merely to give annual awards, but aimed to publicize human rights abuses throughout the world, seeking to end them by shining the light of public attention into the darkest areas of international life. Along with Caroline, Maria was the other best known Kennedy woman of her generation. She had been dropped as coanchor of the *CBS Morning News* soon after her marriage. Now in Los Angeles, she was a mother of two daughters, Katherine Eunice and Christina Maria Aurelia, and coanchor of NBC's *Sunday Today*.

Rose was far too weak to sit through the lengthy evening. The following day three hundred and seventy guests arrived for a mammoth celebration on the lawn before the great house. The event was a bewildering juxtaposition of heartfelt emotion and unseemly rudeness. Eunice was upset that the tent that had been set up on the grounds was too full of light to show properly a film on Rose's life. In front of scores of guests, she berated Herb Kramer of Special Olympics, who was dying of cancer. The film was eventually shown, and it was a deeply moving documentary on Rose's life that brought tears to the eyes of many in the audience. There were tears too when Maureen McGovern sang "My Wild Irish Rose" and "The Rose of Tralee," and thirty-one-year-old Mark Swiconek, a Special Olympian, read his tribute to Rose.

Ted was in his cups again, and so was Pat. Joan was sober; two years before she had pleaded no contest to a drunken-driving charge when she ran into a chain fence in Barnstable, on Cape Cod, near Hyannis Port. Ted was not one to sit around for lengthy speeches and awards. In the middle of the afternoon he went out on his boat with two young women. He returned in time to say good-bye to some of the guests, attempting to kiss one woman on the mouth, a gesture that she found offensive, as did her husband. And through much of it, the guests were told Rose sat up in her wheelchair on the second floor of the house, looking down on the events below.

If Rose had been able to understand, she would have been simultaneously proud and saddened by the lives of her daughters. Pat no longer had to pretend to her mother that her life was something other than what it was. She had always wanted to do something in the arts, and she settled for being a friend of artists. She was a social fixture at charity auctions, fundraisers for the arts, and other elite affairs of Manhattan. "Pat is impressed by talent and achievement," said the journalist Dotson Rader, one of her closest friends. "She knows all sorts of rich people but she has very few friends who have money. She likes to be around writers, and painters, people in the arts."

Pat was one of the names that the society reporters usually mentioned in their accounts of parties and affairs. Pat lived in a classic old New York building at Sutton Place South, the entrance of which the doorman treated as if it were a bank vault. Her gracious apartment looked out on the East River and was a glorious venue for parties, as was her summer house in the exclusive precincts of Southhampton, on Long Island.

Those who read about her in the newspapers could easily have envisioned Pat's life as enviable, one elegant party after another. They did not see her as she returned alone by herself in the evening to her apartment building on the East Side wobbling on her high heels. Nor did they talk to her in the afternoons or evenings when her breath smelled of liquor and she slurred her words into meaningless garble.

Pat was the most gentle of the Kennedy sisters, with a shy vulnerability that she had long ago learned to expose to almost no one. She, like her mother, was consumed with maintaining her youthful visage and figure, with all the craft of art and science. She could not abide the idea of getting fat. She attended a splendid dinner party given by Judith Green in honor of Frank Sinatra. Dinner included hearty portions of pasta, and afterwards Sinatra stood up and sang while Peter Duchin played the piano. It was a night to be savored, but Pat left, went upstairs to her guest bedroom, put on her swimming suit, and did laps in the pool, working off her excessive dinner.

Peter had died of failing liver and kidneys in December of 1984, victim in part to the wages of alcoholic abuse, but it was a lesson that Pat did not learn. Her children loved her with a deep and certain love, and in their small ways tried to protect her. To her small coterie of friends, she was a woman of overwheming generosity, whose idea of charity was not celebrated public benefice, but help to those for whom she cared. Rose had not wanted Pat to remarry, but there were few eligible men out there for a woman in her sixties anyway, and she was escorted by a series of platonic friends, including Rader.

Rader had been Tennessee Williams's lover, and he escorted Pat to the opening night of the playwright's last play, *Clothes for a Summer Hotel*. Afterwards at the cast party she attempted to encourage the sixty-nine-year-old artist, but he read the dreary first reviews as the obituary for his career. "We've got to do something to help him," Pat told Rader. "Let's get some of his friends together at my place and try to cheer him up."

Pat and Williams's lives resonated with one terrible similarity. Like Rosemary, Williams's own sister, Rose, as a young woman had been given one of the earliest lobotomies, a tragedy that he wrote about in his poignant drama, *Suddenly Last Summer*. Pat empathized with Williams's artistic plight, and she offered to give a dinner party for him. That was what she knew best how to do, to serve up good cheer and encouragement. Pat usually wore bright colors, and had dyed her hair red, as if that alone could banish black moods and life's darkness. For Williams's party she ordered so many flowers that her apartment was like a garden in bloom, and put an enormous balloon in the foyer with the words HURRAY FOR TENNESSEE!

The other guests were Williams's theatrical friends, including Eli Wallach, and social friends such as Jan Cushing. There was a curious anonymity about celebrities, and Pat was more comfortable speaking the predictable patter of the famous than talking to someone who might want to say *something*. The guests had been told that Williams was despondent, and that they were there to lift his spirits. During cocktails the playwright ran out on the balcony and was about to throw himself to his death in the East River seven floors below, when Wallach pulled him back.

Liquor was the sweetest solace of all to Williams as it was to Pat, and during dinner as they downed drink after drink, the playwright's mood lifted. Pat could not turn her own mournful memories to art the way Williams could, but she read his emotional state as clearly as the wrinkles on her hands, and as she sat on his right she was there for him in a way that was as simple as it was meaningful. He turned to her and held her elegant long hand, stroked her hair, and told her how beautiful she was.

"We're all doomed," Williams said, as he sat there. "Doomed. Dying ducks in a winter freeze."

For Pat the memories of her marriage with Peter lived in the faces of their four children. Pat continued to live her life in New York City and Southampton. In New York she was a founder of the National Committee for the Literary Arts, arranging a series of author lectures and scholarships. She was involved as well with the refurbishment of the exhibits at the Kennedy Library, but such activities did not fill up her personal life. She had never been able to find a man with whom she could even think seriously about building a new life together. In the late 1980s, she began a relationship with a television producer, a man of public virtues, full of anecdotes and lively repartee. He proved, however, to be emotionally destructive, tearing away at whatever shards of self-confidence Pat still had. When he stayed at her house on Long Island, he sometimes left in the night, and Pat suspected that he was out looking for other, younger women. Pat began drinking almost uncontrollably, so seriously in fact that for a while her own brother, Ted, and her children vowed to avoid her until she got control of her drinking. The family had tried almost everything. They were faced with a terrible dilemma. Pat needed to be in an institution, but they feared that as soon as Pat checked into a facility a patient or employee was bound to sell her story to the tabloids. That had happened with Joan, and indeed would happen later with other family members. The family, despite everything that had happened to Joan, continued to have this dread fear of revelation as the greatest of evils. Such exposure would only deepen Pat's pain. She ended up spending most of her time at home. She was in such pathetic shape that for a Fourth of July celebration at Jean's Long Island home, her younger sister asked that Pat not attend. Finally, in June 1989, she was driving on Hampton Road near her great house on Long Island when she ran into a telephone pole. The police gave her a breath analyzer test and arrested her for driving under the influence of alcohol.

Pat's friends and family saw that this minor accident did what all their heartfelt lecturing could not do: convince her to attempt to get some control over her drinking. To the Kennedys it was public disgrace that was the highest humiliation, and Pat seemed unwilling to see herself made a public spectacle like Joan. Pat stopped her most extreme drinking, and though she continued to be a heavy drinker, she was no longer such a danger, to herself and to others.

Of all her daughters, Jean was the only one to blame Rose

for the unhappiness of much of her adult life. Thus it undoubt-edly would have made Rose immensely proud to see what her youngest daughter was doing with her life. Jean often appeared jealous of the way Eunice dominated the women in the family. She wanted her own achievements in the world, never forget-ting what Eunice had done. In 1974 when Jean began Very Special Arts to foster art for the handicapped, she had con-sciously mimicked Special Olympics. She had her own celeb-rities from Mickey Mouse to Andy Warhol, and her own arts festivals that Jean said were "supposed to be a culmination of art experiences for the child throughout the year." Jean's orga-nization, unlike Special Olympics, received its major funding from the federal government, more than five million dollars between 1976 and 1980 alone. There was, moreover, in the early years what appeared to be an unseemly extravagance. In the fall of 1979, for instance, the National Committee of Arts for the Handicapped that ran Very Special Arts held its annual meeting in Washington at a cost of about sixty thousand dol-lars. The two-day event culminated in a dinner for over two hundred people at the Kennedy Center, featuring poached salmon and pears in Cassis for dessert. The national Special Arts Festival held that same year cost four times its projected cost of sixty thousand dollars.

"It [the criticism] wasn't a big deal," Jean said. "It was all from someone on the board who was upset because we dropped him. It was like a one-day story." In the next years, Jean developed Very Special Arts into a major program across America, reaching outside the United States as well. The suc-cess of the program showed not only what handicapped indi-viduals could do, but what a woman in her late fifties could do, a woman who had never had a career outside her family. Suddenly, Jean was a public person in her own right. During her brother's political campaigns, she had read the gracious lit-tle remarks she was asked to give and stood shaking hands at receptions, but she had not given real speeches. "I was not raised to speak, and I didn't particularly like to give speeches," she reflected. "Now, I don't mind them at all because I do a lot of it with Very Special Arts."

Jean had a confidence about herself that was totally new. "It's a lot of hard work, and terrific work, challenging work," she reflected. A full-time staff in Washington backed up the chairwoman, but Jean was the impetus behind the organization. Jean filled benefit committees with the names of America's media and cultural elite, from Tom Brokaw to Michael Collins, Lauren Hutton to Itzhak Perlman. It was a heady business, flying to Ireland to inaugurate that country's program, and to Paris for a benefit that included a concert by the Paris Philharmonic Orchestra, the event presided over by Madame Danielle Mitterrand, wife of the French president.

In June of 1989, the first International Very Special Arts Festival brought together more than a thousand handicapped individuals from fifty states and fifty-one countries. The group was given a reception at the White House attended by President George Bush, and the closing gala was filmed by NBC for an hour-long program that *The New York Times* called "a healthy dose of good old-fashioned uplift . . . [and] an encouraging reminder that there are still uncommonly decent and generous impulses to be found in the country at large."

For Jean these were good times, if only Steve had not been dying of cancer. In her family, Jean had gone through so many tragedies, moments of monumental despair, and now with her mother's lingering illness and Steve's sickness, a shadow hung over even the most glorious of moments. As much as she liked to pretend otherwise, Steve had always had his other lives, his other women, but as he declined, she saw that he was at the center of so much of their lives. The image of the Smiths as a happily married couple had been a façade behind which they had lived their often separate lives. Jean, however, was there for her husband in the last months of his life. She was there walking beside him on empty beaches in the Caribbean, there sitting beside him in his hospital room, there not simply playing the devoted wife but being one. For the family Steve had been the one to call. He was the one who could make it right, and as he became more ill the family began to realize how crucial his role had been in their fortunes. In August of 1990, a month after Rose's one-hundredth birthday celebration, Steve died.

Jackie rarely visited Hyannis Port any longer. She had always retreated from the shrill shouts and frenetic activities of the compound. In 1981, on an isolated spit of land on Martha's Vineyard, she built what was truly her home. The estate, its worth estimated at three million dollars, rested in the midst of 375 acres of land, secure from the sight of the curious. Each summer she invited the Kennedys for a party in the 3,100-square-foot house, but that was the primary contact she had with her old family, except for public gatherings, fund-raisers, and library events. The house was built in the traditional style of New England homes, without great windows looking out on the sea, but with small panes held by wooden pegs instead of nails, and it was here that she lived with solitude and peace.

Jackie and Maurice talked about marriage, but though he had separated from his wife, he never took that step. In the late 1980s Maurice moved in with Jackie, and they lived together as man and woman in a manner that would have confounded Rose or most of the women of her generation. Jackie had been in analysis for years, but she found, in her life with Maurice and her work as an editor, a life of peace and security that she had never known before. She had always understood that the essence of elegance is simplicity, and it was an elegant life she led now. There was elegance in her exquisite apartment, elegance in her summer home, elegance in her occasional dinner parties, elegance in her sense that each moment of her life was to be savored, be it a walk with her grandchildren, a passage of a book to be edited, a *bon mot* to be savored. She even stopped her chain smoking.

In the library of her apartment, she kept a powerful telescope with which she could sit high above the city watching the strollers in Central Park, matrons hailing cabs, and deliverymen hurrying into the buildings along Fifth Avenue. In her house on the Vineyard, she and Maurice often went bird watching, tromping through the dunes and brush, hoping to spy an exotic species that she would capture for a moment in the lenses of her binoculars, as others for so long had sought to capture her.

Eunice and Sarge attended mass every morning. Those who saw them there, so vitally energetic and unobtrusively pious, sometimes assumed that they had reached a blessed state of serenity. Anthony asked his father, "Why do you go to church every day?" Sarge replied, "I'm so weak and I need so much help."

Eunice and Sarge built a large house for themselves in the Maryland suburbs. They knew that it would be their last house. Sarge loved modern art and the walls were full of abstract paintings, as well as Andy Warhol's portrait of Maria. Eunice preferred religious art, and there were antique Madonnas and other profoundly Catholic art to satisfy her sensibilities. There were framed letters from Jack, a full-length portrait of Joe Jr., and all sorts of other family photographs in silver frames. There was little evidence of the awards and honorary degrees that Eunice had received, including in 1984 the Presidential Medal of Freedom, the national's highest civilian award, given her by President Reagan. When the plans for the outdoor swimming pool were shown to Eunice, she revised them to make the pool accessible to the disabled, and added a shower area for the Special Olympians whom she intended to invite to use the facility.

Sarge had had triple bypass surgery and was suffering from prostate cancer, but he still played a good game of tennis, and went out and played catch with his sons. Eunice was a good tennis player too, and though she and Sarge played doubles well together, they made an even better team at Special Olympics. Sarge had taken over as chairman of the board of Special Olympics International and he was an inexhaustible source of ideas and initiatives, flying off around the world, returning to his office as if jet lag did not exist.

Eunice was the honorary chairman of Special Olympics International, but there was nothing honorary about the many hours she spent in the executive offices on New York Avenue each week. She vowed that she would retire from Special Olympics, but the two Shrivers kept a tight grasp on the organization. Special Olympics Inc. was legally part of the Joseph P. Kennedy Jr. Foundation, and they ran this major international social organization as a family charity.

From her office in downtown Washington, Eunice worked at a frenetic pace. She sometimes didn't remember things the way she used to remember. That was a new burden on her hapless secretaries, who often lasted no longer than a box of Kleenex. Members of her staff knew of the enormous contributions Eunice had made. They wondered how she could be so noble about the great things of life and so petty about the insignificant. She had done magnificent work developing Special Olympics, but she seemed unable to allow any new leadership to evolve. Eunice almost never went down to their floor at the Special Olympics office from the executive suite above, her main contact with the staff often a curt imperious command on the telephone pushing them on to some new endeavor.

Eunice's whole vision of life began and ended with the family, and she saw the fruition of that vision in the lives of her own children. She saw her youngest son, Anthony, almost every day. He was in his mid-twenties and was as handsome as his sister Maria was pretty. He had all the markings of a self-indulgent, self-satisfied young heir. Instead, he had an office at Special Olympics for a program he was developing called Best Buddies, which fostered friendships between college students and those with retardation. Anthony had his own best buddy in Rosemary, whom he visited regularly, and he sought to institutionalize that experience in hundreds of college and university campuses.

Anthony was not one for details. His little office was a shambles, papers strewn across the floor, but he was energetic and inspiring especially to members of his own generation. And Best Buddies was growing rapidly. Eunice was immensely proud of her youngest son. As for Anthony, he understood how profoundly his parents had shaped his values and the life he intended to live. At times he found it less than ideal working twenty yards away from his mother, her shadow hovering over his every move.

Eunice talked to her other three sons regularly as well. Timmy oversaw public school prevention programs for drugs, pregnancy, AIDS, and violence in New Haven public schools, and Eunice also saw in Timmy her social visions being fulfilled. She talked to him about education and change and the omnipresent problems of class. Mark ran Choice, a social program in Baltimore. That too was a fulfillment of Eunice's ideas of social usefulness.

Her eldest son, Bobby, had tried a number of businesses and professions. He was in his mid-thirties and was living out in Los Angeles working for Special Olympics. He had inherited his father's gifts of salesmanship and had helped convince many of the most popular singers in America to contribute songs to a unique Christmas album that earned about twenty million dollars for Special Olympics. Bobby won accolades for that effort but at the Washington office he was singularly unpopular, his abrasive sense of entitlement irritating even the most loyal of the family associates. "I told him he should take a Dale Carnegie course," said Jay Emmett, the director of public affairs for Special Olympics International. The larger problem surrounding Bobby involved not his personality but the fact that his special projects office in Los Angeles had been given a budget of more than one million dollars over two years, with a $150,000 annual salary for Bobby. That made him the second highest paid employee in the entire organization and created serious morale problems. Eunice had been warned that this largess opened Special Olympics up to charges of family favoritism and the abuse of contributors' money. She felt her son, her Bobby, had earned his splendid office and that anyone else who raised that amount of money would earn an even larger salary. She refused to back down, and the staff learned that as much as Eunice loved Special Olympics, she loved her son more. But at the end of 1993, the salary ended and a new lower-paid employee took Bobby's place.

Maria was Eunice's only daughter and she talked to her every day. "What drives Maria, whether she realizes it or not is her mother," said Theo Hayes, her oldest friend. "She wants to see her mother's approval before anyone else's." Maria had begun her high-profile career in network journalism by doing celebrity interviews. Eunice not only watched every program, but she told her friends to watch, and then asked them their opinions, passing on their remarks to Maria.

With Arnold as her husband, Maria had access to practically every celebrity in America. She could probably have made herself enormously and easily successful doing immensely popular programs that were more entertainment than journalism. Her mother had taught her that fame by itself meant nothing, and that she should make a difference in the world. Maria set out to use celebrity, rather than have it use her. On her hour-long specials, she interviewed the celebrities of the moment, whose marquee names drew a large television audience, but she also had examinations of social problems, and interviews with serious political figures and others. "When I started these prime-time specials, it was always with an eye, 'Well, if I put on somebody like Michael Jordan or Danny DeVito, people might tune in,' " she reflected. "But I could also put two other stories that they wouldn't necessarily see in prime time that would become something that they would be interested in and it would have a social conscience." From there Maria moved to thematic shows including a controversial hour on gay life in America.

Maria was a political woman of a new generation, using her power and celebrity with subtle force. She and Arnold traveled in the highest circles in Hollywood, and Maria's friends included those who were both interesting and useful. At the NBC commissary in Burbank, she could as easily grab a coffee or sandwich with Brandon Tartikoff, then the network entertainment president, as with her young assistant. If she were a man, Maria might have used her power to maximize her exposure on television, turning herself into a brand name. Instead, she negotiated a contract that allowed her to do only occasional specials, work out of her house, be a mother and wife as well as a television journalist. She had always been reluctant to talk about herself, but she understood that in her world celebrity was the fuel of power. She was obsessed by her image in the looking glass of the media, and her face smiled out on the cover of magazines from *Good Housekeeping* to *Vanity Fair*.

Maria had almost called her program *Cutting Edge with Maria Shriver* and that's where both she and her mother wanted to be. She was at times a victim of her enthusiasms, infused with a gullibility that assumed an interview was the same thing as the truth. She did a touching interview with Lyle Alzado, the former Los Angeles Raider football player, in which he denied that he had ever taken steroids. Arnold had taken steroids to help build up his bulk, and it would not have taken a massive investigation to realize the extent to which athletes were using the dangerous drug. A year later Alzado returned for another interview. He was dying of brain cancer, and he blamed it on the massive doses of steroids that he had taken over the years. "I thought I'd get into trouble," he told Maria. "I lied to you because I was afraid."

Eunice was constantly asking her daughter what was happening, discussing the latest cultural trend, social conditions in Watts, the voucher systems in schools. When Eunice came out to Maria's sprawling eight-thousand-square-foot house in Malibu with its tennis court, swimming pools, and Chagalls, Mirós, and Wyeths on the walls, she didn't even think of relaxing. Maria was awed by Eunice's energy and endless commitments. Here she was almost seventy and still flogging herself onward, up at five in the morning, on the phone to her office in New York, whipping off faxes, writing articles. By eight-thirty she was ready to head out with Maria's two daughters for a trek somewhere. Then she would be off investigating a social issue or a Special Olympics program. In the afternoon she might swim with the two children, but then she would be pestering Maria to invite somebody interesting over for cocktails or dinner.

Of all the aspects of her formidable mother that Maria

loved, nothing filled her with such emotion as watching Eunice as a grandmother. Maria left Katherine Eunice and Christina with Eunice. She returned and found the outdoor furniture had all been turned over, the pillows piled up and around, creating a gigantic playhouse. In the middle of the imaginary house sat Maria's daughters with Eunice playing Sally, their imaginary little friend.

Eunice had not wanted Maria's first daughter to be named after her. "In this day and age you can't do that to a child," Eunice had said definitively, and Maria had compromised by making "Eunice" her second name.

One day Maria was driving with her daughter when Katherine asked: "Mummy look at me. Who am I?"

Maria turned just enough to see her daughter making the most extraordinary grimace, her jaw clenched, her teeth showing. "I don't know. Who?"

"I'm Grandma."

As Maria grew older, she found that she more and more resembled her mother. Eunice had been sick so much of her life that the family would joke about what she would have accomplished if she had been healthy. Maria had a multitude of health problems herself, including a serious struggle with meningitis, but she soldiered on, pretending that she was fine.

One day she headed off for a parents' meeting at Katherine's school. As always she was balancing home and career, running off at the last minute. She put on leggings, combat boots, and a jacket, and looked like a motorcycle moll. Rushing into the assembly, Maria realized that the room was full of impeccably suited fathers and mothers in an abundance of Chanel suits and headbands. She thought for a moment of the way her mother had come to get her from school, hopelessly rumpled and unchic, a walking embarrassment. And she said to herself, *"I've become my mother."*

Eunice had the primary concern for Rosemary. Since Rose's illness, the oldest Kennedy sister had become more a part of the family than she had since the lobotomy. Three or four times a year Rosemary flew from Milwaukee to Palm Beach, Hyannis Port, Washington, or New York City to visit her relatives, and usually at least once a year Eunice flew out to Wisconsin. Eunice took Rosemary into the Special Olympics office, to mass on Sunday, and on drives in the countryside.

It took a whole new language of understanding to be able to

relate to Rosemary, and no one in the family spoke it as well as Anthony. Of all the young Kennedys, he was the one who made the trip out to Jefferson, Wisconsin, to visit his aunt. When Anthony eventually took the headquarters of his Best Buddies organization to Miami, he built a special room in his house so that when Rosemary visited she would feel comfortable. Caroline had a way with Rosemary too. When she and her two daughters visited Palm Beach in the winter, they made a birthday cake for Rosemary and decorated it with strawberries. Rosemary's birthday was in September, but Rosemary adored parties. The family gave her several birthday parties each year, and Caroline sent her a tape full of birthday music.

Rosemary was well into her seventies. She was in such good health and lived such a sound life that she might well outlive all her siblings. As she aged, the challenge for Eunice and the nuns was to be able to understand whatever infirmities she might have. One day she suddenly refused to walk, and then refused to swallow her food. It took Sister Margaret Ann's astute sense of Rosemary to realize that she was having problems with her knee. Rosemary, Sister Margaret Ann, and Alan K. Borsari, the Alverno director, flew down to Chicago for Rosemary's operation. Eunice arrived from Washington to be with her sister too. The group spent several days acclimating Rosemary to the hospital and her room, and a staff person from St. Coletta's slept in the bed next to her. It was the kind of exquisitely sensitive care that few of those with retardation received. Rosemary did not become frightened at these new surroundings, and made a remarkable recovery.

Sister Margaret Ann was a woman of deep and simple faith. She had worked in the cafeteria at St. Coletta's before being assigned to Rosemary. It had taken Rosemary a year to be comfortable with Sister Margaret Ann, but now after a decade together they had a rapport that was profound and often wordless. In the more than four decades that Rosemary had been at St. Coletta's, much had changed at the institution. There were only about thirty nuns left, and the school was run by lay administrators and staff, dependent largely on government monies for its financing. In 1983 the Kennedys gave a million dollars to renovate Alverno House, putting in a therapeutic pool and enlarging the chapel.

Rosemary's trust fund allowed her to have exemplary care. She had four people watching over her. Sister Margaret Ann spent more time with her than anyone else. Sister Leona lived in Rosemary's house, and worked part-time overseeing her. A college student came in evenings and early morning hours, while a fourth woman spent three nights a week doing ceramic work with Rosemary and being with her for supper. The team was supervised by Alan Borsari, who drew on other specialists including physical therapists and nurses.

Rosemary's daily routine was almost always the same. "I'll go into her room at six-thirty and turn on the light," said Sister Margaret Ann. "Rosemary's very cooperative. She helps you turn her out of bed. Usually I put her shoes on right away, and she will push her foot into the shoe. And then I take her to the washroom and wash her up. She's been putting her foot out for shoes all these years. She doesn't dress herself but she helps me. Her arms go out and her feet go out, and she will button her buttons. I will take out a couple things and make sure they match, and I'll let her choose. I know that when I buy something new she will choose the new thing. She is aware of things, and she loves jewelry. She loves to dress up. She really has a magnetic personality. I go to the mother house and everybody asks 'Where's Rosemary?' Eunice calls her 'Rosie' a lot but they call her both here."

Rosemary didn't get angry so often any longer. Borsari believed that Rosemary may have found other ways to get people's attention, or simply had mellowed with age. She had a pattern of life that she did not like to see changed. At mass she would not leave her pew until another resident walked by, and the two elderly women left the chapel together. "She knows her prayers by heart, like 'Hail Mary' and the meal prayer," said Sister Margaret Ann. "I think those memories are from before her surgery. I think mass means a lot to her. The world 'Jesus' means a lot to her."

After mass, Rosemary had some kind of planned activity, guided by an aide. She might play volleyball with a balloon or put cones on a stake. Usually she went to her cottage for lunch, but when she took her meal in the cafeteria, she had several women whom she wanted at her table. After eating they might hold hands, or simply sit and look at picture cards. Rosemary enjoyed going into the warm water of the pool with the therapist, and sometimes when the session was over, she wanted to get back into the water.

After lunch another resident might be invited over to spend time with Rosemary, or she might walk back to Alverno House to take part in the adult day-care program. In the evenings,

Rosemary usually was at home, although occasionally Sister Margaret Ann took her out to dinner, to a movie, or turned on the television set.

"She likes music and she likes to dance," said Sister Margaret Ann. "When you ask her if she wants to dance, she will say no, but if you tease her, she will start. I have several pictures of her dancing with different people. There's a picture on the wall of Rosemary in a long dress with her mother waiting to be presented to the king. I think she remembers, but it's hard to tell because she can't tell you. But if you have a program like the Academy Awards with long dresses, she loves it, and she sits there watching so happy."

For Eunice what loomed ahead most dramatically was the International Special Olympic Games in Minneapolis in the summer of 1991. It was a gigantic undertaking, by all estimates the largest athletic event in the world that year, and hardly a day went by when she was not involved with one question or another. The staff at Special Olympics knew that neither Eunice nor Sarge was half as healthy as the images they presented to the world. And they assumed that this would be the last International games in which the Shrivers would still dominate the organization.

If anything, Eunice worked at even a more hectic pace, her demands driving secretaries to tears, and other staff members at times to momentary distraction. For Eunice the day was never long enough, and that an hour was limited to sixty minutes seemed entirely arbitrary and unfair. She always had a score of matters on her mind. The Shrivers had a driver, but Eunice insisted often on driving back and forth from the office in Washington. She drove with willful abandon, rushing through yellow lights as if she were a one-woman presidential motorcade, honking her horn at poky drivers, accelerating past. The quickest way between her home and the downtown office took her along Canal Road, a narrow, winding route shaded with great trees. For many drivers the road was a welcome respite from the crowded thoroughfares of the city, but Eunice roared along as if she were in a sports car rally. In the middle of January 1991, she was driving by herself when she suddenly accelerated across the center line apparently trying to pass, and collided with a van.

The other driver was not hurt, but Eunice lay enmeshed in a tangled mass of steel and glass. She was in such a condition

that when the authorities called Sarge, he had the impression
that she had died or was dying. It took the Jaws of Life to
extract Eunice from her car. She had two broken arms, a shattered elbow, a seriously damaged hip socket, a mass of lacer-
ations, and other complications. She was taken to Sibley
Hospital in Washington, but she insisted on being flown by
helicopter to Johns Hopkins Hospital in Baltimore. Eunice
knew the hospital's reputation, and it was fitting that she
should be treated at the Baltimore institution since it had benefited from the Kennedy largess over the years, including the
renowned Kennedy Institute for Handicapped Children, named
after Jack.

Eunice was laden with casts and bandages, and was scheduled for at least two major operations. She was sixty-nine
years old and by all the laws of time and nature, the accident
should have marked her life, leaving her if not a partial invalid
then at least relegated to a cautious and sedentary old age.
Within days, the staff at Special Olympics began hearing her
familiar nasal twang on the phone, hardly giving the person
time for a greeting before she rushed into the matter at hand.
Hundreds of letters poured into the hospital and the Shrivers'
home, and Sarge answered almost every one with a personal-
ized note. The Shrivers gave out practically no information on
the accident; many people did not even know about it, and
among those who did know few realized how close to death
Eunice had been.

For the Kennedy women of the young generation, these were
the marrying years, and hardly a spring went by when there
was not at least one wedding that brought together the family.
In 1987 Pat's second daughter, Victoria, had married Robert
Pender, a Washington attorney, and, like her older sister Sydney, was living a gratefully unpublicized life as a wife and
mother of three daughters. Her cousin Kerry was a much more
public Kennedy, and her 1990 wedding was the most spectacular and publicized since Maria's and Caroline's. Ethel's
daughter had an immense sense of entitlement as a Kennedy.
When she was attending law school in Boston, one of her
housemates, Brad Blank, was a fanatic Boston Celtics fan.
Kerry had no interest in the sport, but when the playoffs arrived, Brad convinced Kerry that she should watch at least one
televised game with him, and he lovingly instructed her on the
niceties of the sport and the glorious tradition of the Celtics.

Brad thought that he had created a new fan, but the next evening Kerry shrugged off his invitation to watch and left the house. When Brad turned on the television to watch the game, the camera scanned across the notables at Boston Garden, including Kerry sitting in the front row next to her Uncle Ted.

In June of 1990, Kerry married Andrew Cuomo, the son of the governor of New York, in a resplendent wedding at St. Matthew's Cathedral, where Jack's funeral had taken place. "The Kennedys have a history of overwhelming their in-laws, but there was a general feeling that, in the Cuomos, they had met their match," wrote Mary McGrory. "This obviously is a merger, not a takeover." For a Kennedy, Andrew was a political Prince Charming, a serious, determined young man of innovative ideas. In New York he had founded Housing Enterprise for the Less Privileged (HELP). After their honeymoon, the newlyweds set up shop in two suites of offices in Manhattan, Andrew on his floor running HELP and Kerry on the floor above heading the Human Rights program of the foundation that bore her father's name.

In September, in the same Our Lady of Victory Church where Caroline had married four years before, thirty-year-old Kara wedded Michael Allen, a Washington architect. Kara had often blanched under the kleig lights of publicity that had followed her as Ted's only daughter, and like her two brothers she had had a difficult time growing up. She had been working as a producer for WBZ-TV's *Evening Magazine* in Boston, but with her husband's business in the capital, she moved to Washington and went to work as the director of media relations for Very Special Arts.

For Rose and her daughters, divorce had been unspeakable and practically unthinkable but the young generation felt differently. In 1990 Joe II and Sheila separated after ten years of marriage, and she filed for divorce. Courtney's marriage to Jeff Ruhe, a television executive, lasted a decade as well before ending that same year.

In late March of 1991, a week before Easter, Jean flew into West Palm Beach with her daughter, Kym, from Colorado where they had been vacationing. The six Kennedy families divided up the use of the Palm Beach house each winter season, and these were Jean's three weeks. Her children were largely grown up, and these days would be a rare opportunity to see her daughters and sons, and to relax without any elaborate social schedule. The children would all be leaving after Easter, and after that she had invited a group of her New York friends to come down.

Jean settled into the bedroom on the second floor of the old house, a large end room that faced out on the ocean and a patio near the pool. It was her mother's bedroom, but Jean knew that her mother would never be in Palm Beach again. Jean had a chance for a few more days with Kym, who headed off in the middle of the week to Disney World with a group of friends. Her eldest son, Steve, left early as well. Her daughter Amanda arrived as well as her youngest son, thirty-year-old Willie, who was completing his final year at Georgetown Medical School. Jean had invited another family, the Barrys. Bill Barry had been Bobby's bodyguard, and he had stayed close to the family, in recent years providing security for Ted on a trip to the Middle East. He arrived with his wife, Mary Lou, their son, Stephen, and his wife, Carol.

Ted flew in Wednesday evening. Later that evening Ted's youngest son, Patrick, arrived from Rhode Island, where in 1988 at the age of twenty-one, he had been elected to the state legislature. Ted was fifty-nine years old, four years younger than Jean, and what had been a gigantic difference in age when they were little children now seemed hardly noticeable. There was within the family still the same sexual dichotomy that there had been for three generations, a dichotomy that merely exaggerated what was found elsewhere in society. Ted had not seen his favorite sister for a while but he nonetheless headed out with Patrick and the two Barrys to enjoy the nightlife of the community.

The group drove to Au Bar, a disco nightclub that had become Palm Beach's favorite singles bar. There were other men of Ted's age in the darkened room. There were many young women too. Patrick arrived back at the house by himself at around midnight. His father arrived also, as did two young women. In the early morning hours Patrick called a cab for one of the women. The Kennedys' other new acquaintance was in no condition to drive her own car. "What I understand, I wasn't there," Patrick recalled, "Dennis [Spear, the caretaker] drove the woman back in her car and found a means of transportation back to the house on his own."

Jean was in the house that Wednesday evening while Ted and Patrick entertained their guests. Jean was perfectly used to her brother's behavior, and the fact that he and his son should bring women back to the house was perfectly acceptable. She would never even have considered heading out to the bars with Amanda hunting for an evening's companionship. She cringed at the idea of even setting foot in Au Bar.

After dinner Friday evening, the young people went out on the patio to play charades and other word games. That was the kind of activity that her brothers and sisters had enjoyed when she was growing up, an innocent pleasure that was an anathema to the self-consciously sophisticated youths of today. While Willie, Patrick, and the others amused themselves, shouting out their answers, Jean sat with Ted and the Barrys. It was Good Friday, and Jean and Ted had not spent any time alone since Steve's death. The conversation turned inevitably to a melancholy reflection on the loss of Steve and other Kennedys. Jean was a woman of self-contained emotionality. Since Steve's death she had simply worked harder at Very Special Arts, and kept her social calendar full, giving herself as little time as possible for reflection. Ted seemed to suffer the loss even more intensely. Ted was always called the last brother, but as long as Steve was alive, he had not felt that way. Steve had become another sibling to him, and Ted had not felt the obligations of family rested on him alone. Ted had faith in Steve, Steve who could fix anything, Steve who always saw a way out, Steve who was always there. Since his divorce and Steve's death, Ted had at times seemed rudderless, balancing his often distinguished work in the Senate with mindless drinking and revelry.

After their long, intense talk, Jean went to bed. The next morning she got up early and went for a five-mile walk along the beach. Along her route she traversed a short public beach, but most of the shore was empty except for an occasional stroller, and she was lost within her solitude. This was the kind of walk her mother had taken all of her life. When Jean returned, she went for a swim. All her adult life she had been angry with Rose. Yet as she reached her sixties, Jean had taken on certain aspects of her mother, from her concern for discipline and health to her unwillingness to talk about her personal life. After lunch, she went shopping, and then watched Ted playing tennis. Sunday she attended early mass; played tennis with Willie, Patrick, and Ted; had lunch at the house with friends who included Ted's former lover, Helga Wagner; took Willie to the airport; and then went for a walk on the beach with Bill Barry, Ted, and Patrick. When police arrived at the estate Sunday afternoon, Jean was not even told that the authorities were making inquiries involving her son. Monday morning she flew out of West Palm Beach to attend a Very Special Arts fund-raiser in New York with guests expected to include her sister Pat, Ted Jr., Lauren Bacall, Tom Brokaw, Norman Mailer, and E. L. Doctorow. Afterwards, Jean planned to return immediately to Florida.

When Jean arrived in New York, she learned that Willie was being accused of raping a woman he had brought back to the Palm Beach home late on the evening of Good Friday. Jean had been asleep in the house then, and she had not even known that Willie, Ted, and Patrick had gone out to Au Bar. During the weekend she had spent hours with her son and Ted, and yet according to her sworn deposition, she had been told nothing of the events that night.

Willie had had sex with Patricia Bowman, a woman he had met at Au Bar. After she left, Willie had told his cousin Patrick that she had acted strangely and threatened to accuse him of rape. He had told his mother nothing, though, and for two days pretended to Jean that this was just another Easter vacation in Palm Beach.

In New York Jean saw her son's picture on the cover of the tabloids. "BACHELOR PARTY!" a headline blared. "TEDDY'S SEXY ROMP!" Ted's associates were appalled that he was being pulled down into the muck with his nephew, and his first statement was an innocuous one that sought to distance him from Willie. Other family members believe that Jean was livid that Ted would treat her son as if he were nothing more than a political problem, and she brought all the force of her anger upon her favorite brother. Soon afterwards, Teddy made a second statement, boldly asserting Willie's innocence.

Jean was drawn into the maelstrom of controversy as well. She had nothing to do with the events, but she was forced to give a deposition. Her inquisitor was Moira Lasch, a humorless Palm Beach county prosecutor, who whenever she looked at the Kennedys saw lies and obstructions and dissembling. Bludworth, the Palm Beach County state's attorney, had been accused of undue leniency toward the Kennedys when David had died, but not this time. Lasch and her associates obtained enough evidence to charge Willie with a felony charge of sexual battery, the Florida term for rape, and a misdemeanor charge of battery. Early in May, when Willie surrendered to the

Palm Beach police to be booked, Jean was there by his side, wading through the scores of reporters and television cameras.

Jean pushed the rest of her life and obligations and interests to the side and devoted herself entirely to Willie's defense, agonizing over his legal team, paying for private investigators to find negative material on her son's accuser, watching over the war of rhetoric in the media. "I'm distressed that someone is trying to ruin his life and career when he's trying to help people," Jean told reporters. Other family members knew that Willie was a troubled young man. So did numerous women. As the weeks went by, a number of women came forward to offer witness to his past conduct. Several of them were afraid or did not want their names sullied with the muck of publicity. They hurled their charges of alleged rape and sexual misconduct behind the shield of anonymity. Three other women gave depositions and by so doing became potential witnesses in the trial. To Jean these were more of her son's tormentors, shrews who were willing to say anything for the sake of publicity, their charges pathetic attempts at revenge on her noble son who had spurned them.

Despite what Jean thought, unless these three women—a doctor, a medical student, and a law student—were sociopaths, they were compelling witnesses to the private life of her youngest son. They were professional women who knew that the Kennedy lawyers would attempt to soil their reputations, dredging up every embarrassment in their past. They had nothing to gain. They spurned offers to sell their stories to the tabloids. They sought no moment in the light of the media. Yet still they came forward.

These women were not describing typical date rapes where the man refused to halt sexual activity that had mutually begun, but a man who had pounced on them with hardly more foreplay than if he had entered their bedrooms by jimmying up a window and forcing himself on them.

The three women knew that the defense would attempt to destroy their credibility, but they perhaps did not know how soon that process would begin. During their depositions with Willie's lawyers, all three women got a taste of what would face them if they ever appeared in court in West Palm Beach. One woman swore that when she was a medical student at Georgetown, Willie had invited her back to his house for a pool party. He had been alone and had "grabbed me tightly around both wrists and threw me over the back edge of the couch." The woman was now a married doctor, a woman of unblemished reputation whose mother had warned her about giving a deposition. She was asked by Mark Seiden, one of Willie's attorneys, if she were "physically aggressive during sexual encounters" and whether she had "sex in a projection booth in a classroom in Georgetown." The second woman had been dating Ethel's second youngest son, Matthew "Max," when Willie offered to let her stay over at the Smith town house in Manhattan. There he supposedly "tackled" her and "he tried to kiss me and in the struggle that followed, they [his hands] were on my breasts and trying to get up my dress." This woman also was now married. In recent years she had held a series of responsible positions and was now a law student in Boston. She was asked under oath by Seiden, "Since you have been sixteen years old, have you ever been accused of untruthfulness?" and whether she had "ever stolen anything from a family member in order to sell it and buy drugs?" to which she replied no. The third woman accused Willie of raping her when she was drunk in his apartment. She was asked by Willie's attorney, "Have you ever had intercourse on the first date?" and "Have you ever had intercourse when you have been intoxicated before?"

The Kennedy women were united in backing Willie. Joan was still very much a part of the family, defined by her relationship with the Kennedys. In the divorce she had kept the house on Squaw Island, within walking distance of the old family home where her former husband now stayed. Joan was inordinately proud that she and Ted got along so well, proud that she was still a Kennedy. Joan had entered the family like a beautiful, exotic butterfly, drawn to the bright flame of the Kennedys, gliding into the heat and fire. She had been burned and had glided out again, but she was drawn back, no matter how often her wings were singed, unwilling to turn away toward a world outside that appeared to be nothing but darkness.

Willie was the Kennedy accused of rape, but it was her former husband who had been put into the media pillory, caricatured in the tabloid press as an aging satyr, a pied piper of licentiousness who had led Willie out into the night world. Joan knew, however, that if Ted had not awakened Willie and Patrick to go out with him for a drink, this latest scandal would never have happened. Willie was the accused, but her Patrick was a victim too. He was a sickly asthmatic young man who had had his own problems with drugs, and had been sucked into this shame as well, his name and reputation befouled. If only Ted had not gone out with the two young men that evening, then there would be no photographers hiding in the grass along the private beaches, no reporters haunting the streets of the village, no one interrupting her life and the lives of the other Kennedys. Everything that Ted or any of them did would not be suspect as self-serving manipulation.

On Mother's Day, Ted took Rose out for a walk in her wheelchair accompanied by Ted Jr. They were surprised by a photographer jumping out of a parked car. Ted could hardly run away, and the man took a picture that appeared in newspapers across America. Ted always took his mother for a walk when he was home, but some of their critics believed that the Kennedys did not perform even the most elemental human acts of kindness without some other motive.

"When things get really tough, there's another emerging tradition: bring out matriarch Rose," wrote Margery Eagan in the *Boston Herald*. "A laughing senator and Ted Jr. pushed her wheelchair. But there was something almost cruel about exposing the helpless frailty of this old woman wrapped in a blanket, a woman once so proud, impeccably dressed and coifed."

In the middle of May, Joan drove up alone to Boston from the Cape. She had made the trip innumerable times before, but not with an open bottle of vodka at her side. By the time she reached the outer suburbs, her Buick was weaving back and forth across three lanes of Interstate 93, a high-speed expressway. The drivers following her were too frightened to attempt to pass, and traffic was backed up for miles behind. When state police troopers in two cruisers finally stopped her, they could tell immediately that she was intoxicated. The Breathalyzer analysis reportedly revealed that her blood-alcohol level was .18 percent, almost double the legal definition of drunkenness.

Joan had been arrested for drunken driving before, but this time was like a desperate shriek in the night, a sound so loud and pitiful that it could not be ignored. By the time she appeared in court the next day to surrender her driver's license, her makeup was impeccable, her blond hair perfectly groomed. At the age of fifty-four, she looked almost girlish, but her eyes had a strange blankness to them. As she stood in this courtroom in Quincy to plead guilty and to receive a suspended ninety-day sentence if she would spend at least two weeks in a rehabilitation program, she had no one with her but a lawyer—not Ted, not her former sisters-in-law, not her daughter, and not her sons, no one.

Ted was going through times of emotional desperation himself. A half hour before Hurricane Bob struck the coast of Massachusetts in August of 1991, Ted headed out in his boat for a sail. "I just couldn't believe it," Larry Newman recalled. "The only thing that I could think of is that the guy had a death wish. The guy wants to die."

28

"We Tried"

On July 20 Eunice sat high above the field of the Metrodome in Minneapolis, looking down on over six thousand athletes from 107 countries marching into the gigantic stadium for the 1991 International Special Olympics Games. In the aftermath of her accident, Eunice's ravaged face was as pale as her white linen suit. While Sarge and the other notables stood and applauded the national and state teams marching around the track, Eunice remained seated. Since the accident she had been back in the office for several months. She still had not completely recovered, and it was a miracle that she was here at all, though as Eunice saw it, nothing compared to the miracle of those who marched below.

It was a colossal victory parade yet not a race had been run, not a medal awarded, the applause crescendo upon crescendo, great waves of sound. Eunice and Sarge had perfected the use of celebrities to bring attention to these games, and many famous Americans marched with the athletes, from Evander Holyfield to Hulk Hogan, Warren Beatty to Kirstie Alley, Wayne Gretzky to Don Johnson. Eunice applauded Chris Burke with special relish when he walked out on the track with the New York delegation. Chris was a former Special Olympian himself, a young man with Down's syndrome. He was a hero and role model to thousands of young people. His achievements symbolized how much the American consciousness had changed since Special Olympics had begun. Burke was a star of the television program *Life Goes On*, the first person in America with retardation to be a major celebrity in his own right. The *Life* magazine that had refused to do a story on the first Special Olympics games put Burke on its cover in 1989.

Eunice applauded her sons Timmy, who came marching in with the Connecticut delegation, and Mark, leading the group from his state of Maryland. Her son-in-law Arnold strutted in with the California delegation to an enormous round of applause, looking up and waving at Eunice and Sarge and a pregnant Maria. When it came time to introduce the dignitaries, the audience rose as one person to give Eunice an ovation. Among the forty-four thousand spectators were thousands of parents, family, and friends of the Special Olympians. They knew that this might be seventy-year-old Eunice's last international games. In clapping and cheering they were commemorating everything she had done and meant to those with mental retardation in America and throughout the world. As much as Eunice sought recognition and credit, she was embarrassed by it, and the applause had hardly begun before Eunice squelched it, sitting down, motioning the audience to still itself. She shrank away from praise, as if it were a bad omen, writing finality to all that she felt she had left to accomplish.

To Eunice, Special Olympics was about family, about her family, about the family of Special Olympics, and the family of women and men everywhere. These games were a great marker in the long road of her life, a symbol of all that she had done to justify her father's mandate. If not for Willie's indictment, most of the media interest in the Kennedys this summer would have been on these games. It was deeply painful to her that her family had again become a subject of ridicule, the Hyannis Port hillbillies, America's best known dysfunctional family. That was not the family she saw, not Maria, Timmy, Mark, Bobby Jr., and Anthony. That was not how she perceived her sisters' and brothers' lives and those of her nieces and nephews. It was not what her parents meant to her. She was perpetually bewildered that outsiders and critics imagined that she and her parents and sisters and brothers did not love one another.

On the second day of the games Eunice gave a short address at the reception for the families of the Special Olympians. There were no press people here this day, and her talk was deeply heartfelt, opening herself up emotionally as she rarely did in public.

I look at all of you and think how proud my mother and father would be here tonight. They raised nine of us and taught each to do our best as you teach your children. We tried. In public service, business, law, and in this work. How proud Dad would be to see that his foundation created this movement. And my mother, who is celebrating her 101st birthday today, would feel a special thrill to be here with all the parents, for she, too, had a special child, my sister Rosemary. My three brothers, who entered public service and died in it, would love the competitions, love the remembrance that Rosemary was once a very fine swimmer, and most of all, love that we all could be here together as family with you. No individual is a success without a team, a family. Tonight, every single person here is a member of the Special Olympics family because each one of us believes in the team. Each one of us knows that sacrifice has brought us here and that only the most determined kind of family love will keep us here.

Where we are exactly is face-to-face with a miracle in the truest sense. It happened through the toughness, anger, and determination of parents. You as parents forged a movement in the molten emotions of your hearts. You, like my own mother, looked at the lonely rooms of twenty-five years ago and said we can do better. Today, you survey crowded playing fields and stadiums around the world. This is your miracle. Ladies and gentlemen, tonight is as great a miracle of love and family as can be imagined. I thank and praise you all for this miracle.

The closing ceremonies for the International Special Olympics Games took place in front of the ivory white State Capitol in St. Paul, Minnesota. The great cylinder of the Olympic torch rose behind the temporary stage, the cauldron burning brilliantly, and all across the great lawn sat the Special Olympians. The Greeks wore blue-and-white warm-up suits, the team from Guadeloupe in dazzling red, the Austrians in purple. As they waited, the athletes exchanged pins, swapped jackets and pants, and wandered off to say good-bye to new friends, all the colors blending into this brilliant mosaic of peoples and nations.

As the evening began, the powerful strains of Aaron Copland's "Fanfare for the Common Man" played across the crowds. The stage was full of public men in dark suits, and Eunice in a green dress, and board member Loretta Claiborne in her blue Pennsylvania state warm-up suit. If ever there was a time for Eunice to speak, it was now. Instead, Sarge walked to the microphone, followed by Ted, who had almost nothing to do with Special Olympics, and whose controversial presence irritated staff members. Eunice knew that Ted needed some positive moments in the media. He was Eunice's brother, and her family came before the larger family of Special Olympics.

"Tonight, I bring a very special greeting of the grandmother of the Special Olympics, the mother of my sister Eunice, who founded the Special Olympics, and the mother of Rosemary, our retarded sister, who inspired the Special Olympics," Ted began. "My mother, Rose Fitzgerald Kennedy, was a hundred and one last Monday. She asked me, 'Where are you going today, Teddy?' I said, 'I'm getting on a plane. I'm flying halfway around the country. I'm going to see some of the finest athletes in the world.' She said, 'You're going to the Twin Cities and you're speaking to the Special Olympians.' "

None of that was true, and even if it had been it would not have mattered to most of the Special Olympians. Most of these athletes from other countries knew very little about Rose and Ted and the whole saga of the Kennedys. Special Olympics had reached far beyond the Kennedys, and when the great torch was extinguished, the glow remained long after the flame had died out.

Shortly before nine o'clock on December 2, 1991, Jean arrived at the Palm Beach County Courthouse accompanying Willie for the first day of his trial. Her other son, Steve, and two of her daughters, Kym and Amanda, were also in the battered station wagon as it pulled up in front of the building. On the street corner stood peddlers hawking souvenir T-shirts including one with the words HOT TIME! HOT TRIAL! over a caricature of naked Willie and Ted sitting in a frying pan.

Although most of her friends considered sixty-three-year-old Jean shy, she thought of herself as perfectly normal, but normal did not mean comfortable running this gauntlet of gesticulating reporters. They screamed out the name "Will, Will," calling her son by the more formal appellation that his defense team had decided was appropriate. As Jean walked into the building, the snouts of cameras circled the main entrance, and poked down on the clamorous scene from the second and third floors of the parking garage next door, while inside the media room scores of other reporters sat writing their stories or kibitzing.

Jean wore a lime-green linen dress, white pumps, and tiny pearl earrings, and looked as if she might be going to a society luncheon and not to a trial that could send her son to prison. She sat with the rest of her family in the courtroom behind thirty-one-year-old Willie. The Smiths were albinolike in their paleness. Six-foot, two-inch-tall Willie wore a brown houndstooth check jacket. With his long lashes and narrow, almond shaped eyes, there was a feline quality to him, his large nose above a mouth so narrow that he sometimes appeared to have no lips at all. Jean had only a vague resemblance to her son. As she had aged, she had grown more masculine in appearance, her features as abrupt as her manner was deliberate. In the courtroom Jean's face was purged of emotion. She yawned during prosecutor Lasch's description of Willie's supposed violence. She cocked her ear at the mention of Willie's using marijuana, as if she might learn something here today. When Lasch went on to say what Willie had done "to lure her [Patricia Bowman] to his house" Jean tried to suppress her smile, but it was simply too amusing to bear.

When Jean was young, it was almost unthinkable that a woman could go to a man's house in the middle of the night and then charge him with rape, but that was changing in large part because women were in positions of increasing power in America. In the Kennedy family alone, Kathleen, Caroline, and Kerry all had law degrees, and though none of them were formally practicing, by definition they were aware of the evolution of legal concerns over sexual conduct. So were the other Kennedy women of the new generation. The second youngest Kennedy woman of that generation, twenty-two-year-old Rory, had majored in women's studies at Brown University, and was deeply involved with the issues that would be brought forth in this trial. That did not mean that the young Kennedy women followed every dictum of supposed sisterhood, or that the mere presence of a woman guaranteed new sensitivities, but without women walking in the corridors of power, it was unlikely that Willie would have been indicted. And now women stood at the center of determining his fate.

In this courtroom, the presiding judge was forty-three-year-old Mary E. Lupo, a graduate of the same Manhattanville College where Jean had matriculated. With her long ebony hair, red lipstick, powder-white skin, and black judicial robes, Lupo was the most dramatic feature of the whole courtroom. The prosecutor Moira Lasch was a woman as was her associate,

Ellen Roberts. Lasch was a graduate of the Stone Ridge Country Day School of the Sacred Heart outside Washington that Kathleen and Maria had attended. In her formal blue suit and straight brown hair, the forty-year-old prosecutor looked like a pristine, proper French schoolgirl and had the Sacred Heart reticence to look a man in his eyes. Willie's main lawyer was Roy E. Black, but the defense expert in jury selection was a woman, Cathy E. Bennett. She was dying of cancer but she said that she so much believed in Willie's innocence that she was spending some of her last precious months on this case. Almost half the journalists covering the trial were women and many police officers and expert witnesses were as well. Beyond that, of the six jurors who would decide ultimately on Willie's guilt or innocence, four were women.

Judge Lupo swore in the jury. Then in a crucial setback to the prosecution, the judge ruled that the testimony of the three women who accused Willie of various degrees of sexual assault was not admissible. She also ruled that as a potential witness, Jean could not be in the courtroom, and Jean walked out into the corridor.

That evening at the old house on North Ocean Boulevard, the Kennedy women got together. Eunice, Pat, and Ethel had flown down to sit as spectators in silent support of Willie. His sisters, Kym and Amanda, were there as well, and for a few days Chris Lawford and other Kennedy cousins. Jean and her two sisters often went off by themselves for long talks. The atmosphere was not one of foreboding, with Eunice and Pat nervously reassuring their sister that everything would be all right. It was more like a sorority, the rooms resounding with tales and laughter. The women had what one close observer of them in the house called, "this arrogant self-confidence of their position." Jean was certain that Willie would be found not guilty. The women read the press clippings with immense interest. When they saw Eunice and Ethel described as these dowdy ladies, Jean laughed with wry amusement. As much as they could be cavalierly dismissive of servants, when Roy Black or another powerful man arrived at the house, they became what to one guest seemed like young girls, playing up to the man as they had long ago been taught. Pat had a richly original wit, and she was the resident clown, charming the male guests with her constant asides.

In the morning Jean drove in the old station wagon with Willie, and again walked through the gauntlet with her son. It was unnecessary, and would not change a juror's vote, but it was a symbol of her belief in her son, an attempt to buttress Willie's courage with her own. Though Willie had had his share of nannies and maids watching over him, his mother was here for Willie now.

The other Kennedy women took turns sitting in the three family seats, women supporting a man, a role that was generations old. Ethel kept dozing off, waking up as her head hit her shoulder. Kym and Amanda got up at dawn most days and stood in a line outside the courthouse to obtain two of the scarce public seats. They sat as far back in the courtroom as possible; they shrank back from attention as if they were being struck.

On the morning of the third day of the trial, Willie stopped before a battery of cameras and microphones, and introduced Eunice to the hundreds of reporters and spectators. Until now the media had largely ignored Eunice, Ethel, and Pat, letting them slip away unnoticed and unquestioned. "I'm very happy to be here with my sister Jean," Eunice began, standing there in the Florida drizzle, hunched over the microphones. "She is a very courageous woman. She has raised four very wonderful children. . . . She has also started Very Special Arts, which is an international program that gives arts to all disabled people. So I am very happy to be here for her."

Jean was not on trial, and there was a strange discontinuity to Eunice's remarks. "As for William, he has the same kind of loyalty from his cousins. . . . Most of them are coming down here to stay with him," she went on. "That loyalty was taught by our parents, so to all of those who are going to watch this trial over the next—this rather sad trial, I think—over the next two weeks, I wish you a happy Christmas and the gift of loyal family relationships. Thank you very much."

To Eunice, it was not Willie who was on trial here but the Kennedys, and she was avowing not simply the family's innocence but its goodness. To many of those assembled, her statement sounded like a schoolmarmish lecture; all anyone cared about here was what had happened at the Kennedy estate early that Saturday morning of Easter weekend eight months ago.

Eunice's statement would have been quoted more in the papers, but her words lost their newsworthiness when that afternoon Bowman was called to testify. Most of the media had neither mentioned her by name nor shown her picture, and today the television networks superimposed a gray blob over her features. The tabloids portrayed Bowman as a sexy heiress who had dressed for her evening at Au Bar in Victoria's Secret panties and bra, as if that itself were an invitation to licentiousness. As Eunice and Ethel could see, this woman in a dowager's conservative blue suit, and almost no makeup, was nothing like that image. She looked older than her thirty-one years, and had unhappiness etched into her downcast frown lines. She had the face of a woman who had learned too much about life and men, a woman who was likely to be picked up at a singles bar toward the end of the evening.

Bowman testified in a voice that was at first an almost scholarly monotone, and ended up a wrenchingly tearful monologue, prompted by Lasch's gentle questioning. Willie stared at the woman hardly blinking, while Eunice and Ethel looked down as Bowman explicitly described the alleged rape in words they had most assuredly rarely heard.

Bowman was a single mother with a sick child who had purchased a new dress for her evening on the town. She said that she had literally bumped into Willie at Au Bar. Willie appeared an exemplary young man, several cuts above the social flotsam of Palm Beach with whom she was intimately acquainted. When she learned that he was a medical student, she said that she discussed her daughter with him, and drove him back to the Kennedy estate thinking of him not as a potential romance but a platonic friend.

Bowman said that Willie invited her for a tour of the estate. On the beach he allegedly started to take off his pants to go for a naked swim. "He tackled me and I was on the ground and he was on top of me," Bowman said, her voice trembling with emotion. "He had me on the ground and I was trying to get out from underneath of him because he was crushing me and he had my arm pinned, and I was yelling 'no' and 'stop' and I tried to arch my back to get him off of me, but he slammed me back on the ground and . . . then he pushed my dress up and he raped me, and I thought he was going to kill me."

Bowman sounded not like a witness in a trial, but an ancient, wounded truth teller who had found her way back from a place of terrible darkness to confront Willie with his crime. In his rebuttal, Black attempted to tear asunder this fabric of truth, playing back bits and pieces of her various depositions, badgering her with his snideness, but her testimony had the minor inconsistencies of life, and she confronted Black with her righteous anger. "What he did to me was wrong!" she exclaimed. "I don't want to live the rest of my life in fear of that man! And I don't want to be responsible for him doing it to someone else!"

Jean had to rely on her sister and sister-in-law to tell her what Bowman looked like and other details of the day in court. The Kennedy house did not have cable television, and although the reception was grainy, the local stations broadcast most of the crucial testimony. On the afternoon that Ted testified, she stayed at the estate while Pat took one of the family seats in the courtroom, wearing a short skirt and flaming red hair.

Jean knew how high a price her younger brother had paid for his minor role in the events that infamous Easter weekend. This had become Ted's trial too. His reputation was so besmirched that in the recent Senate Judiciary hearings over Anita F. Hill's charges of sexual harassment against Supreme Court nominee Clarence Thomas, Ted had sat almost silent rather than risk snide asides from his Republican colleagues, and guffaws from the media. He had even given a speech admitting "faults in the conduct of my private life."

Ted knew all about Willie's dark reputation, and privately he was infuriated that his nephew had dragged him down into this muck of scandal, making him the subject of daily ridicule. For Ted, family was the ultimate loyalty, the highest patriotism, and he felt he had to defend not simply Willie, but Jean, Pat, and Eunice, and their parents as well. Thus as Ted strode into the courtroom, he was prepared to be a player in two great dramas taking place, one playing for the benefit of the jury and the world, and a second one for his family: Willie and Pat in the courtroom, and the other Kennedys watching on television. "Steve Smith was Will's father," Ted said. "When Jean married Steve, we had another brother, and when Steve was gone something left all of us when we buried him." To another man these would have been simply the elemental truths of life and death and would not have elicited the profound emotions they did in the senator from Massachusetts. Ted was a man who did not talk openly or easily about his own feelings, not to his family, and not to this courtroom with much of the country watching on television. He was doing so in defense of his family, and as he spoke Willie had tears in his eyes. Ted discussed his actions Good Friday evening and why he had awakened Patrick and Willie and asked them to go out with him. He explained how he had sat with Jean and William Barry out on the veranda and talked about the past. "The conversation was very emotional; it brought back a lot of special memories to me," Ted said, his voice tight with sentiment. "At the end of the conversation I was not able to think about sleeping."

Black tried to get Ted to talk again about his conversation that evening out on the veranda. Ted was a public man in a public place, but he could not talk anymore without risking breaking down. He paused to get hold of himself. "I think I described it earlier," Ted said.

Jean had only a walk-on role in the lives of the Kennedy men that infamous Easter weekend, and she had only a cameo to play in the West Palm Beach courtroom. She wore a light blue linen jacket wrinkled in the back, and large glasses that propped on her nose made her beaked features look owlish. When her brother had testified he had presented a self-confident, self-composed image, and the prosecutor and the judge treated him as deferentially as if he were a king. Jean was visibly nervous as she was sworn in. She said that she had been responsible for pushing Willie to come down to Palm Beach for Easter because "it was the first vacation without my husband." She knew nothing about the events that evening, however, and could only testify that she had heard no screams outside her bedroom window.

Afterwards, Jean returned to the Palm Beach mansion and was there as Willie testified, his graphic language broadcast across the nation. Jean had all the sexual reticence in public discourse of her Sacred Heart education, and she heard Willie speak with the argot of the locker room. She was proud of her son as a potential doctor, a healer of women and men, and she listened to what even by his own words was a sordid tale. This was a man's world, Steve's and Ted's and Bobby's and Jack's, a world to which she had no passport.

Willie described how Bowman had picked him up at Au Bar, brushing against him and dancing suggestively, the two of them kissing on the dance floor. Jean had been brought up never to go to places such as Au Bar, places full of what she considered predatory women preying on Kennedy men for sex and advantage. Willie told how Bowman offered to give him a ride back to the estate.

Willie said that Bowman had removed her pantyhose in the car while he waited in the parking lot. That too was the kind of brazen gesture unthinkable to a woman of Jean's station and morals. On the beach Willie alleged they had sex. "She unbuttoned my pants, I took her panties off . . . with her help," Willie said. That too was perfectly in character. "I put my hands on her and uh she was uh excited." After Willie went for a swim, they supposedly had sex again in the backyard. "I know that Roy Black used the words 'acts of love.' Those weren't my words. I think, probably, I would have said 'sex.' " It was there that Willie allegedly called Bowman "Cathie." "The minute I said it, I knew it was a mistake," Willie said. "She sort of snapped and told me to get the hell out of her." Only then did Bowman become upset and begin to threaten Willie, calling him by the name Michael. "She started out by saying that I was a really nice guy and that she really had a good time and that it was a really wonderful time," Willie said. "And then she said, 'You could have any person in the place.' And she started shaking and crying and she said, 'You don't even want me. And, Michael, you raped me.' "

Jean viewed the world outside her little nucleus of family and friends as an often malevolent place, full of betrayers, seducers, and predators. To her Bowman was just another in that long line of dangerous outsiders. Willie was a compelling witness, his testimony as credible as Bowman's, but even as he told it, this was a base tale, exposing the life of a Kennedy man, and Jean's son. She was a grieving widow, after all, and what had Willie done, as he told his story, but brought a woman back to the house and had sex with her beneath his mother's window. She had testified that she had heard no screams, no shouts. She had heard no moans and gasps either. She had slept alone through the night, as she had slept alone through many nights.

Jean was there the next day in the courtroom when the jury reached its verdict after only seventy-seven minutes. There was little clear physical evidence, and it came down ultimately to Willie's word against Bowman's. By any standard of reasonable doubt if Willie was not innocent, he was at least not guilty, and so the jury found him. "I'm so happy," Jean said as she left the courtroom. "I'm so relieved." Jean stood beside Willie as he faced the reporters on the courthouse steps. "I want to say thank you most of all to my mother," he said with passionate intensity. "I don't think it's possible for a child ever to repay the debt they own their parents. I only hope I can be as good a parent to my children as my mother has been to me."

* * *

Soon after the Kennedys flew north, Eunice told Ted that the next International Special Olympics Games would be held in Dallas in the summer of 1995. Ted and most of the other Kennedys had never returned to Dallas since Jack's death, though they often visited Los Angeles where Bobby had died. In his book on the assassination, William Manchester had helped to create an image of the Texas city as a malevolent place. The author described Dallas as a city with "a stridency, a disease of the spirit . . . [in which] the harlots and the grafters had gone, but the killers were multiplying." The city had its full share of fanatics, but in the years since, it had become clear that the assassination itself could as easily have taken place in Chicago, New Orleans, or anywhere else as in Dallas.

Even if the city's reputation had been unfairly bespattered, it was still the city where Jack had died. These Dallas games would provide civic goodwill and exemplary public relations. They would be considered penance to the Kennedy family. The Dallas civic leaders put together an extraordinarily generous and ambitious, multimillion-dollar plan and Eunice knew that these next games would be the greatest in the history of Special Olympics.

Ted was distraught over the Oliver Stone film *JFK*, and the display of his brother's autopsy photos in the media, the ugly wreckage of the past backing up into his life like sewage. He could not tolerate the idea of returning to Dallas, or having Eunice and other family members do so either, all those memories brought alive again. He thought of Special Olympics as a Kennedy charity, and he set himself up against his sister and her dreams. "He said that if they went there he would withdraw his support for Special Olympics and the family's support," recalled a top official at Special Olympics International. "That put us in a difficult position but Ted was adamant, absolutely adamant." For Eunice again came the choice between her larger family and the smaller one, between Special Olympics and Ted. She might have called Ted's bluff and gone ahead with the Dallas plans, but that was not Eunice. She gave in to her brother, shielding him from public responsibility for the decision, forcing Special Olympics to begin their search for a city all over again. In the end, Special Olympics International settled on a proposal from New Haven, Connecticut, from a group headed by Timmy Shriver.

* * *

Scuttling Eunice's plans for Special Olympics Games in Dallas was not proper brotherly conduct, but his sister knew how deeply Ted mourned his brothers, and how each remembrance, each well-meant anecdote, each memorial was a knife in his heart. In recent years Ted had lived a life of almost unbearable loneliness, covered up by an often threadbare veneer of good cheer. Wherever he went, he had people wanting something from him, holding out their hands, beseeching him for a moment of his time, a snippet of his power, a touch of his self, and he moved through his days as if he were in a constant campaign, a smile, a gesture, a word, and then moving on, never allowing himself time for the darkness of contemplation. He was at times full of that arrogant sense of entitlement that was the common disease of old politicians, and he could be brutally abrupt to associates, but he was equally a man of tender concerns for family and friends. He was drinking too much, though he always managed to get up in the morning. He figured he would never marry again. Then he began dating thirty-eight-year-old Victoria "Vicki" Anne Reggie.

Vicki was not a virginal maiden from Manhattanville but a divorced attorney with two small children. Ted had known Vicki as a family friend, but he had only begun to date her the previous year. At the time, her father, a retired judge, was under indictment for allegedly having profited illegally from loans made by a defunct bank. In Ted's more ambitious days, he never would have thought of marrying a woman who came with such a dowry.

With her gracious dark good looks and vivacious smiles, Vicki hardly looked like the typical law partner in a Washington firm. She was a woman with steady strength. She had not chased after Ted, and he had learned quickly that she was not a woman he could easily bamboozle or manipulate. Ted asked Vicki to marry him, and in July of 1992 the ceremony took place not in some great church but in front of the fireplace in Ted's home in McLean, the couple married not by a prince of the church but by a family friend, A. David Mazzone, a U.S. district judge.

Ted was a Kennedy man, but this was not a Kennedy marriage, not as it had been for the men of his generation. There were those who thought Ted had married Vicki as a shrewd political gesture before his 1994 reelection campaign, but those who thought that did not hear him asking Vicki's advice, calling her office several times a day, or see him whispering to her. She was a woman with bedrock strength, and he leaned on her as he had never leaned on Joan, and nestled into the marriage. He continued to drink heavily, and he was not about to stop and confront his own private devils, still running to stay ahead of the dark shadows of the past. But now when Ted went sailing, it was not out on violent seas, but usually with his bride on a sun-dappled afternoon. For years he had disciplined himself never to put his arm around a woman or to kiss her where the photographers might record his intimacy. He was married now but he approached his bride as gingerly as if affection were a felony. He had to be advised by a member of his staff that it was fine and good and normal to put his arm around Victoria when they walked up from a sail, or kiss her when he felt like it.

During the summer of 1992 Jean made a trip to Ireland. She traveled widely, including a visit to the imposing American ambassador's residence in Dublin. When she returned, Jean told her younger brother about her visit. As they talked, they discussed the possibility that Jean might return there as the ambassador, musing about the idea as if it were a moment's fantasy. "It sort of developed as a wisp of a thought," Ted recalled. "We had all been to Ireland and we talked about that house and how wonderful it would be to live there. We were chatting about it as if we were dreaming."

"It just came to me in a flash," Jean recalled. "I think my husband gave me the idea. It's from heaven. I mean I think he [Steve] must have in some kind of way because it just hit me that it would be a really good idea at this point in my life. And I think it sort of fit, you know. I knew how crazy they [the Irish] were about Jack and I thought, 'Why not try?' You know, I really wasn't very optimistic I'd get it. There would have to be a lot of people wanting it, people who had worked very hard in the campaign."

Jean had just gone through the humiliation of Willie's trial, an experience that would have driven many people into a cloistered life. Instead, after the election of President Bill Clinton, Jean decided that she was seriously interested in pursuing the ambassadorship. With her interests in the arts and her stewardship of Very Special Arts, she would have been a brilliant choice as cultural attaché in Ireland or any other embassy. She had, however, shown no interest in international politics before, nor any but the most tepid sort of curiosity in her Irish past. What upset Jean, however, was the criticism that she was nothing but a dilettante whose only credential was her family name. "They said I did charity work," Jean reflected. "But if I were a man, they would have said I ran an international organization. I mean it all takes planning."

Ted was a politician and he knew that in supporting his sister, he might set off a firestorm of criticism. *The Boston Globe* touted a woman for the position, not Jean but Elizabeth Shannon, a close friend of Ted's, and the widow of a former ambassador to Dublin. Shannon had written or cowritten three books about Ireland and had a long active involvement in the country. The other main contender for the Irish post was former Congressman Brian Donnelly of Dorchester, a man admired by Irish-Americans in Boston. In the House, Donnelly had worked diligently and often single-handedly on Irish matters, his most notable achievement being the "Donnelly visa" that gave special immigration quotas to the Irish. Donnelly's supporters believed that the man they called the "patron saint of Ireland" deserved the position as a capstone to a notable career, and they would remember Ted's defection.

Ted knew that he was more politically vulnerable now than he had ever been. He may have had an enviable record of legislative accomplishments in the Senate but a *Boston Globe* poll in February showed that almost as many Massachusetts voters viewed him unfavorably as favorably, 40 percent to 41 percent. With his reelection coming in 1994, he could hardly afford to risk alienating a large bloc of Irish-Americans. Jean was his sister, however, and in an act of great devotion, he set out to make her the new ambassador. He used all of his influence with the new President. When Clinton agreed that she would be his choice, he went to see his colleagues on the Senate Foreign Relations Committee. Ted was a man of the Senate, who relished the exaggerated courtesies of that institution. He saw to it that when Jean came up for her confirmation hearings there would be no tough questioning in front of the cameras by the Republican opposition.

In the weeks that the nomination was under discussion, Jean fled from the media as if she feared one untoward word might doom her. Ted shepherded Jean through the whole process, and he was with her at the White House on St. Patrick's Day when Clinton formally nominated Jean. He was there beside her for her confirmation hearings as well, sitting there along with Eunice and Pat.

Jean had diligently prepared herself for the hearings, and she displayed none of the embarrassing ignorance of some political appointees. She was a poised, articulate sixty-five-year-old American woman. "Her life has been touched by sadness," said Senator Claiborne Pell of Rhode Island. "It is nice to see it touched by joy and challenge."

Jean was the least sentimental of the Kennedys, a taciturn woman who kept her emotions locked away behind walls of irony, wit, distance, and mistrust. She knew, however, that she had achieved something that none of the Kennedy women had ever achieved before, not even Eunice. Jean had a full measure of that emotional fiber that ran through the women in the family. She had survived it all: the tragedy of Rosemary; the deaths of Joe Jr., Kathleen, Jack, and Bobby; the decades of life with her charming philanderer of a husband; the humiliation of her relationship with Alan Jay Lerner; the shame of Chappaquiddick; Willie's indictment and trial. She had endured as she believed her family had endured.

Jean knew almost nothing about her Irish roots, and the first Kennedy woman, Bridget Murphy, who 143 years ago had sailed from Liverpool to Boston. Like almost all the women of her time, Bridget had lived her life anonymously, considering her greatest achievement the success of her only son, Jean's grandfather, P. J. Kennedy. Bridget had worked as a servant, and Jean's family had been too close to the sweat and grime of their immigrant roots to celebrate the life of the first Kennedy matriarch. Jean's own father had despised what he considered all the sentimental Irish malarkey about his forbears, despised it when he was referred to as an "Irish-American." Of all the members of Jean's generation, only Jack had from his youthful days loved Ireland with a deep and certain love, loved the green meadows, loved the melodic language, loved the stories of his family's past.

That Jean was returning to Ireland now as ambassador was a triumph not simply for her or for Ted, but for four generations of women. As Jean looked back on her past, she was her mother's daughter, choosing her own times to remember, her recollections sweet with tender memories. "I think of it all the time, what a wonderful upbringing I had," Jean said. "People talked about our tragedies but we had such a happy family. We had so much support. We knew what the rules were. We weren't confused like the women are today. They have options but they're really terrified about whether to do this or that. It's very confusing. And I found my childhood stimulating and fun and interesting and wonderful, surrounded by love and care, and a lot of good people, and I couldn't have improved on it. And look where I am now. I don't know how you could fault my family life in any way, really. I can't look back and say anything."

Bridget had to combine her life as a mother with a career running a modest store. In some respects, life had come full circle, and many of the young women in the family now were making the same kind of choice that Bridget had been forced to make. Kathleen had been seeking a position in the Clinton administration, heading the Peace Corps perhaps or the President's new program in domestic service; that didn't work out and she won a more modest post as deputy assistant attorney general in the Department of Justice that her father had once headed. At the age of forty-two, she still hungered for political office. She faced the melancholy prospect that "there may not be a time" for her to run. She was the most politically impassioned Kennedy of her generation, but it was her brother, Joe II, who sat in Congress, her young cousin, Patrick, who in 1994 was running for the House of Representatives from Rhode Island, another cousin, Mark Shriver, who was running for the state legislature in Maryland, not Kathleen, and not any other Kennedy woman. Then in June she was chosen as a Democratic candidate for Maryland's lieutenant governor and won a difficult, challenging race. Kathleen's sixteen-year-old daughter Meaghan was old enough to be a congressional page, a fact that Kathleen contemplated with pride and wonderment over where all the years had gone. Unlike Kathleen, Meaghan had been brought up to believe that she could do anything a boy could do, and if she one day contemplated running for office, she would consider it part of the natural mandate of her life, shouldering herself forward among women and men alike.

Maria considered dropping out of television after the birth of her third child, but she continued attempting that ever-precarious balance of career and home. Caroline's book on the Bill of Rights, *In Our Defense*, was an admirably serious work, a timely reminder of the basis of American liberties. She too continued to be a full-time mother while serving as president of the board of the Kennedy Library Foundation, serving on the board of the Profile in Courage Award, and writing a book on the First Amendment, fulfilling what she considered the mandates of her father's life.

Pat's two eldest daughters, Sydney and Victoria, both re-

mained wives and mothers, but unlike their mother and grandmother, this was a chosen role, not a narrow pathway beyond
which they dared not wander. Their younger sister, Robin,
worked in stage production off-Broadway, was involved in en-
vironmental projects, and showed no great concern either to
exploit the Kennedy name or to join her sisters as a wife and
mother. Her cousin, Courtney, had remarried to an Irishman,
Paul Hill. He had served fifteen years in prison for a crime he
did not commit, the bombing of a Guildford pub by Irish Republican Army terrorists, but this was a marriage that linked
the family to a distant rebel past. Courtney's sister, Kerry, had
come to Washington, and was a leading activist for international human rights serving as executive director of the RFK
Memorial and Center for Human Rights. Of the young generation of Kennedys, only Jean's adopted daughter, Amanda,
took any great interest in the family history, writing a book
about her paternal grandfather while finishing a Ph.D. in education at Harvard. Her younger sister, Kym, the youngest of all
the Kennedy grandchildren, was a student at Brown University.

Since the days that Rose had stood and watched the placard-
carrying suffragists in the streets of Boston, there had never
been a feminist in the family until Rory. At the age of twenty-
four, Rory was the first Kennedy woman to identify herself
with women's issues. She saw her life as representing not a
radical break from the past but part of a natural continuum.
"Even if I have different politics than Eunice, and Eunice has
different politics than Grandma, and even if I have different
politics from my sister Kathleen, there is continued respect for
people who have charted the way," Rory said. "It's to the
credit of the women in the family that attitudes have changed,
and to a certain extent to the credit of the men as well, but it
has definitely been a battle that has had to be fought, and continues to be fought."

Rory was working in Washington producing a series of videos on subjects such as the criminalization of crack mothers.
Rory, like several of her cousins, was benefiting from grants
from the Kennedy Foundation. That had been Eunice's idea,
setting aside funds to involve the young generation in worthy
projects involving mental retardation, furthering her own ideals
of what it meant to be a Kennedy.

To her videos, as to her life, Rory brought her feminist vision. "It's not that the boys in my family were horrible, but an
indicator of a larger social phenomenon," Rory asserted. "The

battle isn't fought in our family simply over who sits at the head of the dinner table and who feels free to speak at Thanksgiving. It's fought out in the world against institutions that limit women, that we demand that women are represented in a more empowering way, that the church show more respect for women, that women be allowed to be priests, that we have all our reproductive rights, that we get respect from medical doctors and hospitals. That's the struggle, not simply for the Kennedy women, but for all women."

In Boston, Joan lived in an exquisite apartment on Beacon Street, overlooking the Charles River. She had suffered a short relapse in March of 1993, but she was sober again, though she knew that her sobriety was measured out not only a day at a time, but an hour at a time and sometimes even a minute. She wondered sometimes why *she* was the Kennedy woman publicly pilloried for her drinking when several of her sisters-in-law had problems, and over the years seven or eight of her nephews and nieces had come to her seeking help with their own addictions. She was still hoping to become a music teacher, and she was taking her practice teaching at the same Boston Latin School that Fitzgerald and Joe had once attended. She was proud that both her own daughter, Kara, and Teddy Jr.'s wife, Katherine "Kiki" Gershman Kennedy, were pregnant and she would soon be twice a grandmother. Fifty-seven-year-old Joan unabashedly relished the prospect of being a grandmother. She looked with fascination at the past now, intrigued by the lives of the strong Kennedy women of generations past, of Mary Augusta especially, with whom she had certain similarities, and at Bridget, and all that they had endowed the family. She wanted her grandchildren to know their own grandmother not through rude headlines as a pathetic victim of a patriarchal family, but as a woman of strength and substance, who had struggled willfully to live her own life. That was the woman she wanted to be, the image of herself that she held aloft, guiding her onward. In the middle of April 1994, she flew down to Washington to spend a weekend with Kara and her husband, Michael Allen. One evening she joined her pregnant daughter and son-in-law to see a new film, *The House of the Spirits*. Joan loved the movie and its portrayal of powerful women. As they left the theater Kara hugged her mother and said: "That's what we are, Mom, strong women." "What are you girls talking about?" Michael asked, and the two Kennedy women continued down the street arm in arm.

The Kennedy women were linked to their family past in a myriad of ways, and to the lives of four generations of American women. Bridget's story resonated with the themes of a million immigrant lives. Mary Augusta's social ambition and cultural attainment was a common thread among the second-generation American women of her generation, as much as was Josie's life, relegated to the parameters of home and hearth. Rose had grasped at the ideals of professional motherhood that were a common currency of her time. Her daughters and daughters-in-law had almost all married in the fifties, and in their narrow adherence to their husbands' ambitions, they too were women of their time. The opportunities and freedoms that were the natural birthright of the young Kennedy women had developed over at least a century and a half, won not simply by ballots and marches and fervent demands, but by the social evolution of individual lives. For the most part these women had not been present at the great events of their time, but they had made their mark on their children, and on the family themes of public ambition and social contribution, leaving as part of their legacy a young generation of Kennedy women who lived in a world of possibility.

These young Kennedy women still lived in a society where men claimed special prerogatives for their gender. John's celebrated affair with Daryl Hannah suffered because the movie actress feared that John was truly his father's son, a Kennedy man incapable of loyalty to one woman. When Joe II married Elizabeth Kelly, a member of his congressional staff with whom he had a long-term relationship, he sought an annulment to wipe the slate clean of the unseemly stain of divorce that barred him from the sacraments of his church. With one magical wave of the ecclesiastical wand, the archdiocese of Boston could do away with his decade of marriage to his former wife. Joe II was a man of notable ambition, and he had decided to risk the momentary wrath of an unlikely alliance of feminists and traditionalists to make himself once again pure in the eyes of his church and the multitude of Catholic voters. No Kennedy woman had ever spoken out against her husband or ex-husband, but there was a righteous anger in Sheila Rauch, and she vowed to fight her former husband, fight him for her children's name, for her own life and history and marriage, opposing those who to her mind were "lying before God."

Jean was of an older generation. For most of her life she had stood back and watched as her brothers and husband and other men dominated the stage, but not any longer, not now. Late in June she flew off to Ireland, the island that beckoned her as once the skyline of Boston had beckoned her great-grandmother. She had hardly settled into her new post when Willie got in a brawl in a bar in Arlington, Virginia, after he was apparently taunted as an alleged rapist, bringing yet more embarrassment to the family name. As much as Jean enjoyed the authority and pomp of her position, she was lonely away from her family, and at Christmas she implored Ted to fly over to spend a few days with his sister.

Jackie was still a Kennedy woman too, a presence at major occasions at the Kennedy Library, lunching with Hillary Rodham Clinton in New York, and sailing with the new president and first lady on Martha's Vineyard.

During the Christmas holidays in 1993, Jackie was sailing in the Caribbean when she couldn't get over a persistent cough, noticed that her lymph nodes had swollen, and felt stabbing pain in her abdomen. She flew back to Manhattan where doctors diagnosed her as suffering from a form of cancer known as non-Hodgkins lymphoma. She began receiving chemotherapy and steroid drugs, while continuing to work three days a week as a book editor.

Jackie wanted to keep the matter private, but she knew that the tabloids would learn of her illness, splashing the news in garish headlines, her condition the common parlance of conversation in supermarket checkout lines across America. And so the story was given out to *The New York Times*, minimizing the seriousness of her condition, and the woman who as a young bride had fought for her husband's health now waged her own struggles, with Maurice Tempelsman, Caroline, and John at her side.

The cancer spread to her brain and spinal cord, and the radiation treatment and powerful anti-cancer drugs that were part of her therapy were almost as debilitating as the illness. Maurice was there with her and for her at this time, as no man had ever been there for her before. Jack had loved Jackie for her beauty and her style and her grace and her youthful wit. Onassis had married her for her celebrity and her power. Maurice loved her for herself, for her soul and her depth. He had made no vow to love her in sickness and in health, but no marital vow, no eternal pledge of fidelity would have made the devotion that he gave her any greater. As Maurice realized the seriousness of Jackie's condition, he gave up most of his business life, moving his office into her apartment on Fifth Avenue. The couple did not want the world to know how ill Jackie had become. On several occasions Maurice served as her medical surrogate, visiting cancer specialists, learning about experimental procedures, because the media would have been alerted if Jackie herself had investigated them.

Jackie had always maintained a tiny island of privacy in the midst of the sea of celebrity. On the third Sunday in May she wanted to go out with Caroline and Maurice and walk once again through Central Park, though she knew they would be plagued by photographers and reporters. Maurice had seen long ago that celebrity was a pathetic adornment, and Jackie's fame was to be endured, a storm of flashbulbs and rude shouts, that he tolerated as his price of entree into Jackie's world. It angered him that a legion of photographers and reporters had camped outside the door at 1040 Fifth Avenue. He considered them a race of sickly voyeurs, waiting to see Jackie stumble, waiting to capture some grotesque image that was not Jackie, not *his* Jackie.

Jackie knew that this would probably be the last time she would ever walk in Central Park. She wore tan slacks and a pink long-sleeve sweater, a scarf around her neck, a brown wig, and large dark glasses, and held on to Maurice's arm. Caroline in jeans and running shoes walked slightly ahead, carrying her father's namesake, one-year-old Jack, in her arms. Jackie had loved to jog around the reservoir, loved strolling with her grandchildren, loved sitting on a park bench with Maurice. The photographers and celebrity reporters followed them into the park, not like a pursuing, gesticulating pack, but staying back as if they felt that theirs was an unseemly business, and they were merely the surrogates for a voyeuristic public. The cameras had always loved her, and in its way they loved her today. They did not show her halting step, or a face grimacing with pain. They showed Jackie and Maurice as an elderly New York couple, meandering through the park on one of the first brilliant Sundays of spring.

Jackie was debilitated, weak, and disoriented. The next day she entered New York Hospital–Cornell Medical Center with pneumonia. The doctors examined her again, discovered that the cancer had spread to her liver, and told her that there was nothing more they could do except dull her pain and treat her pneumonia. Jackie loved life, not half of life, not a tenth of life. She asked that the treatment be stopped even for the pneumonia. On Wednesday she returned home for the final time. The family gathered, and outside the apartment house the crowds stood waiting behind police lines. On Thursday the Kennedy women were among those who arrived at the house to see her. Eunice, Pat, and Ethel all made the journey. And in the evening of May 19, 1994, Jackie died, with Caroline, John, and Maurice at her bedside.

On Saturday, two days after Jackie's death, Eunice gave the commencement address at Loyola College in Baltimore. The speech had already been written, and she added words of her own about Jackie, but it was about the great themes of her life, and to her mind the lives of Catholic women, that she spoke:

> For us—and to my wonderful and big, extended family— Jackie always reminded us that loyalty to one another was to be fiercely practiced and protected. To America, she embodied the beauty of art, of music, of design, and, more than anything, the beauty of family. These were the gifts to us and to the world. . . . We know that God chose a family to bring his message of love, salvation, and peace to all of us on earth. . . . I hope that every woman here will seriously consider Mary, Mother of God, as a role model. She was a true revolutionary. She had a child out of wedlock, and had to give birth to him in a stable with animals and shepherds as her only support system, along with Joseph, the foster father. She raised her son in the Jewish tradition, yet watched him convince his countrymen that he was God on earth. . . . Pray to her. . . . When we ask God "what do you want from me?" the answer is often one we don't like because it calls for sacrifice. It calls for action. It asks us to examine our consciences. . . . No restoration of God to His proper place in our life on earth, or the expansion of spiritual values is possible without your commitment and mine to prayer, service, family and love.

Caroline wanted the funeral to be private. She did not want to hear the shutters of a hundred cameras, or have her tears captured on film, to be peddled on street corners. John took charge of the guest list and other arrangements and early on

Monday morning, the day of the funeral, the family agreed to allow the audio portion of the service to be transmitted outside St. Ignatius Loyola Roman Catholic Church, where Jackie had been baptized and confirmed.

Thirty-one years ago Jackie had memorialized all that was good and noble and true about Jack at his funeral, and this morning Caroline and John sought to do the same for their mother. Though she had given few instructions about her funeral, she had given her children as their greatest entitlement a sense of rightness, and they understood what they must do, and how their mother must be remembered. She had lived for beauty, for the beauty of her children and culture, of family and friends and faith, of the preservation of the beauty of the world around her, and of the preservation of her own personal beauty too.

In the eighty-minute-long service there were words of grace, music of poignant beauty, prayers of heartfelt depth, but no moment so captured Jackie as did Maurice's reading of a favorite poem, "Ithaka" by C. P. Cavafy, in a deep, cultivated voice, resonant with feeling.

> As you set out for Ithaka
> hope your road is a long one,
> full of adventure, full of discovery.
> Laistrygonians and Cyclops,
> angry Poseidon—don't be afraid of them:
> You never find things like that on your way
> As long as you keep your thoughts raised high,
> As long as a rare excitement
> stirs your spirit and your body.
> Laistrygonians and Cyclops,
> wild Poseidon—you won't encounter them
> unless you bring them along inside your soul,
> unless your soul sets them up in front of you.

The Kennedy women were all there for the funeral, including Jean, who had flown from Ireland and Maria who had arrived from Los Angeles. As Eunice sat there in the stilled church, she thought of all the funerals she had gone to in the past, of all the men and women who had gone before, and never had she seen such praise for a woman's life, such emotion over her death. Suddenly, all the rancor and pettiness that permeated most public discourse was gone, and she wondered why it required an occasion such as this for people to reach out for what was good and noble in one another.

Joan sat next to Eunice, who continued to pull her into the warm embrace of the family. The poem was so powerful, so full of Jackie, that Joan realized she had goose pimples. Joan had always identified with Jackie more than any other woman in the family. This morning she thought of how good her former sister-in-law had been to her, and how much they shared in common. She looked out across the church at her former husband sitting next to his new wife, and she reflected on all the years of marriage. And she thought how she was so proud she had never publicly spoken out against Ted, and Jackie had never said anything negative about Jack, and how that was something else the two women had in common.

> Hope your road is a long one.
> May there be many summer mornings when,
> with what pleasure, what joy,
> you enter harbors you're seeing for the first time;
> may you stop at Phoenician trading stations
> to buy fine things,
> mother of pearl and coral, amber and ebony,
> sensual perfume of every kind—
> as many sensual perfumes as you can,
> and may you visit many Egyptian cities
> to learn and go on learning from their scholars.

For Caroline the most overwhelming impression of these past four days was how deeply the world cared about her mother. Caroline adored Jackie, but she had no idea how much the world cared, as neither, perhaps, had the world. Outside in the street hundreds stood, most of them reverentially quiet, many listening to the service on transistor radios. All across America millions in their offices and homes were listening to these words on television.

> Keep Ithaka always in your mind.
> Arriving there is what you're destined for.
> But don't hurry the journey at all.
> Better if it lasts for years,
> So you're old by the time you reach the island,
> wealthy with all you have gained on the way,
> not expecting Ithaka to make you rich.

For Kathleen, this service was not memorializing some grand historic personage, but her Aunt Jackie. Kathleen thought of her father, and she reflected on how close Bobby and Jackie had become after Jack's death, and how wonderful that had been for her father. Bobby had promised to take her to Europe after her high school graduation, but he had died. That summer Jackie had invited Kathleen to visit her in Greece. She remembered all this and more, the images of events flashing through her mind, but most of all she felt the immense sadness of this day. She had read the columnists and editorial writers, and heard the television commentators, all talking knowingly about the end of Camelot. To her, Camelot had ended long ago. There had been so many funerals, so much sadness in her family, so much sadness.

> Ithaka gave you the marvelous journey.
> Without her, you wouldn't have set out.
> She has nothing left to give you now.
> And if you find her poor, Ithaka won't have fooled you.
> Wise as you will have become, so full of experience,
> you'll have understood by then what these Ithakas mean.

That was how the poem ended, but Maurice had written his own final words, his own private poem to his Jackie.

> And now the journey is over.
> Too short, alas too short.
> It was filled with adventure and wisdom
> laughter and love, gallantry and grace.
> So farewell, farewell.

Jack's funeral had been a coming of age of America as an imperial power, able to bury its martyred dead with majesty and ceremony. Jackie's funeral was a different coming of age for America, a nation memorializing a woman who had led no great armies, spoke no noble rhetoric, painted no immortal paintings, led no mammoth enterprises. She had tried to walk in beauty, leaving her touch on the White House, and on the way that her compatriots looked at their own culture. She had been the soul of whatever was true about Camelot, an elegant missionary of style and substance, who had left her mark on the social fabric of her nation, while remaining, first of all, a mother. She had grown up in a time when marrying well was a woman's high calling, and she had ended her life as a successful book editor, living with a married man, whom she loved and who loved her, and most Americans accepted that as fine and good.

Jackie had been a Kennedy woman by marriage. And now she would be one forever. She was laid to rest in Arlington National Cemetery beside Jack, the eternal flame that she had lit for him three decades ago burning now for her as well. When in the years to come Americans visit Arlington to pay their respects to the nation's honored dead, and stand silently in front of the eternal flame, they will think not only of Jack but of Jackie, of all that had been, and of all that might have been.

Rose was a hundred and three years old. She could not speak any longer, not even a word. The family had not told her about Jackie's death but she doubtless sensed that something had happened. All of her expression had gone into her eyes, and some family members could read them and the way she turned her head in approval or disapproval, pleasure or dismay, and believed that she understood far more than the nurses realized. The family had prepared a series of especially edited documentaries on the Kennedys for their mother with all the tragedy and misfortune cut away. Often the nurses played them on the video recorder, and Rose watched, her tiny eyes never turning from the screen. Rosemary was young and beautiful, her ebullient smile lighting up the screen. Joe Jr. did not die in the plane exploding over England. Kathleen lived on eternally young, her laughter cascading across the decades. Jack never flew to Dallas, Bobby never reached Los Angeles on his presidential campaign, and Teddy never drove across a tiny bridge on the island of Chappaquiddick. Joe was always loyal and strong and good. And Jackie was still alive. There were only the times to remember here, the good times, the times when life was full of infinite promise and hope. The films were full of sudden cuts and ellipses, but Rose did not appear to notice, and as she watched the screen, it seemed that there was another loop of film playing within her head with all the scenes still intact.

One day Eunice's old friend, Nancy Coleman, looked out the window of her house in Hyannis Port and saw a strange group moving slowly up the road. She recognized the tall, gaunt figure of Eunice, her nervous energy apparent in her every stride. She saw that her old friend was pushing a wheelchair containing the tiny figure of her mother bundled up in blankets. Then Coleman saw that Rosemary was at Eunice's side. Rosemary appeared stolid and impassive, limping slightly, her head down against her chest, shuffling along holding her younger sister's arm. Someone was talking, and as they passed, Coleman saw that Eunice was carrying on a conversation with her mother and sister as if they still understood, and they continued down the road, off in some other world.

Eunice and Ted continued to take Rose for walks in Hyannisport, but there was only a faint glow of that spirit that had helped to animate their lives. In the middle of January 1995, Rose suffered a relapse and, in the dead of a New England winter, the family gathered in the compound on Cape Cod. Rose finally succumbed on the afternoon of January 22. She was a hundred and four and a half years old, and as much as her children had known her death was coming, they were unprepared for the emotional burden of this moment.

There had never been a public family so adept at the rituals of death as the Kennedys. Rose's funeral this frigid January morning was as exquisitely fitting a memorialization as Jack's and Bobby's funerals were so many years ago. The service took place not in a great cathedral but in the more humble abode of St. Stephen's, the parish church in the North End of Boston where Rose had been baptized over a century ago. Outside in the bitter wind hundreds of Bostonians stood silently in tribute.

Rose had outlived three of her sons, one of her daughters, one of her daughters-in-law, one of her sons-in-law, one of her grandsons, and all of her friends. But she had helped to bring forth a great family, and they came forward one after another to pay their tributes, to say a prayer, repeat a scriptural passage, record a memory or two.

Of Rose's children, Pat was supposed to speak first, but when the moment arrived, she could not move; her eldest daughter, Sydney, came forward instead. Rose would doubtlessly have admired her granddaughter's sense of public ritual and the seamless way she took over from her mother. Sydney leaned slightly over the podium and read the passage from Ecclesiastes that had given Rose so much solace.

For everything there is a season, and a time for
every matter under heaven;
A time to be born and a time to die; a time to plant,
and a time to pluck up that which is planted;
A time to kill and a time to heal; a time to destroy,
and a time to build . . .

The distinguished audience in the small church had come today not to honor a personage of great public achievement but
to pay tribute to a mother of another era. Her life of denial and
discipline and unquestioning faith was as much gone from the
world as were the horses and carriages of her childhood. There
would be a time to pore over the foolscap of her life, to weigh
out the pluses and the minuses, and to pry open the self-
deceptions, but that time was not today. The audience here and
the commentators on television watched in reverential silence.

A time to weep and a time to laugh; a time to
mourn and a time to dance;
A time to scatter stones and a time to gather;
a time to embrace,
and a time to be far from embrace.

Rose had lived far more than the biblical three score and
ten, and for the family there was not the tragic sense of Jack's
or Bobby's funeral, of still-youthful men struck down in the
summers of their lives. Rose had lived long, too long perhaps,
and there was relief that her suffering was gone. But there was
deep sadness, for she was her children's last link to all that had
been, to all the promise, to all the dreams. They were old now,
and so were their dreams.

Eunice came forward clutching crumpled pages of legal
notepaper on which she had written words. Her face was so
lined that it was like some ancient map of life, with endless
byways and directions. She was too intense and single-minded
to speak with the measured cadences of a great orator. She had
many, many things to say, and so she said them, each sentence,
each idea, as if she had fulfilled some hidden obligation. She
was not so eloquent as Ted, her words did not have the poetic
resonances of other readers', but she spoke her own intimate
truths.

All of Eunice's life, she had been moved by what was best
in her mother. She was blind to what was wrong and low about

her family, blind to its excesses and faults. She reached for what was good and noble in her mother, as others reached for what was good and noble in her own life and work.

"My mother was my greatest teacher," Eunice said, peering out of square black spectacles. "She made me laugh and she helped me to learn. And in learning I experienced love. She kept maps around the house and she always quizzed me. 'Now Eunice, where is Pakistan? Where's Wales?' She knew many poems by heart. She taught us to listen to Dad's dinner-table conversations about politics, conversations which seemed boring to a small child but later became the basis for our life's work. But as smart as she was, she would never let us forget our special sister Rosemary. We went to dances together, sailing together, swimming together. My admiration for this quality of my mother, and my great friendship with my sister Rose inspired me and helped me and helped to lead me to my life's work. Mother's acts of intelligence, inclusion, respect, and love of motherhood created unbreakable bounds of love and support between my brothers and sisters. Her acts of goodness were this child's schoolroom. They were my mother's heart and I loved them, and she loved all of you. And I pray that her heart will be with you always."

Rose Fitzgerald Kennedy was buried next to her husband in Holyhood Cemetary in Brookline.

Acknowledgments

In recent years a number of Kennedy biographers have portrayed themselves as members of an intrepid race, throwing their grappling hooks over the hoary walls of Camelot, fighting their way past intellectual eunuchs and other retainers, breaking into the family closets, then retreating into the night, their arms full of dark truths. I too charged ahead toward Camelot, but when I approached I found that the walls had crumbled, the moat was dry and the bridge was down, the guardians of myth were buried or impotent, reams of material were lying around unread, and most of the closets had long since been rifled. I searched in vain for the massive myth-making machinery that I was told was hidden somewhere, and at times I felt more like Dorothy meeting the wizard in the Emerald Palace than an author intruding into the hallowed halls of Camelot.

The walls of Camelot were breached long ago, and I intend here neither to knock over another ruined wall, nor to build the castle up again, but to attempt to look at the lives of the Kennedy women as they were and are.

In this multigenerational context, many of the truisms of psychological determinism fall apart. The personalities and ambitions of the daughters and sons of Rose and Joseph P. Kennedy cannot have been rigidly determined by their supposedly frigid mother and singularly ruthless father unless Rose's and Joe's personalities were equally determined by *their* parents. What one sees is a subtle matrix between the environment in which these women lived—meaning the social, cultural, and historical context of their lives—and their heredity, not simply the family blood, but the social heredity, the distinctive traits inculcated within the home. In the end, it is astounding how so much of the Kennedy character and personality continues generation after generation and how the women in the family struggle against many of the same problems.

I have written about matters that are sensitive and personal, about individuals who are deeply troubled, but I have attempted to do so with understanding.

Few people are neutral about the Kennedys, and doubtless some of the family's fervent admirers will feel that I have focused with inordinate interest on the negative and the unseemly. The Kennedys' worst critics will probably feel that I have been far too kind, pulling as many punches as I have struck. I only hope that in these many pages, I have conveyed at least something of the deep fascination that I feel for these women and their lives. These five years of researching and writing *The Kennedy Women* have been the most fulfilling period of my professional career. I have learned a great deal about the struggles of a unique group of American women over the past 170 years, and I also hope that this book will add to the hidden history of over half the human race.

Soon after I began my research, I met with Melody Miller, Senator Edward Kennedy's longtime spokesperson, to tell her about my project. Miller has known the family since her teenaged years. She worked for Jacqueline Kennedy answering letters after the death of President Kennedy, and on both Robert and Edward Kennedy's Senate staffs, and she is the institutional memory of the family. She spends much of her time vigorously and honestly portraying the more positive aspects of the Kennedys. "All that I ask you is to walk a mile in their moccasins," Miller said.

That has been my goal throughout researching and writing *The Kennedy Women*. My debts to others are immense. I began the serious research in Boston, Massachusetts, with the assistance of Michael Foster, an extraordinarily energetic and creative young man. Foster has a master's degree in history from Northeastern University, and he made this book his own, working with enormous diligence and resolve, not only in various archives but helping with the interviews as well. It was no easy matter researching lives that were considered largely unworthy of any but the most cursory regard by history, and we spent days coming up with a nugget or two of information about Bridget Murphy Kennedy, Josie Hannon Fitzgerald, or Mary Augusta Hickey Kennedy. While Foster and I were immersed in our work, Vesna Obradovic Leamer, my wife, spent many hours at various libraries going through old newspaper collections and obtaining other material. She is my first reader and my closest friend. Anyone who knows us is perfectly aware that without her support and love the book would not have been written. My daughter, Daniela Leamer, is another inspiration to me, as is my father, Laurence E. Leamer.

I benefited as well from the research facilities at the John F. Kennedy Library in Dorchester, whose staff greeted us with courtesy and helpfulness. I would like especially to thank Maura Porter, Susan D'Entrement, Ron Whealan, Allan Goodrich, the chief audiovisual archivist, William Johnson, the chief archivist, and Sheldon Stern, the resident historian. At the archives of the Archdiocese of Boston, Ronald Patkis was a generous guide, as was Richard Wolfe at the Countway Library of Medicine. In Washington, I was especially helped by the late Dr. Herbert Kramer, the director of communications and assistant to the chairman both of the Joseph P. Kennedy Jr. Foundation and Special Olympics International. Kramer cared immensely about Special Olympics and the foundation's work for those with retardation. He was an articulate guide and became a close friend. His memorial is not simply *Conversations at Midnight*, the book that he and Kay Kramer, his wife, wrote when he was dying, but the continuing work of Special Olympics.

Although *The Kennedy Women* is a work of history, I still suffer from the journalistic conceit that the best way to learn about living people is to talk to them. I resolved to track down anyone who knew the Kennedys in their earlier years in Brookline, Riverdale, and Bronxville. The singular truth is that almost none of these people had ever been approached before, though they had intimate knowledge of the Kennedy family. *The Kennedy Women* then is full of interviews with individuals speaking for the first time about the Kennedys.

In these pages I have neither invented dialogue nor pretended to be able read another's thoughts. When I do presume to say what an individual is thinking, it is because I have interviewed that person specifically about his or her thoughts at a certain moment, or have access to written documentation. In either case, the source is listed in the endnotes where the reader is welcome to judge whether I have used my evidence properly. I write for instance about what Joan Kennedy, Eunice Kennedy Shriver, and Kathleen Kennedy Townsend were thinking at Jacqueline Onassis's funeral in May of 1994. Four days after the funeral I interviewed the three women and asked them what they had been thinking during the funeral.

I have attempted not simply to interview everyone possible but to place the various Kennedy women within a social, cultural, and historical context. To do this I have benefited immensely from the fine work of numerous academic historians and scholars. These contributions are duly acknowledged in the endnotes and bibliography.

I was extraordinarily fortunate in getting to know Mary Lou and Kerry McCarthy. They are the Kennedy family's resident historians, and they bring to the subject erudition, insight, candor, and concern. Kerry McCarthy has graciously allowed me to quote extensively from her two excellent unpublished books, one on P. J. Kennedy, and the second on her Great-aunt Rose Kennedy. I had many interviews with Luella Hennessey Donovan, for four decades the Kennedys' nurse. Without question over the years Donovan has been the most intimate observer of the family outside the immediate relatives. She has never before spoken so extensively about the Kennedys. She talked with frankness and perception, and I am profoundly grateful that this good and generous woman would be so trusting of a new acquaintance.

When I began this book, I had neither access to the Kennedys nor much of a prospect of gaining it. Nonetheless, when I wrote the Kennedys asking for interviews, I was not asking perfunctorily so that upon publication I could announce the subjects had spurned me and that I had gone ahead with my heroic and decidedly unauthorized book. I truly wanted those interviews, and I persisted in requesting them.

I had completed most of my initial research when Eunice Kennedy Shriver agreed to talk to me. I interviewed Mrs. Shriver several times in Washington, D.C., and Orlando, Florida. She also gave me access to Kathleen Kennedy's unpublished letters.

I am grateful that most of the family members who are major subjects of this book did, indeed, talk to me and answer questions, some of which they must have found impertinent, intrusive, or just plain painful. One of the major themes of this book is how difficult it is for the Kennedys to talk intimately about themselves and their pasts, largely because that has become a means of psychological survival. I met with Senator Edward Kennedy in his private office in the Capitol, and he mused emotionally about his mother and his life in ways that he has rarely done before. I met with Jean Kennedy Smith in her Very Special Arts office in Washington, and she too dealt with matters that were not easy for her to discuss. Patricia Kennedy Lawford invited me to her home in Manhattan and she responded to my questions. When I first talked to Joan Kennedy in a telephone interview, she was understandably reticent to speak with much candor. But when I saw her again, in her apartment on Beacon Street in Boston, she was startlingly honest. Also, I was the first author or journalist to travel to St. Coletta's in Jefferson, Wisconsin, to interview those responsible for the care of Rosemary Kennedy.

The young generation of Kennedy women was helpful as well. Kathleen Kennedy Townsend never turned aside my questions when I would drive up to her Baltimore office. Kerry Kennedy Cuomo was articulate in discussing her work, and so was Rory Kennedy. Maria Shriver is adept at the craft of interviewing, and when she finally found time to talk, she gave me not simply her time but her intense attention, insights, and personal family anecdotes. Her brothers, Robert Shriver and Anthony Shriver, were extremely helpful as well.

This is not, however, in any way an authorized book. None of the Kennedys or their associates have seen the manuscript, nor has had any control over the contents.

I would especially like to thank Patricia Coughlan, the widow of Robert Coughlan, the author of Rose Kennedy's autobiography. Her husband was a wonderful raconteur and a talented writer and stylist, and Mrs. Coughlan provided access to Coughlan's papers, which included much of the research he employed in writing Mrs. Kennedy's book. Coughlan was a wonderful interviewer and a superb journalist, and his papers were invaluable.

Other than the Kennedy Library, I am grateful for research materials obtained at: Mugar Library, Boston University; George H. Beebe Communication Reference Library, Boston University; O'Neill Library, Boston College; Burns Library, Boston College Archives; Massachusetts Historical Society; Countway Library of Medicine; Holy Cross College archives; Concord Public Library; New England Conservatory; Suffolk County Registry of Deeds; Norfolk County Probate Office; Rosemont College Library; the Schlesinger Library; the Archives of the Sisters of Notre Dame de Namur; Boston School Committee headquarters; Acton Historical Society; Boston Public Library; Barnstable Public Library; library of

Cape Cod Times; University of Notre Dame archives; Manhattanville College archives; Riverdale Country Day School archives; Library of Congress; District of Columbia Library; Harvard University Libraries; Yale University archives; West Palm Beach Public Library; Palm Beach County Library; Santa Monica, California, Library; UCLA Graduate Research Library; American Film Institute Library; Archives of the Archdiocese of Boston; Seeley Mudd Manuscript Library at Princeton University; Special Collections at Arizona State University Library; Choate School archives; Wellesley College archives; Columbia University Oral History Project; Franklin D. Roosèvelt Library; Department of Special Collections of Stanford University Library; British Museum; Irish National Library; Wexford, Ireland Library; the French National Library, Paris, France; the library of *Paris-Match*, Paris; the libraries of *The Boston Globe* and the *Boston Herald*. I also extensively employed CompuServe.

In London Angela Lambert not only gave me an especially insightful interview and provided me with dozens of names and phone numbers, but allowed me to copy her research materials for her book, *1939: The Last Season of Peace*. Other authors, journalists, and writers who were helpful include Robert Andrews, Stephen Banker, Charles Bartlett, Ed Becker, Paul Ciotti, Robert Coughlan, Doris Kearns Goodwin, John Greenya, Nigel Hamilton, Carter Harrison, V. V. Harrison, Burton Hersh, Murray Kempton, Ronni Kern, Barbara Kevles, Fletcher Knebel, Eirik Knudsen, Doug Kriegel, Betty Lasky, Suzannah Lessard, Axel Madsen, Barbara Matusow, Lynne McTaggart, Dan Moldea, Joseph Morgenstern, Khoi Nguyen, Dotson Rader, Kristina Rebelo, Arthur Schlesinger Jr., Ted Schwartz, James Seymore, Dick Shea, David Shumacher, Hugh Sidey, James Spada, Baroness Garnett Stackelberg, Gore Vidal, Frank Waldrop, Richard Whalen, and Craig Wolf. Three friends who read the manuscript are Diane Huffman, Kerry McCarthy, and Maco Stewart, each offering valuable suggestions. My mother, Helen Leamer, also carefully read the manuscript.

Many of the hundreds of interviews did not find their way into the text, but they were useful nonetheless. A few of the people I talked to asked to remain anonymous, for in most instances what I considered legitimate reasons, and I want to thank them as well. Other individuals provided various services and help, and they too deserve acknowledgment. Among those who contributed to *The Kennedy Women* are: Mollie Acland, Dr. Ray Adams, Mikki Ansin, Jan Amory, Manuel Angullo, Dani Asher, Larry Ashmead, Simon Audrey, Elizabeth Augenblick, Larry Baker, Mary Battis, Harriot Benoist, Mrs. Peter Bensen, Mother Binney, Joey Bishop, Danny Blaney, Brad Blank, Marvin Blank, Elizabeth Boggs, Peter Bonventre, Alan K. Borsari, Patricia Breen, Mrs. Emile Bregy, Dr. Ruth Brenner, Patricia Broderick, Diane Broughton, Ann Brown, Lady Browne, Ann Buchwald, Robert Bunshaft, Charles Burke, Ada Burns, Dan Burns, Harmon Burns III, Andrea Cahn, Winifred Campbell, Virginia Carpenter, Mary Boylan Carter, Patsy White Carter, Dr. Sally Cassidy, Oleg Cassini, Mary Lyon Chatfield-Taylor, Loretta Claiborne, Anne Coffey, Fred Cohen, Martha Cole, Nancy Coleman, Jane Kenyon-Stanley Compton, James Connor, William Connors, Dr. Robert Cooke, Marion Coolen, Barbara Cooper, Dorothy Costabile, Pat Coughlan, Francis Cowden, Marcia Coyle, David Crockett, Mary Mann Cummins, Ann Curtin, John Henry Cutler, Gloria Somborn Daly, Mrs. Wilfred Daly, Bob Davidoff, Renee de la Chapelle Perna, Dorothy Dunn Dempsey, Ann Denove, Jacqueline Desobury, Joanna Despotopoulou, Margaret Louise Marnie DeVine, Wyatt Dickerson, Audrey Dines, Janet Donovan, William Douglas-Home, Joan Dreifus, Margaret Driscoll, George Duff, Andrew, Duke of Devonshire, The Duchess of Northumberland, Gunnar Dybwad, Milt Ebbins, Richard Edwards, Tom Egerton, Barbara Eccles Eggert, June Emery, Jay Emmett, Ann Fitzgerald Farrell, Paul "Red" Fay, Mike Feldman, Lady Maureen Fellowes, Joe Finneran, Fred Fitzgerald, Charlotte Fitzgibbon, Lady Virginia Ford, Robert Fosdal, Sarah Foster, Harry Fowler, Frank Fox, Sister Joanne Frey, Madeleine Furth, Alan Gage, Buddy Galon, Barbara Gamarekian, Betty Gargan, Joseph Gargan, Elinor Gates, Jeremy Gilmore, Lady Elizabeth Glendevon, Delayne Gold, Fred Good, Barbara Goodman, Frederika Goodman, Milton Gould, Arthur Grace, Flo Grace, Dorothy Grandfield, Mary Gravolos, Judith Green, Florence Groseenbacher, Nancy Lane Gulliver, Edwin Guthman, Lisa Gwirtzman, Lord Haig, Kay Halle, Marrose Hanavan, Geraldine Hannon, Alice Harreys, Pamela Harriman, Ruth-Ann M. Harris, Jane Hennelly, Barbara Hicks, Sally Roche Higgins, Charlotte Hogan, Lady Hood, Claude Hooton Jr., Maria Hooton, Mary Hubbard, Marian Hunt, Dick Hurley, Herbert Hurwitz, Sister Gabrielle Husson, Doris Hutchings, Margaret

Hutchinson, Eddie Jaffe, Constance Metcalfe Jaggi, Cynthia Jay, Shirley Jobe, Mrs. M. C. Johnson, Virginia Johnston, Mrs. Thomas Joyce, Arthur Kassell, Marilyn Katleman, Nancy Keefe, Dot Keegan, Betty Kelly, Fran Kelly, Tom Killefer, Phyllis Kirk, Harvey Klemmer, Dr. Edward Kolodny, Mirko Kontic, Kay Kramer, Paul R. Leahy, Janet Leigh, Peter Levathes, Flor Lewis, Evelyn Lincoln, Dick Livingston, Mary Lou Linhart, Ernest Macaneany, Lady MacMillian, Sister Joan Magnetti, James Mahoney, Royal Marcher, Sister Margaret Ann, Leonard Mayo, Kerry Mazzone, Cynthia McAdoo, Francis McAdoo, Peter McCabe, Virginia McCann, Sister Caritas McCarthy, Peggy McDonald, Marceille McFarland, Eleanor McGrath, Elizabeth McInerney, Mildred "Brownie" McLean, Thede McKinstery, Chris McNickle, Colette McNickle, Bruce McPherson, Mrs. John Miller, Chris Montague, General Robert Montague, Paul Morgan, Suzanne Morton, Joan Mulgrew, Joe Naar, Larry Newman, Sancy Newman, Wendy Oates, Dejan and Alexsandra Obradovic, Mirko Obradovic, Jack O'Brien, John J. O'Connell Jr., Sister Elizabeth O'Conner, Justine O'Donnell, Dorothy Ogilvie, Chrystal O'Hagan, Ivanka Ostojie, Fred Otash, Jim O'Toole, Dr. John Pearce, Charley Peters, Esther Peterson, Rhona Peyton-Jones, David Phelps, Chuck Pick, David Powers, Mrs. Roderick Pratt, Sister Mary Quinlan, Sister Janet Reberdy, Coates Redmon, Jewel Reed, Amie Reichert, Marilyn Riesman, Sandy Richardson, Marie Ridder, Mrs. Robert Nagle, Raleigh Robinson, Professor Ray Robinson, Terri Robinson, Wayne Rosso, Leonie Rudd, John Ryan, Mary Ryan, Peter Sabiston, Chuck Sachs, Miriam Sargon, Mrs. Edward Schmidt, Ilya Schneider, Del Sharbutt, John Sheehan, Paul Shefrin, Mrs. Eileen Sherwin, Dutch Shutler, Bob Slatzer, George Smathers, Robin Smith, Ned Spellman, Mickey Spillane, Nancy Steiner, Daniel Stewart, Patricia Seaton Stewart, Helen Steverman, Glenn Stout, Mimi Strong, Margaret Sullivan, Countess of Sutherland, Bill Sutton, Lee Tomic, Michael Tomic, Margery Tracy, Dorothy Tubridy, Dick Tuck, Dr. Elliot Valenstein, Margaret Van den Heuval, Linda Vandergraft, Willia Volin, Helga Wagner, Mary Ward, Paul Wasserman, Betty Wertenbaker, John White, Bonnie Williams, Page Wilson, Kelly Wolfington, Jim Wright, Paul Wurtzel, Marilyn Wurzburger, Ursula Wyndham-Quin, and George Zitnay.

As an author, I have benefited from the highest level of professional assistance. My literary attorney, Kenneth Norwick, has provided good counsel for many years. My British agent, Abner Stein, did excellent work. Don Spencer did a superb job of transcribing dozens of interviews. Pam McClintock helped with research in New York. The idea for this book came from my literary agent, Joy Harris, and that is only one indication of the unique regard she shows to her authors. Another sign of it is that she sent this project to Diane Reverand at Villard, who as editor-in-chief and publisher has shown detailed concern for every aspect of *The Kennedy Women*. Her assistants, Melanie Cecka and Hilary Black, helped watch over the book's production and Jacqueline Deval brought her special touch to the publicity, as did Becky Simpson and Lynn Goldberg. Heather Kilpatrick performed the legal review, concerned not simply with narrow legalisms, but with the quality of work. Dennis Ambrose shepherded *The Kennedy Women* through production with an awesome command of detail.

The book is dedicated equally to Joy Harris and to her husband, Bob Tavetian. Bob is a superb artist whose images remain embedded in the minds of any who see his work. He deserves this dedication simply for sitting stoically through too many author-agent dinners, but he has his own unique literary sensitivities, and I immensely value his judgments and his friendship.

Notes

Abbreviations

AAB	Archives, Archdiocese of Boston
AKP	Arthur Krock Papers, Seeley G. Mudd Manuscript Library, Department of Rare Books and Special Collections, Princeton University Libraries, Princeton, New Jersey. Used by kind permission of Seeley G. Mudd Manuscript Library.
ALP	Angela Lambert Research materials. Used by kind permission of Angela Lambert.
AS	Arthur Schlesinger Jr. *Robert Kennedy and His Times* (Boston: Houghton Mifflin, 1978).
ASK	Arthur Schlesinger Jr. *A Thousand Days: John F. Kennedy in the White House* (Boston: Houghton Mifflin, 1965).
ASP	Arthur Schlesinger Jr. papers at John F. Kennedy Library
ASU	Peter Lawford's papers at the Special Collections, Arizona State University Library. Used with the kind permission of Arizona State University Library.
BA	*Boston American*
BCA	Boston College Archives
BG	*Boston Globe*
BH	*Boston Herald*
BHCL	Boston Herald Cuttings Library
BK	Barbara Lynne Kevles Papers and Other Historical Materials in John F. Kennedy Library. This is the first-time use of these papers, with the kind permission of Barbara Lynne Kevles.
BP	*Boston Post*
BSP	*Boston Sunday Post*
BT	*Boston Traveler*
BUCL	George H. Beebe Communication Reference Library of Boston University
BUH	Burton Hersh. *The Education of Edward Kennedy* (New York: Morrow, 1972).

CA	Gail Cameron. *Rose: A Biography of Rose Fitzgerald Kennedy* (London: Michael Joseph, 1972).
CH	Peter Collier and David Horowitz, *The Kennedys* (New York: Summit Books, 1984).
CSA	The Choate School, Andrew Mellon Library, John F. Kennedy Collection
CU	Columbia University Oral History
DEK	David E. Koskoff. *Joseph P. Kennedy* (Englewood Cliffs, NJ: Prentice Hall, 1974).
DKG	Doris Kearns Goodwin, *The Fitzgeralds and the Kennedys* (New York: Simon and Schuster, 1987).
EKS	Eunice Kennedy Shriver
FBIFOI	Federal Bureau of Investigation Freedom of Information Files
FC	Rev. John J. Cavanaugh CSC oral history, 1973, found in oral history collection (UORL) Notre Dame University archives. With the kind permission of University of Notre Dame Archives.
FDRPL	Franklin D. Roosevelt Library, Hyde Park, N.Y.
FNL	French National Library, Paris, France
GA	"The Kennedys of Massachusetts" by Edward L. Galvin in *The Irish in New England* (Boston: New England Historic Genealogical Society, 1985).
GS	Gloria Swanson. *Swanson on Swanson* (New York: Random House, 1980).
HCA	John F. Fitzgerald clippings, Holy Cross Archives, College of the Holy Cross
HCL	Henry Cabot Lodge II papers, Massachusetts Historical Society
HS	Hank Searls. *The Lost Prince: Young Joe, The Forgotten Kennedy* (New York: New American Library, 1969).
IA	Inga Arvad
INL	Irish National Library, Dublin, Ireland
JCB	Joan and Clay Blair. *The Search for JFK* (New York: Berkley/Putnam, 1976).
JFK	John Fitzgerald Kennedy
JFKPL	John F. Kennedy Library
JFKOL	John F. Kennedy Library Oral History series
JMB	James MacGregor Burns. *John Kennedy, A Political Profile* (New York: Harcourt Brace, 1960).
JPK	Joseph P. Kennedy
JPKJR	Joseph P. Kennedy Jr.
KK	Kathleen Kennedy
KKL	Kathleen Kennedy letters. Copyright is owned by Eunice Kennedy Shriver, all rights reserved. Used by kind permission of Eunice Kennedy Shriver.
KKT	Kathleen Kennedy Townsend

KMPK	Kerry McCarthy manuscript of "P. J. Kennedy: The First Senator Kennedy" used by kind permission of Kerry McCarthy.
KMRK	Kerry McCarthy manuscript of "Summers with My Aunt," used by kind permission of Kerry McCarthy.
LB	Laura Bergquist Knebel Papers at Boston University, used by kind permission of Fletcher Knebel.
LBJPL	Lyndon B. Johnson Library
LMT	Lynne McTaggart. *Kathleen Kennedy* (New York: Dial Press, 1983).
MB	Michael Beschloss. *Kennedy and Roosevelt* (New York: Norton, 1980).
MCA	Manhattanville College Archives
NH	Nigel Hamilton. *JFK: Reckless Youth* (New York: Random House, 1992).
NPS	National Park Service Oral History with Rose Kennedy
NYT	*The New York Times*
PBF	Paul B. Fay Jr. *The Pleasure of His Company* (New York: Harper & Row, 1966).
PFP	Paul B. Fay Jr. Papers, Department of Special Collections, Stanford University Library, Stanford, California. Used by kind permission of Paul B. Fay Jr.
RCA	Rosemont College Archives
RCP	Robert Coughlan Papers. Used by kind permission of Patricia Coughlan.
REFK	Rose Elizabeth Fitzgerald Kennedy
RK	Rose Fitzgerald Kennedy. *Times to Remember* (New York: Doubleday, 1974).
RW	Richard J. Whalen. *The Founding Father: The Story of Joseph P. Kennedy* (New York: New American Library, 1964).
RWP	Richard J. Whalen Papers at the John F. Kennedy Library. Used by kind permission of Richard J. Whalen.
SU	Stanford University Archives, Stanford, California.
WCA	Wellesley College Archives, Wellesley, Massachusetts

2	"You see . . .": Interview, REFK. RCP.
3	"Your sons have gone . . .": Interview REFK, *The David Frost Show*, July 5, 1971.
4	*"Oh brave . . .":* quoted in James Mansfield Cleary. *Proud Are We Irish: Irish Culture and History as Dramatized in Verse and Song* (1966), p. 163.
4	old women in: Nicholas Furlong and John Hayes. *County Wexford in the Rare Oul' Times.* Vol. 1 (1985), p. 16.
4	Bridget was born: Massachusetts Vital Records. Boston City Hall.
4	as many as thirty thousand: Robert Kee. *The Green Flag: Volume One: The Most Distressful Country* (1972), p. 115.
4	the rebel leaders: ibid., pp. 124–125.

5   rained half: Kerby A. Miller. *Emigrants and Exiles: Ireland and the Irish Exodus to North America* (1985), p. 9.

5   between 1845 and: R. F. Foster. *Modern Ireland 1600–1972* (1988), p. 320.

5   about a million people: Foster writes that "sophisticated computation estimates excess deaths from 1846 to 1851 as between 1,000,000 and 1,500,000; after a careful critique of this, other statisticians arrive at a figure of 1,000,000." Foster, p. 324.

5   "the young and old . . .": Miller, pp. 285–287.

5   "though we are . . .": Miller, p. 287.

5   At the beginning: *Wexford Independent*, January 6, 1849. INL.

5   Another woman: *Wexford Independent*, January 31, 1849. INL.

6   Few partook: Hasia R. Diner. *Erin's Daughters in America: Irish Women in the Nineteenth Century* (1983), pp. 21–22.

6   all a woman's work: Robert E. Kennedy Jr. *The Irish: Emigration, Marriage, and Fertility* (1973), p. 54.

6   "females in Ireland": Maragaret Mac Curtain and Donncha O Corráin, eds. *Women in Irish Society: The Historical Dimension* (1979), p. 28.

6   If she had had some genteel: Diner, pp. 11–12 or see Miller, p. 57.

7   Bridget sailed: KMPK. The oral history of the Kennedy family, as recorded in Kerry McCarthy's history of Patrick Joseph Kennedy, says that Bridget Murphy met Patrick Kennedy, her husband-to-be, on a ship sailing to Boston. In the voluminous records of passengers at the Boston Public Library, there is only one Patrick Kennedy listed in the appropriate time frame, sailing on the *Washington Irving*. There is, however, no Bridget Murphy. What appears in these pages then is the most likely account.

7   forty-nine single women: *Washington Irving* ship registry, BPL.

7   slightly more than: Diner, p. 31 and Foster pp. 351–353.

7   "servant": *Washington Irving* ship registry, BPL.

7   Kanakas from: Workers of the Writers' Program of the Work Projects Administration in the State of Massachusetts. *Boston Looks Seaward: The Story of the Port 1630–1940* (1941), p. 121.

7   keep them from the women: The situation was so notorious that a decade later Congress passed an act specifically to protect women like Bridget Murphy. The law stated that any sailor who "under promise of marriage, or by threats, or by the exercise of his authority, or by solicitation, or the making of gifts or presents, seduces . . . any female passenger, shall be guilty of a misdemeanor." Reverend John Francis Maguire. *The Irish in America* (1868), pp. 181–82.

7   "Ship fever": Marcus Lee Hansen. *The Atlantic Migration
     1607–1860* (1940), p. 256.

7   about 6 percent: ibid.

8   tall and handsome: KMPK.

8   she could only read: In the 1870 Boston census, Bridget Mur-
     phy Kennedy said that she could read but not write. Boston
     Vital Records and GA, p. 26.

8   Three days later: *Washington Irving* ship registry, BPL.

8   second greatest of American ports: Samuel Eliot Morison. *The
     Maritime History of Massachusetts 1783–1860* (1979), p. 225.

9   buildings of Quincy grainite: ibid. pp. 228–230.

9   a month and a day: *Washington Irving* ship registry. BPL.

9   There to meet Bridget: KMPK.

9   sound of anvils: William H. Sumner. *A History of East Boston*
     (1858), p. 503.

9   among the 8,552: Oscar Handlin. *Boston's Immigrants: A
     Study in Acculturation* (1941), p. 60.

10   *"don't remain . . .":* The editors saw their Irish coreligionists
     living "huddled togerther in close rooms and cellars—whole
     families occupying only one apartment, and inhaling disease
     and death in every breath of tainted air they draw. Those who
     can get work, get at best but precarious employment—at work
     one week and idle the next. Hundreds and thousands go on
     festering in their idleness and poverty—till they become help-
     less and desperate." *Boston Pilot*, September 8, 1849, p. 15.

10   over 15,000: Andrew Buni and Alan Rogers. *City on a Hill.*
     (1984), p. 76.

11   between a dollar: Handlin p. 72.

11   "A married man . . .": Dr. Daniel W. Cahill, as quoted in
     George Potter, *To the Golden Door: The Story of the Irish in
     Ireland and America* (1960), p. 509.

11   scuffling in the employment line: KMPK.

11   the moment they married: Timothy J. Meagher, "Sweet Good
     Mothers and Young Women Out in the World: The Roles of
     Irish American Women in Late Nineteenth and Early Twenti-
     eth Century Worcester, Massachusetts," *U.S. Catholic Histo-
     rian*, 5(3–4) 1986, p. 326.

11   dying on September 24, 1855: There was no Catholic
     cemetery in East Boston and for six dollars Bridget and Pa-
     trick purchased a plot in the Catholic cemetery in Cambridge,
     a plot that would be big enough for at least another Kennedy.

12   "arsenical.": Dennis Ryan. *Beyond the Ballot Box: A Social
     History of the Boston Irish, 1845–1917* (1983), p. 48.

12   copper pots: *Boston Pilot*, October 6, 1849.

12   "to take . . .": *East Boston Argus-Advocate*, July 24, 1879.

12   "Who among . . .": *Boston Pilot*, August 11, 1849.

12   their modest standard of living: In 1852 the tax assessor re-

ported the Kennedys' personal wealth at three hundred dollars, a decent amount for a working man and his family. The tax assessor's report for 1856 listed their wealth at only one hundred dollars. Assessor's report for 1852 for Ward 2 in East Boston, BPL; Assessor's Report for 1856 for Ward 2 in East Boston, BPL.

12 The Kennedy household: 1860 Census, Ward 2, East Boston, 25 June 1860, p. 203.

13 lustful "concupiscence": cited by Ryan, p. 47.

13 "to let it have its full fling": quoted in Ryan, p. 47.

13 On Sundays the two-thousand-pound bell: Sumner, pp. 657–658, and *East Boston Argus-Advocate* souvenir edition, May 1897, p. 13.

14 they named their son Patrick Joseph Kennedy: Baptismal and marriage book for The Church of the Holy Redeemer, AAB.

14 784 people: City Registrar's Report, B.C.D. 1859 (Document for the year 1858), No. 1, p. 28.

14 not hereditary: Selman A. Waksman. *The Conquest of Tuberculosis* (1964), pp. 38–39.

14 lived just fourteen years: Handlin, p. 115.

14 dying at a rate: Robert E. Kennedy Jr., p. 47.

15 a few dollars: Two years later in the 1860 census, Bridget Kennedy's personal estate was valued at only seventy-five dollars. 1860 Census, Ward 2, East Boston, June 1860, p. 203, Boston Vital Records.

15 On November 22, 1858: Mass. Vital Records, (122:80), also cited in GA, p. 25.

15 door to door: William Shannon. *The American Irish* (1963), p. 37.

15 priests couldn't even visit: Peter C. Holloran. "Boston's Wayward Children: Social Services for Homeless Children, 1800–1930," Boston University Dissertation, 1982, p. 154.

15 "physically and mentally sound,": quoted in Holloran, p. 182.

15 breaking threads: Ryan, p. 51.

16 seven other families: Census of 1860 quoted in GA, p. 26.

16 70 percent: Judith Rollins. *Between Women: Domestics and Their Employees* (1985), p. 52.

16 practically a servant race: Barbara Miller Solomon. *Ancestors and Immigrants: A Changing New England Tradition* (1956), p. 57.

16 the highest ratio: Daniel Sutherland. *Americans and their Servants* (1981), p. 47.

16 "biddy,": Potter, p. 513.

16 "Lizzie resembled . . .": Samuel Eliot Morison. *One Boy's Boston, 1887–1901* (1962), p. 16.

17 loneliness would be on them: David M. Katzman. *Seven Days a Week: Women and Domestic Service* (1978), pp. 15–16.

17   As late as 1908: Diner, p. 110.

18   By the end of the century: "The Leadership of Nuns in Immigrant Catholicism" by Mary Owens O.P., in Rosemary Radford Ruether and Rosemary Skinner Keller, eds. *Women and Religion in America: Vol. 1: The Nineteenth Century* (1981), p. 101.

18   sold more rye whiskey: Many poor widows sold liquor without licenses, an offense that Irish-American police and ward politicians usually ignored and often condoned. This custom of widows running "shebeens," kitchen grog shops, had begun in Ireland and was a recognized part of Irish immigrant life. Roy Rosenzweig. *Eight hours for what we will: Workers and leisure in an industrial City, 1870–1920* (1983), p. 43. and Perry R. Duis. *The Saloon: Public Drinking in Chicago and Boston: 1880–1920* (1983), p. 60.

18   lost to history: Bridget was doubly ignored, as an immigrant and as a woman, leaving not even a shadow on the history of her time. In 1897, *The East Boston Argus-Advocate* devoted a special issue to a seventy-page history of the island. The edition included one hundred photos of the most prominent people in East Boston's history. The editors included ninety-nine portraits of posed and somber men, several photos of industrial enterprises, and only one picture that had any women in it: the staff at the Maverick House including a few maids and female cooks. *East Boston Argus-Advocate* souvenir edition, May 1897.

19   "get up to let your brother . . .": Meagher, p. 335.

19   "Look at that boy . . .": *Boston Pilot*, December 1, 1849. p. 1.

19   skirt maker: 1870 census as cited in GA, pp. 26–28. There is no record of Margaret M. Kennedy's employment.

19   "a high class locality . . .": Robert A. Woods and Albert J. Kennedy. *The Zone of Emergence: Observations of the Lower Middle and Upper Working Class Communities of Boston, 1905–1914* (1962), p. 189.

19   "If you are . . .": George Deshon. *Guide for Young Women, Especially for Those Who Earn Their Own Living* (1897), pp. 151–153.

20   his ideal of a young Christian: Father Deshon wrote that the street was full of dangers and "downcast eyes accompany the chaste spirit, and indicate an inward purity." The young Catholic woman should have no illusion about a romantic marriage or she was bound to be disappointed. That suitor who came to her "in his Sunday's best, his shoes shining and his hair brushed and oiled" will within the bounds of holy matrimony "look dirty and coarse, his hair all disorder." Words once soft and tender will turn harsh: " 'Why haven't you done this? Why don't you do better?' " Even worse was the woman mar-

ried to a man who turned out to be a drunkard, his wife "bloated, coarse-looking ... with a lot of ragged children bawling and fighting.... And it was all her own fault. She knew enough about him when he was paying her attentions to put her on her guard." Deshon, p. 299.

20   "Pat's boy": KMPK, and interview, Kerry McCarthy.

21   read books: KMPK.

22   Notre Dame Academy: *Winthrop Sun* June 1, 1923.

22   November 23, 1887: *East Boston Argus-Advocate*, November 26, 1887, and GA, p. 30.

22   wooden gothic Church: Robert H. Lord, John E. Sexton, and Edward T. Harrington. *History of the Archdiocese of Boston*, Vol. III (1944), p. 264.

22   proudest thoroughfare: *East Boston Argus-Advocate*, December 19, 1874.

22   on December 20, 1888: *East Boston Argus-Advocate*, December 29, 1888, p. 8.

23   "a woman of ...": ibid.

24   among the poorest families: In 1872 when Josie was seven years old, there were seventeen men in Acton worth over $10,000, while her father's property was valued at only $225, consisting of a house worth $150, three-fourths of an acre of land valued at $50, and two swine worth $25. *Valuation List of Real and Personal Estates in the Town of Acton*, September 1, 1972, Boston: Tolman and White, 1872.

24   the honor roll: *The Annual Report of the School Committee of the Town of Acton for the School Year 1875–6*, p. 12; *The Annual Report of the School Committee of the Town of Acton for the School Year 1874–5*, p. 12.

24   absent or tardy: *The Report of the School Committee from February 26, 1870, to February 27, 1871*, p. 13.

24   Two of the Hannon children: DKG, p. 81.

25   Years later Josie's mother: ibid., p. 82.

25   raise a family: Interview, Geraldine Hannon.

25   took to the bottle: DKG, p. 83 and interview, Geraldine Hannon.

25   fall of 1878: DKG, p. 77.

25   "condescension of ...": BP, September 15, 1907.

25   "The first time ...": John Henry Cutler. *"Honey Fitz": Three Steps to the White House* (1962), p. 43.

25   picked twelve: ibid., p. 44.

25   Fitzgerald was born: Cutler, p. 35.

26   "sitting in front ...": BP, November 11, 1915, p. 34.

26   fifty-five-year-old: Harvey Rachlin, *The Kennedys: A Chronological History 1823–Present* (1986), p. 14.

26   "I thought my life ...": BP, December 21, 1913.

26   "all six of my brothers,": Cutler, 42.

26   privately bitter: "I never learned why the two older brothers didn't take more responsibility," Rose Kennedy said decades later, "but the fact was that my father became the mainstay of the family and continued to be so until the youngest boys were ready to take care of themselves." RK, p. 9.

27   For much of its history: Rev. Joseph J. C. Petrovits. *The New Church Law of Matrimony* (1919), p. 225.

27   "Each week when John F. . . .": DKG, pp. 88–89.

27   "deficient, delinquent . . .": A. Osborne. President's annual address. Proceedings of the Association of Medical Officers of American Institutions for Idiotic and Feebleminded Persons, 1884, p. 392, quoted in R. C. Scheerenberger. *A History of Mental Retardation* (1987), p. 117.

28   about two years: DKG, p. 88.

28   "He seems to have regarded . . .": RK, p. 11.

29   "The minute he saw me . . .": DKG, p. 105.

29   Fitzgerald belonged: Cutler, p. 42.

29   "perfectly beautiful": RK, p. 15.

30   Fitzgerald had three times: Minutes of the Young Men's Christian Association of Boston College 1887 to 1892. BCA.

30   As a bachelor: Cutler, p. 57.

30   "Every time I went . . .": George Kibbe Turner, "The Mayor of Boston," *Collier's*, November 16, 1907, p. 16.

31   "treat[ing] her . . .": Theodore Lidz. *The Person: His and Her Development Throughout the Life Cycle* (1983 ed.), p. 68.

32   By 1880: Arthur Mann. *Yankee Reformers in the Urban Age* (1954), p. 3.

32   more Italians: The Irish population had begun to decline as early as 1895 when there were 6,800 Irish, 7,700 Italians, and 6,200 Jews. Paula J. Todisco. *Boston's First Neighborhood: The North End* (1976), 29.

32   "Once Mother . . .": quoted in DKG, p. 103.

33   More than a hundred: Anne McCarthy Forbes. "West Concord: Survey of Historical and Architectural Resources" (1989) and Laurence E. Richardson, "Westvale-Warnerville-Prison Village" (undated). Both documents in Concord Public Library.

33   a property that included a: CA, p. 33.

33   thumbs pointing to heaven: Interview, Geraldine Hannon.

33   a litany of "Father says this": CA, p. 38.

33   "Young women learned . . .": Nancy M. Theriot. *The Biosocial Construction of Femininity: Mothers and Daughters in Nineteenth-Century America* (1988), p. 79.

34   past the yellow Thoreau-Alcott: *Concord: A Pilgrimage to the Historic and Literary Center of America* (1922), p. 26.

34   in 1863: Townsend Scudder. *Concord: American Town* (1947), p. 289.

34   farmers in town: Scudder, p. 289.

34   would lose their jobs: Schudder, p. 291.

35   "Going to mass . . .": RK, p. 14.

35   "theater box . . .": RK, p. 16.

35   a finger of smoke: RK, p. 12.

36   "I want to present this . . .": "Recollections" by John F. Fitz-
      gerald in BG, January 14, 1914, p. 35.

36   "knew right then . . .": CA, p. 35.

36   "saturated with . . .": Albert Lane, *Concord Authors at Home*
      (1902), p. 11.

36   "western air": *Concord Enterprise*, October 26, 1899.

36   building had been enlarged: "Report of the Committee on En-
      largement of the West Concord School House," Concord Town
      Report, 1900–1901, Concord Public Library.

37   "wonderful years . . .": RK, p. 11.

37   "mother returning . . .": REFK reflections on Early Childhood.
      RCP.

37   in early 1900: *Concord Enterprise*, February 22, 1900.

37   Her brother, John Edmond: Interview, Geraldine Hannon.

38   "Sometimes I wondered . . .": RK, p. 14.

38   "primal images . . .": Denise L. Carmody and John T.
      Carmody. *Roman Catholicism: An Introduction* (1900), p. 202.

38   "When she was happy . . .": RK, p. 13.

39   Her tenth birthday party: *Concord Enterprise*, July 27, 1890.

39   "Fitzgerald gave . . .": *Concord Enterprise*, July 24, 1901.

40   "What's a congressman's daughter . . .": CA, p. 36.

40   "Father knew . . .": DKG, p. 105.

41   He had put the title: Suffolk County Registry of Deeds, Vol.
      2948, pp. 22 and 23.

41   assessed at $16,400: *Dorchester Beacon*, February 13, 1904,
      p. 6.

41   "He was seldom . . .": REFK reflections on Early Childhood.
      RCP.

42   twice as many girls: In 1905, 698 girls attended Dorchester
      High and only 329 boys. Documents of the School Committee
      of the City of Boston for the year 1905, No. 8, p. 4.

42   a teaching class: Lawrence J. McCafrey, "Irish America" in
      The Wilson Quarterly, Spring 1985, p. 83.

42   five hours a day: Documents of the School Committee of the
      City of Boston for the year 1906, High Schools, Introduction,
      p. 5.

42   she carried home thick tomes: Authorized textbooks, School
      Document No. 10, Documents of the School Committee of the
      City of Boston for the Year 1907, pp. 25–26.

43   dances held: *Dorchester Beacon*, November 5, 1904, p. 2.

43   "I was never allowed . . .": RK, p. 27.

43   died of acute gastritis: BP, September 15, 1905, p. 1.

43   "Do you know . . .": BT, October 10, 1952.

44   "I don't even care . . .": BP, September 30, 1906.

44   "the corporations . . .": BP, November 11, 1905, p. 8.

44   "a business of trading . . .": quoted in Cutler, p. 93.

45   "No, I can't . . .": BA, November 15, 1905, p. 3a.

45   the paper ran: BP, October 22, 1905.

45   "thought politics interfered . . .": BP, November 19, 1905, p. 34b.

46   "Papa will be . . .": BP, November 19, 1905, p. 34b.

46   story on Rose: BP, November 18, 1905, p. 8.

46   "ideal American family": BP, November 19, 1905, p. 34b.

47   "I am glad . . .": BP, December 13, 1905, p. 7.

47   "1,500 dances . . .": CA, p. 46.

47   "startled beholders . . .": BP, November 22, 1906, p. 9.

47   "Me for the pretty . . .": BP, October 2, 1907.

47   "None of the . . .": BP, July 3, 1906.

48   "Fitzgerald really . . .": Interview, Geraldine Hannon.

48   more Irish-Americans: Cutler, p. 83.

48   three time as many nuns: James M. O'Toole. "Militant and Triumphant: William Henry O'Connell and Boston Catholicism, 1859–1944," Ph.D. Dissertation, Boston College, 1987, p. 98. (Note: a revised, expanded version of this thesis was published as a book.)

49   More than two thousand: BH, April 19, 1906, and BG, April 19, 1906.

50   Some seniors had even: Dorchester Beacon, July 28, 1906, p. 7.

50   a simple long-sleeved muslin gown: BP, June 24, 1906, p. 11.

50   The Post photographer: BP, June 24, 1906, p. 11.

50   Although the class president: Dorchester Beacon, June 23, 1906, p. 1.

51   "He spoke of the fact . . .": Dorchester Beacon, June 30, 1906.

51   "her schoolmates are unanimous . . .": RK, p. 28.

51   the family got on: The Fitzgeralds had begun their annual pilgrimages to Old Orchard at least as early as 1901 when their vacation was recorded in the social notes of the Concord Enterprise. Concord Enterprise, September 4, 1901.

51   "one of the finest . . .": Biddeford Daily Journal, July 19, 1906, p. 3.

52   "pitching duties . . .": George Kibbé Turner, "The Mayor of Boston," Collier's, November 16, 1907, p. 16.

52   "I can still picture . . .": DKG, p. 124.

52   mere catching of a ball: BP, August 18, 1906.

52   "I shall always remember . . .": DKG, p. 124.

53   recording secretary: BP, April 21, 1907, p. 14.

54   attending her spring class: undated clipping of Dorchester High Centennial Celebration. BH.

55   "Why that wasn't . . .": unidentified clipping from 1911 in BUCL.

55   In the depths: November 1, 1905, p. 25.

55   "I wanted . . .": Interview, Kerry McCarthy.

56   Ruth Evans: Interviews with Ruth Evans's daughters, Mrs. Francis Cowden and Mrs. Mary Gravalos.

56   "a dyed-in-the-wool . . .": Interview, Mrs. Peter Benson.

56   The church was deeply fearful: The religious press was full of ominous warnings. In all America, reported *The Sacred Heart Review* on July 20, 1907, there were 1,557 Catholic women and 5,830 men attending 269 non-Catholic colleges. That was a minuscule number but the church considered it a threat, a harbinger of secular modernity.

56   "spiritually contaminated": Early in 1907 Archbishop Farley of New York told the Daughters of the Faith the story of a young woman who after only six months in a women's college had refused to go with her mother to confession on Holy Thursday. It was a frightening specter that Archbishop Farley placed before the Daughters of the Faith, and the church laid the blame not only on the wayward maiden. "Any Catholic parent who thus exposes his or her daughter to the loss of the priceless gift of faith will be indirectly responsible if that daughter becomes an apostate from the religion of her fathers," said *The Ava Maria* on May 4, 1907.

56   "the development of . . .": John Tetlow, "The Eastern Colleges for Women: Their Aims, Means, and Methods," *Education*, July 1, 1881, p. 548.

56   daily morning prayers: *Wellesley College Calendar 1907–1908*, p. 21, WCA.

57   the Fitzgerald family: *Boston Journal*, August 16, 1907.

57   an absentminded: BG, August 16, 1907.

57   missed Fitzgerald's head: BP, August 16, 1907.

58   been fatally injured: *Biddeford Daily Journal*, August 16, 1907.

58   Many spectators: *Boston Journal*, August 16, 1907.

58   "It is simply . . .": *Boston Journal*, August 16, 1907.

58   prepared to flee: *Boston Journal*, August 16, 1907.

58   All that was left: *Biddeford Daily Journal*, August 16, 1907.

59   As the tide rose: Robert A. Dominique. *Greetings from Old Orchard Me: A Picture Post Card History* (1981), p. 52.

59   they did not return: It is possible that Fitzgerald returned for occasional gatherings, but the family no longer came to the resort for their summer vacations. Interview, Danny Blaney, local historian.

59   "pleasant place": RK, p. 17.

60   They were standing: letter from John F. Fitzgerald to Cardinal O'Connell, October 20, 1939. AAB.

60   O'Connell had let it be: Robert O'Leary, "Brahmins and Bullyboys: William Henry Cardinal O'Connell and Massachusetts Politics," *Historical Journal of Massachusetts*, January 1982, p. 9.

61   on October 1, 1907: *Wellesley College Calendar 1907–1908*, WCA.

62   "I was accepted . . .": quoted in CA, p. 46.

62   "My greatest . . .": quoted in DKG, p. 144.

62   "There was screaming . . .": Interview, Kerry McCarthy.

62   For Bishop O'Connell: Louise Callan. *The Society of the Sacred Heart in North America.* (1937), p. 615.

62   From Hugh O'Brien: *100 Years of Continuous Sacred Heart Education in Boston and Newton.* Newton: Newton Country Day School, 1980, unnumbered.

63   the students sat: Callan, p. 614.

63   "hostile to Catholicism": *100 Years of Continuous Sacred Heart Education in Boston and Newton.*

63   "for young Catholic . . .": Callan, p. 614.

63   "I never thought . . .": DKG, p. 146.

64   "thousand-dollar tune": Interview, Bruce MacPherson.

64   under Alfred De Voto: *The Neume*, The New England Conservatory of Music, 1912, p. 22.

64   she received A's: Registry Archives, The New England Conservatory of Music.

65   "big, comfortable . . .": DKG, p. 138.

65   to be convicted: DKG, pp. 172–173.

65   "We held a conference . . .": Cutler, p. 119.

65   the first mayor: BP, December 27, 1907.

66   "thousands throughout the city . . .": *The Finance Commission of the City of Boston, Reports and Communications* (1909), pp. 254–258.

66   Fitzgerald often dropped in: RK, p. 55.

67   "I was in love . . .": Interview, Kerry McCarthy.

67   a student either had to be: Interviews, Sister Mary Quinlan and Sister Gabrielle Husson.

67   "both girls are very ambitious . . .": BP, July 17, 1908.

68   On July 18, 1908: BP, July 19, 1908.

69   "dandy time": Postcard from REFK to Miss Emily Hannon, August 22, 1908, JFKPL.

69   "We are here . . .": Postcard from REFK to Mr. John E. Hannon, postmark obscured, in archives at JFKPL.

69   "suggestive of Dutch painters . . .": Mary O'Leary. *Education with a Tradition: An Account of the Educational Work of the Society of the Sacred Heart* (1936), p. 249.

69   occasion of wrenching: V. V. Harrison, *Changing Habits* (1988), p. 19; Mary Colum, *Life and the Dream* (1947), p. 17; and Antonia White, *Frost in May* (1933), p. 8.

69   "Nothing could . . .": Interview, Sister Gabrille Husson.
69   bore such titles: Colum, p. 46.
70   "You cannot read that book . . .": Colum, p. 20.
70   Rose placed a photo: RK, p. 35.
70   "We try . . .": RK, p. 36.
70   "Coeur sacré . . .": *Règlement des Pensionnats and Plan D'Études de la Société Du Sacré-Coeur de Jésus* (1852), p. 18.
71   thirty-five minutes: *Règlement*, p. 19.
71   special cotton bath dresses: Colum, p. 25.
71   The rules instructed: The *Règlement des Pensionnats (Rules of the Boarding School)* proclaimed: "Elle se lavent les pieds tous les quinze jours" (They wash their feet every two weeks), p. 20.
71   modeled in part: The 1805 *Programme des Études* states that "we have adopted the method which Racine admired in the School of St. Cyr, the method of the immortal Fénelon, whose lesson, so delightful in their simplicity, will always surpass all modern theories."
72   "I knew that we had . . .": quoted in DKG, p. 183.
72   "a year ought . . .": RK, p. 36.
73   "the loneliness . . .": DKG, p. 177.
73   "a purplish bluish color": quoted in DKG, p. 176.
73   "for several months": Letters from REFK to Josie Fitzgerald, RK, pp. 35 and 36.
73   almost all the students: Colum, p. 24.
73   a girl neglected: Interview, Dr. Sally W. Cassidy, to whom this incident occurred.
73   the students stood: This account of the weekly assembly is based on interviews with Sisters Mary Quinlan and Gabrielle Husson of the Sacred Heart.
74   "wearing hair shirts . . .": Colum, p. 35.
74   "small iron . . .": White, p. 232.
74   "nuns were . . .": V. .V. Harrison, p. 117.
75   *Friedhof:* O'Leary, p. 251.
75   "We were terribly . . .": undated 1911 clipping, BUCL.
76   "if I am extremely . . .": RK, p. 37.
76   "jumped and talked . . .": RK, p. 38.
76   On New Year's Eve: RK, p. 38.
77   "It was not in my nature . . .": quoted in DKG, p. 185.
77   "Deprived of . . .": DKG, p. 186.
77   "I decided to forgive . . .": Interview, Kerry McCarthy.
77   "When I got to Blumenthal . . .": Interview, Kerry McCarthy.
77   "The girls take cooking . . .": Unidentified 1911 clipping. BUCL.
78   One of Rose's: CA, p. 55.
78   "will to courage . . .": CA, p. 56.

78   "Besides prayer . . .": Speech of REFK at the ground breaking of the Physical Education Building, Manhattanville College, March 11, 1956, MCA.

79   "The lover of . . .": quoted in Margaret Williams, RSCJ. *The Society of the Sacred Heart: History of a Spirit 1800–1975* (1978), p. 184.

79   "it would be too much . . .": RK, p. 39.

79   "not a thing . . .". RK, p. 40.

79   "There are lots of things . . .": quoted in DKG, p. 188. Two other Boston sisters were also at Blumenthal, Miriam and Margaret Finnegan. RK, p. 32.

80   "tears and open arms": RK, p. 41.

80   "Perhaps it is a paradox . . .": "Recollections" by John F. Fitzgerald, BP, January 18, 1914, p. 42.

80   "The thing . . .": Unidentified clipping circa early 1911, BUCL.

80   "Our mother greeted . . .": RK, p. 43.

80   the *Boston Post* reported: BP, August 21, 1909, p. 1.

81   "moody and selfish": *The Sacred Heart Review*, March 29, 1890, p. 6.

81   that openness was: "Family members themselves may be so out of touch with their feelings that their inarticulateness in therapy is most often not a sign of resistance to therapy . . . but rather a reflection of their blocking off their inner emotions even from themselves . . ." wrote Dr. John K. Pearce and Monica McGoldrick Orfanidis, who as therapists have worked extensively with Irish-Americans. "Hostility within the family is dealt with by a silent building up of resentments, culminating in silently quitting off the relationship, a form of social excommunication for interpersonal wrongdoing. . . . Feelings can sometimes be so buried in personal relationships that the family develop a sullen, dour atmosphere, and a puritanical rigidity, reflecting deeply hidden resentments." "Family Therapy with Irish Americans" by John K. Pearce, MD, and Monica McGoldrick Orfanidis. *Working papers in Irish Studies presented at a colloquium, Northeastern University*, January 27, 1983, *Working Papers*, 83:1, pp. 43 and 47.

81   "a dissatisfied person . . .": Interview, Geraldine Hannon.

81   "really a pill": CA, p. 39.

82   "Taking my cue . . .": RK, p. 44.

82   in 1847 to the old Lorillard: *Manhattanville College Catalog, 1986–87*, p. 3. MCA.

82   The school was: It was an expensive school, the costs for her year including tuition, residence fees, physician's fee, washing, apron, gymnastic suit and shoes, fencing lessons, suit and foil totaled $610.19. Rose Fitzgerald bills. MCA.

82   She studied: Rose Fitzgerald's curriculum is taken from her
      bill for the year. MCA, and from Callan, pp. 765–766.

82   "modern pagan fads": Ryan, p. 73.

82   the only course: Manhattanville bulletin for 1905. MCA.

83   why boys' voices: Ryan. p. 73.

83   "Let the Mayor sing . . .": BP, January 18, 1914. p. 42.

84   The largest crowd: HCA scrapbook #65, February 10, 1910.

84   Upon graduation: "Academy of the Sacred Heart of Jesus An-
      nual Distribution of Prizes," June 18, 1910, MCA.

84   "a full participant . . .": RK, p. 45.

84   "over which they had perfect . . .": Nathan C. Chiverick, in
      Alexander Williams. *A Social History of the Greater Boston
      Clubs* (1970), pp. 129–130.

85   "an observer from London . . .": RK, p. 52.

85   "Some of the Irish . . .": Interview, REFK. RCP.

86   in 1909: Cleveland Amory. *The Proper Bostonians* (1947),
      p. 277.

86   "Oh, I'm twenty!": Unidentified clipping from BUCL.

87   looked at Rose: BG, January 3, 1911.

89   The next morning: The account of Rose Fitzgerald's debut is
      based on coverage in the BP, BG, BA, *Boston Evening Rec-
      ord, Boston Journal*, and the *Boston Evening Transcript* from
      January 1 to January 3, 1911; and an unidentified, undated
      clipping from the BUCL clipping file from an interview on
      January 1, 1911. The *Transcript*, the preferred paper among
      Boston's Brahmin society, treated the event in a short article
      above a story entitled "FORTY-SIX CHINAMEN FINED."

89   to teach sewing: Angela Morgan, "A Mayor Who 'Came
      Back,' " *Cosmopolitan.* October 1913, p. 487.

89   She did some: RK, p. 47.

90   "for a major disaster . . .": RK, p. 60.

90   "clean the place out": HCA clipping dated February 3, 1911.

90   "a new South . . .": BP, February 18, 1911.

91   a choir whose: *Boston Journal*, February 18, 1911.

91   "It is not . . .": BG, Februrary 19, 1911.

92   one observer felt: BA, February 17, 1911. p. 5.

92   His new clothes: BP, February 17, 1911.

92   "This was the greatest . . .": BP, February 23, 1911, p. 2.

92   skating on Scarboro: CA, p. 65.

93   "The others, we 'sat out' . . .": RK, p. 64.

93   "I had read . . .": Interview, REFK. RCP.

94   He had promised: clipping, April 16, 1911. HCA.

94   The red, white, and blue: Souvenir card from HA.

95   several days before the game: RW, p. 27.

95   "My father . . .": RK, p. 61.

96   "amazingly quickwitted woman": Quoted in DKG, p. 227, and
      interviews, Mary Lou and Kerry McCarthy.

96   He sported a new: Interviews, Kerry and Mary Lou McCarthy.

96   "set her cap": KMPK.

97   "never married . . .": quoted in Diner, p. 58.

97   listed his occupation: Mary Augusta Hickey Copy of Record of Birth, Massachusetts Division of Vital Statistics, year 1857, Vol. 107, page 72, no. 3227.

97   he was a contractor: *Winthrop Sun*, June 1, 1923.

97   December 6, 1857: GA, p. 30.

97   an average age: Harvey Green. *The Light of the Home: An Intimate View of the Lives of Women in Victorian America* (1983), p. 21.

97   a marvelous success: KMPK.

97   "a young man of common sense . . .": *Supplement to The Sacred Heart Review*, April 20, 1889, p. 1.

97   She would never: *The Sacred Heart Review* warned: "The girl who enjoys the excitements of the streets and the insinuating banter of the young men she meets there, may perhaps do no wrong at first, but how long will such companionship exist before the good in her nature is perverted, before she considers piety prudery and purity priggishness?" *The Sacred Heart Review*, April 20, 1889.

98   walked as if her head: KMPK.

98   his son would be called: KMPK.

98   more Americanized: This was a struggle that went on in many Irish-American homes. In one of his sketches Peter Finley Dunne, the brilliant satirist of the Irish-American experience, has Mr. and Mrs. Hogan arguing over the naming of their tenth child. "Ye'll be namin' no more children iv mine out iv dime novels," says Hogan. "And you'll name no more iv mine out iv th' payroll iv th' bridge department," she counters. "D'ye think I'm goin to sind th' child out into th' wurruld with a name that'll keep him from anny employment but goin' on the polis foorce?" Charles Fanning, "Mr Dooley in Chicago: Finley Peter Dunne as Historian of the Irish in America," in *American and Ireland, 1776–1976: The American Identity and the Irish Connection*, edited by David Noel Doyle and Owen Dudley Edwards (1980), pp. 157–158.

98   did not want their son saddled: KMPK.

98   March 11, 1891: GA, p. 31.

99   home to the likes of: BP, December 12, 1937, p. 2A.

99   "Always, she . . .": BP, December 12, 1937.

99   "very quiet man . . .": Interview with JPK by George Bookman, for *Time* spring 1960. RWP.

99   "teach by example . . .": *The Sacred Heart Review*, August 26, 1916, p. 179.

99   making his father's career: Like Bridget Murphy Kennedy, Mary Augusta Kennedy hardly exists in the history of her

time. At her own wedding, she was the only woman listed as a guest, not even her mother or mother-in-law, though the *East Boston Argus-Advocate* printed a lengthy list of "prominent" male guests. A year later on December 1, 1988, the *Argus-Advocate* reported "a number of Representative P. J. Kennedys' friends assembled at his residence and presented him with a handsome reclining chair, it being the first anniversary of his wedding." There was no mention whether Mary Augusta attended "the first anniversary of his wedding" or not. The *Argus-Advocate* did note that "the occasion was enlivened by songs and recitations," an enlivenment probably provided by Mary Augusta Kennedy.

100   Coffee had to be: Susan Strasser. *Never Done: A History of American Housework* (1982), p. 29.

100   "renowned for her pies . . .": Interview, Kerry McCarthy.

100   setting them apart: By the turn of the century, about a quarter of American bread was commercially baked, but not in homes like the Kennedys'. Harvey Green, p. 60.

100   "P. J. always . . .": KMPK.

101   "valve disease . . .": Massachusetts Vital Records 1902, Volume 53, p. 196.

101   they represented: KMPK and interviews, Mary Lou and Kerry McCarthy.

101   there were circles: KMPK.

102   worked hard: CH, p. 460.

102   "What can I do . . .": Interviews, Kerry McCarthy and Mary Lou McCarthy.

102   Joe remembered: Interview, Kerry McCarthy.

103   From 1889: P. J. Kennedy's quiet career in East Boston real estate is outside the scope of this manuscript, but it makes a fascinating microcosm of the mesh of politics and business in Boston. On June 26, 1889, for instance, Kennedy purchased a property from Charles F. Quigley for thirteen hundred dollars that Quigley had purchased earlier that same day for eight thousand dollars. Whatever reason Quigley took such a loss is not recorded in the Suffolk County Registry of Deeds, Volume 1885, p. 337.

103   "I've already voted . . .": JMB, p. 17.

103   the most powerful: *East Boston Argus-Advocate* souvenir edition, May 1897, pp. 53–54. BPL. East Boston Branch.

103   loaned out at a neat profit: Interview with banker by Richard Whalen. RWP.

103   he rode the electric car: KMPK.

104   "She guided and stressed . . .": Interview, Mary Lou McCarthy.

104   "She left the door . . .": Interview, Kerry McCarthy.

104   "She was the power . . .": Interview, Marnie DeVine.

104   family altar: KMPK.

104   sent her son: On April 9, 1959, JPK wrote the Sisters of Notre Dame de Namur: "I can never forget that my first schooling was taken care of by your wonderful order in the school at the Assumption Church." Archives of Sisters of Notre Dame de Namur, Ipswich, Massachusetts.

104   "neglect on the part . . .": *Course of Study in the Academies and Parochial Schools of the Sisters of Notre Dame* (1895), p. 130. From archives of the Sisters of Notre Dame de Namur, Ipswich, Massachusetts.

104   They taught the children: The Brothers of Mary. *The Polite Pupil: For the Use of Catholic Parochial and High Schools* (1912), pp. 9–11. In the archives of the Sisters of Notre Dame de Namur, Ipswich, Mass. (This book codified moral teaching that was used in parochial schools.)

105   "A cheerful temper . . .": *Krone's Paragon System of Penmanship* (1888). In archives of the Sisters of Notre Dame de Namur, Ipswich, Massachusetts.

105   "Mozart would have . . .": *Course of Study in the Academies and Parochial Schools of the Sisters of Notre Dame*, p. 126.

105   "Be, at least . . .": *The Sacred Heart Review*, June 29, 1889, p. 4.

106   "If you are asked . . .": KMPK.

106   world of newspaper: David Nasaw. *Children of the City* (1985), p. 150–152.

106   "Each wave . . .": quoted in JMB, p. 7.

106   On the Fourth: BP, July 5, 1895.

107   raised pigeons in a coop: RW, p. 21.

107   "They used to say . . .": Interview, Henry O'Meara. RWP.

108   Joe asked Elcock: Interview, Walter Elcock Jr., RWP.

108   "constant bickering . . .": quoted in RW, p. 24.

108   "in a very roundabout . . .": quoted in RW, p. 24.

108   Boston's new bishop: RW, p. 25.

109   "He had a pal . . .": Letter Henry J. O'Meara to Richard Whalen, February 19, 1964, RWP.

109   Joe's primary concern: RW, p. 25.

109   His roommate: RW, p. 26.

110   "fun-loving companion . . .": Interview, Arthur Goldsmith. RWP.

110   The Kennedys bought: The precise date of the Kennedy move to Winthrop is not revealed in public documents.

110   "the triumph of . . .": Duis, p. 204.

110   No Jewish peddlers: Sari Roboff. *East Boston* (1976), p. 26.

111   Loretta played: KMPK.

111   "had seen the show . . .": Edward M. Kennedy, ed. *The Fruitful Bough: A tribute to Jospeh P. Kennedy* (1965), p. 11.

112   rumor that filtered: BG, August 17, 1911.

113   "Why in France . . .": BP, August 17, 1911, p. 1.

113   "a very tangible . . .": BP, August 17, 1911, p. 1.

113   "What do you suffragettes . . .": Cutler, p. 147.

114   "If women stir up . . .": quoted in Eileen Mary Brewer, *Nuns
-      and the Education of American Catholic Women, 1860–1920*
       (1987), p. 107.

114   "We have suffered . . .": Margaret Deland, "The Change in the
       Feminine Ideal," *The Atlantic*, March 1910, p. 299.

114   "Don't you wish . . ." BP, November 12, 1911.

115   "the busiest . . .": BA, June 11, 1911.

115   "the secret springs . . .": *Cosmopolitan*, October 1913, p. 487.

115   "Corned beef and cabbage . . .": Cutler, p. 160.

116   "with all the fair maidens . . .": clipping in HCA, June 11,
       1911.

116   such venerable institutions: Amory, pp. 354–355.

117   "They are not intended . . .": quoted in *The Sacred Heart Re-
       view*, June 22, 1912, p. 4.

117   the Abbotsford Club: CA, p. 61.

117   into the Ace of Clubs: The organization was originally called
       the Lenox Club and met Monday afternoons at the Hotel
       Lenox, but the name was soon changed, as well as the meeting
       date and place. The first article about the club refers to the
       group as the Lenox Club. BP, November 12, 1911.

117   "foster an . . .": "History of the Ace of Clubs," courtesy of the
       Ace of Clubs.

117   Years later Rose admitted: Interview, Joan Kennedy.

117   Vida Scudder: BP, April 7, 1912, p. B1.

117   Katherine Conway: BP, December 29, 1912, p. B1.

117   "After we listen . . .": BP, November 12, 1911, 2nd section,
       p. d.

118   "Please don't think I am . . .": BP, November 12, 1911.

118   "I get enough . . .": BP, November 12, 1911.

118   "Did I sound . . .": CA, p. 64.

118   "Rather soon . . .": RK, p. 48.

118   meeting not even a single: DKG, p. 203.

118   "one or two . . .": Rose Fitzgerald recollections on Childhood.
       RCP.

119   "These noble . . .": *Sermons and Addresses of His Eminence
       William Cardinal O'Connell, Archbishop of Boston*, Vol. IV.
       "Catholic Mothers" speech at Boston College Alumni Banquet
       at Hotel Somerset, June 10, 1912, p. 83.

119   chosen to stand: BP, January 28, 1912, p. B1.

120   "Every Christian . . .": BH, February 18, 1912. AAB.

121   "instantly decrease . . .": quoted in Kathy Peiss. *Cheap
       Amusements: Working Women and Leisure in Turn-of-the-
       Century New York* (1986), p. 102. The author is indebted to
       Peiss's book for much of this analysis of dance-hall life.

121   Joe knew the banned: RK, p. 69.

121   "You were never ...": Interview, REFK. RCP.

121   forbade Oscar Wilde's: Unmarked clipping dated January 8, 1914, HCA.

121   mayor abhorred: Clipping, December 3, 1913, HCA.

122   Yeats anticipated the possibility: BG, November 17, 1911, p. 9.

122   "If they start ...": BP, November 17, 1911, p. 1.

122   The mayor had sent: BG, November 16, 1911, p. 13.

123   "degrading spectacle": BP, November 17, 1911, p. 1.

123   She squirmed: DKG, p. 205.

124   "It was splendid ...": BP, November 17, 1911.

125   "stern face ...": DKG, p. 200.

127   Rose lay awake: ibid.

127   "There was not the smallest ...": BP, May 25, 1913.

127   "There were no 'scenes' ...": RK, pp. 62–63.

129   of Indian summer: *The Republic*, November 10, 1914, p. 8.

130   "I'd always wanted ...": BG, September 28, 1944, quoted in DEK, p. 22.

130   as the newlyweds: CA, p. 69.

130   The *Post* photographer: BP, October 4, 1914, p. 11.

131   She smiled with exuberant: BG, October 8, 1914, p. 1.

131   "only the relatives ...": BA, October 4, 1914, p. 30.

131   "the prettiest romance ...": BP, October 4, 1914.

131   a small wedding: RK, p. 69.

131   Suddenly, she pulled: Interview, Geraldine Hannon.

132   "hilarious": BP, October 8, 1914, p. 11.

132   "the wealthiest town ...": Bruce A. Phillips. *Brookline: The Evolution of an American Jewish Suburb* (1990), p. 3.

132   sixty-five hundred dollars: RW, p. 42.

132   from Howard Kline: *Brookline Chronicle*, December 1, 1966.

132   they had already: NPS, p. 12.

133   "delicate synthesis ...": Bruce A. Phillips, p. 2.

133   silver flatware: NPS, p. 28.

133   mistress of the home spent: Half a century later Rose could still describe the paintings on the walls in the living room and the pattern on the silverware in the dining room. Yet all she could remember of the kitchen were the white curtains emblazoned with tiny red hearts. "Historical Furnishing Plan for the JFK home in Brookline." NPS.

133   The Kennedys had neighbors: The *Jewish Advocate* for October 2, 1915, contained an ad: "WANTED—Jewish girl or woman to do general housework in German family of three adults in apartment. Must be good cook. Kosher household. Call on Monday at 77 Beals Street." Bruce Phillips, p. 19. The Precinct 2 Public Records for Brookline, 1916, list Benjamin Stern at that address.

135   On the morning of July 25, 1915: In her autobiography, REFK gives the wrong date for her first son's birth, July 28, 1915, RK, p. 77.

136   "Feeling fine ...": BG, July 26, 1915, p. 1.

136   "Of course, he ...": *Boston Journal*, July 26, 1915, p. 4.

136   "When a mother ...": REFK reflections on Children General. RCP.

137   For Rose as for other women: L. Emmett Holt, M.D. *The Care and Feeding of Children* (1894). First published in 1894, *The Care and Feeding of Children* had by 1915 gone through eight revised editions, three of them in the previous four years. Sheldon Stern, the resident historian at the Kennedy Library, has confirmed that REFK specifically used the book.

137   "studied the latest ...": *Reader's Digest*, April 1939, p. 84.

137   "the common currency ...": Mary Cable. *The Little Darlings: A History of Child Rearing* (1975), p. 165.

137   "lack of precision ...": Mrs. Burton Chance. *The Care of the Child* (1909), pp. 20–21.

137   must be fed: Holt (1894 edition), p. 35.

137   "The young mother ...": Katherine G. Busbey. *Home Life in America* (1910), p. 32.

138   "They are made ...": Holt (1894 edition), p. 57.

138   "the mother should ...": Holt (1923 edition), p. 51.

139   resented men like Joe: RW, p. 51.

139   In her memory: RK, p. 80.

139   developed an ulcer: RK, p. 80.

139   ready for bed: RK, p. 80.

140   Mary Augusta weighed: Interview, REFK. RCP.

141   "intense, secretive ...": *Fortune*, September 1937, p. 140.

141   "the American woman ...": quoted in Frederick Lewis Allen, *Only Yesterday* (1931), p. 74.

141   "sex o'clock ...": Steven Mint and Susan Kellogg. *Domestic Revolutions: A Social History of American Family Life* (1988), p. 111.

141   "I hope you ...": quoted in ÐKG, p. 304.

141   "He'd say ...": Interview, REFK. RCP.

141   "I had heard ...": Interview, REFK. RCP.

142   "Now, listen ...": DKG, p. 392.

142   "She taught us ...": Interview, Kerry McCarthy.

143   "avoid fatigue ...": BP, September 22, 1918, p. 4.

143   Dr. Good arrived late: Interview, Luella Hennessey Donovan.

143   Rose Marie Kennedy: Record of birth, September 13, 1918.

143   "I was patient ...": RK, p. 151.

143   "Nobody knows ...": Interviews, EKS. RCP.

144   a terrible disillusionment: Interview, Luella Hennessey Donovan.

144   "the centre ...": BP, March 25, 1917, p. 11.

145   America's first great: See Jack S. Blocker, Jr. *American Temperance Movements: Cycles of Reform* (1989), and Ruth Bordin, *Franics Williard: A Biography* (1986).

145   "the commonest and saddest . . .": Abraham Myerson. *The Nervous Housewife* (1920), p. 2.

147   "black web . . .": BP, January 18, 1920, p. 39a.

147   "the buoyant spirit . . .": BP, January 16, 1921, p. 53.

148   "You've made your commitment . . .": quoted in DKG, p. 307.

149   friend who had gotten divorced: Felicia Warburg Roosevelt. *Doers and Dowagers* (1975), p. 90.

150   "frantic terror": quoted in DKG, p. 309.

150   Joe was in: Interview, REFK. RCP.

150   "I had never . . .": DKG, p. 310.

151   "really our eldest daughter": "Notes for Diary." Used by permission of Eunice Kennedy Shriver.

151   other children found: "Notes for Diary." Used by permission of Eunice Kennedy Shriver.

151   "her early letters . . .": "Notes for Diary." Used by permission of Eunice Kennedy Shriver.

151   "Although we delighted . . .": RK, p. 92.

151   "My first four children . . .": KMRK.

151   "Years ago everyone nursed . . .": Interview, REFK. RCP.

152   "Little Partner . . .": quoted in RK, p. 91.

152   oversaw the furnishing: DKG, p. 314.

152   including a chauffeur: CA, p. 92.

153   "would have been bored . . .": RK, p. 91.

153   "Gee, *you're* a . . .": RK, p. 93.

153   Only because she had forgotten: RK, p. 94.

153   "A mother knows . . .": REFK reflections on Children General. RCP.

154   "I looked upon child rearing . . .": REFK reflections on Children General. RCP.

154   "superior achievement or . . .": RK, p. 143.

155   "You will find . . .": REFK reflections on Children General. RCP.

155   "I think that if the Kennedy children . . .": JFK, ed. *As We Remember Joe* (1945), pp. 3–4.

156   choosing books: RK, p. 110.

156   an exaggerated pattern of motherly conduct: In its extremes, it led, as Myerson wrote in 1920, to "women who made the dinner table less a place to eat than a place where a child was pilloried for his manners—pilloried into sullen, appetiteless state." Myerson, p. 102.

156   obsession with fat: Interview, Luella Hennessey Donovan.

157   "I gained a pound . . .": Letter KK to RK, May 19, 1927. Used by permission of EKS.

157   It was an obsession: When the Kennedy's next youngest

daughter, Patricia, was twelve years old and a svelte 115 pounds, she wrote her mother that she was "awful fat" and would have to go on a diet. Letter Pat Kennedy to REFK, May 13, 1936. RCP.

157 "You tell them that their father . . .": Interview, Paul R. Leahy.

157 an Irish peasant woman: LMT, p. 8, and interview, Luella Hennessey Donovan.

157 The homes of Brookline and Boston were still full: "These nurses gave the 'well-bred' children of my generation an intimate touch with a life of which the carefully groomed and mamma-raised suburban kids of today are unhappily ignorant," writes the historian Samuel Eliot Morison, a son of the Brahmin elite. "The nurses not only showed us how the poor lived, but imparted folklore and wisdom that cannot be got from books." Morison, *One Boy's Boston* p. 17.

158 "She kept busy right up . . .": Interview, Margaret Driscoll.

158 "I'd just tell them . . .": NPS, p. 19.

158 "It [physical punishment] . . .": REFK reflections on Children General. RCP.

159 how "cruel" Rose had been: RK, p. 133.

159 "My mother never really held me . . .": Thomas C. Reeves. *A Question of Character: A Life of John F. Kennedy* (1991), p. 32.

160 "We didn't talk . . .": Interview, Luella Hennessey Donovan.

160 "American efficiency": RK, p. 84

160 "We were really organized": quoted in RK, p. 135.

161 checked off her children: RK, p. 119.

161 "We would talk . . .": NPS, p. 50.

161 Tudor-style church: *St. Aidan's Seventy-fifth Anniversary*, Brookline, 1985.

161 It had been built primarily by the small: Interview, Reverend Leonard A. Coppenrath, pastor of St. Aidan's Parish.

161 "I remember the beautiful squirrel . . .": *Brookline Citizen*, November 17, 1988.

161 "They used to say . . .": Interview, Dot Keegan.

162 "destroyed every . . .": Letter from Father Joseph Kennan to His Eminence, Cardinal O'Connell, October 1, 1924. The archives of the Archdiocese of Boston contains a whole series of letters from parishioners, fellow priests, artisans, and workers complaining about Father Creagh. AAB.

162 Rose and Joe were both out: "The most important thing I have to tell you," Joe Jr. wrote his parents, "is that I was confirmed yesterday by Cardinal O'Connell." HS, p. 47.

163 "awful worldliness . . .": quoted in James M. O'Toole. *Militant and Triumphant: William O'Connell and the Catholic Church in Boston, 1859–1944* (1992), p. 175.

163   "proofs of the Cardinal's sexual . . .": quoted in O'Toole, *Militant*, p. 191.

163   caught lying to Pope: O'Toole, *Militant*, p. 193.

164   not admitted to the back rooms: BP, November 31, 1922, p. 26.

164   "tremulous voice": BG, November 6, 1922, p. 11.

164   On election day: BG, November 7, 1922, p. 1.

164   "Tell the people . . .": BG, November 8, 1922, p. 12.

165   "The women's clubs . . .": BP, November 8, 1922.

165   "My babies were rocked . . .": BUH, p. 20.

165   an estate of $13,539: Administration of the Estate of Mary A. (Hickey) Kennedy. Suffolk County Probate File No. 208,343.

165   a Kennedy family funeral: This account of the funeral is based on *The Winthrop Sun*, June 1, 1923; and the *East Boston Argus-Advocate*, May 26, 1923.

166   died the next morning: BP, September 26, 1923.

166   "there was widespread . . .": BP, January 13, 1924, p. B11.

166   "Hi, Jack": Interviews, Paul Leahy and Helen Leahy Steverman.

166   "this rubbing of elbows . . .": REFK reflections on Children General. RCP.

166   "like roughnecks": RK, p. 119.

167   "My mother sent everybody . . .": Interview, EKS.

167   "He didn't want to be bothered . . .": Interview, REFK. RCP.

167   drove herself to the hospital: RK, p. 79.

167   "where they initiate new members . . .": RK, p. 93.

167   "little devils": *Brookline Citizen*, November 17, 1988.

168   "My mother wouldn't let me play . . .": Interview, Robert Bunshaft.

168   "there would be after school . . .": RK, p. 97.

168   "My husband did not think . . .": REFK reflections on Children General. RCP.

168   "I knew he worked hard . . .": RK, p. 79.

169   "Child birth was something . . .": Interview, REFK. RCP.

169   not even obliged: Joseph Kennedy had been in Florida for the birth of Kathleen as he would be for that of his youngest son, Edward. Interview with Rose Kennedy, RCP.

169   "I woke up one morning . . .": DEK, p. 26.

170   "I'm sure it's normal . . .": quoted in RK, p. 122.

170   Margaret McQuaid was impressed: HS, p. 40.

170   Rosemary was given the Binet: A 1919 Massachusetts law required the mental examination of all students considered more than three years behind in mental development. George M. Kline, M.D., Commissioner, Department of Mental Disease, Massachusetts. "Accomplishments and Immediate Aims in Massachusetts in Community Care of the Feeble-Minded," *American Association for the Study of the Feeble Minded Pro-*

ceedings and Addresses of the Forty Eighth Annual Session.
New York: Johnson Reprinting, 1924, p. 35.

170   "there shall be no closing . . ." Report of the School Committee of Brookline Massachusetts for the year ending December 31, 1920 (1921), p. 419.

170   sign of moral deficiency: Rose's generation had one
overwhelming, compelling, transcendent image of those with
mental retardation. That was the cautionary tale of the Kallikak family, written about in a famous study by Henry Herbert
Goddard in 1912. Goddard was the director of the research
laboratory of the training school for Feeble-Minded Girls and
Boys at Vineland, New Jersey. In this capacity, he had given
an intelligence test to an eleven-year old girl, Deborah, whom
he classified as "a high-grade feeble-minded person."

Goddard called her family the Kallikaks, after the Greek
words for good and evil. He supposedly traced her family
roots back to Martin Sr., a young man of good family, living
at the time of the American Revolution. One evening at a tavern Martin Kallikak impregnated the "feeble-minded girl" and
then went off after the war to marry a woman of good family.
Thus were born the two lines of the family. From that casual
mating at the tavern sprung a race full of the immoral and the
sickly, prostitutes, alcoholics, epileptics, feebleminded, criminals, brothel owners. The pictures in his book of the living
generation are the very stereotyped image of the degenerate,
thick lipped, heavily browed, their eye slits open wide enough
only to project malevolence. The other side of the family, the
good side, was a race of doctors, lawyers, judges, professional
men, only two alcoholics among them. Goddard's conclusion
was obvious.

Goddard himself by 1928 had begun to retract some of his
more extreme positions, admitting to the American Association for the Study of the Feeble Minded that "the danger is
probably negligible" that "moron parents are likely to have
imbecile or idiot children." It would be more than half a century later, however, before Professor Stephen Jay Gould of
Harvard University and his colleague Steven Selden would determine that Goddard had retouched the photos of the Kallikaks to create these images of malevolence. In 1985, in *Minds
Made Feeble: The Myth and Legacy of the Kallikaks*, J. David
Smith showed that Goddard's methodology was as retouched
as the photographs, concluding that "the Kallikak study is fiction draped in the social science of its time."

170   Children with low scores: Report of the School Committee,
pp. 420–421.

171   concept of the "moron": Walter E. Fernald, M.D., Superintendent, Massachusetts School for the Feeble-Minded,

Waverly, Mass., "Thirty Years Progress in the Care of the Feeble-Minded," *American Association for the Study of the Feeble Minded Proceedings and Addresses of the Forty Eighth Annual Session Held at Washington D.C., May 30–June 2, 1914*, New York: Johnson Reprint, 1924, p. 206.

171 "No one who understands . . .": Henry Herbert Goddard, Ph.D. *Feeble-Mindedness: Its Causes and Consequences* (1914), p. 14.

171 "sunny in disposition . . .": Walter E. Fernald, M.D., Superintendent, Massachusetts School for the Feeble-Minded, "The Growth of Provision for the Feeble-Minded in the United States," *Mental Hygiene*. Vol. 1, No. 1, January, 1917, p. 42.

172 in twelve states 901 "feebleminded": Harry H. Laughlin, D. Sc., "The Eugenical Sterilization of the Feeble-Minded," *American Association for the Study of the Feeble Minded Proceedings and Addresses of the Fiftieth Annual Session Held at Toronto, Canada, June 3–5, 1926*. New York: Johnson Reprint, 1926, p. 214.

172 "Our family thought . . .": Interview, Geraldine Hannon.

172 "dusk of mankind": quoted in J. David Smith, p. 3.

172 "He was much more emotional . . .": quoted in RK, p. 152.

173 "the rich man's exceptional child . . .": Mrs. M. A. Hare, "The Value of the Private School in the Training of Sub-Normal Children," *American Association for the Study of the Feeble Minded Proceedings and Addresses of the Forty-Seventh Annual Session held at Detroit, Michigan, June 15–18, 1923*. New York: Johnson Reprint, 1923, p. 84.

173 "I rejected it except . . .": RK, p. 152.

173 "I think there's so much made . . .": quoted in RK, p. 154.

173 even cousins and other relatives: Interviews, Joe Gargan and Charles Burke.

173 the Kennedys hired a special governess: Interview, Mr. Fred Good, son of Dr. Fred Good.

174 One man joked over the dinner table: Interview, Mrs. Pauline Wasby.

174 "You remembered them . . .": Interview, Paul Leahy.

174 "My parents hated . . .": Interview, Dorothy Ogilvie.

174 "We would play with our dolls . . .": Interview, Helen Steverman.

174 turning the purchasing of goods: Christine Frederick, an expert on household efficiency, applauded the housewife who "does not hesitate to throw out of her house much that is still useful, even half-new, in order to make room for the newest 'best,' " Quoted in Maxine Margolis, *Mothers and Such: Views of American Women and Why They Changed* (1984), p. 158.

175 What set Joe apart: This analysis is based on a discussion with Senator Edward Kennedy.

175   The money grew in this: RW, p. 74.

175   "We did keep a close ...": RK, p. 114.

175   allowances of ten cents: RK, p. 114.

175   "When my father came home ...": Interview, Helen Leahy Steverman.

175   Rosemary sent hers to the Catholic: Letter of Mrs. Bastien, a former employee of the Kennedy family, dated March 6, 1959. RCP.

176   "Youth, slim youth ...": *Vogue*, February 15, 1925, p. 41.

176   to Mary Murphy's dress shop: Interview, Margaret Driscoll.

176   Several years later Catherine Hickey went: Interviews, Kerry McCarthy and Mary Lou McCarthy.

177   The club had a few Catholic: Interview, John Henry Cutler.

177   "to see old faces": DKG, p. 326.

178   "It was petty and cruel ...": quoted in RW, p. 59.

179   looked down with righteous disdain: "The standards ... have been so low that it is common knowledge that many of the Motion Pictures exhibited in Massachusetts have been of such a character as to be hurtful to many who have seen them," the Leauge of Catholic Women stated in 1922. AAB.

180   "Most of all ...": *Motion Picture World*, December 11, 1926, quoted in Betty Lasky. *R.K.O.: The Biggest Little Major of Them All* (1984), p. 14.

180   "the screen's ... leading family man": Terry Ramsaye, "Intimate Visits to the Homes of Famous Film Magnates," *Photoplay*, 1927 (only date). JFKPL.

180   Eunice was suffering: DKG, p. 368.

181   glad to be away: "A new order of things has arrived ..." the *New York Herald Tribune* wrote. "Joe is going so fast just now that before another year it may be necessary to identify John F.'s name in the newspapers with the phrase 'father-in-law of Joseph P. Kennedy.'" *New York Herald Tribune*, September 16, 1928.

181   Joe had met Gloria a few months: GS, p. 346.

182   "He had the most ambitious ...": GS, p. 351.

182   "P. T. Barnum presenting Lavinia ...": GS, p. 366.

183   "He moved so quickly ...": GS, p. 369.

183   on February 20, 1928: GA, p. 34.

183   "What can you possibly think ...": RK, p. 76.

184   "Joe was the one who was ...": Interview, Jean Smith for *Time*, 1960. RWP.

185   more than twenty years old: "History of the Riverdale Country School," published and edited by the 1957 Riverdalian Staff, Archives of Riverdale Country School.

185   "large and distinguished audience": *The Riverdale Review*, December 1928.

185   same style cloth coat: Class picture October 1928, archives of Riverdale Country Day School.

185   "Rosemary just plugged along . . .": Interview, Doris Hutchings.

185   "The Kennedy family was not very happy . . .": Written statement prepared by Dr. Lynn L. Fulkerson.

186   "She was one hundred percent mother . . .": Interview, George Duff.

186   Kathleen played on one side: Interview, Doris Hutchings.

186   "We just followed around . . .": Interview, Margaret Van den Heuval.

186   discovered yet another creature comfort: Betty Lasky, pp. 55–57. See also Roland Flamini. *Scarlett, Rhett, and A Cast of Thousands* (1975), p. 146.

187   "When he was in control . . .": GS, p. 381.

187   "I remember at one point . . .": Interview, Mrs. Gloria Somborn Daly.

187   "said to be the largest . . .": *The Bronxville Review*, April 20, 1929.

187   deed listed her: Westchester County Registry of Deeds, library 2938, pp. 90–91 and 104–105.

187   "the stock market crowd": *Bronxville: Views and Vignettes* (1974), p. 93.

187   movie theaters were closed: *The Bronxville Review*, July 7, 1934.

188   "the one Jew in town": Stephen Birmingham, *The Right People* (1958), p. 164.

188   There were twenty bedrooms: CA, p. 107 and HS, p. 52.

188   a messy youth who left behind: HS, p. 53.

188   "I tried to have my children . . .": REFK reflections on Children General. RCP.

188   "On the weekends we played . . .": Interview, Manuel Angullo.

189   "I remember going ice-skating . . .": Interview, EKS, RCP.

190   expected to take care of his sisters: Interviews, Mary Lou McCarthy and Kerry McCarthy.

190   "I would guess that his father . . .": Interview, James Landis. RWP.

191   The Kennedys had rented: Joseph and Rose Kennedy purchased the house and land from Beulah A. B. Malcolm on October 31, 1928. The property consisted of the house and three quarters of an acre and a second small piece of land. The Kennedys purchased several more adjoining lots in 1929 followed by other purchases by various family members to complete what became known as "the compound." Deed dated October 31, 1928, State of New York, and Deed between Lucy Scudder Green, and Joseph P. Kennedy for February 2, 1929.

191   "2500 Western Electric sound . . .": *The Barnstable Patriot,
       The Hyannis Patriot, Cape Cod Item,* and *Chatam Monitor,*
       May 2, 1929, p. 9.

191   "probably the first private . . .": clipping from unnamed Bos-
       ton newspaper, June 9, 1929, p. 25, BUCL.

191   next-door neighbor: Madelaine W. and Frederick G. Blackburn
       lived on the north side of Irving Avenue, next door to the
       Kennedys. Barnstable County Registry of Deeds, Book 456, p.
       593.

192   Blackburn went up: Interview, Harry Fowler.

192   One afternoon Geraldine returned: Interview, Geraldine
       Hannon.

192   Of course, she knew: In her autobiography and in all her pub-
       lic utterances, REFK pretended that Gloria Swanson was
       merely her husband's business associate. In an off-the-record
       discussion with the journalist and family friend, Laura
       Bergquist, she more candidly discussed the actress's relation-
       ship with JPK. LB.

193   "You see, you fool . . .": quoted in DKG, p. 396.

193   The townspeople stood on the beach: Leo Damore. *The Cape
       Cod Years of John Fitzgerald Kennedy* (1967), p. 21.

193   visit the clubhouse: ibid.

193   "We had these two fan clubs . . .": Interview, Nancy Coleman.

194   she wrote to little Gloria: KK to "Dear Daddy," January 31,
       1930.

194   asking how little Gloria: KK to "Dearest Daddy," March 23,
       1930.

194   "sweet and motherly . . .": GS, p. 400.

194   "Joe Kennedy had compromised . . .": GS, p. 403.

195   in 1922 alone expending: DKG, p. 386.

195   "She was the great celebrity . . .": RK, p. 187.

195   Rose related later that one day: RK, pp. 202–203, and DKG,
       p. 415.

195   "We all sat around . . .": REFK recollections for Robert
       Coughlan. RCP.

195   meeting may have taken place only: No record of this meeting
       exists in the voluminous public files of the Archdiocese of
       Boston, nor in the William O'Connell scrapbooks at the St.
       John's Seminary Library. But certain key documents have
       been restricted from view.

195   "full of errors . . .": Interview, Gloria Somborn Daly.

196   certain measures to end: Lasky, pp. 55–57.

196   developed an ulcer: RW, p. 97.

196   checked into Boston's Lahey: CH, p. 55.

196   "Well, you know . . .": Axel Madsen. *Gloria and Joe* (1988),
       p. 207, and Ralph Martin. *A Hero For Our Time* (1984), p. 31.
       Martin tells the anecdote in his book without using Alice Har-

rington's name. Madsen says that his agent heard the story directly from Harrington at a Chicago party during the course of research for Madsen's book.

196 "surrounded daily by some . . .": RK, p. 187.

196 to Paris seventeen times: HS, p. 55, also Nancy Gager Clinch. *The Kennedy Neurosis* (1973), p. 77.

196 "My husband said . . .": Interview, REFK. RCP.

197 "Nobody believed her . . .": RK, p. 117.

197 "Soon after Mrs. Kennedy left . . .": Interview, Nancy Coleman.

197 "The story around school . . .": Interview, Alan Gage.

198 "When Joe Kennedy used to have . . .": Interview, Paul Morgan.

198 "Of course, all of us kids . . .": Interview, Jane Cash.

198 "Gloria Swanson was over . . .": Interview, Manuel Angullo.

200 The plumber had supposedly been: Interview, Paul Morgan.

199 "I remember my mother . . .": Interview, Manuel Angullo.

199 "Forty is a dangerous age . . .": Interview, Harvey Klemmer.

200 "She was just terrific . . .": Interview, Manuel Angullo.

200 "She was quite a woman . . .": Interview, Paul Morgan.

200 "My earliest memories . . .": Interview, Senator Edward Kennedy.

200 "She wasn't a bring-them . . .": Interview, Paul Morgan.

201 "THANK YOU. TWENTY YEARS. . . .": DKG, p. 426.

202 "I kicked him . . .": off-the-record interview.

202 "When I'm sixty I hope . . .": Interview with one of JFK's closest friends.

202 "Pat and Eunice were always saying . . .": quoted in CH, p. 58.

202 "If Daddy was running . . .": Interview, EKS.

203 "Daddy did not come home . . .": KK to "Dear Mother," February 13, 1932. Used by permission of EKS.

203 "You were in charge of us . . .": RK, pp. 80–81.

203 "What Joe said, in effect . . .": RW, p. 166.

204 "a condition similar to the one . . .": Letter Mrs. Joseph P. Kennedy to Mrs. St. John, January 1932. CSA.

204 "you procure from the local . . .": Letter Mabel M. Malone for Mrs. Kennedy to Mrs. St. John, January 21, 1932. CSA.

204 "The fact has come to my . . .": Letter Mrs. Joseph P. Kennedy to Mrs. G. C. St. John, September 6, 1932, CSA.

204 "I can easily understand . . .": HS, p. 66.

204 "I never even heard that Jack . . .": Interview, EKS.

205 "Joe and I had . . .": RK, p. 167.

206 included the daughters: *Convent of the Sacred Heart Alumnae Directory*, 1989.

206 Even the scholarship students: Interview, Sister Gabrielle Husson.

206   "I had ski pants on . . .": Letter KK to "Dearest Mother," Jan. 13, 1934. Used by permission of Eunice Kennedy Shriver.

206   "The whole family would come . . .": Interview, Mary Lyon Chatfield-Taylor.

207   "Oh, oh, girls . . .": Interview, Mary Lyon Chatfield-Taylor.

207   "I miss you . . .": KK to "Dearest Mother," January 13, 1934. Used by permission of Eunice Kennedy Shriver.

208   "the dear old fire-trap": KK to "Daddy Dearest," December 2, 1934. Used by permission of Eunice Kennedy Shriver.

208   "would get out of breath": KK to "Dearest Mother," December 17, 1933. Used by permission of Eunice Kennedy Shriver.

208   an ailment that in a milder: "The asthma is coming," KK wrote REFK in a postscript to her letter on January 13, 1934. "I can feel it." Used by permission of Eunice Kennedy Shriver.

208   Pat had a series of allergies: Pat Kennedy letter to REFK, May 13, 1936. RCP.

208   "about four days out of seven": HS, pp. 66–67.

208   "a very fine spirit": quoted in DKG, p. 485.

208   "Wherever Kathleen went, sunshine . . .": Off-the-record interview with a Noroton classmate.

208   "doing something crazy": Interview, Sister Gabrielle Husson.

209   "We'd walk down the big . . .": Interview, Elizabeth Rivinus Augenblick.

209   occasionally bypassing the nuns' censorship: "I am enclosing a letter which is just meant to be dropped in the mail box," KK wrote her mother. "It is perfectly alright and the whole school is doing it." KK to "Dearest Mother," December 6, 1934. Used by permission of Eunice Kennedy Shriver.

209   "She really thinks you . . .": quoted in DKG, p. 486.

210   "Here I am . . .": KK to "Dearest Mother." Dated Monday. Used by permission of Eunice Kennedy Shriver.

210   "the richest group . . .": Janet Erskine Stuart, *The Education of Catholic Girls* (1911), pp. 26–28.

211   "special influence depends . . .": Sacred Heart doctrine as quoted in Stephen Birmingham, *Real Lace: America's Irish Rich* (1973), p. 241.

211   "Except for the gardener . . .": Interview, Suzannah Lessard.

212   Except for questions of faith: Interview, Herb Kramer.

212   "To us they were heroes . . .": RK, p. 167.

213   "I had a firm talk . . .": DKG, p. 497.

213   "I would do anything . . .": quoted in DKG, p. 497.

213   "Pray very hard . . .": quoted in DKG, p. 497.

214   "The reason I . . .": letter REFK to Mr. Steele quoted in *The Kennedy Years*, p. 11 and letter from Mr. Steele or Mr. St. John to Mrs. Joseph P. Kennedy, January 13, 1934. CSA.

215   "Years ago, we decided ...": *The Reader's Digest*, April 1939, p. 84.

215   "the glue that held ...": RK, p. 150.

215   "He ruled the roost": Interview, Sancy Newman.

216   "Joe knew what he wanted ...": Interview, Thomas Corcoran conducted by N. Bryan for *Time*, November 18, 1962, RWP.

216   pounded his shoe once: CA, p. 12.

216   "We don't want any losers ...": RK, p. 143.

216   "Don't come in second ...": RK, p. 143.

216   "I remember racing fourteen ...": Edward M. Kennedy, *Fruitful*, p. 217.

217   "If we live long enough ...": Oral History of Eddie Dowling, p. 312. CU.

217   "The older boys would ...": Interview, Pat Kennedy. RCP.

217   he would call her "Jeanah ...": HS, p. 97.

217   Rose set up a bulletin: RK, p. 104.

218   "Rose was like a Hollywood mother ...": Interview, Harry Fowler.

218   "Father wasn't awfully interested ...": Interview, EKS.

219   none of them sailed: HS, p. 59.

220   "There wasn't any real damage ...": Damore, *Cape*, p. 35.

220   "trying to help": ibid.

220   for seven years in a row: *The Barnstable Patriot*, September 5, 1940, p. 6.

221   could save the other half: JPK, *I'm for Roosevelt* (1936), p. 3, quoted in RW, p. 112.

221   "I'm as much concerned ...": Louis Lyons, "Joe Kennedy Sticks His Neck Out," *The Boston Sunday Post*, undated clipping at FDRPL.

221   "I can well remember ...": Reflections of Married Life. RCP.

221   "It is the finest home ...": quoted in Margaret Truman. *Bess W. Truman* (1982), p. 142.

221   conservative Republican Bronxville: Bronxville was a profoundly Republican bastion; in 1933 in the Kennedy's election district there were 330 enrolled Republicans and only 62 Democrats, including Joe, Rose, and three of their servants.

221   "I think of you ...": Undated letter from REFK to JPK. Courtesy of EKS

222   "Mother, Hope looks ...": KK to "Dearest Mother and Daddy," November 27, 1935. Used by permission of Eunice Kennedy Shriver.

223   The nuns noticed that Kathleen: From a Sacred Heart Nun (name illegible) to "Dear Mrs. Kennedy," December 8, 1935. Used by permission of Eunice Kennedy Shriver.

223   "I do not know all the ...": KK to "Dearest Mother," December 13, 1935. Used by permission of Eunice Kennedy Shriver.

223   "every time I think of that darn brother . . .": quoted in DKG, p. 491.

223   "We weren't so restricted . . .": Off-the-record interview with a student at Neuilly.

223   "I have never been in such . . .": KK to "Darling Mother and Dad," October 25, 1935. Used by permission of Eunice Kennedy Shriver.

224   "Thanks awfully for your letter . . .": KK to "Dear Johnny," Sunday the 8th. Used by permission of Eunice Kennedy Shriver.

224   She tried on her evening gowns: KK to "Dearest Mother and Daddy," October 31, 1935. Used by permission of Eunice Kennedy Shriver.

224   Kathleen vowed that she would not return: KK to "Dearest Mother," February 3, 1936. Used by permission of Eunice Kennedy Shriver.

225   "rather sad at the prospect . . .": quoted in DKG, p. 491.

225   the trip would cost: KK to "Dearest Mother and Daddy," October 31, 1935. Used by permission of Eunice Kennedy Shriver.

225   would be able: KK to "Dearest Mother and Daddy," November 27, 1935.

225   "Mother and I have no objection . . .": JPK to KK, January 20, 1936. Used by permission of Eunice Kennedy Shriver.

226   School lets out the tenth . . .": KK to "Mother dearest," February 11, 1936. Used by permission of Eunice Kennedy Shriver.

226   "really are not as bad . . .": KK to "Mother and Daddy dear," February 23, 1936. Used by permission of Eunice Kennedy Shriver.

226   "When you said you thought . . .": KK to "Dearest Mother," February 17, 1936. Used by permission of Eunice Kennedy Shriver.

226   the young man and his mother: KK to "Dearest Mother and Daddy," March 13, 1936. Used by permission of Eunice Kennedy Shriver.

227   "We have all decided . . .": KK to "Family," March 30, 1936. Used by permission of Eunice Kennedy Shriver.

227   "It is not very funny . . .": KK to "Darling Mother and Dad," March 29, 1936. Used by permission of Eunice Kennedy Shriver.

227   "Just saw a parade . . .": KK to "Darling Mother and Dad," April 2, 1936. Used by permission of Eunice Kennedy Shriver.

227   "The girls are very jealous": KK to "Daddy dear," April 18, 1936. Used by permission of Eunice Kennedy Shriver.

227   "Mother shall be here . . .": KK to "Bobby dear," April 26, 1936. Used by permission of Eunice Kennedy Shriver.

227   "She looked so pretty . . .": quoted in DKG, p. 493.

228   "Traveling with Kathleen . . .": quoted in DKG, p. 493.

228   "EXPECT LEAVE FOR MOSCOW . . .": *McCalls*, May 1961, p. 105.

228   "The masses really were better . . .": RK, pp. 209–210.

228   "Well, darling, I miss . . .": quoted in DKG, p. 493.

229   "seemed rather funny . . .": KK to "Mother Dearest," June 8, 1936. Used by permission of Eunice Kennedy Shriver.

229   "Don't eye the Frenchmen . . .": Letter from KK to "Darlings'—Miss Cahill (included)," June 30, 1936. RCP.

230   never did he even give her a kiss: HS, p. 58.

230   Jack darted back to the men's room: Interview, Manuel Angullo.

230   Jack could not even bring himself: Interview, Manuel Angullo.

230   "Jack was a very naughty boy": Quoted in *McCalls*, May 1961, p. 196.

230   It was here at the age of seventeen: JCB, p. 34.

230   a brothel in West Palm Beach: Larry Baker, a classmate of JFK at Choate, recalls the Christmas vacation when a group of students drove down to Florida together. According to Baker, Jack insisted on going to the brothel even before he went to his parents' home. Interview, Larry Baker.

231   kept her picture atop: LMT, p. 20.

231   could not admit to Rose and Joe: "Kathleen would say how she hated to go to Palm Beach at Easter because her friends were in New York," recalled one friend. "But I guess her father insisted that everyone go down."

231   *"Dearest Daddy—I didn't have . . .":* KK to "Dearest Daddy," dated Tuesday. Probably January 1937. Used by permission of Eunice Kennedy Shriver.

232   *Mother—Hope this . . .":* KK to "Dearest Mother," dated Friday. Used by permission of Eunice Kennedy Shriver.

233   "Will Hays came in and saw . . .": LMT, p. 19 and JCB., pp 72–73.

233   "thought she would have left home": quoted in LMT, p. 19.

234   "That was a nice little . . .": Interview, Peter Grace.

234   the first Irish-born mayor of New York: Birmingham, *Real Lace*, p. 192.

235   "Mrs. Kennedy was very interested . . .": Interview, Peter Grace.

235   "surrounded by critics . . .": *Fortune*, September 1937, p. 59.

235   flying back to Washington: *Hyannis Patriot*, July 15, 1937, p. 6.

235   The boat began a series: Interview, Mary Lou McCarthy.

236   "All my ducks . . .": Quoted in Peter Collier and David Horowitz, "The Kennedy Kick," *Vanity Fair*, July 1983, p. 50.

236   "I think she probably had . . .": Interview, Tom Egerton.

236 "Eunice [who] was not . . .": Rose Kennedy recollections for Robert Coughlan. RCP.
237 "Puny Eunie": LMT, p. 14.
237 She slept with eye pads: LMT, p. 14.
237 "Listen, Ten, don't you . . . .": LMT, p. 14.
237 "All right, now . . .": CA, p. 95.
237 She was fond of measuring: KMRK.
237 winning five races: BP, March 20, 1938, p. 16.
238 "I didn't like Jean at all . . .": Interview, Mary Lou McCarthy.
238 "Rosemary would have . . .": *Los Angeles Times*, November 20, 1987, part 5, p. 12.
238 "I would take her as crew . . .": EKS, "Hope for Retarded Children," *Saturday Evening Post*, September 22, 1962, p. 71.
238 "I think she was partly . . .": Interview, EKS. RCP.
239 "Rose seemed to enjoy . . .": Undated letter from JFK to REFK. RCP.
239 "Why don't other boys . . .": "Rose Kennedy: 'Rosemary Brought Us Strength,' " *Catholic Digest*, March 1976, p. 36.
239 "a mother suffers more for a child . . .": Associated Press, October 31, 1963, file "Mrs. Joseph P. Kennedy 1963." BUCL
239 "Rosemary, you have the best . . .": *Catholic Digest*, op. cit., p. 37.
240 slow, but she was not stupid: This phrase and basic insight in the life of one with retardation is from Mark Swiconek, a Special Olympics athlete, a member of the Connecticut Board of Special Olympics and a talented after-dinner speaker. Much of America had an opportunity to hear Swiconek when he spoke at the opening ceremonies of the International Special Olympic Games in Minneapolis in July 1991.
240 erupt in an inexplicable fury: Interview, Sancy Newman.
240 twenty quarts a day: CA, p. 91.
240 Eunice and her friends: Interview, EKS.
240 "There was so much to be thankful . . .": Interview, EKS.
241 "They were golden years . . .": Interview, Nancy Tenney Coleman.
241 "Joe was the high honcho . . .": Interview, Bill Mulcahy.
241 Joe ordered the projectionist: RK, p. 117.
241 "I can remember . . .": Interview, Harry Fowler.
242 pinching Kathleen's friends: LMT, p. 18.
242 "I think only a Roman Catholic . . .": quoted in JCB, p. 16.
242 "Dear, it's time . . .": RK, p. 131.
242 a little note: Interviews, Mary Jo Gargin Clasby and Richard Clasby. RCP.
243 "Arrange flowers?": LMT, p. 16.
243 "Mother thought it was a wonderful . . .": Interview, Pat Kennedy Lawford, RCP.
243 "had been travelling in Europe . . .": BP, September 22, 1936.

243   "Aunt Rose was marvelous . . .": Interview, Joe Gargan.

244   in November of 1936: RK, p. 204.

244   "one of the nation's leading . . .": RK, p. 204.

244   "Who would ever think to see . . .": Recollections for Autobiography. RCP.

245   no one was allowed to sit: As the years went by the chair appeared more nondescript, but it stayed there, next to the piano, and Rose would say that yes that was the chair where Cardinal Pacelli had sat, Cardinal Pacelli who the world would come to know as Pope Pius XII. According to Harry Fowler, in the 1940s, the parents of a young woman whom Jack was thinking of marrying were visiting the Kennedy's summer home in Hyannis Port, Massachusetts. The mother walked over to the old chair and begin to ease herself down onto the plush seat. "Oh don't sit there," Rose said, crying out in alarm. "That's where Pope Pius XII sat." The woman looked bewilderingly at the chair and then at Rose. "Perhaps, Mrs. Kennedy," the woman said, her sarcasm lightly garbed in civility, "you should put a red velvet rope over the chair."

245   At the end of July: unidentified clipping "Mrs. Joseph Kennedy Takes European Trip," July 29, 1937, BUCL.

245   "Mother always took trips . . .": Interview, EKS.

245   "Bobby, have you . . .": CA, p. 112.

246   "Patricia was such . . .": "My Happy Life with 17 Kennedy Babies" by Luella R. Hennessey as told to Margot Murphy. *Good Housekeeping*, August 1961, p. 55.

246   young woman was Catholic: BP, March 20, 1938, p. 28.

247   "dispensing with Henry . . .": RK, p. 211.

247   Rose felt that the chairmanships: REFK on Married Life. RCP.

247   "What has the President . . .": RK, p. 212.

247   "THE KENNEDY . . .": *Life*, December 20, 1937.

247   the President had sensed: Harold Ickes wrote in his diary on June 30, 1934: "The President has great confidence in him because he has made his pile, has invested all his money in Government securities, and knows all the tricks of the trade. Apparently he [Roosevelt] is going on the assumption that Kennedy would now like to make a name for himself for the sake of his family but I have never known many of these cases to work out as expected." Harold Le Claire Ickes. *The Secret Diary of Harold L. Ickes: The First Thousand Days 1933–1936*, Vol. 1 (1953), p. 172.

248   *"My dear Mr. President . . .":* Undated letter from RK to President Franklin Roosevelt. FDRPL.

248   "Boston blue bloods . . .": BG, December 12, 1937.

248   "I have to buy 200 . . .": BG, December 12, 1937. REFK had a large wardrobe but as she told Anne Elizabeth of the *New Bedford Standard Times*, "I buy on an average of 200 dresses

and suits a year for them." *New Bedford Standard Times*, March 13, 1938.

249   "Mrs. Kennedy asked Mother Patterson . . .": Interview, Sister Quinlan.

250   "Of course we are excited . . .": BG, January 25, 1938.

250   was stricken with appendicitis: NYT, February 9, 1938.

250   "to keep the children . . .": *Good Housekeeping*, p. 114.

250   "I had had an old family nursemaid . . .": REFK reflections on Married Life. RCP.

250   "Of all the surprising things . . .": quoted in RK, p. 216.

252   Rose remembered that she had been: RK, p. 217.

252   a legion of photographers: NYT, March 9, 1938.

252   "We're just going to act . . .": AP, March 9, 1938, BUCL.

252   "As I approached London . . .": RK, p. 217.

253   Peter Grace had done everything: Interview, Peter Grace and LMT, p. 23.

253   "London will be just grand": *Daily Express*, March 16, 1938.

254   "as vivacious as a screen-star": quoted in CA, p. 115.

254   "remarkable woman . . .": *Vogue*, August 3, 1938, p. 60.

254   "The men usually know . . .": quoted in DEK, p. 126.

254   On the first floor: *Vogue*, August 3, 1938, p. 43.

254   Eunice and Rosemary arrived: "2 More Kennedys, Rosemary, Eunice Will Sail Tomorrow for London Home" by AP, April 19, 1938, BUCL.

255   "they were like birds of paradise . . .": CH, p. 84.

255   shouting "Hey, hey": CH, p. 84.

255   making a coat and skirt: *Parents Magazine*, September 1939, p. 62.

255   the most popular girl: Anne Elizabeth, "Chatter," *New Bedford Standard Times*, June 11, 1939.

255   "She was a clever girl . . .": Interview, Mother Binney.

255   woefully behind in algebra: *Parents*, op. cit.

255   "Well, five . . .": *Parents*, op. cit.

256   felt so terribly alone: Interview, Luella Hennessey Donovan.

256   sent off to a Montessori: DKG, p. 539.

256   attending the Gibbs Boys' School: BT, April 14, 1938. BUCL.

256   "Rose," Joe said: RK, p. 221.

258   "There was something about seeing . . .": DKG, p. 527.

258   "talk Chamberlain's language": MB, p. 163.

258   "Joe later told me . . .": RK, p. 224.

259   ambassador yelled at Rose: Interview, Harvey Klemmer.

259   "She was absolutely remarkable . . .": Interview, Page Wilson.

259   "She was a rather shadowy . . .": Interview, Jane Compton.

259   "I found him extremely . . .": Interview, Hon. Mrs. Sarah Norton Baring.

259   "Oh, Eunice . . .": Interview, Lady Roderic Pratt.

260 "Mr. Kennedy was the center . . .": Interview, Luella Hennessey Donovan.

261 in a black organdy dress: RK, p. 231.

261 "The whole thing was a façade": Interview, Harvey Klemmer.

262 he occasionally used his staff: LMT, p. 28 and interview, Page Wilson.

262 "He even watched . . .": Interview, Luella Hennessey Donovan.

262 "I remember it . . .": Interview, Jane Compton.

262 "He was a filthy . . .": Interview, Lady Maureen Fellowes.

262 "spend[ing] Sunday with a volcano": Christopher Sykes. *Nancy: The Life of Lady Astor* (1972), frontispiece.

263 "How can you . . .": Sykes, p. 248.

263 "Very chummy . . .": quoted in DKG, p. 541.

265 "undemocratic": BG, April 10, 1939, p. 1.

265 "go down in history . . .": Dewitt MacKenzie, "Kennedy's Daring Ends Nightmare," Associated Press, April 11, 1938. BUCL.

265 "We were expected . . .": Letter from Mrs. Peter Tabor to Angela Lambert, April 30, 1988. ALP.

266 they had been secretly locked: "Windsor Knot" by Christopher Hitchens, NYT *Magazine*, May 12, 1991, p. 28.

266 mothers got together: Angela Lambert, *1939: The Last Season of Peace* (1989).

267 practiced with a curtain: Anne de Courcy. *1939: The Last Season* (1989), pp. 34–36.

267 "Have to practice . . .": quoted in DKG, p. 543.

267 Rose feared that she might: DKG, p. 543.

268 "felt a little like Cinderella": RK, p. 228.

268 "Oh, Rosemary, you're going . . .": Interview, Luella Hennessey Donovan.

269 Rose waved back: RK, p. 228.

269 one driven by a debutante: NYT, May 21, 1938.

269 a momentary frown: RW, p. 212.

269 trailed along the floor: De Courcy, p. 38.

270 she tripped: Off-the-record interview with an embassy staff member.

271 the mother of Lady Maureen: Interview, Lady Maureen Fellowes.

271 their signature song: de Courcy, p. 18.

272 "everything was wonderbar": quoted in DKG, p. 544.

272 "That's what all men do": quoted in LMT, p. 62.

272 "getting up to mischief": LMT, p. 156.

272 "I knew what happened to animals . . .": Interview, Hon. Mrs. Sarah Norton Baring.

273 an absolute abhorrence: When Kathleen Kennedy traveled to Rome to visit two of her friends from Noroton, Charlotte

McDonnell and her sister Anne, the three young women went on crowded sightseeing bus. "Stoppa the bus!," Kathleen screamed, as one of the passengers pinched her. "Stoppa the bus!" It was an obnoxious business surely, but Kathleen had reacted with absolute horror, as if she had been violated in some unspeakable way. LMT, p. 62.

273   "One could see pathetic faces . . .": quoted in Lambert, p. 113.

274   "If someone else had done that . . .": *Vanity Fair*, July 1983, p. 51.

274   "Could I have . . .": Interview, William Douglas-Home.

274   "Kick was the merriest . . .": Interview, William Douglas-Home.

274   promised Douglas-Home: LMT, pp. 43–44.

274   "How could I . . .": Helen Long. *Change into Uniform* (1978), p. 18.

274   "Your devoted . . .": DKG, p. 542

275   "Grace is wildly . . .": DKG, p. 543.

275   "always bubbling over . . . .": Interview, Peter Grace.

275   "We were close": Interview, Peter Grace.

276   the painting of the First Duke: Duchess of Devonshire. *The House: A Portrait of Chatsworth* (1982), pp. 22–35, and Peter Brown and Karl W. Schweizer, eds. *The Devonshire Diary* (1982).

276   "plain in the manners, negligent in his dress": Duchess of Devonshire, p. 24.

277   the family migrated: Duchess of Devonshire, p. 44.

277   "the worst dressed . . .": Interview, Andrew, Duke of Devonshire.

277   "He was a frustrated . . .": Sir Henry Channon. *Chips: The Diaries of Sir Henry Channon* (1967), p. 547.

277   He enjoyed sitting: Duchess of Devonshire, p. 73.

277   "I think it's fair . . .": Interview, Andrew, Duke of Devonshire.

280   singing of the German: RK, p. 39.

281   the 400,000 German Social Democrats: William Manchester. *The Last Lion: Alone: 1932–1940* (1988), p. 339.

281   "filled with sadness . . .": RK, p. 238.

282   Rose had heard the rumor: REFK's diary for September 25, 1938 reports that "Mike Scanlon phoned from London, said trenches were being dug in Hyde Park." RK, p. 238. William Manchester writes that "There were even rumors . . . that trenches were being dug in Hyde Park." Manchester, *Last Lion*, p. 346.

282   "like some bird . . .": William L. Shirer. *Berlin Diary: The Journal of a Foreign Correspondent 1934–1941* (1988), pp. 144–145.

282   "Everyone feels relieved . . .": REFK diary, RCP, and RK, p. 239.

282   "what a great day ...": DKG, p. 562.

282   "have to live together ...": quoted in RW, p. 248.

283   "Have you thought ...": quoted in RW, p. 248.

283   "That was the beginning ...": RK, p. 243.

283   Bobby sprained: *Daily Telegraph*, December 30, 1938.

283   "It sure looks ...": Interview, Luella Hennessey Donovan.

283   Ted amused: Interview, Edward Kennedy. RCP.

284   *"My dear Mr. President ...":* REFK to President Roosevelt, RDRPL.

284   "We hope to stay ...": quoted in RW, p. 258.

285   "Well, why ...": quoted in CH, p. 115.

285   "studying to be a kindergarten ...": Condensed from *Woman's Day, Reader's Digest*, April 1939, p. 83

285   "an interest in social welfare ...": *Parents Magazine*, September 1939, p. 62.

285   "I have always ...": quoted in DKG, p. 594. (BG wrote on December 7, 1941, that Rosemary was "teaching kindergarten in the Academy of the Assumption in London.")

286   "I am going ...": quoted in "Rose RK" by Marguerite Higgins, *McCall's*, May 1961, p. 102.

286   a piece of brown wrapping: CA, p. 102.

287   "retained his kindness ...": RK, p. 244.

287   "Oh, will Joe never ...": William Phillips Diary MS, entry of March 6, 1939, quoted in DEK, p. 190.

287   another seat was found: JCB, pp. 61–62.

287   "I told my sister ...": NYT, March 14, 1939.

288   "See that?": quoted in CH, p. 101.

288   "You mustn't pay ...": CH, p. 101.

288   shooting one of the Kennedys: DKG, p. 585.

289   "It was so frightening ...": Interview, Lady MacMillian, the former Kathleen Ormsby-Gore.

289   "She ordered Baltimore ...": Associated Press, May 4, 1939. BUCL.

289   printed in English: CA p. 122.

290   "about twenty-seven minutes ...": RK, p. 246.

290   "I think the queen was ...": *The David Frost Show*, Westinghouse Broadcasting Company, July 5, 1971, interview with Mrs. Joseph P. Kennedy, transcript p. 15.

291   "Their Majesties were delighted ...": RK, p. 249.

291   "To Mrs. Kennedy, of whom we did not ...": *Daily Telegraph*, June 22, 1939.

291   "She isn't seeing anyone ...": *New Bedford Standard Times*, June 11, 1939.

291   her mother was in the United States: *Daily Express*, June 19, 1939.

291   "Despite the none too good ...": *Tatler*, July 12, 1939.

292 "Eunice would never . . .": Interview, Luella Hennessey Donovan.

292 "There wasn't any jealousy . . .": Interview, EKS.

292 "I hated those parties": Interview, EKS.

293 "They [the Kennedys] all had . . .": Lambert, p. 133.

293 easy to talk to . . .": Lambert, p. 133.

293 "I remember going . . .": Interview, the Countess of Sutherland.

294 "It was a wonderful . . .": Interview, the Duchess of Northumberland.

294 It was an evening: The following evening, July 13, 1939 the last Court of the Season took place, but it was not the equal of the presentation the previous evening. Lambert, p. 174.

294 "each one as big . . .": Oral history, Admiral and Mrs. Alan G. Kirk. CU.

294 "I'm very sorry . . .": Oral history, Admiral and Mrs. Alan G. Kirk, p. 126. CU.

294 "The day I had planned . . .": EKS Recollections. JFKPL.

295 On the Fourth of July: De Courcy, p. 210.

295 at an Independence Day banquet: List of Guests and Plan of Tables at Independence Day Banquet & Ball of the American Society in London, July 4th, 1939. James Landis papers, box 2, Library of Congress.

295 "reprimanded Kick . . .": RK, p. 250.

296 within minutes a melee: De Courcy, p. 205.

296 "nearly as big as . . .": quoted in NH, p. 268.

296 "I have seen . . .": Channon, p. 253.

296 "I suffered the same . . .": quoted in Lambert, p. 170.

296 pink malmaisons and huge: Lambert, p. 169.

296 Behind their table stood: Hugh Montgomery-Massingbred. *Blenheim Revisited: The Spencer-Churchills and their Palace* (1985), p. 177.

297 a 180-feet-long: Montgomery-Massingbred, p. 85.

297 leaving their minks: Lambert, p. 171.

297 "Let's ask this man . . .": *Tatler*, July 12, 1939, quoted in Lambert, p. 138.

297 strolling Tyrolean: De Courcy. p. 210.

297 "Oh look at that poor . . .": Interview, Mollie Acland.

298 "What fun we had!": JFK, *As We Remember Joe*, p. 53.

298 "told his son to die . . .": quoted in DKG, p. 585.

298 Joe Jr. had gotten: NYT, August 1, 1939.

298 splendid rose gardens: NYT, July 22, 1939.

299 It would be a two-day-long: *Daily Express*, August 16 and 17, 1939.

299 "Kathleen and Billy were . . .": Interview, Jane Compton.

299 wrecked their dilapidated rented car: NH, p. 270.

299   Rose ruled that her: Interview, Luella Hennessey Donovan and *Good Housekeeping*, August 1961, p. 116.

299   Rose watched the Kennedy sons: Interview, REFK. RCP.

299   "I could barely swim . . .": Interview, Senator Edward Kennedy. RCP.

300   Marlene Dietrich descended: *The Tatler*, August 16, 1939, p. 280.

301   The children heard the news: Interview, Jane Kenyon-Slaney Compton.

301   "It's the end . . .": quoted in MB, p. 190.

301   passersby were carrying: "Letter from London" by Mollie Panter-Downes, September 3, 1939, quoted in *The New Yorker Book of War Pieces* (1947), p. 3.

301   "When the sirens . . .": Clipping dated September 18, 1939 in files of *New Bedford Standard Times*.

301   "I thought later . . .": RK, p. 252.

302   the great house turned into: The Duchess of Devonshire, p. 68.

302   he would be damned: Interview, Luella Hennessey Donovan.

302   "They were all so gay . . .": Interview, Tom Egerton.

302   Joe Jr. took passage: HS, p. 145.

302   Jack flew home: NH, p. 355.

303   Eunice had an eleven-inch: Clipping dated September 18, 1939 in *New Bedford Standard Times* files.

303   "all great fun": RK, p. 256.

303   Thomas Mann: *The New York Times*, September 19, 1939.

304   "returning to . . .": *Vanity Fair*, July 1983, p. 53.

304   "moral roustabout": Birmingham, *Real Lace*, p. 97.

304   on her twenty-fifth wedding anniversary: NYT, October 8, 1939, p. 9.

305   "At the end of September": RK, p. 257.

305   the Germans were subjecting: Cesare Salmaggi and Alfredo Pallavisini, compilers. *2194 Days of War* (1977), p. 28.

305   "just the same.": KK to JPK, September 26, 1939, quoted in RK, p. 256.

305   decided to attend Finch: KK to JPK, September 26, 1939, quoted in RK, p. 256.

305   "a series of Gotham . . .": clipping dated November 27, 1939, *Cape Cod Times* library.

305   "One evening in Cambridge . . .": Interview, Richard Edwards.

306   When Pat learned: RK, pp. 168–169.

306   "By then Mother decided . . .": quoted in RK, pp. 268–269.

307   a curriculum half of which: *Manhattanville College of the Sacred Heart Bulletin of Information*, 1939. MCA.

308   "must never be separated . . .": "Principles Versus Prejudices: A Talk Given to the Alumnae on Class Day, May 31st, 1938,"

quoted in Mary J. Oates. *Higher Education of American Catholic Women* (1987), p. 394.

308   She roomed by herself: Interview, Barbara Eccles Eggert.

308   "I remember her brilliance": Interview, Mrs. Margery Tracy.

308   Eunice always sat: Interview, Nancy Lane Gulliver.

309   "The chief topic of ...": RK, p. 265.

309   "he couldn't stand it anymore.": DKG, p. 595.

309   "My darling ...": Marguerite Higgins, "Rose Fitzgerald Kennedy," *McCall's*, May 1961, p. 102.

309   "after a while she is bound ...": JPK to Arthur Krock, September 15, 1939. AKP.

309   "The job is now terribly boring ...": JPK to Arthur Krock, November 3, 1939. AKP.

310   "Between you and me ...": quoted in RK, p. 258.

310   "It all seems ...": KK to JFK, September 18, 1939, quoted in DKG, p. 606.

310   his eyes filled with tears: Interview, Harvey Klemmer.

310   his hair had begun: BG, December 11, 1939.

310   in the fine restaurants: DEK, p. 233.

311   "based on some fundamental ...": J. Victor Perowne, January 29, 1940, British Foreign Office 371, PRO, quoted in MB, p. 192.

311   St. Leonard's: *Daily Telegraph*, October 19, 1939.

311   "Wouldn't you like ...": interview, Page Huidekoper Wilson.

311   "all the family ...": JPK to Arthur Krock, November 3, 1939. AKP.

312   "It will be good ...": D. Gibbs to JPK, January 10, 1940, quoted in DKG, p. 594.

312   "in no uncertain words": quoted in RK, p. 157.

312   "it seemed wise": RK, p. 258.

313   "I see in the paper ...": DKG, p. 594.

313   on December 6, 1939: United Press, December 6, 1939, JPK file 1939. BUCL.

313   Inside the building: BP, December 7, 1939.

314   "which to be effective ...": Dr. Sara M. Jordan to Roosevelt, December 13, 1939, President's Personal File, container No. 207 re: Joe Kennedy. FDRPL.

314   "You would be surprised ...": quoted in AS, (paperback edition), p. 35.

314   "Joe dear": quoted in AS, p. 35.

314   "It is easy enough ...": AS, p. 35.

314   they had moved beyond: In a month and a half in London, the author interviewed thirty-nine women who were debutantes in 1938 and 1939 and knew the Kennedys. Most of that material is peripheral to the main themes of this book, but not the sense of what a profound impact the war had on these women's

lives, and how over half a century later they are such intriguing individuals, still so deeply touched by the war years.

315 a vote was taken: KK to JPK, May 21, 1939, quoted in DKG, p. 607.

315 wrote a pro-isolationist editorial: NH, p. 290.

315 "Kick is very ...": JFK to JPK, Spring 1940. JFKPL.

315 "to continue her art studies": AP story in BG, May 28, 1940.

316 "She mentioned the terrible ...": BG, June 2, 1940.

316 "It would be difficult for ...": "Letter from London" by Mollie Panter-Downes, June 2, 1940, *The New Yorker Book of War Pieces*, p. 37.

316 "get something that likes lovin' ": JFK to KLB, October 23, 1939, quoted in NH, p. 295.

316 "Well Jack's tied up ...": CH, p. 92.

316 "first boy completely approved ...": quoted in DKG, p. 606.

317 "the wedding of the century": Birmingham, *Real Lace*, p. 96.

317 "Jack was autographing ...": Damore, *Cape*, p. 57.

318 "These were still days ...": Oral history, Charles Spalding. JFKPL.

318 the cable that arrived: *Barnstable Patriot*, July 18, 1940, p. 4.

318 "telling everyone ...": quoted in DKG, p. 607.

318 "really awfully nice": JK to JPK, quoted in RK, p. 270.

319 "It was embarrassing ...": Interview with a close friend of JFK.

319 Rose sent her: RK, p. 266.

319 feet were bloody: CA, British edition, p. 84.

319 she asked Luella if she could: This account of Rosemary's visit to Falmouth is based on interviews with Luella Hennessey Donovan.

320 it looked as if the Kennedys: RK, p. 265.

320 on the sports pages: NYT, September 4, 1940.

320 "plenty homesick": JPK to Eunice Kennedy, August 2, 1940, quoted in RK, p. 270.

320 "forgotten to shave ...": JPK to Edward M. Kennedy, September 11, 1939, quoted in RK, p. 273.

321 "about 30 yds. away": John W. Wheeler-Bennett. *King George VI: His Life and Reign* (1958), p. 468.

321 "Haven't the slightest ...": JPK to JFK, September 10, 1940. JFK personal correspondences, 1933–1950, Box 4A, JFKPL.

321 "There has been plenty of bombing ...": quoted in RK, p. 272.

321 "the Chancellery would operate ...": Diary entry for September 13, 1941 in James Leutze, ed. *The London Journal of General Raymond E. Lee* (1971), pp. 55–56.

321 calling the embassy: Lee diary for September 22, 1941 in Leutze, p. 67.

321 "had lost his nerve": DEK, p. 257.

321   "Kennedy has the speculator's smartness . . ." Lee diary for
       September 17, 1951 in Leutze, p. 62.
322   "Kick and Jack both had . . .": Interview, Francis McAdoo.
322   "Kick talked . . .": Interview, Cynthia McAdoo.
322   "Joe felt that at . . .": REFK recollections of Married Life.
       RCP.
322   no longer even deeming: DEK, p. 269.
323   "In a moment . . .": BP, October 28, 1940, p. 9B.
323   "KENNEDY ANGRY AT PRESIDENT": BP, October 24, 1940.
323   because of her great . . .": quoted in MB, p. 217.
324   "an indictment of President . . .": MB, p. 213.
324   "The President sent you . . .": Arthur Krock private memoran-
       dum, December 1, 1940. AKP.
325   A White House chauffeur: Time report, October 28, 1940 in
       RWP.
325   brought up as a Catholic: James F. Byrnes. All In My Lifetime
       (1958), p. 16.
325   "that Roosevelt didn't want . . .": Krock memorandum, De-
       cember 1, 1940. AKP.
325   "This is goodbye . . .": Landis MS, quoted in NH, p. 364.
326   "Joe did most of the . . .": AS, p. 38.
327   "what the President could possibly . . .": Byrnes, p. 126.
328   "would not lead . . .": RK, p. 275.
328   "I'm willing to spend . . .": BG, November 10, 1940.
328   "England was virtually . . .": BT, November 26, 1940.
328   "I never want to see . . .": This account of the meeting be-
       tween Kennedy and Roosevelt is based on MB, p. 229, which
       itself is based on extensive documentation including inter-
       views with James and Franklin Roosevelt Jr.
329   "stomach problems . . .": JCB, p. 109.
329   "We had everything . . .": Interview, Kerry McCarthy.
330   "For God's sake . . .": Interview, Page Wilson.
331   "a hey-you kind of job": Interview, Frank Waldrop.
331   candidate for disability: JFK clinical record, Naval Hospital,
       Charleston, South Carolina, diagnosis and patient's record
       dated April 13, 1942. JFKPL.
331   Joe used his: NH, p. 406.
331   taking up residence: NH, p. 409.
332   "When they joked . . .": Interview, Frank Waldrop.
332   "boy who was supposedly brilliant . . .": IA to JFK, Janu-
       ary 20, 1942. JFKPL.
333   "big bag of wind": LMT, p. 97.
334   "It delighted her . . .": Interview, John White.
335   men she may have wanted: "Can you imagine what it must
       have been like to know your daughter was walking the streets
       in the darkness of the night, the perfect prey for an unsuspect-
       ing male?" said Ann Gargan, the Kennedy niece who took

care of Joe during the last years of his life. Quoted in DKG, p. 640.

335   "they're gone as a person ...": Interview, John White.

335   Kathleen discussed the surgery: Interview, Kerry McCarthy.

335   "Oh, Mother, no ...": Interview, Kerry McCarthy.

335   "I think he knew ...": Interview, Luella Hennessey Donovan.

336   350 to 500 lobotomies: Elliot S. Valenstein, ed. *The Psychosurgery Debate: Scientific, Legal and Ethical Perspectives* (1980), p. 25.

336   "The doctors told ...": Interview, EKS. RCP.

337   "often behaved like a barker ...": Valenstein, *The Psychosurgery Debate*, p. 22.

337   Joe would not have had: Many responsible researchers cautioned that "in thinking of psychosurgery, we must ... realize we are substituting one disease for another, and although this may be a perfectly justifiable procedure in severe cases, it can never be used in those individuals whom we wish to return to a reasonable high economic and social life." Others made a far harsher argument. Editorialized the *Medical Record* in 1940: "In the name of Madam Roland who cried aloud concerning the many crimes committed in the cause of 'liberty' we would call the attention to these mutilating surgeons to the Hippocratic oaths." Quoted in Valenstein, *The Psychosurgery Debate*, p. 30.

337   Freeman kept meticulous: See Walter Freeman, M.D., and James W. Watts, M.D. *Psychosurgery: Intelligence, Emotion and Social Behavior Following Prefrontal Lobotomy for Mental Disorders* (1942).

337   patients were far older: At the age of twenty-three, Rosemary was younger than all but one of the sixty-seven patients whose ages Freeman and Watts listed in their 1942 book, *Psychosurgery*.

337   Freeman had his own caveats: "Not always does the operation succeed," he wrote in his 1942 book, *Psychosurgery*. "And sometimes it succeeds too well, in that it abolishes the finer sentiments that have kept the sick individual within bounds of adequate social behavior. What may be satisfactory for the patient may be ruinous to the family." Freeman and Watts, unpaged preface.

337   "The operation erases any ...": Interview, Luella Hennessey Donovan.

337   "some patients have been ...": Freeman and Watts, p. 85.

338   "precision operation": Elliot S. Valenstein. *Great and Desperate Cures: The Rise and Decline of Psychosurgery and Other Radical Treatments for Mental Illness* (1986), p. 149.

338   tragically changed: Valenstein, *Great*, p. 151.

338   black silk sutures: Freeman and Watts, p. 85.

338   Rosemary was shipped: During the course of the author's research, an acquaintance told him that his friend, Dr. Jonathan Slocum, had once guiltily confided to him that Rosemary had been at Craig House, an institution that Slocum then headed. On the author's visit to St. Coletta's, he learned that Rosemary Kennedy did not arrive at her current home in Jefferson, Wisconsin, until July of 1949. He called Luella Hennessey Donovan and asked her where Rosemary Kennedy had been in the forties. Donovan said that she had been at Craig House. The author then called Dr. Slocum who said that he did not discuss patients. Finally, he asked Eunice Shriver, who said that she had no recollections of where her sister had been during those years.

338   Craig House, a private psychiatric hospital: This description of Craig House is based on interviews with two journalists who had close knowledge of the facility, Dick Shea of the *Beacon News* and Craig Wolf of the *Poughkeepsie Journal.*

339   often considered poor therapy: Interview, Dr. Robert Cooke.

339   Then she mentioned Joe and each: The letters are dated December 5, 1941; January 5, 1992; January 12, 1942; February 2, 1942; February 10, 1942; February 16, 1942; March 27, 1942; October 9, 1942. Rose Kennedy does not mention all of her eight children in every letter but never does she write of Rosemary.

339   Bobby was at Portsmouth Priory: AS, p. 44.

340   "The house was no longer . . .": REFK to "my darlings," December 5, 1941. JFKPL.

340   "When you all were . . .": REFK to "Dear Children," January 5, 1942. JFKPL.

340   "We got sidetracked . . .": Interview, Senator Edward Kennedy.

341   "will go along . . .": REFK to "Dear Children," January 12, 1942. JFKPL.

341   "He . . . shakes his head . . .": REFK to "Dear Children." February 16, 1942. JFKPL.

341   "I nominate Jean . . .": REFK to "Dear Children," January 12, 1942. JFKPL.

341   Rose sent them: REFK to "Dear Children," March 27, 1942. JFKPL.

341   "changed too often": Interview, REFK. RCP.

341   "That was hard . . .": Interview, Senator Edward Kennedy.

342   She missed so many: Interview, Barbara Dunn Goodman.

342   students whispered: Interview, Mrs. Lucille Sidenberg.

342   "Others gossiped": Interview, Mrs. Ann Dixon Curtin.

342   "My mother . . .": Interview, EKS.

342   "We sent her . . .": REFK recollections on Married Life. RCP.

342   "everything is well . . .": EKS to "Dear Mother and Dad,"

January 5, 1942. JFK personal correspondence, 1933–1950, box 4a. JFKPL.

342   "Some of the male . . .": REFK to "Dear Children," February 2, 1942. JFKPL.

342   had shelled a refinery: *The Stanford Daily*, February 24, 1942, p. 1.

343   she was writing Rose asking: REFK to "My darlings," January 12, 1942. JFKPL.

343   "Hi, girl": Interview, Virginia Carpenter.

343   "an Eastern custom": REFK to "Dear Children," March 27, 1942. JFKPL.

343   When she went off on a ski: undated letter EKS to "Dear Mother," JFKPL.

343   "I didn't really . . .": Interview, EKS.

343   "All I heard . . .": Interview, Charlotte Cecil Walter.

343   "Eunice was hell-bent . . .": Interview, Virginia Carpenter.

344   "an interesting and varied . . .": REFK to "Dear Children," March 27, 1942. JFKPL.

344   locked into their rooms: *Quad.* Stanford Yearbook for 1942, p. 357.

344   "a letter from the Federal . . .": NH, p. 427.

345   Kathleen commandeered: LMT, p. 107.

345   "One of Ex-Ambassador . . .": quoted in NH, p. 438.

345   Joe arrived at the newspaper: John White diary.

346   "But of course . . .": IA to JFK, January 19, 1942, JFK personal box 4a, JFKPL.

346   "Betty is more . . .": IA to JFK, January 27, 1942. JFKPL.

346   "Daddy wouldn't approve": KK to "Dear Twinkle-Toes [JFK]," January 28, 1942. JFKPL.

346   arriving late for her: Letter to Michael Foster from Mrs. Thomas J. Joyce, July 24, 1991.

346   "when the dorms . . .": Interview, Mrs. Thomas Joyce.

347   "the Communistic program . . .": *The Rambler*, November 4, 1941.

347   She had what her classmates: Interview, Sister Caritas McCarthy.

347   "Write me . . .": Pat Kennedy to "Dear Jack," February 14, 1942. JFK personal correspondence, 1933–1950, box 4a, JFKPL.

347   ever more flagrant: "At one party Joe spotted some young girl and said to her, 'Would you like to go to Bermuda?' " John White recalled. "And she said, 'Well maybe.' He said 'Come on.' And before she knew it, they were on a plane to Bermuda and back practically before the party was over."

347   become terribly upset: LMT, p. 112.

348   "Sometimes I feel . . .": quoted in LMT, p. 91.

348   "Tonight for . . .": John White's diary courtesy of John White.

348   John thought of her as Claudette Colbert: LMT, p. 110.

349   "Inga was much wiser . . .": Interview, John White.

349   "To you I need not . . .": IA to JFK. Wednesday. (By textual analysis probably dated January 28, 1942.) JFKPL.

350   "Maybe your gravest . . .": ibid. JFKPL.

350   "You have . . .": IA to JFK, ibid. JFKPL.

350   "Anyone as brainy . . .": IA to JFK, February 23, 1942. JFKPL.

350   "If you feel . . .": IA to JFK, March 11, 1942. JFKPL.

350   "What I give you . . .": IA to JFK, "Monday," probably February 9, 1942. JFKPL.

351   "their ability to . . .": Lyn Mikel Brown and Carol Gilligan. *Meeting at the Crossroads: Women's Psychology and Girls' Development* (1992), p. 215.

351   "Inga seemed very sad . . .": KK to "Dear John F." Undated, JFK personal correspondence, 1933–1950, box 4a.

351   "Please do not mention . . .": quoted in DKG, p. 639.

352   "Your father again . . .": REFK to "Dear Children," February 2, 1942. JFKPL.

353   "It was all very gay . . .": REFK to "Dear Children," March 27, 1942. JFKPL.

353   "I was caught . . .": RK, p. 285.

354   "dinner with future Pres. . . .": KK to JFK. Undated. JFK personal correspondence 1933–1950, box 4a.

354   "hadn't any ambitions . . .": quoted in JCB, p. 128.

354   Kathleen showed Betty letters: Interview, Betty Coxe Spalding, quoted in JCB, p. 128.

354   "one shouldn't marry . . .": KK to "Dearest Family," November 11, 1943. Courtesy of Eunice Kennedy Shriver.

354   "But I thought . . .": Interview, Page Huidekoper Wilson.

354   "I would advise . . .": JFK to KK, March 10, 1942, JFKPL.

355   Norton spent most of the war: Interview, Sarah Norton Baring.

355   Killing Johnson and thirty-three: Lambert, p. 210.

355   "Well, then, let's go . . .": LMT, p. 87.

355   "You had to go out . . .": Interview, Lady Ford.

355   In March Kathleen went: KK to Joseph P. and Rose Kennedy, March 20, 1942. JFKPL.

356   having to spend days in bed: ARV record, March 6, 1942 (H468). JFKPL.

356   "fusion of the . . .": Medical record of Lieutenant JFK, USNR, December 15, 1944, JFKPL.

356   "wouldn't show he was pleased": KK to Mrs. Mead, quoted in JCB, p. 155.

357   with the Fifth Marines: Richard B. Frank. *Guadalcanal: The Definitive Account of the Landmark Battle* (1992), p. 48.

357   "Well how's every little . . .": Pat Kennedy to "Dear Jack," July 10, 1942. JFKPL.

357   George Mead was one: Richard Tregaskis. *Guadalcanal Diary*, quoted in JCB, p. 155.

357   "The love in our hearts . . .": LMT, p. 120.

358   "Your words meant more . . .": LMT, p. 120.

359   hardly recognized: KK to "Dearest Family," June 27, 1943. Courtesy of EKS.

359   "the most pathetic . . .": KK to REFK, June 27, 1943, quoted in RK, p. 289.

359   five thousand she: Neil Potter and Jack Frost. *The Mary: The Inevitable Ship* (1961), p. 155.

360   "personal service": LMT, p. 129.

360   "most of the Red Cross . . .": KK to REFK, June 27, 1943 quoted in RK, p. 289.

361   "As a matter of fact this job . . .": JFK to KK, June 3, 1943 quoted in DKG, p. 650.

361   searching the waters: HS, p. 196.

362   twenty-seven hundred professional staff: George Korson. *At His Side: The Story of the American Red Cross* (1945), p. 259.

362   "by putting the squeeze . . .": Tim McInerny to JPK, July 28, 1943 quoted in DKG, p. 665.

362   "Everyone is very surprised . . .": KK to JFK, July 3, 1943. Courtesy of Eunice Kennedy Shriver.

362   "As we get a day . . .": KK to Frank Waldrop, quoted in LMT, p. 135.

362   "You wouldn't recognize . . .": KK to LB, March 25, 1943, quoted in DKG, p. 667.

363   fifteen hundred cots: BG, May 7, 1944, p. 5.

363   "The boys around the club . . .": KK to "Dearest little Kennedys," July 14, 1943. Courtesy of Eunice Kennedy Shriver.

363   "We are very nice . . .": KK to "Dearest Family," August 24, 1943. JFKPL.

363   "There's heavy betting . . .": KK to "Dearest little Kennedys," July 14, 1943. JFKPL.

364   "I can't understand . . .": KK to "Dearest Jack," July 29, 1943. Courtesy of Eunice Kennedy Shriver.

365   "There was such resentment . . .": Off-the-record interview with a contemporary of KK.

365   Tony Rosslyn, who: DKG, p. 667.

365   "She was after . . .": Interview, Rhona Peyton-Jones.

365   they had days off: LMT, p. 136.

365   "As you said . . .": LMT, p. 136.

365   "You must remember . . .": JPK to KK, September 8, 1943, quoted in DKG, pp. 666–667.

366   "of herself when . . .": quoted in DKG, p. 667.

366   "I was amazed . . .": REFK to "Dear Children," May 13, 1943. Courtesy of Eunice Kennedy Shriver.

366   "Well, take care . . .": quoted in RK, p. 292.

367   "worried to death . . ." KK to JFK, September 10, 1943, quoted in RK, p. 293.

367   In October: AS, pp. 56–57.

367   an estimated four million: David Hinshaw. *The Home Front* (1943), p. 43.

367   Roosevelt had signed: *Nation at War: Shaping Victory on the Home Front.* Reprinted from Compton's Pictured Encyclopedia 1942, p. 12s.

367   he gave an informal lecture: *The Rambler*, March 2, 1943, p. 1. RCA.

367   conservative church leaders feared: Joseph B. Schuyler Jr. wrote in *The Catholic World*: "You hear the President praise women's attention at work, as contrasted with men's. And yet one wonders. Is business going to. be of the same mind when millions of men return from the services to reclaim their old jobs? Will women remain satisfied with the lower divisions of labor? Just ask them! And if they are not will men be willing to compete with women in the job of earning a living? Will they complacently sit by, as women bring home the pay envelopes from jobs that the men once surrendered to go to war? Not if men are men! Industry is disturbed now at union demands; what will happen when strikes, collective bargaining, etc. are furthered by women?" Joseph B. Schuyler Jr., "Women at Work," *The Catholic World*, April, 1943, p. 29.

368   At morning mass: *The Rambler*, June 7, 1943, p. 6. RCA.

368   "Pat is a study . . .": *The Rambler*, February 20, 1945, p. 3. RCA.

368   She appeared a creature: Letter to Michael Foster from Mrs. Thomas J. Joyce, July 24, 1991.

369   "She seemed very mature . . .": Interview, Sister Caritas McCarthy.

369   "Mrs. Kennedy ran the most orderly . . .": Interview, Joan Mulgrew.

369   "He [Ted] and I were the babies . . .": Ralph Martin. *Hero*, p. 30.

369   "There was no gas . . .": Interview, Ann Fitzgerald Farrell.

370   "His speech was on what you . . .": Interview, Renee de la Chapelle Perna.

370   "I think what I got mostly . . .": Interview, Jean Kennedy Smith.

370   "She was a lot of fun": Interview, Mary Mann Cummins.

371   "You took my hand and squeezed . . .": Letter from Stanley, Irene, Stacey, Jerry, and Mickey Kyinksi to Mr. and Mrs. Joseph Kennedy. August 26, 1968. LB.

371   "To Ambassador Joe Kennedy, father . . .": quoted in HS, p. 203.

372   the marriage was formally dissolved: David Williamson and

Patricia Ellis, eds. *Debrett's Distinguished People of Today* (1988), p. 616.

373 "Dear Ex-Boss ...": quoted in *Vanity Fair*, p. 57.

374 "You talk to me ...": quoted in HS, p. 217.

374 "People swarmed in": quoted in RH, p. 294.

374 "Kick handled herself to perfection ...": quoted in HS, p. 217.

374 What struck Wyndham-Quin: Interview, Lady Roderic Pratt.

375 "I want to do the right ...": quoted in DKG, p. 674.

376 "let all the rest of us ...": JPK to KK, March 8, 1944, quoted in DKG, p. 676.

376 "When both people have been handed ...": REFK to KK, February 24, 1944, quoted in DKG, p. 675.

376 "She thinks you would ...": quoted in DKG, p. 675.

377 "I think something ...": KK to parents, March 4, 1944, quoted in DKG, p. 675.

377 "Billy wanted to marry her badly ...": *Vanity Fair*, p. 57.

377 "He never should have come ...": Interview, Lady Maureen Fellowes.

378 "The by-election was a grave error ...": Interview, Andrew, Duke of Devonshire.

378 "I was known as ...": KK to "Dearest Family," February 22, 1944. JFKPL.

378 "Young man, you ought ...": *London Sunday Express*, February 13, 1944.

378 "Can you milk a cow?": *Evening Standard*, February 9, 1944.

379 "Lord Hartington will have to explain ...": quoted in HS, p. 224.

379 "I must say I haven't ...": KK to "Dearest Family," February 22, 1944. JFKPL.

380 "It has been a fierce fight ...": *London Express*, February 19, 1944, also HS, p. 225.

381 "Moral courage ...": *As We Remember Joe*, p. 54.

381 Fifteen years ago the Catholic: KK to REFK, May 9, 1944, quoted in DKG, p. 680.

381 went to see Father Torbert: LMT, p. 155.

382 "a routine physical checkup": NYT, May 7, 1944, p. 44., also Associated Press, May 6, 1944.

382 "will bring her [Kathleen] ...": BT, May 4, 1944, p. 1.

382 "HEARTBROKEN. ...": quoted in DKG, p. 677.

382 "I thought it would have ...": quoted in DKG, p. 677.

383 "As far as Kick's soul ...": quoted in DKG, p. 678.

383 Kathleen rushed breathlessly: NYT, May 7, 1944, p. 44.

383 Bruce purchased material in part: Letter from Lady Bruce to REFK, May 28, 1965. RCP.

385 "You would rejoice ...": quoted in DKG, p. 679.

385 "finished in Boston": quoted in DKG, p. 680.

385 "I was only ...": Interview, Lady Anne Tree.

385 "Listen, you God damn ...": KK to her parents, May 9, 1944, quoted in DKG, p. 681.

385 they walked the half mile: BG, May 7, 1944, p. 1.

386 "Her heathen friends have ...": quoted in LMT, p. 164.

386 "I'm sorry, but I don't feel ...": BG, May 6, 1944, pp. 1-2.

387 "Duchess of Devonshire, [she] ...": BG, May 7, 1944.

387 "WITH YOUR FAITH ...": quoted in DKG, p. 680.

387 "[Now] every morning ...": quoted in DKG, p. 680.

388 "At the moment I am a camp ...": quoted in LMT, p. 165.

388 "At the moment I am living ...": quoted in LMT, p. 165.

389 "absolutely terrified": quote in DKG, p. 686.

389 "the most perfect month": quoted in DKG, p. 682.

389 "I am going to do something ...": quoted in DKG, p. 686.

383 On the morning: *Barnstable Patriot*, June 8, 1944, p. 3.

390 a forlorn young woman: Ralph G. Martin. *Henry and Clare: An Intimate Portrait of the Luces* (1991), p. 133–135.

390 In January Ann had been riding: NYT, January 12, 1944, p. 25.

390 "become a different place ...": Luella R. Hennessey as told to Margot Murphy, "My Happy Life with 17 Kennedy Babies," *Good Housekeeping*, August 1961, p. 116.

390 saw the names of young men: Damore, p. 66.

392 "We've got to carry ...": quoted in RK, p. 301.

392 Joe telephoned: Interview, Mary Lou McCarthy.

392 "splintering into ...": quoted in DKG, p. 691.

392 "I'm so sorry ...": quoted in LMT, p. 175.

393 Kathleen stood: BG, August 17, 1944.

393 "abdominal symptoms": NH, p. 664.

393 "It's a great treat ...": quoted in LMT, p. 176.

394 "I remember ...": JCB, p. 345.

395 "The humor ...": Interview, Red Fay.

396 "An American's ...": JFK to IA, September 26, 1943, NH p. 616.

396 "I can still see ...": *The Times of London*, September 23, 1944. Letter to the editor.

397 he rode into the Belgium: KK to "Dearest family," February 17, 1945. KK correspondence 1942–1947. JFK personal files 1933–1950, box 4a. JFKPL.

397 "Come on, you fellows ...": DKG, p. 695.

397 by the back door: Interview, Frans Mangelscots, conducted by Henriette Claessens-Heuten, NH, p. 862.

398 Washington had banned: Richard R. Lingeman. *Don't You Know There's A War On?* (1970), p. 120–121.

399 "a great cloud ...": Interview, Patsy Carter.

399 "What have you ...": LMT, p. 186.

399 "So ends the story ...": quoted in DKG, p. 696.

400   "never met anyone so desperately . . .": *Vanity Fair*, July 1983, p. 60.

400   "I guess God . . .": quoted in RW, p. 375.

401   "Do what you think": KK to "Dear Jackie," December 22, 1944. JFKPL.

401   "looking to see . . .": *Vanity Fair*, p. 60.

401   "the ability to not . . .": quoted in DKG, p. 697.

401   "It's such a wonderful . . .": *Vanity Fair*, p. 60.

402   "I was surprised . . .": Interview, REFK. RCP.

402   "Rose was so important . . .": Interview, David Powers. RCP.

402   At the VFW: Interview, Dave Powers, RCP, and RK, p. 315.

403   "I can feel Pappy's . . .": PBF (paperback edition), p. 132, and interview with Paul Fay.

403   They stayed a few: Interview, Bill Sutton.

403   In the evenings: Oral history, William F. Kelly. JFKPL.

403   repeated every word: Oral history, Mary McNeely, JFKPL, quoted in JCB, p. 469.

403   "Eunice would have . . .": quoted in JCB, p. 524.

404   "Women compose . . .": BG, November 11, 1945.

404   Brighton women's club: Oral history, Thomas Broderick, JFKPL, and interview with Bill Sutton.

404   the first woman veteran: *Greenfield Recorder*, April 12, 1946. JFK scrapbooks 1946–1951, JFKPL.

404   The thirty-five-year-old lawyer: AP, April 11, 1946.

404   "We thought there was little . . .": Oral history, John J. Droney. JFKPL.

404   "Falvey was a fresh . . .": Oral history, Samuel Bornstein. JFKPL.

405   "Perhaps the best . . .": Interview, Billy Sutton.

406   race of "social climbers": quoted in JCB, p. 472.

406   "Any guy who would . . .": Interview, Billy Sutton.

406   expressed himself dubious: RK, p. 319.

407   radio station WBZ: BP, November 3, 1946, p. 12.

407   "Eunice, you . . .": Oral history, John Droney. JFKPL.

407   "Jean was about . . .": Interview, REFK. RCP.

407   Jean and Eunice joined: Damore, pp. 91–92.

408   Jack spent much of the time: Dineen, p. 85.

408   "When we were . . .": Interview, Mary Lou McCarthy.

409   "scary": AS, p. 95.

409   swung her from the second story: Lester David, *Ethel* (1971), pp. 6–7.

410   "This is ridiculous . . .": Interviews, Mary Cummins and Jean Kennedy Smith.

410   As revenge: Interview, Mary Cummins.

410   "Mother didn't . . .": Interview, Jean Kennedy Smith.

411   Interracial Forum: The College Journal 1937–1948. MCA.

411   "You may feel . . .": *The Centurion*, March 1949, p. 3. MCA.

411   "We had a Happy Husband Hunting . . .": Interview, Charlotte Hogan.

412   "I can remember Jean . . .": Interview, Betty Street Vanderbilt.

412   "Mother said . . .": *Time* reporting June 7, 1960. RWP.

412   "Jack wanted me . . .": Interview, Paul Fay.

413   "If that girl had been born . . .": quoted in CH, p. 159.

413   A few months before, representatives of: Oral history, James V. Bennett. JFKPL.

414   A picture of Eunice: *Newsweek*, January 27, 1947, p. 29.

414   "She is a pretty girl . . .": *Washington Times Herald*, February 26, 1947.

414   "complete disorder": Oral history, Joseph W. Alsop. JFKPL.

414   discovering the ancient leavings: CH, p. 158.

414   subsisted on cream of tomato: Bill Sutton quoted in JCB, p. 515.

415   She brought home troubled girls: Joseph F. Dinneen, *The Kennedy Family* (1959), p. 126.

415   "Eunice was really more interested . . .": Interview, Charles Bartlett.

415   When he could manage it, he was elsewhere: Interview, Bill Sutton.

415   "It's fair to say . . .": Interview, EKS.

416   told his friend Peter: Interview, Peter Hoguet.

417   "smitten": Robert A. Liston. *Sargent Shriver: A Candid Portrait* (1964), p. 55.

417   She thought nothing: Liston, p. 55.

417   "In those days . . .": Interview, John White.

417   "being so old . . .": Barbara Kevles, "The Kennedy Who Could be President," *'Ladies' Home Journal*, March 1976, p. 156.

417   Horton went to bed: DKG, p. 724.

418   "He did something . . .": JCB, pp. 521–522.

419   pouring a quart of milk: Interview, John White.

419   "One night they had us . . .": Interview, Frank Waldrop.

419   "I never thought . . .": Peter Lawford's unpublished autobiography. ASU.

419   "skinny, scrawny . . .": JCB, p. 558.

420   "We found the original . . .": Interview, Pamela Harriman.

420   "For then I can imagine . . .": Anthony Eden to KK, January 10, 1948. JFKPL.

420   "Gaiety, like . . .": Angela Lambert. *Unquiet Souls: The Indian Summer of the British Aristocracy* (1985), p. 21.

421   "king dandy and . . .": quoted in LMT, p. 207.

421   been the chairwoman: *Daily Express*, June 13, 1946.

423   "I liked Peter . . .": Interview, Andrew, Duke of Devonshire.

423   "You don't know him": quoted in LMT, p. 217.

423 "I think there would ...": Interview, Jane Kenyon-Stanley Compton.

423 "like Joseph ...": quoted in CH, p. 166.

423 he was somewhat envious: DKG, p. 734.

423 Rose and Pat unexpectedly: *Evening Standard*, September 25, 1947.

424 cortisone, had recently been: Russell L. Cecil, ed. *A Textbook of Medicine* (1947), p. 1357.

424 "That young American friend ...": Interview, Pamela Harriman. See also DKG, p. 734.

424 "He used to turn green ...": Oral history, Joseph Alsop. JFKPL.

424 "He had leukemia ...": Interview, REFK. RCP.

426 "It was passion....": CH, p. 168.

426 "more fulfilled ...": Interview, Patsy White Carter.

427 "a perfectly hair-raising ...": Oral history, Joseph Alsop. JFKPL.

427 "*You* made Kathleen leave ...": LMT, p. 226, and interview, John White.

427 "As she talked of Fitzwilliam ...": Interview, John White.

428 "We all knew that Jean's sister ...": Interview, Margaret Hutchinson.

431 "No American, man or ...": quoted in LMT, p. 239.

432 people walking through: On September 9, 1965, REFK wrote her children a letter quoting paragraphs of a letter she had received from the Duchess of Devonshire: "I think you would be touched if you could see the hundreds of holiday folk who come here to see darling Kick's grave ..." Robert Kennedy papers at JFKPL. On the author's own visit in 1990, the church vicar remarked on the continuing visits to KK's grave.

433 Joe had learned about St. Coletta's: DKG, p. 642. Just two years previously under Cushing's patronage a branch of the school had opened in Massachusetts. Sister Mary Theodore Hegeman, O. S. F. *A History of St. Coletta School* (St. Coletta School, Jefferson, Wisconsin).

433 visitors usually stayed in Serra Home: Hegeman, p. 11.

433 the first of July: This date is based on the records at St. Coletta's as stated by Alan K. Borsari, Alverno director.

433 "They say Rosemary was very uncontrollable ...": Interview, Sister Margaret Ann.

434 "I am still very grateful ...": quoted in DKG, p. 643.

434 Rose visited Rosemary: Interviews, Luella Hennessey Donovan and Kerry McCarthy.

434 "In the back of my mind ...": Interview, Sister Margaret Ann.

434 wreaked such damage: AS, p. 96.

435 Joe danced with his new: David, p. 48.

435 "she probably wouldn't arrive ...": BP, October 5, 1950.

435   "In spite of his age . . .": DKG, p. 748.

436   "We had such a very good time . . ." Interview, Jean Kennedy Smith.

436   had initially hoped to arrive: *Boston Daily Record*, May 11, 1950, p. 4.

436   "Girls give each other bracelets . . .": EKS transcribed notebooks. James Landis papers at the Library of Congress.

437   asked to paint their rooms: EKS notebook, p. 1 *op. cit.*

437   "See her more and . . .": EKS notebook, p. 12 *op. cit.*

437   "I didn't know quite . . .": Interview, EKS.

437   "I used to say that I'm the . . .": Interview, Sargent Shriver. BK.

438   "Never in my . . .": BG, May 11, 1950.

438   at the Conference: BG, May 10, 1950.

438   Pat was spending a good deal: Interview, Mary Ann Orlando.

438   "Do you like him?": Interviews, Mary Lou, Kerry, and Matt McCarthy.

439   "I learned a lot": Interview, EKS.

439   Eunice had left an eighteen-thousand-dollar: BG, April 29, 1950, and May 26, 1950.

440   "Pat said you'll have a much . . .": Interviews, Mary Jo Gargan Clasby and Richard Clasby. RCP.

440   Pat moved to southern California: Interview, Patricia Lawford Kennedy.

440   she had introduced him to Pat: Peter Lawford unpublished autobiography. ASU.

441   they separated even before: James Spada. *Peter Lawford: The Man Who Knew Too Much* (1991), p. 161.

441   Joe invited McCarthy: Roy Cohn. *McCarthy* (1968), p. 66.

441   "We came away . . .": BP, October 7, 1951.

442   wrestling with female criminals: Dineen, p. 136.

442   "photographs of yourself with . . .": JFK to "Dear Eunice," April 30, 1952. JFK prepresidential papers, box 102. JFKPL.

442   "I've written to Pat and Eunice . . .": JFK to "Dear Mother," May 7, 1952. JFK prepresidential papers, box 103. JFKPL.

442   "I don't want . . .": JFK to "Dear Jean," June 28, 1952. JFK prepresidential papers, box 103. JFKPL.

442   "You never meet . . .": Jean Smith interview for *Time*, June 1960. RWP.

443   "I'm crazy about Jack . . .": *Providence Standard-Times*, October 18, 1952. JFK prepresidential papers, box 119. JFKPL.

443   "However, upon considering . . .": "Ted" to "Dear Mother and Dad," undated. RCP.

443   *"Reception To—"*: *Quincy Patriot-Ledger*, undated clipping, JFK prepresidential papers, box 119. JFKPL.

444   "Certainly I can appreciate . . .": *Boston Advertiser*, November 2, 1952, JFK prepresidential papers, box 118, and *Worces-*

ter Record, October 29, 1952, JFK prepresidential papers, box 19. JFKPL.

444   "have been kissed ...": Irwin Ross, "The Senator Women Elected," *Cosmopolitan*, December 1953, p. 81.

444   "her visit to Paris": *New Bedford Standard-Times*. October 19, 1952, JFK presidential papers. JFKPL.

445   "There go the Kennedy sisters": *East Boston Leader*, July 11, 1952, JFK prepresidential papers, box 118. JFKPL.

445   thirty-three teas: DKG, p. 766.

445   "as if it were an exclusive ...": quoted in DKG, p. 766.

445   a thousand women: *Salem Democrat*, August 25, 1952. JFK prepresidential papers. JFKPL.

445   "watchdogs of government": *Worcester Telegram*, June 9, 1952. JFK prepresidential papers. JFKPL.

445   "better let go ....": *Holyoke Democrat*, September 20, 1952. JFK preadministration papers. JFKPL.

445   Kennedy's campaign was based: On October 25, 1952, Cabell Phillips reported in *The New York Times Magazine:* "Kennedy is putting his greatest emphasis after the women's vote on the labor vote."

445   the highest percentage: *Congressional Quarterly News Feature*, October 3, 1952, pp. 964–965, JFK prepresidential papers, box 101. JFKPL.

445   he polled Boston voters: PMS Analysis of Poll, September 5, 1952. HCL.

446   "He gave the pitch ...": Oral history, Edward C. Berube. JFKPL.

446   called in questions: *The Standard-Times*, October 16, 1952, JFK prepresidential papers, box 119. JFKPL.

446   "Maybe you don't ...": "A Weekly Look: Between the Lines," unidentified newspaper clipping, JFK prepresidential papers, box 118. JFKPL.

446   68,753 votes: NYT, November 6, 1952.

447   "a directory of Who's Who ...": BG, May 24, 1953.

448   "Somebody decided that ...": Interview, Paul Fay.

448   One mirthful soiree: Interview, EKS. BK.

449   Jack was attracted enough: Interview, Charles Bartlett.

449   "We were a gang of girls ...": Interview, Sally Roche Higgins.

450   "Now listen to me ...": Interview, Frank Waldrop.

451   "The women chased him ...": Interview, Evelyn Lincoln.

451   "both too young and too old ...": JFK to Red Fay. PFP.

451   "You're all black ...": Interview, Jacqueline Onassis. RCP.

451   Rose thought that the charming thank-you: Interview, REFK. RCP.

452   "Where do you think you're ...": Interview, Jacqueline Kennedy Onassis, September 2, 1972, RCP, and RK, p. 347.

452 "I remember she was . . .": ibid.

453 "She wasn't as fast . . .": Interview, Richard Clasby. RCP.

453 "My sisters are direct . . .": LB.

453 "not in the usual sense 'religious' ": FC.

453 "if you don't believe . . .": Oral history, Father John Cavanaugh. JFKPL.

454 So Joe ran up to a policeman: Interview, Joe Gargan. RCP.

454 "I always thought . . .": Interview, Jacqueline Onassis. RCP.

455 "How can you live . . .": Interviews, Marie Ridder and an off-the-record confirmation.

455 "I warned them . . .": Interview, REFK. RCP.

455 When Rose went to meet Mrs. Auchincloss: Interview, Jacqueline Kennedy Onassis, RCP, and RK, p. 350.

456 "a tendency . . . to think I am not good enough . . .": JFK to Red Fay, June 24, 1955. PFP.

456 "Now you're going to have to speak . . .": Oral history with George A. Smathers, Senate Historical Office, August 1, 1989, p. 19.

457 "I couldn't help feeling . . .": Unedited Red Fay manuscript. PFP.

457 Jack wrote a lengthy: Interview, Evelyn Lincoln.

457 "The pressures of . . .": Paul Fay (paperback), p. 141.

457 supposedly suggesting: Interview, Jewel Reed.

458 "Jackie, isn't . . .": An unrehearsed interview with Jacqueline Kennedy Onassis for the University of Kentucky "John Sherman Cooper History Project." Conducted by Terry L. Birdwhistell on May 13, 1981.

459 "She would switch . . . . . .": KMRK.

459 "The more I hear Jack . . .": *Holyoke Transcript-Telegram*, April 20, 1954. JFK Library clippings. JFKPL.

459 "Jack would be traveling . . .": Interview, Jacqueline Kennedy, University of Kentucky.

459 "She didn't play . . .": Interview, REFK. RCP.

460 "Gosh, Jackie . . .": FC.

460 "It was very . . .": Interview, REFK. RCP.

461 "The only thing . . . .": Oral history, Grace Burke. JFKPL.

461 Lem Billings could: DKG, p. 776.

461 the rumor was: Oral history interview with Howard E. Shumann, legislative and administrative assistant to Senators Paul Douglas and William Proxmire 1955–1982, Senate Historical Office.

461 "How is Jack?": Telephone conversation of Senator Lyndon Johnson with Mr. Joe Kennedy, November 10, 1954, at four o'clock presumably transcribed by Johnson's secretary. LBJPL.

463 "Look, Oleg . . .": Oleg Cassini. *In My Own Fashion: An Autobiography* (1987), p. 305.

463   "When the moment . . .": Interview, Oleg Cassini.

463   "Where does she . . .": Interview, Red Fay.

463   Fay watched one day: unedited manuscript of Red Fay in Myrick E. Land Papers, box 5, Boston University Special Collections.

464   "Why don't we go . . .": Interview, Harry Fowler.

465   "They both believed . . .": Interview, Jean Kennedy Smith.

465   "I knew Father . . .": Interview, Jean Kennedy Smith.

466   "She has the maturity . . .": BP, November 8, 1953. BUCL.

466   foundation donated $620,000: NYT, August 12, 1954, p. 12.

466   "We lined . . .": Interview, Jean Kennedy Smith.

466   "Jean worked . . .": Interview, Ann Denove.

467   "The one with the best . . .": *New York Herald Tribune*, December 12, 1960.

467   "Do let me . . .": Pat Kennedy to Peter Lawford, February 21, 1953. ASU.

467   "She was one of the *purest* . . .": quoted in Spada, p. 162.

468   "He seems like a nice . . .": quoted in Spada, p. 163.

469   "had no intention . . .": BH, February 15, 1954.

469   "Peter was being courted . . .": Interview, Joe Naar.

470   "The spark was never . . . .": Interview, Milt Ebbins.

470   "I think he loved . . .": Interview, Patricia Seaton Stewart.

470   mother had dressed: Spada, p. 31.

470   He was about ten years: Spada, p. 46.

470   "Then my nanny . . .": Patricia Seaton Lawford with Ted Schwarz. *The Peter Lawford Story* (1990), p. 17.

471   "If there's anybody . . .": Spada, p. 164, also Peter Lawford unpublished autobiography, ASU, and Dineen, p. 159.

471   appreciating Joe's: Peter Lawford unpublished autobiography. ASU.

471   "Pat's father couldn't control . . .": Interview, Milt Ebbins.

472   "Do you think . . .": quoted in Spada, p. 166.

472   "Lady May never . . .": Interview, Buddy Galon.

474   "You're lucky I didn't . . .": quoted in Spada, p. 173.

474   "She cut most of the . . .": Interview, Royal Marcher, Jr.

475   "I'm one of the few . . .": Interview, Dick Livingston.

477   "Pat tried on a couple . . .": Interview, Peter Sabiston.

478   "This sounds good . . .": Spada, pp. 176–177.

478   "The three sisters hadn't seen . . .": Interview, Claude Hooton Jr.

479   "I think that Peter just . . .": Off-the-record interview.

479   "We left Russia with a vast . . .": BG, October 13, 1955.

479   If she felt as aged: Western Union Telegram from Jean Kennedy to Mrs. Peter Lawford, May 1955. ASU.

479   his grandfather William Cleary: *Time* file for cover story on JFK. RWP.

480   "Daddy gave me the choice . . .": CH, pp. 215–216.

480	Jean flashed an: BP, May 20, 1956, p. 1.
480	"I was up at Hyannis Port . . .": FC.
481	"should be married. . .": JMB. p. 182.
482	"This brings a lot . . .": BG, August 3, 1956.

480 Jean flashed an: BP, May 20, 1956, p. 1.

480 "I was up at Hyannis Port . . .": FC.

481 "should be married. . .": JMB. p. 182.

482 "This brings a lot . . .": BG, August 3, 1956.

482 concerned with questions of race and poverty: It was not until 1975, when Sargent Shriver made his own race for the Democratic presidential nomination, that he pointed out that he "was involved with minorities and their problems before the Kennedys." *Washington Star*, September 10, 1975.

482 "I'm perfectly satisfied . . .": *Chicago Daily News*, August 3, 1956. Files of JFKPL.

483 "Don't feel sorry . . .": BH, August 18, 1956.

483 cried when Jack: George Smathers oral history, Senate Historical Office.

483 sprinting away: Maxine Cheshire and John Greenya. *Maxine Cheshire, Reporter* (1978), p. 35.

483 "expecting a child soon": *New Bedford Standard-Times*, August 19, 1956.

483 "Why don't you . . .": George Smathers oral history, Senate Historical Office, p. 83.

484 she asked her husband: DKG, p. 785.

484 "women [were] either prostitutes . . .": Handwritten note late in 1955, JFK personal papers, box 40. JFKPL.

484 "I would like . . .": J.V. Bouvier, III, to Senator JFK, June 13, 1956, JFK prepresidential papers, box 521. JFKPL.

484 "bronzed and smiling": REFK to Clare Boothe Luce, August 23, 1956, JFK prepresidential papers, box 503. JFKPL.

485 stay at different hotels: REFK to Clare Boothe Luce, August 23, 1956, JFK prepresidential papers, box 503. JFKPL.

485 "exhaustion and . . .": undated untitled clipping at JFKPL with headline "EXHAUSTION BLAMED IN KENNEDY BABY LOSS."

485 "You knew that . . .": quoted in AS, p. 143.

485 "Jackie lost her baby!": REFK to Clare Boothe Luce, August 23, 1956, JFK prepresidential papers, box 503. JFKPL.

485 "She [Jackie] was very . . .": George Smathers oral history, Senate Historical Office.

486 "I know it must have . . .": Interview, REFK. RCP.

486 "The old man . . .": Interview, Oleg Cassini.

486 he voted for Eisenhower: AS, p. 146.

486 arguably working harder: JMB, p. 193.

487 "You're better than . . .": *San Francisco Chronicle*, October 5, 1956.

487 "Just as their teen daughters mob Presley . . .": L. Gary Clemente to "Dear Jack," October 29, 1956, and clipping, "Dem Ladies Mob 'Elvis' Kennedy," JFK prepresidential papers, box 521. JFKPL.

487 "Even his friends admit . . .": Address by EKS at South Bend, Indiana, October 19, 1956. JFKPL.

487 "Eunice is the one . . .": Interview, George Smathers.

488 "Well, Dad . . .": DKG, pp. 787–788.

489 She sent down: Paul E. Murphy to Robert F. Kennedy, April 15, 1957. Robert F. Kennedy. Preadministration working papers, box 42–45. JFKPL.

489 "*Dear Bobby . . .*": REFK to Robert F. Kennedy, May 9, 1957. Robert Kennedy papers. JFKPL.

489 "One of his slogans . . .": Later Years Index, p. 35. RCP.

490 a Kennedy operative made: Francis X. Morrissey to Robert F. Kennedy, March 28, 1958, Robert F. Kennedy preadministration working papers, box 44. JFKPL.

490 "where his Daddy . . .": Undated letter (presumably 1957) from Joseph P. Kennedy to Robert Kennedy, from Villa Les Fal Eze, Kennedy Family Correspondence, Robert F. Kennedy preadministration papers, box 42. JFKPL.

490 Christmas list in: In the fifties there was an openly symbiotic relationship between the media and government, and the Kennedys were only unusual in the extent that they exploited this relationship. Francis Morrissey, for instance, wrote Jack Kennedy on January 4, 1957, that he had had an unflattering reference about Robert Kennedy taken out of a column by Westbrook Pegler. Later that same year Clark Mollenhoff, an investigative reporter for *Look*, wrote Robert Kennedy the kind of flattering letter that a journalist of the contemporary generation would probably not have written. The Christmas list and these letters are in the Robert F. Kennedy preadministration working papers, box 44. JFKPL.

490 "Kathleen arrived . . .": Interview, Anne Coffey.

491 "I've got to go at a thing . . .": BUH, p. 100.

491 "weak as a cat": quoted in BUH, p. 104.

492 "It was so exciting . . .": Interview, Joan Kennedy.

493 "I couldn't have planned . . .": Interview, Joan Kennedy.

493 "A friend of mine . . .": Interview, Dan Burns.

494 "She asked me . . .": Interview, Joan Kennedy.

495 Finishing sixty-seventh in her class: MCA.

495 one student, Delayne Dedrick Gold, recalled: Interview, Delayne Gold.

495 Joan had found it: Interview, Joan Kennedy.

495 "All our dates . . .": Interview, Joan Kennedy.

497 "Joan's father, Mr. Bennett, arranged . . .": Interviews, Mary Lou McCarthy and Joan Kennedy.

497 "But the funny . . .": Interview, Joan Kennedy.

498 "It was always . . .": Jacqueline Kennedy Onassis interview, RCP.

498 "At home with the Kennedys": Videotape at JFKPL.

500   the greatest victory: DKG, p. 793.

501   After the honeymoon: Interview, Joan Kennedy, and Interview, Joan Kennedy RCP.

502   "Daddy, I'd like to . . .": Interview, EKS.

502   not one university: Herbert J. Kramer, "The Joseph P. Kennedy Jr. Foundation—A Retrospective," unpublished research paper.

503   "If we had wanted . . .": Interview, EKS.

504   with an entourage: Oral history, Robert E. Cooke. JFKPL.

504   "I don't think it's her Catholicism . . .": Interview, Dr. Robert Cooke.

504   "I think that Eunice . . .": Interview, Mary Ann Orlando.

505   "Ethel, you are . . .": Unedited Red Fay manuscript, Myrick E. Land Papers, Boston University Department of Special Collections.

505   "I was around . . .": Interview, Peter Sabiston.

506   "When Peter . . .": Interview, Milton Ebbins.

506   "These stories kept coming . . .": Interview, Fred Otash. See also Spada, p. 220.

507   "Boy, did you . . .": Peter Lawford unpublished autobiography. ASU.

507   "Guess what?": Peter Lawford unpublished autobiography. ASU.

509   "Well, I guess . . .": Peter Lawford unpublished autobiography, ASU.

510   Campbell recalled that Pat could not: Judith Exner as told to Ovid Demaris, pp. 55–56.

510   "Her Catholic . . .": Patricia Seaton Lawford, p. 147.

511   "take very good care . . .": JPK to Peter Lawford, June 25, 1956. ASU.

511   "He was so cheap . . .": Interview, Fred Otash.

511   "Peter was my closest . . .": Interview, Milton Ebbins.

513   "feeling like Scarlett . . .": Exner, p. 602.

513   "I was there . . .": Interview, Milton Ebbins.

513   "There were all these bimbos . . .": David Heymann, *A Woman Named Jackie* (1989), p. 231.

514   "it was almost . . .": Judith Exner, as told to Ovid Demaris. *My Story* (1977). p. 142.

514   "He's gone . . .": Interview, Marie Ridder.

514   "If Pat Lawford . . .": Exner, p. 113.

516   "The most important thing for a . . .": Robert J. Levin, "Senator Kennedy's Wife: If He Wins, How Much Does She Lose?" *Redbook*, April 1960.

516   no more than three days: Associated Press, May 20, 1960.

517   "That little bitch . . .": Red Fay unedited manuscript. PFP.

517   "I don't think . . .": Robert J. Levin, "Senator Kennedy's Wife."

517 "I am sorry . . .": clipping, May 16, 1960, BUCL.

518 "the public life above . . .": undated letter from Jacqueline Kennedy to Fletcher Knebel, Fletcher Knebel papers Boston University Special Collections.

518 "I'm sure there must be . . .": Robert J. Levin, "Senator Kennedy's Wife."

518 "Really Fletcher! . . .": undated letter from Jacqueline Kennedy to Fletcher Knebel, Fletcher Knebel papers, Boston University Special Collections.

518 "for the ladies to become . . .": Robert Sargent Shriver Jr. to Mrs. Edith Sampson, May 19, 1960, The Schlesinger Library, Radcliffe College.

518 "He thought it was great . . .": *Washington Star*, October 11, 1960. Whether women volunteers had the name Kennedy or not, they were largely an invisible race in the campaign, invisible to the campaign leaders, invisible to the journalists who followed the campaign, and largely invisible to history. Indeed, Rose Kennedy, her daughters, and other major women volunteers were considered such nonentities by Theodore H. White, author of the classic *The Making of the President 1960*, that their names do not even merit listing in the index. Although the Kennedy women actively campaigned in West Virginia, in *his* list of volunteers, White gave the names and backgrounds of nine men "plus girls, drivers, typists, press men, chauffeurs, TV men."

519 "as remarks of Grandpa Fitzgerald . . .": REFK diary, November 3, 1959. Campaigning Index, p. 11. RCP.

519 "The efficiency with which . . .": REFK diary of June 23, 1960. Campaigning index, p. 9. RCP.

519 "She looked like a woman . . .": Oral history, Patrick Lucey, JFKPL.

519 part of a plan surreptitiously to visit: Interviews, Judge Danforth and Father Runde.

520 "I could get in trouble . . .": *Washington Star*, February 26, 1960.

520 "All this massing of the family . . .": "Family Campaign Strategy for '60," *The Washington Evening Star*, March 4, 1960.

520 "It just seemed that they were . . .": Oral history, Marguerite Benson, JFKPL.

521 "Well, get a load of . . .": *Rochester Democrat & Chronicle*, October 14, 1960. MCA.

521 "We've lost that one": *Time* file, June 3, 1960, RWP.

522 "Oh, he's the Catholic . . .": Interview, Dorothy Tubridy.

522 "Jack liked to have a female . . .": Interview, Joan Kennedy.

523 "It makes you wonder . . .": Hugh Sidey file, and interview with JFK, June 6, 1960. RWP.

524 Florence Mary Kater was obsessed: Kater sent copies of let-

ters to J. Edgar Hoover (April 3, 1963); Robert Kennedy (April 2, 1963); Jack Paar (October 28, 1961); and to Hedda Hopper, the prominent Hollywood columnist. Hedda Hopper collection at American Film Institute Library.

524   decided there was no truth: Hugh Sidey file and interview with JFK, June 6, 1960, for *Time*. RWP.

524   "In the last year I got . . .": *Time* file on Jean Smith, June 7, 1960. RWP.

524   each woman asking what her sisters: Interview, Hugh Sidey.

525   "We said it was for Eunice . . .": Interview, Pat Lawford.

525   The party was a synergistic: "Kennedy Clan to Fete Eunice on 40th Birthday," UPI, July 9, 1960, BUCL.

525   badly twisted her ankle: BT, July 11, 1960.

526   Pat and Jean were there: *Lowell Sun*, July 11, 1960, MCA.

526   arrived late, with Eunice: AP, July 11, 1960, BUCL.

526   startled at the parade: Interview, Daniel Stewart.

526   Jack escaped out the: Oral history, James McShane. JFKPL.

526   "The girls are in there . . .": Oral history, James McShane. JFKPL.

527   formed a semicircle: PBF, p. 48.

527   residents were bothered: AP, August 11, 1960.

527   "enthralled by it": Jacqueline Kennedy to Arthur Schlesinger, July 24, 1961, ASP.

528   "Bobby always spat . . .": Interview, Charles Peters.

528   over three million more voting-age women: "Feminine Interest in New Frontier Called Wide," NYT, August 11, 1960.

528   reporters tallied up: Laura Bergquist and Stanley Tretick. *A Very Special President* (1965), p. 60.

528   Jack appointed Margaret Price: "The Woman at Kennedy's Elbow," *The Christian Science Monitor*, August 11, 1960.

528   "There was really no room . . .": Oral history, Barbara Coleman. JFKPL.

529   a slight that had not gone: Joan Braden, *Just Enough Rope* (1989), p. 109.

529   "I'm sure I spend less . . .": AP, September 15, 1960.

529   "the pleasant, homey . . .": *The Christian Science Monitor*, September 27, 1960.

529   They could not even join: Doris Fleeson, "Women are Not Admitted," BG, November 22, 1961.

529   "They were all just as gentle . . .": Oral history, Barbara Coleman. JFKPL

530   "There was no question . . .": quoted in Heymann, p. 220.

530   "She had a kind of image . . .": Oral history, Barbara Coleman. JFKPL.

530   "as hard as the girls . . .": Oral history, Peter Dugal. JFKPL.

531   in three days the two Kennedy: "Chicago News, September 13, 1960.

531   "I don't know if . . .": Oral history, Barbara Coleman. JFKPL.
532   "That night Frank is having . . .": Interview, Dick Livingston.
532   did not want to share: Braden, p. 110.
532   Sinatra campaigned actively: Spada, p. 228.
532   "You may think . . .": *Look Magazine*, "The Kennedy Women," October 11, 1960.
532   "She changes her hair . . .": *Newark News*, October 12, 1960.
533   "I'm not here . . .": *Tampa Times*, October 20, 1960.
533   "It is true that the women . . .": BG, November 2, 1960.
534   "jumping up and . . .": Theodore White, p. 18.
534   "Oh, Bunny . . .": Theodore White, p. 18.
534   "Good night, Mr. President": RK, p. 377.
534   "the longest night in history": NYT, November 10, 1960.
534   Jack had received only 112,881 votes: White, p. 350.
534   "It was a joke": Interview, Jean Smith.
534   women had voted in larger numbers: Jane Jaquette, ed. *Women in Politics* (1974), p. 15.
535   "Our dresses clash . . .": NYT, November 10, 1960.
535   was in Boston Hospital: Oral history, EKS. JFKPL.
535   "There was nothing . . .": Interview, EKS.
535   "Yes, we really ought to . . .": Oral history, EKS. JFKPL.
536   placed on the desk: UPI, November 23, 1961, Kennedy family file. LBJPL.
536   "Sammy called Sinatra . . .": Interview, Dick Livingston.
536   "I remember a meeting . . .": Interview, Mike Feldman.
537   "What I wanted . . .": Letter from Jacqueline Kennedy Onassis dated June 1973. RCP.
537   she gave birth to a six-pound: *Washington Star*, November 25, 1960.
537   "most things are made easier . . .": Eleanor Roosevelt to Mrs. John Fitzgerald Kennedy, December 1, 1960. FDRPL.
538   "panic" as first lady: Jackie Kennedy to Mrs. Roosevelt, December 5, 1960. FDRPL.
538   "designer-couturier": Cassini, p. 299.
539   "I think she was under . . .": Interview, Oleg Cassini.
539   "Just send me an accounting . . .": Cassini, p. 308.
539   "I knew I wasn't up to it . . .": Mrs. Onassis to RK, June 1973. RCP.
540   a single man, Richard Pavlick, carrying: ASK, p. 161.
540   "I did not wish to harm . . .": U. E. Baughman, "Kennedy's Closest Call," *Washington Post*, February 17, 1962.
541   "If I go into the study . . .": RK, p. 382.
541   "Your house was in turmoil": Mrs. Onassis to REFK, June, 1973. RCP.
541   When she saw an improper neckline: RK, p. 382.
542   "Well, the trouble is . . .": Interview, Evelyn and Tom Jones. RCP.

543   "an intellectual . . .": Cassini, p. 311.

542   "will be a wreck . . .": Cassini, p. 309.

543   a brutal and vulgar barracks-room jargon: This political argot was not unique to the Kennedys; indeed, most Americans would first hear it spoken a decade later on the Watergate tapes by the Quaker-born President Richard Nixon and several of his Mormon aides.

543   "What am I going to do about Bobby?": Interview, George Smathers. Smathers's account parallels the story told by Clark Clifford in his memoirs.

543   "So that's it gentlemen . . .": CH, p. 257.

543   "I guess I was just . . .": Interview, Jackie Kennedy Onassis. RCP.

544   flew back alone: "First Lady-To-Be Flies to Capital," *Palm Beach Post*, January 19, 1961.

545   only been painted green: Herbert S. Parmet. *J.F.K.: The Presidency of John F. Kennedy* (1983), p. 82.

545   "I am Mrs. Kennedy, the president's mother . . .": Interview, REFK, RCP.

546   "That day I was going . . .": Interview, REFK, RCP.

546   she thought of the words: RK, p. 388.

546   "Thanksgiving to almighty God . . .": Interview, REFK. RCP.

547   "The period . . . was not a happy time . . .": Letter from Mrs. Onassis, dated June 1973, RCP.

547   "Mrs. Eisenhower said": ibid.

547   "seemed genuinely to enjoy . . .": NYT, January 22, 1961.

548   "I had been in my room . . .": Letter from Mrs. Onassis, June, 1973. RCP.

548   so badly sprained her ankle: AP, January 17, 1961. BUCL.

548   six thousand Democratic women: BG, January 19, 1961. BUCL.

548   Jean's preinaugural party: BG, January 18, 1961.

549   "I hope Sinatra will live . . .": Unedited Red Fay manuscript. PFP.

549   A prostitute had supposedly ended up dead: Interview, Pat Seaton Lawford and Lawford and Schwarz, pp. 137–138.

549   "Hey, come on, you should . . .": Interview, Milt Ebbins.

550   "covered up": UPI, January 30, 1961, BUCL.

550   three men in their thirties: UPI, February 2, 1961.

550   "She certainly knows . . .": UPI, February 6, 1961. BUCL.

550   Pat avoided the police: UPI, February 6, 1961. BUCL.

550   the three Lawford children: *Newsweek*, March 6, 1961, p. 100.

550   "The police told me . . .": AP, February 7, 1961. BUCL.

550   Hogan announced that only: BH, February 9, 1961.

551   Margaret Price, the new vice chairman: Cynthia E. Harrison, "A 'New Frontier' For Women: The Public Policy of the Kennedy Administration," *The Journal of American History*, December 1980, p. 635.

551   "men sometimes needed . . .": Patricia G. Zelman. *Women, Work, and National Policy: The Kennedy-Johnson Years* (1982), p. 25.

551   "nothing but sex objects": Zelman, p. 27.

552   "Mr. Eisenhower named eight women . . .": BG, March 9, 1961.

552   "I talked President Kennedy . . .": Interview, Esther Peterson.

552   He listed the commission: Harrison, "A 'New Frontier'," p. 644.

552   "tremendously suppressed affection on both sides": Oral History, Barbara Ward. JFKPL.

552   at least a half dozen of the cabinet: Interview, Mike Feldman.

552   "My impression of President Kennedy . . .": Oral history, Barbara Ward. JFKPL.

553   "John Hersey, John . . .": Oral history, John Hersey. CU.

553   "Jackie walked upstairs . . .": REFK diary note of April 19, 1961. RCP.

553   Eunice became ill: "Kennedy Sister in Hub Surgery," March 14, 1961, clipping at BUCL.

554   "They would say, 'Lay low, hunker down . . .' ": Interview, Coates Redmon.

554   state visit: ASK, p. 526.

554   "So that's what you look like . . .": Interview, William Douglas-Home, also Oral History, William Douglas-Home. JFKPL.

554   "I think I had my maximum . . .": Interview, EKS.

555   "It took me three days . . .": Oral History, EKS. JFKPL.

555   "Mr. Shriver, your wife is listed . . .": Interview, Leonard Mayo.

556   "livid, screaming" Eunice: Oral history, Edwin Bayley. JFKPL.

556   "The big problem was that mental . . .": Oral history, Dr. Patrick Doyle. JFKPL.

556   "Jack, this group interested in mental . . .": Oral History, EKS. JFKPL.

557   "You talk to her . . .": Oral history, Leonard Bernstein. JFKPL.

557   "Has my sister been giving . . .": Transcript of Kennedy Library Conference on the Role of the Presidency in Mental Health and Mental Retardation, November 14, 1983. JFKPL.

558   "The girl can't just rush . . .": Interview, REFK. RCP.

558   "So many people . . .": An unrehearsed interview with Jacqueline Kennedy Onassis, May 13, 1981, University of Kentucky.

558   "You know, you were . . .": Oral history, Laura Bergquist Knebel. JFKPL.

558   She wrote him handwritten missives: Jacqueline Kennedy to Arthur Schlesinger Jr., undated note. ASP.

559   "Look at that damn . . .": Paul Fay unedited manuscript. PFP.

560   "Unfortunately, last summer . . .": quoted in *Washington Post*,
        May 26, 1994.

560   the first time since 1904: Philip B. Kunhardt Jr., ed. *Life in
        Camelot: The Kennedy Years* (1988), p. 196.

560   "I couldn't help comparing . . .": Oral history, Leonard
        Bernstein. JFKPL.

561   "immeasurable lustre": Letter from Jackie Kennedy to REFK.
        Courtesy of Eunice Kennedy Shriver.

561   "He was very much concerned . . .": Dr. Max Jacobson unpub-
        lished manuscript. Courtesy of Mrs. Ruth Jacobson.

562   "her charm, her beauty . . .": *Boston Traveler*, May 18, 1961.

563   *"Vive Jacqui! Vive Jacqui"*: Carl Sferrazza Anthony. *First La-
        dies: Volume II* (1991), p. 41.

563   the reign of Louis XVI: ASK, p. 350.

563   "was so loquacious . . .": Dr. Max Jacobson unpublished
        manuscript. Courtesy of Mrs. Ruth Jacobson.

563   wore a Givenchy gown: ASK, p. 354.

564   "I now have more confidence . . .": Anthony, p. 42.

564   flew to Greece for a private: *Washington Post*, June 7, 1961.

564   Jacobson returned to his seat: Dr. Max Jacobson unpublished
        manuscript. Courtesy of Mrs. Ruth Jacobson.

564   Eunice had finally gone on her way: The following June,
        Bobby Kennedy was worried enough about the doctor's min-
        istrations that he had his executive assistant, Andrew
        Oehmann, take a bottle with Dr. Jacobson's name on it to be
        examined by the FBI laboratory. The analysts found that the
        specimens contained vegetable oil and water, and did not con-
        tain barbiturates or narcotics, not mentioning amphetamines.
        When Bobby heard the results, he expressed his appreciation
        and "indicated he wanted this matter kept most confidential."
        Memo from Mr. Conrad and C. A. Evans to Mr. Belmont,
        FBIFOI; Memo from C. A. Evans to Mr. Belmont, June 11,
        1962, FBIFOI.

564   "I'll tell you something . . .": Interview, Charles Bartlett.

564   "I think Jack was a hard . . .": Interview, Charles Bartlett.

565   Loewe came to the White House: Oral History, Edward
        McDermott, JFKPL.

566   "Jackie would say . . .": Interview with Joan Kennedy.

566   In May *Newsweek: Newsweek*, May 15, 1961.

567   "some people are . . .": An unrehearsed interview with
        Jacqueline Kennedy Onassis, May 13, 1981, University of
        Kentucky.

567   "You are right . . .": JFK to Laura Bergquist, July 23, 1961.
        LB.

568   "We had a reception . . .": ibid.

568   "You know when a dog . . .": Interview, Milt Ebbins.

568   "Pat would get mad . . .": Interview, Dick Livingston.

569   Pat traveled to the Cape: RK, p. 410.

570   By the time they arrived: BH, UPI, August 17, 1961.

570   decided against joining: BH, August 18, 1961.

570   "Say, Pat, let's go . . .": Interview, Milt Ebbins and Spada, p. 275.

570   On September 26 while Jack and Jackie: BH, September 27, 1961.

571   a live fish into the swimming: BT, January 12, 1961.

571   the children competed in everything: Ethel Kennedy, "Keep Fit!" *This Week*, December 17, 1961.

571   Ethel put the chestnut horse: *Washington Star*, October 25, 1961.

572   "I had a baby boy . . .": Interview, Jean Kennedy Smith.

572   "Love and bunny hugs . . .": undated letter to Lyndon Johnson from Jean Smith, early June 1961. LBJPL.

572   calling him "Mr. President": RK, pp. 398–399.

572   she walked out on the White House: "Impressions of the Mother of the President," Later Years Index, p. 1. RCP.

572   "It's sort of a leitmotif . . .": Interview, REFK. RCP.

573   "He was a man of great talent . . .": Interview, Oleg Cassini.

573   "It's so incredible about Jack . . .": Interview, Frank Waldrop.

573   "I don't think they ever communicated . . .": Frank Saunders with James Southwood. *Torn Lace Curtain* (1982), p. 153.

574   Rose started play in the middle: FC.

574   Joe drove to the airport: *Palm Beach Post*, December 16, 1961.

574   she developed multiple sclerosis: Edward Kennedy, ed., *The Fruitful Bough*, p. 268.

575   "Was he able . . .": Saunders, p. 119.

577   he did not recognize: *New York Daily News*, December 20, 1961.

577   "They want to concentrate . . .": Interview, Dr. Henry Betts. RCP.

578   "I'm going dear, I'm going": Saunders, p. 135.

578   "His children told me . . .": Interview, Dr. Henry Betts. RCP.

578   "She was awfully good . . .": Interview, Luella Hennessey Donovan.

579   Rose read on, oblivious to the scene: Rita Dallas with Jeanira Ratcliffe. *The Kennedy Case* (1973), pp. 56–57.

579   "What have I done?": ibid., p. 57.

579   "I called the White House . . .": Interview, Luella Hennessey Donovan.

580   "I'm praying for . . .": Dallas, p. 87.

580   "Oh, Daddy, Daddy . . .": Dallas, p. 106.

581   "Grandpa, remember . . .": Dallas, p. 103.

581   "Ann did not make . . .": Interview, Dr. Henry Betts. RCP.

581   She started again giving: *Worcester Gazette*, February 1, 1962; *Fitchburg Sentinel*, January 20, 1962.

581   In late April she traveled to Paris: AP, BG, May 6, 1962.

582   "I don't understand . . .": Dallas, p. 113.

582   "Now I can stay here now . . .": Interview, Dr. Henry Betts. RCP.

583   "No! No! No!": Dallas, p. 115.

583   she insisted that they wear: Dallas, p. 150.

584   "tour has turned into . . .": Marjorie Hunter, "It's Just a Little Visit to India," NYT News Service. BH, February 26, 1962.

584   At a luncheon in Rome: George Dixon, "Gift to 'Crash Kennedy' " clipping dated March 22, 1962, JFKPL.

585   Ethel toppled: BG, June 21, 1962.

585   "The swimming pool thing was poor . . .": Interview, REFK. RCP.

585   "Teddy was less inhibited . . .": Interview, REFK. RCP.

585   "We started campaigning . . .": Interview, Joan Kennedy.

586   "Ted explicitly asked us . . .": *Boston Record*, October 22, 1962.

587   "I hoped that Ted . . .": *Boston Record American*, October 23, 1962.

587   "My mother-in-law campaigned . . .": Interview, Joan Kennedy.

587   he belted out a chorus: BT, November 5, 1962.

587   "Live in town . . .": BT, January 16, 1963.

588   "I can't get over it . . .": *Boston Traveler*, January 23, 1963, p. 16.

589   Fred Otash and two of his former associates: Interview, Fred Otash; see also Spada pp. 3–5, 286–287.

590   "Everybody complains about my relationship . . .": Interview, Charles Bartlett.

590   Otash said that with their electronic surveillance: Interview, Fred Otash.

590   "I recall a party . . .": Interview, Joe Naar.

590   "That god damn Pearson . . .": Red Fay Manuscript in Myrick E. Land Papers, box 5, Boston University Department of Special Collections.

591   "They dined in a popular . . .": Spada, p. 282.

591   "Hello, Pat, I'm Lee Remick": Spada, p. 283.

591   "Jean would suddenly start crying . . .": Interview, Milt Ebbins.

592   "I am sorry to have to . . .": This letter on the stationery of the Hotel Carlnia in Courchevel, France, is in the possession of Peter Lawford's widow, Patricia Seaton Stewart. The letter is undated and the postmark on the envelope is illegible. But since the one occasion when Patricia Lawford is known to

have been in Courchevel was in the spring of 1962, that is the apparent date of the letter.

593   "both disturbed and abusive": Interview, Milton Gould.

594   Don Pack, a photographer friend: Spada, p. 314.

594   "Pat became very close ...": Interview, Patricia Seaton Stewart.

595   The threesome stayed: Anthony Summers. *Goddess: The Secret Lives of Marilyn Monroe* (1985), p. 284.

595   "Pat's in Hyannis ...": Earl Wilson, "Peter Lawford Certain Marilyn Not a Suicide," BH, August 7, 1962.

596   "Peter, don't do it!": Interview, Milt Ebbins.

596   phone calls including one to Joe Naar: Interview, Joe Naar; see also Spada, p. 323.

596   "I am shocked ...": "Lawfords Not Invited to Funeral," BH, August 9, 1962.

596   "I blame the changes ...": Interview, Joe Naar.

596   "At the accident the cop ...": Interview, Milt Ebbins.

597   overheard by Matty Jordan: Spada, p. 333.

598   "I don't think of my parents ...": Interview, Maria Shriver.

598   "I remember growing up ...": Interview, Maria Shriver.

599   "Nobody else's mother ...": Interview, Maria Shriver.

599   "One Down's syndrome boy was ...": Interview, Chris McNickle.

600   Many of those in the mental: Interview, Elizabeth Boggs.

600   "I spoke to my father and Jack ...": Interview, EKS.

600   "Early in life Rosemary ...": *Saturday Evening Post*, September 22, 1962.

600   When Luella showed the article: Interview, Luella Hennessey Donovan.

601   As Eunice rightfully suggested: Interview, EKS.

601   "Eunice, the only way you're going ...": Transcript of JFKPL Conference on the Role of the Presidency in Mental Health and Mental Retardation, November 14, 1983. JFKPL.

602   "Of the two hundred thousand ...": *Washington Post*, May 10, 1963.

602   "You should put more fire ...": *Washington Post*, May 10, 1963, C1.

602   "That's a good idea ...": Oral history, EKS. JFKPL.

603   Hackett proposed a cabinet-level: AS, p. 444.

603   It had been Eunice's idea: EKS, then, had been the gadfly behind a program that become the clearest antecedent to VISTA, the massive domestic volunteer program begun during the Johnson administration. Sargent Shriver became the first head of VISTA, but by then EKS was on to other pursuits, her role largely forgotten.

603   "patients were left naked ...": AS, p. 445.

604   "There is no lady bountiful ...": Interview, Sarge Shriver. BK.

604   "My mother wanted to have . . .": Interview, Maria Shriver.
604   "Shriver doesn't give a damn . . .": quoted in *Washington Post*, August 6, 1972.
605   Eunice visited a home for those: BG, June 29, 1963.
605   " 'Do you know it is impossible . . .": Red Fay manuscript in Myrick E. Land Papers, box 5, Boston University Department of Special Collections.
605   returning to his roots: To Dr. Thomas J. Kiernan, the Irish ambassador to Washington, the visit represented the closure of the era of the famine, Jack's triumph the triumph of the Irish people. "I think he appeared to the people as an ending to the famine," Kiernan reflected, "as a triumph out of the famine. The famine, although it happened a hundred years ago, remained in the consciousness of the people." Oral history, Dr. Thomas J. Kiernan. JFKPL.
578   "The outpouring of love . . .": Interview, Jean Kennedy Smith.
606   greeted Jack with a hug: BG, June 28, 1963.
607   "It was magic . . .": Saunders, p. 210.
607   He was so taken: Interview, Melody Miller.
608   "How's it going . . .": Dallas, p. 143.
609   not even attending Josie's: BG, November 1, 1963.
609   "Pat drank a bottle . . .": Saunders, p. 195.
609   she had miscarried: BG, May 17, 1963.
609   kept her pregnancy secret: *Washington Star*, April 21, 1963.
609   "Everybody asks me about . . .": LB.
610   she directed that a baby's room: J. B. West with Mary Lynn Kotz. *Upstairs at the White House: My Life with the First Ladies* (1973), pp. 271–272.
610   Eight minutes after her physician: JFK to Fred Korth, Secretary of the Navy, August 12, 1963, Pierre Salinger Papers, box 10. JFKPL.
610   At 6:25 A.M. on the third: Transcript of news conference with Pierre Salinger, August 9, 1963, Salinger Papers. JFKPL.
610   Eunice left Hyannis Port: BG, September 9, 1963.
610   "Did John Kennedy have . . .": Interview, Mike Feldman.
611   "They were trying to blackmail . . .": Interview, Evelyn Lincoln.
611   "Hoover hated . . .": Interview, Edwin O. Guthman.
612   overseeing efforts in New York: AP, BG, January 17, 1963.
612   "I've no idea . . .": BT, April 25, 1963.
612   "He'd make a wonderful . . .": BG, April 22, 1963.
613   Lincoln had become convinced: Interview, Evelyn Lincoln.
614   When she arrived back: BG, September 23, 1963.
614   she announced that: ibid.
614   "Where did you get that?": Interview, Evelyn Lincoln.
614   "Kennedy said to me . . .": Interview, Evelyn Lincoln.
615   "improper for the wife . . .": *Newsweek*, October 28, 1963.

615 "Touring with her sister . . .": BG, October 29, 1963.

615 "an alive and vital person": Ben Bradlee. *Conversations with Kennedy* (1975), p. 219.

616 "Now does anybody want . . .": Interview, Sister Joanne Frey.

617 "You know, last night . . .": William Manchester. *The Death of a President: November 20–November 25, 1963* (1967), p. 120.

618 "How pleasant . . ." ibid., p. 154.

618 at St. Coletta's, Rosemary sat: *New York Herald Tribune*, November 23, 1963.

618 "Something's happened . . .": Manchester, p. 208.

619 "these things happen. It's not going . . .": Interview, REFK. RCP.

619 "Don't worry . . .": Dallas, p. 14.

619 "Jack is having . . .": RK, p. 442.

619 "It looks bad . . .": Manchester, p. 209.

620 "Joey, we must go on . . .": Interview, Joseph Gargan.

620 At Maria's third-grade class: Marie Brenner, "Growing Up Kennedy," *Vanity Fair*, February 1986, p. 58.

620 his first instincts: Manchester, p. 199.

620 Pat had been with her maid: Manchester, p. 145 and 256.

620 Peter was up at Lake Tahoe: Spada, p. 344.

620 A multitude of people: Spada, p. 348.

621 Ebbins walked: Interview, Milt Ebbins.

621 "Oh, Jesus . . .": Saunders, p. 232.

622 "Daddy, Daddy, there's been . . .": Dallas, p. 19.

622 "in the usual sense . . .": FC.

622 Eunice buried her head: There are several contradictory accounts of the manner in which JPK learned about JFK's death. This rendering of the story is based firstly on REFK's tape-recorded recollections to Robert Coughlan. Mrs. Kennedy confided to the author of her autobiography that her daughter, EKS, told her husband of JFK's death. But in Mrs. Kennedy's published autobiography, as in William Manchester's largely authoritative book, Ted Kennedy told Mr. Kennedy the following morning. REFK's original account to Coughlan is confirmed by Rita Dallas's recollections in *The Kennedy Case*, and also by Frank Saunders in *Torn Lace Curtain*. Saunders remembers how the family pretended that the Kennedy patriarch was not told until the next day. The shame, if there is any, is not in Senator Kennedy's deep grief, but in the apparent belief in the family and presumably with the senator himself that he had not acted as he should have acted. The author specifically asked EKS her own recollections, telling her that if she did not contradict him he was going to say that she had told her father upon her arrival in Hyannis Port. EKS declined to make any comment.

623   "I think Miss Shaw . . .": Oral history, Mrs. Janet Auchincloss. JFKPL.

623   "Who is that?": Oral history, Mrs. Janet Auchincloss. JFKPL.

624   "Jackie, what can I . . .": FC.

624   "We don't want to hear . . .": Interview, Milt Ebbins, and Spada, p. 349.

624   The following evening Bobby: Manchester, p. 555.

625   "If Jackie can do it . . .": Manchester, p. 540.

625   Rose was on the verge: Manchester, p. 582.

625   "the service was sad . . .": Manchester, p. 586.

625   "John, you can salute . . .": ibid., p. 590.

625   Jackie took Mary Ryan: Interview, Mary Ryan.

626   his Navy dog tags: Dave Powers confirms that Mary Ryan was given one of John F. Kennedy's two sets of dog tags. The other set was given to Richard Cardinal Cushing. Richard Cardinal Cushing Oral History. JFKPL.

626   "Mommy, did they love . . .": FC.

628   "Sister, we were just riding . . .": Interview, Sister Joanne Frey.

628   family flew up to Hyannis Port: RK, p. 448.

629   "History . . . it's what those bitter . . .": Theodore H. White. *In Search of History: A Personal Adventure* (1978), p. 523.

629   "Strange for someone to want . . .": Interview, Gloria Guinness. RCP.

630   "I will tell you one thing . . .": Interview, Charles Bartlett.

630   "Noon was the only time . . .": Interview, John Linehan.

630   time with her sister-in-law: RK, p. 455.

631   Rose never talked to her son: Interview, REFK. RCP.

631   One evening at a dinner party: Interview, Coates Redmon.

632   "He was with her a great . . .": Interview, REFK. RCP.

632   "After Jack's death, Jackie . . .": Interview, Paul "Red" Fay.

632   "I was saying something . . .": Interview, Murray Kempton.

632   With Jackie he exchanged personal notes: The Lyndon Baines Johnson Presidential Library contains an eclectic collection of documents concerning Jacqueline Kennedy and other Kennedys, from obscure newspapers to the *National Enquirer*, the tabloid that is generally not considered presidential reading material.

633   Eunice had not let even a week: Leonard Mayo remarks at 1983 Conference on Mental Retardation. JFKPL.

633   walked hand-in-hand: BG, September 16, 1964.

633   "I don't ever remember . . .": Interview, Patti Blair Brown.

634   In April she flew up: BG, April 11, 1964.

635   "Hi, Joansie . . .": James MacGregor Burns. *Edward Kennedy and the Camelot Legacy* (1976), p. 121.

635   "She's the first candidate's wife . . .": Jane Clancy, "The Phenomenal Joan," November 8, 1964, clipping at BUCL.

635   In July after her summer camp: BG, July 23, 1964.
635   Eunice traveled to Philadelphia: BG, August 21, 1964.
635   a lesson she had learned: BG, November 7, 1965.
635   "feeling fine": BG, August 24, 1964.
636   "the member of the Kennedy clan . . .": *New York World Tele-gram*. Illegible date on this 1964 clipping in Robert Kennedy Papers. JFKPL.
636   "He was having an affair . . .": Off-the-record interview.
636   Staff members saw the candidate and Jackie: Interview, V. V. Harrison.
636   "Jackie would call all the time . . .": Off-the-record interview with a woman who worked for several years as a secretary to Bobby Kennedy.
636   "The former First Lady and . . .": *New York Express*, October 19, 1964.
636   Bobby had reportedly vetoed: *New York World-Telegram*, August 28, 1964, box 34, RFK Senate Papers, 1964 Campaign. JFKPL.
636   "RFK does not want much . . .": Unsigned press memo in Senatorial Campaign folders in Robert Kennedy papers. JFKPL.
637   "Robert F. Kennedy's secret weapon . . .": *New York World Telegram*, October 27, 1964, Robert Kennedy papers. JFKPL.
637   "I know you were expecting . . .": *New York Post*, September 30, 1964.
637   spent the morning at Kenneth's: Schedule of Mrs. Joseph P. Kennedy for October 19, Robert Kennedy Senate campaign papers, Robert Kennedy papers. JFKPL.
637   attended two exclusive campaign: Schedule of Mrs. Joseph P. Kennedy for October 20, Robert Kennedy Senate campaign, Robert Kennedy papers. JFKPL.
638   "You mean I'm never . . .": Spada, p. 364.
639   a separation agreement: Separation agreement between Patricia K. Lawford and Peter S. Lawford, December 17, 1965. ASU.
639   "I think I did the best joke . . .": Interview, Dick Livingston.
640   Marcher called over a waiter: Interview, Royal Marcher.
641   "Even during the divorce . . .": Doris Shapiro. *We Danced All Night: My Life Behind the Scenes with Alan Jay Lerner* (1990), p. 73.
642   "could see her smile . . .": Shapiro, p. 108.
642   a clerk to hold: Shapiro, p. 110.
642   "Who was it?": Shapiro, p. 162.
643   Jean sat next to the lyricist: Gene Lees. *Inventing Champagne: The World of Lerner and Lowe* (1990), p. 239.
643   "a very romantic figure": Lees, p. 240.
644   "What Jean got . . .": This account of the relationship between

Jean Smith and Alan Jay Lerner is based on an on-the-record interview with Milt Ebbins, an off-the-record interview with an intimate observer of most of the events, four other off-the-record interviews, and the previously noted books by Doris Shapiro and Gene Lees.

644   "I think Steve loved . . .": Interview, Jan Amory.

645   "I thought you should see this": REFK to RFK, September 17, 1965. Robert Kennedy papers, Senate Correspondence, personal file, 1964–1968. JFKPL.

645   "I'm so embarrassed": Interview, Charles Bartlett.

645   a crowd of three hundred: BG, July 2, 1965.

645   "Bloody Mary and a cheeseburger": *Time*, January 8, 1965.

646   "start working to soften . . .": Confidential Memo from "Liz" to "The President," April 1, 1966, 10:45 A.M. LBJPL.

646   "Tear this up . . .": "LBJ/mf," April 1, 1966, 9:30 P.M. LBJPL.

646   "I was just wondering . . .": Jacqueline Kennedy to Lady Bird Johnson, April 8, 1966. LBJPL.

646   "How incredibly thoughtful . . .": Jacqueline Kennedy to President Lyndon Johnson. LBJPL.

646   Fourteen-year-old Kathleen penned: KK to President and Mrs. Johnson, September 6, 1965. LBJPL.

647   "Jacqueline often fears . . .": ASK, p. 103.

647   "But the world has no right . . .": undated letter JFK to "Dear Arthur." ASP.

647   "Oh, Jack, I'm so sorry . . .": The manuscript of *A Thousand Days* is in Arthur Schlesinger Jr. papers at the JFKPL. In the finished book, Schlesinger emotionally distances Jack Kennedy from the material, making the president's thoughts the author's interpretation. Schlesinger writes: "He was never worried; he loved her as she was." ASK, p. 103.

647   with the stipulation: On May 9, 1966, Fay's editor Evan Thomas wrote Robert Kennedy that he had agreed to show Kennedy the finished manuscript and that he was under the impression that Fay knew about the stipulation. PFP.

648   "I don't want to read . . .": PFP.

648   "Leave it": Fay manuscript in Myrick Land Papers, box 5, file 20, Boston University.

648   Eunice was instrumental; Memo from Jack Valenti to Lyndon Johnson, August 31, 1965; and Eunice K. Shriver to Jack Valenti, April 30, 1965. LBJPL.

648   Manchester's questions written: Memo from Jack Valenti to Lyndon Johnson, May 11, 1965. LBJPL.

649   "It is not difficult to understand . . .": BH, December 18, 1966.

649   "Do you know what . . .": Interview, Gloria Guinness. RCP.

649   one of the best dressed: Mary Cremmen, "Chic Rose, 76, Fashion First," BG, January 4, 1965.

649   Rose traveled to several: Helen Keyes, "Europe Remembers," *This Week*, May 23, 1965.

650   Ted sometimes got down: Interview, Wyatt Dickerson.

650   "someone as nice . . .": Poem by Caroline Kennedy. RCP.

651   "You were always tense . . .": Interview, John Ryan, RCP, confirmed by author interview.

652   "Why Ted!": AS, p. 901.

652   repeated Ethel's refrain: AS, p. 902.

652   Pat was not so vocal: Jack Newfield. *Robert Kennedy: A Memoir* (1969), p. 195.

652   "This is going to cost . . .": ibid., p. 203.

652   Jackie was not quiet: AS, p. 907.

652   "At stake is not simply . . .": quoted in AS, p. 918.

652   "If Joe were himself . . .": Interview, Gloria Guinness, RCP.

653   "Do you know . . .": AS, p. 921.

653   "Looks like we're going . . .": Dallas, p. 301.

654   In February of 1967: Peter Hamill, "The Woman Behind Bobby Kennedy," *Good Housekeeping*, April 1968, p. 164, and AP, May 19, 1967.

654   board small planes: *Washington Daily News*, April 17, 1968.

654   he got the stewardesses: Interview with Richard "Dick" Tuck.

655   "I believe in discipline . . .": NYT, April 20, 1968.

655   "I think Mrs. Kennedy . . .": *D.C. Examiner*, May 2–4, 1968.

655   A few weeks after Kopson's: AP, May 2, 1968, and *New York Post*, May 3, 1968, Robert Kennedy files. JFKPL.

655   "Most of the wives . . .": James J. Kilpatrick, "Matching up at Bobby's," April 23, 1968, unidentified clipping. JFKPL.

655   Sarge had just been named: NYT, April 19, 1968.

656   believed she was campaigning: Interview, EKS.

656   "I felt a little torn . . .": Interview, EKS.

656   "Jean did better in Salt Lake . . .": Pat Lawford, ed. *That Shining Hour* (privately printed), p. 282.

656   "It's our own money . . .": *Women's Wear Daily*, May 9, 1968.

657   "Oregonians couldn't care less . . .": Oral history, Edith Green. JFKPL.

657   She not only visited: Unpublished manuscript on Joan Kennedy by Laura Bergquist Knebel, LB.

657   reorganized the campaign: Newfield, p. 274.

658   Diane Broughton had: Interview, Diane Broughton.

658   "Jean literally pushed me . . .": Diane Broughton, "William Kennedy Smith, the Accused," *Thumper*, November/December 1991, p. 3.

659   romped on the foggy beach: AS, p. 980.

659   "For Christ's sake . . ." David, p. 187.

660   "And now on to Chicago . . .": Robert Blair Kaiser. *"R.F.K. Must Die"* (1970), p. 24.

660   "Take care of Ethel": Warren Rogers. *When I Think of Bobby: A Personal Memoir of the Kennedy Years* (1993), p. 154.

661   Seventeen-year-old Irwin Neal Stroll fell: Police interview with Irwin Neal Stroll, Courtesy of Dan Moldea, and Kaiser, p. 32.

661   Broughton put a blanket: Interview, Diane Broughton; *Los Angeles Times*, May 2, 1984, Part V; *Los Angeles Herald Examiner*, April 29, 1984. Theodore White told the United Press International that David was left alone in the hotel room and that he found the young man "awake before the television screen, devastated at the sight he had just seen." White was a man of distinguished reputation, and variations of his account found their way into a number of books about the Kennedys. When David Kennedy died in April of 1984, numerous newspaper, magazine, and television stories repeated the story of David alone on the evening of his father's assassination. When Broughton gave her account of that evening, she found herself accused of exploiting a casual relationship with the Kennedy children. Steve Smith was one of the few people who knew the truth, and on May 24, 1984, wrote Broughton thanking her for "setting the record straight." The author has a copy of this letter. David was taken from the bungalow to a room at the Beverly Hills Hotel where he stayed with a number of Kennedy friends. It is possible that White saw him there hours later and believed that David had been left alone.

661   Jean forced her way: Rogers, p. 163.

661   she struck the man: Behrmann police interview and untitled clipping "Amid Shouts of victory, the torch," RFK Papers, box 6, '68 presidential campaign, 1968. JFKPL.

662   pushed her shoulder down: Rogers, p. 165.

662   "Do you feel as badly . . .": Saunders, p. 321.

662   Eunice kept her scheduled appointment: *Le Monde*, June 7, 1968. FNL.

663   "Ted more than anyone else . . .": *Good Housekeeping*, September 1969, p. 77.

663   "No, it can't have happened . . .": Francine Klagsbrun and David Whitney, eds. *Assassination: Robert F. Kennedy: 1925–1968* (1969), p. 47.

663   Ted stood in the bathroom: Background interview.

663   "The Church is . . .": quoted in AS, p. 983.

663   By six-thirty P.M. the machine: "Surgeon gave no hope for RFK," Boston(A), undated clipping, Robert Kennedy files. JFKPL.

663   they planned the funeral: Jean Stein and George Plimpton, eds. *American Journey: The Times of Robert Kennedy* (1970), p. 340.

664   pushed Sarge away: Interview, Herbert Kramer, who worked on Sargent Shriver's unfinished autobiography.

664   "My brother need not . . .": quoted in James MacGregor Burns. *Edward Kennedy and the Camelot Legacy* (1976), pp. 147–148.

664   "I came away from this . . .": Interview, Andrew, Duke of Devonshire.

666   first sexual experience: CH, p. 361.

667   Kathleen taught English: Interview, KKT.

667   "Oh, has our sister hurt . . .": CH, p. 362.

668   Eunice had suggested making the games national: Mrs. Shriver is not without competitors for the title of founder of Special Olympics. Her most vociferous challenger is Anne Burke, a Chicago attorney who as a youthful physical-education instructor for the Chicago Park Districts went to the Kennedy Foundation with the idea of summer games. "Eunice is not the founder of the Special Olympics," Burke told the *Chicago Tribune* on August 22, 1991. Herbert Kramer, the longtime publicist for the foundation, recalled the meeting early in 1968 where Burke's plan was discussed and how Mrs. Shriver expanded the concept into a far more ambitious program than the one envisioned by Burke. Another candidate with a considerable right to claim partial credit is Dr. Frank Hayden, a Canadian academic who as a Kennedy Foundation consultant played an instrumental role in developing the early ideas of Special Olympics. In essence, however, Mrs. Shriver *is* the founder of Special Olympics in a political sense. That first year she put together the money through the Kennedy Foundation, and had the power of her name to attract media attention and corporate help. Unquestionably, without her quarter of a century of dedicated interest, Special Olympics would never have become an organization in which people would consider it worthwhile arguing over who deserved to be considered its founder.

668   At her own home: Interview, EKS.

669   editors were not ready: Interviews with Herbert Kramer and EKS.

669   she was tearing around: *Time*, April 25, 1969, p. 47.

669   a Gallup poll named her: *Time*, April 25, 1969, p. 46.

670   "O.K., everybody, let's have . . .": *Time*, April 26, 1969, p. 47.

670   The main exception: Pat Lawford, ed., *That Shining Hour*, p. 224.

671   "Isn't she coming back . . .": Interview, V. V. Harrison.

671   "I pay you to teach them . . .": Off-the-record interview with a Washington tennis pro.

672   "I knew he had been here . . .": Interview, REFK, RCP.

672   totally inexplicable choice: Interview, REFK, RCP.

672 "She romanced him right on . . .": Interview, Larry Newman.
673 "I've known about it . . .": Saunders, p. 332.
673 "Of all the people . . .": Interview, Jacqueline Onassis. RCP.
673 heart-shaped rubies: *Washington Post*, October 24, 1968.
673 "aide de camp": Peter Evans, *Ari: The Life and Times of Aristotle Onassis* (1986), p. 17.
673 "Johnny loved to talk . . .": Interview, Rita Whitely.
674 "Now each house . . .": Interview, Jacqueline Onassis. RCP.
675 The young women were warned: Interview, Wendy Oates.
675 "Just a minute, I have to wait . . .": Interview, James Connor.
675 please forget buying: Interview, Gloria Guinness. RCP.
675 "a warm and loving man": Pat Lawford, ed. *That Shining Hour*, unpaged dedication.
676 "bereft of even that minimal spark": Interview, REFK. RCP.
676 "They're going to shoot . . .": quoted in BUH, p. 378.
676 accepted an invitation to attend: "Personal Notes of Mrs. Joseph P. Kennedy Regarding Ted's Tragic Accident, July, 1969," Saturday, July 19, 1969. RCP.
677 "I'm telling you the truth . . .": Dallas, p. 338.
677 "I never discussed . . .": Interview, REFK. RCP.
677 last name he did not even know: Interview, Teri Robinson, former assistant press secretary to Senator Edward M. Kennedy.
677 the diver who discovered: Damore, pp. 214–215.
678 "I always try to be . . .": Personal notes of Mrs. Joseph P. Kennedy regarding Ted's Tragic Accident, July, 1969. RCP.
678 "Where's Teddy? . . .": Dallas, p. 340.
678 led the dazed, bewildered Ted: Dallas, p. 339.
679 "I couldn't understand . . .": Damore, p. 142.
679 "How do you plead? . . .": Damore, p. 191.
680 ordered them out: Dallas, p. 342.
680 directed her to leave: Damore, p. 203.
680 healthy enough that on the day: Interview, Harry Fowler.
681 Joan narrated: BH, August 6, 1969. BUCL.
681 afterwards vowed to be: BG, August 6, 1969. BUCL.
681 "In England the hotel maître d' passed . . .": Laura Bergquist manuscript, LB, and Interview, Joan Kennedy. Joan Kennedy confirmed that her mother became ill.
682 Joan suffered her third miscarriage: BG, August 29, 1969.
682 "It was after Chappaquiddick . . .": Interview, Joan Kennedy.
683 "You'd think that there would be . . .": Interview, Herbert Kramer.
684 The end was near: Dallas, pp. 350–352.
685 Jackie had not even stopped: ibid., p. 351.
685 Rose sat with the others: Dallas, p. 352.
686 "Nobody's ever going to . . .": Interview, Jacqueline Kennedy Onassis. RCP.

686	"I don't go . . .": Interview with Joseph Morgenstern, a former editor of *Newsweek*, present at the luncheon.
687	"Now that she's all alone . . .": Interview, Jacqueline Kennedy Onassis. RCP.
687	"She wasn't this gay, divine . . .": Interview, Gloria Guinness. RCP.
688	"We went ashore . . .": Interview, Gloria Guinness. RCP.
689	"always very nervous": Interview, KKT. RCP.
689	"A French secretary . . .": Interview, Sarge Shriver. BK.
690	everywhere they went they were late: Interview, Mary Ann Orlando, and *Washington Star*, November 9, 1969.
690	"One gathers that when . . .": *Washington Star*, November 9, 1969.
690	"We lived in the vast . . .": Marie Brenner, "Growing Up Kennedy," *Vanity Fair*, February 1986, p. 114.
690	the children had no idea: *Paris Match*, June 6, 1969, p. 12. FNL.
691	"My husband can make it . . .": KKT, Interview. RCP.
691	"Mother was a great traveler . . .": Interview, Jean Kennedy Smith.
692	As Chris Lawford recalled: CH, p. 373.
692	They untied boats: CH, p. 373.
692	"children tied up the family cook . . .": Interview, Harry Fowler.
692	"Those kids didn't see . . .": Interview, Larry Newman.
692	"I am a widow here . . .": Interview, Harry Fowler.
693	"You've dragged your family's . . .": CH, p. 382.
693	Bobby listened to his father: CH, p. 383.
694	Chris wrote his father: Christopher to Dear Daddy, April 10, 1972. ASU.
694	she asked to try on: Lawford and Schwartz, p. 235.
694	"it was not one . . .": Christopher to Dear Petro, April 4, 1976. ASU.
695	"Do you love . . .": Interview, Mr. and Mrs. Jim Connor.
696	"Grandma, do you want . . .": Interview, KKT. RCP.
696	Rose was intrigued enough: Interview, Mary Sanford. RCP.
697	living in the same corridor: Interview, KKT.
697	"I would define the Hard Society . . .": *Vogue*, May 1969, p. 140.
698	"Oh Mummy!": LB.
698	as ready for play as for work: Interviews, Herb Kramer and a former Kennedy Foundation official.
699	"It was never expected . . .": Interview, KKT.
699	"I'm glad women are working . . .": Laura Bergquist, "Kathleen Kennedy: Here Comes a Whole New Generation of Kennedys," LBP.
700	"I didn't say so but . . .": Interview, KKT.

700   "I wanted to get away . . .": Interview, KKT. LBP.

700   "NEVER": Interview, REFK. RCP.

701   "I don't want him to be president . . .": Interview, REFK. RCP.

701   McGovern's seventh choice: "Acceptance Speech by Sargent Shriver," *Vital Speeches*, August 8, 1972.

701   Eunice made a few campaign junkets: *Washington Star*, September 8, 1972.

701   fifteen-hour days: *US News and World Report*, October 30, 1972.

701   "He is tearing through . . .": *Washington Star*, October 15, 1972.

702   friends considered it an achievement: BG, August 8, 1972.

702   "I haven't finished . . .": BG, October 9, 1972.

702   "This will be quite . . .": *Washington Star*, November 8, 1972.

702   She was presented with the "Staszak Award": *The Washington Star*, November 8, 1972.

704   "My sons . . .": Interview, Joe Gargan.

704   Every morning during the winter: Interviews, Robert and Pat Coughlan.

705   "I think Rose realized that . . .": Interview, Robert Coughlan.

705   "She relived . . .": Interview, Jim Connor.

706   "That was a great mistake . . .": Interview, REFK. RCP.

706   "was the captive of her family": Interview, Robert Coughlan.

707   "I would get there . . .": Interview, Joan Kennedy.

708   "There are times of real despair . . .": Harrison Rainie and John Quinn. *Growing Up Kennedy: The Third Wave Comes of Age* (1983), p. 234.

709   "It's strange, but for some reason . . .": Joan Braden, "Joan Kennedy Tells Her Own Story," *McCall's*, August 1978.

709   "When I started having a drinking problem . . .": Interview, Joan Kennedy.

709   when she returned: Interview, Joan Kennedy.

710   "As both a priest . . .": Interview, Joan Kennedy.

710   "They have council . . .": Interviews, Joan Kennedy and Del Sharbutt.

711   "I think she welcomed us . . .": Interview, Charles Burke.

711   "They weren't going to spend . . .": Interview, Herbert Kramer.

711   set among cheap plastic flowers: BG, March 7, 1974.

711   When she returned from Paris: Gibson, p. 69.

711   one New Year's Eve not with Joan: BG, March 7, 1974.

711   "Whenever he could . . .": Interview, Jim Connor.

712   "goal oriented": *Chicago Tribune*, Jan 7, 1976.

713   Gloria had been at St. Coletta's: *Chicago Tribune*, January 7, 1976.

713   "Her mind is completely gone . . .": Interview, REFK. RCP.

713   "Bronxville": Interview, Sister Margaret Ann.

713   "When we returned . . .": Interview, Jim Connor.
713   "I saw them in the living . . .": Interview, Bob Davidoff.
714   in the winter of 1975: Photograph by Bob Davidoff.
714   "Kerry, look at Rosie's hair . . .": KMRK.
715   Not until almost five hours: AP, October 6, 1975.
715   "Are you looking for Eunice?": *Chicago Tribune*, October 6, 1975.
715   She spent an hour or more: Interview, Brad Blank.
715   "I just find Rosemary to be . . .": Interview, Anthony Shriver.
716   Blank cringed: Interview, Brad Blank.
716   grew dangerously dependent: Gibson, p. 46 and off-the-record interview with a Kennedy family member.
716   "Sometimes when I get all . . .": Interview, REFK. RCP.
717   no interest, and practically no knowledge: Interviews, Doris Kearns Goodwin and Kerry McCarthy.
717   "I want to maintain my posture . . .": KMRK.
717   "I appreciate your interest . . .": KMRK.
719   His former wife, Athina Livanos Onassis Blandford, died: Peter Evans. *Ari: The Life and Times of Aristotle Onassis* (1986), p. 293.
719   lunch at La Caravelle with Jack Anderson: ibid., p. 263.
720   have his wife wiretapped: Interview, Fred Otash and Heymann, p. 560.
720   "I met with Onassis and Meyer at P. J. Clarke's . . .": Interview, Fred Otash.
721   "Sometimes I just want to shake . . .": KMRK.
721   "She's divorced . . .": Interview, REFK, RCP, and REFK diary quoted in interview, RCP.
721   "Well, what was I to do?": Gibson, p. 40.
722   "Imagine!": KMRK.
722   "That's supposed to be funny . . .": Interview, Jean Kennedy Smith.
723   "I am sure you realize . . .": 1972 letter from REFK to Ted Kennedy. Original on wall of Edward Kennedy's senatorial office.
723   "The reason is . . .": REFK to Ted Kennedy, January 13, 1975. Original on wall of Edward Kennedy's senatorial office.
723   "by 1974 the house had changed . . .": Gibson, p. 102.
723   "My daughters are nice . . .": Interview, Kerry McCarthy.
724   "During one period in Hyannis Port . . .": Interview, REFK. RCP.
724   "Family friends insist . . .": BH, September 9, 1975.
725   "If you're not going to run . . .": BG, August 18, 1975.
725   "Poor Sarge, I hope he . . .": CH, p. 415.
725   "Teddy didn't do shit . . .": CH, p. 415.
726   "She's a perfectionist. . . .": Interview, Maria Shriver.
727   "The old man told them . . .": Interview, Dr. Herbert Kramer.

728   "I'm letting you off . . .": Interview, Maria Shriver. RCP.

728   "She was about as wide . . .": Interview, Jim Connor.

728   "Why can't you be thin . . .": Interviews, General Robert and Mrs. Robert Montague.

728   "My daughter wants . . .": Barbara Kevles, "The Kennedy Who Could Be President," *Ladies' Home Journal*, March 1976, p. 156.

728   "I think Mother has struggled . . .": Interview, Anthony Shriver.

729   In September of 1972: RK, p. 510.

729   five Secret Service agents: BG, September 13, 1972.

729   "I remember this one mean-spirited person . . .": Interview, John Sheehan.

729   Caroline was known by the: Off-the-record interviews with staff of the Concord Public Library.

729   had some overdue books: *Chicago Tribune*, November 28, 1973.

730   "The people behind me . . .": Interview, Caroline Kennedy. RCP.

730   "Joe exited her home . . .": KMRK and interviews with Kerry and Mary Lou McCarthy.

731   "The child is burning up": KMRK.

731   "Patrick was a severe . . .": Interview, Joan Kennedy.

732   "I tried to talk about . . .": Joan Braden, "Joan Kennedy Tells Her Own Story," *McCall's*, August 1978, p. 190.

732   she arrived drunk in Palm Beach: Interview, Jim Connor.

732   appeared in a silvery leather: *Washington Star*, September 23, 1970.

732   hot pants under a short, slashed skirt: *Washington Evening Star*, March 16, 1971.

733   "small signs of rebellion": Unpublished article on Joan Kennedy by Laura Bergquist Knebel. LB.

733   She told her secretary, Marcia Chellis: Marcia Chellis. *The Joan Kennedy Story: Living with the Kennedys*. New York, Simon and Schuster (1985) (paperback ed.), p. 42.

733   an interview to *Good Housekeeping*: *Chicago Tribune*, May 17, 1972.

733   "bored to tears . . .": Boston (UPI), October 18, 1972. BUCL.

733   "When one grows up feeling . . .": Joan Braden, "Joan Kennedy Tells Her Own Story," *McCall's*, August 1978, p. 193.

734   rammed into the rear of a vehicle: *Washington Star-News*, October 10, 1974, and November 6, 1974.

734   "Oh really, don't they have . . .": KMRK.

735   "It may be self-evident . . .": Interview, Joan Kennedy.

735   "We helped Ted out . . .": Interview, Luella Hennessey Donovan.

735 "Eunice has always been so supportive . . .": Interview, Joan Kennedy.

736 made a point of sitting: *National Enquirer*, April 13, 1976.

736 "violated every canon of honorable journalism": *Washington Star*, April 11, 1976, p. B3.

736 "She was a rag mop . . .": BUH, paperback and Burton Hersh, interview.

736 Joan moved up to an apartment: Joan Braden, "Joan Kennedy Tells Her Own Story," *McCall's*, August 1978, p. 193.

737 "barge in": Lester David, "Joan Kennedy: Her Search for Herself," *Ladies' Home Journal*, May 1979.

737 "Ted comes up . . .": Braden, p. 193.

737 at home drunk: Off-the-record interviews with two of Senator Kennedy's closest friends, and *Time*, November 5, 1979, p. 19.

737 "I don't know . . .": Lester David, "Joan Kennedy: Her Search for Herself," *Ladies' Home Journal*, May 1979, p. 111.

738 "There is nothing we can prescribe . . .": Richard E. Burke. *The Senator: My Ten Years with Ted Kennedy* (1992), pp. 190–191.

739 "The 1980 campaign was my high water . . .": Interview, Joan Kennedy.

740 Jean had pushed: Interview, Kerry McCarthy.

740 "One day it may be different . . .": Rainie, p. 20.

741 "The sensational pieces . . .": Jacqueline Kennedy to Laura Bergquist, Nov. 9, 1978. LB.

743 "That was ages ago . . .": BG, December 6, 1979.

743 "The senator looked embarrassed . . .": *Washington Post*, December 14, 1979.

744 "the man for the women of 'America' ": NYT, February 24, 1980.

744 she made campaign appearances: BG, July 21, 1980.

744 "I know you helped . . .": quoted in Davis, p. 759.

744 "Do you know what time it is?": Interview, Edward Kennedy. BK.

745 "And that night . . .": Chellis, p. 122.

745 "I want Eunice with me . . .": Burke, p. 228.

745 Jean had the unenviable task: Davis (paperback), p. 762.

746 "All right, then . . .": Background interview with campaign worker, confirmed by Pat Lawford.

746 "Sheila Rauch Kennedy, [who] was considered the best of all": Davis, p. 768.

746 driven up in his brown BMW to Harlem: *New York Post*, September 7, 1979, *Miami Herald*, September 18, 1979.

746 "White James": *New York Post*, September 7, 1979.

746 hustled to Boston: CH, p. 424.

746 sitting in a dreary room by himself: CH, p. 440.

746 been arrested in Aspen trying: CH, p. 438.

747   "who does not deserve . . .": CH, p. 437.

747   "One of the things I admire . . .": Interview, Melody Miller.

748   called his young son: Interview, Melody Miller.

748   "So, what's the good news?": CH, p. 442.

750   flew on alone: Interview, Joan Kennedy.

750   "Have you all had . . .": This account of Thanksgiving 1982 in
       Hyannis Port is based on an interview with the journalist
       Dotson Rader. Rader, a close friend of Pat Lawford's, had
       been asked by the Kennedy family to go around the United
       States determining what a broad range of Americans thought
       about Ted Kennedy running again for president. Rader gave
       his report to the Kennedys that Thanksgiving and was there
       for family meals and discussions.

753   "When I'm introduced . . .": Sydney Lawford to "Dear
       Daddy," March 20, 1980. ASU.

753   considered him a pathetic failure: Interview, Pat Seaton Stew-
       art.

754   "white as a sheet, cold as an ice cube . . .": Washington Post,
       September 26, 1983.

755   "own state of mind": Interview, Joan Kennedy.

756   switched the place cards: Interview, Pat Seaton Lawford.

758   Rose collapsed during dinner: Miami Herald, April 21, 1984.

759   "neuro-electric therapy": Gibson and Schwarz, p. 195.

759   David had hoped that it might help: Palm Beach Times,
       May 3, 1984.

759   "David, this is very sad . . .": Boston Herald, October 13,
       1984.

760   The employee looked at him standing: Palm Beach Times,
       May 24, 1985, and Palm Beach Daily News, May 25, 1985.

760   the security guard turned him away: Palm Beach Daily News,
       October 25, 1984.

760   "really was in bad shape . . .": Deposition of Howell
       VanGerbig Jr., as reported in Miami Herald, May 18, 1985.

760   the talk over the dinner table: Caroline Kennedy's deposition
       as excerpted in Miami Herald, January 15, 1985.

760   "Mrs. Kennedy from Boston": Sun-Sentinel, April 26, 1984,
       Palm Beach Daily News, February 20, 1985.

761   Caroline and Sydney arrived back: Palm Beach Times, Janu-
       ary 15, 1985.

761   Caroline remembers that they said: Caroline Kennedy deposi-
       tion as detailed in Palm Beach Daily News, January 15, 1985.

761   An observer watched as Sydney began to cry: BG, April 27,
       1984.

761   "as quickly as possible . . . so . . .": Palm Beach Daily News,
       October 25, 1984.

762   Dorr had eagerly volunteered: Palm Beach Daily News, De-
       cember 4, 1985.

762   injected into his groin: *Orlando Sun Sentinel*, May 25, 1984.

762   pleaded nolo contendere, were fined: *Palm Beach Daily News*, December 4, 1985.

762   significant traces of cocaine and Demerol: *Palm Beach Post*, April 25, 1985.

762   "clean up": *Miami Herald*, April 25, 1985.

763   "Do you know if anybody . . .": *Miami Herald*, October 16, 1984.

763   "It sounds like [by the way] you're . . .": *Orlando Sun Sentinel*, January 15, 1985.

764   "Every time I see her . . .": Interview, Caroline Kennedy. RCP.

764   working on an oral-history documentary: BG, July 2, 1983.

764   "interviewed miners, miners' wives and . . .": Caroline Bouvier Kennedy résumé on file at the library of the BG.

764   Associated Press was buying some: *Washington Post*, February 21, 1974.

765   call a halt to the sale: *Washington Post*, March 3, 1974.

765   "Everyone hates me! . . .": *Chicago Tribune*, November 23, 1975.

765   Caroline came within minutes of being killed: BG, October 25, 1975.

767   tears in her eyes: *Chicago Tribune*, July 20, 1986.

767   Maria talking authoritatively: Winzola McLendon, "Caroline Kennedy: Living Down a Legend," *McCall's*, November 1974, p. 42.

767   "I saw the impact . . .": Interview, Maria Shriver.

768   invited to fly back with the family: Nancy Lloyd, "Maria Shriver: Up Close and Personal," *Good Housekeeping*, February 1993, p. 102.

768   "When one has money . . .": Wendy Leigh, *Arnold* (1990), p. 178.

769   Maria flew off to New York: *Los Angeles Times*, August 31, 1985.

769   "Maria was first-rate with celebrities . . .": Peter McCabe, *Bad News at Black Rock* (1987), p. 235.

770   the whispered story was that Maria was pregnant: Marvin Kitman, "Blues at 'The CBS Morning News,' " *The New Leader*, July 14, 1986.

770   "I think I was obsessive . . .": Interview, Maria Shriver.

771   "following the stream . . .": *People*, June 6, 1983.

771   "I didn't want . . .": *People*, June 6, 1983, p. 63.

771   austere, primitive house: Interview, Bob Davidoff.

772   "David massaged . . .": Susan Issacs, "What's It Really Like to Be a Kennedy," *Parents*, November 1980, p. 91.

772   "It takes a while to change attitudes . . .": Interview, Kathleen Kennedy Townsend.

772   "made all the difference": quoted in Harrison Rainie, "To Be Young, Female and Kennedy," *Women's Day*, April 2, 1985.

773   "A professor with a Harvard Ph.D. . . .": KKT, "A Rebirth of Virtue: Religion and Liberal Renewal," *Washington Monthly*, February 1982, p. 24.

773   an essay titled "The Forgotten Virtue of Voluntarism": KKT, "The Forgotten Virtue of Voluntarism," *The Washington Monthly*, October 1983, pp. 10–16, 48–50.

773   "she could be the first female president of the United States": Interview, Charles Peters.

773   "When we were young, my mother used to say . . .": Barbara Matusow, "Move Over, Teddy," *Washingtonian*, November 1988, p. 161.

774   seventy-year-old Victorian house: NYT, January 7, 1986, p. B6.

774   "personally advocated acts of violence . . .": *Philadelphia Inquirer*, November 21, 1984.

775   her appearance was scrutinized: *The Washington Post*, March 5, 1986.

776   ropes of pearls: Interview, Marty Mazzone.

776   "I'm obviously pro-choice . . .": Interview, KKT.

776   "The other day someone said . . .": Sara Martin, "A New Kennedy on the Campaign Trail," *The Washington Women*, August 1986, p. 22.

777   "What we need and want . . .": Maureen Orth, "Carrying the Torch," *Vogue*, July 1986, p. 88.

777   a family income in 1985 of $174,434: *Washington Post*, April 24, 1986.

777   "the challenge for Kathleen Kennedy Townsend is to get elected . . .": *Vogue*, July 1986, p. 91.

777   more than ten thousand doors: *The Philadelphia Inquirer*, September 7, 1986, p. A1.

777   "Forget it. . . .": *Vogue*, p. 91.

780   "The church is very chauvinistic . . .": Interview, KKT.

781   Congress passed a resolution: *USA Today*, July 14, 1990, p. 10A.

781   "Go ahead and eat, Mother . . .": Two off-the-record interviews including one with a nurse involved with REFK's care.

781   "We didn't tell Rose . . .": Interview, Joan Kennedy.

782   "Are you sure this is . . .": NYT, July 13, 1990.

782   "Ted made these quotes up": Interview, EKS.

782   "There's a presence about her . . .": Interview, Senator Edward Kennedy.

782   "I'm like old wine . . .": *Washington Post*, July 16, 1990.

783   she berated Kramer: Interviews with four of the guests.

783   brought tears to the eyes of many in the audience: BG, July 16, 1990.

783   McGovern sang: NYT, July 16, 1990, p. B5.

784   "Pat is impressed . . .": Interview, Dotson Rader.

784   wobbling on her: Interview, Larry Ashmead.

784   attended a splendid dinner party: Interview, Judith Green.

786   founder of the National Committee: Interview, Dotson Rader.

786   she ran into a telephone pole: Newsday, June 27, 1989.

787   four times its projected cost: Washington Post, November 30, 1980.

787   "I was not raised to speak . . .": Interview, Jean Kennedy Smith.

787   the names of America's media and cultural elite: PR Newswire, September 12, 1989, Compuserve.

788   flying to Ireland: Irish Times, November 1, 1984.

788   more than a thousand handicapped individuals: Newsday, June 21, 1989, p. 2.

788   "a healthy dose of good old-fashioned uplift . . .": NYT, September 8, 1989.

788   estimated at three million: New Bedford Standard-Times, November 15, 1981.

789   "Why do you go to church every day?": Interview, Anthony Shriver.

791   twenty million dollars: Figure provided by David Phelps.

791    $150,000: Salary figure confirmed by David Phelps.

792   "What drives Maria, whether she realizes it or not is her mother . . .": Nancy J. Perry, "Hail Maria," L.A. Style May 1993.

792   "When I started . . .": Interview, Maria Shriver.

792   grab a coffee or sandwich with Brandon Tartikoff: Interview, Doug Kriegel.

793   Cutting Edge with Maria Shriver: L.A. Style.

793   "I lied to you . . .": Los Angeles Times, June 28, 1991.

793   sprawling eight-thousand-square-feet house: Jean Vallely, "The Promoter," GQ July, 1986, p. 180.

794   "I've become my mother": L.A. Style.

795   Kennedys gave a million dollars: BG, July 25, 1983, and interview with Alan K. Borsari, Alverno Director.

796   "I'll go into her room . . .": Interview, Sister Margaret Ann.

796   Borsari believed that: Interview, Alan K. Borsari.

797   accelerated across the center line: Washington Times, January 17 and January 20, 1991.

797   when the authorities called Sarge: Interviews, General Robert Montague and Chris Montague.

798   two broken arms: Washington Times, January 20, 1991.

798   two major operations: Baltimore Sun, January 22, 1991.

799   "The Kennedys have a history . . .": Washington Post, June 12, 1990.

799   She had been working: BG, September 9, 1990.

800   Ted flew in Wednesday evening: Deposition of Senator Edward M. Kennedy, May 11, 1991, in re: investigation of William Kennedy Smith, "What I understand . . .": Deposition of Patrick J. Kennedy, May 1, 1991, in re: investigation of William Kennedy Smith.

801   She cringed at the idea: In her deposition in re: investigation of William K. Smith on April 30, 1991, Mrs. Smith was asked "You never went to Au Bar or any of those other places?" She replied: "No, thank God."

802   guests expected to include: BG, March 30, 1991.

803   "I'm distressed that someone is trying . . .": *Chicago Tribune*, May 12, 1991.

803   "grabbed me . . .": Deposition of ——— M.D., October 26, 1991 State of Florida Plaintiff, vs. William Kennedy Smith, Defendant.

804   "physically aggressive . . .": Deposition of October 26, 1991, p. 135.

804   "sex in a projection . . .": Deposition of October 26, 1991, p. 138.

804   "he tried to kiss me and in the struggle . . .": Deposition of ———, taken October 5, 1991, in State of Florida, Plaintiff, v. William Kennedy Smith, Defendant, p. 55.

804   "Since you have been sixteen years old . . .": Deposition of October 5, 1991, p. 150.

804   "Have you ever had intercourse . . .": Deposition of October 5, 1991, p. 155.

805   "When things get really tough, there's . . .": BH, May 16, 1991, p. 6.

806   "I just couldn't . . .": Interview, Larry Newman.

807   over six thousand athletes: Saint Paul *Pioneer Press*, July 21, 1991, p. 1.

807   the *Life* magazine: *Life*, November 1989.

808   "I look at all of you and think . . .": EKS: Family reception remarks, July 22, 1991, Minneapolis, Minnesota.

811   Jean tried to suppress her smile: The author was in the courtroom for most of the crucial moments in the trial, as described in this book. The courtroom descriptions are for the most part based on the author's own observations and tapes of the proceedings when he was present.

811   graduate of the same Manhattanville: NYT, December 6, 1991.

812   graduate of the Stone Ridge Country Day School: NYT, December 8, 1991.

813   "I'm very happy . . .": *The Miami Herald*, December 5, 1991.

814   "He tackled . . .": *The Miami Herald*, December 5, 1991.

814   "What he did to me . . .": *Sun-Sentinel*, December 6, 1991.

815   Ted had sat almost silent: NYT, December 7, 1991.

815   privately he was infuriated: Interviews with two close associ-
       ates of Senator Edward Kennedy.

818   "a stridency . . .": Manchester, p. 43.

818   Dallas civic leaders put together: *The Houston Post*, February
       9, 1992.

819   figured he would never marry: NYT, October 1, 1992.

820   "It sort of developed . . .": Interview, Senator Edward Ken-
       nedy.

820   "It just came . . .": Interview, Jean Kennedy Smith.

821   "They said I did charity work . . .": Interview, Jean Kennedy
       Smith.

821   *The Boston Globe* touted: BG, December 14, 1992.

821   "patron saint of Ireland": BG, March 13, 1993.

822   "Her life has been touched . . .": BG, June 10, 1993.

822   "I think of it all the time what . . .": Interview, Jean Kennedy
       Smith.

824   "Even if I have . . .": Interview, Rory Kennedy.

825   "That's what we are . . .": Interview, Joan Kennedy.

826   "lying before God": Interview, Sheila Rauch Kennedy,
       Primetime Live, ABC Television, January 7, 1994.

827   flew off to Ireland: *Chicago Tribune*, June 24, 1993.

827   The cancer spread: NYT, May 20, 1994.

829   Thursday the Kennedy women: *New York Daily News*,
       May 21, 1994.

829   "For us—and to my . . .": EKS commencement address to
       Loyola College graduating class, May 22, 1994. Courtesy of
       Special Olympics International.

830   As Eunice sat: The reflections of EKS are based on an inter-
       view conducted by the author on May 27, 1994, four days af-
       ter the funeral.

831   Joan sat: The reflections of Joan Kennedy during the funeral
       are based on an interview conducted by the author on May 27,
       1994, four days after the funeral.

831   For Caroline: Caroline Kennedy's reflections on her mother's
       death are based on interviews with intimate associates of the
       family.

832   For Kathleen: Kathleen Kennedy Townsend's thoughts during
       the funeral are based on an interview conducted by the author
       on May 27, 1994, four days after the funeral.

833   the nurses played them: This scene with REFK is based on an
       interview with Kerry McCarthy, who saw her great-aunt for
       several days in December of 1993.

833   looked out the window: Interview, Nancy Coleman.

Bibliography

Abbott, Edith. *Historical Aspects of the Immigration Problem*. New York: Arno Press, 1969 (c 1926).

Abbott, Edith. *Immigration: Select Documents and Case Records*. New York: Arno Press, 1969 (c 1924).

Adam, Ruth. *A Woman's Place*. London: Chatto & Windus, 1975.

Adams, George. *East Boston Directory*. Boston: Adams, 1849.

Adams, William Forbes. *Ireland and Irish Emigration to the New World from 1815 to the Famine*. New Haven: Yale University Press, 1932.

Ainley, Leslie G. *Boston Mahatma: A Biography of Martin Lomasney*. Boston: Bruce Humphries, Inc., 1949.

Akenson, Donald. *Being Had: Historians, Evidence and the Irish in North America*. Port Credit, Ontario: P. D. Meany, 1985.

Aldrich, Nelson W. *Old Money: The Mythology of America's Upper Class*. New York: Knopf, 1988.

Allen, Frederick Lewis. *Only Yesterday*. New York: Harper & Row, 1931, Perennial Library edition.

Allston, Margaret. *Her Boston Experiences: A Picture of Modern Boston Society and People*. Boston: Curtis, 1899.

Alsop, Joseph. *FDR, 1882–1945: A Centenary Remembrance*. New York: Viking, 1982.

Alsop, Joseph and Robert Kintner. *American White Paper: The Story of American Diplomacy and the Second World War*. New York: Simon and Schuster, 1940.

Amory, Cleveland. *The Proper Bostonians*. New York: E.P. Dutton & Company, Inc., 1947.

Anderson, Bonnie S. and Judith P. Zinnser. *A History of Their Own: Women in Europe from Prehistory to the Present*, Vol. II. New York: Harper & Row, 1988.

Anthony, Carl Sferrazza. *First Ladies: Volume II*. New York: William Morrow, 1990.

Anthony, Katharine. *Mothers Who Must Earn*. New York: Survey Associates and The Russell Sage Foundation, 1914.

Appleton, William S. *Fathers and Daughters: A Father's Powerful Influ-*

ence on a Woman's Life. New York: Doubleday, 1981, Berkley edition, 1984.

Arensberg, Conrad. *The Irish Countryman: An Anthropological Study*. New York: Macmillan, 1937.

Arensberg, Conrad and Solon Kimball. *Family and Community in Ireland*. Cambridge: Harvard University Press, 1940.

Argyll, Margaret Campbell, Duchess of. *Forget Not*. London: W.H. Allen, 1975.

Aries, Phillipe. *Centuries of Childhood: A Social History of Family Life*. Translated from the French by Robert Baldick. New York: Vintage Books, 1962.

Ashmore, Ruth. *Side Talks with Girls*. New York: Charles Scribner's Sons, 1903.

Associated Press. *Triumph and Tragedy: The Story of the Kennedys*. New York: Morrow, 1968.

Atkinson, Clarissa W., Constance H. Buchanan, and Margaret R. Miles, eds. *Immaculate and Powerful: The Female in Sacred Image and Social Reality*. Boston: Beacon Press, 1985.

Baldrige, Letitia. *Of Diamonds and Diplomats*. Boston: Houghton Mifflin, 1968.

Banks, Joseph Ambrose. *Victorian Values: Secularism and the Size of Families*. London: Routledge and Kegan Paul, 1981.

Banks, Olive. *Becoming a Feminist: The Social Origins of "First Wave" Feminism*. Athens, GA: University of Georgia Press, 1987.

Barrows, Esther G. *Neighbors All: A Settlement Notebook*. Boston: Houghton Mifflin, 1929.

Beard, George. *American Nervousness: Its Causes and Consequences*. New York: G.P. Putnam's Sons, 1881.

Beard, Mary Ritter. *Women's Work in Municipalities*. New York: D. Appleton-Century, 1915.

Beckett, J. C. *A Short History of Ireland*, sixth edition. London: Hutchinson, 1979.

Beebe, Lucius. *Boston and the Boston Legend*. New York: Appleton Century, 1935.

Bergquist, Laura and Stanley Tretick. *A Very Special President*. New York: McGraw-Hill, 1965.

Beschloss, Michael R. *Kennedy and Roosevelt: The Uneasy Alliance*. New York: Norton, 1980.

Birmingham, Stephen. *Jacqueline Bouvier Kennedy Onassis*. New York: Grossett & Dunlap, 1978.

Birmingham, Stephen. *Real Lace: America's Irish Rich*. New York: Harper & Row, 1973.

Birmingham, Stephen. *The Right People*. Boston: Little, Brown, 1958.

Bishop, James. *The Day Kennedy Was Shot*. New York: Funk & Wagnals, 1968.

Blanc, Marie Thérèse. *The Condition of Women in the United States: A Traveler's Notes*. Boston: Roberts Brothers, 1895.

Bliss Jr., Edward, ed. *In Search of Light: The Broadcasts of Edward R. Murrow 1938–1961.* New York: Knopf, 1967.

Blocker, Jack S. *American Temperance Movements: Cycles of Reform.* Boston: Twayne Publishers, 1989.

Blodgett, Geoffrey. *The Gentle Reformers: Massachusetts Democrats in the Cleveland Era.* Cambridge, MA: Harvard University Press, 1966.

Blythe, Ronald. *The Age of Illusion: Glimpses of Britain Between the Wars, 1919–1940.* Oxford: Oxford University Press, 1983.

Boorstin, Daniel J. *The Image: A Guide to Pseudo-Events in America.* New York: Atheneum, 1971.

Bordin, Ruth. *Francis Willard: A Biography.* Chapel Hill, NC: The University of North Carolina Press, 1986.

Bordin, Ruth. *Women and Temperance: The Quest for Power and Liberty, 1873–1900.* Philadelphia: Temple University Press, 1981.

Boyer, Peter J. *Who Killed CBS?: The Undoing of America's Number One News Network.* New York: Random House, 1988.

Braden, Joan. *Just Enough Rope.* New York: Villard, 1989.

Bradlee, Ben. *Conversations with Kennedy.* New York: Norton, 1975.

Brady Anna, compiler. *Women in Ireland: An Annotated Bibliography.* Westport, CT: Greenwood Press, 1988.

Braun-Ronsdorf, Margarete. *The Wheel of Fortune, Costumes since the French Revolution, 1789–1929.* London: Thames and Hudson, 1964.

Brewer, Eileen Mary. *Nuns and the Education of American Catholic Women, 1860–1920.* Chicago: Loyola University Press, 1987.

Briggs, Asa. *A Social History of England, 1815–1865.* New York: Viking, 1983.

Brooks, Van Wyck. *The Flowering of New England.* New York: E.P. Dutton & Co., Inc., 1936.

The Brothers of Mary. *The Polite Pupil: For the Use of Catholic Parochial and High Schools.* Dayton: 1912.

Brown, Dorothy M. *Setting a Course: American Women in the 1920s.* Boston: Twayne, 1987.

Brown, Lyn Mikel and Carol Gilligan. *Meeting at the Crossroads: Women's Psychology and Girls' Development.* Cambridge: Harvard University Press, 1992.

Brown, Peter D. and Schweizer, Karl W., eds. *The Devonshire Diary: William Cavendish Fourth Duke of Devonshire Memoranda on State of Affairs 1759–1762.* London: Offices of the Royal Historical Society, 1982.

Brown, Thomas. *JFK: History of an Image.* Bloomington, IN: Indiana University Press, 1988.

Brown, Thomas N. *Irish-American Nationalism 1870–1890.* Philadelphia: J.B. Lippincott, 1966.

Brownlee, W. Elliot. *Dynamics of Ascent: A History of the American Economy.* New York: Knopf, 1979.

Buck, Pearl S. *The Kennedy Women: A Personal Appraisal.* New York: Harcourt, 1969.

Buetow, Harold A. *Of Singular Benefit: The Story of Catholic Education in the United States.* New York: The Macmillan Company, 1970.

Bugg, Lelia Hardin. *The People of Our Parish: Being Chronicle and Comment of Katharine Fitzgerald, Pew-Holder in the Church of St. Paul the Apostle.* Boston: Marlier, Callanan, & Company, 1900.

Bullitt, Orville H., ed. *For the President: Personal and Secret Correspondence Between Franklin D. Roosevelt and Wilkliam C. Bullitt.* Boston: Houghton Mifflin, 1972.

Buni, Andrew and Alan Rogers. *City on a Hill.* Boston: Windsor Publications, 1984.

Burke, Richard E. *The Senator: My Ten Years with Ted Kennedy.* New York: St. Martin's Press, 1992.

Burns, James MacGregor. *Edward Kennedy and the Camelot Legacy.* New York: Norton, 1976.

Burns, James MacGregor. *John Kennedy: A Political Profile.* New York: Harcourt, 1960.

Busbey, Katherine G. *Home Life in America.* New York: Macmillan, 1910.

Busey, Samuel C. *Immigration: Its Evils and Consequences.* New York: De Witt & Davenport, 1856.

Butler, Elizabeth Beardsley. *Women and the Trades.* New York: Charities Publication Committee and the Russell Sage Foundation, 1909. (Part of *The Pittsburgh Survey: Findings in Six Volumes,* edited by Paul U. Kellogg.)

Butlin, R. A., ed. *Development of the Irish Town.* London: Croom Helm, 1977.

Byington, Margaret. *Homestead: The Households of a Mill Town.* New York: The Russell Sage Foundation, 1910.

Byrne, Rev. Stephan. *Irish Emigration to the United States.* New York: Catholic Publication Society, 1873.

Byrnes, James F. *All In My Lifetime.* New York: Harper and Brothers, 1958.

Cable, Mary. *The Little Darlings: A History of Child Rearing.* New York: Scribner's, 1975.

Caffrey, Kate. *'37–'39: Last Look Round.* London: Gordon & Cremonesi, 1978.

Calhoun, Arthur W. *A Social History of the American Family,* Vol. III. Cleveland, OH: The Arthur H. Clark Company, 1919.

Callan, Louise. *The Society of the Sacred Heart in North America.* London: Longmans, Green and Co., 1937.

Cameron, Gail. *Rose: A Biography of Rose Fitzgerald Kennedy.* New York: Putnam, 1971.

Campbell, Helen. *Prisoners of Poverty: Women Wage-Workers, Their Trades and Their Lives.* Boston: Robert Brothers, 1895.

Carmody, Denise L. and John T. Carmody. *Roman Catholicism: An Introduction.* New York: Macmillan Publishing Company, 1990.

Carr, William H. A. *Those Fabulous Kennedy Women.* New York: Wisdom, 1961.

Cassini, Oleg. *In My Own Fashion: An Autobiography.* New York: Simon and Schuster, 1987.

Cecil, Lord David. *The Young Melbourne.* London: Constable, 1939.

Cecil, Russell L., ed. *A Textbook of Medicine.* Philadelphia and London: W.B. Saunders Co., 1947.

Chambers, William. *Things as They Are in America.* London: W & R Chambers, 1854.

Chance, Mrs. Burton. *The Care of the Child.* Philadelphia: Penn, 1909.

Chellis, Marcia. *The Joan Kennedy Story: Living with the Kennedys.* New York: Simon and Schuster, 1985.

Cheshire, Maxine. *Maxine Cheshire, Reporter.* Boston: Houghton Mifflin, 1978.

Chuilleanáin, Eiléan Ní, ed. *Irish Women: Image and Achievement: Women in Irish Culture from Earliest Times.* Dublin: Arlen House, 1985.

Churchill, Winston. *The Second World War.* Vol 1, *The Gathering Storm.* Vol. 2, *Their Finest Hour.* Vol. 3, *The Grand Alliance.* Boston: Houghton Mifflin, 1948, 1949, 1950.

Churchill, Winston S. *Step by Step: 1936–1939.* New York: Putnam's, 1939.

Churchill, Winston S. *The Unrelenting Struggle.* Boston: Little, Brown, 1942.

Cita-Malard, Suzanne. *Religious Orders of Women.* Translated from French by George J. Robinson. New York: Hawthorn Books, 1964.

Clark, Dennis. *Hibernia America: The Irish and Regional Cultures.* New York: The Greenwood Press, 1986.

Clark, Sue Ainsllie and Edith Wyatt. *Making Ends Meet: The Income and Outlay of New York Working Girls.* New York: George H. Doran Company, 1918.

Clarke, Edward Hammond. *Sex in Education; or A Fair Chance for the Girls.* Boston: J. R. Osgood & Co., 1873.

Cleary, James Mansfield. *Proud Are we Irish: Irish Culture and History as Dramatized in Verse and Song.* Chicago: Quadrangle Books, 1966.

Clifford, Deborah Pickman. *Mine Eyes Have Seen the Glory: A Biography of Julia Ward Howe.* Boston: Little, Brown, 1979.

Clinch, Nancy Gager. *The Kennedy Neurosis.* New York: Grosset & Dunlap, 1973.

Clinton, Catherine. *The Other Civil War: American Women in the Nineteenth Century.* New York: Hill and Wang, 1984.

Cogan, Frances B. *All-American Girl: The Ideal of Real Womanhood in Mid-Nineteenth Century America.* Athens, GA: The University of Georgia Press, 1989.

Cohn, Roy. *McCarthy.* New York: New American Library, 1968.

Cole, Donald B. *Immigrant City: Lawrence, Massachusetts, 1845–1921.* Chapel Hill, NC: University of North Carolina Press, 1963.

Cole, Wayne S. *America First: The Battle Against Intervention, 1940–1941.* Madison, WI: University of Wisconsin Press, 1953.

Cole, Wayne S. *Charles A. Lindbergh and the Battle Against American In-

tervention in World War II. New York: Harcourt Brace Jovanovich, 1974.

Coles, Robert. *Privileged Ones: The Well-Off and the Rich in America*. Boston: Little, Brown, 1977.

Collier, Peter and David Horowitz. *The Kennedys: An American Drama*. New York: Summit Books, 1984.

Collier, Richard. *Eagle Day: The Battle of Britain, August 6–September 15, 1940*. New York: Dutton, 1966.

Colum, Mary. *Life and the Dream*. Garden City, NY: Doubleday, 1947.

Commonwealth of Massachusetts: State Department of Health. *The Food of Working Women in Boston*. Boston: Wright & Potter Printing Co., 1917.

Condren, Mary. *The Serpent and the Goddess: Women, Religion, and Power in Celtic England*. New York: Harper & Row, 1989.

Connell, K. H. *Irish Peasant Society*. Oxford: Clarendon, 1968.

Conway, Jill. *The Female Experience in 18th and 19th Century America: A Guide to the History of American Women*. Princeton: Princeton University Press, 1985.

Cook, Blanche Wiesen. *Eleanor Roosevelt*. Vol. One 1884–1933. New York: Viking, 1992.

Corry, John. *Golden Clan: The Murrays, the McDonnells, and the Irish American Aristocracy*. Boston: Houghton Mifflin, 1977.

Cott, Nancy F. *The Bonds of Womanhood*. New Haven: Yale University Press, 1977.

Cott, Nancy F. and Elizabeth H. Pleck. *A Heritage of Her Own: Toward a New Social History of American Women*. New York: Simon and Schuster, 1979.

Course of Study in the Academies and Parochial Schools of the Sisters of Notre Dame. Cincinnati: Notre Dame Press, 1895.

Craig, Gordon A. and Felix Gilbert, eds. *The Diplomats, 1919–1939*. Princeton: Princeton University Press, 1953.

Cramer, Rev. W. *The Christian Mother: The Education of Her Children and Her Prayer*. Translated by a Father of the Society of Jesus. New York: Benzinger Brothers, 1870, 1880 edition.

Crawford, Mary Caroline. *The College Girl of America*. Boston: L.C. Page & Co., 1905.

Crawford, Mary Caroline. *Famous Families of Massachusetts*. 2 Vols. Boston: Little Brown, 1930.

Crawford, Mary Caroline. *Romantic Days in Old Boston*. Boston: Little Brown, 1922.

Crawford, Mary Caroline. *Social Life in Old New England*. Boston: Little Brown, 1914.

Crewe, Quentin. *The Frontiers of Privilege*. London: Collins, 1961.

Cross, Robert D. *The Emergence of Liberal Catholicism in America*. Cambridge: Harvard University Press, 1958.

Cullen, James B. *The Story of the Irish in Boston*. Boston: J. B. Cullen, 1889.

Cullen, Mary, ed. *Girls Don't Do Honours: Irish Women in Education in the 19th and 20th Centuries*. Dublin: Women's Education Bureau, 1987.

Cullinan, Elizabeth. *House of Gold*. Boston: Houghton Mifflin Company, 1970.

Cunnington, Cecil Willett. *Feminine Attitudes in the Nineteenth Century*. New York: The Macmillan Company, 1936.

Curran, Robert. *The Kennedy Women: Their Triumphs and Tragedies*. New York: Lancer, 1964.

Cusack, Mary Frances. *Advice to Irish Girls in America*. New York: F. Pustet, 1886.

Cutler, John Henry. *"Honey Fitz": Three Steps to the White House*. Indianapolis and New York: The Bobbs-Merrill Company, Inc., 1962.

The Dallas Morning News, November 22: The Day Remembered As Reported By. Dallas, TX: Taylor, 1990.

Dallas, Rita with Jeanira Ratcliffe. *The Kennedy Case*. New York: Putnam's, 1973.

Dally, Ann. *Mothers: Their Power and Influence*. London: Weidenfield and Nicolson, 1976.

Daly, Mary. *The Church and The Second Sex*. New York: Harper Colophon edition, 1975.

Damore, Leo. *The Cape Cod Years of John Fitzgerald Kennedy*. Englewood Cliffs, NJ: Prentice-Hall, 1967.

Damore, Leo. *Senatorial Privilege: The Chappaquiddick Cover-Up*. Washington, DC: Regnery, 1988.

Damrell, Charles S. *A Half Century of Boston's Building*. Boston: Louis P. Hager, 1895.

David, Lester. *Ethel: The Story of Mrs. Robert F. Kennedy*. New York: World, 1971.

Davies, Marion. *The Times We Had*. Indianapolis: Bobbs-Merrill, 1975.

Davis, John. *The Bouviers: Portrait of an American Family*. New York: Farrar, Straus, 1969.

Davis, John. *The Kennedys: Dynasty and Disaster*. New York: McGraw Hill, 1984.

Davis, Kenneth S. *The Hero: Charles A. Lindbergh and the American Dream*. Garden City, NY: Doubleday & Company, Inc., 1959.

Day, Dorothy. *Loaves and Fishes*. New York: Curtis, 1972 (c 1963).

De Bedts, Ralph F. *Ambassador Joseph Kennedy 1938–1940: An Anatomy of Appeasement*. New York: Peter Lang, 1985.

De Courcy, Anne. *1939: The Last Season*. London: Thames and Hudson, 1989.

Degler, Carl N. *At Odds: Women and the Family from the Revolution to the Present*. New York: Oxford University Press, 1980.

Dehey, Elinor Tong. *Religious Orders of Women in the United States*. Hammond, IN: W.B. Conkey, 1913.

Demarco, William. *Enclaves: Boston's Italian North End*. Ann Arbor, MI: UMI Research Press, 1981.

Deshon, George. *Guide for Catholic Young Women, Especially for Those*

Who Earn Their Own Living. New York: Catholic Book Exchange, 1897 (c 1868).

Diner, Hasia R. *Erin's Daughters in America: Irish Immigrant Women in the Nineteenth Century*. Baltimore: Johns Hopkins University Press, 1983.

Dinneen, Joseph. *The Kennedy Family*. Boston: Little, Brown, 1959.

Dinneen, Joseph F. *The Purple Shamrock: the Hon James Michael Curley of Boston*. New York: W.W. Norton, 1949.

Ditzion, Sidney. *Marriage Morals and Sex in America: A History of Ideas*. New York: Octagon Books, 1975.

Doan, James E. *Women and Goddesses in Early Celtic History: Myths and Legend*. Boston: Northeastern University, 1967.

Dolan, Jay P. *The Immigrant Church: New York's Irish and German Catholics, 1815–1865*. Baltimore: Johns Hopkins Press, 1975.

Dominque, Robert A. *Greetings from Old Orchard Me: A Picture Post Card History*. Wilmington, MA: Hampshire, 1981.

Donnelly, Mabel Collins. *The American Victorian Woman: The Myth and the Reality*. New York: Greenwood Press, 1986.

Doyle, David Noel and Owen Dudley Edwards, eds. *America and Ireland, 1776–1976: The American Identity and the Irish Connection*. Westport, CT: Greenwood Press, 1980.

Drake, Samuel Adams. *The Old Boston Taverns and Tavern Clubs*. Boston: Cupples, 1886.

Drudy, P. J. *The Irish in America: Emigration, Assimilation and Impact*. Cambridge: Cambridge University Press, 1985.

Dublin, T. *Women at Work*. New York: 1979.

Duchess of Devonshire. *The House: A Portrait of Chatsworth*. London: Macmillan, 1982 (paperback 1987).

Dudden, Faye E. *Serving Women: Household Service in Nineteenth-Century America*. Middletown, CT: Wesleyan University Press, 1983.

Duff, John B. *The Irish in America*. Belmont, CA: Wadsworth Publishing Co., 1971.

Duis, Perry R. *The Saloon: Public Drinking in Chicago and Boston: 1880–1920*. Urbana and Chicago: University of Illinois Press, 1983.

Echols, Alice. *The Demise of Female Intimacy in the Twentieth Century*. Ann Arbor, Michigan: University of Michigan, 1978.

Edel, Matthew, Elliott D. Sclar, and Daniel Luria. *Shaky Palaces: Home-ownership and Social Mobility in Boston's Surburbanization (sic)*. New York: Columbia University Press, 1984.

Ellacott, S. E. *A History of Everyday Things in England*, Vol. V. London: Batsford, 1968.

Epstein, Barbara Leslie. *The Politics of Domesticity: Women, Evangelism, and Temperance in Nineteenth-Century America*. Middletown, CT: Wesleyan University Press, 1981.

Espaillat, Arturo. *Trujillo: The Last Caesar*. Chicago: Henry Regnery Company, 1963.

Evans, E. Estyn. *Irish Folk Ways*. London: Routledge & Kegan Paul, 1957.

Evans, E. Estyn. *The Personality of Ireland*. Cambridge: Cambridge University Press, 1973.

Evans, Peter. *Ari: The Life and Times of Aristotle Onassis*. New York: Summit, 1986.

Evans, Sara M. *Born to Liberty: A History of Women in America*. New York: The Free Press, 1989.

Exner, Judith, as told to Ovid Demaris. *My Story*. New York: Grove Press, 1977.

Faderman, Lillian. *Surpassing the Love of Men: Romantic Friendship and Love Between Women From the Renaissance to the Present*. New York: William Morrow, 1981.

Fay Jr., Paul B. *The Pleasure of His Company*. New York: Harper & Row, 1966.

Fellman, Anita Clair and Michael Fellman. *Making Sense of Self: Medical Advice Literature in Late Nineteenth-Century America*. Philadelphia: University of Pennsylvania Press, 1981.

Fenwick, S. J. and Benedict Joseph. *Memoirs to Service for the Future*, edited with an introduction by Joseph M. McCarthy. Yonkers, NY: U.S. Catholic Historical Society, 1978.

Fields, Suzanne. *Like Father, Like Daughter: How Father Shapes the Woman His Daughter Becomes*. Boston: Little, Brown, 1983.

Fitzgerald, John F. *Letters and Speeches of the Honorable John F. Fitzgerald Mayor of Boston, 1906–07, 1910–13*. Boston: Printing Department, 1914.

Fitzpatrick, Brendan. *Seventeenth-Century Ireland: The Wars of Religion*. Dublin: Gill and Macmillan, 1988.

Fitzpatrick, David. *Irish Emigration 1801–1921*. Dundalk: Studies in Irish Economic History No. 1, 1984.

Flamini, Roland. *Scarlett, Rhett, and A Cast of Thousands*. New York: Macmillan, 1975.

Fleming, Thomas J. *All Good Men*. Garden City, NY: Doubleday & Company, Inc., 1961.

Flower, Benjamin O. *Civilization's Inferno, or, Studies in the Social Cellar*. Boston: Arena, 1893.

Forbes, A. and J. W. Greene. *The Rich Men of Massachusetts*. Boston: Fetridge and Co., 1851.

Forbes, Anne McCarthy. *West Concord: Survey of Historical and Architectural Resources, Concord, Massachusetts*. Concord, MA: Concord Historical Commission, January, 1989.

Formisano, Ronald P. and Constance K. Burns. *Boston 1700–1990: The Evolution of Urban Politics*. Westport, CT: Greenwood Press, 1984.

Foster, R. F. *Modern Ireland 1600–1972*. New York: Viking Penguin, 1988.

Fowler, Marian. *Blenheim: Biography of a Palace*. New York: Viking, 1990.

Frank, Richard B. *Guadalcanal: The Definitive Account of the Landmark Battle*. New York: Random House, 1990 (paperback edition 1992).

Fraser, Flora. *The English Gentlewoman*. London: Barrie & Jenkins, 1987.

Frederic, Mrs. Christine. *The New Housekeeping: Efficiency Studies in Home Management*. Garden City, NY: Doubleday, 1918.

Frederick, Christine. *Household Engineering: Scientific Management in the Home*. Chicago: American School of Home Economics, 1920.

Freeman, Walter, M.D., and James W. Watts, M.D. *Psychosurgery: Intelligence, Emotion and Social Behavior Following Prefrontal Lobotomy for Mental Disorders*. Springfield, IL: Charles C. Thomas, 1942.

Frischauer, Willi. *Jackie*. London: Michael Joseph, 1976.

Frischauer, Willi. *Onassis*. New York: Meredith, 1968.

Frothingham, Charles W. *Six Hours in a Convent—or The Stolen Nuns!* Boston: Graves & Weston, 1857.

Furlong, Nicholas. *County Wexford in the Rare Oul' Times*, Vol. 1. Wexford: Old Distillery Press, 1985.

Galbreth, Lillian. *The Homemaker and Her Job*. New York: D. Appleton-Century Co., 1927.

Gallagher, Mary Barell. *My Life with Jacqueline Kennedy*. New York: McKay, 1969.

Garland, Joseph E. *Boston's Gold Coast: The North Shore, 1890–1929*. Boston: Little, Brown and Company, 1981.

Gay, Peter. *The Education of the Senses (The Bourgeois Experience: Victoria to Freud, vol. 1)*. New York: Oxford University Press, 1984.

Gay, Peter. *The Tender Passion (The Bourgeois Experience: Victoria to Freud, vol. 2)*. New York: Oxford University Press, 1986.

Gehman, Richard. *Sinatra and His Rat Pack*. New York: Belmont, 1961.

Gentry, Curt. *J. Edgar Hoover: The Man and the Secrets*. New York: Norton, 1991.

Gibson, Barbara with Caroline Latham. *Life with Rose Kennedy*. New York: Warner Books, 1986.

Gibson, William. *A Mass for the Dead*. New York: Atheneum Publishers, 1968.

Gilbert, Martin and Richard Gott. *The Appeasers*. Boston: Houghton Mifflin Company, 1963.

Goddard Ph.D., Henry Herbert. *Feeble-Mindedness: Its Causes and Consequences*. New York: Macmillan, 1914.

Goodwin, Doris Kearns. *The Fitzgeralds and the Kennedys*. New York: Simon and Schuster, 1987.

Graves, Robert and Alan Hodges. *The Long Week End: A Social History of Great Britain, 1918–1939*. New York: The Macmillan Company, 1941.

Graves, Robert and Alan Hodge. *The Long Week End: A Social History of Great Britain, 1919–1939*. London: Faber and Faber, 1940.

Greeley, Andrew M. *The Catholic Experience: An Interpretation of the History of American Catholicism*. New York: Doubleday, 1967.

Greeley, Andrew M. *That Most Distressful Nation*. Chicago: Quandrangle, 1972.

Greeley, Dana McLean. *Know These Concordians*. Concord: 1975.

Green, Constance McLaughlin. *Holyoke, Massachusetts: A Case History of the Industrial Revolution in America.* New Haven: Yale University Press, 1939.

Green, Harvey. *The Light of the Home: An Intimate View of the Lives of Women in Victorian America.* New York: Pantheon, 1983.

Green, Martin. *The Problem of Boston: Some Readings in Cultural History.* New York: W.W. Norton, 1966.

Gunn, Thomas B. *The Physiology of New York Boarding Houses.* New York: Mason Brothers, 1857.

Hageman, Alice L., ed. *Sexist Religion and Women in the Church: No More Silence!* New York: Association Press, 1974.

Halbert, Stephen and Brenda Halpert, eds. *Brahmins and Bullboys: G. Frank Radway's Boston Album.* Boston: Houghton Mifflin, 1973.

Hale, Edward Everett. *Letters on Irish Emigration.* Boston: Phillips, Sampson, 1852.

Hale, Edward Everett. *A New England Boyhood.* Boston: Little, Brown, 1927.

Hall, Florence Howe. *The Correct Thing in Good Society.* Boston: Estes and Lauriat, 1888.

Hall, Florence Howe. *Social Customs.* Boston: Estes and Lauriat, 1887.

Hammond, William A. *Cerebral Hyperaemia; the Result of Mental Strain or Emotional Disturbance; the So-Called Nervous Prostration or Neurastnenia.* Washington: Brentano's, 1895.

Handlin, Oscar. *Boston's Immigrants: A Study in Acculturation.* Cambridge, MA: The Belknap Press of Harvard University Press, 1941, 1959.

Handlin, Oscar. *The Uprooted.* Boston: Little, Brown, 1951.

Hansen, Marcus Lee. *The Atlantic Migration 1607–1860,* report by Harper Torchstone, 1961. Cambridge, MA: Harvard University Press, 1940.

Hardyment, Christina. *Dream Babies: Three Centuries of Good Advice on Child Care.* New York: Harper & Row, 1983.

Hareven, Tamara K. *Family and Kin in Urban Communities 1700–1930.* New York: New Viewpoints, 1977.

Harris, Barbara J. *Beyond Her Sphere: Women and the Professions in American History.* Westport, CT: Greenwood Press, 1978.

Harrison Rainie and John Quinn. *Growing Up Kennedy: The Third Wave Comes of Age.* New York: G.P. Putnam's Sons, 1983.

Harrison, V. V. *Changing Habits: A Memoir of the Society of the Sacred Heart.* New York: Doubleday, 1988.

Harrisson, Tom. *Living Through the Blitz.* New York: Schocken Books, 1976.

Hayden, Dolores. *Redesigning the American Dream: The Future of Housing, Work, and Family Work.* New York: W.W. Norton & Company, 1982.

Hecht, Ben. *A Child of the Century.* New York: Simon and Schuster, 1954.

Hellerstein, Erna Olafson, ed. *Victorian Women: A Documentary Account* of Women's Lives in Nineteenth-Century England, France, and the United States. Stanford: Stanford University Press, 1981.

Herbst, Winfrid. Girlhood's Highest Ideal: Helpful Chapters to Catholic Girls at the Parting of the Ways. St. Naziani, WI: The Society of the Divine Savior, 1924.

Herlihy, Elizabeth M., ed. Fifty Years of Boston: A Memorial Volume. Boston: Boston Tercentenary Committee, 1932.

Hersh, Burton. The Education of Edward Kennedy. New York: Morrow, 1972.

Heymann, David. A Woman Named Jackie. New York: Lyle Stuart, 1989.

Hiner, N. Ray and Joseph M. Hawes. Growing Up in America: Children in Historical Perspective. Urbana, IL: University of Illinois Press, 1985.

Hinshaw, David. The Home Front. New York: G.P. Putnam's Sons, 1943.

Hitchcock, James. Catholicism and Modernity. New York: Seabury Press, 1979.

Hoffert, Sylvia D. Private Matters: American Attitudes toward Childbearing and Infant Nurture in the Urban North, 1800–1860. Urbana, IL: University of Illinois Press, 1989.

Holmes, Oliver Wendell. Dr. Holmes's Boston, ed. by Caroline Ticknor. Boston: Houghton Mifflin, 1915.

Holt, L. Emmett. The Care and Feeding of Children: A Catechism for the Use of Mothers and Children's Nurses. New York: Appleton, 1894 (also 1923 edition).

Hopper, Hedda. From Under My Hat. Garden City, NY: Doubleday, 1952.

Horney, Karen. The Neurotic Personality of Our Time. New York: W.W. Norton, 1937.

Horowitz, Helen Lefkowitz. Campus Life: Undergraduate Cultures from the End of the Eighteenth Century to the Present. New York: Alfred A. Knopf, 1987.

Hough, Richard and Denis Richards. The Battle of Britain: The Greatest Air Battle of World War II. New York: W.W. Norton, 1989.

Howard, Brett. Boston: A Social History. New York: Hawthorn, 1976.

Howe, Helen. The Gentle Americans. New York: Harper & Row, 1965.

Howe, M. A. De Wolfe. Boston, The Place and The People. New York: Macmillan, 1903.

Howe, M. A. De Wolfe. Memories of a Hostess. Boston: Atlantic Monthly Press, 1922.

Hyde, Francis Edwin. Cunard and the North Atlantic, 1840–1973. Atlantic Highlands, NJ: Humanities Press, 1975.

Ickes, Harold L. The Secret Diary of Harold L. Ickes: The First Thousand Days 1933–1936. New York: Simon and Schuster, 1953.

Ickes, Harold L. The Secret Diary of Harold L. Ickes. Vol. 2. The Inside Struggle, 1936–1939. New York: Simon and Schuster, 1954.

Ickes, Harold L. The Secret Diary of Harold L. Ickes. Vol. 3. The Lowering Clouds, 1939–1941. New York: Simon and Schuster, 1954.

Jaquette, Jane, ed. Women in Politics. New York: John Wiley, 1974.

Jenkins, Alan. *The Forties*. New York: Universe Books, 1977.

Jones, Kenneth Paul, ed. *U.S. Diplomats in Europe, 1919–1941*. Santa Barbara, CA: ABC-Clio, 1981.

Josephson, Hannah. *The Golden Threads: New England's Mill Girls and Magnates*. New York: Duell, Sloan and Pearce, 1949.

Josephson, Matthew. *The Money Lords*. New York: Weybright and Talley, 1972.

Jullian, Marcel. *The Battle of Britain*. New York: Orion, 1967.

Kahn Jr., E. J. *The Merry Partners: The Age and Stage of Harrigan and Hart*. New York: Random House, 1955.

Kaiser, Robert Blair. *"R.F.K. Must Die."* New York: Dutton, 1970.

Kantor, David and William Lehr. *Inside the Family: Toward a Theory of Family Process*. San Francisco: Jossey-Bass, 1976.

Katzman, David M. *Seven Days a Week: Women and Domestic Service in Industrializing America*. New York: Oxford University Press, 1978.

Kay, Jan Holtz. *Lost Boston*. Boston: Houghton Mifflin, 1980.

Kee, Robert. *The Green Flag: Volume One: The Most Distressful Country*. London: Penguin, 1972.

Kee, Robert. *In the Shadow of War*. Boston: Little, Brown, 1984.

Kelley, Mary. *Private Woman, Public Stage: Literary Domesticity in Nineteenth Century America*. New York: Oxford, 1984.

Kenneally, James J. *The History of American Catholic Women*. New York: Crossroad, 1990.

Kennedy, Caroline and Ellen Alderman. *In Our Defense: The Bill of Rights in Action*. New York: Morrow, 1991.

Kennedy, Edward M., ed. *The Fruitful Bough: A Tribute to Jospeh P. Kennedy*. Privately printed, 1965.

Kennedy, John F., ed. *As We Remember Joe*. Cambridge, MA: privately printed at the University Press, 1945.

Kennedy, Senator John F. *Profiles in Courage*. New York: Harper, 1955.

Kennedy, Joseph P. *I'm for Roosevelt*. New York: Reynal and Hitchcock, 1936.

Kennedy, Robert F. *The Enemy Within*. New York: Harper, 1960.

Kennedy Jr., Robert E. *The Irish: Emigration, Marriage, and Fertility*. Berkeley: University of California Press, 1973.

Kennedy, Rose. *Times to Remember*. Garden City, NY: Doubleday, 1974.

Klagsbrun, Francine and David C. Whitney, eds. *Assassination: Robert F. Kennedy: 1925–1968*. New York: Cowles, 1969.

Kluckhohn, Frank. *America Listens*. Derby, CT: Monarch, 1962.

Korson, George. *At His Side: The Story of the American Red Cross*. New York: Coward-McCann, 1945.

Koskoff, David E. *Joseph P. Kennedy: A Life and Times*. Englewood Cliffs, NJ: Prentice-Hall, 1974.

Krock, Arthur. *In the Nation: 1932–1966*. New York: Paperback Library, 1969.

Krock, Arthur. *Memoirs: Sixty Years on the Firing Line*. New York: Funk and Wagnalls, 1968.

Krone's Paragon System of Penmanship. New York: Krone Brothers, 1888.

Kuenhel, Rev. Reynold. *Conferences for Married Women*. New York: Joseph F. Wagner, 1919.

Kunhardt Jr., Philip B. ed. *Life in Camelot*. Boston: Little, Brown, 1988.

Lacey, Robert. *The Queens of the North Atlantic*. New York: Stein and Day, 1976.

Lambert, Angela. *The Last Season of Peace*. New York: Weidenfeld & Nicolson, 1989.

• Lambert, Angela. *Unquiet Souls: The Indian Summer of the British Aristocracy*. London: Macmillan, 1984 (paperback 1985).

Lane, Albert. *Concord Authors at Home*. Concord, MA: The Erudite, 1902.

Lane, Francis E. *American Charities and the Child of the Immigrant: A Study of Typical Child Caring Institutions in New York and Massachusetts between the Years 1845 and 1880*. Washington, DC: The Catholic University of America, 1932.

Lane, Roger. *Policing the City: Boston 1822–1885*. Cambridge MA: Harvard University Press, 1967.

Larcom, Lucy. *A New England Girlhood*. Boston: Houghton Mifflin & Co., 1889.

Lash, Joseph P. *Eleanor and Franklin*. New York: W.W. Norton, 1971.

Lasky, Betty. *R.K.O.: The Biggest Little Major of Them All*. Englewood, NJ: Prentice-Hall, Inc., 1984.

Lasky, Victor. *J.F.K.: The Man and the Myth*. New York: Macmillan, 1963.

Laslett, Peter and Richard Wall, eds. *The Household and Family in Past Time*. Cambridge, Eng.: Cambridge University Press, 1972.

Latham, Caroline and Jeannie Sakol. *The Kennedy Encyclopedia*. New York: NAL, 1989.

Lawford, May and Buddy Galon. *Bitch!—The Autobiography of Lady Lawford*, Brookline, MA: Branden, 1986.

Lawford, Patricia Seaton with Ted Schwarz. *The Peter Lawford Story*. New York: Carroll & Graf, 1988.

Leach, William. *True Love and Perfect Union: The Feminist Reform of Sex and Society*. New York: Basic Books, 1980.

Lees, Gene. *Inventing Champagne: The Worlds of Lerner and Lowe*. New York: St. Martin's, 1990.

Leigh, Wendy. *Arnold*. New York: Congdon & Weed, 1990.

Leighton, Isabel, ed. *The Aspirin Age, 1919–1941*. New York: Simon and Schuster, 1949.

Lender, Mark Edward and James Kirby Martin. *Drinking in America: A History, The Revised Edition*. New York: The Free Press, 1987.

Leutze, James, ed. *The London Journal of General Raymond E. Lee: 1940–1941*. Boston: Little, Brown, 1971.

Lewis, Dio. *Our Girls*. New York: Harper & Brothers, 1871, reprinted by Arno Press, 1974.

Lidz, Theodore. *The Person: His and Her Development Throughout the Life Cycle*. New York: Basic Books, 1968.

Lindbergh, Charles L. *The Wartime Journals of Charles A. Lindbergh*. New York: Harcourt Brace Jovanovich, 1970.

Lingeman, Richard R. *Don't You Know There's a War On?* New York: Putnam, 1970.

Lippman Jr., Theo. *Senator Ted Kennedy: The Career Behind the Image*. New York: W.W. Norton, 1976.

Liston, Robert A. *Sargent Shriver: A Candid Portrait*. New York: Farrar, Straus, 1964.

Long, Helen. *Change into Uniform*. London: Terence Dalton, 1978.

Longford, Lord. *Kennedy*. London: Weidenfeld and Nicolson, 1976.

Lord, Robert H., John E. Sexton and Edward T. Harrington. *History of the Archdiocese of Boston: In the Various Stages of Its Development*, 3 Vols. New York: Sheed & Ward, 1944.

Mac Curtain, Margaret and Donncha O Corráin. *Women in Irish Society: The Historical Dimension*. Westport, CT: Greenwood Press, 1979.

MacManus, Seumas. *The Story of the Irish Race*. New York: The Irish Publishing Co., 1921.

MacPherson, Myra. *The Power Lovers: An Intimate Look at Politicians and Their Marriages*. New York: Putnam, 1975.

Madsen, Axel. *Gloria and Joe*. New York: Morrow, 1988 (paperback edition 1989).

Maguire, Reverend John Francis. *The Irish in America*. Report, New York: Arno, 1969; 1st pub., London: Longmans, Green, and Company, 1868.

Malzberg, B. *Social and Biological Aspects of Mental Disease*. Utica: St. Hospital's Press, 1940.

Manchester, William. *The Death of a President: November 20–November 25, 1963*. New York: Harper & Row, 1967.

Manchester, William. *The Glory and the Dream: A Narrative History of America, 1932–1972*. New York: Bantam, 1980.

Manchester, William. *The Last Lion: Alone: 1932–1940*. Boston: Little, Brown, 1988 (paperback 1989).

Manchester, William. *Portrait of a President: John F. Kennedy in Profile*. Boston and Toronto: Little, Brown & Company, 1962.

Mann, Arthur. *Yankee Reformers in the Urban Age*. Cambridge, MA: The Belknap Press, 1954.

Marcus, Sheldon. *Father Couglin*. Boston: Little, Brown, 1973.

Margolis, Maxine. *Mothers and Such: Views of American Women and Why they Changed*. Berkeley: University of California, 1984.

Martin, Ralph. *A Hero For Our Time*. New York: Ballantine, 1984.

Martin, Ralph G. *Henry and Clare: An Intimate Portrait of the Luces*. New York: G.P. Putnam's, 1991.

Martin, Ralph G. and Ed Plaut. *Front Runner, Dark Horse*. Garden City, NY: Doubleday, 1960.

Matthaei, Julie A. *An Economic History of Women in America*. New York: Schocken Books, 1982.

Matthews, Glenna. *Just a Housewife: The Rise and Fall of Domesticity in America*. New York: Oxford University Press, 1987.

McCabe, Lida Rose. *The American Girl at College*. New York: Dodd, Mead & Co., 1893.

McCabe, Peter. *Bad Day at Black Rock*. New York: Arbor House, 1987.

McCaffrey, Lawrence J. *The Irish Diaspora in America*. Washington, DC: The Catholic University of America Press, 1984.

McCarthy, Joe. *The Remarkable Kennedys*. New York: The Dial Press, 1960.

McCarthy, Mary. *Memories of a Catholic Girlhood*. New York: Berkley Publishing, 1957.

McCluskey, Neil G., ed. *Catholic Education in America: A Documentary History*. New York: Columbia University, 1964.

McGee, Thomas D'Arcy. *A History of the Irish Settlers in North America from the Earliest Periods to the Census of 1850*. Boston: American Celt, 1951 (copyright 1852).

McSorley, Edward. *Our Own Kind*. New York: Harper & Row, 1946.

McTaggart, Lynne. *Kathleen Kennedy: Her Life and Times*. New York: Dial Press, 1983.

Meagher, Timothy J. *From Paddy to Studs: Irish-American Communities in the Turn of the Century Era, 1880 to 1920*. New York: Greenwood Press, 1986.

Mewick, Donna. *Boston Priests, 1848–1910: A Study of Social and Intellectual Change*. Cambridge, MA: Harvard University Press, 1973.

Meyers, Joan, ed. *John Fitzgerald Kennedy: As We Remember Him*. New York: Atheneum, 1965.

Miller, Kerby A. *Emigrants and Exiles: Ireland and the Irish Exodus to North America*. New York: Oxford, 1985.

Mindel, Charles H., Robert W. Habenstein, and Roosevelt Wright Jr. *Ethnic Families in America: Patterns and Variations*, Third edition. New York: Elsevier, 1988.

Minnigerode, Meade. *Some American Ladies*. New York: Putnam, 1926.

Mintz, Steven and Susan Kellogg. *Domestic Revolutions: A Social History of American Family Life*. New York: The Free Press, 1988.

Mokyr, Joel. *Why Ireland Starved: A Quantitative and Analytical History of the Irish Economy 1800–1850*. London: Allen & Unwin, 1983.

Montgomery-Massingbred, Hugh. *Blenheim Revisited: The Spencer-Churchills and Their Palace*. New York: Beaufort Books, 1985.

Morison, Samuel Eliot. *The Maritime History of Massachusetts 1783–1860*. Boston: Houghton Mifflin, 1921, Northeastern University edition, 1979.

Morison, Samuel Eliot. *One Boy's Boston, 1887–1901*. Boston: Houghton Mifflin, 1962.

Mosley, Sir Oswald. *My Life*. New Rochelle: Arlington House, 1968.

Muggeridge, Malcolm. *The Thirties*. London: Hamish Hamilton, 1940.

Myerson, Abraham. *The Nervous Housewife*. New York: Arno Press, 1972 (copyright 1920).

Nasaw, David. *Children of the City*. Garden City, NY: Anchor Press, 1985.

Nation at War: Shaping Victory on the Home Front. Reprinted from Compton's Pictured Encyclopedia, 1942.

Neidle, Cecyle S. *America's Immigrant Women*. New York: Hippocrene Books, 1975.

Newfield, Jack. *Robert Kennedy: A Memoir*. New York: Dutton, 1969.

The New Yorker Book of War Pieces. New York: Reynal & Hitchcock, 1947, reprint Schocken.

Nicolson, Harold. *Diaries and Letters 1930–1964*. London: Penguin, 1984.

Nunnerly, David. *President Kennedy and Britain*. London: The Bodley Head, 1972.

O'Brien, James, ed. *The Vanishing Irish: The Enigma of the Modern World*. New York: McGraw-Hill, 1953.

O'Connell, D. D., Most Rev. *Souvenir or Receptions and Banquets to Most Rev. William H. O'Connell, D.D. as Coadjutor Archbishop of Boston*. Boston: Washington Press, 1906.

O'Connell, William. *Recollections of Seventy Years*. Boston: Houghton Mifflin, 1934.

O'Connell, William. *The Letters of His Eminence Archbishop of Boston*. Cambridge, MA: Riverside Press, 1915.

O'Connor, Edwin. *The Edge of Sadness*. New York: Bantam Books, 1970.

O'Connor, Edwin. *The Last Hurrah*. New York: Bantam Books, 1970.

O'Connor, Thomas H. *Bibles, Brahmins and Bosses: A Short History of Boston*. Boston: Trustees of the Public Library of the City of Boston, 1984.

O'Connor, Thomas H. *Fitzpatrick's Boston 1846–1866*. Boston: Northeastern University Press, 1984.

O'Donnell, Kennedy P. and David F. Powers. *Johnny, We Hardly Knew Ye: Memories of John Fitzgerald Kennedy*. Boston: Little, Brown, 1972.

O'Faolain, Sean. *The Irish: A Character Study*. Old Greenwich, CT: The Devin-Adair Company, 1949.

O'Grady, Joseph P. *How the Irish Became American*. New York: Twayne Publishers, Inc., 1973.

O'Hanlon, Rev. J. *Irish Emigrant's Guide for the United States*. New York: Arno Press, 1976 (c 1851).

O'Leary, Mary. *Education with a Tradition: An Account of the Educational Work of the Society of the Sacred Heart*. New York: Longmans, Green & Company, 1936.

O'Reilly, Bernard. *The Mirror of True Womanhood: A Book of Instruction for Women in the World*. New York: Peter F. Collier, 1878.

O'Toole, James. *Guide to the Archives of the Archdiocese of Boston*. New York: Garland, 1982.

O'Toole, James M. *Militant and Triumphant: William O'Connell and the Catholic Church in Boston, 1859–1944*. Notre Dame: University of Notre Dame Press, 1992.

Oates, Mary J. *Higher Education for Catholic Women: An Historical Anthology.* New York: Garland Publishing, 1987.

Ogden, Annegret S. *The Great American Housewife: From Helpmate to Wage Earner, 1776–1986.* Westport, CT: Greenwood Press, 1986.

One Hundred Years of Continuous Sacred Heart Education in Boston and Newton. Newton, MA: Newton Country Day School, 1980, unnumbered.

Pagels, Eliane. *Adam, Eve and the Serpent.* New York: Random House, 1988.

Palmer, Phyllis. *Domesticity and Dirt: Housewives and Domestic Servants in the United States, 1920–1945.* Philadelphia: Temple University Press, 1989.

Parmet, Herbert S. *Jack: The Struggles of John F. Kennedy.* New York: Dial, 1980.

Parmet, Herbert S. *J.F.K.: The Presidency of John F. Kennedy.* New York: Dial, 1983.

Peiss, Kathy. *Cheap Amusements: Working Women and Leisure in Turn-of-the-Century New York.* Philadelphia: Temple University Press, 1986.

Perrett, Geoffrey. *Days of Sadness, Years of Triumph.* New York: Coward, McCann & Geoghegan, 1973.

Peterson, J. Jeanne. *Family, Love and Work in the Lives of Victorian Gentlewomen.* Bloomington, IN: Indiana University Press, 1989.

Petrovits, Rev. Joseph J. C. *The New Church Law of Matrimony.* Dissertation Submitted to the Faculty of Sacred Sciences at the Catholic University of America in partial fulfillment of requirements for the Doctorate in Canon Law. Philadelphia: John Joseph McVey, 1919.

Phillips, Bruce A. *Brookline: The Evolution of an American Jewish Suburb.* New York: Garland, 1990.

Phillips, Cabell. *From the Crash to the Blitz, 1929–1939.* New York: Macmillan, 1975.

Phillips, Cabell. *The 1940s: Decade of Triumph and Trouble.* New York: Macmillan, 1975.

Pilat, Oliver. *Drew Pearson: An Unauthorized Biography.* New York: Warner Pocketbooks, 1973.

Plimpton, George and Jean Stein, eds. *American Journey: The Times of Robert Kennedy.* New York: Signet, 1970.

Post, Emily. *Etiquette.* New York: Funk and Wagnalls, 1942.

Potter, George. *To the Golden Door: The Story of the Irish in Ireland and America.* Boston: Little, Brown, 1960.

Potter, Jeffrey. *Men, Money and Magic: The Story of Dorothy Schiff.* New York: Coward, McCann & Geoghegan, 1976.

Potter, Neil and Jack Frost. *The Mary: The Inevitable Ship.* London: Harrap, 1961.

President's Committee on Mental Retardation. *Changing Patterns in Residential Services for the Mentally Retarded.* Washington: U.S. Government Printing Press, 1976.

President's Committee on Mental Retardation: *Report to the President:*

Mental Retardation: Century of Decision. Washington: U.S. Government Printing Office, 1976.

Priestly, J. B.: *All England Listened*. New York: Chilmark Press, 1967.

Puch, David G. *Sons of Liberty: The Masculine Mind in Nineteenth-Century America*. Westport, CT: Greenwood Press, 1983.

Rachlin, Harvey. *The Kennedys: A Chronological History 1823–Present*. New York: Pharos, 1986.

Radway, G. Frank. *Brahmins and Bullyboys*. Boston: Houghton Mifflin, 1973.

Rainie, Harrison and John Quinn. *Growing Up Kennedy: The Third Wave Comes of Age*. New York: G.P. Putnam's Sons, 1983.

Ranke-Heinemann. *Eunichs for the Kingdom of Heaven*. New York: Doubleday, 1990.

Redmon, Coates. *Come As You Are: The Peace Corps Story*. San Diego, CA: Harcourt Brace Jovanovich, 1986.

Reeves, Thomas C. *A Question of Character: A Life of John F. Kennedy*. New York: Macmillan, 1991.

Reglèment des Pensinnats and Plan D'Études de la Société Du Sacré-Coeur. Orléans: Imprimerie D'Alex, Jacob, 1852.

Rhodes, James Robert, ed. *Chips: The Diaries of Sir Henry Channon*. London: Harmondsworth, 1970.

Roboff, Sari. *East Boston*. Boston: The Boston 200 Corporation, 1976.

Rogers, Warren. *When I Think of Bobby: A Personal Memoir of the Kennedy Years*. New York: HarperCollins, 1993.

Rollins, Judith. *Between Women: Domestics and Their Employers*. Philadelphia: Temple University Press, 1985.

Roosevelt, Felicia Warburg. *Doers and Dowagers*. New York: Doubleday, 1975.

Rose, Phyllis. *Parallel Lives: Five Victorian Marriages*. New York: Knopf, 1983.

Rosenberg, Charles C. *The Cholera Years*. Chicago: The University of Chicago Press, 1962.

Rosenzweig, Roy. *Eight Hours For What We Will: Workers and Leisure in an Industrial City, 1870–1920*. Cambridge, Eng.: Cambridge University Press, 1983.

Ross, Margorie Drake. *The Book of Boston: The Victorian Period 1837 to 1901*. New York: Hastings House Publishers, 1964.

Rothman, David J. and Shelia M. Rothman, eds. *The Dangers of Education: Sexism and the Origins of Women's Colleges*. New York: Garland Publishing, 1987.

Rothman, Sheila M. *Woman's Proper Place: A History of Changing Ideals and Practices, 1870 to the Present*. New York: Basic Books, 1978.

Ruether, Rosemary Radford and Rosemary Skinner Keller, eds. *Women and Religion in America: Vol. 1: The Nineteenth Century*. San Francisco: Harper & Row, 1981.

Rugoff, Milton Allan. *America's Gilded Age: Personalities in an Era of Extravagance and Change 1850–1890*. New York: Holt, 1989.

Rumbarger, John J. *Profits Power and Prohibition*. Albany: State University of New York, 1989.

Russell, Francis. *The President Makers: From Mark Hanna to Joseph P. Kennedy*. Boston: Little, Brown, 1976.

Ryan, Dennis. *Beyond the Ballot Box: A Social History of the Boston Irish, 1845–1917*. East Brunswick: Associated University Presses, 1983.

Ryan, Dorothy and Louis J. Ryan. *The Kennedy Family of Massachusetts: A Bibliography*. Westport, CT: Greenwood Press, 1981.

Sainte-Foi, Charles. *Mission and Duties of Young Women*, translated by Charles I. White. Baltimore, MD: Kelly, Piet & Co., 1879.

Sainte-Foi, Charles. *The Perfect Woman*, translated from the French of Charles Sainte-Foi by Zephirine N. Brown. Boston: Marlier and Company, Ltd., 1901.

Salaman, Redcliffe. *The History and Social Influence of the Potato*. Cambridge, Eng.: Cambridge University Press, 1985 (c 1949).

Salinger, Pierre. *With Kennedy*. New York: Doubleday, 1966.

Salmaggi, Cesare and Alfredo Pallavisini, compilers. *2194 Days of War*. New York: Windward, 1977.

Saunders, Frank with James Southwood. *Torn Lace Curtain*. New York: Holt Rinehart and Winston, 1982.

Scheerenberger, R.C. *A History of Mental Retardation*. Baltimore: Brookes, 1987.

Scheper-Hughes, Nancy. *Saints, Scholars, and Schizophrenics: Mental Illness in Rural Ireland*. Berkeley, CA: University of California Press, 1979.

Schlesinger Jr., Arthur M. *The Age of Roosevelt*. Vol. 1, *The Crisis of the Old Order, 1919–1933*. Vol. 2, *The Coming of the New Deal*. Vol. 3, *The Politics of Upheaval*. Boston: Houghton Mifflin, 1957, 1958, 1960.

Schlesinger Jr., Arthur M. *Robert Kennedy and His Times*. Boston: Houghton Mifflin, 1978.

Schlesinger Jr., Arthur M. *A Thousand Days*. Boston: Houghton Mifflin, 1965.

Schoor, Gene. *Young John Kennedy*. New York: Harcourt, Brace & World, Inc., 1963.

Schrier, Arnold. *Ireland and the American Emigration 1850–1900*. New York: Russell & Russell, 1970 (copyright 1958).

Scudder, Townsend. *Concord: American Town*. Boston: Little, Brown and Company, 1947.

Searls, Hank. *The Lost Prince: Young Joe, the Forgotten Kennedy*. New York: World Publishing Co., 1969.

Seidenberg, Robert. *Marriage Between Equals*. Garden City, NY: Doubleday, Anchor Press, 1973. Orig. titled *Marriage in Life and Literature*. New York: Philosophical Library, 1970.

Seller, Maxine, ed.; *Immigrant Women*. Philadelphia: Temple University Press, 1981.

Sexton, John E. *Cardinal O'Connell: A Biographical Sketch*. Boston: The Pilot Publishing Company, 1927.

Shackleton, Robert. *The Book of Boston*. Philadelphia: The Penn Publishing Company, 1916.

Shannon, William V. *The American Irish*. New York: Macmillan, 1963.

Shannon, William V. *The Heir Apparent: Robert Kennedy and the Struggle for Power*. New York: Macmillan, 1967.

Shapiro, Doris. *We Danced All Night: My Life Behind the Scenes with Alan Jay Lerner*. New York: William Morrow, 1990.

Sheean, Vincent. *Between the Thunder and the Sun*. New York: Random House, 1943.

Sheed, Wilfrid. *People Will Always Be Kind*. New York: Dell Publishing Co., 1973.

Sherwood, Robert E. *Roosevelt and Hopkins: An Intimate History*. New York: Harper, 1948.

Shirer, William L. *Berlin Diary: The Journal of a Foreign Correspondent, 1934–1941*. Boston: Little, Brown, 1988.

Shirer, William L. *The Rise and Fall of the Third Reich*. New York: Simon and Schuster, 1960.

Shkolnik, Ester. *Leading Ladies: A Study of Eight Late Victorian and Edwardian Political Wives*. Modern European History Series, edited by W. H. McNeill and Peter Stansky. New York: Garland, 1987.

Shulman, Irving. *Jackie! The Exploitation of a First Lady*. New York: Trident Press, 1970.

Shurfleff, Nathaniel B. *A Topographical and Historical Description of Boston*. Boston: Noyoes, Holmes, and Company, 1872.

Sidney, Margaret. *Old Concord: Her Highways and Byways*. Boston: D. Lothrop, 1892.

Slater, Peter Gregg. *Children in the New England Mind in Death and in Life*. Hamden, CT: Archon, 1977.

Slatzer, Robert F. *The Life and Curious Death of Marilyn Monroe*. Los Angeles: Pinnacle, 1975.

Slevin, Jonathan and Maureen Spagnolo. *Kennedys: The Next Generation*. Bethesda, MD: National Press, 1990.

Smith, Gene. *Dark Summer: An Intimate History of the Events That Led to World War II*. New York: Macmillan, 1987.

Smith, J. David. *Minds Made Feeble: The Myth and Legacy of the Kallikaks*. Rockville, MD: Aspen Systems Corporation, 1985.

Smith-Rosenberg, Carroll. *Disorderly Conduct: Visions of Gender in Victorian America*. New York: Alfred A. Knopf, 1985.

Solomon, Barbara Miller. *Ancestors and Immigrants: A Changing New England Tradition*. Chicago: The University of Chicago Press, 1972 (c 1956).

Sorenson, Theodore. *The Kennedy Legacy*. New York: Macmillan, 1969.

Spada, James. *Peter Lawford: The Man Who Knew Too Much*. New York: Bantam, 1991.

Spalding, John Lancaster. *The Religious Mission of the Irish People and Catholic Colonization*. New York: Catholic Publication Society Co., 1880, reprinted by Arno Press, 1978.

Spofford, Harriet Prescott. *The Servant Girl Question.* Boston: Houghton Mifflin Co., 1881; reissued by Arno Press and *The New York Times*, 1977.

Spoto, Donald. *Marilyn Monroe: The Biography.* New York: HarperCollins, 1993.

Stage, Sarah. *Female Complaints: Lydia Pinkham and the Business of Women's Medicine.* New York: W.W. Norton, 1979.

Stein, Jean and George Plimpton. *American Journey: The Times of Robert Kennedy.* New York: Harcourt Brace Jovanovich, 1970.

Stivers, Richard. *The Hair of the Dog: Irish Drinking and American Stereotype.* University Park, PA: Pennsylvania State University Press, 1976.

Stock, Phyllis. *Better Than Rubies: A History of Women's Education.* New York: G.P. Putnam's Sons, 1978.

Story, Ronald. *Harvard and the Boston Upper Class, The Forging of an Aristocracy 1800–1870.* Middletown, CT: Wesleyan University Press, 1985 (c 1980).

Strasser, Susan. *Never Done: A History of American Housework.* New York: Pantheon, 1982.

Stuart, Janet Erskine. *The Education of Catholic Girls.* London: Longmans, Green and Co., 1911.

Stuart, Janet Erskine. *The Society of the Sacred Heart.* London: Convent of the Sacred Heart, 1914.

Sullivan, Rev. John F. *The Fundamentals of Catholic Belief.* New York: P.J. Kenedy & Sons, 1925.

Sullivan, Robert E. and James M. O'Toole, eds. *Catholic Boston: Studies in Religion and Community, 1870–1970.* Boston: Roman Catholic Archbishop of Boston, 1985.

Summers, Anthony. *Goddess: The Secret Lives of Marilyn Monroe.* New York: Macmillan, 1985.

Summers, Anthony. *Official and Confidential: The Secret Life of J. Edgar Hoover.* New York: Putnam's, 1993.

Sumner, William H. *A History of East Boston.* Boston: J.E. Tilton and Company, 1858.

Sutherland, Daniel. *Americans and their Servants.* Baton Rouge, LA: Louisiana State, 1981.

Sykes, Christopher. *Nancy: The Life of Lady Astor.* London: Collins, 1972.

Tager, Jack and John W. Ifkovic, eds. *Massachusetts in the Gilded Age: Selected Essays.* Amherst, MA: The University of Massachusetts Press, 1985.

Tannen, Deborah. *You Don't Understand: Women and Men in Conversation.* New York: Morrow, 1990.

Taylor, Telford. *The Breaking Wave: The Second World War in the Summer of 1940.* New York: Simon and Schuster, 1967.

Taylor, Telford. *Munich: The Price of Peace.* Garden City, NY: Doubleday, 1979.

Ternune, Mary. *Eves Daughter; or Common Sense for Maid, Wife, and Mother*. New York: J.R. Anderson & H.S. Allen, 1882.

Thayer, Mary Van Rensselar. *Jacqueline Bouvier Kennedy*. New York: Doubleday, 1961.

Theriot, Nancy M. *The Biosocial Construction of Femininity: Mothers and Daughters in Nineteenth-Century America*. New York: Greenwood Press, 1988.

Thernstrom, Stephan. *The Other Bostonians: Poverty and Progress in the American Metropolis, 1860–1870*. Cambridge, MA: Harvard University Press, 1964.

Thernstrom, Stephan. *Poverty and Progress: Social Mobility in a Nineteenth-Century City*. Cambridge, MA: Harvard University Press, 1964.

Thompson, Robert E. and Hortense Myers. *Robert F. Kennedy: The Brother Within*. New York: The Macmillan Company, 1962.

Thornton, Tamara Plakins. *Cultivating Gentlemen: The Meaning of Country Life Among the Boston Elite, 1785–1860*. New Haven: Yale University Press, 1989.

Tierney, Gene. *Self-Portrait*. New York: Wyden Books, 1979.

Time-Life Books, ed. *This Fabulous Century: 1940–1950*. Alexandria, VA: Time-Life Books, 1969.

Todisco, Paula J. *Boston's First Neighborhood: The North End*. Boston: Boston Public Library, 1976.

Travell, Janet. *Office Hours: Day and Night*. New York: World Publishing Company, 1968.

Trout, Charles H. *Boston: The Great Depression and the New Deal*. New York: Oxford University Press, 1977.

Truman, Margaret. *Bess W. Truman*. New York: Macmillan Publishing Company, 1982.

Tull, Charles. *Father Coughlin and the New Deal*. Syracuse: Syracuse University Press, 1965.

Turner, E. S. *The Phoney War*. New York: St. Martin's Press, 1961.

Tyack, David B. *One Best System: A History of American Urban Education*. Cambridge, MA: Harvard University Press, 1974.

Valenstein, Elliot S. *Great and Desperate Cures: The Rise and Decline of Psychosurgery and Other Radical Treatments for Mental Illness*. New York: Basic Books, 1986.

Valenstein, Elliot S., ed. *The Psychosurgery Debate: Scientific, Legal and Ethical Perspectives*. San Francisco: W.H. Freeman, 1980.

Verbrugge, Martha. *Able-bodied Womenhood: Personal Heath and Social Change in Nineteenth Century Boston*. New York: Oxford University Press, 1988.

Vidal, Gore. *Homage to Daniel Shays: Collected Essays 1952–1972*. New York: Random House, 1972.

Vogel, Morris J. *The Invention of the Modern Hospital: Boston 1870–1930*. Chicago: University of Chicago Press, 1980.

Von Bremscheid, Rev. Matthias. *The Christian Maiden*. Translated from the German by Members of the Young Ladies Sodality Holy Trinity Church, Boston. Boston: Angel Guardian Press, 1905, second edition.

Waksman, Selman A. *The Conquest of Tuberculosis*. Berkeley: University of California Press, 1966.

Warbasse, Elizabeth. *The Changing Legal Rights of Married Women in 1800–1861*. New York: Garland Press, 1987.

Ward, David. *Cities and Immigrants: A Geography of Change in Nineteenth-Century America*. New York: Oxford University Press, 1971.

Ward, Margaret. *Unmanageable Revolutionaries: Women and Irish Nationalism*. London: Pluto Press, 1983.

Ware, Susan. *Holding Their Own: American Women in the 1930s*. Boston: Twayne, 1982.

Ware, Susan. *Modern American Women: A Documentary History*. Chicago: The Dorsey Press, 1989.

Warner, Sam Bass. *Streetcar Suburbs: The Process of Growth in Boston, 1870–1900*. Cambridge, MA: Harvard University Press and The M.I.T. Press, 1962.

Watt, Donald Cameron. *Why War Came: The Immediate Origins of the Second World War, 1938–1939*. New York: Pantheon Books, 1989.

Wayman, Dorothy G. *Cardinal O'Connell of Boston: A Biography of William Henry O'Connell 1859–1944*. New York: Farrar, Straus and Young, 1954.

Weatherford, Doris. *Foreign and Female: Immigrant Women in America, 1840–1930*. New York: Schocken, 1986.

Wecter, Dixon. *The Saga of American Society*. New York: Charles Scribner's Sons, 1937.

Weller, The Reverend Philip T., translator and editor. *The Roman Ritual: Vol. II Christian Burial, Exorcism, Reserved Blessings, Etc*. Milwaukee, WI: The Bruce Publishing Company, 1952.

Wertz, Richard and Dorothy Wertz. *Lying-In: A History of Childbirth in America*. New York: Schocken Books, 1977.

West, J. B. with Mary Lynn Kotz. *Upstairs at the White House: My Life with the First Ladies*. New York: Coward, McCann and Geoghegan, 1973.

Whalen, Richard. *The Founding Father: The Story of Joseph P. Kennedy*. New York: New American Library, 1964.

Wheeler-Bennett, John W. *King George VI: His Life and Reign*. New York: St. Martin's, 1958.

White, Antonia. *Frost in May*. New York: Dial Press, 1980 (c 1933).

White, Theodore H. *America in Search of Itself: The Making of the President 1956–1980*. New York: Harper & Row, 1982.

White, Theodore H. *In Search of History: A Personal Adventure*. New York: Warner Books, 1978.

White, Theodore H. *The Making of the President 1960*. New York: Atheneum, 1961.

Whitehall, Walter Muir. *Boston in the Age of John Fitzgerald Kennedy*. Norman: University of Oklahoma Press, 1966.

Whiting, Lillian. *Boston Days*. Boston: Little Brown, 1911.

Wicker, Tom. *Kennedy Without Tears*. New York: William Morrow and Co., 1964.

Williams, Alexander W. *A Social History of the Greater Boston Clubs*. Boston: Barre Publishers, 1970.

Williams, Margaret, RSCJ. *The Society of the Sacred Heart: History of a Spirit 1800–1975*. London: Darton Longman, 1978.

Williamson, David and Patricia Ellis, eds. *Debrett's Distinguished People of Today*. London: Debrett's Peerage Limited, 1988.

Wills, Garry. *The Kennedy Imprisonment: A Meditation on Power*. Boston: Little, Brown, 1981.

Winsor, Justin, ed. *The Memorial History of Boston, 1630–1880*, 5 Vols. Boston: Ticknor & Co., 1880.

Winter, C.W.R. *The Queen Mary: Her Early Years Recalled*. New York: W.W. Norton, 1986.

Wittke, Carl. *We Who Built America: The Saga of the Immigrant*. New York: Prentice-Hall, 1940.

Wittke, Carl. *The Irish in America*. Baton Rouge: Louisiana State University Press, 1956.

Wolf, Albert Benedict. *The Lodging House Problem in Boston*. Cambridge, MA: Harvard University Press, 1913.

Wolfensberger, Wolf, Bengt Nirje, Simon Olshansky, Robert Perske, and Philip Roose. *The Principle of Normalization in Human Services*. Toronto: National Institute on Mental Retardation, 1972.

Woodham-Smith, Cecil. *The Great Hunger: Ireland 1845–1849*. London: Hamish Hamilton, 1962.

Woods, Robert A. and Albert J. Kennedy. *The Zone of Emergence*, Second edition. Cambridge, MA: M.I.T. Press, 1962.

Woods, Robert A., ed. *Americans in Process: A Settlement Study*. Boston and New York: Houghton Mifflin, 1902.

Woods, Robert A. *The City Wilderness: A Settlement Study*. New York: Arno Press, 1979 (c 1898).

Workers of the Writers' Program of the Work Projects Administration in the State of Massachusetts. *Boston Looks Seaward: The Story of the Port 1630–1940*. Boston: Bruce Humphries, Inc., 1941.

Wright, R. L. *Irish Emigrant Ballads and Songs*. Bowling Green, OH: Bowling Green University, 1975.

Wright, Carroll D. *The Working Girls of Boston*. Boston: Wright and Potter, 1884.

Zelman, Patricia G. *Women, Work, and National Policy: The Kennedy-Johnson Years*. Ann Arbor, MI: UMI Research Press, 1982.

Index

Ace of Clubs, 117–18, 135, 147–48, 158, 166, 249–50, 405

Adams, Henry, 527

Adams, John Quincy, 247

Admirable Crichton, The (Barrie), 726

Alcoholics Anonymous, 710, 736

Alcott, Louisa May, 34, 39, 137, 729

Allen, Kara Kennedy, 531, 585, 680, 729–30, 737, 747, 799, 825

Allen, Michael, 799, 825–26

Allen, Robert S., 328

Alsop, Joseph, 414, 424, 427, 530

Alzado, Lyle, 793

Ambrose, Margaret, 413

America, 114, 117

Amory, Jan Cushing, 644, 785

Anderson, Jack, 550–51, 719–20

Angullo, Manuel, 188–89, 199, 200, 201

"Appeasement at Munich" (Kennedy), 296, 317

Arnaz, Desi, 466

Arvad, Inga, 332, 344–46, 348–51, 354, 360, 361, 383, 414, 423, 449, 450

Astor, Nancy, 262–63, 295, 354, 366, 384, 385

"At Home with the Kennedys," 498–500

Auchincloss, Hugh, 449, 623

Auchincloss, Janet Bouvier, 449, 453, 455–56, 458, 483, 623

Augensblick, Elizabeth Rivinus, 209

Avedon, Richard, 567

Ball, Lucille, 466

Barat, Madeleine Sophie, 62

Baring, Sarah Norton, 259, 272

Barnett, Betty, 760, 763

Barrie, J. M., 726

Barron, Patrick, 9, 11, 101

Barron, Tom, 101–2,

Barry, Bill, 660, 800, 801, 815

Bartlett, Charles, 415, 449, 564–65, 590, 630

Baudelaire, Charles, 452

Bayley, Edwin R., 556

Bay of Pigs invasion, 553, 559

Bazilauskas, Victor F., 662

Beale, Betty, 690

Beck, David, 489

Benedict XV, Pope, 163

Bennett, Candy, 495

Bennett, Cathy E., 812

Bennett, Constance, 193, 195

Bennett, Harry, 495, 497, 681

Bennett, Joan, *see* Kennedy, Joan Bennett

Bennett, Virginia "Ginny," 495, 496, 681, 735

Benson, Marguerite, 520
Bentley, Helen, 775, 777, 778
Bergquist, Laura, 558, 567, 733, 741
Berle, Milton, 536
Berlin, Irving, 374
Bernard, Ena, 670–71
Bernstein, Felicia, 557
Bernstein, Leonard, 557, 560–61, 733
Berube, Edward C., 446
Betts, Henry, 577–78, 580–81, 582
Billings, Kirk LeMoyne "Lem," 621, 666, 678, 698, 718
  JFK's friendship with, 207, 210, 263, 267, 275, 296, 305, 316, 345, 355, 362, 364, 419, 423, 431, 459, 461
Bingham, Robert Worth, 247
Birdwell, Russell, 186
Bishop, Joey, 512
Bitch (Galon), 472
Black, Roy E., 812, 814, 816, 817
Blackburn, Madelaine, 191–92
Blandford, Athina Livanos Onassis, 719
Blank, Brad, 715–16, 798–99
Bludworth, David, 763, 802
Born, John, 763
Bornstein, Samuel, 404
Borsari, Alan K., 795, 796
Boston:
  Catholic community in, 10, 18, 30, 48–49, 60–61, 63, 67, 82, 108, 114, 118–21
  East, 9–23, 47, 99–104, 110, 256
  Irish immigration to, 7, 8–12, 31–32, 48–49, 106, 252
  North End of, 2, 10, 26, 29, 31, 32, 40, 43, 89, 115
Boston *American*, 45, 115
Boston College, 61, 108
Boston Globe, 88, 130–31, 144, 248, 285, 299, 323, 328, 386–87, 430, 447–48, 743, 821

Boston Herald, 483
Boston Latin School, 26, 53, 54, 107, 108, 825
Boston Pilot, 10, 12, 19, 62, 163
Boston *Post*, 45–46, 50, 67, 80, 90, 99, 112–13, 125–27, 130, 131, 144, 166, 323, 442, 466
Boston Traveler, 382, 490
Boutin, Bernard L., 560
Bouvier, Jacqueline, *see* Kennedy, Jacqueline Bouvier "Jackie"
Bouvier, Janet, 449, 453, 455–56, 458, 483, 623
Bouvier, John, III "Black Jack," 449, 453, 456–57, 484
Bowman, Patricia, 802, 811, 813–15, 816–17
Braden, Joan, 557, 737
Braden, Tom, 557
Bradlee, Ben, 615
Bradlee, Tony, 615
Britt, May, 536
Brokaw, Ann Clare, 390
Brothers, Joyce, 737
Broughton, Diane, 658
Brown, Lyn Mikel, 351
Brown, Patti Blair, 633–34
Bruce, Marie, 374, 376, 383–84, 385, 387
Buchwald, Art, 669, 670
Bullitt, William, 228
Bunshaft, Robert, 168
Burden, Amanda, 733
Burke, Anne, 668
Burke, Charles, 189, 711
Burke, Chris, 807
Burke, Grace, 461
Burke, Margaret Louise Kennedy, 98, 111, 131, 189, 190, 408
Burke, Richard, 738, 739, 744, 745
Burns, Dan, 493
Burns, James MacGregor, 525
Burt, Elizabeth, 125–27
Busbey, Katherine G., 138
Bush, George, 788
Byrnes, James F., 325, 326–27

Callas, Maria, 615
Camelot, 565, 629, 649, 653, 673, 832
Cameron, Gail, 700
Campbell, Judith, 512–14, 524, 611
Camus, Albert, 631
Capote, Truman, 561
Caroline, 520, 544, 574, 579–80
Carpenter, Liz, 645–46
Carpenter, Virginia, 343–44
Carter, Jimmy, 725, 738, 740, 743, 745, 748
Carter, Rosalynn, 743
Casals, Pablo, 560–61
Cassidy, Howard, 668
Cassini, Oleg, 462–63, 486, 538–39, 541, 542, 559, 573, 645, 754
Catholics, Catholicism:
  in Boston, 10, 18, 30, 48–49, 60–61, 63, 67, 82–83, 108, 114, 118–21
  clubs for, 116–18
  corruption in, 163
  education as viewed by, 56, 60–61, 70–75, 78–79
  in England, 254–55, 258, 276–77, 278–79
  marriage as viewed by, 27–28, 97
  in New York, 233, 234
  sexuality as viewed by, 13, 53–54, 82
  social involvement of, 307–8, 411
  women in, 12, 19–20, 48–49, 78–79, 113–14, 119–21
Caulfield, John Thomas, 21
Cavafy, C. P., 830–32
Cavanaugh, John J., 453, 460, 622, 623–24
Cavendish, Andrew, 277–78, 378, 400, 423, 431, 664
Chamberlain, Neville, 256–57, 258, 280, 281–82, 300–301, 316, 325

Channon, Henry "Chips," 277, 296
Charlie (JFK's dog), 608
Chatfield-Taylor, Mary Lyon, 206
Chellis, Marcia, 733, 745
Cheshire, Maxine, 483
Chicago Merchandise Mart, 416, 438
Choate School, 203–4, 213
Christopher Hour, The, 466–67, 478
Christophers, 411, 465–67, 478
Churchill, Pamela, 419, 424
Churchill, Winston S., 295, 297, 316, 322, 432, 614
Church of England, 258, 279, 374–75, 380–81
Church of the Most Holy Redeemer, 23, 98, 108
Claiborne, Loretta, 809
Clark, Blair, 513
Clark, Tom C., 413–14
Clasby, Richard, 453
Cleary, William, 479
Clinton, Bill, 820, 821
Clothes for a Summer Hotel (Williams), 785
Coffee, Catherine, 115
Coffey, Anne, 490
"Coffee with the Kennedys," 446
Cohen, Wilbur, 557
Colbert, Claudette, 348
Cole, Nat King, 525, 548
Coleman, Barbara, 528, 530
Coleman, Nancy Tenney, 193–94, 197, 237, 241, 322, 833–34
Coleman, Zeke, 316, 356
Colleran, Bill, 591
Collins, Patrick A., 43
Colum, Mary Magiore, 72, 74
Columbia Trust Company, 103, 127, 130, 176, 408
Co-Madres, 775
Como, Perry, 492
Compton, Jane, 259, 262, 299, 301, 401, 423
Conboy, Katherine "Kico," 157–58, 184, 250, 256

Confidential, 506
Connally, John, 618, 621
Connelly, George, 190
Connelly, Loretta Kennedy, 68, 189–90, 714
Connelly, Mary Lou, 438–39
Conniff, Frank, 468, 469
Connor, James, 675, 695–96, 705, 710, 732
Conway, Katherine, 117
Cooke, Robert, 504
Cooper, Gary, 507
Cooper, John Sherman, 458
Cooper, Rocky, 507
Copland, Aaron, 809
Corcoran, Thomas "Tommy the Cork," 216
Coughlan, Robert, 704–7, 713, 716
Cox, Channing H., 164
Coxe, Betty, 346, 354, 355
Creagh, John T., 162, 168
Crimmins, John "Jack," 677
Crosby, Bing, 590
Cuomo, Andrew, 799
Cuomo, Kerry Kennedy, 659, 666, 783, 798–99, 811, 824
Curley, James, 97, 128–29, 435, 527
Cushing, Richard, 405, 408, 433, 457, 503, 610, 672

Daladier, Edouard, 282
Dallas, Rita, 578, 580, 583, 684
Daly, Gloria Somborn, 187, 194, 195, 197
Dammann, Mother, 307, 308
D'Arcy, Martin, 381
Dauth, Ingo, 457
David, Lester, 737
Davidoff, Bob, 713
Davies, Marion, 457, 526
Davis, Daniel, 423
Davis, John H., 746
Davis, Sammy, Jr., 512, 536
Day, Dorothy, 307
Death of a President, The (Manchester), 648–49

de Gaulle, Charles, 562, 563–64, 626, 690
DeGuglielmo, Lawrence "DeGug," 405–6
de la Falaise, Henri, 182–83, 194–95
Deland, Margaret, 114
Democracy (Adams), 527
Democratic National Committee, 528, 551
Democratic National conventions:
  in 1956, 481–83, 485, 487
  in 1960, 525–27
  in 1972, 700–701
  in 1980, 748–49
Denove, Ann, 466–67
Depression, 199–200, 220–21, 311, 449
de Sapio, Carmine, 550
Deshon, George, 19–20
DeVine, Marnie, 104
De Voto, Alfred, 64
Diaghilev, Sergei, 452
Dickens, Charles, 42, 224
Dickerson, Wyatt, 650
Didion, Joan, 699
Dietrich, Marlene, 300, 561
DiMaggio, Joe, 596
Donnelly, Brian, 821
Donovan, Edward J., 45
Donovan, George, 735
Dorchester High School, 42–43, 50–51, 54, 56, 63, 138
Dorr, David Lindwood, 762
Douglas-Home, William, 274, 354, 365
Doyle, John H., 47
Doyle, Patrick J., 556
Drayne, Richard, 735
Driscoll, Margaret, 158
Droney, John, 404, 407
Drouin, Mark, 562
Duchin, Peter, 784
Duff, Margaret, 186
Dugal, Peter, 530
Dukakis, Michael, 772
Duke, Angier Biddle, 624

Dunn, Barbara, 342
Dunn, Elizabeth, 252, 268, 271, 282
Dutton, Fred, 651

Eagan, Margery, 805
Eagleton, Thomas, 701
Ebbins, Milton, 469–70, 471, 476, 478, 506, 511–12, 513, 549, 568, 570, 591, 596–97, 621, 624, 640
Eden, Anthony, 297, 420
Edwards, India, 551
Edwards, Richard, 306
Egerton, Tom, 236, 302
Eisenhower, Dwight D., 446, 448–49, 450, 481, 486, 524, 539, 547, 551–52, 553, 560, 566
Eisenhower, Mamie, 539, 547
Elcock, Walter, 108
Elizabeth, Princess of England (later Elizabeth II), 256, 276, 281, 421
Elizabeth, Queen of George VI, 248, 256–58, 262, 266–70, 290–91, 294–95, 304
Emerson, Ralph Waldo, 42, 85
Emmett, Jay, 791
Evans, Ruth, 55, 88

Fairbanks, Charles Warren, 70
Falvey, Catherine, 404
"Fanfare for the Common Man" (Copland), 809
Farrell, Ann Fitzgerald, 369
Fascism, 227, 298
Fay, Anita, 457, 504
Fay, Red, 394–95, 403, 412, 448, 451, 457, 463, 504, 516–17, 527, 549, 605, 632, 647–48
Federal Bureau of Investigation (FBI), 344, 349, 471, 611–12
Federal Penitentiary for Women, 436–37
Fejos, Paul, 332

Feldman, Meyer "Mike," 536–37, 552, 557, 601–2, 610–11
Fellowes, Maureen, 262, 271, 377–78
Field, Patsy White, 340, 347, 398–99, 426, 427
Finian's Rainbow, 431
Finnegan, Miriam, 80, 173
Fisher, Bob, 90, 109
Fisher, Eddie, 492
Fitzgerald, Agnes, 28, 33, 36, 40, 46, 49, 54, 68–80, 90, 112, 144, 153, 169, 228, 243
Fitzgerald, Eunice, 33, 37–38, 138, 140, 146, 151, 166, 361
Fitzgerald, Fred, 135–36, 243
Fitzgerald, F. Scott, 141
Fitzgerald, Henry, 44
Fitzgerald, James, 26, 44
Fitzgerald, John F., Jr., 33, 37, 46
Fitzgerald, John Francis "Honey Fitz":
    affairs of, 30–31, 47–48, 80, 90, 128, 129, 146–47, 193, 201–2
    background of, 25–26, 126
    birth of, 25
    congressional campaign of, 144–45
    as congressman, 31, 40, 44, 402
    corruption charges against, 44, 64–66, 67, 81–82, 129, 144–45, 174
    death of, 435
    Dorchester mansion of, 41, 114–15, 124–26, 131–32
    education of, 26, 825
    in Europe, 67–69, 80
    as family man, 115, 124–27, 129
    funeral of, 435
    as grandfather, 135–36, 605
    health of, 128–29
    as Irish–American, 115, 128, 134
    JFK and, 164, 201, 202, 317
    Joseph Jr. and, 135–36, 164, 201, 202, 407–8

Joseph Sr. and, 66–67, 90,
    109–10, 127, 131–32, 137,
    179, 181, 192, 195–96, 201,
    299, 326, 519
as Josie Fitzgerald's second
    cousin, 25, 27–28, 48–49, 172
as mayor, 43–48, 49–50, 53, 60,
    61, 64–66, 81–84, 91, 103,
    113–15, 121, 123–30, 174,
    452, 587, 691, 750
at Old Orchard Beach, 51–52,
    57–59
in Palm Beach, 89–92, 299
personality of, 2, 25–26, 33, 58,
    90, 120, 435
P. J. Kennedy and, 44, 52,
    102–3
as politician, 29–30, 31, 34–35,
    38–39, 40, 41–42, 43–48, 54,
    61–62, 65–66, 81–84, 85–86,
    88, 92, 144–45, 164–65, 527,
    568, 587
press coverage of, 44–47, 65,
    80, 115, 124–27, 130, 136
Rosemary and, 316
Rose's relationship with, 28–29,
    33–37, 40, 43, 51–55, 61–62,
    63, 83, 89–92, 113, 114,
    121–22, 130, 131–32, 134,
    139, 145, 148, 202, 250, 291,
    382, 448
Senate campaign of, 128–29
in state legislature, 29
Ted and, 435, 496, 587
wealth of, 41, 64–65, 86
women's suffrage as viewed by,
    113–14
Fitzgerald, Josephine Hannon "Jo-
    sie":
background of, 24–25
as Catholic, 24, 37–38, 48–49
Fitzgerald's funeral and, 435
as Fitzgerald's second cousin,
    25, 27–28, 48–49, 172
marriage of, 28, 29–31, 40–48,
    80–81, 90, 102, 115, 125–27,
    128, 129, 826

personality of, 25, 28, 29, 31,
    32, 37, 42, 81, 124–25, 164
physical appearance of, 124, 156
Rose's relationship with, 28, 31,
    37–38, 39–40, 52, 54, 79, 86,
    87, 126–27, 129, 130,
    146–47, 156, 159, 193, 608
self-control of, 25, 81, 115–16
in women's clubs, 117, 119
Fitzgerald, Polly, 445
Fitzgerald, Rosanna Cox, 26
Fitzgerald, Rose Elizabeth, see
    Kennedy, Rose Fitzgerald
Fitzgerald, Thomas, 26
Fitzgerald, Thomas Acton, 33, 94,
    138, 140, 608
Fitzgerald, Thomas J., 26
Fitzroy, Mary, 279
Fitzwilliam, Olive "Obby"
    Plunkett, 422, 425
Fitzwilliam, Peter, 421–23, 424–32
Flagler, Henry Morrison, 91
Flame of Hope project, 650
Fleeson, Doris, 551–52
Flynn, Nick, 18
Fonda, Henry, 525
Ford, Henry, II, 233, 317
"Forgotten Virtue of Voluntarism,
    The" (Townsend), 773
Fowler, Harry, 218, 241–42, 464,
    680, 692
Frankenheimer, John, 659
Fraser, Hugh, 298, 354, 419, 765
Freckles (RFK's dog), 654
Frederick, Christine, 160
Freeman, Walter, 336–38
Frey, Joanne, 616–17, 628
Friedan, Betty, 744
Frost, David, 3, 730
Frost in May (White), 74
Fulkerson, Lynn L., 185–86

Gable, Clark, 348
Gage, Alan, 197
Galeazzi, Enrico, 227
Galon, Buddy, 472
Garbo, Greta, 198

Gardner, Ava, 469, 470, 507
Gardner, Isabella Stewart, 122, 123–24
Gargan, Ann, 243, 574–75, 578, 579, 580–83, 619, 676–77
Gargan, Joseph F., Jr. "Joey," 243, 243–44, 454, 574, 620, 680, 683
Gargan, Mary Jo, 243, 440, 477
Garland, Judy, 470, 521, 525, 620
George, Phyllis, 769
George VI, King of England, 248, 256–58, 261, 267, 269–70, 289–91, 294–95, 304, 321
Gershe, Leonard, 569
Giancana, Sam, 514, 595, 611
Gibbens, W. Blair, 596–97
Gibbs, Dorothy, 312
Gibson, Barbara, 711, 721, 723
Gilliat, Virginia, 372
Gilligan, Carol, 351
Glenn, John, 665, 667
Gloria (Rosemary's friend), 713
Goddard, Henry Herbert, 171
Gold, Delayne Dedrick, 495
Goldsmith, Arthur, 110
Goldwater, Barry, 611–12
Good, Frederick L., 135, 143, 144, 181, 183
Good Housekeeping, 600, 733, 737, 793
Goodwin, Doris Kearns, 62
Goodwin, Richard, 678
Gould, Milton, 593
Grace, Michael, 233
Grace, Peter, 233–35, 253, 275, 278, 305
Grady, Ronan, 107
Graham, Katharine, 686
Granby, Charles, 384
Green, Edith, 657
Green, Judith, 784
Greene, Graham, 162
Greene, Marie, 140, 286
Greene, Vin, 140
Grier, Roosevelt, 667, 768

Guide for Catholic Young Women (Deshon), 19–20
Guild, Rab, 474
Guinness, Gloria, 629–30, 649, 652, 675, 687–88
Guinness, Loel, 629–30
Gundersen, Karen, 643
Guthman, Edwin O., 611

Hackett, David, 603
Haig, Irene, 279
Haile Selassie, Emperor of Ethiopia, 626, 628, 691
Halifax, Edward Frederick Lindley Wood, Lord, 256, 347
Hals, Frans, 134
Hannah, Daryl, 826
Hannon, Elizabeth, 24–25
Hannon, Emily, 68–69
Hannon, Geraldine, 48, 81, 172, 192
Hannon, John Edmond, 25, 37, 69
Harrington, Alice, 196
Harrison, V. V., 74
Hartington, Kathleen "Kick" Kennedy, Lady:
    allowance of, 175
    Arvad and, 332, 344–45, 350–51
    asthma of, 208, 223
    birth of, 150, 151
    Cambridge University visited by, 225–26, 228–29
    as Catholic, 305, 316, 333–34, 375–77, 380–83, 385–88, 399, 400, 402, 422
    correspondence of, 222–29, 267, 275, 387, 393, 419
    dating by, 203, 205, 224, 229, 234–35, 253, 271–79, 298–99, 305, 333–34, 348, 412
    death of, 430–32, 833
    as debutante, 3, 262–73, 291, 293, 294, 712
    denial by, 209
    diary of, 389, 399–400,

dispensation for marriage sought by, 375–77, 381
education of, 185, 205–210, 222–27, 228–29, 236, 306, 317, 333, 369, 375
emotional reticence of, 264, 322, 334, 348, 401, 423, 427
engagement of, 382–83
in England, 3, 225–26, 228–29, 252, 253, 262–79, 301–2, 310, 359–67, 371–401, 419–23
Eunice's relationship with, 224, 292–93, 334, 425, 427
European trips of, 222–29, 245
Fitzgerald and, 201
on French Riviera, 298–99, 301
French studied by, 223
friends of, 222–23, 259, 262, 282, 288–89, 311, 317, 346, 354–55
gravesite of, 431–32, 607
at Hans Crescent, 362–67, 371–72
in Harlem, 230–31
Hartington's death and, 397–401, 421, 426, 664
Hartington's romance with, 276–79, 288, 293, 295, 299, 302, 318, 354, 363–64, 375–83, 422
honeymoon of, 385–89
Ireland visited by, 419–20
as Irish–American, 419–20
in Italy, 226–27
JFK's relationship with, 186, 207, 209–10, 222–23, 230–31, 315, 316–17, 322, 331–32, 348, 350–51, 353–54, 356, 364, 366–67, 393–95, 419–20, 423, 425, 427
Joseph Jr.'s death and, 392–96
Joseph Jr.'s relationship with, 298, 353, 371–74, 380–81, 396

Joseph Sr.'s affairs as viewed by, 194, 233, 262, 347
Joseph Sr.'s relationship with, 202, 203, 209, 225, 235–36, 253, 288, 295, 310, 314–15, 322, 330–32, 365, 375–76, 382, 384–85, 387, 395, 398, 423, 425, 426, 427, 429, 471
marriage of, 317, 354, 375–77, 380–88, 390, 393, 400–401, 425
memorial to, 491
in Montana, 322
morality of, 373–74
nickname of, 151, 235
in Paris, 222–28, 429–30
Pat's relationship with, 346–47
personality of, 1, 150–151, 168, 203, 210, 223, 227, 236, 263, 264, 274–75, 364, 365, 394, 420, 431–32
physical appearance of, 151, 236, 295, 421, 727
political awareness of, 164, 282, 298, 302, 378, 379, 387
popularity of, 272–79
press coverage of, 253, 274, 282, 299, 365, 386–87, 430, 431
Red Cross work of, 318, 359–67, 375
as reporter, 330–31, 333, 335, 340, 344, 351–52, 353, 354, 360, 413, 450
RFK's relationship with, 395
as role model, 184–85, 188
Rosemary and, 203, 206–7, 266–71
Rose's relationship with, 155, 203, 209, 225, 226–28, 242–43, 272, 298–99, 322, 376–77, 381–83, 385, 386–88, 423, 425, 426, 428–29, 431, 833
in Russia, 228, 479

at Sacred Heart schools, 205–11,
222–28, 236, 306, 317, 369,
375
in Scotland, 282
self-improvement by, 223–24
sex as viewed by, 333–34, 336,
348, 360
sexuality of, 229–31, 236
snobbishness of, 362, 420
social life of, 228–29, 262–79,
305–6, 316, 354, 366,
372–74, 380, 420–23, 766
in Spain, 298, 302
in Switzerland, 225–26
touch football played by, 1, 186,
188–89, 318
in Washington, D.C., 330–31,
333, 335, 340, 344, 351, 352,
353, 354, 360, 361, 413
wedding of, 383–88
weight of, 156–57, 224
wit of, 222, 224, 263–64, 274
Hartington, William "Billy" Cavendish, Lord:
death of, 397–401, 421, 426,
664
Kathleen's engagement to,
382–83
Kathleen's marriage to, 317,
354, 375–77, 380–88, 390,
393, 400–401, 425
Kathleen's romance with,
276–79, 288, 293, 295, 299,
302, 318, 354, 363–64,
375–83, 422
military service of, 377–78,
379–380, 384, 386, 393,
396–401
political campaign of, 377–80,
396
Harvard University:
JFK as student at, 296, 313,
316–17, 352
Joseph Jr. as student at, 217,
222, 313, 331, 352
Joseph Sr. as student at, 64, 66,
67, 93–95, 108–11, 127, 697

RFK as student at, 367, 411
Ted as student at, 435, 443
Haskett, Sheila, 712
Hayden, Frank, 668
Hayes, Theo, 792
Hays, Will H., 180, 233
Healy, Patrick, 13
Hearst, William Randolph, Jr., 372
Heffernan, Mary Hannon, 27
Hennessey, Luella, 160, 246, 250,
256, 260, 268, 271, 282, 292,
299, 302, 319–20, 335, 337,
476–77, 538, 540, 578, 580,
600, 669, 735
Hersey, John, 396, 553
Hibbard, George Albee, 65
Hickey, Catherine, 101, 130, 176
Hickey, Charles, 130
Hickey, James, 130
Hickey, John, 101, 130
Hickey, Margaret, 101
Higgins, Sally Roche, 449–50
Hill, Anita F., 815
Hill, Paul, 824
Hilsman, Roger, 657
Hitler, Adolf, 247, 252, 278, 280,
281, 301, 303, 332, 344, 345,
706
Hoffa, Jimmy, 589
Hogan, Charlotte Murdoch, 411
Hogan, Frank S., 550–51
Hoguet, Eleanor "Ellie," 228
Hoguet, Peter, 416
Holliday, Judy, 468, 470
Holmes, Burton, 64
Holocaust, 281, 289
Holt, Emmett L., 137, 571
Home Life in America (Busbey),
137–38
Hooton, Claude E., Jr., 478, 678
Hoover, J. Edgar, 471, 523, 611
"Hope for Retarded Children" (E.
Shriver), 600–601
Hopper, Hedda, 196, 591
Hornung, Paul, 668
Horowitz, David, 759
Horton, Rip, 418

Houghton, Arthur, 141
House of the Good Shepherd, 439, 442
Hugo, Victor, 72
Huidekoper, Page, 259, 311, 330, 344, 354
Humphrey, Hubert H., 522
Humphrey, Muriel, 530, 531
Hurok, Sol, 303
Husson, Gabrielle, 69
Hutchings, Doris, 185, 186
Hutchinson, Margaret, 428

In Our Defense (C. Kennedy), 782, 823
International Special Olympics Games (1991), 797, 807–10
Irish–Americans:
  alcoholism of, 10–11, 12, 20
  "Brahmin" prejudice against, 16–17, 18, 32, 34, 48, 84–85, 89, 107, 108, 114, 116–17, 133, 177–78
  immigration of, 7, 8–12, 31–32, 48–49, 252
  as laborers, 9–11, 15–16, 19
  marriages of, 5–6, 8, 10–11
"Ithaka" (Cavafy), 830–32
"I Think Continually of Those Who Were Truly Great" (Spender), 740

Jacobs, George, 509
Jacobson, Max, 561–62, 563–64, 631, 642, 643
Jacobson, Nina, 564
Jaffe, Eddie, 405
Jakubik, John, 702
"Joan Kennedy: Her Search for Herself" (David), 737
John, Augustus, 385
John F. Kennedy Library, 630, 634, 649, 739–41, 746, 782, 786, 823
Johnson, Lady Bird, 531, 536, 548, 646
Johnson, Lyndon B., 461, 536
  Eunice and, 633, 648, 652, 655, 656
  Great Society program of, 633
  Jackie and, 645, 646
  JFK's assassination and, 632–33, 648
  RFK and, 632, 645–46, 648, 656
  as vice president, 548, 572
  Vietnam policy of, 645, 651, 656
Johnson, May, 161
Johnson, Rafer, 667, 668
Johnson, Samuel, 42
Johnson, Snakehips, 354, 355
Jordan, Matty, 597
Jordan, Sara M., 313
Joseph P. Kennedy Jr., 407
Joseph P. Kennedy Jr. Foundation, 408, 466, 502–4, 505, 535, 612, 668, 669, 704, 790, 824
Joseph P. Kennedy Jr. Memorial trophy, 571
Joyce, Mrs. Thomas, 346

Kane, Lawrence, 21
Kater, Florence Mary, 524
Keating, Kenneth, 636
Keegan, Dot, 162
Kefauver, Estes, 482
Keller, James, 347, 370, 411, 465–66
Kelley, Ann, 202
Kelley, Pam, 694
Kelly, Gene, 548
Kelly, Grace, 462
Kempton, Murray, 632
Kennedy, Bridget Murphy:
  as Catholic, 13, 18–20
  death of, 22–23, 165
  emigration of, 6–9, 822
  as first Kennedy woman, 3, 605, 823, 825, 826
  as maid, 16
  marriage of, 10–15, 98
  as mother, 11–14
  personality of, 18–20

P.J. Kennedy's relationship with, 15–16, 18–19
store owned by, 17–18, 20, 106
in Wexford County, Ireland, 4–6, 8, 11–12
as widow, 15–16, 100
Kennedy, Caroline Bouvier, *see* Schlossberg, Caroline Kennedy
Kennedy, Christopher George, 609, 658, 659
Kennedy, David Anthony, 477, 655, 659, 661, 666, 671, 692–93, 698, 718
    death of, 760–63, 781, 802
    drug problem of, 693–94, 746, 758–63
Kennedy, Douglas, 707, 758, 759
Kennedy, Edward Moore, Jr., 585, 707–9, 737, 754, 805, 825
Kennedy, Edward Moore "Ted":
    affairs of, 501, 513, 531–32, 589, 676, 709, 711, 733–35, 742–43, 744, 800–801
    assassination as threat to, 676, 701, 738, 747–48
    birth of, 200, 203
    as Catholic, 287, 685
    in Chappaquiddick accident, 676–83, 686, 707, 738, 742, 747, 822, 833
    David Kennedy's death and, 761
    divorce of, 750, 755, 781, 801, 804
    drinking by, 683, 783, 819
    education of, 256, 339, 341, 435, 443, 483, 489, 491, 501
    emotional reticence of, 480, 495, 496, 736, 743–44, 815–16
    in England, 252, 254, 256
    Ethel's relationship with, 669
    as father, 701, 707–8, 731
    First Communion of, 287
    first marriage of, 2, 491, 493, 494–95, 500–501, 531, 587–89, 676, 708, 734–39, 742–45, 749–50, 831

Fitzgerald and, 496, 587
on French Riviera, 299–300
health of, 558, 635
in Hollywood, 472
Jackie's second marriage and, 672
Jean's ambassadorship and, 820–22, 827
Jean's relationship with, 341, 369, 480–81, 800–801
JFK's assassination and, 620, 621–22, 625, 626, 630, 818
as JFK's campaign manager, 498
JFK's legacy and, 635, 652
JFK's political career supported by, 496, 498, 520, 526, 531–32, 613
JFK's presidency and, 613
JFK's relationship with, 501, 585, 613
Joan's drinking problem and, 732–39
Joseph Sr.'s death and, 685
Joseph Sr.'s relationship with, 500, 504–5, 650, 676
in law school, 483, 489, 491, 501
military service of, 443
name of, 217
in Palm Beach, 340–41, 711–12, 800–805
Pat's relationship with, 287, 786
personal courage of, 747
personality of, 435, 491, 495–96, 497, 679, 683, 806, 819
Pius XII met by, 245, 287
in plane crash, 634–35, 676
political advisors of, 678, 679, 746–47, 821
as politician, 491, 496, 520, 587, 652, 683, 725, 748–49
presidential campaign of, 700, 723, 725, 738–39, 742–50, 772

press coverage of, 491–92, 497, 742, 749, 802, 805, 810
RFK's assassination and, 663–64, 665, 677
RFK's presidential campaign and, 676
Rose's autobiography and, 706
Rose's one hundreth birthday and, 1, 781–82
Rose's relationship with, 1, 200, 494, 586–87, 676, 711–12, 731–32, 750, 758, 761, 781–82, 805, 810, 833
second marriage of, 819–20
Senate campaigns of, 584, 585–87, 612–13, 630, 634–35, 730, 772, 821
as senator, 587–89, 634, 679, 681, 683, 738, 821
sense of humor of, 443, 480–81
Shriver's presidential campaign and, 725
skiing by, 283
Smith as campaign manager for, 586, 612, 725, 746–47
Smith trial and, 800–805, 810, 815–16
Squaw Island house of, 730–31, 736, 804
as surrogate father, 666, 676
at Sydney Lawford's wedding, 754
weight of, 443
as youngest sibling, 237, 243–44, 245, 306, 323, 391, 480, 491
Kennedy, Elizabeth Kelly, 826
Kennedy, Ethel Skakel:
abortion opposed by, 698
background of, 409, 654
as Catholic, 698, 699, 780
children of, 443, 477, 487, 490, 499, 501, 659, 666, 692–94
Eunice's relationship with, 693
Hickory Hill home of, 486, 499, 551, 571–72, 631, 655, 670, 697

horses as interest of, 410, 571
at Hyannis Port, 452–53, 607, 693
Jackie's death and, 829
Jackie's relationship with, 452–53, 455, 458, 653
Jean's relationship with, 409–13, 493
JFK's assassination and, 624, 631
at JFK's inauguration, 548
JFK's political career supported by, 443, 482, 531, 533
JFK's presidency and, 551
Joseph Sr.'s death and, 685
Joseph Sr.'s relationship with, 435, 505
Joseph Sr.'s stroke and, 580
Kathleen Townsend's relationship with, 771–72, 775–76
marriage of, 2, 434, 446–47, 486, 499, 631, 640, 654
as mother, 490–91, 571, 654–55, 658, 666, 670–71, 692–93, 754, 760, 761
personality of, 409–10, 584–85, 653
political awareness of, 455
pregnancies of, 436, 452–53, 569, 607, 609, 654, 669
press coverage of, 584
RFK as viewed by, 608, 654, 670–71
RFK's affairs and, 455
RFK's assassination and, 660–65, 666
at RFK's funeral, 663–65
RFK's legacy and, 669–71
RFK's presidential campaign and, 652, 653, 654–55, 656, 659–61
RFK's romance with, 412–13
RFK's Senate campaign and, 638
as RFK's widow, 669–71
Rose's relationship with, 2, 410, 455, 692, 710, 731–32

at Sacred Heart school, 409,
410–11
Smith trial and, 812, 813, 814
social life of, 584–85, 655
Ted's presidential campaign and,
738–39
tennis played by, 452–53, 669,
671
wedding of, 434–35
Kennedy, Eunice Mary, see
Shriver, Eunice Kennedy
Kennedy, Francis Benedict, 98
Kennedy, Jack "London Jack," 271
Kennedy, Jacqueline Bouvier
"Jackie":
at Aspen, 645
background of, 449–50, 452–53
in Canada, 562
Caroline's relationship with,
566–68, 616–17, 674,
729–30, 763–65, 766–67
Caroline's wedding planned by,
766–77
as Catholic, 449, 451, 455, 663
cesarian section of, 610
Chappaquiddick accident and,
678
clothes of, 538–39, 540–41, 542,
559, 617, 622–23, 648
correspondence of, 537
culture of, 559–64
death of, 827–33, 834
divorce threatened by, 486, 517
as editor, 741, 754, 789
education of, 452, 459
emotional reticence of, 449–50
Ethel's relationship with,
452–53, 455, 458, 653
feminism as viewed by, 686
Fifth Avenue apartment of, 789
as first lady, 536–42, 553,
557–68, 569, 570, 584,
604–5, 613–18, 685
funeral of, 829–833
gravesite of, 833
in Greece, 614–15, 673–75
honeymoon of, 457–58

horses as interest of, 450, 557,
593
at Hyannis Port, 452–53, 494,
498–500, 517, 527, 566–68,
607, 609–10, 628–29, 674,
686–87, 788
ill health of, 538, 539–40,
543–44, 547–48, 561–62
intelligence of, 452, 459–60
Jean's relationship with, 517,
630
JFK's affairs and, 455, 484, 505,
514, 564, 613
JFK's assassination and, 617–18,
622–27, 630, 631–33,
648–49, 653–54
JFK's engagement to, 451,
453–56
JFK's first meeting with, 449
JFK's forty-fifth birthday and,
593–94
at JFK's funeral, 624–27, 830
at JFK's inauguration, 543–44,
546–49
JFK's legacy and, 647–49,
669–70
JFK's political career supported
by, 461–62, 481, 482–83,
486, 498–99, 514, 516–20,
528–30, 532, 534–35,
613–14, 617–18
JFK's romance with, 450
JFK's vice-presidential nomination and, 481, 482, 485
as JFK's widow, 630, 631–32,
645, 669–70, 672–73, 686–87
Joan's relationship with, 566,
587
John's relationship with, 566,
615–16, 674
Joseph Sr.'s death and, 684
Joseph Sr.'s relationship with,
451–52, 460, 462–63, 486,
539, 654, 684
Joseph Sr.'s stroke and, 577, 580
Kennedy sisters and, 452–55,
458–59, 472, 530

LBJ and, 645, 646

marriage of, 446–47, 448–49, 451, 456–57, 458–64, 481, 486, 516, 562, 564, 613–14, 827, 831

Martha's Vineyard estate of, 788–89

miscarriages of, 485, 537

as mother, 566–68, 616

in New York City, 633, 789

in Palm Beach, 540–42, 695

in Paris, 563–64

personality of, 449–50, 451, 452–53, 454–55, 458–60, 580

as photographer, 450, 765

physical appearance of, 449, 617

poetry written by, 459

political awareness of, 455, 536, 567–68, 645

post-Onassis life of, 741–42, 754, 755–56, 766–67, 788–89, 827–29

pregnancies of, 481–85, 525, 529, 532, 534, 537, 604–5, 609–10, 613–14

press coverage of, 456, 516–17, 529–30, 546–47, 615, 636, 645, 673, 741, 827, 828, 829–30

privacy needed by, 566–68, 673, 741, 788–89, 828

public image of, 529–30, 535–40, 541, 542, 562, 563–64

RFK's assassination and, 653, 663

RFK's presidential campaign and, 652, 653, 659

RFK's relationship with, 458, 485, 631–32, 636, 645, 653, 674, 832

RFK's Senate campaign and, 636, 637

Rose as viewed by, 455, 686, 687

Rose compared with, 458, 613

Rose's relationship with, 451–52, 454, 455, 459, 498, 541–42, 561, 672–73, 674–75, 685–87

Rose's views on, 455–56, 460, 486

second marriage of, 672–75, 684, 719–20, 827

snobbishness of, 532

social life of, 458–60

Squaw Island house of, 566, 607, 610

at Sydney Lawford's wedding, 754, 755–56

Ted's presidential campaign and, 745

touch football played by, 453, 459

voice of, 449, 453, 686

in Washington, D.C., 449–50, 458–60, 486, 536–41, 547–48

wealth of, 673–74, 684, 720, 741

wedding of, 448–49, 450, 455–57

White House redecorated by, 559–60, 646

White House tour of, 539–40

as wife, 516–18

Kennedy, James, 8

Kennedy, Jean Ann, see Smith, Jean Kennedy

Kennedy, Joan Bennett:
background of, 492, 495

Chappaquiddick accident and, 679–80, 681–82

divorce of, 750, 755, 781, 801, 804

drinking problem of, 588–89, 676, 682, 709–10, 733–39, 742–43, 783, 786, 805–6, 825

engagement of, 496–97, 500

Eunice's relationship with, 709, 735–36

feminism supported by, 744

as grandmother, 825

at Hyannis Port, 494, 749–50

Jackie's death and, 831

Jackie's relationship with, 566, 587

JFK's assassination and, 620, 630

at JFK's inauguration, 548

JFK's political career supported by, 522, 525–26, 531–32, 613

JFK's presidency and, 613

Joseph Sr.'s relationship with, 496, 497, 500–501, 504–5

marriage of, 2, 491, 494, 496–97, 500–501, 531, 587–89, 676, 708, 734–39, 742–45, 749–50, 831

miscarriages of, 609, 634, 682

as mother, 707–9, 730–31, 735, 737

personality of, 497, 588–89

physical appearance of, 492, 494, 496, 522, 531, 588, 709, 733, 735, 805

political awareness of, 586, 588, 613, 739

pregnancies of, 609, 634, 680, 682

press coverage of, 733, 734–35, 736, 737–38, 749

RFK's assassination and, 662–63

RFK's presidential campaign and, 657, 659

Rose's relationship with, 2, 494–95, 501–2, 587, 676, 730–32, 734–35, 781

at Sacred Heart school, 492–95

as senator's wife, 587–89, 634, 732, 739

at Sydney Lawford's wedding, 754, 755

Ted's affairs and, 500–501, 513, 531–32, 589, 676, 709, 711, 733–35, 742–44, 800–801

Ted's presidential campaign and, 738–39, 742–45, 747–50

Ted's romance with, 491–97

Ted's Senate campaigns and, 585–87, 613, 630, 634–35

television work of, 492

in Washington, D.C., 587–89

wedding of, 500–501

Kennedy, Joanna, 11, 16, 19, 21

Kennedy, John, 11

Kennedy, John Fitzgerald:

Addison's disease of, 423–24, 535

adolescence of, 215

affairs of, 202, 230–31, 295, 316, 332, 348–51, 383, 418, 424, 450–51, 455, 464, 471, 484, 505, 512–15, 523–26, 542, 564–65, 610–12, 613, 615

as altar boy, 162, 166, 167

as Anglophile, 605

assassination attempt against, 540–41

assassination of, 617–34, 648–49, 653, 665, 818, 833

in auto accident, 299

back problems of, 444, 460–64, 562–63, 567, 630

birth of, 138

books about, 524–25, 647–49

campaign biography of, 525

in Canada, 561–62

as Catholic, 162, 166, 167–68, 255, 316, 402, 404, 487–88, 521–22

childhood of, 143, 145–146

at Choate, 203–4, 213

congressional campaign of (1946), 402–407

as congressman, 413–15, 418–19, 424

daily schedule of, 610–11

dancing class taken by, 230

dating by, 205, 332, 345, 348–51

education of, 203–4, 213, 222–23, 296, 313, 317, 329, 342, 352

emotional reticence of, 160, 264, 349–50, 379, 417, 423, 535

in England, 222–23, 295, 301

Eunice's relationship with, 204–5, 255, 407, 414–19, 424, 458, 535, 554–55, 556–57
as family man, 481–86, 499–500
as father, 517, 518
Fitzgerald and, 64, 201, 202, 317
forty-fifth birthday of, 593–94
on French Riviera, 299, 483–86
friends of, 207, 240–41, 394–95, 412, 647–48
funeral of, 624–27, 830
golf played by, 566–67
gravesite of, 626, 663, 833
at Hyannis Port, 607–9, 686
ill health of, 138, 143, 146–47, 150, 155, 203–05, 208, 223, 237, 331, 349, 356, 393, 419, 423–24, 435, 444, 460–64, 535, 540, 562–63, 567, 619, 630
inaugural address of, 546
inauguration of, 536, 542, 544, 545–49
intelligence of, 491, 523
Ireland visited by, 419–20, 605–6, 626
as Irish–American, 405–6, 419–20, 605–6
irresponsibility of, 220
isolationism as viewed by, 315, 316–17
Joseph Jr.'s death and, 392, 393–95, 400–401, 408
Joseph Jr.'s relationship with, 155, 217, 371, 380
Joseph Sr.'s affairs as viewed by, 202, 233, 242, 316, 484
Joseph Sr.'s relationship with, 150, 167, 202, 203, 209–10, 321, 327, 331–32, 345, 366, 395, 484, 504–5, 523, 543, 573, 609
Joseph Sr.'s stroke and, 577, 579
journalism as interest of, 403
Kathleen's death and, 431

Kathleen's grave visited by, 606–7
Kathleen's relationship with, 186, 207, 209–10, 222–23, 230–31, 315, 316–17, 322, 331–32, 348, 350–51, 353–54, 356, 364, 366–67, 393–95, 419–20, 423, 425, 427
Kennedy family as viewed by, 522–23
Lawford's relationship with, 549, 590–91, 596–97, 611
legacy of, 628–29, 635–36, 637–38, 647–50, 652, 669–70, 739–40, 763–65, 782–83
at London School of Economics, 222
loyalty to, 552–53
Manichaean view of, 442
marriage of, 447, 448–49, 450–51, 457, 458–60, 481, 485–86, 516, 561–62, 564–65, 613–14, 827, 831
Monroe and, 590, 592–93, 594
musicals liked by, 431, 565, 629
name of, 138
in Naval Reserves, 331, 339, 345, 356–57
New Frontier program of, 549, 551, 554, 561
Onassis as viewed by, 614–15, 624
pain injections for, 561–62, 563, 564
in Palm Beach, 540–42
in Paris, 563–64
Pat's relationship with, 357, 597
personality of, 160, 222, 264, 274, 322, 348–49, 379, 417, 423, 485–86, 535, 609
political acumen of, 218, 293, 315, 316–17, 530, 536–37, 539, 562, 567, 648
popularity of, 584, 626–27

as president, 1, 217, 526–27,
    535–36, 540–46, 551–59,
    563–64, 572–74, 585,
    600–605, 612–13
as president-elect, 535–37, 539
presidential campaign of, 486,
    487–88, 497, 502, 512,
    514–35
presidential reelection campaign
    of, 597, 612–13, 615–16,
    617–18
press coverage of, 345, 396,
    443–44, 445, 522–24, 526
at Princeton, 223
as PT-109 skipper, 357, 361,
    366–67, 394, 553, 716
Pulitzer Prize awarded to, 490
RFK as campaign manager for,
    443, 772
RFK's relationship with, 407,
    443, 543, 609–10, 772
Rose as viewed by, 153, 159,
    215, 345–46, 523
Rosemary's relationship with,
    214, 239, 267, 319, 334, 349,
    519, 600, 712
Rose's relationship with, 149,
    153, 173, 184, 203–5,
    345–46, 366, 390, 424,
    455–56, 484, 523, 572–73,
    712, 833
Senate campaigns of, 442–45,
    496, 497–500
as senator, 456, 458–59, 465
senior thesis of, 296, 317
as sibling, 184
Smith as campaign manager of,
    612
social life of, 316, 417–19
in Stevenson campaign, 486–87
Ted's relationship with, 501,
    585, 613
as vice-presidential candidate,
    481–83, 484, 487
at Vienna summit, 562
as war hero, 366–67, 371, 380,
    389, 396

in Washington, D.C., 331–32,
    344–45, 413, 414–15
wit of, 222–23, 274
women as viewed by, 484,
    518–19, 543, 551–52
Kennedy, John Fitzgerald, Jr.
    "John John":
    birth of, 537, 544, 548
    Caroline's relationship with,
        617, 740
    ill health of, 540
    Jackie's death and, 829–30
    Jackie's relationship with, 566,
        616, 674
    JFK's assassination and, 622–23,
        624–26, 628–29, 630
    LBJ's letter to, 646
    love life of, 826
    physical appearance of, 740
    press coverage of, 566, 567
    Rose's relationship with, 572
    Ted's presidential campaign and,
        746
Kennedy, Joseph Patrick, Jr.:
    adolescence of, 215
    affairs of, 230, 276, 295,
        372–73, 377, 380, 383
    as altar boy, 162, 167
    birth of, 135–36, 138
    book of reminiscences about,
        400–401
    as Catholic, 162, 168, 380–81,
        382, 385
    childhood of, 136–38
    confirmation of, 162–63
    correspondence of, 416
    dating by, 205
    death of, 389–90, 391–96, 405,
        407–8, 665, 833
    education of, 204, 217, 222,
        313, 331, 352
    as eldest sibling, 155, 184
    in England, 222, 276, 295, 301
    Eunice's relationship with, 394,
        407–8
    European trips of, 245, 283

Fitzgerald and, 135–36, 164, 201, 202, 407–8
on French Riviera, 299
friends of, 240–41
as isolationist, 301–302, 315
Jean's relationship with, 184, 217
JFK's relationship with, 155, 217, 371, 380
Joseph Sr.'s affairs as viewed by, 242
Joseph Sr.'s relationship with, 167, 202, 217, 327, 377
Kathleen's marriage and, 380–81, 383, 385, 400–401
Kathleen's relationship with, 298, 353, 371–74, 380–81, 396
in law school, 313, 331
in London, 222, 371–74
at London School of Economics, 222
as Navy pilot, 331, 339, 357, 361, 371, 373, 380, 389–90
political acumen of, 218, 385
portrait of, 790
robustness of, 136, 138, 143, 151, 167–68, 203, 208
as role model, 184, 188
Rosemary's relationship with, 214, 239, 267, 285, 319, 712
Rose's relationship with, 155, 188, 203, 381, 387, 390, 712, 833
in Russia, 228, 479
at St. Moritz, 283, 285
in Spain, 286, 298
sports of, 1, 216–17, 219, 283
Kennedy, Joseph Patrick, Sr.:
affairs of, 105, 110, 121, 141–42, 152–53, 181–87, 192–99, 202, 232–33, 241–42, 244, 261–62, 295, 316, 345, 347, 383, 418, 454–71, 477–78, 484–85, 486, 506, 613, 674, 682
alcohol avoided by, 85

aloofness of, 160, 161
as ambassador to Great Britain, 2, 247–328, 329
ambitions of, 180, 216
anger of, 259, 325–27, 638
appeasement supported by, 280–83, 287–89, 301, 303, 317, 323, 706
Arvad as viewed by, 345–46, 351
authority of, 156–57, 186–87, 216, 242, 260–61
automobiles owned by, 132, 174, 177, 197
as banker, 127, 130, 134, 176
baseball played by, 54, 93–95, 107
at Bethlehem Steel, 139, 140–41
birth of, 22, 98
"Brahmins" as viewed by, 107, 175
British criticism of, 283, 288–89, 314, 315, 321
in Bronxville, 187–250
in Brookline, 132–80
"bullpen" of, 215
as Catholic, 53, 64, 93, 104, 108, 111, 130, 142, 162, 177, 179–80, 187, 242, 324, 375–76, 382, 453, 622
Chamberlain and, 258, 300–301, 325
Chappaquiddick accident and, 676–77, 681, 684
childhood of, 99–108
in Cohasset, 177–78
death of, 609, 684–85
defeatism of, 321, 329
democracy as viewed by, 328–29
as diplomat, 253–54, 257–61, 323–24
in East Boston, 99–103, 110, 256
education of, 53, 54, 64, 66, 67, 93–95, 104, 107–9, 110, 127, 697, 825

Ethel's relationship with, 435,
    504–505
Eunice's relationship with, 179,
    200–203, 292, 308–9, 318,
    321, 394, 413–14, 448, 504,
    535, 600, 684, 808
as family man, 179–80, 187,
    192, 261, 280–81, 309–13,
    320–21, 327
as family patriarch, 1, 145,
    215–19, 243, 260–61, 309–11,
    408, 471, 489–90, 504–5,
    524–25, 613, 650–51, 677,
    711
as father, 150, 168–69, 202–3,
    227
as film producer, 179–80, 186,
    189, 194–95, 196–97, 200,
    207
Fitzgerald and, 66–67, 90,
    109–10, 127, 131–32, 137,
    179, 181, 192, 195–96, 201,
    299, 326, 519
golf played by, 574
as grandfather, 607, 650–51
health of, 196, 199, 310, 313
in Hollywood, 179–80, 186–87,
    196–97, 200
at Horizon House, 579–83
at Hyannis Port, 215–17, 235,
    583, 621–22, 662, 676–77,
    681, 684–85
as Irish–American, 54, 98,
    104–5, 822
as isolationist, 254, 257,
    280–81, 288–89, 291, 293,
    301, 314, 327, 329, 330, 331,
    340, 411
Jackie's relationship with,
    451–52, 460, 462–63, 486,
    539, 654, 684
Jean's relationship with, 184–85,
    407, 411, 412, 480
Jews as viewed by, 328
JFK's assassination and, 621–22
JFK's political career supported

by, 402, 403, 405, 407,
    487–88, 503, 519, 526
JFK's presidency and, 543, 573,
    574
JFK's relationship with, 150,
    167, 202, 203, 209–10, 321,
    327, 331–32, 345, 366, 395,
    484, 504–5, 523, 543, 573,
    609
Joseph Jr.'s death and, 391–92,
    394–95, 407–408
Joseph Jr.'s relationship with,
    167, 202, 217, 327, 377
Kathleen's death and, 430–31,
    432
Kathleen's marriage and,
    375–76, 382, 385, 387
Kathleen's relationship with,
    202, 203, 209, 225, 235–36,
    253, 288, 295, 310, 314–15,
    322, 330–32, 365, 375–76,
    382, 384–85, 387, 395, 398,
    423, 425, 426, 427, 429, 471
Lawford's relationship with,
    468, 471
in London blitz, 318, 320–21,
    325
as Maritime Commission chair-
    man, 235, 236
marriage of, 66–67, 77, 79, 127,
    129–49, 152–53, 162–63,
    169, 192–99, 201, 329, 353,
    573–74, 577–83, 687, 705,
    750–51
Mary Augusta's relationship
    with, 95, 96, 99, 104–6, 107,
    111, 130, 139, 311
name of, 98, 106
in Palm Beach, 150, 153,
    181–83, 200, 283, 329, 543,
    573–79, 583
at papal audience, 286–87, 324
Pat's relationship with, 310, 318,
    368, 471, 477–78, 511, 595
personality of, 54, 94–95,
    104–10, 112, 130, 160, 161–
    62, 182, 197, 353, 392, 768

physical rehabilitation of, 577, 579–83

P. J. Kennedy's relationship with, 108–9, 139, 189–90

political acumen of, 218, 221, 280–81, 322–29

populist reputation of, 264–65, 267–69, 289

press coverage of, 130–31, 180, 247, 253, 300, 313, 323, 328, 345

Prince's Gate residence of, 254, 281, 310, 320

private movie theater of, 191, 241–42

radio address of, 325, 327

real estate ventures of, 176–77

resignation of ambassadorship by, 322–29

RFK's assassination and, 662

RFK's presidential campaign and, 652

RFK's relationship with, 395, 490, 505, 573, 638

in Riverdale, 180–87

Rose as viewed by, 321, 351

Rosemary's relationship with, 213, 312–13, 334–37, 433–34, 524–25, 600–601

Rose's views on, 121, 139–40, 141–42, 146–49, 179–80, 192–93, 215, 221–22, 241–42, 250–51, 283, 285, 309, 312–13, 314, 322, 329, 352, 353, 751, 833

at royal occasions, 256–59, 261, 264–65, 267–70

at St. Leonard's estate, 311

as SEC chairman, 221, 235, 247

shrewdness of, 95, 106–109

Shriver's relationship with, 416, 447–48

social life of, 109, 110–11, 130, 140, 160, 177, 182, 216

as stockbroker, 141, 152, 169, 176–77, 190, 199

stroke suffered by, 575–83, 607, 609, 646, 650–51, 676–77

success of, 104, 106, 107–9, 110–11, 130, 139, 140–41, 152, 174, 176–78, 179

Ted's relationship with, 500–501, 504, 650, 676–77

Trafalgar Speech of, 282–83

trust funds established by, 175, 712, 777, 795

ulcer of, 196, 313

vacations of, 150, 153, 181

in Washington, D.C., 221, 235, 246–47, 283, 323–29

wealth of, 2, 109, 140–41, 174–78, 180, 187–88, 190, 199–200, 220–21, 408, 466, 504–5, 519, 613

weight of, 156, 196, 310

at Windsor Castle, 256

in Winthrop, 110

Kennedy, Joseph Patrick "Joe II," 443, 492, 501, 662, 663, 665, 666, 667, 761

adolescent problems of, 692–93, 693–94, 718, 730

in auto accident, 694, 730

divorce of, 799, 826

at JFK Library dedication, 740–41

political career of, 730, 748, 772, 773, 775, 777, 823

Kennedy, Kara Ann, 531, 585, 680, 729–30, 737, 747, 799, 825, 826

Kennedy, Katherine Gershman "Kiki," 825

Kennedy, Kathleen Agnes "Kick," see Hartington, Kathleen "Kick" Kennedy, Lady

Kennedy, Kathleen Hartington, see Townsend, Kathleen Kennedy

Kennedy, Kerry, 659, 666, 783, 798–99, 811, 824

Kennedy, Loretta, 68, 189–90, 714

Kennedy, Margaret, 11, 16, 21

Kennedy, Margaret Louise, 98,
    111, 131, 189, 190, 408
Kennedy, Mary, 11, 16, 19, 21
Kennedy, Mary Augusta Hickey:
    background of, 21–22, 95, 96,
        97–98, 826
    death of, 165–66, 311
    Joseph Sr.'s relationship with,
        95, 96, 99, 104–6, 107, 111,
        130, 139, 311
    at Joseph Sr.'s wedding, 131
    marriage of, 21–22, 96–104, 111
    personality of, 96, 97–102, 825
    in Winthrop, 110–11, 165
Kennedy, Mary Courtney, 487,
    501, 658, 659, 799, 824
Kennedy, Mary Loretta, 98, 111,
    131, 392, 408
Kennedy, Matthew "Max," 659,
    804
Kennedy, Michael LeMoyne, 490,
    659
Kennedy, Patricia, see Lawford,
    Patricia Kennedy
Kennedy, Patrick:
    background of, 8–9, 606, 822
    as cooper, 11
    illness and death of, 14–15, 20,
        23
    marriage of, 10–15, 98
Kennedy, Patrick Bouvier, 610,
    613–14
Kennedy, Patrick Joseph, 671,
    730–31, 737, 748, 800–801,
    802, 804–5, 815, 823
Kennedy, Patrick Joseph "P.J.":
    as banker, 103, 128, 190
    birth of, 13–14
    Bridget's relationship with,
        15–16, 18–19
    death of, 190, 435
    education of, 18–19, 20
    estate of, 190
    Fitzgerald and, 44, 52, 102–3
    Joseph Sr.'s relationship with,
        108–9, 139, 189–90
    liquor business of, 102

    marriage of, 21–22, 96, 104, 111
    personality of, 20, 103–4
    as politician, 21, 44–45, 54, 66,
        95, 96, 99, 101–3
    real estate ventures of, 103–4
    in state legislature, 21, 96
    taverns owned by, 21, 66, 97,
        102
Kennedy, Robert F., Jr., 501, 662,
    663–64, 665, 666–67,
    692–94, 698, 718, 748, 754
Kennedy, Robert Francis:
    affairs of, 455, 590, 593–594
    anger of, 638, 674
    anti-Communism of, 465
    assassination of, 653, 660–65,
        666, 676, 759, 818, 833
    as attorney general, 2, 543, 551,
        584, 590, 603, 608, 631, 635,
        774
    birth of, 169
    as Catholic, 237, 632
    as chief counsel in Senate labor
        investigations, 489, 490
    as congressman, 465
    education of, 256, 339, 367,
        411, 435
    in England, 252, 254, 256
    as father, 658, 697, 701
    funeral of, 663–65
    gravesite of, 663–65
    at Hyannis Port, 454, 567
    intelligence of, 491
    Jackie's relationship with, 458,
        485, 631–32, 636, 645, 653,
        674–832
    Jean's relationship with, 412–13,
        480, 642
    JFK's assassination and, 620,
        623, 624, 625, 626, 631–32
    as JFK's campaign manager,
        443, 772
    at JFK's inauguration, 549
    JFK's legacy and, 637–38
    JFK's political career supported
        by, 407, 443, 520, 526, 532,
        533

JFK's presidency and, 543, 553
JFK's relationship with, 407,
    443, 543, 609–10, 772
Joseph Sr.'s relationship with,
    395, 490, 505, 573, 638
Joseph Sr.'s stroke and, 577, 580
Kathleen's relationship with, 395
in law school, 435
LBJ and, 632, 645–46, 648, 656
legacy of, 669–71, 740, 774,
    776, 778, 780
marriage of, 2, 434, 446–47,
    486, 499, 631, 640, 654
memorial mass for, 671
memorials for, 669, 671, 675,
    740–41, 774–75, 783
Monroe and, 590, 593, 594
in Naval Reserve, 367, 391
personal courage of, 608
personality of, 608, 610, 638,
    639, 656, 674
pneumonia of, 246
as politician, 520, 656–57, 694,
    774
presidential campaign of,
    651–61, 667, 676
press coverage of, 490, 636–37
Rose's relationship with, 246,
    489–90, 712, 833
Senate campaign of, 635–38
Shriver as viewed by, 528, 656
as sibling, 318
Smith as campaign manager for,
    636
social life of, 584, 585
sports of, 1, 238, 283
in Stevenson campaign, 487
Kennedy, Rory Elizabeth Kather-
    ine, 669, 707, 811, 824–25
Kennedy, Rose Fitzgerald:
acquisitiveness of, 174
alcohol avoided by, 85
aloofness of, 137, 157, 158–60,
    160, 161, 192, 245, 353
as ambassador's wife, 247–328,
    329, 581
ambition of, 79–80, 117–18

appendicitis of, 250–51
art owned by, 463
at Ascot, 261
authority of, 137, 156–57, 216
in auto accident, 167
autobiography of, 3, 93, 132,
    168–69, 228, 704–7
at Berlin Opera, 76
biography of, 700
birth of, 2
"Brahmins" as viewed by,
    117–18, 123–24
in Bronxville, 187–250, 286,
    287, 304–40, 353
in Brookline, 132–80, 181
in California, 153
Caroline's relationship with,
    541–42, 572, 730, 764
as Catholic, 34–35, 37–38,
    48–49, 53–54, 56, 61–80,
    82–83, 89, 113–21, 124, 131,
    142, 145, 148, 154–55,
    161–63, 168, 177, 216,
    244–45, 249, 286–87,
    304–305, 317, 375–76,
    380–81, 405, 425–29, 465,
    587, 662, 688, 722
Chappaquiddick accident and,
    676–77, 678–79, 682–83,
    707, 833
charity ball founded by, 118,
    147–48, 158, 166
childhood of, 28–51, 205
as Child of Mary, 76, 77–79, 83,
    89, 148
child-rearing practices of,
    135–38, 153–61, 166–69
clothes of, 114–15, 161, 175–76,
    196, 248–49, 261, 649
in Cohasset, 177–78
in Concord Junction, 33–41, 54,
    156, 181, 729
correspondence of, 69, 72–73,
    204, 213–14, 248, 256, 284,
    323
daily walks of, 695, 717

daughter's boyfriends as viewed
    by, 224, 226, 235, 242
death of, 834–36
as debutante, 86–89, 131, 180
declining health of, 1, 740, 744,
    750–51, 754, 757–58, 760,
    761–62, 781–83, 833–34
decorum admired by, 289–90
denial by, 192–93, 194, 249–50,
    575–76, 582–83, 833
diary of, 168, 256, 260, 295,
    519, 541, 553, 672, 721
as disciplinarian, 157, 158–60,
    166, 168, 728
discontent of, 144
in Dorchester, 41–43, 49–51, 54,
    56, 63, 114–16, 124–27,
    131–32, 146–49, 181, 205
duty as important to, 120
education of, 36–37, 38–40,
    42–43, 49–51, 53, 56–57,
    60–64, 67, 69–80, 82–83, 84,
    86–87, 88, 89, 114, 116,
    118–19, 137, 146, 168, 192,
    205, 212, 222, 248, 249, 383,
    587, 722
efficiency of, 160
in Egypt, 286
in England, 80, 252–303
England as viewed by, 284
Ethel's relationship with, 2, 410,
    455, 692, 710, 731–32
in Ethiopia, 691
Eunice's relationship with, 243,
    352–53, 675, 717–18,
    720–21, 724, 740, 758, 781,
    833–34
European trips of, 67–69,
    112–14, 134, 194–95, 196,
    201, 222, 227–28, 245–46,
    629–30, 687–89, 691, 711
fame of, 707, 717–18, 730
as family matriarch, 1–2, 154,
    158–59, 218, 242–43, 260,
    285, 369, 505, 517, 523,
    644–45, 674–75, 694–96,
    704–12, 716–24, 730,

750–51, 757–58, 781–82,
    805, 833–34
family newsletters of, 339, 343,
    352, 696
film about, 2–3, 783
Fitzgerald's death and, 435
Fitzgerald's relationship with,
    28–29, 33–37, 40, 43, 51–55,
    61–62, 63, 83, 89–92, 113,
    114, 121–22, 130, 131–32,
    134, 139, 145, 148, 202, 250,
    291, 382, 448
flower arranging by, 243
on French Riviera, 280,
    298–301
French studied by, 42, 63, 70,
    72, 117
friendships of, 56, 88–89, 118,
    629–30
furnishings selected by, 134,
    152, 191
generosity of, 695
golf played by, 574, 575–76
as grandmother, 2, 3, 572–73,
    609, 696, 716, 730–31
handwriting of, 214
Hartington's death and, 400
honeymoon of, 132
hospitalizations of, 167, 386
as hostess, 259–60, 292
at Hull, 135–36
at Hyannis Port, 1–2, 582–83,
    608–9, 692, 716–19, 723–24,
    761–62, 781–83, 788, 833–34
independence of, 54–56, 76–77,
    121–22
as Irish–American, 35, 37, 54,
    68, 81, 85–86, 121–24, 137,
    252
Jackie as viewed by, 455–56,
    460, 486
Jackie compared with, 458, 613
Jackie's death and, 833
Jackie's relationship with,
    451–52, 454, 455, 459, 498,
    541–42, 561, 672–73,
    674–75, 685–87

Jackie's second marriage and, 672–73, 674–75

Jackie's view on, 454–55, 685–87

Jean's relationship with, 184, 676, 691, 704, 721–22, 723, 750–51, 761, 786–87, 801

jewelry owned by, 131, 198

Jews as viewed by, 196–97, 322

JFK's assassination and, 619–20, 621, 625, 626, 629–30, 631, 632, 833

at JFK's inauguration, 545–46, 548

JFK's legacy and, 629–30, 649–50

JFK's political career supported by, 402, 405, 406, 443–44, 446, 498–500, 519, 525–26, 527, 533, 535

JFK's presidency and, 1, 541, 572–73, 585

JFK's relationship with, 149, 153, 173, 184, 203–5, 345–46, 366, 390, 424, 455–56, 484, 523, 572–73, 712, 833

Joan's relationship with, 2, 494–95, 501–2, 587, 676, 730–32, 734–35, 781

John's relationship with, 572

Joseph Jr.'s death and, 391–92, 394–95, 444, 582

Joseph Jr.'s relationship with, 155, 188, 203, 381, 387, 390, 712, 833

Joseph Sr. as viewed by, 121, 139–40, 141–42, 146–49, 179–80, 192–93, 215, 221–22, 241–42, 250–51, 283, 285, 309, 312–13, 314, 322, 329, 352, 353, 751, 833

Joseph Sr.'s courtship of, 53–54, 57, 64, 66–67, 68, 70, 83, 89, 90–91, 92–93, 109–10, 112, 127, 129, 299

Joseph Sr.'s death and, 609, 684–85

Joseph Sr.'s stroke and, 575–83, 609, 646, 651, 677, 761

Joseph Sr.'s views on, 321, 351–52

as Joseph Sr.'s widow, 3, 685–86

Josie Fitzgerald's relationship with, 28, 31, 37–38, 39–40, 52, 54, 79, 86, 87, 126–27, 129, 130, 146–47, 156, 159, 193, 608

Kathleen's death and, 431, 582

Kathleen's marriage and, 376–77, 381–83, 385, 386–88, 390, 582

Kathleen's relationship with, 155, 203, 209, 225, 226–28, 242–43, 272, 298–99, 322, 376–77, 381–83, 385, 386–88, 423, 425, 426, 428–29, 431, 833

Kathleen Townsend's relationship with, 688–91, 696

marriage as viewed by, 113, 152

marriage of, 67, 77, 79, 127, 129–49, 152–53, 163, 168–69, 192–99, 201, 329, 353, 573–74, 577–83, 687, 704–5, 750–51

memory of, 608

morality of, 120–21, 127–28, 209, 218, 286–87, 289–90, 306, 373

as mother, 2–3, 79, 135–38, 143, 145–46, 148–49, 150–51, 153–61, 166–69, 184, 186, 200, 203, 227–28, 245–46, 249, 571, 721–22, 727–28

in New York City, 82–83, 84

at Old Orchard Beach, 51–52, 57–59, 91–92

one hundredth birthday of, 1–2, 781–83, 788

optimism of, 167, 352

in Palm Beach, 89–92, 153, 181,
299, 340–41, 425, 541–42,
694–96, 705, 710–12, 761–62
at papal audience, 286–87
Pat's relationship with, 243,
245–46, 346, 476–77, 595,
721, 723, 750–51, 781,
784–85
as pedagogue, 118, 153, 155–56,
218
personality of, 2–3, 36, 49–51,
54, 55–56, 59, 62, 67, 69,
72–73, 77, 81, 82, 84, 93,
115, 137, 149, 180, 200,
249–51, 454–55, 687–89,
694–96
physical appearance of, 2,
35–36, 46, 50, 131, 156, 180,
196, 608, 687, 716
piano played by, 64, 144, 240,
494, 751
political awareness of, 40, 44,
45–46, 50, 55, 65, 82, 91,
114, 115, 124–25, 127,
247–48, 258–59, 281,
282–84, 323–29, 444,
535–36, 824
pregnancies of, 135–36, 138,
142, 169, 180, 181, 183, 197
press coverage of, 46, 50–51,
86–87, 89, 92, 112–13,
114–15, 118, 130–31, 144,
252, 253–54, 284, 291, 303,
386–87, 533, 737, 781
privacy needed by, 152, 253,
717
reading by, 39–40
RFK's assassination and, 662,
664, 833
RFK's presidential campaign
and, 652–53, 656, 657
RFK's relationship with, 246,
489–90, 712, 833
in Riverdale, 180–87
Rosemary's relationship with,
143–44, 149, 172–74,
200–201, 212, 213–14, 239,

284–85, 334, 335, 337, 338,
339, 434, 582, 712–14, 833
routine as important to, 137,
155–57, 240, 454, 575–76,
608, 694–95, 717
at royal occasions, 256–58, 261,
264–65, 266, 267–70,
289–91, 294–95
in Russian, 228, 479
at Sacred Heart schools, 62–64,
67, 69–80, 82–83, 84, 89,
114, 116, 137, 146, 168, 192,
205, 212, 222, 248, 249, 587,
722
at St. Moritz, 283–85
in Scotland, 281–82
self-control of, 3, 66, 69, 72, 78,
81, 82, 84, 115, 137, 153,
156, 159, 167, 218, 250, 353,
526, 579, 705–6, 721, 722–23
self-criticism of, 118
self-improvement philosophy of,
118, 523
sense of humor of, 489, 706
sex life of, 141, 142–43,
152–53, 196
shrewdness of, 93
social life of, 36, 42–43, 49–57,
64, 67, 83, 84–92, 112,
114–27, 140–49, 158, 160,
174, 177, 185, 192, 199, 248,
261, 266–67, 289–91, 694–95
social work by, 89, 117
Swanson and, 184, 192–99, 706
at Sydney Lawford's wedding,
754, 755, 757
Ted's presidential campaign and,
700–701, 744, 748
Ted's relationship with, 1, 200,
494, 586–87, 676, 711–12,
731–32, 750, 758, 761,
781–82, 805, 810, 833
Ted's Senate campaigns and,
586–87
twentieth wedding anniversary
of, 201
in Washington, D.C., 323–29

wedding of, 129–32, 139, 287
weight of, 156–57
as wife, 135, 139–40, 146–49,
    152–53, 167, 168–69,
    179–80, 196, 244, 249,
    258–59, 260–61
at Windsor Castle, 256–58
as woman, 2–3, 38, 55–56, 59,
    76–77, 78–80, 112–13, 115,
    145, 153
in women's clubs, 116–18, 135,
    144, 147–48, 158, 166,
    249–50, 405
writing ambitions of, 351
Kennedy, Rose Marie "Rosemary":
allowance of, 175
anger of, 240, 320, 334, 434,
    796
birth of, 143, 144
Caroline's relationship with,
    714, 795
in Chicago, 715
at Craig House, 338–39, 433
as debutante, 3, 265, 266–71,
    294, 712
education of, 170, 173–74, 185,
    212–14, 239–40, 256
in England, 3, 256, 265, 266–71,
    294, 302, 311–13; 315
epilepsy of, 238
Eunice's relationship with, 152,
    189, 238, 284, 319, 320, 336,
    341–42, 599, 600–601, 635,
    714–16, 794–95, 796, 808–9,
    834
Fitzgerald and, 316
at Hyannis Port, 713–14, 834
JFK's assassination and, 618
JFK's relationship with, 214,
    239, 267, 319, 334, 349, 519,
    600, 712
Joseph Jr.'s relationship with,
    214, 239, 267, 285, 319, 712
Joseph Sr.'s relationship with,
    213, 312–13, 334–37,
    433–34, 524–25, 600–601

Kathleen and, 203, 206–7,
    266–71
Kennedy family's attitude to-
    ward, 319, 334, 338–39, 390,
    433–34, 600, 750
letters of, 706
lobotomy performed on, 335–39,
    341–42, 349, 383, 434, 600,
    750, 785, 794–95
mental retardation of, 143–44,
    145–46, 170–74, 208,
    212–14, 238–40, 250,
    312–13, 319–20, 334–39,
    502–3, 525, 599, 600–601,
    635, 809, 810
at Palm Beach, 713–15
personality of, 1, 239–40,
    284–85, 312, 319–20,
    334–35, 712–14, 796–97
physical appearance of, 143,
    239, 268, 284, 312, 712
Rose's relationship with,
    143–44, 149, 172–74,
    200–201, 212, 213–14, 239,
    284–85, 334, 335, 337, 338,
    339, 434, 582, 712–14, 833
at Sacred Heart school, 212–14
at St. Coletta residence, 433–34,
    503, 519, 600, 618, 712–13,
    714, 715, 795–97
at St. Moritz, 284–85
social life of, 239, 267, 271,
    284–85, 491
at special camp, 319
in Washington, D.C., 331,
    334–38
weight of, 157, 312
Kennedy, Sheila Rauch, 746, 799,
    826
Kennedy, Victoria Anne Reggie,
    819
Kennedy family:
aloofness of, 160, 192
Boston accent of, 188
Bouvier family and, 455–57,
    547
British opinion on, 253–54

as Catholics, 154, 155, 156, 161–63, 168, 174, 217, 244–45, 250, 308, 387, 405

childhood friends of, 168, 174, 188–89, 201, 215–16, 219, 240–41

competitiveness of, 166, 169, 216–17, 219, 220, 237

contradictions in, 453

dinnertime of, 157, 217–18, 302, 718

documentaries on, 833

education of, 156, 166–67, 168, 175, 185, 186, 205

emotional reticence of, 81, 157, 159–160, 607

in England, 246–303

exemplary behavior expected of, 155–60, 166–67, 168

extended family of, 163, 237–38, 243–44

family feeling of, 221, 255, 292, 318, 710

Fitzgerald family and, 129–32, 547, 718, 750

Fitzwilliam affair and, 426–27, 428, 430–31

on French Riviera, 298–301

health records of, 160, 180, 203–4

hereditary traits of, 151, 169

humble origins of, 15–16, 17–18, 177–78

Hyannis Port compound of, 1–2, 191–94, 197, 215–22, 235–42, 245, 291, 317–18, 357, 390–93, 407–8, 498–99, 607–10, 704

introspection lacked by, 454–55, 496, 707–8

as Irish–Americans, 161–62, 174, 217, 254, 419–20, 605, 822–23

irresponsibility of, 188, 219–20, 439–40

JFK's views on, 523

Joseph Sr.'s stroke and, 576–78, 579–80

male predominance in, 19–20, 33–34, 154–55, 164–70, 188, 203, 212, 217, 489–90, 608, 663–64, 666, 667, 686, 718–19, 720, 826–27

morality of, 161

myths about, 523, 705, 717

older vs. younger siblings in, 151, 154–55, 156

at papal audience, 286–87

photographs of, 180, 247, 252, 300, 303, 320

politics as central to, 164–65, 517

press coverage of, 247, 252, 260, 285, 300, 303, 317, 320, 522–23

reputation of, 2, 174, 185, 191–99, 217, 219, 247, 285, 300, 304, 323–24, 325, 327, 329, 335, 401, 405, 431, 433–34, 446, 469, 615–16, 644–45, 679–80, 682–83, 804–5, 813, 815

Rosemary as viewed by, 319, 334, 338–39, 390, 433–34, 600, 750

sailing by, 216, 217, 219, 220, 320, 392

self-reliance of, 184–85, 196–97, 215, 478–79

servants of, 133, 135, 157, 184, 188, 246, 250, 256, 413

shrewdness of, 18–19, 20

Shriver family and, 447

Skakel family and, 409, 434–35

smiles of, 160, 303

social status of, 116–17, 173, 177–78, 185–86

stoicism of, 153, 159–60, 167, 222, 250–51, 261, 283, 349–50

success as important to, 216–17, 240–41

in swimming meets, 216–17, 391

tennis played by, 216, 217, 391

touch football played by, 1, 186, 191, 318, 667

wealth of, 21, 174–75, 504–5, 613, 656

Kennedy Institute for Handicapped Children, 798

Kennedy men:
Joseph Sr.'s affairs and, 202, 242, 262, 295
Joseph Sr.'s influence on, 201, 217, 218, 241, 286
Kennedy women vs., 19–20, 33–34, 154–55, 164–70, 188, 203, 212, 217, 489–90, 608, 663–64, 666, 667, 686, 718–19, 720, 826–27
Rose's influence on, 351, 383
toughness of, 233–34
women as viewed by, 229–30

"Kennedy's Woman Problem: Women's Kennedy Problem" (Lessard), 742

Kennedy women:
boyfriends of, 224–26, 242, 262, 412
celebrity of, 305–6, 645
clothes of, 248–49
competitiveness of, 219
denial by, 242
Jackie's death and, 830
JFK's assassination and, 618–34
JFK's legacy and, 647
JFK's political career supported by, 402–7, 443–46, 481–82, 497–500, 516–35, 612–13
JFK's presidency and, 551–53, 584, 592–94, 610, 612–13
Joseph Jr.'s death and, 407–8
Joseph Sr.'s affairs and, 193–94, 202–3, 242, 262, 418
Joseph Sr.'s influence on, 215–17, 218–19, 236, 295, 309–10, 412, 577, 684–85
Kennedy men vs., 19–20, 33–34, 154–55, 164–70, 188, 203, 212, 217, 489–90, 608, 663–64, 666, 667, 686, 718–19, 720, 826–27
RFK's presidential campaign and, 652–58
RFK's Senate campaign and, 636–38
Rose's influence on, 3, 242–43, 250–51, 383, 541, 689, 691, 734–35
Smith trial and, 811, 812–13
Ted's presidential campaign and, 738–39, 746
Ted's Senate campaign and, 586
weight as concern of, 155, 156–57, 728, 729–30

Kenniston Day Camp, 635
Khrushchev, Nikita, 562
Kickham, Charles Joseph, 4
Kilpatrick, James J., 655
King, Martin Luther, Jr., 626, 656
Kirk, Mrs. Alan, 294
Klemmer, Harvey, 199, 259, 261–62
Kline, Howard, 132
Knebel, Fletcher, 518
Koch, George, 65
Kopechne, Joseph, 679
Kopechne, Mary Jo, 677–83
Korean War, 444
Kramer, Herbert, 683, 711, 726–27, 783
Krock, Arthur, 242, 309, 311, 317, 330

Ladies' Home Journal, 154, 160, 351, 538, 737
Lally, Frank, 100
Lally, Jenny, 100
Lally, Lottie, 100
Lambert, Angela, 420
Landis, James, 437
Lane, Thomas, 103
Lasch, Moira, 802, 811, 814
Laski, Harold, 222
Last Hurrah, The (O'Connor), 527

Lawford, Christopher Kennedy, 476–77, 666, 692–94, 698, 718, 746, 755, 812

Lawford, May, 468, 472, 473

Lawford, Patricia Kennedy:
  affairs of, 511–12
  allergies of, 208, 243
  allowance of, 175
  appendectomy of, 245–46
  birth of, 169
  as Catholic, 472, 510–11, 514–15
  Chappaquiddick accident and, 678
  dating by, 440, 462
  divorce of, 597, 612–13, 638–39, 721, 752, 784–85
  dramatics as interest of, 368
  drinking problem of, 472, 511, 569, 589, 596–97, 609, 675, 694, 757, 783, 784, 785, 786
  education of, 254–55, 256, 306, 339, 346–47, 367–69, 402, 593
  emotional reticence of, 568–69
  engagement of, 468–72
  in England, 252, 254–55, 256
  friends of, 390–91
  in Hollywood, 467, 506–8, 525, 532
  honeymoon of, 473–74
  at Hyannis Port, 454, 595, 596, 607
  Jackie's death and, 829
  Jean's relationship with, 479, 591–92
  JFK as viewed by, 347
  JFK's affairs and, 505, 512–15
  JFK's assassination and, 620–21, 624, 625, 631–32, 665
  at JFK's inauguration, 544, 548–49
  JFK's political career supported by, 402, 404, 408, 445, 446, 514–15, 520, 521, 525, 531, 533–34, 612–13
  JFK's presidency and, 536, 553, 569, 570–71, 597, 612–13
  JFK's relationship with, 357, 597
  Joseph Sr.'s death and, 685
  Joseph Sr.'s relationship with, 310, 318, 368, 471, 477–78, 511, 595
  Joseph Sr.'s stroke and, 579–80
  Kathleen's relationship with, 346
  Lawford's affairs and, 506, 510–11, 549–51, 591–92, 597, 612–13
  Lawford's romance with, 440–41, 467–72
  marriage of, 2, 317, 436, 472–79, 493, 499, 505–15, 525–26, 568–71, 589–97, 620–21, 638–39, 720, 755, 786
  Monroe and, 592–96
  as mother, 477, 507–8, 569, 570, 571, 639
  in New York City, 636–37, 783–86
  personality of, 246, 255, 470, 473, 474, 475–76, 568–69
  physical appearance of, 246, 255, 306, 318, 347, 449, 511, 592–93, 727, 754
  pregnancies of, 476–77, 481, 506, 569
  press coverage of, 550, 591
  RFK's assassination and, 662, 663, 664–65
  RFK's presidential campaign and, 652, 656, 659
  RFK's Senate campaign and, 636–39
  Rose's relationship with, 243, 245–46, 346, 476–77, 595, 721, 723, 750–51, 781, 784–85
  in Russia, 479
  at Sacred Heart schools, 254–55, 256, 306, 346–47, 592

sex as viewed by, 470, 506,
    510–11
Smith trial and, 812, 813, 815
social life of, 390–91, 474–75
at Sydney Lawford's wedding,
    754, 755, 756–57
Ted's presidential campaign and,
    745–46
Ted's relationship with, 287, 786
tennis played by, 368
wealth of, 468, 478, 511, 639
wedding of, 457, 472–73
weight of, 318, 347, 391, 784
Lawford, Peter:
    acting career of, 419, 468, 478,
        570, 590, 638
    affairs of, 506, 510–11, 549–51,
        591, 597, 612
    background of, 467–68
    death of, 784
    divorce of, 597, 612–13,
        638–39, 721, 752, 784–85
    drinking by, 568, 589, 592,
        596–97, 612, 638, 639,
        725–53, 757, 784
    drug problem of, 639–40, 694,
        752–53, 757
    Eunice's relationship with, 419,
        440
    honeymoon of, 473–74
    JFK's assassination and, 620–21
    at JFK's inauguration, 548–49
    JFK's relationship with, 549,
        590–91, 596–97, 611
    Joseph Sr.'s relationship with,
        468, 471
    marriage of, 2, 317, 436,
        472–79, 493, 499, 505–15,
        525–26, 568–71, 589–97,
        620–21, 638–39, 720, 755,
        786
    Monroe and, 592–96
    Pat's engagement to, 469–72
    Pat's letter to, 592
    Pat's romance with, 440–41,
        467–72
    RFK's views on, 638

sex life of, 470, 471, 506, 511,
    568
at Sydney Lawford's wedding,
    753, 756–57
Ted's affairs and, 531–32
Lawford, Robin Elizabeth, 569,
    570, 754, 824
Lawford, Sydney, 467
Lawford, Sydney Maleia, 487,
    633, 758
    David Kennedy's death and,
        760–61, 763
    marriage of, 752–57, 782, 798,
        823–24
    wedding of, 752–57
Lawford, Victoria Francis, 507–8,
    633, 754, 798, 823–24
Laycock, Angie, 373
Laycock, Robert, 373
Leahy, Paul, 174
Lee, Raymond, 321
Legg, Vera, 56
LeHand, Missy, 325
Leigh, Janet, 536
Lelong, Lucien, 195
Lemmon, Jack, 468
Lerner, Alan Jay, 561
    Jean's relationship with, 641–44,
        822
Lessard, Suzannah, 211, 742–43
Leukemia Society, 571
Leveson-Gower, Elizabeth, 293,
    295
Lidz, Theodore, 31
Life, 247, 260, 320, 366, 456, 628,
    669, 781, 807
Life on the Mississippi (Twain),
    700
Lincoln, Abraham, 176, 634
Lincoln, Evelyn, 450, 451, 457,
    611, 613, 614
Lindbergh, Charles, 260, 314
Lindsay, Janie, 347–48
Linehan, John, 630
Lipton, Thomas, 80, 134
Little Women (Alcott), 39–40, 137

Livingston, Dick, 475, 477, 532, 536, 568, 639–40
Lodge, George, 586
Lodge, Henry Cabot, Jr., 442, 443, 445
Loewe, Frederick, 565
Lomasney, Martin, 40, 44, 97
Long, Helen, 274
Lovat, Lord, 570
Lowell, Ralph, 178
Luce, Clare Boothe, 260–61, 360, 390, 485
Luce, Henry, 260
Lucey, Patrick L., 519
Luft, Sid, 521
Lupo, Mary E., 811, 812
Lyons, Louis, 328

McAdoo, Cynthia, 322
McAdoo, Francis, 322
McCabe, Peter, 769
McCall, Father, 34, 37
McCall's, 737, 767, 781
McCarthy, Caritas, 369
McCarthy, Eugene, 651, 657
McCarthy, Joseph, 418, 441, 447, 461–62
McCarthy, Kerry, 62, 100, 104, 459, 714, 716–17, 718–19, 721, 722, 723, 730, 734–35
McCarthy, Kevin, 717
McCarthy, Mary Lou, 104, 176, 238, 408, 722
McCarthy, Matt, 438
MacClean, Jimmie, 219, 220
Macdonald, Torbert, 229, 231, 299, 300, 346
McDonnell, Anne, 233, 317
McDonnell, Charlotte, 225, 232–33, 316–17, 426
McDonnell, James, 233
McGovern, George, 701–3
McGovern, Maureen, 783
McGowan, Ann, 10
McGrory, Mary, 701, 702, 799
McInery, Tim, 362
McIntyre, Francis, 472

McKelvy, James Peter, 752, 755–56
McKelvy, Sydney Lawford, *see* Lawford, Sydney Maleia
McKinley, William, 36, 46
McLaughlin, Charles "Chick," 94–95
McNamara, Robert, 624, 677
McNickle, Chris, 599–600
MacPherson, Myra, 743–44
McQuaid, Margaret, 170
McShane, J. P., 526–27
Mafia, 508, 514, 589, 595, 611
Mahoney, Humphrey, 21, 101
Mailer, Norman, 754, 802
Manchester, William, 648–49, 818
Mandela, Nelson, 742
Mankiewicz, Frank, 663
Mann, Mary "Dickie," 370, 410
Mann, Thomas, 303
Marchant, Peter, 762, 763
Marcher, Royal, Jr., 474–75, 640
Margaret Ann, Sister, 433–34, 795–97
Markham, Paul, 680, 683
Martin, Dean, 512, 532
Maryland Student Service Alliance, 778–79, 780
Mather, Cotton, 32
Mather, Increase, 32
Mather, Samuel, 32
Mathew, Bishop, 376
Mathias, Bob, 668
Maxwell, Elsa, 300
Mayer, Louis B., 505
Mayo, Leonard, 555, 601–2
Mazzone, A. David, 819
Mead, George, 355–58, 379
Means, Marianne, 724
Meyer, John W., 673, 720
Miller, Bill, 761
Miller, Melody, 747
Milne, A. A., 320
Misérables, Les (Hugo), 72
Mitchell, Michael, 60, 65
Mitford, Deborah "Debo," 278
Mitford, Diana, 278

Mitford, Jessica, 278
Mitford, Unity, 278
Mitterrand, Danielle, 788
Moniz, Egas, 336
Monroe, James, 247
Monroe, Marilyn, 448, 590, 592–96
Montague, Chris, 728
Montague, Robert M., Jr., 728
Montessori, Maria, 285
Moore, Eddie, 177, 181, 183, 184, 217, 285, 311, 313, 315, 682
Moore, Mary, 184, 311, 315
Morgan, Paul, 198, 200
Morgenthau, Henry, Jr., 246–47
Morison, Samuel Eliot, 16
Moschiano, Douglas, 760, 763
Mosely, Oswald, 279
Moynihan, Daniel Patrick, 657
Mudd, Roger, 742, 743
Mueller, Anastasia, 434
Mulcahy, Bill, 241
Mulgrew, Joan, 369
Munich agreement, 282, 295, 316
Murphy, Mary, 176
Murphy, Paul, 366
Murray, Margot, 492, 493
Mussolini, Benito, 247, 303
Myerson, Abraham, 145

Naar, Joe, 469, 590, 596
National Committee for the Literary Arts, 786
Nawn, Harry, 66
Nawn, Hugh, 66, 89, 93, 112
Nazism, 278, 280–83, 288–89, 303, 316, 347, 411
Neal, Bob, 569
Nehru, Jawaharlal, 554
Nervous Housewife, The (Myerson), 145
New Deal, 220, 522
New Housekeeping, The (Frederick), 160
Newman, Larry, 672, 692, 806
Newman, Mary Francis "Sancy" Falvey, 215–16, 692

Newsweek, 414, 416, 566, 686
New Yorker, 220, 396, 553
New York Times, 141, 303, 304, 320, 336, 535, 547, 556, 584, 655, 788, 827
New York World-Telegram, 253, 637
Niarchos, Stavros, 569
Niarchos, Tina, 569
Niemann, Marion, 759
Nixon, Pat, 528–29, 530
Nixon, Richard M., 418, 447, 528–29, 534, 553, 693, 701, 702, 724
Nolan, Peter, 715,
Norton, Sarah, 355

O'Brien, Edward J., 135
O'Brien, Hugh, 32, 62
O'Brien, Michael, 12
O'Byrne, Elizabeth, 494–95
O'Callaghan, Marguerite, 56, 88
Ocean's Eleven, 508, 512
O'Connell, James, 163, 195
O'Connell, William H., 48–49, 60–61, 62, 67, 82, 108, 119–21, 123, 129–30, 161, 163, 179, 287, 305, 383
O'Connor, Edwin, 527
Ogilvie, Dorothy, 174
Ogilvy, Jean, 273, 274
O'Leary, Ted, 181
Olmsted, Frederick Law, 133
O'Meara, Henry J., 107, 109
On a Clear Day You Can See Forever, 642–43
Onassis, Alexander, 719
Onassis, Aristotle:
    Jackie's marriage to, 672–75, 684, 719–20, 827
    Jackie's relationship with, 614–15, 624
    JFK's views on, 614, 624
    will of, 720
Onassis, Jacqueline Kennedy, *see* Kennedy, Jacqueline Bouvier "Jackie"

O'Neill, Eugene, 495
O'Neill, Maggie, 779
O'Reilly, John Boyle, 62
Orlando, Mary Ann, 504
Ormsby-Gore, David, 362
Ormsby-Gore, Kathleen, 288–89
Ormsby-Gore, Sylvia "Sissy," 362
Otash, Fred, 506, 511, 589, 590, 720
Other Side of Paradise, The (Fitzgerald), 141
Owens, Jesse, 668

Pacelli, Eugenio, 244–45, 286–87, 324, 375, 457
Pack, Don, 594
Panter-Downes, Mollie, 316
Patterson, Cissy, 344, 353
Pavlick, Richard, 540
Pearl Harbor attack, 340, 342, 344
Pearson, Drew, 328, 486, 550, 590–91
Pell, Claiborne, 822
Pender, Robert, 798
Peters, Charles, 528, 530, 773
Peterson, Esther, 552
Peyton-Jones, Rhona Wood, 365
Pink Lady, The, 110, 111
Pitcairn, Mary, 418
Pius X, Pope, 60, 119
Pius XI, Pope, 286
Pius, XII, Pope, 244–45, 286–87, 324, 375, 457
Playboy of the Western World, The (Synge), 121–24
Plimpton, George, 657
PM Magazine, 746, 769
Polk, Virginia Brand, 355
Powers, Dave, 402
President's Commission on Mental Retardation, 535–36, 554–57, 601, 646
Presley, Elvis, 487, 534
Price, Margaret, 528, 551
Profile in Courage Award, 782–83, 823
Profiles in Courage (Kennedy), 463–64, 485, 490

Prohibition, 145, 177
Pupton, Daniel, 7, 9
Pygmalion (Shaw), 565

Queen Kelly, 186, 189, 196, 197
Quigley, John J., 21
Quinlan, Mary, 249
Quinn, Sally, 769

Rader, Dotson, 784, 785
Radziwill, Lee, 458, 584, 614, 615, 663
Reader's Digest, 285, 396, 436
Reagan, Ronald, 743, 790
Redgrave, Vanessa, 689
Redmon, Coates, 554
Reed, James, 394–95
Reed, Jewel, 394
Reggie, Victoria Anne "Vicki," 819–20
Remick, Lee, 591–92
Reston, James, 649
Revere, Paul, 32
Richardson, Derek, 225–26, 229
Ridder, Marie, 514
Ridder, Walter, 417, 514
Riverdale Country School, 185, 203, 205, 341
R.K.O., 196
Roach, Mary, 12
Robert F. Kennedy Human Rights Award, 774–75
Robert F. Kennedy Memorial Center for Human Rights, 783, 824
Robert F. Kennedy Memorial Foundation, 669
Roberts, Ellen, 812
Roosevelt, Eleanor, 247, 248, 328, 537–38, 551, 552, 604, 646
Roosevelt, Franklin D., 139, 408
 Joseph Sr.'s discussion with, 301, 313–14, 322–28
 Joseph Sr.'s support for, 220–21, 232, 235, 246–48, 340
 Joseph Sr.'s views on, 220–21, 257, 330

leadership of, 290
marriage of, 537–38, 604
reelection campaign of (1940),
    323–28
Rose's letters to, 248, 284,
    323–28
war strategy of, 367
Roosevelt, Frank D., Jr., 522, 614
Roosevelt, James, 347
Roosevelt, Suzanne, 614
Roosevelt, Theodore, 560
Rosemont College, 339, 346,
    367–69, 402
Ross, George "Barney," 394–95
Rosslyn, Tony, 354, 365, 419
Rostow, Walter, 552
Rubirosa, Odile Rodin, 650–51
Ruhe, Jeff, 799
Ryan, John, 651
Ryan, Mary, 606, 626
Ryan, Mary O'Connell, 173
Ryan, Mr. (plumber), 198

Sabiston, Peter, 478, 505
Sacred Heart Review, 44, 97, 99,
    105
St. Aiden's Church, 161–62, 168,
    181
St. Bernard's Church, 34, 37
St. Elizabeth's Hospital, 245–46,
    250, 335, 336
St. John, George, 204, 213
St. Patrick's Cathedral, 447, 480
Salinger, Pierre, 651
Salomé (Wilde), 121, 452
Sampson, Edith, S., 518
Sanford, Mary, 696
Sargent, John Singer, 123
Saturday Evening Post, 600–601
Saunders, Frank, 574, 575, 607
Schaefer, William Donald, 778
Scherrer, Jean-Louis, 753
Schlesinger, Arthur, Jr., 527,
    558–59, 585, 647, 653, 657
Schlossberg, Caroline Kennedy:
    as author, 782–83, 823
    as Catholic, 766

in Concord, 729–30, 764, 765
David Kennedy's death and,
    760–61, 763
education of, 542, 568, 616–17,
    628, 633–34, 729, 811
Jackie's death and, 828–30, 831
Jackie's relationship with,
    566–68, 616–17, 674,
    729–30, 763–65, 766–67
JFK's assassination and, 623,
    624, 626–28, 630, 633–34,
    649
JFK's legacy and, 740, 763–65,
    782–83
JFK's political career and, 499,
    517, 518, 541
John's relationship with, 617,
    740
Joseph Sr.'s relationship with,
    650
on Kennedy Library board,
    739–40, 782–83, 823
LBJ's letter to, 646
marriage of, 766–67, 782–83
in Palm Beach, 537, 541,
    760–61, 763
as photographer, 764–65
physical appearance of, 740, 765
press coverage of, 541, 566–67,
    763–64
privacy needed by, 740
Rosemary's relationship with,
    714, 795
Rose's relationship with,
    541–42, 572, 730, 764
at Sacred Heart school, 633–34
at Sydney Lawford's wedding,
    754
Ted's presidential campaign and,
    746
wedding of, 766–67, 798
weight of, 729
Schlossberg, Edwin, 766–67
Schlossberg, John, 828
Schlossberg, Rose, 782
Schlossberg, Tatiana, 782
Schulberg, Budd, 659

Schwarzenegger, Arnold, 768–69, 770, 792–93

Schwarzenegger, Christina Maria Aurelia, 783, 794, 808

Schwarzenegger, Katherine Eunice, 783, 794

Schwarzenegger, Maria Shriver, 499, 566, 598, 607, 620, 714, 830

  Caroline's relationship with, 767

  as Catholic, 767

  education of, 690, 767, 812

  Eunice's relationship with, 598, 604, 612, 726, 727–28, 768–69, 792, 793–94

  marriage of, 770, 782, 783, 792, 793, 808

  physical appearance of, 718, 767, 791

  at Sydney Lawford's wedding, 754

  Ted's presidential campaign and, 746, 747

  in TV journalism, 768, 769–70, 783, 792–93, 823

  wedding of, 770, 798

  weight of, 728, 729, 767

Scudder, Vida, 117

Seaton, Patricia, 470, 510, 594, 752

Seiden, Mark, 804

Seigenthaler, John, 657

Shakespeare, William, 42, 82, 282, 352, 368

Shannon, Elizabeth, 821

Shapiro, Doris, 641, 642

Sharbutt, Del, 710

Shaw, George Bernard, 262, 565

Shaw, Mark, 567

Shaw, Maude, 498, 616, 623

Shearer, Norma, 300

Sheehan, John, 729

Sheen, Fulton, 368, 427

Shirer, William, 282

Shriver, Anthony Paul Kennedy, 638, 715–16, 728, 789, 791, 794–95, 808

Shriver, Eunice Kennedy:

  abortion opposed by, 697–98

  allowance of, 175

  as ambassador's wife, 656, 662, 675, 689–90, 693

  in auto accident, 797, 807

  birth of, 151

  at Blenheim Palace, 296–98

  boyfriends of, 418, 441, 462

  as Catholic, 237, 255, 343–44, 448, 504, 622, 697–98, 774, 789

  Chappaquiddick accident and, 678, 679, 680

  in Charlottesville, 435, 438

  in Chicago, 448

  children of, 476, 499, 609, 610, 693

  as debutante, 291–98

  education of, 185, 210–12, 224, 254–55, 256, 293, 306, 307–9, 339, 341–44, 352–53, 369, 390, 437–38

  in England, 254–55, 256, 291–98, 308

  Ethel's relationship with, 693

  European trip of, 441–42

  friends of, 259, 288–89, 390

  as grandmother, 794

  Hartington's death and, 398

  at Hyannis Port, 607, 693, 721, 833–34

  ill health of, 236–37, 341–44, 352, 353, 415, 417, 535, 553–54, 638, 725, 728, 794, 797

  intelligence of, 294–95, 308, 343

  Ireland visited by, 606

  Jackie as viewed by, 532–33

  Jackie's death and, 829, 830–31

  Jean's relationship with, 437, 787

  JFK's assassination and, 618–19, 620, 621–22, 623, 625

  at JFK's inauguration, 544, 548

  JFK's legacy and, 650

JFK's political career supported by, 402–8, 439, 443–46, 481–83, 487, 518, 526, 527, 532–35, 612

JFK's presidency and, 535–36, 551, 554–57, 564, 600–605, 612

JFK's relationship with, 204–5, 255, 407, 414–19, 424, 458, 535, 554–55, 556–57

Joan's relationship with, 709, 735–36

Joseph Jr.'s relationship with, 394, 407–8

Joseph Sr. as viewed by, 216, 416, 418, 504

Joseph Sr.'s death and, 684, 685

Joseph Sr.'s relationship with, 179, 200–203, 292, 308–9, 318, 321, 394, 413–14, 448, 504, 535, 600, 684, 808

Joseph Sr.'s stroke and, 580–81

at Justice Department, 413–15

Kathleen's death and, 431

Kathleen's relationship with, 224, 292–93, 334, 425, 427

Lawford's relationship with, 419, 440

LBJ and, 633, 648, 652, 655, 656

Maria Schwarzenegger's relationship with, 598, 604, 612, 726, 727–28, 768–69, 792, 793–94

marriage as viewed by, 438–39

marriage of, 317, 416–17, 436, 447–48, 502, 504, 527–28, 554, 604, 789–90

mental retardation as concern of, 502–4, 505, 535–36, 554–57, 599–605, 612, 633, 635, 646, 667–69, 689–90, 725–27, 769, 787–98, 807–10, 818–19, 824

as mother, 566, 599, 693, 716, 727–28

nickname of, 224, 237

at Peace Corps headquarters, 554

personality of, 1, 151–52, 168, 169, 180, 208, 210–11, 236–37, 255, 291–93, 342–44, 414, 416–17, 448, 503–4, 604, 666, 718, 727, 778, 783

physical appearance of, 293, 407, 414, 607, 701–2, 721, 727, 745, 777, 794

political awareness of, 164, 218, 403–4, 487, 520, 534, 586, 675, 724, 824

pregnancies of, 609, 634, 638

Presidential Medal of Freedom awarded to, 790

RFK's assassination and, 662, 665

RFK's presidential campaign and, 652, 655–56

RFK's relationship with, 603

RFK's Senate campaign and, 636–38

Rose as viewed by, 160, 167, 216, 245, 250–51, 711, 809, 835–36

Rosemary's relationship with, 152, 189, 238, 284, 319, 320, 336, 341–42, 599, 600–601, 635, 714–16, 794–95, 796, 808–9, 834

Rose's autobiography and, 674

Rose's relationship with, 243, 352–53, 675, 717–18, 720–21, 724, 740, 758, 781, 833–36

at Sacred Heart schools, 211–12, 224, 254–55, 256, 292–93, 306, 307–9, 339, 341–43, 369, 438–39

sailing by, 219, 220, 394

Shriver's presidential campaign and, 724–25

Shriver's vice-presidential campaign and, 701–3

skiing by, 343, 353

Smith trial and, 812, 813, 815
social life of, 238–98, 352–53,
    390–91, 417–19, 598
social work by, 436–39, 442,
    603–4, 640
in swimming meets, 216
at Sydney Lawford's wedding,
    754
Ted's presidential campaign and,
    738–39, 744–45, 747, 748
tennis played by, 309, 353, 790
touch football played by, 1, 255,
    702
in Washington, D.C., 402,
    413–19
wedding of, 447–48, 456, 480
weight of, 157, 236–37, 728
Shriver, Maria, see
    Schwarzenegger, Maria
    Shriver
Shriver, Mark Kennedy, 634, 791,
    808, 823
Shriver, Robert Sargent, Jr.
    "Sarge":
  as ambassador to France,
    655–56, 662, 664, 675, 683,
    689–90, 693
  as Catholic, 415, 448, 789
  Eunice as viewed by, 535, 555,
    604
  Eunice's romance with, 415–17,
    438, 447–48
  as father, 598, 693, 727
  as head of Peace Corps, 1–2,
    543, 551, 554, 602–3, 604
  as head of War on Poverty, 633,
    646, 652
  JFK's assassination and, 618–19,
    620, 625
  JFK's political career supported
    by, 518, 526
  JFK's views on, 417, 528, 602
  Joseph Sr.'s relationship with,
    416, 447–48
  Kathleen's views on, 224, 415
  marriage of, 317, 416–17, 436,

    447–48, 502, 504, 527–28,
    554, 604, 789–90
  personality of, 416–17
  political career of, 482, 527–28,
    612
  presidential campaign of,
    724–25
  RFK's assassination and, 662,
    664
  Rose's relationship with, 716
  Special Olympics supported by,
    725–26, 790, 797–98, 807,
    808, 810
  as vice-presidential candidate,
    701–2
Shriver, Robert Sargent, III, 476,
    499, 566, 598, 607, 692–94,
    725, 791–92, 808
Shriver, Timothy, 607, 618, 791,
    808, 818
Sidey, Hugh, 523, 524
Sinatra, Frank, 506–9, 512, 513,
    595, 638, 784
  JFK's relationship with, 525,
    527, 531–32, 535, 548–49,
    589–90
Skakel, Ann, 409, 654
Skakel, Ethel, see Kennedy, Ethel
    Skakel
Skakel, George, 409, 410, 654
Skakel, George, Jr., 654
Skakel, Kathleen, 654
Skakel, Pat, 411, 413, 654
Slattery, Jack, 198
Smathers, George, 403–4, 456,
    483, 485, 543
Smith, Amanda Mary, 644, 800,
    810, 812, 813, 824
Smith, Earl, 542
Smith, Florence, 542
Smith, Jean Kennedy:
  adopted children of, 644
  as ambassador to Ireland,
    820–23, 827
  birth of, 183–84
  boyfriends of, 412, 413

Chappaquiddick accident and, 678, 822

as debutante, 412

education of, 254, 255–56, 307, 339, 341, 369–70, 409–11, 465, 721

in England, 252, 254–56

Ethel's relationship with, 409–13, 493

Eunice's relationship with, 437, 787

European trip of, 436, 439, 441

friends of, 369–70

in Hollywood, 466–67, 478

Ireland visited by, 605, 820–23, 827

irresponsibility of, 440

Jackie's death and, 830

Jackie's relationship with, 517, 630

Jackie's second marriage and, 672

JFK's assassination and, 622–23, 625, 630

at JFK's inauguration, 544, 548

JFK's political career supported by, 407, 408, 442, 444, 482, 483, 497, 499, 520–21, 524, 526, 533–34, 612

JFK's presidency and, 605–7, 612

Joseph Jr.'s death and, 407–8

Joseph Jr.'s relationship with, 184, 217

Joseph Sr.'s death and, 684, 685

Joseph Sr.'s relationship with, 184–85, 407, 411, 412, 480

Joseph Sr.'s stroke and, 580

Kathleen's grave visited by, 607

Kennedy family as viewed by, 718

Smith trial and, 800–804, 810–17, 820, 822

Lerner's friendship with, 641–44, 822

marriage of, 1, 412, 591, 612, 636, 640–41, 643–44, 706

mental retardation as concern of, 723, 787–88, 799, 802, 813, 820–21

as mother, 572

in Palm Beach, 340–41, 799–804, 810–17

Pat's relationship with, 479, 591–92

personality of, 184, 237, 255–56, 306–7, 369–70, 640–41, 658, 721–22

political awareness of, 520–21, 612, 640

press coverage of, 524, 810

Red Cross work of, 318

RFK's assassination and, 662, 663–64, 665

RFK's presidential campaign and, 652, 656, 659

RFK's relationship with, 412–13, 480, 642

RFK's Senate campaign and, 637–38

Rose's autobiography and, 706

Rose's relationship with, 184, 676, 691, 704, 721–22, 723, 750–51, 761, 786–87, 801

in Russia, 479

at Sacred Heart schools, 254–56, 306, 307, 341, 369–70, 409, 410–11, 465, 722

sailing by, 237

Smith's affairs and, 526, 636, 640–41, 644, 651, 755

social work by, 442, 465–67

at Sydney Lawford's wedding, 754, 755

Ted's presidential campaign and, 738–39, 748

Ted's relationship with, 341, 369, 480–81, 800–801

Ted's Senate campaigns and, 586

tennis played by, 238

wedding of, 480

weight of, 217

wit of, 370

Smith, Kym Maria, 644, 799, 800, 810, 812, 813, 824
Smith, Merriman, 615
Smith, Stephen Edward:
  affairs of, 526, 636, 640–41, 644, 651, 755
  background of, 479–80
  Chappaquiddick accident and, 678
  death of, 788, 801, 815, 820
  JFK's assassination and, 625, 630
  as JFK's campaign manager, 612
  JFK's political career supported by, 497, 526
  JFK's presidency and, 551, 572
  Joseph Sr.'s relationship with, 480
  Lawford divorce and, 640
  marriage of, 1, 412, 591, 612, 636, 640–41, 643–44, 706
  RFK's presidential campaign and, 657, 659
  RFK's relationship with, 636, 640
  as Ted's campaign manager, 586, 612, 725, 746–47
Smith, Stephen Edward, Jr., 499, 572, 612, 800, 810
Smith, William Kennedy, 533, 571–72, 612, 671, 718–19
  rape trial of, 800–805, 810–17, 820, 822, 827
Soden, Mark, 388, 392
Solymossy, Ilona, 428, 429
Sorensen, Theodore, 463, 651, 678, 680
Spaatz, Katherine "Tatty," 360
Spalding, Charles, 317–18, 329, 346, 356, 357
Spanish Civil War, 247, 286
Spear, Dennis, 800
Special Olympics:
  Eunice's support for, 667–69, 689–90, 725–27, 769, 787–98, 807–10, 818–19, 824

Ted's support for, 810, 818
Spellman, Francis J., 304, 318, 375–76, 382, 388, 447, 480, 501
Spencer-Churchill, Sarah, 296–97
Spender, Stephen, 740
Spindel, Bernard, 720
Spock, Benjamin, 137, 571
Stanford University:
  Eunice as student at, 342–44, 352–53, 390
  JFK as student at, 329, 342
Staszak, Joseph, 702
Steinem, Gloria, 744
Stern, Benjamin, 133
Stevenson, Adlai, 446, 481, 482, 487, 553
Steverman, Helen Leahy, 166, 174, 175
Stewart, Daniel, 526
Stoddard, Lothrop, 172
Stone, Galen, 140–41
Stone, Oliver, 818
Stroll, Irwin Neal, 661
Stuart, Janet Erskine, 79, 210–11
Sullivan, Frank, 89
Sullivan, John H., 103
Sumner, William Graham, 652
Sutton, Billy, 405, 406, 413
Swanson, Gloria:
  at Hyannis Port, 193–94
  Joseph Sr.'s affair with, 181–83, 186–87, 192–99, 345, 418, 674
  marriage of, 182–83, 194–95
  Rose and, 183–84, 192–99, 706
"Sweet Adeline," 83, 91, 126, 181, 250, 326, 587, 751
Swiconek, Mark, 783
Synge, J. M., 121–24

Tabor, Juliet "Mollie" Acland, 265
Taft, William Howard, 91
Tale of Two Cities, A (Dickens), 42, 224
Tartikoff, Brandon, 793
Taylor, Charles, 166
Tempelsman, Lily, 742

Tempelsman, Maurice, 741–42, 756, 766, 789, 827–33
That Shining Hour (P. Kennedy Lawford), 675
Thayer, Mary Van Rensselaer, 538
Theriot, Nancy M., 33–34
Thom, Kate, 394
Thom, Leonard, 394
Thomas, Clarence, 815
Thomas, Evan, 647
Thoreau, Henry, 34
Thousand Days, A (Schlesinger), 647–48
Tierney, Gene, 449, 462
Time, 522–23, 524–25, 645
Times to Remember (R. Kennedy), 3, 93, 132, 168–69, 228, 704–7
Timilty, Joseph F., 371, 386, 525
"Toodles" (cigarette girl), 128, 129
Toomey, David J., 163
Townsend, David, 699–700, 707, 771, 772, 773, 774
Townsend, Kathleen Kennedy, 443, 490–91, 492, 501
    abortion issue as viewed by, 697–99, 776, 779–80
    as Catholic, 697–700, 776, 779–80
    children of, 740, 771–72, 774, 777
    education of, 688, 691, 697, 699, 771, 772, 811, 812
    essays of, 772–73
    Ethel's relationship with, 771–72, 775–76
    Jackie's death and, 832
    marriage of, 699, 707, 771–72, 773, 774, 782
    political career of, 772–80, 823
    RFK as viewed by, 663, 664, 665, 666–67, 670
    RFK's legacy and, 740, 773–74, 776, 778, 780
    Rose's relationship with, 688–89, 691, 696

Ted's presidential campaign and, 746, 772
Townsend, Maeve Fahey, 772
Townsend, Meaghan Anne, 771, 776, 823
Townsend, Rose Katherine, 774
Townshend, Peter, 429–30
Tracy, Margery Mullen, 308
Travell, Janet, 544, 564
Tree, Anne, 385
Tretick, Stanley, 566–67
Truman, Bess, 221
Truman, Harry S., 221, 524
Tsongas, Paul, 725
Tubridy, Dorothy, 522
Tuck, Richard "Dick," 654
Turner, Lana, 469, 470
Turnure, Pamela, 524
Twain, Mark, 123, 700

United World Brethren, 437

Vanderbilt, Betty Street, 412
VanGerbig, Howell, Jr., 760
Very Special Arts, 723, 787, 788, 799, 802, 813, 820
Vietnam War, 645–46, 651–52, 656
VISTA program, 602–4, 633
Vogue, 176, 452, 698, 777
Von Stroheim, Eric, 186

Wagner, Helga, 679, 801
Wagner, Robert, 508
Waldrop, Frank, 330–32, 344, 345, 353, 347, 388, 393, 419, 450
Wallach, Eli, 785
Walsh, James, 550
Walsh, John, 610, 618, 623
Walter, Charlotte Cecil, 343
Walters, Barbara, 706, 770
Walton, William, 560
Ward, Barbara, 552
Warhol, Andy, 770, 789
Washington Post, 686, 764
Washington Press Corps, 529–31

Washington Times-Herald, 388
   Jackie as photographer for, 450,
      765
   Kathleen as reporter for, 330–
      32, 335, 339, 344–45, 351–5,
      353, 354, 360, 413, 450
Watergate scandal, 724, 725
Watts, James, 336–38
Waugh, Evelyn, 381, 386
Wellesley College, 56–57, 60–62,
   63, 79, 88, 119, 168, 383
White, Antonia, 74
White, Byron "Whizzer," 275
White, Charlie, 378–80
White, John, 333–34, 335, 336,
   345, 347–49, 354, 360–61,
   398, 414, 417, 427
White, Theodore, 628–29, 746
White, William S., 520
Whitely, Rita, 673
Whittaker, Jim, 669
Why England Slept (Kennedy), 317
Wilde, Oscar, 121, 452
Williams, Andy, 669, 707
Williams, John J., 10, 28, 48, 60
Williams, Rose, 785
Williams, Tennessee, 561, 785
Willie (office boy), 113
Willkie, Wendell, 324
Wilson, Earl, 595
Wilson, Patricia, 372–73, 380
Wilson, Robin Filmer, 372
Wilson, Woodrow, 630
Winchell, Walter, 345
Winfrey, Oprah, 768, 770
women:
   as Catholics, 12, 13, 19–20,
      48–49, 78–79, 113–114,
      118–21
   clubs formed by, 116–18, 147
   divorced, 147–148, 149
   education of, 42, 63
   in England, 314–315, 364–65
   JFK supported by, 444–46, 450,
      487, 500, 518–19, 528–31
   JFK's views on, 483–84, 516,
      518–19, 543, 551–52

   as journalists, 529–31, 767–68
   as nuns, 49, 74–75
   in politics, 2–3, 43, 164–65,
      551–52
   as Protestants, 114, 147
   as teachers, 37, 42
   voting by, 113–14, 145, 404–7,
      498–99, 518–19, 528–31
   see also Kennedy women
Women's Army Auxiliary Corps
   (WAAC), 367, 404
Wood, Natalie, 508
Wood, Richard, 365
World War I, 138–39, 140, 354,
   396
World War II:
   Eunice's views on, 303
   German invasion of Poland in,
      300–1, 305
   Japanese invasion of Philippines
      in, 356, 357
   Joseph Sr.'s views on, 301,
      309–15, 340, 353
   Kathleen's views on, 288–89,
      301, 314–15, 354–58
   Kennedy family and, 280–83,
      288–89, 300–303, 315–16
   London bombed in, 316, 318,
      320–21, 325, 354–55
   Nazi–Soviet pact in, 300–301
   Operation Overlord in, 377, 388
   Rose's views on, 301, 314, 318,
      370–71
   U-boat operations in, 389
   U.S.–British alliance in, 280–83,
      288–89, 295, 300–303,
      320–21, 328
   U.S. entry into, 340, 342, 344
Wyndham-Quin, Ursula, 259, 292,
   374

Yarmolinsky, Adam, 657
Yeats, William Butler, 122
Yellow Cab Company, 169
Young, Betty, 230

Zanuck, Darryl F., 570